ALSO BY RICHARD REEVES

The Reagan Detour

Passage to Peshawar

*American Journey: Traveling with
Tocqueville in Search of
Democracy in America*

Convention

A Ford, Not a Lincoln

PRESIDENT KENNEDY

PROFILE OF POWER

≡

RICHARD REEVES

SIMON & SCHUSTER
New York • London • Toronto
Sydney • Tokyo • Singapore

SIMON & SCHUSTER
Simon & Schuster Building
Rockefeller Center
1230 Avenue of the Americas
New York, New York 10020

SIMON & SCHUSTER and colophon are registered trademarks of
Simon & Schuster Inc.

Designed by Levavi & Levavi
Photo research by Natalie Goldstein
Manufactured in the United States of America

1   3   5   7   9   10   8   6   4   2

Library of Congress Cataloging-in-Publication Data
Reeves, Richard.
President Kennedy : profile of power / Richard Reeves.
p.   cm.
Includes bibliographical references (p.) and index.
1. Kennedy, John F. (John Fitzgerald), 1917–1963.   2. United
States—Politics and government—1961–1963.   3. Presidents—United
States—Biography.   I. Title.
E842.R358   1993
973.922'092—dc20

[B]   93-24805
                                                   CIP

ISBN: 0-671-64879-9

The excerpt from "The Oracles" on page 179 is taken from The
Collected Poems of A. E. Housman. *Copyright 1922 by Henry Holt
and Company, Inc. Copyright 1950 by Barclays Bank Ltd.
Reprinted by permission of Henry Holt and Company, Inc.*

This book is for Fiona O'Neill Reeves

And for her mother, Catherine O'Neill

And her grandmothers, Dorothy Forshay Reeves
and Bridget Ruddy Vesey

John F. Kennedy's favorite book was Melbourne *by David Cecil, the biography of William Lamb, Viscount Melbourne, who was prime minister of Great Britain for seven years, from 1834 to 1841, serving as the political mentor of Queen Victoria. The book was published in 1939 and this is part of Cecil's description of the young William Lamb:*

"To be a thinker one must believe in the value of disinterested thought. William's education had destroyed his belief in this, along with all other absolute beliefs, and in doing so removed the motive force necessary to set his creative energy working. The spark that should have kindled his fire was unlit, with the result that he never felt moved to make the effort needed to discipline his intellectual processes, to organize his sporadic reflections into a coherent system of thought. He had studied a great many subjects, but none thoroughly; his ideas were original, but they were fragmentary, scattered, unmatured. This lack of system meant further that he never overhauled his mind to set its contents in order in the light of a considered standard of value—so that the precious and the worthless jostled each other in its confused recesses; side by side with fresh and vivid thoughts lurked contradictions, commonplaces and relics of the conventional prejudices of his rank and station. Even his scepticism was not consistent; though he doubted the value of virtue, he never doubted the value of being a gentleman. Like so many aristocratic persons he was an amateur.

"His amateurishness was increased by his hedonism. For it led him to pursue his thought only in so far as the process was pleasant. He shirked intellectual drudgery. Besides, the life he lived was all too full of distracting delights. If he felt bored reading and cogitating, there was always a party for him to go to where he could be perfectly happy without having to make an effort. Such temptations were particularly hard to resist for a man brought up in the easygoing, disorderly atmosphere of Melbourne House, where no one was ever forced to be methodical or conscientious and where there was always something entertaining going on. If virtue was hard to acquire there, pleasure came all too easily."

PRESIDENT KENNEDY

Introduction

The Emperor, Ryszard Kupscinski's book about the fall of Emperor
Haile Selassie of Ethiopia, begins with the writer searching through
Addis Ababa for the men who once were Selassie's court. Each tells his
story of life around the King of Kings, from the man who took down
every spoken word, the Minister of the Pen, to the high and rich officials
whose lives could be made or broken by a glance or the hint of a frown
in public from the man at the center of the world they knew.

It was a marvelous portrayal of life at court, the circle around power.
Reading it, though, I found myself wondering what this all looked like
to Selassie. What was it like at the center? Knowing little of emperors
or Ethiopia, I began to think about what it was like to be the President
of the United States. Though I had written books on three Presidents
and had talked and corresponded with a fourth over the years, I realized
that most of what I knew, or thought I knew, was basically the testimony of the men and women of White House courts, the circles around
the power of each of those Presidents.

Eventually those thoughts focused on John F. Kennedy, the 35th
President. I thought there were enough witnesses and enough records to
try to reconstruct his world from his perspective. I was interested in
what he knew and when he knew it and what he actually did—sometimes day by day, sometimes hour by hour, sometimes minute by minute. The timing was right, it seemed to me. Kennedy came to power at

the end of an old era or the beginning of a new, which was important because his words and actions were recorded in new ways. The pulse of communication speeded up in his time. At the beginning, his presidency was recorded by stenographers and typists; secretaries listened in and took notes during telephone calls. There were things we never see anymore: carbon paper, stencils, mimeographs, vacuum tubes and flashbulbs. Three years later, there were transistors, television sets in almost every home and tape recorders and Xerox machines in offices. Because of jet airliners, Americans suddenly lived only six hours from Europe.

The timing also seemed right to me because of the availability of new information and insight. The end of the Cold War resulted in new sources of documents and interviews, particularly in Moscow. A central reality of Kennedy's presidency was being the first modern Commander-in-Chief who came to office facing the possibility that a potential enemy had the military power to destroy the United States; the size of the Atlantic and the Pacific could not stop nuclear missiles launched from the Soviet Union. The Freedom of Information Act has opened new windows to the extraordinary events of those years—in Moscow and Washington, in Berlin, Birmingham, and Havana. Although far too much information is still hidden by government classification procedures and the defensiveness of the Kennedy family, it is now possible to separate fact from imagery in relations between Kennedy and the other significant men of power in the early 1960s, including former President Eisenhower, Premier Khrushchev, Charles de Gaulle, Harold Macmillan, Fidel Castro, Ngo Dinh Diem, Martin Luther King, Jr., and the President's own men, particularly Robert Kennedy and Robert McNamara.

Looking back, it seemed to me that the most important thing about Kennedy was not a great political decision, though he made some, but his own political ambition. He did not wait his turn. He directly challenged the institution he wanted to control, the political system. After him, no one else wanted to wait either, and few institutions were rigid enough or flexible enough to survive impatient ambition-driven challenges. He believed (and proved) that the only qualification for the most powerful job in the world was wanting it. His power did not come from the top down nor from the bottom up. It was an ax driven by his own ambition into the middle of the system, biting to the center he wanted for himself. When he was asked early in 1960 why he thought he should be President, he answered: "I look around me at the others in the race, and I say to myself, well, if they think they can do it why not me? '*Why not me?*' That's the answer. And I think it's enough."

Kennedy's public persona was generational. He was the first of the men who did the fighting during World War II to become Commander-in-Chief. When Lieutenant (junior grade) John Kennedy, U.S. Navy, came back a hero, he moved first into a position prepared for him by a rich father whose own ambitions had evolved into plans for his children. The son was elected commander of a new Veterans of Foreign Wars post, named for his brother, a pilot killed in action over Europe: the Joseph P. Kennedy, Jr., Post of Boston. A year later he was a candidate for Congress with streetcar posters that read: "The New Generation Offers a Leader." By the end of the 1950s, the young veterans, the junior officers and enlisted men, 16 million of them, were in their thirties and forties. And they were frustrated. They had been expected to come back from their conquering roles, accept the cheers, and then act their age. Wait their turn.

Of all of them, it was Jack Kennedy who moved most boldly. The great shared experience of his generation was a major factor in neutralizing the fact that he was only the second Roman Catholic to run for President, and the first, New York Governor Al Smith, had been crushed in 1928. But the war had changed and was still changing America, a country almost one-third Catholic by then. One Nation Indivisible was an idea the United States needed to win: We're-all-in-this-together was made visual in patriotic World War II movies showing tough Irish and Italian kids from Brooklyn fighting alongside all-American towheads from Iowa. Last names were not such a big deal anymore to the young men coming home, and there could be no better answer to innuendo that Catholicism was somehow un-American than the one Kennedy used: "No one asked me my religion in the South Pacific."

Kennedy decided to run for President after the 1956 Democratic National Convention. Adlai Stevenson, the party's nominee, had thrown open the race for Vice President, and Kennedy, a thirty-nine-year-old second-term senator, could not resist going for it. He came close, finally losing the balloting to Senator Estes Kefauver. "I know now that you don't get far in public life until you become the total politician," he said after twenty-four thrilling hours of competing for delegate votes. "That means you've got to deal, not just with voters, but with the party leaders, too. From now on I'm going to be the total politician."

Three weeks after the convention, Dr. Janet Travell, who had been treating his back problems with massive injections of novocaine for the past five years, asked him: "You weren't really disappointed when you lost the nomination, were you?"

"Yes, I was," he answered. "But I learned that it should be as easy to get the nomination for President as it was for Vice President. Until then, I thought I would have to work first toward the vice presidency."

There was, he realized, no certain reward for such things as patience and loyal service, so he began the transformation to total politician by going to twenty-six states to campaign for the Stevenson-Kefauver ticket —and for himself. He courted the old pols and sought out young veterans of World War II, setting up a political network that responded to him above party. When Stevenson was defeated by President Eisenhower, Kennedy told an old friend, Charles Bartlett, the Washington correspondent of the *Chatanooga Times:* "Now, this is the time for me."

"You have plenty of time. Why not wait?" said Bartlett.

"No, they will forget me. Others will come along."

Kennedy stayed on the road, organizing friends from school and the war, using seed money from his father, Joseph P. Kennedy, who was worth $200 million or so. Getting national press attention was an essential part of the strategy, and the way to do that was to win a few primaries. He was not as interested in trying to collect bunches of delegates controlled by state political leaders as he was in appearing to be the inevitable nominee, impressing newspaper and magazine reporters and editors that he was the choice of Democrats outside Washington.

"Come out with me," he said in late 1959, to Bartlett. "You'll be surprised at the reaction I'm getting."

After only three 1960 primary victories, in New Hampshire, Wisconsin, and West Virginia, over only one campaigning opponent, Minnesota Senator Hubert Humphrey, Kennedy had the nomination won. He needed only a Southern running mate not totally offensive to the North, and the blessing of Adlai Stevenson. But Stevenson would not bend to him, still hoping for another run in 1960. "A bitter old man with a little thing," Kennedy said of him in private, describing what his party's most dignified leader looked like coming out of a shower. Stevenson returned the feeling, though his language was more polite: "That young man! He never says 'please' and he never says, 'I'm sorry.' "

Actually Kennedy understood manners and all the rules of appropriate behavior. But he did not necessarily believe they applied to him. His entreaties to Stevenson for support were polite and respectful. Up to a point. A few days before the 1960 convention, he asked Stevenson again. "No, I can't do that," Stevenson answered once more. Kennedy said, "Look, I have the votes for the nomination. If you don't give me your support, I'll have to shit all over you. I don't want to do that but I can, and I will if I have to."

For his running mate, he chose the one man who could do the most for him in November, Lyndon Johnson of Texas, the Majority Leader of the Senate. Many of his supporters were shocked and his campaign manager, Robert Kennedy, was enraged. So the total politician sowed confusion, putting out inside stories that he had never really wanted Johnson, or that he had thought Johnson would not accept an offer, or that the invitation had been meant as nothing but courteous ritual—whatever version they wanted to believe.

His Republican opponent, Vice President Richard Nixon, was only forty-seven years old himself, but he was an old man's idea of a young man, eager to please his elders. Former Lieutenant (senior grade) Nixon's Navy photo showed him standing stiff and unsmiling in full dress blues. Kennedy's campaign photo showed him at the wheel of PT-109, the little patrol boat he commanded in the South Pacific. He was bare-chested and grinning, wearing a fatigue cap and sunglasses.

Something else worked for Kennedy, something new: the growing penetration of television into the life of the nation. It was a studio medium then, with bulky equipment and hot lights and heavy stage makeup. In a Chicago studio, Kennedy and Nixon debated on September 26, 1960. Whatever the words spoken that night, Kennedy seemed cooler, healthier, and wittier than Nixon. He *looked* as presidential as the man who had been Vice President for the past eight years.

There were only three themes in Kennedy's general election campaign, as it was analyzed by Walter Lippmann, the most cerebral of the country's syndicated columnists: "The military power of the United States is falling behind that of the Soviet Union: we are on the wrong end of a missile gap. The American economy is stagnating: we are falling behind the Soviet Union and behind the leading industrial nations of Western Europe in our rate of growth. The United States is failing to modernize itself: the public services, education, health, rebuilding of the cities, transportation, and the like, are not keeping up with a rapidly growing urbanized population."

In hundreds of interviews with the men and women who were around John Kennedy, the story that I tend to remember first was told by Abram Chayes, a Harvard Law School professor who became counsel to the Department of State. He was waiting for the candidate at Washington National Airport one hot August afternoon in 1960, on board the *Caroline,* a twin-engined Convair that was the campaign plane. The two-year-old daughter for whom the plane was named was there along with a half dozen other small children, two pregnant women—Jacqueline Kennedy and Jean Kennedy Smith—and another professor, Walt Rostow, an economist from the Massachusetts Institute of Technology.

Kennedy arrived two hours late for the short flight to a weekend at Hyannis Port. The pilot cranked the propellers into action as soon as he saw Kennedy walk into the airport's private North Terminal. Inside the plane, the passengers watched him at the pay telephones, making one more call, then another and another.

Finally, he came up the stairway to the plane, kissing his wife and sister then strapping them into the plane's two beds, buckling the children into their seats with a flash of conversation for each, leaving lighted little faces in his busy wake. He did the same with the men, focusing on each for a moment. Then, surrounded by smiles and happy chatter, he settled in his seat, a large swivel chair in the center. The stewardess came back with a bowl of his favorite fish chowder, someone handed him the afternoon newspapers, and his barber began to cut his hair as the professors reported to him on their specialties and the issues of the day.

It was almost as if those around him were figures in tableaux, who came alive only when John Kennedy was in place at the center. He was an artist who painted with other people's lives. He squeezed people like tubes of paint, gently or brutally, and the people around him—family, writers, drivers, ladies-in-waiting—were the indentured inhabitants serving his needs and desires.

On November 8, 1960, Kennedy received 34,226,731 votes to 34,108,157 for Nixon, winning an Electoral College majority of 303 to 219. Over the next three years, he often stuck a slip of paper into his pocket to remind himself of that tiny popular vote margin: 118,574 votes.

This book is a narrative of what President John F. Kennedy did at crucial points of his three years in power. What I searched for was what he knew or heard, said or read. In this account all of what he says, and is said to him, is taken from recordings, documents, journals, notes, and interviews. In the instances where someone's thoughts are mentioned, it is because they told me what they had been thinking, or they told someone else at the time, or they recorded their thinking in journals or memoranda. In some cases, usually in tape-recorded meetings and telephone conversations, I have edited out "uhs," repetitions, and confusing errors of grammar.

The two essential Kennedy books, *A Thousand Days* by Arthur Schlesinger, Jr., and *Kennedy* by Theodore Sorensen, were written within two years of the President's assassination. Both of those eyewitness books see his presidency as a tale of personal growth, with Kennedy making early mistakes, learning from them to gain a sure control of the power of his position, and then to go on to later triumphs. The Kennedy I found certainly did not know what he was doing at the beginning, and in some ways never changed at all, particularly in a certain love for chaos, the kind that kept other men off-balance.

The man at the center was a gifted professional politician reacting to events he often neither foresaw nor understood, handling some well, others badly, but always ready with plausible explanations. He was intelligent, detached, curious, candid if not always honest, and he was careless and dangerously disorganized. He was also very impatient, addicted to excitement, living his life as if it were a race against boredom. He was a man of soaring charm who believed that one-on-one he would always prevail—a notion that betrayed him when he first confronted the premier of the Soviet Union.

Kennedy was decisive, though he never made a decision until he had to, and then invariably he chose the most moderate of available options. His most consistent mistake in governing, as opposed to politics, was thinking that power could be hoarded for use at the right moment—but moments and conditions defied reason. He had little ideology beyond anti-Communism and faith in active, pragmatic government. And he had less emotion. What he had was an attitude, a way of taking on the world, substituting intelligence for ideas or idealism, questions for answers. What convictions he did have, on nuclear proliferation or civil rights or the use of military power, he was often willing to suspend, particularly if that avoided confrontation with Congress or the risk of being called soft. If some would call that cynicism, he would see it as irony. "Life is unfair," he said, in the way the French said, *C'est la vie.* Irony was as close as he came to a view of life: things are never what they seem.

"No one ever knew John Kennedy, not all of him," said Charlie Bartlett.

That was obviously the way Kennedy wanted it. All his relationships were bilateral. He was a compartmentalized man with much to hide, comfortable with secrets and lies. He needed them because that was part of the stimulation: things *were* rarely what they seemed. He called people when he wanted them, for what he wanted then. His children came at the clap of his hands and were swooped up and taken away at a nod to a nanny. After his election, he said his White House organization would look like a wheel with many spokes and himself at what he called "the vital center."

"It was instinctive at first," he said. "I had different identities, and this was a useful way of expressing each without compromising the others."

There was an astonishing density of event during the Kennedy years. In October of 1962, the President was still grappling with the riots that began with the admission of the first Negro to the University of Mississippi when he was shown the aerial photographs that proved the Soviets were putting nuclear missiles into Cuba. In one forty-eight-hour period in June 1963, he gave the speech of his life trying to break the world's nuclear siege, America was changed by a church bombing in Alabama, and the world was changed by a monk burning himself to death on a street in Saigon. On an August day when more than two hundred thousand Americans were marching for civil rights in Washington, Kennedy was giving the orders that led to the assassination of an annoying ally, the president of South Vietnam.

John F. Kennedy was one of only forty-two men who truly knew what it is like to be President. He was not prepared for it, but I doubt that anyone ever was or will be. The job is sui generis. The presidency is an act of faith.

On the morning after the new President's first night in the White House, Charlie Bartlett asked him if he had slept in Abraham Lincoln's bed, and Kennedy answered that he had: "I jumped in and just hung on!" He was still hanging on three years later.

Chapter 1

In the weeks between his election and inauguration as the thirty-fifth President of the United States, John F. Kennedy spent as much time as he could relaxing in the sun at his father's house in Palm Beach, Florida. On the first Saturday night of December, at a casual dinner in the big kitchen with a few friends and members of his campaign staff, someone asked him whether he was nervous about his first meeting with President Dwight Eisenhower, the next Tuesday. Kennedy jumped up laughing. "Good morning, Mr. K-e-e-nnedy," he said, imitating Eisenhower, who sometimes mispronounced his name. Then he swept an imaginary hat from his head, bowed, and said: "Good morning, Mr. Eeeee-senhower."

Three days later, the forty-three-year-old President-elect, the youngest ever elected, was driven to the North Portico entrance of the White House to meet the seventy-one-year-old President, the oldest man ever elected. Kennedy opened the door of his limousine before it had even stopped and bounded up the six stairs alone, carrying his hat. He caught Eisenhower by surprise. The President, attended by a covey of aides, whipped off his own hat and started to reach out his hand, but Kennedy beat him to the handshake, too. "Good morning, Mr. President," he said.

"Senator," Eisenhower replied. The Marine Band struck up "The Stars and Stripes Forever."

. . .

It was the first formal encounter between two men of surpassing charm from different generations. The cameras clicking furiously were focused on the two most famous smiles in the land. The general who had commanded all of the Allied troops in Europe during World War II was born in the nineteenth century. At Kennedy's age, he was a major in the Army. His famous grin and calm public manner had convinced many of his countrymen that he was a nice guy and a lousy politician. Those who knew him well thought the opposite. Kennedy lived along a line where charm became power. Men and women fell in love with him. And politics, the career he had chosen, was a business that magnified charm and institutionalized seduction.

Kennedy and Eisenhower had a certain contempt for each other. Kennedy's campaign attacks had been muted and indirect because of Ike's popularity, but Eisenhower still took them personally. Privately, Kennedy called Ike "that old asshole," the wisecracking Navy officer mocking the commander. Eisenhower, using words of his generation, had called Kennedy "that young whippersnapper" or "Little Boy Blue."

The two men had met for the first time fifteen years earlier in Potsdam, Germany, at the end of World War II, but General Eisenhower did not remember being approached by an ex-lieutenant, junior grade, who was working as a special correspondent for the Hearst newspapers. And Senator Kennedy's status in Washington before the 1960 election might be measured by the fact that he had never met with the President in eight years in the Senate.

Their meeting on December 6 was officially unofficial. No notes were taken and no aides sat in. The senator looked at the President's bare desk as they sat down and asked him where he put his papers. Halfway through the question, he realized there were no papers. Eisenhower did not work that way. He did not like details and he preferred talking to reading.

They talked for more than an hour, mostly about national security and foreign affairs. Eisenhower realized quickly what was on Kennedy's mind and he didn't much like it. His questions were about the structure of decision making on national security and defense. It was clear to Ike that Kennedy thought his structure was too bureaucratic and slow— with too many debates and decisions outside the President's reach and control. Eisenhower thought Kennedy was naive, but he was not about to say that, and so he began a long explanation of how and why he had built up what amounted to a military staff apparatus to collect and feed information methodically to the Commander-in-Chief and then coordinate and implement his decisions.

"No easy matters will ever come to you as President. If they are easy, they will be settled at a lower level," Eisenhower told him. It was not an idea that appealed to Kennedy. He wanted to see it all.

"I did urge him to avoid any reorganization until he himself could become well acquainted with the problem," Eisenhower dictated to his secretary later. But clearly Kennedy was not interested in organization charts, or in organization itself, for that matter. Ike's bent toward order was exactly the kind of passive thinking he wanted to sweep away. He had no use for process, with its notemaking, minute taking, little boxes on charts showing the Planning Board and the Operations Coordinating Board. He did not think of himself as being on top of a chart; rather, he wanted to be in the center, the center of all the action.

The other matter the President wanted to discuss was "burden-sharing." Alone and in a shorter session with Cabinet members that followed, Eisenhower told his successor that it was time to start bringing the troops home from Europe. "America is carrying far more than her share of free world defense," he said. It was time for the other nations of NATO (the North Atlantic Treaty Organization) to take on more of the costs of their own defense. Their economies were more productive than ever in their histories and the costs of American deployment were creating a trade imbalance, draining gold from the United States Treasury. Americans, in uniform and out, were spending and buying more overseas than foreigners were spending here. Kennedy nodded. Eisenhower sounded just like his father, who had always drummed into him that nations are only as strong as their currencies.

At the end of the day, the two men had impressed each other in a grudging sort of way without really agreeing on much. Kennedy was surprised to find Eisenhower so knowledgeable, but that confirmed his conviction that Eisenhower's problem was that he had not understood the real powers of the office. Ike, too, found Kennedy surprisingly well informed about many things, but being President was not one of them.

Kennedy told his brother Robert, who had waited in the limousine, that he knew now how Ike had become President; there was a surprising force to the man. Eisenhower wrote almost the same words about Kennedy in his diary that night, though he worried that he did not begin to understand the complexity of the job. It seemed to him that Kennedy thought the presidency was about getting the right people in a few jobs here and there.

He got it. Kennedy believed that problem solving meant getting the right man into the right place at the right time. If things went wrong, you put in someone else. His man for the transition from candidate to President was his personal lawyer, Clark Clifford, who had served on

President Truman's staff. In August, three months before the election, Kennedy had said to him, "I don't want to wake up on November 9 and have to ask myself 'What in the world do I do now?' "

But he did wake up as President-elect asking that question, surrounded by transition memos—literally surrounded, because he liked to work in bed—from Clifford, from college professors, from national security intellectuals and high-minded social reformers, from management consultants. Most of it was a waste of time: lists of three hundred appointments that could be delayed until after the inauguration were not worth much to a politician whose first priority was to begin a new campaign to win over some of the 34 million people who voted against him.

Kennedy had celebrated victory in his house at Hyannis Port with a joke about his wife and Toni Bradlee, the wife of a friend, Ben Bradlee, the Washington bureau chief of *Newsweek* magazine. Both women were pregnant. "Okay, girls, you can take out the pillows now. We won!" But he looked tired and subdued when he met with four hundred reporters in a National Guard Armory near Hyannis Port. "The New Frontier" the candidate had proclaimed during the campaign was approached rather timidly that morning. He announced that his first telephone calls as President-elect had been to the crustiest dons of Washington's old frontiers: J. Edgar Hoover, director of the FBI, and Allen Dulles, director of the CIA. He had asked them both to stay on.

Then he had to lie. When a reporter asked about rumors that he had Addison's disease, an adrenal gland failure often considered terminal, Kennedy replied without hesitation, "I never had Addison's disease. In regard to my health, it was fully explained in a press statement in the middle of July, and my health is excellent." The campaign statement was not true. Kennedy had received the last rites of the Catholic Church at least four times as an adult. He was something of a medical marvel, kept alive by complicated daily combinations of pills and injections.

The necessity to project an image of tirelessness during the campaign was a tremendous physical strain on Kennedy—and a personal triumph. But he was a wreck when it was over. Sometimes he was barely coherent in the month after the election. He spent most of November and December at the Palm Beach house his father had bought for $100,000 in 1933. There, and later at his house on N Street in Georgetown, he began to put together a government, beginning with Clifford's simple memos, which read like high school texts and were basically lists from McKinsey and Company, the management consultants who had done an almost identical transition study for Eisenhower in 1952. "The occupants of 71 to 74 positions in the Executive Branch and agencies will vitally influence the President-elect's power to govern," one began. "The most important posts are State, Treasury, Defense, Justice, and the UN."

Kennedy interviewed strangers for hours every day—falling asleep during an interview with a candidate for Secretary of Agriculture—trying to decide whether to give them some of the most powerful jobs in the world. "We can learn our jobs together," he told one, Robert McNamara, who was president of the Ford Motor Company, when McNamara told him he didn't know anything about government. "I don't know how to be president, either."

He had read about McNamara, who was a Republican, in *Time* magazine on December 2 and met him six days later. McNamara asked the first question: "Did you really write *Profiles in Courage* yourself?" Kennedy insisted he did and then offered McNamara his choice of two of the most important Cabinet seats, Treasury or Defense. McNamara came back a week later saying he preferred Defense, then handed Kennedy a letter detailing his conditions, which included the right of final approval of all appointments in his department.

Kennedy glanced at the paper, then handed it to Robert Kennedy, sitting beside him on the loveseat. "Looks okay," his brother said.

"It's a deal," said John Kennedy. He repeated what he had said at their other meeting: "We'll learn together."

"Jesus Christ, this one wants that, that one wants this," he grumbled as he shuffled notes on the way to play golf in Palm Beach. "Goddamn it, you can't satisfy any of these people. I don't know what I'm going to do about it all."

His father, Joseph P. Kennedy, who was sitting in the front seat, turned around and said: "Jack, if you don't want the job, you don't have to take it. They're still counting votes up in Cook County."

By the second week in December, with newspapers needling him about the slow pace of announcements, Kennedy's Georgetown living room looked like a doctor's office, with men shuttling in and out every twenty minutes or so, while reporters and cameras waited outside in the cold.

He met his Secretary of State, Dean Rusk, who was the president of the Rockefeller Foundation, for the first time on the same day he met McNamara. One of Rusk's qualifications was that he was not Adlai Stevenson. "Aren't you going to choose Stevenson?" Rusk had asked him when Kennedy called. "No," Kennedy replied. "Adlai might forget who's the President and who's the Secretary of State."

He also passed over David K. E. Bruce, a former Ambassador to France and West Germany, because he thought that at sixty-two he was too old. The man he really wanted was Senator William Fulbright of Arkansas, the chairman of the Senate Foreign Relations Committee. "It would be nice to have someone in the Cabinet I actually knew," he told Robert Kennedy when Fulbright's name was on the table, or the loveseat. But his brother thought the senator from Arkansas would be unacceptable to black African leaders (and perhaps to American Negroes) because he had signed the Southern Manifesto, an anti–civil rights declaration, in 1957.

When he came down to Washington for his interview, Rusk didn't know that by process of elimination the big job was almost his already. He was surprised when Kennedy called him the next day with the offer. "Wait a minute . . . ," Rusk said. He began telling Kennedy the amount of his mortgage payments and that he had only a few thousand dollars in the bank, saying he could not afford to take a cut from his $60,000 Rockefeller Foundation salary to the $25,000 paid Cabinet members. Kennedy was taken aback. "All right," he replied. "I'm going to Palm Beach tomorrow. You come down." There were a couple of calls to Rockefeller brothers, beginning with Nelson Rockefeller, the governor of New York, and by the time Rusk arrived in Florida, the Rockefeller Foundation had provided a financial package to supplement Rusk's government salary. When Rusk got to the Kennedy mansion, the *Washington Post,* lying at Kennedy's feet, had a headline saying he would be Secretary of State. It had been leaked by Kennedy himself to Philip Graham, the paper's publisher.

As Rusk sat there, Kennedy picked up a telephone and called Stevenson to ask him to be Ambassador to the United Nations. Rusk listened, dazzled, as Kennedy worked on Stevenson—flattering, stroking, prodding. As Kennedy described the job, Rusk thought there would be nothing left for him and the President to do. Finally, Stevenson said yes, he would serve under Rusk.

Kennedy chose Walter Heller of the University of Minnesota as chairman of the Council of Economic Advisers mostly because he was not from Harvard or Yale. There were too many Ivy Leaguers around him already. Heller had met Kennedy in October before he spoke to a Minneapolis rally. The candidate was running an hour late and was changing his shirt when Senator Hubert Humphrey brought Heller in.

"You're an economist?" Kennedy asked. "Tell me, do you really think we can make this 5 percent growth rate in the platform?"

"It'll be pretty tough," said Heller, meaning it would take massive government stimulus. Kennedy asked three more questions: Is accelerated depreciation an effective way to increase investment? Why has the German economy grown so fast in the face of high interest rates? Can a tax cut be an effective stimulus? Heller had never seen anything like it. As soon as Kennedy began talking, the other dozen men in the room stopped, falling away, but still straining to hear what he was saying to the outsider.

The next time Heller saw Kennedy was in December, in the Georgetown living room. Kennedy nodded toward the dining room where C. Douglas Dillon, Eisenhower's Undersecretary of State, was on the telephone. "I've asked him to be Secretary of the Treasury," Kennedy told Heller. Dillon was calling to get Ike's permission to join the enemy. Eisenhower tried to discourage him, telling him he was being used by liberals who would inevitably undermine sound money principles.

"I think Dillon will accept and I need you as a counterweight," the President-elect told Heller. "He has conservative leanings, and I know your leanings are liberal." Kennedy had that 5 percent growth he had promised on his mind, his promise to "Get the country moving again!" Heller's mission was to figure out how to make it happen. Dillon's mission would be to make sure Heller did not go too far and take Kennedy with him.

As he was leaving, Heller asked: "What about a tax cut?" Kennedy said he was not against it, but that he could not do it just after calling on Americans to sacrifice.

What he told Dillon a moment later was that he needed the confidence of the financial community, and Dillon as former chairman of Dillon, Read Company was a member of the highest standing. "I'll put up Walter Heller because I have to for political reasons," Kennedy told him. "But I will do nothing without your recommendation. I will always refer to you as my chief financial adviser."

"How can you do this?" asked Kennedy's next visitor, Democratic Senator Albert Gore, Sr., of Tennessee. Not only was Dillon a Republican, he had given $30,000 to Richard Nixon's campaign. "If you want someone rich from Wall Street, pick Averell Harriman."

"Too old," said Kennedy.

Besides, he was trying to put together a bipartisan government, with Republicans as his shields on defense and economics. "Sound" was the image he wanted to project.

"Don't worry about this," he told Gore. Kennedy said he was going to appoint a liberal Harvard professor, Stanley Surrey, to be the assistant secretary in charge of tax policy.

"That's not going to work," said Gore, who had sat next to Kennedy in the Senate. "You're going to be busy with a million things. Don't you know that? Dillon will make the policy. Nobody's going to listen to some assistant secretary."

"Albert," Kennedy said, "I got less than 50 percent of the vote. The first requirement of the Treasury job is acceptability to the financial community."

Finally, he chose Minnesota Governor Orville Freeman for Secretary of Agriculture after a thirty-second, one-question interview in the downstairs bathroom of the Georgetown house. The question was: Would he accept an undersecretary from the South? Freeman said, "Yes." Kennedy said, "All right, let's go out," and they walked out to the street for the announcement.

Working down a list of the most important sub-Cabinet jobs with Dean Rusk by his side, Kennedy called Paul Nitze, one of the brightest but least personable of the Wall Street lawyers who had become the intellectual scouts of the Cold War.

"Paul, I have a friend of yours sitting next to me, and he has agreed to become my Secretary of State. He would like you to be his Undersecretary for Economic Affairs. . . . I would like you to become either my National Security Adviser or Deputy Secretary of Defense."

"How long do I have to make up my mind?" Nitze asked.

"Thirty seconds."

"I choose Deputy Secretary of Defense."

"Fine, thank you, Paul."

But McNamara held Kennedy to their deal, and vetoed Nitze. Then McNamara called Nitze again and asked whether he would step down a level, to an Assistant Secretary of Defense. Stung, Nitze called the private Palm Beach number Kennedy had given him. A woman answered and came back in a minute to say: "Mr. Kennedy doesn't wish to speak with you."

The next day, Kennedy let *The New York Times* know "on background"—meaning the paper could use the information but not his name—that Franklin D. Roosevelt, Jr., would be appointed Secretary of the Navy. The leak was intended for an audience of one. But McNamara, who was the one-man audience, was too new at the game to get the message. He wondered how the *Times* had got it so wrong. He did not know FDR, Jr. He had no intention of naming him to anything.

"Bob?" The call came a few days later. "Jack Kennedy. I was wondering if you saw that story in the *Times* about Frank Roosevelt? Have you talked to him?"

"No."

"Do you know how I won the West Virginia primary? What he did for me there?" Kennedy had thought he might lose in West Virginia, and probably be knocked out of the race, until Franklin Roosevelt's son had come down to campaign for him. It was as if the son of God had come to give the Protestants permission to vote for this Catholic.

"I understand," McNamara said. "But I hear he's a drunk and a womanizer."

"Maybe," Kennedy said, "you could just talk to him."

McNamara telephoned Roosevelt in New York and flew up for lunch. He was barely back in his Washington hotel room when the telephone rang. "How did it go?" asked Kennedy.

"Good. Fine," McNamara said. "But I can't appoint him."

"Why not?"

"He's a drunk and a womanizer."

Kennedy sighed. "I guess I'll have to take care of him some other way," he said.

On December 15, Kennedy told Robert Kennedy to come to Georgetown for breakfast. They had discussed a Cabinet job, perhaps Attorney General, or maybe a place in the sub-Cabinet, in the Defense Department with McNamara, but Robert had decided to go back to Massachusetts, perhaps to run for governor. "No," John Kennedy said at breakfast. "You will be Attorney General.

"I need you . . . I believe McNamara will make a great contribution, but I don't know him," he went on. "Dean Rusk . . . the truth of the matter is I've had no contact with him. I need someone I know to talk to in this government." It was true, though John Kennedy hadn't wanted his brother in the Cabinet until his father had insisted: "I want Bobby there. It's the only thing I'm asking for and I want it."

"So, that's it, General," he said, standing up. "Let's go." They went out onto the N Street stoop.

"Nine strangers and a brother for a Cabinet," said Fred Dutton, one of Kennedy's talent scouts.

On January 19, 1961, the eve of the inauguration, Kennedy and Eisenhower met for a second time. They were alone for forty-five minutes, and Ike talked about being President. He began with the black vinyl satchel, "the Football," which contained nuclear options, commands, and codes, officially called "Presidential Emergency Action Documents." It was carried by military officers who handed it off to each other in eight-hour shifts, like quarterbacks and halfbacks. The President carried a laminated plastic card in his wallet to identify himself to electronic systems and begin choosing among deadly options outlined in the thirty thick looseleaf pages in the Football. In a couple of minutes, he could activate the command links to junior officers in the squadrons of bombers always in the air and on alert, to the missile silos under the Great Plains and in European fields, to the submarines under the Atlantic and Pacific. Then, those lieutenants could turn the keys and push the buttons to blow up the world, or the part of the world marked in red on National Security Council maps: the Soviet Union and China and their Communist allies.

"Watch this," Eisenhower said, picking up a telephone and ordering: "Opal Drill Three!" They were standing by the French doors behind the President's desk. Three minutes later a Marine helicopter settled on the lawn behind the Oval Office. Kennedy loved it.

"I've shown my friend here how to get out in a hurry," the President said as they walked into the Cabinet Room for an official working session with the old and new secretaries of State, Defense, and Treasury. Eisenhower and Kennedy sat side by side at the head of the table. Secretary of State Christian Herter sat next to Rusk on one side, and Secretary of Defense Thomas Gates was next to McNamara on the other. Next to them, Secretary of the Treasury Robert Anderson sat with Dillon. On the other side, Eisenhower's transition chief, General Wilton Persons, sat with Clark Clifford.

The agenda was as formal as the arrangement of the chairs. Kennedy had requested discussion in four categories: "(1.) Trouble Spots—Berlin, Far East (Communist China and Formosa), Cuba; (2.) The National Security Set-up—including how the Pentagon is working; (3.) Organization of the White House; (4.) President's Confidential Comments regarding Macmillan, De Gaulle, Adenauer."

Eisenhower's talking paper on Cuba had been written by Robert Hurwitch, the State Department's Cuba desk officer, who had also prepared Kennedy's paper. Following instructions from his once and future bosses, Hurwitch handed a one-page memo to Eisenhower and a two-page version to Kennedy.

As Eisenhower began to speak, Kennedy interrupted. He was looking over at Persons, who was writing furiously. "Mr. President," he said, "I did not understand that notes were to be taken at this meeting."

Eisenhower cocked his head toward Persons, who remarked, "Everything a President says is recorded. This is historical record."

Kennedy glanced at Clifford, who pulled a pencil from his pocket and began taking notes on the back of his copy of the meeting agenda, continuing on the back of press statements prepared before the session began.

"Thailand is a valuable ally," Clifford wrote as Eisenhower began, "because Communist-dominated Laos would expose T's borders. Military training under French is poor. Would be a good idea to get U.S. military instructors in there. [Thailand] . . . Morale not good in Democratic forces, Ike says Communist forces always appear to have better morale—Commie philosophy inspires them to be dedicated. If a political settlement cannot be arranged *then we must intervene.* (Herter)."

"If Laos should fall to the Communists," Eisenhower said, glancing at his papers, "then it would be a question of time until South Vietnam, Cambodia, Thailand and Burma would collapse. The United States would accept this task with our allies, if we could persuade them, and alone if we could not, our unilateral intervention would be our last desperate hope.

"This is one of the problems I'm leaving you that I'm not happy about," he said, looking directly at Kennedy. "We may have to fight."

"How long would it take to put a division into Laos?" Kennedy asked.

Eisenhower looked to Gates. "Twelve to seventeen days," answered the Defense Secretary. That was from the United States, but there were U.S. troops that could be moved in more quickly from bases in Japan and Okinawa or the Philippines.

"This is the cork in the bottle of the Far East," Eisenhower said; "if Laos is lost to the free world, in the long run we will lose all of Southeast Asia. . . . You are going to have to put troops in Laos. With other nations if possible—but alone if necessary."

"If the situation was so critical," Kennedy asked, "why didn't you decide to do something?"

"I would have, but I did not feel I could commit troops with a new administration coming to power."

Kennedy asked the President whether he would prefer a coalition government including Communists in Laos or military intervention by SEATO (the South-East Asia Treaty Organization), which had been put together by the United States as a Pacific mutual defense alliance in the manner of NATO. Eisenhower and Herter double-teamed him. Eisenhower said coalitions never worked; the Communists always ended up in control. Herter added that SEATO would not work either. Thailand, the Philippines, and Pakistan might be willing to join with U.S. troops in Laos, but the British and the French, who were also SEATO members, had already made it clear that they would quit that alliance before sending troops to Asia.

"What do you recommend as the next step to be taken?" Kennedy asked.

The most desirable solution, Herter said, would be a coalition government without Communists, but he did not think that was possible. "The government's armed forces—our side—has [sic] been unwilling to fight, despite our logistical support. . . . The Thais, the Philippines, the Pakistanis, who are counting on SEATO for their own self-defense against Communist aggression, are concerned that SEATO is a paper tiger . . . I can't see any alternative for us but to honor our obligation."

Eisenhower then said he was sure the Thais, the Filipinos, and the Pakistanis would join in the fight. But he doubted anyone else would.

"What about China?" Kennedy asked. The President said he thought the Chinese would be cautious about the possibility of provoking a major war. Kennedy had the uncomfortable impression that Ike was enjoying this.

"It's a high-stakes poker game," Eisenhower said. "There's no easy solution."

McNamara asked only one question. He wanted an appraisal of the United States' limited war requirements versus limited war capabilities.

Eisenhower and Gates handed him a National Security Council study that had been completed two weeks earlier. It listed five places the United States might be drawn into war at some level: Laos, Korea, Formosa, Iran, and Berlin.

"We can handle one limited war, a Korean war situation," Gates said. "But not two. And any number of small wars. Small wars are no problem."

Eisenhower looked dubious. He said he did not like the phrase "limited war." "In other words," he said, "when do you go after the head of the snake instead of the tail?"

In answer to a list of questions from Rusk about "trouble spots," Herter began with Berlin. He said more and more refugees were fleeing from East Germany to West Berlin every day, and sooner or later the Communists had to do something to stop that.

When Herter went back to Laos, Eisenhower interrupted to offer his opinion about the country next door, South Vietnam. There was no similar danger there, but there was always a possibility of a coup overthrowing the country's anti-Communist leader, Ngo Dinh Diem.

"Should we support guerrilla operations in Cuba?" Kennedy asked.

"To the utmost," said Eisenhower.

The President-elect had been briefed twice by the CIA on the training of anti-Castro guerrillas in Guatemala. He had the impression that the operations would involve infiltration of small sabotage teams. Eisenhower said there were no final plans.

"We cannot let the present government there go on," Eisenhower said. Treasury Secretary Robert Anderson offered his own perspective: "Large amounts of United States capital now planned for investment in Latin America are waiting to see whether or not we can cope with the Cuban situation."

Kennedy asked about atomic weapons in other countries.

"Israel and India," Herter replied. The Israelis had a nuclear reactor capable of producing ninety kilograms of weapons-quality plutonium by 1963. He advised Kennedy to demand inspection and control before there were atomic bombs in the Middle East. In India, he said, the Russians were helping build a reactor.

The meeting ended before noon, twenty-four hours before John Kennedy would take the oath as President. As they got up, eight of the ten men in the room moved away from the two at the center. The outgoing President picked that moment to tell his successor quietly that whatever was said during the campaign about Soviet missile and nuclear strength (he obviously meant Kennedy's "missile gap" charges), the United States had a strategic edge because of nuclear-firing submarines along the coasts of the Soviet Union: "You have an invulnerable asset in Polaris. It is invulnerable."

John Kennedy was considered a pretty cool fellow, the most detached and rational of politicians. But he was amazed at Eisenhower's calmness as he talked of nuclear submarines, war, and disaster. "Equanimity" was the word Kennedy used later, talking to Robert Kennedy about the meeting. He thought there was something frightening about Eisenhower. There was also something politically intimidating about succeeding a man of such great popularity. The new President was determined never to cross his predecessor. Ike's approval was not necessary, but his public disapproval would be devastating.

Eisenhower knew that, of course, and now he reminded Kennedy. "I'm going to try to support you every way I can on foreign policy," he said. "But there is one point on which I would oppose you strongly— the seating of Communist China in the U.N. and bilateral recognition."

That took care of that. Kennedy thought it was stupid not to have diplomatic relations with the Communist government in China. But relations with Eisenhower were a more compelling concern.

It was snowing as Kennedy left the White House, a visitor for the last time.

Chapter 2

"Ask not what your country can do for you—ask what you can do for your country," said John F. Kennedy. Then he paused, took another bite of bacon, and reached for his coffee.

This was the second morning rehearsal of his Inaugural Address. The first time had been in the bathtub, with his words echoing off the tiles. Then it was on to the bacon and eggs. January 20, 1961, was quite a day for this American Catholic—three strips of bacon on a Friday morning. Because of the inauguration of the first Catholic President of the United States, the pope had given Roman Catholics in the Washington area a special dispensation from the Church's stricture against eating meat on Fridays.

An hour later, Kennedy stepped out into the eight inches of snow that had fallen overnight to go to mass at Holy Trinity Church near Georgetown University. His way was cleared by soldiers who had been shoveling snow all night into seven hundred Army trucks. Kennedy had been up pretty late himself, coming home at 4:00 A.M. after moving from celebration to celebration, his limousine guided through the streets by running Secret Service men waving flashlights. Bundled-up people were grouped around fires on the great Mall from the White House to the Lincoln Memorial. "Turn the lights on in here," he said on the way to one party early in the evening, "so they can see Jackie." She had gone home before he went on to "The Gala," a variety show put on by Frank

Sinatra at the city's Armory. The stars of the show, Ethel Merman, Jimmy Durante, Gene Kelly, and others, had trouble making it there from their hotels and it had lasted until almost 3:00 A.M., when Kennedy went on to Paul Young's restaurant for a late dinner hosted by his father.

"Have you ever seen so many attractive people in one room?" Kennedy had said as he walked into the restaurant with his friend, Paul Fay, Jr., an ensign on Lieutenant Kennedy's boat, PT-109, twenty years before. His assignment for this night and the next day and night was to escort a twenty-eight-year-old actress named Angie Dickinson, with whom Kennedy slipped away to private rooms a couple of times during the ceremonies.

After mass that Friday morning, Kennedy picked up his wife and together they went to the White House at eleven o'clock to meet President and Mrs. Eisenhower for coffee. Kennedy and Eisenhower rode together up Pennsylvania Avenue to the Capitol. Their relationship was slightly awkward, and Kennedy chatted a little nervously about *The Longest Day,* a book on D-Day, the Allied invasion of Europe in 1944. Eisenhower said he knew about the book but hadn't read any of it. Kennedy was surprised. But of course Ike had been there, commanding the operation.

There were twenty thousand people on the East Plaza of the Capitol. It had not been easy for most of them to get there, even with the Army working through the night. The temperature was ten degrees below freezing, exceptionally cold for Washington. The sky was a bright and clear blue, and the sun reflected everywhere off the new snow.

The day's *Washington Star* caught the generational mood in its humor column, "Potomac Fever": "Ike leaves office as popular as ever. People like the way he keeps the White House free of the taint of government. . . . President Kennedy swears to uphold the Constitution. From now on, no Kennedy will serve more than two terms, waiting his turn until his older brother is through."

There were indeed sixteen Kennedys among the one hundred and five men and women on the platform. Most of them were there by title, beginning with President Eisenhower, former President Truman, Vice President Nixon, and the Chief Justice of the Supreme Court, Earl Warren, who would administer the oath of office. The only outsiders were Marian Anderson, who would sing "The Star-Spangled Banner," and Robert Frost, the eighty-six-year-old New England poet, who had trouble reading in the white glare of the day, so he set aside the new poem he had composed for the occasion and recited one he had written in

1942 called "The Gift Outright": "Such as we were we gave ourselves outright . . . To the land vaguely realizing westward . . ."

Just below the podium, in Reserved Section 1-A, were six hundred and thirty-five places set aside by Kennedy himself for his oldest friends, political and personal. It was a warren of Kennedy connections and secrets. Most of the men and women in 1-A did not know each other; all the lines led only to the man at the center. There were seats for Ted Sorensen, who had drafted the speech, and for Mayor Richard Daley, who it was said had drafted the Chicago voters who elected Kennedy; for George Meany of the AFL-CIO and Walter Reuther of the United Auto Workers, honored for their commitment to party and candidate. Angie Dickinson sat next to "Red" Fay. Behind them was a New York physician named Max Jacobson. Dr. Jacobson had begun to travel with Kennedy after he had helped him prepare for the television debates with Richard Nixon by injecting him with mixes of vitamins, painkillers, human placenta, and amphetamines. Doctors came and went around Kennedy. In a lifetime of medical torment, Kennedy was more promiscuous with physicians and drugs than he was with women.

The momentary confusion caused by Robert Frost's problems ended Kennedy's worry that the poet might steal the show. "He's a master of words. I have to be sure he doesn't upstage me," Kennedy had said to his Interior Secretary, Stewart Udall, when Udall had told him that Frost wanted to speak. "They'll remember what he said and not what I said. Maybe we can have him just recite a poem."

Then it was his time. Kennedy took off his overcoat and set down his silk topper. He stood before Chief Justice Warren to take the oath of office, looking spectacularly young, ruining the more mature image he had wanted to project and had thought formal dress would give him. His words made small clouds in the cold air.

"Let the word go forth from this time and place, to friend and foe alike, that the torch has been passed to a new generation of Americans. . . .

"Let every nation know, whether it wishes us well or ill, that we shall pay any price, bear any burden, meet any hardship, support any friend, oppose any foe to assure the survival and success of liberty. . . .

"Now the trumpet summons us again—not as a call to bear arms, though arms we need—not a call to battle, though embattled we are— but a call to bear the burden of a long twilight struggle year in and year out. . . . And so, my fellow Americans: ask not what your country can do for you—ask what you can do for your country. . . ."

"A long twilight struggle." The speech was about the Cold War, the ideological, political, economic, and overt and covert military contest for control of most of the world. The victors of World War II, the United States and other Western powers and the Union of Soviet Socialist Republics, had become adversaries, then enemies within three years of its end. Victory had deteriorated into struggle between the ideas and forces of the West, democracy and free-market capitalism, led by the Americans, and the forces of the East, communism and totalitarianism, socialism and central planning, led by the Soviets.

But it was also a speech meant to inspire an anxious country, a call to national action in the manner of the man Kennedy most admired, Winston Churchill. America was not weak, far from it, but for the first time in almost two centuries, a serious adversary could reach Americans across the great shining seas that protected the United States. The Soviets had tested their first thermonuclear weapon, a hydrogen bomb, in 1953, and then, in 1957, had startled the world by successfully orbiting a satellite in space. *Sputnik* they called it—"The East"—a high-flying, visible, and beeping symbol of Soviet achievement and power. Obviously, the country with the rockets to put that into space had the capability to deliver nuclear warheads into the heart of America. That was the fear button that Kennedy had pushed in the campaign, declaring that the Soviets not only had nuclear capability, but that they had more missile capacity than the United States did. That was the "missile gap" he had exploited even after he had been given classified military information indicating there was no such thing.

The Communists were preaching the historical inevitability of their cause. Much of the world listened and many listeners believed. Some leaders of the forty new countries in Asia and Africa, created from the colonies of the old European powers—nineteen new flags were raised at the United Nations in 1960 alone—were choosing Moscow's guidance over Washington's. Many thought socialist systems simply worked better. Some calculated that Soviet police techniques, applied in their countries, could keep them in power longer than American-style elections, free speech, and assembly.

As Kennedy took office, the economic growth rate of the Soviet economy was estimated at 6 to 10 percent a year, compared with 2 or 3 percent in the United States. After eight years of Republican tight-money policies aimed at keeping inflation below 2 percent, American unemployment was at 7 percent and the country had gone into recession early in 1960. "We have to get this country moving again" was Kennedy's most common campaign line, in response to the boasting of the Soviet leader, Nikita Khrushchev, who had proclaimed: "We will bury you! . . . Your grandchildren will live under Communism."

The foreign policy Kennedy was inheriting from Eisenhower, and from Truman before him, had two essentially unquestioned central goals: containing communism and preventing world war. Truman had mandated the first goal, ringing the borders of the Communist sphere with U.S. military power and alliances. Soviet science had triggered the second, bringing fear of devastation to Americans for the first time.

Kennedy believed in that consensus. Preparing for his second meeting with Eisenhower, he had studied a long report by the RAND Corporation, a think tank associated with the Air Force, entitled "Political Implications of Posture Choices." He had underlined just one sentence: "Political history does not support that it is more dangerous to be strong than to be weak, more dangerous to threaten than to betray fear, more dangerous to be as 'provocative' as an Adenauer or a De Gaulle than to be as conciliatory as a Macmillan."

In his inaugural speech that judgment became: "We dare not tempt them with weakness. For only when our arms are sufficient beyond doubt can we be certain beyond doubt that they will never be employed. . . ." He had concluded that Eisenhower's doctrine of "Massive Retaliation"—that Communist attack on U.S. installations or allies anywhere in the world would be met by American nuclear attack on the Soviets—could not prevent or deter smaller Communist thrusts around the world. The old orders of colonialism and military dictatorship were breaking up in Latin America and Asia and Africa—and local Communists were often significant factors in those emerging countries. The United States, Kennedy was declaring, needed more capability, must be ready to move quickly in small wars, too—needed new military options, to contain communism without blowing up the world, something like "Flexible Response," the doctrine articulated by former Army Chief of Staff General Maxwell Taylor, whose career had been blocked by Eisenhower.

"The torch is passed to a new generation," Kennedy said at his inaugural, "born in this century, tempered by war, disciplined by a hard and bitter peace . . . granted the role of defending freedom in its hour of maximum danger." His slogan for his first campaign, for Congress, in 1946, "The New Generation Offers a Leader"—had evolved into "The New Frontier." The 16 million young men who had gone to war in the 1940s were taking over from the generals and the admirals, and this was their new adventure. They could finish the job of remaking the world in America's image.

In Section 1-A, a former Air Force lieutenant named Harris Wofford, now a law professor at Notre Dame and a civil rights adviser to the new President, was sitting directly below Kennedy. He was thrilled by the speech, but he was still listening for two words.

Wofford was a practicing idealist who had shocked his Southern family, old Alabama aristocracy, by going to a Negro college. He was too stiff and too earnest, boring actually, following Gandhi rather than Churchill, to get close to the man he was now serving. He had left his job as staff director of the U.S. Civil Rights Commission two years before to work for Kennedy. He had edited a book of Kennedy speeches, written a few new ones, and had spent a lot of time calming down Eleanor Roosevelt liberals and Negroes who wanted Kennedy to take public stands on civil rights that would match his private assurances. Wofford was straining to hear the new President say something about civil rights.

"You can't do this," he had told Kennedy the day before, when he had seen the final draft of the Inaugural Address. That day, January 19, twenty-three Negro students had sat down and demanded to be served at the segregated lunch counters of the two biggest department stores in Richmond, Virginia, one hundred miles to the south. There was not a single word on civil rights in the speech, not a single word on economics or on any domestic concern at all. "There's an equal rights struggle here at home, too," Wofford had said. "You have to say something about it. You have to."

"Okay," Kennedy said, and wrote in two words, so that one sentence ended, ". . . unwilling to witness or permit the slow undoing of those human rights to which this nation has always been committed and to which we are committed today *at home* and around the world."

That was it. Two words about home in a speech about the world. That was one of thirty-one changes Kennedy had made in the speech in the last few hours. For his own conclusion, Kennedy edited Abraham Lincoln, who had ended his Inaugural Address: "In your hands, my dissatisfied fellow countrymen, and not in mine, is the momentous issue of civil war."

"Let us begin," concluded Kennedy. "In your hands, my fellow citizens, more than mine, will rest the final success or failure of our course."

Within an hour, the new President's men were rushing into the White House. The place was empty. There was not a single piece of paper on a desk, in a cabinet or in a drawer. There was not a picture on the wall or a book on the shelves in the Oval Office. The United States is born anew with each President. Pierre Salinger, the thirty-five-year-old press secretary, was one Kennedy assistant able to walk into an office, because his space was already defined by rows of typewriters, teletypes, mimeograph machines, klieg lights, and the other paraphernalia of modern communications. But the desks and file cabinets he inherited were as empty as the rest. "It's a place without history," Salinger thought as he looked around.

When Kennedy got there, he satisfied his curiosity about something.

He walked through with his brother, Edward, and his brother-in-law, Stephen Smith, turning over chairs and other furniture. "Look at this. Reproductions," he said again and again. "Sears, Roebuck stuff."

Back outside, he was soon bored reviewing the inaugural parade. He called over one of his new military aides, Army Major General Chester Clifton, and said, "There must be more we can do up here. Why don't you think of something?"

"Yes sir," Clifton said. "You've got your whole Cabinet and the Joint Chiefs of Staff. Why don't I bring them up one at a time to stand with you and review some of the sections of the parade?"

"That's a great idea, General . . ." Then Kennedy saw there were no Negroes in the detachment of marching cadets from the Coast Guard Academy. "Call the commandant and tell him I don't ever want to see that happen again," he said to Richard Goodwin, a young speechwriter from the campaign. Goodwin picked up a phone and did just that, thinking, "With just a telephone like this we can change the world!"

Inside the White House, some of Kennedy's men were reading the first official paper he sent them, a forty-page transcript of a secret speech by Soviet Premier Khrushchev that he had just read himself the day before. The speech, given to leaders of Communist governments and parties from around the world in Moscow on January 6, seemed to be a guide to the patient expansion of communism by supporting guerrilla insurgencies, limited warfare under the umbrella of nuclear stalemate. This is part of what Kennedy read and passed on:

For New Victories of the World Communist Movement

Our time, whose main content is the transition from capitalism to social-ism initiated by the Great October Socialist Revolution, is a time of strug-gle between the two opposing social systems, a time of socialist revolutions and national-liberation revolutions, a time of the breakdown of imperialism, of the abolition of the colonial system . . . the balance of forces in the world has changed radically in favor of socialism. . . .

Now about national-liberation wars. Recent examples of wars of this kind are the armed struggle waged by the people of VietNam and the present war of the Algerian people, which is now in its seventh year. These wars, which began as uprisings of colonial peoples against their oppressors, developed into guerrilla wars. . . .

What is the Marxist attitude to such uprisings? It is most favour-able. . . . The Communists support just wars of this kind whole-heartedly and without reservations. . . .

In recent years the initiative in world affairs has belonged to the Soviet Union and the other socialist countries. . . . The positions of the U.S.A.,

Britain and France have proved to be especially vulnerable in West Berlin.
. . . They cannot fail to realize that sooner or later the occupation regime
in that city will end. . . . Should they balk, we shall take resolute measures. We shall then sign a peace treaty with the German Democratic
Republic to end the occupation regime in West Berlin, and thereby remove
the thorn from the heart of Europe. Comrades, we live in a splendid time.
. . . Men of the future, Communists of the next generation, will envy us.

President Kennedy had attached a memo to the copies he sent to
members of the National Security Council: "Read, mark, learn and
inwardly digest. . . . Our actions, our steps should be tailored to meet
these kinds of problems."

For the moment, though, they were tomorrow's problems. Tonight
was for the inaugural balls. John and Jacqueline Kennedy went from
one to another. He sat at dinner for a time with Arthur Krock, the *New
York Times* columnist who was an old friend of his father's, and who
had worked with him in 1940 transforming his senior thesis at Harvard
into a book called *Why England Slept,* modeled on Churchill's 1937
book, *While England Slept.* The columnist said he thought the inaugural
speech was the finest political document written in the country since
Woodrow Wilson.

"Are you going to write that?" Kennedy asked. He did not think of
himself as a great speaker. For years he had raced through his scripts
with Boston speed and accent, without emphasis or emotion. Finally, at
the beginning of 1960, he had hired a dramatics coach who led him in
voice exercises every morning. One drill was barking like a seal for two
minutes, which Kennedy did in the bathtub. Home alone in Washington,
he would put on a silk bathrobe, pour himself a brandy, light up a cigar,
and speak along with records of Winston Churchill's greatest speeches.

Churchill was his literary model as well. John Kennedy projected
himself as a different kind of politician, one who not only read books,
rare enough in his chosen profession, but wrote them. His two books,
Why England Slept and *Profiles in Courage* (1955), were both best-
sellers and owed a great deal to Churchill, as well as to Krock and to
Ted Sorensen, respectively.

Kennedy made it home that night to the White House at 3:00 A.M.,
and slept in Lincoln's bed. Five hours later he was propped up on
pillows reading *The New York Times,* with headlines he could have
written himself:

> Kennedy Sworn In, Asks "Global Alliance"
> Against Tyranny, Want, Disease and War,
> Republicans and Diplomats Hail Address

Nation Exhorted
Inaugural Says US
Will "Pay Any Price"
to Keep Freedom

Says US Is Ready
for Soviet Talks

Khrushchev Sees
Hope for Accord

Castro Suggests
Amity with US

UN Delegates Praise Speech
Acclaim the "Quest for Peace"
Some Diplomats Believe Kennedy Talk
Heralds Relaxation of Tensions

2 Doctors Find Kennedy
Is in Excellent Health

The *Times* health story was based on a release from his press office saying that a new physical examination by his internist, Dr. Eugene Cohen, and his back doctor, Dr. Janet Travell, who was now his new White House physician, showed that Kennedy's "health continued to be excellent." He had certainly looked great, laughing and waving the night away—with time out for some actress-hopping. But as he partied, physicians and technicians were bringing in the prescriptions and paraphernalia of his secret medical life. The treatment for his Addison's disease, a total failure of the adrenal glands, named for the British doctor who first discovered it, was cortisone injections, pills, and pellets implanted in his thighs. For emergencies, his father had since 1947 put caches of cortisone and other medications in bank safety deposit boxes all over the world.

Indeed, Kennedy was a famous Addisonian, at least in the medical literature. What made him notable in the profession was a back operation he survived on October 21, 1954. Senator Kennedy had gone into New York Hospital that fall for two spinal fusions in an attempt to relieve his constant back pain. "I'd rather be dead than spend the rest of my life on these goddamned crutches," he had told one of his doctors. Death was a very real possibility—"This is the one that cures you or kills you," he said to one of his men, Larry O'Brien. Addisonians, with weakened immune systems, had rarely survived the trauma of major surgery. The operation was described in the November 1955 issue of the *American Medical Association Archives of Surgery,* the patient described only as "A man 37 years of age."

"A man 37 years of age had Addison's disease . . . managed fairly successfully for several years on a program of desoxycorticosterone acetate pellets of 150 mg implanted every three months and cortisone in doses of 25 mg daily orally. Owing to a back injury, he had a great deal of pain which interfered with his daily routine," the report began, then went on to say that the surgeons did not want to proceed because it was just too dangerous. But the patient insisted. The report ended: "No Addisonian crisis ever developed."

There was gallantry to Kennedy's consistent lying about his health and his success in persuading press and public that he was a man of great energy. "Vigor" was the cliché used by the press. In truth, boy and man, he was sick and in pain much of the time, often using crutches or a cane in private to rest his back, and taking medication, prescribed and unprescribed, each day, sometimes every hour. He had trouble fighting off ordinary infections and suffered recurrent fevers that raged as high as 106 degrees. As candidate and President, Kennedy concealed his low energy level, radiating health and good humor, though he usually spent more than half of most days in bed. He retired early most nights, read in bed until 9:00 A.M. or so each morning, and napped an hour each afternoon.

Besides all that, Kennedy had persistent venereal disease, a very uncertain stomach that restricted him to a bland diet all his life, some deafness in his right ear, and a baffling range of allergies that sometimes laid him out. Joining the Navy, he had lied about the fevers and his debilitating back problems, and had somehow managed to get in without a physical examination. In politics, the spinal problems he had suffered since childhood became "old football injuries" or "war injuries," and the fierce fevers he had suffered all his life became "malaria from the war." *

Kennedy's health had come up during the campaign as an issue only once. Lyndon Johnson, then an opponent for the Democratic nomination, had repeated rumors that were circulating but not published. Pierre Salinger had come to Kennedy to ask what he should say if

---

* Kennedy had one great stroke of medical luck. In 1939, it was discovered that cortisone could maintain Addisonians in relatively normal lives. "That young American friend of yours, he hasn't got a year to live," Sir Daniel Davis, a prominent British physician, told Pamela Churchill, Winston's daughter-in-law, after she brought Congressman Kennedy to the London Clinic on September 21, 1947. Addison's disease, pronounced Dr. Davis, who did not know about the new treatment discovered in 1939, prolonging the lives of Addisonians. In 1949 the Mayo Clinic discovered that cortisone, taken daily by injection or orally, allowed Addisonians to live almost normal lives. Pellets of a drug called DOCA (desoxycorticosterone acetate) could be implanted into the thigh or back to release the hormones necessary to sustain life for three months at a time—and then could be replaced.

There were several common side effects associated with Addison's disease and its treatment. Addisonians often took on skin coloration that looked like a permanent tan, and their hair stayed thick and brown for life. Their faces tended to puff up after taking the cortisone. And they suffered reduced resistance to infection. An enhanced sense of confidence and personal power was common, and many cortisone users noticed increased sexual desire.

the press began raising questions. "Tell them I don't have Addison's disease."

"They're saying you take cortisone," Salinger said.

"Well, I used to take cortisone, but I don't take it anymore."

So, the new President was an Addisonian, a liar—and a brave stoic, too. His friend Paul Fay had once watched Kennedy getting ready to inject himself in the thigh, as he did most days, and said: "Jack, the way you take that jab, it looks like it doesn't even hurt."

Kennedy lunged over and jabbed the needle into Fay's thigh. His friend screamed in pain.

"It feels the same way to me," Kennedy said.

Chapter 3

JANUARY 28, 1961

One of the President's first official visitors at the White House was Paul-Henri Spaak, the retiring Secretary-General of NATO, who came to receive the Medal of Freedom. Kennedy was too impatient to rehearse things like that. He quickly read the proclamation, presented the medal, circled the Oval Office shaking hands with various ambassadors and stepped out the door. He had no idea where he was, saw another door, and went in—to the bathroom. He stayed there in solitary dignity until Spaak and the others left his office.

But he was where he wanted to be, where only thirty-three men had been before.* Just over a year earlier, when he had first announced his candidacy, he had called the job "the vital center"—the center of the center of the action. "In the very thick of the fight," was where a president must be, he said that day, "... prepared to exercise the fullest powers of his office—all that are specified and some that are not." Now he was there, and like other modern presidents beginning with Franklin D. Roosevelt during World War II, he began his day in the office with intelligence briefings.

"Look, I've only got a half hour today. Do I have to read it all?" he asked one of his assistants, Walt Whitman Rostow, who was handing

---

* Kennedy was the thirty-fifth President, but only the thirty-fourth man to hold the office, because Grover Cleveland's two separate terms are considered separate presidencies, the twenty-second and twenty-fourth.

him a thick folder across his desk as he began his eighth day in the job.

"Yes, I think so," replied Rostow, a Yale economics professor serving under former Harvard dean McGeorge Bundy at the National Security Council, or what was left of the Council. Kennedy had already begun breaking up the White House bureaucracies that Eisenhower had constructed to screen the stacks of diplomatic, military, and intelligence papers produced by the government, and then to distribute the President's reactions and orders back into the larger bureaucracies that are the operating arms of the executive branch of the United States government. Kennedy wanted to see everything himself. One of his first calls from the Oval Office was to the CIA director, Allen Dulles. He was interested, he told him, in more than the agency analyses that had satisfied Eisenhower. He wanted the most important raw intelligence data sent to Bundy and Rostow every morning. Ike approved decisions; Kennedy intended to make them.

That morning, January 28, Rostow handed the President some unchecked and unedited data, a twenty-five-page report entitled "Lansdale's Trip, January 1961." The trip had been to Vietnam, and the report had been passed from the CIA and Eisenhower's Secretary of Defense to McNamara, and on to the White House.

"This is going to be the worst one yet," Kennedy said, after skimming the pages. He stopped at the recommendation: "The U.S. should recognize that Vietnam is in critical condition and should treat it as a combat area of the Cold War, as an area requiring emergency treatment."

"I'll tell you something," he said, looking up at Rostow. "Eisenhower never mentioned the word Vietnam to me." *

"Get to work on this, Walt. And . . ." He asked Rostow to get him some books on guerrilla warfare.

"Lansdale" was Brigadier General Edward Geary Lansdale, United States Air Force. No one was exactly sure how he had got that rank. He was a CIA operative, the real-life model for a central character in one of the most popular books of the day, a novel called *The Ugly American*. It had been on the best-seller lists during the presidential campaign, selling 5 million copies, more than a few of them bought by Senator John F. Kennedy, one of six prominent Americans who had signed a full-page advertisement in *The New York Times* announcing that they had sent copies to all U.S. senators.

---

* In fact, Eisenhower had mentioned Vietnam to Kennedy a couple of times in their meeting on January 19, the day before the inaugural. But the emphasis then was on Laos.

The book, written by Eugene Burdick, a political science professor, and William Lederer, a captain in the U.S. Navy, was advertised as "fiction based on fact." It was a series of simple stories, most of them about clumsy and arrogant Americans being outwitted by Communists of all nationalities in the battle for the hearts and minds of the people of a country in Southeast Asia called Sarkhan—a fictionalized Vietnam. There were a couple of American heroes. One was the man in the title, an engineer named Homer Atkins who showed peasants how to make irrigation pumps using local materials. Another was Colonel Edwin Barnum Hillandale, who won over natives, playing "ragtime" harmonica in village squares.

General Lansdale was the model for Colonel Hillandale. In the mid-1950s, he had been the CIA station chief in Saigon, the capital of South Vietnam, and a friend and adviser to the country's president, Ngo Dinh Diem. Before that he had been an adviser and friend to Ramón Magsaysay, defense minister and then president of the Philippines. The two had worked together to beat back the Communist-led Huk insurgency in those islands. Lansdale was a legend, either the United States' premier agent in Asia, or a shifty, swaggering pain-in-the-ass with a knack for making friends and getting his way in faraway and chaotic places. Graham Greene, the British novelist, also modeled a character on Lansdale in his 1956 novel *The Quiet American*—an American agent in Saigon named Pyle, described this way by a British correspondent: "I never knew a man who had better motives for all the trouble he caused. . . ."

"The Ugly American" was a symbol of U.S. frustration in trying to influence the boundaries and politics of the new countries carved out of the old colonies around the world. In the book, Sarkhanese regularly say things like this to Americans: "The side with the most brains and power wins. That's not your side anymore. . . . You haven't got the power or the will or anything." President Eisenhower had read the novel, too, and a story got out that as a result he had ordered a top-to-bottom review of American foreign aid programs. In 1959, twenty-one pieces of legislation introduced in the Congress cited *The Ugly American*.

"The picture as we saw it. . . ," Burdick and Lederer wrote in a non-fictional epilogue, "is of an Asia where we stand relatively mute, locked in the cities, misunderstanding the temper and the needs of the Asians. We saw America spending vast sums where Russia expends far less and achieves far more. We have been losing—not only in Asia but everywhere."

The Lansdale report Kennedy read on January 28 made some of the same points; but its most forceful arguments related to the general's old friend President Diem, whose country had been created by an international conference in Geneva in 1954, the year the French colonial army was defeated by Vietnamese revolutionaries led by a Communist from the north of the country, Ho Chi Minh. The old French colony had been divided into two countries, North Vietnam, with Ho as leader, and South Vietnam, which was largely financed by the U.S. government. The United States, in fact, had been paying the bills for the French colonial army during its war against Ho's Communists.

"We must support Diem until another strong executive can replace him legally," Lansdale had written after returning to Washington two days before Kennedy's inaugural. "President Diem feels that Americans have attacked him almost as viciously as the Communists, and has withdrawn into a shell. . . . If the next American official to talk to President Diem would have the good sense to see him as a human being who has been through a lot of hell for years—and not as an opponent to be beaten to his knees—we would start regaining our influence with him in a healthy way."

The Vietnamese leader was a devout Roman Catholic who had lived for years at a seminary in New Jersey, in voluntary exile to protest French rule of his country. Senator Kennedy, along with Francis Cardinal Spellman of New York and Senator Mike Mansfield of Montana, had been among the prominent American Catholics who had persuaded Eisenhower's Secretary of State, John Foster Dulles, to support Diem as the first leader of the new South Vietnam.

From that beginning, Diem had been called an American puppet. But he was no puppet—which was the U.S. government's problem in South Vietnam. The man would not take orders. The Americans wanted to use Diem to block communism in Southeast Asia, but it became more and more obvious, particularly after Diem won election as president in 1955, that he saw the Americans as rich and necessary friends with their own agenda. The first U.S. representative to the new country, General J. Lawton Collins, had been in Saigon less than a month when he cabled the State Department: "Diem still presents our chief problem. . . . Time may be approaching rapidly when some thought should be given to possible alternatives to Diem."

Six years later, that was the situation facing Kennedy as he read Lansdale's report. American diplomats and soldiers did not have enough leverage to force Diem to do anything because the United States was in Vietnam only by an invitation that Diem could withdraw at any time.

Kennedy picked up the phone as he finished the report and called McNamara, telling him to find Lansdale. It was not hard. The general, it turned out, was on McNamara's staff, far down, with the title "Liaison Officer"—between Defense and the CIA.

"Get down here right away!" said McNamara, when he found the general at home in Virginia at nine o'clock that Saturday morning. Before Lansdale was out the door, the phone was ringing again and this time it was the President. Kennedy told Lansdale that he loved his account of the anti-Communist heroics of a Catholic priest named Nguyen Loc Hoa who had fled to Vietnam from Communist China. Father Hoa, who had been a lieutenant colonel in Chiang Kai-shek's Nationalist Chinese army, had organized several hundred followers in a fortified village called Binh Hung to fight the Viet Cong, the Communist guerrillas. Kennedy had an idea for Lansdale: "We should get this into the *Saturday Evening Post.*"

Lansdale thought it might be someone imitating Kennedy's Boston accent. But he checked with a friend in McNamara's office, and within an hour he was at the White House. Two minutes later, he was brought to the Cabinet Room. The President smiled and nodded, pointing him to a chair, as others in the room whispered to each other, "Who's that?" Allen Dulles, Lansdale's boss, was standing in front of a map of Cuba with a pointer.

Kennedy was amused by the obvious discomfort around the Cabinet table. When Dulles finished talking about guerrilla landings on Cuban shores, the President turned to Lansdale: "I want to thank you for giving me a sense of the danger and urgency of the problem in Vietnam. Did Mr. Rusk tell you I'd like you to go over to Vietnam as our ambassador?"

Mr. Rusk certainly had not, and he was appalled at the idea of the CIA's best known agent in Asia representing the State Department. Dulles and McNamara looked as if they felt the same way. But this was Kennedy's style: The right man is the best policy—find the right man for the right spot.

Kennedy, however, did not give an actual order then and there. He turned to J. Graham Parsons, Assistant Secretary of State for the Far East, to summarize a report entitled "Basic Counterinsurgency Plan for Viet-Nam," a series of recommendations calling for $42 million in new aid to Diem and the Army of the Republic of South Vietnam (ARVN). The plan was the last presidential paper produced on Vietnam under Eisenhower, who had sent several hundred U.S. military advisers into the country.

"Beginning in December 1959 and continuing to the present, there has been a mounting increase throughout South Viet-Nam of Viet Cong terrorist activities and guerrilla warfare," the report began.

This activity has included armed propaganda and leaflet distribution; taxing of the population for food, money, and medicines; kidnapping and murder of village and hamlet officials, road and canal ambushes; and armed attacks. . . . Politically, discontent with the Diem Government has been prevalent for some time among intellectuals and elite circles and has been rising among the peasantry. . . . Criticism of these elements focuses on Ngo family rule, especially the roles of the President's brother, Ngo Dinh Nhu, and Madame Nhu.

If the GVN [Government of South Vietnam] does not take immediate and extraordinary action to regain popular support and to correct the organizational and procedural weaknesses . . . the Viet Cong can cause the overthrow of the present GVN government in the months to come.

The paper concluded: "Mission: Defeat Communist insurgency efforts in SVN."

The President quickly approved the Basic Counterinsurgency Plan, providing the $42 million, most of it for soldiers' pay and weapons, increasing the size of the ARVN by 20,000 men and the size of the paramilitary Civil Guard by 32,000 men. Next to $660,000 set aside for "Psychological Operations," Kennedy scribbled, "Why so little?"

Then Kennedy told Dulles he wanted guerrilla operations organized inside North Vietnam. Finally, he asked Lansdale to describe his recent conversations with Diem. The general said that the Vietnamese president thought U.S. plans were too elaborate, that he had only three men in his entire government with the executive ability to carry out an order without coming back to him. More ominously, he said, Diem believed that some American diplomats were very close to the Vietnamese paratroopers who had tried to assassinate him on November 11, 1960. Then Lansdale made the kind of judgment call for which he was famous, the kind of remark that guaranteed that Rusk and the State Department would do everything they could to keep this man out of Saigon: "The people in our Embassy are defeatist. . . ."

"We must change our course in these areas," said the President as he stood up. "We must be better off there in three months than we are now."

Back at the State Department, Rusk asked Parsons what he knew about Lansdale. Notes on the conversation read: "Lansdale = Col. Hillandale. Able performance in Manila. Close to Diem. Lone wolf and operator. Tagged as operator. Flamboyant. . . . Not a team player."

His suspicions confirmed, Rusk felt free to try to block the appointment. The President, after all, had not specifically ordered him to send Lansdale to Saigon. Power unused was usually power lost, even for a President.

Back home in Virginia, Lansdale was writing a long letter to his friend Diem, exaggerating just a bit:

> President Kennedy had me in for a long talk. . . . He was warmly interested and asked many questions. I am sure that you can count on him as an understanding friend and that you will be hearing further about this. . . . However, there will be some here who will point out that much of the danger of your present situation comes about from your own actions. They say that you try to do too many things yourself, that you refuse to give real responsibility to others and keep interfering with what they do, that you feel you are infallible personally. . . .

"They" were Rusk and more than a few of his deputies at the State Department, and they were saying a few things about Lansdale, too. The Secretary derailed the appointment by persuading the President that the United States needed a fresh look at Diem and his government. Instead of Lansdale, he recommended Frederick Nolting, the deputy chief of the U.S. Mission to NATO in Paris. Kennedy agreed. Rusk called Nolting in and told him that the President wanted him to find out what kind of man Diem really was. He wanted him to get close to the South Vietnamese president and to report back to him and the President on whether or not Diem was the right man, the man the United States should go with. Or, should they find someone else?

The first time Kennedy met with Nolting and other new American ambassadors, he reached into his pocket, pulled out a wrinkled piece of newsprint, and began reading to them: "I've got a clipping here from *The New York Times* and it says, 'The American embassy here is not terribly well regarded. They all seem to stay in the embassy and not get out into the countryside or to meet all types of people.' . . . Now I hope that no such thing is going to be written about any one of you men here, present today. Remember you're ambassador to the country, to the whole country . . . don't get desk-bound."

He did not want to be desk-bound himself. On his second Friday night as President, Kennedy rounded up a couple of friends to go to a theater near the White House for the eight o'clock showing of a movie he wanted to see, *Spartacus*. When it ended and the lights came up, he saw that one of the people in front of him was Secretary of Agriculture Orville Freeman. He tapped him on the shoulder and said: "Haven't the leaders of the New Frontier got anything better to do with their time than spend it going to the movies?"

"I'll walk you back to the Army-Navy Club," Kennedy said a couple of nights later to Red Fay, after they had had a quick dinner at the

White House. They walked along, Kennedy swinging a cane he was using for his back, Secret Service agents trying to look inconspicuous as they maneuvered to put themselves between the President and other strollers on 16th Street.

"If that fellow over there suddenly pulled a gun, what would you do to safeguard the life of the beloved President?" Kennedy asked Fay.

"Dive for cover," Fay said. Then he asked, "Do you worry about the possibility?"

"I guess there is always the possibility, but that is what the Secret Service is for." But he had already begun scheming to lose his protectors, using back doorways, scaling fences, and lying on the floor of cars to shake them when he wanted to be alone. There were often women involved in these hide-and-seek games with the Secret Service and others, but not always. John Kennedy could not stand being cornered.

Even now that he was President, he was still determined not to be trapped by procedures. He liked a certain disorder around him, it kept his people off balance, made them try a little harder. He dismantled Eisenhower's military-style national security bureaucracy, beginning with the Operations Coordinating Board, a small unit responsible for systematically channeling foreign policy information to and from the President. In an executive order Kennedy said, "We plan to continue its work by maintaining direct communication with the responsible agencies, so that everyone will know what I have decided, while I in turn keep fully informed of the actions taken to carry out decisions." His use of the National Security Council itself was casual enough that when General Earle Wheeler, the chief staff officer of the Joint Chiefs of Staff, was handed National Security Action Memorandum 22—the twenty-second formal national security order approved by the President —he realized he had never seen numbers 5 to 21. "The lines of control have been cut," Wheeler said to his staff. "But no other lines have been established."

That was the Kennedy way. Lines of power, the President said, were supposed to be like the spokes of a wheel, all coming from him, all going to him. He preferred hallway meetings and telephone calls to desk officers in the State Department or to startled professors and reporters. Anyone who had just been to countries in crisis, or had written something that had interested him, might be woken by a Boston-accented voice saying: "This is Jack Kennedy, can you tell me . . ." Some of them hung up on him, thinking it was a joke.

"Why have there been no National Security Council meetings?" Kennedy was asked in his first television interview from the Oval Office.

"These general meetings are a waste of time," he replied. "Formal meetings of the NSC are not as effective, and it is much more difficult to decide matters involving high national security if there is a wider group present." He said that he preferred one-on-one meetings or seeing small groups of people. In fact, the best way for Cabinet members to see their boss was to hang around his secretary's office, catching him when he popped out of his office looking for newspapers.

Short conversations and long hours substituted for organization. Kennedy was not interested in being told what he already knew, and he did not like rehearsals, preferring to be briefed as he was walking or riding to the next event. And boredom was the worst sin. Sometimes its name was Adlai Stevenson or Chester Bowles, the well-meaning, long-winded dons of American liberalism.

Bowles, a former congressman and governor of Connecticut, had been appointed Undersecretary of State as a reward for being the first liberal to endorse Senator Kennedy in 1960. That was important then, because many liberals distrusted Kennedy and despised his father, the former chairman of the Securities and Exchange Commission and Ambassador to England, whom they considered among other things to be anti-Semitic. But Bowles, like Harris Wofford and sometimes Arthur Schlesinger, Jr., just drove Kennedy nuts. Bowles walked out of the Oval Office one day the first week, passing John Kenneth Galbraith, the economist, who was nothing if not wonderful company. "Come on in here, Ken," said Kennedy, adding when the door closed, "Chet was just telling me there are four revolutions going on in the world. The first one was the revolution of rising expectations. I lost track of the three others. Do you know what they are?"

John Kennedy was known as a quick study—there were stories about his "speed-reading" up to fifteen hundred words per minute—which was a positive way to describe a short attention span. Except for economists, advisers rarely had to explain things twice to Kennedy. His first question was almost always his best. He could suck people dry in minutes, without a second thought. He had picked up Harris Wofford on a street in Georgetown for the short ride up to Capitol Hill during the presidential campaign and said: "Tell me the ten things I have to know about this goddamned civil rights mess."

"We're not looking for business" was the last thing Eisenhower's liaison, General Persons, had told Kennedy. The new White House, though, had opened for business on its first day. And the first order of business was unambiguous. This was how the candidate had put it during the campaign: "I have heard all the excuses, but I believe not in an America that is first 'but,' first 'if,' first 'when,' but first, period. . . .

The first vehicle in space was called Sputnik, not Vanguard. The first passengers to return safely from outer space were named Strelka and Belka, not Rover or Fido. . . . I want to be known as the President at the end of four years, as one who not only held back the Communist tide but who also advanced the cause of freedom and rebuilt American prestige."

Part of that business was business itself. In the first week, Fred Dutton, the secretary to the Cabinet, brought in a memo to the President from the Secretary of Labor: "Arthur Goldberg suggests that an incidental item which you may want is the fact that in the fourth quarter of 1960 the Soviet Union came much too close to the level of U.S. in steel production—18.6 million net tons to 18.87 million net tons." The day was coming when they would surpass the United States. One set of government growth projections, based on CIA estimates, indicated that the gross national product of the Soviet Union would be triple the U.S. GNP by the year 2000.

Kennedy had come to office in the great tradition of American presidents, more or less blissfully ignorant of economics. Part of his official biography presented him as a graduate of the London School of Economics, a student of the great Marxist scholar Harold Laski; but that was not true. He had enrolled there in 1935, before beginning college, but never attended because his health had broken down again that year.

"Whatever happened to that guy we hired to teach us economics?" Charlie Bartlett, a newspaper columnist who was a friend from prep school days, had asked Kennedy one day just after the election. Several years before, the two of them, the young congressman and the young correspondent from the *Chattanooga Times,* had spent Tuesday nights in a small private seminar with a professor from American University.

"I don't know," answered Kennedy. "I imagine he jumped out of the window when he heard I was elected."

Senator Kennedy was only comfortable with economics as politics, working the grain of American obsession with communism. In that, he was no different from the politicians of Eisenhower's generation, using the fear that the Russians were coming. It was the easy way, sometimes the only way, to persuade Americans to pay for raising the educational level of the nation or building an interstate highway system. Eisenhower had slipped the magic word "Defense" into the titles of new laws that greatly expanded the role of the federal government during the 1950s: the National Defense Education Loan Act and the National Defense Highway Act.

Six days into the Kennedy presidency, Walter Heller, the chairman of his Council of Economic Advisers, gave a detailed background briefing to economic reporters on the new administration's plans to deal with the continuing recession that had begun early in 1960, giving them precise figures and goals worked out by the Kennedy administration. Those numbers began to appear in newspapers around the country, which is where the President saw some of them for the first time.

"Never do that again," he told Heller, the politician lecturing the professor. "Forget those numbers. Numbers can come back to haunt you. Words can always be explained away."

During those first days in office Kennedy also discovered that the numbers in Congress did not add up for him. He was having breakfast with Sam Rayburn, the Speaker of the House, who told him: "Mr. President, I don't believe we have the votes to expand the Rules Committee."

"Larry," said the President, turning to Lawrence O'Brien, his congressional liaison. "What is this? We can't lose this one, Larry. The ball game is over if we do."

There were eight Democrats and four Republicans on Rules, the committee that controlled the schedule of the House, which meant total control over the release of proposed legislation for debate by the full House. The President had the power to command the national agenda by summoning press and television coverage, but Rayburn was telling him that he did not have the power to make the Congress even consider his legislative proposals. He could be blocked by four Republicans and two senior Southern Democrats, Howard Smith of Virginia, the chairman of Rules, and William Colmer of Mississippi. When those two voted with the Republicans, producing a 6–6 tie, liberal legislation died right there.

Kennedy had taken for granted Rayburn's power to change that by calling a vote of the entire House of 263 Democrats and 174 Republicans to expand Rules from 12 to 15 members. Then Rayburn, who came to the House in 1913 and had been Speaker for sixteen years, could appoint two new Democrats, younger and more liberal, producing 8–7 votes that would get the Kennedy legislation to the floor. But now, the Speaker was advising the President that the old coalition between Republicans and Southern Democrats was still the real majority party in the House. As a matter of fact, they were even stronger than before because even many of the moderate Democratic congressmen owed nothing to a president of the majority party—national registration was 47 percent Democratic, 30 percent Republican—who won by just one-tenth of 1 percent. Most of the Democrats in Congress had been hurt rather than helped by having Kennedy at the top of the party's ticket.

Kennedy sent O'Brien back to the House to find out what had to be done to get a majority of the 435 members. Part of the price to get a few conservative Democratic and moderate Republican votes, O'Brien reported when he came back, was a balanced budget pledge. Kennedy did it immediately, issuing a statement: "A new administration must of necessity build upon the spending and revenue estimates already submitted. Within that framework, barring the development of national defense needs or a worsening economy, it is my current intention to advocate a program of expenditures, including revenues from a stimulation of the economy, which will not of and by themselves unbalance the earlier budget."

Heller and Kennedy's other economic advisers, particularly Paul Samuelson of the Massachusetts Institute of Technology, were devastated. They were getting ready to urge the President to cut taxes in order to stimulate the economy, still in mild recession. But Kennedy was more concerned with the Rules vote and two other political imperatives. He could not reduce taxes after an inaugural that called for bearing any burden; and he was not going to be seen as a big spender compared with Eisenhower, who genuinely believed that government was best that not only governed least but spent least.

So, as Kennedy was getting an economics education from them, the professors were getting a political education from him. Two days later, on January 29, Heller gave an on-the-record press briefing on anti-recession measures. One frustrated reporter had finally asked: "How can we judge a stimulating effect without knowing the cost?"

"How did you answer that?" Kennedy asked Heller.

"Fast talk and rapid gestures," Heller said.

"Good job," said the President.

On his eleventh day in office, January 30, Kennedy delivered his first State of the Union Address to enthusiastically applauding members of Congress packed into the House of Representatives. It was a wartime speech without a war, composed in the stirring and urgent rhythms of Churchill and Lincoln:

"I speak today in an hour of national peril and national opportunity. . . . We shall have to test anew whether a nation organized and governed such as ours can endure. . . ."

He said the economy was in trouble, he hinted that the Russians were coming, and he deliberately confused the question of the missile gap with fudge words. "It has been publicly acknowledged for several years that this nation has not led the world in missile strength. . . .

"Each day we draw nearer the hour of maximum danger, as weapons spread and hostile forces grow stronger . . . the tide of events has been running out and time has not been our friend. . . . It is one of the ironies of our time that the techniques of a harsh and repressive system should be able to instill discipline and ardor in its servants—while the blessings of liberty have too often stood for privilege, materialism and a life of ease.

"We cannot escape our dangers—neither must we let them drive us into panic or narrow isolation. . . . There will be further setbacks before the tide is turned. But turn it must. The hopes of mankind rest upon us."

The next day, January 31, in the same great room, Sam Rayburn stepped down briefly as Speaker to stand on the floor like any other member to plead the President's case on expanding the Rules Committee. He ended: "Let us move this program." He won, and the President won, by a vote of 217 to 212.

Chapter 4

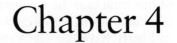

FEBRUARY 10, 1961

"**K**ENNEDY DEFENSE STUDY FINDS NO EVIDENCE OF A 'MISSILE GAP' " read a two-column headline on the front page of *The New York Times* on February 6, 1961.

"What the hell is this?" Kennedy said, calling Secretary of Defense McNamara from his bedroom.

"Well, Mr. President. . . . " The Secretary was not talking as fast as usual.

McNamara told Kennedy that he had invited some Pentagon correspondents to his office for drinks at six o'clock the evening before. It was his first "backgrounder," and he had answered questions on the customary condition that the reporters present would not identify him as the source. "NFA—Not for Attribution" was the term of art in Washington. The Secretary rather casually had told the reporters that there was really no difference in the number of operational Soviet and American nuclear missiles. And if there was a gap, the United States was ahead.

That, of course, was the opposite of what Kennedy had said during the campaign. "We are facing a gap on which we are gambling with our survival," was one of his alarming campaign lines. He used it even after classified briefings by General Earle Wheeler, who told him that the United States was not behind any country in nuclear delivery capability. There was no missile gap. But the argument was already central to the campaign and to his entire political career, and closing that gap was the highest priority of his campaign rhetoric.

"The bottom line on the missile gap," McNamara told the angry President on the morning of February 6, was that the United States could absorb a full-scale Soviet attack—intercontinental missiles, bombers, and submarine-launched missiles—and after all that, the United States would still have enough nuclear capacity remaining to destroy every city in the Soviet Union, kill 100 million Soviets, and demolish 80 percent of Soviet industrial capacity.*

Since the election, Kennedy had never really asserted that there was any kind of a missile gap. He talked around the subject when he had to, as he had done in his State of the Union Address. But on the day after McNamara's briefing, the President sent out his press secretary, Pierre Salinger, to deny McNamara's clumsy truth-telling: "These stories are incorrect. Absolutely wrong. No such studies have been completed and no such finding has been made. . . ."

At his televised press conference the next morning, February 8, the third of his term, Kennedy said: "It would be premature to reach a judgment as to whether there is a gap or not a gap." Then, back in the office, he dictated a memo to his national security adviser, McGeorge Bundy: "Could you let me know what progress has been made on the history of the missile gap controversy . . . I would like to know its genesis: what previous government officials put forth their views and how we came to the judgment that there was a missile gap."

One of the appointments that was delayed that morning, as the President worked out a storyline to cover McNamara's indiscretion, was with Father Theodore Hesburgh, the president of the University of Notre Dame. Hesburgh had been appointed by Eisenhower to the new U.S. Civil Rights Commission and Kennedy asked him to stay on. Hesburgh, who did not particularly like Kennedy, guessed that the reason he was being kept around was to avoid any civil rights debate, even the

---

* The "missile gap" dialogue was partly based on the assumption that the Soviet Union had greater capability to manufacture new missiles than the United States and would leave the United States trying to catch up during the early 1960s; but, in fact, the Soviets never tried to speed up missile production and may not have been capable of doing so. Spy satellites later in the Kennedy administration revealed that CIA estimates of Soviet strength were indeed much too high and that in 1960 the Soviets may have had only three ICBMs. U.S. studies in 1963 indicated that actual Soviet ICBM strength in 1961 was 3.5 percent of official U.S. estimates.

McNamara had used CIA numbers, which tended to overestimate Soviet strength. These were the estimates of February 1961: The Soviets had thirty-five operational intercontinental ballistic missiles (ICBMs) and two hundred long-range bombers, most of which had neither the range nor equipment to get close to the United States; the United States had sixteen Atlas ICBMs, sixty Thor medium-range missiles in Great Britain, thirty-two Polaris missiles on nuclear submarines, and six hundred long-range bombers which could be refueled in the air and reach any target in the Soviet Union. And the United States was in the process of placing thirty Jupiter medium-range nuclear missiles in Italy and fifteen Jupiters in Turkey, less than one hundred miles from the Soviet border.

kind that might be triggered by speculation over who would get his job. When they met, Kennedy was quick, charming, and informed, at least statistically. He corrected Hesburgh on the number of Negroes in state university graduate schools in the South. Hesburgh said there were none; Kennedy replied that he knew of one in a law school.

"There are things here that are just not right," Hesburgh said, beginning with another statistic: the number of Negroes in the Alabama National Guard was zero.

"Look, Father," Kennedy said, surprising Hesburgh with his candor, "I may have to send the Alabama National Guard to Berlin tomorrow and I don't want to have to do it in the middle of a revolution at home."

Kennedy drew people to him by being direct, speaking candidly in a way older politicians rarely did. No mean politician himself, the priest understood immediately not only that Kennedy thought civil rights was peripheral but that he intended to keep it that way if he could, at least until after he was up for reelection in 1964.

In fact, Kennedy was most concerned about domestic racial troubles as a foreign policy problem. He didn't want to see the problems give the country a bad name abroad. Before his meeting with Hesburgh, the State Department's new chief of protocol, Angier Biddle Duke, had reported to the President that some progress was being made among restaurant owners along Route 40 in Maryland, the road from New York City south to Washington. The State Department was trying to persuade those owners to end their practice of refusing service to dark-skinned diplomats or even use of a bathroom as they traveled between the United Nations and the capital.

"Can't you just tell the Africans not to drive on Route 40?" Kennedy asked. "Tell the ambassadors I wouldn't think of driving from New York to Washington." The President, of course, flew—above it all.

But Hesburgh pressed Kennedy. He wanted some show of commitment. There had been no White House liaison to the Civil Rights Commission since 1958, and Hesburgh asked for one, a name he could use, a number he could call.

"I already have a special assistant who's working on that full time."

"Who?"

"Harris Wofford. "

"Really?" said Hesburgh. He had seen Wofford, who was a friend and a former assistant, that morning, and Wofford had said nothing like that.

A few minutes after Hesburgh left, Wofford got a call telling him to get to the White House as soon as possible. He was greeted there by a man he didn't know who was holding a Bible.

"You Wofford?" asked the man, whose name was William Hopkins. "Raise your right hand, please."

"What for?"

"I'm supposed to swear you in."

"For what?"

"I don't know," said Hopkins. "I just got word from the President to come up and swear you in this minute as a Special Assistant."

"But I haven't seen the President. I don't know what this is all about."

"I don't know about you," Hopkins said, "but I take my orders from the President. Raise your right hand, please."

Also at the February 8 news conference, the President had been asked about racial troubles in New Orleans. A reporter said: "Three months ago a Federal court in New Orleans ordered two public schools there desegregated. Since then, what is apparently an organized campaign of intimidation has kept most white children out of those schools and effectively frustrated the court order. During the campaign you spoke of using your moral authority as President in the civil rights field. Can you tell us what you plan to say or do to help the New Orleans families who evidently want to obey the Constitution but are afraid to do so?"

"I want to make sure that whatever I do or say does have some beneficial effect and, therefore, it is a matter which we are considering," Kennedy answered. ". . . It is my position that all students should be given the opportunity to attend public schools regardless of their race, and that is in accordance with the Constitution. It is in accordance, in my opinion, with the judgment of the people of the United States. So there is no question about that."

The reporter persisted: "But you do not have anything to say specifically about New Orleans today or about what has happened there—for example, last week the man who had tried to send his children to school and then in fear left town?"

"That is a matter which we are carefully considering," Kennedy tried again. "On the general question, there is no doubt in my view: students should be permitted to attend schools in accordance with court decisions. The broader question of course is, regardless of the court decisions, I believe strongly that every American should have an opportunity to have maximum development of his talents, under the most beneficial circumstances, and that is what the Constitution provides. . . .

"On the question specifically of what we can usefully do in New Orleans in order to provide a more harmonious acquiescence with the court decision, I would feel that we could perhaps most usefully wait until we have concluded our analysis of it."

Kennedy was not a bigot. In fact, like many of his generation, he thought prejudice was irrational, a waste of emotion and time. "I'll tell you something about that," he said one day to a young White House aide named Daniel Patrick Moynihan. "I can't get used to Harry Truman talking all the time about 'the niggers.' " During his campaign, Kennedy had moved his entourage out of a hotel in Paducah, Kentucky, when the manager had refused a room to a Negro reporter, Simeon Booker of *Jet* magazine.

For Kennedy, civil rights, Negro demands, were just politics, a volatile issue to be defused. Careless days growing up in England, the effortless C's of a young gentleman at Harvard, serving in a Navy without Negroes and then going to Congress before he was thirty years old, had left him with no particular feelings and great voids of knowledge about the day-to-day lives and cares and prejudices of his fellow Americans. Moynihan had been a naval officer, too, but he had grown up on the poorer, meaner kind of Irish streets of the West Side of Manhattan in a neighborhood called Hell's Kitchen. He had walked out of Kennedy's office thinking that it was too bad the new President had not run a primary campaign in a state with large numbers of Negro voters. Kennedy usually knew what he had to know, but the only Negro he spent time with was his valet for the past fourteen years, George Thomas. The man had literally been a gift from Arthur Krock, who had repaid past favors from Joe Kennedy by sending Thomas over to take care of Congressman Jack Kennedy. It was the kind of thing one did for a young prince who did not know about such things as going to the cleaners or getting shoes resoled.

Kennedy had won well over 70 percent of the Negro vote, almost double what Stevenson had gotten against Eisenhower in 1956. He had won some of that vote, which may have won the election for him, with a single telephone call to the wife of the Reverend Martin Luther King, Jr., on October 20, 1960. Harris Wofford and Sargent Shriver, who was married to one of Kennedy's sisters, had persuaded him to do it after Dr. King, the best known of the Negro rights leaders, had been sentenced to four months of "hard labor" in a Georgia jail for a traffic violation.

"Hard labor" for a Negro rabble-rouser in segregated Georgia sounded like death to the preacher's wife, Coretta King, who had called Wofford for help. Kennedy had picked up a telephone—saying, "What the hell? It's the decent thing to do." He told Mrs. King that he was thinking of them and would like to help. He hung up and began talking about something else.

Now, four months later, after three weeks in the White House, Kennedy said to Wofford, with a noticeable lack of enthusiasm: "Well, I guess I have to start meeting with the civil rights people." It was political duty, a diversion from the priority business of promoting and winning freedom around the world. "Bring them in."

On February 10, three days after his meeting with Hesburgh, Kennedy met with some of the men he called the "Honkers," his private term for the most liberal Democrats, particularly those from New York City and Cambridge, Massachusetts. Here they were—the officers of Americans for Democratic Action (ADA), the organizational standardbearers of the liberalism of Eleanor Roosevelt and Stevenson. ADA was determined and proud to lobby and speak for government planning and for the rights of Negro Americans, though the delegation was as white as Father Hesburgh.

Robert Nathan, an economist, spoke first, arguing that Kennedy had to break the recession the country was in with a heavy dose of deficit spending. The President didn't flinch openly when Nathan said $50 billion in debt added to the $81 billion federal budget should do the job of providing jobs for all Americans.

"Well, there's a problem with that," Kennedy said, leaning back, knowing that only a Harvard economist could propose a 60 percent increase in the federal budget with an earnest face. "With the seven percent unemployment we have now, ninety-three percent of the people in the country are employed. That other seven percent isn't going to get enough political support to do it. I don't believe that, right or wrong, there's any possibility of doing the kind of all-out economic operation that you want."

"Bob, I want you to keep this up," he said pleasantly to Nathan. "It's very helpful now for you to be pushing me this way."

Everyone smiled, and Joseph Rauh, the general counsel of the United Auto Workers, and a founder of ADA, took the moment.

"Well, Mr. President, I hope the spirit with which you have treated Bob's pressure from the left, on the issue for which he speaks for the ADA, will go equally for the issue on which I speak for the ADA—civil rights."

"Absolutely not," Kennedy said, annoyed. Rauh was shocked by the sudden hardening of the President's face. "It's a totally different thing. Your criticism on civil rights is quite wrong."

"Oh, shit," Rauh thought, as Kennedy began to list Negroes in the administration and said that his brother, the Attorney General, was preparing a number of voting rights suits in Southern states. "Oh, shit. Nothing is going to happen. How did we let this happen?"

Rauh was crushed. He did not speak again, trying instead to figure out Kennedy's anger. He concluded that he had made a mistake by challenging the President's morality, while Nathan had only argued about his judgment. He was still replaying the words in his head when he left, passing Senator Russell Long of Louisiana in the hallway.

But Senator Long was not there to talk about race relations in New Orleans or anyplace else; he had come to introduce the President to the Queen of the Mardi Gras, his own daughter Katherine. A photographer came in to preserve the moment. Photographs were political coin. Kennedy took photographs seriously, spending hours looking at himself on glossy paper before deciding which image the public might see. During the campaign, he had taken the time for three photo sessions with one of his few Negro campaign workers, a Milwaukee city councilwoman named Vel Phillips. He had wanted to make sure she looked dark enough.

Chapter 5

"The word 'politics.' I have no great liking for that," President Eisenhower once said. Reminded of that, President Kennedy responded: "I do have a great liking for the word 'politics.' It's the way a President gets things done."

And in his first weeks in power, workaday politics was often the first thing on Kennedy's mind when he came downstairs from the presidential apartments on the upper floors of the White House to his office in the long and low West Wing. His first stop was usually the desk of his secretary, Evelyn Lincoln, where he dictated a short list of things-to-do, which she distributed, in turn, to his staff and Cabinet members, including items like this in February: "Remind me to call Bill Bates and thank him for his vote" . . . "Ask Larry O'Brien to speak to me about what progress they are making in hiring Gene Robinson, who Smathers is interested in" . . . "Ask Ralph Dungan to speak to me about what progress has been made on the Teno Roncallo appointment. If Teno isn't going to do it we should consider Joe De Gugliemo" . . . "I understand that Dean Acheson is interested in having his son appointed District Attorney of Washington. Will you ask Kenny O'Donnell to talk to Byron White. If it can be done and he is good I would like to do it. If it can't be done I would like to know about it" . . . "Landis: Senators Kefauver and Gore informed me that there have been five increases in rates in the Tennessee gas transmission without any action by the Federal Power Commission. Are they getting away with murder? If so, what can we do about it?"

Then, usually at 9:30 A.M. or so, Kennedy walked into the Oval Office for the first scheduled business of the day, his daily Cold War briefing. "Good morning. Is this one of ours or one of theirs?" he would say to whomever had collected and sifted through CIA reports and overnight cables from U.S. embassies around the world.

Most days that was national security adviser McGeorge Bundy or his deputy, Walt Rostow. There were rarely surprises. Almost all of the same information was in *The New York Times* or one of the half dozen other newspapers he had skimmed over breakfast in bed upstairs—or he might have picked it up in his early morning phone calls. That was the information—along with good gossip—that Kennedy valued most. He preferred the observations of people he knew over official government reports. And, most days, the news and gossip were more up to the minute. Rostow might be talking about a detailed plan to stop communism in Asia, but Kennedy might cut him off, saying, "What do you want me to do about it today?" If there was no quick answer, he was ready to move on.

His campaign biographer, Williams historian James MacGregor Burns, had noticed that impatience long before. When he tried to impress Kennedy with ponderings about deeper meanings, Kennedy lost interest, sometimes snapping: "What good are ideas, unless you make use of them?"

The first morning call on February 23, the day after Washington's Birthday holiday, was from Robert Kennedy. "You're not going to believe this," said the Attorney General. He read the President a note an FBI messenger had brought over from J. Edgar Hoover: "After observing your car in the Department garage, I would like to thank you for coming to work on February 22, a national holiday. The spirit you demonstrated—the spirit of Valley Forge and Monte Cassino—will, we hope, spread through the entire Department of Justice. Keep up the good work."

"He's frightening . . . rather a psycho," said Robert Kennedy privately of the FBI director, whose bureau was part of the Justice Department. John Kennedy knew exactly what kind of man Hoover was. The director was a friend of his father's, and he knew that Hoover had been keeping a file on him since he had been a twenty-five-year-old Navy officer assigned to the Pentagon in 1942. The file listed the women he had slept with, telling the father, among others, that one of his son's girlfriends was believed (incorrectly) to be a Nazi spy. Kennedy had reappointed Hoover because he considered him more dangerous as a vindictive opponent outside the government than an obsequious or vaguely threatening presence inside. The brothers thought they could control the FBI chief until there was a way to move him out and keep him quiet about the intelligence he had gathered over the years on them and thousands of other prominent Americans. That was something, too, that had to wait, probably until after the 1964 election.

The next call was from Red Fay, his buddy. Fay, along with his wife and four-year-old daughter, had been shaken up in a crash landing in New Jersey in the early morning hours. The Fays were on a Navy plane flying from New York to Washington for his swearing in as Undersecretary of the Navy—a gift from Kennedy, who liked having him around. "What were they doing on that Navy plane?" was the first question Kennedy asked.

"I cleared it with John Connally before I left," said Fay. Connally was the new Secretary of the Navy. "He granted me approval."

"Fortunately for John, when we lose a half-million-dollar plane, the Navy is just one plane shorter. But the President of the United States is minus one plane plus a hell of a lot of general public support because an Undersecretary of the Navy is flying around in a Navy plane with his wife and child."

Fay didn't know what to say.

"Well," said his friend the President. "I'm pleased no one was seriously hurt or killed. We'll hold your swearing in tomorrow instead of today."

That same day, Kennedy sent off a secret letter to Soviet Premier Khrushchev, who had been giving clear signals that he was open to a one-on-one meeting with the new President. One of those signals had been the release, on February 8, of two U.S. Air Force officers who had been detained since the crash of their plane, an RB-47 bomber, on Soviet territory in July of 1960. Despite the fact that he had campaigned against summit meetings, saying that raising hopes of accommodation weakened U.S. resolve in the twilight struggle, Kennedy wanted to meet Khrushchev. He was determined to convince him from the start that the new generation would not back down anyplace the United States deemed "vital" to national security—not Europe, not Cuba, not Southeast Asia. He wanted no misunderstandings about that. He noted the conciliatory signs, and wrote to the Soviet leader, using his title as Chairman of the Council of Deputies of the Soviet Union:

Dear Mr. Chairman:
   . . . I agree with your thought that if we could find a measure of cooperation on some of these current issues this, in itself, would be a significant contribution to the problem of insuring a peaceful and orderly world.
   I hope it will be possible, before too long, for us to meet personally for

an informal exchange of views in regard to some of these matters. . . .
You may be sure, Mr. Chairman, that I intend to do everything I can
toward developing a more harmonious relationship between our two
countries.

The letter was taken to Moscow and delivered to Khrushchev by
Llewellyn Thompson, the U.S. ambassador. Thompson had quickly
picked up the sense that the Soviets planned to increase pressure to get
the Americans (and the French and British) out of Berlin, the old German capital. What was Berlin had been divided into four sectors with
the defeat of Nazi Germany in 1945, sectors occupied by military units
of the Soviet Union, the United States, Great Britain, and France. There
were now, in effect, two Berlins: Soviet-occupied East Berlin, and West
Berlin, which stood alone as an enclave controlled by the United States
and its allies deep inside East Germany, the part of the country occupied
and controlled by the Soviets since the end of World War II. "All my
diplomatic colleagues who have discussed the matter appear to consider
that in the absence of negotiations Khrushchev will sign a separate peace
treaty with East Germany and precipitate a Berlin crisis this year,"
Thompson reported back to the White House in a "Top Secret—Eyes
Only" cable. "We must at least expect the East Germans to seal off the
Sector boundary in order to stop what they must consider intolerable
continuation of refugee flow."

Kennedy thought Berlin was the most dangerous place in the world.
If there were to be a nuclear war, it would probably begin there. The
Americans were convinced that if the Communists began a military
drive to control Europe, it would start in Berlin. The Soviets believed
the West planned to reunite and rearm Germany as a bulwark against
the historically inevitable spread of Communist doctrine. Divided Berlin
was the symbol and the capital of the Cold War. It was first on a list of
nineteen national security "tasks" prepared by Bundy and approved
by Kennedy on February 24. The President was replacing the formal
organization of Eisenhower's National Security Council with small ad
hoc task forces, their number rising and falling with his perception of
crises. The task forces would be unofficial, temporary, never functioning
long enough to generate their own bureaucracies or get around the
direct control of the man in the Oval Office. The first two of the tasks
in Bundy's draft to the President were defined as: "Certain urgent situations"—the crisis of the day, whether Berlin, Cuba, Laos, or Vietnam,
and ". . . Problems of military force and policy; e.g., the deterrence of
guerrilla warfare."

That second task was an attempt to beat the Communists at their own game, on the ground, among the people. It was an institutionalizing of *The Ugly American*. There would be more "Special Forces" soldiers wearing green berets. Under the provisions of his second National Security Action Memo, Kennedy had authorized a $19-million budget augmentation to train three thousand more elite troops in unconventional warfare and counterinsurgency techniques. And there would be unarmed young Americans in the field, too, using shovels and textbooks to win the hearts and minds of villagers threatened by Communist insurgents anywhere in the world.

On March 1, a cable went out to the U.S. Embassy in Saigon that read like the novel. It advised Americans in Vietnam to emphasize contacts with peasants and study the work of General Lansdale in the Philippines, then stated: "White House ranks defense Viet-Nam among highest priorities US foreign policy. Having approved Counter-Insurgency Plan, President concerned whether Viet-Nam can resist Communist pressure during the 18–24 month period before plan takes full effect.... Start immediately, with or without GVN participation as judged best by Ambassador, preparation overall Operations-Plan for driving Viet Cong from Viet-Nam...."

The same day, Kennedy issued an executive order creating the Peace Corps, headed by his brother-in-law Sargent Shriver. Young Americans would fan out over the world to live in mud huts and shanties, doing good. "They will live at the same level as the citizens of the countries which they are sent to, doing the same work, eating the same food, speaking the same language," stated the order—teaching the less fortunate about personal hygiene and democracy, crop rotation and the English language. Robert Kennedy had another idea one morning at a task force meeting: "Why don't we organize American businessmen overseas to demonstrate against the Communists? They could counter anti-American student protests."

"What do you think of the idea of our Peace Corps?" Kennedy, with a certain pride of authorship, asked Jawaharlal Nehru, the Indian prime minister. A good plan, Nehru replied, privileged young Americans could learn a lot from Indian villagers. Whether or not Nehru was joking, and he almost certainly was not, Kennedy was not amused.

But the most dramatic American anti-Communist action was much closer to home, and it had begun in secret a year before Kennedy took office. The CIA was training Cuban exiles to overthrow Premier Fidel Castro.

Candidate Kennedy had been briefed twice about the CIA plans, but he knew few of the details, except that there were more than a thousand Cubans being trained by the CIA in Guatemala. The operation had been authorized in March 1960 by Eisenhower, who had instructed: "Everyone must be prepared to swear that he has not heard of it." The idea was to duplicate the U.S. role in the covert overthrow of two leaders who might have been hostile to American interests, Premier Mohammad Mossadegh of Iran, in 1953, and President Jacobo Arbenz Guzman of Guatemala, in 1954.

But the operation was never as secret as the CIA maintained. The best briefing Kennedy had gotten on Cuba before he took office was in *The New York Times* of January 10, 1961. The paper ran a three-column headline on page one: "U.S. HELPS TRAIN AN ANTI-CASTRO FORCE AT SECRET GUATEMALAN BASE." Datelined Retalhuleu, Guatemala, accompanied by a map, the story began: "In the Cordillera foothills a few miles from the Pacific, commando-like forces are being drilled in guerrilla warfare tactics by foreign personnel, mostly from the United States. . . ."

Alongside the continuation inside the paper was an advertisement for coverage of the same open secret placed by the *Times'* downscale competition, *The New York Daily News:* "Castro's Black Future" . . . "35,000 saboteurs ready to strike from within. 6,000 Cuban patriots ready to storm ashore."

A month later, when he had been President for three weeks, Kennedy read another piece on the exiles in the *Times,* and dictated a morning memo to Mac Bundy: "Has the policy for Cuba been coordinated between Defense, CIA [and State]? Have we determined what we are going to do about Cuba? . . . If there is a difference of opinion between the agencies I think they should be brought to my attention."

On March 11, CIA Director Dulles and the agency's chief of operations, Richard Bissell, were called to the White House to give a detailed briefing on their plans. The Joint Chiefs were in the Cabinet Room, as were Bundy, Rusk, and McNamara. Arthur Schlesinger, just back from a trip to South American capitals, was invited by Kennedy. He was shocked by what he heard from Dulles and Bissell, and thought the President was, too. The CIA men had laid out plans for a small but full-scale invasion of Cuba with 750 men recruited from the 100,000 Cuban exiles living in Miami, who were to come ashore on the south coast of the island near the small city of Trinidad. The landing, which would take place after a series of air strikes, Bissell said, was modeled after the Allied invasion of Anzio, the Italian port city where seventy thousand American and British soldiers landed in 1944. Neither he nor Dulles mentioned that the Allied invaders had been pinned down for four months on their beachhead.

"Too spectacular," Kennedy said after a few minutes. "It sounds like D-Day. You have to reduce the noise level of this thing."

"You have to understand . . ." Bissell began at one point. The President interrupted him, saying he understood perfectly. He was concerned about the politics of the invasion. He wanted the least possible political risk—even though that meant military risks would be greater. There could be no intervention by U.S. forces and he wanted to be able to deny, plausibly, any U.S. involvement. He wanted a more remote landing spot and he wanted to be able to call off the whole thing up to twenty-four hours before the landing.

The two men from the CIA looked at each other. They would go along with anything the President said. They assumed that once troops were on the ground and American prestige was on the line, he would agree to anything, throw in anything, men and matériel, whatever it took to win. "When you commit the flag, you commit it to win," was the way President Eisenhower had put it, when he had sent U.S. planes over Guatemala after the 1954 invasion looked as if it were collapsing.

If the new President said he wanted this one quiet, too, that was fine with the CIA. It would start quiet. Dulles and Bissell stayed quiet themselves, deciding not to point out that the hope of success of an uprising against Castro required as noisy an invasion as possible. The people on the island had to know what was going on, had to believe the Americans were coming before they would risk their lives against Castro's army and police. Anyway, with any luck, the Cuban leader might be dead by the time the exiles landed. The CIA was pursuing parallel assassination plans to eliminate Castro as the invasion began. If the invaders could not hold on against Castro's 200,000 men, both regular troops and militia, Bissell said, they could escape into the nearby Escambray Mountains and wage a guerrilla war.

Dulles made a couple of final points. He wanted the President to understand that there would be a political price, as well as a military price, for calling off the invasion. "Don't forget one thing," the director interjected, as the meeting was beginning to wind down. "We have a dispersal problem. If we take these men out of Guatemala, we will have to transfer them to the United States, and we can't have them wandering around the country telling everyone what they have been doing." Then Dulles said that more than one hundred Cubans were in Czechoslovakia being trained as jet pilots. When they came back and Russian MiGs were on the island, an invasion of Cuba would really be like World War II. Or, World War III.

Kennedy did not press Dulles or Bissell. He thought highly of the CIA. The agency was quicker and more responsive than the State Department, and more attentive than the military. And he trusted Bissell, who had done most of the briefing, and then had personally collected every scrap of paper in the room. Kennedy didn't know what presidents were supposed to say or do in such situations.

"They're not queer at State, but . . . ," he remarked once to his friend Charlie Bartlett. "Well, they're sort of like Adlai . . . I don't care what it is, but if I need material fast or an idea fast, CIA is the place I have to go. The State Department takes four or five days to answer a simple yes or no."

"You can't beat brains," he would say, and Bissell obviously had them. The agency's deputy director for operations was a former economics instructor at Yale, and a formidable intellect, a confident man whose secret triumphs included the development of the U-2 spy plane, the high-flying reconnaissance machine he took from idea to prototype in just eight months from December 1954 to August 1955. The entire project had been secret—at least to the American people—until May 1960, when Soviet surface-to-air missiles finally shot one down from 80,000 feet, captured its CIA pilot, Francis Gary Powers, and showed him to the world on television.

After the briefing, Bissell mentioned that Undersecretary of State Chester Bowles had asked him to come over as his chief deputy. Kennedy called Bowles. "You can't have him," he said.

"Why not?" asked Bowles.

"He's going to take Allen Dulles' job on July 1."

The next day Bundy circulated National Security Action Memorandum 31: "The President expects to authorize US support for an appropriate number of patriotic Cubans to return to their homeland. He believes that the best possible plan, from the point of view of combined military, political and psychological considerations has not yet been presented, and new proposals are to be concerted promptly. Action: Central Intelligence Agency with appropriate consultation."

Four days later, on March 15, Bissell came back with a different plan. The new landing zone was one hundred miles to the west on the south coast. The place was called Bahía de Cochinos—the Bay of Pigs. Once again, Dulles and Bissell did not answer questions unless they were asked directly. They left in the escape clause from the Trinidad plan— the force could retreat into the Escambray Mountains and reorganize into guerrilla units.

The CIA men were making it up as they went along. They thought they had Kennedy's number already. They were calling this White House "the floating crap game." No regular meetings meant that all the action went with the President; if he was not looking, there was no system and no guarantee that anyone was checking for him. Kennedy was at the center, but he was alone there—and Bissell was going ahead on his own.

"Mr. President, I know you're doubtful about this," said Dulles, who then pricked Kennedy in the perfect spot, pushing the "Ike" button. "But I stood at this very desk and said to President Eisenhower about a similar operation in Guatemala, 'I believe it will work.' And I say to you now, Mr. President, that the prospects for this plan are even better than our prospects were in Guatemala."

That was what Kennedy wanted to hear. He had decided to move first in Latin America. He had the idea that, with Castro out of the way, he could form a kind of club of the Americas. "Club" was exactly the word Kennedy used, talking about inviting progressive leaders from Central and South America to regular get-togethers around the pool at his father's house in Palm Beach. The overthrow of the Communists in Cuba and the announcement of a new ten-year North to South American aid plan, the *Alianza para el Progreso,* would set these Pan-American events in motion.

Richard Goodwin, the young speechwriter who had thought they could change the world with a telephone, came into the Oval Office on the afternoon of March 13 to find the President pacing the floor and practicing Spanish for that night's speech announcing the Alliance to Washington's corps of Latin American ambassadors. "Techo . . . techo; trabajo . . . trabajo; obero . . . obero."

"It's obrero with an 'r,' not *obero,*" Goodwin said. There was nothing he could say about his boss's accent, which was atrocious.

"I have called upon all people of the hemisphere to join in a new Alliance for Progress . . . to satisfy the basic needs of the American people for homes, work and land, health and schools—techo, trabajo y tierra, salud y escuela," Kennedy said in his speech in the East Room of the White House.

When Kennedy saw Goodwin afterward, he asked, "How was my Spanish?"

"Perfect, Mr. President."

"I thought you'd say that."

Almost everybody was saying nice things about Kennedy. His pollster, Louis Harris, completed surveys that same day, March 23, and sent him a report saying: "Public popularity has risen to perhaps record heights"—higher than either Franklin D. Roosevelt and Eisenhower had enjoyed in their early days.

The reaction to the Kennedys in the White House was amazing, considering that more than half the country had voted against him a few months earlier. Once in the White House, Kennedy had to go on national television to ask people to stop sending telegrams and letters congratulating him and his wife.

But for Kennedy the euphoria was muted by events in Laos, the landlocked kingdom of fewer than three million people that Eisenhower had told him was "the cork in the bottle" of Southeast Asia. A civil war had been going on in the place traditionally called Lanxang, "The Land of a Million Elephants," since the French had been driven out of Indochina in 1954. The Royal Lao Government of King Savang Vatthana was being supported by the United States—the entire budget of the Royal Army was paid by the CIA and the Defense Department—in its fight against the insurgents of the Pathet Lao (Patriotic Front), who were supported by the Communists in North Vietnam. So far, the U.S. had put in $300 million, more than $150 for each Laotian, about twice the country's annual per capita income. The king's speeches were written in Washington by the State Department, though the ghostwriters were not responsible for his most famous line: "My people only know how to sing and make love."

"What is our position out there?" Kennedy asked the U.S. Ambassador, Winthrop Brown.

"Well, sir," Brown began, "the policy is . . ."

"That's not what I asked you," Kennedy interrupted. "I said, 'What do you think, you, the Ambassador?' What kind of people are these people: Souvanna and Souphanouvong and Phoumi and the King and Kong Le?"

Brown began to pour out what he knew, his perceptions and frustrations that no one had wanted to hear before. "Laos is hopeless," he said. "It's just a series of lines on a map. Fewer than half the people speak Lao. They're charming, indolent, enchanting people, but they're just not very vigorous.

"The king is a total zero," Brown said. He went on to say that the general the United States was backing, Phoumi Nosavan, had never been near a battlefield and was leading Uncle Sam around by the nose. We were calling Kong Le a Communist but he was actually just a disgruntled soldier, a patriot rebelling against corrupt politicians. Souvanna Phouma, the political leader we were trying to get rid of, was the only Lao with even a remote chance of pulling the country together.

After listening for almost an hour, Kennedy stood up. Brown had given him everything he had, and he left thinking he had met a President who could be trusted to do the right thing. Five days later, Kennedy told Walter Lippmann at lunch, "As far as Laos is concerned, I don't see why we have to be more royalist than the king. India is more directly threatened than we are, and if they are not wildly excited, why should we be?"

But at the same time, his task force on Laos was excited, reporting to him that one village after another was falling to small units of the Pathet Lao—and that he would soon have to decide whether to walk away and let the Communists take over or send in U.S. troops. The numbers discussed by the task force, which was run by Walt Rostow, and those of the Joint Chiefs ranged from ten thousand to sixty thousand U.S. personnel.

The President found a middle way, at least for the moment. He ordered the Seventh Fleet, stationed at Okinawa, to prepare to steam to Thailand with fourteen hundred combat-ready Marines. He moved another 150 Marines to the Thai-Lao border by helicopter, as if they were an advance unit for more to come. Rostow was delegated to brief reporters on background that the President was resolved to face down the Communists in Laos, and the Soviets, too, which produced this three-column front-page headline in *The New York Times* of March 21: "U.S. READY TO FACE ALL RISKS TO BAR RED RULE OF LAOS."

At 6:00 P.M. on March 23, Kennedy went on national television, holding a pointer to large maps of Laos and saying:

"These three maps show the area of effective Communist domination as it was last August, with the colored portions up in the right-hand corner being the areas held and dominated by the Communists at that time; and now next, in December of 1960, three months ago, the red area having expanded; and now from December 20 to the present date . . . the Communists control a much wider section of the country. . . . Soviet planes, I regret to say, have been conspicuous in a large-scale airlift into the battle area . . . plus a whole supporting set of combat specialists, mainly from Communist North Viet-Nam, with the clear object of destroying by military action the agreed neutrality of Laos.

"We strongly and unreservedly support the goal of a neutral and independent Laos. . . . There must be a cessation of the present armed attacks by externally supported Communists. . . . The security of all Southeast Asia will be endangered if Laos loses its neutral independence. Its own safety runs with the safety of us all. . . . I know that every American will want his country to honor its obligations. . . ."

Two days later, Kennedy repeated his tough-sounding warnings on Laos: "No one should doubt our resolution on this point." But, in fact, what he had done in public was to downgrade U.S. policy from supporting a "free" Laos to accepting a "neutral" Laos. In private, with his own men, the President said he did not intend to honor obligations in Laos. The talk and the troop movements, he said, were a bluff. If the United States had to make a stand in Southeast Asia, he said, it would be across the border, in Vietnam.

Chapter 6

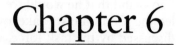

APRIL 4, 1961

"**W**hat do you think about this damned invasion?" Arthur Schlesinger asked the President on the morning of March 28. He meant, what do you *really* think, because the two had been talking about the Cuban operation for almost an hour, going over a draft of the White Paper Schlesinger was writing to explain officially why the government of the United States felt compelled to destroy the government of Fidel Castro in Cuba.

"I think about it as little as possible," Kennedy answered.

The answer went beyond Kennedy's usual irony. Or perhaps he was just saying that because he knew Schlesinger did not like the idea. Kennedy had a gift for convincing others that, whatever he did or had to do, he was at heart with them. Still, this time there seemed to be a flash of self-pity, as if he knew he was losing control of events and had no idea how to regain it.

The next day, Kennedy turned the question to a very different kind of man. "Do you know anything about this Cuba proposal?" Kennedy asked Dean Acheson, who had been President Truman's Secretary of State. At the age of sixty-seven, Acheson was the leader of the Democratic Party's hard-line cold warriors.

"A Cuba proposal? I didn't know there was one," Acheson answered.

Kennedy explained what he knew, emphasizing that the plan had been developed for Eisenhower and involved the secret landing of fifteen

hundred exiles—the number had doubled during the past three weeks
—armed and trained by the CIA with some help from Army and Marine
instructors. Many of the exiles, Kennedy said, already had military
training in the army of Fulgencio Batista, the U.S.-supported dictator
overthrown by Castro on New Year's Day 1959, when his guerrilla
army marched into Havana. The original CIA plan, he told Acheson,
had called for an amphibious landing near Trinidad, and depended on
a popular uprising against Castro, beginning in that city. But Kennedy
wanted a night landing in a more remote region.

Acheson listened with uncharacteristic patience, but then he asked:
"Are you serious?"

"I'm giving it serious thought," the President said. "I don't know if
I'm serious or just . . ." He paused, then continued. "I've been thinking
about it."

Acheson asked him how many men Castro might be able to get to the
beachhead the first day. The answer was twenty-five thousand.

"Well," he said, "it doesn't take Price-Waterhouse to figure out that
fifteen hundred Cubans aren't as good as twenty-five thousand."

The two men were sitting on a bench in the Rose Garden, outside the
President's office. Kennedy had invited Acheson out into the early spring
sunlight after reading the draft of a memo on Berlin he had asked
Acheson to prepare. "It seems more likely than not that the USSR will
move toward a crisis on Berlin this year," Acheson told Kennedy. They
were not particularly comfortable with each other. Kennedy respected
Acheson and thought him a brilliant analyst, but he was put off by his
bitterness and his sarcasm. Acheson, for his part, thought Kennedy was
soft. He had more than once called him a fool.

Kennedy knew what Acheson thought, but he felt he needed him as a
symbol of continuity in U.S. foreign policy. He was the one Democrat
whose presence in the White House would signal that Kennedy was as
determined as Truman or Eisenhower that the Allies would never be
pushed out of Berlin. Whatever Kennedy and Acheson thought of each
other personally, what they agreed on was more important to both. If
there was to be war between the United States and the Soviet Union, it
would likely begin in Berlin, and it would begin because the Soviets
would have misread the intentions and resolve of the new President.

"There is no 'solution' for the Berlin problem short of the unification
of Germany," Acheson's memo stated. "The fight for Berlin must begin,
at any rate, as a local conflict. The problem is how and where it will
end. All courses of action are dangerous and unpromising. Inaction is
even worse. . . . If the USSR is not to dominate Europe, and, by doing
so, dominate Asia and Africa also, a willingness to fight for Berlin is

essential. . . . If a crisis is provoked, a bold and dangerous course may be the safest."

"Dangerous" had a rather precise meaning in Berlin. The United States, Great Britain, and France had a total of fifteen thousand troops in West Berlin. If the Soviets moved to take it by force, the allies had no realistic hope of reinforcing their garrisons by air or along the rail lines and the Autobahn, which ran 110 miles from the West German bases of NATO through East German territory, occupied by hundreds of thousands of Red Army troops. That meant the President of the United States had to decide within hours, perhaps even minutes, whether to use nuclear weapons or surrender West Berlin.

Acheson and Kennedy also knew that it was only a matter of time before the Soviets would test this President—and his first priority was to demonstrate that he was as tough as the men who had preceded him as Commander-in-Chief. He tried to make that point later the same day, issuing a special message to Congress requesting $2.4 billion in new military appropriations, a figure that included $1.8 billion for missile programs—very substantial numbers in a budget that totaled $81 billion for all domestic and foreign expenditures.

In the afternoon, Kennedy saw Senator William Fulbright, the chairman of the Senate Foreign Relations Committee, at a brief White House meeting on foreign aid. "Where are you going for the holiday?" the President asked him. It was the Thursday before Easter.

"Florida," Fulbright said. "Betty and I are going down to see her aunt in Delray."

"Well, I'm going down there to stay with my father," Kennedy said. "How about coming with me on the plane?"

Fulbright not only accepted the invitation, he decided he would use it to confront his friend the President about the reports and rumors on Cuba. He hurried back to the Capitol and called one of his assistants, Pat Holt, into his office and told him to draft a memo to the President making these points: "The invasion is an open secret" . . . "Castro is getting stronger not weaker. Resistance will be formidable and the United States will probably have to use its own armed forces to win" . . . "An invasion will undo thirty years of U.S. work to live down earlier interventions."

Holt wrote twelve pages. After Fulbright and Kennedy had settled down the next day on Air Force One, the Senator handed the pages to Kennedy. The key paragraph, edited and rewritten by Fulbright, said: "Provided that the Soviet Union uses Cuba only as a political and not as a military base ('military' is used here to mean missiles and nuclear weapons, not small conventional arms . . .). The Castro regime is a thorn in the flesh; but it is not a dagger in the heart. . . . To give this activity even covert support is of a piece with the hypocrisy and cynicism for which the United States is constantly denouncing the Soviet Union."

The President read through the memo quickly and looked at the senator for a long moment. Then he nodded but said nothing. Fulbright wanted to ask what he thought, but men rarely ask presidents questions without an invitation. Perhaps Kennedy did not know what to say, or to think. At his feet he had a briefcase filled with raw CIA reports that said exactly the opposite of what Fulbright was trying to tell him: "Anti-Castro terrorists are exploding bombs daily in Havana—twelve in a single day, according to one report . . . armed dissidents are said to be active in Pinar del Río and Las Villas provinces . . . sugar cane fires—allegedly set by saboteurs—may be increasing."

On the Tuesday after Easter, April 4, Kennedy called Fulbright and invited him to fly back to Washington on Air Force One. The President was quiet again, saying nothing about the memo during the flight north. But when they landed at Andrews Air Force Base in Maryland, he asked Fulbright to come with him to the State Department. "There's a meeting about Cuba," Kennedy said. After flying with Kennedy to Washington on Marine One, the presidential helicopter, Fulbright waited around while the President accepted a gold shovel, a gift from the Governor of South Dakota, and swore in Anthony J. Drexel Biddle as ambassador to Spain. Then Kennedy led the senator into a small conference room behind Secretary Rusk's office on the seventh floor of the State Department.

There were a dozen men around a table that almost filled the bare little room. McNamara, Bundy, Dulles and Dillon were there, and so was the chairman of the Joint Chiefs of Staff, General Lyman Lemnitzer. "Meeting on Laos" was listed on their official schedules—to mislead nosy reporters. That was certainly plausible: the Seventh Fleet was moving toward Thailand to back up Kennedy's television threats of military intervention if the Pathet Lao did not agree to a cease-fire. On the day before he had left for Palm Beach, the President had personally told Soviet Foreign Minister Andrei Gromyko that if Laos could not be neutralized a U.S.-Soviet confrontation there might lead to World War III.

There were also men in the conference room whose schedules were not considered important enough to be printed and distributed to the press every day: Schlesinger and Richard Goodwin, and Dick Bissell, of course. Rusk slipped in, hurrying back after greeting British Prime Minister Harold Macmillan, who had arrived at Washington's National Airport for his first meeting with President Kennedy.

Senator Fulbright was not a welcome guest. The Chiefs and the CIA were shocked that the President would bring a member of Congress, especially this one, into an executive meeting. Rusk was sulking for another reason. He couldn't stand the disorder of these things; the absence of hierarchy bothered him. In Kennedy meetings, a Secretary of State and assistant speechwriters, and anybody else who happened by, were lumped together, treated as equals. The Secretary was determined not to speak unless the President formally called on him. Play the village idiot again, he told himself. Rusk, who had worked on guerrilla operations in Burma during the war, thought the whole idea of a successful Cuban invasion was mostly wishful thinking and did not have a chance in hell. He had said that privately to the President, but he kept it to himself at meetings.

It was Rusk's office but Bissell's meeting. Bissell skated through the latest plans. The others tried to impress the President with short, sharp questions. A presidential glance their way could trigger fantasies for weeks. How's the Cubans' morale? What about the markings on the planes?

"Suppose they can't establish a beachhead?" someone asked.

"It's unlikely, but we have a contingency plan," Bissell said. He turned to a uniformed military aide, who drew a document from his briefcase and handed it to him. Then Bissell pointed to a large map of the targeted section of Cuba coastline. "If they can't hold on here," he said, pointing to the Bay of Pigs, "they'll move into mountains here," pointing to a spot about eighty miles away, "and form guerrilla units which we can resupply by air. That's the worst that can happen."

Goodwin asked with uncharacteristic timidity: "How do we know the Cuban people will support the rebels, why do we think they want to overthrow Castro?"

"We have the NIE on that, don't we?" Bissell said with a hint of impatience. He held up a National Intelligence Estimate, a summation issued by a secret twelve-member board charged with the analysis of all intelligence data from the CIA, military intelligence groups, and other agencies as well. Reports indicated that Cuba was on the verge of revolt or chaos:

> The great mass of Cuban people believe that the hour of decision is at hand. . . . They expect an invasion to take place before mid-April 1961 and place great reliance in it. The Castro regime is steadily losing popularity . . . housewives and servants must stand in line for hours to obtain such necessities as soap and lard. . . . Church attendance is at an all-time high as a demonstration of opposition to the government. . . . It is

generally believed that the Cuban Army has been successfully penetrated by opposition groups and that it will not fight in the event of a showdown.

Goodwin, afraid he was making a fool of himself, said nothing more. Nobody else did, either. The President turned to Fulbright, on his right.

The senator was tense. All he had heard before this could be put down as rumors, but these people were talking about real things: landing strips, troop strength, ammunition ships, $40 million spent training the exiles. Fulbright talked for a very long time, nervously repeating the points of his memo, then saying finally: "The real question is whether Castro can in fact succeed in providing a better life for the Cuban people; in making Cuba a little paradise, a real Pearl of the Antilles; and whether he can do a better job in this respect in Cuba than the United States and its friends can do elsewhere in Latin America."

Paul Nitze, the Assistant Secretary of Defense, could not believe what he was hearing from Fulbright and from everyone else around the table. This was like a bull session. The only question that mattered now, he thought, was whether the thing would succeed. Nitze thought the odds were less than fifty-fifty—but that had nothing to do with morality or pearls of the Antilles.

Fulbright plowed on. "If you succeed, what are you going to do with Cuba? We had it once and we let it go. What's the point?" he asked. "If one has faith in the human values of the United States, and if that faith is supported by vigorous and intelligent action, then there is no need to fear competition from an unshaven megalomaniac."

"What do you think?" the President said, looking around the table. He was becoming impatient. His fingers were beginning to move on the table. "Yes or no," he said.

They all said yes, sort of, and quickly, knowing the President wanted to get out of there. Kennedy was too impatient to go all around the table, so three or four men there never had to put their opinions on the line. Rusk's answer was not clear, and the military men tried to emphasize that this was a CIA thing, none of their doing. Many of the men around the table—Nitze among them—found themselves defending the invasion in an instinctive response to the arguments of the outsider, Fulbright.

Adolf A. Berle, a State Department specialist on Latin America since Roosevelt's days, began a longer analysis but was cut off by the President, "Adolf, you haven't voted!"

"Mr. President," Berle said, "there has to be a confrontation with Castro sooner or later, so . . . I say let 'er rip!"

"No," said Fulbright.

But the senator was reassured by the meeting. He was convinced that Kennedy had brought him in as a surrogate to voice his own doubts. He was sure that, beneath it all, the President agreed with him. But Nitze thought that, too. Both of them, and others at the table, were convinced that he had said what Kennedy would have said, or what he wanted to hear.

They were all wrong. The President did not know what he wanted to hear—or do. Kennedy hated the feeling of being trapped. But he was trapping himself by moving toward approving a plan without feeling committed to it. Bissell collected the papers on the table, satisfied that things were going his way and that this thing would work—with or without the President.

"Gentlemen," Kennedy said, standing up. "We better sleep on it." As they left the meeting, he nodded to Fulbright and said quietly, "You're the only one in the room who can say, 'I told you so.' "

After the meeting, Douglas Dillon, who was in on the Cuban planning as a kind of liaison to Eisenhower, took the President aside and told him the invasion was common conversation all over Latin America, and at the United Nations. Kennedy said that didn't bother him, he was mainly concerned about hiding the U.S. hand in the operation. Dillon thought that was crazy. There was no way to hide American involvement. Where else could the exiles get weapons, to say nothing of ships and planes? But he did not say that to the President.

Arthur Schlesinger had sat in a corner throughout the meeting, too junior to vote on small surrogate wars. To many of the others, the professor's status was measured by the fact that his office was in the East Wing of the White House. "With the women," Rusk noted. But Schlesinger was at his typewriter at six-thirty the next morning, banging out another in an endless flow of gracefully written and usually sensible memos to the President. He was against the invasion, though he did not agree with Fulbright's arguments about the morality of U.S. interventions in Latin America.

"If force is used efficiently and effectively, and if the threat to national security is demonstrable and convincing, the controlled use of force for limited objectives might well enhance respect for the United States," he wrote to the President. But he did not think many people could be convinced of a compelling threat from the 7 million people of Cuba and their erratic leader. "People around the world have forgotten the muddling and moralizing conservatism of the Eisenhower period with surprising speed. The United States is emerging again as a great, mature and liberal nation, coolly and intelligently dedicated to the job of stopping Communism. . . . It is this reawakening world faith in America which is at stake in the Cuban operation."

Kennedy told Schlesinger not to worry so much. "I'm trying to make sense out of it," he told him. He had already scaled down the operation, he said, and he could cancel everything up to twenty-four hours before D-Day. Anyway, there would be no real D-Day, no real invasion, just infiltration by the CIA's Cubans. He told Schlesinger that he had to do something with all those Cubans training in Guatemala. "The disposal problem," as Allen Dulles called it.

But Schlesinger did worry. "We seemed destined to go ahead with a quasi-minimum basis," he wrote in his bulging diary. He went to Robert Kennedy, and was shocked to learn that the Attorney General knew nothing of the plan. The younger Kennedy gave Schlesinger one piece of advice he took as an order: Once the President has made up his mind, we support him and we keep our mouths shut!

So much for "we." But "they" were talking. Kennedy already had a memo from Schlesinger reporting on a lunch on April 1 with a correspondent named Harold Handleman from *U.S. News & World Report,* who had recited many of the details of the CIA's "Top Secret" plan. "Obviously if an enterprising magazine writer could pick this all up in Miami in a couple of weeks," Schlesinger stated, "Havana must be well-posted on developments."

Indeed they were. A couple of days later, a Harvard professor named John Plank, just back from Cuba, told Schlesinger that details of the invasion were street gossip in Havana, and had been for weeks. "The people around Fidel are talking about it, too," Plank added.

Schlesinger, by then, was running around like a fireman, trying to stamp out the brushfires in the press. "The attached article entitled 'Our Men in Miami' "—by Karl Meyer, a *Washington Post* editorial writer —"is due to appear in the *New Republic,*" he reported to Kennedy.

"Stop it," the President said.

"Gil Harrison came through like a gentleman and a patriot," Schlesinger reported back after a session with the publisher of the *New Republic.* "He asked no questions and said he would drop the piece, though it must have done violence to his journalistic instinct."

Then someone at *The New York Times* called the President and told him that the next morning's paper would have a front-page story by Tad Szulc, their best Latin American reporter, saying that the invasion the paper had written about in January was now imminent. The lead, as read to him, was: "For nearly nine months Cuban exile military forces dedicated to the overthrow of Premier Fidel Castro have been training in the United States as well as Central America. . . ." Kennedy blew up, banging down the phone and throwing around words like "treason." Calming down, he telephoned the *Times's* publisher, Orville Dryfoos, and asked him to kill the story in the national interest.

But that did not happen. Dryfoos called back and said that some of his editors had threatened to quit on the spot if the story did not run. Still, there was a compromise: the size of the headline was reduced from four columns to one—"ANTI-CASTRO UNITS TRAINED TO FIGHT AT FLORIDA BASES" read the compromise headline—and the story was moved from the top of page one to the middle. Most important, the words "invasion imminent" were taken out of the copy. That did not satisfy the President.

"I can't believe what I am reading," he said the next day when he saw the *Times,* which had also run a two-paragraph Associated Press item repeating a CBS News report that invasion preparations were in the final stages. "Castro doesn't need agents over here. All he has to do is read our papers. It's all laid out for him." The President told Schlesinger to go to the *Times* with a list of inaccuracies in Szulc's story. "The unfortunate fact," Schlesinger reported back, "is that we do not have a strong case against the story as inaccurate." He added that it was being broadcast on Radio Moscow.

By then, fact and hope, truth and deception had been woven into a web so complicated that only two men could have known what was actually going on: Bissell and Kennedy. One of them, the President, did not know, and his national security adviser, Bundy, was beginning to realize that there were serious problems in the new and casual organization of the White House. He sent the President a memo on April 5 under the title "Crisis Commanders in Washington," saying, in effect, that in the most important of current foreign policy crises, no one was in charge:

> Over and over since January 20th we have talked of getting "task forces with individual responsible leaders" here in Washington for crisis situations. At the beginning, we thought we had task forces for Laos, the Congo and Cuba. We did get working groups with nobody in particular in charge, but we did not get clearly focused responsibility. The reason was that the Department of State was not quite ready . . . these Assistant Secretaries, although men of good will, were not really prepared to take charge of the "military" and "intelligence" aspects—the Government was in the habit of "coordination" and out of the habit of the acceptance of individual executive leadership . . . more than once the ball has been dropped because no one person felt a continuing clear responsibility.

However the system broke down, it seemed now that the invasion had a life of its own. Schlesinger took Robert Kennedy's order that the time had come to rally around the boss. His next Cuba memo was called

"Protection of the President," and in it he said: "When lies must be told, they should be told by subordinate officials. At no point should the President be asked to lend himself to the cover operation. There seems to me merit in Secretary Rusk's suggestion that someone other than the President make the final decision and do so in his absence—someone whose head can later be placed on the block if things go terribly wrong." One Schlesinger failure option was to put the blame on the CIA as "errant idealists and soldiers-of-fortune working on their own."

But the President could not be protected from himself. He met with Dulles, Rusk, and McNamara on April 5, the day after the State Department meeting and told them he was going to approve the CIA plan, but he added that under no circumstances would he order American troops or planes into the battle. Three days later, he told Bissell that he could go ahead and schedule the landing. The date Bissell chose was April 16.

For a time, Kennedy put Cuba away somewhere in the compartments of his mind. He spoke mainly about Europe and Laos with Prime Minister Harold Macmillan during his state visit. Among other things, Macmillan wanted the President's impressions of what he half-jokingly called Britain's "Grand Design" for Europe. The prime minister hoped to develop a compromise power-sharing scheme on European security matters that was halfway between the United States' inclination to make unilateral decisions and French President Charles de Gaulle's insistence that France, Britain, and the United States must be equal partners in decision making. But Kennedy was reluctant to talk about that on the first day or so of Macmillan's visit. The reason was that he had not yet read Macmillan's proposals. In fact, he had lost the papers. It took several hours to find them—in Caroline's bedroom.

On April 12, the President's valet, George Thomas, knocked on his bedroom door at eight o'clock in the morning as he always did, and Kennedy called back: "I'm awake."

Thomas called Pierre Salinger and said, "It's okay. He's up." The press secretary then called Kennedy to read him an Associated Press bulletin that began: "The Soviet Union announced today that it had won the race to put a man into space."

A Russian named Yuri Gagarin had orbited the earth three times in a spacecraft called *Vostok*. The Soviet blast-off had been detected by U.S. monitoring stations in Iran and Turkey at 1:35 A.M., Washington time.

By 10:00 A.M., Kennedy was in his office, pacing back and forth, asking Vice President Lyndon Johnson, who had been made chairman of the Space Council to give him something to do on his own: "Is there any place where we can catch them? What can we do? Are we working twenty-four hours a day? Can we go around the moon before them?

Can we put a man on the moon before them? . . . Can we leapfrog? . . .
If somebody can just tell me how to catch up! Let's find somebody,
anybody. I don't care if it's the janitor over there, if he knows how."

"It is a most impressive scientific accomplishment . . . I have already
sent congratulations to Mr. Khrushchev," he said that afternoon at his
news conference.

"Mr. President," a reporter asked, "has a decision been reached on
how far this country will be willing to go in helping an anti-Castro
uprising or invasion of Cuba?"

He answered: "First I want to say that there will not be, under any
conditions, an intervention in Cuba by the United States armed forces.
This government will do everything it possibly can, and I think it can
meet its responsibilities, to make sure there are no Americans involved
in any actions inside Cuba. . . ."

Near the end of the news conference, another reporter asked: "Mr.
President, this question might better be asked at a history class than a
news conference, but here it is, anyway. The Communists seem to be
putting us on the defensive on a number of fronts—now, again, in
space. Wars aside, do you think that there is a danger that their system
is going to prove more durable than ours?"

Kennedy answered: "Well, I think that we are in a period of long,
drawn-out tests to see which system is, I think, the more durable, not
better, but more durable. And we have had a number of experiences
with this kind of competition—a dictatorship enjoys advantages in this
kind of competition over a short period by its ability to mobilize its
resources for a specific purpose. We have made some exceptional scientific advances in the last decade, and some of them—they are not as
spectacular as the man-in-space, or as the first Sputnik, but they are
important. . . . I do not regard the first man in space as a sign of the
weakening of the free world, but I do regard the total mobilization of
man and things for the service of the Communist bloc over the last years
as a source of great danger to us. And I would say that we are going to
have to live with that danger and hazard through much of the rest of
this century."

That was not a new thought for John Kennedy. He had questioned
the crisis capability of democratic government at some length twenty-
one years earlier in his book *Why England Slept,* saying then:

I say, therefore, that democracy's weaknesses are great in competing with
a totalitarian system. Democracy is the superior form of government,
because it is based on a respect for man as a reasonable being. For the
long run, then, democracy is superior. But for the short run, democracy

has great weaknesses. When it competes with a system of government which cares nothing for permanency, a system built primarily for war, democracy, which is built primarily for peace, is at a disadvantage. . . . A democracy will, indeed, be two years behind a dictatorship. The weight of public opinion in the dictatorship, which would ordinarily be inclined on the side of peace, will not be of decisive importance. The dictator is able to know exactly how much the democracy is bluffing, because of the free press, radio, and so forth, and so can plan his moves accordingly.

Chapter 7

On April 11, a Tuesday night, at nine o'clock, NBC had broad-cast an hour-long television special on the First Family, a show as morn-ing-fresh as the sponsor, Crest toothpaste, and warm as new babies, with Jacqueline Kennedy talking about her children and the President describing his hands-on management of the White House, the country, and the world. That may have surprised some of his own men, who were worrying that his management style emphasized style over man-agement. He had called only two Cabinet meetings, then stopped, say-ing, "They're a waste of time." He felt the same way about National Security Council meetings.

But he was certainly doing something right. Polls and praise were going up like rockets around Kennedy—73 percent approval in the latest Gallup Poll—and it seemed nothing could go wrong for him. Congressmen, returning from their Easter break, reported that their constituents were cheering on the President whether they had voted for him or not. A tongue-in-cheek *New Republic* article by James Mac-Gregor Burns, his admiring biographer, said he might be looking too good. "He is not only the handsomest, the best-dressed, the most articu-late, and graceful as a gazelle. He is omniscient; he swallows whole books in minutes; he confounds experts with superior knowledge of their field. He is omnipotent."

President Kennedy stayed in Washington until midday on Saturday,

April 14, still reading and talking about the Cuban invasion. It was scheduled to begin in the early morning hours of Monday, April 16. He still had not given the final go-ahead. He told Bissell again that he wanted the option of calling off the invasion at any time up to noon on Sunday. Among the people Kennedy called on was a Marine colonel named Jack Hawkins, an amphibious-landing expert lent to the CIA. He flew down to the Cubans' training site in Guatemala, where they had named themselves Brigade 2506, and reported back first to the agency, and then to the President, telling him what he needed (or wanted) to hear: "My observations have increased my confidence in the ability of this force to accomplish not only initial combat missions, but also the ultimate objective, the overthrow of Castro. They have more firing experience than U.S. troops would normally receive. . . . This is a truly formidable force. The Brigade officers do not expect help from U.S. armed forces."

After lunch that Saturday afternoon, Kennedy flew by helicopter to Middleburg, Virginia, in the horse country forty miles west of the capital, to join his wife and children at a country house they were renting there for $2,000 a month. Jacqueline Kennedy, who was teaching four-year-old Caroline to ride and care for horses, loved the area and was looking for land to build a home of their own. The rental house, a small estate, was called Glen Ora. Her husband did not much care for horses, or for Glen Ora, either.

Kennedy was an ocean person, greatly preferring Cape Cod or Newport in Rhode Island. So, on Glen Ora weekends, mother and children would leave for the house on Friday or early Saturday morning. The President would delay until lunchtime Saturday, often asking Charlie Bartlett, Ben Bradlee, or Lemoyne Billings, a New York advertising man who was another friend since prep school, to come there with him. He usually took a little walk after lunch, and then, more often than not, went upstairs to his bedroom where he would stay, sleeping or watching television, reading sometimes, as Jackie and Caroline rode or groomed their horses. He usually reappeared around eight o'clock for a drink, a daiquiri, if his stomach was not bothering him, and dinner. Later there was backgammon or checkers, games Kennedy turned into complicated gambling contests, with twenty dollars or so at stake. Or, he just chatted with whomever was around. On the nights there were games, the host won. If he was losing at checkers or backgammon, he would cough and scatter the pieces of the game, saying, in the way of apology: "Oh shit! Now we'll have to start all over again."

On Sundays at Glen Ora, Kennedy went to mass in the morning, then often played a little golf at the Fauquier Springs Country Club if he felt up to it. Sometimes he drove through the rich, rolling hills, occasionally stopping to see friends. Or, he just watched more television, football games and the Washington interview shows, "Meet the Press" and "Face the Nation"—then calling astounded and flattered officials or reporters to critique their performances on camera. He was bored out there.*

This weekend was different. As he prepared to take off for Glen Ora, a B-26 bomber, World War II surplus with Cuban Air Force insignia and dozens of bullet holes in the body and wings, landed at Miami International Airport. There had been bombings of Cuban airfields that morning, and Cuban delegates were already demanding a special session of the United Nations to investigate the air attacks. In Miami, the pilot stepping down from the B-26 said he was defecting and had decided to say *adios* with a few bombs. Actually his name was Mario Zuñiga; he was being paid $225 a month by the CIA. The bullet holes had been made by CIA men shooting .45-caliber pistols.

Another B-26 with Cuban markings landed at Key West a few hours later, as Adlai Stevenson was speaking before the U. N. General Assembly, reading the statement dictated to him by the State Department about the incident, indignantly denying Cuban charges that the bombing was prelude to invasion. Castro's Cubans were right, of course. The CIA owned the two planes that had landed in Florida and eight others that had bombed and strafed Cuban fields trying to destroy the Cuban Air Force's forty or so old American planes. They all came from a secret field in Nicaragua, where the exile Cuban Brigade, fourteen hundred men brought by trucks from Guatemala, were being loaded onto four old freighters. By sunset Saturday, the men of Brigade 2506 were at sea, crossing six hundred miles of the Caribbean between Puerto Cabezas, Nicaragua, and the south coast of Cuba.

Stevenson was unwittingly telling the lies in New York, but even the State Department men who had briefed him did not know the truth.

---

* One of the best kept secrets of the Kennedy campaign was that he loved golf as much as Eisenhower did. But he did not play in public because he was using Ike's golfing as a symbol of age and a passive approach to governing. He was good, too, but no one was ever sure how good, because he was too impatient to finish a full eighteen holes, usually quitting after nine holes or even after two or three.

During the campaign, Kennedy had sneaked off one day with Red Fay for a secret round in Monterey, California. Kennedy hit a long and true seven-iron from the tee that landed ten feet from the pin on a short hole. "Go, Go, baby!" yelled Fay, cheering for a hole in one as the ball rolled.

"No! No!" yelled Kennedy.

"What's wrong with you?" Fay said.

"If that ball had gone into the hole, it would be all over the country . . . another golfer trying to get into the White House." Then Kennedy looked over at their caddies and whispered to Fay: "I wonder what it would have cost me to have our two trusted caddies keep quiet."

Safely elected, he played a dozen times between the election and his inaugural, usually at Palm Beach. Senator Stuart Symington played an abbreviated round there with the President-elect and reporters asked him about how he thought Kennedy would do over eighteen holes. "He wouldn't score too well," Symington said. "But he'd hit some magnificent shots."

Stevenson told the United Nations that the planes that had bombed the Cuban airfields were part of Fuerza Aerea Revolucionaria (FAR), Castro's air force. As he said that, Stevenson held up a photograph of the B-26 that had landed in Miami, showing the bullet holes and the red star of FAR.

On Sunday morning, the President went to mass in Middleburg, borrowing ten dollars from Lem Billings for the collection as he always did. He almost never paid back. Then he played some golf with his youngest sister, Jean, and her husband, Stephen Smith. Finally, at 2:00 P.M., two hours after the noon deadline he had given Bissell, he telephoned Rusk and told him to give the CIA the go-ahead. He told Rusk to be sure to repeat his press conference pledge that no Americans would intervene. Kennedy had given his word, in public. In his mind, each decision on the invasion was a trade-off between military and political considerations. He chose a minimum of political risk, which meant a maximum military risk.

Then he called Salinger and instructed him: "I want you to stick close to home tonight, Pierre. You may have some inquiries from the press about a military affair in the Caribbean. If you do, just say you know only what you have read in the newspapers." Then Kennedy got up and walked out of the house, carrying a golf club, his driver. By himself, he set up balls in a row, hitting one after another deep into a neighbor's cornfield.

The last thing Kennedy did before he went to bed Sunday night was to call Rusk again and tell him to order the cancellation of a dawn air strike by the entire exile air force of sixteen B-26s, a planned second shot at Castro's airfields, even though overflights that afternoon had indicated that only five FAR planes had been disabled in the first strike. He still wanted to keep the noise level down.

On Monday morning at Glen Ora, the phone next to the President's bed rang at 5:15 A.M. It was Rusk. The invasion of Cuba had begun thirty minutes before, he said. The Cuban exiles, Brigade 2506, had landed at and around the Bay of Pigs. Already, Rusk said, the CIA wanted to call in American planes to cover the men hitting the beach. They wanted to call in jets from the U.S.S. *Essex,* an aircraft carrier steaming fifty miles off the island. The B-26s were no help now because it would take them three hours to fly from Nicaragua to Cuba.

"No," Kennedy told Rusk again. Tell the CIA: No Navy jets; no more B-26s. He had said there would be no direct involvement of U.S. armed forces and he meant it. No. No. No. Then he told the Secretary, who was only a messenger to the CIA now, that he wanted the *Essex* and U.S. destroyers farther away from Cuba, over the horizon, out of sight.

At 9:00 A.M. the President boarded a helicopter with his wife and children and headed back to Washington. The invasion failed before he reached his office. At about nine-thirty that Monday morning, Castro's FAR planes sank two freighters carrying ten days of reserve ammunition and much of the expedition force's communications equipment. The planes that made the difference—three old T-33 jet trainers—were made in the United States. They had been supplied to the Batista government by the U.S. government and inherited by Castro.

But Kennedy did not know that yet. Communications from the ships and the beachhead to officials in Washington lagged by as much as twelve hours, despite the fact that ham radio operators in Atlanta, Georgia, and in places along the East Coast were picking up transmissions from the beach. Bissell told Kennedy that the agency was hearing from the panicky men on the beach that they were being attacked by Soviet MiG-15s flown by Czech pilots. The CIA, it turned out, had not known that Castro had turned the old trainers into fighter-bombers, equipping them with machine guns and bomb racks. There were many things America's spymasters did not know, among them that Fidel Castro had a favorite fishing spot near the isolated swamp and shoreline of the Bahía de Cochinos. He planned to develop the area as a workers' resort. He knew the terrain, he knew the people of the area, and when they called the alarm, the Cuban leader had quickly moved in thousands of troops to encircle the little exile force.

"I don't think it's going as well as it should," the President said in one of his first calls that Monday morning, to his brother Robert. His tie was pulled down a little and he was talking faster than usual. Robert Kennedy was a hundred miles away, in Williamsburg, Virginia, to speak to a convention of newspaper editors. "Come back here," his brother said.

By noon the next day, Tuesday, April 18, messages from the beachhead were desperate. Brigade 2506 was totally outnumbered and outgunned. Some fought bravely, but more than a thousand surrendered. Some said they had never had enough ammunition. Many of them had believed that they would hit the beach with the U.S. Air Force above and U.S. Marines behind them. There was no uprising of the Cuban people. Castro, who did indeed read the same newspapers as Kennedy, had arrested virtually all the potential rebels in his country, thousands of men and women. And the potential for rebellion had been low to begin with. The Cuban Revolutionary Council, a dozen pre-Castro politicians organized by the CIA as political cover for the invasion, was seen by many anti-Castro Cubans as just a motley collection of servants of the old dictatorship. The CIA's B-26s had only enough fuel to stay over the beachhead for less than forty minutes because the flight to and from

Nicaragua was a 1,000-mile, six-hour round trip. They were no match for Castro's three American-made jets and two British-made Sea Furys.

"We are under attack by two Sea Fury aircraft and heavy artillery," the Brigade commander on the beach, a former Cuban Army lieutenant named José Pérez ("Pepe") San Román, broadcast at 1:45 P.M. Tuesday. "Do not see any friendly air cover as you promised. Need jet support immediately. Pepe." In his last message, when a final call for U.S. aid was denied, San Román said: "And you, sir, are a son of a bitch."

In Washington, Kennedy and his men continued trying to publicly play at business as usual, as if they believed the cover stories that the invasion was strictly a Cuban affair. They sensed disaster, but it had not happened yet, and most of official Washington, including other politicians and the press, was still in the information dark. Inside the White House, crisis followed the President from room to room. The meetings finally broke up for a while that evening when the President and some of the men in the Cabinet Room had to change into white tie and tails for a grand White House reception to honor members of Congress. Four hundred and fifty men and women wandered through the house that night, impressed that the Kennedys had opened the closed doors and taken down the tourist ropes that kept visitors, including congressmen, confined to a few public rooms. It seemed gracious and calm to most of them.

John and Jacqueline Kennedy appeared at just after ten, at the top of the stairway into the front entrance hall of the President's house. The Marine Band in the East Room struck up a popular Broadway song, "Mr. Wonderful."

Kennedy seemed totally at ease, mingling with his guests, sipping a little champagne. Shortly before midnight, however, he slipped away, going to the Cabinet Room where his men were waiting. Their faces were grim. Those who had planned and sold the invasion, including Dick Bissell, were insisting that the invasion could still succeed—if only the President would send U.S. Navy jets to control the air over the beachhead and bring up a U.S. destroyer to knock out Castro's tanks.

"Right," said Admiral Arleigh Burke, chief of staff of the Navy. "Let me take two jets and shoot down those enemy aircraft."

"No," Kennedy said again. "I don't want the U.S. to get involved in this."

"Hell, Mr. President," Burke said. "We are involved."

"Admiral, I don't want the United States involved in this," the President said again.

"It's time for this outfit to go guerrilla," said General Lyman L. Lemnitzer, Chairman of the Joint Chiefs of Staff. That was the CIA back-up plan: Disperse and head for the Escambray Mountains.

"They're not prepared to go guerrilla," said Bissell. The mountains were eighty miles away, and the men were trapped in the swamps with more than twenty thousand of Castro's soldiers waiting between the beach and the high ground. It had all been a lie. There was no way through the swamps and Castro had been waiting for them. The Cuban leader had weapons the Americans did not know about. There was no uprising. The unwritten plan, it seemed, had always been for the President, Eisenhower or Kennedy, to send in the Air Force, the Navy, and the Marines if the Cuban exiles could not handle Castro's men. Kennedy felt betrayed. In the days that followed he was seen talking to himself, sometimes startling his men by interrupting conversations with lines like: "How could I have been so stupid?"

The talk went in circles that Tuesday night and early Wednesday morning. So did the men who were called in or just happened to be around. This was a parody of Kennedy's hallway style, men in white tie and tails, men in sportshirts and corduroys hurriedly pulled on when they were awakened at home by calls from the White House switchboard.

"Where is Berle? Find Berle," the President said. He wanted Adolf Berle, the Assistant Secretary of State for Latin America, to go down to Opa-Locka, Florida, to calm down the Revolutionary Council of exiled Cuban politicians fronting for the CIA. The politicians, led more or less by José Miró Cardona, the first president of the Cuban Supreme Court under Castro, were at an abandoned U.S. Air Force Base. They were prisoners for all practical purposes, unaware that the CIA was issuing battle communiqués to the press in their name.

"One of them is threatening suicide," Kennedy told Berle. "Others want to be put on the beachhead. They don't know how dismal things are."

"I can think of happier missions," Berle said. Kennedy turned to Arthur Schlesinger and said, "You ought to go with Berle."

People were repeating themselves as Berle and Schlesinger left at 2:00 A.M. Bissell and Burke continued to press Kennedy to send Navy jets over the beachhead. Finally, the President did contradict his earlier orders, saying six planes from the *Essex* could be used to fly cover for the Cubans piloting the CIA's B-26s.

"That's a deeper commitment, Mr. President," Rusk said quickly. The President's pledge not to use U.S. forces under any circumstances, made on national television a week before, had originally been the Secretary's idea.

The President put his hand under his nose. "We're already in it up to here," he said.

But Kennedy was consistent on one thing: he stayed focused on political repercussions rather than military considerations. He was splitting the differences between his men, sticking with half-measures, but he was still trying, against all reason, to keep things quiet. At 3:30 A.M. Wednesday morning, he said the jets could go for one run over the beach—to protect a bombing and strafing sortie by the B-26s and allow more ammunition to be landed from the invaders' supply ships. Bissell and Burke jumped up and ran from the room to transmit the orders to the U.S.S. *Essex*, the aircraft carrier.

"Wait," Kennedy called. "Paint out the markings. . . ." The President wanted all U.S. insignia removed from the jets. The futility of it all was dramatized just after dawn. The American jets never found the B-26s, arriving over the beach at six-thirty, an hour before the old bombers from Nicaragua. No one had remembered that Cuba is in the same time zone as New York, but Nicaragua is an hour earlier, in the same zone as Chicago. The exiles on the beach were radioing again that they were under attack from Soviet MiGs, a dozen or more of them. But there were actually just the three T-33s and they shot down two of the unprotected B-26s.

Kennedy sent Mac Bundy off to New York to calm down Stevenson. The U.N. ambassador's personal credibility was critical to control political damage around the world. "Hold his hand," Kennedy said.

After 4:00 A.M., Kennedy went back into his office with Salinger and his appointments secretary, Ken O'Donnell. In the middle of a sentence, he walked away from them, out the French doors and into the Rose Garden. He walked alone out there on the wet grass for an hour, still in his white tie and tails.

Kennedy was crying in his bedroom when he woke up after sunrise that Wednesday morning. His hair was messed and his tie was a little off-center when he came downstairs to the Oval Office, but he sharpened up when he went over to the Cabinet Room for more hours of bad news. At one point he was called from the room and Robert Kennedy, who had not known of the invasion plan until the week before, was pacing back and forth, muttering: "We've got to do something. We've got to do something." He stopped for a moment, glared at the men around the table, and said heatedly: "All you bright fellows have gotten the President into this, and if you don't do something now, my brother will be regarded as a paper tiger by the Russians."

There was silence until Dean Rusk broke it by pounding his left hand over and over on the arm of the President's empty chair.

"What matters now is this man," he said. "We have to save this man!"

Chapter 8

APRIL 22, 1961

José Miró Cardona, president of the Cuban Revolutionary Council, and five council members had been flown to Florida from New York by CIA agents on Sunday night, April 15, just before the landings at the Bay of Pigs. They thought they were going to Nicaragua to see Brigade 2506 before it headed for Cuba. Three of them, including Cardona, had sons in the Brigade. Instead, for more than sixty hours they had been at Opa-Locka, in a small house surrounded by U.S. soldiers, with no idea what was happening on the beaches.

Shortly after 10:00 A.M. on Wednesday, April 19, Kennedy took a phone call from Arthur Schlesinger. He was with the members of the Revolutionary Council. For three hours, Schlesinger said, he and Berle had absorbed the outrage and pain of the Cubans. "We can't do any more here," Schlesinger said. "They're demanding to see you."

"Bring them up here," Kennedy told him. It seemed he had another disposal problem: how to prevent this crew of used politicians, who still had not been told the details of the disaster on the beach, from going public with their sorry tale of American duplicity and stupidity.

It was after four when Schlesinger and Berle led the Cubans into a side door of the East Wing of the White House. The idea was to avoid the reporters and cameras clustered, as always, in the lobby of the West Wing. They were an exhausted bunch, physically and politically, too. A couple of them had not slept for more than forty-eight hours, arguing with each other and their CIA guardians, staring for hours out the windows of the old house at their American guards.

The Cubans were taken to the Oval Office and seated facing each other on couches in front of the fireplace. The President sat in his rocking chair at the end of the couches, facing the fire. Schlesinger had never seen him so drawn. Kennedy began by apologizing for the way the Cubans had been treated. He had not known, he said. He was sorry.

"I know something of how you feel," Kennedy said, adding that he knew some of them had sons in the Brigade. "I lost a brother and a brother-in-law in the war."

He showed them a photograph of Joseph P. Kennedy, Jr., who was twenty-nine years old when the bomber he was piloting blew up over the English Channel in 1944. He asked if they had pictures, and one of them, Dr. Antonio Maceo, took out a small photo of his nineteen-year-old son.

"Does this look like a mercenary?" Kennedy said, holding up the little picture. The council members looked a bit confused. They did not know that Castro was calling the men of the Brigade "mercenaries." In fact, many were the pampered children of the island's old first families. "The Yacht Club Boys," they were called. Many had seemed to think the invasion was a game: U.S. Marines would do the fighting and they would get the girls in Havana.

Kennedy read them the optimistic cable Colonel Jack Hawkins had sent from the Brigade's training camp in Guatemala. That was what had convinced him, he said, that their sons and the men of the Brigade could win without American troops. The council's "Minister of War," Antonio de Varona, who already knew he had lost a son and was the most haggard of the lot, said then, "You have been taken for a ride, Mr. President, and this Council has been taken for a ride."

Kennedy seemed to nod. He was bitter, too. He believed he had been set up for disaster by the Joint Chiefs of Staff, especially its chairman, Army General Lyman L. Lemnitzer. He told the Cubans they must understand that the United States had to balance many considerations, many commitments, many obligations, around the world. He could not send in troops this time. His commitment to a free Cuba was total. U.S. ships would be moving in after dark to rescue men on the beach or in the water. There would be other times.

Schlesinger, who had been frightened at how tired Kennedy looked when he came in with the council members, thought he had never seen him so impressive.

"As soon as you leave the White House, you are all free men," the

President told them. "Free to go anywhere you want, free to say anything you want, free to talk to anyone you want."

Then Kennedy went to his desk, took out a small stack of photographs of himself, and autographed one for each of the Cubans. As John Plank, who had been called down from Harvard to translate, was leaving, Kennedy said, "You'll stay with the Revolutionary Council?" The professor began to say, "I can't . . ." But instead he said, "Yes, Mr. President."

Plank flew with Cardona and the others to New York secretly. They had agreed not to mention Opa-Locka and to pretend they had never left their headquarters in the Commodore Hotel in Manhattan. That night, the public relations operation set up by the CIA issued a bulletin in the name of the exile council. No translator was needed. The statement, a total lie, was written in English and released in English to the American press: "The recent landings in Cuba have been constantly though inaccurately described as an invasion. It was, in fact, a landing of supplies and support for our patriots who have been fighting in Cuba for months. . . . The major portion of our landing party has reached the Escambray Mountains."

Cardona emerged forty-eight hours later, telling reporters he had never asked for U.S. help and that none was given. But he also hinted of new commitments from Kennedy, and said he expected his country to be liberated within a month. Other council members disagreed, saying it might take three or four months.

By the next day, Thursday, April 20, Kennedy seemed to be himself again in his first appearance after the public learned some of what happened at the Bay of Pigs: a long-scheduled speech to the American Society of Newspaper Editors at the Statler-Hilton Hotel a few blocks from the White House. He tried to elevate the Cuban misadventure into an American Dunkirk, as heroic and momentous as Britain's last stand on the continent of Europe in 1940—and once again he returned to the dismal theme of *Why England Slept*, the shortcomings of democracy.

"The hour is late. . . ," said the President. "If the self-discipline of the free cannot match the iron discipline of the mailed fist—in economic, political, scientific and all other kinds of struggles as well as the military —then the peril to freedom will continue to rise . . . The advantages of a police state—its use of mass terror and arrests to prevent the spread of free dissent—cannot be overlooked by those who expect the fall of every fanatic tyrant.

"The message of Cuba, of Laos, of the rising din of Communist voices in Asia and Latin America—these messages are all the same: The complacent, the self-indulgent, the soft societies are about to be swept away with the debris of history. Only the strong, only the industrious, only the determined, only the courageous, only the visionary who determines the real nature of our struggle can possibly survive.

"We dare not fail to realize that this struggle is taking place every day, without fanfare, in thousands of villages and markets—day and night—and in classrooms all over the globe. We intend to profit from this lesson. . . . We intend to reexamine and reorient our forces of all kinds, our tactics and other institutions. I am determined upon our system's survival and success, regardless of the cost and regardless of the peril."

As if to emphasize his point, after the speech Kennedy established a secret Vietnam Task Force, headed by Deputy Secretary of Defense Roswell Gilpatric. The chief operating officer was General Lansdale. The charge was just a few words: "To prevent Communist domination of Vietnam."

"It was the worst experience of my life," Kennedy said of the Cuban fiasco later that afternoon of the meeting with the Cubans—to, of all people, Richard Nixon. "Believe it or not, they're ready to go out and fight again, if we will give them the word and the support."

Nixon had been called in as part of a series of unity meetings. Kennedy wanted the symbolic presence and public support of both political friends and foes to show the nation and the world that Americans were rallying around the President, right or wrong.

"What would you do now?" Kennedy asked his old opponent.

"I would find a proper legal cover and I would go in," Nixon replied. "There are several justifications that could be used, like protecting American citizens living in Cuba and defending our base at Guantánamo. The most important thing at this point is that we do whatever is necessary to get Castro and Communism out."

"I just don't think we can take the risk," Kennedy said. He shook his head, telling Nixon that both Walter Lippmann and Charles Bohlen, one of the State Department's most respected Soviet-watchers, were telling him that Khrushchev was cocky after this American debacle. "There is a good chance that if we move on Cuba, Khrushchev will move on Berlin."

"I will publicly support you to the hilt," Nixon said. The two men talked for almost an hour about Cuba and Berlin, and Southeast Asia. Kennedy said one of the first things he had to do now was reassure President Diem of South Vietnam that the Cuban disaster did not mean the United States would abandon that far part of the world to the Communists. To make that point, he had to consider sending more U.S. troops to Vietnam, as trainers for Diem's army.

Nixon and Kennedy, past and assumed future adversaries, talked on about the effect of Cuba on the politics of 1964. That was their business, after all, the thing they had in common, and they both understood the cycles of military action and its effect on voters—first the cheers and parades, then the coffins and the anger. To Nixon, Kennedy seemed depressed. "The way things are going," Kennedy said, "and with all the problems we have, if I do the right kind of job, I don't know whether I'm going to be here in 1964."

The former Vice President said nothing. The President stood up and paced, saying, "It really is true that foreign affairs is the only important issue for a President to handle, isn't it? I mean who gives a shit if the minimum wage is $1.15 or $1.25, in comparison to something like this?"

It was the closest Kennedy and Nixon had ever been to the kinship of competitors. But Kennedy was not himself. And he was still distracted later that day when he greeted another visitor, Dr. Martin Luther King, Jr. As much as Kennedy wanted to understand King's motivations and politics, there always seemed to be something more important going on, and civil rights rated with the minimum wage this particular day.

King's meeting with the President was for the record supposed to be "accidental," though it had been planned weeks before. King was in Washington for a meeting with Robert Kennedy and his civil rights staff, a secret meeting in a private dining room at the Mayflower Hotel. When it was over, King had gone to the White House, unannounced and unscheduled, with his friend Harris Wofford. On schedule, the President had come by Wofford's office and had bumped into King.

"It's good to see you," said the President, who had met with King only once, during the campaign to ask his advice on winning more of the Negro vote. The preacher said then that Kennedy had to do something quick and dramatic. Two months later, when King was jailed in Georgia, Kennedy had telephoned to comfort his wife.

"I've been keeping up with you and with your work," the President said this time. "My brother's been keeping me apprised of certain developments and if you ever need me, you know the door is always open to you."

But it was the back door or, sometimes, the side door. Kennedy had told Wofford that he wanted to see King unofficially, that is, away from photographers and reporters—any time he was in town. He had given the same instructions about Nelson Rockefeller to his Deputy Secretary of Defense, Roswell Gilpatric, who was a close friend of the New York governor, the Republican Kennedy thought would probably be his opponent in 1964. He wanted to see Rockefeller unofficially any time the governor was in town. He wanted to know King and Rockefeller better than he did, size them up. The King appointment was one of many each day not recorded in White House calendars or schedules, though those books *seemed* to cover every minute of the President's life. Their apparent excess of detail served to bury the minutes and encounters the President preferred to conceal or forget.

By Friday morning, he was a politician back at work, preparing for a news conference. Schlesinger, Salinger, and Goodwin came at nine o'clock to prepare Kennedy for a barrage of questions on the failed invasion. The President cut them off. He said he was not going to take any questions on Cuba. "Memory is short," he said. "If we just sit tight for about three weeks, things will cool off and we can proceed from there."

An hour later, he began his news conference with this statement: "I know that many of you have further questions about Cuba. . . . But I do not think that any useful national purpose would be served by my going further into the Cuba question this morning."

That was about it. The President obviously had not been able to control events, but he had the power to control the flow of information and the first interpretation of events. Now he used that power, leaving the press and public with fragments, unable to figure out exactly what had happened, predisposed to take the President's word. Only one reporter defied Kennedy's injunction on questions, asking whether it was true that Rusk and Bowles were against the invasion. But the others seemed embarrassed by that defiance of the President at a time when Americans had to stick together. And Kennedy deflected it easily, saying, "There's an old saying that victory has a hundred fathers and defeat is an orphan. . . . I am the responsible officer of this government."

Back in the Oval Office again, he was angry that anyone had questioned him at all. "What the hell do they want me to do—give them the roll call vote? . . . Say we took the beating of our lives? That the CIA and the Pentagon are stupid? . . . We're going to have to straighten this out, and soon."

First, though, he had to find out what had happened. The next morning, Saturday, April 22, he met with Maxwell Taylor, the retired Army Chief of Staff who had first championed "Flexible Response." Taylor was in New York now, the chairman of Lincoln Center for the Performing Arts. The President wanted him to take a leave of absence to work with Robert Kennedy in preparing a report for him alone on what had gone wrong at the Bay of Pigs, and what he should do about it.

Taylor was stunned by what he saw when he arrived at the Oval Office at ten o'clock that morning. Vice President Johnson, McGeorge

Bundy, and several other men were gathered around the President. The scene reminded him of something he had seen fifteen years before: a command post overrun by the enemy during the Battle of the Bulge. He saw the same glazed eyes, heard the same slow speech. Kennedy showed him the operational map for the Bay of Pigs operation, and Taylor had trouble believing it was real. It was a plan doomed to failure, he thought, fifteen hundred amateurs attempting the most difficult of military operations, an amphibious invasion on a hostile shore. His first conclusion was that he would have used at least a division of regular troops— fifteen thousand men—to hold that beachhead. "It's a hell of a way to learn things," Kennedy said of his on-the-job training.

After seeing Taylor, the President boarded a helicopter, flying to Camp David for the most important of his unity meetings, lunch with former President Eisenhower at the heavily wooded presidential retreat in the Catoctin Mountains, seventy miles and thirty minutes away. Kennedy had never seen the place, which Ike had named for his grandson. The two men ate lunch at Aspen Cabin and Kennedy described the mess of the Cuban plan, the failures in intelligence, timing, and tactics. He was more candid than Eisenhower had expected, but he seemed bewildered to the five-star general who had commanded the largest amphibious invasion in history. Then, as they walked the paths of the 125-acre reservation, the general gave the former lieutenant the tongue-lashing of his life.

"No one knows how tough this job is until after he has been in it a few months," Kennedy said, kind of ruefully.

"Mr. President," Eisenhower said. "If you will forgive me, I think I mentioned that to you three months ago."

"I certainly have learned a lot since," Kennedy said.

"Mr. President," Ike said, "before you approved this plan, did you have everybody in front of you debating the thing so you got the pros and cons yourself and then made the decision, or did you see these people one at a time?"

Kennedy smiled and said, "Well, I did have a meeting . . . I just approved a plan that had been recommended by the CIA and by the Joint Chiefs of Staff. I just took their advice."

"Mr. President, were there any changes in the plan that the Joint Chiefs of Staff had approved?"

"Yes, there were. . . . We did want to call off one bombing sally."

"Why was that called off?" Ike demanded. "Why did they change plans after the troops were already at sea?"

"Well," Kennedy responded, "we felt it necessary that we keep our hand concealed in this affair; we thought that if it was learned that we were really doing this and not these rebels themselves, the Soviets would be very apt to cause trouble in Berlin."

"Mr. President, that is exactly the opposite of what would really happen," Eisenhower said. "The Soviets follow their own plans, and if they see us show any weakness that is when they press us the hardest. The second they see us show strength and do something on our own, that is when they are very cagey."

"Well, my advice was that we must try to keep our hands from showing in this affair."

"Mr. President," repeated Eisenhower, "how could you expect the world to believe that we had nothing to do with it? Where did these people get the ships to go from Central America to Cuba? Where did they get the weapons? Where did they get all the communications and all the other things that they would need? How could you possibly have kept from the world any knowledge that the United States had been involved? I believe there is only one thing to do when you go into this kind of thing, it must be a success."

"Well, I assure you that, hereafter, if we get in anything like this, it is going to be a success."

"Well, I am glad to hear that," said Eisenhower.

That was in private. In public, the two men came back from their walk to face the reporters and cameras assembled outside the electric fence patrolled by a platoon of Marines.

Kennedy began, saying, "I asked President Eisenhower here to bring him up to date on recent events and get the benefit of his thoughts and experience." Eisenhower dutifully added: "I am all in favor of the United States supporting the man who has to carry the responsibility for our foreign affairs."

After that, as Eisenhower recorded in his diary that night: "He took me in his car to the heliport and suggested a golf game in the near future."

Back in Washington that afternoon, Kennedy was still angry, at least in private, where he did his shouting about his generals and admirals with tiers of service ribbons advertising their experience: "Those sons-of-bitches with all the fruit salad just sat there nodding, saying it would work" . . . "I've got to do something about those CIA bastards" . . . "How could I have been so stupid?"

He told Allen Dulles that he and Bissell, men he had respected and liked, would have to leave after things quieted down. "In a parliamentary system I would resign," the President told Bissell. "In our system the President can't and doesn't. So you and Allen must go." He thought he would make his brother, Robert, head of the agency, but not yet. He needed Dulles's Republican credentials to ensure against all-out partisan criticism of the Bay of Pigs operation.

Pacing his office later, alone with his friend Red Fay, the President said: "I sat around that day and all these fellas all saying 'This is gonna work, and this won't go,' saying 'Sure, this whole thing will work out.' Now, in retrospect, I know damn well that they didn't have any intention of giving me the straight word on this thing. They just thought that if we got involved in the thing, that I would have to say 'Go ahead, you can throw all our forces in there, and just move into Cuba.' . . . Well, from now on it's John Kennedy that makes the decisions as to whether or not we're going to do these things."

Or rather, John Kennedy and his own men. He turned instinctively to the people who got him into office. He told his brother and Ted Sorensen, neither of whom had been involved in Bay of Pigs planning, that they were now to consider themselves experts on foreign policy and defense. He took the lesson that he could not trust other people's people. "You see Kenny there?" he said once as O'Donnell slept on a plane. "If I woke him up and asked him to jump out of this plane for me, he'd do it. You don't find that kind of loyalty easily." Of Mrs. Lincoln, his secretary, the President said that if he called to inform her that he had just cut off Jackie's head and wanted to get rid of it, the devoted secretary would appear immediately with a hatbox of appropriate size.

Robert Kennedy was more than a brother. He had no hidden agenda, no other loyalty than to John Kennedy. Among his many services, he played the political wife, intuitive judge of who could be trusted and who could not, a role rejected by Mrs. Kennedy. The brothers could share personal assessments of other men and women without the distortion of separate ambition or goals. John Kennedy summed up part of his dependence on his brother by saying: "With Bobby, I don't have to think about organization. I just show up."

As a new foreign policy adviser, Robert Kennedy's first advice was to forget about making him CIA director. That would be the end of the President's plausible deniability regarding the less wholesome of CIA operations. He began to sit in on foreign affairs deliberations as a sort of surrogate President. On April 27, he was at a National Security Council meeting, screaming at Undersecretary of State Bowles, who was already in disfavor for telling reporters he had been against the Bay of Pigs landings. Bowles had the bad luck to be sitting in for Rusk that day and presenting two turgid State Department papers. One of them reported that Castro was now securely in power. Bowles said that only a full-scale U.S. invasion could dislodge him now, which was something the Kennedys did not want to hear.

"This is worthless," Robert Kennedy shouted, throwing down one of the State Department reports. "What can we do about Cuba? This doesn't tell us anything." He went on like that for almost ten minutes. "You people are so anxious to protect your own asses that you're afraid to do anything. All you want to do is dump the whole thing on the President.

"We'd be better off if you just quit and left foreign policy to some one else," he finished, glaring at Bowles.

The President sat silently as if nothing were happening. He tapped the metal part of his pencil's eraser against his front teeth as Bobby went on and on. Sitting behind Ted Sorensen, Richard Goodwin realized for the first time that there could be rage and more behind the controlled and easy manner of John Kennedy. He had no doubt that Robert Kennedy was communicating exactly what his brother wanted said, probably repeating what the President was saying when the two of them were alone.

A week after that meeting, the President formalized the sense of the White House by approving a "Record of Action" that began:

"Agreed that U.S. policy toward Cuba should aim at the downfall of Castro, and that since the measures agreed below are not likely to achieve this end, the matter should be reviewed at intervals with a view to further action. . . .

"Agreed that the United States should not undertake military intervention in Cuba now, but should do nothing that would foreclose the possibility of military intervention in the future."

He also approved another item at the same time: "Efforts should be made to reassure Sarit and Diem that we are not abandoning Southeast Asia; noted that the Secretaries of State and Defense would be sending recommendations to the President promptly on U.S. training troops in Viet Nam."

There were meetings, too, in Havana and Moscow. The Soviets assumed that there would be another invasion of Cuba, a real one next time with U.S. troops. After a conversation with Anastas Mikoyan, First Deputy of the Soviet Council of Ministers, Secretary Rusk reported to Kennedy that the Soviets were more committed to Castro than Americans knew. "Cuba means a great deal to old Bolsheviks like Khrushchev and me," Mikoyan had told Rusk with surprising passion. "This is the first time a country has gone Communist peacefully."

President Kennedy had some passion of his own about Cuba now. He had commanded men in combat himself and he felt it was his responsibility to get the men of Brigade 2506 out of Castro's prisons. More than a thousand of them had been captured.

"I put those men in there," he told Goodwin. "They trusted me. And they're in prison now because I fucked up. I have to get them out. . . . Whatever it takes."

That Sunday night, April 30, the President saw the page proofs of *Time* magazine, the pages the editors were given to make final corrections before the edition went to press. The first section of the magazine, "The Presidency," began: "Last week as John F. Kennedy closed out the first 100 days of his administration, the U.S. suffered a month-long series of setbacks rare in the history of the Republic. First came the Russians' man-in-space triumph. Then the shockingly bungled invasion of Cuba. Finally, and belatedly, came the sickening realization that U.S.-backed Laos was about to go down the Communist drain."

Kennedy was determined to turn that kind of talk around, but he still thought he could do it on the cheap, with some hard thinking, a little bluff, and a few good men—or even all by himself. He thought that he could straighten out a few things himself if he just had a reasonable opportunity to get together one-on-one with Khrushchev. He had charmed a lot of men in his time. He was beginning to recover his optimism and humor. Assuming, correctly, that Arthur Schlesinger was taking notes for a book on his presidency, Kennedy told him he had a title for him: "Kennedy: The Only Years."

Maybe. But maybe not. The nation rallied around its humiliated President. The national Gallup Poll that came out after the Bay of Pigs, on the same day as *Time,* reported that 83 percent of respondents approved of the job Kennedy was doing as President, and only 5 percent disapproved—his approval rating had jumped ten points.

"Jesus, it's just like Ike," Kennedy said, reading the poll. "The worse you do, the better they like you."

Chapter 9

On the morning of April 26, President Kennedy had been working with Ted Sorensen, editing the speech he planned to give the next night in New York to the American Newspaper Publishers Association. He was going to ask those publishers to work with the government in a voluntary censorship plan. "In the interest of national security," he would tell them. Then, just after noon, he was shown a cable from Ambassador Winthrop Brown in Vientiane, Laos:

> Muong Sai has fallen . . . I do not see how we can afford to let enemy continue his forward movement. . . . See no way to stop him except by use of B-26s, probably followed up by U.S. or SEATO Troops . . . I realize that such action would blow whole cease-fire negotiations wide open . . . but see no alternative.

Almost no one in Washington, including the President, really knew where or what Muong Sai was. But what Kennedy did know was that his bluff in Laos did not seem to be working. The Pathet Lao certainly did not seem to be impressed with the movement of U.S. ships and troops to Thailand and the Laotian border.

Kennedy spent more than four hours the next day, April 27, in meetings on Laos, first three hours with his own men, officially convened as the National Security Council, and then an hour with congressional leaders. As he took off for New York that afternoon, the White House issued a statement saying: "Discussions revolved around the question of what the approach of the United States and other nations interested in maintaining the integrity of an independent Laos is to be should the Communist rebels prove completely unwilling to grant a cease-fire and work toward a peaceful solution." The first edition of *The New York Times* came out that night with its lead headline: "KENNEDY CONFERS ON ACTION IN LAOS IF TRUCE BID FAILS . . . Situation Called Grim."

At the Waldorf-Astoria, the President wanted to look back at what happened in Cuba the week before. He had no great love for the seventeen hundred people in the grand ballroom of the Waldorf. These were the men who ran newspapers that had endorsed Nixon by better than three to one. They also owned hundreds and hundreds of local radio and television stations around the country. He blamed Franklin D. Roosevelt for that, thinking that FDR's greatest mistake as a politician had been to allow publishers to get those licenses to use the public airwaves. Publishers were rich businessmen and rich businessmen were almost all Republicans.

"Our way of life is under attack. Those who make themselves our enemy are advancing around the globe," the President told the newspaper owners in a style that generally matched their own editorials. In fact, many of them were suspicious that Kennedy himself was one of the attackers of their way of life. "Soft on Communism" was their shorthand for most national Democrats. Many of the papers owned by the men (and a couple of widows) in the audience were calling for following up the failure of the Bay of Pigs with a full-scale invasion of Cuba. The Memphis *Commercial Appeal* had said that week: "The American who holds back is already doomed. The well-armed Red gravediggers are knocking on our door." The *Charleston News and Courier* made it personal: "Not much time remains for the education of John F. Kennedy. In his first great crisis, he bungled horribly." In Hearst newspapers around the country, columnist George Sokolsky asked: "Do we have to stand still until Soviet Russia has established a missile and submarine base in Cuba?"

The President went on: "We are opposed around the world by a monolithic and ruthless conspiracy that relies primarily on covert means for expanding its sphere of influence—on infiltration instead of invasion, on subversion instead of elections, on intimidation instead of free choice, on guerrillas by night instead of armies by day. Its preparations are concealed, not published. Its mistakes are buried, not headlined. Its dissenters are silenced, not praised. No expenditure is questioned, no rumor is printed, no secret is revealed.

"In time of war, the government and the press have customarily joined in an effort, based largely on self-discipline, to prevent unauthorized disclosures to the enemy. In time of 'clear and present danger,' the courts have held that even the privileged rights of the First Amendment must yield to the public's need for national security. . . . I do ask every publisher, every editor, and every newsman in the nation to reexamine his own standards and to recognize the nature of our country's peril."

He wanted the press to join in recognizing that the twilight struggle with communism around the world was as clear and as present a danger as World War II had been. He called for "self-discipline," then asked the publishers themselves to join with the government in establishing Cold War news guidelines.

"Every newspaper now asks itself, with respect to every story: 'Is it news?' All that I suggest is that you add the question: 'Is it in the national interest?' "

The publishers clapped politely only twice, once when he said he was not asking for editorial support on every decision, and once when he finished. It was not his view of communism that turned them off; most of them agreed totally with that. It was the fact that he wanted to tell them how to run their businesses. Some of the newspaper owners thought Kennedy was hysterical that night, and the next day's editorial reaction was not polite. "In days of peril especially, the country needs more facts, not fewer," said *The New York Herald Tribune. The New York Times* said the same: "In this time of 'clear and present danger' it is more essential than ever that people be fully informed of the problems and the perils. . . ."

The President stayed in New York after his speech, making a show of visits the next day to the thirtieth President, Herbert Hoover, who was eighty-five years old, and to General Douglas MacArthur, who was eighty-one. Both of them did their duty, loyally backing the President in his hour of need. Then he had lunch, by way of apology for the bodyguard of lies around the Bay of Pigs, with Adlai Stevenson and the Secretary-General of the United Nations, Dag Hammarskjöld, at the Waldorf Towers. Hoover, MacArthur, and Stevenson all lived there.

Kennedy was tremendously impressed by MacArthur, the United States' other retired five-star general, commander of all U.S. troops in the Pacific during World War II. Kennedy had spent years, as both officer and civilian, making fun of the general's vanity and arrogance, but he changed his mind just before meeting the old soldier—when he read the citation for the Congressional Medal of Honor, the nation's highest decoration for bravery, won by thirty-eight-year-old Brigadier

General MacArthur in France in World War I. Courage above all impressed Kennedy and he actually took notes as the general spoke, writing: "He does not feel we should intervene at this time in Cuba because it does not represent a military danger to us although the time may come when we may have to do so" . . . "Believes it would be a mistake to fight in Laos" . . . "He thinks our line should be Japan, Formosa and the Philippines." The general, who disliked Eisenhower, once his aide de camp, made Kennedy feel better by blaming Ike for Cuba and most everything else, saying: "The chickens are coming home to roost and you live in the chicken house."

At his own penthouse apartment in the Carlyle Hotel, the President met with local Democratic powers, the party's leaders in Brooklyn and the Bronx, City Council president Joseph Sharkey and Representative Charles Buckley, to talk about local patronage and the city's upcoming mayoralty election. Then he took a helicopter to Idlewild Airport and boarded Air Force One to go to Chicago, taking along two Illinois congressmen, Roland Libonati and Daniel Rostenkowski, to talk a little more local politics—Chicago politics this time—before he spoke that night at the annual $100-a-plate Cook County Democratic Dinner. Wars, small or big, won or lost, were part of Kennedy's business, but so was repaying favors. He owed the mayor of Chicago, Richard J. Daley, who had done as much as one politician could do for another in the making of the President in 1960. Nixon, for one, always believed that Daley's help included rounding up a few thousand crucial votes, just enough to carry Illinois, from Democrats who had died between presidential elections.

The President arrived at the Conrad Hilton Hotel in Chicago just before 5:00 P.M. "The President remained in his suite until 7 P.M.," according to the mimeographed schedules handed out by the White House press later to reporters downstairs. Actually, he had slipped out of the Hilton for twenty minutes of sex with a young woman named Judith Campbell in another hotel, the Ambassador East. Campbell, who was twenty-six years old, had been introduced to Kennedy during the campaign by his brother-in-law, actor Peter Lawford, and Lawford's buddy Frank Sinatra, a former lover. She was a woman with many friends, it seemed. When Kennedy flew back to Washington the next day, she flew to Miami to stay with another lover, Sam Giancana, the organized crime boss of Chicago.

Back in the White House, the President had to refocus on Laos. Since his March 23 speech, the number of Marines on alert in Okinawa had increased from fourteen hundred to ten thousand, all ready to board Seventh Fleet ships for the twenty-five-hundred-mile journey across the

Pacific to Thailand and then six hundred miles across that country and part of Laos to confront the Pathet Lao and their North Vietnamese allies.

Kennedy had also had some success in lining up reluctant SEATO allies to join in a possible U.S. invasion. Pakistan agreed to send eight thousand troops, which made Kennedy an admirer of its military dictator of the time, Ayub Khan. Four other SEATO allies, Thailand, the Philippines, Australia, and New Zealand, promised to send troops—but not many. Prime Minister Macmillan agreed, reluctantly, to send a British battalion from Hong Kong. President de Gaulle had told Kennedy that France would not send troops back to Indochina under any circumstances.

Among the papers on the President's bed each morning was the *Daily Intelligence Briefing,* ten pages or so each day on events round the world from 6:30 A.M. one day to 6:30 A.M. the next. The Laos section was often the longest. Reading it these mornings, Kennedy did not know whether to laugh or cry. The American-paid Royal Army would break ranks to pick flowers or go swimming. Many Laotian soldiers had never seen tanks but were sure they could be stopped by sharpened bamboo sticks tipped with phallic symbols. Once, both sides left a "battlefield" together to join the fun at a local water festival. One morning the report solemnly estimated that 90 percent of Laotians believed the world was flat and Laotians were the only people on it.

"Well, we made good soldiers of the Koreans," General Lyman Lemnitzer, Chairman of the Joint Chiefs of Staff, told the President during a late April meeting. "Why can't we make good soldiers out of the Laotians?"

The answer was that no people on earth, flat or round, could be much more different than the driven and disciplined Koreans and the lovemaking Lao. There was even doubt that the Pathet Lao, the toughest force in the field, would continue fighting without the prodding of North Vietnamese battalions behind them. And, despite those words, the U.S. military, which had been unable to win "limited" war in Korea, was less than eager to become involved in a land war anywhere in Asia. The Joint Chiefs were now talking of Laos in terms of "all or nothing." Stay out completely or send in more than a hundred thousand combat troops and be ready to use nuclear weapons if the Chinese Communists—who were reported to be building roads into Laos, a country that had few —responded by sending troops, too. Military confidence in the new administration was not helped when McNamara enthusiastically proposed arming the Royal Laotian Air Force with 100-pound bombs to scatter the Pathet Lao and North Vietnamese, apparently without knowing the Royal Army had only six planes, each capable of carrying only two bombs in a country with more than twice the land area of Cuba.

Kennedy, though, was already on a different wavelength. Humbled in Cuba and warned by MacArthur, he was determined not to send combat troops into Laos. The movement of troops and ships was a bluff. He thought Lemnitzer was a fool. Remembering that Thomas Gates, Eisenhower's Secretary of Defense, had told him in January that a U.S. division could be in Laos and ready to fight in twelve days, Kennedy asked Lemnitzer: "How will they get in there?"

"They can land at two airports," said the General. The places named were Savanaket and Peske.

"How many can land at those airports?" Kennedy asked.

"If you can have perfect conditions, you can land a thousand a day."

"How many Communist troops are in the area?"

"We would guess three thousand."

"How long will it take them to bring up more?"

"They can bring up five or six thousand, eight thousand, in four more days."

"What's going to happen," asked the President, "if on the third day you've landed three thousand—and then they bomb the airport? And then they bring up five or six thousand more men. What's going to happen? Or if you land two thousand—and then they bomb the airport?"

This was Kennedy once burned, or so he thought. "We would have troops in Laos right now if it weren't for the Bay of Pigs," he told Sorensen after that session with his generals.

This time, ignoring the Joint Chiefs, the President sent out Averell Harriman to Moscow and to Vientiane, the royal capital of Laos, to get any kind of deal he could—not to win anything, just to keep talking. "We must never face the President with the choice of abandoning Laos or sending in troops," Harriman told Ambassador Brown. "This is our job, to keep him from having to make that choice."

The idea was to talk tough, move fleets and battalions around, but avoid actually sending in the Marines. The *Saturday Evening Post* got it exactly right in an article by Keyes Beech, writing from Saigon: "What the President is engaged in is a tactical retreat under cover of a show of American strength, which may save face but will not save Laos." One Kennedy order was to have the hundreds of U.S. military advisers in Laos who had been pretending to be civilians put on their uniforms to show American resolve, a costume change in a comic-opera war.

"If we have to fight in Southeast Asia, let's fight in Vietnam," the President told his men in Washington. "The Vietnamese, at least, are committed and will fight. Vietnam is the place."

"No long faces," Kennedy would tell them as he regained his composure after the Bay of Pigs. But there were long nights of doubt and debates in Washington. Some of his people were disillusioned, doubting their leader for the first time, realizing that his shining confidence was only personal, perhaps political, but not necessarily presidential.

Some of them doubted themselves, too. In spite of his curt public bravado, even Robert McNamara was having a crisis of confidence, thinking that the debacle was his fault, that he was just an automobile company executive who knew nothing about his job. "Zero," he thought. But it was a thought he kept to himself.

He may have been right about that. Secretaries of Defense, and Presidents, too, make it up as they go along. Two weeks after the failure at the Bay of Pigs, McNamara had sat through an hour of discussion at a Cuba Task Force meeting at the State Department, stood up, put his hand on Richard Goodwin's shoulder, and said: "The only thing to do is eliminate Castro."

"You mean. . . ?"

"I mean it, Dick," McNamara said, still holding Goodwin. "It's the only way."

McGeorge Bundy, the national security adviser, gave the President a letter of resignation after the failure of the Bay of Pigs. Kennedy rejected it and told the former Harvard dean to get control of the flow of information into the Oval Office—what the President knows and when he knows it. Bundy immediately moved from grand quarters in the Executive Office Building to an old storage area in the basement of the White House, a step up because it was a step closer, nearer to the center than the EOB next door. Then he began writing a long memorandum to the President that began: "I hope you'll be in a good mood when you read this. . . ."

> Cuba was a bad mistake. But it was not a disgrace and there were reasons for it. . . . We do have a problem of management; centrally it is a problem of your use of time. . . . What follows represents, I think, a fair consensus of what a good many people would tell you—O'Donnell, Sorensen, R. Kennedy, Rusk. . . . We can't get you to sit still. . . .
>
> The National Security Council, for example, really cannot work for you unless you authorize work schedules that do not get upset from day to day. Calling three meetings in five days is foolish—and putting them off for six weeks at a time is just as bad.
>
> Truman and Eisenhower did their daily dozens in foreign affairs the first thing in the morning, and a couple of weeks ago you asked me to begin to meet you on this basis. I have succeeded in catching you on three mornings, for a total of about 8 minutes, and I conclude that this is not really how you like to begin the day. Moreover, 6 of the 8 minutes were

given not to what I had for you but what you had for me from Marguerite Higgins, David Lawrence, Scotty Reston, and others. The newspapers are important, but not as an exercise in who leaked and why; against your powers and responsibilities, who the hell cares who told Maggie? . . .

Bundy went on like that, scolding his boss:

Right now it is so hard to get to you with anything not urgent and immediate that about half of the papers and reports you personally ask for are never shown to you because by the time you are available you clearly have lost interest in them. . . . Above all you are entitled to feel confident that (a) there is no part of government in the national security area that is not watched over closely by someone from your own staff, and (b) there is no major problem of policy that is not out where you can see it and give a proper stimulus to those who should be attacking it.

What Kennedy now wanted, Bundy knew, amounted to a miniature and personal National Security Council apparatus inside the White House—staffed by Robert Kennedy, campaign people, and the three newcomers most important to him now, McNamara, Bundy, and Maxwell Taylor. The President had re-created some of the official little agencies he had eliminated by an executive order back in February, including the Foreign Intelligence Advisory Board. But Bundy and most everyone else still had to chase him through the hallways to get their messages to the President.

Bundy's sorting of raw intelligence cables was done early each morning in a windowless twenty- by forty-foot room in the West Wing of the White House. The International Situation Area, called the Situation Room, was reached by passing a security guard and National Security Council typists at small desks. The space was small but the impact was enormous, as thousands of electronic reports came to the same place every day, reducing the influence of intelligence officials from the CIA director on down. The President now often saw CIA field reports before the director did.

A table in the center could seat twelve men hip to hip and twenty of their assistants pressed against the wall. But down there with them were scrambler phones and teletypes reaching most of the world, and maps of American military deployment moving up and down. The telephones to President de Gaulle, Prime Minister Macmillan, Chancellor Konrad Adenauer, and other leaders of the day were activated by plastic cards, similar to the ones carried by the military officer who followed the President with "the Football."

The room gave men at the table, especially the man at the head of the table, the impression that only they knew what was going on in the world—except maybe in Laos. When Kennedy's questions shifted from Cuba to Southeast Asia, he asked Senator Mike Mansfield, like himself an organizer of American Friends of Vietnam, what he thought, and the senator from Montana, speaking as one politician to another, emphasized the domestic consequences of action in that part of the world: "If the intervention involves U.S. forces, the initial approval, such as it is, will start to disappear as soon as the first significant casualty lists are published. And it will not be long before approval of 'stand-firm' gives way to the disapproval of 'Kennedy's War' and, 'What are we doing in Laos?' "

"How can I send troops to Laos when I didn't send them to the Bay of Pigs?" Kennedy had asked Richard Nixon and almost everyone else he saw during the last week of April. On April 26, in South Vietnam, President Diem had been reelected with more than 90 percent of the vote. At a National Security Council meeting the next day, Allen Dulles had told Kennedy that there was no point in discussing the numbers, stating the obvious: "It was rigged."

The President was trying to huff and bluff his way out of Laos. The ten thousand Marines boarded ships at Okinawa, with a fanfare of uncoded radio transmissions indicating they were headed for Southeast Asia—five thousand destined for Laos, five thousand for South Vietnam. The Communists both in Moscow and Hanoi assumed they were all headed for Thailand and then into Laos. Then Averell Harriman was sent to New Delhi to deliver a simple message to Prime Minister Nehru and through him to the Soviet Union: Laos would not be abandoned even if American forces had to intervene. But Harriman also told Nehru that President Kennedy was more flexible than Eisenhower and was now prepared to accept a truly neutral Laos after the Russians ended their airlifts of weapons and supplies to the Pathet Lao.

A deal was in the works. In Moscow, Premier Khrushchev was apparently willing to accept Laotian neutrality over Chinese-influenced communism. In Hanoi, the capital of North Vietnam, President Ho Chi Minh was not willing to take the chance that the Americans meant it, that they might be ready to commit their own troops in Southeast Asia. U.S. troops in the region could set back North Vietnamese ambitions of a united and Communist Vietnam for decades. So, Kennedy sent Harriman on to Geneva to try to negotiate anything he could to end American commitment in Laos. And he did that. The Soviets, the Americans, and everyone else involved agreed to a cease-fire document on May 5, leaving enforcement to the winking supervision of a United Nations control commission. On paper, Laos was now neutral as the Communists prepared slowly and, Kennedy hoped, quietly, to win the civil war.

"The cease-fire in Laos came as a cold war defeat for the U.S. . . ." began the coverage in *Time* magazine that week. "Laos—with a Communist sympathizer at the head of the government, with Communists in posts of government power, and with Communist troops already holding half the nation—will quickly go behind the Iron Curtain. . . . Kennedy had declared he would 'pay any price' to 'assure the survival and success of liberty.' But the price in Laos seemed too high. . . . If the U.S. is to save South Viet Nam, it must be willing to get far more deeply involved—to the point of fighting, if necessary."

"Sons of bitches," said the President, tossing the early bound edition of the magazine. "If they want this job they can have it tomorrow."

But he knew he was on notice from America's hard-liners, from Acheson to *Time*. No troops in Cuba, negotiations in Laos; he had to get tough somewhere. Soon.

Vietnam was the place he chose. He had ticked off the reasons at a National Security Council meeting on April 29. It was a more unified nation; it included a million refugees from communism in North Vietnam; its military was larger and better trained; it had direct access to the sea, increasing the usefulness of U.S. naval and airpower; it had no border with Red China.

The working paper for the meeting was a twenty-three-page "Program of Action to Prevent Communist Domination of South Vietnam." The principal authors of the "Top Secret" document were the Deputy Secretary of Defense, Roswell Gilpatric, and General Lansdale, the chairman and operations officer of the informal Vietnam Task Force reporting directly to the President.

Fact was imitating fiction: the Ragtime Kid, General Lansdale, Colonel Hillandale, was now making policy, and commenting on it, too. On May 20th, the Lansdale report that had so impressed Kennedy in his first days as President was published in the *Saturday Evening Post* under the title "The Report the President Wanted Published." The byline read: "By An American Officer." It was Lansdale's description of Father Hoa's struggle to keep the Viet Cong out of his village, Binh Hung, at the southern tip of Vietnam.

Among the Lansdale and Gilpatric recommendations presented to the President on April 29 was one to send more U.S. military personnel into South Vietnam, in violation of the 1954 Geneva Accords that had ended French rule in Indochina. Those agreements limited the number of foreign military advisers in South Vietnam to the same number the French had there at the end: 685 men. More trainers than that would be needed if Kennedy were to agree to a new request from President Diem for U.S. funding and training to increase the size of the South Vietnamese Army (ARVN) from 150,000 to 170,000 men.

"A state of guerrilla warfare now exists throughout the country," Lansdale reported.

> The number of Viet Cong hard-core Communists has increased from 4400 in early 1960 to an estimated 12,000 today. . . . Casualties on both sides totalled more than 4500 during the first three months of this year. 58% of the country is under some degree of Communist control, ranging from harassment and night raids to almost complete administrative jurisdiction. . . . They have announced publicly that they will "take over the country before the end of 1961."
>
> The situation is thus critical, but it is not hopeless. The need is . . . to impress on our friends, the Vietnamese, and on our foes, the Viet Cong, that come what may, the U.S. intends to *win* this battle.

The President approved more than fifty of the recommendations made by Lansdale and Gilpatric, violating the Geneva Accords, training South Vietnamese guerrilla units to go into both Laos and North Vietnam, and setting up a plan to "Penetrate political forces, government, armed services and opposition elements to measure support of government, provide warning of any coup plans and identify individuals with potentiality of providing leadership in event of disappearance of President Diem."

Kennedy also approved a recommendation to finance the training of "Special Forces" in the South Vietnamese Army, men who would wear the green berets of U.S. Special Forces, the highly publicized symbols of the President's attraction to guerrilla warfare and counterinsurgency. The Commander-in-Chief had personally overruled Defense Department orders to end the wearing of the green berets in the U.S. Army. The Pentagon did not want visible elite units, thinking they undercut the morale of "ordinary" soldiers. Kennedy wanted them; they were his troops, and he was inclined to use them.

On May 5, Kennedy was at another meeting of the National Security Council. Those around the big table in the Cabinet Room had been diverted from a discussion of the Lansdale recommendations, though, and were now talking about the possibility of a Communist takeover of British Guiana, a small colony on the north coast of South America, when Evelyn Lincoln, the President's secretary, walked in and whispered to him.

"Two minutes," she said.

"Two minutes to launch," the President said, and stood up.

He walked into Mrs. Lincoln's office, followed by Johnson, Rusk, McNamara, Taylor, Sorensen. Mrs. Kennedy appeared through another door and her husband said, "Come in and watch this." They all gathered around a small television set, tensely watching the final preparations for the first U.S. attempt to put a man in space. Unlike the Soviets' secret ninety-minute orbit of Yuri Gagarin twenty-three days before, Kennedy had decided to let the world watch the launch of Captain Alan Shepard, a Navy pilot.

Shepard would be in space only fifteen minutes, if he got there, riding an arc like a cannon shot, 115 miles up and then a drop into the ocean, 302 miles from where he blasted off. The television screen showed his spaceship, bravely named *Freedom 7,* a little cone on top of a smoking Atlas missile at Cape Canaveral on the Atlantic coast of Florida. Johnson was on a direct telephone line to the Cape. The Atlas lifted off in a belching, flaming roar, and then it was gone from the screen.

The President waited, like every other American. He was as tense as anyone else about this, afraid that his decision to publicize would prove another mistake. Confidential reports to the White House rated the chances of a successful flight at 75 percent; the probability that Shepard would survive was rated 90 to 95 percent. There seemed to be no sound in the room.

A door suddenly burst open. "The astronaut is in the helicopter," said an assistant press secretary, Andrew Hatcher, bumping into the President. "The pilot says he appears normal and in good shape."

"It's a success," said Kennedy, who needed one. He heard cheers going up around the building. He was smiling. He had not been doing much of that lately.

Afterward, he called Johnson aside.

"Lyndon, I still want you to go to Vietnam," Kennedy said, for the third or fourth time that week. "You've just got to go out there."

"Mr. President," Johnson answered, "I don't want to embarrass you by getting my head blown off in Saigon."

His Vice President was a proud, moody, and difficult man. But that did not change the fact that he was the Vice President and Kennedy could not have won Texas in 1960 without him and could not have won the presidency without Texas. More than once the President had chewed out his own people for making fun of Johnson.

"I just want you to know one thing," he said to Kenny O'Donnell one of those times. "Lyndon Johnson was Majority Leader of the United States Senate, he was elected to office several times by the people. He was the number one Democrat in the United States, elected by us to be our leader. I'm President of the United States. He doesn't like that. He thinks he's ten times more important than I am, he happens to be that kind of a fellow. But he thinks you're nothing but a clerk. Just keep that right in your mind. . . .

"Elected officers have a code, and no matter whether they like each other or hate each other. . . . You have never been elected to anything by anybody, and you are dealing with a very insecure, sensitive man with a huge ego. I want you literally to kiss his ass from one end of Washington to the other."

Code or no code, though, Kennedy thought that maybe Johnson really was a coward. He didn't know whether to be disgusted or amused. But he showed nothing.

"Don't worry, Lyndon," he said. "If anything happens to you, Sam Rayburn and I will give you the biggest funeral Austin, Texas, ever saw."

Johnson finally left for South Vietnam on May 9, carrying a letter from President Kennedy to President Diem, which significantly changed the relationship between the two countries. The President of the United States was offering to move from providing assistance to assuming responsibility in a joint effort to defeat the Communists in South Vietnam:

> Since I took office my colleagues and I have watched developments in Viet-Nam with attention and concern. . . . We are prepared to initiate in collaboration with your government a series of joint, mutually supporting actions in the military, political, economic and other fields. We would propose to extend and build on our existing programs including the Counter-Insurgency Plan and infuse into our actions a high sense of urgency and dedication . . . the steps already taken to implement the Plan have made it possible for us to have approved Military Assistance Program support of the 20,000 increase of your regular force. . . . We would also be prepared to consider carefully with you, if developments should warrant, the case for a further increase in the strength of your forces beyond the 170,000 limit now contemplated. . . .

Kennedy had told Johnson that his mission was to persuade President Diem and the world that the Vietnamese leader had both the support and the respect of the Americans—a duty Johnson dispatched with gusto, referring publicly to Diem as the "Winston Churchill of Southeast Asia."

Diem responded to Kennedy's letter with what he called "an interim letter" that the President saw on May 16. It stated that "the government of Vietnam accepts the proposals in your letter to initiate, in collaboration with the Government of the United States, the series of joint, mutually supporting actions to win the struggle against communism in Vietnam . . . I was most deeply gratified by this gracious gesture . . . particularly as we have not become accustomed to being asked for our own views as to our needs."

The next day, May 17, President Kennedy made his first foreign trip —to Canada. He too issued a Churchillian declaration of American, or North American, purpose before that country's Parliament: "For our historic task in this embattled age is not merely to defend freedom. It is to extend its writ and strengthen its covenant. . . ." But that was not the purpose of the visit. In private talks, Kennedy tried to persuade Prime Minister John Diefenbaker to change his country's policy against the stationing of U.S. missiles and nuclear warheads on Canadian soil. Then the two men walked out onto the lawn in front of Government House in Ottawa for the ceremonial planting of a small oak tree from the United States.

The President was talking to Diefenbaker about the chance that he might be meeting soon with Chairman Khrushchev and, without bending his knees, lifted a silver shovelful of dirt, then felt the pain. He had thrown his back out and he knew the pain was going to get worse. He brought his right hand up to his forehead as the first twinge struck him. By the time he was on Air Force One for the trip home, Kennedy could barely move. The pilot was told to radio ahead to make sure the President's crutches were at Andrews Air Force Base when he landed.

Back home, on his crutches, Kennedy approved a new statement on May 23 concerning the U.S. goal in Southeast Asia: "To prevent Communist domination of South Vietnam; to create in that country a viable and increasingly democratic society, and to initiate, on an accelerated basis, a series of mutually supporting actions of a military, political, economic, psychological and covert character designed to achieve this objective . . . to keep Viet-Nam free."

That paragraph was the lead of "The Presidential Program for Viet-Nam," the final product of the Lansdale-Gilpatric recommendations, which included several points: (1) "Seek to increase the confidence of President Diem and his government in the United States"; (2) "Attempt to strengthen President Diem's popular support within Viet-Nam by reappraisal and negotiation, under the direction of Ambassador Nolting"; (3) "A full examination will be made of the size and composition of forces which would be desirable in the case of a possible commitment of U.S. forces to Viet-Nam."

The President also reversed an Eisenhower policy that restricted American activities in South Vietnam to the capital, Saigon, and directed

Americans from the ambassador on down to operate under the orders of the government of President Ngo Dinh Diem. Eisenhower had played this one by the book. So in a way did Kennedy, but this time the book was *The Ugly American*. General Lansdale's report to Kennedy had emphasized outreach to the countryside. What that meant, he had told Kennedy, was the creation of a secret army of Meo tribesmen, hill people, several thousand of them financed by the CIA, to harass North Vietnamese movement on the "Ho Chi Minh Trail," a jungle path through Laos used to supply guerrilla units in the south.

"Develop agricultural pilot-projects—show-places—throughout the country, with a view toward exploiting their beneficial psychological effects," was another Lansdale recommendation to the President that could have come from the novel: "This project would be accomplished by combined teams of Vietnamese Civic Action personnel, Americans in the Peace Corps, Filipinos in Operation Brotherhood and other Free World nationals."

On the evening of May 23, the President had a drink and a long talk with Arthur Krock. He was feeling good about the events of the day. His confidence was coming back like the color in his face. He told Krock about the possibility of a meeting with Khrushchev. Among other things, Kennedy thought he could pin responsibility on Khrushchev for the fact that neither side could agree on a treaty banning tests of nuclear weapons after years of on-and-off negotiations and pious cross-talk about the dangers of testing.

Most Americans had forgotten, the most knowledgeable among them choosing to forget, that it was Khrushchev who had first proposed negotiations on a test ban, in February 1955. This was after the discovery that the fallout from an American test in March 1954—not the bomb but the radioactive debris carried in the atmosphere—had killed or maimed Japanese fishermen and islanders hundreds of miles from the test site on Bikini Atoll. The Americans had said they would discuss test bans only as part of a comprehensive disarmament plan, which had meant no serious negotiations. Now, after seven years of anti-nuclear demonstrations around the world, and U.S. and Soviet charge and countercharge, Kennedy wanted to make a personal appeal for a treaty. Maybe the two of them, two politicians, could work something out.

That same week he also asked Theodore White, the author of *The Making of the President, 1960,* who had lived in China for years, what he thought might come of a face-to-face meeting on Southeast Asia with Communist China's Chairman Mao Tse-tung.

He was feeling like a President again.

Chapter 10

MAY 15, 1961

President Kennedy found out there was a revolution in his country by reading *The New York Times* on May 15, 1961. That Monday morning, under the headline: "BI-RACIAL BUSES ATTACKED, RIDERS BEATEN IN ALABAMA," the paper published an Associated Press story that began:

> ANNISTON, Ala.—A group of white persons today ambushed two buses carrying Negroes and whites who were seeking to knock down bus station racial barriers. A little later, sixty miles to the west, one of the buses ran into another angry crowd of white men at a Birmingham bus station. The interracial group took a brief but bloody beating, and fled.

An Associated Press photograph showed a Greyhound bus burning, the fire producing a thick column of oily black smoke over Alabama Route 78 just outside Anniston, a small city halfway between Birmingham and Atlanta, Georgia. The Greyhound had been followed from the Anniston bus terminal by fifty cars filled with white men carrying clubs and knives and lead pipes. One of the cars had pulled alongside the bus and someone had thrown a firebomb into an open window of the Greyhound.

"Both buses were carrying members of the Congress of Racial Equality (CORE) on a swing through the Deep South, testing segregated facilities in bus stations," continued the *Times* story. "They call themselves 'Freedom Riders.' "

The passengers in the bus, ten men and three women, seven Negroes and six whites, organized in Washington by CORE, were testing Southern enforcement of a December 1960 ruling by the U. S. Supreme Court that racial segregation was illegal in facilities serving interstate travelers. The Court, citing federal interstate commerce laws, had ordered the desegregation of waiting rooms, restaurants, and bathrooms in terminals used by buses that regularly crossed state lines.

James Farmer, the new leader of CORE, wanted to make a name for the small organization, and for himself. He had been inspired by Kennedy's words about change and freedom, he said. He was convinced that this new President wanted to end American segregation. So, on May 4, 1961, the thirteen Freedom Riders had begun their journey from Washington, buying tickets on two buses headed south, a Greyhound and a Trailways. Their goal was to reach New Orleans by May 17, the seventh anniversary of the 1954 Supreme Court decision ordering the desegregation of public schools in the South.

The buses ran into no trouble, and no press coverage, either, as they rolled through Virginia, the Carolinas, and Georgia. The riders ignored "White" and "Colored" signs in the terminals, and local officials and local people ignored them. But in Rock Hill, South Carolina, as Navy Captain Alan Shepard was being hailed by the President, a retired Navy captain named Albert Bigelow, a fifty-five-year-old white Freedom Rider, was being beaten to his knees by a cursing crowd in the Rock Hill Greyhound terminal.

Then, sixty miles west of Atlanta, the Greyhound crossed the state line between Georgia and Alabama. In Anniston, fifteen miles farther west, the Greyhound's tires were slashed in the terminal. Leaving town on Route 78, heading for Birmingham, eighty miles away, the bus began to wobble as the tires lost air. When the firebomb exploded, the bus was surrounded by the carloads of white men. The six riders on board were beaten, then escaped in cars driven by local Negroes, who had followed the white caravan.

That was the story and picture the President saw on the morning of May 15. He was angry—this was exactly the kind of thing the Communists used to make the United States look bad around the world. And he was mad because he knew nothing about the rides or the riders. In the beginning, at least at the White House, no one knew who the people on the buses were, or what they were doing. Farmer had sent a press release to the Justice Department but it got lost somewhere. Simeon Booker, the *Jet* magazine reporter, had told Robert Kennedy about the riders before they took off, but the Attorney General had other things on his mind. He was spending most of his time with Maxwell Taylor investigating the Bay of Pigs failure.

The follow-up story came in on the AP wire. The Trailways bus, carrying the seven other riders, had had some trouble in Anniston, too, but had managed to make it to the highway. But there was a mob waiting for those riders at the Trailways terminal in Birmingham. The riders and some local Negroes who happened to be in the wrong place at the wrong time were beaten, chased through the terminal and the streets, which were empty of police. Then the mob went after local reporters and photographers who were trying to record the event. Birmingham's police commissioner, Eugene Connor, nicknamed "Bull," said later that there were no police at the terminal because his men were all home celebrating Mother's Day.

The thirteen Freedom Riders were defeated, four of them in hospitals. The rest ended up at the Birmingham airport, surrounded by hostile police and whites spitting and cursing. They were trying to get on a plane to New Orleans, but each time one was announced, telephoned bomb threats kept it on the ground. Booker telephoned Attorney General Kennedy from the airport, saying: "It's pretty bad down here and we don't think we're going to get out. Bull Connor and his people are pretty tough."

But bad as it was, it seemed to be ending. The President agreed with his brother's idea of sending someone to Birmingham to make sure the Freedom Riders got out of there safely. Then they would try to get Alabama's Governor John Patterson to take the lead on calming people down. Patterson had been their man in Alabama during the campaign, their one important southerner. Robert Kennedy said he would send his administrative assistant John Seigenthaler, the only southerner in his own office, to help get the Freedom Riders to safety—and then to meet with Patterson.

"What do you want me to do?" asked Seigenthaler.

"Hold their hands and let them know we care," Robert Kennedy said.

"They were in bad shape, but he got them out," Kennedy reported the next morning to his brother. It seemed easy for a moment, at least from a distance.

Seigenthaler, a former reporter for the *Nashville Tennessean,* knew better. He thought he was watching the beginning of a new civil war in the South. And he was shocked by the federal reaction. He was the federal reaction! Driving to see Governor Patterson in Montgomery, he thought about it: Here comes the United States government, a thirty-one-year-old newspaper reporter in a rented car.

The President called in Harris Wofford and said: "Can't you get your goddamned friends off those buses? Stop them."

It was an embarrassment, and the President was concentrating on more important things. His priorities that May 15 were reflected in the headlines of *The New York Times*. The lead that morning read: "KENNEDY WEIGHS MEETING IN JUNE WITH KHRUSHCHEV." He was preparing for his first overseas trip as President at the end of the month, to France and England—and he had just received a cable from Moscow reporting that Nikita Khrushchev had agreed to meet him in Vienna the first week in June. That was a way to get the Bay of Pigs behind him—sitting down one-on-one with the Soviet leader, and impressing him and the world with the resolve and determination of the United States in Berlin, in Southeast Asia, anywhere communism moved.

It was a tense, testing time for Kennedy, and it had little to do with Negro activists and excited white liberals looking for trouble and headlines. "TWO EFFORTS FAIL AT TALKS ON LAOS," was the *Times* headline from Geneva, where a new international conference on Southeast Asia was beginning that day. The newspaper did not know it, but three days earlier, on May 11, Kennedy had secretly formalized his decision not to try to "save" Laos at the conference or on the battlefield. All he wanted now was a cease-fire and neutrality for a while. "Johnson Renews Pledges of U.S. Support for Chiang" was next over a story from Taipei, Taiwan, as the Vice President stopped there on his way to Saigon. Two weeks before the Anniston incident, Kennedy had received a memo from McNamara entitled "Military Planning for a Possible Berlin Crisis" and it had confirmed his worst fear—that the real plan of the United States and its allies was to counter almost any Soviet military action in Berlin with nuclear weapons. And, that same day, again secretly, he ordered five hundred more American troops into South Vietnam.

On May 17, before he took off for his twenty-four-hour visit to Canada, the President had met in his bedroom with the Attorney General and his two top assistants, Byron White and Burke Marshall, to talk about the Freedom Riders. Kennedy moved the group to the sitting room next door, sitting in his pajamas with eggs and toast and juice in front of him. But he never touched the food and let the others do most of the talking.

The brothers had already agreed on two things, speaking on the phone in their grunted code: First, that this whole thing and the people behind it were a giant pain-in-the-ass—especially James Farmer of CORE—and second, that the federal government was on the side of the riders, that was the law and that was right. The first was politics. Kennedy thought this kind of agitation was going to make it more difficult for him to deal with the southerners in Congress. The second was history. He thought that the nation was not ready yet to deal with the demands of Negroes, but if it came to confrontation, he and the power of the U.S. government had to be on their side.

So now he wanted to avoid confrontation. "Not helpful," Robert Kennedy said when he called civil rights leaders and tried to bully them into getting the riders back home and leaving the civil rights struggle in friendly federal courts. The political priority was simple and direct, to keep the President himself out of what he himself kept calling "this Goddamned civil rights mess."

"There's going to be another bus," Robert Kennedy reported unhappily to the President on May 19, when John Kennedy was back in the White House on crutches. Negro college students from Nashville, organized by a young woman named Diane Nash, had driven to Birmingham to take up the unfinished journey to New Orleans. "Seigenthaler knows the girl, but he couldn't stop them," Robert said.

"It was like talking to a brick wall," reported Seigenthaler, who had first met Nash when she was involved in successful demonstrations during the spring of 1960 to integrate department stores in Nashville. "She never listened to a word. She said nothing could stop them now: 'We're going to show those people in Alabama who think they can ignore the President of the United States.' "

The President they were quoting actually wanted them to go back home, and did not understand the reach and resonance of his own words. People were listening to him in a way they listen only to a President. The country was moving again. Kennedy would have to catch up or try to stop this parade. The students from Nashville told Seigenthaler that they were answering the call to do something for their country, ready to bear any burden. Within a few hours they began paying a price, as more than a thousand white citizens of Birmingham came to the Greyhound terminal there to curse and jeer them.

"This has to go forward," Nash told Seigenthaler. "Nobody is going to turn us around."

"You won't make it to New Orleans. You're going to get your people killed," he said.

"Then others will follow," she replied.

All of that reported to the President, Burke Marshall was in his bedroom to brief him on legal options. He was a new face to the President, Robert Kennedy's choice as Deputy Attorney General for Civil Rights, chosen to avoid appointing Harris Wofford. The brothers wanted someone who could be objective about civil rights, so they had picked a bright Washington lawyer whose specialty was corporate anti-trust matters. The President thought it was not fair to Wofford, but he did not want a civil rights advocate. He wanted someone more detached, as he was himself. Marshall laid out the law for Kennedy, coolly presenting the extreme options: a President could send in the Army to force a state to obey federal laws or he could do nothing, saying these were state matters. The only major law enforcement organization between those extremes was the Federal Bureau of Investigation, but the FBI, itself a segregated force under J. Edgar Hoover, could not be trusted where civil rights were concerned.

"Hoover's on the other side," Robert Kennedy agreed.

The FBI's traditional constituency in the South were state and local police forces, the sheriffs and police chiefs its agents worked with, and traded information with, on a daily basis. There was collusion between police and the Ku Klux Klan and other white supremacy organizations in Birmingham and Montgomery, and the FBI was close to being party to that. FBI informers had passed along intelligence that there would be a Mother's Day mob in Birmingham. They had also told agents that Connor's police would not go to the terminal until fifteen minutes after the first Freedom Riders bus arrived; in other words, the mob had fifteen minutes to beat up the riders. Hoover did not tell any of that to his immediate superior, the Attorney General, nor to the President.

Troops were the worst option. Kennedy was determined not to send in the regular Army, or to federalize the Alabama National Guard units. He had criticized Eisenhower for sending the 82nd Airborne into Arkansas in 1957 to enforce federal court orders to admit Negro children to Central High School in Little Rock. He thought that was the domestic equivalent of massive retaliation; the paratroopers in full combat gear, with fixed bayonets, were photographed guarding little Negro school-girls, producing dramatic images that had embarrassed the United States around the world— a powerful propaganda windfall for the other side. Marshall told him that if he were to send in troops in Alabama this time, he would have to issue a presidential proclamation of a breakdown of public order. And that would put Kennedy personally and publicly on the line for whatever happened next.

Then Byron White, the Deputy Attorney General, once the country's most admired football star and the naval intelligence officer who had debriefed Kennedy after his PT-109 was sunk, came up with a third way. It was the kind of thinking Kennedy liked, from the kind of man he liked. White suggested creating a civilian force of U.S. marshals.

"Marshals" sounded impressive. But, in fact, they were just federal officials who happened to carry badges, a motley group of agents and clerks from the Treasury Department's Bureau of Alcohol, Tobacco and Firearms Control, U.S. Border Patrol officers from Texas, and federal prison officials and guards from around the South. Most of them were middle-aged men who had never fired a gun on duty.

"Not yet. Not yet. Let's let it go, let it go a while," John Kennedy said each time his brother, and the others pacing the offices of the Justice Department, said it was time to send in their marshals. The President wanted to talk with Governor Patterson, the single southerner who had supported his national political aspirations since 1956. Kennedy picked up the telephone on May 18, four days after the Anniston attack on the Freedom Riders, and asked the White House operator to get Governor Patterson. Moments later the operator called back to say that Patterson's office said the governor was unavailable, he had gone fishing in the Gulf of Mexico.

The President called again the next day. This time there was no fish story. Patterson simply refused to take the call. Finally, during a telephone conversation with Robert Kennedy later the same day, he agreed to meet face to face with "a personal representative of the President of the United States." So, Seigenthaler rented another car in Birmingham that Friday and headed for Montgomery.

"There's nobody in the whole country that's got the spine to stand up to the goddamned niggers except me," Patterson told Seigenthaler, when they met Friday night, May 19. "I believe I'm more popular in this country today than John Kennedy is for the stand I've taken."

Seigenthaler and Patterson worked out a statement declaring that the governor, not the President, was responsible for maintaining order in Alabama. Seigenthaler telephoned the text to the White House: "The State of Alabama has the will, the force, the men, and the equipment to give full protection to everyone in Alabama, on the highways and elsewhere."

Within hours, the President's personal representative was beaten and bloody, his unconscious body halfway under his rented car down the hill from the Alabama Capitol. The new Freedom Riders, organized in Nashville, had left Birmingham at eight-thirty Saturday morning, escorted by Alabama Highway Patrol cars, with the patrol's single airplane flying overhead. The bus had left only after Robert Kennedy had personally persuaded Greyhound officials to find a driver willing to make the run to Montgomery. "I am—the government is—going to be very much upset if this group does not get to continue their trip," the Attorney General said. He did not have to say that the government had a great deal of power over the bus company's business in the rest of the country.*

---

* The Attorney General did not know it but his telephone conversations were being recorded in Alabama. Governor Patterson passed them along to state newspapers—including a sentence that made it sound like the Kennedys had something to do with organizing the rides. There was some ironic laughter inside the White House over the idea the Kennedys planned the rides, but millions of Americans believed it after hearing the Alabama tapes.

The Highway Patrol cars turned around at the city limits of Montgomery and the bus pulled into the Greyhound terminal at 10:15 A.M. The place seemed almost empty. But there were white men hiding everywhere and within a couple of minutes they appeared, surrounding the riders, beating them with baseball bats and lead pipes, smashing the equipment of newspaper photographers and television cameramen.

Seigenthaler happened to be driving by the terminal after having breakfast with John Doar, a Justice Department attorney who was trying a civil rights case in the city. He tried to rescue two Freedom Riders, young white women being chased by white men swinging bats and clubs. He had stopped and tried to get them into his car, but he was the one who was clubbed to the ground. From a window of the Federal Building across the street, Doar was on the phone with Burke Marshall and Byron White, describing what he could see of the scene at the bus station. White and Doar had met when "Whizzer" White was the star of the Pittsburgh Pirates of the National Football League, and Doar was the team's water boy. "Oh there are fists, punching!" Doar said. "It's terrible! It's terrible! There's not a cop in sight! People are yelling, 'There those niggers are! Get 'em! Get 'em!' It's awful."

Robert Kennedy called Seigenthaler, who was in a Montgomery Hospital that afternoon, and said the President had decided to send in White and his little army of U.S. Marshals. "You did what you had to do," said the President when he called Seigenthaler later.

Then the President did what he had to do, with no enthusiasm and some resentment. The Freedom Riders had made their point. It was pointless to go on like this, he thought, this bunch was not doing themselves or their country much good. "My fundamental belief," was the way his brother had put it as he took office as Attorney General, "is that all people are created equal. Logically, it follows that integration should take place today everywhere. . . . But other people have grown up with totally different backgrounds and mores, which we can't change overnight."

Martin Luther King, Jr., came back to Montgomery that Sunday night. The Alabama capital was where he had made his name, as a thirty-one-year-old preacher who had led the Negro boycott of the city's segregated buses four years earlier. This time he was leading a meeting at the First Baptist Church, a week after the Anniston attack, to celebrate the courage of the Freedom Riders. A few of the riders, including James Farmer, were among the fifteen hundred people singing and cheering in the church. The sound inside covered a lot of the noise made by the crowd of thousands of whites surrounding the building. In between the crowd and the churchgoers, on the steps of the church, stood the representatives of the federal government, a dozen brave and frightened men, armed only with nightsticks and wearing new yellow "U.S. Marshal" armbands.

The rest of the 550 marshals were outside the city at Maxwell Air Force Base, commanded by Byron White and Chief U.S. Marshal James McShane, a onetime Boston policeman who had won his federal position by loyal service as John Kennedy's bodyguard and chauffeur. Regular Army units were on alert one hundred miles away at Fort Benning, Georgia. And so was the Alabama National Guard, still under Governor Patterson's control.

In Montgomery, inside the church, Martin Luther King was comparing that hot night to nights in Hitler's Germany. The Negroes had been inside for four hours, afraid to go out into the white crowd. As the rocks and bottles, and the curses, began to fly, the marshals at Maxwell headed for the city, ordered there by Attorney General Kennedy, who was on the phone with King inside First Baptist. They came in red, white, and blue trucks marked "U.S. MAIL."

And they made it just in time. "They're here!" shouted King on the telephone to Robert Kennedy, who was using his office in the Justice Department as a war room. The President was at Glen Ora, seemingly disengaged from such mundane tasks as enforcing federal court orders. In fact, he was making the decisions, talking constantly with his brother on an open line. At midnight Sunday night, Robert Kennedy relayed a complaint from one of his assistant attorney generals at Maxwell. William Orrick had told him they were getting no help from the FBI. Within an hour, the agent-in-charge of the Montgomery field office was there, with four agents and a plea to Orrick never to complain again. The President had called J. Edgar Hoover, and the director had called the agent out of bed. The next morning, the FBI arrested four men in connection with the firebombing of the first Freedom Riders bus in Anniston.

In Montgomery, the streets around the First Baptist Church were foggy with tear gas, the marshals' principal weapon against the charging mob. Pretty soon everyone was coughing and crying—the white crowd, the marshals, and, worst of all, those in the barricaded church. Some of them were now trying to break out of the building, willing to take their chances with the mob. That was when White made a telephone call to Washington, asking the President to declare a state of public disorder—the official declaration required to bring in the Army.

That call, and everything else happening at Maxwell, was being reported to Governor Patterson by the switchboard operators at the Air Force Base. Before regular Army troops could be moved, Patterson made his own move, ordering the Alabama National Guard to the First Baptist Church. The weekend warriors, part of the Army Reserve, but under state command since 1776, marched from armories that displayed no American flags—Confederate flags were everywhere—and pushed through the mob, bayonets unsheathed. They surrounded the church, half with bayonets pointed at the white crowd, half looking toward the church. The marshals withdrew to their mail trucks.

Kennedy, for a brief but deceptive moment, had what he wanted. The state of Alabama was on the line now rather than the federal government. The President and the Attorney General seized the moment, orchestrating newspaper stories of federal-state cooperation. Reporters were told there had never been much of a chance of using the regular Army. A lie, of course, but the President still hoped to have it both ways.

John Kennedy went to bed, leaving his brother to calm down Reverend King.

"You betrayed us. You shouldn't have withdrawn the marshals!" King shouted so loudly that Robert Kennedy had to hold the phone away from his ear.

"Now, Reverend," he said. "You know just as well as I do that if it hadn't been for the United States Marshals, you'd be dead as Kelsey's nuts right now."

King turned away from the phone, asking: "Who's Kelsey? Anyone know Kelsey?"

It ended as the Negroes walked out of the First Baptist Church in the dawn's early light in Montgomery; or so it seemed for the moment in Washington. The Freedom Riders in the church regrouped and headed for Birmingham one more time, and then on to Jackson, Mississippi, three days later as part of a National Guard convoy under the command of General Henry Graham, who was still reporting to Governor Patterson.

Before the riders and their Guardsmen, rolling along now at seventy miles an hour, got to Birmingham, a new group of fourteen students appeared at the Greyhound terminal in Montgomery and bought tickets for Birmingham and Jackson. "Tell them to call it off," the President told Harris Wofford one more time.

"I don't think anybody's going to stop them now," Wofford replied.

"Are your constituents happy?" Kennedy would ask him after that, smiling without warmth. But Wofford's constituents—established civil rights advocates, Negro and white men who knew their manners—were also already falling behind the movement. On Friday, May 19, Wofford brought the Peace Corps' National Advisory Council into the Cabinet

Room for a little pep talk. As they waited for the President, Harry Belafonte, the singer, Eugene Rostow, the dean of Yale Law School, and a couple of others were complaining among themselves that Kennedy seemed to have neither the conviction nor the courage to stand with the young riders from Nashville, who were then in Birmingham trying to get a bus to take them to Montgomery and on to New Orleans. But they shut up as soon as the President, smiling and joking, walked among them. Finally, Wofford announced that there were men in the room who had strong feelings about what was going on in Alabama.

There was a long moment of silence which was broken by Belafonte. "Mr. President, I know how much you're doing in civil rights," he said. "I deeply respect your leadership in civil rights. I trust you in civil rights. And I know all these other things are going on. But perhaps you could say something a little more about the Freedom Riders."

"There is a need now for moral leadership," added Rostow.

"Have you read my statement in the newspapers?" Kennedy asked. He was angry.

A guard ran after the group as they left and caught them at the White House gate. The President wanted to see Wofford.

"Who the hell was that man with Harry Belafonte?" Kennedy snapped at him. He said he was Walt Rostow's brother. "What in the world does he think I should do? Doesn't he know I've done more for civil rights than any President in American history? How could any man have done more than I've done?"

"This is too much!" Robert Kennedy told Wofford on Sunday, after he'd heard more complaints from Martin Luther King, Jr., demanding more federal action in Alabama. "I wonder whether they have the best interest of their country at heart? Do you know that one of them is against the atom bomb?—Yes, he even picketed against it in jail! The President is going abroad and this is all embarrassing for him."

The day's *New York Times* had some of the same concerns, although its editorial did blame the mobs, not those who were mobbed.

In Birmingham and Montgomery the United States has lost another battle in the global cold war. The hoodlums, the screaming women, the citizens who stood and watched have done much to aid the Communist cause throughout the world. . . .

The African, the Middle Easterner, the Asian, the Latin American, must be expected to exaggerate and misinterpret what happened in Alabama. We know that we were seeing something that ninety-nine out of 100 Americans condemn as utterly immoral. . . . But in other lands they will see—if they have not done so already—the photographs of men beating Negroes or other unarmed white men and women. They will read the details—and there will be no need for the most skillful Red propaganda to embroider the facts—and they must be expected to ask themselves what the United States really stands for.

President Kennedy was feeling sorry for himself in a peculiarly presidential way. He was preparing for the most important meeting of his life in less than two weeks, a face-to-face meeting with the leader of communism, and he was being nagged and nitpicked and nibbled to distraction by his own people—by the Negroes and the liberals, the newspapers *and* the conservatives. "What gets me is that all these people seem to want me to fail," he said one evening to Hugh Sidey of *Time* magazine. "I don't understand that. If I don't succeed there may not be another President."

As he saw it, he was taking real risks with the tolerance of the southerners in Congress, and there was no reasonable political point in getting too far ahead of the American people. The first Gallup Poll to evaluate public reaction to the Freedom Rides had reported that, whatever *New York Times* editorial writers thought, 63 percent of those questioned disapproved of the whole idea. It was just troublemaking. Senator Prescott Bush, a liberal Republican from Connecticut, attached an anti-segregation amendment onto the Kennedy administration's school aid bill. The amendment was defeated 61 to 25.

Kennedy wanted to be fair. But to Reverend King and the others it was not a question of fairness, it was a question of right and wrong. They saw it as a moral confrontation. They wanted a moral commitment from the President of the United States.

The President offered a political solution. He urged King to support and promote federal voter registration projects. If Negroes could vote, politicians would respond. No, said King, not enough.

King asked Kennedy to greet the Freedom Riders when they returned to Washington. No. He asked him to declare a Second Emancipation Proclamation. No. Wofford and Burke Marshall suggested that Kennedy go on television to say "a few stout words on this racial crisis." No.

John Kennedy decided that it should be Robert Kennedy who would speak publicly about recent racial upheaval. The Attorney General gave his first televised interview, live on the NBC network for twenty-two minutes at 10:00 P.M., prime time. The Freedom Riders? "They performed a service bringing a problem to attention," he said. "Now it's before the courts. . . . Are we going to let this be settled in the streets instead of the courts? . . . Frankly, a lot of people have never had their name in the papers. I have no sympathy with segregationists, but segregation is far better than having it decided in the streets, with beatings."

The Kennedys were playing their game of good cop–bad cop. Robert was the tough guy, trying to get the Freedom Riders out of the South. "Curiosity seekers, publicity-seekers," he called some of them. On May 24, Robert Kennedy issued a statement saying: "A cooling-off period is needed."

Patience. "Wait," Martin Luther King responded. "Wait means 'Never!' " The travelers on the road to freedom were not listening to Robert Kennedy's words. They thought they had heard John Kennedy's music.

Chapter 11

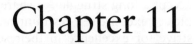

MAY 25, 1961

"The Constitution imposes upon me the obligation to 'from time to time give to the Congress information of the State of the Union," President Kennedy said, as he began a nationally televised address to a joint session of Congress on May 25, 1961. "While this has traditionally been interpreted as an annual affair, this tradition has been broken in extraordinary times." He paused for a beat. "These are extraordinary times."

The President was giving his second State of the Union Address in four months, and he was asking for a second special increase in military spending on top of the $2.4 billion, mostly for new missiles and warheads, he had asked for at the end of January. He called this one a "Special Message to the Congress on Urgent National Needs," requesting an additional $2 billion for military purposes, this time emphasizing the weaponry of conventional warfare and military assistance to countries threatened by "wars of national liberation."

"New helicopters, new armored personnel carriers, and new howitzers," he said, "must be obtained now." And he wanted more Marines, a reorganized Army prepared for smaller wars, and money to organize a national civil defense program, beginning with the location of possible bomb shelters in basements, subway stations, mine shafts, and caves across the country.

The senators and representatives cheered as the President said the

American people must sacrifice—"pay the price for these programs . . . accept a long struggle . . . share their resources with less fortunate people . . . exercise self-restraint rather than push up wages and prices . . . strive for excellence in their schools, in their cities, in their physical fitness." Then they roared their approval when Kennedy said he would leave within the week to meet with Soviet Chairman Khrushchev in Vienna. The young American champion was ready to take on the fat little premier in Moscow. The President's men thought it would be like his triumphant television campaign debates all over again.

The performance and the confidence were extraordinary that night. The day before, the President had called in Hugh Sidey to complain about *Time* magazine's evaluation of his prospects against Khrushchev: "Jack Kennedy, his New Frontier foreign policies currently in a state of some disarray, was taking a chance . . . the Communists are pretty cock-a-hoop these days, sure that they can toy with the nuclear talks, conquer Laos, wreck the U.N., and maybe start something in Berlin."

On the day of the speech, Kennedy read a similar warning in a cable from Llewellyn Thompson, the U.S. Ambassador to Moscow, reporting on a meeting with Khrushchev. The Soviet premier had suggested that Thompson attend a particular performance of an American ice show appearing in the Soviet Union as part of a cultural exchange. When he arrived, Thompson was escorted to a private room where Khrushchev told him that he was determined to sign a separate peace treaty with East Germany, trying to create a new country with the sovereign power to order the United States and its allies out of West Berlin.

"This would end our occupation rights and East Germans would control communications," Thompson wrote Kennedy, reporting Khrushchev's words. "He realized this would bring period of great tension but he was convinced would not lead to war. I told him . . . it was my duty as ambassador to see that he was under no misunderstanding of our position and that if he signed separate treaty and force was used to interfere with our communications it would be met with force. He replied if we wanted war we would get it but he was convinced only madmen would want war and western leaders not mad . . . I said we could not stop him from signing peace treaty but important question was whether our rights were interfered with."

"He's not dumb," Kennedy said of Khrushchev, after a week of study and briefings on his adversary. "He's smart. He's"—the President couldn't find the word, so he clenched his left fist and shook it in the air above his head—"He's tough!"

And Kennedy said his job was to be as tough, too. He had to warn Khrushchev on Berlin: The United States will fight! He added that he wanted Khrushchev to know something else: "I'll go the last mile" to try to prevent new testing of nuclear weapons by both countries—and to find a way to prevent China from developing its first nuclear bomb.

Kennedy received a second warning from Thompson. The ambassador, in language more direct than many diplomatic cables, wrote: "I consider Khrushchev has so deeply committed his personal prestige and that of Soviet Union to some action on Berlin and German problems that if we take completely negative stand . . . this would probably lead to developments in which chances of war or ignominious Western retreat are close to 50–50."

The problem, as Thompson analyzed it for Kennedy, was that both sides believed the other would not really go to war over Berlin, which meant that either side might push the other too far. He said Kennedy's job was going to be difficult: "Convincing Khrushchev on one hand that we will fulfill our commitment to people of Berlin and on other that it is not our intention to saw off limb on which he has crawled."

The ambassador closed by counseling patience. "It would not be to our advantage to revert to all-out cold war or have Soviet Union swing over to Chinese policy," he wrote. "Time is on our side. I consider this the more true in view of real possibility eventual split between Soviet Union and Red China."

Smart or dumb, Khrushchev was a politician. He shared Kennedy's confidence that he would prevail in any one-on-one encounter. The two leaders had already agreed secretly to meet alone for several hours in Vienna, with only interpreters in the room. That business was handled by Robert Kennedy and a Soviet agent named Georgi Bolshakov, who was in Washington officially as an information officer in the Soviet Embassy, editing an English-language magazine called *Soviet Life*. He was ranked fortieth of the sixty-seven names on the embassy's protocol list.

"Who is he, really?" asked Kennedy. A major or colonel in GRU, Soviet military intelligence, answered the CIA. More important, the agency told Kennedy, Bolshakov was a friend of Aleksei Adzhubei, the editor-in-chief of *Izvestia*, who was Khrushchev's son-in-law. Bolshakov was quite the guy, gregarious and irreverent, and he had good friends in the Washington press corps, particularly Kennedy's good friend Charlie Bartlett, and Frank Holeman of *The New York Daily News*. Both regularly reported to Robert Kennedy on their conversations with the Russian.

Holeman brought Bolshakov to the Attorney General's office two weeks before the scheduled summit meeting. The Russian and Robert Kennedy walked outside for a while on Pennsylvania Avenue, then sat down on the grass in a park there.

"Look here, Georgi," Robert Kennedy said. "I know pretty well about your standing and about your connections with the boys in Khrushchev's entourage. I know you're on intimate terms with Adzhubei and others. I think they wouldn't mind getting truthful firsthand information from you, and I presume they'll find a way of passing it on to Khrushchev."

They talked for four hours, running back into the Justice Department building when they were caught in a thunderstorm. The Attorney General told Bolshakov that Khrushchev would be making a mistake if he believed the President was weak or inexperienced. That was the big thing, he said. Berlin was the big headache for both of them, he said, and the President wanted an agreement of some kind in Vienna, because he was worried about a war starting over miscalculations or misjudgments.

The cheers Kennedy got from the congressmen, when he said he was ready for Khrushchev, were topped a few minutes later when he went on:

"If we are to win the battle that is now going on around the world between freedom and tyranny, the dramatic achievements in space which occurred in recent weeks should have made it clear to us all, as did the Sputnik in 1957, the impact of this adventure on the minds of men everywhere. . . ." He paused.

"I believe this nation should commit itself to achieving the goal, before this decade is out, of landing a man on the moon and returning him safely to earth. No single space project in this period will be more impressive to mankind."

An American on the moon! The place went wild. It was unbearable to see the United States beaten in space. Newsreels still questioned whether the Russian, Yuri Gagarin, had really been up there; perhaps this was an elaborate hoax. *Time* magazine, for one, had disdainfully called the Soviet cosmonaut "Gaga."

The pledge represented a total reversal in Kennedy's thinking. As a senator, he had been ready to vote to kill the space program. He had agreed with Eisenhower that it was a waste of money. As President, he had been ready to dismantle the National Aeronautics and Space Administration (NASA). He had chosen a science adviser, Jerome Wiesner, president of the Massachusetts Institute of Technology, who opposed the whole idea of men in space, because he thought instruments could do the job and they didn't talk back. The only thing that had prevented Kennedy from trying to push space off the American agenda early in his term was the enthusiasm of Vice President Johnson—which had something to do with the fact that NASA was headquartered in

Houston. On March 22, three weeks before Gagarin's flight, Kennedy had told James Webb, the director of NASA, that he had decided against giving new funding to Project Apollo. The American moon project was to be put on indefinite hold.

But the Gagarin flight, or, perhaps, world reaction to the flight, had shaken Kennedy badly. After he had allowed NASA to go ahead with Alan Shepard's suborbital flight, and it worked, he was ready to deal with space as a political contest. That idea was reinforced the day after Shepard's flight when Habib Bourguiba, president of Tunisia, was the guest of honor at a state dinner in the White House. Kennedy saw Bourguiba talking with Jerome Wiesner and walked over to them. "You know, we're having a terrible argument in the White House over whether we should put a man on the moon," the President said to the Tunisian leader. "Jerry here is against it. If I told you you'd get an extra billion dollars a year in foreign aid if I didn't do it, what would be your advice?"

"I wish I could tell you to put it in foreign aid," Bourguiba replied. "But I cannot."

Another pretty fair politician, Lyndon Johnson, sent Kennedy a memo saying: "This country should be realistic and recognize that other nations, regardless of their appreciation of our idealistic values, will tend to align themselves with the country which they believe will be the world leader—the winner in the long run. Dramatic accomplishments in space are being increasingly identified as a major indicator of world leadership."

Kennedy had gotten the message. He had recently written a space memo to Johnson that read: "Are we working 24 hours a day on existing programs? If not, why not?"

One of the men Kennedy turned to was Wernher von Braun, who had worked on German V-2 rocket projects during World War II and been brought to the United States to design rockets for the U.S. Army— and who had, in fact, designed the missile that put the first American satellite into space.

"Can we beat the Russians?" the President asked him.

"We have a sporting chance . . . ," von Braun answered. "With an all-out crash program I think we could accomplish this objective in 1967/68."

Winning in space was a political imperative. It would cost $562 million in the coming fiscal year, Kennedy told the Congress in his speech, between $7 billion and $9 billion altogether. They cheered that, too.

The race to the moon, though it captured the headlines, was almost an aside to the President's principal message, which was that the United States under Kennedy was prepared to escalate and expand the Cold War anywhere in the world. He did not talk of containing communism, he talked of defeating it wherever it appeared. He described programs and goals that reflected his image of Soviet and Chinese strategies and tactics: "The adversaries of freedom . . . have fired no missiles, and their troops are seldom seen. They send arms, agitators, aid technicians and propaganda to every trouble area. But where fighting is required, it is usually done by others, by guerrillas striking at night, by assassins striking alone. . . ."

Assassination was much on the President's mind as he prepared for his trip to Europe—first, two days of meetings in Paris with President Charles de Gaulle, and then to Vienna, the neutral ground for his Khrushchev meeting. The killing of the right man, a leader, was, after all, the most concentrated form of unconventional warfare, the ultimate use of leveraged covert action, the essential surgical strike. That was why it was called "Executive Action" in the jargon of secret meetings.

Before the Bay of Pigs, Kennedy and his aides had been moving forward confidentially on both the evaluation and the implementation of three assassination plans they had inherited from the Eisenhower administration. The CIA had been plotting to "eliminate" two leaders in the Caribbean: Fidel Castro and Generalissimo Rafael Leónidas Trujillo Molina of the Dominican Republic, a brutal dictator tolerated by the United States until he had reacted to cuts in U.S. aid by opening conversations with Castro. U.S. plots against Castro had been going on for almost a year, when it was not clear whether he was a Communist or not, but *was* clear that he was expropriating Cuban properties of U.S. corporations. He had also taken over hotels and gambling casinos owned and operated by American gangsters.

Since June 1960, the CIA had been working with those gangsters in attempts to kill the Cuban leader. The plotting against Trujillo, the dictator the United States had helped into power thirty-one years before, the owner of 60 percent of his country's principal asset, sugar cane fields, had begun a month before. On January 12, 1961, eight days before Kennedy's inauguration, President Eisenhower had approved a shipment of arms from the CIA to Dominicans intent on killing Trujillo.*

Kennedy had been President for only three weeks when he received a memo from Rusk saying: "Our representatives in the Dominican Repub-

---

* The third man was Patrice Lumumba, the deposed leftist prime minister of the Congo, considered a Communist by many U.S. officials, who was murdered by his own countrymen just before Kennedy took office, though his death was not confirmed until February 1961.

lic have, at considerable risk to those involved, established contacts with numerous leaders of the underground opposition. . . . The CIA has recently been authorized to arrange for delivery to them outside the Dominican Republic of small arms and sabotage equipment." Two days later, on February 17, the CIA told the White House that the Dominican plotters were ready to move. "Their action," Rusk said, "will end either with the liquidation of Trujillo and his cohorts or with a complete roll up of the internal opposition."

The failure of the Cuban invasion confused Kennedy. He was even more afraid of "noise"—of having the obvious revealed to the world. One of the last notes the President wrote to his secretary, Evelyn Lincoln, before leaving for Paris and his summit meetings late on Memorial Day, May 30, read: "Get an up-to-date report on what we are doing about the Dominican Republic."

The last official thing he had done about the assassination plot was to approve a coded cable that same day to the CIA station in Ciudad Trujillo, saying: "We must not run risk of U.S. association with political assassination, since U.S. as a matter of general policy cannot condone assassination. This last principle is overriding and must prevail in doubtful situation. . . ." But the last sentence made it clear that what the President wanted was plausible deniability: "Continue to inform dissident elements of U.S. support for their position."

He was too late to stop the plotting, as he had known when he said the United States could not condone such things. In the week after the noisy Bay of Pigs humiliation, Kennedy had said he wanted to slow down the plotting in the Dominican Republic. But the CIA station there had cabled back in code: "We doubt statement U.S. government not now prepared to cope with aftermath will dissuade them from attempt." The President had then repeated his new caution for the record at the National Security Council meeting on May 5. "The United States should not initiate the overthrow of Trujillo before knowing what kind of government would succeed him," he said. Those words were transmitted, in code, to Henry Dearborn, who was the U.S. deputy chief of mission in Ciudad Trujillo and the link between the CIA and the Dominican dissidents.

"Too late," Dearborn had answered. The U.S. government, he said in code, had been "nurturing the effort to overthrow Trujillo and had assisted the dissidents in numerous ways, all of which were known to the State Department." The "dissidents," as the State Department called the potential assassins, were actually a family named De La Maza seeking revenge for the killing of a son by Trujillo. They had asked the U.S. Consulate for weapons in mid-March.

"The members of our club," Dearborn cabled in an almost childlike code, "are now prepared in their minds to have a picnic but do not have the ingredients for the salad. Lately they have developed a plan for the picnic, which just might work if they could find the proper food. They have asked us for a few sandwiches, hardly more. . . . Last week we were asked to furnish three or four pineapples for a party in the near future, but I could remember nothing in my instructions that would have allowed me to contribute this ingredient."

Guns, ammunition, and hand grenades. The weapons were delivered to Dearborn in a U.S. diplomatic pouch. He gave them to the assassins.

Before he took off for Paris, the first European stop on his trip to the Vienna summit with Khrushchev, President Kennedy spent a day in New York. Still trying to charm Eleanor Roosevelt and her active constituency, he kept a long-standing invitation to speak at a fund-raising dinner for her Roosevelt Cancer Foundation at the Waldorf-Astoria Hotel.

The day in New York also gave him a chance to meet for the first time Israel's prime minister, David Ben-Gurion, who was also in New York on a fund-raising trip, meeting American Jews whose generosity was critical to the survival of his twelve-year-old state. They met against a background of suspicion. Jewish Democrats, particularly in New York, did not yet fully trust the son of a man who had been accused of being both anti-Semitic and pro-Nazi. Nor did John Kennedy, comfortably surrounded by Jewish staff members, trust all Jews, particularly New Yorkers. "I had the damnedest meeting in New York last night," he had said to his friend Charlie Bartlett one day in the early fall of 1960. "I went to this party. It was given by a group of people who were big money contributors and also Zionists and they said to me, 'We know that your campaign is in terrible financial shape!' . . . The deal they offered me was that they would finance the rest of this campaign if I would agree to let them run the Middle Eastern policy of the United States for the next four years."

Kennedy greeted Ben-Gurion with talk of gut-level politics. It usually worked, politician to politician. This time it didn't. "You know I was elected by the Jews," Kennedy said. "I was elected by the Jews of New York. I have to do something for them. I will do something for you." Ben-Gurion was offended. He was the founder and leader of a nation, not a politician from Brooklyn.

"I go as the leader of the greatest revolutionary country on earth," the President said before boarding Air Force One that night. The "leader" part, though, had not yet been quite accepted in other countries. The foreign minister of France, Couve de Murville, speaking of Kennedy's trials in Cuba and Laos, had been heard to say of the summit meeting with Khrushchev: "It's rather like fighting a championship bout after your last two sparring partners have knocked you out."

Before Khrushchev, Kennedy would be tested by three days with Murville's imperious boss. He had spent almost as much time doing his homework on America's grand and grandiose ally, President Charles de Gaulle, as he had on Khrushchev. With Churchill and Eisenhower retired and writing their memoirs, de Gaulle was the surviving titan of the World War II command generation, a strong man guided by a sense of France and its role in the world that bordered on mysticism. "Why is de Gaulle screwing us? What does he want?" Kennedy had asked more than once when he was considering NATO affairs. From Kennedy's perspective, the French lived under the protection of the U.S. military but never hesitated to take an anti-American line in promoting de Gaulle's goal of making France the leader of continental Europe and an equal partner of the Americans and the British. "The Anglo-Saxons," he called the two English-speaking nations. His interest was France—a France he did not want to seem dependent in any way, which meant a France with independent nuclear striking force.

The President's briefings on de Gaulle were direct: "De Gaulle is basically solid on East-West issues, although he is difficult to deal with because of his desire to enhance French prestige. . . . He also wants a voice in nuclear decisions. This we have resisted, believing it would endanger our alliances. We have also resisted French efforts to enlist our support in their national nuclear and missile program, preferring to approach this problem on a multilateral basis in order to prevent the further proliferation of nuclear capabilities. The French will not be bound by any agreements we make with the Soviets on nuclear test suspension."

It was cool in Paris, 58 degrees, when Air Force One touched down at Orly Airport at 10:17 on the morning of May 31. Kennedy and his wife had slept in their separate bedrooms on the specially outfitted Boeing 707 during the six-hour flight from New York.

"He was the youngest senator in the United States," said Léon Zitrone, the commentator at Orly for French government television. "He has but recently entered into this new presidential career and will no doubt develop and learn much more about it in the future." Zitrone and his colleagues in Paris referred to the thirty-one-year-old Jacqueline Kennedy as "la femme-enfant," the woman-child.

A certain official coolness was also to be expected when Kennedy stepped out to greet the seventy-year-old French president. In *Le Monde* the day before, André Fontaine, the political editor, who sometimes spoke for the French president, warned that de Gaulle simply did not believe that the United States intended to defend Europe against a Soviet invasion. The French president thought that NATO did not have enough troops and conventional weapons to stop the Soviets from marching across the continent. In nationalistic shorthand: No American President would trade Chicago for Lyon or Hamburg. The United States, de Gaulle believed—and he was not alone—would not use nuclear weapons against the Soviet Union to fight for Europe at the risk of nuclear retaliation against the U.S. mainland. The French president also planned to tell Kennedy that Khrushchev shared that opinion—especially after Kennedy had let his surrogates die at the Bay of Pigs.

The leading French conservative paper, *Le Figaro*, was even rougher on Kennedy: "Laos, the menace hanging over Vietnam, the Cuban fiasco, racial upheavals in the South with the deplorable effect which they produce on young nations whose friendship the Kennedy administration is trying so hard to cultivate, the continuing Russian lead in space. . . . The young President is paying dearly the price of his lack of experience and the likeable disorder which he has installed in the White House."

"DE GAULLE WILL ASK KENNEDY IF HE WOULD RISK BERLIN WAR" headlined the Paris edition of *The New York Herald Tribune*.

But at Orly Airport, de Gaulle, waiting on a red carpet lined with hydrangeas and roses, under fifteen French and fifteen American flags, instantly changed the tone of the visit. On his way to the airport, he had seen his people lined up ten deep along the roads and streets to see and cheer Kennedy. De Gaulle stunned his nation by greeting Kennedy with obvious enthusiasm—and by speaking in English, which he usually refused to do. "Have you made a good aerial voyage?" he said as Kennedy reached the bottom of the plane's stairs.

The Kennedys' triumph was apparent from the moment the limousines pulled out of Orly for the ten-mile ride to the Quai d'Orsay, the French Foreign Ministry on the Left Bank of the Seine. As de Gaulle had sensed, his countrymen were fascinated by the sight and the idea of this young man, with the beautiful wife and young children, in control of the most powerful nation in the world. The Kennedys were escorted by fifty motorcycle policemen in uniforms grander than those worn by American admirals. In front of the city's gold statue of Jeanne d'Arc, the motorcade was joined by the plumed cavalry of the Garde Républicaine. They crossed the river to the Left Bank, where only ten years before Jacqueline Bouvier had studied at the Sorbonne. Kennedy, standing in an open car, happily pointed out a Harvard banner to the seated de Gaulle. Students along the Boulevard Saint-Michel chanted a play on Kennedy's name and the French numbers from one to ten—"Kenned-un, Kenne-deux, Kenne-trois"—ending with a roared "Kenne-dix!" Kenne-dee!

"You had more than a million people out there," de Gaulle said, through a translator this time. "You saw this morning how happy Paris was to see you. I do not need to add anything to this."

The French were smitten by the Kennedys. The papers were filled with adoring anecdotes, enthusiastically supplied by the White House and in one instance by the French minister of culture, the writer André Malraux. He said he had walked with Kennedy through the Hall of Statuary in the palace of the Sun King, Louis XIV, at Versailles and that Kennedy's glance had fallen on one sculpture an instant longer than the rest. "Interesting," the American had said softly.

"That one," said the minister, "is the only real one here. The rest are copies."

Luck. Or magnificent briefing. Kennedy radiated good fortune and youth in Paris, but he was in terrible pain, hurting still from the muscle spasms in his back that had begun two weeks before, in Ottawa. He was able to hide the crutches, and the pain, too, from everyone but his closest staff. Even Ted Sorensen did not realize how bad it was this time, until he saw Kennedy slowly and painfully lowering himself into the steaming water in a gold bathtub in the King's Chambers of the Palais d'Orsay. Heat, particularly wet heat, loosened the muscles in spasm.

Kennedy's doctors knew of the agony, although they did not all know of each other. His two White House physicians, Admiral George Burkley and Dr. Janet Travell, had flown with him on Air Force One. Burkley was assigned to the President by the government. Travell had treated his back for years, injecting novocaine deep into his muscles, sometimes several times a day. Unknown to the two doctors included in the official presidential party, another physician also made the trip, Dr. Max Jacobson, the amphetamine doctor who had treated Kennedy during the 1960 campaign.

On May 12, 1961, the President had called Jacobson to Palm Beach asking him to look at Mrs. Kennedy, who was suffering from headaches and continuing bouts of depression after the birth of John F. Kennedy,

Jr., in late November 1960. Sitting on a porch there, Kennedy had told Jacobson that he wanted his wife to make the European trip, but that she was in no shape to do anything now. Was there anything the doctor could do? Eleven days later, on May 23, Jacobson was called to Washington again, this time to treat the President's back pain after the tree planting in Canada.

"I feel much better," Kennedy had told him after his shot. "I would like you to come with me to Europe next week. Will you rearrange your schedule? . . . You can send a bill."

"I will come, of course," the doctor said. But he said he would never send a bill, not to the leader of the country that made it possible for him and his family to escape Nazi Germany before the war. Later that day, Jacobson saw Mrs. Kennedy, who said she would be going to Paris and Vienna, too. Then, Dr. Jacobson later told friends, she showed him a vial of Demerol, the opium-based painkiller. She said she had found it in her husband's bathroom and believed he was getting it from one of his Secret Service guards. She wanted to know whether he could get the President to stop using it, and Jacobson said he would try. The painkiller, he said, was not only addictive but would affect the President's thinking.

Dr. Jacobson came on board Air Force One at the American Airlines freight terminal at Idlewild Airport, seeing Kennedy alone for a few minutes before the plane took off for Paris. Then the physician and his wife flew separately to Paris, the only passengers on a chartered jet. In Paris, the Jacobsons were put up at the Hôtel Napoléon. He called on the President each day.

"I don't care if it's horse piss. It works," Kennedy told Robert, when his brother learned of the Jacobson treatments and wanted the concoctions to be tested by Food and Drug Administration chemists.

After a long soak and medication, Kennedy was driven to the Elysée Palace, the residence of the president of France, for his first conversation with de Gaulle. It began exactly as Ted Sorensen, who had made his first trip to Europe to prepare for Kennedy's visit, had said it would in a short memo he had radioed to Air Force One: "Evidently what the General wants is to be sure that we are as determined as he on this one. . . . Are we determined to maintain the nuclear strength on the continent and use it? Are you personally the man to deal with Khrushchev? Is the United States really mature? etc."

Much of what the French leader said could have been taken from the transcript of his conversations with President Eisenhower. De Gaulle proposed again a three-power directorate for European affairs—France, the United Kingdom, and the United States. Kennedy responded exactly as Eisenhower had, turning it down, promising full consultations on all issues of interest to France, and pledging that the United States would respond to a Soviet attack on Western Europe as an attack on the United States itself, defending the continent with nuclear weapons.

The two presidents talked for almost an hour before lunch. They were comfortable with each other, which surprised them both and astonished their assistants who kept whispering in two languages: "They get along. . . . They get along." De Gaulle, like Eisenhower before him, was obviously impressed with the power of Kennedy's personality. But they were talking at each other; there was little attempt at persuasion. One man outlined his position, it was translated, then the other did the same.

Their differences aside, Kennedy was thrilled to be sitting in the Elysée, in front of a fireplace dominated by the "N" crest of Napoleon III. He told de Gaulle he thought he could calm down Soviet demands and threats over the presence of American, British, and French occupation troops in West Berlin. His principal concern, he said, was that a Soviet miscalculation in Berlin could lead to war. So he was willing to tell Khrushchev that the allies would consider talking about some aspects of the status of the old German capital—as long as the United States, France, and Great Britain retained the military access assured under occupation agreements.

De Gaulle disagreed. "There is nothing to negotiate with the Russians.

"Russia does not want a war," the French leader continued. Khrushchev had been threatening war over Berlin every six months for three years, he said. But it was obviously a bluff. There would be no war if the allied occupiers of West Berlin, particularly the United States, stood firm.

De Gaulle seemed to think Kennedy was foolish to be meeting with the Soviet leader at all. He, however, never used the word "Soviet." Communism, ideology, are frauds, he said, knowing how desperately serious Americans were about such things. Nationalism, he said, is the problem. Leaders use ideology to serve their own purposes. Lenin's communism was different from Stalin's, and Stalin's different from Khrushchev's. But "Russia" is real, de Gaulle said. The Russians may or may not always be Communists, he said, but they will always be Russians. Mother Russia will always try to expand to the west and the south; she will always hold back if she is convinced the Western nations will fight. Your job, Mr. President, is to make sure Khrushchev believes you are a man who will fight.

"Stand fast when Khrushchev summons you to change the status of

Berlin," de Gaulle said. "This is the most useful service you can render the whole world."

"Tenir bon," he repeated. "Tenir le coup." Hold on, be firm, be strong. Wait them out. One day, communism will fall of its own weight.

Kennedy smiled when de Gaulle ended the morning by saying: "You can listen to your advisers before you make up your mind, but once you've made up your mind don't listen to anyone."

At lunch, the presidents were joined by their wives. De Gaulle focused on Mrs. Kennedy, obviously charmed by her questions about French history and art. The two had reached the eighteenth century when Kennedy interrupted to ask about more recent history: What was Churchill like? What was Roosevelt like? De Gaulle said Churchill was a wild man, changing from day to day, and that they had argued violently, but he felt a rapport with the Englishman. Roosevelt, he said, was colder; they never argued, but he felt he had never connected with the American leader.

In the afternoon, there was rapport without agreement. De Gaulle had chosen to begin with Berlin in the morning. In the afternoon, Kennedy said he would like to talk first about Southeast Asia. "I know you think Laos is a peripheral area which can be abandoned. . . ," he began.

"You will find that intervention in this area will be an endless entanglement," responded de Gaulle. "Once a nation has been aroused, no foreign power, however strong, can impose its will upon it. You will sink into a bottomless military and political quagmire, however much you spend in men and money."

"I hope you will not say that in public," Kennedy said.

"Of course not," the Frenchman replied. Then, realizing his words had not convinced Kennedy, he added: "I never speak to the press. Never."

De Gaulle added another thought about that part of the world. Perhaps, he said, the Russians are backing the Pathet Lao insurgents in Laos so heavily because they, too, are nervous about Chinese expansion. That idea was too much for Kennedy. The Americans still saw a monolith they called the "Sino-Soviet bloc." Kennedy's response was clever but wrong: He said he thought the Soviet Union and China were like Caesar and Pompey, they would become enemies again only after vanquishing the common foe.

"Rusk is trying to reach you. He says it's urgent," Kennedy was told as he left the Elysée Palace for the short ride across the Seine to his apartments. It was raining, but there were still crowds along the streets to cheer him or just get a glimpse of his car.

"Trujillo is dead," the Secretary of State told the President on a secure telephone line to the King's Chamber of the Palais d'Orsay from a conference room in the State Department.

"He was assassinated last night going to one of his houses."

"Were we involved?" Kennedy asked.

"I don't think so," Rusk said. "There's some confusion."

Kennedy had to cut it short. He and de Gaulle were scheduled to ride together up the Champs-Elysées to the tomb of The Unknown Soldier, under the Arc de Triomphe. The tall Frenchman arrived downstairs, stepping out of his car under umbrellas held high in the pouring rain.

"Let's take the open car," Kennedy said, and de Gaulle ordered the top of the convertible Citroën limousine taken down. Kennedy was stripping off his raincoat; de Gaulle immediately did the same. The two presidents, soaking wet within moments, waved and smiled as their open car turned into a long alley of black umbrellas and cheering men and women for the ride across the river to the Arch.

Back in the King's Chamber after the ceremony, drying himself after another fifteen minutes in the gold tub, Kennedy told Rusk back in Washington that the United States had a single, overriding priority in the Dominican Republic: "Do whatever is necessary to prevent a Communist takeover." At the May 5 meeting of the National Security Council, he had ordered the administration's Cuba Task Force to prepare contingency plans for invasion and occupation of the Dominican Republic and Haiti, the dictatorship that shared the island of Santo Domingo with Trujillo's country. He wanted U.S. Navy ships deployed, according to plan, around the Caribbean island. Just over the horizon, Kennedy said.

He called Kenny O'Donnell into the large bedroom. His appointments secretary was the perfect President's man. Later that same night, O'Donnell and another aide, Dave Powers, would realize that they could not get to their rooms without going through the King's Chamber. But by then the President was already in bed. So, getting down on all fours, they crawled across the carpet of Kennedy's room to reach the door on the far side.

"Call Pierre," Kennedy told O'Donnell. The press secretary was at the Hôtel Crillon, just across the Seine on the Place de la Concorde, headquarters these days for the world's press.

Salinger had a press briefing scheduled for 7:00 P.M., where he would fend off questions about the day's talks by saying only that Kennedy and de Gaulle were in "general agreement on Berlin." A reporter asked when Rusk would be arriving.

"He isn't coming right away," Salinger said. "Because, you know, of the situation in the Dominican Republic."

"What situation?"

"You know, Trujillo's being killed."

The reporters did not know—and they were not supposed to know until Kennedy himself had a better idea of what had happened and what might happen next. The President still did not know when or where the assassination had taken place.

A hundred reporters battled each other to get to the telephones and transmit the news to the world in a dozen languages. By the time Salinger caught up with the President at the dinner President de Gaulle was giving for fifteen hundred people at the Elysée Palace, Kennedy had received another call from Washington saying that new intelligence indicated Trujillo might still be alive.

"Do you know what that means, Pierre?" Kennedy said.

"Yes, Mr. President. It means he's dead or I am."

"That's right."

But Trujillo was dead. He had been gunned down with American-supplied weapons as he drove out of Ciudad Trujillo in a light blue Chevrolet Belair on the Avenida George Washington. It had happened while Kennedy was flying to Paris. It had been sixteen hours later before the State Department learned of the shooting, and Rusk had immediately called the President.

Rusk also warned Kennedy that General Ramfis Trujillo, the dictator's son and the commander of the Dominican Air Force, was in Paris, apparently making a regular run to deposit more of his country's stolen treasure into foreign banks and vaults. There was reason to believe he might try to murder Kennedy in revenge for his father's assassination. The son, thirty-two years old, was an experienced and brutal killer who, it was said, had a meat locker in his home in Ciudad Trujillo where he hung the bodies of executed political opponents for the amusement of dinner party guests. Within an hour, more than fifteen thousand French police and American officials were searching the city for the younger Trujillo. But Ramfis, it turned out, was making his own desperate search: he was indeed roaming Paris, but he was trying to charter a plane to take him back to the Dominican Republic to seize power and search out his father's killers.

At the Elysée dinner, Kennedy rose to toast de Gaulle. He ignored a formal text pledging that U.S. troops would stay in Europe as long as they were needed, ready to do whatever was needed, and decided to be personal: "I sleep in a French bed. In the morning my breakfast is served by a French chef . . . I am married to a daughter of France."

Rusk was now flying to Paris, and Undersecretary of State Bowles, the department's number-two man, had taken over the "Operations

Center" in the Secretary's conference room, at least until Robert Kennedy marched in. As he had after the Bay of Pigs, the President's brother went after Bowles. "You're a gutless bastard," Robert Kennedy yelled when he realized that Bowles was reluctant to bring U.S. warships closer to the Dominican coast.

It was the Attorney General's first crisis as a foreign affairs expert. "Let Bobby play around," was what the President had told Rusk. "If he gets in your way, let me know."

After midnight, when Kennedy got back from the Elysée to the King's Chamber and again lowered his aching back into steaming water, angry calls were coming from Washington one after another—from Bowles, from his brother, and from McNamara, who was siding with Robert Kennedy against the cautious Undersecretary.

"They want to send in the Marines," Bowles told the President, referring to Robert Kennedy and McNamara. Burned once in the Caribbean, the President preferred to err on the side of caution, and he said that to the Undersecretary.

"Well, I'm glad to hear it," said Bowles, "and in that case, would you clarify who's in charge here?"

"You are," the President said.

"Good. Would you mind explaining that to your brother?"

The next morning, his second day in Paris, the President bumped into Averell Harriman at the U.S. Embassy. Not by accident. Harriman had been jockeying for position near presidents since Franklin D. Roosevelt. This time he had invited himself to Paris from Geneva, where he had been negotiating with the Soviets over Laos. But Harriman, sixty-nine years old now and hard of hearing, was both too rough and too slippery to stay away from the center for very long. Advising at the highest level was no business for the polite or faint-egoed. Harriman was neither. He had served two presidents, Roosevelt and Truman, and he told his assistants that when a President looks your way, you have just seven seconds to make your point.

He had paced for hours that morning inside the doorway of the U.S. Embassy, muttering to himself, ignoring everyone else. When the President came through the door, Harriman took his elbow, which Kennedy did not appreciate at all, and said, "Mr. President, I have just one question: Do you want a settlement on Laos or not?"

"Yes. Get us out of there any way you can," Kennedy answered, his voice rising. Harriman had gotten his seven seconds, but he wanted more. That night he persuaded the President's sister, Eunice Shriver, to bring him to the palace at Versailles for the formal dinner in the Hall of Mirrors for just one hundred fifty people. He told her it was desperately important that he talk with the President before the meetings with Khrushchev in Vienna.

"I hear there is something you want to say to me," Kennedy said to Harriman, who had managed to end up just three seats away from him.

"Have fun with Khrushchev," Harriman said. "Don't let him frighten you.

"Remember that he's just as scared as you are. Don't let him rattle you, he'll try to rattle you and frighten you, but don't pay any attention to that. . . . His style will be to attack and then see if he can get away with it. Laugh about it, don't get into a fight. . . . Have some fun."

Another Harriman moment was over. The President looked away.

After dinner, President de Gaulle led the guests to a brief performance by the Paris Opera Ballet in the Louis XV theater, a room of such exquisite proportion and decoration that spectators had the sensation of being inside a perfect jewel. One of the Americans there, who was without a seat, was a *Washington Star* reporter named Mary McGrory. Looking for someplace to stand after the first act, she stumbled into the small holding room under the King's box and found herself face to face with her President.

"Pretty impressive, isn't it?" Kennedy said. "A little different than Fred Waring and Lawrence Welk at the White House. We've got to start doing something different."

"How are you getting along with de Gaulle?" McGrory said, surprised that Kennedy was obviously sticking with her rather than de Gaulle or anyone else in the room. He was not comfortable and not quite so charming in a language he did not understand and spoke in a way that no one else could, either.

"Do you want to meet him?" Kennedy asked, pulling her along. "General, I'd like you to meet a friend of mine. This is Mary McGrory of *The Washington Star*."

De Gaulle looked off into the middle distance, not amused at the idea of having a reporter as a friend. Kennedy chatted on, all in English.

McGrory thought, not for the first time, that despite his poise and manners, Kennedy was a shy man. He preferred people to come to him, feeling a sense of control when they did. But, she realized, he had no control whatever in that room, where everyone else was speaking in a strange tongue.

"My, where did you learn to speak French?" Kennedy said with a bit of edge in his voice to another reporter, George Herman of CBS. The President then proceeded to introduce Herman to de Gaulle three times. The general, a foot taller than Herman, sniffed at the air above him as if something had gone bad.

It was misty as the black Citroën limousines pulled away from the palace at midnight. Twice, Kennedy asked his driver to stop as his car moved through the gardens and fountains of the long-ago kings and queens. He stepped out each time with his wife and walked a ways. The second time, de Gaulle walked up and joined them. The two men shook hands.

"Apotheosis at Versailles," headlined *France-Soir* the next day. "Versailles at Last Has a Queen" was another headline. They were an extraordinarily handsome couple. She had won over the French forever by appearing in a white silk bell-skirted gown designed by one of their own, Hubert de Givenchy.

That day, after their sixth long meeting, de Gaulle thrilled Kennedy by saying, "I have more confidence in your country now." In his own notes of the visit, the Frenchman wrote without much grace that this American represented the next generation of world leaders: "Enjoying the advantages of youth, but suffering the drawbacks of a novice."

Kennedy spent his last night in Paris with his own men. Rusk had finally arrived, joining Bundy, Llewellyn Thompson, Charles Bohlen, and Harriman for Kennedy's last briefings before the Khrushchev encounter. In a final press conference, with 540 reporters from everywhere in the world, he left with a smile and a little joke, beginning: "I am the man who accompanied Jacqueline Kennedy to Paris. . . ."

His wife had conquered all Paris, and de Gaulle and Malraux as well. "What a cruel fate," she said to the culture minister as they toured Malmaison, the home of Napoleon's Josephine, and looked at a portrait of the empress. "She must have been an extraordinary woman."

"What she was," Malraux said, "was a real bitch!"

That was said more than once about Mrs. Kennedy, too, though it never seemed to bother her.

Early in the administration, Kennedy, who avoided confrontation with his wife, had sent Angier Biddle Duke, his chief of protocol, to talk to Mrs. Kennedy about the role of First Lady. "Tell her," the President had said, "the responsibility of the wife of the President in regards to visitors and things."

"What do you want to do, Mrs. Kennedy?" Ambassador Duke had begun.

"As little as possible," she said. "I'm a mother. I'm a wife. I'm not a public official."

"Tell her it's hurting me politically," Kennedy said to Duke, when his wife accepted expensive gifts from foreign heads of state. The issue of the moment was horses offered by the king of Saudi Arabia and the prime minister of Ireland. "The Arabs give her these horses and then the Israelis come along with an old Bible worth about $12."

"I understand what you're saying, Angie," Mrs. Kennedy had replied after hearing out Duke. "But there's a problem."

"What's that?"

"I want the horses," she said.

But there was no problem in Paris, and the man who accompanied Jacqueline Kennedy was delighted. "Well," he told her, "I'm dazzled." He even forgot about how mad he was when he had found out she was bringing two truckloads of dresses, jewelry, and accessories to Paris and Vienna, or that she had sent locks of her hair ahead so that the hairdressers of each capital would be prepared to meet her needs.

"Stop that plane!" called a French official running across the tarmac toward Air Force One just before nine o'clock the next morning at Orly. The Kennedys froze halfway up the steps to the plane, holding their smiles and waving hands. A station wagon roared up behind the Frenchman, filled with trunks and valises, with more tied onto the roof. One of Mrs. Kennedy's maids had gotten lost on the way to the airport. The man who accompanied Jacqueline Kennedy to Paris dropped his smile for a moment. The plane took off for Vienna a few minutes late.

Chapter 13

"**R**usk, you make a hell of a substitute for Jackie," President Kennedy said happily as he waved to the crowds along the roads and sidewalks on his route from Schwechat Airport into the center of Vienna. The Secretary of State, seated next to Kennedy in a bubble-topped black Chrysler, had never seen anything like it: seventy thousand Austrians were cheering in a driving rain.

"Look," Kennedy said, pointing to a sign held up by some American students: "INNOCENTS ABROAD SAY HOWDY."

Kennedy was confident. The meetings with President de Gaulle had been a perfect dress rehearsal, a test of his credibility as a world leader. He laughed when he read a column in the Paris edition of *The New York Herald Tribune* the day he left that city. "JFK intends to act not only as his own foreign minister," wrote Marguerite Higgins, "but as his own Soviet expert, French expert, Berlin expert, Laotian expert, nuclear test ban expert, etc. . . ."

The Bay of Pigs was behind him, both politically and personally. He had been willing to take the blame in public, although he believed his real mistake was in not having seen through men whose titles were more impressive than their advice, strangers with impressive résumés. He blamed them in private. And, in a way, because he had never been truly committed to the plan, Kennedy blamed Eisenhower. Now that was over, and what he was committed to was making sure the Soviet leader did not underrate American resolve.

"Khrushchev must not misunderstand Laos and Cuba," he had said as he was doing his homework for the Vienna meeting, "as an indication that the United States is in a yielding mood on such matters as Berlin."

Kennedy had a simple agenda. He wanted to meet Khrushchev, size him up, talk to him politician-to-politician about the dangers of military miscalculation in a nuclear world. The political systems that produced the two leaders were different, but they were in the same business and Kennedy had no doubt they would understand each other. He assumed that the Russian was no madman either, and that they had a common interest in not wanting to blow up the world. The best way to avoid war by accident or miscalculation was for each man to understand the vital interests of the other—and work to avoid dangerous shifts in the existing balance of power.

Kennedy's mission, though he would never have put it that way, was to preserve the status quo. He wanted Khrushchev to understand the vital interests of the United States as the dominant country in most of the world—what this President was prepared to defend—and then the two of them could work out some arrangement to avoid clashes where national interests and ambitions intersected, particularly in Berlin.

The State Department had seemed to agree. Kennedy's briefing papers concluded that while Khrushchev might use bluster and threat on occasion, the Russian was also looking for a relaxation of tensions. "Khrushchev would prefer the talks end on a note of accord, and may make some conciliatory gestures for this reason. . . . It seems likely that he will generally assume an attitude of reasonable firmness, coupled with a pitch for improved US-Soviet relations."

All that, a mirror of his own expectations, seemed reasonable to Kennedy. He had done his homework on Khrushchev's personality, even if much of what he had heard seemed unreal. It was hard for him to make sense of something Walter Lippmann had told him after the columnist had met with Khrushchev in April: The Russian leader believed that American presidents were only tools of the greatest capitalists, and that Kennedy took his orders from Nelson Rockefeller because the Rockefellers had more money than the Kennedys. Khrushchev, said Lippmann, had told him that he knew who ran the United States, "the Monopolists"—he had met fifty of them with Averell Harriman when he visited New York in 1957.

The President had laughed and turned to more reasonable things, focusing on briefings about the Soviet leader's political personality. Lippmann, who had been telling presidents what to do for forty years, told him the Russian reminded him of Al Smith, the governor of New York who was the first Roman Catholic to run for President, thirty-two years before Kennedy. Khrushchev, said Lippmann, had a sense of what every man in his constituency was thinking, and he had a gift for explaining government, budgets, and all that in anecdotes and common language his people understood.

Kennedy's focus was on Khrushchev the man, a wild sort who had shocked the world only a year before by taking off his shoe and banging it on the desk in front of him during a debate in the U.N. General Assembly. CIA psychologists had sent the President character sketches with advice like this on the Soviet leader: "He is more aggressive when he's tired, watch for swelling of the vein on his left temple, that's the signal to take it easy."

As a senator and candidate, Kennedy had been skeptical of summits. "I would not meet with Mr. Khrushchev unless there were some agreement at the secondary level," he had said, "which would indicate that the meeting had some hope of success, or useful exchange of ideas."

He had been in office only three weeks when the first feelers came from Khrushchev for an early meeting. He had jumped at the chance, writing to the Soviet leader on February 22 to suggest a meeting, and he wrote again when Khrushchev repeated the invitation after the Bay of Pigs. The chairman had emphasized that he was not interested in talking about that embarrassing piece of business. The challenge, the action, was irresistible to Kennedy. And it must have been irresistible to Khrushchev, too. The timing was right: triumphant in space, on the move in a half dozen countries around the world, Soviet power and influence were at a peak, and Khrushchev wanted the Americans to acknowledge that before the world.

The first meeting was scheduled to begin just twenty minutes after the President arrived at the residence of the U.S. Ambassador to Austria, H. Freeman Matthews. The President's men were already circulating among reporters outside, telling them how ready their President was, repeating that this would be like the Kennedy-Nixon debates of last year. The American entourage almost ran down the steps from Air Force One, scattering to their hotels as the President was rushed off to pay a courtesy call on the president of Austria, Dr. Adolf Schärf.

Dr. Max Jacobson was not listed as a member of the official presidential party, but he was in the entourage and on the White House housing list, rooming with the President's military attachés. As he did back in the United States, the doctor responded to calls and messages from "Mrs. Dunn," a simple code name for the White House. There was a call soon after Air Force One landed in Vienna.

"Khrushchev will be here any minute," Kennedy said to Jacobson as the doctor prepared an injection in an upstairs bedroom of the residence.

"This could go on for hours. I can't afford any complications with my back."

"You won't have that for an excuse," the doctor said.

A few minutes later, Kennedy was pacing the halls downstairs when the cars bringing Khrushchev and his party rolled slowly through the gates at 12:45 P.M. As the cars stopped, Kennedy burst out the front door, running down the steps. It was the same race he had won with Eisenhower at the White House six months before. But Khrushchev was quicker than he looked, and he was double-timing, too, as they met for one of the most photographed handshakes of all time.

"Another one," the photographers shouted.

"Tell the Chairman," Kennedy said to his interpreter, Alexander Akolovsky, "that it's all right with me if it's all right with him." It was. Khrushchev grinned and stuck out his hand again. The leader of the Soviet Union, sixty-seven years old and fat as a sausage, came up to the nose of the trim President of the United States. No hats; they were both bareheaded in the rain.

"My wife," said Kennedy, who was not much for small talk, "says that Gromyko looks so kind, so pleasant that he must be a nice man."

Khrushchev laughed on cue, looking over at his foreign minister, the dour Andrei Gromyko. "Really?" the chairman said. "Some people say Gromyko looks like your Richard Nixon."

Kennedy got stuck with the small talk, reminding Khrushchev that they had met in Washington in September 1959.

"I remember. I remember how young you looked," the Russian said. "Would you like to exchange ages? Or split the difference?

"We cast the deciding vote when you beat that son-of-a-bitch Nixon," Khrushchev said.

"How?"

"We waited to release the spy pilots until after the election. So Nixon could not claim he knew how to deal with the Russians."

Kennedy protested the Soviet leader's remark to Lippmann that the Rockefellers and other rich families told him what to do. "None of those men supported me," Kennedy said.

"They are clever fellows," said Khrushchev.

Inside, the two leaders faced each other across a large coffee table in the music room, a homey sitting room, fifteen by twenty feet, with glass doors looking out over the garden. Each man had his interpreter just behind him. Rusk, Llewellyn Thompson, Charles Bohlen, and Assistant Secretary of State for European Affairs Foy Kohler sat behind Kennedy. Andrei Gromyko; Mikhail Menshikov, the Soviet Ambassador to the United States; and Anatoli Dobrynin, chief of the Americas Countries

Division of the Soviet Foreign Ministry, were behind Khrushchev. The first thing the Soviet chairman noticed was that Kennedy rarely looked at his aides, much less talked to them. He was different from Eisenhower, who rarely spoke without turning to his team, especially his Secretary of State, John Foster Dulles.

Kennedy said what he had come to say: The great danger in this dangerous world was a miscalculation of motives or resolve that led to war between the two great nuclear powers. What they should do now, he said, was agree that neither side would try to upset the complicated balances of power around the world. Their responsibility, his and Khrushchev's, was to find a way to compete without direct confrontation in areas where both had interests, without affecting each other's vital security interests or prestige.

Khrushchev's response, as recorded by American note takers, was harsh and angry: "The West and the United States as its leader must recognize one fact: Communism exists and has won its right to develop. . . . Mr. Dulles based his policy on the premise of liquidation of the Communist system."

No, it is the opposite that is true, said Kennedy, trying to turn the argument around: "You wish to destroy the influence of my country where it has traditionally been present," he complained. "You wish to liquidate the free system in other countries."

Khrushchev ignored that, saying that it was not the Soviets but the people of other countries who were fighting for change—as the capitalists had begun their fight with the French Revolution. Now, he said, the capitalists, and Kennedy as their leader, wanted to preserve the status quo. And from there the Soviet leader took over, bullying, goading, and trapping Kennedy again and again. The President was on a slippery slope with this tough old dialectitian. Kennedy was arguing against change.

"If I understand you correctly, Mr. President," said Khrushchev, "you wish to erect something in the way of a dam on the road of the development of the human mind. This is not possible. . . . Ideas have never been destroyed and this is proven in the whole course of human development. . . . If you seek to destroy ideas, then this will inevitably lead to conflict. . . . If you are able to assure, under your system, a higher standard of economic development, then victory will be with you and we will recognize it. If, however, the socialist system assures a higher standard of economic development of industry and culture, then we will win. I am speaking now, of course, not about military victory, but about victory in the plane of ideas.

"From your words," he continued, "I draw the conclusion that you wish to transfer to us the responsibility for the growth of influence of

Communist ideas in the whole world. In order that there should not be any conflict between us, you wish that these ideas not be propagated beyond the already existing socialist countries. But I repeat, Mr. President, that ideas cannot be stopped. . . . The Spanish Inquisition burned people who disagreed with it but ideas did not burn and eventually came out as victors. Once an idea is born it cannot be chained or burned."

Kennedy was having trouble getting into the conversation, much less persuading or impressing. The notes recorded: "The President interjected that Mao Tse Tung had said that power was at the end of the rifle."

Khrushchev said he did not believe that, because Marxists were against war. Then he went back to where he had been, saying the United States wanted the Soviet Union to sit like a schoolboy with his hands folded on the desk. "The Soviet Union supports its ideas and holds them in high esteem," he said. "It cannot guarantee that these ideas will stop at its borders."

"The President said that he understood Mr. Khrushchev's point of view but that he was anxious to give him our views," the record reports. "His own main ambition, the President said, is to secure peace."

"Mr. Khrushchev responded by saying . . . that he did not quite understand what kind of conditions, in the US view, the USSR should maintain in order to ensure peace. He wondered what the meaning of 'miscalculation' was. He said the Soviet Union would defend its vital interests and the United States might regard some of such acts as 'miscalculations.' "

"There was a man who bossed his son," Khrushchev went on, reciting another Russian story, this time without warmth or humor. "Then his son grew up, but the father didn't realize it and took him by the ear. 'Look here, father,' said the son. 'I'm grown up. I have children of my own. You can't treat me the way you used to.'

"We have grown up," said the leader of the Soviet Union. "You're an old country. We're a young country."

"If you look across the table, you'll see that we're not so old," Kennedy replied.

But the American President's arguments did seem old and defensive. He was taken by surprise, caught in the web of Communist cant. He was defending traditional spheres of influence, defending colonialism, defending old-line dictators, tripped into defending ideas he did not believe in and men he despised. Balance of forces, balance of power. Defending the status quo, he had stumbled through the mirror. He was on the other side, arguing against revolution, against change. The Marxist coal miner was tying him in knots.

"The people in those countries will decide the outcome of this,"

Khrushchev said. These governments will be overthrown by the people for the most basic of reasons: "To rise up against moral constraint, moral oppression, or moral bondage a man must have a highly developed and highly refined conception of what human freedom is all about. Most people still measure their own freedom or lack of freedom in terms of how much meat, how many potatoes, or what kind of boots they can get for one ruble."

Kennedy agreed. Of course.

"Don't blame the Soviet Union then," the Soviet leader said to the American President.

Kennedy came out of the music room looking pale. It had taken just a little more than an hour. Looking at the smaller man, Kennedy wondered if this was what Napoleon was like.

They broke for lunch at two o'clock.

"Is it always like this?" Kennedy asked Llewelyn Thompson, who was one of the men seated behind him at the first session.

"Par for the course, Mr. President," the ambassador said. He did not mean it. The old American Soviet hands—Thompson, Bohlen, and Kohler—caught each other's eyes for a moment, a bad moment. Thompson told his State Department colleagues that he was shocked that Kennedy just sat there taking one shot after another from the Russian.

At lunch, though, Kennedy did most of the talking, smiling and showing the kind of grace under pressure that he so admired. There were two summits, the private and the public; what happened, and what the world saw and was told was happening. The President shone in public. The two leaders laughed together through the meal. Kennedy asked Khrushchev what were the two medals he wore and the chairman answered, "Lenin Peace Prizes."

"I hope you get to keep them," Kennedy said, or so his men immediately reported to American reporters, who quickly broadcast the clever exchange to the world.

Khrushchev had his laugh in the garden outside the music room as the two leaders walked for a few minutes at three o'clock before returning to their official table inside. Kennedy asked Khrushchev how he found the time for the hours-long conversations he had with visiting Americans like Senator Hubert Humphrey and Walter Lippmann. The chairman said the Soviet system was more decentralized than it seemed. He explained that he made overall policy decisions but leaders of the Soviet Republics made operating decisions. The President said most of his time was taken up in contacts and consultations with various branches of the U.S. government.

"Well," said Khrushchev, "why don't you switch to our system?"

Back inside, this time with only their translators, they took up their debate about capitalism, communism, and revolution. Kennedy again tried to explain what he meant by "miscalculation."

"We have a common task," said the President, saying that about the only thing they agreed on during that first session was that nuclear war could destroy all civilization. The two of them now—and President Eisenhower after 1957—were the first men ever to face off with that kind of power, and the capability to deliver it. Explaining himself more clearly than he had earlier, Kennedy repeated that Washington and Moscow had to avoid moves that might force the other to react with force.

Khrushchev took off again, saying that it was not the Soviet Union fomenting revolution around the world, the problem was the United States always looking for outside forces in local upheaval. Cuba was his first example. According to the U.S. transcript, Khrushchev said:

"A mere handful of people, headed by Fidel Castro, overthrew the Batista regime because of its oppressive nature. . . . The President's decision to launch a landing in Cuba only strengthened the revolutionary forces and Castro's own position, because the people of Cuba were afraid that they would get another Batista and lose the achievements of the revolution. Castro is not a Communist but U.S. policy can make him one."

"It was a mistake," Kennedy said. But if Castro used his country as a base to undermine other governments in the Western Hemisphere, that would imperil the United States itself.

"Can six million people really be a threat to the mighty U.S.?" Khrushchev asked.

"Would you tolerate a regime friendly to the United States, with military bases, on your border in, say, Poland?" Kennedy countered.

"Of course not."

"Well, that is the way we feel about Cuba," Kennedy said.

But Khrushchev was still in control, taunting Kennedy, asking how the United States could oppose Castro but support Generalissimo Franco, the dictator in Spain. He said that both sides, the Soviets and the Americans, were supplying arms in Laos, but the U.S. weapons would end up in the hands of the Communists—just as the weapons the United States supplied to Chiang Kai-shek in China had ended up in the hands of Mao Tse-tung and his troops. Finally at the bottom of the sixth page of the sixteen-page U.S. transcript, the note taker wrote what looked like a double-entendre: "The President rejoined . . ."

Part of that rejoinder, according to the notes, was: "The reason for this policy is that if Franco should be replaced and if the new regime were to associate itself with the Soviet Union, the balance of power in Western Europe would radically change and this is, of course, a matter of great concern to us."

Kennedy brought up Laos, saying that the United States had made mistakes there. His candor must have surprised Khrushchev, who treated it as weakness, ideological retreat. At one point Kennedy picked up on that, saying, "We admit our mistakes. Do you ever admit you're wrong?"

"Yes," Khrushchev said. "In the speech before the Twentieth Party Congress I admitted Stalin's mistakes . . ."

"Those weren't your mistakes . . ." Kennedy interrupted.

All the United States wanted in Laos was neutrality and independence, Kennedy repeated. Khrushchev said that's all the Soviets wanted, too—and that Rusk and Gromyko should be talking about that.

Then he knocked Kennedy onto the defensive again, bringing up American alliances with the old colonial powers of Western Europe, starting with Portugal, which was desperately trying to put down rebellion in Angola. "The USSR regards this situation as a popular war against colonialists," Khrushchev said. "The U.S. has no colonies but it supports colonial countries, and this is why the people are against it. There was a time when the United States was a leader in the fight for freedom. As a matter of fact, the Russian Czar refused to recognize the United States for twenty-six years because he regarded the United States as an illegitimate creature. Now the United States refuses to recognize New China—things have changed, haven't they?"

Kennedy protested that the United States had voted with African countries and with the Soviet Union against Portugal, and against Belgium in the case of the Belgian Congo, in the United Nations.

"Timid . . . voice is very quiet. Basically, U.S. policy is support for Colonialist powers," Khrushchev replied. "These are sacred wars. . . ." He brought up Algeria, where France was fighting to maintain its control. "What should the Algerian people do? Wait for France? The fact is that Algeria should belong to Algerians. . . . Such wars will go on. The United States itself rose against the British. But now the U.S. has changed its position and it is against other people following suit."

Kennedy protested that, as a senator, he had spoken for Algerian independence in 1956, causing quite a stir at the time. "I am for change," he said. Khrushchev laughed at him.

Khrushchev's January 6 speech came up and he repeated some of it. There were three kinds of war. Nuclear, he ruled out. Conventional, which his side, communism, would win: "We will put five divisions where you put only one." And wars of national revolution—"holy wars," Khrushchev called them—nothing could stop such wars, and the Soviets would support them. The United States was on the wrong side of history, opposing the will of the peoples of the world.

"No, there will be no nuclear war," Khrushchev said, a danger signal because it meant he believed the United States would not use nuclear weapons to preserve the status quo in Western Europe—and that was the only way the West could stop an invasion by the Soviets and their allies.

Then the Russian challenged the legitimacy—and the morality, too —of the American commitments around the world. He attacked the ring of U.S. and NATO forces surrounding the Soviet Union. If the United States considered Cuba a danger and a provocation, how did he think the Soviet Union felt about U.S. troops in Iran, in Turkey, in Pakistan, in South Korea, in Southeast Asia, in Taiwan? He said if he ran China, he would have attacked Taiwan long ago.

Kennedy responded by paraphrasing Churchill's 1945 commitment to preserving and defending the British Empire. He did not become President of the United States to undo American commitments around the globe. The prestige of the United States, the balance of power in the world, depended on the United States honoring those commitments.

"The United States has delusions of grandeur," Khrushchev said. "Megalomania."

They came back to Laos at the end. It seemed that the Soviet leader had no passion about the place or what happened there—or perhaps he wanted a U.S.-Soviet agreement that would effectively limit Chinese influence there—and he immediately agreed to Kennedy's suggestion that they join together to try to bring about a neutral settlement in the lethargic civil war there. "We'll lock our foreign ministers in a room and tell them to find a solution," he said.

"You were going into Laos in April or May, weren't you?" Khrushchev asked. He was referring to the movement of U.S. ships and Marines heading that way when what the President had really hoped for was a cease-fire and negotiations. So, Kennedy's bluff had worked!

Both men were visibly tired when they walked out of the music room at 6:45 P.M.—after three hours and forty-five minutes of talk. Kennedy brushed by Dr. Jacobson, who had been sitting in a window seat in a vestibule outside the music room. "Are you all right, Mr. President?"

"I'm fine," Kennedy said. "Do you mind if I take time for a piss?"

"How did it go?" Evelyn Lincoln asked the President when she saw him later in the living quarters upstairs.

"Not too well."

"He treated me like a little boy," Kennedy said later, pacing his room at the ambassador's residence in a rage, cursing at Khrushchev and at himself. "Like a little boy."

Nothing seemed to go right. Two hours after the end of the afternoon session, he and Khrushchev were together again before a state banquet in the Schonnbrunn Palace, once the glittering seat of the Austro-Hungarian Empire. The empire was gone and Austria was a small, neutral country, rigidly neutral after Soviet troops had left in 1955, the only time they had left a country they'd occupied after the war. The imperial gold leaf and crystal still glittered everywhere as the leaders arrived for a gala dinner. Kennedy, Khrushchev, and Austrian President Adolf Schärf all rose from the long sofa they shared as the two wives arrived —followed by photographers.

"Would you shake hands with Mr. Kennedy?" one called to Khrushchev.

The Russian was focused on Mrs. Kennedy. "I'd like to shake hands with her," he said.

His own wife ("motherly" routinely preceded Nina Khrushchev's name in the Western press) sat down on the sofa, where Kennedy had been seated before he stood. A few beats later, he stepped back and began to sit on Mrs. Khrushchev's lap.

Hearing the gasps, Kennedy, bad back and all, stopped an inch or two short. Her husband barely noticed. He was talking to Mrs. Kennedy, first joking, then telling her seriously that her husband was wise to reverse his order to send troops into Laos. Kennedy interrupted to say he had never done that, but Khrushchev widened his eyes as if he knew better.

There were gasps across town, too, as the American team began to go over the minutes of the day's sessions. Kennedy, they realized, had barely defended himself, or U.S. positions.

"He's a little bit out of his depth, isn't he?" said Bohlen, one of the note takers in the first session. George Kennan, an old Soviet hand who was ambassador to Yugoslavia, thought the President had seemed tongue-tied, totally unsure of himself. "Shattered" was Harriman's word.

"He's dancing," said Assistant Secretary of Defense Paul Nitze. "All he's doing is dancing."

Khrushchev, out at the Soviet ambassador's residence in the suburb of Purkersdorf, told his people just about the same thing: "He's very young . . . not strong enough. Too intelligent and too weak."

The Americans who had sat behind Kennedy were shocked. They had briefed Kennedy about Khrushchev the man, never thinking he might have trouble with Khrushchev the Communist. After all, the President had studied at the London School of Economics, or so he said. But it was obvious now that he knew very little about Marxism or the ideas that drove the man on the other side of the table. He was also having trouble with Khrushchev's violent mood swings. When Kennedy had said that if there were free elections in Poland the Communists might be voted out, Khrushchev had turned on him in fury. "The United States recognizes the government of Poland," Khrushchev said, his face reddening. "Poland is more democratic than the United States. Its elections laws are more honest than those in the United States."

There were three thousand people waiting the next morning, Sunday, June 4, to applaud Kennedy as his car drove up to the Soviet Embassy with Rusk, Bohlen, and Thompson for the second day of the summit. The President smiled and waved, the picture of self-confidence.

At 10:15 A.M. the leaders sat down on a sofa, with their aides nearby around an oblong table.

Kennedy carried the small talk at the beginning of the second day, asking Khrushchev about the place where he was born, and the chairman described his village, called Kursk, just inside Russia on the border of the Ukraine. He said deposits of iron ore had just been found there, perhaps 300 billion tons of ore, compared to 5 billion in all of the United States.

"So, why do you care about Laos?" the President asked with a laugh.

You're the one with the commitment in Laos, Khrushchev responded, you were sending in Marines and rescinded the order. "There was no order," Kennedy snapped. Now it was Khrushchev's turn to laugh. He said he only knew what he read in the newspapers.

After that exchange, Kennedy said: "Look, Mr. Chairman, you aren't going to make a communist out of me and I don't expect to make a capitalist out of you, so let's get down to business."

They shifted to the business of banning the testing of nuclear weapons. Neither country had tested for three years, and Khrushchev told Kennedy that the Soviet Union would not be the first to resume. But, as far as any treaty was concerned, the Soviet Union would not accept U.S. or U.N. inspections on its territory. He had no intention of inviting U.S. espionage and, as far as the United Nations was concerned, it was another American tool, and that was being proved again in the Congo.* He repeated two Soviet positions: A test ban had to be part of a general

---

* In the Republic of the Congo, formerly the Belgian Congo, U.N. troops had played a significant role in the political demise of the new country's first prime minister, Patrice Lumumba, who was supported and supplied by the Soviets. Khrushchev blamed Secretary General Dag Hammarskjöld—which was why he was pounding his shoe in New York in September of that year.

disarmament agreement; and U.N. inspectors and the United Nations itself had to be directed by a "Troika," a three-member directorate named for the traditional three-horse Russian sleigh teams—with one Communist, one Westerner, and a neutral chairman, each with veto power.

That was going nowhere. The Soviet Union had all the advantages, Kennedy said, because the United States conducted most of its affairs in the open.

"What about Allen Dulles?" Khrushchev cracked. "Isn't the CIA secret?"

"I wish it was," Kennedy said, laughing again.

"We're back where we started," the American said when Khrushchev again began talking about general disarmament. The President said a test ban was like the Chinese proverb: "A journey of a thousand miles begins with one small step."

"You seem to know the Chinese very well," said Khrushchev with a smile.

"We may both get to know them better," countered Kennedy.

"I know them well enough now," the Russian said, and Kennedy laughed.

Then Khrushchev began to talk about Berlin. "The bone in my throat," he said, his voice rising. There was a rage in the man, Kennedy thought—just underneath the jokes and the clowning.

The chairman had reason to be angry and frustrated. In East Berlin, communism was bleeding to death. There was a real question whether Marxism could survive along an open border with glittering capitalist prosperity—and that was what it was like between East and West Berlin. Each day a thousand or more East Berliners or other East Germans took trains or buses into West Berlin, or walked across that border with no intention of coming back. Refugees from communism, they were the brightest and best of the East, educated and skilled people. There was a joke being told in Vienna as Khrushchev and Kennedy talked: "Khrushchev died and went to heaven. But St. Peter told him to go to hell. Then, a few days later, a couple of devils, from hell, knocked on the door to heaven. St. Peter demanded to know why they were there and the devils said, "We are the first refugees."

"Sixteen years have passed since World War II," said Khrushchev, according to the American notes, reminding Kennedy that 20 million Soviets died in the war begun by the Germans. "Now two German states exist," he said. What he left unsaid was that the Russians, like many Europeans, never again wanted to face a unified Germany. Too much history, too many wars. United States policy, though, supported a united Germany.

"The USSR will sign a peace treaty with the German Democratic Republic [East Germany]. . . . The USSR would be prepared to join the U.S. in ensuring all the conditions necessary for preserving what the West calls West Berlin's freedom. However, if the US rejects this proposal . . . the USSR will sign a peace treaty unilaterally and all rights of access to Berlin will expire because the state of war will cease to exist."

The gauntlet was thrown. Kennedy responded that he appreciated Khrushchev's frankness. Then he said, more slowly, "Here, we are not talking about Laos. This matter is of greatest concern to the US. We are in Berlin not because of someone's sufferance. We fought our way there, although our casualties may have been not as high as the USSR's. We are in Berlin not by agreement of East Germans but by contractual rights. . . . U.S. national security is involved in this matter because if we were to accept the Soviet proposal US commitments would be regarded as a mere scrap of paper. Western Europe is vital to our national security and we have supported it in two wars. If we were to leave West Berlin, Europe would be abandoned as well. . . . We cannot accept that."

Khrushchev, growing angrier, countered that the Soviet Union could not accept a world where Hitler's generals, the men who fought for *Lebensraum* from Berlin to the Urals, in Russia itself, were now high commanders in NATO. "The USSR will sign a peace treaty and the sovereignty of the GDR will be observed. Any violation of that sovereignty will be regarded by the USSR as an act of open aggression . . . with all the consequences ensuing therefrom." Diplomatic code words for war.

Would this peace treaty block access to Berlin, Kennedy asked. "Yes," said Khrushchev.

That is a unilateral abrogation of the four allies' 1945 agreement, the President said, and the United States could not accept that.

"The West has been saying that I might miscalculate," said Khrushchev. "But ours is a joint account and each of us must see that there is no miscalculation. If the US wants to start a war over Germany let it be so. . . . If there is any madman who wants war, he should be put in a straitjacket. So this is the Soviet position. The USSR will sign a peace treaty at the end of this year."

The President said he wanted Khrushchev to understand one thing: "The signing of a peace treaty is not a belligerent act. . . . However, a peace treaty denying us our contractual rights is a belligerent act. What is a belligerent act is transfer of our rights to East Germany. . . . The US is committed to that area and it is so regarded by all the world. If we accepted Mr. Khrushchev's suggestion the world would lose confidence in the US and would not regard it as a serious country. It is an important strategic matter that the world believe the US is a serious country."

Khrushchev stood up first. The meetings were over. He handed Kennedy two aides-mémoire, seven pages that laid out most of what he had just said. Dean Rusk drew in his breath when he saw that, thinking that if the Soviets made those papers public, it was the signal that they were deadly serious about trying to drive the United States out of Berlin.

The two leaders walked side by side into lunch and a sort of closing ceremony, each one with a half dozen of their ministers and aides. The mood was grim. Small talk was on the order of Khrushchev saying that he had heard Kennedy was under pressure from his military people to resume nuclear testing after the three-year moratorium observed voluntarily by the two countries. Before Kennedy could answer, the Soviet premier said he was certainly under that kind of pressure, but he would not do any testing unless the United States did so first. He also said he wanted to restrain his scientists from planning a moon shot, because it was so expensive. "Why don't we do it together?" Kennedy said. "No," Khrushchev said, he could not talk about things like that until there was disarmament.

Khrushchev, who was the host for the lunch, toasted the American President at length, saying there were obviously real tensions between them but that things would work themselves out by the grace of God or common sense, depending on your religion.

Kennedy joked that Khrushchev had told him that when he was forty-four, Kennedy's age, he was a member of the Moscow Planning Commission, hoping one day to be chairman. So, Kennedy said, he hoped he could make it to the Boston Planning Commission when he was sixty-seven.

"Perhaps," Khrushchev interrupted, "you mean the planning commission of the whole world?"

"No," Kennedy said. "Just Boston, that would be fine."

He then gave Khrushchev a gift, a model of America's most famous warship, the *Constitution*, "Old Ironsides," which was still berthed in Boston, almost two hundred years after firing its last volley. The range of those guns, the President said, was just a half mile. Countries could recover from wars in a matter of months. But with nuclear weapons, they could be destroyed for generations. "We can't let that happen," he said.

Khrushchev understood. He had told his assistants the night before that he liked Kennedy, he thought him intelligent and sensitive. The question was whether to believe that the intelligent and sensitive man who had begun an invasion of Cuba, and then abandoned his troops there, had the will to launch a nuclear attack.

It was time for the formal goodbyes.

"No," Kennedy said to Rusk. "We're not going . . . I'm not going to leave until I know more." He sent the Secretary of State to tell Foreign Minister Gromyko that he wanted to talk to the chairman one last time, alone. For ten minutes.

As the President and the chairman went back upstairs with their translators, Kennedy said to Rusk, "This is the nut-cutter."

"We can destroy each other," Kennedy began, as they sat down.

"Yes, Mr. President, I agree."

Once again, Kennedy said he hoped the Soviet leader would not present him with situations that so deeply involved the national interests of the United States. He emphasized that the critical American interest in Berlin was access rights. The Soviets could sign a treaty or do anything they liked as long as they did not threaten Allied occupation rights in West Berlin.

"Force would be met by force," Khrushchev warned Kennedy, saying the Soviets were preparing for that and he should, too. "If the US wants war that's its problem."

"It is up to the U.S. to decide whether there will be war or peace," said the Russian, according to the American transcript. "The decision to sign a peace treaty is firm and irrevocable and the Soviet Union will sign it in December if the US refuses an interim agreement."

"The President concluded the conversation," noted the transcript, "by observing that it would be a cold winter."

What Kennedy actually said was stronger: "Then, Mr. Chairman, there will be war. It will be a cold winter."

"**H**ow was it?"

"Worst thing in my life. He savaged me," said the President.

The question had been asked by James Reston, the Washington bureau chief of *The New York Times,* who was interviewing Kennedy at the United States Embassy in Vienna. The President walked into the room ten minutes after he left Khrushchev for the last time. The blinds were pulled so that no one could see that Reston was inside while fifteen hundred of his colleagues were outside, waiting for a promised joint statement on the summit. So the room was dark, but Kennedy didn't seem to notice. He slumped on a couch and pulled his hat down over his eyes.

"I think I know why he treated me like this. He thinks because of the Bay of Pigs that I'm inexperienced. Probably thinks I'm stupid. Maybe most important, he thinks that I had no guts."

Reston thought that Kennedy was practically in shock, repeating himself, blurting out things he would never say in other circumstances. The gentleman from the *Times* was shocked himself, thinking this had nothing to do with him, that he just happened to be the first person the President was talking to after a kind of trauma. The reporter noted: "Not the usual bullshit. There is a look a man has when he has to tell the truth."

"So we've got a problem," Kennedy said more coolly after a few minutes, beginning to sound like himself again. "We have to see what we can do that will restore a feeling in Moscow that we will defend our national interest. I'll have to increase the defense budget. And we have to confront them. The only place we can do that is in Vietnam. We have to send more people there."

"If you could think only of yourself, it would be easy to say you'd press the button. And easy to press it, too," the President said two hours later on Air Force One as he flew to London for a meeting with Harold Macmillan. He was sitting on his bed in his undershorts with Kenny O'Donnell and a couple of other aides. His eyes were red and watery, his back hurt. "It's so damned hard. You can't just think about yourself. There are generations involved. It really doesn't matter as far as you and I are concerned. I've had a full life. What really matters is all the children. . . ."

"That son-of-a-bitch. Son-of-a-bitch," O'Donnell muttered. "Give him an inch he wants a mile. The son-of-a-bitch."

As the Americans were leaving Vienna, the joint statement was issued and it was, to quote Reston, one paragraph of the usual bullshit: "President Kennedy and Chairman Khrushchev have concluded two days of useful meetings during which they have reviewed the relationships between the U.S. and the USSR. . . . The President and the Chairman reaffirmed their support of a neutral and independent Laos . . . and in this connection they have recognized the importance of an effective ceasefire. The President and the Chairman have agreed to maintain contact."

The Viennese were already telling a summit joke that was closer to the mark. "Khrushchev says: 'Give me your watch and your wallet.' Kennedy says: 'No.' Khrushchev says: 'Be reasonable. Let's negotiate. Just give me your wallet.' "

Kennedy's visit to London was partly personal, the christening at Westminster Cathedral of the first child of Jacqueline Kennedy's sister, Lee Radziwill, wife of Stanislaus Radziwill, an exiled Polish prince. There was a round of parties after the ceremony, but without the usual gaiety. The men huddled in corners. "It was just a disaster," said Paul Nitze at the home of Frank Wisner, the CIA station chief in London. "Khrushchev was frightening. I'm scared to death about what will happen next."

In the garden of the Radziwills' house, Kennedy stood for a while with the columnist Joseph Alsop, a family friend. "I just want you to know, Joe," he said. "I don't care what happens, I won't give way. I won't give up, and I'll do whatever's necessary. I will never back down, never, never, never."

The official part of the London visit was dinner with the Queen and a report on the summit to Prime Minister Harold Macmillan. Macmillan waited for Kennedy at the doorway of Admiralty House, where a formal meeting had been arranged with a dozen advisers from each country sitting across from each other, with the Prime Minister and the President in the center of each row. Macmillan looked hard at Kennedy—the President seemed depressed, probably in pain. "Mr. President," said the Prime Minister, "you've had a tiring day, don't let's have this. Why not come up to my room and we will have a little chat?" As he wrote later in his diary, "He seemed rather relieved, and he came up at about half past eleven and we sat down till about three in the afternoon. I gave him some sandwiches and whisky, and that was all. He just talked. . . .

"Rather stunned—baffled perhaps would be fairer . . ." Macmillan wrote, "surprised by the almost brutal frankness of the Soviet leader. The Russians are (or affect to be) 'on top of the world.' They are now no longer frightened of aggression. They have at least as powerful nuclear forces as the West. . . . They have a buoyant economy and will soon outmatch Capitalist society in the race for material wealth. It follows they will make no concessions. . . ."

"The President was completely overwhelmed by the ruthlessness and barbarity of the Russian Chairman," the prime minister wrote in a note to Queen Elizabeth. "It reminded me in a way of Lord Halifax or Neville Chamberlain trying to hold a conversation with Herr Hitler. . . . For the first time in his life Kennedy met a man who was impervious to his charm."

Kennedy had even complained to Macmillan as they sat upstairs about the way the press in Vienna had written about his wife. Seeing the prime minister smile at that, Kennedy said: "How would you react if somebody said, 'Lady Dorothy is a drunk'?" Macmillan said, "I would say, 'You should have seen her mother.' "

Kennedy had stared for a moment, and then laughed for the first time since he had arrived.

As Air Force One took off on the night of June 5 for the flight from London to Washington, the President called in his secretary, Evelyn Lincoln, and asked her to file the papers on the desk in front of him. One small slip had fallen to the floor. There were two lines on it, a quote from Abraham Lincoln in Kennedy's handwriting:

> *I know there is a God—and I see a storm coming;*
> *If He has a place for me, I believe I am ready.*

Chapter 15

When Air Force One landed at Andrews Air Force Base on the morning of June 6, President Kennedy stopped on his way through the little terminal and telephoned his friend Charlie Bartlett.

Bartlett's father's business had included importing magnesium from the Soviet Union, and he had told Kennedy for years, "Every man has his Russian"—a friend who could make sense of people and ways of that vast country.

"Charlie, I want you to know something," the President said. "I've got my own Russian now. He's tough. It's very scary."

In the White House, Kennedy asked for some statistics before reporting to the nation on his travels to Europe, first to a private meeting with congressional leaders, and then a national television address scheduled for that evening.

This was his first question: How many Americans would die in an all-out nuclear exchange with the Soviet Union?

The answer came back from the Pentagon: 70 million dead, about half the nation.

How many would die if just one enemy missile got through and hit somewhere near a city? The answer this time was 600,000. "That's the total number of casualties in the Civil War," he said. "And we haven't gotten over that in a hundred years."

"Goddamnit, Ros, use your head . . ." Kennedy snapped an hour later during the meeting with congressional leaders, when Roswell Gilpatric said allied policy was to use nuclear weapons in defense of Berlin. "What we are talking about is seventy million dead Americans."

He lost his temper again in the middle of the meeting, after he had said the country would have to consider a civil defense program to minimize nuclear casualties, and a couple of the Republican leaders had replied that that could be awfully expensive. They were responsible, after all, for controlling government spending.

"Responsible?" Kennedy said. "And what about my responsibility? I'm the one who has to push the button, if it goes that far. I'm convinced it won't go that far, but I can't guarantee it. Do the House and Senate want me to give way in the end?"

"He's shaken," was the conclusion the Senate Majority Leader, Mike Mansfield, carried back to his office after the congressional leadership briefing. The President, Mansfield told his staff, thinks there is a serious chance of war. He said that he and the rest of the leadership had left as shaken as the President.

"There are limits to the number of defeats I can defend in one twelve-month period," Kennedy was telling his own men. "I've had the Bay of Pigs, and pulling out of Laos, and I can't accept a third."

"We can't let Khrushchev get away with this," were the words Fred Dutton, secretary of the Cabinet, used to describe the White House mood that day. "It's more than the Cold War. It's saving Kennedy's presidency."

"I will tell you now that it was a very sober two days," the President said on television that night at seven o'clock, from the Oval Office. "Our views contrasted sharply but at least we knew better at the end where we both stood. . . . We have wholly different views of right and wrong. . . . We have wholly different concepts of where the world is and where it is going.

"Our most somber talks were on the subject of Germany and Berlin. I made it clear to Mr. Khrushchev that the security of Western Europe and therefore our own security are deeply involved in our presence and our access rights to West Berlin . . . and that we are determined to maintain those rights at any risk . . . we and our allies cannot abandon our obligations to the people of West Berlin.

"I am not fearful of the future. We must be patient. We must be determined. We must be courageous. We must accept both risks and burdens, but with the will and the work freedom will prevail."

"Sober" and "somber" were the words being pushed by the men of the White House to describe the summit dialogue to reporters, though all the while emphasizing that the Kennedy-Khrushchev confrontation was a tough-minded draw. "There is no reason to believe that the President was outclassed in nerve, self-confidence or candor by the Soviet Premier," wrote Richard Rovere in his "Summit Diary" in *The New Yorker*, as if in response to James Reston's guarded but pessimistic reporting—not revealing he saw Kennedy—in the *Times*.

The President, unfortunately, knew that Reston had it right. He was in pain and depressed. Neither conditions were helped by CIA reports that day, that the Pathet Lao was again on the move in the highlands of Laos, attacking and taking a hamlet called Padong. In the *Washington Star* that same day, he read a United Press International dispatch from Moscow that began:

"Premier Khrushchev sang, danced and played a drum tonight at a reception given by the Indonesian Embassy on visiting President Sukarno's sixtieth birthday. Fresh from what he obviously considered his diplomatic success in Vienna, Khrushchev romped with Asian princes. ... UPI correspondent Henry Shapiro said Khrushchev looked more relaxed and exuberant than he had seen him in years."

Whatever the Russian leader thought, the American leader was brooding over the unthinkable: He might be the man who had to push the button and destroy the world.

Nobody seemed to understand that. Because no one else was President. He could not stop talking in the days after he returned home. "If Khrushchev wants to rub my nose in the dirt, it's all over," he told James Wechsler, editor of *The New York Post*. He saw a pregnant woman, Marion Ridder, the wife of a newspaperman who had been a friend since Harvard, and said: "I question whether it's really right to bring children into this world now."

Kennedy saw his first fight as convincing people, abroad and at home, that he would not give way. He was incensed by a Marguerite Higgins column in *The New York Herald Tribune* under the headline "The Next to the Last Straw," quoting "high German officials" saying: "Why do we doubt? Not because of anything that President Kennedy has said or done about Germany. ... But elsewhere, in Laos for instance, the president has said something was the last straw, then retreated."

Time magazine, reporting on post-Vienna surveys by its correspondents around the country, said that two major facts emerged: "FIRST FACT: A great majority of Americans are prepared to risk war over Berlin rather than back down to the Reds. ... SECOND FACT: There is a widespread feeling that the Administration has not yet provided ample leadership in guiding the U.S. along the dangerous paths of the cold war."

The *Denver Post* reported that seven out of ten Coloradans favored war over retreat. Walter Lippmann, in an interview on CBS television, was asked whether an open country like the United States could compete with the secretive dictatorships of communism, and he answered: "That's the drama of our age. Many of us think the Kennedy administration has to get going and moving rapidly or we won't be able to do it. . . . He's not sure of himself." *The New York Times* called editorially for "military measures . . . an armed forces alert . . . unmistakable evidence of our determination to draw a line." The State Department's *Daily Opinion Survey* reported to the President that "the general feeling is that the Soviet leader remains unconvinced of our determination to risk aggression."

Kennedy stayed in Washington for only forty-eight hours. On June 8, press secretary Salinger told reporters of the President's back problems, which the White House had been able to keep secret since the middle of May. He said Kennedy was on crutches, as he had been before his operation in 1954, and would be going down to Palm Beach to rest and recuperate. Through three weeks of excruciating pain, hot baths, and medication upon medication, John Kennedy had fooled the world. But he was fooling himself, too. The injections of novocaine for pain and amphetamines for energy were masking the severity of his back problems.

On the trip home from London, Secretary Rusk had told Kennedy his conviction that the seriousness of Soviet intentions to move against the allies in Berlin could be calculated by whether or not Khrushchev decided to go public with the two secret aides-mémoire on Berlin he had given the President in Vienna. If the chairman released the documents affirming his intention to negotiate a separate peace treaty with East Germany then, Rusk said, the United States had to assume the Soviets were ready for confrontation and crisis in Berlin—and there could be war. On June 10, a Saturday, as Kennedy tried to recuperate in Florida, the Soviets released the texts of their aides-mémoire.

"The Soviet government advocates the immediate conclusion of a peace treaty with Germany," they began. "The question of a peace treaty is the question of the national security of the USSR. . . . Occupation rights, of course, would discontinue with the conclusion of a peace treaty, no matter whether it is signed with both German states or only with the German Democratic Republic, inside whose territory West Berlin lies. . . . It is necessary to establish a deadline period not exceeding six months."

So, the United States would prepare for war. The President had all but come to that conclusion already. It was a bad time for him. He was in pain and he was depressed about the trip and now there was the

Soviets' formal public threat. Kennedy told the columnist Joe Alsop, who was in Palm Beach that weekend, that he thought there was a one-in-five chance of a nuclear exchange—beginning with an incident in Berlin or with Chinese troops moving into Laos. In both cases, he thought the United States had little in effective means of military response short of nuclear weapons. "The only plan the United States had for the use of strategic weapons was a massive, total, comprehensive, obliterating attack upon the Soviet Union," said McGeorge Bundy's analysis. "An attack on the Warsaw Pact countries and Red China [with] no provision for separating them out. . . . An attack on everything Red."

That was the plan. The President wanted to change that strategy, but it was still all he had. Before leaving for Paris, he had approved a secret directive to NATO which summarized the situation in Central Europe and the working plan for its defense in the event of Soviet attack:

> There are now 22 NATO ready divisions in the Central Region, which reduce to 20 on an equivalent scale with the 50–55 he [the enemy] could employ against us. Present NATO forces could not stop such an attack by conventional weapons. . . . First priority must be given to preparing for the more likely contingencies, i.e., those short of nuclear or massive non-nuclear attack. [But] it must be clearly understood that tactical and strategic nuclear weapons would be used when it becomes necessary to do so to avoid being driven from the Continent.

The United States would use nuclear weapons to prevent Soviet occupation of Western Europe. One of the reasons for keeping this secret was that the American people believed the United States would never be the first to use nuclear weapons. But that was not true, not in Kennedy's mind, particularly not after the previous week. Kennedy talked to Joe Alsop about his lonely, even helpless sense of tragedy after Vienna. The columnist responded with verses from A.E. Housman, the poet's lines about the attempt of Xerxes to impose the Oriental despotism of Persia on Athens in 480 B.C.:

> *The King with half the East at heel is marched from lands of morning;*
> *Their fighters drink the rivers up, their shafts benight the air.*
> *And he that stands will die for nought, and home there's no returning.*

Kennedy permitted Alsop to write about some of their conversations. "The Most Important Decision in U.S. History—And How the President Is Facing It" was the headline of his article in the *Saturday Review*.

The decision, as Alsop phrased it, was "Whether the United States should risk something close to national suicide in order to avoid national surrender."

That was the way the President saw it. One way to arouse and prepare Americans, he had decided, was to push a civil defense program. First, though, he had to try to convince himself that there really was something individual citizens could do to survive nuclear war. Before Vienna, he had attempted to neutralize demands for civil defense—particularly from Governor Nelson Rockefeller of New York—by saying the administration would be "looking hard" at a national program. Now, though, Kennedy decided to promote civil defense, to adopt the logic of something Rockefeller had told him early in May: "A strong program is needed to stiffen public willingness to support U.S. use of nuclear weapons if necessary."

The President passed the new word in a memo to Bundy: "I think we should ask the Civil Defense people to come in next week with an emergency plan. What could we do in the next six months that would improve the population's chance of surviving should a war break out? What should we ask the citizens to do at this time and what should be required of them in case of attack?"

Kennedy may not have been converted, but he was scared. And he was ready to frighten almost everyone else in the country and much of the world. His alarm resonated as he set out to plan a massive program of fallout shelters in places public and private. Food and water were ordered for storage deep in train stations, and do-it-yourself shelter plans were prepared to tell Americans how to live underground in their own backyards.

"Did you build your shelter yet?" he asked Red Fay.

"No," Fay said, and laughed. "I built a swimming pool."

"You made a mistake," the President said.

On June 13, Kennedy received a 154-page compendium of mistakes, Maxwell Taylor and Robert Kennedy's report of the Bay of Pigs investigation. There was a single copy to prevent leaks, and it could be read only in a locked room with an observer present to be sure no notes were taken.

The document concluded with a dry summary of Kennedy's management: "The Executive branch of the government was not organizationally prepared to cope with this kind of paramilitary operation. . . . There was no single authority short of the President capable of coordinating the actions of the CIA, State, Defense, and USIA. Top-level direction was given through ad hoc meetings of senior officials without consideration of operational plans in writing and with no arrangement for recording conclusions and decisions reached."

Those were Taylor's words. Robert Kennedy's were more pointed. "We will take action against Castro," he remarked when the investigation was completed. "It might be tomorrow, it might be in five days or ten days, or not for months. But it will come."

It was more than a week after Kennedy's television report on summitry in Vienna and the dangers of Berlin, on June 15, that Khrushchev went on Soviet television to alert or alarm his people to the coming crisis. "The conclusion of a peace treaty with Germany cannot be postponed any longer," he said. The status of Berlin had to be changed before the end of the year, or else . . . "Hundreds of millions of people would be killed," he added after the speech.

It was already June 16 in Washington and Kennedy was back in the city. Flat on his back, he had been lifted into Air Force One by an airport cherry picker normally used by mechanics working on the engines. And he was working from his bedroom most of the time. One of the first things he did was call in the old hard-liner Acheson to ask him to prepare a plan to counter the Soviet pressures in Berlin.

On June 22, after a couple of days with a sore throat, the President was hit with a debilitating fever, probably from a viral infection. His temperature reached 105 degrees as doctors and aides gave him massive doses of penicillin and cold sponge baths through the night to bring it down to 101 degrees. That was what the thermometer showed in the morning as he stepped painfully out of the elevator from the second-floor living quarters of the White House, handing his crutches to a Secret Serviceman, and walking slowly into a meeting with the prime minister of Japan, Hayato Ikeda.

Day after day, the President's aides clustered around his bed, as he puffed on a cigar or sorted through stacks of newspapers and "Top Secret" reports. One of his meetings after his temperature returned to near normal was with Judith Campbell, the girl Frank Sinatra had sent him, who was able to minister to his sexual needs without disturbing his atrophying back muscles.

"There is no serious concern about the President's health," said a statement issued by Dr. Travell, and widely printed and reprinted by newspapers and magazines. But there certainly was serious talk among those who actually saw Kennedy upstairs. His aides worried over his mood post-Vienna. One of the most cheerful and voluble of them, Walt Rostow—"Walt sure uses a lot of words, doesn't he?" Kennedy said more than once—tried to cheer up the boss with memos like this one:

In these five months I have often been reminded of 1942. Then, too, many things were sliding against us: the Philippines, Singapore, the Russian Front, the Western Desert, the Battle of the Atlantic. But the tide was turned in a series of wholly defensive victories: Midway, Guadalcanal, Stalingrad, the containment of the U-boats. . . . In Truman's duel with Stalin, too, there were turning points which took the form of defensive victories: the Berlin Airlift and Korea. . . .

As we head into our crucial months of crisis . . . to turn the tide we must win our two defensive battles: Berlin and Viet-Nam. In Europe I believe that if Berlin is held . . . then the Russians will have to think about some different way to deal with East Germany. It is the instability of East Germany which has led them to try to solve the problem of West Berlin at some risk. . . . In Asia, if Viet-Nam can be held, not merely will Thailand, Cambodia, and probably Laos, stay out of Communist hands, but we shall have demonstrated that the Communist technique of guerrilla warfare can be dealt with.

These were the worst of times in the Kennedy White House. Much of the world simply believed that he was not tough enough to stand up to Khrushchev in Berlin. Prime Minister Macmillan, who had been brooding ever since seeing the President after Vienna, wrote in his diary: "I 'feel in my bones' that President Kennedy is going to fail to produce any real leadership. The American press and public are beginning to feel the same. In a few weeks they may turn to us. We must be ready. Otherwise we may drift to disaster over Berlin—a terrible diplomatic defeat or (out of sheer incompetence) a nuclear war."

Dismay over Kennedy was strongest among many of his own military men, particularly the commander of the Strategic Air Command (SAC), Air Force General Curtis LeMay, a World War II hero, a tough talker with a big cigar in his mouth, who commanded planes capable of carrying more than ten thousand nuclear bombs. Kennedy despised the man. During the campaign, only a year ago, Kennedy had cut short a tour of SAC headquarters outside Omaha, Nebraska, when he realized that LeMay had ordered his men to give him the kind of sanitized walkthrough usually reserved for local city councilmen and garden clubs. In the White House, Kennedy had walked out on LeMay again, more than once. Walking out on generals was a Kennedy specialty. "The uniforms" seemed incapable of listening, or understanding, and they could not stop once they swung into canned briefings, not even to take questions from their Commander-in-Chief.

"I don't want that man near me again," Kennedy said after one of his walk-outs on LeMay. McNamara and his men learned not to bring the general's name up. "He has a kind of fit if you mention LeMay," Roswell Gilpatric warned one of his assistants as they went to a White House meeting. But on June 19, Kennedy announced that he was promoting LeMay to the Joint Chiefs of Staff as commander of the Air

Force. There were two reasons. He could not afford to have the man out of uniform, traveling the country and giving speeches about how weak the President was—which was surely what LeMay would do if he were retired. And he believed that whatever he thought of LeMay's company, the general was the kind of man you wanted around if there was a real war. Kennedy quoted another Air Force general who told him: "LeMay's like Babe Ruth. Personally he's a bum, but he's got talent and the people love him."

A few days later, Kennedy telephoned Maxwell Taylor and asked the retired general to come back to the White House in a new position, military adviser to the President. Part of the job would be to keep the Joint Chiefs away from Kennedy.

By the end of June, Kennedy seemed to have regained his confidence and he was getting ready for the struggles ahead in Berlin and in Saigon. On June 29, he approved the text of a letter to President Diem in Saigon stating that the United States was ready to back him in increasing the size of the Army of the Republic of South Vietnam again, this time from 170,000 to 200,000 men. The same day he summoned several members of the National Security Council and influential Democratic senators, including Foreign Relations Chairman William Fulbright and Majority Leader Mike Mansfield, to a secret White House meeting, at which they were allowed to read the thirty-three-page Acheson recommendations on Berlin policy, which began with the former Secretary of State's summary: "Khrushchev [is] now going further than the USSR had ventured since 1948, because he believes that the U.S.A. [will] not use nuclear weapons to stop him, and could not do so otherwise."

The President's assurances to Diem were in response to a letter the South Vietnamese leader had sent him on June 14 requesting funds and training for 270,000 men, his formal reply to the letter Kennedy had sent with Vice President Johnson in late May. Diem estimated the cost of training and paying the new troops at $175 million over two and a half years. "We now know that as a small nation we cannot hope to meet all of our defense needs alone and from our own resources. We are prepared to make the sacrifices in blood and manpower to save our country and I know that we can count on the material support from your great country which will be so essential to achieving final victory."

On Berlin, Acheson's tone was apocalyptic. The United States, he said, could only impress Khrushchev by convincing him that the price of taking West Berlin was nuclear war. "He cannot be persuaded by eloquence or logic, or cajoled by friendliness. No negotiation can accomplish more than to cover with face-saving devices submission to Soviet demands."

Acheson also made it quite clear that he thought the current Berlin crisis was essentially the result of Kennedy's weakness and blundering:

West Berlin has been protected, in the last analysis, by the fear that interference with the city, or with access to it, would result in war between the United States and the Soviet Union. . . . The capability of U.S. nuclear power to devastate the Soviet Union has not declined over the past two years. The decline in the effectiveness of the deterrent, therefore, must lie in a change in Soviet appraisal of U.S. willingness to go to nuclear war. . . .

It has become an issue of resolution between the U.S.A. and the U.S.S.R., the outcome of which will go far to determine the confidence of Europe—indeed, of the world—in the United States. It is not too much to say that the whole position of the United States is in the balance. . . .

Acheson told Kennedy he must make an early and secret decision to prepare for war. "War," he emphasized, "in this case means nuclear war."

Chapter 16

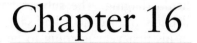

In the weeks following the Vienna meeting, more than twenty thousand people fled from East Germany to West Germany. They were mostly men and most were young, half of them under twenty-five. Many were professionals: engineers, teachers, physicians, technicians. Almost all passed through the ninety or so streets, roads, and railroad lines crossing the twenty-eight-mile border between Soviet-occupied East Berlin and West Berlin.

The number of refugees from East to West always increased in times of crisis and rumor. The exodus had been greatest during and after two Berlin crises: the eleven-month Berlin Airlift beginning in the summer of 1948, and in June 1953, when a workers' revolt in the eastern sector was put down by Soviet troops and tanks.*

---

* On June 24, 1948, the Soviet Union, after withdrawing from the joint Allied commissions governing Germany and Berlin, severed all land and water routes between Berlin and the U.S.-, British-, and French-occupied sectors in the western part of the country. The Western Allies supplied the city by air for eleven months. There were a total of 277,728 flights, which brought in 2,343,301 tons of food and other supplies. On May 12, 1949, the Berlin Blockade ended in defeat for the Soviets, but both the country and its capital city were effectively divided.

More than 330,000 East Germans fled in 1953 alone. The fifteen-year total was 4 million or more. From 1954 to the summer of 1961, reception centers in West Berlin (where most but not all of the refugees registered to obtain West German citizenship and relocation benefits) recorded the names of 3,371 medical doctors—one of every five in East Germany—16,724 teachers and 17,082 engineers and technicians. Most were young men alone or young families. The per capita income of the 2 million West Berliners was more than double the East German average—and the Soviet-occupied sector regularly suffered shortages of most everything except potatoes. The food shortages were even worse after the forced collectivization of East German farms in the spring of 1960. But the most common reason for flight listed in the reception center paperwork was not food; it was "Education." Young parents said they did not want their children taught in Communist schools.

Sooner or later the Communists were going to have to try to stop the hemorrhaging. The subject had come up during the Kennedy-Nixon debates and Kennedy had said, "The next President of the United States, in his first year is going to be confronted with a very serious question on our defense of Berlin. Our commitment to Berlin. There's going to be a test of our nerve and our will. The United States must meet its commitment on Berlin." He had said too that he believed that if the Soviets gained control of West Berlin, all of Western Europe would eventually become neutral. "They're fighting for New York and Paris when they struggle over Berlin," he said late in 1959. "We would fight."

Now he was that next President, preparing himself and the American people for war over Berlin. He had to assume that it would quickly become nuclear war. Back from Vienna, Kennedy read a "Top Secret" analysis of the course of confrontation over Berlin by a thirty-seven-year-old Harvard professor named Henry Kissinger, a consultant to the White House on Germany, with this summary note by McGeorge Bundy: "The current strategic war plan is dangerously rigid and, if it continues without amendment, may leave you very little choice as to how you face the moment of thermonuclear truth. . . . In essence, the current plan calls for shooting off everything we have in one shot, and it is so constructed as to make any more flexible course very difficult."

This was the most dangerous time in the most dangerous place. Khrushchev seemed euphoric after Vienna, repeating one of his own earthier analyses of the situation: "Berlin is the testicles of the West. Every time I want to make the West scream, I squeeze on Berlin." But, in fact, the problem was his. If neither side could accept defeat in Berlin, just maintaining the political and military status quo meant victory for the United States and its allies. Khrushchev was being pressured too by hard-liners in his government who thought that for all his bluster he was too weak to confront the West. If Kennedy worried about being trapped in a corner, Khrushchev already was.

It was the Russian who needed a way out in Berlin. But neither Khrushchev nor the East German Communist leader, Walter Ulbricht, could figure out a way to stop the continuing public renunciation of communism. East Germany was supposed to be a Communist show-place, the most prosperous and creative of the countries and areas the Red Army occupied after 1945. East Berlin, with a population of 1.3 million, for all its shortages was the richest of communism's satellite capitals. Some of that prosperity came from at least fifty thousand *Grenzgänger,* "border-crossers," who lived in the cheap housing of the East and worked for the fat wages of the West. Despite the daily defections, and with a loss of about $15 billion in plant and equipment in the late 1940s when factories were moved bolt-by-bolt from Eastern Germany to the Soviet Union as war reparations, East Germany was, in June 1961, the sixth largest economy in the world, even if the waiting list to buy small washing machines and refrigerators was as long as two years. The only countries producing more were the United States, the Soviet Union itself, Great Britain, France, and West Germany, which had a population of 53 million people.

Of the 17 million people left in East Germany, only 45 percent were male, and there was a ratio of only four workers for each three children and old-age pensioners. But Germans on both sides of the city, and on both sides of the three-mile-wide "Death Strip" of barbed wire and guntowers along the 98-mile-long semicircular western boundary between West Berlin and East Germany, had seen worse in the 1940s. Europeans high and low tried to stop the world in July and August, with some success, and thousands upon thousands of East Germans almost certainly planned to make their move as soon as Europe's vacationing ended on the last day of August.

There did seem to be time. Khrushchev, after all, was not talking about forcing the peace treaty issue until the end of the year. And Berliners, still a cocky and sardonic bunch, were used to crisis. The United States had not even answered the Soviet aides-mémoire by the middle of July, and the only one who seemed excited about that was President Kennedy, who had not adjusted to the ways of summer in his own State Department. There had still been no direct answer to the cable that Ambassador Llewellyn Thompson had sent from Moscow to the Secretary of State and the President back in March, saying that he expected the Soviets would sooner or later close off East German sector boundaries to stop the refugee flow. The principal question Thompson had raised before Vienna was still unanswered after the summit: "What action [do we] propose to take if East Germans close Sector boundary . . . without disturbing Allied access?"

That cable was classified "Top Secret (Eyes Only)," to be seen only by the President and the Secretary of State. But there was nothing secret about Khrushchev's problem in East Germany. The President had also seen a cover story in *The Reporter* magazine entitled "The Disappearing Satellite." The author, George Bailey, recounted the statistics of the East German exodus and concluded:

There are some indications that the Soviet Union and its East German minions have finally drawn the ultimate conclusion: the only way to stop refugees is to seal off both East Berlin and the Soviet Zone by total physical security measures. . . . Khrushchev will ring down the Iron Curtain in front of East Berlin—with searchlights and machine gun towers, barbed wire, and police dog patrols. Technically, this is feasible. . . . The West's main problem is to provide some way out for the Soviets with as little loss of face and as many guarantees of security as possible.

"Is this true?" the President said after reading the article. "Check this out."

It was obviously true, but so far no one in the White House or State Department seemed to have worked out what it meant: a simple political way out of military confrontation in Berlin. When Kennedy had come back from Europe in June, one of his first questions was whether West Berlin could survive another siege if the Soviets cut off allied road and river access to the city as they had in the summer of 1948. On the day he returned from London, he had asked the Joint Chiefs of Staff for a report on the levels of military and civilian emergency supplies in West Berlin.

General Lyman Lemnitzer, chairman of the Joint Chiefs of Staff, answered: "As a result of the stockpiling program undertaken after the 1948 blockade, West Berlin has on hand about $200,000,000 worth of food, fuel, and raw materials. It has sufficient basic foods to provide a year's supply at an estimated rate of consumption of 2,950 calories per person per day."

The U.S. occupation forces, the Chiefs said, had enough ammunition for eighteen days of fighting without resupply, food for 180 days, medical supplies for 210 days, and gasoline for 300 days. West Berliners themselves, 2.3 million people, had food, coal, and fuel for at least a year and medical supplies for six months. That included 3,224 tons of canned pickles, 82 tons of baby food, and 143 tons of feed for zoo animals.

Even as the President prepared for war, he was being criticized by much of the press for timidity. "Look at this shit," Kennedy said, when he read an article in *Time*, which week after week repeated questions about his strategic manhood:

There is a danger that the president has misread the U.S. mind—and that the American people are in fact more than ready and more than willing to take whatever action is necessary in the international struggle against Communism. . . . In that fiery spirit and in the determination of the U.S. to throw back the challenges of Communism at whatever cost, lies the great opportunity for President Kennedy—but it is an opportunity that he must seize upon unhesitatingly and with boldness.

Newsweek made him even madder. That magazine reported on Berlin defense proposals by the Joint Chiefs of Staff that had not yet reached the White House:

(1.) Evacuation of some 250,000 U.S. dependents in exposed positions in West Germany and France. (2.) Reinforcement of the five American divisions and their supporting units in West Germany (about 250,000 troops) shipping one or more additional divisions from the U.S.; Declaration of limited emergency; call-up of four National Guard divisions; step-up of draft calls. (3.) Commandeering of commercial airlines to move U.S. paratroopers and other soldiers to Germany. (4.) Some demonstration of U.S. intent to employ nuclear weapons; this might be accomplished by resumption of atomic weapons tests or by moving atomic weapons now in the NATO area stockpile to advanced "ready" positions.

"This shit has got to stop. We've got to stop this," the President said, flinging a copy of *Newsweek* across his bedroom. He called up J. Edgar Hoover, ordering him to send FBI agents to the Pentagon to find out who was talking to *Newsweek*.

On June 29, the day Dean Acheson had come in with his Berlin recommendations, Kennedy came downstairs to his office with his usual run of morning memos for Evelyn Lincoln, beginning with one for Fred Dutton: "Speak to me about the Negro unemployment. I think we should do something about it." For McGeorge Bundy, he had another complaint about the State Department: "I want a report . . . I asked Secretary Rusk about this, on whose idea it was for me to send the letters to the MidEast Arab leaders. The reaction has been so sour I would like to know whose idea it was, what they hoped to accomplish and what they think we have accomplished."

Then with Acheson's "Top Secret" report as the touchstone, the President began scheduling meetings on Berlin. "He's imprisoned by Berlin, that's all he thinks about," said Secretary of the Interior Stewart Udall, who, along with most other Cabinet members, was finding it impossible to reach the President. Kennedy was locked up much of the time with Acheson, Rusk, McNamara, his brother, the Joint Chiefs, and men from the CIA.

From the beginning, the Berlin meetings were dominated by Acheson. The former Secretary of State was a speaker of great power and relentless certainty, and it was his report that was the White House's working document. There were no other papers on the table at first, and Acheson began by totally dismissing any political or diplomatic alternatives to his hard military line. "Until this conflict of wills is resolved, an attempt to solve the Berlin issue by negotiation is worse than a waste of time and energy," he had written. "It is dangerous. This is so because what can be accomplished by negotiation depends on the state of mind of Khrushchev and his colleagues. At present, Khrushchev has demonstrated that he believes his will will prevail because the United States and its allies will not do what is necessary to stop him. He cannot be persuaded by eloquence or logic, or cajoled by friendliness."

Acheson's hard-line arguments divided not only Kennedy's men but also the congressional leaders the President called in that same day.

The Joint Chiefs of Staff and the CIA, through Allen Dulles, generally backed Acheson and the idea that a build-up of massive allied forces would intimidate the Soviets into backing down. Maxwell Taylor and Walt Rostow in the White House backed Acheson, and so did U. Alexis Johnson and Foy Kohler, the State Department's most respected "Europeanists," and Paul Nitze in Defense. Acheson also had foreign allies, most importantly Charles de Gaulle in Paris and Konrad Adenauer in Bonn. The other side had an impressive roster, too, but they had no paper to match the Acheson Report, and they had trouble beating something with nothing. Rusk was openly skeptical, the openness unusual for him. So were Averell Harriman and Chip Bohlen. Undersecretary of State Chester Bowles was against military-driven options in general, as was his protégé, Abram Chayes, the department's counsel.

Chayes ended up with the assignment of considering negotiating alternatives to Acheson's recommendations. He took on the task with enthusiasm, particularly after Kennedy said to him privately, "If the issue is talking to the East Germans or having a war, we are obviously going to talk with the East Germans." That did not impress Acheson, who turned to the young counsel and said: "Abe, you'll see. You try, but you will find that it just won't write."

Ted Sorensen and Arthur Schlesinger both opposed Acheson, but they had nothing on paper. So did Senators William Fulbright, Mike Mansfield, and Hubert Humphrey—all three called into the White House that day. They had a foreign ally in Harold Macmillan, who agreed essentially that Khrushchev was not challenging the United States as much as he was trying to preserve Soviet control of the occupied countries of Eastern Europe.

The President said very little during the meetings of June 29. And, as at the Bay of Pigs meetings, what Kennedy did say tended to convince each of the other men there that he was the one speaking the President's unspoken thoughts.

"What do I do if Khrushchev calls for another summit meeting on Berlin this summer?" Kennedy asked at one point.

"Suggest preliminary meetings at a lower level," Acheson answered. "There are plenty of elderly unemployed people like me who can be sent to interminable meetings."

As the days of early July went by with meeting after meeting on Berlin, Schlesinger had the sinking feeling that he was reliving the days before the invasion of the Bay of Pigs. Acheson's Berlin recommendations, like the CIA's Cuban plans, were taking on a life of their own. In the absence of alternative ideas, he envisioned World War III, beginning with U.S. Army tanks and trucks rolling down the Autobahn to break into Berlin through Soviet barriers. His apprehension grew when Georgi Kornienko, the counselor of the Soviet Embassy, asked to see him on July 5.

It was impossible for Schlesinger or anyone else to figure out what was really going on with Kornienko, the number-two man in the Soviet Embassy, and Georgi Bolshakov, the Red Army intelligence officer posing as a magazine editor. But they had to assume that their words were messages, usually confusing ones, from Khrushchev, so that the Soviet leader could sound out Kennedy without committing himself to anything. On July 5, Kornienko complained that President Kennedy was wrong to ignore Soviet guarantees in Berlin.

"He doesn't trust you," Schlesinger told the Russian.

"Why don't you propose your own guarantees?" Kornienko said.

What did that mean? Schlesinger didn't know, but the conversation did persuade him to bring a memo over to Kennedy just before lunch the next day, stating, "Are we not running the risk of directing most of our planning to the least likely eventuality—i.e., an immediate blockade of West Berlin?" He said the Berlin issue was being defined in the crudest and most dangerous way: "Are you chicken or not? When someone proposes something that seems tough, hard, put-up-or-shut-up, it is difficult to oppose it without seeming soft, idealistic, mushy. Yet, as Chip Bohlen has so often said, nothing would clarify more the discussion of policy toward the Soviet Union than the elimination of the words 'hard' and 'soft' from the language. People who had doubts about Cuba suppressed those doubts lest they seem 'soft.' It is obviously important that such fears not constrain free discussion of Berlin."

Kennedy listened, then told him, "Then tell me what you think we should be doing."

He was leaving for Hyannis Port at five o'clock that Friday, July 8, to spend a long weekend discussing Berlin with Rusk, McNamara, and Maxwell Taylor, who had commanded U.S. forces in West Berlin from 1949 to 1951.

Schlesinger rushed back to his office in the East Wing, calling for Abe

Chayes and Henry Kissinger, who were both already at lunch. It was three o'clock before the two of them made it over to Schlesinger's office. The three men from Harvard could see the President's helicopter on the lawn, ready to take off at five o'clock. Chayes and Kissinger paced, dictating and thinking out loud, as the resident historian, who seemed able to write as fast as the President was supposed to be able to read, banged away at his typewriter with a cigar jutting into the air.

He made the deadline, running back to the West Wing with a five-page memo that McGeorge Bundy pushed into the bulging old briefcase filled with Kennedy's weekend reading as the helicopter warmed up. For better or worse, the memo—framed as questions the President might want to ask McNamara and Rusk—was the paper Acheson had told Chayes could not be written. Discussing the Acheson Report, Schlesinger wrote:

> The paper indicates no relationship between the proposed military action and larger military objectives . . . it does not state any political objective other than the present access procedures for which we are prepared to incinerate the world. It is essential to elaborate the cause for which we are prepared to go to nuclear war. Where do we want to come out if we win the test of wills? German unification, for example: what is our real intention with regard to this traditional objective?

The adrenaline was flowing in Schlesinger's East Wing office as the Marine One rose above the White House lawns. "Well, now what can we do next?" he asked.

"Get the Secretary of State a set of answers to the questions we asked in the memo," said Chayes.

The President spent Saturday, July 8, at Hyannis Port with Rusk, McNamara, and Taylor. They cruised in circles on Joseph Kennedy's boat, the *Marlin,* with McNamara and Taylor occasionally diving off for quick swims as the sun broke through the gray Cape Cod sky in mid-afternoon. Rusk was in a business suit, looking slightly uncomfortable. He looked even more uncomfortable when, during one of McNamara and Taylor's swims, Kennedy demanded to know why the State Department still had no official answer five weeks after the Vienna summit to the Soviet aides-mémoire. Rusk discussed the problems of consulting with allies and complained that Ralph Dungan of Bundy's staff had put a first draft of the State Department response in his office safe and then gone on vacation for two weeks. No one knew the combination.

"I want that damn thing in ten days," the President said.

It was not a happy day. Alone with his Defense Secretary, Kennedy wanted to know why McNamara had assured him only two months ago that the United States had adequate ground forces to meet predictable crises. It was obvious now that such forces were not ready or available in Germany. Kennedy had more questions than his men had answers, even to surprisingly basic questions: "If we mobilize a million men, what would we do with them—how many would be logistic support units, etc.? . . . Would we send the million to Europe, how long would it take to get them over, how many ships, if by sea, how many would we plan to send by plane? . . . How many days would it take to get all of them there? . . . Where would they be positioned in Europe when they get there?"

"I want all those answers in ten days," he told McNamara, echoing his order to Rusk. Time was much on his mind. He told McNamara that if he had to approve the use of nuclear weapons in a Berlin crisis, he wanted a month to think about it, not an hour—which was how much time he thought he would have if the Red Army moved in Germany.

The President's mood was not helped when one of his military aides, Army General Chester Clifton, met the *Marlin* as it returned to the Kennedy compound in the late afternoon. The general handed the President a cable reporting that Khrushchev had just given a speech to the new graduates of the Soviet military academies, announcing that he was canceling the scheduled demobilization of 1.2 million of the 3 million Soviet men in uniform. The Soviet Union, he said, would increase defense spending by one third to match increases announced and proposed by Kennedy. The speech had been televised nationally and the Soviet leader was wearing the uniform of a lieutenant general of the Red Army, the rank he had attained as a political officer in World War II.

In Washington, late on the afternoon of July 13, the President called together an expanded National Security Council—twenty-five men, including Acheson, Taylor, and Kissinger. Rusk brought in a cable he had just received from Allan Lightner, the United States' ranking diplomat in West Berlin:

Official Senat refugee figures for first four days, July 9–12, current week show 4,979 refugee arrivals in Berlin for daily average of 1,245 . . . Sudden phenomenal increase in refugee flow has many causes, including deterioration in economic conditions, shortages of food . . . [and] intensified USSR/GDR propaganda for "Free City of West Berlin." All these have contributed to incipient "Gate Closing Panic" (*Torschlusspanik*) in East German populace whose fears have grown that control of travel to and within Berlin about to be greatly intensified.

McNamara was ready with some of the data the President had ordered him to produce within ten days. He proposed what amounted to a two-thirds increase in the size of the armed forces by the end of the year. He wanted 450,000 new uniformed personnel and 40,000 new civilian defense personnel at a cost of $4.3 billion—raising the number of combat-ready Army and Marine divisions from the current fourteen to twenty-two by January 1, 1962. He said the Joint Chiefs believed those actions, combined with a Declaration of National Emergency—legally necessary to call up reserves—would provide them with what they needed, which, he said, was "The capability to initiate military measures to reopen access to Berlin. . . . Sufficient forces to wage non-nuclear warfare on a scale which would indicate our determination and provide some additional time to begin negotiation before resorting to nuclear warfare. . . . Increased readiness for the use of nuclear weapons should escalation to this level become necessary."

Acheson and Lyndon Johnson backed McNamara, as Kennedy listened. But Rusk responded that it might be better to go to Congress for a resolution authorizing the call-up of the reserves—"National Emergency" sounded too close to war.

"I wouldn't go to Congress," said the Vice President, who rarely spoke at such meetings. "They expect the President to take the lead."

The President then adjourned the meeting, going into his office with eight men: Johnson, Rusk, McNamara, Dillon, Taylor, Allen Dulles, General Lyman Lemnitzer, and Edward R. Murrow, the director of the United States Information Agency (USIA). Each had been shown a "Top Secret—Eyes Only" memo, written by Bundy, outlining "Military Choices in Berlin," from a Declaration of National Emergency to reinforcement of troops to use of nuclear weapons. As that session began to break up, Rusk asked Kennedy what, at the end of the day, mattered to the United States in Berlin.

"Two things," the President answered. "Our presence in Berlin and our access to Berlin."

East Berlin, or access to it, was not worth a war, Kennedy said, repeating what he had already told Abe Chayes. After those two meetings, the President talked with Sorensen and Schlesinger, and asked them to approach Berlin as a political problem rather than a military confrontation. Each came back saying the same thing: The political problem was finding a way to let Khrushchev back off from his ultimatums without humiliation. On July 17, Sorensen sent Kennedy a memo, warning: "We should not engage Khrushchev's prestige to a point where he felt he could not back down from a showdown." Schlesinger sent his the next day, saying about the same thing: "Should not explicit attention be given to the problem of providing an escape hatch for Khrushchev? We must not shove him against a closed door. . . . Our plans should therefore include a sketch as to how we think Khrushchev is going to get out of the hole he has dug for himself."

Kennedy agreed with that. The trick was to signal accommodation, the dialogue of politicians, without appearing irresolute in the dialogue between military commanders-in-chief. Sorensen, the speechwriter, was telling Kennedy to make a speech. A speech would force the State Department and Defense Department to resolve their differences and arguments under deadline pressure. Once the President spoke publicly, that was it. There was not much point in trying to persuade the President *after* he committed himself on national television. Speeches are policy; the drafting of speeches are the making of policy. By July 18, the President had informed Sorensen that he would speak to the nation on Tuesday night, July 25.

So the deadline was set to announce a Berlin policy, in one week. "This is probably the most important NSC meeting that we have had," Bundy said in a memo to the President on the morning of July 19. He said the President had to decide whether to be specific on a couple of critical points in the speech: "The first is whether we should make clear that neither the peace treaty nor the substitution of East Germans for Russians along the Autobahn is a fighting matter. . . . The second is whether we should extend serious feelers to the Soviets with respect to the elements of an eventual settlement of the crisis."

Shuttling between the Justice Department and the White House that day, Robert Kennedy thought there was a one-in-five chance of war. He knew his brother thought it was close, too. The problem was still to convince Khrushchev that the United States would fight for West Berlin. Georgi Bolshakov was talking to Robert Kennedy almost every day, telling him that Khrushchev was listening to his ambassador in Washington, Mikhail Menshikov. "Smiling Mike," as the Americans called Menshikov, was telling Moscow that President Kennedy did not have the guts for war.

"He does, I know," Robert Kennedy said to Bolshakov. "Tell Khrushchev that."

The President held his fourteenth news conference late that morning. He began by reading a long summary of the official U.S. answer to the aides-mémoire given him by Khrushchev in Vienna. "The real intent of the June 4th aides-mémoire," he said, "is that East Berlin, a part of a city under four power status, would be formally absorbed into the so-called German Democratic Republic (East Germany) while West Berlin, even though called a 'free city' by the Soviets, would lose the protection presently provided by the Western Powers and become subject to the will of a totalitarian regime."

There were a dozen questions on Berlin and four on the future of Undersecretary of State Bowles, who rumor had it was being forced out as State's number-two man. "Mr. Bowles has my complete confidence," said Kennedy. In fact, he had decided to move the Undersecretary out because he could not get along with Robert Kennedy, but Bowles had stalled the maneuver by leaking stories to *The New York Times* that prompted Mrs. Roosevelt and other liberals to come to his defense. One of the Berlin questions quoted Ambassador Menshikov as telling Khrushchev in secret cables back to Moscow: "When the chips are down, the American people won't fight for Berlin." Kennedy answered: "This is a very basic issue, the question of West Berlin. . . . We intend to honor our commitments."

The NSC meeting was later that day. Kennedy told McNamara and the Joint Chiefs that he was, more or less, splitting their requests for more men and money down the middle. He said he was not going to declare a national emergency, seeing that as his last public step not his first. But he would triple draft calls and ask for a congressional resolution giving him stand-by authority to call up Reserves—providing six new combat-ready divisions and supporting air groups ready for European deployment. He would ask the Congress for another $3.2 billion in new military appropriations, rather than the $4.3 billion recommended by the Joint Chiefs. He would emphasize a steady non-nuclear build-up in Europe: "Escalation."

McNamara and his men were not happy. The Chiefs wanted the Secretary of Defense to argue for what they officially called "Plan A," the toughest of the military scenarios, which gave them authorization to use tactical nuclear weapons. The President skipped to "Plan C," the most moderate alternative. McNamara immediately switched sides, becoming the chief advocate for the Kennedy alternative. He took the lead in defending Kennedy's decisions against tense arguments by Acheson. At a later meeting the same day of one of the smaller "Working Groups" created to implement Berlin policy, Acheson reacted to mention of Kennedy's name by saying: "Gentlemen, you might as well face it. This nation is without leadership."

The speech he was to give on July 25 was Kennedy's weapon, and he hoped to use it to mobilize the American people—and to persuade the Soviet leader that the United States was ready for war. He wanted to raise Moscow's calculation of risk in Berlin. The draft calls and public statements about a civil defense program would be the strategic equivalent of sending the Seventh Fleet steaming toward Thailand to try to win a cease-fire in Laos. So would be the seemingly matter-of-fact talk of using nuclear weapons to stop the Soviets in Germany.

Kennedy had been impressed by a long memo prepared for him by Thomas C. Schelling, one of the most respected of the defense intellectuals who evolved as an enormously influential class in the Cold War. Schelling's memo to the President had argued that the real purpose of nuclear weapons was to be used as chips in a calculated game of threat and risk. Played well in that game, the purpose of nuclear weapons was to prevent their use. "The purpose of nuclears is to convince the Soviets that the risk of general war is great enough to outweigh their original tactical objectives, but not so great as to make it prudent to initiate it preemptively. . . . It is a war of nuclear bargaining. Destroying the target is incidental to the message the detonation conveys to the Soviet leadership."

The President decided to go to Hyannis Port the weekend before the speech. He left Washington on Friday, July 21. He still had not decided about one final signal of U.S. resolve. "The Berlin surcharge" had been Robert Kennedy's idea: a one-year, 1 percent increase in all personal and corporate income taxes to raise an estimated $2.5 billion to pay for the defense of West Berlin and whatever happened next.

The money wasn't the issue with Robert Kennedy, or with his brother, either. Most of the politicians in the administration liked the idea as a political signal. The economists, though, were appalled. Walter Heller and Paul Samuelson thought they had been winning their patient campaign to move John Kennedy from Economics 101 to becoming the first American leader to accept and implement the economics introduced a generation ago by John Maynard Keynes. But Kennedy had not signed on yet. He still believed in balanced budgets, or he said he did, because most other Americans did. Now he was supposed to talk about raising taxes for political reasons at precisely the time Keynesian economics dictated reducing them to get the country moving again. Heller and Samuelson hit the telephones like Paul Revere, lining up colleagues to warn the President that the country was just beginning an economic recovery cycle and that raising taxes—no matter why or how—would reduce corporate investment and private spending after a time of hoarding to prepare for war or rationing. It would drive the country back into recession. They wanted to press their arguments in terms Kennedy understood: a Berlin surcharge would increase both inflation and unemployment.

"If consumers and firms respond to the crisis with a surge of scare buying and inventory accumulation, inflation could be touched off," Heller told the President. "This is what happened in 1950, upon the outbreak of the Korean conflict. Consumers reduced their saving from 5.9 percent of disposable income in the second quarter of 1950 to 2.8 percent in the third. The possibility of similar behavior in 1961 must be faced."

The President had invited one of the most liberal of the economists he knew, Seymour Harris, to hitch a ride up to Cape Cod that Friday afternoon. Heller, Samuelson, and Harris worked up a small plot, and as Air Force One touched down at Otis Air Force Base, Harris got up the courage to say: "Mr. President, any rise of taxes at the beginning of a recovery would be disastrous."

On Sunday, Kennedy telephoned Samuelson and said, "Can you come over here to Hyannis tomorrow morning? Fly to Washington with me, talk about this surtax idea?"

"It will simply take the money out of the GNP," Samuelson said on the plane. "It will delay full employment."

"Okay," Kennedy said. "I want you to come with me to a meeting at the White House."

The Berlin tax died. Kennedy called in his brother, Heller and Dillon, Secretary of Health, Education and Welfare Abraham Ribicoff, Rusk and Bundy, and told them to forget about any kind of tax talk until the end of the year. "You were wrong," he said to Robert Kennedy after the others left. "Admit it."

Ted Sorensen went back to work on the speech. The thinking on short-range policy, as the final draft was being written, was laid out by Rusk in a secret cable to the U.S. Ambassador to West Germany, Walter Dowling, with copies to the ambassadors in London, Paris, and Moscow. It emphasized again that it was the Soviets who had the problem in Berlin:

> We believe Soviets watching situation even more closely than we, since they are sitting on top volcano. . . . Department has impression either of two contingencies could arise. First, and more likely, if refugee flood continues, East German regime might take measures designed to control it. They could do this either by tightening controls over travel from Soviet Zone to East Berlin or by severely restricting travel from East to West Berlin. Second, situation in zone could deteriorate sufficiently to lead to serious disorders.

On the day before the speech, the President cabled Macmillan, laying out the situation as he saw it: "Our central problem at this juncture is to protect our mutual vital interests without war if possible and to put ourselves in the best possible position if war should be forced upon us.

... This is a time of clear and imminent danger. I do not believe that we can convince the Soviets of our willingness to face the greater risks which may be ahead unless we are ready to bear the burdens of a period of growing peril."

On the day he was to give the speech, July 25, Kennedy called in Hugh Sidey, the White House correspondent from *Time*. "Let's go swim," he said.

"I don't have a bathing suit," Sidey said.

"That's okay," Kennedy said. "In this pool you don't need one. It's a little hot, but I need it for my back."

The narrow pool, fifteen feet wide and fifty feet long, had been built in 1933 by Franklin D. Roosevelt, another President who needed to swim regularly in hot water, in his case to exercise muscles crippled by polio. The water was heated to 80 degrees. There was a mural of sailboats in the harbor of St. Croix in the Virgin Islands covering one long wall—a gift from the President's father to make the place a little brighter.

The President slowly lowered himself down a ladder into the water. He swam and walked back and forth in the pool for almost an hour, pushing away a blue plastic boat that belonged to his daughter Caroline, talking to Sidey mostly about Berlin and the speech he would give that night. The most discouraging thing about what had happened at Vienna, and since, was that he and Khrushchev had not come close to finding philosophical common ground to discuss the effects of a nuclear exchange.

"That son of a bitch won't pay any attention to words," Kennedy said. "He has to see you move."

Then, on crutches, he hobbled through the White House to the elevator up to the living quarters. He came back down the same way just before 10:00 P.M., ready to read his speech on American moves in Berlin and around the world, military moves to impress the son of a bitch in the Kremlin.

Chapter 17

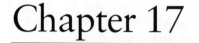

"Which door will he come through?" "I'm getting nothing. Hurry." "Dammit, who turned off that light?"

The Oval Office was filled with the voices and confusion and clutter of cables and machines of television. It was practically a military medium itself, the new correspondents and technicians of television made up of armored brigades compared with the familiar little patrols of pencil-and-paper reporters.

The pencil press pool selected by Pierre Salinger to report back to all White House correspondents was relegated to a corner. Tom Wicker of *The New York Times* and Cecil Sutherland of the *Washington Star* were joined by a gentleman from Tass, the Soviet news agency. President Kennedy walked through them a minute or so before 10:00 P.M., sweating immediately from the heat of klieg lights and vacuum tubes. The air conditioning had to be turned down because the big boom microphones picked up the humming of the machinery. The office had the nervous feel of the stage of a Broadway theater before the curtain went up.

"Good evening," Kennedy began.

"Seven weeks ago tonight I returned from Europe to report on my meeting with Premier Khrushchev. . . .

"In Berlin, as you recall, he intends to bring to an end, through a stroke of the pen, first our legal rights to be in West Berlin—and secondly our ability to make good on our commitment to the two million free people of that city. That we cannot permit.

"West Berlin . . . has become—as never before—the great testing place of Western courage and will. . . . We are clear about what must be done—and we intend to do it.

"I want to talk frankly with you tonight about the first steps that we shall take. These actions will require sacrifice on the part of many of our citizens. We intend to have a wider choice than humiliation or all-out nuclear action . . . if that should require more men, or more taxes, or more controls, or other new powers, I shall not hesitate to ask for them."

The President laid out the final moves and numbers that had been decided on during the days and nights of White House meetings: $3.25 billion in new defense expenditures; Army personnel increased by 125,000 new men to a 1 million total; 29,000 new Navy personnel; 63,000 new Air Force personnel; draft calls tripled; new authorization to call up reservists and extend duty tours. He added a call for $207 million for civil defense, meaning that in six months in office he had asked for $6 billion in new defense spending, increasing the defense budget to $47.5 billion. He called the nation to arms:

"The immediate threat to free men is in West Berlin . . . an attack upon that city will be regarded as an attack upon us all. We cannot separate its safety from our own. . . . But that isolated outpost is not an isolated problem. The threat is worldwide. . . . There is also a challenge in Southeast Asia, where the borders are less guarded, the enemy harder to find, and the dangers of communism less apparent to those who have so little. . . .

"I hear it said that West Berlin is militarily untenable. And so was Bastogne. And so, in fact, was Stalingrad. Any dangerous spot is tenable if men—brave men—will make it so.

"We will at all times be ready to talk, if talk will help. But we must also be ready to resist with force, if force is used upon us. Either alone would fail. Together, they can serve the cause of freedom and peace.

"And let me add that I am well aware of the fact that many American families will bear the burden of these requests. Studies or careers will be interrupted; husbands and sons will be called away; incomes in some cases will be reduced. But these are burdens which must be borne if freedom is to be defended—Americans have willingly borne them before —and they will not flinch from the task now.

"The steps I have indicated tonight are aimed at avoiding that war. To sum it all up: we seek peace—but we shall not surrender. . . .

"In the thermonuclear age, any misjudgment on either side about the intentions of the other could rain more devastation in several hours than has been wrought in all the wars of human history.

"In these days and weeks I ask for your help. . . . All of us, I know, love our country, and we shall all do our best to serve it."

Kennedy was sweating and tense when the television lights were turned off and the Oval Office's air conditioning turned back on after thirty-one minutes. But his words had done the job. More than a thousand telegrams reached the White House by the next morning, running about 20 to 1 in support of the President.

The mail to the White House ran better than 100 to 1 in support. A national Gallup Poll indicated that 85 percent of Americans were willing to risk war to keep U.S. troops in West Berlin. More than 67 percent favored sending U.S. troops to fight their way into Berlin if the city was closed off by the Soviets or East Germans. The Congress immediately and overwhelmingly passed the new legislation needed to approve the President's round of increased defense expenditures, bringing the new total to the peak expenditures of the Korean War. The Senate went further than Kennedy, voting 81 to 0 for $750 million for new manned bomber programs, money the President had not asked for. *The New York Herald Tribune*'s Don Ross, reporting from a town of 4,200 in upstate New York called Hoosick Falls, wrote an "Open Letter to Khrushchev" on the paper's front page, saying: "They are determined, even the little old ladies rocking on the porches, that you shan't have Berlin. 'Mr. Big Mouth' one little old lady said when she heard your name. If you have any notion, sir, as you are said to have, that Americans are too fat and comfortable to risk a fight over Berlin, you should come here and talk to these Americans and get your thinking straightened out about Americans in general."

"It's your greatest triumph," Sorensen told the President. From his home in Independence, Missouri, Harry S Truman sent a telegram that night: "Great speech. I don't know when I've been happier. . . . Keep it up." The next morning, a *New York Times* editorial said: "In a speech at once solemn, determined, and conciliatory, President Kennedy last night reasserted American leadership of the free world. . . . We are confident that the American people and free men everywhere will support him."

But, if most Americans rallied round the President, there were some who read his messages differently. In Berlin, staying up to hear Kennedy at 4:00 A.M., Major General Albert Watson, commander of U.S. troops in the city, was shaken by all the references to *West* Berlin rather than just Berlin. He thought that was a signal to the Soviets and the East Germans, a deliberate signal, that they could seal off their sectors of the city without American interference.

And East Berliners began crossing the border to the West in the largest numbers since Soviet troops had violently put down street demonstrations against the East German government in 1953. More than three thousand men, women, and children fled East Berlin in the twenty-four hours after Kennedy spoke. On the eastern side of the boundary that cut across the city, East German policemen and soldiers began taking young men off trains and buses crossing into West Berlin. *Torschlusspanik:* East Germany was headed toward chaos. The new refugees from the East to West Berlin included a justice of the Supreme Court and the medical director of the city's largest hospital. The refugees reported that Communist Party hacks, minor officials in the provinces, were threatening that the streets into West Berlin would soon be blocked.

The most important man in the audience of hundreds of millions, Nikita Khrushchev, heard more than one message, too. On the night Kennedy spoke, the Soviet leader was at his dacha on the Black Sea with an important American guest, John J. McCloy, the former U.S. High Commissioner in Berlin, a Republican serving now as Kennedy's chief disarmament adviser. McCloy was in Moscow to plan for a joint Soviet-U.S. disarmament conference. The chairman had invited him down for a couple of days by the seashore.

Kennedy received McCloy's report, an "Eyes Only" cable from the U.S. Embassy in Moscow, on the morning of Saturday, July 29:

> Khrushchev was cordial on Wednesday but firm in reiterating his Vienna position. Really mad on Thursday after digesting President's speech. Used rough war-like language. . . . Will sign peace treaty no matter what; occupation rights thereupon cease, access cut off. . . . If you attempt force way through we will oppose by force; war bound to be thermonuclear and though you and we may survive all your European allies will be completely destroyed. . . . All this followed by offers to negotiate peace terms, guarantee access and settle German problem.

Press reaction from around the world, as reported to the President by the CIA in the forty-eight hours after the speech, included: "Noncommunist reaction . . . is generally favorable, with West European commentators stressing both the firmness of the American position and the expressed desire for negotiations. Soviet bloc comment stresses that the President has chosen the alleged threat to West Berlin as an excuse for an American military build-up." Soviet commentators were repeating the analysis of *The New York Times* that the U.S. military build-up was not designed so much to defend Berlin as to give the West the ability to fight any kind of war anywhere in the world. Radio Moscow, broadcast abroad but not in the Soviet Union itself, said: "The United States is openly preparing for war. . . . If a Third World War breaks out, no ocean will protect America. It is very dangerous to play with fire in the age of hydrogen bombs and ballistic rockets."

"What this means," the CIA quoted a Tass commentary, "is active opposition to national liberation movements in Africa, Asia and Latin America. Only this can explain the words of the President about the need for creating a sea and airlift capability to move forces quickly and in large numbers to any part of the world."

In the United States, thousands of Americans reacted first to Kennedy's lines about civil defense. "I hope to let every citizen know what steps he can take without delay to protect his family in case of attack," he had said near the end of his speech. Ordinary Americans began digging holes behind their houses, personal shelters from the deadly radioactive fallout after a nuclear attack. Others sold them the shovels and lead panels and canned food and water they all thought could save them and their families. Guns sold well, too. In newspapers and magazines, and in churches, civil defense was the subject of national moral debate: Was it right or wrong to arm yourself and your family in order to protect your shelter against neighbors who were too foolish or too lazy to build their own?

As frightening as the President's words were to many people at home and around the world, the contradictions were deliberate—the hard and soft images that were transmitted in background briefings for the influential Washington commentators. "Actually," wrote James Reston in *The New York Times* the morning after the speech, "there has been far more private discussion here of negotiation with the Russians than either the statements of our officials or the headlines of the press would suggest. The determination of the Kennedy Administration not to be bullied into dishonorable concessions had to be established first."

Three important Democratic senators were among the Washingtonians discussing negotiations. Majority Leader Mike Mansfield, Foreign Relations Chairman J. William Fulbright, and Hubert Humphrey all raised the question of whether refugees from East Germany were worth nuclear war. Fulbright created the most excitement, saying on "Issues and Answers" on ABC television, Sunday July 30, that the Soviets and the East Germans could solve their own problems at any time they chose. "I don't understand why the East Germans don't close their border," the senator said. "The truth of the matter is that the Russians have the power to close it in any case . . . without violating any treaty."

That same day, the Sunday edition of *The New York Times*, considered another voice of the U.S. government by Khrushchev, reported with authority if without named sources: "The ceding of control of access routes to the East Germans would not lead to a military showdown so long as there were no interference with Allied military traffic. . . ."

On Monday, July 31, McCloy, called back to Washington by Kennedy, went over his Khrushchev conversations with the President, emphasizing the number of times the Soviet leader brought up the flow of refugees out of East Germany. Khrushchev's message, as McCloy delivered it, was that unless the exodus was stopped it could lead to war. The Khrushchev scenario amounted to an extraordinary plea for Kennedy's understanding of the domestic politics of communism. It began with a revolt in the East German Republic, probably triggered by food shortages. That would be followed by West German military intervention to aid anti-Communist demonstrators, then a Soviet move to block West German troops, and confrontation between the superpowers. Khrushchev's point—McCloy reported to Kennedy—was that stopping the refugee exodus was as important to the United States as it was to the Soviet Union.

Four days later, NATO foreign ministers, including Secretary Rusk, met in Paris. By coincidence, the premiers of the countries of the Warsaw Pact, the Communist mirror image of NATO, were meeting in Moscow. The U.S. position on Berlin leaked, of course, with the Paris edition of *The New York Herald Tribune* reporting, accurately, what it called Kennedy's "three essentials": no change in allied occupation of West Berlin; free access to the city from West Germany; and the freedom of the people of West Berlin.

The furious Berlin debate after Kennedy's speech crystallized the real concerns of both sides. The Soviets and East Germans were looking for a way to stop the refugee flow into West Berlin. The United States and its allies wanted no change in their legal access to West Berlin and then into East Berlin.

Khrushchev's official response was broadcast on Soviet television on August 7. He repeated that the Soviet Union was determined to sign a peace treaty with East Germany—giving the East German government legal control over its own boundaries. "The agreements between the USSR and the Western Powers on the question of access to West Berlin during the occupation period will become null and void." That was the one thing Kennedy said the United States could not tolerate. But then Khrushchev, twice, mirrored Kennedy's "soft" line: "I should like once more to repeat that in concluding a peace treaty with the GDR [East Germany] we do not intend to infringe upon any lawful interests of the Western Powers. Barring access to West Berlin or a blockade of West Berlin are entirely out of the question."

"Nothing new" was the official White House response. But the next day's *New York Times* quite clearly printed a message from Washington: "If Mr. Khrushchev is prepared to offer concrete guarantees that no effort will be made by the East Germans to interfere with the free flow of traffic into Berlin, officials said, this would remove the immediate threat of a military clash."

Then, on August 9, the U.S. Ambassador to West Germany, Walter Dowling, and the U.S. minister in West Berlin, Allan Lightner, briefed U.S. chiefs of mission in the rest of Europe on the results of the Paris meetings, saying, according to Lightner's notes: "The other side might stop the German refugees from entering East Berlin at the zonal border by erecting some drastic controls there, but there was also the alternative of putting the border control right through the middle of the city. . . ."

That same day, Khrushchev went back to direct threats. This time he wanted to frighten Europeans, trying to crack or at least shake the Western coalition. "If Adenauer thinks he can achieve reunification of the German nation by war and we are attacked, there will be no German nation left after that, all Germany will be reduced to dust," he said at a Moscow reception for the second Soviet cosmonaut, Gherman Titov. It had been another triumph for Soviet science—three days earlier Titov had completed seventeen orbits of the earth in twenty-five hours. But Khrushchev himself had to solve a common Soviet technological problem after his speech. A Soviet ballpoint pen he was handed to autograph invitations did not work. "Here, mine writes," he said. "It's American."

On August 10, the premier extended his threats to all of Europe: "The laws of war are cruel. Hundreds of millions of people will die. . . . Defending our security, we will have to strike at the NATO military bases wherever they are situated, even if they are in the orange groves. . . . Then not only the orange groves of Italy but also the people who created them and who have exalted Italy's culture and arts, people in whose good feelings we believe, may perish. . . . We know there are military bases in Greece directed against the Soviet Union. We are threatened with war even by such countries as Greece, Italy, Norway, Denmark, Belgium and Holland, not to mention France, Britain and West Germany. . . . If the imperialist states unleash a war, they will force us, in self-defense, to deal crushing blows. . . . In a future thermonuclear war, if it is touched off, there will be no difference between the front and the rear."

On that same day, at a White House press conference, one reporter asked, "Mr. President, Senator Fulbright suggested that the border might be closed. Could you give us your assessment of the danger and could you tell us whether this Government has any policy regarding the encouragement or discouragement of East German refugees moving West?"

"The United States Government does not attempt to encourage or discourage the movement of refugees and I know of no plans to do so," Kennedy answered. He had ignored the first part of the question about closed borders.

But the kind of signal Kennedy seemed to be waiting for came after the news conference. As he was getting ready to leave Washington for a weekend in Hyannis Port, the Soviets announced that the new military commander in Berlin would be Marshal Ivan Koniev, "the Tank," as he was called, one of the great Soviet heroes of World War II, the conqueror of Prague and Dresden. He was an old man, called out of retirement. His sudden appearance at a meeting of the military commanders of the four occupying powers made it look as if the Soviets were preparing to fight. But Koniev's words made it clear Moscow had received Washington's signals.

"We are hearing about substantial military transport activity in your command," said a Western general at a reception that evening in Potsdam.

"Gentlemen, you can rest easy," Koniev replied. "Whatever may occur in the foreseeable future, your rights will remain untouched and nothing will be directed against West Berlin."

That was exactly what the Warsaw Pact had been discussing in secret during several days of meetings that had begun in Moscow on August 3. After listening to the pleas from East German leader Walter Ulbricht, Khrushchev had secretly agreed to a three-year-old East German plan called "Operation Chinese Wall" to put up barriers along the twenty-seven-mile line separating East Berlin from West Berlin. The leaders had approved a secret resolution stating: "The governments of the Warsaw Pact member states call on the German Democratic Republic to establish . . . effective control around the whole territory of West Berlin."

But, Khrushchev said, the barrier could only be barbed wire at first, to see how the allies would react. "That much," Khrushchev told Ulbricht, "and not a millimeter more." It meant there would be no East German or Soviet actions to try to take over West Berlin, or even to disrupt life on the western side of the barriers.

One morning that same week, after a swim, the President walked with Walt Rostow along the colonnade that connects the Oval Office and the living quarters of the White House. As usual, Rostow was talking, but Kennedy was not listening. He was talking more or less to himself.

"This is unbearable for Khrushchev," Kennedy said. "East Germany is hemorrhaging to death. The entire East bloc is in danger. He has to do something to stop this. Perhaps a wall. And there's not a damn thing we can do about it."

Chapter 18

At St. Francis Xavier Church in Hyannis Port the priest cut short the ten o'clock mass on Sunday, August 13. It was just too hot inside the church. The President and Mrs. Kennedy were back in the family compound before eleven, changing into lighter clothes for a short trip on the *Marlin*. A little after noon, they set out for Great Island for lunch with friends.

The *Marlin* was out only fifteen minutes when a Secret Service agent on board took a radio call from "Watchman"—the code name of Brigadier General Chester Clifton, Kennedy's Army aide. The general had been swimming near the President's house in Hyannis Port when a Signal Corps major from the temporary White House communications office, two miles away at the Yachtsman Hotel, had come running down the beach and walked right into the surf in full uniform. Clifton, back on land, ripped open a brown envelope and read a yellow telex from the State Department's Operations Center in Washington. It was from Rusk:

East German regime took extensive security precautions morning August 13 when implementing decision prevent travel East Germans West Berlin. Between 4:00 and 5:00 A.M., VOPOs [East German *Volkspolizei*, paramilitary state police] at sector crossing points were heavily reinforced. Barbed wire and other barriers were laid. . . . Kampfgruppen units en-

tered almost all buildings on streets adjacent to East/West sector lines. . . .
Many Soviet-licensed cars making observation tours.

The troop movements and the laying of the wire along the twenty-seven-mile sector border dividing the city had begun at 2:30 A.M. Berlin time, according to Allan Lightner in Berlin. That was 9:30 P.M. Saturday night in Washington and Hyannis Port. It had taken the East Germans three and a half hours to complete their work. But it had taken more than twelve hours to get the word to Kennedy.

"How come we didn't know anything about this?" the President asked Clifton when the *Marlin* docked.

He was angry, but the general could not tell whether it was about the barrier itself, or the lack of details about what was actually happening in Berlin. In fact, Dean Rusk had deliberately held off telling the President anything at first because he did not have answers for the barrage of questions he knew would come from Hyannis Port. State and Defense Department planning and intelligence were based on the presumption that any walls or barriers would be an attempt to blockade West Berlin, but the Communists had blockaded East Berlin—as Kennedy had been more or less inviting them to do for weeks with repeated American statements about "access rights." Khrushchev and East German President Walter Ulbricht had responded in kind over those weeks, as more and more refugees fled west. The Soviet chairman had repeatedly emphasized at the Warsaw Pact summit and later that whatever the Soviets and East Germans did there would be no interference with existing allied occupation rights.

Kennedy took a golf cart to his house above the beach and called Rusk at home. He asked first whether Soviet troops were near the dividing line. He also wanted to know whether the border guards were attempting to block access into East Berlin. No, Rusk answered, there were no Soviets in sight; the operation was obviously designed to block access from East Berlin to West Berlin. The trains—the elevated U-Bahn and the S-Bahn subway—were still running through the city, but East German passengers were being removed from the cars at the last stations inside the eastern sector. East Germans trying to cross into West Berlin in automobiles or by foot were being turned back forcibly at the eighty streets and other crossing points along the sector boundaries. There was no interference at all with official allied access.

"Okay," said the President, who knew Rusk had been planning to go to the Washington Senators–New York Yankees game at Griffith Stadium. "Go to your ball game. I'm going sailing."

Before catching up with his wife, Kennedy approved a deliberately casual State Department communiqué: "Statement Regarding Travel Restrictions in Berlin." Rusk signed the paper, which was handed out to the press in Washington. "Available information," it read, "indicates that measures taken thus far are aimed at residents of East Berlin and East Germany and not at the Allied position in West Berlin or access thereto. . . . These violations of existing agreements will be the subject of vigorous protest through appropriate channels."

That was it from Hyannis and Washington that Sunday. The VOPOs and their barbed wire and jackhammers, breaking up concrete to put in fenceposts, stayed on their own side of the boundary. The Warsaw Pact issued a statement emphasizing: "These measures will not affect the valid conditions for traffic and control on the connection routes between West Berlin and West Germany."

A traffic problem. The President had no intention of rushing back to Washington, quite the opposite. He was being photographed cruising on Nantucket Sound as if he hadn't a care in the world, the simplest way to signal that the United States was not going to war over the paperwork at border crossings.

Kennedy returned to Washington on schedule the next morning at ten-thirty, letting McGeorge Bundy sit in for him at the regular morning intelligence briefing by Robert Amory of the CIA. The Monday editions of *The New York Times*—only a few thousand final Sunday editions reported the border closing—recounted Sunday's events in a dozen stories led by a four-column headline on the top of page one: "SOVIET TROOPS ENCIRCLE BERLIN TO BACK UP SEALING OF BORDER; U.S. IS DRAFTING VIGOROUS PROTEST."

Bundy had a "Secret" written summary of those same events ready for Kennedy when he reached the White House. It summarized the discussions about the advisability of allied negotiations with the Soviet Union on the long-range status of Berlin, then shifted to what Bundy called "the border closing episode." The national security adviser said he could see no point in reprisals, and ended, "Incidentally, I find agreement in both Joe Alsop and George Kennan to these three conclusions: (1) this is something they have always had the power to do; (2) it is something they were bound to do sooner or later, unless they could control the exits from West Berlin to the West; (3) since it was bound to happen, it is as well to have it happen early, as their doing and their responsibility."

The President's first memo was a short, calm note to McNamara: "With this weekend's occurrences in Berlin there will be more and more pressure for us to adopt a harder military posture . . . I would appreciate it if you would plan to discuss this matter with me this week after you have made a judgment on it."

At Pierre Salinger's press briefing at 4:40 P.M. that Monday, August 14, he began with an announcement that the President had signed HR845, a bill reducing from sixty-five to fifty the age at which Congressional Medal of Honor winners could begin collecting their veterans' pensions. Only after thirty-four other questions did a reporter bring up Berlin, asking if there had been any personal messages between Kennedy and Khrushchev concerning the border closing. "I do not want to be quoted on it," Salinger said. "But no, the answer is no."

"This is the end of the Berlin crisis," Kennedy was saying then, relaxing with Kenny O'Donnell. "The other side panicked—not us. We're not going to do anything now because there is no alternative except war. It's all over, they're not going to overrun Berlin."

Right. But as in Cuba four months earlier, when he had been persuaded that there would be an anti-Castro uprising, the President this time misjudged the reaction of West Berliners. He had never considered the reaction of the people who lived there. Berliners, in every way, lived on the edge. His briefing memos had stressed the law, not the pain. When the mayor of West Berlin, Willy Brandt, told a huge crowd gathered at his City Hall that the allied commanders in Berlin were sending a letter of protest to the Soviet commander on the other side of the barriers, the crowd booed and jeered him.

Bundy handled most of the press briefings that Monday, private sessions "on background," in the jargon of the trade. He met with Murray Marder of the *Washington Post* whose front-page story on Tuesday, August 15, was headlined: "REDS TIGHTEN SEAL-OFF IN BERLIN; U.S. OFFICIALS MINIMIZE DANGER OF WAR OVER COMMUNIST CLAMP-DOWN."

On the front page of *The New York Times* the same day, without citing Bundy as the source, Max Frankel transmitted the White House line:

> Highly qualified Administration sources summarized the day's findings as follows:
> . . . Only extreme counter-measures by the West could undo the Communists' action. These would probably lead to war and are not justified so long as the West is assured continued access to West Berlin.
> . . . On balance, it is probably a good thing that East Germany will not be entirely depopulated of citizens who oppose Communist rule. The continued flights of refugees would have made East Germany even less stable and dangerous . . . Thus, while Washington cannot endorse or approve of the erection of final barricades across the center of Germany and

Europe, it recognizes the situation as a mere extension of what it has been willing to accept throughout the last decade.

Allen Dulles came to the White House to report to the President that same day on reactions of the citizens of West Berlin. His notes record part of that discussion:

"Sudden fear . . . sudden drop in morale of the West Berliners as they saw the tanks and barbed wire across the exit points and along the sector boundary . . . resentment against the Western occupying Allies, particularly the United States, when no immediate action was taken. . . ."

The President heard the same from Ambassador Dowling in Bonn: "Crisis of confidence in Berlin. Viewed objectively, West German and West Berlin reaction to sealing of Berlin Sector border is highly emotional and disproportionate to the gravity of the situation. It exists, however, and must be reckoned with. . . . My suggestion would be a personal message from President to people of Berlin in which he might say to them that they are much in his thoughts, that he will take all appropriate and peaceful means to restore integrity of Berlin as a whole city."

There was suddenly a new class of Berlin refugees: hundreds of *West* Berliners were leaving each day, fearful that the Americans were going to abandon them between the Iron Curtain and the new barricades through Berlin. Edward R. Murrow, the director of the United States Information Agency, was in West Berlin when the border was closed. After more than forty-eight hours without U.S. action, he cabled the White House: "There is a real danger that Berliners will conclude they should take themselves, their bank accounts and moveable assets to some other place. What is in danger of being destroyed here is that perishable quantity called hope."

On Tuesday night, August 15, Murrow's old network, CBS, showed Americans the first film of the East Germans stringing barbed wire. CBS correspondent Daniel Schorr and producer Av Westin had been at a café near the border between West Berlin and East Berlin when the VOPOs began stringing their barbed wire in the early hours of Sunday morning. They had rushed their film in orange network bags to Schipol Airport, and it was on the air in the United States less than seventy-two hours later.

But by then, the barbed wire was mostly gone, replaced by a three-foot-high concrete block wall—for the first time, the term was "the Wall." In Berlin, anger was drifting toward depression. On Wednesday in front of City Hall, Brandt told a mass rally of 300,000 Berliners that he had sent a personal letter to President Kennedy demanding action instead of words. "KENNEDY: YOU CAN'T STOP TANKS WITH WORDS," one poster waved back at Brandt.

"There has been a serious attack on the life of West Germany. The illegal sovereignty of the East German government has been acknowledged by acceptance," Brandt telexed the White House. "The failure to act will cause a crisis of confidence in the Western powers . . . an increasingly menacing military display in the East. . . . Instead of flight to West Berlin, we might then experience beginning of flight from Berlin. . . . There will be further action that will turn West Berlin into a ghetto."

"Look at this! Who does he think he is?" Kennedy responded angrily. He saw it as cheap campaign talk at his expense—Brandt was the Social Democrat candidate for chancellor against Adenauer, a Christian Democrat, in West German parliamentary elections scheduled for September 17.

"You're wrong. It's not a campaign trick," said Marguerite Higgins, who came in at lunchtime on Friday. She was there not as a reporter but as a self-appointed and well-connected advocate for action in Berlin. "The Firebug," Bundy called her, because he thought she would burn down a town for the sheer excitement—and a good story! But the President thought more of her, and he showed her the letter from Brandt. "He's right," she said. "The suspicion is growing in Berlin that you are going to sell out the West Berliners."

"Well then, I have good news for you," the President said. "I'm sending General Clay to Berlin . . . and the Vice President with him."

Higgins knew that already. She had been at dinner with Lucius Clay when Kennedy called him the night before. The general was a hero to West Berliners, the commander of U.S. troops in Europe during the Berlin Airlift in 1948. The other two men at the table were Vice President Johnson and Speaker of the House Sam Rayburn.

Johnson did not want to make the trip, as he had not wanted to go to Vietnam. "Why me?" he asked, when the President told him what he wanted him to do. "There'll be a lot of shooting and I'll be in the center of it." Rayburn was bucking up his protégé's courage, warning Johnson not to say anything like that again to the President.

Late that afternoon the President called in the Vice President and General Clay. He responded immediately to Clay's suggestion that he order a motorized Army Battle Group down the Autobahn, 110 miles through East Germany, from Helmstedt, West Germany, to West Berlin —to show West Berliners American resolve, and the Soviets that access to the city was still the American baseline. If things went according to plan, Johnson and Clay would be there to greet the first U.S. troops.

The action could look like the liberation of Paris in 1944. By nine o'clock that night, Johnson and Clay were on an Air Force jet—and fifteen hundred soldiers, the First Battle Group of the 18th Infantry Regiment, were getting ready to roll to Berlin.

The Vice President and the retired general were an odd couple leading an odd crew. Johnson was accompanied by a pair of flashy secretaries no one believed were there for typing. Real typists were in the back of the plane with State Department and White House men, writing out the encouraging words that Johnson would deliver to Berliners. Clay, a conservative Republican and the chairman of Continental Can Company, was chatting about the old days with Chip Bohlen of the State Department. They both avoided talking about the fact that Bohlen in 1948 had recommended ceding all of Berlin to the Soviets, while Clay was insisting that the Soviet blockade of the city could be defeated by an around-the-clock airlift of food and essential supplies to keep 2 million people going.

The appearance of Johnson and Clay that Saturday, August 19, six days after the barbed wire was laid, was a triumph. All of West Berlin's 2.2 million people, it seemed, were in the streets. Thousands chanted: "Der Clay, der Clay, der Clay ist hier!" Johnson's speeches, written by Walt Rostow and edited personally by Kennedy, were cheered even before the words were translated into German. "To the survival and to the creative future of this city we Americans have pledged, in effect, what our ancestors pledged in forming the United States, 'our lives, our fortunes, and our sacred honor.' "

The next morning Johnson offered not words but his body, driving and walking the streets of West Berlin, mobbed and cheered everywhere, handing out bags of ballpoint pens with his name inscribed on them. Repeatedly, the man who had been reluctant to go almost leaped into the crowds. His guards were terrified, but Johnson was in his element.

When his ballpoint pens ran out, Johnson began reaching into bags of U.S. Senate Gallery passes, with a facsimile of his signature as president of that body, flipping them to cheering Berliners. He bumped Bohlen from his bedroom at Ambassador Dowling's house and installed one of his secretaries. He delivered a message written by President Kennedy to Mayor Brandt: "Make it clear to him that in these next months it will be very important to avoid hasty criticism of each other." Johnson made it very clear, then he dispatched an apologetic Willy Brandt on one errand after another, saying: "Wasn't it you who were saying two days ago in front of City Hall that what you wanted was action, not words? Well, goddamit, that's the way I feel about it, too."

The first action Johnson wanted was for someone to get him a set of china by the old Berlin company that had served Frederick the Great, Staatliche Porzellanwerke. Brandt said the works were closed. Johnson said he wanted action, make them open up. "Where did you get those nifty shoes?" he asked Brandt later that day. "I want a pair just like them." The mayor started to protest again that it was Sunday, that shops were closed in Germany. "Weren't you the one," Johnson began, "who was in front of City Hall saying . . ."

The china and two pairs of the shoes were sent to the LBJ Ranch in Johnson City, Texas.

One hundred and ten miles to the west, the real action of the day, the test of Western military access to Berlin, began at 6:30 A.M. in Helmstedt. Trucks of the First Battle Group, 18th Infantry, United States Army, crossed the border and were stopped moments later at the Soviet checkpoint at Marienborn by a nervous Red Army captain named Beleav.

Five thousand miles away, President Kennedy was practically listening in on the tense dialogue between U.S. and Soviet officers. In the White House, Kennedy's military aide, General Clifton, was on one end of a radio-telephone system patched together by the Signal Corps. On the other end was the leader of the convoy, Colonel Grover S. Johns, Jr. The link went from Johns to regional Army headquarters in West Germany and then to Clifton, who was listening through headphones from late Saturday night until Sunday afternoon in Washington. Each fifteen minutes for fourteen hours, Clifton called the President with a summary of action.

"The new Berlin Desk Officer," they were calling the President, with a touch of mockery, in the State Department. He had personally approved Colonel Johns for the probe to Berlin after reviewing his service record and reading the citations for the three Silver Stars he was awarded for bravery in World War II. "Talking to Kennedy right now is like talking to a statue," said his Cabinet secretary, Fred Dutton. But the President's word to his own men was that if there was going to be a war, he would be the one to start it rather than some trigger-happy sergeant on the Autobahn. It said something about Kennedy as Commander-in-Chief that Colonel Johns's orders were to do whatever he had to do to get to Berlin, but the battle group's ammunition was in sealed boxes on the trucks.

The reports to the President were recorded this way by the Joint Chiefs of Staff:

Advise the Soviets that the convoy of approximately 350 vehicles and 1600 personnel would arrive at the Marienborn checkpoint at 6:30 a.m.

and that it would be divided into six serials. Shortly before the arrival of the first serial at Marienborn a Soviet staff vehicle with the Soviet checkpoint staff commander at Marienborn showed up at the checkpoint. The Soviet officers stated that they were prepared to clear the convoy, although they appeared to take a serious view of the matter.

Captain Beleav, claiming that he could not count the men in the trucks, required all personnel to fall out and line up in front of the vehicles. He systematically wrote down the serial number and type of each vehicle and the number of personnel in each one . . . added up the number on an ancient abacus. The first serial was then allowed to proceed at 7:45 a.m. The second serial proceeded through the checkpoint at 10 a.m. . . .

It was also observed that the VOPOs were out in force on the Autobahn . . . posted at all bridges, crossings, parking lots and were running up and down in official vehicles on the other side. . . . The VOPOs did not interfere in any way with the U.S. convoy. . . .

At the Babelsberg checkpoint the Soviets acted with relative speed in clearing the first and second serials, the first going through in a little over an hour, completed at 12:38 p.m. and the second in half an hour, completed at 1:45 p.m. The Soviets then held up the third serial, claiming that the convoy had two men and one vehicle more than indicated. . . . It was explained to the Soviets that the two men had been picked up by the third serial due to a breakdown. The Soviets used this as a pretext for detaining the convoy. . . . A message from USCOB Berlin [stated] that if the convoy were not released within fifteen minutes, the heaviest vehicle would be ordered to go through the barrier and proceed to Berlin without clearance. . . .

The Soviet major became nervous and released the third serial. Following this the fourth serial cleared the Soviet checkpoint at 7:13 p.m. . . . Fifth serial. A Soviet captain Pertsov climbed up on the tailgate of one of the vehicles in order to inspect the contents. The American MP on duty ordered him down immediately. The captain then threatened to turn the convoy back to a ramp where he could inspect the vehicles. Such an action would have created considerable confusion. The Soviet major in charge was told that the U.S. Provost Marshal would not permit Soviet officers on the vehicles and they would also not turn the convoy around. . . . The fifth was finally cleared at 7:49 p.m. These actions would suggest that the Soviets were under orders to delay the entry of American troops into Berlin as long as possible, probably in order to prevent their participation in the parade and reception by the population of the city. The sixth was cleared at 8:10 p.m.

The next message was from Allan Lightner, the U.S. minister in Berlin: "First unit of American Battle Group ordered into Berlin was met by VP . . . commander said only comparable welcome 'was when we liberated France.'

"Please tell the President," Lightner said, "that I consider the VP's Berlin visit to have been an overwhelming success in restoring Berlin morale and dispelling mood of despair prevalent in earlier part of week. In brief, it was most significant event in Berlin history since lifting of blockade. . . ."

At a press conference a week later, Kennedy was asked about a remark by former Vice President Nixon that the reinforcement of the garrison in West Berlin was "a useless gesture"—and that, in fact, the Soviets had succeeded in making East Berlin part of East Germany in violation of the Four-Power Agreement at the end of World War II.

"I'm quite aware that Berlin is, from a military point of view, untenable, if it were subjected to a direct attack by the Soviet Union," the President answered. "What we hope will prevent that direct attack is the awareness of the Soviet Union that we mean to defend our position in West Berlin, and that American troops, who are not numerous there, are our hostage to that intent."

After it was over, Walter Lippmann wrote a column saying: "The Western Powers were caught unprepared . . . the preoccupation of the President's advisers with the memory of Stalin's blockade in 1948 prevented them from preparing adequately for the formidable measures short of war which were available to Khrushchev."

The President called the columnist to the head table at a White House dinner for the president of the Sudan to tell him: "You were wrong, Walter!"

Chapter 19

Vice President Johnson reported to President Kennedy as soon as he and Clay returned from West Berlin on August 21. One thing he told Kennedy was that the leaders of West Germany and the public there considered the Berlin crisis essentially a confrontation between the United States and the Soviet Union. The last paragraph in Johnson's long written report read: "After having travelled through Asia, Africa, and Germany, the most important conclusion I have is the fantastic dependence that the Free World places on the United States. . . . We have a responsibility that has no parallel in all of history."

The President had come to the same conclusion on his own. The British had agreed to send three armored cars and a few soldiers along with the U.S. Army Battle Group that made the run along the Autobahn from Helmstedt to Berlin, and that only after the President had practically begged Prime Minister Macmillan for the symbolic assistance. The French had refused to send a man. It was Khrushchev who had backed down this time. But now Kennedy saw the experience as evidence of a harsh truth: "The West" was a euphemism for the United States. With all the neat trimmings of NATO and endless meetings and memos, the Western burden was the American burden.

"I want to take a stronger lead on Berlin negotiations," Kennedy told Rusk as the East Germans built their wall higher and higher. "I no longer believe that satisfactory progress can be made by four-power discussion alone. I think we should promptly work toward a strong U.S. position . . . and should make it clear that we cannot accept a veto from any other power."

"I read the Cyprus report," he told Bundy in a morning memo the day Johnson returned home. "It seems to me that if the situation is as desperate as we hear it is that we cannot continue to rely upon our policy of hoping that [other] powers will shoulder the principal share of the Western burden."

"I would like to stay out of some of these fights, but it is a luxury we can't afford," he said later, when the subject turned to West Irian, the western half of the island of New Guinea, where Indonesia and its old colonial masters from the Netherlands were fighting a small war—and the Dutch wanted the Americans to take over their side.

" 'Over-extended commitments' is a phrase with a lot of appeal," he remarked to Sorensen during one of those end-of-the-day, highest-level bull sessions Kennedy liked before going upstairs to dinner. "But how do we withdraw from South Korea or from Vietnam? I don't know where the non-essential areas are. I can't see how we can withdraw from South Korea, Turkey, Iran, Pakistan."

Vietnam was not at the top of that list, but now he had to focus on Southeast Asia just to catch up on developments there during the summer of Berlin's discontent. The President had ordered one study after another on South Vietnam, trying to find the way to help or persuade President Diem to save his country the American way.

In mid-June, Kennedy had sent out an economics mission headed by Dr. Eugene Staley, the president of Stanford Research Institute. Staley and a dozen men from the U.S. government were charged with evaluating Diem's economic programs. They had come back with what amounted to a military finance plan, saying: "Security requirements must, for the present, be given first priority"—endorsing Diem's request for American funding for 100,000 more men in the Army of Vietnam, bringing its strength up to 270,000. In July, a working paper for the President had been prepared by an interim Southeast Asia Task Force, headed by the Deputy Assistant Secretary of State for the Far East, John Steeves. It recommended covert action to disrupt supply lines used to bring war matériel from North Vietnam into the South. If that did not work, Steeves's group said, the North Vietnamese should be warned that the next U.S. step would involve military retaliation against North Vietnam.

On July 28, the President had met with Rusk, Bundy, Taylor, Rostow, and members of his Southeast Asia Task Force to consider a Taylor-Rostow recommendation that he must choose among three broad strategies: "(1) Disengage from the area as gracefully as possible; (2) Find out as soon as possible a convenient political pretext and attack with American military force the regional source of aggression in Hanoi; (3) Build as much indigenous military, political and economic strength as we can in the area, in order to contain the thrust from Hanoi, while preparing to intervene with U.S. military force if the Chinese Communists come in or the situation otherwise gets out of hand."

At that meeting, Deputy Undersecretary of State U. Alexis Johnson had told the President that another way to relieve the pressure on South Vietnam would be to invade and occupy southern Laos, cutting off the Ho Chi Minh Trail. The President mostly listened. He almost never announced decisions at meetings, which was one reason almost everyone around the table went away thinking he agreed with them.

On August 11, Kennedy had endorsed most of the Staley recommendations, but had finally agreed to pay for the equipment and training of only 30,000 new troops, bringing ARVN to a strength of 200,000 men, rather than the 270,000 new men Diem requested.

Then, on August 29, during another long White House meeting on Southeast Asia, the President authorized the CIA to add 2,000 more Meo tribesmen to the 9,000-man army the agency had secretly organized in the Vietnamese highlands. The tribal army was not secret in Vietnam, of course, only in the United States. At the same time, Kennedy increased the number of U.S. military trainers in Laos to five hundred men, serving now as low as company level of the Royal Army. He also approved plans for the use of unmarked U.S. and Philippine Air Force planes for aerial reconnaissance over the southern part of the country. Then the President asked McNamara and Lemnitzer for details of a next step, if he decided to send U.S. troops into southern Laos to block the Ho Chi Minh Trail into South Vietnam.

Under existing contingency plans, Lemnitzer said, the first force would be 13,000 men—and the number would go up rapidly if the North Vietnamese responded by sending in troops. Taylor interrupted: "It's inconceivable to me how we can do something like this *and* ship six new divisions to Germany and do something like this without total mobilization."

Two days later, on August 31, Kennedy sent a note to McNamara, saying that the United States might need more men in uniform than he had anticipated in his three military build-up speeches. And, for the first time, he said he might have to send combat troops to Vietnam: "I would like to have you present your analysis of the military situation with recommendations as to any further expansion of our military forces in the light of the events of recent weeks."

Kennedy seemed to be seeing himself more clearly as Commander-in-Chief. His distrust of the United States' oldest allies, Great Britain and France, was matched by his feelings toward some of the country's biggest military names. More and more, he was reaching new conclusions about the military structure and posture of the United States. One of those conclusions was unique and may have been shared only by his principal adversary, the premier of the Soviet Union: No President (or premier) was actually going to use nuclear weapons if the enemy had the capacity to retaliate in kind, as the Americans and Soviets did. The bombs and missiles were not usable weapons. They amounted only to massive deterrence against attack. And, despite the doubts of President de Gaulle, the existence of U.S. missiles almost certainly meant no Soviet leader would use nuclear weapons against Western Europe. Kennedy knew now that the missile gap overwhelmingly favored the United States. Still, that did not matter much. After Vienna, he had concluded that for all practical purposes there was no such thing as nuclear superiority. There was no difference between superiority and parity or anything remotely close to parity.

During the long Berlin summer, two of the President's ranking generals, LeMay and Lemnitzer, had told him they would need authorization to use nuclear weapons to defend Berlin or to stabilize Southeast Asia. Kennedy had walked out of both those meetings.

"These people are crazy," he said one of those times, throwing his hands into the air. He looked back toward the Cabinet Room, filled with generals and admirals, and said to no one in particular: "I told you to keep them away from me."

Nothing former Lieutenant (junior grade) Kennedy had learned in his rise to Commander-in-Chief had changed his gripes about the failings of admirals and generals. In fact, his experience as their commander lowered Kennedy's estimation of many of the highest-ranking men he commanded. When he had decided to send the battle group down the Autobahn into Berlin, he had discovered that the troops were not on the border between West Germany and East Germany, as he had been told, but forty-eight hours away from the takeoff point in Helmstedt.

The troops and the planes and the ships never seemed to be where they were supposed to be—or where generals and admirals said they were. *The Ugly American* was still his guidebook when he turned his mind to Southeast Asia and focused on new kinds of military and paramilitary capability to counter wars of national liberation. As for nuclear weapons, the President wanted more than just the constitutional title of Commander-in-Chief. Four days after the barbed wire was strung across Berlin, he had ordered Maxwell Taylor to prepare a short and direct paper entitled: "Guidance for Berlin Contingency Planning." Taylor's last sentence read: "The planners should be told to produce plans for these seven situations to include command arrangements which will keep all decisions to use nuclear weapons with the President."

On August 30, Kennedy announced at a news conference that Lucius Clay had agreed to return to West Berlin as his personal representative. His official rank would be ambassador, but everyone who knew Clay and his style thought he would act as a proconsul and try to take command of both civilian and military affairs. It was not an easy appointment. Clay was not only Republican, he was Eisenhower's friend and chief fund-raiser. He was used to giving orders, not taking them. Bundy had warned Kennedy that he could end up in a losing battle with his own general, as President Truman had when he fired General Douglas MacArthur for insubordination as the commander of Allied forces in Korea in 1951. But it was a pure Kennedy appointment, another hedge against Republican criticism. And he thought Clay was the one American who could make a difference in Berlin.

Before Clay accepted the job, he had set one condition: Never under any circumstances would he deal with Robert Kennedy.

"I understand," said the President. He had laughed.

Back at the White House that day, the President was with his brother when he was handed an Associated Press bulletin.

"Fucked again," said the President to the Attorney General. Premier Khrushchev had just announced that the Soviets were resuming atmospheric tests of thermonuclear weapons. Hydrogen bombs.

"I want to get off," said Robert Kennedy.

"Get off what?"

"Get off the planet."

"The bastards. That fucking liar," John Kennedy repeated later that same day when he was handed a yellow CIA telex reporting seismic evidence of a thermonuclear explosion above ground in Siberia.

The surprise was not complete, but almost so: only two days before, U.S. military intelligence had picked up local Soviet radio transmissions in Siberia warning aircraft to stay away from designated areas on August 30, usually a sign that testing was imminent. Carl Kaysen, Bundy's principal national security deputy, and Jerome Wiesner, the President's science adviser, brought Kennedy the news, saying Soviet tests would be a great propaganda opportunity for the United States.

"What are you? Peaceniks?" Kennedy said. "They just kicked me in the nuts. I'm supposed to say that's okay?"

The Soviet test preparations had obviously begun before Khrushchev had told Kennedy in Vienna that the Soviet Union would not be the first to resume nuclear testing after the informal moratorium observed by both powers for the past three years. It took a lot longer than eighty-five days to prepare a test like this one.

After he cooled down, Kennedy said that perhaps the Russian had not lied, perhaps he just had not been able to resist or manipulate the pressure from his generals and scientists to begin testing again. "Hard-liners" was the term on both sides for those who believed more bombs were the only real defense against each other. Kennedy knew all about that. The American military and some scientists had been pushing for new U.S. tests. And, in fact, the President had secretly ordered preparations to resume testing, to be ready to respond to the politics of the moment.

Kennedy had shared some of his thoughts on testing with Harold Macmillan in a long letter in which he thanked the British leader for public support after his Berlin speech at the end of July. The subject of the letter, classified "Top Secret," was not Berlin. It was nuclear testing. "What we have all feared is the fact [that] we simply cannot be sure, without a control system, that the Soviets are not testing, and if they are testing, they can be learning important things," Kennedy wrote. "I remain most reluctant to take a firm decision to resume testing . . . I think we ought to make one more try in Geneva. . . . I am not very hopeful that it will be possible to wait much beyond the first of the year. If we do resume, it will be underground, unless and until the Soviets resume atmospheric tests."

"May I hear how all this strikes you?" Kennedy politely asked Macmillan. He did not tell the prime minister that one of the first things he had done after returning from Vienna was to order the Defense Department and the Atomic Energy Commission to prepare to resume nuclear testing, a process that usually took six months. He had ordered the paperwork on that decision withdrawn, so he would have the option of saying he had made the preparation decision later than he had actually had.

"The President met this morning with members of the National Security Council and Congressional leaders. . . ," began the official White House reaction to the August Soviet test on August 30. "The Soviet action was primarily a form of atomic blackmail, designed to substitute terror for reason in the present international scene."

Kennedy called Glenn Seaborg, chairman of the Atomic Energy Commission, to ask how soon the United States could schedule a test. "One or two weeks, Mr. President," Seaborg answered—if they did not take the time to install diagnostic equipment at the Nevada test site. A political blast takes less time.

That weekend, Kennedy invited James Reston of *The New York Times* to Hyannis Port for an interview, after which they were walking along the beach, talking less formally. Reston asked him about his vision of the future, what kind of world he would like to help make. Kennedy looked at Reston for a long moment, seeming a little sad. "I haven't had time to think about that yet," he answered.

Chapter 20

"In view of the continued testing by the Soviet Government, I have today ordered the resumption of nuclear tests, in the laboratory and underground, with no fallout," President Kennedy announced on September 5, 1961, six days after the first Soviet test. "We must now take those steps which prudent men find essential."

There was no scientific or military reason for the United States to test until early 1962 or even into 1963. The National Security Council had reported that to the President three weeks before the first Soviet shot. But there were political reasons now. In the six days, the Soviets exploded two more hydrogen bombs after their first 150-kiloton shot into the atmosphere above Siberia.

Some of Kennedy's men, including Adlai Stevenson at the United Nations, tried to talk Kennedy out of matching the Soviet testing. The United States, they argued briefly, could score a propaganda victory around the world by not testing now. But he was under much greater pressure to resume testing from the Joint Chiefs of Staff, from Congress, from the Atomic Energy Commission—and from the American people who, according to Gallup polls, favored new U.S. testing by better than two-to-one margins even before the Soviets had broken the moratorium both sides had observed since 1958. Personally, Kennedy did not want to resume testing. In meetings with scientists, he asked fewer questions about megatonnage than about radioactive fallout.

"Where would we be if testing had continued at the 1958 rate?" he asked Dr. Charles Dunham, director of the Atomic Energy Commission's Division of Biology and Medicine.

"Civilized man would have been in trouble," Dunham said.

"How does the radioactive fallout get to the earth?" he asked his science adviser, Jerome Wiesner.

"The clouds are washed out by rain," answered Wiesner.

Kennedy looked out through the French doors into the garden. It was a rainy day and he asked: "You mean it's in the rain out there?"

"Yes," Wiesner said. He stood, awkwardly, waiting. Kennedy did not speak for a long time.

But neither fallout nor propaganda nor technology was the problem as the President saw it. Certainly personal feelings were no part of it. He felt he must not look weak. He felt, too, that Stevenson's reluctance to test was one of the reasons why he and not Stevenson had made it to the White House.

"Shit, I have no choice," he told Stevenson. "They spit in our eye three times. We have to do this."

"But we're ahead in the propaganda. . . ," Stevenson replied.

"What does that mean?" Kennedy answered. "I don't hear of any windows being broken because of the Soviet decision. The neutrals have been terrible. . . . All this makes Khrushchev look pretty tough. He has had a succession of apparent victories—space, Cuba, the Thirteenth of August in Berlin, though I don't regard that as a Soviet victory. He wants to give out the feeling he has us on the run. . . . The decision has been made. I'm not saying it was the right decision. Who the hell knows? But it's the decision that has been taken."

Two of the neutrals came to Washington on September 12: President Sukarno of Indonesia, short and volatile, and President Keita of Mali, a tower of dignity almost seven feet tall. Their mission was to inform Kennedy of the results of the Conference of Non-Aligned Nations, just completed in Belgrade, Yugoslavia. As usual, the neutrals had found more fault with the United States than with the Soviet Union. Usually, the Americans just gritted their teeth and smiled. But this time, the President had no patience with them. They had condemned the United States' underground tests, which had not happened yet, while more or less ignoring the Soviet Union's atmospheric blasts, which were going off every couple of days.

Sukarno and Keita laid that out for Kennedy.

"Are you finished?" he asked. "Well, let me tell you that I, on behalf of the people of the United States, subscribe 100 percent to the objectives of the conference in spite of the tone of the language. . . . I support your views. Now you have a much harder job—you go and sell this to Chairman Khrushchev in Moscow. Is there anything further you want to say?"

Three days later, on September 15, the White House issued a statement saying: "President John F. Kennedy announced that the United States conducted an underground nuclear weapons development test of low yield at the Nevada Test Site at 1 p.m., Washington time. . . ." It was a 6-kiloton bomb from the U.S. stockpile—a "proof test." Without instrumentation, the only thing tested was whether or not the device would go off. It did, but it was nothing more than a loud political statement.

The same thing was partly true of the Soviet blasts, the State Department's intelligence bureau reported to the White House:

> The USSR has sound military-technical grounds for renewed weapons testing—the achievement of a lower weight to yield ratio of warheads, the development of an anti-missile missile, and the demonstrative explosion of a "super bomb." However, it appears that the primary reason for deciding to test at this time is to serve Soviet political aims regarding Berlin. . . . Otherwise, Moscow would have chosen to refrain from nuclear testing until U.S. resumed underground tests (which the Soviets had good reason to believe was not far in the offing), thus throwing the political onus on the U.S.

The Soviets were acting out of weakness. The game of "missile gap" was ending. Khrushchev had been bluffing: he had used the heroic efforts of Soviet space scientists, and the ambitions of Kennedy the candidate, to convince most of the world that Soviet weapons, technology, and productivity were equal to or better than anything the Americans had. The endgame had begun in August 1960, when the United States, after twelve secret failures, finally succeeded in putting into orbit its first spy satellite, the Central Intelligence Agency's Corona. The public had been told that the device was a weather satellite, called Discoverer 13. In January, just about the time Kennedy was inaugurated, Corona had begun parachute-dropping cans of film taken over Russia into nets on Air Force planes. The spy satellite's cameras were designed to focus on known Soviet missile installations—known because Khrushchev had boasted about them over the years. There was nothing there but farmland and wilderness. No missiles; no silos; no factories.

By the end of the summer of 1961, there was film from a new satellite, this one publicly called Discoverer 29, which was capable of "seeing" and photographing the ground through cloud cover. From the new film, the CIA and McNamara and Gilpatric concluded that the Soviets had only a few primitive ICBMs, perhaps just four 100-ton SS-6s, which were more than twice as heavy as the biggest American rocket, the Atlas. They knew, too, that the Soviet monsters were kept on extremely low alert. Warheads were stored separate from the delivery vehicles, and it took three hours to fill each of them with liquid fuel. They were all standing at the same place, a Siberian testing site called Plesetsk.

In addition to those missiles, the Soviets had two hundred bombers capable of carrying nuclear weapons, but with limited probability of reaching targets in the United States. They also had seventy-eight missiles on submarines that would have to get within 150 miles of U.S. shores to have any chance of hitting American coastal cities. Those subs were rarely at sea, staying instead in the safe harbor of Soviet ports.

Of course, Kennedy knew all that. The United States, with 185 ICBMs, and with more than 3,400 nuclear warheads on submarines, and bombers capable of striking deep into the Soviet Union, had overwhelming nuclear superiority. But he also knew that there was no guarantee that some Soviet missiles would not hit American targets, even if the United States launched a first strike.

The thing was to make sure that Khrushchev knew that Kennedy knew the Soviet leader had been bluffing. He told McNamara to invite Pentagon correspondents for another round of Scotch-and-soda and off-the-record conversation, to set the record straight. This time McNamara would deliberately let them know that the missile gap heavily favored the United States. The idea was to change the tone of American defense reporting, to emphasize the "new" strength of the U.S. military. McNamara called in the reporters, and midway into his second Scotch, he told them: "Our means of delivery and our nuclear power exceeds theirs—any place, at any time, in any way."

It was only then, on September 13, 1961, after eight months in office, that Kennedy finally sat down for a two-hour briefing on the United States' most guarded secret, the plan for nuclear war. It was officially called SIOP-62—Single Integrated Operational Plan for Fiscal Year 1962. The military did not volunteer its own information and plans when it had reason to believe that presidents might change them. What presidents didn't know couldn't hurt the military, or so reasoned generals and admirals who saw presidents come and go. Kennedy knew the general outlines of the SIOP, which had been described to him by Bundy as "a massive, total, comprehensive, obliterating strategic attack . . . on everything Red." Once a president said yes to touching a nuclear button, his power shifted to the military. The chain of command was a gigantic and deadly snake with a life of its own if the Commander-in-Chief opened the cage.

The chairman of the Joint Chiefs of Staff, Lemnitzer, did the briefing himself, setting up easels with thirty-eight flip charts of target and deployment maps. There were 3,729 targets on the cards, which would, according to plan, be destroyed by 1,060 bombs or warheads. At all times, the President was told, 1,530 missiles and bombers were on full alert, meaning they could be launched or sent within fifteen minutes of a presidential command. Another 1,737 weapons were on "non-alert" status, meaning they could be fired or sent within six hours of command.

After a presidential order or stand-by authorization was given, Lemnitzer said, "the JCS will designate E-Hour and the appropriate execution option"—"E" as in execution. Then he said: "Under any circumstances—even a preemptive attack by the US—it would be expected that some portion of the Soviet long-range nuclear force would strike the United States."

Ending his presentation, Lemnitzer demonstrated the rigidity Kennedy most hated about the military: "It must clearly be understood that any decision to execute only a portion of the entire plan would involve acceptance of certain grave risks. . . . There is no effective mechanism for rapid rework of the plan, after order for its execution, for a different set of conditions than for which it was prepared."

Kennedy was tapping his front teeth with the fingernail of his thumb for the last twenty minutes of Lemnitzer's show, a sign to those who knew him that he was either bored or furious. And there was nothing boring about the plan.

"Why do we hit all those targets in China, General?" Kennedy asked. The Chinese had no missiles, no nuclear delivery systems.

"It's in the plan, Mr. President," said the general.

Kennedy was gripping the arms of his chair so tightly that his knuckles showed white. As he walked out of the room with Dean Rusk, he said: "And we call ourselves the human race."

Nevertheless, Kennedy had initiated and was presiding over one of the great military build-ups of all time. He knew it was not a direct response to a real Soviet threat; it was the result of runaway American politics, exaggerated threats of communism, misunderstood intelligence, inflated campaign rhetoric, a few lies here and there, and his own determination never to be vulnerable to "soft on Communism" charges that Republicans regularly used to discredit Democrats. He had created a bipartisan national security government. McNamara, Bundy, and Gilpatric were among the many Republicans around him.

In 1961, he had explicitly challenged the Soviets into an escalating arms race, doubling the production of Polaris missile submarines from ten a year to twenty, increasing the number of Strategic Air Command nuclear-armed bombers in the air on alert at all times from 33 percent to 50 percent, signing off on one thousand new U.S. intercontinental ballistic missiles, each one with a charge eighty times more powerful than the atomic bomb dropped at Hiroshima. That was considered a compromise; General LeMay and the Air Force had wanted three thousand new ICBMs.

Khrushchev also had generals who were demanding more, but the Soviets had less of everything. By August 1961, Kennedy was beginning to realize too that his own warnings about the Soviet economy overtaking U.S. production were as exaggerated as had been his missile gap rhetoric. Walter Heller, chairman of the Council of Economic Advisers, had done quick calculations for him showing that the United States' better than two-to-one advantage in gross national product was exactly the same as it had been over czarist Russia in 1913. The Soviets, in fact, were not gaining on the United States, and some of the President's men were playing with the idea that a sustained arms race could break the Soviet economy—and communism with it.

The President was not above taunting Russians about that. That same August, Khrushchev's son-in-law, Aleksei Adzhubei, was slipped in the back door of the White House with Georgi Bolshakov—avoiding any possibility of photographs showing the President fraternizing with the enemy. He had met Yuri Gagarin, the first cosmonaut, the same way the month before. To Adzhubei, the editor of *Izvestia,* he said: "You've made remarkable economic advances. But you're like a high-jumper. He can raise the bar a foot at a time until he reaches a certain height, say six feet. But for the next foot he must raise it by inches and then by fractions of inches. . . . We'll all be around in 1978 to find out whether Mr. Khrushchev's estimates [of Soviet growth] are correct."

Kennedy saw clearly the linkage between defense and economics. One of his first innovations as President had been to establish a bureau in the Pentagon to push the sales of U.S. weaponry around the world, as one way to improve the country's foreign trade balance, the "gold drain," as he called it.

Militarily, Kennedy's goal now was not more missiles but "Flexible Response," as defined by Maxwell Taylor as an alternative to the "Massive Retaliation" doctrine of the Eisenhower years. "Strengthen the alternatives between inaction and nuclear war," was the expression McNamara used in one of a series of "Military Build-Up" memos that went back and forth to and from the President in September. Kennedy wanted a series of escalating military and political options that began with Colonel Hillandales on the ground, and ended with SIOP in the air. He initiated and protected the guerrilla option; the military was demanding that he preserve wipe-them-out nuclear capability.

"It is absolutely essential that the Soviets be forced to act and move at all times in full awareness that if they use force they risk general war with nuclear weapons," General Lauris Norstad, the commander of NATO, told the President on September 18. "I am sure you agree that nothing we do should suggest that our goal is to confine the fight for Allied rights in Europe to Europe." In other words, the United States must continually warn the Soviets and assure the Europeans that an attack on Hamburg was indeed an attack on Chicago, meaning U.S. missiles would fly in retaliation.

As he added missiles, Kennedy also added men. He ordered the Army expanded from fourteen divisions to sixteen. All of them were to be combat-ready, which meant tremendous increases in weapons and ammunition purchases and airlift capacity. "Airlift" became a high military priority with Kennedy after he had asked McNamara how long it would take to move a U.S. infantry division to Vietnam, and the answer had come back: "Two months."

"Unconventional warfare" was another term Kennedy popularized in his fascination with creating small highly trained guerrilla or counterinsurgency units. He was reading Mao Tse-tung on warfare, sometimes quoting the Chinese leader in the middle of casual conversation. " 'Guerrillas must move among the people as fish swim in the sea,' " he said for no apparent reason one Saturday at lunch, surprising his wife as they ate alone at Glen Ora.

He wanted American fish swimming out there, too. "Special Forces," the Green Berets, would live off the land, training guerrillas. The Air Force, seeing which way the wind was blowing from the White House, officially changed the name of its own special forces to "Jungle Jims."

The President also picked up some of Robert Kennedy's ideas about training policemen and paramilitary cadres around the world to control and counter the success of Communists and students in street demonstrations and riots. On September 5, the day he announced that the United States would resume thermonuclear testing, Kennedy also asked McNamara for plans to establish "police academies" in both Latin America and the United States, with American officers and FBI agents as instructors on fighting subversion. "Teach them how to control mobs and fight guerrillas," he said. "Increase the intimacy between our armed forces and the military of Latin America."

Undersecretary of State Bowles was one of the few New Frontiersmen who objected to that emphasis. He wrote a memo to the President suggesting that the United States should train policemen and soldiers around the world as builders and defenders of democracy. "There can be no successful action by guerrillas unless there is a dissatisfied rural population which can provide them a base of operations," said Bowles. "Our aid programs have woefully underemphasized an integrated attack on rural poverty and despair."

Bundy sent that memo to him with a note on top: "Bowles has volunteered certain of his personal views. . . . If you agree, I will acknowledge receipt of the memorandum, expressing your interest, etc." And in fact the President did not read it.

Kennedy dictated a morning memo in mid-September to Bundy and McNamara: "If we mobilize a million men (thinking of the Berlin situation), what would we do with them—how many would be combat troops, how many would be logistic support units, etc.? Would we send the million to Europe, how long would it take to get them over, how many ships, if by sea, how many would we plan to send by plane? How many days would it take to get them all there? Where would they be positioned in Europe when they get there?"

That same day, September 18, *Life* magazine was on America's newsstands with the headline: "A LETTER TO YOU FROM PRESIDENT KENNEDY. HOW YOU CAN SURVIVE FALLOUT—97 OUT OF 100 PEOPLE CAN BE SAVED."

The President's science adviser, Wiesner, was angry enough about that to tell Kennedy in a memo that the *Life* coverage was not true: "In my opinion, this article gives the American people an entirely false and misleading estimate of the protection that would be provided by fallout shelters, and of potential mortalities in the event of large-scale thermonuclear attack on this country."

Kennedy ignored that, though he had known it was true since checking nuclear casualty estimates the day he returned from the Vienna summit. In letters to the governors of the fifty states, Kennedy wrote: "In simple terms, the goal is to reach for fallout protection for every American as rapidly as possible. Protection against this threat is within the reach of an informed America willing to face the facts and act." To McNamara, he had written, as a National Security Action Memorandum, "I would appreciate receiving a weekly report on what progress we are making on Civil Defense. Do you think it would be useful for me to write a letter to every home owner in the United States giving them instructions as to what can be done on their own to provide greater security for their family?"

Whether or not it could work, civil defense could be part of bearing any burden. Arthur Schlesinger had said that in a memo to the President: "For years, internationalists have been yearning for some means of making questions of foreign policy less abstract or remote and bringing these questions home to every household in the land. Now, at last, there is such an issue. Civil defense has become the focus for all anxieties over foreign policy. When people read about American and Russian [confrontation] they feel they can do something about it themselves—they can decide whether or not to build a shelter."

But Schlesinger did have one reservation about civil defense, pointing out that emphasizing homeowners in civil defense planning looked as if it were designed to save the middle and upper classes. Poor people did not have backyards or basements to build private shelters.

(Schlesinger also took the opportunity to ask the President if it was all right if he wrote a film column for a magazine called *Show*. In the midst of meetings on nuclear testing, Kennedy dictated an answer to Schlesinger: "The President says it is fine . . . as long as you treat Peter Lawford with respect.")

On September 18, Kennedy was trying to decide whether or not to address the opening session of the United Nations General Assembly on September 25, when news from Africa made up his mind for him: U.N. Secretary-General Dag Hammarskjöld had been killed in a plane crash in the Congo, where U.N. troops were still trying to end the civil war that had begun with independence in 1960.

Pierre Salinger went to New York to make arrangements for the press corps that would follow the President. As soon as he checked into the Carlyle Hotel, he received a telephone call from Georgi Bolshakov. The Russian intelligence agent said he had to see Salinger. He came through a side door to avoid the press corps in the lobby. With him was Mikhail Kharlmalov, the chief press officer of the Soviet Foreign Ministry, who was in New York with his boss, Foreign Minister Andrei Gromyko. As Kharlmalov walked into Salinger's suite, he said: "The storm in Berlin is over."

With Bolshakov translating, the Foreign Ministry spokesman said he was carrying a message from Khrushchev to Kennedy, which he asked Salinger to pass on to the President: "There was intense pressure on Khrushchev from within the Communist bloc to recognize East Germany . . . the danger of a major military incident in Berlin was too great to delay a settlement very much longer. He hopes your President's speech to the UN won't be another warlike ultimatum like the one on July 25. He didn't like that at all."

"Good news," said Kennedy, when Salinger passed on the message. "He's not going to recognize the Ulbricht regime—not this year at least."

Kennedy read over his speech again, and instructed Salinger to assure the Russians, and presumably their leader, that his tone would be moderate. In fact, he had already received other indications that Khrushchev wanted to turn down the heat on Berlin, and that he also wanted another summit meeting. One of those hints had been delivered by C. S. Sulzberger of *The New York Times,* who had interviewed the Soviet leader early in September. The *Times* reported this on its front page on the morning before the U.N. session began: "[The Soviets have] indicated in a number of quiet ways that their threat and deadline on Germany might be subject to another temporary delay. Communist diplomats were reported as saying that the West did not have to feel itself under an artificial 'deadline' if serious negotiations were undertaken."

Why? Kennedy assumed that the Soviet chairman believed the Americans would fight for Berlin. Or, as Sulzberger and Llewellyn Thompson each told him, there were power struggles between hard-liners and soft-liners in the hidden political processes of the Kremlin. Either way, the President wanted to appear firm but open to talk. At the United Nations, he declared that the United States would never agree to the replacement of Secretary-General Hammarskjöld by a "Troika," the Soviet-proposed three-member executive with representatives of the West, the Communists, and the neutral nations.

He stressed both the need for a nuclear test ban and the firmness of U.S. commitments in Berlin and Vietnam, and concluded with soaring hyperbole: "The events and decisions of the next ten months may well decide the fate of man for the next ten thousand years. . . . Ladies and gentlemen of this Assembly, the decision is ours. Never have the nations of the world had so much to lose, or so much to gain. Together we shall save our planet, or together we shall perish in its flames."

Chapter 21

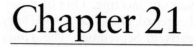

At the end of the summer of 1961, Theodore H. White delivered *The Making of the President, 1960* to his publisher and decided to take a look for himself at what was happening in Asia. He knew much of the continent well, having lived in China in war and peace in the 1930s and early 1940s, first as an aide to the Chinese leader Chiang Kai-shek, then as a *Time* magazine correspondent. He was shocked at what he saw in Vietnam, and upon return asked his old friend Arthur Schlesinger, Jr., to deliver an urgent fourteen-page letter to his newer friend, the President. It was a blunter assessment than the ones Kennedy usually saw:

> The situation gets worse almost week by week. I say this despite the optimistic bullshit now hitting the papers. The guerrillas now control almost all the southern delta—so much so that I could find no American who would drive me outside Saigon in his car even by day without military convoy.
>
> There is a political breakdown here of formidable proportions. . . . If we mean to win, perhaps we must do more. But what? If there is another coup against Diem by his army, should we support it? If there is no natural coup and we are convinced that Diem is useless, should we incubate one? If we feel bound by honor not to pull or support a coup, shall we lay it on the line to Diem and intervene directly . . . or should we get the Hell out and make another line or policy elsewhere?

What perplexes the hell out of me is that the Commies on their side, seem to be able to find people willing to die for their cause. I find it discouraging to spend a night in a Saigon night-club full of young fellows of 20 and 25 dancing and jitterbugging . . . while twenty miles away their Communist contemporaries are terrorizing the countryside.

The President also got unofficial counsel from a British counterinsurgency expert, Robert K. G. Thompson, the man credited with devising British strategy in turning back a Communist insurgency in Malaya during the 1950s. Thompson proposed fortifying villages and villagers against the Viet Cong in what he called "strategic hamlets." The "new" idea was quite similar to an old French plan to create what they called *agrovilles*. "The overall aim of any counter-insurgency plan must be to win the people," stated Thompson in a report that went first to President Diem in Saigon and then to the Americans. "The killing of communist terrorists will follow from that. . . . Protection, confidence, intelligence and kills would be a constantly expanding circuit."

White's former employer, *Time* magazine, run by another old China hand, Henry Luce, who had been born there, the son of Christian missionaries, was calling for action, too. Vietnam, said *Time*, was the burden Kennedy must ask America to bear:

The Viet Cong, which is what the Communist Vietnamese are called, are everywhere: furtive little bands of Communist guerrillas, dressed in black peasant pajamas or faded khakis tossing grenades into isolated villages in the rice fields in the south. . . . South Viet Nam has been U.S. sponsored from the start; its government is militantly anti-Communist, and its soldiers are willing to fight. If the U.S. cannot or will not save South Viet Nam from the Communist assault, no Asian nation can ever again feel safe in putting its faith in the U.S.—and the fall of all Southeast Asia would only be a matter of time.

Pressure was building for a greater U.S. commitment to Vietnam. The flow of classified paper, and the President's attention, both escalated after September 18, when three battalions of Viet Cong, about one thousand men, seized Phouc Vinh, a provincial capital fifty-five miles from Saigon, and held it for six hours. In that time, the Viet Cong had captured one hundred rifles and six thousand rounds of ammunition, freed two hundred and fifty suspected Communists in the local jail, and publicly beheaded the province chief and his chief deputy for "crimes against the people." The Viet Cong, believed to have about twelve thousand full-time guerrillas living off the land, had assassinated fourteen hundred village officials in a year and controlled a third of the country-side during the day and much more at night.

Within two weeks of the Phouc Vinh raid, President Ngo Dinh Diem, in conversations with U.S. Ambassador Frederick Nolting, brought up for the first time the idea of a mutual defense treaty between his country and the United States. And for the first time, he brought up the possibility of inviting in American combat troops or "combat trainers."

During the first five days of October, Kennedy received separate warnings of impending disaster in South Vietnam from both Rusk and McNamara. A State Department "Situation Summary" on October 1 said the number of Viet Cong "regulars" had increased from seven thousand to seventeen thousand since the beginning of the year. On October 5, the Joint Chiefs reported: "The time is now past when actions short of intervention by outside forces could reverse the rapidly worsening situation. . . . There is no feasible military alternative of lesser magnitude which will prevent the loss of Laos, South Vietnam and ultimately Southeast Asia."

"We cannot afford to be preoccupied with Berlin to the extent that we close our eyes to Southeast Asia. . . ," was the way the Joint Chiefs report began.

Berlin, though, was no longer quite the obsession it had been for the President. The Democratic Anti-Fascist Protection Wall, as the East Germans called it, was an ugly thing, thirteen feet high, backed up by five hundred watchtowers and a plowed and mined death strip patrolled by soldiers and dogs. But it had solved the refugee problem, and tension was decreasing along that East-West border.

And Khrushchev had reached out to Kennedy again. On September 29, while the President was staying at his mother-in-law's summer home, Hammersmith Farm in Newport, Rhode Island, Pierre Salinger received another call from Georgi Bolshakov. The GRU man was excited. He said he wanted to charter a plane and come up to Newport. He had something important for the President's eyes only.

"Tell him 'No,'" Kennedy said. He had visions of Khrushchev's messenger walking through ranks of American reporters, all of them looking for a story to break the journalistic boredom of Newport. "You go down to New York."

"You wouldn't say 'no' if you knew what I had," the Russian replied. Salinger flew to New York the next day and met him at the Hotel Carlyle. Folded inside the day's New York Times, Bolshakov carried a twenty-six-page letter from Khrushchev to Kennedy—a personal letter, rambling, but candid and conciliatory. Finally, Khrushchev proposed that the two leaders deal one-on-one, using private letters to bypass old bureaucracies, hostilities, and suspicions. Salinger distilled the content into three sentences:

"You and I, Mr. President, are the leaders of two nations that are on a collision course. But because we are reasonable men, we agree that war between us is unthinkable. We have no choice but to put our heads together and find ways to live in peace."

Khrushchev had written that Kennedy could ignore the letter and that would be the end of it, no one would ever know it happened. But Kennedy answered with ten pages of his own thoughts, talking of his family and children and a better world, saying that he welcomed a private correspondence free of Cold War polemics.

Kennedy was now convinced that the storms over Berlin were beginning to break up. A week later, on October 6, Soviet Foreign Minister Andrei Gromyko came to the White House, after conferring with Rusk for two days. Kennedy saw it as a chance to use Gromyko to demonstrate a skill the Soviet leader seemed to prize, making political points with parables and folktales. The subjects of the day were Berlin and the search for a successor to Dag Hammarskjöld. On Berlin, the President talked seriously again of miscalculation and war, but he also turned aside Gromyko's talk of new arrangements and understandings, saying: "You've offered to trade us an apple for an orchard. We don't do that in this country."

When Gromyko brought up again the Soviet proposal to replace the office of U.N. Secretary-General with a three-man troika, the President reached for a book, thumbed through to a marked page, and handed it to the Soviet foreign minister. "I have a delightful little book for you here," Kennedy said. "It's in Russian. I'm sure you'll enjoy it."*

It was a Russian fable, *The Swan, the Pike, and the Crab,* by Ivan Krylov, about the impossible attempts of those three creatures to pull a cart—"The Swan took flight. . . . The Pike pulls into the water . . . the Crab keeps backing. . . . Now which of them was right, which wrong, concerns us not: The cart is still upon the selfsame spot."

Gromyko did not change expression as he read it.

"Are you going to make this public?" Gromyko asked.

"No," Kennedy said. "But you might want to share it with Chairman Khrushchev."

Gromyko smiled, a rare event. Whether or not the fable made any difference, within a week Khrushchev dropped the troika proposal and decided to join the U.S. in support of U Thant of Burma for Secretary-General.

---

* The book was discovered and sent to the White House by Walter Bestermann, a staff assistant of the House Judiciary Committee, who recalled the fable from his childhood in Poland.

Kennedy, more confident on Berlin now, was able to concentrate on Vietnam. During the first two weeks of October, he turned first to McNamara. The Department of Defense, with an unofficial nod from the President, became the lead agency in dealing with Vietnam. Ambassador Nolting, only five months on the job, realized that he was out of favor with Kennedy's men, and he felt that it was because he had followed the President's orders to evaluate Diem and was now seen as too close to the South Vietnamese president. He concluded that Kennedy relied much more on news reports and the impressions of intimates than he did on the yards of cables he sent from the embassy each day.

He was right. What Teddy White thought carried more weight than anything Nolting, perhaps even Rusk, had to say. And White was telling Kennedy: "The State Department and its competitive instruments have in the years since I worked with them become so tangled as to be almost unfit for any policy-making purpose or decision." He suggested that it might be time to go back to an older system, when ambassadors were not professional diplomats tiptoeing up State's career ladder but energetic men known for their political skill and intuition. He said Kennedy should think about finding an Assistant Secretary of State with enough rank to stand up to the military and the CIA and "to shake the whole China service out of its sloth."

That was about what Kennedy had been thinking. He had begun to think that the right man for the Assistant Secretary job was Averell Harriman.

Ambassador Nolting tried to defend Diem and himself, cabling Washington: "Our present policy of all-out support to the present government here is, I think, our only feasible alternative. Diem is right and sound in his objectives and completely forthright with us." But Nolting —and the whole State Department, for that matter—had little impact compared to McNamara and Kennedy's traveling friends. "It's going to be difficult to put a Ford engine in an ox-cart," Nolting said one day to the Defense Secretary.

"We can do it," said the Secretary, the former president of the car company.

The "engine" had to be U.S. troops. The Joint Chiefs of Staff concluded, on October 9, that U.S. Army units were needed to cut Viet Cong supply lines. They recommended a force of 22,800 men from the South-East Asia Treaty Organization, including 13,200 from the United States, with the rest coming from Australia, New Zealand, Thailand, Pakistan, and the Philippines. The Chiefs added two contingencies to the plan. If North Vietnam responded by sending in regular troops, SEATO would need 200,000 men, including 129,000 Americans. If

China sent in troops, SEATO would need 278,000 men, including 150,000 Americans. In that case, the Chiefs said, the United States would also have to consider using nuclear weapons against military targets in China.

The consensus was to take the first step, to send in 10,000 men. Walt Rostow offered a rationale, in a memo shrewdly calculated to complement the President's bent toward leveraged counterinsurgency action: "It is somehow wrong to be developing these capabilities [Special Forces] but not applying them in a crucial active theater. In Knute Rockne's old phrase, we are not saving them for the Junior Prom."

On October 11, Kennedy called together the Vietnam Task Force he had created after the disorganization of the Bay of Pigs invasion. U. Alexis Johnson prepared a working paper for Kennedy, "Concept for Intervention in Vietnam," synthesizing the ideas of the Joint Chiefs, of Taylor, and of Rostow, and listing arguments for and against direct military intervention by the United States and whichever SEATO allies could be persuaded to send in men:

"This initial action"—based on sending 22,800 troops as soon as possible—"to arrest and hopefully to reverse the deteriorating situation in Vietnam . . . cannot be taken without accepting as our real and ultimate objective the defeat of the VietCong, and making Vietnam secure in the hands of an anti-Communist government."

The paper listed a dozen "pros" and "cons" of sending combat troops. The "pros" included raising South Vietnamese morale and the "cons" the open renunciation of the United States observance of the Geneva Accords of 1954. The United States, officially only an observer at the conference, had declined to sign the accords but had pledged to honor them.

There was no meeting of minds on those points, or on many others discussed that day. But one thing Kennedy did authorize was an operation code-named "Farm Gate," sending several hundred "Jungle Jims" to South Vietnam along with a dozen old planes able to fly slowly over the jungle on reconnaissance and attack missions. American officers in civilian clothes would do the flying, with Vietnamese military observers on board to camouflage the President's first orders to send Americans into battle in Vietnam.

Beyond that, Kennedy just did not know what to do. Enemies and events were moving very quickly, and again he was looking for more information, new information. He ended the October 11 meeting by ordering Maxwell Taylor to go to Vietnam and take a long, hard look at the insurgency and counterinsurgency. He told him to take a small group with him, including Walt Rostow and General Lansdale, and to leave as soon as possible. "Bear in mind," he told Taylor, "that the initial responsibility for the effective maintenance of the independence of South Vietnam rests with the people and government of that country."

The President wanted Taylor to concentrate on three options: the SEATO intervention; "U.S. Presence," a small combat force moved in to deter aggression by the North Vietnamese, who presumably did not want to take on the United States; or stepped-up U.S. assistance and training for the government and military of South Vietnam.

"High administration sources said today . . . the President remains strongly opposed to the dispatch of American combat troops to South Vietnam," reported *The New York Times* in a front-page story on the mission. The high source was Kennedy himself, whose written instructions to Taylor were somewhat different: "As part of your appraisal, I should like you to evaluate what could be accomplished by the introduction of SEATO or United States forces into South Vietnam, determining the role, composition and probable disposition of such forces."

After that meeting, the President went to a small gymnasium that had been built for him next to the White House swimming pool and began forty minutes of stretching routines that had been prescribed for him by a New York orthopedic surgeon named Dr. Hans Kraus. There had been a power struggle during the summer between his two principal physicians, Admiral George Burkley, his official government doctor, and his back doctor, Dr. Janet Travell. Dr. Burkley thought the President's back was getting worse rather than better. By August, he had begun to describe how Kennedy moved to other doctors. It was obvious to him that the President was moving with a kind of stiff caution, often getting up from chairs with difficulty, using his hands to take weight off his back. His body was getting softer and he was spending more time walking and paddling in the White House pool, heated now to 87 degrees. Burkley was not the only one who had noticed. Some Secret Servicemen, the President's guardians, were speculating among themselves that the President would be in a wheelchair during a second term.

The doctors he consulted told Burkley that the problem was almost certainly Dr. Travell's treatment. She was injecting her novocaine mixtures into the President's back as often as five and six times a day. The deep injections were extremely painful, but Kennedy badly wanted the couple of hours of relief that followed. Burkley, a cautious and conservative man, was worried, with good reason, that the novocaine was having less and less effect and the next painkilling step would be narcotics.

Kennedy was not shy about medication. He was used to it, practiced at self-prescription and self-injection. The corticosteroid injections and

time-release capsules implanted in his thigh every three months to treat
Addison's disease kept him alive and functioning one day at a time. At
lunchtime every day he also took pills of the same substance, desoxycorticosterone acetate, called DOCA. These were the medications that had
been stored in safety deposit boxes in banks around the world by his
father, ready for emergency use. DOCA allowed John Kennedy to live a
relatively normal life, but there were side effects, the most visible of
them his year-round tan and the puffiness of his face that changed his
looks from day to day. Another possible side effect was heightened
sexual desire, but there were those, many of them, who said that Kennedy, like his father before him, had that long before he had Addison's.

"That isn't my face, that's not me," Kennedy said one morning as he
stopped at a White House mirror and pressed his fingers into his cheek-
bones on the way to his office after a cortisone injection. The corticoste-
roids also gave him a rush, a feeling for a while that he was ready to
take on the world—which was his job. He got the same surge and more
from the amphetamine mixes that Dr. Jacobson was injecting into him,
coming to the White House or Palm Beach or wherever the President
was two or three times some weeks. The side effects of those treatments
were more dangerous: an exaggerated sense of power and capabilities,
and the debilitating symptoms of classic paranoid schizophrenia, then
slow death by poisoning. It was not Kennedy's doctors but his brother
Robert Kennedy who suspected such dangers and tried to get rid of Dr.
Jacobson. That was when the President had told Robert Kennedy he
didn't care if the stuff was horse piss; it worked.

The admiral had been arguing more and more frequently with Dr.
Travell about the number of novocaine shots she was giving the President. Finally, he had ordered Dr. Travell to bring Dr. Kraus in to examine the President. She refused.

"You do it," he said. "Or I'll go to the President and do it myself."

After weeks of argument, Travell had called Dr. Kraus in late September. "You are going to be a cripple if you do not exercise," said Dr.
Kraus after examining Kennedy. A blunt little Austrian, once the trainer
of that country's Olympic ski team, he told Kennedy that his back
muscles would get stiffer and stiffer, and that his abdominal muscles,
the back's principal support, were atrophying and almost useless. He
recommended three hour-long therapy-and-exercise sessions a week.

The President did not want to do that. He was afraid White House
reporters would see Kraus coming and going and begin writing about
his health problems.

"It's your decision," Kraus said. "But you will only get worse. What
will they write then?"

Admiral Burkley had set up the little gymnasium in the basement of the White House, and Kennedy had begun gentle stretching routines there three days a week with Kraus, at first for half an hour. A new sound system pumped out the country and western music and show tunes that he liked.

At lunch one day that week, Kennedy told Arthur Krock that the Pentagon, both the Chiefs and McNamara, was pushing him to send troops into Southeast Asia—and that he would like to find a way to avoid doing that. He was thinking about writing to Khrushchev and asking him to hold back the North Vietnamese.

"The President still believes," Krock wrote in his diary, "in what he told the Senate several years ago—that United States troops should not be involved on the Asian mainland, especially in a country with the difficult terrain of Laos and inhabited by people who don't care how the East-West dispute as to freedom and self-determination was resolved. Moreover, said the President, the United States can't interfere in civil disturbances created by guerrillas, and it was hard to prove that this wasn't largely the situation in Vietnam."

Chapter 22

"Thereree have been charges," said a reporter at the President's October 11 news conference, "that we have not adequately maintained the strength or the credibility of our nuclear deterrent and that we also have not fully convinced the leaders of the Soviet Union that we are determined to meet force with force in Berlin or elsewhere. What is your reaction to those charges?"

Kennedy's reaction was to get mad. He could not seem to escape that question. Once again he went over the statistics: a 14 percent increase in defense spending; a 50 percent increase in Polaris submarine construction; a 100 percent increase in Minuteman missile production; a 50 percent increase in the number of strategic bombers on fifteen-minute alert; a 75 percent increase in troop airlift capacity; a 150 percent increase in anti-guerrilla forces; an increase in M-14 rifle production from 9,000 per month to 44,000 per month. All of that in just nine months.

"They don't get it," he said to Pierre Salinger after the session. More important, he was not sure Nikita Khrushchev got it either. The Soviet leader was still telling the world that the Soviet Union was at least as powerful militarily as the United States, using Kennedy's own words at Vienna against him, repeating the President's statements that the forces of the great powers were equal. The Americans saying "equal," the chairman said, was proof that the Soviets were actually ahead. Was

Khrushchev bluffing? Probably, but Kennedy could not be sure—and much of the world obviously believed the bluster from Moscow.

So, still peppering his staff with memos telling them to figure out a way to explain away his old "missile gap" speeches, the President decided to lay out the true extent of U.S. military superiority. He considered giving a major speech on American might, but finally concluded that the resonance of the presidential voice would make it sound like a declaration of war. Even a McNamara speech might be too much. So, he decided on the Deputy Defense Secretary, Roswell Gilpatric. It turned out that Gilpatric had a speech scheduled before the National Business Council at the Greenbriar Hotel in Hot Springs, Virginia, on October 21—a date that coincided with the fifth day of the Twenty-Second Communist Party Congress in Moscow, a forum Khrushchev was certain to use to trumpet Soviet strength and achievements. Then Kennedy appointed himself Gilpatric's editor, going through the text line by line and number by number.

The Soviet leader did precisely what Kennedy thought he would do in his opening speech to the Congress on October 17. He announced that the Soviet Union was about to explode the largest bomb in the history of the world, a 50-megaton thermonuclear device. But then, near the end of the speech, after talking for more than five hours straight, Khrushchev shocked the Communist leaders and most of the world:

"Recently, while attending the United Nations General Assembly, Comrade Gromyko had talks with the Secretary of State and the President of the United States. He also had talks with the Minister of Foreign Affairs and the Prime Minister of England. These talks left us with the impression that the Western powers were showing a certain understanding of the German problem and the question of West Berlin on a mutually acceptable basis. . . .

"Some Western spokesmen say that our proposals that a German peace treaty be concluded this year are an ultimatum. But this is an erroneous contention. . . . The question of a time limit for the signing of a German peace treaty will not be so important if the Western powers show a readiness to settle the German problem; we shall not in that case absolutely insist on signing the peace treaty before December 31, 1961."

The winter, it seemed, would not be so cold. Kennedy was one of the least surprised men in Washington, because of the September 29 letter from Khrushchev, and because he had been right when he had decided better a wall than a war. Rusk gave the formal U.S. response, opening a news conference the morning after with a smile, saying: "I know that you will wish to know whether I have any comments on Chairman Khrushchev's speech of yesterday." He did, focusing on the removal of the Berlin deadline, saying that it would reduce Soviet-American tensions. For the moment, except for a routine condemnation of plans for the 50-megaton atmospheric test, the Americans ignored the rest of Khrushchev's bombast. The President decided, though, that Gilpatric should go ahead with his speech on U.S. sabers, not quite rattling them but describing them in detail.

"Our confidence in our ability to deter Communist action, or resist Communist blackmail, is based on a sober appreciation of the relative military power of the two sides," Gilpatric said at Hot Springs.

"The fact is that this nation has nuclear retaliatory force of such lethal power that an enemy move which brought it into play would be an act of self-destruction on his part. The U.S. has today hundreds of manned intercontinental bombers capable of reaching the Soviet Union, including six hundred heavy bombers and many more medium bombers equally capable of intercontinental operations because of our highly developed in-flight re-fueling techniques and world-wide base structure. The U.S. also has six Polaris submarines at sea carrying a total of 96 missiles, and dozens of intercontinental ballistic missiles. Our carrier strike forces and land-based theater forces could deliver additional hundreds of megatons. The total number of our nuclear delivery vehicles, tactical as well as strategic, is in the tens of thousands; and, of course, we have more than one warhead for each vehicle. . . .

"Our forces are so deployed and protected that a sneak attack could not effectively disarm us. . . . In short, we have a second strike capability which is at least as extensive as what the Soviets can deliver by striking first. Therefore, we are confident that the Soviets will not provoke a major nuclear conflict. . . .

"The Iron Curtain is not so impenetrable as to force us to accept at face value the Kremlin's boasts," Gilpatric concluded. "The United States does not intend to be defeated."

Chairman Khrushchev saw the full text of the Gilpatric speech on Sunday, October 22, at the Party Congress in Moscow. He decided immediately that the Americans had to be answered and delegated that job to his defense minister, Marshal Rodion Malinovsky, a comrade from the Battle of Stalingrad. The Soviet marshal did so within hours, repeating but not challenging Gilpatric's statistics of destruction, then stating: "The imperialist powers are hatching mad plans of armed attack on the Soviet Union. . . . What is there to say to this petty speech? Only one thing: The threat does not frighten us!"

As Malinovsky spoke, the Soviets detonated a 30-megaton thermonuclear device in Siberia. But the words from Washington seemed to have more impact than the explosion. Not only had Kennedy set the record straight and called Khrushchev's bluff, he had finally hit where the Soviet leader was most vulnerable—on China. The Gilpatric speech had dismissed the current Soviet test series as an attempt to impress, not the United States, but Communist China. It had taken the President and most of the foreign policy establishment of the United States a long time to figure out that communism was not as monolithic as American Cold War rhetoric. The Soviet Union and the People's Republic of China had been drawing apart in a manner similar to, if much more important than, the tense separation between the United States and France. And for some of the same reasons. The cliché of the "Sino-Soviet bloc" had been evolving into the "Sino-Soviet split" ever since the late 1950s when the Soviets refused to give nuclear technology to the Chinese, just as the United States had tried to prevent or slow down French development of nuclear weapons. Both the United States and the USSR preferred their allies gathered under a single nuclear umbrella—with the superpowers holding the two umbrellas.

As if to make that point, the chief Chinese delegate to the Congress, Premier Chou En-lai, left Moscow as Malinovsky spoke. Chou, in effect, was walking out on Khrushchev's party because of the chairman's attacks on China's ideological allies, the hard-line Stalinist leaders of Albania.

That night, Sunday, October 22, as the world realized the Soviets and the Americans were stepping back a bit in Berlin, the U.S. minister in that city, Allan Lightner, and his wife, decided to go to East Berlin for a performance by a visiting Czechoslovakian opera company. As he passed through the wall at Checkpoint Charlie on Friedrichstrasse, the minister was stopped by East German VOPOs demanding to see his papers. The VOPOs had harassed allied officials before and Lightner followed standard procedure—refusing to accept East German authority and asking to see a Soviet officer. This time, though, the VOPOs refused to call in the Soviets. After about forty minutes of sitting there, Lightner gunned his engine and tried to race through the barriers. The East Germans surrounded him.

Just then four U.S. M-48 tanks clanked up to Checkpoint Charlie, followed by two armored personnel carriers carrying men of the Second Battle Group. That was standard procedure, too. After another half hour, under orders from General Clay, eight U.S. soldiers, bayonets fixed, marched the few yards into East Berlin and took up positions around Lightner's car. The East Germans stepped back and with the soldiers walking alongside, Lightner drove slowly up the Friedrichstrasse for a block on the Communist side, then turned around and drove back into West Berlin. Then he turned around and did the same thing again, asserting U.S. access rights with the American soldiers still walking alongside. By then word had gotten back to Washington, where it was still Sunday morning.

"What's he doing?" President Kennedy said angrily to Rusk, once again envisioning war by miscalculation. The Secretary of State said he did not believe there was any problem greater than an overzealous VOPO officer. No Soviets had been involved. "Yeah?" Kennedy grumbled. "We didn't send him to Berlin to go to the opera."

Kennedy called Clay, officially the "Personal Representative of the President," resident full time in Berlin. The general said he was personally giving the orders, and that the United States would have no credibility in Berlin, Germany, or the world if he backed down in the face of East German pretensions. The President's only choice, then, was to go along with his man or order him to back down—an order that almost certainly meant that Clay would quit and raise hell back in the United States. Kennedy wished him luck.

General Clay had arrived back in Berlin late in September. In case there was anyone who did not notice, one of the first things he had done was try to drive into an exclave called Steinstücken, a part of West Berlin that was actually within the city limits of East Berlin, and therefore on the wrong side of the Wall. VOPO guards stopped his car. Clay turned around, drove back into West Berlin, got into a helicopter, and flew over the Wall to Steinstücken, where the 180 trapped West Berliners ran from their houses cheering *"Der Clay."*

He stepped out of the copter and announced that a contingent of U.S. Military Police would be stationed in the exclave until a road was opened to allow them to go back and forth to West Berlin. Back on the other side of the Wall, he ordered Army Engineers to build a replica of the Wall in a remote part of one of the city's forests. U.S. tanks with bulldozer fronts were practicing knocking it down when General Bruce Clarke, the commander of all U.S. troops in Europe, discovered it and ordered his men to knock it down and leave it down. "Take your cotton-picking hands off my troops," said General Clarke, looking at Clay's red telephone to the White House. "If you don't like that, call the President and see what he says."

Clay did not do that and no one else told Kennedy about Clay's secret wall. But the East Germans and the Soviets knew about it, and they thought the bulldozer tanks might soon be coming their way.

On Wednesday morning, October 25, Clay ordered another carload of U.S. diplomats into East Berlin, testing whether the VOPOs were going back to the old system of waving through cars with official American occupation license plates. The East Germans stopped the car. Within a few minutes, Clay called ten M-48 tanks to the Friedrichstrasse checkpoint, Checkpoint Charlie, with their guns pointed at the VOPOs inspection offices. The tanks had bulldozer fronts. Three U.S. jeeps, each carrying four soldiers with fixed bayonets, came through the checkpoint, formed up in front and behind the diplomat's car, and drove up the Friedrichstrasse without incident. The East Germans and a half dozen Soviet officers just watched.

The next day, Thursday, October 26, thirty-three Soviet tanks, with markings and insignia painted over, came into East Berlin and arranged themselves in the streets off the Friedrichstrasse. On Friday, another official U.S. car, carrying civilians, was stopped by the VOPOs. The arguments began again—and ten of the Soviet tanks pulled up to their side of Checkpoint Charlie, confronting the ten American tanks thirty yards away. It was the first nuclear-age American-Soviet confrontation: soldiers and weapons eyeball to eyeball.

Clay picked up the telephone at his side in the map room of American occupation headquarters, on a street named Clayallee in honor of his heroics of 1948.

"How are things up there?" It was the President.

"Fine," Clay said. "We're equal. We have ten tanks there.

"Mr. President," he said suddenly, looking at a piece of paper handed to him, "I'll have to rectify that statement. The Russians have brought up twenty more tanks. This is proof of the accuracy of their information. That is the number of tanks we have in Berlin. Thirty. So we'll bring up our remaining tanks as well."

"Are you nervous?" Kennedy asked.

"Nervous? No, we're not nervous here. If anybody's nervous, Mr. President, it will probably be people in Washington."

"Well," Kennedy said, "there may well be a lot of nervous people around here, but I'm not one of them."

The nation *was* nervous. "What to Do in Case of War" was the cover line of the current issue of *Nation's Business*. "Examine the Methods of Transportation Your Company Uses. Would a War-caused Oil Shortage Cripple Your Operations?" The *New Republic,* a voice of Democratic liberalism, put Nikita Khrushchev on its cover with a Hitler mustache painted on his face. Inside, Sidney Hyman wrote that "the timing required of the President in the days immediately ahead could involve the end of man's time on earth."

In the White House, many believed something like that—and some thought Kennedy had unwillingly and unwittingly put the question of war and peace into the hands of a man he barely knew. Clay was taking hard-line chances with the peace of the world, willing to risk most anything to crush the Soviets. If Kennedy was in fact less nervous than those around him, it was because he believed he had finally established one-on-one contact with Khrushchev. He told his brother Robert Kennedy to call in Georgi Bolshakov and make a deal with Khrushchev: You take yours out within the next twenty-four hours and mine will be gone thirty minutes later.

Bolshakov said he would get the message to Moscow as quickly as he could, but he could promise nothing. "I only know what I'm told to know," he told Robert Kennedy, and the President's brother responded in kind. "Don't ask me what I think, Georgi. I just deliver the messages to my brother and he doesn't tell me what he does with them."

Twenty hours later, on the morning of October 28, the Soviet tanks backed off. Khrushchev had given the order to Marshal Ivan Koniev, the Russian hero called out of retirement in a move to counter Clay's appointment. Koniev's subordinates balked, not wanting to hand the Americans a victory. Move the tanks out of sight from the west, behind buildings on side streets, the marshal ordered. Khrushchev had told him the U.S. tanks would withdraw within the hour. "I guarantee it," the premier had said. "This is not worth a war." And it happened just that way. There was not going to be a peace treaty or a war over Berlin.

On the last day of October, the Soviets detonated their 50-megaton bomb. Western calculations put the actual strength of the blast as the equivalent of more than 60 megatons. The test provided a propaganda harvest for the West as the United Nations and neutral leaders led by Nehru of India protested the horrors of radioactive fallout.

Two days later, on November 2, at a meeting of the National Security Council at the White House, McNamara recommended that U.S. atmospheric tests begin as soon as possible. "If we don't," he said, "the Soviets will catch us sooner or later." Edward R. Murrow at USIA wanted the opposite. He said world anger at the Soviets would be even more intense if Kennedy announced that the United States had no intention of doing the same thing.

"That's not possible, Ed," Kennedy said.

That day, the President announced that the United States would resume atmospheric testing as soon as it was ready—probably in April of 1962—and added:

"This much can be said with certainty now: In terms of military strength, the United States would not trade places with any nation on earth. . . . The United States does not find it necessary to explode 50-megaton nuclear devices to confirm that we have many times more nuclear power than any other nation on earth and that these capabilities are deployed so as to survive any sneak attack and thus enable us to devastate any nation which initiates a nuclear attack on the United States or its Allies. . . .

"We have taken major steps in the past year to protect our lead—and we do not propose to lose it."

Chapter 23

President Kennedy had met for hours with Taylor and Rostow before they left Washington on October 17 for their inspection tour of South Vietnam. By choosing those two men, the President was making it clear that the United States had no intention of withdrawing from Southeast Asia. These were his tough guys. "The question," in Taylor's words, "was how to change a losing game and begin to win, not how to call it off."

"As we understand your position," Taylor and Rostow said in a formal memo to Kennedy, "you would wish to see every avenue of diplomacy exhausted before we accept the necessity for either positioning U.S. forces on the Southeast Asian mainland or fighting there. . . . Should we have to fight, we should use air and sea power to the maximum and engage minimum U.S. forces on the Southeast Asian mainland."

Kennedy told Taylor about his own experiences in Vietnam, which he had visited for a day in 1951 as a young congressman on an around-the-world tour. He had begun that day in Saigon with the commander of the 250,000 French troops fighting Viet Minh guerrillas. General Jean de Lattre de Tassigny had assured him that his soldiers could not lose to these natives. He had ended the evening on top of the Caravelle Hotel with a young American consular officer named Edmund Gullion. The sky around the city flashed with the usual nighttime artillery and mortar bombardment by the Viet Minh.

"What have you learned here?" Kennedy asked the diplomat.

"That in twenty years there will be no more colonies," Gullion had said. "We're going nowhere out here. The French have lost. If we come in here and do the same thing we will lose, too, for the same reason. There's no will or support for this kind of war back in Paris. The homefront is lost. The same thing would happen to us." *

In Congress, after that 1951 trip, Representative Kennedy had spoken of the $50 million a year the United States was then giving France in aid of its Vietnam operation: "We have allied ourselves to the desperate effort of a French regime to hang onto the remnants of an empire. I am frankly of the belief that no amount of American military assistance in Indochina can conquer an enemy which is everywhere and at the same time nowhere. . . . The forces of nationalism are rewriting the geopolitical map of the world."

But by 1956, Senator Kennedy had helped organize American Friends of Vietnam, saying in a speech then: "Vietnam represents the cornerstone of the Free World in Southeast Asia, the keystone to the arch, the finger in the dike. Burma, Thailand, India, Japan, the Philippines, and obviously Laos and Cambodia are among those whose security would be threatened if the Red tide of Communism overflowed into Vietnam. . . . The United States is directly responsible for this experiment—it is playing an important role in the laboratory where it is being conducted. We cannot afford to permit that experiment to fail. . . . If we are not the parents of little Vietnam, then surely we are the godparents."

Now, briefing the ten members of his group before leaving on October 17, Taylor emphasized that the President had asked for his personal views and advice. They would be consulted and could make suggestions, but it was his trip and his report. The four-star general particularly wanted to impress that on the one-star general Kennedy put on the team: Ed Lansdale. But Lansdale could not contain himself. He quickly began offering suggestions, beginning with this one: Recruit two thousand or so young veterans of Chiang Kai-shek's Nationalist Chinese Army in Taiwan, give them weapons and Vietnamese names, then grant them timber concessions in the jungle and "Let them fight their way to the trees," mopping up any Viet Cong in their way. "Human defoliation," Lansdale called it.

Taylor told Lansdale he would not be in the official meeting with President Diem. "But we're friends. . . ," said Lansdale. Taylor was talk-

---

* When they parted, Gullion asked Kennedy: "What are you going to do?" The congressman replied: "Run for senator or governor. Whatever opens up and looks good." Kennedy's trip ended in Japan, where he was hit by a 106-degree fever. He received the last rites of the Catholic Church there, but was brought home finally by his traveling companion, Robert Kennedy, then twenty-five years old. When he became President, Kennedy appointed Gullion Ambassador to the Congo.

ing to reporters when the American party arrived at Tan Son Nhut Airport on October 18. He did not see Diem's private secretary invite Lansdale to dinner that night at the Presidential Palace. Diem surprised Lansdale by saying that he wanted U.S. combat troops in Vietnam. He was not as direct the next day with Taylor, but the general got the idea. Diem said he had to reconsider his opposition to foreign troops.

"Why have you changed your mind?" Taylor asked.

"Because of Laos," Diem replied. He thought the United States had abandoned the men it supported across the border, though he did not say that to Taylor. Like European leaders, Diem had come to believe that American casualties were the best guarantee that the United States would not go home after any attack. He was telling Lansdale this time that his people needed some sign of formal commitment by the United States, a physical guarantee.

On October 25, after four days in Saigon listening to President Diem, and to ARVN generals complaining about Diem, Taylor spent most of one day flying over rice-growing areas of the Mekong Delta. The fields had been ruined by the worst flooding in years. Back in Saigon, Taylor sent an "Eyes Only" cable to Kennedy recommending that the flood be used as a pretext for sending in six to eight thousand U.S. troops. He added: "It will be necessary to include some combat troops for the protection of logistical operations and the defense of the area occupied by U.S. forces. Any troops coming to VN may expect to take casualties."

Flying home one week later, on November 1, Taylor stopped at the Philippine hill resort of Baguio. He sent two "Eyes Only for the President" cables repeating the call for troops more specifically and citing both advantages and disadvantages of the proposal:

> As an area for the operations of U.S. troops, SVN is not an excessively difficult or unpleasant place to operate. While the border areas are rugged and heavily forested, the terrain is comparable to parts of Korea where U.S. troops learned to live and work without too much effort [and] NVN is extremely vulnerable to conventional bombing. [But] if the first contingent is not enough to accomplish the necessary results, it will be difficult to resist the pressure to reinforce . . . there is no limit to our possible commitment (unless we attack the source in Hanoi).

The next day in Washington, Kennedy told Senate Majority Leader Mike Mansfield that Taylor was going to recommend sending in troops.

"South Vietnam could be a quicksand for us," said Mansfield. He wrote the President a quick note saying he could see only four possible results: "1. A fan-fare and then a retreat. 2. An indecisive and costly conflict along the Korean lines. 3. A major war with China while Russia stands aside; 4. A total world conflict."

On the other hand, Democratic Senator Stuart Symington of Missouri, who was in Saigon, cabled Kennedy at the same time to say: "It seems to me we ought to try to hold this place. Otherwise this part of the world is sure to go down the drain."

Maxwell Taylor and the other members of the commission to Vietnam reported personally to the President on November 3. He and other commission members were shown into the Oval Office at four o'clock in the afternoon, but Kennedy was late coming back from a long lunch with the president of Senegal. Taylor walked around the office, saying his daughter would ask him every detail of what it looked like. Then he sat himself down in the President's rocking chair, trying it out. That's when Kennedy walked in. Taylor snapped to attention, but his hips were too wide for the chair and it came up with him. He wriggled out of the thing and Kennedy pretended not to notice.

The title across the cover page of Taylor's report was "A Limited Partnership." He repeated his call for sending six thousand or more U.S. troops to South Vietnam, arguing: "It is evident that morale in Vietnam will rapidly crumble if the sequence of expectations set in motion by Vice President Johnson's visit and climaxed by General Taylor's mission are not soon followed by a hard U.S. commitment to the ground in Vietnam. . . . In Washington, as well, intelligence and back-up operations must be put on a quasi-wartime footing. . . . The initiative proposed here should not be undertaken unless we are prepared to deal with any escalation the communists might choose to impose.

"There is reason for confidence if the right men are sent to do the right jobs," Taylor said finally, in a phrase tailored for Kennedy. In private, the President asked Taylor and Rostow how long the Diem government could hold on without American help. He was shocked by the answer: "Three months."

Troops in and Diem out were arguments at the crux of the dialogue the President heard. "No one action, not even the removal of Diem, is the key to success in Vietnam," Taylor told Kennedy.

Rostow asked Taylor later what he thought Kennedy would do and the general answered: "I don't know. He's instinctively against introduction of U.S. forces."

The anti-Diem argument was summarized for the President by a member of the Taylor mission, William Jorden of the State Department's Policy Planning Council, who wrote:

There is near paralysis in some areas of administration. Small decisions that would be handled by minor officials in one of the ministries of most governments are taken to the Presidency. . . . A chance remark in a cafe can produce a jail sentence. Men are held indefinitely without indictment or even the placing of charges. . . . Brother Nhu holds power second only to that of Diem himself. Brother Can rules the northern provinces like an oriental satrapy from his base in Hue. Archbishop Thuc, as the President's elder [brother], is listened to respectfully by the President. . . . Madame Nhu presides over the women of South Viet Nam like an Empress. . . . Even persons long loyal to Diem and included in his official family now believe that South Viet Nam can get out of the present morass only if there is early and drastic revision at the top.

Rusk weighed in with an anti-Diem argument from Tokyo, cabling the President that he thought the South Vietnamese president was "a losing horse."

The number-three man at State, George Ball, had a different take, saying a small number of U.S. troops would have no real impact on events in Vietnam. "Taylor is wrong," he told Kennedy on November 7. Ball knew Southeast Asia relatively well. As a lawyer in private practice, he had once handled French legal matters in Indochina. Vietnam was not a small country, he said, it ran more than a thousand miles from north to south, with a population of over 30 million, more than ten times the population of Laos.

"Within five years, we'll have three hundred thousand men in the paddies and jungles and never find them again," he told the President. "That was the French experience. Vietnam is the worst possible terrain both from a physical and political point of view."

Kennedy didn't like that. "George, I always thought you were one of the brightest guys around here," he said. "But you're just crazier than hell. That just isn't going to happen."

Kennedy was touchy on Vietnam now. Former President Eisenhower had just given two foreign policy speeches, praising the administration for steadfastness in Berlin, but criticizing Kennedy on Cuba and Vietnam. "Indecision and uncertainty," said Ike. The big problem as Kennedy saw it—Vietnam as a domestic issue—was addressed by McNamara and Rusk in a joint memo analyzing Taylor's recommendations: "The loss of South Vietnam would stimulate bitter domestic controversies . . . and would be seized upon by extreme elements to divide the country and harass the Administration."

Kennedy told them to produce a working paper for a National Security Council meeting in the next few days. Then he went off to his eighteenth news conference, in the State Department Auditorium, where there was not a single question about Vietnam.

The President touched, as newspapers say, "on a wide range of concerns." He praised negotiators trying to work out an equitable trade balance with the country's second largest trading partner, Japan. The Japanese were complaining that the difference between exports and imports was running close to $1 billion a year in favor of the United States. He laughed off a question by Mae Craig, of the *Portland Press Herald* in Maine, who asked him what he was doing about campaign promises of equal rights and equal pay for women. He deftly (and untruthfully) dodged a question about his 180-degree turn on the missile gap by saying that during the campaign he was only quoting Eisenhower's concerns. But no reporter asked about Vietnam.

Three days later, on November 11, Rusk and McNamara delivered their NSC working paper, summarizing this way:

> The fall of South Vietnam to Communism would lead to the fairly rapid extension of Communist control, or complete accommodation to Communism, in the rest of mainland Southeast Asia and in Indonesia. The strategic implications worldwide, particularly in the Orient, would be extremely serious. The chances are against, probably sharply against, preventing the fall of South Viet-Nam by any measures short of the introduction of U.S. forces on a substantial scale—without serious interference with our present Berlin plans. . . . We should be prepared to introduce United States combat forces if that should become necessary for success. Dependent upon the circumstances, it may also be necessary for United States forces to strike at the source of the aggression in North Viet-Nam.

Being "prepared" was a way to meet the President's desire to blur and defer the question of combat troops. But in the end, they concluded: "We now take the decision to commit ourselves to the objective of preventing the fall of South Viet-Nam to Communism and that, in doing so, we recognize that the introduction of United States and other SEATO forces may be necessary to achieve this objective."

Kennedy crossed that out. He did not want to go that far. He received a note that same day from Averell Harriman, who was dealing with the Soviets on a Laos settlement in Geneva: "There are some indications that the Soviet Union would be interested in the establishment of a peaceful and stable situation in Southeast Asia, at least for a time." The CIA was reporting similar small hints from the Chinese and from Viet Cong sources, too. There was no doubt that keeping the Americans out was a principal priority of the North Vietnamese, and perhaps of the Soviets.

Reading Harriman's cable, Walt Rostow, who had a sense of the President's political insecurities, had a countermemo on the way to him in less than an hour: "If we postpone action in Vietnam in order to engage in talk with the Communists, the image of U.S. unwillingness to confront Communism—induced by the Laos performance—will be regarded as definitely confirmed. There will be real panic and disarray. . . . The moves we now make will be examined on both sides of the Iron Curtain with the greatest care as a measure of this Administration's intentions and determination."

Kennedy called his men together in the Cabinet Room on November 15. He sided with Taylor and McNamara—up to a point. He had effectively decided that, operationally, Vietnam was a military issue. But he was not willing to send in U.S. combat troops, he said. Not now. Not yet. He agreed to almost every other recommendation in Taylor's report. More advisers, more pressure on Diem to act less like a Mandarin emperor and more like an American-style democrat, and more helicopters flown by Americans in an attempt to gain control of South Vietnamese troop movement.

Notes on the November 15 meeting were taken for Vice President Johnson by his military aide, Colonel Harold Burris, who caught Kennedy's seeming ambivalence:

> He questioned the wisdom of involvement in Viet Nam since the basis thereof is not completely clear. By comparison he noted that Korea was a case of clear aggression. . . . The conflict in Vietnam is more obscure and less flagrant. The President then expressed his strong feeling that in such a situation the United States needs even more support of allies in such an endeavor as Vietnam in order to avoid sharp domestic partisan criticism as well as strong objections from other nations of the world. The President said that he could even make a rather strong case against intervening in an area 10,000 miles away against 16,000 guerrillas with a native army of 200,000, where millions have been spent for years with no success. . . .

The President also agreed to the use of herbicide defoliants—commercial weedkillers containing cacodylic acid and several kinds of butyl—sprayed from U.S. planes in an operation code-named "Ranch Hand." The idea was to clear underbrush within two hundred feet of roads through ambush country. Then, in a second phase—food denial—the weedkiller would be used to destroy fields of rice, manioc, corn, and sweet potatoes in Viet Cong territory. Presented with three defoliant options, Kennedy, as he almost always did, selected the compromise choice, allocating $10 million for roadside defoliation and then food denial, "with prior consideration and authorization by Washington." He bypassed the first option, a $75 million Air Force plan to kill anything green over 32,000 square miles of South Vietnam, almost half the country.

At the end of the long meeting, after hearing General Lemnitzer argue again that communism must be stopped in Vietnam or it would engulf most of Asia, Kennedy said again that he was not sure he could justify sending troops around the globe to Vietnam while there was a Communist government ninety miles offshore in Cuba. "Mr. President," Lemnitzer said, "speaking for the Joint Chiefs, we feel we should go into Cuba, too."

Kennedy's decisions that day were executed in instructions to Nolting in Saigon. He was ordered to tell Diem that the United States was prepared to join the government of South Vietnam "in a sharply increased joint effort to cope with the Viet Cong threat." The procedure outlined was a letter from Diem to Kennedy citing efforts at government reform and asking for new U.S. assistance. "The President's reply would be responsive to Diem's request...," Nolting was told. There was a catch, though. "We would expect to share in the decision-making process in the political, economic and military fields as they affected the security situation."

"If this doesn't work," Kennedy said, as he stood up to end the meeting, "perhaps we'll have to try Walt's Plan Six...." He nodded over to Rostow—the "Air Marshal," as Rostow was called, wanted to attack North Vietnam.

As a check on his tough guys, Kennedy also told John Kenneth Galbraith to take a look at Vietnam on his way back to his ambassador's post in India. Galbraith could write reports as fast, as colorful, and as certain as Rostow's. He did not disappoint, cabling the President on November 21 that troops were not the problem. Diem had "a comparatively well-equipped army with paramilitary formations numbering a quarter million men . . . facing a maximum of fifteen to eighteen thousand lightly armed men. If this were equality, the United States would hardly be safe from the Sioux.... The only solution must be to drop Diem.... While no one can promise a safe transaction we are now married to failure.... We should not be alarmed by the army as an alternative. Civilian rule is ordinarily more durable and more saleable to the world. But a change and a new start is of the essence...."

Ambassador Galbraith left a very unhappy colleague in Saigon. "Nolting while not in favor of dumping Diem," Galbraith continued, "has said that a nod from the United States would be influential." Nolting did not know that Galbraith had told Kennedy back in the White House that he should drop Nolting, too, and replace him with Averell Harriman. In his own note to Kennedy a couple of days earlier, Harriman had said: "We must make it clear to Diem that we mean business about internal reform. This will require a strong ambassador who can control all U.S. activities (political, military, economic, etc.) and who is known by Diem to have the personal intimacy and confidence of the President. . . ."

Fighting back for Taylor and those who would send in troops, Rostow read Galbraith's cable and sent Kennedy a memo on November 24: "The Viet-Nam situation confronts us with the question of whether we shall or shall not accept the mounting of a guerrilla war across a frontier as legitimate. I wish it were not so; but the New Frontier will be measured in history in part on how that challenge was met."

Rostow had done it again. "History" was a trigger word for Kennedy. Politics was a mistress, coming by every day, delightful and undemanding, but history was the goddess Kennedy pursued with notes and short calls to Sorensen or Schlesinger: "Get that down for the book." He meant the book he would write after eight years. "There are limits to the number of defeats I can defend in one twelve-month period," he had told Galbraith. "I've had the Bay of Pigs, pulling out of Laos, and I can't accept a third."

He told Rostow he did not need stacks of memos to understand political consequences, that was his business. American withdrawal and Communist triumph would destroy him and the Democratic Party in a replay of the "Who Lost China?" debate that had plagued President Truman in the early 1950s. "Diem is Diem and he's the best we've got," Kennedy told Rusk in frustration, as the South Vietnamese president began ignoring the demands of Washington.

Diem was keeping the U.S. proposals secret, saying of the American conditions that they would make him look like a stooge, handing the nationalism issue to the Communists. At the same time the press in Saigon shifted to an anti-American line, protesting U.S. pressure on Diem with headlines such as "Vietnam Not a Guinea Pig for Capitalist Imperialism to Experiment On."

Despite what he said to Taylor and Nolting, President Diem and his family seemed to have the impression that they could do whatever they wished, and that the United States would go along rather than accept the public humiliation of withdrawing. Rusk agreed that there was no turning back now for Kennedy, not after the President had decided to openly violate the Geneva Accords and their limit of 685 U.S. advisers.

"We will honor our commitments," the Secretary of State told NATO foreign ministers in Brussels, briefing them secretly on the situation in Southeast Asia. "We will not be a virgin in the Atlantic and a whore in the Pacific."

But Kennedy would not yet decide. The domestic political consequences of withdrawal were too much to risk, and he knew what would happen if he gave the military a go-ahead on combat troops. "They want a force of American troops," he told Roger Hilsman, the chief of the State Department's intelligence bureau. "They say it's necessary to restore confidence and maintain morale. But it will be just like Berlin. The troops will march in; the bands will play; the crowds will cheer; and in four days everyone will have forgotten. Then we will be told we have to send in more troops. It's like taking a drink. The effect wears off, and you have to take another."

Kennedy knew all that, but he was sipping. Public letters between the presidents were exchanged on December 15. "Vietnam is not a great power," wrote Diem. "We must have further assistance from the United States if we are to win the war now being waged against us." The President answered: "We are prepared to help the Republic of Viet-Nam to protect its people and independence. We shall promptly increase our assistance to your defense effort."

That week, two U.S. helicopter companies arrived in Vietnam, thirty-three aircraft and four hundred men. The President did not want them used in combat immediately because of ongoing negotiations over Laos. A system was put in place to allow him to make day-to-day decisions on the use of U.S. combatants without leaving a paper trail. It was outlined in a memo from one of his military advisers on December 19: "If there is no reaction from the White House, Saigon will be given an affirmative answer. Mr. Bundy is aware of this procedure which I gather is an agreed approach to avoid pinning down the President."

By the end of December, there were 2,067 American military advisers in Vietnam. On December 20, they were given the first official authorization to use their weapons—in self-defense. On December 22, 1961, Specialist 4th Class James Thomas Davis of Livingston, Tennessee, was killed in the jungle. He was the first.

Chapter 24

Sitting with President Kennedy in the Oval Office on November 3 with the other members of the Taylor mission to South Vietnam, General Edward Lansdale had thought that he would finally be going back to Saigon. President Diem, after all, had officially asked for him to serve as an adviser again and as a liaison between the two governments. He should have known better. Neither Dean Rusk nor Robert McNamara had any intention of letting him get a job that could make him more powerful than the U.S. ambassador, or the commander of the U.S. military forces in the country.

As the President ended the meeting, he turned to Lansdale and said: "Stay here a minute."

"Drop everything else you're doing," Kennedy said when they were alone. "I want you to work on Cuba."

"Get off your ass about Cuba!" Robert Kennedy shouted at Lansdale and everyone else in the room the next day, November 4. The Attorney General was the chairman of something called the "Special Group (Augmented)," which was really a White House team trying to get rid of Fidel Castro any way they could. He wanted Lansdale as his operating officer and he got him.

"The Cuban problem carries top priority in the U.S. government," Robert Kennedy said. "No time, money, effort or manpower is to be spared."

The Attorney General's own notes on November 4 said: "McNamara, Dick Bissell, Alexis Johnson, Paul Nitze, Ed Lansdale (the Ugly American). McNamara said he would make latter available for me—I assigned him to make survey of situation in Cuba—the problems and our assets. My idea is to stir things up on island with espionage, sabotage, general disorder, run & operated by Cubans themselves. . . . Do not know if we will be successful in overthrowing Castro but we have nothing to lose in my estimate."

Robert Kennedy thought the CIA and everyone else in the bureaucracies were ignoring the President on Cuba, ignoring the charge he and Maxwell Taylor had laid out in their report to his brother back on June 13 on what to do after the Bay of Pigs: "There can be no long-term living with Castro as a neighbor. His continued presence within the hemispheric community as a dangerously effective exponent of Communism and anti-Americanism constitutes a real menace capable of eventually overthrowing the elected governments in any one or more of weak Latin American republics."

On November 8, Robert Kennedy met with Tad Szulc, the *New York Times* correspondent who had unearthed the timing and details of the Bay of Pigs invasion, and asked him to come over to the White House the next day.

"Why didn't you tell me the truth about the Bay of Pigs? That it was going to be a disaster?" asked the President.

"Even if I could have gotten in here, which I couldn't, you would have had me arrested," said the reporter.

"You're probably right," said Kennedy. He laughed.

The President asked Szulc about his conversations with Castro over the years, what kind of man he was. He asked whether there was a possibility of a dialogue with the Cuban leader. Szulc did not have that much to add to what he had written—unlike politicians, reporters don't hold back the real story if they know it—and he could not figure out why he was there. Perhaps they were considering him for a job. He thought Kennedy seemed a much tougher man than the young congressman he had known years ago. "Hardened" was the word that came to mind.

"What would you think if I ordered Castro to be assassinated?" the President asked.

"I don't think that's a good idea," Szulc said. He was uncomfortable. The idea of assassination was stupid, he thought. "That would not necessarily change things in Cuba. Personally, I don't think the United States should be a party to political assassinations."

"I agree with you completely," the President said. He said he was just testing Szulc, that he too thought it was morally wrong. So did his brother, Kennedy added. He talked for quite a while about how wrong it would be.

"I'm glad you feel the same way," the President said finally to Szulc. "That's the kind of thing I'm never going to do. We can't get into that kind of thing, or we would all be targets." Back in his own office, Szulc prepared notes of the conversation, writing: "JFK said he raised the question because he was under terrific pressure from advisers (think he said intelligence people, but not positive) to okay a Castro murder, said he was resisting pressures."

Most other people in the government whose duties included Cuban affairs would have said that it was the Kennedys who were putting pressure on them about getting rid of Castro. "Bobby is a wild man on this," said Richard Bissell, who was still running CIA covert operations eight months after the Bay of Pigs. And Szulc was not the first person the President had asked about an assassination. Even before the April invasion, Kennedy had asked the same questions of his friend George Smathers, a senator from Florida whose constituents included more than one hundred thousand Cuban exiles. Kennedy had said the job would be easy but he wondered what would happen next. Smathers answered that if the United States got caught, there would be trouble all over Latin America.

The job was not easy. If it were, Castro might have been dead before Kennedy took office. The CIA had been working on assassination plots and sabotage in Cuba since at least December 1959. A dozen plots involved Cuban politicians, American gangsters, and anyone else who had ended up losers after Fidel Castro had overthrown Fulgencio Batista on New Year's Day, 1959, and had begun expropriating the property of U.S. citizens, including the casinos owned by big-name criminals. Shortly after Kennedy was inaugurated, Bissell supervised a project code-named "ZR/RIFLE" to develop a "stand-by assassination capability," run by a CIA agent as famous as Lansdale. That was William Harvey, whose exploits included Operation Prince, a tunnel from West Berlin into the central switching station of the East Berlin telephone system, tapping every call.

The Kennedy pressure on the CIA and other agencies was mostly verbal. There was a real effort to keep orders and intent out of the official record. National Security Action Memorandum 100 on October 5, under the title "Contingency Planning for Cuba," consisted of only twenty words: "In confirmation of oral instructions conveyed to Assistant Secretary of State Woodward, a plan is desired for the indicated contingency."

The "contingency" was the assassination of Castro. "A contingency plan in connection with the possible removal of Castro from the Cuban scene," was the wording in the minutes of a Cuban Special Group meeting. Maxwell Taylor told a staff member that in transmitting information on NSAM-100 he preferred that "the President's interest in this matter not be mentioned."

The question, though, was still: What would be accomplished by killing Castro? "The Situation and Prospects in Cuba" which had been prepared by the CIA, also on October 5, concluded that assassination of the leader might actually strengthen Cuban Communists: "His loss now, by assassination or by natural causes, would have an unsettling effect, but would almost certainly not prove fatal to the regime. . . . Principal surviving leaders would probably rally together in the face of a common danger."

In public as in private, the President attempted to distance himself from assassination talk, which was common conversation, not only in the White House but in newspapers and at Georgetown dinner parties. On November 16, six weeks after signing NSAM-100, Kennedy made a speech at the University of Washington in Seattle, saying for the record: "We cannot, as a free nation, compete with our adversaries in tactics of terror, assassination, false promises, counterfeit mobs and crises." But moments later in that speech, he repeated the frustration that regularly moved him to secretly promote some of those tactics: "We possess weapons of tremendous power—but they are least effective in combatting the weapons most often used by freedom's foes: subversion, infiltration, guerrilla warfare, civil disorder."

From Seattle, the President flew to Arizona for some more speechmaking and then on to Bonham, Texas, for the funeral of Speaker Sam Rayburn on November 18. That night he flew to Los Angeles, making another speech, and rendezvousing briefly with Judith Campbell.

While Kennedy was in the West, the United States closed the books on the assassination of President Trujillo of the Dominican Republic, who had been murdered on May 30 with guns supplied by the CIA. The late dictator's son, Ramfis Trujillo, had left the country after murdering six of the men involved in the assassination. They had been taken from prison and he had shot them himself, then left for exile in Paris. Two of his uncles, Petan and Hector Trujillo, had moved into the National Palace, ready to seize power from the elected president Joaquín Balaguer, who was backed by the United States. On November 19, they woke to see two U.S. aircraft carriers, the *Valley Forge* and the *Franklin D. Roosevelt*, and a missile cruiser, the *Little Rock*, riding three miles outside the harbor. The U.S. consul, John Calvin Hill, arrived to give the Trujillo brothers a choice dictated by the U.S. President: Leave now or the U.S. Marines will land. They were put on a chartered Pan American plane and taken to exile in Florida.

On November 30, the President sent a memo to Secretary of State Rusk, ordering him to "Use our available assets to help Cuba overthrow the Communist regime." That day he officially appointed Lansdale as executive director of the Special Group (Augmented), "The Cuba Project," run by Robert Kennedy, with an action arm called "Operation Mouse."

"We are in a combat situation. We have been given full command . . . putting American genius to work," said Lansdale, beginning the work of recycling ideas he had tried in the Philippines and Vietnam, coming up with idea after idea, including a covert campaign to convince Cuban Catholics that there would be a second coming of Jesus Christ on their island, but only if Castro were removed.

The President himself was focused on Latin America again a month later, but it was still as if all of Central America and South America, 200 million people, were visible only over the shoulders of the military fatigues Castro wore most of the time. On December 16, Kennedy flew to Bogotá, Colombia, and then on to Caracas, Venezuela—choosing two countries with elected presidents, Alberto Lleras Camargo and Romulo Betancourt—to proclaim again the high goals of the Alliance for Progress. The Secret Service, responsible for protecting the President, and the CIA had tried to persuade Kennedy to cancel the trip, reminding him, as if he did not remember himself, that Vice President Nixon had been stoned by angry mobs in Caracas only two years earlier. "I'll go," Kennedy had said, shrugging his shoulders.

As Air Force One landed in Caracas and the pilot said the local temperature was in the eighties, Kennedy told his Air Force attaché, General Godfrey McHugh, who was responsible for many of his personal arrangements, that next time he better get it right; the suit he was wearing was too heavy for the heat. Then he turned to Richard Goodwin, who had argued for the trip. "Well, Dick, if this doesn't work out, you might as well keep going South."

It worked out far beyond anyone's imagination. Diplomats said they had never seen anything quite like it. The most powerful man in the world was young; he was Catholic; he had a dark and beautiful wife who spoke Spanish to the crowds. And he was there. Anything seemed possible. "Do you know why those workers and campesinos are cheering you like that?" President Camargo asked as Kennedy's open car inched through ecstatic crowds in Bogotá. "It's because they believe you are on their side."

So did Kennedy.

"We have made many mistakes in our relations with Latin America," he said that night, promising a new day. "The leaders of Latin America, the industrialists and the landowners are, I am sure, also ready to admit past mistakes and accept new responsibilities."

Kennedy was deluding himself and millions of other people on what the United States wanted, and would accept, south of the Rio Grande. The real goal, sometimes the only goal, was stopping Castro and communism. Shortly before the President decided to go south himself, Cheddi Jagan, a dentist trained in Chicago, had been elected prime minister of Guyana, a tiny country with a population of 600,000 that had been British Guiana on the north coast of South America. A month or so later Jagan was in Washington, seeking $40 million in U.S. foreign aid. Coming to Kennedy was part of the ritual followed by new leaders in 1961—a year in which thirty-three new countries were created as European colonialism collapsed around the world. A flag, a visit to Washington, a steel mill from the Soviets, were the symbols of sovereignty. The State Department cut down Jagan's request, recommending $5 million in aid for Guyana. Kennedy agreed and a meeting between the two presidents was scheduled for a Wednesday.

On the Sunday morning before they were to meet for the first time, the President caught the last half of Jagan's interview on "Meet the Press"—and he didn't like what he heard. The Guyanan said he was a Marxist but not a Communist, that like President Kennedy he admired the British socialist Harold Laski. But Jagan refused several obvious invitations to criticize the Soviet Union. Kennedy picked up the phone and called Rusk, saying: "Hold the aid until after I talk to him."*

Kennedy told Jagan that he was not against socialism and he was not intent on forcing private enterprise on nations that did not want it. "We consider ourselves pragmatists," he said. But in Latin America, Kennedy's pragmatism focused on finding practical ways to get rid of Communists or anyone who looked or sounded anything like one. Before he had left for Bogotá and Caracas, he had ordered McNamara to set up the first of his secret Police Academies on U.S. Army property in the Panama Canal Zone. The project to train South American and Central American police forces in riot control and intelligence and interrogation techniques was code-named "1290-D." "We're going to get control of the streets away from the communists down there," said Robert Kennedy, the real force behind the academies. "One or two good men, trained properly, can make the difference."

---

* Kennedy did not like what he heard then, either, and later approved a covert program channeling $1 million through the AFL-CIO to Guyanan labor unions to overthrow Jagan.

"Gestapo stuff," thought Robert Amory, a CIA liaison to 1290-D. He did not say that out loud, of course. The Attorney General was running these operations day to day, and it was bureaucratically assumed that his orders came from his brother.

The president of Argentina, Arturo Frondizi, the most pro-American leader that country had ever elected, told Kennedy during a visit to Palm Beach after the President returned from Caracas: "You must understand that Castro is just a representative of the illness of poverty and previous repression."

"Yes," Kennedy answered. He might have said the same thing himself before he was President. "But he is undermining other countries that are trying to get on their feet. We must stop him."

The President himself was looking pretty good. The foreigners who had cheered him were probably the same people who had stoned Vice President Nixon in 1958, and he was holding his own and then some at home after a year with far more trouble than achievement. His approval rating in the national Gallup Poll was at 77 percent. In an odd but significant memory trick of democracy, the *San Francisco Chronicle*'s year-end poll of Californians showed that when asked for whom they voted the year before, 59 percent of the respondents answered, "Kennedy," to 32 percent who said, "Nixon." Actually, Nixon had won California in 1960.

Kennedy's problems were in the House of Representatives, where Southern Democrats held the balance of power and were almost unanimously opposed to the agenda of Northern liberals, the basic national Democratic Party platform, which included increased foreign aid, civil rights, federal aid to education and medical care for the aged. "It's just hell being a Southern Conservative Democrat with a left-wing Democrat as President," was the answer one House member gave on a survey of congressional attitudes conducted by *U.S. News & World Report* after the end of the first session of the 87th Congress.

It was hell for Kennedy, too, who was considered a left-winger only in the deepest South. The Democrats had lost twenty-three House seats with Kennedy at the top of the ticket. And 303 of the House's 435 members had received more votes in 1960 than John Kennedy in their home districts. They thought they had a better idea of what their people wanted than did the President from Boston.

Kennedy's first congressional victory, the expansion of the House Rules Committee, had not changed such hard realities of Congress. The old alliance between Southern Democrats and Republicans was still the working majority in the entire House. The only Kennedy bills of importance they supported were the military appropriations bill and a

$6 billion moderate- and low-income housing bill that represented new federal money going into most districts across the country.

The southerners and other conservatives in both parties were almost unanimously opposed to civil rights legislation. They did not even want to talk about it, and Kennedy had dealt with that by not proposing any. Nor did he make good on a campaign promise to end racial segregation in new federal housing with "a stroke of the pen"—by signing anexecutive order. On November 22, he had met with the Civil Rights Commission and assured them he was just about ready to sign the order. At least that's what Father Hesburgh and the five other members of the commission had thought after the meeting. Kennedy had told him he planned to work on it over Thanksgiving weekend. In fact, up in Hyannis Port that Saturday, the President asked Sorensen what he was thinking about when he wrote that promise into a campaign speech.

"It wasn't me," Sorensen said.

"Oh, I guess nobody wrote it," Kennedy replied.

He signed nothing, talking instead about the problems he already had with the southerners in Congress, problems he expected to get worse after Rayburn's death. The new Speaker, John McCormack, was from Massachusetts, but he was not particularly close to the Kennedys, nor did he have much sway over the southerners.

On civil rights, Kennedy was working from a long options memo prepared for him by Sorensen and Assistant Attorney General Lee White. It was a list of thirty presidential actions and possible consequences shown in separate columns:

Require desegregation in schools receiving aid under impacted-area program.	Larry O'Brien's people believe this would doom aid-to-education legislation. HEW ready to explore this, but leery of acting now.
Prohibit discrimination in direct Federal Housing programs: Public Housing, Urban Renewal, and VA direct loans. Also any lending companies who discriminate would lose the right to guarantees of their loans by VA, FHA, and Farmers Home Adm.	Civil Rights commission recommended including banks insured by FDIC. . . . Sen. Sparkman and Cong. Rains are, of course, strongly opposed to any Housing order. And quite clearly the bill to create Dept. of Urban Affairs would be lost if order issued.

In a separate memo to the President on desegregating National Guard units, the Defense Department said: "It is anticipated that forced integration of National Guard units would result in some or all of the Southern states either deactivating units or in states rejecting Federal funds and equipment. . . . It also must be noted that action of this type will place the Department in a difficult position with Congress. The chairman and the ranking members of the Armed Services Committees in both houses are from Southern states, as are the key members of the Appropriations Committees. . . ."

Kennedy reacted to that as most politicians would. He decided not to decide. There was no point in losing and making enemies in the process. "First things first," Sorensen told someone who asked about inaction on civil rights. "He concentrates on what he has to concentrate on. There's no reflection and no torment."

Timing was all. And civil rights and Congress were not the President's biggest political problem by any means—or so he thought. Kennedy's real political troubles, as he saw them, both foreign and domestic, centered on whether he was tough enough with the Russians and their friends in Cuba. In November, during a series of lunches with newspaper executives from around the country, he had had to sit still when the publisher of the *Dallas Morning News,* E. M. Dealey, said: "We need a man on horseback to lead this nation, and many people in Texas think that you are riding Caroline's bicycle."

"I'm just as tough as you are, Mr. Dealey," Kennedy had responded, as eighteen other publishers sat there in embarrassment. "I have the responsibility for the lives of 180 million Americans, which you have not . . . and I didn't get elected by arriving at soft judgments."

But there was trouble just then with one of his most visible symbols of toughness. "Civil Defense is rapidly blossoming into our number one political headache, alienating those who believe we're doing too much or too little," Ted Sorensen told the President in a memo, after Congress had appropriated $207 million for the program. "The fatality level from a major nuclear attack will be distressingly high even in the event of a massive shelter program . . . and it will neither deflect an attack by our enemies (who are influenced by the vulnerability of our retaliatory force, not the invulnerability of our citizens), nor will it help the President feel freer to engage in a course leading to a nuclear exchange. On the contrary, it may only spur the enemy into developing even more destructive weapons."

The most prolific of Kennedy's academics, Galbraith and Schlesinger, offered their thoughts in long memos to the President after seeing a draft copy of a proposed government booklet entitled "Fallout Protection." Galbraith wrote that "the present pamphlet is a design for saving Republicans and sacrificing Democrats. These are the people who have individual houses with basements. . . . There is no design for civilians who live in three-deckers, tenements, or low cost apartments. . . ."

Schlesinger said he still thought civil defense was a great way to enlist civilians in the Cold War, but that the nation was getting crazy:

> It is an invitation to barbarism. It has already led to the divisive and degrading debate over a shelter-owner's right to murder neighbors seeking entrance to his shelter. . . . The Civil Defense Co-ordinator of Riverside County, California, has warned people to arm themselves in order to save their community from refugees fleeing a bombed Los Angeles. . . . The CD pamphlet distributed door-to-door by Cub Scouts in Nutley, N.J., says: "The Civil Defense Organization is the most obvious and most opportune instrument for recording each individual's committed stand on the question of appeasement or resistance to active Party-line Communism. Either you belong now—committed to your nation's defense—or you do not belong."

And for those defeatists who argued that shelters would not change the fact that the world would be destroyed, Adam Yarmolinsky, an assistant to Secretary McNamara, told an interviewer: "It would be a different world, but no more hostile than the one faced by Robinson Crusoe when he emerged from his shipwreck."

At the end of his South American trip, the President flew from Bogotá to Palm Beach, arriving on December 18. Both his wife and his father were there, and he relaxed for a day, flying back to Washington on the morning of the 19th. He was back at the White House by nine-fifteen the following morning and had just finished his exercises and a National Security Council meeting when he was called from the Cabinet Room for a telephone call from Robert Kennedy. Their father had collapsed on the golf course at the Palm Beach Country Club. Joseph Kennedy was seventy-three, and he had suffered a massive stroke. The last rites of the Catholic Church had already been administered by a priest at St. Mary's Hospital. The President flew down late that afternoon, but it was almost forty-eight hours before his father even seemed to recognize him.

He stayed a day in Palm Beach this time, then flew to Bermuda for a day-long conference with Harold Macmillan. The President needed a site for atmospheric tests and the British had one, Christmas Island, an uninhabited reef in the Pacific. Kennedy pressured Macmillan to allow U.S. testing there in exchange for allowing British underground tests in Nevada of warheads for a new air-to-ground missile being developed by the United States for the British. "Skybolt" was designed to turn Royal Air Force bombers into missile launchers, a cheap way for Great Britain to upgrade its nuclear capability. Macmillan, who was more opposed to new testing than any other world leader, resisted, saying he had to take the matter up in Cabinet.

The two Anglo-Saxons, as de Gaulle called them, were becoming friends against all odds. In his diary that night, Macmillan, who was twenty-three years older than Kennedy, wrote:

> He is courteous, amusing, and likes jokes or a neat turn of phrase. . . .
> There is a marked contrast between President Kennedy "in action" on a specific issue (e.g., Congo, West Irian, Ghana), and his attitude to larger issues (the nuclear war, the struggle between East and West, Capitalism and Communism, etc.). In the first, he is an extraordinarily quick and effective operator—a born "politician" (not in a pejorative sense). On the wider issues, he seems rather lost. . . .
> In health, I thought the President *not* in good shape. His back is hurting. He can not sit long without pain. . . .

Flying back to Palm Beach, Kennedy began a routine of seeing his father twice a day at St. Mary's, but then his back went out completely and he was in bed again, surrounded by his doctors—Burkley, Travell, Kraus, and Preston A. Wade, who had performed his 1954 back operation. The surgeon agreed with Burkley that their patient needed more exercise and less medication.

Kraus looked at Travell. He thought that she had tried, yet again, to keep him away from this meeting.

"I will not treat this patient, if she touches him again," he said, glaring at Travell. "Even once."

The President nodded.

From then on, Dr. Travell administered procaine shots only when she was authorized by Burkley or Kraus. "You understand?" Burkley told her. "You keep your hands off the President."

Kennedy took the exercises more seriously after that, going through the routine five times a week with Navy therapists. Secret Service technicians installed a red telephone in Kraus's New York office and one in his car for emergencies—and then rigged the instruments with scrambling devices to prevent tapping or eavesdropping after Kraus's offices in New York were broken into in what seemed to be a search for Kennedy's records. The same thing had happened to Dr. Travell and to another of Kennedy's physicians, Dr. Eugene Cohen, during the 1960 campaign. Robert Kennedy, for one, rejected the President's notion that the break-ins were the work of Republicans or Soviet spies. He had become convinced they were the work of J. Edgar Hoover's FBI.

It had been an amazing year: the Bay of Pigs, the Freedom Rides, the Vienna summit, the Berlin Wall, the escalation in Vietnam. Ted Sorensen told Kennedy during the last week of 1961 that a couple of reporters had talked about writing books on the Year of the New Frontier. The President looked at him and said: "Who would want to read a book on disasters?"

"Sure it's a big job," he had said in an interview at the end of 1960, before he had taken office. "But I don't know anybody who can do it any better than I can. Besides, the pay is pretty good." At the last National Security Council meeting of 1961, the President began by opening the agenda folder and reading down a list of problems. He said with a small smile, "Now, let's see, did we inherit these, or are these our own?"

Chapter 25

"Strengthening the Economy" was the opening theme of Kennedy's State of the Union message on January 11, 1962. "The task must begin at home. For if we cannot fulfill our own ideals here, we cannot expect others to accept them." He called the Cold War "a global civil war." He framed his domestic proposals in the context of competition with the Soviet Union, even in his own personal competition with the leader of the Soviets:

"At home, we began the year in the valley of recession; we completed it on the high road of recovery and growth. . . . At year's end the economy which Mr. Khrushchev once called a 'stumbling horse' was racing to new records in consumer spending, labor income and industrial production. . . . Let us not forget that we have suffered three recessions in the last seven years. The time to repair the roof is when the sun is shining. We need Presidential standby authority, subject to Congressional veto, to adjust personal income taxes downward . . . to slow down an economic decline before it has dragged us all down. . . .

"We can show the whole world that a free economy need not be an unstable economy, that a free economy need not leave men unemployed. . . . Above all, if we are to pay for our commitments abroad, we must expand our exports. . . ."

Kennedy ended exactly where he had begun a year before, restating the world view of his Inaugural Address: "It is the fate of this generation

—of you in the Congress and of me as President—to live with a struggle we did not start, in a world we did not make. But the pressures of life are not always distributed by choice. And while no nation has ever faced such a challenge, no nation has ever been so ready to seize the burden and the glory of freedom."

On January 17 and 18, the President presided over two days of meetings with the senators and representatives of his party. The agenda of those sessions was politics: the selling of the achievements of the first year of his presidency, and preparations for what he expected to be the focus and the most important event of his second year—the midterm congressional elections on November 6, 1962.

He began by talking about Gallup polls showing strong public approval of him and of a couple of administration initiatives. Seventy-six percent of respondents favored the higher minimum wage enacted in March of 1961, and 71 percent approved of the Peace Corps, created in February 1961. Asked how they would vote if the Kennedy-Nixon election were held now, 62 percent of the respondents said they would vote for Kennedy, compared with just under 50 percent who actually did so on November 8, 1960.

"This year's program will be popular, too," Kennedy told them. Sixty-seven percent of respondents favored an increase in Social Security taxes to pay for subsidized medical care for the elderly. There was also high support for federal aid to education, partly in response to the fact that 71 percent of Gallup's Americans expected their children to go to college, though 49 percent had no savings to pay tuitions.

Six of the eight items the President discussed involved domestic issues rather than foreign situations. He concentrated on the bread-and-butter concerns of Americans and American politicians in election years. But that 6-to-2 ratio was almost the exact opposite of the way he had spent his time during his first year in the White House. His days had been spent on foreign affairs and matters of national security. Periodically, he would tell Sorensen and O'Donnell that they had to keep people away from him so that he could clear his desk and concentrate on a domestic agenda. But it never happened. Larry O'Brien and the others who worked Capitol Hill would sometimes commiserate with each other about what happened after the helicopter took off from the White House lawn on Friday afternoons. There would be a weekend of charming pictures of the President and his young family, sailing, running along the beach, petting Caroline's pony Macaroni, and then a week of grumbling from senators and congressmen who wanted to be petted, too.

So these meetings were for political stroking. Most of the members bored Kennedy, as they had even when he was one of them. Whenever he could get away with it, Kennedy shrugged off congressional concerns, and most domestic issues, too, handing them off to Sorensen and O'Brien and to Sorensen's assistant, Myer Feldman, who was charged with almost all domestic matters, except for civil rights and major economic issues.

"If Mike Feldman is a crook, we're all in big trouble," Kennedy once said, as he walked away from a paper stack of domestic pleas and complaints.

Sorensen had prepared a briefing paper for the congressional meetings, laying out the political line the President was selling, beginning with a negative achievement which underlined just how defensive he was about the "soft on Communism" charges that Republicans had been throwing at Democrats since the 1950s:

"1. There has been no finding of communism or corruption in government. . . . 2. There has been no serious inflation, and without controls. . . . 3. Budget balances (for fiscal 1963). . . . 4. No Korean-type war. . . . 5. No appeasement. Increased Ike's defense budget 15%. . . . 6. Religion and Youth no longer issues. . . . 7. Prosperity returning. . . . 8. Farmers happier."

Happy farmers were not a principal Kennedy goal. "Did you understand anything I was saying? I sure didn't," he had asked Feldman, after his first agricultural speech of the 1960 campaign. And after his last, at the South Dakota State Fair, he had remarked to Richard Goodwin: "Well, that's over. Fuck the farmers after November."

He soon understood that, as President, his voice was the most important in the country on domestic issues, but he had to negotiate endlessly on each of them—with business, with labor, with governors, and particularly with Congress. In foreign affairs, especially national security affairs, he was seldom challenged. Americans tended to suspend disbelief when their President spoke about the world. On foreign policy, the President often was, for all practical purposes, the United States of America.

But Kennedy was too good a politician to be bored by the economy. Politics is a pocketbook business for voters, and the 1962 vote was what the January meetings were about. The country had gone through three recent recessions—in 1953, 1958, and a 1960 recession that had continued through the first half of 1961. He worried that another economic slump might make him a one-term President.

His most important teacher at the White House was Walter Heller, the chairman of his Council of Economic Advisers, backed up occasionally by Heller's mentor, Paul Samuelson of the Massachusetts Institute of Technology. They were both disciples of John Maynard Keynes, whose *General Theory of Employment, Interest and Money* was published in 1935. Kennedy, Harvard Class of '40, had been drilled in pre-Keynesian presumptions, including the classic conventional wisdom that deficits were bad because they led to inflation. Not so, said Keynes, and "the Master's" followers, Heller and Samuelson, were devoted to persuading Kennedy that cuts in personal income taxes would increase consumer spending and stimulate the economy enough, without inflation, to fulfill his pledge to get the country moving again—and ensure himself a second term.

They were winning him over, though he could not go that far yet in public. "I asked people to sacrifice," he said to Heller early on, "and you want me to start by announcing that I'm reducing their taxes?" Besides that, tax cuts would increase the national debt, which was already $284 billion. From day one of his presidency, one of Kennedy's most rigid political goals was to hold the yearly deficit below $12.8 billion, the high during Eisenhower's eight years.

There was no question in Kennedy's mind, and little argument from anyone else, that the struggle with communism would be the focus of the history of his times. As 1961 ended, he had begun an address to historians meeting in Washington by quoting Churchill's prediction that history would be kind to his role in World War II: "Because I intend to write it!"

And Kennedy intended to do the same, with the help of Sorensen and Schlesinger. He had invited one of the historians, David Donald of Princeton, an expert on Abraham Lincoln, to the White House and asked him: "How do you go down in history books as a great president?"

The gateway to history for Kennedy was journalism, a business he and a new communications technology, television, seemed to be changing forever. He had held nineteen televised press conferences during 1961. "News Conference" was the White House's designation, an accurate one, because it was used by the President to deliver news and to react to news. The press preferred the old name, "Press Conference," trying to elevate themselves to the dominant role. More and more correspondents came and they dressed better and asked questions twice as long as they had in pre-television days.

It was Kennedy's show. He was the man in the arena—charming, informed, caring, and witty—gracefully drawing reporters into his cape or even pricking them with his sword on occasion. His dominance in that arena changed the journalism of Washington and, to a large extent, that changed the presidency and government itself. When Kennedy took office, there had been only a few dozen men and women regularly covering the White House full-time. There were hundreds now as 1962 began. One after another, news organizations shifted their men and women to where the action was. Reporters like Peter Lisagor of the *Chicago Daily News* or Sander Vanocur of NBC News had begun covering the Kennedy administration in the traditional way, checking in daily with the big departments; but within the year, they were covering only Kennedy. The President was gaining more and more control over information going out of the government, information that used to be distributed by Cabinet secretaries, appointees, and civil servants with their own agendas. Reporters and editors, and Republicans, grumbled periodically about "news management," but for the gentlemen and ladies of the press it was fair exchange, a lovely affair. And many White House regulars were becoming celebrities themselves.

Kennedy liked reporters. He was the first modern president who did not call them "the boys." He and Robert Kennedy had got to know many of them during their service to a big running story, as a member and counsel of the Senate Labor Committee during its highly publicized 1957 hearings on connections between organized labor and organized crime. Senator Kennedy had learned their language. He was candid in private—not necessarily honest, but extraordinarily direct. There was a bonding in such sharing of secrets, a jargon of intimacy, close and compromising at the same time. His aides, all of them men, competed in describing sitting in business suits on toilets taking orders as he took long steaming baths to relieve the pain in his back—unaware that Kennedy might be demonstrating his mastery over them. During the 1956 convention, Abram Chayes had picked up a telephone in Kennedy's hotel suite. It was Jacqueline Kennedy, and Chayes had gone into Kennedy's bedroom and found him reading in his underwear. "I'll take it out there," Kennedy said, and began to walk into the big sitting room. "Wait," Chayes said. "You can't go out there in your shorts, there are reporters and photographers there." Kennedy walked into the sitting room, saying just loud enough for all to hear: "Abe, I know these fellows. They're not going to take advantage of me."

They rarely did. He talked with reporters about their work and frustrations rather than his own, and he was sensitive to their needs and their limitations. He brought stenographers and banks of typists to national politics, providing transcripts of speeches and press conferences almost as soon as they ended. It was easier for reporters to stick to his words rather than their own notes. He was shameless in exploiting his family and children, using them to take over the slots newspapers usually reserved for photos of local kids and their puppies. It was all within the context of a rule cited by his friend, Senator Smathers: "If they were for Kennedy, Kennedy was for them."

He democratized the business of news as he concentrated it, allowing more reporters and photographers more access than ever before, but directing their attention away from the edges of government to the very center. He favored correspondents over columnists, offering younger men and women from the big newspapers, the newsmagazines, and the television networks a measure of fame—fortune followed—that had been the preserve of the lions of an older generation.

"You have lunch with Lippmann or Reston and they go back and knock the shit out of you to prove their integrity," Kennedy told Charlie Bartlett. "The hell with them."

One of the beneficiaries of Kennedy's press style was a young Time-Life correspondent named Hugh Sidey who was given a column called "The Presidency." He prowled the White House, stopping in to see Salinger, Sorensen, O'Donnell, O'Brien, Feldman, Goodwin—and Kennedy himself, too. They all talked to him. And they all said the same things, sometimes word for word. One of the stories that Sidey wrote concerned Kennedy's publicized prowess in "speed-reading."

Eunice Shriver, the President's sister, had sat next to Henry Luce, the founder and editor of *Time,* at a dinner party. She told him that her brother had taken a course in something called "Speed-Reading" and could read entire books in a single sitting. Luce assigned Sidey to find out what it was all about. The reporter called an institute where Kennedy had enrolled but had not completed a course in speed-reading, and was told that the President probably read at seven or eight hundred words a minute, twice the average for men his age.

Kennedy didn't like that. He told Sidey that Ken Galbraith had once timed him reading a twenty-six-page memo in ten minutes, which worked out to a thousand words a minute. Thinking about it, though, Kennedy still thought that was too low.

"How about twelve hundred?" Sidey asked.

"Okay," Kennedy finally said. That was it. *Time* published that number, and other magazines and newspapers took up the story of the phenomenal reading skills of the man in the White House.

His first news conference of 1962 had been on January 15. Most of the sessions were in the afternoon when the bulk of the television audience was made up of women at home. The question that drew the shortest answer that day was:

"Mr. President, are American troops now in combat in Vietnam?"

"No."

That was not true. Americans were flying the helicopters that had been shipped into South Vietnam from U.S. bases in the Philippines a month before. Vietnamese pilots sat next to the Americans so that any U.S. casualties could be announced as accidents on training missions.

The Jungle Jims selected to fly the helicopters and six specially rigged C-123s spraying defoliant on roads and rice paddies were asked ten questions before being chosen for what was officially designated "extended temporary duty in country 77." A single no meant automatic rejection. The last two questions were: "(9.) Would you wear civilian clothes?" and "(10.) Would you go knowing that if you were captured your government would disclaim any knowledge of you?"

On January 18, after his final political meeting with Democratic congressmen, the President formally authorized war, or a form of war, in Southeast Asia by signing a National Security Action Memorandum that said: "The Function of the Special Group (C.I.) will be as follows: To insure proper recognition throughout the U.S. Government that subversive insurgency ('wars of liberation') is a major form of politico-military conflict equal in importance to conventional warfare. . . . Hereby assign to the cognizance of the Special Group (Counter-Insurgency) the following countries: Laos, South Viet-Nam, Thailand." *

That same day Kennedy sent out another aide for a Vietnam evaluation, this time Roger Hilsman, chief of the State Department's intelligence bureau, who had run guerrillas in Burma as a young Army officer during World War II. He reported back to Kennedy that the helicopter gunships were proving that counterinsurgency could work. "Fantastic mobility," he said. "Roaring in over the treetops, a terrifying sight to the superstitious Viet Cong peasant . . . they simply turned and ran— and, flushed from their foxholes and hiding places, and running in the open, they were easy targets. . . ."

That good news was quickly leaked from the White House to *Time* magazine, which reported to the nation on the new successes of U.S. military technology: "The remarkable U.S. military effort, mounted in the few short months since Washington decided last October to hold South Viet Nam at all costs . . . a steady stream of huge Globemasters unloads tons of electric generators, radar equipment, trucks and Quonset huts. More than 80 H-21 Shawnee helicopters. . . ." What chance could an enemy have? "The typical VietCong soldier is a thin, unkempt young man hardly reaching a G.I.'s armpit and weighing scarcely 100 lbs. . . . His uniform is the same black calico shirt and trousers worn by all Vietnamese peasants."

But such accounts of the war were beginning to be countered by new

---

* Special Group (CI) and the Special Group (Augmented) were essentially task forces, and many important Kennedy administration figures, particularly Robert Kennedy and Maxwell Taylor, were members of both groups. The other members of SG (CI) were Alexis Johnson, Roswell Gilpatric, Lyman Lemnitzer, John McCone, McGeorge Bundy, and AID Administrator David Bell. The difference in the SGs was that SG (CI) was dealing with insurgencies in friendly countries, principally South Vietnam, while SG (A) was dealing with an unfriendly country, Cuba.

young reporters, who had been assigned to Vietnam as the U.S. presence was becoming more visible—particularly a reporter from *The New York Times*, David Halberstam, and *Time* magazine's own man on the scene, Charles Mohr. The President himself took notice of changes in coverage. "Why are we having so much trouble with reporters out there?" he asked John Mecklin, the embassy's press officer back on home leave. He then ordered up a new Saigon press policy. He wanted "maximum feasible cooperation and guidance" for correspondents, with the goal of directing them away from "undesirable" situations and stories. The President was trying to keep bad news from Americans, but the real effect of keeping the press away from unpleasantness was that he himself might be the last to know what was happening in Southeast Asia if he depended only on official reports.

Even Hilsman was disillusioned a couple of days later when he monitored an all-day operation, on January 21, by the Army of the Republic of South Vietnam (ARVN) covertly supported by U.S. pilots. The objective was the village of Binh Hoa, seventeen miles west of Saigon near the Cambodian border, believed to be a storage area for Viet Cong munitions and a haven for VC guerrillas. The place was bombed for an hour by Vietnamese planes with American pilots and then five ARVN battalions moved in, finding no Viet Cong. The day's work produced five dead and eleven wounded civilians—plus one dead and three wounded Cambodians from a few stray bombs dropped accidentally on a village on the wrong side of the border.

"How can things like this go on happening?" Kennedy said to Hilsman when he reported back. "I've been President for a year."

This was not the Bay of Pigs again. Kennedy was in charge now, and he wanted to know everything, from the length of jungle airstrips in Laos to the weight and feel of the weapons being sent to the little Vietnamese, many of whom also stood armpit-high to their American advisers. He told the Joint Chiefs to bring over samples of the weapons being used in Southeast Asia, lifting the heavy new Army M-14 rifle, which had an effective range of 500 yards, then asking to try the lighter carbine he had been trained to use in the Pacific. "You know, I like the old carbine," he said. "You aren't going to see a guy five hundred yards in the jungle."

There was another weapon President Diem wanted to use against the Viet Cong: napalm, a jellied gasoline that could be dropped from planes to burn extensive areas of vegetation. Kennedy had approved napalm use at the end of 1961. Tanks of the jellied gas were part of the cargo of the Globemasters flying into Saigon almost every day now.

The big transports also flew in the drums of herbicides and chemicals for "Operation Ranch Hand," the roadside clearance and food denial missions. Ships carrying two hundred thousand more gallons of defoliants had left Oakland, California, on December 15, 1961. Those drums were marked as civilian cargo for the United States Mission in Saigon to avoid inspection by the International Control Commission enforcing the Geneva Accords. They had arrived in Saigon on January 8. The whole operation was illegal under the accords, but Kennedy, like the North Vietnamese and Soviet suppliers of the Viet Cong guerrillas, had long since decided to ignore those restrictions, and the risk of political "noise" that had frightened him so much only eight months earlier at the Bay of Pigs.

The President had approved specific defoliation plans on January 3, personally selecting the first targets: sixteen of the sixty miles of Route 15, the highway between Binh Hoa and Vung Tau. Three C-123s, outfitted for spraying at Olmstead Air Force Base in Pennsylvania, had been flown from the Philippines to Saigon on January 7. The planes and their crews were kept in a fenced area at the edge of Tan Son Nhut Airport —again to avoid ICC inspection—but everyone near the airport knew what was going on because vapors immediately began to kill off the shrubbery and flame trees near the C-123s. "Our ultimate objective," Hilsman said, "is to turn the Vietcong into hungry bands of outlaws devoting all their energies to staying alive."

The U.S. Air Force pilots, nineteen of them at first, had moved together into a single apartment building near the center of Saigon, leaving their fifty ground-crew personnel in tents at the airport. Ambassador Frederick Nolting had given a cocktail party for the pilots. They flew the first of the Kennedy-approved sorties on January 13.

Three weeks later, after evaluating the first defoliant flights, Kennedy —who did not know that ordinary folks in both Saigon and Hanoi knew all about what was classified "Top Secret" in Washington—approved more extensive missions along three more highways and to clear fields of fire around three South Vietnamese military bases.

This was counterinsurgency. The key now was to find the right people, hard thinkers to run the show in Vietnam. On February 2, the President upgraded the Military Advisory and Assistance Group to the Military Assistance Command, Vietnam, with a new commander, a Max Taylor protégé, General Paul Harkins. He was given co-equal status with Ambassador Nolting. Kennedy wanted a general in his forties, but none of them that young had the rank to take over an official command. McNamara tried to reassure the President, saying, "Although General Harkins is fifty-seven years old, he is physically active."

On February 18, Robert Kennedy was in Saigon for two hours on a refueling stop between Indonesia and India on a world tour. "We are going to win in Vietnam," he said there. "We will remain until we do. . . . I think the United States will do what is necessary to help a country that is trying to repel aggression with its own blood, tears, and sweat."

"They're Boy Scouts with guns," thought Michael Forrestal, the son of the U.S.'s first Secretary of Defense, James Forrestal, who was in Vietnam as a young assistant to the Assistant Secretary of State for the Far East, Averell Harriman. Counterinsurgency was an acquired taste for some. When the Army ordered all of its schools to devote 20 percent of their class time to counterinsurgency, including the training of finance officers and cooks, Robert Amory, a CIA liaison, came back to the agency saying: "They're talking about how to wire typewriters to explode or how to make apple pies with hand grenades inside."

The President, though, did acquire the taste. He had visited Fort Bragg, North Carolina, in the fall to watch Green Beret training. The show he saw was described this way by one of the participants, a Special Forces sergeant:

> It was mass rehearsals from morning to night—talk-throughs, walk-throughs, and, finally, dress rehearsals. . . . A man wearing a rocket contraption—jets roaring, he flew across the water and landed in front of the President. Scuba divers swam to shore from the dummy submarine; sky divers trailing colored smoke tracked in. . . . A thousand men who had been hiding in the brush across the lake stood and removed fatigue shirts, and in their white T-shirts, shooting off hand flares, ran screaming and yelling to the water's edge. They represented the number of guerrillas the twelve-man team can organize and direct. . . . Much of the equipment shown, including the rocket, had never been seen before and probably would never be seen again.

Chapter 26

Beginning on December 20, 1961, the United States had scheduled ten attempts to put a man in orbit around the earth to match the Soviet flight of Yuri Gagarin on April 11, 1961. Each time the launch had been canceled because of bad weather or minor equipment failures. The tenth failure occurred on January 27, 1962, when a Marine pilot, Lieutenant Colonel John Glenn, sat in a capsule, *Friendship 7,* which was attached to the tip of an Atlas intercontinental ballistic missile—where a nuclear warhead was usually bolted on. The next try was scheduled for February 20.

President Kennedy turned on the television set in his bedroom at 7:15 A.M. that day. More than 100 million other Americans were watching the same live broadcast from Cape Canaveral on the Atlantic Ocean in Florida. Millions around the world saw a long shot of the ninety-five-foot-high rocket, the United States' standard strategic missile, twice as heavy as the Redstone rocket that had taken Alan Shepard on his up-and-down ride. Smoke and oxygen vapor poured from small ports on its side. The television picture was the big difference, a big gamble: Kennedy had decided that U.S. space shots would not be done in secret, as Soviet shots were, so that only successes could be reported. The whole world was watching the few dots at the top of the screen that were *Friendship 7.* Glenn had climbed in just after 6:00 A.M.

The President watched with the sound off, eating breakfast, reading his newspapers. He jotted down a couple of notes for the good-luck and God-bless telephone conversation he hoped to have with Glenn as the astronaut passed over Washington itself, 160 miles above the continent, whirling by at more than 17,000 miles per hour—if everything went according to plan. He went downstairs for a nine o'clock meeting in the Cabinet Room with Democratic congressional leaders. Another silent television showed the same scene, the rocket sitting there smoking, through one delay after another. The President never sat down. He stood as he listened to the men from Congress go through the list of administration bills sitting in committee at the beginning of this second session of the 87th Congress.

The rocket finally lifted off at 9:36 A.M. No one spoke. In New York, fifteen thousand people stood silently in Grand Central Station, watching giant television pictures of the slow, flaming rise of *Friendship 7*. In Des Moines, Iowa, the employees of Younkers department store congregated in the television section to watch. There was no call to the city police department's main switchboard for the next twenty-seven minutes. That had never happened before.

Glenn was a very cool character. He had flown 149 combat missions in World War II and the Korean War. His idea of fun—and a demonstration of his skill—was to come alongside the jets of other pilots in his squadron and gently tap the bottom of their wings with the tip of his own, at 600 miles per hour. "That man is crazy," one of the other pilots, the great baseball player Ted Williams, had said. Glenn's pulse rate had stayed normal, 70 beats per minute, until the actual moment of lift-off, when it rose to 110 beats per minute, compared to 139 and 170 for the two Americans who preceded him into space on suborbital flights, Shepard and Virgil Grissom.

He was a forty-year-old all-American boy, a churchgoing family man from a small town in Ohio. Straight as an arrow. Lyndon Johnson, the biggest booster of the space program in the government, was practically counting the votes that the shot would produce. "If only he were a Negro," he said. Kennedy laughed. It became his favorite Johnson story.

"The clock is operating. We're under way," Glenn said after lift-off to the millions of people hearing his calm voice. It was all totally new. The astronaut ate applesauce from a tube to see whether it was possible to eat in a state of weightlessness. "It's all positive action," he reported. "Your tongue forces it back in your mouth and you swallow normally."

"Just to my right, I can see a big pattern of light, apparently right on the coast," Glenn said as he approached Australia. It was the city of Perth, where every resident had turned on all their lights and used bedsheets as reflectors to direct beams into the sky. Weightless, he reported that he was able to urinate into the bag attached to his leg.

Then there was trouble. The tiny rockets designed to automatically keep *Friendship 7* in a steady attitude were misfiring. The capsule was drifting to the right, 20 degrees, then bouncing back to normal, bouncing from side to side in a 20-degree arc, rather than holding steady. Small golden flakes seemed to be flying past Glenn's little window on the world. He could not figure out what was happening, but on the ground NASA controllers knew that the heat shield on the bottom of his bell-shaped vehicle was breaking up. If the shield broke off, or if it could not be maneuvered to take the impact and heat of reentry into the atmosphere, the capsule and its pilot would be burned up, probably totally vaporized.

The President canceled the phone call, not wanting to be remembered as congratulating a man before his certain death. He waited like everyone else, until Glenn used manual controls to fly the capsule through the atmosphere and down to a soft parachute landing in the Atlantic Ocean near Bermuda at 2:43 P.M. He had orbited the earth three times in four hours and fifty-six minutes, coming down within range of helicopters waiting to take him on board the U.S.S. *Noa*, a cruiser named for a midshipman killed in the Philippines during an insurgency against American rule in 1901. After the landing, the President stepped outside into the Rose Garden to pose for waiting cameras and wait for a ship-to-shore telephone call from the new hero.

"He wants to see you," Kenny O'Donnell said to Hugh Sidey, one of the reporters outside the Oval Office.

"You've done it again," Kennedy snapped at Sidey back inside the office.

"Done what?" Sidey said.

Sorensen and Salinger walked in holding copies of *Time*. Kennedy grabbed one and said, "Where did you get this story?"

He tapped a sentence in a long story about the number of magazines featuring the President, his wife, and his daughter Caroline on their covers: "On the cover of *Gentlemen's Quarterly*, a slick symposium of the latest men's fashions, was a specially posed photograph of President Kennedy himself, modelling a trimly tailored dark grey suit."

Sidey grinned. He couldn't stop grinning, not because he thought anything was funny. He was nervous. *GQ* had a reputation as a magazine favored by homosexuals—"A fag rag," in Robert Kennedy's words.

"I'm not kidding," John Kennedy said. "I'm goddamn sick and tired of it. This is all a lie. I never posed for any magazine, never posed for any picture."

"We'll correct it," Sidey said. But that didn't stop Kennedy.

"I never posed for any picture. Anybody who read this would think I was crazy. Any President who would pose for *Gentlemen's Quarterly* would be out of his mind. People remember other people for one thing. I remember Arthur Godfrey only because he buzzed that tower." The President went on for a minute about Godfrey, a television personality who flew his own plane and had been fined once for flying too close to an airport control tower.

"What are you trying to do to me?" Kennedy asked, scaring Sidey now. "What do you think you're doing?"

"Mr. President, Mr. President," said one of his military aides, Tazewell Shepard, running into the office. "Colonel Glenn is on the line."

"All right, Sidey, stand there and see if you can get this right," Kennedy said, glaring at him.

"Hello, Colonel Glenn," said the President, his voice and mood totally changed. He was boisterous. "We are really proud of you. You did a wonderful job. We are glad you got down in very good shape. I've just been watching your mother and father on television and they seem very happy. . . . Well, I'm coming down to Canaveral on Friday. . . ."

When he hung up, Kennedy turned back to Sidey. "Now, get this . . ." And he started all over again with his angry complaints.

When they met, Glenn wanted to talk about numbers and science. Kennedy wanted to know how it felt, how hot it was, how hard was the landing? He wanted to hear about the personal experience. It was Glenn's courage that interested him.

A week later, on February 27, after Colonel Glenn had been honored at the White House, Robert Kennedy and Kenny O'Donnell received identical memos from J. Edgar Hoover saying that Judith Campbell was a regular companion of two organized crime figures, Sam Giancana and Johnny Roselli. Giancana was a high-ranking mobster, the organized crime chieftain in Chicago, and Roselli worked for him. Both men had been approached by the CIA in their on-and-off schemes to use gangsters to assassinate Fidel Castro.

It was not the first time Hoover had let the Kennedys know they were, in effect, under FBI surveillance. A typical memo to the White House read like this one: "I have received information which I feel will be of interest to you. . . . In as much as this information originated through a highly delicate source available to this bureau, I would appreciate it if you would handle the above information on a need-to-know basis."

"He's sending me stuff on my family and friends and even me, too," said Robert Kennedy, Hoover's official superior. "Just so I'll know they are into all this information."

"J. Edgar Hoover has Jack Kennedy by the balls," Vice President Johnson told friendly reporters over drinks.

Maybe. But the Kennedys still thought they controlled the situation, at least until Hoover called for an appointment with the President after sending the February 27 memo. The President loved gossip and the FBI specialized in collecting it. Some he thought was funny. When Hoover had wanted to know why the President was not taking action on an ambassador who was literally caught with his pants down jumping out the window of a lady's bedroom in Europe, Kenny O'Donnell passed along the word that Kennedy would make an effort to hire ambassadors who could run faster.

The FBI director appeared at the White House for lunch on March 22. He brought a memo that had been prepared for him two days earlier:

Subject: JUDITH E. CAMPBELL
         ASSOCIATE OF HOODLUMS
         CRIMINAL INTELLIGENCE MATTER

This is being submitted as the Director may desire to bear this information in mind in connection with his forthcoming appointment with the President.

Information has been developed that Judith E. Campbell, a free-lance artist, has associated with prominent underworld figures Sam Giancana of Chicago and John Roselli of Los Angeles.

A review of telephone toll calls from Campbell's Los Angeles residence discloses that on November 7 and 15, 1961, calls were made to Evelyn Lincoln, the President's secretary at the White House.

Telephone toll calls were charged to residence Campbell rented in Palm Springs, California, to Evelyn Lincoln at the White House on November 10, 1961, and November 13, 1961. Campbell was also charged with a call to Mrs. Lincoln on February 14, 1962, from Cedars of Lebanon Hospital in Los Angeles, where Campbell was a patient at the time.

The last line of the memo said that an informant reported that Frank Sinatra "referred to Campbell as the girl who was 'shacking up with John Kennedy in the East.' "

The events that led to the March 22 encounter had begun on October 31, 1960, before Kennedy was elected. The FBI had discovered an illegal wiretap in the Las Vegas hotel room of a comedian named Dan Rowan, and then, in the course of time, had figured out that it had been put there by CIA operatives at the request of Giancana. The mobster, who was under almost constant investigation and surveillance by the FBI, was working for the CIA—or at least he told them he was. He had been given $150,000 by the CIA in 1960 to distribute as part of a Castro assassination attempt. The agency was pressuring the FBI not to file charges in the wiretap case.

The CIA and Giancana had been in bed together. But what worried Giancana was that Rowan, the Las Vegas comedian, was in bed with one of his girlfriends, a singer named Phyllis McGuire of a popular group, "The McGuire Sisters." The CIA had hired a former FBI agent named Robert Maheu to deal with Giancana—they wanted deniability, too—and Maheu had installed the wiretap so that Giancana could find out what was going on between McGuire and Rowan.

"You are the chief gunman for the group that succeeded the Capone mob," Robert Kennedy had charged Giancana during a 1958 interrogation when he was counsel to the Senate Rackets Committee. As Attorney General he had gotten the first word of criminal "national security" operations four months after his brother became President. On May 22, 1961, FBI Director Hoover had sent him a memo saying:

> Colonel Edwards advised that in connection with CIA's operation against Castro he personally contacted Robert Maheu during the fall of 1961 for the purpose of using Maheu as a "cut-out" in contacts with Sam Giancana, a known hoodlum in the Chicago area. Colonel Edwards said that since the underworld controlled gambling activities in Cuba under the Batista government, it was assumed this element would continue to have sources and contacts in Cuba, which perhaps could be utilized successfully in connection with the CIA's clandestine efforts against the Castro government. . . . Edwards said that since this is "dirty business," he could not afford to have knowledge of the actions of Maheu and Giancana.

Dirty business it was. Only after Hoover came to the White House on March 22, 1962, did John Kennedy sever his relationship with Judith Campbell, making the last of seventy telephone calls through the White House switchboard to her number that afternoon.

The logistics of Kennedy's liaisons with Judith Campbell and dozens of other women in the White House and in hotels, houses, and apartments around the country and around the world required secrecy and devotion rare even in the annals of the energetic service demanded by successful politicians. The arrangements were frequent. "I wonder how it is for you, Harold?" Kennedy had said to the flabbergasted Harold Macmillan during their Bermuda meeting at the end of 1961. "If I don't have a woman for three days, I get terrible headaches."

The routine of clandestine comings and goings had to be taught to the willing among the women Kennedy regularly propositioned, often within a couple of minutes of introduction. Some of the action was somewhat graceful—or at least roses were sent with a card that said: "Friends of Evelyn Lincoln." Some of it was in the back seats of cars. Many of the women he asked said yes, but if they did not, Kennedy asked again. He propositioned Mary Meyer, a Washington artist and the sister-in-law of his friend Ben Bradlee, during a reception at the White House just before Christmas of 1961, but it was six weeks later before she finally agreed and became the most frequent of the President's secret visitors. The delivery duty was shared by old friends and by almost everyone in the White House from the military attachés and typists—some of whom had made the backstairs trip a few times themselves—to members of the Cabinet.

His friends and the closest assistants, a few of them appalled by the whole business, pretended it was not happening or treated it as if it were the boss's hobby. After all, it took less time than tennis, and partners were often easier to find. It was a rite of passage for some, an excited feeling that they had been accepted into a private Kennedy circle. The women, secretaries and stars, the wives of friends, were symbols and rewards of aggressive privilege. Sneaking around, cleaning up the mess, covering up was all part of the game. Sharing secrets drew men together. "We're a bunch of virgins, married virgins," said one young staff member, Fred Dutton, the secretary of the Cabinet. "And he's like God, fucking anybody he wants to anytime he feels like it."

It was a male world, and a pretty crude one at that. "Happening babes," the women were called. When a reporter he knew, Laura Bergquist Knebel of *Look* magazine, had gotten an exclusive interview with Fidel Castro, the President peppered her with questions about the Cuban's sex life: "Where are the dames? . . . Who does he sleep with? . . . I hear he doesn't even take his boots off." Then he said he heard she had the hots for Che Guevara, not noticing or caring how much he had hurt her.

"That's just the way Jack is; it doesn't really matter," said the wife of one of Kennedy's older male friends. "Everyone at court knows it. No one minds, of course, unless they're jealous of the ones he chooses —or they feel bad for Jackie. But there aren't many who do." Then she passed along the latest story of the cognoscenti: The two young women seen around Hervé Alphand, the French ambassador, aren't his nieces, at all; they are plants who are supposed to get close to Jack because the French are so concerned about the President's friendship with David Ormsby-Gore, who had been named, at Kennedy's personal request to Macmillan, British ambassador in October of 1961.

It was all good fun to most who knew—part of the thrill of being inside one of the President's closer circles. Keeping the secrets was part of the price of admission, and those who knew didn't tell those who didn't. The Secret Service, who were supposed to be with the President, or at least outside his door, at all times, made their deal between the election and the inaugural, but they had had to lock Kennedy out of the Hotel Carlyle to get his attention. When Kennedy was in New York, he used the family penthouse atop the hotel, coming and going as he pleased through a service door without walking through the lobby. The first time the men charged with guarding him had realized that the President-elect was not upstairs where he was supposed to be, they had ordered hotel employees to lock all entrances except the main one on Madison Avenue. Kennedy came in the main door a few minutes after midnight, grinned, and said: "Is there anything you'd like to talk about?"

Some of the fun ended with Hoover's formal visit to the Oval Office. Two weeks later, on April 4, the CIA's formal request to the FBI to forgo prosecution of Giancana and Maheu was worded this way: "Any prosecution in the matter would endanger sensitive sources and methods used in a duly authorized intelligence project and would not be in the national interest."

On May 7, Robert Kennedy was visited by the general counsel of the CIA, Lawrence Houston. Houston told the Attorney General, for the record this time, details of the gangster assassination schemes, most of which involved trying to poison Castro, and said they had all been terminated. That's what Houston said, but it was not true. The CIA had reactivated the Mafia plotting, giving more poison capsules to Giancana's man, Johnny Roselli.

But what Robert Kennedy heard that day—plus the gossip he knew was going around that the Kennedy Justice Department would never prosecute Giancana because he was a buddy of Jack Kennedy's buddy Sinatra—was enough to send him to the Oval Office to tell his brother that he had to forget his plans to go to Sinatra's house in Palm Springs, California, for sun and fun in early June.

"Johnny," the Attorney General said to his brother. "You just can't associate with this guy."

FBI memos kept Hoover advised as the Attorney General adjusted his brother's travel plans:

"Lido Hotel, Palm Springs advised SA [Special Agent] . . . of a possible visit of President Kennedy in Palm Springs during the weekend of 3/23/62 . . . Sinatra reportedly has this house adequately wired for teletype facilities, has five private telephone lines, and enough cable available to handle a switchboard."

The next report to Hoover said: "Special Agent at Palm Springs has been advised by the Palm Springs Police Department that they have been contacted by the Secret Service . . . that the President is going to stay at Bing Crosby's residence."

Chapter 27

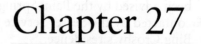

"Terrific! This is terrific," President Kennedy said at the end of a telephone conversation with his Secretary of Labor, Arthur Goldberg, on March 31. Goldberg was in Pittsburgh, reporting that the United States Steel Company and the United Steelworkers union had just agreed to a new contract that would raise employee wages and benefits by a total of 10 cents an hour. That was less than a 2.5 percent increase. That, Goldberg said, meant no steel strike and no increase in steel prices. And, Kennedy added, no quick jump in inflation.

"Terrific, Arthur. Terrific job." They worked out a statement, which Kennedy read in telephone calls to the company's chairman, Roger Blough, and the union's president, David McDonald: "The settlement you have announced is both forward looking and responsible. It is obviously non-inflationary and should provide a solid base for continued price stability."

It was a satisfying piece of work for Kennedy. Eight months before, in August 1961, he had received a memo from Walter Heller, chairman of his Council of Economic Advisers, warning him that a steel strike or a sharp rise in the price of steel or steelworkers' wages, or both, was the greatest single threat to economic stability during his presidency. "Steel bulks so large in the manufacturing sector of the economy," Heller told him, "that it can upset the applecart all by itself."

Kennedy was a politician, not an economist. "You can't just talk to me in abstract terms," he had once snapped at Paul Samuelson. "You've got to make it in terms of human beings." He knew little of banking or corporate America or, for that matter, of the lives of his countrymen. He was forever asking workmen or drivers how much they were paid or how much rent they paid, how much refrigerators cost, how they paid for college. The only paychecks John F. Kennedy ever got came from the government—from the Navy and Congress—and they were donated to charity without his ever touching them. He once told his father that one of his former assistants was going to law school at night and making good money during the day: $5,000 a year. "Good God," Joe Kennedy said. "How can you say a thing like that? You've been spending fifty thousand dollars a year on incidentals."

"Now tell me again how do I distinguish between monetary and fiscal policy?" the President asked Heller more than once in the first couple of months of the administration. "Well," Heller had answered, "monetary is 'M,' like Martin"—William McChesney Martin, chairman of the Federal Reserve Board. "So remember Martin and think of the Federal Reserve."

Kennedy knew what he did not know, but he also knew what he wanted: more growth than the 3 percent a year increase in gross national product during the 1950s while European economies were growing at 5 percent. He knew also what he would not accept politically: a deficit bigger than Eisenhower's biggest, $12.8 billion in 1958. He believed that it was inflation, not unemployment, that was politically dangerous. He wanted unemployment reduced, but sometimes expressed the rather un-Democratic view that 7 percent unemployment meant that 93 percent of the country was working and relatively content.

With inflation on his mind, Kennedy had begun talking regularly to Blough and McDonald late in 1961, trying to persuade them that their restraint was the key to checking inflation, then running at 2.5 percent a year (almost double the 1.4 percent average during Eisenhower's second term). "Wage restraint" . . . "price stability" . . . "statesmanship" were phrases he repeated again and again to the two men.

U.S. Steel, which accounted for more than one quarter of American steel production, traditionally set the pay scales for the other eleven steel companies of any size. In February, the President had pressured both sides to begin negotiations for a new contract that would become effective in June—on the theory that the earlier they began, the less chance there was for a strike, and the sooner they had a contract, the less chance that it would be inflationary. In six weeks, he had his prize.

The contract signed on April 6 was a victory for Kennedy. The President had defined the national interest and had persuaded management and labor to modify their own agendas for the sake of the country. Within four days, the eleven other principal steel companies had signed practically identical contracts with the steelworkers' union.

On April 10, Roger Blough asked to see the President and an appointment was set for five forty-five that day. Earlier that afternoon, Charlie Bartlett called the White House to say that a friend at U.S. Steel had told him the company wanted to raise prices. That did not seem possible. Kennedy thought he knew Blough pretty well. "I've been breaking my ass trying to get along with these people," Kennedy had sort of bragged to Ben Bradlee.

"Perhaps the easiest way I can explain the purpose of my visit is to give you this," said Blough as he entered the Oval Office. He handed the President a mimeographed copy of a four-page statement that had just been given to the press. It began:

"For the first time in nearly four years, United States Steel today announced an increase in the general level of its steel prices. The 'catchup' adjustment, effective at 12:01 A.M. tomorrow, will raise the price of the company's steel products by an average of about 3.5 percent—or three-tenths of a cent per pound."

Kennedy looked up after reading that paragraph. "You have made a terrible mistake," he said. "You double-crossed me."

The President was furious. He called Goldberg and told him to come to the White House immediately. Blough was shocked by Kennedy's anger. He protested that he had never said he would not raise prices. Goldberg arrived, arguing against price increases as he walked in the door. "Wait a minute, Arthur," said Kennedy. "Read the statement. It's already done."

"Isn't that a hell of a note? What if we roll them back?" Kennedy said to Goldberg after Blough was shown out. "He fucked me. They fucked us and we've got to try to fuck them." He was pacing the office, calling in one aide after another. He got David McDonald on the phone: "Dave, you've been screwed and I've been screwed."

"This is war," Goldberg said. "I might as well quit. There's nothing I can do now. I simply won't be able to talk to labor again if this holds."

"My father told me businessmen were all pricks," Kennedy said, "but I didn't really believe he was right until now. I wish he were here now," he said, walking back and forth across the office. "What makes businessmen tick? Why did Blough do this? Does he think he can get away with it? He must have been misled. God, I hate the bastards.

"I think steel made a deal with Nixon, not to raise prices after the election," Kennedy went on. "Then came the recessions and they didn't want to raise prices. Then when we pulled out of the recession they said,

'Let Kennedy squeeze the unions first, before we raise prices.' . . . And they kicked us right in the balls."

Evelyn Lincoln came in several times to remind the President that he had to get ready for the congressional reception that evening. It was the second of his administration. The night of the first one, the year before, American-trained Cuban exiles were being gunned down on the beaches of the Bay of Pigs. Now this. "Jesus," he said, still pacing. "I'll never have another one of these receptions."

The next morning in bed, Kennedy read James Reston's column in *The New York Times*. The President, Reston wrote, needed a crisis a year, and this was the time for it. "Doesn't he know I need his help with this?" Kennedy said. "What's wrong with these people?" he said a couple of times that day. "Don't they understand that if I fail America fails?"

He was considering asking Congress for special legislation to freeze steel prices, and a draft of the Steel Price Emergency Act of 1962 was on his desk within hours. But he decided to begin by appealing to public opinion. A news conference had already been scheduled for that afternoon, April 11. By then, five more steel companies—Bethlehem Steel, Republic, Jones & Laughlin, Youngstown, and Wheeling—had announced pricing schedules identical to those of U.S. Steel. The President read out an angry opening statement:

> The simultaneous and identical actions of United States Steel and other leading steel corporations, increasing steel prices by some six dollars a ton, constitute a wholly unjustifiable and irresponsible defiance of the public interest.
> In this serious hour in our nation's history, when we are confronted with grave crises in Berlin and Southeast Asia, when we are devoting our energies to economic recovery and stability, when we are asking Reservists to leave their homes and families for months on end and servicemen to risk their lives—and four were killed in the last two days in Vietnam —and asking union members to hold down their wage requests; at a time when restraint and sacrifice are being asked of every citizen, the American people will find it hard, as I do, to accept a situation in which a tiny handful of steel executives whose pursuit of private power and profit exceeds their sense of public responsibility can show such utter contempt for the interests of one hundred eighty-five million Americans.

Reporters were literally gasping. Kennedy heard them, and he poured it on:

"It would add, Secretary McNamara informed me this morning, an estimated one billion dollars to the cost of our defenses, at a time when every dollar is needed for national security and other purposes. It would make it more difficult for American goods to compete in foreign markets, more difficult to withstand competition from foreign imports, and thus more difficult to improve our balance-of-payments position and stem the flow of gold.

"Some time ago I asked each American to consider what he would do for his country and I asked the steel companies. In the last twenty-four hours we had their answer."

Around the country the press went about the business of collecting responses as strong as the President's rhetoric. In South Carolina, the vice president of a construction company in Greenville, George McDougal, said: "I just figured that this is the way Hitler took over." From New Hampshire, Robert Frost said: "Oh, didn't he do a good one! Didn't he show the Irish all right?"

Back in the Oval Office, the President took personal charge of a campaign against U.S. Steel. Reporters were called with questions to ask Blough at a press conference he had scheduled for the next day. Cabinet members were assigned statements to make regarding the effects of the price rise on everyone from automobile manufacturers to small farmers. The Justice Department would talk of grand jury investigations of steel executives. Friendly senators and congressmen were asked to hold anti-trust hearings.

At the Defense Department, McNamara checked procurement schedules and found that a $5.5 million steel-plate order for Polaris submarines was divided between U.S. Steel and Lukens Steel, a small company which had not yet announced price increases. He announced immediately that Lukens would be given the entire order. Walter Heller calculated that the government used so much steel that it could shift as much as 9 percent of the industry's total business away from the six companies that had announced price rises to six that were still holding back. On Capitol Hill, Senator Estes Kefauver and Representative Emanuel Celler quickly did their part for the President by announcing congressional investigations of the steel companies' pricing policies.

Robert Kennedy, as usual, hit the hardest, summoning a federal grand jury and sending FBI agents to offices and homes of steelmen. The pretext was an Associated Press story the President had read on April 10 in the *Washington Star* reporting on the annual meeting of Bethlehem Steel in Wilmington, Delaware. The AP quoted the president of Bethlehem, Edwin Martin, as saying: "There shouldn't be any price rise. We shouldn't do anything to increase our costs if we are to survive. We have more competition domestically and from foreign firms."

On April 11, Martin denied the AP report and announced that Bethlehem was matching the U.S. Steel price increases, penny for penny. As far as Robert Kennedy was concerned, that looked like price fixing. He convened the grand jury, and also ordered FBI agents in Philadelphia and Wilmington to call on reporters who had covered the Bethlehem Steel meeting to determine Martin's exact words to the company's shareholders.

"We're going for broke," Robert Kennedy told his men. "Their expense accounts and where they'd been and what they were doing . . . I told the FBI to interview them all—march into their offices . . . subpoenaed for their personal records. . . subpoenaed for their company records. . . . We can't lose this."

FBI agents took the Attorney General at his word, telephoning steel executives in the middle of the night. In Philadelphia and Wilmington, agents were at reporters' doors beginning at three o'clock on the morning of April 12, asking for notes taken at the Bethlehem meeting.

Later that morning, Roger Blough held his press conference in New York. He opened with a long statement, talking of profits as the prerequisite of new jobs and of modernization to compete with the new steel mills of Japan and Western Europe. Then he said that his responsibility was to the owners of U.S. Steel, millions of American shareholders, and he minimized the inflationary impact of the price increases—65 cents added to the price of a refrigerator, $8.33 added to the price of a medium-sized car.

"Gentlemen, I have touched upon a few matters here, in the hope that [this] will lead to a greater understanding and a more thoughtful appraisal of the reasons for that action. Now, gentlemen, I am ready for your questions."

He never had a chance. The press was not gentle. The first question was from Walter Cronkite of CBS, and it set the tone: "You say that no commitment was asked or given, during the wage negotiations regarding price increases. Yet at your joint news conference with Mr. McDonald, he mentioned the non-inflationary nature of the agreement, and the newspapers, radio and television played that as the biggest feature of the agreement. I wonder if you can tell us why there was no denial at that time, or in this week that has passed, on your part that an agreement—whether an increase was intended?"

He was asked why he was defying the President and the national interest, why he was helping foreign competition, why he was increasing the defense budget. The last question was: "Delaney, CBS News. Some significance has been attached to the fact that the steel companies in 1960 did not raise prices under a Republican administration. Would you comment on that?"

Blough answered that last question with his only humor of the day: "Well, I think you gentlemen can readily see that I do not know anything about politics."

"Listen to this," the President said that afternoon, holding a telegram from the New York City office of the FBI. "Listen. Quote: 'J. F. Tenant, general counsel of United States Steel, informed us today that he is too busy to talk to agents from the bureau.'

"Who the fuck do they think they are?" Kennedy demanded.

In the middle of all that, the Bureau of the Budget sent over an analysis of the effect of the steel price rise on gross national product, tax revenues, and the overall federal budget: "Would increase GNP by (roughly) $2.8 to $2.85 billion. Very roughly, then, in fiscal 1963, Budget receipts would rise $900 million. Budget expenditures would rise $600 million. The Budget surplus would gain $300 million." That data was discarded.

Then Evelyn Lincoln popped her head into the Oval Office and said: "It's the Governor of Delaware calling from Wilmington." The President picked up the phone, said, "Hello, Governor"—and listened with a mystified look on his face before hanging up in about forty-five seconds.

Before Sorensen or the others could ask what happened, Kennedy called out: "Mrs. Lincoln, what the hell was that all about?"

"They just installed a direct-dial line between Delaware and Washington and he wanted to make the first call, to the White House," she said. "It was set up a long time ago."

Kennedy laughed at that. But within hours he was angry again after watching the fifteen-minute NBC Nightly News. He thought anchorman Chet Huntley was being too kind to big steel. He picked up the phone and got Newton Minow, chairman of the Federal Communications Commission: "Did you see that goddamn thing on Huntley-Brinkley? I thought they were supposed to be our friends. I want you to do something about that. You do something about that."

That night at 11:00 P.M., Charlie Bartlett's friend, who was Hal Korda, a public relations man at U.S. Steel, called Bartlett and said Blough was about ready to surrender. Bartlett called the White House, but the President was downstairs at a dinner for the Shah of Iran. Forty-five minutes later, Kennedy called Bartlett and said, "Okay, tell your friend I said let's make peace."

The next morning, April 13, Inland Steel Company in Chicago became the first company to announce that it would not raise prices. Two hours later, Edgar Kaiser, the chairman of Kaiser Steel, called the White House and asked to speak to the President. After a couple of minutes of conversation, Kennedy, who was having lunch, asked Mrs. Lincoln to come back on the line and take down a statement which began: "Edgar F. Kaiser, chairman of the board, Kaiser Steel Corporation, today announced that his company will not raise its mill prices at this time. . . ."

U.S. Steel was bending—or trying to. The President sent Clark Clifford to New York to join Arthur Goldberg, who was meeting with Blough's staff, many of whom despised Goldberg from his days as counsel to the United Steelworkers. Blough himself refused to deal directly with Goldberg. After a first round of conversations, Clifford telephoned the White House to say: "Blough and his people want to know what you would say if they announce a partial rollback of the price increases, say 50 percent?"

"I wouldn't say a damn thing," Kennedy told him. "It's the whole way."

An hour after Kaiser's statement, with the President flying to Norfolk, Virginia, to watch naval maneuvers, Bethlehem Steel announced that it was rescinding its increases. The news was telephoned to Blough at the Hotel Carlyle in New York, where he was meeting with Clifford and Goldberg.

The U.S. Steel chairman left the hotel to meet with his own people, and at five-thirty, he sent out a press release stating that the company would rescind the price increases announced three days before.

The President was on a submarine, the U.S.S. *Thomas A. Edison*, when that happened. He got the news as he transferred to a cruiser, the U.S.S. *Northampton*. "We have met the enemy and they are ours," said Clifford, quoting Oliver Hazard Perry after a victory over the British in the War of 1812. "They have capitulated, Mr. President."

"The Babe has been at the plate and just hit that Big Steel pitcher for a home run," said Dave Powers, the President's chief coat-holder, who was with him on the *Northampton*. "Let's do the job right and knock him right out of the box."

Kennedy told him to knock off the victory talk. He did not need hard feelings or enemies in steel or any other business. No gloating. But he could not resist in private. Paul Fay, his Undersecretary of the Navy, came into his quarters as Kennedy was doing Dr. Kraus's stretching exercises. Doing a series of sit-ups, Kennedy said: "If any one person deserves the credit . . . it's that damned Clark Clifford. Since he represents so many of them in Washington, he had immediate entrée. Can't you just see Clifford outlining the possible courses of action the Government can take if they showed signs of not moving? Do you know what you're doing when you start bucking the power of the President of the United States? I don't think U.S. Steel or any other of the major steel companies wants to have Internal Revenue agents checking all the expense accounts of their top executives. Do you want the government to go back to hotel bills that time you were in Schenectady to find who was with you? Too many hotel bills and night club expenses would be hard to get by the weekly wives' bridge group out at the Country Club."

Now, he told Fay and Powers, it was time to get back to being President of all the people. He did that the next day, cruising on the *Northampton* through nine miles of U.S. Navy ships steaming by in double lines. Unfortunately, though, a missile show planned for the President went bad, with one Sidewinder missile after another veering wildly and crashing into the sea. Not one missile fired from the ships and from Phantom jets hit the radio-controlled drone planes flying in straight lines overhead.

"God Almighty, what the hell kind of Navy are you running," Kennedy said to Fay. "If I were going to ask the President of the United States and all the top members of the diplomatic corps to watch a surface-to-air missile shoot, I damn well would make sure the missiles hit the drone. . . . If you're going to put on an operation like that, have some sort of fallback to make sure that plane exploded if the last missile even came near it."

His own laughing gave away a joke as he told Fay of a supposed conversation with a South American diplomat during the Sidewinder show: "Mr. Ambassador, you have the opportunity of seeing our great ships of war and our great weapons systems, and I want you to know that these systems are for sale to you. Would you like to have some of those Sidewinder missiles?"

"Oh, Mr. President, you are so wonderful," the ambassador said. "You have these wonderful planes, these wonderful ships, and these missiles. I know that it would be very good for our Navy, but could you sell us some of those marvelous little drones that just keep going. . . ."

Then lunch arrived.

"It's cold," Kennedy said, pushing the soup aside after one spoonful. "Where is the rest of the meal?"

A Filipino steward served chicken.

"My God, this is fried chicken! Where's the chief steward?

"Chief, I gave orders around here that the President of the United States doesn't eat fried foods. This is fried chicken. You have two choices. You can broil chicken or you can fry it. My request was that you broil it. And what do I get? Fried chicken. I don't think I was asking too much."

The great steel victory turned cold quickly, too. The President did his best to guide the coverage, letting Hugh Sidey of *Time* know that the book on his bedstand during the week was *On Moral Courage* by Sir

Compton MacKenzie. But *Time* also lamented a general trend toward thinner profits and fatter paychecks over a decade, and hit the President harder on the ruthlessness of his governing, collecting quotes from all over the country: "Said University of Chicago Economist Milton Friedman: 'It brings home dramatically how much power for a police state resides in Washington.' . . . David Lawrence, the editor of *U.S. News & World Report,* called it 'quasi-Fascism' . . . [that] had led the public into believing that price increases are sinful or unpatriotic."

Lawrence's syndicated column appeared in *The New York Herald Tribune,* and so did a cartoon by John Fischetti showing Pierre Salinger, who had been in the Soviet Union during the fight, reporting back to Kennedy: "Khrushchev said he liked your style in the steel crisis."

"The fucking *Herald Tribune* is at it again," Kennedy said that morning in an angry telephone call to his press secretary. Then he canceled the twenty-two *Trib* subscriptions that came to the White House each morning. But soon enough he himself finally realized that he did have problems of both style and substance with American business. After the crisis, Kennedy got a memo from Walter Heller. "The real remedy," Heller said, "may well be to break up the coalition of companies called 'U.S. Steel.' "

"We may have already bit off more than we can chew," Kennedy said to James Tobin, another member of his Council of Economic Advisers. On April 30, he gave a long and defensive speech to the U.S. Chamber of Commerce, punctuated with assurances such as: "This administration, I assure you, shares your concern about the cost-profit squeeze on American business. We want prosperity, and in a free enterprise system there can be no prosperity without profit."

Meanwhile the pre-dawn FBI raids were giving the President more immediate trouble, political trouble. Robert Kennedy, who had ordered the FBI action, angrily blamed J. Edgar Hoover for carrying out the raids in ways sure to embarrass the President. But the image of police knocking on doors in the dark fit too well with perceptions of a ruthless streak and even a contempt for the niceties of American law in the Kennedy brothers. The *Los Angeles Times* compared President Kennedy to Mussolini.

Canceling the *Herald Tribune* was another stupid thing to do. Cartoonists and comedians around the country were making fun of the President—and his aides made things a bit worse by whispering that, of course, the President read the *Trib* secretly. But Kennedy managed to turn the laughter around at his next press conference. He answered a hostile question about the cancellation with a parody of a popular cigarette commercial that used the line: "Are you smoking more and enjoying it less?" His line was: "Well, I'm reading more and enjoying it less."

Then he added a line on his view of the press: "They are doing their task . . . and I am attempting to do mine, and we are going to live together for a period and then go our separate ways."

He joked about his victory over the sons of bitches of American business at a small family party later. Toasting his brother, the President said that he had just talked with the president of Republic Steel, James Patton. "I was telling Patton what a son of a bitch he was . . .

"And he was proving it," Kennedy continued after the laughter stopped. "Patton asked me, 'Why is it that all the telephone calls of all the steel executives in all the country are being tapped?' And I told him I thought he was being wholly unfair to the Attorney General. . . . And he asked me, 'Why is it that all the income tax returns of all the steel executives in the country are being scrutinized?' And I told him that, too, was wholly unfair, that the Attorney General wouldn't do any such thing. . . .

"And of course, Patton was right."

"They were mean to my brother," said Robert Kennedy, jumping up to keep the joke going. "They can't do that to my brother."

Of course, it was not really a joke. The FBI and the CIA had installed dozens of wiretaps and listening devices on orders and requests from the Attorney General. Transcripts of secret tapes of steel executives, congressmen, lobbyists, and reporters routinely ended up on the President's desk. The targets ranged from writers who criticized the President —Hanson Baldwin of *The New York Times;* Lloyd Norman of *Newsweek;* Bernard Fall of Howard University; and Victor Lasky, a conservative author—to members of Kennedy's own staff: his Air Force assistant, General Godfrey McHugh; and Robert Amory, the CIA's man on the National Security Council. And the White House had had its own taping system installed by the Secret Service with help from military aides early in 1962, on Kennedy's orders. When he thought of it, the President used hidden switches in the Oval Office, the Cabinet Room, and his living room in Hyannis Port to secretly record meetings and phone calls. Among other reasons, the President wanted the transcripts as notes for his own memoirs.

Chapter 28

Two best-selling books caught President Kennedy's attention during the spring of 1962, both of them concerned with military matters. *Seven Days in May* by two Washington newspaper men, Fletcher Knebel and Charles Bailey, was a fictional thriller about an attempted military coup against an American president. *The Guns of August*, by Barbara Tuchman, was a serious piece of work that touched on one of Kennedy's persistent worries: war by miscalculation. It chronicled the way kings and prime ministers, marshals and generals, had stumbled into World War I in August of 1914. In speeches and conversation, he repeated an exchange in the book between two German leaders talking about the war: "How did it all happen?" and the answer, "Ah, if one only knew."

"Could it happen here?" asked Red Fay, who had read *Seven Days in May*, as he and the President were cruising off Hyannis Port.

"It's possible," Kennedy said. "But the conditions would have to be just right. If the country had a young President, and he had a Bay of Pigs, there would be a certain uneasiness. Maybe the military would do a little criticizing behind his back. Then if there were another Bay of Pigs, the reaction of the country would be, 'Is he too young and inexperienced?' The military would almost feel that it was their patriotic obligation to stand ready to preserve the integrity of the nation and only God knows just what segment of Democracy they would be defending. . . .

"Then, if there were a third Bay of Pigs it could happen," said the President. His friend looked shocked and Kennedy added: "It won't happen on my watch."

Back on shore, Kennedy called in one of his military aides, General Chester Clifton. Quoting from the book, the real President asked about the man with "the Football," the nuclear strike codes. "The book says one of those men sits outside my bedroom door all night. Is that true?"

"No," Clifton replied. "He's downstairs in the office area. . . . He'll be upstairs—we've timed it many times—he can make it even if he has to run up the stairs and not use the elevator—in a minute and a half. If he knocks at your door some night and comes in and opens the valise, pay attention. . . ."

After he read *The Guns of August,* the President called up his Secretary of the Army, Elvis Stahr, Jr., and asked him to come over to the White House. He handed the Secretary a copy of the book. "I want you to read this," he said. "And I want every officer in the Army to read it."

Stahr had the book placed in every one of the officers' day rooms on U.S. military bases around the world. Commanders were informed that the Commander-in-Chief wanted them and their men to read it.

John Kennedy distrusted the military, at least its commanders. Part of it was the perception of the lieutenant seeing the big brass giving orders to men they did not know in places and situations they did not understand. He felt something like that about the Joint Chiefs of Staff, persuaded they had misled him, even betrayed him, in the weeks leading up to the Bay of Pigs. Most of the Chiefs seemed narrow or stupid to him.

"You can't beat brains," he said of those he listened to most on national security affairs. Robert McNamara, McGeorge Bundy, and Maxwell Taylor were the men he entrusted with one of his fundamental goals: gaining civilian control over the military. Taylor was the only active or former senior officer with regular access to the Oval Office. One of his qualifications was that most other senior officers disliked him, which was a big part of the reason that Taylor, a former Army Chief of Staff, had never become Chairman of the Joint Chiefs.

The generals and admirals did not think much of Kennedy's ideas, either. One of them, retired Admiral Arleigh Burke, could now say anything he wanted to, and was doing just that.

"America and the West in general have a guilt complex about power," he had told a Daughters of the American Revolution convention late in April 1962. "It frustrates our every use of power. In Cuba, Suez, in Korea, currently in Laos, we half use it in a compromise between dream and reality. . . . In a schizoid manner we have balanced a

Department of Defense with a Committee on Disarmament, ballistic missiles with the position that war is unthinkable. Basically, we oscillate between an unpalatable reality and an act of faith. . . . No one really knows what we will do because we ourselves do not know."

"God, 30-Knot Burke! To think I used to admire these people," Kennedy said. He not only wanted a new kind of military strategy, he had a vision, a rather romantic one, of new kinds of soldiers: Green Berets and intellectual Colonel Hillandales. Max Taylor was the model. Kennedy liked to make the point that his chief military adviser spoke French and German and Spanish. The official White House line, repeated often to reporters, was that if you asked Taylor about a problem in the Middle East, he wanted to know how Xerxes had handled it.

On the Saturday that he and Red Fay were cruising, Kennedy had to face up to another military crisis in Southeast Asia. On May 5, several companies of Pathet Lao troops—reportedly supported by some of the nine thousand North Vietnamese troops in Laos—overran a provincial capital, Nam Tha, in northern Laos. They chased out 5,200 men of the Royal Laotian Army commanded by the United States' man, General Phoumi Nosavan, who was as incompetent as he was anti-Communist. For four months, against the advice of several hundred Americans who were roaming the country under various covers, the royal government had been reinforcing Nam Tha, which was only twenty miles from the border with China. Phoumi was inviting attack in the rainy season when it would be impossible to supply or reinforce his men. The cease-fire was broken, the United States' friends were in panicked retreat, and, once again, Kennedy had to decide whether to move troops into Laos.

That was the question at his May 9 news conference, and he answered: "We are hopeful that we can bring about a restoration of the cease-fire. I agree it's a very hazardous course, but introducing American forces which is the other one—let's not think there is some great third course—that is also a hazardous course."

The next day he ordered the Seventh Fleet to steam into the Gulf of Thailand. "To signal Moscow," he said at a National Security Council meeting that day. It was exactly the kind of posturing military men most disliked. The Joint Chiefs told the President that the obvious next step, troop commitment in Thailand along the border of Laos, had to be backed up with command authority for any contingency, including military authority to use nuclear weapons if the Chinese called the U.S. bluff and moved troops toward the U.S. positions. The generals and admirals let it be known, through the Pentagon press corps, that they thought the President was playing games. Of course that was exactly what he was doing, playing move and counter, bluff and feint. He was trying to avoid defeat or the appearance of defeat. Their business, as they saw it, was victory. Kennedy, in turn, saw them as men who were willing to blow up the world to win—with some sergeant or lieutenant having the authority to push the Commander-in-Chief into world war.

Averell Harriman, who had negotiated the cease-fire the Pathet Lao had openly broken at Nam Tha, agreed with the Pentagon up to a point: moving the fleet was an empty gesture without committing some troops. Ships alone might tempt the Communists to make a final move to take over all of Laos. They had to be persuaded that U.S. troops just might go in.

Harriman had moved up to Assistant Secretary of State for the Far East, in a title shuffle after Kennedy had finally pushed Chester Bowles out of Washington into a made-up job as special ambassador to all the new countries of Asia and Africa. With his sometime sidekick, Roger Hilsman, Harriman telephoned the White House, determined to persuade Kennedy not to move the fleet until he had decided whether or not to offload the U.S. Marines. Kennedy listened to their argument as a crowd of foreign students congregated behind him in the Rose Garden. "Okay, do that, stop the fleet," the President said over his shoulder to McGeorge Bundy as he strode outside to greet the students.

Bundy telephoned Hilsman, and he telephoned General George Decker, acting Chairman of the Joint Chiefs. "My God," the general said. "The message to move has already gone out. . . . Be sure and give me a little memo about this."

Within an hour Kennedy focused on what had happened and was angry with Harriman and Hilsman and the whole State Department. "What the hell is going on there?" he yelled into the phone at an assistant when he could not find Hilsman or Harriman. "Do you know that Roger Hilsman has just stopped the Seventh Fleet?"

Kennedy did get Hilsman a few minutes later and asked him why he had wanted to stop the ships. The State Department's intelligence chief repeated the fear that it might tempt the Communists instead of frightening them. Laos, after all, had no coastline, so U.S. ships were out of sight—even though U.S. troops were to be greatly feared.

"Well," said the President. "Something has happened politically which makes it a little less tricky." He had just heard from his new CIA director, John McCone, another Republican, that former President Eisenhower was willing to back him on any action in Laos. "That should take care of our concerns. . . . You and Mac Bundy talk it over between you and you and he decide whether to stop the Fleet or send the Fleet. Just issue the orders and let me know."

The President ended the conversation by asking Hilsman to try to do something to prevent the Pentagon from telling the press about his own indecision. "We have to figure out how this is to be described from the Pentagon. Otherwise they'll leak it and we'll look stupid."

Hilsman called the duty officer at the Joint Chiefs and told him to stop the second message and send in the fleet.

"Yes, sir," said the officer. "Right away. Where are we going?"

"Thailand," Hilsman said. The officer came back on the line and said the second message calling back the fleet had not yet gone out. "Then tear it up," Hilsman said.

"It's torn up," Hilsman said, calling the White House again. "It doesn't exist."

When he got home that Saturday night, Hilsman wrote himself a long memo about what happened as the President called out the fleet, called it back, and then sent it out again. At one point he broke the narrative to say: "When do I have time to think?—driving to and from work, sitting in meetings . . . shaving."

"You want to read something fantastic?" Kennedy said, pulling a two-page cable from his pocket, reading it out loud himself as he relaxed with a Scotch-and-water with friends at the end of the day. It was from the U.S. military mission in Vientiane, a field report from an American adviser with Laotian troops: "We're still holding Houei Sai, but no thanks to the Royal Laotian Army, whose performance is just plain gutless. While the battle for the airstrip was raging, the Royal Laotian forces were swimming in a nearby stream."

"Phoumi is a total shit," the President said of the man America was backing. In Nam Tha, American military advisers had escaped by helicopter on May 6 as the Pathet Lao had entered the town. That escape plan had been devised after dozens of other Americans were captured by the Pathet Lao or the North Vietnamese when they were abandoned in earlier firefights. In at least three earlier engagements, Americans had been left behind when the Royal Laotian Army fled without telling its advisers. Kennedy received another cable, this one from a U.S. military adviser reporting back from Nam Tha: "The morale of my battalion is substantially better than in our last engagement. The last time, they dropped their weapons and ran. This time, they took their weapons with them."

This time they ran sixty miles in forty-eight hours, across the Mekong River into Thailand, where they were airlifted back to Vientiane. Without surrogates, who were again in flight, Kennedy decided he had to once again show the American flag. On May 14, nine days after the Pathet Lao had overrun Nam Tha, the first of three thousand U.S. troops, units that had been training in Thailand, moved into positions along the border on the Thai side of the river.

Newspapers were excited by speculation that the United States would "introduce" troops into Laos. But, in fact, there were already several hundred Americans in Laos, most of them lying about why they were there. Even the President of the United States was not sure what they were doing. The lies got bigger and bigger as information trickled up. *The Times* of London reported that CIA agents in Laos were working against U.S. policy and against the forming of a neutral government. Pierre Salinger asked Kennedy whether he should deny it. "The story, I assume, is untrue," the President said. "Do they offer any evidence?"

The most important secret dealing, though, was between the President and Khrushchev—as it had been in Berlin the year before. The two leaders were negotiating once again through Georgi Bolshakov.

"My brother feels he has been double-crossed," said Robert Kennedy to the Russian, explaining that the President had relied on Premier Khrushchev's assurances at Vienna regarding a neutral Laos. Bolshakov met Robert Kennedy again on May 22, a week after the Marines had taken up their positions along the Thai border, and said he carried Khrushchev's personal assurances to the President that there would be no more large-scale military action in Laos.

"Georgi said that Khrushchev understood that the reason the troops were sent in was because of the possibility of an outbreak in Laos," Robert Kennedy told his brother. "Therefore, now that the agreement had been made in Laos . . . Mr. Khrushchev hoped that it was possible for the United States to withdraw its troops from Thailand." The President told his brother to tell his Russian that U.S. troop withdrawal would begin in ten days. The secret channel that had worked in Berlin when U.S. and Soviet tanks faced off had worked in Southeast Asia this time.

The President sent Harriman off to Geneva to try to negotiate the neutralization of Laos—taking some political fire as an appeaser. Kennedy practically worked out the terms himself in daily telephone calls to the American team in Switzerland. Within a few days it became apparent that both the Soviets and the United States still wanted a settlement, as they had wanted one in 1961—and for the same reasons. The Soviets wanted to close off the Laotian conflict before the Chinese became involved too deeply, and Kennedy had long since concluded that "the Land of a Million Elephants" was not worth intervention. Phoumi Nosavan, the United States' man, was holding out for a better deal in a coalition government, but he fell in line, too, when Harriman, acting on Kennedy's orders, told him the United States was pulling out no matter what he did.*

---

* The "Declaration and Protocol on Neutrality in Laos" was signed on July 23, 1962, by representatives of fourteen countries.

So it seemed certain now that if there were going to be a showdown in Southeast Asia, it would be in Vietnam, the real-life Sarkhan of *The Ugly American*. In Washington, the debate was once again a question of whether the United States had the right man out there. Was Ngo Dinh Diem tough enough? Was he competent enough? Was he flexible enough? That last question was really about whether he would take American orders.

"He's a losing horse in the long run," John Kenneth Galbraith told Kennedy when the President asked him to make a second trip to Saigon. "We cannot ourselves replace Diem. But we should be clear in our mind that almost any non-Communist change would probably be beneficial and this should be the guiding rule for our diplomatic representation in the area. . . . This could expand step by step into a major, long-drawn-out indecisive military involvement. There is consequent danger we shall replace the French as the colonial force in the area and bleed as the French did."

Harriman, though, still supported Diem. "I get a little tired of people who expect the Vietnamese to have a Jeffersonian democracy," he told Kennedy after the Geneva conference. "We don't have that in a lot of places in this country. Is there a Jeffersonian democracy in Mississippi?"

As Kennedy and Khrushchev secretly worked out a Laos deal, President de Gaulle called one of his rare news conferences and announced: "France's defense is once again a national defense. As regards the defense of France, the battle of Europe and even world war as they were imagined when NATO was born, everything is now in question. . . ." The French, who had been testing nuclear bombs in the Sahara Desert since February 1960, intended to develop their own nuclear arsenal, he said, missiles and warheads separate from the NATO arsenal and umbrella provided by the United States.

It seemed that Kennedy's dream of a test ban treaty, signed and enforced by the United States and the Soviet Union, had become a nightmare. On May 17, at his own news conference, the President said: "We test and test and test, and you finally get weapons which are increasingly sophisticated. But the fact of the matter is that somebody may test ten or fifteen times and get a weapon which is not nearly as good as these megatons weapons, but nevertheless, they are two to three times what the weapon was which destroyed Hiroshima or Nagasaki, and that was dreadful enough."

"I am haunted by this," he said in private. He thought that nuclear proliferation was the greatest single problem of the world in the 1960s, and that the single most compelling reason for a test ban was to prevent Communist China from developing a bomb. But like most Americans, he ignored or did not understand the feeling in other countries that "the Bomb" was seen as the icon of national adulthood. Kennedy had hoped to persuade de Gaulle that France did not need its own nuclear force. The United States, he said, would always be there to protect Western Europe. But the more Kennedy talked, the more de Gaulle was convinced that he was right to believe that the first and perhaps last stage of a nuclear exchange would involve Soviet missiles destroying Western Europe and U.S. missiles leveling Eastern Europe. Besides, who was Kennedy to talk? The United States had resumed atmospheric testing on April 25.

On June 6, the President had an opportunity to articulate his vision of the kind of military he wanted when he traveled to West Point, New York, to give the commencement address at the U.S. Military Academy.

"Whether it is Viet Nam or Laos or in Thailand, whether it is a military advisory group in Iran, whether it is a military attaché in some Latin American country during a difficult and challenging period. . . . Whatever your position, you will need to know and understand not only the foreign policy of the U.S. but the foreign policy of all countries scattered around the world. . . . You will need to give orders in different tongues and read maps by different systems. You will be involved in economic judgments which most economists would hesitate to make. You will need to understand the importance of military power and also the limits of military power. . . . In many countries, your posture and performance will provide the local population with the only evidence of what our country is really like. In other countries, your military mission, its advice and action will play a key role in determining whether those people will remain free."

That was quite different from the perspective of the speaker invited to West Point by the commandant, General William Westmoreland, just the month before. "Your mission remains fixed, determined, inviolable —it is to win our wars," said General Douglas MacArthur in his last address to cadets. "Everything else in your professional career is but corollary to this vital dedication."

Chapter 29

May 29, 1962, was John F. Kennedy's birthday. One of his presents was $3 million of the principal of the $10 million trust fund his father had established in his name. Since he was twenty-one, Kennedy had lived on the interest paid on that $10 million, one of eight similar funds set up by Joseph P. Kennedy for each of his children.

John was forty-five years old, but still very much the rich boy who never paid his own bills. His father had set up an office in New York to handle such details and Kennedy rarely carried money in the pockets of his custom-made clothes. He just borrowed cash from whoever happened to be around. They could send a bill to New York, if the amount was worth the trouble.

He called his parents "Mother" and "Father," not "my mother" or "my father" the way most Americans did. When his own children burst happily into his office, he would sweep them up and then after a few moments of play clap his hands to call their nanny or press the button he had to call her in to take them away again. He donated his $100,000 salary as President to charities, beginning with the Boy Scouts and Girl Scouts of America.

Kennedy was also cheap in the way rich people often are, periodically checking up on White House spending, which was supplemented by his own money. "Why are we giving them French champagne? Isn't New York champagne good enough?" he asked during one of his personal economy drives. He did not drink much champagne, but when he did, insisted on Dom Pérignon. One night after a state dinner he cruised the White House kitchen to confirm his suspicions that champagne glasses and bottles were being taken away half full—the staff, of course, was taking them home—and ordered that henceforth glasses would not be refilled until they were empty, and new bottles would not be opened until the bottles at tables were emptied. "I don't want to see five bottles opened at the same time," he said.

When he focused on it, he was also tight with public money in ways large and small. The first papers he saw from the Bureau of the Budget recorded expenditures in tenths of millions—$12.4 million was the standard style—and he sent them back saying he wanted the figures spelled out to $12,400,000. "I want every zero put in there," he said. "I want those guys to realize they're spending real money." Those guys included Robert Kennedy, who one weekend that spring had sent the Secret Service on a nationwide search for a damper plate that broke as he was sailing off Maine with a couple of friends. "Goddammit," the President said when he heard about it. "Don't ever let that story out. It must have cost . . . all the people who went to work on that damper plate, the cost would probably be about $100,000."

"Good morning, George," were usually John Kennedy's first words of the day as the valet laid four morning newspapers on his bedstand. Thomas, a fifty-five-year-old Negro, had been a gift from Arthur Krock, who repaid past debts to Joseph Kennedy by sending his own valet to take care of Joe's son when he came to Washington in 1947 as a young bachelor used to being taken care of by servants. Thomas laid out the first suit of the day. Kennedy had a habit of changing clothes from the skin out as often as four times a day, sometimes using six shirts. He was surprised once when Ben Bradlee told him that he and a lot of other men wore the same shirt two days in a row. The President owned eighteen suits, with European-cut, two-button jackets different from the three-button models worn by most American men. If Kennedy's back was troubling him, Thomas would help him into his clothes.

Kennedy had celebrated this birthday in public ten days before, raising a million dollars for the Democratic National Committee at a giant gala in Madison Square Garden in New York on the night of May 19. Fifteen thousand people had bought tickets priced from $3 to $1,000 to be there as he sat in a box in front of the stage, smiling through the night of entertainment by some of the biggest stars of New York, Hollywood, and the world: Jack Benny, Maria Callas, Harry Belafonte, Ella Fitzgerald, Peggy Lee, Henry Fonda, Jimmy Durante, Mike Nichols and Elaine May.

"The amazing thing to me," Benny had said, looking over at the President, who was happily puffing a cigar, "is that a man in a rocking chair could have such a young wife." The crowd roared with laughter, and so did Kennedy, whose wife had stayed in Virginia, going to the Loudoun County Hunt horse show with her daughter Caroline, winning a third-place ribbon on a horse named Minbreno.

The most memorable lady of that evening was Marilyn Monroe, the reigning sex goddess of American films, who was literally sewn into a $5,000 flesh-colored, flesh-pressing gown, embroidered with rhinestones, with nothing underneath but the world's most famous body. A Monroe poster had filled the wall at the foot of John Kennedy's bed as he recovered from his back operation at New York Hospital in 1954. The senator's friends had tacked a poster of the star in shorts upside down, so her legs were spread apart for the recuperating patient.

"Happy Birthday to you, Happy Birthday to you," Monroe sang in Madison Square Garden, in a whispery voice both seductive and little-girl. It was a performance people remembered.

"Happy Birthday, Dear Mr. Pres-i-dent. Happy Birthday to you!"

Then, to the tune of "Thanks for the Memory," she sang:

> Thanks, Mr. President, For all the things you've done,
> The battles that you've won,
> The way you deal with U.S. Steel,
> And our problems by the ton,
> We thank you so much.

She led the crowd in another chorus of "Happy Birthday." Then Kennedy came up to the stage and responded: "Thank you. I can now retire from politics after having had 'Happy Birthday' sung to me in such a sweet, wholesome way."

Marilyn Monroe was trouble. She was telling people in Hollywood of an affair with the President—with his brother-in-law Peter Lawford handling the arrangements for liaisons at a Santa Monica beach house and apartments and hotels in Los Angeles. "I think I made his back feel better," she said. Sometimes she talked of marrying the President. Kennedy was worried that the press, particularly *Time* and *Newsweek,* might be looking into those stories. Rumors and talk about women or his health did not particularly bother Kennedy; at least they did not change his behavior, so long as they were not published. He understood an important fact about the press and scandal: respectable journals generally avoided being the first to report on rumors or evidence concerning sex. But he knew that once something had been printed, no matter where, newspapers and magazines quickly quoted each other, using the first publication as a peg for their own reports. His political opponents would do the same thing, hiding behind any ink on any paper. The idea was to stop the first mention.

After the Madison Square Garden party, there had been enough rumors about the President and the movie star that Kennedy felt he should send out some of his men to try to kill any stories in the works, even in gossip columns. One of those he turned to was the inspector general of the Peace Corps, a former *New York Post* reporter named William Haddad. Haddad was not a regular Oval Office visitor, but knew his way around New York journalism.

"See the editors," Kennedy said. "Tell them you are speaking for me and that it's just not true."*

By Kennedy's actual birthday, Tuesday, May 29, he had other things on his mind. The lead headline in *The New York Times* was "STOCK PRICES DIVE IN SHARPEST LOSS SINCE 1929 BREAK—$20,800,000,000 of Value Erased. Turnover, the Fifth Busiest in History, Makes Ticker 141 Minutes Late." The stock market had dropped more than 35 points on Monday. The Dow Jones average, which had been steadily declining since Kennedy's election, dropped from 611.78 to 563.24 before bouncing back 12 points or so at the end of the trading day. It was the deepest one-day drop in stock prices since the Crash of 1929.

"Blue Monday," they were calling it on Wall Street—or "the Kennedy Crash," saying it was Kennedy's fault, caused by mistrust of him or a delayed response to the President's attack on U.S. Steel. Whatever the cause, the value of all the stocks on the exchange was down more than 25 percent overall in six months. The joke of the day, told bitterly on Wall Street, was that when old Joe Kennedy heard about the drop, he began to speak again, for the first time since his stroke, and his first words were: "To think I voted for that son-of-a-bitch."

There were no jokes in Washington. It was a political crisis of the first order at 1600 Pennsylvania Avenue. Too many businessmen were convinced the administration was simply anti-business. In late May, just before the crash, Allison R. Maxwell, Jr., the president of Pittsburgh Steel, had been cheered by a thousand executives at the annual convention of the American Iron and Steel Institute when he said: "This administration is heading toward a form of socialism in which the pretense of private property is retained while, in fact, prices, wages, production and distribution are dictated by bureaucrats."

"No, no," Kennedy told his own men in private. "I'm not against

---

* "He lied to me," Haddad would say years later. "He used my credibility with people I knew."

business—I want to help them if I can. They're our partners—unwilling partners. But we're in this together. I want business to do well. If they don't, we don't. . . . But look at the record. I spent a whole year trying to encourage business. And look what I get for it. . . . What do they mean by all this 'anti-business' stuff anyway? I don't get it. Point out to me a single instance in the last year when I've said anything that's anti-business. Ike could have tried to give business a tax break. But he didn't do it. I'm at least trying. We're going to give them better depreciation credit."

Perhaps he was protesting too much. He did find businessmen boring and had contempt for what he called "chasing the dollar." That, of course, was a race that had been run and won for him by his father.

Kennedy tried to protect himself politically on White House dealings with businessmen and business groups in exactly the same way he protected himself on national security. Except for Walter Heller as chairman of the Council of Economic Advisers, the Democratic President had appointed Republicans to front-line economic positions: Douglas Dillon as Secretary of the Treasury and William McChesney Martin as chairman of the Federal Reserve. "Walter," he said one day, inviting Heller to come down to the White House pool while he swam and had a massage, "I understand your problems with Bill Martin in terms of policy, but you get along with him well personally, don't you?"

"Yes, that's true," said Heller, a little disconcerted. He had never seen a naked President before.

"Good," the President said. "Frankly I need Martin and Dillon. I need these Republicans to maintain a strong front as far as the financial community is concerned."

The President wanted to be seen as pro-business in the sense that he was willing to try anything that might promote business investment and economic growth above the 2.3 percent rise in GNP in 1961. He regularly compared that number with the 6 and 7 percent growth announced each year by the Soviet Union. And he was pro-business in very fundamental ways. When Chalmers Roberts, the White House correspondent of the *Washington Post,* asked him what exactly it was average Americans could do for their country, Kennedy said, "Restrain their wage demands." But if he and the financial community were trying to get to the same place, they were going there in different ways. Businessmen wanted, above all, reduced government spending—at least non-defense spending—and a balanced federal budget. Heller's school of one, in private, was more and more interested in his teacher's Keynesian arguments for a cut in personal and business income taxes.

Heller thought that the balanced budget was the problem, not a solution. He believed lower tax rates would not only stimulate the economy by putting more money in people's pockets, but that the resulting economic growth would increase overall tax revenues. Heller and Samuelson pushed Kennedy hard and often for a cut in the corporate rate of 52 percent, and in personal income tax rates, imposed to finance World War II. The personal rates now escalated rapidly from 20 percent on the first $2,000 of a taxpayer's earnings, to 50 percent on anything between $32,000 and $36,000, up to a confiscatory rate of 91 percent on marginal income above $400,000 a year. Heller argued that the rates discouraged initiative—i.e., making more money—and took too much cash out of the overall economy. Business required investment and it was in competition with government for those same dollars. Kennedy was close to convinced Heller was right.

But while the President studied with Heller, the Dow Jones average was in decline. It had dropped steadily from an all-time peak of 734.91 on December 13, 1961, to under 690 just before April's steel showdown. Then it had declined to 611 at the beginning of trading on May 28. Heller warned his boss that a "Kennedy Bear Market" was a real possibility. "It's none too soon to start considering concrete sources of action in case it turns out that our forecasts were too optimistic," he had told the President a month before the crash. If Kennedy was beginning to sound like Heller, at least in private, the economist was beginning to sound like the politician, advising the President that he and the council were determined to keep the economy moving no matter what economics books taught: "We aren't about to . . . stick our heads in the sand, and lose elections."

When the Dow Jones average settled at 576 on "Blue Monday," Heller had a memo on Kennedy's desk that began: "A Quickie Tax Cut? —A tax cut would be the most effective governmental action that could be taken in the present situation to support the economy and bolster consumer and investor confidence."

Heller liked the phrase "performance gap." He defined it as the difference between the economy operating at full employment—that is, with unemployment at 4 percent or less—and at the current rate of about 5.5 percent. He calculated that difference, the performance gap, in 1961, at $50 billion—and 5 million jobs. "Current levels of Federal expenditures and tax rates," the professor told the President, "bring the budget into balance substantially below full employment." From there on, the budget moved into surplus, meaning from that point on the government was taking more money out of the economy than it was putting in. Businessmen attacked government deficits, said Heller, without understanding that tax revenue shortfalls kept money in the private economy.

Government deficits, said the President's man, mean new private investment and new jobs.

Kennedy got it. But he also understood the American commitment to puritan economics—"Neither a borrower nor a lender be"—and he was not yet willing to take the political heat of being seen as a borrower, a lender, and a spender. Early on, he had told Paul Samuelson that publicly pushing for a tax cut was asking for it: "The Republicans would kick us in the balls on that one."

"Suppose," Kennedy said, "that I ask for something, a bold program, and I don't get it?"

"Then you've fought the good fight," Samuelson replied.

"That's vanity, Paul, not politics," the President said, opening the door from his office to the hallway. Kennedy made it a practice to stand in the middle of the Oval Office to greet people he thought might talk too long. Then he would drift toward the door, opening it when he had heard enough.

For the moment, he decided to stick with the advice of his Republicans, particularly Treasury Secretary Douglas Dillon, who dreamed of reforming the almost impenetrable complexity of federal tax codes at the same time rates were cut. Kennedy also listened to the even more conservative dicta of Robert Lovett, his consultant on Wall Street. "Do nothing. Say nothing," Lovett told him when Kennedy telephoned him on Monday morning, as soon as he heard the Dow Jones was plunging. Lovett told Kennedy that what was happening was long overdue, a correction in the market caused by the fact that most stocks were bloated, overvalued in anticipation of inflation. Average price-earnings ratios on Blue Monday were 26 to 1, compared with 17 to 1 before the beginning of a steady bull market that lasted four years, under both Eisenhower and Kennedy, until the December 1961 peak.

The same advice was also coming from Kennedy's left. The President called Ken Galbraith, on home leave at his farm in Vermont, and the ambassador dictated a memo: "Hold rigidly to the explanation that the market is accommodating itself to the end of inflation. . . ." He sent Kennedy a copy of his book on the 1929 Crash.

McGeorge Bundy also slipped a memo into the pile on the President's desk on the day after, Tuesday, May 29. "It's not my department," he said. "But I'm strongly against a TV speech from you now on the stock-market flap. What we have at the moment is panicky selling, and if you take to a national TV hookup you can only add to the panic. . . . Be calm and let the calmness spread."

Dillon was designated to articulate publicly the official story in political terms: The drop in share prices was a belated recognition by Wall

Street that inflation had been defeated by Kennedy. The U.S. Steel confrontation was the final proof that there would be no destructive wage-price spirals while this man was President. Stable prices would make American goods more salable around the world, said Dillon. That cheerful interpretation was reported almost word for word on the front page of *The New York Times,* under the headline: "WASHINGTON SEES MARKET REACTING TO OVERPRICING."

The official price stability story also served the political purpose of elevating the Kennedy–U.S. Steel battle from a personality clash to what was called inside the White House "the Economic Battle of the Bulge." Winners write the history, Kennedy understood.

The storm passed quickly, though there was a sense that more might be coming. On Tuesday, the Dow Jones average, which had dropped below 554 in the morning, climbed steadily to close at 603.96. An hour later, Kennedy boarded a helicopter with White House chef René Verdon and a big chocolate cake for a flight to Glen Ora and a birthday dinner with his wife and children. Reporters in Washington had one question left, though: Did the President see the birthday gift from Frank Sinatra, a rocking chair covered in chrysanthemums?

"No," Pierre Salinger said. "It was sent straight to Children's Hospital with other birthday flowers and the President never saw it." A deliberate snub, the press reported.

In a news conference on June 7, after the market had calmed itself, Kennedy announced that he would submit a tax reform package when the next Congress convened in January 1963. "An across-the-board reduction in personal and corporate income tax rates which will not be wholly offset by other reforms," he said. "In other words, a net tax reduction."

The Democratic President tried to reach out to business on June 11, in a commencement speech at Yale University. After the hood of an honorary Doctor of Laws was lifted over his head and placed on his shoulders, the 1940 Harvard graduate charmed the New Haven crowd with a clever opening: "It could be said now that I have the best of both worlds, a Harvard education and a Yale degree."

It was an extraordinary performance. The President, student of Heller and Samuelson, had become a disciple of Keynes. He came, he said, to speak of "Myths"—"particularly the myth and reality in our national economy." The big three he set out to debunk were:

"The myth here is that the government is big, and bad. . . .

"The myth persists that Federal deficits create inflation and budget surpluses prevent it. . . .

"Third, the matter of confidence, business confidence, or simply confidence in America."

1.

January 20, 1961. The inauguration of the thirty-fifth President, watched by his wife and the thirty-fourth President. The two men were impressed by each other's force of personality. Ike's nickname for Kennedy was "Little Boy Blue." Kennedy's name for Eisenhower was what lieutenants (j.g.) call the big brass, the "old asshole."

(*Top*) March 23, 1961. "The safety of Laos runs with the safety of us all . . . I know that every American will want his country to honor its obligations."

(*Right*) May 16, 1961. National Security Adviser McGeorge Bundy said: "I hope you'll be in a good mood when you read this. . . . We do have a problem of management. We can't get you to sit still."

(*Above left*) November 25, 1961. Georgi Bolshakov (right), meeting with President Kennedy at Hyannis Port, was identified as "a Soviet editor." In fact, he was a major in Soviet intelligence, Khrushchev's secret envoy to the Kennedys.

5.

May 15, 1961. Kennedy learned there was a revolution in America when he saw this photograph of a Freedom Riders' bus afire in Alabama. He said to his civil rights adviser: "Can't you get your goddamned friends off those buses?"

6.

May 7, 1963. FBI Director J. Edgar Hoover between the Kennedy brothers. Robert Kennedy said of him: "Rather a psycho. . . . But it's a danger we can control. He serves our interest."

7.

8.

(*Top*) June 4, 1961. Khrushchev and Kennedy in Vienna. "Worst thing in my life," Kennedy said. "He savaged me . . . thinks I have no guts. . . . We have to confront them. The only place we can do that is in Vietnam."

(*Bottom*) June 1, 1961. Presidents Kennedy and de Gaulle talked in the Great Hall at Versailles as ten thousand security men searched for an assassin.

9.

(*Left*) June 5, 1961. Dr. Max Jacobson, Kennedy's amphetamine doctor, was in the presidential party in Vienna and London. "I don't care if it's horse piss. It works," Kennedy remarked.

10.

(*Above*) June 22, 1961. Dr. Janet Travell, Kennedy's back doctor. George Burkley, a White House doctor, told her, "You're making him a cripple. . . . Keep your hands off him!"

11.

(*Above right*) June 16, 1961. Kennedy returned from Europe. He had once said: "I'd rather be dead than spend the rest of my life on these goddamned crutches."

(*Left*) August 13, 1961. Marguerite Higgins of *The New York Herald Tribune,* who accused Kennedy of selling out Berlin and murdering President Diem of South Vietnam. McGeorge Bundy called her the "firebug."

(*Below*) August 18, 1963. *Der Clay.* General Lucius Clay, Kennedy's proconsul in Berlin, with West Berlin mayor Willy Brandt and Vice President Lyndon Johnson.

12.

(*Below*) September 30, 1961. Clay looking over the Berlin Wall. The commander of the U.S. troops there would tell him: "Take your cotton-picking hands off my troops. If you don't like that, call the President and see what he says."

13.

14.

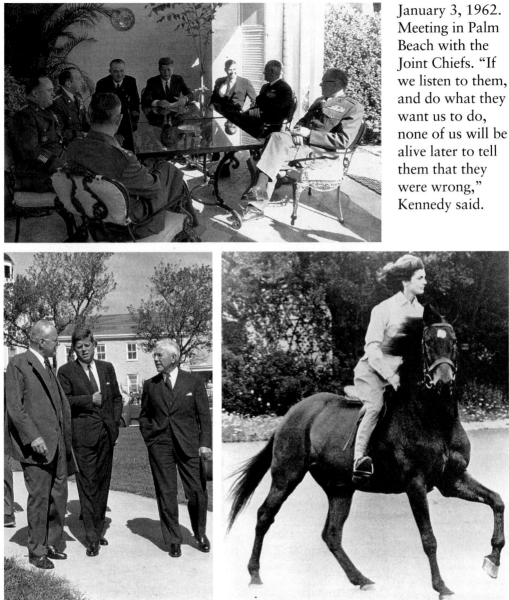

January 3, 1962. Meeting in Palm Beach with the Joint Chiefs. "If we listen to them, and do what they want us to do, none of us will be alive later to tell them that they were wrong," Kennedy said.

15.

16.

17.

(*Above left*) September 27, 1961. Kennedy replaced CIA Director Allen Dulles (*left*) with John McCone (*right*). Dulles and McCone were two of the many Republicans Kennedy put in top ranks of his administration. Said McCone when assassination of Fidel Castro was brought up by Secretary of Defense McNamara: "I could get excommunicated for something like this."

(*Above right*) Jacqueline Kennedy, riding Sardar, a gift from the king of Saudi Arabia. Her husband wanted her to give it back, saying: "Israelis come along with an old Bible worth about twelve dollars." Jackie said: "I want the horses."

18.

19.

(*Top*) February 20, 1962. Kennedy and Lyndon Johnson with congressional leaders watching the launch of Colonel John Glenn, the first American to go into space orbit. Johnson said, "If only he were a Negro."

(*Bottom*) October 18, 1961. General Edward Lansdale (*center*) at Tan Son Nhut Airport in Saigon, the model for Colonel Hillandale of *The Ugly American,* a book Kennedy lived by, and for Pyle in *The Quiet American* by Graham Greene.

20.

21.

22.

(*Far left*) April 14, 1961. Arthur Schlesinger, Jr., wrote the memo "Protection of the President": "When lies must be told, they should be told by subordinate officials. At no point should the President be asked to lend himself to the cover operation."

(*Left*) October 18, 1962. Ted Sorensen, the speechwriter, walked out with Kennedy after he met with congressional leaders. Kennedy said, "If they think they can do this job better than me, they can have it."

September 30, 1962. Federal marshals escort James Meredith into the University of Mississippi. "Where are they getting [these ideas]?" Kennedy asked a Negro politician. "From you," the man replied.

September 9, 1962. Robert Frost was Kennedy's poet-laureate until he met with Khrushchev and reported that the Russian thought Americans were "too liberal to fight." Kennedy refused to speak to him again, ignoring pleas from the eighty-eight-year-old poet's deathbed.

23.

November 10, 1962. The President and Mrs. Kennedy at Eleanor Roosevelt's funeral along with ex-presidents Truman and Eisenhower. On the way back to Washington, Kennedy and Chief Justice Earl Warren sat together, laughing over newspaper clippings reporting Richard Nixon's defeat in his race for governor of California and his "last press conference."

24.

25.

October 24, 1962. A White House meeting during the Cuban missile crisis. At the height of the crisis, Kennedy asked Prime Minister Harold Macmillan, "Should I take out Cuba?"

26.

27.

(*Top*) June 11, 1963. A Vietnamese monk burned himself to death on a Saigon street in protest against the government of President Ngo Dinh Diem. This photograph by Malcolm Browne of the Associated Press would contribute to an American takeover of the country. The State Department soon told Kennedy: ". . . one more burning bonze will cause domestic U.S. reaction which will require strong public statement . . . that might precipitate coup in Saigon."

(*Bottom*) May 3, 1963. In Birmingham, Alabama, Martin Luther King, Jr., used schoolchildren in demonstrations, and local police used dogs and firehoses to break up Negro civil rights demonstrations. Kennedy said: "It makes me sick!"

28.

29.

30.

31.

(*Top left*) Mary Meyer, a Georgetown artist and the sister-in-law of Kennedy's friend Ben Bradlee, was slipped into the White House by the President's aides during 1963 whenever Mrs. Kennedy was away. (*Top right*) Judith Campbell (shown here in 1975) met Kennedy in several cities during 1961 and 1962—and was also involved with gangster Momo "Sam" Giancana. (*Bottom right*) January 20, 1961. Actress Angie Dickinson was escorted by Kennedy's PT-109 buddy, Paul Fay, during the inaugural. She and the new President managed to slip away together a couple of times between ceremonies and parties. (*Bottom left*) May 29, 1962. On Kennedy's forty-fifth birthday, Marilyn Monroe, whose name would become linked with those of both John and Robert Kennedy, was the featured attraction of celebrations at Madison Square Garden and here, later, at a small party in New York. Said Kennedy at the Garden event: "Thank you. I can now retire from politics after having had 'Happy Birthday' sung to me in such a sweet, wholesome way."

June 26, 1963. Crowds greeting Kennedy in West Berlin (*left*) were so enthusiastic that German Chancellor Konrad Adenauer—shown at the Berlin Wall with Kennedy and Mayor Willy Brandt (*below left*)—later asked a worried question: "Does this mean that Germany could have another Hitler?"

32.

33.

The President's reception the next day in Ireland (*below*) was spirited, but he was there only to share tea with distant relatives and pass off the whiskey to assistants, who dutifully drank it down and handed the boss an empty glass.

34.

35.

36.

37.

(*Top left*) July 24, 1963. At a Rose Garden ceremony for state leaders of the American Legion's Boys Nation, Kennedy stopped to shake hands with an assertive seventeen-year-old from Arkansas, William Jefferson Clinton, who would become the forty-second President.

(*Top right*) July 15, 1963. Premier Khrushchev and Undersecretary of State Averell Harriman opened the first session of negotiations on what became the Limited Test Ban Treaty. In secret briefings and documents, Harriman was told to explore "radical steps, in cooperation with the USSR, to prevent further proliferation of nuclear capabilities [and] Soviet, or possibly joint US–USSR, use of military force against China"—presumably a joint airstrike against China's nuclear facilities.

(*Bottom*) August 28, 1963. Kennedy agreed to meet with the civil rights leaders of the March on Washington only after the event ended without violence or disorder—wanting to be associated with it only if it succeeded.

October 2, 1963. General Maxwell Taylor and Secretary of Defense Robert McNamara reporting to the President on a joint mission to Vietnam. U.S. options had come down to two, said McNamara: "Reconciliation with Diem or a coup to overthrow Diem." In Saigon, he had come to the conclusion, with help from Henry Cabot Lodge, that Diem must go, that the United States was better off with a military government than an ineffective dictator.

38.

39.

September 2, 1963. Walter Cronkite's interview with Kennedy was featured on the first half-hour national news broadcast on American television. Kennedy said of Diem: "In my opinion, in the last two months the government has gotten out of touch with the people."

October 28, 1963. President Diem and U.S. Ambassador Henry Cabot Lodge, three days before the South Vietnamese leader was assassinated. As he went about the business of eliminating Diem and his brother Ngo Dinh Nhu, Lodge said, "They are essentially a medieval, Oriental despotism of the classic family type."

40.

41.

42.

43.

Kennedy began 1963 believing that his 1964 Republican opponent would be Governor Nelson Rockefeller of New York (*top right*) or Senator Barry Goldwater of Arizona (*bottom right*). He looked forward to the campaign, saying of Rocky: "No guts," and of Barry: "No brains."

The government, he said, was growing slower than almost every other American institution. There was a budget deficit approaching $10 billion, but inflation was less than 1 percent. And it was simple-minded to attribute all the fits and starts of business cycles to a lack of confidence in the national administration.

However convincingly he made those three points, there was an underlying theme that showed that, despite the ringing rhetoric of many of his public statements, Kennedy seemed to think he was a man born too late: He believed there were no great problems to be solved, no great dragons to slay, no great compromises to be made. Pragmatism and the tuning and polishing of machinery of government might be important and necessary, but they were boring.

"Calhoun in 1804 and Taft in 1878 graduated into a world very different from ours," he said, referring to Yale alumni John Calhoun and William Howard Taft. "They and their contemporaries spent entire careers grappling with a few dramatic issues on which the Nation was sharply and emotionally divided, issues that occupied the attention of a generation at a time: the national bank, the disposal of public lands, nullification or union, freedom or slavery, gold or silver. . . . The central issues of our time are more subtle and less simple. They relate not to basic philosophy or ideology but to ways and means of reaching common goals—to research for sophisticated solutions to complex and obstinate issues.

"The differences today are usually matters of degree. . . . What is at stake in our economic decisions today is not some grand warfare of rival ideologies which will sweep the country with passion but the practical management of a modern economy. What we need is not labels and clichés, but more basic discussion of the sophisticated and technical questions . . . political labels and ideological approaches are irrelevant to the solutions. . . . The point is that this is basically an administrative or executive problem."

Any illusions the President entertained about winning over business with words were gone by the next morning, when he was shown a cartoon in the *Philadelphia Bulletin*. A portly character labeled "American Business" was shown walking into his office with a black eye, saying, "So help me—I was hit by a myth."

Time magazine wrote that "President Kennedy and his advisers place boundless faith in his powers of persuasion on TV screens ('We don't need the press anymore,' said a New Frontiersman last week. 'We've got TV.') and public platforms. So it must have come as a disappointment to the administration that the Yale speech notably failed to reassure the business community."

Proving *Time* right, Ted Sorensen, who had drafted the Yale speech, told Kennedy afterward: "Most big businessmen are, by conviction, habit and association, Republicans or Harry Byrd Democrats inherently opposed to this administration and its policies.... Any steps taken for the primary purpose of pleasing the business community should be largely psychological, not substantive." Maybe try to charm them, Sorensen added—"Luncheons or black-tie stag dinners for business leaders in small groups of eight or ten, to exchange views."

Three days after the Yale appearance, at a news conference on June 14, the President got even, at least on the national laugh meter. A reporter asked about the feeling that big business was using the stock market slump to put Kennedy on the defensive. Sort of, the reporter said, "We have you where we want you!"

"I can't believe I'm where business—big business—wants me," said the President of the United States, as the reporters laughed.

Chapter 30

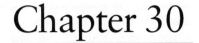

The Massachusetts Democratic Convention endorsed a candidate for John F. Kennedy's old Senate seat on June 12, 1962: his brother Edward Moore Kennedy, who had become old enough to qualify for the job on February 22, his thirtieth birthday. To keep the seat warm for "Teddy," the President had arranged for the appointment of one of his Harvard roommates, a Gloucester businessman named Benjamin Smith, to replace him in the Senate after January 20, 1961. His task was to hold the job until the youngest Kennedy was eligible to run for it.

"Teddy smiled sardonically," *Time* magazine said in reporting his reaction as he watched his principal opponent, state Attorney General Edward McCormack, concede defeat to the convention delegates. "Bobby and I smile sardonically," John Kennedy joked at a little celebration dinner in the White House two nights later. "Teddy will learn how to smile sardonically in two or three years, but he doesn't know how yet."

Ben Bradlee joined in with the family mockery, making a couple of cracks about Teddy and the senatorial qualifications of a man just three years out of law school.

"What do you mean?" the President asked coldly. "He has to win three separate contests—the convention, a Democratic primary, and then the election."

Winning was the real qualification for elective office, the politician told the reporter. Teddy had not waited his turn. Why should he? Candidates were self-selected and campaigns revolved around the men who dared. The role of staff and friends was to arm and protect the gladiator in the arena. Teddy's campaign was being run from the White House, with Sorensen supplying questions and answers for news conferences in small towns in western Massachusetts. Over in the Justice Department, under Robert Kennedy's supervision, records were being searched to see if there was anything that could be used against Eddie McCormack. In the archives of Robert McNamara's Pentagon, aides were searching to see if there was anything hurtful in the old folders containing McCormack's service records, just in case. That was the kind of material the Kennedys used only if things were going badly.

"We're ready with plenty of material to choke old Eddie off," Teddy told his brother one weekend in Hyannis Port before a debate with McCormack. The President, leaning on his crutches in a corner of the big living room of Joseph Kennedy's house, said nothing as Teddy showed off some of the material. Finally, he said: "Listen, Eddie, you forget any personal attack on Eddie McCormack. You're going to need all the supporters that McCormack has right after the debate. Let McCormack attack you as much as he wants. You're running for United States Senator. Stay on the issues and leave the personal attacks out. He'll be gone and forgotten when you are a United States Senator."

From another corner, Joseph Kennedy in his wheelchair raised his finger in a counting motion, and forced out the words: "You do what Jack says."

When a presidential aide named Milton Gwirtzman reported to the President that his brother had not done well in the debate at the convention, Kennedy responded with a touch of anger: "Don't tell him that. Don't give him a dispassionate analysis. He's the candidate. He's the one under the gun. You've got to make him feel good."

The President had already done a bit of staffwork for his brother, meeting with *Boston Globe* editors and reporters who had allowed him to do some editing on the most dangerous story of his brother's campaign. The *Globe* had investigated a campaign rumor that had turned out to be true: The youngest Kennedy had been thrown out of Harvard for cheating. The editors had told the President what they had and had negotiated back and forth with him for a couple of days. "We haven't spent as much fucking time on anything since Cuba," Kennedy joked after a long session with the *Globe*'s Washington bureau chief, Robert Healy. The President and the bureau chief worked out a statement, which Edward Kennedy repeated in a staged interview, admitting that another student had taken a freshman Spanish exam for him. The *Globe* broke the cheating story on March 30, under the gentlest of headlines: "Ted Kennedy Tells About Harvard Examination Incident."

"There has been considerable criticism of the candidacy of your brother Ted . . . ," a reporter began his question at a news conference two weeks after the Massachusetts convention. "It is said that there are going to be too many Kennedys in Washington. Would you comment . . . ?"

The President was not amused, answering: "He had a very vigorously contested convention. He is going to have a primary in September. He will have a very vigorous fight in November. And I would think the people of Massachusetts could make a judgment as to his qualifications and as to whether there are too many Kennedys." *

No matter how friendly or candid he was with some reporters, John Kennedy was in a different business. He was a politician and he never forgot that, even if some reporters sometimes did. He looked forward to the 1962 political season as a chance to fight for a prize he had not won in 1960, effective control of the Congress. The formal counts of party membership looked good for a Democratic President: 263 Democrats and 174 Republicans in the House, and 64 Democrats and 36 Republicans in the Senate. But on most issues and votes, the effective majority party in the Congress was the old coalition of Republicans and conservative Democrats, mostly southerners, many of them primarily concerned with tamping down Negro demands for legal and real equality.

Besides that, Kennedy's relations with the House, where he had served without particular distinction, were not helped by the fact that Eddie McCormack was the nephew and protégé of John McCormack of Massachusetts, the new Speaker of the House. One of the questions at Kennedy's June 27 news conference focused on those troubles: "Mr. President, speaking generally about your legislative program, do you feel that it has had the proper degree of support from the Democratic majorities in the House and Senate?"

"No," said the President. "We should realize that some of the Democrats have voted with the Republicans for 25 years, really since 1938, and that makes it very difficult to secure the enactment of any controversial legislation. . . . You can water down bills and get them by. But important legislation, medical care for the aged and these other bills are much more difficult. . . . That is why this election in November is an important one, because if we can gain some more seats, we will have a workable majority."

---

* In the Democratic primary on September 18, Edward Kennedy won 69 percent of the vote. A *New York Times* editorial called the victory "demeaning to the dignity of the Senate and the democratic process."

The first question had concerned a new Supreme Court ruling the day before prohibiting prayer, Bible reading, and other religious observances in public schools.

"I think that it is important for us if we are going to maintain our constitutional principle that we support the Supreme Court decisions even when we may not agree with them," the President said. "In addition, we have in this case a very easy remedy and that is to pray ourselves. . . . We can pray a good deal more at home and attend our churches with a good deal more fidelity."

Kennedy was looking forward to midterm campaigning, rallying Democratic troops for his kind of Democrats, which basically meant younger Northern Democrats. But, no matter how well he did on the road, Kennedy's news conferences were his real campaign theater. They were central to his style and his presidency, presenting him as he wanted to be seen, quick and knowledgeable, but also forcing him to pay attention to situations and people who bored him.

The President's work on each conference began the night before when Pierre Salinger delivered briefing papers on expected questions, some of them sure things planted with friendly reporters. The next morning began with a breakfast briefing in his bedroom with Johnson, Rusk, McNamara, Sorensen, Bundy, and Salinger asking him twenty or thirty likely questions. "I can handle that," he would say, moving on, or he would try an answer and listen to criticism. There was an updating and a little rehearsal at about 3:00 P.M., as he dressed after his afternoon nap. At night, whenever he could, he would excuse himself from dinners or receptions to watch replays of the day's conference at nine o'clock, critiquing the show. "That lighting is terrible, we have to do something about it," he would say to his own image. "Now, look, that camera angle is killing me."

The coming together of President and television was a new kind of American politics. "We couldn't do it without TV," Kennedy told Salinger, but neither of them knew what that meant. He had come to office at the end of politics' industrial age. The dominant visual medium as he began the 1960 campaign was black and white photography. People could rarely move faster than two hundred miles per hour on propeller-driven airliners. But Kennedy had sensed a new politics as a farmer might feel a coming change in the weather. The great newspaper reader, the politician who seemed to hear the cocking of a camera at a hundred yards, was gripped by the fact that he could reach millions of Americans without first offering himself to the machines controlled by Henry Luce at *Time* in New York or E. M. Dealey at the *Morning News* in Dallas. This was a political miracle.

The most difficult questions were on civil rights, particularly the one that was repeated every couple of months about when he intended to keep his campaign promise to end racial discrimination in public housing with "a stroke of the pen"—by signing an executive order legally prohibiting that discrimination. It had last been asked on July 5:

"Mr. President, I believe you've been in office about seventeen months and still haven't signed that order against racial segregation in federally financed housing. Could you tell us when you do plan to sign that?"

"I will announce it when we think it would be a useful and appropriate time."

"You will sign it before the end of your term?"

"I have said already . . . I will point out that we have carried out a great many activities in the field of civil rights. . . ."

He was having enough trouble with Congress already. He had won his first fight there just days after taking office when Speaker Rayburn persuaded just enough of his colleagues in the House to expand the membership of the House Rules Committee. But that was a defensive victory: preventing Southern Democrats from joining Republicans to keep White House legislation off the House floor. It was no small accomplishment, but the President and his men, led by Larry O'Brien, had not gotten much further.

After a year and a half in office, Kennedy was asked: "Mr. President, you have given Congress an awful lot to chew in this session and some of them are getting a little impatient, this being a campaign year. . . . Do you propose to give them some top priority list and say, that is it?"

"Well . . . ," Kennedy answered. "Going down the list: medical care for the aged, youth employment, aid for higher education, the trade bill. . . . There's a good many of great importance."

The list went on, but the President was blocked at almost every turn.

The idea of some sort of national health plan for Americans sixty-five and older—the United States was the only industrialized country without one—had been debated in Congress since Theodore Roosevelt's 1912 campaign for President. Roosevelt failed, and Kennedy did, too. His program was called Medicare. It was to be financed by a half-percent increase in Social Security taxes, providing 90 days of hospital care and 180 days of nursing home care for 17 million Americans over sixty-five. After three weeks of Senate debate, and determined and expensive opposition by the American Medical Association, Medicare was voted down in the Senate on July 17, by a 52–48 vote. Twenty-one Democrats, mostly southerners, sided with the Republicans.

Kennedy was on television within the hour, using network cameras which were now held in readiness around the clock in the White House in case the President wanted to say something to the nation. "This is a most serious defeat for every American family. . . . Nearly all the Republicans and a handful of Democrats joined with them to give us today's setback. I hope that we will return in November a Congress that will support a program like medical care for the aged."

He was mad as hell. In the middle of the Medicare struggle, the president of the AMA, Dr. Leonard Larson, asked for a meeting with the President to discuss their differences. "Forget it," Kennedy said. Why not? A meeting suggested compromise, he said, and a photograph suggested a meeting of equals. He was not of a mind to give either to Dr. Larson. He had the same reaction when Walter Heller asked him to pose for the cameras at a reunion of past chairmen of the Council of Economic Advisers, including Truman's man, Leon Keyserling, and Eisenhower's, Arthur Burns. "Burns and Keyserling are kicking me in the balls every day and I'm not going to give them a platform to do it more successfully," he told Heller.

Being seen with Kennedy had taken on international status within a few months of his inaugural. The State Department received so many requests for state visits from presidents, kings, and prime ministers that a new category of "unofficial" visits was devised to give Kennedy a break from rounds of toasting and twenty-one-gun salutes. Martin Hillenbrand, the U.S. minister in Bonn, informed Kennedy that not only were West German politicians lining up for visits to Washington but back home they broadcast the number of minutes each spent in the White House, the record being twenty-six minutes, rumored to include eight in the Men's Room. Harriman reported back to the White House from halfway around the world that the best way to keep Indonesia's President Sukarno on his best behavior was to hold out the chance that Kennedy might visit Djakarta if Sukarno played the good boy.

The President's next news conference was on July 23, and it changed world history. At least that was what Pierre Salinger thought. The only thing he could compare it to was the first atomic bomb. The first ten minutes of the conference were shown live in Europe. The television signals from Washington were bounced off the new Telstar communications satellite built by the American Telephone and Telegraph Company and launched into space by the U.S. government six weeks before, on June 10. The last words transmitted from the satellite to London were something Kennedy had said time and time again in speeches and newspaper interviews: "The United States will not devalue its dollar. And the fact of the matter is the United States can balance its balance of payments any day it wants if it wishes to withdraw its support of our defense expenditures overseas and our foreign aid."

"Mr. President," Salinger said, as Kennedy left the State Department Auditorium used for news conferences. "Mr. President, the price of gold on the London markets is breaking." All the printed words of the most powerful man in the world over eighteen months had not produced that result. Ten seconds of the man live on television had changed the value of money in most of the world.

Chapter 31

$\mathbf{B}$y late summer 1962, Kennedy was persuaded that Walter Heller was right about the benefits of a cut in income tax rates, or correct economically; but it was still an intellectual exercise for the President, not a political commitment.

When he had taken office, the economy was in recession, but that was politically an "Eisenhower recession." A mild recovery had begun in February 1961, measured in statistics showing a growth rate of about 2 percent in the gross national product. During the summer of 1962, automobile sales and new housing starts began declining and Kennedy began worrying about a recession before the midterm elections—this one with his name on it. If Heller had a magic bullet to kill recessions— using Keynesian theory to stimulate economic activity—there was still the question of when to fire it, and whether and when Congress would let him pull the trigger. Maybe the smart thing to do was to hold his fire until 1963. The worst "Kennedy recession" would be one during the 1964 presidential campaign.

Ted Sorensen had summarized the politics of the economy in a memo to the President on July 12:

> A tax cut is a massive economic weapon. It can be used once. We have promised a tax cut effective January 1; a bill this year could hardly be effective before October 1. . . . Therefore, I am for a tax cut only when

we can be certain: 1. That both employment and production are on a decline that will be both substantial and continuing; 2. That a cut in income taxes will not go largely into savings instead of consumption; 3. That the resultant deficit will not be as large as Eisenhower's $12.8 billion in fiscal 1958. . . .

At his news conference on August 1, Kennedy was reminded of how effectively his predecessor had upheld the old-time all-American conventional economic wisdom that deficit spending was a root of all evils. "Mr. President," a reporter said, "the Gallup Poll published today shows that 72 percent of those polled are opposed to a tax cut if it means the government will go further into debt. Can you tell us what factor this will be in your decisions about the tax cut?"

"Well, as I've said before, we are going to wait until we get the July figures," Kennedy responded. "We'll make a judgment as to whether these numbers indicate we're in a plateau or whether we are in more serious economic difficulty."

He was also asked that day about another deficit, the balance of payments. The United States was buying more than it was selling to other countries, running an international trade deficit of about $5 billion a year ($1.6 billion of that was NATO expenses in Europe), giving foreign suppliers and governments the power to claim their debts in gold-backed U.S. dollars.

"A constant concern," Kennedy said in answering the question about the balance of payments. "We hope by the end of next year to bring our balance of payments into balance. . . ." At one meeting, discussing the gold drain, Kennedy had looked up and said: "So what happened in the 1950s was that we collected A-bombs while the Europeans rounded up gold."

"Our businessmen, workers and farmers are in need of new markets —and the fastest growing market in the world is the European Common Market," he had said when he introduced the Trade Expansion Act of 1962, greatly expanding presidential power to reduce tariffs to promote trade. "Its consumers will soon be 250 million people. . . . Think of the opportunities in a market where, compared to the ratio of ownership in this country, only one-fourth as many consumers have radios, one-seventh television sets, one-fifth automobiles, washing machines and refrigerators! To share in that market we must strike a bargain—we must have something to give the Europeans—we must be willing to give them increased access to our markets. . . ." Then he added Japan to the equation, saying that the island country, our former enemy, had to sell to survive. Some way had to be found to balance U.S.-Japan trade, reducing the $500 million gap between U.S. exports to Japan and what the Japanese were able to sell in the United States.

It was a busy summer in the Capital, busyness being a trademark of the Kennedy years. People carried folders and papers as they walked, looking as if they were going someplace important, doing something important. But on the day after the President's pledge to end the gold drain, the nation and much of the world was otherwise engaged: On August 5, Marilyn Monroe was found dead in her home in Los Angeles, at the age of thirty-six. It had been only ten weeks since she had starred at the President's birthday gala. There had been some titillating rumors of an affair with Kennedy—and, like Judith Campbell, the star regularly telephoned the White House and spoke with the President—but such talk lasted much longer and spread much further in Hollywood than in Washington. Both cities were self-absorbed, taken with their own importance, and Washington did care and talk about theories of trade and taxes, which was why it bored so many people.

In his official house, the President had achieved a working balance between his fervent Keynesian, Walter Heller, and his more traditional Republican, Douglas Dillon. Kennedy intellectually accepted Heller's schemes to produce a net tax reduction, while also endorsing Dillon's dreams of a tax-neutral but sweeping tax reform—closing and opening the myriad maze of loopholes in the Internal Revenue Code. Dillon was a strongman of the administration, too, and an effective link to Republicans in Congress, since the day in January 1961 when he first appeared before the Joint Internal Revenue Committee. That was one day after his deputy, Stanley Surrey, following presidential orders, appeared before the committee and was greeted by Senator Robert Byrd, a West Virginia Democrat, who asked where the Secretary was, then said: "This is an affront to the Congress." He stood up, along with four other senators and Representative Wilbur Mills, saying they would return when the President sent the Secretary rather than an assistant— and that was exactly what Senator Albert Gore had told Kennedy would happen when the President-elect had said Dillon would not speak for the new administration.

The July economic numbers were better than the June indicators, but still mixed, and so was the President, able to argue both sides in the Heller-Dillon debates. He was clear in his own mind about the difference between what he thought and what he thought could be done. One day, paying homage to Eisenhower's penny-saved, penny-earned economic puritanism, he said: "I take some pride in the fact that we kept last year's deficit well below that incurred in the recession of 1958." The next night, talking to Charlie Bartlett, he said: "Everybody talks about our deficit. Everyone wants us to cut spending. They don't seem to understand that it's the deficit, the spending that's keeping the economy pumped up. I love that deficit."

In mid-August, the mild Kennedy recovery from the mild 1960–61 Eisenhower recession definitely seemed to be losing whatever momentum it had. Samuelson told Kennedy he thought the odds on a new cycle of recession were fifty-fifty; that would be the fifth downturn since the end of World War II. Why? Why was economic growth stuck below 3 percent—and declining? Heller's answer, again, was: Tax rates are too high, so the budget balances before there is full employment. From that point on, the government is taking more from the spending stream than it is pumping in—and the stream slows down.

The economy, in the jargon of the day, was not operating at "full capacity"—the country was only producing 85 or so percent of what could be done at "full employment," that is, if unemployment was at 4 percent or less, rather than moving around between 5 and 7 percent. Crawford Greenewalt, the chairman of Du Pont-Nemours, the country's dominant chemical company, saw the President on August 9 and told him that Du Pont was operating at 80 percent of capacity—which meant that if consumer demand increased, all the company had to do to increase sales by $600 million was open its valves wider.

Congress, though, looked at the economy from another direction, generally favoring bigger spending over smaller taxing. Many members preferred new highways and hospitals to tax cuts, because they could influence the spending and take the credit for visible construction. Tax talk just reminded voters of how much they were paying. The President did most of his congressional negotiating with the chairman of the House Ways and Means Committee, Wilbur Mills of Arkansas, who was against a quick tax cut, mainly because he thought it would be defeated in the Congress. Mills and Kennedy had sat down for a long session on the evening of August 6, with the President reading to the chairman from a British magazine, *The Economist:* " 'Nothing would harm the world economy and confidence in the dollar more than a premature slide of the American economy in a recession.'

"In other words, we're too restrained," Kennedy said, looking up from the magazine.

"Let me make this point with you," Mills replied. "Let us assume half the people in the United States were sophisticated and fully informed. . . . You have fifty percent that say, 'Yes, this is a good thing.' But then you've got a division in that fifty percent as to how it's to be done. . . . You've got business on the one hand, if they want a tax cut, wanting one type of a tax cut. You've got the labor groups on the other hand wanting a tax cut, but a different kind of tax cut."

"Look," Kennedy said, "Paul Samuelson says the downturn will take place in the fourth quarter. Let's assume that he's wrong, and that we're all right this year on the plateau, and the unemployment figures stay below six percent. Then we get to the winter of 1963, the thing runs out of gas. . . . We're about to have a recession in the winter of 1963. Wouldn't we be better off, if I go up and ask for a tax cut now, and Congress isn't going to give it to us? It's going to complicate the running for office of a lot of fellows who have to defend: the President's asked for a tax cut; it shows the economy's desperate; it shows the Democrats have failed to bring the economy back. . . . And a lot of bastards will come out and say they're not for a tax cut and some will break with me."

"Your judgment is right," Mills said.

"Ah, but let's say we also know that," Kennedy went on, suggesting that Congress be called back into session in November, after the elections, if economic indicators had not improved. "And then at least if the Congress didn't, it would be—the responsibility would be, uh, wouldn't be ours."

"Why don't we keep this to ourselves," the President finally said. "I'll be working on some satisfactory way of putting our case, and we can just keep this to ourselves, so we don't get the press. . . ."

Kennedy decided to put his case to the country on television on August 13. Walter Heller, writing now like an economic campaign manager, made one more pitch on August 9, in a memo entitled "The Range of Tax Cut Choices Before Us":

> A 1962 tax cut: Our last chance (a) to take out advance insurance against a "Kennedy recession"; (b) to have a tax cut reduce, not increase, the FY 1964 deficit; (c) to give Democratic congressional candidates a more activist economic policy to brandish in the 1962 elections. . . . Slack and recession produce budget deficits; and these deficits become roadblocks to the use of tax cuts, our major weapon in fighting slack and recession. Early action can break this vicious circle, visibly improve the economy in 1963–64, and shrink the FY 1964 deficit.

That was the first choice Heller offered. He had six of them in the memo; the last was along the line taken by Dillon, who wanted more time to combine tax cuts with tax reforms. At the White House they joked that the President always agreed with Heller but always supported Dillon. "No Action now," was Heller's number six. "Issue a reassuring statement explaining why (a) it is not urgent to cut taxes today; (b) a tax cut next year is essential; (c) stand-by authority is vital."

The President chose number six. He went on national television the night of August 13, by coincidence the first anniversary of the Berlin Wall. It also happened to be a tremendous day for the Soviet Union, which announced a space spectacular that *The New York Times* recorded with a three-line banner across the top of page one, the kind of headline usually reserved for presidential elections: "TWO SOVIET SPACE CRAFT CIRCLING EARTH IN ADJACENT ORBITS AFTER NEW LAUNCHING; PILOTS KEEP IN TOUCH BY SIGHT AND RADIO." The day's front-page news also included an account of racial tensions in the small city of Albany, Georgia, where the Reverend Martin Luther King, Jr., was leading a sustained protest against segregation in that small city.

The President began the speech by congratulating the Soviets, then saying to Americans: "We are behind and we will be behind for a period in the future, but we are making a major effort now. . . ." A moment later he began his most trying speech to date, showing a mind-numbing array of charts, saying: "When I came into office in January 1961 this country was in a recession. We have made a recovery. . . ."

He did manage to sum up the argument against the current high tax-rate schedule in one sentence: "During the last 15 months, for example, of the current expansion of our economy, Federal purchases have added $7 billion to the economy, but Federal taxes have siphoned out $12 billion. . . ."

He ended by saying he would seek a cut in those rates—but not until January 1963.

"It was a C-minus," Kennedy said, when the cameras and microphones were shut off. He told Heller that he still wanted to get as much stimulus as possible with or without a tax cut: "I don't care if you paper over one or two or even three billion dollars of deficit."

In official Washington on August 14, the morning after the President's national economics lesson, telephones and alarm bells were ringing secretly all over town, and across the Potomac River in Arlington and Langley, Virginia, at the Pentagon and the Central Intelligence Agency. The subject was assassination.

The first calls were made by William Harvey, the CIA agent who had run ZR/RIFLE, the agency's program to develop stand-by assassination capability. He was in charge of Task Force W, an agency unit created at the beginning of 1962 to try to overthrow Castro. He was in a rage over a short memorandum that had been sent out the day before by General Lansdale, chief of operations of "Operation Mongoose," the action arm of Robert Kennedy's interdepartmental Special Group (Augmented), the "Cuba Project." Mongoose had been created at the end of 1961 with this goal: "In keeping with the spirit of the Presidential memorandum of 30 November 1961, the United States will help the people of Cuba overthrow the Communist regime from within Cuba and institute a new government with which the United States can live in peace." A Mongoose guideline had added: "In undertaking to cause the overthrow of the target government, the U.S. will make use of indigenous resources, internal and external, but recognizes that final success will require decisive U.S. military intervention."*

The Lansdale memo that enraged Harvey was only a call for a Mongoose meeting later on August 14, but it was classified "TOP SECRET, SPECIAL HANDLING, NOFORN":

> In compliance with the desires and guidance expressed in the 10 August policy meeting on Operation Mongoose. . . . We will hold an Operational Representatives work session in my office, at 1400 hours, Tuesday, 14 August. Papers required from each of you for the Tuesday meeting:
> Mr. Harvey: Intelligence, Political (splitting the regime), including liquidation of leaders. . . .

The SG(A) had been meeting almost every day in early August as Mongoose (named for the animal that kills poisonous snakes) tried to shift from Phase I, the gathering of intelligence and organizing networks of operatives, to a stepped-up phase of sabotage and paramilitary operations. It was after the August 10 meeting of the SG(A), attended by Rusk, McNamara, McCone, USIA director Edward R. Murrow, and McGeorge Bundy, that Lansdale had sent out his memo calling for the next session.

Harvey's angry memorandum on the memorandum was to Richard Helms, who had succeeded Richard Bissell in February as the CIA's deputy director for plans. It was Bissell who had assigned Harvey to Task Force W at the end of 1961, telling him he was under more and more pressure from the White House to get rid of Castro. Now Harvey told Helms:

"Reference is made to our conversation on 13 August 1962, concerning the memorandum of that date from General Lansdale. Attached is a copy of this memorandum. . . . The question of assassination, particu-

---

* Mongoose, including the CIA component called Task Force W, cost more than $100 million a year and involved more than four hundred Americans and two thousand Cubans, a fleet of small boats, and some airplanes operating from U.S. Air Force bases in Florida. The August 1962 planning was, officially, "Phase I" of the Kennedy plan to get Castro: gathering intelligence and establishing espionage and sabotage networks to set the stage for the kind of incident that could plausibly trigger invasion—but, the guidelines stated, "political, economic and covert actions will be undertaken short of those reasonably calculated to inspire a revolt within the target area, or other development which would require U.S. armed intervention." The President wanted to avoid military action if he could. But he also wanted to be ready this time; the Joint Chiefs of Staff, spectators at the Bay of Pigs, were ordered to create detailed invasion plans.

larly of Fidel Castro, was brought up by Secretary McNamara at the meeting of the Special Group (Augmented) in Secretary Rusk's office on 10 August. It was the obvious consensus at that meeting, in answer to a comment by Mr. Ed Murrow, that this is not a subject which has been made a matter of official record."

So, as he had after the Bay of Pigs, McNamara was talking about the assassination of Castro, but this time it was on paper. The Lansdale memo Harvey sent to his superiors at the CIA read: "Upon receipt of the attached memorandum, I called Lansdale's office and . . . pointed out the inadmissibility and stupidity of putting this type of comment in writing in such a document. I advised . . . that, as far as CIA was concerned, we would write no document pertaining to this and would participate in no open meeting discussing it."

Harvey never had any doubt in his own mind that in planning for Castro's demise he was acting on orders from the highest authority, the President. But Bissell, the man who had assigned him, had been replaced by Helms, and Harvey wanted to cover his moves with the new boss. Besides, his big boss, John McCone, the director of the CIA, had challenged McNamara immediately after the August 10 meeting.

"The subject you just brought up," McCone had said. "I think it is highly improper. I do not think it should be discussed. It is not an action that should ever be condoned. It is not proper for us to discuss and I intend to have it expunged from the record."

McCone, a conservative Republican who made a fortune building ships during World War II, was a late and devout convert to Roman Catholicism. What he had said to McNamara was passed around the White House with a touch of wonder: "I could get excommunicated for something like this."

So, liquidation was off the record. But it was never off the table. "It was made abundantly clear to everybody involved in the operation that the desire was to get rid of the Castro regime and to get rid of Castro," said Helms. "No limitations were put on this injunction."

"Massive activity," that was what the President wanted, said Robert Kennedy at an SG(A) meeting on October 4.

Chapter 32

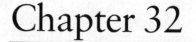

J ohn McCone was still thinking about Cuba when he returned to his office after the August 10 meeting of the Special Group (Augmented). It was not Castro that concerned him; he had said his piece about assassination to McNamara. He was bothered by scraps of intelligence coming his way about more and more Soviet ships bringing more and more Soviet soldiers or technicians into Cuban ports. Refugees, foreign diplomats, and letters from Cubans to relatives in Florida—that mail was routinely intercepted and opened by the CIA—reported that a dozen or more ships had come into Havana and smaller ports during the last days of July and the first of August. The landings were usually at night. Roads to dockside areas were blocked and Cubans were cleared from waterfront areas as hundreds of young men and large crates were offloaded.

A letter from Havana: "I was an eyewitness. . . . Yesterday July 26 the Russian ship *Maria Ulanova* entered the port. It was painted white. It disembarked about 500 men, in my opinion they were military technicians." From Mariel: "Two ships in Cabañas and two in Mariel disembarked approximately 600 men each, with the peculiarity that the Russians themselves unloaded the baggage and cargoes. . . . A Norwegian merchant ship that was going to enter the harbor was detoured."

The captain of the Norwegian vessel had stopped next at New Orleans and reported to U.S. Navy officials there that he had seen a 15,000-

ton Russian ship carrying about two thousand men, many in uniform. A refugee arriving in Miami reported driving by a long truck convoy in the early morning hours of August 5: "After about every third truck there was a long flatbed pulled by a tractor-like vehicle. On each vehicle there was a round object as tall as a palm tree and covered by a tarpaulin. . . . Going through Matanzas, I saw between 250 and 300 men, foreigners, standing near parked trucks near the Penas Altas bar, which was closed at that hour."

McCone was going to the West Coast that weekend, but before leaving, he decided to dictate a memo for delivery to the President on Monday. The stories he was seeing and hearing, he wrote, had convinced him that where there was smoke there was fire. He was reasonably sure that the trucks were carrying SA-2s, Soviet surface-to-air missiles, defensive weapons which could be part of a coastal defense system. The SA-2s, if they existed, were considered part of a defensive build-up by the State Department and military intelligence—a Soviet response to Castro's continuing demands for weaponry to defend against the American invasion he was sure would come someday.

McCone wrote Kennedy that he disagreed with that analysis. The SAMs were being put in to protect something bigger. "The only construction I can put on the missiles going into Cuba is that the Russians are preparing to introduce offensive missiles. I question the value of SAMs except as a means of making possible the introduction of offensive missiles."

Ballistic missiles, McCone wrote. The Soviets might be in the process of placing medium-range ballistic missiles and intermediate-range ballistic missiles with nuclear warheads within ninety miles of the United States. MRBMs with ranges of perhaps 200 miles could reach Miami; IRBMs with a range of almost 1,500 miles could reach Washington from Cuba. Khrushchev was a gambler after all. The Soviet leader could be responding to the cool and detailed boasting of the President and his Secretary of Defense about U.S. nuclear might by emulating the U.S. strategy of bringing nuclear missiles right up to the borders of the enemy.

Better than anyone else in the world, Khrushchev knew those American boasts were true. And he had to suspect that the balance was tipping faster and faster—that the Soviets could never catch up. The United States was nearing the end of twenty-four-blast nuclear test series in the South Pacific; one of the shots, called "Starfish," a 1.4-megaton weapon, had exploded 250 miles above the sea on July 9, lighting up the night skies from Hawaii to Australia. Perhaps Khrushchev thought he could dramatically change the balance of threat with just a few middle-range delivery systems at the doorstep to the United States—as the United States had missiles aimed at Moscow from Great Britain, Italy, and Turkey. McCone repeated that he had no proof of Soviet intentions.

That's preposterous, said the President's men that Monday, August 13. Roger Hilsman, the State Department's intelligence chief, ridiculed the sketchy reports as "Guess what my cousin saw" intelligence—the kind that had convinced the CIA in April 1961 that the island would rise in revolt after exiles landed at the Bay of Pigs. The State Department and the Defense Department were arguing that Khrushchev might be crazy, but he's not that crazy. They told Kennedy, in essence: The Soviets are cautious and suspicious, they don't take chances, and they don't trust their allies, particularly the Cubans. They have never put offensive missiles on foreign soil. Never. There were no nuclear weapons in Eastern Europe. The communications gear spotted at Mariel and Cabañas is almost certainly matériel for coastal defenses of the kind the Soviets installed in Egypt and Syria and Iraq. The equipment piling up on Cuban docks might be for an earth station to track future orbital space flights —and to listen in on U.S. space talk and launchings from Cape Canaveral, two hundred miles to the north on Florida's east coast. All of that, they said, takes a lot of technicians, particularly when you're dealing with people as easy-going as the Cubans.

Four days later, McCone met with Rusk and McNamara. He repeated that the best hard intelligence the CIA had indicated that the Soviets on Cuba might be there to install surface-to-air missiles, technically defensive weapons, and to train Cubans to use them. But, he added, one reason to put in such missiles might be to shoot down high-flying U-2 spy planes to blind American surveillance of the construction of offensive sites—launching pads for MRBMs. Rusk and McNamara were not persuaded. McCone was a wolf-crier; his religious anti-communism made his urgency a little suspect. So did the fact that he was distracted by wedding plans and was getting ready to leave the United States to go to the South of France on his honeymoon early in September.

Five days later, on August 22, McCone went to the White House himself. He brought a four-page Current Intelligence Memo that stuck strictly to what the agency considered hard intelligence. But it pointed out that nothing quite like this had ever happened in the Soviet bloc. It said, in part:

As many as 20 Soviet vessels may have already arrived in Cuba since late July with military cargoes. Five more Soviet vessels have left Black Sea ports under conditions suggesting they are en route to Cuba with additional military equipment. Most reports on these shipments have referred to large quantities of transportation, electronic and construction equipment, such as communications and radar vans, trucks of many varieties, mobile generator units, tracked and wheeled prime movers, cranes, trailers, and fuel tanks. Eyewitnesses who saw the material being transported from the port areas report that much of the transportation was done at night and even that town street lights were turned off as the convoys passed through. . . .

The speed and magnitude of this influx of bloc personnel and equipment into a non-bloc country is unprecedented in Soviet military aid activities; clearly something new and different is taking place.

Kennedy knew that Cuba was only part of what was new and different. In July, before the Cuban build-up began, he had told Rusk, McNamara, McCone, and Lyman Lemnitzer to work together to study Soviet responses to the U.S. military build-up. They had reported back to him that it was clear the Soviets were attempting to mirror-image new U.S. defense spending with secret military development and production of their own. And they were failing and succeeding at the same time. The Soviet Union was falling further behind as the United States began turning out land- and submarine-fired missiles as if they were Chevrolets: hundreds, then thousands of solid-fuel missiles, which meant instantaneous-firing Minutemen with ranges of 6,000 miles, and Polaris submarine missiles, each one with more destructive power than all the bombs dropped in World War II.

But, the four-man group reported, comparisons aside, the Soviets had, in fact, significantly increased their own strategic strength and could be expected to be less cautious in foreign affairs as time went on. They told the President:

> Their appraisals of risks may change now that their capability has become real and is growing. . . . The Soviets will almost certainly test Western, and particularly American, reactions in order to judge whether their gains in strength have so inhibited the US as to widen the scope of action which they can undertake without substantial risk of war. . . . We judge the greatest hazard to be in the Soviet calculation (or miscalculation) of the risks of particular courses of action as Soviet military capabilities grow. A dangerous change in the calculus of risks would of course be most likely if the Soviets thought they had obtained a temporary military superiority, especially in the field of ICBMs. . . .

McCone's hunch was that the testing might begin in Cuba. He reasoned that Khrushchev perhaps thought he could gain a cheap and temporary military superiority by putting the United States under the nuclear gun ninety miles offshore—in effect, turning MRBMs into ICBMS. The Soviets could double the number of missiles targeting the United States and evade U.S. missile detection systems, which were all pointed north toward the Soviet Union itself. The President listened but was not convinced. At a news conference that same afternoon, he was asked whether he had information to indicate that the Communist bloc troops and equipment were being landed in Cuba.

"Yes," he answered. "New supplies definitely in large quantities. Troops? We do not have information, but an increased number of technicians."

"What is the significance of this, in your opinion?"

"Well, we are examining it now."

His first announcement that day, before the questions, had been that two U.S. nuclear-powered submarines had met under the North Pole, then surfaced together, 850 miles from Soviet territory. The military implications of the rendezvous were obvious. The Soviets were surrounded by submarines carrying Polaris missiles, the "invulnerable asset" that President Eisenhower had described to President-elect Kennedy. Now, President Kennedy had also just been told of the results of the latest Atlas missile test firing. The missile, fired from Vandenberg Air Force Base in California, had traveled 7,000 miles to the Philippine Sea and hit just 100 yards short and 400 yards to the right of the marked target.

Nevertheless, uncertain about what exactly was new and different in Cuba, Kennedy issued a National Security Action Memorandum, NSAM-181, the next day, August 23, a "Top Secret and Sensitive" document written by Bundy and available in full to only five men—Rusk, McNamara, Robert Kennedy, McCone, and Max Taylor:

> The President has directed that the following actions and studies be undertaken in the light of evidence of new bloc activity in Cuba.
> • What action can be taken to get Jupiter missiles out of Turkey? (Action: Department of Defense)
> • What information should be made available in the US and abroad with respect to these new bloc activities in Cuba? (Action: Department of State, in consultation with USIA and CIA). . . .
> • The line of activity projected for Operation MONGOOSE Plan B-plus should be developed with all possible speed. (Action: General Taylor)
> • An analysis should be prepared of the probable military, political and psychological impact of the establishment in Cuba of either surface-to-air missiles or surface-to-surface missiles which could reach the US. (Action: White House, in consultation with Department of State, Department of Defense and CIA)

• A study should be made of the advantages and disadvantages of making a statement that the US would not tolerate the establishment of military forces (missile or air, or both?) which might launch a nuclear attack from Cuba against the US. (Action: Department of State, in consultation with Department of Defense)

• A study should be made of the various military alternatives which might be adopted in executing a decision to eliminate any installations in Cuba capable of launching nuclear attack on the US. What would be the pros and cons, for example, of pinpoint attack?, general counter-force attack, and outright invasion? (Action: Department of Defense)

To facilitate coordination of these efforts, I should like to receive an immediate report from action Departments. . . . Insofar as practicable . . . these assignments should be made from among senior officers already informed of MONGOOSE.

There will be a further meeting with the President about September 1 to review progress. . . . The President emphasized again the sensitive character of these instructions.

The first item on Mongoose eliminated the limit set on Phase 1 of the operation, the order to stop short of inspiring a revolt. This was, in effect, a signal from the President that the United States was prepared to invade Cuba. He had personally overruled the Special Group (Augmented), chaired by his brother Robert Kennedy, which had decided, on August 10, against implementing Plan B-plus. He made the decision on August 20, after Maxwell Taylor reported to him that the SG(A) saw no possibility that Castro could be overthrown without the direct intervention of United States troops.

Tracking the military build-up in Cuba was becoming an important industry in Washington, with wildly varying numbers. During the first six weeks of 1962, only one Soviet passenger ship had docked in Cuba. There were now reports of ten ships in the past six weeks. The President was told that twenty Soviet cargo ships had unloaded military vehicles and men and sealed crates in June, then thirty more in July and fifty-five in August. Cubans were being permanently evacuated from dockside areas, and certain villages had been emptied across the country. Schools were being vacated to provide housing for soldiers. The State Department and CIA estimated that there were five thousand Soviet troops on the island. Newspapers were onto the story, whatever it was, interviewing Cuban exiles in Miami and anonymous national security types in Washington.

But Cuba was not dominating the headlines, as it had at times during the past couple of years. Most information on the military build-up was still government-generated and distributed. At his August 29 news conference, Kennedy began by announcing that Justice Felix Frankfurter was retiring from the Supreme Court. He said he would nominate his Secretary of Labor, Arthur Goldberg, to fill the vacancy. Then he declared that the United States welcomed a sudden and surprising Soviet announcement in Geneva that a nuclear test ban treaty could be negotiated by the end of the year.

There were three questions on Cuba at the press conference, coming after ten on Berlin, foreign aid, the midterm elections, and a Supreme Court decision on pornography. The first concerned a statement by Republican Senator Homer Capehart of Indiana, who had said two days earlier that there were thousands of Soviet troops in Cuba and that the time had come for a U.S. invasion to clean them out of there: "It is high time the American people demand that President Kennedy quit 'examining the situation' and start protecting the interests of the United States."

Kennedy tried to push the question aside. "We've no evidence of troops," he answered, then more or less repeated the line that had provoked Capehart and other Republicans. "However, we are continuing to watch what happens in Cuba with the closest attention. . . ."

The reporter persisted, saying: "Mr. President, did you answer my question or Mr. Capehart's suggestion that we invade Cuba? What was the answer?"

Kennedy was annoyed. "I think it would be a mistake to invade Cuba," he said. "An action like that, which could be very casually suggested, could lead to very serious consequences for many people."

"Mr. President," asked another reporter, ". . . Some of us were told at the State Department the other day that these are military technicians, and are the people who are probably going to operate missiles, similar to Nike missiles. Is this . . ."

Kennedy cut the question off: "I don't know who told you that at the State Department, that they're going to operate Nike missiles, because that information we do not have at this time. . . . On the question of troops, as it's generally understood, we do not have evidence that there are Russian troops there. There is an expanded advisory and technical mission."

As he spoke that day, August 29, a U-2 spy plane, a spectacular advance in reconnaissance technology the Soviets had not been able to match, was flying an east-to-west pattern 80,000 feet over Cuba, back and forth above the 800-mile-long island—looking for hard photographic evidence of what the Soviets were doing. The flight had been delayed, postponed day after day, by cloud cover over most of the island. But, finally, the photographs were ready and were studied on August 31. Kennedy was shown the first hard evidence of surface-to-air missile sites, launching pads under construction near Mariel for the same Soviet SA-2 missiles that had shot down the U-2 over the Soviet Union in May 1960. McCone asserted again that they must be protecting something. SA-2s were worthless against planes flying below 10,000 feet, so they were not there to defend against invasion from the sea. They were there, he said, in an attempt to end U-2 reconnaissance.

Kennedy was still being briefed on the intricacies of aerial photography and missile ranges when a Republican senator blew open the secrecy and the political cover of the White House's rather unhurried and methodical analysis of Soviet and Cuban intentions.

Senator Kenneth Keating, a New York Republican, had seen and heard some of the "soft" evidence of Soviet activity in Cuba, the refugee interviews and intercepted letters about midnight unloading of ships. So, in fact, had anyone else who read newspapers and magazines. *Time* magazine was printing classified CIA and State Department dispatches practically word for word—the documents were being handed out by anonymous mid-level officials hoping to pressure the President to make some move to block the Cuban build-up.

"18,000 SOVIET TROOPS IN CUBA," headlined *The New York Daily News*—the tabloid's figure was dismissed as sensationalism.*

What Keating had was the power to make the build-up, and the White House's calm reaction, evidence that John Kennedy just did not have the guts to stand up to the Communists even when they were only ninety miles away—precisely the charges that Kennedy believed were his greatest political problem.

"I am reliably informed," Keating said on the Senate floor that August 31, "that between August 3rd and August 15th, at the Cuban port of Mariel, 10 to 12 large Soviet vessels anchored at the former Marante docks. The dock area previously had been surrounded by construction of a high cinder block wall. The Soviet ships unloaded 1,200 troops. . . . Through August 13, five torpedo boats have been unloaded and now are moored at nearby La Base. . . . What are the Soviets planning to do with their new island fortress? What are they going to build with all this new equipment? What will the army of technicians be required to maintain? So far we have had a number of answers, but in my judgment none of them tells the true story."

"Those CIA bastards," Kennedy said, when he was told of Keating's speech. He was sure Keating's numbers had come from the intelligence agency. "I'm going to get those bastards, if it's the last thing I ever do."

The midterm elections Kennedy was counting on to give him a Congress he could work with were only sixty days away, Cuba was an issue

---

* In fact, the *News* numbers were far closer than lower White House estimates. Thirty years later, in conferences between American and Soviet officials, it was revealed that there were 40,000 Soviet military personnel in Cuba by the summer of 1962.

again, and once again, there was talk that this President was soft on communism. "Mr. Kennedy," reported *The New York Times* of September 3, "is caught between Cuban charges that he is planning to invade the island and mounting Congressional demands that he should do precisely this."

The President called the Democratic congressional leaders together, telling them: "I wanted to acquaint you with what is taking place in Cuba, which is not my favorite subject. We have a new CIA report. . . ."

On September 4, after an announcement in Moscow that the Soviet Union had agreed to new arms shipments along with more advisers and technicians to Cuba, the Soviet Ambassador to Washington, Anatoli Dobrynin, invited Robert Kennedy to tea to assure him that Soviet intentions in Cuba were strictly defensive. Did the Americans really think the Soviet Union would put itself in a position to be drawn into world war, nuclear war, by a country like Cuba?—and, again, that nothing, nothing at all would be done that could embarrass his brother before the midterm elections.

Two days later, Dobrynin invited Ted Sorensen to the Soviet Embassy and dictated a message to the President that he said came directly from Khrushchev: "Nothing will be undertaken before the American Congressional elections that could complicate the international situation or aggravate the tension in the relations between our two countries. This includes a German peace settlement and West Berlin. . . . The Chairman does not wish to become involved in your internal political affairs."

"What about Cuba?" Sorensen asked, emphasizing that the President was already aggravated by political attack. "He repeated several times," Sorensen immediately reported to the President, "they had done nothing new or extraordinary in Cuba—that the events causing all the excitement had been taking place somewhat gradually and quietly over a long period of time." Still aggravated, the President asked Robert Kennedy to bring in his Russian, Georgi Bolshakov, the agent-editor.

"Hello, Georgie," said the President. "I know you are off to Moscow for a vacation, and I'd like you to communicate something to Premier Khrushchev."

He told the Russian that Ambassador Llewellyn Thompson in Moscow had informed him that Khrushchev was personally upset by U.S. military planes flying low over Soviet cargo ships headed for Cuba. "Tell him I've ordered those flights stopped today," Kennedy said. "I believe that the outlook for American-Soviet relations is good. The signing of a treaty on banning nuclear tests will be the next milestone along the road to their improvement. The treaty could mark the initial stage of our two countries' disarmament, and we would spare our children and grand-children the threat of war. . . . Tell Khrushchev I hope I'll be seeing him again in the near future."

Outside, in the private alley between the White House and the Execu-tive Office Building, called Executive Avenue, Robert Kennedy delivered the rest of the message. Without mentioning Senator Keating or missiles, the Attorney General was asking the Russians not to embarrass his brother: "Goddamn it, Georgie, doesn't Premier Khrushchev realize the President's position? Doesn't the Premier know that the President has enemies as well as friends? Believe me, my brother really means what he says about American-Soviet relations. But every step he takes to meet Premier Khrushchev halfway costs. . . . If the Premier just took the trou-ble to be, for a moment at least, in the President's shoes he would understand him."

Then Robert Kennedy surprised Bolshakov, saying he feared for his brother's life. "In a gust of blind hate, 'they' may go to any length. . . ." Bolshakov assumed his friend was talking about American right-wingers of some sort.*

The Keating speech pushed Cuba onto the front pages again. On television, Keating was attacking our "Do-nothing President." Kennedy responded as coolly as possible, issuing a statement that same day, September 4, as he took a short vacation at his wife's family's home in Newport, Rhode Island:

"Information has reached this government in the last four days from a variety of sources which established without doubt that the Soviets have provided the Cuban government with a number of anti-aircraft defensive missiles with a slant range of twenty-five miles which are similar to early models of our Nike. . . .

"The number of Soviet military technicians now known to be in Cuba or en route—approximately 3,500—is consistent with assistance in setting-up and learning to use this equipment. . . . There is no evidence of any organized combat force in Cuba from any Soviet bloc country . . . or of the presence of ground-to-ground missiles; or of other significant offensive capability either in Cuban hands or under Soviet direction and guidance. . . .

"Were it to be otherwise the gravest issues would arise. . . . The United States in conjunction with other Hemisphere countries will make sure that, while increased Cuban armaments will be a heavy burden to the unhappy people of Cuba themselves, they will be nothing more."

---

* Robert Kennedy was a suspicious man. He had asked the FBI to examine wine sent as a gift to President Kennedy from Premier Khrushchev to check for poison or personality-altering drugs. "No drugs or poisons were identified," reported the FBI lab. "The wine was consumed in the examination."

Then Kennedy, who was in Newport to watch the America's Cup sailing races, sat down to talk with *Newsweek*'s Ben Bradlee. He had been summoned to see Kennedy family files and FBI reports to try to knock down a story called "John's Other Wife." It concerned a recurring rumor that John Kennedy had been married before he met Jacqueline Bouvier. Bradlee was allowed to see reports of an FBI investigation of the story. The rumor was false, but it was being circulated in nasty little pamphlets around the country.

It was the first time Kennedy had spoken to his old neighbor and friend since Bradlee had been quoted in a *Look* magazine article early in August on press coverage of the White House: "It's almost impossible to write a story they like. Even if a story is quite favorable to their side, they'll find one paragraph to quibble with."

In return for seeing the "Other Wife" files, Bradlee, after checking with his bosses in New York, had given Kennedy a personal veto over the wording of the *Newsweek* article. But any hopes Bradlee had that this meant the end of his social exile were dashed when the British ambassador, David Ormsby-Gore, asked Bradlee whether he was coming to the day's race.

"No, he's not coming," Kennedy said, and turned away.

Chapter 33

SEPTEMBER 30, 1962

KENNEDY PLEDGES ANY STEPS TO BAR CUBAN AGGRESSION
President Sees No Evidence of "Significant" Increase
in Castro's Military Power

The President's "Statement on Soviet Military Shipments to Cuba" was the lead story of *The New York Times* on September 5, 1962. Another front-page story reported the Soviet Union's protest of a violation of its airspace by a U.S. bomber over the Pacific coast of Siberia. The missiles and warplanes shared the top of the page with two photographs of Negro children. One group was the first of their race to be admitted to St. Frances De Sales School in New Orleans; the other was being turned away at the doors of the high school in Albany, Georgia. Inside the paper were more than two dozen stories on the integration or resistance to integration of school districts across the South. One photograph showed "No Niggers Please" written across the doors of Albany High.

Kennedy's assertion that the missiles photographed in Cuba were short-range antiaircraft weapons was an attempt to calm the war talk coming from Senators Keating and Capehart and their CIA sources. He was contemptuous of the two Republicans. It was, he thought, ridiculous to think that the Soviets would dare to try to install nuclear missiles within ninety miles of the United States. In Moscow, the Soviets responded to the American headlines by repeating claims that Cuba was in imminent danger of invasion from the United States. Tass, the Soviet news agency, mirrored Kennedy's words, saying: "Weapons going to Cuba are designed exclusively for defensive purposes."

On September 8, Kennedy received a secret cable from Secretary of the Interior Stewart Udall, who had spent a long afternoon talking with Premier Khrushchev at the Soviet leader's villa on the Black Sea. " 'Now as to Cuba—here is an area that could really lead to some unexpected consequences,' " Udall quoted Khrushchev. " 'I have been reading what some irresponsible Senators have been saying on this. A lot of people have been making a big fuss because we are giving aid to Cuba. But you are giving aid to Japan. Just recently I was reading that you have placed atomic warheads on Japanese territory and surely this is not something the Japanese need. So when Castro comes to us for aid, we give him what he needs for defense. . . . Only for defense. However, if you attack Cuba, that would create an entirely different situation.' "

Kennedy had sent Udall to the Soviet Union to accompany Robert Frost, who had been adopted as the unofficial poet laureate of the administration. The eighty-eight-year-old writer had been invited to Moscow for a week of readings and meetings with Soviet poets, and Khrushchev invited him to spend a day at his retreat at Petsunda in Soviet Georgia. In fact, the premier had come to the poet's bedside in a guest house because Frost was not feeling well. The two of them had talked for ninety minutes, lusty conversation shifting from agreement on poetry to differences on politics. "A noble rivalry" was proposed by the poet for Communists and capitalists. "No more propaganda and no more name-calling." They shook hands, and Frost said he looked forward to passing on Khrushchev's thoughts and ideas to Kennedy as soon as possible.

Secretary Udall met with Khrushchev for more than two hours. Most of their conversation was on Cuba. "The President has made his position clear," Udall said in response to Khrushchev's mild threats. "A few people in Congress may call for an invasion of Cuba, but the President makes the policy."

"Yes, I know," Khrushchev said. "It's up to me to make the decision on going to war, but fools in airplanes do exist, I realize. . . . You have surrounded us with military bases."

The Premier specifically mentioned U.S. Jupiter missiles in Turkey, lined up along the Soviet border. President Eisenhower had ordered them put there in 1959, partly to draw Turkey into NATO planning and partly to quiet Democrats like Senator Kennedy who were demanding the United States do something to neutralize big Soviet ICBMs. An intermediate-range missile on the border was essentially a strategic weapon, capable of reaching as deep into the Soviet Union as an ICBM in North Dakota, and able to get to the target a lot quicker. Eisenhower had been surprised that the Soviets did not react more vehemently to

U.S. missile installations in Turkey and Italy. In June 1959, Ike had said privately that putting the Jupiters in Turkey was like the Soviets putting intermediate-range missiles in Cuba or Mexico. He said, privately again, that for once Khrushchev was absolutely right in accusing the United States of provocations; that if Soviets had done something like that, the United States would have had to take military action.

"I will convey your messages to President Kennedy," Udall said, as he and Khrushchev parted on September 8. "He is a strong leader—a courageous man, a man of steel, as you are. You, the President and I myself were all participants in the last World War."

"Yes, good!" Khrushchev said. "If the press asks what we talked about tell them electric power plants."

"Please," the Soviet leader said as they parted, "give my best personal regards to the President, his family, and his daughter from me and my wife."

"He's a great man. . . . Rough and ready," Frost said to Udall, as they began their trip home that night. "He knows what power is and he knows how to take hold of it."

Frost's ten-day visit had been front-page news across the United States, and a crowd of reporters and cameras were waiting for him and Udall when they arrived at Idlewild International Airport in New York on September 9. Frost was obviously tired, but he agreed to sit down before a bouquet of microphones, saying he looked forward to passing along what he had heard to Kennedy, including a private message from the premier to the President. Then he said: "Khrushchev said he feared for us modern liberals. He said we were too liberal to fight. I suppose he thought we'd stand there for the next hundred years saying, 'On the one hand—but on the other hand.' "

"Why did Frost say that?" the President demanded of Udall. The President was furious. It was the kind of thing Keating and Capehart were saying, that Kennedy was soft! The Secretary said he didn't know, that he was not sure Khrushchev actually said anything like that, that Frost had misunderstood a favorite Khrushchev story about the young writer, Maxim Gorky, asking the old one, Leo Tolstoy, about sex. Tolstoy's answer was something like, "The desire is the same, it's the performance that's different."

The President was under increasing pressure to get tough. The CIA was asking for permission for more U-2 flights. One had been canceled on September 6 because of bad weather. There was cloud cover over most of Cuba—it was the beginning of the tropical storm season—and U-2s could not photograph what their pilots could not see. The President was not enthusiastic about the overflights, worrying about a repeat of the 1960 shooting down of Francis Gary Powers over the Soviet Union. The Cuban overflights were much riskier now with SAM missiles on the island. That point was dramatically made later on the same day Frost and Udall returned. The Chinese shot down a U-2 from Taiwan with a Soviet-made missile.

"Rockets Will Blast the United States if It Invades Cuba," was the headline across the top of the front page of *Revolución* in Havana on September 12. To the White House, that sounded like routine Cuban bluster. Castro and even Khrushchev did not seem to be Kennedy's biggest problem at the moment. It was Keating he was concerned about. McGeorge Bundy's memo to the President before his September 13 news conference said: "The Congressional head of steam on this is the most serious that we have had. It affects both parties. . . . The immediate hazard is that the Administration may appear to be weak and indecisive."

The President opened the news conference with a statement on Cuba and on the Soviet shipments: "I would like to take this opportunity to set the matter in perspective. . . . It is Mr. Castro and his supporters who are in trouble. So it is not surprising that in a frantic effort to bolster his regime he should try to arouse the Cuban people by charges of an imminent American invasion. . . . I will repeat the conclusion that I reported last week: that these new shipments do not constitute a threat to any other part of this hemisphere. . . . We shall neither initiate nor allow aggression in this hemisphere. . . . I have indicated that if Cuba should possess a capacity to carry out offensive actions against the United States, that the United States would act."

He was asked next about Robert Frost and reports that the poet was carrying a private message from Khrushchev, and he responded: "I have not received his message, though I hope to see him shortly. . . ." Actually, Kennedy had no intention of seeing Frost. He was still angry that the old man had added to the impression that he was weak and indecisive.

The President was also asked about his request the week before, on September 7, for congressional approval of standby authorization to call up as many as 150,000 Ready Reserve troops to active duty. On background, his men had told reporters that that had more to do with Berlin than with Cuba. That had not convinced Castro, who continued to tell the people of Cuba and the world that a U.S. invasion was in preparation. Yet, at home, the President was being criticized not for doing too much, but for seeming to do nothing. "The press boys bobbled their lines," wrote William Randolph Hearst, Jr., publisher of the newspapers his father had created from San Francisco to New York. "They neglected to ask the question, 'Why not blockade?' "

In fact, U.S. military preparations were under way in the Caribbean —maneuvers, contingency plans, and such—but they were more visible abroad than at home. Such things were kept secret from the American people, even though they were noisy enough to be picked up by Cuban and Soviet intelligence networks. At the beginning of August, the Special Group (Augmented) running Operation Mongoose, and acting for the President, had asked the Joint Chiefs of Staff for a paper on "Consequences of US Military Intervention in Cuba" and, specifically, for a sustained military occupation plan. On September 7, the Air Force had begun extensive training exercises near Cuba for possible action designed "To achieve complete destruction of the Cuban air order of battle." Kennedy knew such maneuvers might lead the Cubans to believe the Americans were coming. But that was fine, it would keep them off balance.

There were a couple of civil rights questions about Negro voter registration efforts in Albany, Georgia. "I think—and I'm sure this is the view of the people of the States—the right to vote is very basic," Kennedy answered. "I commend those who are making the effort to register every citizen. They deserve the protection of the United States government, the protection of the State, the protection of local communities . . . and if it requires extra legislation and extra force, we shall do that."

The right to vote was the easy way out for Kennedy on civil rights. Americans in the North were united on that. The tough calls had to do with integrating schools and neighborhoods. On September 17, he read a letter from Representative Martha Griffiths, a Michigan Democrat, pleading with him not to move on civil rights until after the midterm elections:

> There is not time enough left before the election for the white areas to understand the full implications of this order; throw the rocks and settle down.
>
> Most white people have resigned themselves to the fact of integration, but the suburbs of Detroit believe it will be years before it applies to their exact area. . . . No Democratic Congressman, from suburbia, to whom I have talked, believes he is in any danger of losing colored votes; but he does feel such an order could cost white votes.
>
> In case the counsel of those seated less close to the fire than I am prevails, however, and I lose this election . . . Can I have the next Supreme Court vacancy, where I can legislate in safety far from the prejudices of the precincts?

The President would do what he could to postpone the reckoning, but he was a prisoner of events. The federal government was being drawn into the legal maneuvers of a young Air Force veteran who had been inspired by Kennedy's Inaugural Address—and decided that what he could do for his country was become the first Negro to attend the University of Mississippi. Just before the news conference, Supreme Court Justice Hugo Black had dismissed the final legal attempt by the state of Mississippi to block the admission of James Meredith, who had applied when the university offices opened on January 21, 1961, the morning after Kennedy's inauguration. Now, said Meredith in legal triumph, he was going to drive up to the school in Oxford, Mississippi, in a new gold Thunderbird. Justice Department attorneys convinced him to forget the Thunderbird as they tried to negotiate a peaceful entry with officials of the university and the state on the first day of classes. That was scheduled for September 25.

On September 19, the President was given a Special National Intelligence Estimate (SNIE). This was the top-of-the-line paper, approved by a secret analysis committee involving the entire government, the CIA and FBI, State and Defense, the National Security Agency and the Atomic Energy Commission. It was delivered to him at 9:30 A.M. by one of his Army aides, General Clifton, with his usual *Intelligence Checklist,* a small secret morning newspaper with a circulation of about twenty. There were usually a dozen headlines like "Ivanov G.R.U. Agent in London." Kennedy read it every day but was never fully convinced it was as accurate or timely as, say, *The New York Times.*

The President's nine-page SNIE, one of only five copies, confirmed his own conclusion that the Soviet leader's actions in Cuba were more political than military. The paper ended by saying:

> We believe the USSR values its position in Cuba primarily for the political advantages to be derived from it, and consequently that the main purpose of the present military buildup in Cuba is to strengthen the Communist regime there against what Cubans and the Soviets consider to be a danger that the US may attempt by one means or another to overthrow it. . . . They evidently recognize that the development of an offensive military base in Cuba might provoke U.S. military intervention and thus defeat their present purpose.

Kennedy left the next day, Thursday, for a long weekend at Hyannis Port. A celebration commemorating the one hundredth anniversary of the Emancipation Proclamation was scheduled for Washington that weekend. He left a recording of a short speech to be played at the Lincoln Memorial: "Despite humiliation and deprivation, the Negro retained his loyalty to the United States and to democratic institutions . . . by a quiet and proud determination to work for long-denied rights within the framework of the American Constitution. It can be said, I believe, that Abraham Lincoln emancipated the slaves, but that in this century since, our Negro citizens have emancipated themselves."

Kennedy was sailing when his words were broadcast. The rhetoric was standard stuff—unless Negroes took it to heart in American places like Mississippi, where only 60,000 of the 1 million of them there could vote and none had ever been allowed into the state university. On Tuesday, September 25, James Meredith was driven into Jackson, the state capital, by two federal officials, John Doar, now the number-two man in the Civil Rights Division of the Justice Department, and the Chief U.S. Marshal, James McShane. They were charged with enforcing the orders of the Fifth Circuit of the United States Court of Appeals that the state of Mississippi had no legal power to prevent Meredith's admission to the public university. He was blocked that day by Governor Ross Barnett, who appointed himself, temporarily, as the registrar of the university. Barnett turned away the federal men and Meredith after they had pushed their way through a crowd of jeering state legislators and two thousand other citizens of Mississippi.

"Which one is Meredith?" said Barnett to great laughter, looking past the man he was refusing, the only Negro in sight. The governor's words were being reported around the state by television—and by telephone to Attorney General Kennedy in Washington. Robert Kennedy had been on the phone with Barnett for hours over the past ten days. He was attempting to orchestrate a political deal allowing the peaceful admission of Meredith, something that would get this over as quickly as possible with political pride preserved all around. The President and the governor were both skillful politicians, nominally members of the same party, but toiling in different fields—Kennedy had won only 37 percent of Mississippi's vote against Nixon and an unpledged slate of anti–civil rights electors.

The situation the next morning was reported this way in *The New York Times* and the *Jackson Daily News:*

In New York: "U.S. IS PREPARED TO SEND TROOPS AS MISSISSIPPI GOVERNOR DEFIES COURTS AND BARS NEGRO STUDENT."

In Jackson: "THOUSANDS SAID READY TO FIGHT FOR MISSISSIPPI."

Then the same thing happened that day, but this time in Oxford, the seat of the university, where Lieutenant Governor Paul Johnson blocked Doar, McShane, and Meredith. On Thursday, September 27, after more hours on the telephone, the Attorney General again thought he had his deal: Meredith would arrive that day with two dozen marshals and Barnett would personally block his way—until forced to yield at gunpoint.

Meredith was on his way to Oxford again the next day, by car from

Memphis in Tennessee, as Barnett and Robert Kennedy worked out details.

"General," said the governor, "I was under the impression they were all going to pull their guns. This could be very embarrassing. We got a big crowd here, and if one pulls his gun and we all turn, it would be very embarrassing. Isn't it possible to have them all pull their guns?"

"I hate to have them all pull their guns," the Attorney General said. "I think it could create harsh feelings. Isn't it sufficient if I have one man draw his gun and the others keep their hands on their holsters?"

"They must all draw their guns," the governor countered. "Then they should point their guns at us and then we could step aside.

"You understand we have had no agreement," he added. Barnett wanted what was called "plausible deniability" in Washington.

"That's correct," said the Attorney General. But the deal they did have collapsed over how many guns would be drawn on the governor of Mississippi. Meredith and the marshals were twenty miles from Oxford when Robert Kennedy ordered his men to turn around and take Meredith back to the Naval Air Station outside Memphis. That night the Defense Department ordered a DEFCON-3 alert—Army units from New York to Florida and Texas were ready to move within four hours.*

For the President, once court orders had been issued, negotiations and political charade were greatly preferable to the obvious alternatives: Giving in to Barnett or sending in the U.S. Army. Dealing with American race relations had seemed easier and simpler to him when he was just Senator Kennedy. In 1957, he had criticized President Eisenhower when he had sent the Army into Little Rock, Arkansas, after local officials defied federal court orders to desegregate schools there. Kennedy's argument then was that Ike had let matters drift until he had no choice but to send in troops—an order that produced photographs and film clips of U.S. paratroopers pointing M-1 rifles at white parents to get Negro children into the school buildings. Now President Kennedy was determined there would be no photo opportunities on his watch that would embarrass the United States all over the world.

From the President's perspective, the problem with civil rights was that the Negroes and their white friends were pushing the most fundamental kind of attack on the status quo. Their righteous expectations, in that view, were based on an unrealistic political premise, thinking that the President alone had the power to persuade millions of free people—the whites—to do something they did not want to do. The time

---

* DEFCON-3 represented a medium military alert between DEFCON-5, no alert, and DEFCON-1, which was war.

was not right, he said again and again, more than once to the United States Civil Rights Commission, a semi-autonomous body created by President Eisenhower. The commission, appointed by Ike to deflect some of the heat generated in Little Rock, now wanted to schedule public hearings on discrimination complaints in the state producing more of them than any other, Mississippi.

"You're making my life difficult," Kennedy said to John Hannah, the chairman of the commission, and his staff director, Berl Bernhard. "I've read this law and I know you can do anything you want to, but I would appreciate it if you didn't."

So far, he had been able to hold off public action by Hannah and Bernhard, who were both white. But Negroes, including James Meredith, were beginning to take things into their own hands. "Negroes are getting ideas they didn't have before," said Kennedy's one Negro adviser, Louis Martin, a publisher of Negro newspapers in Chicago who was serving as deputy chairman of the Democratic National Committee.

"Where are they getting them?" the President asked.

"From you! You're lifting the horizons of Negroes."

Negroes, it seemed, did not want to wait their turn, either. Kennedy was learning that he did not have the power, either, to stop the march of millions of Negro men and women determined to make themselves free. When one of his other assistants said he was risking a great deal to get one Negro into one school, "I have no choice," said the President, which was the same thing he told Governor Barnett. "I don't have the power to call off Meredith."

On this one, the President wanted to appear to be exercising minimum power. He wanted to be seen as doing his constitutional job of enforcing the orders of the Fifth Circuit of the United States Court of Appeals—acting only as the nation's chief executive fulfilling his oath to uphold the laws of the land. He was as interested in getting this over with as Barnett was. The governor wanted to look as if he stood up to the northerners in order to protect and preserve what the white folks of Mississippi called "traditions" or "our way of life" until he was crushed by superior power. The President wanted to use a minimum of power; most of all he wanted to avoid calling out troops to get one Negro into Ole Miss.

Kennedy continued to hold back, letting his brother be the public voice of the administration. "I concur in your judgment to stay out of it personally for the time being," Ted Sorensen wrote in a note to the President—from the hospital. The thirty-three-year-old speechwriter was developing ulcers. "The defiance should be against the majesty of the United States, not John F. Kennedy. Similarly I assume you will not hold a press conference until all this is over. There are too many questions you should neither evade nor answer directly."

Sorensen also advised the President to think about going after the things white Mississippians cared most about, money and football: "The businessmen backing the Governor may be more nervous if the big NASA, defense and other Federal contracts in that state were held up for fear that violence may interfere with their being carried out. . . . The students may be less enthusiastic if Ole Miss lost her accreditation, some of her football opponents for this fall, or her eligibility for post-season bowl games."

On Friday, September 28, the judges of the Fifth Circuit in New Orleans began the legal endgame. Governor Barnett was scheduled to answer contempt of court charges that morning, but he did not appear and was found guilty in absentia. The judges gave him four days to purge himself of the contempt—get Meredith registered by Tuesday—or be fined $10,000 a day and taken into the custody of the Attorney General of the United States.

The next day, Saturday, the President told Evelyn Lincoln to place a call to the governor. While he waited, he joked, playing for laughs from his brother and his men from the Justice Department sitting in the Oval Office. He pretended to rehearse his lines: "Governor, this is the President of the United States—not Bobby, not Teddy, not Princess Radziwill . . ."

The phone rang. "And now—Governor Ross Barnett," said John Kennedy, playing master of ceremonies as he reached for the phone.

"Go get him, Johnny boy," said his brother.

"This is not my order, I just have to carry it out," the President told Barnett on the telephone. "I didn't put him in the University, but, on the other hand, under the Constitution. . . . So I want to get together and try to do it with you in a way which is the most satisfactory and causes the least chance of, uh, damage to the people in Mississippi. . . . I don't want to do it in any way that causes, uh, difficulty to you or anyone else."

"You don't understand the situation down here," said the governor. "I took an oath, you know, to abide by the laws of this state."

"The problem is, Governor, that I've got my responsibility, just like you have yours . . ."

"I realize that, and I appreciate that so much . . ."

"What I want is to try to work this out in an amicable way. We don't want a lot of people down there getting hurt or killed."

There was a little more back and forth that day, and finally Barnett said: "I appreciate your interest in our poultry program and all those things."

The President began to laugh softly. Finally he had to put his hand over the phone. He hung up and turned to his brother and said: "You've been fighting a sofa pillow all week."

"He's a rogue," Robert Kennedy said.

Back on the phone with Barnett an hour later, the President said: "I'd like to get assurances from you about, that the state police down there will take positive action to maintain law and order."

"They'll do that," said Barnett, who was also telling Kennedy that Oxford was filling up with Mississippians carrying shotguns and pistols. "We'll have two hundred and twenty highway patrolmen. . . ." Barnett continued.

"Right," the President said.

"And they'll be absolutely unarmed," said the governor. "Not a one of 'em'll be armed."

With the prospect of unarmed state police trying to hold back armed mobs, the President gave up pillow fighting. Robert Kennedy continued the conversations with Governor Barnett, who took time out to go to the Saturday night football game in Jackson between Ole Miss and the University of Kentucky. The governor was being cheered by the crowd at the game when the President called an assistant attorney general named Norbert Schlei to his living quarters on the third floor of the White House at midnight (10:00 P.M. in Jackson) to sign the legal documents and orders necessary to send troops into Mississippi.

"Is this pretty much what Ike signed in 1957 with the Little Rock thing?" He was reading the papers by the light of a reading lamp on a small table.

"Essentially," Schlei said.

"Where do I sign?"

Kennedy snapped off the lamp and took off his reading glasses, standing in the light from a hallway. He rapped the little table and said, "You know this was General Grant's table."

Schlei was thinking about that as he started down the stairs—the table belonged to the commander of Union troops in the Civil War!—to tell the reporters waiting in the lobby about the proclamation. "Wait!"—he heard the President's voice and looked back to see him leaning over the railing at the top of the stairs.

"Don't tell them about General Grant's table," Kennedy said.

On Sunday afternoon, Robert Kennedy thought again that he had a deal with Governor Barnett, and the President was preparing to go on national television to proclaim the end of the crisis. The brothers had finally pinned down the governor by threatening to release the tapes of their earlier negotiations showing that Barnett had been collaborating with the White House all along. The phone conversations would destroy him politically in Mississippi.

"We've got it all down, Governor," Robert Kennedy said.

"You don't mean the President is going to say that tonight," Barnett said.

"Of course he is," the Attorney General said. "You broke your word to him."

Barnett quickly suggested that federal agents move Meredith immediately onto the Ole Miss campus in Oxford, while he himself was leading anti-Meredith rallies in Jackson. By 6:30 P.M. in Oxford (eight-thirty in Washington) Meredith was on the campus, brought secretly to a room in Baxter Hall, a dormitory building. Three hundred federal marshals commanded by Assistant Attorney General Nicholas Katzenbach—an ad hoc force of Treasury agents, border patrolmen, and federal prison guards from around the country, each wearing a white helmet and yellow armband—circled the Lyceum, the campus's main administration building. There were a thousand students and other locals there, too, being held back by Mississippi Highway Patrolmen. They thought Meredith was inside in the registrar's office.

Katzenbach put a dime in a pay telephone and made a collect call to the Cabinet Room in the White House, while television cameras were being set up in the Oval Office. The President intended to report to the nation on the crisis, at 10:00 P.M. Washington time. Kennedy asked what was going on outside. They're chanting, he was told.

"What are they chanting?"

"Go to hell, JFK!"

"I think they've got it in pretty good shape," Robert Kennedy reported. He said that General Edwin Walker was on the campus, whipping up students, calling integration a plot of the anti-Christ. Walker was a Korean War hero who had led the U.S. troops in Little Rock in 1957, but was dismissed from the Army in 1961 for trying to indoctrinate troops in West Germany with his own brand of ultra-conservative politics.

"Imagine that son of a bitch having been commander of a division?" said the President.

"Have you read *Seven Days in May?*" someone asked.

"Yeah," Kennedy said. "The president was awfully vague. But I thought the general was a pretty good character."

It was quiet for a while, at least in the White House. The President began talking about a column by James Reston he had heard was going to be in the next day's *New York Times,* saying that Soviet leaders had no interest in inviting Kennedy to Moscow. "It's an inaccurate story," Kennedy said. "We ought to knock it down tonight—that's just kicking Reston in the balls, isn't it?"

He picked up another paper and was commenting on articles when he heard his brother on the open line to Oxford, exclaiming, "The state police have left?"

The Mississippi troopers, two hundred or so of them, began leaving at about 7:30 P.M., Mississippi time*—a half hour before the President was to go on national television to proclaim peace. The crowd, more than two thousand now, was closing in on the marshals. A Coke bottle landed at the feet of one marshal; another bottle filled with gasoline, a Molotov Cocktail, smashed in flames on the steps of the Lyceum. People out in the dark around the building were collecting bricks and iron bars from a construction site nearby. "Bob," said Ed Guthman, the Attorney General's executive assistant, who was manning the pay telephone in the Lyceum, "we may have to use tear gas."

"How many agents do you have down there?" the President asked his brother. "Where are they? Are they in the administration building with Meredith?"

"No," Robert Kennedy answered. "Meredith is in another building."

"I think you ought to get those MPs. . . . I don't see what you've got to lose, if they're at the airport. You can always send them back," the President said.

Then he went back to the text of his speech, going over it with Sorensen, who had left the hospital to write the first draft. At two minutes to ten o'clock, Washington time, the President was at his desk in the Oval Office, strapped in, as it were, as television technicians made their final light and sound tests.

Next door in the Cabinet Room, Robert Kennedy was still on the line with Guthman, who told him: "I'm sorry to report that we've had to fire tear gas. We had no choice."

Burke Marshall, the Assistant Attorney General for Civil Rights, went next door to try to tell Kennedy that they might have a riot on their hands, but the President was already on the air.

"Good evening, my fellow citizens . . . ," he began.

"Mr. James Meredith is now in residence on the campus of the University of Mississippi. This has been accomplished thus far without the use of National Guard or other troops. . . . Even though the Govern-

---

* There was a two-hour difference in time between Washington, D.C., and Oxford during the summer, because of daylight saving time in Washington. When it was 10:00 P.M. in the Capital, it was 8:00 P.M. in Oxford.

ment had not originally been a part of this case . . . my obligation under
the Constitution and statutes of the United States was and is to implement the orders of the court with whatever means are necessary. . . .
There is in short no reason why the books on this case cannot now be
quickly and quietly closed in the manner directed by the court. Let us
preserve both the law and the peace. . . .

"Thank you and good night."

The Lyceum was under siege by the time the President finished—
"Like the Alamo," his brother told him—and he immediately ordered a
unit of the Mississippi National Guard, on active duty under federal
control since his midnight order the day before, to move to the campus
from their armory in Oxford. Reports were now being logged in at the
White House every few minutes: 11:23—Marshal shot through leg . . .
11:42—state trooper hurt bad . . . 11:55—Highway Patrol still without orders to return . . . 12 midnight—gunfire spreading . . . 12:10—
only 67 local National Guardsmen immediately available.

The rioters were charging the Lyceum behind stolen bulldozers and
fire engines. On the fringes of the mob, reporters were being attacked
and cameras smashed. An Associated Press correspondent was
wounded, shot twice. A man from Agence France Presse—the whole
world was watching—was killed, shot in the back. A construction
worker from Oxford, apparently just watching the action, was killed,
shot in the head. But the marshals had still not fired a shot.

There was something close to panic at the White House. The U.S.
government was undermanned and overwhelmed in the battle, again.
"This reminds me a little bit of the Bay of Pigs," said Kenny O'Donnell.
"Yeah," said the President. "I haven't had such a good time since the
Bay of Pigs." Robert Kennedy made a face and then a mock announcement about the failure of this operation: "The Attorney General announced today that he's joining Allen Dulles at Princeton Univers . . ."

Katzenbach was on the line, asking for permission to start firing in
self-defense. "No," said the President. "They are not to fire under any
conditions"—except, he said, to protect Meredith's life. He didn't want
a lynching.

"Stay right by Meredith," Robert Kennedy told Katzenbach. "Shoot
anybody that puts a hand on him."

"Where's the Army? Where are they? Why aren't they moving?" the
President was demanding, yelling on the telephone at his Secretary of
the Army, Cyrus Vance, who had told him it would take one hour to
move the first Military Police units from the Memphis Naval Air Station,
eighty miles away. The reports from Vance had the President in a fury:
12:13—Army regulars in Memphis still on ground . . . 12:24—still not

airborne . . . 1:02—troops on way . . . 1:47—mistake earlier, troops still in Memphis . . . 2 o'clock—troops in air . . .

"People are dying in Oxford," Kennedy said to the field commander of the troops in Memphis, General Creighton Abrams. "This is the worst thing I've seen in forty-five years. I want the MP battalion to enter the area."

One hour, then two passed, and the siege of the Lyceum continued. Meanwhile, the President and Governor Barnett were back on the phone again.

"Mr. President, please," said Barnett. "Why don't you, why can't you give an order up there to remove Meredith?"

"How can I remove him, Governor, when there's riot in the street? He may step out of that building and something happen to him."

"I'll go up there myself and get a microphone and tell him you have agreed . . . for 'em to be removed," Barnett said.

"No, no. Now, wait a minute, Governor . . . Call me from up there. Then we'll decide what we're going to do before you make any speeches about it."

"People are wiring me and calling me saying, 'Well, you've given up,' Barnett said, talking politician to politician. "I said, I had to say, 'No I'm not giving up . . . I have courage and faith and, and we'll win this fight.' You understand. That's just to Mississippi people."

"I understand," the President answered. "But I don't think anybody, in Mississippi or anyplace else wants a lot of people killed. . . . Let's get the maximum number of your state police to get that situation so we don't have sporadic firing."

"What are we going to say about all this?" asked Robert Kennedy. "We're going to have a hell of a problem about why we didn't handle the situation better. . . . I think we're gonna have to figure out what we're gonna say. . . . I just think that we're going to take a lot of knocks, because of people getting killed. . . . The fact that I didn't get the people up there in time. . . . The point we want to get over, you know, is that the Governor made this arrangement. We didn't sneak him in. I think that's going to be the cry that we snuck him in unprepared."

"Damn Army!" he said, after talking to Vance and Abrams. "They can't even tell if the MPs have left yet."

"I have a hunch that Khrushchev would get those troops in fast enough," said O'Donnell. At 3:33 A.M., the White House was told the troops had not left the Oxford airport.

The President nodded. "They always give you their bullshit about their instant reaction and their split-second timing, but it never works out. No wonder it's so hard to win a war."

"This one is a ball-breaker," John Kennedy said to Dr. Max Jacobson, who had been flown down from New York to Washington to treat the President before his television appearance. The doctor's pilot, as usual, was his patient, Mark Shaw, a well-known photographer, who owned a twin-engined Cessna. The two of them shuttled back and forth between New York and Washington on presidential call.

The first U.S. Army regulars, Military Policemen, finally reached the campus after 4:00 A.M., October 1. By dawn, there were 16,000 soldiers in Oxford, which had a population of 10,000. Two men were dead, 166 marshals and 40 soldiers were injured, 200 were arrested, including General Walker. The President told his brother to find out from the Solicitor General, Archibald Cox, what authority he needed to arrest Governor Barnett.

President Kennedy stood up at 5:30 A.M. "I'm going to bed," he said. "I want to be called if anything happens."

Four hours later, with a bodyguard of six federal marshals, and a squad of soldiers waiting outside in two U.S. Army trucks, James Meredith attended his first class at Ole Miss—in Colonial American History. There were 23,000 soldiers camped around Oxford.

Robert Kennedy turned out to be wrong about the politics of that bloody Sunday night in Mississippi—at least in the short term, which was what counted with midterm elections only a month away. The President did not have to explain anything. Crisis, once again, was its own reward. Americans rallied around the President.

Three days after Meredith's first class at Ole Miss, the President got a memorandum from his pollster, Lou Harris, that began:

> I am frank to say that I have never seen the temper and mood change so drastically as this election outlook. . . . In key Northern industrial states, sentiment is behind you 2-1/2 to 3–1 on Mississippi. We happened to be checking New York State day by day in continuous polling over the Mississippi events and in two days time, the Jewish vote (21 percent of the state) jumped 12 points from 61 to 73 percent Democratic. The Negro vote went from 65 to 84 percent Democratic. The Catholic vote moved up 2 points and the White Protestant vote went up 3. Every Democrat running for major office should put front and center that this country needs firm and resolute leadership such as the President demonstrated in the Mississippi case.

The events in Oxford had taken place in the middle of the potentially more dangerous moves in the triangular tension between the United States, Cuba, and the Soviet Union. Harris's polls took account of that.

"Some of the edge has been taken off the Cuban issue by Mississippi, but tensions are still high on foreign policy," Harris continued. "In Michigan within the past week, a majority of 82–18 percent wanted a blockade of Cuba, although a majority of 68–32 percent oppose going to war there. . . . You can say that on Cuba, they (the Republicans) have been shooting from the hip and in the process have gone a long way toward undermining abroad the notion that we Americans are united in our firm and steadfast stand against Communism."

During the first week in October, the President ordered the Navy to prepare for a blockade of all shipping to and from Cuba—a contingency plan—and he received a "Top Secret" report from the Secretary of Defense on further contingency planning to knock out the SA-2s, Soviet surface-to-air antiaircraft missiles, installed in Cuba. "It is not necessary to build a model of an SA-2 for training purposes," McNamara told Kennedy in a memo. "The Navy plans to attack SA-2 targets at low levels using four divisions of A-4D's (4 aircraft per division) armed with 250-pound, 500-pound, and 2,000-pound low-drag bombs and napalm. All crews are proficient in the delivery techniques planned. . . . Target folders are in the hands of crews; and crews are familiar with their assigned targets."

As soon as John McCone was back from his honeymoon, stories began appearing which argued, as he had, that SA-2s were not a problem but whatever they were protecting might be. The October 1 issue of *Aviation Week,* which appeared the day James Meredith was actually registered, reported precisely what McCone had been telling the President: "Strategists consider the present arms build-up in Cuba the first step toward eventual construction of the intermediate-range ballistic missile emplacements. . . . SA-2s were aimed at preventing aerial photographic reconnaissance." ·

In fact, there had been no U-2 overflights for more than a week. Cuba was again hidden under the clouds of the hurricane season. Besides that, the President, wanting to avoid another Powers incident, had ordered the CIA to turn over Cuban flights to Air Force pilots—the idea was that if a U-2 was shot down, the White House could defend it as routine military action rather than a spy operation. But training new pilots to fly the extraordinary spy plane set surveillance schedules back several more days.

The Russian intelligence officer, Georgi Bolshakov, was also back in Washington after his vacation. In Moscow, he had been asked by Khrushchev personally if he thought the United States would go to war over Cuba. "Yes," Bolshakov had replied, mentioning pressure from reactionary forces that might go as far as killing Kennedy—at least that was what he had been told. "They can't mean it," Khrushchev had said. "Is he President or isn't he? If he is a strong President he has no one to fear."

Bolshakov called Robert Kennedy, saying he had a verbal message from the premier to the President. He met with him on October 4 and again on October 6. He was surprised that the Attorney General seemed cool and tense. "It's like this, Georgie," said Robert Kennedy, who sat formally in a suit and tie behind his desk at the Justice Department, making it clear this was an official meeting. "The President is very busy right now. . . ."

The Russian recited Khrushchev's message to the President:

"The Soviet leaders welcome the President's moves aimed at reducing tensions and bringing the relations between our two countries back to normal. However, they cannot but call the President's attention to the fact that the situation has been worsening of late chiefly owing to the American government's hostile actions in the Caribbean with regard to Cuba. . . . Premier Khrushchev is concerned about the situation being built up by the United States around Cuba, and we repeat that the Soviet Union is supplying to Cuba exclusively defensive weapons intended for protecting the interests of the Cuban revolution and not for perpetrating an aggression against any state, the U.S. included. The Soviet leaders are perfectly well aware of President Kennedy's position, will not take any action with regard to the United States before the elections to Congress due in November 1962 and hope that after the elections we shall get down to a new round of active negotiations."

Robert Kennedy asked Bolshakov to repeat the part about defensive weapons, and he wrote it down carefully. The next day, October 7, Charles Bartlett invited Bolshakov to lunch and asked him to recite Khrushchev's message once more for the President. Bartlett wrote it all down, too, then said that the President was extremely concerned that Khrushchev was misinterpreting American action and resolve in the Caribbean.

In the Caribbean, and along the southern Atlantic coast, the United States was openly escalating military planning and actions obviously targeting Cuba, including amphibious invasion exercises around Puerto Rico through the summer and early fall. The last exercise involving 7,500 Marines was aimed at the overthrow of a dictator named "Ortsac"—Castro spelled backwards. The Air Force transferred combat aircraft to Key West and other southern Florida bases from other parts of the country and, on September 18, the Air Force had begun training exercises simulating attacks on Cuba. More than 70,000 men participated in the largest exercise—"Operation Swift Strike II"—and both

Castro and Khrushchev stepped up charges that a U.S. invasion was in the works.

The plans for an invasion were being updated. If the President gave the order, 100,000 men massed from North Carolina to Key West would invade Cuba eight days later. Beginning on October 6, troops, aircraft, and support equipment were pre-positioned, ready to execute one of three military options: "CINCLANT Oplans 312–62, 314–61 and 316–61"—the plans, respectively, for the air strikes, small amphibious landings, or a full-scale invasion of Cuba, with estimated casualties (killed, wounded, and missing) of 18,484 men in the first eleven days. The target date for maximum readiness for the Oplans—and for a separate naval blockade of the island—was October 20.

A memorandum from Secretary of Defense McNamara on October 8 outlined contingencies that might lead to the invasion: "The positioning of bloc offensive weapons on Cuban soil. . . . Soviet action against Western rights in Berlin. . . . A substantial popular uprising in Cuba, the leaders of which request assistance in recovering Cuban independence. . . . A decision by the President that the affairs in Cuba have reached a point inconsistent with continuing US national security."

On October 10, the White House asked for and got permission from the British government to stockpile armaments in the Bahamas for use in a possible invasion, with two conditions: "1) Nothing is to be put in writing, 2) Facilities are not to be put to active use without prior agreement of British Government."

That same day, Senator Keating pushed the President aside again, taking centerstage in Washington by telling the Senate: "Construction has begun on at least half a dozen launching sites for intermediate range tactical missiles. Intelligence authorities must have advised the President and top government officials of this fact, and they must have been told that ground-to-ground missiles can be operational from inland Cuba within six months."

"Keating's a nut," the President told James Reston. Then Bundy briefed Reston on the White House version, basically telling him about Operation Mongoose. On October 12, the columnist wrote:

> What is going on is something quite different from the black and white picture of the Cuban controversy presented from the political platforms. In those angry talks it appears that the issue of American Cuban policy is between those who want to invade or at least blockade Cuba on the one hand, and those who want to "do nothing" on the other. . . . There is a missing element in the debate—subversion, which is going on all the time on that island. . . . In present circumstances, there will be no invasion, and no blockade, and no acquiescence in Soviet control of Cuba. But

there will be total surveillance of Cuba and there will be more turmoil in Cuba than Castro has yet experienced or imagined.

On October 14, the President went out to Indiana to campaign against Senator Capehart, who was being challenged for reelection by a young Democrat named Birch Bayh. It was a Sunday and also happened to be the first day the cloud cover over Cuba broke enough to send out a U-2. In Indianapolis, Kennedy was saying: "These self-appointed generals and admirals who want to send somebody else's son to war ought to be kept home by the voters and be replaced by somebody like Birch Bayh, who has some understanding of what the twentieth century is all about."

The President then went on to Buffalo, New York, for more campaign speechmaking, getting back to Washington at 1:45 A.M. on Monday. The lights of at least one government office were on despite the hour. Inside the National Photographic Interpretation Center in the center of the city, military and intelligence men were developing and studying the photographs taken from the U-2, piloted by an Air Force major, Rudolf Anderson, Jr. It was not until eight o'clock on Monday night, while the President was having dinner in the White House with his disabled father —Mrs. Kennedy was on a four-week holiday in Italy, providing the press of the world with lively pictures that the President thought were hurting him politically—when the photographic interpreters finally concluded that they were looking at pictures of eight ballistic missile launch pads under construction in a remote area in the west of Cuba.

It was almost 9:00 P.M. before McGeorge Bundy, who was hosting a dinner at home for Chip Bohlen before Bohlen left to take up his new post as Ambassador to France, was informed. Bundy thought the President was probably tired from his campaign trip and decided that there was no point in bothering him before morning. At 8:45 A.M. on Tuesday, October 16, the first photographs under his arm, he knocked on the President's door. Kennedy was sitting on the edge of his bed, wearing a bathrobe and slippers, surrounded by the papers and newspapers he had been reading.

"Mr. President," Bundy said, "there is now hard photographic evidence, which you will see, that the Russians have offensive missiles in Cuba."

Kennedy told Bundy to set up a meeting that morning, reeling off names, the first his brother. He called the Attorney General. "We have some big trouble. I want you over here."

Robert Kennedy was already in his office, waiting for Richard Helms, who was coming with a Soviet defector he had asked to meet.

"Dick, is it true? Dick, is it true?" Robert Kennedy asked Helms a moment later. "Did the Russians put missiles in Cuba?"

"Yes, it's true."

"Shit!"

Chapter 34

"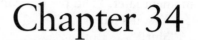e are probably going to have to bomb them," the President had said, after he looked at the U-2 photographs that Bundy had brought to his bedroom.

An hour later, he walked into Kenny O'Donnell's office and said: "You still think the fuss about Cuba is unimportant?"

"Absolutely. The voters won't give a damn about Cuba."

"I want to show you something," he said, laying out the photos. O'Donnell, just as Kennedy before he had been briefed, could make no sense of them. He looked confused, and then Kennedy explained: "It's the beginning of a launching site for a medium-range ballistic missile."

"I don't believe it."

"You better believe it," said Kennedy. The tone was ironic, but he knew he had made the greatest mistake of his life and he would probably pay for it by being defeated for reelection. The 1962 midterm elections would be a dark preview. "We've just elected Capehart in Indiana and Ken Keating will probably be the next President of the United States." He thought he was going to go down as the Commander-in-Chief who looked the other way while the Soviets put nuclear missiles ninety miles from the United States.

"Not a word about this to anyone," Kennedy said finally. "We want to look as though nothing unusual is going on around here."

"I'm going to see Gromyko here, Thursday," the President told Pierre

Salinger that morning when the press secretary brought in the week's schedule. "I don't know what he wants.

"Another thing. I expect a lot of traffic through here this week—Rusk, McNamara, Stevenson, the Chiefs of Staff. If the press tries to read something significant into it, you're to deny anything special is going on."

The heavy traffic began at eleven-thirty that morning, when the fourteen men Kennedy had chosen to help him deal with the crisis began to move into the Cabinet Room. Some of them—Rusk, McNamara, and Taylor—had been working through the night with their staffs to formulate possible diplomatic and military responses to the discovery of the missiles. The President came in a few minutes later, talking to his daughter Caroline, who was almost five years old now.

"Have you been eating candy?" asked the President. She did not answer.

"Caroline, have you been eating candy?" No answer.

"Answer me. Yes, no, or maybe."

She ran off into the garden and her father sat with his back to the window at the center of the long table, looking across at models of sailing ships and a small bust of Abraham Lincoln.

"Okay," he said.

The aerial photographs, standing on a row of easels, were interpreted by Arthur Lundahl of the National Photographic Interpretation Center: "There's a medium-range ballistic missile launch site and two new military encampments on the southern edge of Sierra del Rosario in west central Cuba. . . ."

"How do you know this is a medium-range ballistic missile?" asked Kennedy after a bit.

"The length, sir."

"There are two missiles involved," said Sidney Graybeal, a CIA analyst. Photo analysts, measuring the crates and canvas-covered tubes, had identified the missiles as a Soviet R-12 and R-14. Both were well known to them—the U.S. designations were SS-4 and SS-5—with estimated ranges of 630 miles and 1,100 miles, respectively.*

"Is this ready to be fired?" asked the President.

"No, sir."

"How long have we got . . . how long before it can be fired?" he asked. The men around the table looked at each other. No one knew. General Marshall Carter, a deputy director of the CIA, saying that he was guessing, answered: "Two weeks. Maybe one."

---

* The American designations meant these were the fourth and fifth classes of Soviet missiles identified by U.S. intelligence.

"Would you care to comment on the position of nuclear warheads?" asked McNamara.

"Sir, we've looked very hard," Graybeal said. "We can find nothing that would spell nuclear warhead. The mating of the nuclear warhead would take about, uh, a couple of hours."

"Don't you have to assume these are nuclear?" asked Rusk.

"There must be some storage site there," said McNamara. "It should be one of our important objectives to find that storage site."

At that moment, the President knew for sure from photographs only that there were at least sixteen Soviet ballistic missiles in Cuba near launch pads still under construction. They were fairly primitive weapons by American standards. It would take hours to fuel them and make ready for launch—if they already had nuclear warheads installed. That seemed extremely unlikely even if there were warheads on the island. The preliminary estimates of their ranges meant they could deliver nuclear warheads in a great circle that included Miami, Atlanta, Houston, New Orleans, Mexico City and all of Central America—and Washington, D.C. The question of whether or not nuclear warheads were on the island was irrelevant; Kennedy had to assume they were there, somewhere on the 800-mile-long island. He had already decided, as soon as Bundy had shown him the aerial photos, that the United States had to get the missiles out. There was no conversation or debate on that, he had to get them out, one way or another.

There were almost certainly more pads and missiles, but clouds still covered the island when two U-2s overflew it that morning. Kennedy asked the military men if they had reconnaissance planes that could fly under the cloud cover. The answer was yes. But there was a good chance the Cubans might shoot down one or more of those and the whole world would know what was happening.

The President asked for Rusk's recommendations.

"We have to set in motion a chain of events that will eliminate this base," he replied. "I don't think we can sit still . . . I think that, by and large, there are these two broad alternatives: one, the quick strike; the other, to alert our allies and Mr. Khrushchev that there is an utterly serious crisis in the making here, and that, facing a situation that could well lead to general war; that we have an obligation to do what has to be done but do it in a way that gives everybody a chance to . . . back down."

The President nodded to McNamara.

"There are two propositions I would suggest," said the Secretary of Defense. "My first is that if we are to conduct an air strike, we must agree now that we will schedule that prior to the time these missile sites become operational. Because, if they become operational before the air strike, I do not believe we can knock them out before they can be launched. Secondly, I would submit the proposition that any air strike must be directed not solely against the missile sites, but against the missile sites plus the airfields plus the aircraft which may not be on the airfields but hidden by that time, plus all potential nuclear storage sites. A fairly extensive air strike."

General Taylor, who had been back in uniform since October 1, when Kennedy appointed him to replace General Lemnitzer as Chairman of the Joint Chiefs of Staff, said the Chiefs would be meeting through the afternoon to develop specific recommendations for an air strike or invasion. The air strike, he said, would have to be followed by a naval blockade to prevent any replacement or repair of damage to the missile sites. As to invasion, the general said, "Cuba is deep mud."

"How effective can the take-out be?" Kennedy asked.

"It'll never be a hundred percent, Mr. President," said Taylor. "We hope to take out a vast majority in the first strike, but this is not just one thing, one strike, one day, but continuous air attack."

"I don't believe, myself, that the critical question is whether you get a particular missile before it goes off," said Rusk. "Because if they shoot those missiles we are in general nuclear war."

"What is the reason for the Russians to set this up . . . ?" the President asked. "It must be that they're not satisfied with their ICBMs."

Rusk answered: "Khrushchev knows that we have a substantial nuclear superiority. . . . We don't really live under fear of his nuclear weapons to the extent that, uh, he has to live under fear of ours. Also we have nuclear weapons nearby, in Turkey and places like that."

"How many weapons do we have in Turkey?" Kennedy asked.

"About fifteen," said McNamara.

"Berlin is very much involved in this," said Rusk. "I'm beginning really to wonder whether maybe Mr. Khrushchev is entirely rational about Berlin. They may be thinking that they can either bargain Berlin and Cuba against each other, or that they could provoke us into a kind of action in Cuba which would give an umbrella for them to take action with respect to Berlin."

Then the topic turned to a public warning, really the question of whether to make public any of this information. Also whether the United States should consult with its allies or with the Organization of American States (OAS). Kennedy asked Dillon for his thoughts, and the Treasury Secretary, who had been Undersecretary of State in the Eisenhower administration, answered: "Getting us wide out in the open, OAS action and telling people in NATO, would appear to me to have the danger of forcing the Russians, uh, Soviets to take a position that if anything was done, they would have to retaliate. . . . Whereas a quick action, with a statement at the same time saying this is all there is to it, might give them a chance to back off and not do anything."

The President agreed with that. The attack had to be a surprise, and warning anyone was warning everyone. "You can't sort of announce that in four days we're going to take them out. They may announce within three days they're going to have warheads on them; if we come and attack, they're going to fire them. Then what'll we do? . . . Of course, we then announce, well, if they do that, then we're going to attack with nuclear weapons."

"What about this?" asked Robert Kennedy. "We should also think of whether there is some other way we can get involved in this through Guantanamo Bay or something or whether there's some ship that, you know, sink the *Maine* again or something."

Secrecy was the one decision they made. Vice President Johnson made his contribution by stating that Congress should be ignored, too. "I realize it's a breach of faith," said the former Majority Leader of the Senate. "But we're not going to get much help out of them."

The meeting lasted just over an hour, then the President closed the discussion, telling McNamara to send out as many U-2 flights as he thought necessary. He told the men around the Cabinet table that he was inclined to favor taking the missiles out with an air strike:

"We ought to meet tonight again at six, consider these various proposals . . . I don't think we've got much time on these missiles. Maybe we just have to just take them out, and continue our other preparations. I think we ought to, beginning right now, be preparing to. . . . Because that's what we're going to do anyway. We're certainly going to do number one; we're going to take out these missiles. Uh, the questions . . . number two, which would be a general air strike. That we're not ready to say, but we should be in preparation for it. The third is the general invasion. At least we're going to do number one, so it seems to me that we don't have to wait very long."

The President stood up and went upstairs. He changed his clothes and came back down for a formal lunch with Hasan al-Rida al-Sanusi, the Crown Prince of Libya. After lunch, he invited U.N. Ambassador Adlai Stevenson to come upstairs. He was showing Stevenson the aerial photographs when his wife walked into the sitting room. Jacqueline Kennedy liked Stevenson as much as her husband disliked him, so there was some cheek-kissing before she left.

"We'll have to do something quickly," Kennedy told Stevenson. "I suppose the alternatives are to go in by air and wipe them out, or to take other steps to render the weapons inoperable."

"Let's not go into an air strike until we have explored the possibilities of a peaceful solution," Stevenson said quickly. Stevenson was shaken by the President's casual manner, as two years before Kennedy had been shocked by Eisenhower's casual talk of nuclear weaponry. He was, after all, talking about the deaths of millions of people. That night Stevenson wrote Kennedy a long, rambling memo with one sentence underlined: *"I feel that you should make it clear that the existence of nuclear arms anywhere is negotiable before we start anything."*

Kennedy's feeling was close to the sentiment of some lines of poetry written by a Spanish bullfighter. He recited it later that afternoon during a brief scheduled speech to a group of editors and television people at a foreign policy conference sponsored by the State Department:

> *Bullfight critics row on row*
> *Crowd the enormous plaza de toros,*
> *But only one is there who knows,*
> *And he is the one who fights the bull.*

General Carter of the CIA opened the 6:30 P.M. meeting by saying that the processing of film taken that morning during two U-2 overflights of Cuba was still under way. But, he said that in addition to the sixteen MRBMs already identified, there were apparently at least four more medium-range missiles on the island, apparently solid-fuel SS-4s. That would mean a much shorter firing sequence, perhaps a forty-minute countdown, rather than the two hours it took to pump oxygen into the older liquid-fuel SS-4s. It would take them less than ten minutes to reach U.S. targets.

McNamara did most of the talking at first, saying that the Joint Chiefs believed that even a limited air strike—going only for the missiles and their back-up systems—would require several hundred bombing runs.

"What is the strategic impact on the position of the United States of MRBMs in Cuba?" asked McGeorge Bundy.

"Mac, I asked the Chiefs that this afternoon . . . ," said McNamara, "and they said, [it was] substantial. My own personal view is, not at all."

The United States had approximately five thousand deliverable nuclear weapons. U.S. intelligence estimated that the Soviets had three hundred deliverable weapons. The U.S. estimate of the number of Soviet intercontinental missiles targeted at the United States was now seventy-five. Those missiles had relatively primitive guidance systems, and analysts on both sides doubted they could even come close to their presumed targets. The Soviets also had ninety-seven short-range missiles on submarines that had to surface before they could launch the missiles. Most of the Soviet weapons would have to be delivered by 155 heavy bombers, and those airplanes would have to fly a gauntlet of American detection systems and bases across Alaska and Canada. The United States had 156 ICBMs, 144 Polaris missiles which could be fired by submarines without surfacing, and 1,300 bombers in the Strategic Air Command, all nuclear-armed, a third of them in the air at all times.*

"This is a political struggle as much as military . . . ," the President said. "You may say it doesn't make any difference if you get blown up by an ICBM flying from the Soviet Union or one that was ninety miles away"—but he *did* think it made a difference to Cuba and Castro, particularly in the rest of Latin America—"It makes them look like they're co-equal with us. . . ."

But that was obviously not why the Soviets had done it. And what advantage was there for the Soviets?

"It's a goddamn mystery to me," the President said. "I don't know enough about the Soviet Union, but if anyone can tell me any other time since the Berlin Blockade where the Russians have given us clear provocation. They've been awfully cautious really. . . . It's just as if we suddenly began to put a major number of MRBMs in Turkey. Now that'd be goddamn dangerous, I would think."

"Well, we did," said Bundy emphasizing the last word.

"We did it. We did it in England," added U. Alexis Johnson, the Deputy Undersecretary of State, who was sitting next to Rusk. He pointed out that putting medium-range missiles close to national boundaries transformed them from tactical to strategic weapons—perhaps that was what Khrushchev liked about the idea of missiles in Cuba.

The meeting ended inconclusively. John Kennedy left a page of scribbled notes and doodles on the big Cabinet table: "Really . . . really. 16 to 32 (missiles) in the space of a week . . . Khrushchev . . . Soviet submarines . . . submarines . . . submarine . . . blockade . . . Sunday . . . 16 to 32 . . . Friday morning . . . increased risk . . . A million men . . . maintain an alliance."

"Sophomoric babble," Secretary of the Navy Paul Nitze wrote in his

---

* As U.S. and Soviet records were released over the years, it became obvious that even that 17-to-1 United States nuclear advantage over the Soviet Union actually overestimated Soviet strength. During a 1989 Moscow conference on the Cuban missile crisis, the director of the Institute of Military History of the Defense Ministry, General Dimitri Volkogonov, said the number of Soviet ICBMs aimed at the United States in late 1962 was actually only twenty. But only one hit may have been more than the United States was willing to accept. On the other hand, U.S. intelligence had badly underestimated the number of Soviet troops on Cuba, reporting to the President that there were between 8,000 and 20,000 Red Army soldiers. The actual number, according to Soviet officials at the 1989 conference, including former Foreign Minister Gromyko, was 42,000. Some Soviets, including Sergei Khrushchev, son of the late premier, also stated there were warheads on the island during the 1962 crisis—a claim U.S. intelligence never could verify because aerial photography never clearly revealed storage bunkers.

journal about the evening session. The President was not happy either. He thought his men were still trying to impress him rather than hammer out a workable strategy.

Kennedy changed clothes again for a dinner party at the Georgetown home of columnist Joseph Alsop. It was another going-away party for Chip Bohlen. Bohlen was a former Ambassador to Moscow and Kennedy had talked to him earlier in the day about the missiles. At the Alsops, Kennedy and Bohlen paced at the back of the garden. Kennedy said he wanted Bohlen to delay his departure for Paris. Bohlen replied that if he stayed in Washington the Soviets would know that something was up, that the U.S. knew about the Soviet missiles. Susan Mary Alsop watched them—and watched her roast lamb turning browner and drier.

At the table, the President took over, asking the male guests, including Isaiah Berlin, a prominent British scholar of Russian affairs, and the French ambassador, Hervé Alphand, variations on this question: "Historically, how have the Russians reacted to great pressure? When their backs were against the wall?"

"Sitting next to Jack tonight was like sitting next to the engine of a very powerful automobile," Mrs. Alsop told her husband after everyone had left. "He was enjoying himself greatly in some way I don't understand. Something is going on. Didn't you feel it?"

"What are you talking about?" he said.

The next morning, Wednesday, October 17, the President met first with Bundy and CIA Director McCone. "Take Cuba away from Castro," was McCone's personal advice. The phrase appeared in Kennedy's first working paper of the crisis, a summary by Sorensen of the events and discussions of Tuesday:

> The following possible tracks or courses of action have each been considered.
>
> Track A—Political action, pressure and warning, followed by a military strike if satisfaction is not received.
>
> Track B—A military strike without prior warning, pressure or action, accompanied by messages making clear the limited nature of this action.
>
> Track C—Political action, pressure and warning, followed by a total naval blockade, under the authority of the Rio Pact and either a Congressional Declaration of War on Cuba or the Cuban Resolution of the 87th Congress.
>
> Track D—Full-scale invasion, to "take Cuba away from Castro."
>
> Within Tracks A and C, the political actions, pressures and warnings could include one or more of the following:
> a) Letter to Khrushchev

    —Stating if ever offensive bases exist, they will be struck; or
    —Warning that we know they exist, and must be dismantled or
they will be struck; or
    —Summoning him to a Summit, offering to withdraw our
MRBM's from Turkey, etc.

Wednesday's *Washington Post*—whose editors knew nothing of the missile installations or the White House meetings—was filled with speculation about action in Cuba, part of the coverage that had been fueled by Keating and Capehart and other Republicans who were demanding that the President get tough with Castro. A Gallup Poll, reported on page one, indicated that a majority of respondents, 51 percent, believed that an attack on Cuba would lead to World War III.

The men Kennedy chose to be with him during this crisis were shuttling between meetings practically around the clock, at the State Department and in the Executive Office Building next to the White House. Stevenson had joined the group, as had Dean Acheson. Acheson decided almost immediately that the movable sessions were a waste of time.

He thought the problem was Robert Kennedy, that the Attorney General was an inexperienced fool. Robert Kennedy seemed obsessed with morality, or moralism, and with the dangers of killing Soviet technicians and soldiers if the missile sites were bombed. At one point he had said that bombing Cuba would be "Pearl Harbor in reverse." Acheson and some of the others preferred the "Munich" metaphor, the British appeasement of Hitler in 1938. But Robert Kennedy had come back from World War II with both the patriotism and the idealism of a very young warrior. He had been a nineteen-year-old seaman serving on a destroyer named for his oldest brother, *Joseph P. Kennedy, Jr.*, stationed at Guantanamo Bay. Talking about that, he said his other brother was not going to be the "Tojo of the 1960s."

Later that day, Acheson was appalled when he met alone with the President and heard him use the same phrase, "Pearl Harbor in reverse" —as if the United States were planning a sneak attack without provocation.

"I know where you got that," Acheson said to John Kennedy. "It is unworthy of you to talk that way."

The President was indeed getting it from his brother. More than once. "I now know how Tojo felt when he was planning Pearl Harbor," Robert Kennedy had said in a note to his brother that day.

Robert Kennedy aside, most of the group was moving along the bombing track. When the President stopped in to listen to the debate before lunch on Thursday, General Curtis LeMay was laying out bombing plans.

"How will the Russians respond?" Kennedy asked him.

"They'll do nothing," LeMay said.

"Are you trying to tell me that they'll let us bomb their missiles, and kill a lot of Russians and then do nothing?" Kennedy responded. "If they don't do anything in Cuba, then they'll certainly do something in Berlin."

"Can you imagine LeMay saying a thing like that?" the President said back in his office. He said the generals had one thing going for them: "If we listen to them, and do what they want us to do, none of us will be alive later to tell them that they were wrong."

It was his job, the President decided, to walk through business as usual, to divert the attention of the Soviets, the Congress, and the press. He met with the foreign minister of West Germany for an hour and a half, then went to another lunch for the Crown Prince of Libya, this one at the Libyan Embassy. At two-thirty in the afternoon, he flew to Connecticut for an afternoon and evening of campaigning with Abe Ribicoff, who had resigned as Secretary of Health, Education and Welfare to run for the U.S. Senate. The President seemed to have a great time. "Waterbury is either the easiest city in the United States to draw a crowd in, or it has the best Democrats," he told a crowd of fifty thousand. He was still gossiping and laughing about the afternoon on the plane back to Washington. Then his friend Charlie Bartlett mentioned Mexico and saw the air go out of Kennedy's face and frame. "Boy," he said, "I've got problems in that part of the world."

Robert Kennedy and Sorensen were waiting for the President at Andrews Air Force Base at 9:30 P.M. New U-2 photographs showed early stages of the construction of three intermediate-range ballistic missile launch sites. Four SS-5 missiles—their range previously calculated at 1,100 miles—could be launched from each of the pads. Although it was not certain there were SS-5s on the island, the CIA believed they were probably on cargo ships at sea.

Bolshakov had called him, Robert Kennedy told his brother. "He said he had a 'personal message' from Khrushchev to you: 'Under no circumstances would surface-to-surface missiles be sent to Cuba.' "

On the way back to Washington, Robert Kennedy and Sorensen showed the President a map of North America with concentric circles, centered at the western tip of Cuba. It showed the cities within the potential range of both the SS-4s and the longer SS-5s. The SS-5 circle covered almost the entire United States. Using an extended range (or deliberately exaggerated range) of 2,200 miles, double the standard CIA calculation, the map indicated that all but one of country's largest cities could be hit—only Seattle was safely outside the new estimated range—and so could almost all of the capitals of South America. The MRBM range was also extended (or exaggerated), giving the SS-4s a range of more than 1,000 miles, meaning they could reach Washington. "PRBMs," said CIA and Air Force analysts when they saw the exaggerated White House map, "political-range ballistic missiles." There was also one small college town in range. It had been put on the map after Robert Kennedy had made a crack when he saw the first set of photos: "Can these things reach Oxford, Mississippi?"

Sorensen's summary memo to the President the next morning, Thursday, October 18, laid out the options in routine White House style, putting the most extraordinary decision making into the format of ordinary "Yes" and "No" box checking. Kennedy picked it up after he had given the order to airlift a reinforced Marine infantry battalion and a Marine Hawk antiaircraft missile battalion from the West Coast to the U.S. Navy Base at Guantanamo, Cuba.

Two big questions must be answered, and in conjunction with each other:
   1. Which military action, if any:
      —Limited air strike:
      —Fuller air strike:
      —Blockade:
      —Invasion:
   2. Should political action—in particular a letter of warning to Khrushchev—precede military action?
      —If blockade or invasion, everyone says yes
      —If air strike
      —Yes:
      —No:
      —Undecided:
These questions could be focused upon by considering either the Rusk or the Bohlen approaches. Rusk favors the limited or "surgical" air strike without prior political action or warning. Bohlen favors a prompt letter to Khrushchev, deciding after the response whether we use air strike or blockade.

Bomb or blockade? Check the appropriate box.
The meetings, night and day, were becoming repetitive. Dillon, Acheson, and McCone spoke for those who favored bombing, arguing that the political track would do little but give the Soviets time to complete the missile installations. Dillon, the Republican, sat coolly through most of the arguments. He had a bit of contempt for Kennedy's new boys, calculating that the men around the table, talking about the possibility of nuclear war for the first time, were more frightened than men

like himself, Acheson, McCone, and Nitze. The older hands had thought the unthinkable before. The new boys, he thought, did not comprehend the true extent of U.S. military superiority, nor did they understand that the Soviets were more afraid than they were, for good and simple reasons. The Soviets were surrounded by U.S. bases and they remembered something Americans tended to block out: that only the Americans had ever used nuclear weapons against other people.

Robert Kennedy, particularly, annoyed some of the men who had served Presidents Truman and Eisenhower. The Attorney General made it clear that he was there by birth rather than title and was reporting back to his brother on the meanings and moods of the rest of them. He also exercised the right to argue on both sides, moving toward the blockaders, but then interjecting random and contradictory thoughts. The official notes of the Thursday meetings recorded: "The Attorney General said that in looking forward to the future it would be better for our children and grandchildren if we decided to face the Soviet threat, stand up to it, and eliminate it now. The circumstances for doing it at some future time were bound to be more unfavorable, the risks would be greater, the chances of success less good."

But others had their simple moments, too. Dillon passed a note to the President, through Sorensen, asking: "Have you considered the very real possibility that if we allow Cuba to complete installation and operational readiness of missile bases, the next House of Representatives is likely to house a Republican majority? This would completely paralyze our ability to react sensibly and coherently to further Soviet advances."

Rest assured, Sorensen told him, that thought had crossed the boss's mind.

At 5:00 P.M. that day, Andrei Gromyko arrived at the White House. The Soviet foreign minister had asked for the meeting. Kennedy thought this might be it: the Soviets might be ready to make their move, Gromyko might have come to tell him that the United States was under the gun now, too. The President had the latest U-2 photographs of the missile sites in the middle drawer of his big desk made from the wood of a nineteenth-century warship, the U.S.S. *Resolute*.

But Gromyko said nothing about missiles. Perhaps he was there to gauge whether or not the Americans knew anything. Kennedy disliked the foreign minister; his face and eyes barely moved. Most of the talk, formal, cool, and false, was about Berlin. Gromyko repeated Khrushchev's message that the Soviet Union would do nothing to embarrass the President before the American midterm elections on November 6. On Cuba, said the Russian, reading from notes: "I have been instructed to make it clear that the purpose of any arms is by no means offensive."

Kennedy went to his desk then. He pulled out his September 4 statement on offensive weapons in Cuba and read it aloud, slowly, emphasizing the phrase "the gravest issues would arise"—if offensive missiles
were discovered. The man from Moscow said nothing.

"Gromyko, in this very room not over ten minutes ago, told more
bare-faced lies than I have ever heard in so short a time," the President
told Robert Lovett after the meeting. He had called the New York
lawyer, Truman's Deputy Secretary of Defense, and asked him to join
some of the meetings. Lovett had walked into the President's office as
Kennedy was telling Bundy and Llewellyn Thompson, the former U.S.
Ambassador to the Soviet Union, that he had been tempted to show
Gromyko the U-2 photos and get it over with. But secrecy was his first
priority. He was still undecided about what to do.

The President told them that he thought whichever side made the first
announcement of the missiles could dominate the politics of the crisis
by framing the world debate. A Soviet announcement would certainly
emphasize defending Cuba against continued American hostility. The
world might think that was reasonable. Certainly the United States
threat to Cuba was real.

A U.S. announcement would emphasize the threat to itself. Part of
that threat, never publicly acknowledged, was that the United States had
no real defense systems, no radars or antiaircraft installations pointed
to the south. The North Americans had never considered that they might
face a strategic threat from the south.

But Gromyko's repeating of Khrushchev's message about the American elections had persuaded Kennedy of one thing. The Soviets were not
planning to make their move until after November 6. Perhaps Khrushchev thought Kennedy would have to be tougher during a campaign.
He guessed that Khrushchev, who would be in the United States later in
November for the opening of the United Nations session, planned to
say something like this: We have decided to do something about Berlin.
If the United States is thinking of resisting, they should be aware that
we now have nuclear missiles in Cuba ready to threaten Americans as
they have threatened us for the past ten years from bases in Europe and
Turkey.

That Thursday evening, Ted Sorensen gave the President the first
draft of a possible letter to Premier Khrushchev, announcing bombing:

Dear Mr. Chairman:
    My Government has recently obtained full and incontrovertible evi-
dence that offensive weapons and bases of a significant nature and number—specifically, medium range ballistic missiles capable of attacking the

United States mainland and many Latin American countries—are now being assembled in Cuba. . . .

Consequently, the purpose of this note is to inform you that, shortly after the close of your conference with my emissary, I have no choice but to initiate appropriate military action against the island of Cuba. Should you . . . give to my emissary your unequivocal assurance that this work will halt, these missiles, bases and all other offensive weapons [will be] removed, United States military action can be withheld. . . . In this event, I would be glad to meet with you upon your arrival in this country and to discuss other problems on our agenda, including, if you wish, the NATO bases in Turkey and Italy. . . .

All of this—in Moscow, in Havana, and in Washington—was happening in secrecy. Lies were being told in all the capitals to protect the secrets. More than a dozen American news organizations had queried the Defense Department about numerous reports of Soviet IL-28 heavy bombers being shipped to Cuba. On Thursday evening, the Pentagon released a statement through Assistant Defense Secretary Arthur Sylvester saying: "A Pentagon spokesman denied tonight that any alert has been ordered or that any emergency military measures have been set in motion against Communist-ruled Cuba. Further, the spokesman said the Pentagon has no information indicating the presence of offensive weapons in Cuba."

At 9:00 P.M., Robert Kennedy sat on Alexis Johnson's lap as nine men who had been meeting through the afternoon and evening at the State Department climbed into one big car to go over to the White House to brief the President. A caravan of limousines, they thought, might alert reporters that something was going on. The group was still split. "We took a vote," Robert Kennedy told his brother. It was eleven for blockade, six for bombing. He started to tell his brother the line-up, pulling out little slips of paper recording the votes. But the President cut him off, saying: "I don't want to see them. I may choose the wrong policy, and then the people who were right will have it in writing."

Eleven to six was hardly a consensus, and Bundy, who had voted for blockade, changed his mind right there, saying maybe doing nothing was the wisest choice. Go back, try again, the President told them.

Although Robert Kennedy was sure his brother wanted to go with the blockade, the President told Sorensen to write two speeches, one announcing blockade, one announcing bombing.

Sorensen began by reading two speeches, the declarations of war by Woodrow Wilson in 1917 and Franklin D. Roosevelt in 1941.

Up to now, secrecy had been more critical to the President than time because he wanted to control the words that defined the crisis, to tell the world his way. But by the end of the Thursday meetings, he realized that secrecy and time were now the same thing. Hundreds of people in Washington, wives and secretaries among them, knew about the hours and hours of meetings at the White House, the State Department, and the Pentagon. Florida newspapers were reporting news of military movements around the state. He had himself shown the U-2 photographs to the British ambassador, his friend David Ormsby-Gore, telling him of the bombing or blockade choice.

"Blockade" was Ormsby-Gore's vote when Kennedy asked him. The ambassador said that other countries would not see the missiles as a significant threat to the United States. They neither understood nor sympathized with the American feeling that they were entitled to total security, total immunity, the ocean-guarded security the United States enjoyed before the development of nuclear weapons. Bombing would be seen around the world as overreaction. Then he sent a telegram to his prime minister, Harold Macmillan, warning of "an impending crisis."

The next morning, Friday, October 19, Bundy, Acheson, Taylor, and the Joint Chiefs were waiting for the President when he came down to the office. They urged him to order the air strike. Time was running out, they said, even an order at that moment could not be executed until Monday, the 22nd. The number of sorties the Air Force wanted to do the job had risen to eight hundred. U.S. squadrons would head for the known ballistic missile sites, the surface-to-air missile sites, antiaircraft emplacements, and the fields of the Cuban Air Force, which now had its own MiG jet fighters. Cuba had come a long way since using old U.S. jet trainers during the Bay of Pigs. Admiral George Anderson, the chief of Naval Operations, said the only military plan that could succeed was the complete destruction of Soviet power on the island. But then Maxwell Taylor repeated that there was no such thing as complete. "The best we can offer you, Mr. President, is to destroy 90 percent of the known missiles."

Within forty-eight hours, Admiral Anderson told the President, the Air Force and the Navy would have 511 tactical fighters on one-hour alert in Florida, compared to the usual 140. That commitment amounted to one third of the country's tactical fighter resources. Satellite-tracking stations in Moorestown, New Jersey, Thomasville, Georgia, and Laredo, Texas, were being modified and turned around in an attempt to monitor aircraft or missiles rising from Cuba. The United States was close to being ready for war in the Caribbean.

The President, still keeping scrupulously to a normal public schedule, told his brother it was time to break the blockade versus bombing deadlock. The next meeting was scheduled for eleven o'clock in George Ball's conference room at the State Department. The President, on schedule, left the White House lawn by helicopter at 10:35 A.M., headed for Andrews Air Force Base and a day of campaigning in Ohio and Illinois.

The midterm elections were nineteen days away, but there was no joy for the President now in beating up on Republicans. "The campaign is over," he told Robert Kennedy. "This blows it—we've lost anyway. They were right about Cuba."

"These are the issues of the campaign," Kennedy told more than one hundred thousand people in Public Square in Cleveland, not believing a word of it: "Housing, jobs, the kind of tax program we write in the coming session. . . ."

"LESS PROFILE—MORE COURAGE" read a poster held up as Kennedy arrived at the Sheraton Blackstone Hotel in Chicago. Upstairs, in the Presidential Suite, he was stripped to his underwear, ready for a bath before he would go downstairs to a $100-a-plate dinner of the Cook County Democratic Committee. Pierre Salinger came in to say that Carelton Kent of the *Chicago Tribune* wanted a comment on a report that paratroopers were ready to invade Cuba. "Call Kent and tell him that report is all wrong," Kennedy said.

In Washington, the first order of business for the men who convened at eleven o'clock that morning was the question of whether the President should seek a Declaration of War from Congress before hitting Cuba. The Attorney General turned to his assistant, Nicholas Katzenbach, who said it was not necessary. The President could justify any action by saying the United States was acting in self-defense. The next question was whether to seek United Nations sanction for military action. The answer was again no—because it might not be possible to get it. The Assistant Secretary of State for Latin America, Edwin Martin, was up next, and he said the United States could get a substantial majority for a resolution from the Organization of American States if the President himself called other heads of state.

Robert Kennedy was pushing for blockade. The word now was "quarantine." It was being used because it had no precise meaning, as opposed to "blockade," which was an act of war according to international law. The Attorney General pushed ahead as if there were now a consensus on the blockade, though Taylor, Acheson, Bundy, and Dillon continued to argue for an air strike, the sooner the better. Robert Kennedy continued the Pearl Harbor argument with some passion, saying that surprise attacks were not and could not be part of the American heritage. "Sneak attack," he repeated; thousands of Cubans and Russians would be killed without warning. Max Taylor spoke next, saying the Joint Chiefs opposed a "quarantine" because they thought the United Nations would respond reflexively by pressuring the United States not to follow up with an attack if the blockade failed to stop the Soviet build-up. Acheson argued forcefully for a showdown. The United States, he said, was in a test of wills, a direct challenge by Khrushchev: "You must remember we are dealing with a madman."

McCone and Paul Nitze still favored bombing, as did Dillon. Bundy said: "It comes down to this—a blockade will not eliminate the bases, an air strike will."

McNamara said he favored a blockade. He believed the United States would end up having to give up the U.S. missile bases in Turkey and Italy, no great strategic loss, to get the Soviet bases out of Cuba. It was worth it, because no matter how effectively the United States hit Cuba, it was possible, more than possible, that the Soviets could get one or two missiles off the ground, with nuclear warheads, probably headed for Miami or Cape Canaveral. It was possible, too, that the Soviets or the Cubans would respond to the first-wave attack by getting whatever planes and bombs they could into the air, and heading for the United States to retaliate. How could they know that a sky black with American planes represented nothing but a "surgical strike"?

George Ball, who admitted he was still between the options, said that he had learned as commander of an Air Force unit evaluating bombing effectiveness during World War II that there was no such thing as pinpoint bombing; you leveled what you could and hoped for the best. Llewellyn Thompson argued for a blockade with a twenty-four-hour warning to the Soviets to give them time to contact the captains of their ships at sea—and to consider backing down.

Dillon had been staring at Robert Kennedy during the meeting, a little unnerved by his open emotion. He was finally impressed by what he thought the President's brother was trying to say. He was thinking: "He's right; we fought World War II for ideals and we should not change now." Waves of bombers appearing over the horizon at dawn began to register with him, too, as somehow wrong—if not morally wrong, historically self-destructive.

So, Dillon switched sides. He was willing to try blockade first; then if it did not work, we could still bomb, there would be nothing sneaky about it by then.

In the afternoon, the meeting broke into two groups. Rusk, who was presiding in the President's absence, delegated Bundy to head a team to write a bombing scenario, and Undersecretary of State U. Alexis Johnson to head a team writing a blockade option. After some inconclusive discussion of the alternative papers, the meeting ended at seven o'clock that evening. The last sentence of the official notes read: "It was generally agreed that the President should continue on his trip until Sunday morning."

But Robert Kennedy had concluded that Dillon's shift made it possible to put together a blockade or "quarantine" consensus. Sorensen had left the meeting with instructions to write two speeches for the President. But he was writing only one—the quarantine speech.

In the early hours of Saturday, October 20, after the President had given his speech to the Cook County Democrats and gone to a late-night pep talk to Mayor Richard Daley's precinct captains, Robert Kennedy reached him at the Sheraton Blackstone and said it was time to return to Washington.

In the morning, the President, who was scheduled to go to Milwaukee and then on to the West Coast, called in his traveling physician, Admiral George Burkley, and said he was not feeling well, that he thought he might be catching a cold. The doctor said, as he had on other occasions, that traveling and speaking would make it worse. Kennedy, who regularly ignored that kind of advice, surprised the doctor by saying, "You're right, I better go back."

Kennedy told Burkley not to speak to the press, and called in Salinger. "Tell the press," he said, "that I'm returning to Washington on the advice of Admiral Burkley."

"Wait a minute," he said, as Salinger began to leave. "We better be sure we're all saying the same thing." He took the telephone pad next to the bed and wrote: "Slight upper respiratory . . . 1 degree temperature . . . weather raw and rainy . . . recommended return to Washington . . . cancelled schedule."

Kennedy, trying to look as if he was worried about a cold, wore a hat on his way to the plane, one of the few times he had done that in public since he put away his top hat after his inaugural. The man was killing the American hat business. Kennedy, bareheaded, and youth were an image team. He went right to sleep on the plane and was back at the White House just after one-thirty.

Sorensen met him with a draft of the quarantine speech—and a short, slanted memo summing up the four days of secret meetings:

I. There are 2 fundamental objections to air strike which have never been answered:
   1) Inasmuch as no one has been able to devise a satisfactory message to Khrushchev to which his reply could not outmaneuver us, an air strike

means a US-initiated "Pearl Harbor" on a small nation which history could neither understand nor forget.

2) Inasmuch as the concept of a clean, swift strike has been abandoned as militarily impractical, it is generally agreed that the more widespread air attack will inevitably lead to an invasion with all of its consequences.

II. There are 2 fundamental advantages to a blockade which have never been answered:

1) It is a more prudent and flexible step which enables us to move to an air strike, invasion or any other step at any time it proves necessary, without the "Pearl Harbor" posture.

2) It is the step least likely to precipitate general war while still causing the Soviets—unwilling to engage our Navy in our waters—to back down and abandon Castro.

At the White House, John Kennedy went down to the swimming pool with his brother. He paddled around for a half hour, with Robert Kennedy sitting by the ladder telling him where everyone stood. At two-thirty, the President sat down with his advisers. He had still not told anyone but his brother what he thought. But he made it clear this would be the decisive meeting: "You should all hope that your plan isn't the one that will be accepted."

McCone laid out the latest photos and numbers: At least thirty-two SS-4s; launch sites for twenty-four SS-5s, still at sea; twenty-four SAM (surface-to-air) sites, ready to fire ninety-six non-nuclear antiaircraft missiles; forty-two IL-28 bombers, called Beagles by the United States, capable of carrying nuclear bombs; eight to ten thousand Soviet personnel, mostly technicians and guards for missile sites.

McNamara presented the argument for quarantine. Bundy presented the bombing arguments: the goal was removing the missiles and at best the blockade would only prevent new installations. Then no one said anything. They all just looked at the President. Roswell Gilpatric, the Undersecretary of Defense, broke the silence, putting the matter in the words of a politician: "Essentially, Mr. President, this is a choice between limited action and unlimited action, and most of us think it's better to start with limited action."

Kennedy nodded. The goal was not to corner Khrushchev; the whole point was to give him room to maneuver, to back down. But first, he had to do something. The Russians had moved; he had to act. To do nothing amounted to political suicide. He was now on the other side of the charges he had made about Vice President Nixon two years before: "Mr. Nixon hasn't mentioned Cuba very prominently in this campaign. . . . The transformation of Cuba into a Communist base of operations a few minutes from our coast—by jet plane, missile or submarine—is an incredibly dangerous development to have been permitted by our Republican policymakers."

Now Democrats made policy, and he was the man in the arena. And so was the big-talking Russian politician on the other side. Kennedy worried that he understood his adversary's political position too well. He thought Khrushchev was right to try to break the rings of American troops and missiles around the Soviet Union. But such thoughts had nothing to do with this job this day. Whatever the President's nod meant, the men in the room took it as the decision for limited military action: Quarantine.

"What about diplomacy?" Kennedy asked next.

Adlai Stevenson took that as his cue. He was a politician, too, and he focused on political weapons, words. What would the President say in public to Khrushchev? He concentrated on the speech, urging Kennedy to offer something in return for removing the missiles—discussions on the demilitarization of Cuba, perhaps abandoning the U.S. Naval Base at Guantanamo Bay, consider taking the Jupiters out of Turkey and Italy.

McCone was outraged by what Stevenson was saying. The missiles were pointed at our heart, he said, this was no time to be giving up anything. Most of the other men who had been hammering away at each other around the table and around the clock were angry, too. Some thought Stevenson was just a coward in a high place. But the President did not disagree all that much with the ambassador's words, saying at one point that perhaps the only way to get the missiles out of Cuba was "invading or trading"—that the quarantine alone probably could not do that job.

But he thought that it was foolish to begin negotiating by revealing your final terms. He also thought it had taken guts for Stevenson to speak up. Kennedy himself had twice moved toward removal of the Jupiters from Turkey during the past year, but nothing had happened because, after they were in place, the missiles had become symbols of Turkey's international maturity. "The Bomb" was coming to represent international maturity, international manhood; and the President had not followed up his own initiatives.

Dillon, who had been Eisenhower's Undersecretary of State when the decision was made to install the weapons, said: "Well, everyone knows that those Jupiter missiles aren't much good anyway. We only put them in there because we didn't know what else to do with them, and we really made the Turks and Italians take them."

"Did you hear that from Dillon?" Kennedy said in a telephone call to Sorensen after the meeting broke up. "Put that down for the book!"

The memoirs. He also pulled Arthur Schlesinger aside that day, telling him to go to New York with Stevenson, work with him to make sure the ambassador stuck to the official line. "We will have to make a deal at the end," Kennedy told him. "But we must stand absolutely firm now. Concessions must come at the end of the negotiation, not the beginning."

It was history that was on the President's mind that evening. He was standing with Sorensen and Robert Kennedy on a White House balcony, looking out over the Washington Monument and the Lincoln Memorial. "Well," he said, "I guess Homer Capehart is the Winston Churchill of our generation."

Then he turned back to the two men who were most important to him and said, in Irish mordant: "We are very, very close to war. And there's not room in the White House bomb shelter for all of us."

Kennedy telephoned his wife, who was at Glen Ora with Caroline and John Junior, and asked her to come back to Washington that night. He also wanted her to cancel any dinner plans they had for a while, so that the four of them could spend time together each night.

His speech was scheduled for 7:00 P.M., Monday, October 22.

After going to mass at St. Stephen's with his wife on Sunday morning, Kennedy had lunch with his brother and Robert Lovett, who was commuting back and forth to New York each day. Kennedy asked Lovett whether he thought Stevenson was tough enough to handle the Soviets at the United Nations. No, the lawyer said, and Robert Kennedy agreed.

"Who should be there?"

"McCloy," Lovett said.

The White House operators found John McCloy in Frankfurt, West Germany, on his way to a pheasant-hunting excursion in Spain. An Air Force jet was dispatched to bring him back to New York to sit beside Stevenson at the United Nations.

Then the President went downstairs again and joined the continuing crisis meeting, with official note takers recording:

> The President outlined the manner in which he expected Council Members to deal with the domestic aspects of the current situation. He said everyone should sing one song in order to make clear that there was now no difference among advisers as to the proper course to follow. He pointed out the importance of fully supporting the course of action:

> The President then summarized the arguments as to why we must act. . . .

> In September we had said we would react if certain actions were taken

in Cuba. . . . The secret deployment was such a complete change in their previous policy of not deploying such missiles outside the USSR that if we took no action in this case, we would convey to the Russians an impression that we would never act, no matter what they did anywhere.

Next, the President read a list of questions that could be expected when the public and press learned what had happened. The first question was: "Why didn't we act sooner?" The party-line answer: "We needed more evidence of the existence of Soviet strategic missiles in Cuba." "How do we answer if we are asked whether we're preparing to invade?" asked General Taylor. The President responded by saying they must ask the press not to push that line of questioning—"in the interest of national security."

General Clifton, the President's military aide, left a note on the Cabinet table after the meeting: "Is there a plan to brief and brainwash key press within 12 hours or so? *New York Times?* Lippmann? Marquis Childs? Alsop? Key bureau chiefs?"

The press was meanwhile getting closer to the story. "MARINE MOVES IN SOUTH LINKED TO CUBAN CRISIS," headlined the *Washington Post.* After that, the President tried to confuse White House reporters by ordering three men with no connection to Latin American affairs to come over to the White House in the largest limousines they could find. Assistant Secretary of State for Far Eastern Affairs Averell Harriman; Martin Hillenbrand, the State Department's German desk officer; and Assistant Secretary of State for Near Eastern Affairs Phillips Talbot arrived shortly.

"How long do I have to sit here?" grumbled Harriman, who was taken to an empty office to sit for a while to confuse the reporters in the White House lobby.

Kennedy made three press calls himself, enlisting pledges of cooperation from Orville Dryfoos, publisher of *The New York Times,* Philip Graham, president of the *Washington Post,* and Henry Luce of *Time* magazine. James Reston of the *Times,* probably the best reporter in town, had put most of the missile story together, but the President convinced Dryfoos not to publish any of it. Reston agreed, though in hindsight he was persuaded that self-censorship had been a mistake on the Bay of Pigs story. He asked Dryfoos to ask the President to promise that while the *Times* remained silent, the U.S. government would "Shed no blood and start no war."

On Monday morning Kennedy called Eisenhower, who had been briefed by his old friend John McCone. Eisenhower said he thought conventional bombing of the sites would not work, that blockade or a full-scale invasion of Cuba with overwhelming force seemed to him to be the only workable options. Kennedy answered that he would begin with the blockade.

"Whatever you do," Eisenhower said, "you will have my support."

Since the early hours of Monday morning, Air Force jets had been crisscrossing the United States, bringing congressional leaders back to Washington for a 5:00 P.M. White House briefing. In recess, senators and representatives could be hard to find. House Republican Leader Charles Halleck of Indiana was pheasant hunting somewhere in South Dakota, and House Whip Hale Boggs of Louisiana was fishing in the Gulf of Mexico. A military helicopter found Boggs, dropping a note to him in a bottle: "Call Operator 18, Washington. Urgent message from the President."

A voice amplified by a speaker on the helicopter led Boggs's boat to an oil rig, where it picked the congressman up and took him to an Air Force Base. He was strapped into a two-seat fighter and flown to Washington.

The meeting started with a joke. Everett Dirksen of Illinois, the Republican leader of the Senate, said: "That was a nice little speech you gave for Sid Yates in Chicago. Too bad you caught that cold making it."

Kennedy was not in the mood. He made it clear that he was not seeking advice or consent, he was merely informing Congress. McCone showed his photographs, and McNamara filled them in on the discoveries and debates of the past week. When McNamara said some of the missiles were ready to fire, Senator Hubert Humphrey turned to Dean Rusk and said: "Thank God I am not the President of the United States."

Another senator who had once run for President, Richard Russell of Georgia, chairman of the Senate Armed Services Committee, did not like what he was hearing. He was taking notes: "Have been warned again and again . . . Where are military advisers? . . . Khrushchev believes what he says—we are afraid. . . ." When he got a chance to speak, he said:

"The danger to this country is in the missiles already in place. If fired, they could destroy forty of our cities and inflict millions of casualties on our people. The quarantine will not remove that danger. We warned Cuba and Russia time and again by three speeches by President Kennedy and a Joint Congressional Resolution he signed, that establishment of any offensive bases in Cuba would, in effect, be considered an act of war against this hemisphere. The fact that they were warned again and again removed such action from the 'sneak attack' category referred to by Secretary McNamara. The quarantine will earn bitter statements and a series of incidents that could more likely lead to nuclear war than the fait accompli of having done that which we told them we would do."

Kennedy was angered. He said that if Russell had been through the process of meetings . . . but Senator William Fulbright interjected that he agreed with Russell. Kennedy seemed shocked. Fulbright had tried to talk him out of the Bay of Pigs invasion. But it turned out that Fulbright thought the quarantine was more dangerous than bombing or invasion because it would bring American sailors into direct confrontation with Russians. In an odd twist, the leader of the Republican minority in the House, Charles Halleck of Indiana, glared at Fulbright and said: "I'm standing with the President."

As the meeting broke up, Kennedy tried to make a joke, saying to Humphrey: "If I'd known the job was this tough, I wouldn't have beaten you in West Virginia." Humphrey came back: "If I hadn't known it was this tough, I never would have let you beat me."

But Kennedy was still mad. Walking out with Sorensen, he said: "If they think they can do the job better than me, they can have it."

But he had the job. This was the first nuclear confrontation. Millions of people could be dead within hours. Senator Mike Mansfield of Montana, the Senate Democratic Leader, was stunned now at the difference between his old colleague and the rest of them. None of us have anything to do with this, he thought, it's all Jack Kennedy. The meeting, he knew, was a sham, part of constructing a historical record, or a historical defense.

Mansfield, the Senate Majority Leader, by law the fourth highest official in the land, knew that there was nothing he could or should do now. The senator left the White House and called his wife, asking her to meet him at National Airport. Mansfield wanted to go home to Montana, and he told his wife there was something he wanted to tell her involving Kennedy. When the Mansfields landed at Billings later that day, there were soldiers patrolling the runways and the terminal— as there were at other airports all across the country.

Chapter 35

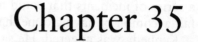

The President was scheduled to address the nation on television at seven o'clock, Monday night, October 22—and the nation still did not know why. "A Day of Mystery in D.C.!" the *San Francisco Examiner* headlined. "There was an air of crisis in the capital," reported *The New York Times* Monday morning. "Is Major U.S. Move in Store for Cuba Next?" asked a headline in the *Miami Herald*. But most speculation focused on Berlin.

Monday morning the President signed National Security Action Memo 196, the document formally and secretly establishing those who had attended the crisis meetings as the Executive Committee (Ex Comm) of the National Security Council. During the day, U.S. Navy ships and planes shuttled between Norfolk, Virginia, and Guantanamo Bay on Cuba's southeastern end, evacuating 2,810 women and children and other noncombatants from the American naval base there. Six thousand Marines and sailors were left to defend the installation, a trophy of the Spanish-American War in 1898. Beginning the evacuation of all Americans from Moscow was the next topic on the table.

At 6:00 P.M., an hour before Kennedy was to go on television, Anatoli Dobrynin, the Soviet ambassador, was called to the State Department. He came in smiling at reporters in the lobby, but he was grim when he came out a few minutes later. "He looks sick," one remarked. Another called out, "What's going on?"

"You can judge for yourself soon enough," the Russian said. In fact, he was carrying a letter from the President of the United States to the premier of the Soviet Union explicitly threatening nuclear war. He was driven back to the Soviet Embassy, where he asked for a telephone line to Moscow. One happened to be open, and he began to dictate Kennedy's words to stenographers in the Kremlin. There was some passion in the message as Kennedy referred back to the words and mood of the Vienna summit:

"I have not assumed that you or any other sane man would, in this nuclear age, deliberately plunge the world into war which it is crystal clear no country could win and which could only result in catastrophic consequences to the world, including the aggressor. . . . I made clear that in view of the objectives of the ideology to which you adhere, the United States could not tolerate any action on your part which in a major way disturbed the existing over-all balance of power in the world.

"I publicly stated that if certain developments in Cuba took place, the United States would do whatever must be done to protect its own security and that of its allies. . . . Despite this, the rapid development of long-range missile bases and other offensive weapons in Cuba has proceeded. I must tell you that the United States is determined that this threat to the security of this hemisphere be removed."

"Good evening, my fellow citizens," the President began at 7:00 P.M. More than 100 million Americans were watching. As Kennedy spoke, twenty-two U.S. Air Force fighters flying in attack formation above Florida turned toward Cuba—in case the reaction to Kennedy's words were rising jets or missiles:

"Cuba . . . Within the past week, unmistakable evidence has established the fact that a series of offensive missile sites is now in preparation on that imprisoned island. The purpose of these bases can be none other than to provide a nuclear strike capability against the Western Hemisphere."

The President spoke for seventeen minutes, using no numbers or specific information on the missiles except the questionable White House numbers on ranges. He said that the medium-range weapons, ready to fire now, could reach and destroy Washington, D.C., the Panama Canal, Cape Canaveral, and Mexico City. The intermediate-range weapons, not yet installed, he said, could hit almost all the major cities from Lima, Peru, north to Hudson Bay, Canada.

"This secret, swift and extraordinary buildup of Communist missiles is a deliberately provocative and unjustified change in the status quo which cannot be accepted by this country, if our courage and our commitments are ever to be trusted again by either friend or foe. The 1930s taught us a clear lesson: aggressive conduct, if allowed to go unchecked and unchallenged, ultimately leads to war.

"I have directed that the following initial steps be taken immediately:

"First: To halt this offensive buildup, a strict quarantine on all offensive military equipment under shipment to Cuba. . . .

"Second: . . . Should these offensive military preparations continue, thus increasing the threat to this hemisphere, further action will be justified. I have directed the Armed Forces to prepare for any eventuality. . . .

"Third: It shall be the policy of this Nation to regard any nuclear missile launched from Cuba against any nation in the Western Hemisphere as an attack by the Soviet Union on the United States, requiring a full retaliatory strike upon the Soviet Union."

Near the end, repeating what he had said to Ex Comm in private, Kennedy inserted a line that meant more to him, to the politics of the crisis, than it did to his vast audience: "The greatest danger of all would be to do nothing."

He walked out of the Oval Office and saw a small man sitting outside. It took him a moment to refocus. "Oh, I'm sorry, doctor," he said. It was Hans Kraus, his back doctor, down from New York for a regular appointment. "I just don't have the time today. I'm sorry I put you through all this trouble."

His tailor, Sam Harris, was there too. The President had forgotten to tell Mrs. Lincoln to cancel an appointment to try on a new suit and topcoat.

Fifty-six American warships were moving south to establish a blockade line along intersecting 500-mile radius circles centered at Havana and at Cape Maisi, the eastern tip of Cuba, near Guantanamo Bay. The arrangement of the ships was a modification of the last blockade enforced by the U.S. Navy—of Cuba in 1898. Now called a "quarantine," it was scheduled to begin at 10:00 A.M. on Wednesday morning, October 24. The President passed the order to begin the countdown for "Operation Scabbards"—the word itself was classified "Top Secret"— the U.S. invasion of Cuba, the eight-day exercise that would end on October 30 with ninety thousand Marines and Airborne troops hitting the island. The Pentagon ordered all U.S. military personnel to DEFCON-3 alert. All military leaves were canceled. More than two hundred ICBMs in silos across the American West were cocked for firing. A dozen Polaris submarines carrying 144 nuclear missiles moved toward the seacoasts of the Soviet Union, setting up an underwater picket fence of nuclear missiles. Sixty B-52s armed with 196 hydrogen bombs were airborne at all times, their pilots carrying sealed envelopes specifying their targets. Six hundred and twenty-eight more bombers armed with 2,026 nuclear weapons were dispersed to military and civilian airfields around the globe.

"This is the first day of the world crisis!" wrote Prime Minister Harold Macmillan in his diary the day after Kennedy spoke. When the U.S. ambassador, David K. E. Bruce, came to show him the first U-2 photographs, Macmillan reacted quickly and revealingly, saying: "Now the Americans will realize what we in England have lived through for the past many years." Dean Acheson had been delegated to show the photos to President Charles de Gaulle in Paris. "Tell President Kennedy that France will be with the United States," said de Gaulle. "It is exactly what I would have done."

"They're scared shitless," said Richard Helms of the people in the White House.* In New York, at the United Nations, a Soviet diplomat named Eduard Ivanian watched the speech with colleagues, then toasted them: "Here lie the Soviet diplomats. Killed by their own bombs."

The world was stunned; there was something new under the nuclear sun—the possibility of obliteration. Americans seemed more frightened than anyone else. As Macmillan had noted, they had never before lived in fear of direct attack. Richard Neustadt, a Columbia University professor who had helped Kennedy with his transition, sent this message for the President: "The reaction among students here . . . was *qualitatively* different from anything I've ever witnessed before. . . . These kids were literally scared for their lives and were astonished, somehow, that their lives could be risked by an *American* initiative."

"In the old days," said Dean Rusk at the Ex Comm meeting Tuesday morning, "you could have a confrontation or a showdown, you could go to sleep and you'd wake up in the morning, and you'd be there, and the city would be there."

Robert Kennedy was watching the Secretary of State closely. He thought the pressure was getting to him. That morning Rusk had awakened his Undersecretary, George Ball, who was sleeping on a couch in his office: "We have won a considerable victory. You and I are still alive," he said.

The Executive Committee of the National Security Council met at ten o'clock on Tuesday morning in the White House. McGeorge Bundy took the notes in his tiny handwriting, recording the first orders:

> The President approved the following contingency plan for action in the event of an incident affecting U-2 overflights . . . it is expected that if there

---

* Helms replaced Richard Bissell as CIA Director of Operations in February 1962. By then, almost a year after the Bay of Pigs, President Kennedy was willing to let Bissell stay in the CIA in a different position, Deputy Director for Administration, but Bissell chose to leave.

is clear indication that the incident is the result of hostile action, the recommendation will be for immediate retaliation upon the most likely surface-to-air site involved in this action. The President delegated authority for decision on this point to the Secretary of Defense . . . [if] the President himself should be unavailable.

CIA Director McCone reported that twenty-three of the twenty-four SAM sites and four of the ten MRBM sites on Cuba were now operational. The target date for activating three IRBM sites under construction was expected to be between December 1 and 15. Twenty-seven Soviet or Soviet-chartered ships were at sea headed for Cuba, nineteen of them believed to be carrying military equipment. They were all being shadowed and monitored by the two hundred and forty U.S. Air Force planes assigned to the quarantine operation. McCone also reported that reconnaissance flights showed work on the missile sites was speeding up, not slowing down. The Soviets too had canceled all military leaves. But, oddly, Soviet and Cuban military planes were parked wingtip-to-wingtip on airfields across the island—easy targets.

"What about ours?" asked the President. Within two hours, over-flights of U.S. installations in Florida and other Southern states showed Air Force and Navy planes parked in the open in exactly the same pattern.

Rusk left the morning meeting to present the American case to the Organization of American States (OAS), the twenty countries of South and Central America organized into a regional political alliance by the United States after World War II. The organization was essentially a twentieth-century attempt to perpetuate the Monroe Doctrine, the 1823 unilateral declaration by the fifth President, James Monroe, that the Americas were closed to European colonialization. President Kennedy personally believed that the declaration was not worth the paper it was written on. He never mentioned it in public. In private, when Norbert Schlei of the Justice Department had recommended that it be used as legal justification to move against Cuba, Kennedy had snapped: "What the hell is the Monroe Doctrine? Don't ever mention it again."

Just before lunchtime, at 11:56 A.M., the bells began dinging on the teletype from the State Department to the Situation Room in the basement of the White House. "ELITE. POLICY. EYES ONLY," were the first words that jumped up from the keys. It was a letter to the President from Khrushchev, delivered to the U.S. Embassy in Moscow three hours before:

I should say frankly that the measures outlined in your statement represent serious threat to peace and security of all peoples. United States has openly taken path of aggressive actions both against Cuba and the Soviet Union and other states. Charter of the United Nations and international norms do not give right to any state whatsoever to establish in international waters control of vessels bound for shores of the Cuban Republic. . . . It is self-understood that we also cannot recognize right of United States to establish control over armaments essential to Republic of Cuba for strengthening of its defensive capacity.

"I hope," the Soviet leader concluded, "that the government of the United States will show prudence. . . ."

"I want to answer this as soon as possible," Kennedy said. "When we get the word from the OAS." That word came just before five o'clock that afternoon. After eight hours of debate, OAS members, often resentful of the bullying patronage of the United States, surprised Washington and shocked Moscow by voting 20 to 0 to condemn the Soviet Union. The vote was unanimous also for a resolution calling for "immediate dismantling and removal from Cuba of all missiles." Some countries even offered ships and men to sail with the North Americans in the Caribbean quarantine.

There were none of the usual contradictory words from Latin American leaders who often publicly attacked Yankee imperialism and privately urged the United States to play policeman of the South. If nuclear missiles in Cuba could reach Denver or Los Angeles, they also could hit Buenos Aires or Rio de Janeiro. In New York, at the same time, the Soviets demanded an emergency meeting of the United Nations Security Council to condemn "the threat to the peace by the United States." As the session began, Ambassador Stevenson immediately and triumphantly announced the OAS action—before Soviet Ambassador Valerian Zorin could charge that the United States was planning to invade Cuba.

It was only after the OAS vote that the President signed the proclamation ordering the blockade to begin at 10:00 A.M. the next morning. The United States also scored another important diplomatic victory when Morocco, Senegal, and Guinea—three West African countries the Soviets needed as refueling stops on airplane transport flights to Cuba—agreed to American requests to deny Soviet landing rights. As Kennedy prepared to sign the proclamation, Evelyn Lincoln came into the Oval Office with a tray of pens, thinking he would use each of them for a bit of his signature, then distribute the pens to the others. He used just one pen this time and put it in his pocket after signing the paper.

Then President Kennedy sent his answer to the letter he'd received from Khrushchev five hours earlier: "I am concerned that we both show prudence . . . I hope you will issue immediately the necessary instructions to your ships to observe the terms of the quarantine, the basis of which was established by the vote of the Organization of American States this afternoon."

At about that time, McNamara was briefing reporters at the Pentagon. It was a tense show; many of the correspondents, as many of their countrymen, had never imagined that nuclear weapons might hit the United States. When the Secretary began to talk about civil defense, the room rocked with laughter. Kennedy's plans for cans of water and peas in basements, and children diving under school desks, suddenly seemed ludicrous.

At the White House, they were laughing, too, though some of the laughter was bitter. Military aides were going from office to office handing out envelopes "To Be Opened in Emergency." In the event of attack, Vice President Johnson was told, there were nineteen locations where he could be picked up by helicopter for a flight to shelters dug deep under the Cactocin Mountains in Maryland. His choices ranged from the street in front of his house in Virginia to the athletic field at McKinley High School in northeast Washington. The reporters on certain lists would be taken to the caves if they were at the White House or could get to the reservoir west of Georgetown. Otherwise, they were as out of luck as their wives or husbands and children.

"You are allowed to bring one secretary," General Clifton said to Larry O'Brien. "Phyllis Maddock," said O'Brien, and Clifton wrote down the name because each one had to be approved personally by the President.

"What about Elva?" O'Brien asked about his wife. The general gave him another packet, marked "TOP SECRET." It contained a sticker Mrs. O'Brien was to put on the windshield of her car, so that traffic would clear out of her way as she headed for a designated gathering place on the George Washington Parkway along the Potomac River. All this was to be done while air-raid sirens wailed.

"Ted," said O'Brien, using Clifton's nickname, "is this a joke?"

Secretary of State Rusk was thinking the same thing. He had already decided that if the missiles were coming, he was not going to Maryland but to Virginia. Not the state—Virginia was his wife's name. If there were survivors, he thought, the first thing they would do was find Kennedy and him and McNamara and hang them from the nearest tree.

On Wednesday morning, October 24, the President talked with his brother for twenty minutes before he was to meet with the rest of the Ex Comm. "It looks really mean, doesn't it?" he remarked. "But then there really was no other choice. If they get this mean on this one in our part of the world, what will they do the next time?"

"I just don't think there was any choice," Robert Kennedy told him. "If you hadn't acted, you would have been impeached."

"That's what I think—I would have been impeached."

In Moscow, the lead headlines of *Pravda* were warlike: "The unleashed American aggressors must be stopped!" . . . "Hands off Cuba!"

The Ex Comm meeting began at 10:00 A.M. So did the quarantine. McCone, as usual, began with an intelligence briefing: "We do not believe the measures to achieve a higher degree of action readiness for Soviet and bloc forces are being taken on a crash basis. . . ." In other words, he said, though Soviet diplomats in Washington and New York were saying their country was preparing for war, there were no indications that that was true.

"Surveillance of Cuba indicates continued rapid progress in completion of IRBM and MRBM missile sites," he continued. "Buildings believed to afford nuclear storage are being assembled with great rapidity."

Then he began to track Soviet ships, going down the list vessel by vessel. Three ships had hatches big enough to load and unload missiles —and they had been joined, overnight, by escorts of Soviet submarines.

"Isn't there some way we can avoid having our first exchange with a Russian submarine?" the President asked. "Almost anything but that."

"No," said McNamara. "There's too much danger to our ships. . . . This is what we must expect." Robert Kennedy had rarely seen his brother look so bad, even with all the illnesses over the years. The President was holding a hand over his mouth, opening and closing his fist.

McCone resumed the briefing, but he was interrupted at ten twenty-five when a messenger brought a note in to him. "Mr. President," he said. "We have a preliminary report that seems to indicate that some of the Russian ships have stopped dead in the water. . . ."

"We're eyeball to eyeball, and I think the other fellow just blinked," Rusk said to Bundy. Perhaps, the President said. He wanted commands issued to the Navy and the commanders around Cuba to hold everything: "Give the Russian vessels an opportunity to turn back."

The focus of the confrontation was slipping from the political to the military, which was making Kennedy even more irritable than he had been over the past few days. He did not trust his generals and they did not trust him. Without informing the White House, Air Force General Thomas Power had raised the Strategic Air Command's readiness alert from DEFCON-3 to DEFCON-2—prepared for immediate action. DEFCON-1 was war. And Power, who obviously had his own ideas about handling a crisis, had deliberately sent the alert in the clear and uncoded so that the Soviets could read it instantly.

McNamara, meanwhile, was trying to persuade Admiral George Anderson, the chief of Naval Operations, the man responsible for overseeing the blockade, that the President saw the crisis as political. This is not a textbook military operation, he said, but the communication of political signals.

"When the ship reaches the line, how are you going to stop it?" McNamara asked the chief, who was sitting in his conference room with a row of his top subordinates, all in full uniform.

"We'll hail it," the admiral said.

"In what language—English or Russian?"

"How the hell do I know? I have faith in my officers," said Anderson, his face glowing with anger. "This is none of your goddamn business. . . . We've been doing this ever since the days of John Paul Jones. If you'll just go back to your quarters, Mr. Secretary, we'll take care of this." He handed McNamara a copy of *The Manual of Navy Regulations,* saying, "It's all in there!"

"I don't give a damn what John Paul Jones would have done," said McNamara. "I want to know what you are going to do, now. What if they don't stop?"

"We'll send a shot across the bow," said the admiral.

"Then what, if that doesn't work?"

"Then we'll fire into the rudder. . . . This is none of your goddamn business, Mr. Secretary. This is what we're here to do."

"You're not going to fire a single shot at anything without my express permission, is that clear?" said McNamara, walking out as Anderson was announcing that the Navy did not need any help from civilians to do its job.

"That's the end of Anderson. I'll never . . . He won't be reappointed," McNamara said to Gilpatric as they walked back to the Secretary's office in another ring of the Pentagon's miles of corridors.

In Moscow on Wednesday afternoon—still morning in Washington —Khrushchev called in an American businessman who happened to be in the Soviet Union to discuss patent law and procedures. William Knox, the president of Westinghouse International, was a friend of Dean Rusk. The premier seemed exhausted, but he talked for three straight hours, telling Knox to deliver a message: If the Americans sank Soviet ships, his submarines would sink U.S. ships—and there would be world war. As Knox was leaving, Khrushchev said something about Kennedy, paused, then added: "How can I deal with a man who is younger than my son?"

That afternoon, Washington time, Kennedy and Khrushchev received identical letters: "An urgent appeal," from the United Nations Secretary-General, U Thant. He proposed a voluntary suspension of both arms shipments to Cuba and the American blockade—for two or three weeks to allow time for negotiations.

Khrushchev said yes. Kennedy said no. "The existing threat," the President replied in writing, "was created by the secret introduction of offensive weapons into Cuba, and the answer lies in the removal of such weapons."

That night, Walter Cronkite reported on CBS News: "At its beginning, this day looked as though it might be one of armed conflict between Soviet vessels and American warships on the sea lanes leading to Cuba. . . ." But there was no confrontation, yet.

"Shouldn't we be celebrating?" asked Charlie Bartlett at dinner in the White House that night.

"No, it's too early for that," said the President.

Far too early, in Kennedy's mind. He had just talked to Prime Minister Macmillan in London, asking a blunt question that had shaken the British leader: "Should I take out Cuba?"

"We're going to have to make a judgment as to whether we're going to invade Cuba, taking our chances, or whether we hold off and use Cuba as a sort of hostage in the matter of Berlin," the President had said. "Then any time he takes an action against Berlin, we take action against Cuba. That's really the choice we now have. . . . If he takes Berlin, then we will take Cuba. . . ."

Macmillan could not tell how serious Kennedy was. Perhaps the President was just testing him. The dialogue—he wrote in his diary that night—reminded him of a popular satirical revue running in London called *Beyond the Fringe*.

After Bartlett and three other guests, including David Ormsby-Gore, the British ambassador, left the White House that night, Kennedy received another letter from Khrushchev at 2:00 A.M. There were four angry pages:

Mr. President . . . By what right have you done this? . . . You are trampling upon the generally accepted norms of law. . . . All this is not only out of hatred for the Cuban people and government, but also a result of considerations of the election campaign in the USA. . . . The actions of the USA with regard to Cuba are outright banditry, or, if you like, the folly of degenerate imperialism . . . an act of aggression pushing mankind toward the abyss of a missile nuclear war. . . . Consequently, the Soviet government cannot give instructions to the captains of Soviet vessels bound for Cuba to observe the instructions of the American naval forces blockading that island. . . . We will then be forced for our part to take the measures which we deem necessary and adequate in order to protect our rights. For this we have all that is necessary.

Kennedy called Bartlett at home: "I got a cable from our friend and he said those ships are coming through, they're coming through tomorrow."

The public Soviet response was spelled out in the lead headlines of *Pravda* that morning, Thursday, October 25, in Moscow: "The aggressive designs of United States imperialists must be foiled. Peace on earth must be defended and strengthened!" . . . "Hands off Cuba!"

The President's answer to Khrushchev's letter, sent out within two hours, was only four paragraphs long. "I regret very much that you still do not appear to understand what it is that has moved us in this matter," his reply began, and then he called the Soviet chairman a liar. "This government received the most explicit assurances from your Government and its representatives, both publicly and privately, that no offensive weapons were being sent to Cuba . . . all those public assurances were false. . . . I hope your Government will take the necessary action to permit a restoration of the earlier situation."

Two ships did go through the quarantine line that morning, October 25. A Soviet oil tanker, the *Bucharest,* and an East German passenger ship were allowed to pass on direct orders from the President after identifying themselves and their cargoes. Most of the Ex Comm wanted the *Bucharest* stopped and boarded because it was the first Soviet ship to cross the line, but the President overruled his men, limiting the action again. "I don't want to put him in a corner. . . ," he said of Khrushchev. "We don't want to push him into a precipitous action."

Kennedy also wanted to keep secret the action, or lack of action, in the Caribbean. But it was on radio and television within an hour, announced by a Pennsylvania Congressman named James Van Zandt as he walked out of a secret State Department briefing. Kennedy was so angry that he walked out of an Ex Comm meeting and tracked down the State Department briefer, the deputy director of intelligence, Thomas Hughes, at Idlewild Airport in New York—"The President is calling American Airlines passenger Hughes. The President is calling American passenger Hughes . . ." which everyone in the airport thought was a joke of some kind. It wasn't. Hughes picked up a courtesy phone and heard the most famous Boston accent in the land: "What the hell is going on?"

The President was angered, too, by Walter Lippmann's column in the *Washington Post*—a column that the Soviets, who believed all newspapers were government instruments, would certainly take as coming from the White House. Lippmann had proposed a face-saving trade: "The only place that is truly comparable with Cuba is Turkey. This is the only place where there are strategic weapons right on the frontier of the Soviet Union. . . . The Soviet military base in Cuba is defenseless and the base in Turkey is all but obsolete. The two bases could be dismantled without altering the world balance of power."

"Shit!" was Kennedy's reaction. Lippmann was right, but that was not the point. The Jupiters in Turkey were almost worthless to the United States; they took hours to fuel and launch, were wildly inaccurate, and could be ruined by a sniper firing a rifle from a public highway. But, as far as the President was concerned, Lippmann was doing the same thing Stevenson had done in private, offering concessions before they were demanded.

Even Averell Harriman, who was rarely called soft, had urged Kennedy in a memo on October 22 to consider removing the Jupiters, not only because they had little military value but because they were so close to the Soviet Union and so humiliating to both military leaders and ordinary Soviet citizens that they might be puffing up the influence of Kremlin hard-liners, might even have been the primary reason Khrushchev was persuaded or forced to put the missiles in Cuba.

Worthless as they might be, the Jupiters were a matter of pride and new stature to the government of Turkey. The Jupiters, Kennedy had just learned, had become operational only a few weeks before. He had also discovered that the maintenance of the first of them had been transferred from the U.S. Air Force to the Turkish Army three days before, on October 22.

Stevenson's advice may not have impressed Kennedy, but the U.N. ambassador looked good to the boss on the afternoon of October 25. Stevenson rolled over the Soviets at a new emergency meeting of the United Nations Security Council, this one requested by Cuba. The Communists could not win at the United Nations; they never had. In the fifteen-year history of the Council, the Soviets had had to use their veto 109 times to stop resolutions or actions pushed by the Americans. The United States, on the other hand, had never once stood alone, had never cast a veto. Still, the Soviets and the Cubans thought they could embarrass the Americans this time, particularly with their ambassador, Valerian Zorin, holding the rotating position of president of the Council.

It did not work out that way. Stevenson mauled Zorin—and he did it again and again as their confrontation was televised all over the world, then repeated and repeated electronically.

"Do you, Ambassador Zorin," said Stevenson, "deny that the

U.S.S.R. has placed and is placing medium- and intermediate-range missiles and sites in Cuba? Yes or no—don't wait for the translation—yes or no?"

"I am not in an American courtroom, sir, and therefore I do not wish to answer. . . ," answered Zorin, looking as if he were in a courtroom. "In due course, sir, you will have your reply."

"You are in the courtroom of world opinion right now, and you can answer yes or no. . . ."

". . . You will have your answer in due course," said the Russian.

"I am prepared to wait for my answer until hell freezes over. . . ," Stevenson said. Then he took the stage, dramatically displaying reconnaissance photos of Cuba to the room and the world.

"Terrific," said Kennedy, who was watching on television. "I never knew Adlai had it in him. Too bad he didn't show some of this steam in the 1956 campaign."

That evening the President personally selected the first ship to be stopped and boarded. She was called the *Marucla*, American-built, Panamanian-owned, Lebanese-registered, Soviet-chartered, captained by a Greek. There was no chance she was carrying military equipment. Two American destroyers fell in behind her that night, the U.S.S. *Pierce* and the U.S.S. *Kennedy,* Seaman Robert Kennedy's old ship.

In Moscow the morning of Thursday, October 26, the headline of *Pravda* was a good deal more conciliatory than the day before: "EVERYTHING TO PREVENT WAR." Below that there was an editorial with the title: "Reason Must Prevail."

At seven-fifty that morning the U.S. Navy boarded the *Marucla*. They found asbestos, newsprint, sulfur, and a dozen trucks.

There was something comic about the boarding party. The Americans were in dress white uniforms and were unarmed, two of them spoke Russian, but no one on the ship did. The Greek captain offered the U.S. officers coffee, which they drank in his cabin while their men tried to figure a way to lower themselves into the cargo ship's holds. Finally they gave up, taking the Greek's word that there was nothing down there worth starting a nuclear war over.

The quarantine seemed to be working well enough. Most of the Soviet ships suspected of carrying military equipment had turned around and were headed home. The U.S. Navy had total control of the sea, forcing six Soviet submarines to surface and identify themselves. They were a rusty bunch, but American cameras filmed every inch of them for intelligence agencies. Yet Kennedy and his aides were worried, many of them depressed: none of this had much to do with the President's goal of getting out the missiles that were already on Cuba. The Joint Chiefs were once again pressing for an air strike and invasion. At noon, at the regular State Department briefing, the department's spokesman, Lincoln White, began by repeating a sentence from the President's speech four days before: "Should these offensive military preparations continue, thus increasing the threat to the hemisphere, further action will be justified."

Kennedy was angry again, calling White to chew him out for using his name in a threat to the Soviets. But a couple of hours later, at the White House, Pierre Salinger repeated the warning, reading from a presidential letter to the United Nations Security Council: "There is no evidence to date indicating that there is any intention to dismantle or discontinue work on these missile sites." The President ordered USIA to begin printing five million leaflets in Spanish to drop over Cuba to explain the reasons for a U.S. attack or invasion.

"We are going to have to face the fact that, if we do invade, by the time we get to these sites, after a very bloody fight, they will be pointed at us," the President told Ex Comm that morning. "And we must further accept the possibility that when military hostilities first begin, those missiles will be fired."

He was thinking in terms of two more days. "If at the end of forty-eight hours we are getting no place and the missile sites continue to be constructed, then we are going to be faced with some hard decisions," he had told Prime Minister Macmillan during their phone call that day. The calls to London had been part of his daily routine since the Monday speech.

After the Lincoln White briefing, the ABC network diplomatic correspondent, John Scali, returned to the State Department press room and decided to eat lunch at his desk, a bologna sandwich. His phone rang. It was Alexander Fomin, a Russian he knew slightly, listed as a counselor at the Soviet Embassy, but believed to be the Washington station chief of Soviet intelligence, the KGB. It is very important, the Russian said, asking Scali to meet him at a restaurant called the Occidental.

"The situation is very serious," began Fomin, who seemed haggard to Scali. He got right to the point. Would Scali check with high State Department sources on a possible deal? The Soviets would remove the missiles under U.N. supervision if the United States would pledge never to invade Cuba.

Scali went to Roger Hilsman, who took him to the Secretary of State's office. It was almost five o'clock. Rusk was inside meeting with Robert Kennedy and Mac Bundy. He came out, listened to Scali, and a few minutes later returned with a handwritten note that the television correspondent memorized: "I have reason to believe that the United States Government sees real possibilities in this and supposes that representatives of the two governments could work this matter out with U Thant and each other. My impression is, however, that time is very urgent."

The Secretary of State brought Scali over to the White House. "What the hell are you doing here? I want you out of here!" Pierre Salinger shouted when he saw the correspondent outside the Oval Office. But Kennedy came out then and told Scali that he did not know quite what to make of Fomin and the proposal, but he wanted to keep the conversation going. He wanted the newsman to indicate there was interest at "the highest level," but not to tell the Russian he had seen the President or to use his name.

It was possible, Kennedy thought, that Fomin was replacing Robert Kennedy's Russian, Georgi Bolshakov. Bolshakov's credibility had been blown when he had delivered Khrushchev's lies about the missiles to the Attorney General in September. But Robert Kennedy believed the Russian agent-editor did not know he was delivering the lie and he still liked the man. He asked Charlie Bartlett to telephone Bolshakov and tell him that the President and he were disappointed in him, and in what happened. Bartlett did it, and moments later his own phone rang. "Boy, you were really rough on Georgie, you didn't have to go that far," said Robert Kennedy, who obviously had a tap on the Russian's phone, or Bartlett's.

By Friday afternoon, the Soviets and the Americans seemed locked in stalemate and the United States was still no nearer the goal of getting the missiles out of Cuba. Most Ex Comm members thought that the President would have to decide very soon—not between blockade and bombing, but between bombing and invasion. He might have to do both, first the bombing. His option paper for the day, which assumed the Soviets had nuclear warheads hidden somewhere in Cuba, listed several strike scenarios, including these two: "This action may force Khrushchev to react strongly and could result in some kind of war. (Khrushchev will not order launch of a missile from Cuba unless he is ready for war essentially on other grounds.) . . . There is a remote possibility that some local Soviet commander may order firing of a missile."

At exactly six o'clock that Friday evening, the State Department teletypes came alive with the first of four sections of a long letter from Khrushchev to Kennedy, the eighth of the series that had begun after the Monday night speech. The letter had been delivered to Ambassador Foy Kohler in Moscow at 4:43 P.M., which was seven forty-three in the morning in Washington. But there had been problems in both transmission and translation, trouble with Soviet telegraph lines and with the language, because, Kohler told waiting State Department personnel in Washington, the letter was long and quite strange—rambling, personal, almost hysterical.

"This reads as if he wrote it himself without anyone else around, without consultation or editing," said Llewellyn Thompson, Kohler's predecessor in Moscow, who was with President Kennedy as he began to read it. "He's worried. He seems to be under a lot of strain."

Chapter 36

"Dear Mr. President:

"I have received your letter of October 25. From your letter, I got the feeling that you have some understanding of the situation which has developed and some sense of responsibility. I value this. . . ."

The translation and transmission of Khrushchev's letter to Kennedy was not completed until nine-fifteen that night. It was ten o'clock the next morning, October 27, before the President and the members of Ex Comm sat down again in the Cabinet Room to consider it. In Moscow, the morning headline of *Pravda* read: "Peoples of all countries, be vigilant; unmask the imperialist warmongers! Struggle more actively for the preservation of a durable and indestructible peace!"

The first order of business at Ex Comm was "Saying Grace"—the name several of them used among themselves to describe CIA Director McCone's droning summaries of overnight intelligence, most of it ship movements and progress reports on the missile site construction. McNamara followed with a report from the Defense Intelligence Agency, a bureau he had created to compete with the CIA: "There is considerable speculation that a power struggle is in progress in the Kremlin between Khrushchev and a more militant and aggressive group."

The State Department's analysis, presented by Rusk, emphasized that the missiles in Cuba had changed the strategic balance of the Cold War. "The missiles in the Caribbean will increase the first-strike missile salvo which the USSR could place on targets in the continental United States by over 40 percent. The strategic significance of the Cuban missile complex is due not only to the substantial quantitative increase in megatons deliverable in a surprise first strike, but also by their effect on the US deterrent striking force. Approximately 40 percent of the SAC bomber force is now located on air bases within range of Soviet MRBMs in Cuba, and almost all of it is in range of the IRBMs . . . this represents a serious dilution of US strategic deterrent capability."

Finally they got to a full reading of Khrushchev's letter:

". . . I see, Mr. President, that you too are not devoid of understanding and a proper evaluation of the character of contemporary war, a sense of anxiety for the fate of the world. What would a war give you? You are threatening us with war. . . . If indeed war should break out, then it would not be in our power to stop it, for such is the logic of war. I have participated in two wars and know that war ends when it has rolled through cities and villages, everywhere sowing death and destruction."

"He's scared," concluded McNamara.

Kennedy nodded. He was, too. The part of him that was always detached was more sympathetic to Khrushchev than he could ever say in public or would ever say to most of these men. He thought that he might be the only other man in the world who understood all of Khrushchev's rambling thoughts. One night during the crisis, trying to relax, he remarked that if he were Khrushchev he would be as angry about missiles and 27,000 U.S. troops in Turkey as the Americans were about Soviet missiles and troops in Cuba.

"It is insane that two men, sitting on opposite sides of the world, should be able to decide to bring an end to civilization," Kennedy said.

In his letter, Khrushchev called the quarantine "piracy." He accused Kennedy of using the crisis to influence congressional elections. He said the Soviets had good reason to fear a U.S. invasion of the island. He even brought up a piece of history unknown to most Americans: A U.S. expeditionary force had been sent to Russia in 1917 to fight the Bolsheviks.

"You are threatening us with war . . . ," Khrushchev continued. Then, abruptly, his tone changed.

However, let us not quarrel now. It is apparent that I will not be able to convince you of this. . . . Do you really seriously think that Cuba can attack the United States and that even we together with Cuba can attack you from the territory of Cuba? Can you really think that way? Is it possible? . . . You can regard us with distrust, but, in any case you can be calm in this regard, that we are of sound mind and understand perfectly well that if we attack you, you will respond the same way. . . . Only lunatics or suicides, who themselves want to perish and to destroy the world before they die, could do this.

"We, however, want to live and do not at all want to destroy your country . . . ," Khrushchev said. Then he offered Kennedy a deal:

If assurances were given by the President and the Government of the United States that the U.S.A. itself would not participate in an attack on Cuba and would restrain others from actions of this sort, if you would recall your fleet this would change everything. . . . The questions of armaments would disappear, since, if there is no threat, then armaments are a burden for every people.

Let us therefore show statesmanlike wisdom. I propose: We, for our part, will declare that our ships, bound for Cuba, will not carry any kind of armaments. You would declare that the United States will not invade Cuba with its forces which might intend to carry out an invasion of Cuba.

Mr. President, I appeal to you to weigh well what the aggressive, piratical actions, which you have declared the U.S.A. intends to carry out in international waters, would lead to. . . . If you did this as a first step towards the unleashing of war, well then, it is evident that nothing else is left to us but to accept this challenge of yours. If, however, you have not lost your self-control and sensibly conceive what this might lead to, then, Mr. President, we ought not now pull on the ends of the rope in which you have tied the knot of war, because the more the two of us pull, the tighter that knot will be tied. And a moment may come when that knot will be tied so tight that even he who tied it will not have the strength to untie it, and then it will be necessary to cut that knot, and what that would mean is not for me to explain to you, because you yourself understand perfectly of what terrible forces our countries dispose.

"These thoughts," Khrushchev closed, "are dictated by a sincere desire to relieve the situation, to remove the threat of war."

The brief optimism ended less than fifteen minutes after the meeting began when Pierre Salinger came into the Cabinet Room holding a ripped sheet of Associated Press copy that was moving on the wires. Kennedy read the lead: "Premier Khrushchev told President Kennedy yesterday he would withdraw offensive missiles from Cuba if the United States withdrew its rockets from Turkey."

"What the hell is this?" said someone down the table.

There was, it turned out, a new letter from Khrushchev—a public letter. It was being read on Radio Moscow—the reading took fifteen minutes—which avoided the telegraph problems that had delayed the first letter for so long. But that also meant the whole world knew the words and offers and demands of the new letter, while only a couple of dozen people in Washington and Moscow knew about the proposals in the first letter. The public language was more formal and more rigid:

> How are we, the Soviet Union and our government, to assess your actions which are expressed in the fact that you have surrounded the Soviet Union with military bases, surrounded our allies with military bases, literally disposed military bases around our country, and stationed your rocket armaments there?
>
> You are worried by Cuba, you say that it worries you because it is a distance of 90 miles by sea from the American coast. However, Turkey is next to us, literally at our elbow. . . . I therefore make this proposal. We agree to remove from Cuba those means which you regard as offensive means. We agree to carry this out and declare this pledge in the United Nations. Your representatives will make a declaration to the effect that the United States on its part, considering the uneasiness and anxiety of the Soviet State, *will remove its analogous means from Turkey. . . .*

The second letter ended with a repeat of the demand for a U.S. pledge not to invade Cuba, and a reciprocal Soviet pledge not to invade Turkey.

"It's very odd, Mr. President," said McGeorge Bundy. "If he's changed his terms . . .

"Let's assume that this is an accurate report of what he's now proposing this morning," the President said. "There may have been changes over there—a change over there. Well now let's say he has changed it. This is his latest position."

"I would answer back saying I would prefer to deal with your—with your interesting proposals of last night," Bundy said.

Kennedy seemed not to hear that. He continued: "We're going to be in an insupportable position on this matter if this becomes his proposal. In the first place, we last year tried to get the missiles out of there [Turkey] because they're not militarily useful, number one. Number two, it's going to—to any man at the United Nations or any other rational man it will look like a very fair trade."

Kennedy began to read aloud again, this time from the rest of the AP report: " 'A special message appeared to call for negotiations and both nations, Cuba and Turkey, should give their consent to the United Nations to visit their territories. Khrushchev said the Security Council of the Soviet Union was solemnly pledged not to use its territory as a bridgehead for an attack on Turkey, called for a similar pledge from the United States not to let its territory be used as a bridgehead for an attack on Cuba. . . .' "

"We've known this was coming for a long time," Kennedy said, looking up. "How much negotiation have we had with the Turks?"

Rusk answered: "We haven't talked with the Turks. The Turks have talked with us." And Turkey had made it clear that it did not want the Jupiters removed, it would be too great a blow to its prestige. It was the kind of thing that had led to the fall of Turkish governments.

"This would be an extremely unsettling business. . . . The Turks feel very strongly about this," said George Ball.

"Well, this is unsettling now, George, because he's got us in a pretty good spot here," said the President, "because most people will regard this as not an unreasonable proposal, I'll just tell you that."

"I don't see why we pick that track when he's offered us the other track, within the last twenty-four hours," Bundy said for the second time. "You think the public one is serious?"

"Yeah," Kennedy said. "I think you have to assume that this is their new and latest position and it's a public one."

"If we talked to the Turks," added Ball, "they would take it up in NATO. This thing would have been all over Western Europe . . . immediately the Soviet Union would know that this thing was being discussed."

"In their own terms," said Bundy, "it would already be clear that we were trying to sell our allies for our interests. That would be the view in all of NATO."

"The fact of the matter is," said Kennedy, "that we received a letter last night from Khrushchev with an entirely different proposal. Therefore we first ought to get clarification from the Soviet Union. . . . Until we have gotten our position a little clearer we ought to go with this— uh—last night business."

Then the President left the room for twenty minutes to meet with a group of governors headed by Nelson Rockefeller on the matter of civil defense. When Kennedy came back, Bundy told him: "While you were out of the room, Mr. President, we reached an informal consensus—I don't know whether Tommy [Thompson] agrees—that this—last night's message was Khrushchev and this one is his own hard-nosed people overruling him—this public one—that they didn't like what he said to you last night. Nor would I, if I were a Soviet hard-nose."

"They've got a very good card," said Kennedy. "This one is going to be very tough, I think, for us. . . . We're going to be forced to take action, that might seem, in my opinion, not a blank check but a pretty good check to take action in Berlin on the grounds we were totally unreasonable. . . . The only thing we've got on him is the fact that now they've put forth varying proposals in short periods of time, all of which are complicated, and under this shield this work goes on."

Dillon added then that there was one sentence he thought was particularly dangerous in this new letter: "It's where he says, 'How are we to react when you have surrounded our country with bases about which your military speak demonstratively?' That opens up our whole base system."

"We may—now let's not kid ourselves; they've got a—God—they've got a very good proposal, which is the reason they made it publicly not privately," said the President. "The only thing that I'm trying to suggest is that all these proposals come; they're all complicated, and what they can do is hang us up in negotiations on different proposals while the work goes on."

Paul Nitze shook his head. He spoke more directly than do most people when they talk to presidents: "That looks like a rationalization of our own confusion. I think you've got to take a firmer line than that. . . . We cannot get into the position of selling out an ally . . . to serve our own interests, i.e., getting the Soviet missiles out of Cuba."

The President replied that perhaps the Turks could be persuaded to make the suggestion to remove the Jupiters. "I'm just trying to cope with what the public problem is about—because everybody's going to think that this is very reasonable."

Edwin Martin, the Assistant Secretary of State for Latin America, tried out an idea: "Suppose that we give him a letter which is addressed to his letter of yesterday and ask U Thant to release them both—he's the fellow to release them—and then he releases correspondence which consists really of an offer from Khrushchev and we—we came back and write . . ."

Bundy interrupted to end the sentence: " 'Thank you.' "

" 'Thank you, yes,' " Martin echoed. "And it doesn't mention Turkey."

The President said that if he were Khrushchev, he would just say he wasn't interested—and then the United States would have to make the next move, a military move. The arguments went on about what to do, what to say, about what, to whom. The quarantine looked good but it was not changing anything. The Soviets seemed to have whatever they needed on Cuba and the construction of the launch sites was speeding up, not slowing down. The Russians were working around the clock. There was one other problem: The morning U-2 flight over Cuba had not returned to Florida.

"The turndown," the President said, trying to figure out what would happen if he turned down the Cuba-Turkey swap, "the turndown puts us in the position of then having to do something. What we're going to be faced with is—because we wouldn't take the missiles out of Turkey, then maybe we'll have to invade or make a massive strike on Cuba which may lose Berlin. . . . And we all know how quickly everybody's courage goes when the blood starts to flow, and that's what's going to happen in NATO, when they—we start these things, and they grab Berlin. And everybody's going to say, 'Well that was a pretty good proposition.' Let's not kid ourselves. Today it sounds great to reject it, but it's not going to, after we do something."

At one-thirty that afternoon, between Ex Comm meetings, Rusk dispatched Roger Hilsman, to go to the White House with the latest draft version of the President's reply to Khrushchev. He delivered the paper to McGeorge Bundy, who was headed to the Oval Office. "Mr. Hilsman," said a guard. "It's your office, on the phone. They say it's urgent."

Hilsman almost fainted, standing there with the phone. A U-2 based in Alaska, said to be on an air-sampling mission in Antarctica, was flying somewhere over the Soviet Union. Soviet fighters had scrambled and were coming up after the spy plane. U.S. Air Force fighters were up, too, trying to find the U-2 and guide it back over the ocean or United States territory. One U-2 was missing in the Caribbean; now one was lost over Russia. Hilsman sat down for a moment to clear his head—he had not slept for thirty-six hours—then he ran over to the Oval Office to tell the President. Kennedy already knew. McNamara had just called him from the Defense Department, after rushing out of a meeting saying, "This means war with the Soviet Union!"

Kennedy's reaction seemed detached: "There's always some son-of-a-bitch who doesn't get the word." On the other side, Khrushchev dictated his reaction as part of his next letter to Kennedy: "How should we regard this? What is this, a provocation? . . . An intruding American plane can easily be taken for a bomber with nuclear weapons, and this could push us toward a fatal step—all the more so because both the United States government and the Pentagon have long been saying that bombers with atomic bombs are constantly on duty in your country."

The President joined Ex Comm again at four o'clock that afternoon. He was beginning to feel cornered. The quarantine had failed. The Cuba-Turkey swap would be interpreted as political defeat for Kennedy —and possibly lead to the break-up of NATO. Certainly it would validate the perceptions of General de Gaulle and others that the United States would never risk its own security or trade its own cities to defend foreigners. And the alternative, air strike and invasion of Cuba to back up his public position, could lead to nuclear war, particularly if the Soviets chose to retaliate in Berlin.

"I don't think there's any doubt he's going to . . . ," the President said of Khrushchev, turning toward Thompson. "Tommy, he's not going to take them out of Cuba."

"I don't agree, Mr. President," said the ambassador. "I think there's still a chance that we can get this line going."

"He'll back down?"

"The important thing for Khrushchev, it seems to me, is to be able to say, 'I saved Cuba, I stopped an invasion.' "

"He must be a little shaken up," Robert Kennedy said, backing up Thompson, "or he wouldn't have sent the message to you in the first place."

"That's last night," the President said.

"Yeah," said the Attorney General, "but I mean it's certainly conceivable that you could get him back to that. . . ."

By now, Bundy, Martin, Stevenson, Thompson, and Robert Kennedy had all suggested variations on the same theme: Answer the first letter, the private letter. Say "Thank you" and ignore the second letter.

"The only thing," said Robert Kennedy, ready to argue against himself as he thought it out, "is that what we're proposing in here is the abandonment . . . the abandonment of Cuba."

The first-letter ploy went right by McNamara. "Hell, that's no offer," he said. "You read that message carefully. He didn't propose to take the missiles out. . . . It's twelve pages of fluff."

That was true. There was more passion than proposition in the private letter. McNamara did not trust passion. The President, though, was now willing to try, to see what his men could do with it.

"I have read your letter of October 26th with great care and welcome the statement of your desire to seek a prompt solution to the problem." The first sentence of the response was easy. In fact, the first few sentences were taken word for word from an answer that had been suggested by Stevenson in the morning. For an hour or so, the meeting became an editing session, as the men around the table tried to come up with language that ignored the missiles in Turkey. They were getting nowhere, partly because the President thought of himself as a master of words. They broke up in giddy laughter when Robert Kennedy turned on his brother and said: "Why don't we try to work it out without you being able to pick . . ."

"Mr. President . . . ," said Maxwell Taylor, when the laughing stopped. The Joint Chiefs of Staff, he said, wanted to begin the invasion within thirty-six hours: "Executed no later than Monday morning the 29th unless there is irrefutable evidence in the meantime that offensive weapons are being dismantled and rendered inoperable; that the execution of the Strike Plan be part of the execution of 3-16, the Invasion Plan."

"That was a surprise," said Robert Kennedy sarcastically. The room broke into laughter again.

"They just feel that the longer we wait now . . . ," said Taylor.

War was close, most of the men in the Cabinet Room thought this Saturday afternoon. The first U.S. combat aircraft might be flying over Cuba by Monday morning; Tuesday morning for sure. But the President held back. "Bobby," he said, "you want to go out now and get this letter sent. . . ." Robert Kennedy and Sorensen went over to the Oval Office to see if they could draft an acceptable answer to Khrushchev's private letter.

Then McNamara reported that U.S. surveillance planes, now flying over the missile sites at low altitude, were being fired on by antiaircraft guns. "The first question we have to face tomorrow morning is, are we going to send surveillance flights in?" he said to the President. "If we send them in with proper cover and they're attacked, we must attack back, either the SAMs and/or the MiG aircraft that come up against them, or the ground fire that comes up."

After some back-and-forth, the President decided that one quickly. He decided not to decide: "Let's wait and see whether they fire on us tomorrow. . . . If we get fired on, then we meet here and we decide. . . ."

He did not have to wait that long. A few minutes later, there was a telephone call for Rusk. He left the room to take it and came back pale, with tears in his eyes: The U-2 missing over Cuba had been shot down by a SAM missile.

"Pilot killed?" asked Robert Kennedy.

"The pilot's body is in the plane," Rusk said. It was Major Anderson, the same man who had first photographed the missile sites.

"We can't very well send a U-2 over there, can we, now?" said the President. "And have a guy killed again tomorrow?"

"We certainly shouldn't do it until we retaliate and say that if they fire again on one of our planes, that we'll come back with great force," said Taylor. But the President had already backed away from retaliation, ignoring his own order that if a reconnaissance plane was shot down, U.S. planes would take out the SAM site that had fired on it.

There was not much more time to buy. McNamara took the floor then. The Defense Secretary crisply laid out an action-reaction scenario leading to nuclear war:

"We've been fired on today. We're going to send surveillance aircraft in tomorrow. Those are going to be fired on without question. We're going to respond. You can't do this very long. We're going to lose airplanes, and we'll be shooting up Cuba quite a bit, but we're going to lose airplanes every day. So you just can't maintain this position very long. So we must be prepared to attack Cuba—quickly. . . . When we attack Cuba we're going to have to attack with an all-out attack. . . . I personally believe that this is almost certain to lead to an invasion. . . . If we do this, and leave those missiles in Turkey the Soviet Union may, and I think probably will, attack the Turkish missiles. . . . We cannot allow a Soviet attack on the—on the Jupiter missiles in Turkey without a military response by NATO. Now the minimum response to a Soviet attack on the Turkish Jupiter missiles would be a response with conventional weapons by NATO forces in Turkey, that is to say Turkish and U.S. aircraft, against Soviet warships and/or naval bases in the Black Sea area. Now that to me is the absolute minimum, and I would say that it is damned dangerous."

The President left the Cabinet Room to meet with General Lyman Lemnitzer, who had become commander of U.S. forces in Europe when he was replaced by Taylor as Chairman of the Joint Chiefs. They discussed the next round of troop movements. The conversation in the Cabinet Room was for a time dominated by Vice President Johnson. He had not spoken at all while the President was present, but now he made some telling points. If the United States was willing to give up the Jupiters in Turkey, why not trade them to save all the lives that would be lost on both sides in an American invasion of Cuba? After all, the great worry of the early Ex Comm meetings was that Khrushchev wanted to trade the Cuban missiles for Berlin, so what was the big deal about a few obsolete missiles in Turkey? "You're going to have a big problem right here in a few more hours, in this country. . . . What are you doing? The President made a fine speech. What else have you done?"

"They want more action?" asked Rusk.

"They don't know what we're doing," Johnson snapped. "They see that there are some ships coming through. There's a great feeling of insecurity."

"Ask yourself," the Vice President said to Llewellyn Thompson, "what made the greatest impression on you today, whether it was his letter last night or whether it was his letter this morning. Or whether it was shooting down the U-2?"

"The U-2," Thompson said.

"Exactly right," Johnson was saying as the President walked back in.

Kennedy seemed removed from the arguments, as if he had already made up his mind. "We can't very well invade Cuba . . . when we could have gotten them out by making a deal on the same missiles in Turkey. If that's part of the record, I don't see how we'll have a good war," he said. Was that a decision? Before anyone could ask, Kennedy told them to get something to eat and come back at nine o'clock.

The two politicians, Kennedy and Johnson, had come separately to the same conclusion: The President of the United States could not risk nuclear war or even send troops to die over fifteen obsolete missiles in Turkey. There was a chance, too, that a third politician, the Russian one in the Kremlin, had made the same kind of decision.

In the two hours between meetings, President Kennedy made his moves. He worked over Sorensen's draft answer to the private letter from Khrushchev, saying, in effect, "Yes, thank you," though he felt sure the Russian would reject it. Then he acted on Rusk's suggestion to consider asking U Thant at the United Nations to suggest the Cuba-Turkey swap, if Khrushchev did indeed turn down the letter.

The President talked alone with his brother after the others left. He wanted him to call Anatoli Dobrynin. At 7:15 P.M. Robert Kennedy and the ambassador agreed to meet within a half hour. The President's letter to Khrushchev would be ready by then.

Both the Attorney General and the ambassador were tired. Both were scared. Neither was sure of what the other was saying—or could do. The final American letter was ready, Robert Kennedy told Dobrynin. It would be sent very soon and it was going to be made public. This was the last chance, he told the ambassador. The U.S. military was pressing for an invasion, and that was what was going to happen if Khrushchev did not agree to take the missiles out, now. He did not know how much longer his brother could hold off the generals and the admirals, he insisted. If Khrushchev did not take the missiles out, the United States would take them out.

"This does not mention the missiles in Turkey," Dobrynin said. That was nothing, Robert Kennedy said, it could be worked out. His brother wanted them out, too—but later, not now, and not in public. Now, he said, Khrushchev had to answer this letter. He had to do it by tomorrow. The President could not stand up to the military for much longer. Did Khrushchev understand that? The Russian thought Robert Kennedy was near tears.

"I am not optimistic," said Dobrynin. "The Politburo is too committed to back down now."

The Soviet ambassador had no reliable telephone or telegraph link with the Kremlin. He wrote a summary of Robert Kennedy's warnings and pleadings and called Western Union. A young Negro came by on a bicycle to pick up the telegram. Dobrynin watched him pedal away, figuring that if he stopped for a Coca-Cola or to see his girlfriend, the world might blow up.

The President was upstairs in the White House with Dave Powers eating roast chicken and drinking milk, which was about the most his tender stomach could handle even under the best of circumstances, when his brother returned. Robert Kennedy was not optimistic. He asked for a chicken leg. Powers continued to eat while the brothers talked in somber tones.

"God, Dave," the President said, "the way you're eating up all that chicken and drinking up all my wine, anybody would think it was your last meal."

"The way Bobby's been talking, I thought it was my last meal."

At 8:05 P.M., the President released his answer to Khrushchev's first letter, with no mention of Turkey or the missiles there. Like the Soviets, Kennedy was now worried about the speed of communications. Rather than trust diplomatic channels, he decided that his letter should be broadcast immediately by the Voice of America to Moscow and everywhere else in the world:

> I have read your letter of October 26th with great care and welcomed the statement of your desire to seek a prompt solution to the problem. The first thing that needs to be done, however, is for work to cease on offensive missile bases in Cuba and for all weapons systems in Cuba capable of offensive use to be rendered inoperable, under effective United Nations arrangements.
>
> Assuming this is done promptly, I have given my representatives in New York instructions that will permit them to work out this weekend . . . an arrangement for the permanent solution to the Cuban problem along the lines suggested in your letter of October 26th. (1.) You would agree to remove these weapons systems from Cuba. . . . (2.) We, on our part, would agree . . . (a) to remove promptly the quarantine measures now in effect and (b) to give assurances against an invasion of Cuba.
>
> There is no reason why we should not be able to complete these arrangements and announce them to the world in a couple of days. The effect of such a settlement on easing world tensions would enable us to work toward a more general arrangement regarding "other armaments" as proposed in your second letter which you made public. . . .

If it did not work, Kennedy had one more mechanism of compromise. Rusk had worked out a way to offer to trade the Jupiters if that was what Khrushchev wanted. The Secretary of State had recruited the president of Columbia University, Andrew Cordier, a former deputy of U Thant's at the United Nations, to personally deliver a note from Kennedy to the Acting Secretary-General asking him, on a signal from the White House, to suggest the Cuba-Turkey swap as his own plan.

The third Ex Comm meeting of the day began at 9:00 P.M. "You do anything about the SAM site that shot down our plane?" Douglas Dillon asked the President.

"We don't know if it did yet, Doug," Kennedy replied, still not ready to do what he said he would do, knock out a SAM site if a missile were fired at a U-2.

McNamara said, "I think the point is that if our planes are fired on tomorrow, we ought to fire back."

No, the President said again. "I think we ought to wait till tomorrow afternoon, to see whether we get any answer—if we haven't got a satisfactory answer back from the Russians then I think we ought to put a statement out tomorrow that we were fired upon, and we are therefore considering the island of Cuba as an open territory, and then take out all these SAM-sites. What do you think?"

"I would say only that we ought to keep some kind of pressure on," answered McNamara. "I believe we should issue an order tonight calling up the twenty-four air reserve squadrons, roughly 300 troop carrier transports, which are required for an invasion, and this would both be a preparatory move, and also a strong indication of what lies ahead."

"I think we ought to do it," Kennedy agreed.

He was used to call-ups; this one, of 140,000 airmen, was the fourth in less than two years. But the President was still not ready to send those men into overt combat, though that was getting close. The next piece of business was to decide what to say to NATO and to the Turks. "Prepare this groundwork for a disaster . . . later in the week, in Berlin or someplace," were his exact words. "We ought to be saying to them that the situation is deteriorating, and if we take action, we think there will be reprisals.

"Let's give an explanation of what we're trying to do. We're trying to get it back on the original proposition of last night, and because we don't want to get into this trade. If we're unsuccessful, then we—it's possible that we may have to get back on the Jupiter thing. If we do, then we would of course want it to come from the Turks themselves and NATO, rather than just the United States."

A messenger came in and Robert Kennedy took the paper. "They say they shot down our U-2"—this was an announcement from Havana—"They say they shot it down. Then we're going to get shot at tomorrow."

"How are you doing, Bob?" the Attorney General asked McNamara as they all stood to leave.

"Well, hard to tell," said McNamara. "You have any doubts?"

"Well, I think we're doing the only thing we can do."

"We need to have two things ready," McNamara said, "a government for Cuba, because we're going to need one . . . and secondly, plans for how to respond to the Soviet Union in Europe, because sure as hell they're going to do something there."

"Suppose we make Bobby mayor of Havana?" someone called out.

It was not funny any more. The President was depressed. Just after midnight, he dictated identical letters to President de Gaulle in Paris and Chancellor Konrad Adenauer in Bonn: "The situation is clearly growing more tense and if satisfactory responses are not received from the other side in forty-eight hours, the situation is likely to enter a progressively military phase."

He was too tired to sleep. So he sat up for a while with Dave Powers. They watched a screening of one of Kennedy's favorite movies, *Roman Holiday,* with Audrey Hepburn and Gregory Peck.

The Ex Comm meeting the next morning, Sunday, October 28, was scheduled for 10:00 A.M. at the White House. Along the Atlantic coast, preparations were under way for the first air strikes against Cuba. They would begin at dawn on Tuesday, October 30.

In Moscow, *Pravda*'s lead headline that morning seemed ambiguous: "We Must Defend and Consolidate Peace on Earth."

A few minutes before nine o'clock that Sunday morning, as the President was reading *The New York Times* in bed before getting up to dress for church, Radio Moscow broadcast word that there would be an important announcement at 6:00 P.M. Moscow time, 9:00 A.M. in Washington. The U.S. government was cranking up its cable machines and code words, but the man in charge got the word just like any other American, by turning on the radio next to his bed and hearing an Associated Press bulletin interrupt the morning music. An announcer in Moscow came on at the hour and read a new letter from Khrushchev to Kennedy. The second paragraph said:

"In order to complete with greater speed the liquidation of the conflict dangerous to the cause of peace, to give confidence to all people longing for peace, and to calm the American people, who, I am certain, want peace as much as the people of the Soviet Union, the Soviet Government, in addition to previously issued instructions on the cessation of further work at building sites for the weapons, has issued a new order on the dismantling of the weapons which you describe as 'offensive,' and their crating and return to the Soviet Union."

Khrushchev ended by saying:

"I regard with respect and trust your statement in your message of October 27, 1962, that no attack will be made on Cuba—that no invasion will take place—not only by the United States, but also by other countries of the Western Hemisphere, as your message pointed out. Then the motives which prompted us to give aid of this nature to Cuba cease. . . . The Soviet Government has sent to New York USSR First Deputy Minister of Foreign Affairs Kuznetsov with a view to assisting

U Thant in his noble efforts aimed at liquidation of the present danger-ous situation."

The President quickly drafted a letter to Khrushchev broadcast by the Voice of America at noon in Washington: "I welcome Chairman Khrushchev's statesmanlike decision. . . . We shall be in touch with the Secretary General of the United Nations with respect to reciprocal mea-sures to assure peace in the Caribbean area."

It was over as quickly as that. By noon, the President was sitting with Pierre Salinger watching television, the CBS network's "Washington Report," where two correspondents, David Schoenbrun and Marvin Kalb, talked of "American victory."

"Tell them to stop that," Kennedy told Salinger.

The press secretary called CBS, and Schoenbrun picked up the tele-phone during a commercial break. "David, I'm speaking from the Oval Office," Salinger said. "The President is right next to me. Please do not let Kalb run on about a Soviet defeat. Do not play this up as a victory for us. There is a danger that Khrushchev will be so humiliated and angered that he will change his mind. Watch what you are saying. Do not mess this up for us."

The reporters did as they were told.

But that night, CBS News could not hold back. A two-hour special on the events of the past two weeks ended with correspondent Charles Collingwood saying: "The danger of war over Cuba seems to have ended with Premier Khrushchev's remarkable letter to Kennedy. More-over it has ended, if it has ended, on our terms—which can only be read as a humiliating defeat for Soviet policy. . . . If the exchange between the President and the Premier can be taken at its face value, there is a possibility that the Cuban crisis may mark something more than just a challenge and retreat in the Cold War, but a genuine turning point in modern history. . . ."

So, life went on. Another voice continued: "This CBS News Special Report, 'The Anatomy of a Crisis,' has been brought to you by the makers of Geritol, the high-potency vitamin, iron-rich tonic, to help you feel stronger."

In Moscow, where people knew far less about the days of missile-rattling than Americans watching CBS, it was already Monday morning. *Pravda's* lead headline was: "We Must Ensure the Peace and Security of All Peoples."

At higher levels, Soviet leaders knew their public backdown meant the end of Nikita Khrushchev's wild and brilliant bluff, the rattling of missiles and might the Soviets never really had. "You got away with it this time, but you will never get away with it again," the deputy foreign minister of the Soviet Union, Vasily Kuznetsov, told John McCloy—meaning that the Soviets would put everything they had into trying to achieve a more convincing military parity with the United States.

"May I congratulate you on your leadership, firmness and judgment over the past tough week," Dean Acheson wrote to the President. "We have not had these qualities at the helm in this country at all times. It is good to have them again. . . ."

In the privacy of his own home, though, the former Secretary of State was calling the strategy a reckless gamble. "Plain dumb luck," he said of Kennedy's triumph.

A few days later, President Kennedy invited the Joint Chiefs of Staff over to his office to thank them personally for their role in the crisis. General Curtis LeMay looked at his Commander-in-Chief and said there was no reason for thanks. "We lost! We ought to just go in there today and knock 'em off!"

The next week, in *Time* magazine, Kennedy read that the reality of his presidency had caught up with his rhetoric—at least the world finally believed the Americans meant what their leader was saying militarily. *Time* reported a conversation in Bonn between Andrei Smirnov, the Soviet Ambassador to West Germany, and Franz Krapf, head of the West German Foreign Office's Eastern section:

"Now, Herr Krapf, as objective diplomats we must admit that American rocket bases in Britain, Italy and Turkey are legally and morally the same as the ones we are dismantling in Cuba, mustn't we?"

"I admit no such thing," Krapf said. "It seems to me they are entirely different."

"Well, you must admit that Chairman Khrushchev acted in a very statesmanlike manner."

"One hopes he will continue to do so," said the German. "One hopes further that after Cuba he will not make the mistake committed by two German governments and hold the illusion that Americans won't fight."

Many illusions were shattered in those two tense weeks, but a significant reality emerged, too. At least two men, the two at the center—Nikita Khrushchev and John Kennedy—realized that no politician in his right mind was going to use nuclear weapons first. The price was too high; the judgment of history would be too severe. On Sunday afternoon, after the Soviet announcement that the missiles would be withdrawn, Kennedy sat down and wrote to Khrushchev again: "I think that you and I, with our heavy responsibilities for the maintenance of peace, were aware that developments were approaching a point where events could have become unmanageable. . . ."

Chapter 37

"This is the night I should go to the theater," John Kennedy said to Robert Kennedy on Sunday night, October 28. It was a bad joke that referred to conversations the brothers had about history and its reverence for Abraham Lincoln, assassinated at Ford's Theater after the Union victory in the Civil War. He thought the resolution of the missile crisis might be the peak of his political life.

After it was over, Kennedy called Tiffany's, the New York jeweler, to make up small Lucite calendars showing the month of October 1962, with the thirteen dates of October 16 to October 28 engraved more deeply than the other days. He wanted to give one to each of the thirty men who had sat on Ex Comm, with their initials in one corner and his, JFK, in another. Walter Hoving, the president of Tiffany's, called back and said he would pick up the cost, but didn't the President think silver might be more appropriate than plastic? Silver it was for Kennedy's men, and for two women, Jacqueline Kennedy and Evelyn Lincoln.

The United States' sense of triumph in Cuba was a new making of the President in more ways than one. The American will, the American nuclear deterrent, and the American President were more credible around the world. At home, Kennedy's personal approval rating, which had been 66 percent in the August Gallup Poll, rose to 77 percent after the Soviets began dismantling the missiles of October.

Khrushchev was also able to claim victory, saying he had saved Cuba from imminent U.S. invasion. On October 30, in a long and very personal letter to Kennedy, the premier said: "To our mutual satisfaction, we may have even sacrificed self-esteem. Apparently there will be scribblers who will engage in hair-splitting over our agreement, will be digging as to who made greater concessions to whom. As for me, I would say that we both made a concession to reason and found a reasonable solution which enabled us to ensure peace for all including those who will be trying to dig up something."

The day before, Kennedy had twice called in his most talented scrivener, the house historian, Arthur Schlesinger, Jr., to put his version of what had happened on the record. The crisis over, the press was already second-guessing the President, analyzing his use of news and newsmen. "The administration's management of the news after the Cuban crisis was more disturbing to people than the controls exercised during the crisis itself," wrote Ted Lewis of *The New York Daily News*. But Kennedy was already moving on to try to control the history, giving those thirteen days an order that rationalized his own decisions. At the first Ex Comm meeting after Khrushchev's withdrawal announcement, Kennedy told all the members they were not to speak to the press without his specific approval. All inquiries were to be directed to Bundy, Sorensen, and Salinger.

Schlesinger's notes that day recorded the President's version of the events of October this way:

He told me he thought it odd that our intelligence community hadn't anticipated the Soviet move earlier. Of course, one reason they hadn't is that they didn't believe Khrushchev would be so stupid as to do something which as much as invited an invasion. The President thought that the Soviet Union had done it for three reasons: that it would help bring Russia and China together; that it would radically redefine the setting in which the Berlin issue would be reopened after the election; and that it would deal the United States a tremendous political blow. . . . The President said they had us either way. If we did nothing, we were dead. If we reacted, they hoped to have us in an embarrassed and exposed position, whether with regard to Berlin or Turkey or the U.N.

Our policy had worked, he said, for three reasons. First, we had overwhelming local conventional superiority; second, no vital Soviet interests were at stake in Cuba, so that they could afford to back down if they had to; and third, they did not have a case that they could plausibly sustain before the world. It was because of these factors that our policy worked —not just because we were tough. . . . He worried that people would take the wrong lessons away from the crisis.

The National Security Council, with all its members meeting that same day without the President, had their own version of what had happened. They did in fact cite toughness, recording these minutes: "If we have learned anything from this experience, it is that weakness, even only apparent weakness, invites Soviet transgression. At the same time, firmness in the last analysis will force the Soviets to back away from rash initiatives."

There had been a noticeable closeness between Kennedy and his wife during the crisis. They had canceled several events, public and private, during those two weeks, spending time alone together and with their children. But early in November, a number of newspaper stories on the Kennedy family revealed the fact that the President had been donating his salary to charity since he entered Congress in 1947. His $100,000 salary as President was being divided, after taxes, among two dozen charities, including the Boy Scouts and Girl Scouts of America, the United Negro College Fund, and the Federation of Jewish Philanthropies. The schedule of contributions was worked out each year during a short money meeting Kennedy had with a family accountant named Thomas Walsh.

"Well, are we making money? Am I living within my income, or am I digging into my capital?" Kennedy would ask.

"You're doing all right," Walsh answered each year.

That was it, until Mrs. Kennedy found out. She confronted her husband, saying they could use the money that was going to charity, particularly since they were building a new $70,000 seven-bedroom home near Middleburg in Virginia on a hill called Rattlesnake Mountain. The property, thirty-nine acres spread between two hunt clubs, the Piedmont Fox Hounds and the Orange County Hunt, had cost another $26,000. Kennedy was so annoyed with his wife's questions that he had Tom Walsh send him a more detailed accounting of his family finances. He was carrying around a letter reporting that he was living off principal, even after putting his valet and his wife's personal maid on the government payroll. One item made him particularly crazy: "Department Stores . . . $40,000."

"What about this?" he asked one evening in the White House, in front of Ben Bradlee and his wife. Jacqueline Kennedy said she did not know anything about it, that it was not as if she had a sable coat or anything like that. Adlai Stevenson called from the United Nations that same night, continuing negotiations to get Russian IL-28 bombers out of Cuba, and as the President talked to his U.N. ambassador, his angry wife turned up the volume of her record player to drown out affairs of state.

On November 6, Election Day, the President flew to Boston to cast his ballot for his brother at the police station near the sloppy one-bedroom apartment on Bowdoin Street that had been his official residence on voting records since 1946. He was one of 53,734,985 Americans to come out that day, just about 65 percent of those eligible. He stayed at the Sheraton Plaza Hotel in the city, taking time to visit with his father in Hyannis Port and with his grandmother, Mrs. John F. Fitzgerald, widow of the mayor of Boston, known as "Honey Fitz."

The Democrats won twenty-five of the thirty-nine U.S. Senate seats up for election that Tuesday, electing six new senators while losing two old ones, a net gain of four. That gave the President's party sixty-two of the one hundred senators, including Edward Kennedy, who won with 57 percent of the vote over his Republican opponent, George Cabot Lodge, the thirty-five-year-old son of Henry Cabot Lodge, the Republican John Kennedy had defeated for the Senate in 1952. In the House of Representatives, the Democrats lost four seats—fewer than the usual drop-off for the presidential party in midterm elections—leaving them with a 259–175 margin in the House. The day's losers included Senator Homer Capehart of Indiana, defeated by just 6,000 votes by thirty-four-year-old Birch Bayh; and former Vice President Richard Nixon, defeated by almost 300,000 votes for governor of California by the incumbent Democrat, Edmund ("Pat") Brown.

The midterm election was no landslide. The Democrats won 52.7 percent of the overall vote, compared with 56.3 percent in the 1958 midterm election and 55 percent of the congressional total in 1960. The turnout was high, 5.8 million voters more than in 1958, but 4.2 million of the new voters cast their ballots for Republicans. The crisis in Cuba —"Cuba II," as it was called in the White House—had obviously helped the Democrats. But there were some in the party who sensed longer-term trends moving against the President's party, a backlash against civil rights in the South, and some fading of the power of big-city political bosses and labor leaders in the North, as working-class families moved to the greener fields of suburbs that traditionally voted Republican.

The results did not change very much in Washington's balance of power. Pre-election polls showed most Democratic candidates losing votes toward the end. If the world had just been saved from nuclear annihilation, the American survivors quickly returned to the politics of wages and taxes—and to uneasy talk of the Negro agitation in the South. "This Congress is so evenly balanced and the change of one or two seats one way or the other can make all the difference," Kennedy had said during the midterm campaign. "All these things are won by one or two votes in the Congress. If you want them, elect a man who'll provide another vote."

"All these things" were his legislative agenda: medical programs for senior citizens, aid for the cities and for education—and civil defense. During the 87th Congress, Kennedy's first two years, the White House had proposed 653 pieces of legislation—about double the Eisenhower rate—and almost half of them, 304 bills, became laws, passed by both houses of Congress and signed by the President. But, domestically, it was not the important half. His proposals for Medicare, for a new Department of Urban Affairs, for increased federal aid to higher education, for mass transit aid, were all defeated. Kennedy's incentive programs for the building of fallout shelters were never even scheduled for hearings in either House, and he had made no attempt to introduce his tax-cut ideas as legislation.

The President did have one significant victory in Congress: passage on October 11 of the Trade Expansion Act of 1962, a controversial piece of legislation he had first introduced as a senator. It gave the President authority to reduce tariffs by as much as 50 percent to promote foreign trade (100 percent in trade with the European Common Market) and also gave him some power to compensate American workers who might lose their jobs if American manufacturers were hurt by competition from Europe and Japan. This seemed unlikely, except in steel, and a few low-technology businesses such as textiles and toys and leather goods.

Kennedy had won on that one by emphasizing the growing competitiveness of products and goods from Western Europe. The United States, in total, was buying more than it was selling to other countries, running an international trade deficit of about $5 billion a year by the end of 1962, giving foreign suppliers and governments the power to claim their debts in the gold backing U.S. dollars.

"The gold drain" was theoretical because none of those countries were actually taking the gold stored in Fort Knox, Kentucky. But Kennedy accepted it as a valid measure of a comparative economic decline. The United States, with by far the greatest domestic market in the world, exported only 4 percent of its gross national product of $540 billion, compared with up to 40 percent for European countries and Japan. Some American businessmen were complaining about Japanese business tactics, to the point that Kennedy had sent Secretary of Commerce Luther Hodges to Tokyo to complain about Japanese "targeting" of American markets and "dumping" of textiles, selling them in the United States at less than the cost of making them. But the President was not so concerned about trade itself. It was hard to imagine that the United

States would ever be spending significant amounts of dollars for foreign goods. What concerned him most were the domestic political effects of unemployment, in Southern textile plants and the shoe factories of New England, for instance. Business was really the business of Republicans, most Democrats thought, and once again, the President turned to the opposition, appointing Eisenhower's last Secretary of State, Christian Herter, to handle the new trade negotiations with the member countries of the Common Market.

"I know everyone thinks I worry about this too much," he said to Sorensen, when the speechwriter asked him if he really thought the United States could lose its gold reserves because more dollars were going overseas—mainly because of the presence of U.S. troops and their dependents around the world—than foreign currencies were being spent in the United States. "But if there's ever a run on the bank, and I have to devalue the dollar or bring home our troops, as the British did, I'm the one who will take the heat. Besides, it's a club that de Gaulle and all the others hang over my head. Any time there's a crisis or a quarrel, they can cash in all their dollars and where are we?"

On the floor of the House and the Senate, the President was actually winning on almost nine out of ten of his proposals, but more often than not his legislation was not making it to the floor. The real action was still in committees chaired by Southern Democrats—half the Kennedy proposals died right there. Some of that was his own fault, a matter of personal style. There was only so much time he was willing to spend with, or even think about, his old colleagues.

Conservative Southern Democrats routinely joined with Republicans in committee to block Kennedy's liberal domestic agenda. The white Southern voters who had sent them to Washington to contain Northern Democrats and their social (or socialist) scheming were also showing more inclination to vote Republican. In the eleven states of the old Confederacy, the Republicans had not put up serious candidates since the Reconstruction period after the Civil War. But, in 1962, Republicans won four new House seats and 31 percent of the total House vote in the South, almost double their 1958 midterm total of 16 percent. In Georgia, Republican candidates ran for Congress for the first time in decades, and won 18 percent of the vote. In Alabama, they attacked Democrats as "Kennedy men" and "liberals" and went from 2.5 percent in 1958 to 29 percent. A Republican businessman named James Martin carried Birmingham and polled more than 49 percent of the statewide vote for the U.S. Senate, losing by only 6,000 votes to the Democratic incumbent, Senator Lister Hill.

In *The New York Herald Tribune,* a paper identified with Northern

Republicanism, columnist Roscoe Drummond wrote: "Beneath the troubled waters of the Democratic Party in the South there is a floating Republican iceberg of unknown size. Enough of it is showing to suggest that it can become a very formidable force. If it keeps growing, the effects will be far reaching. It could render President Kennedy's re-election exceedingly difficult."

This was the new politics of race. Kennedy was the Democratic President who had been so solicitous of Martin Luther King, Jr., during the 1960 campaign, and had sent the U.S. Army into Mississippi so that one Negro could go to the state university. Also, Negro unrest and white fear were moving north. The President read an election-week item in *U.S. News & World Report*: "A story is told that indicates how the civil-rights issue tends to work in practical politics: In a section of a large city having a heavy concentration of Polish descent, a new church has been built costing 1 million dollars, with $700,000 still owed. Now Negroes show signs of moving in and the fear is that, if they move in, white residents will start moving out of the area and the church will be in trouble."

The city was Detroit, part of it represented in the House by Martha Griffiths, the congresswoman who had urged Kennedy not to sign any housing order before the election. Two weeks after the elections, on November 20, two years after promising to do so, he did finally sign Executive Order 11063, announcing at a news conference: "I have today . . . directed Federal departments and agencies to take every proper and legal action to prevent discrimination (on the basis of race, color, creed or national origin) in the sale or lease of housing facilities owned or operated by the Federal government; housing constructed or sold as a result of loans or grants made by the Federal government or by loans to be insured by the Federal government. . . ."

Eleanor Roosevelt died the day after the 1962 election. The widow of Franklin Delano Roosevelt had remained immune to Kennedy's charm. Adlai Stevenson was her man, a protégé, really. She had left the 1960 Democratic National Convention in tears when John Kennedy won the nomination. He was, to her, just Joe Kennedy's overreaching son, an arrogant young man who would not wait his turn. She had gone straight to the airport in Los Angeles, trying to get back to New York as soon as possible. Kennedy had attempted to reach her by telephone at the airport, but she had refused to take the call. He had courted her as best he could during the presidential campaign, promising to consult Stevenson and Chester Bowles, her favorites. But she had refused to sit on the inaugural platform with Kennedy and his family, wrapping herself in a mink coat and an Army blanket in the crowd below the stand.

He took her advice, when she offered it, with a professional smile. "I listened during a rather long drive which I took, to your last press conference and decided that it did not take the place of fireside chats," Mrs. Roosevelt had written to him not long before she died. "I wish you could get someone like my old teacher to help you deepen and strengthen your voice on radio and TV. It would give you more warmth and personality in your voice. It can be learned. . . ."

"It's difficult to change nature, but I will attempt to nudge it," Kennedy wrote back.

President Kennedy used Mrs. Roosevelt only once, appointing her as chairwoman of a Presidential Commission on the Status of Women, created at the end of 1961. The commission's charge was to evaluate the impact of the fact that women had not really returned to home and hearth after taking over men's jobs during World War II. Forty percent of women over the age of sixteen were working, and a third of those working women had children. Republicans and professional women's organizations were energetically advocating an Equal Rights Amendment to the U.S. Constitution guaranteeing female workers the same rights as male counterparts. Liberal Democrats and organized labor both opposed the idea. Kennedy hoped Mrs. Roosevelt's name might be able to push off consideration of equal pay, as opposed to equal rights, legislation that was moving through Congress—delay it at least until after the 1964 election.

Eleanor Roosevelt's funeral was held on November 10, 1962, at Hyde Park, the Roosevelt family seat on a ridge overlooking the Hudson River eighty-five miles north of New York City. The Roosevelts had settled there in 1819, not so long after the Revolution, and Anna Eleanor Roosevelt, a niece of the twenty-sixth President, Theodore Roosevelt, had come there as a bride in 1905. The funeral was for all practical purposes a state occasion, a gathering of political clans. There were three presidents there to honor her: Kennedy, Eisenhower, and Truman. They were seated by party inside St. James's Protestant Episcopal Church. Kennedy, Truman, and Vice President Johnson sat on one side of the aisle; Eisenhower, New York Governor Nelson Rockefeller, and Chief Justice Earl Warren, a former Republican governor of California, were on the other side.

"What do you think I should do about a tax cut?" Kennedy asked Senator Albert Gore in the living room of Eleanor's son John Roosevelt's house after the service.

"Forget it!" said the man from Tennessee.

"But," the President said, "we must have booming times by 1964." His reelection year.

The Washington contingent had flown in two planes to Stewart Air Force Base in Newburgh, New York, the first time the President had used his new fifty-seven-passenger Air Force One, an updated Boeing 707 fan-jet with a range of 7,000 miles. As they were about to take off for the trip back, Kennedy sent a messenger over to the second plane to get Gore. "Will my honorable colleagues excuse me?" the senator asked, bowing as his colleagues joked about his elevation to the presidential party so that he and the President could continue their long-running economic arguments.

"Once taxes are cut, they are not likely to be reimposed," said Gore. The cut would kill exactly the kind of social programs Franklin Roosevelt created. "Congress will always be ready to cut taxes, never ready to raise them. It is a beautiful economic theory about moving taxes up and down, but it is only a theory, utterly impractical in our system. It just won't work!"

"I wish you could talk to Walter Heller," said Kennedy.

"Well, I'll be glad to," said the senator, who found himself on the same side of this argument as Treasury Secretary Dillon, his personal idea of the worst kind of Wall Street Republican. For different reasons, Dillon wanted tax reform before tax cuts, dreaming of eliminating thousands of old rules, incentives and penalties to guide the conduct of American business—replacing them with new ones designed to free up the free enterprise system. "But Walter can talk with equal facility on either side," said Gore of Heller.

"Then listen to him on my side," Kennedy replied.

They were never going to agree. Gore's father was a farmer who went broke and lost his land to the bankers; only big government and big taxes could save men like that. Kennedy's father was a rich man, a financial pirate; the kind of government Gore wanted sometimes put men like that in jail.

As soon as the plane was in the air, Kennedy left his private compartment in the back to prowl the forward passenger section, filled with officials and reporters. He saw Mary McGrory of the *Washington Star* and said: "That was a nice story you wrote about Nixon."

"Thank you, Mr. President," she said. It was obvious to everyone else around, all in danger of falling out of their seats as they leaned out trying to hear his every word, that Kennedy was absolutely delighted that his old rival had blown his top in a post-election press conference. "Now that all the members of the press are so delighted that I have lost," the former Vice President had said to a couple of dozen stunned reporters, "just think how much you're going to be missing. You won't have Nixon to kick around any more, because, gentlemen, this is my last press conference. . . ."

"Unlike some people," Nixon added, in a final dart at Kennedy, "I've never cancelled a subscription to a paper. . . ."

The subscription canceler was grinning and laughing. "I must remember to smile when I get defeated," Kennedy said to McGrory loudly enough for all to hear.

Earl Warren, who disliked his fellow California Republican more than Kennedy did, was sitting alone further up front and he beckoned to Kennedy. He pulled a pile of newspaper clippings from his pocket, all accounts of Nixon's bizarre exit. The President of the United States and the Chief Justice of the United States Supreme Court sat there reading the clips to each other, laughing all the time like a couple of schoolboys.

So Nixon, it seemed, was dead, a political suicide. But he was never the Republican Kennedy most feared as a head-to-head opponent. Nelson Rockefeller was on the cover of the current issue of *Newsweek*, and Bradlee, the magazine's Washington bureau chief, told the President that the New York governor had denied he had ever said he would have beaten Kennedy in 1960, and could do it in 1964.

"Nobody ever had any doubt he could beat me in 1960. I knew that," Kennedy said. But 1964 would be a different story, even though Rockefeller had just won reelection in New York by a half million votes, despite a very messy divorce. Kennedy had already asked Ted Sorensen to have the Justice Department do some checking into the activities of the Rockefeller Foundation and other family enterprises. At the Army-Navy Football Game, on November 26 in Philadelphia, Kennedy sat with Roswell Gilpatric, who had known Nelson Rockefeller and his brothers since they were all children. Kennedy did what he always did with Gilpatric: he questioned him about Rockefeller—about the family, their homes, the foundations, their wives, their children, their hobbies. What about Rocky's girlfriends? There were a lot of them, Gilpatric said.

"How does he get away with it?" asked Kennedy, pressing for details.

Chapter 38

On December 16, 1962, President Kennedy sat in his rocking chair, which was on blocks so it could not move, and answered questions from three television correspondents in the Oval Office for an hour and thirty-five minutes. The session was edited down to one hour and shown the next night on all three networks—CBS, NBC, and ABC—with the title "After Two Years—A Conversation with the President."

It was the President himself who insisted on shooting longer than what would be broadcast. George Herman, the CBS correspondent who supervised the cutting of the film, realized why in the editing room. When Kennedy did not like the wording or the thrust of a question, he gave long and rambling, dull, answers, because he knew those questions would be the first ones on the cutting-room floor, making the final version more to his liking.

And he did like what he saw; so did most everyone else. The *Reporter* magazine called it "Perfect"—the coming of age of television, and of a President. Watching at home, Ben Bradlee thought he saw the future and he did not much like it. Newspapers and magazines could not match this—it was human, serious, and humorous at the same time. He called the President to congratulate him, and Kennedy said: "Well, I always said that when we don't have to go through you bastards, we can really get our story over to the American people."

Television was still a studio medium when Kennedy ran in 1960;

almost everything had come from a few old warehouses and theaters crammed with hot, bright lights and walls of switches. Candidate Kennedy had learned to use all of that, gaining greatly in the most famous of live studio encounters, his campaign debates with Richard Nixon. But the great struggle in those studios and on the campaign trail then was not between candidates; it was the war between the old and the new, print journalism versus television news. In 1960, most newspapers refused to print the speedy election returns fed into the studios of the first two television networks, NBC and CBS, sticking doggedly with the totals of their old supplier, the Associated Press. In 1961, the White House Correspondents Association voted against accepting television reporters as members, deciding that they were not true journalists.

John F. Kennedy was not a television President; he was the President when television established itself as the new American environment—more like the weather than a communications medium. His presidency was at the end of politics' Industrial Age, recorded by black and white photographs, typewriters, carbon paper, and mimeograph machines. Television news was fifteen minutes of headlines read from studios in New York. But the torch was being passed to a new technological generation. Sandor Vanocur, a reporter for *The New York Times*, was thought odd by colleagues when he left the newspaper to become the White House correspondent of NBC News. He was sure he had made the right career decision only when, having disagreed with Kennedy one day about the impact of a particular program, the President called to his secretary: "Mrs. Lincoln! Give me those Nielsens from last week. They were in *Variety*."

William Lawrence of ABC, another former *Times* man, asked the first question on December 16: "As you look back upon your first two years in office, sir, has your experience in the office matched your expectations?"

"Well, I think in the first place the problems are more difficult than I had imagined they were," Kennedy answered. "The responsibilities placed on the United States are greater than I imagined them to be, and there are greater limitations upon our ability to bring about a favorable result than I had imagined them to be. And I think that is probably true of anyone who becomes President, because there is such a difference between those who advise or speak or legislate, and between the man who must select from the various alternatives proposed and say that this shall be the policy of the United States. It is much easier to make the speeches than it is to finally make the judgments, because unfortunately your advisers are frequently divided. If you take the wrong course, and on occasion I have, the President bears the burden of the responsibility quite rightly. The advisers may move on to new advice."

He ended the edited hour by saying: "But I must say after being here for two years, and having the experience of the Presidency, and there is no experience you can get that can possibly prepare you adequately for the Presidency, I must say that I have a good deal of hope for the United States. . . . One hundred and eighty million people, for seventeen years, really for more than that, for almost twenty years, have been the great means of defending first the world against the Nazi threat, and since then against the Communist threat, and if it were not for us, the Communists would be dominant in the world today. . . . I think that is a pretty good record for a country with six percent of the world's population. I think we ought to be rather pleased with ourselves this Christmas."

The President watched himself in Palm Beach on December 17, then flew the next day to Nassau in the Bahamas for two days of meetings with Harold Macmillan. The prime minister had been waiting through the Cuban crisis until it was his turn for American attention—to the point that his own government was in danger of falling. Macmillan, proud of his own "special relationship" with Kennedy, was embarrassed when it became obvious that the United States had consulted no allies before making its moves in Cuba. Then he had been humiliated when Defense Secretary McNamara recommended canceling the production of the self-guided air-to-ground missile called Skybolt.

In 1960, Eisenhower had approved the development of the weapon, which was designed to be carried under the wings of strategic bombers. The cost of the program was $2.5 billion for fifteen hundred copies, one thousand for the U.S. Air Force and five hundred for the Royal Air Force. The British had their own nuclear warheads, but could not afford to develop surface-to-surface missiles. But Skybolt would give them the independent nuclear force delivery system they needed to maintain their status as a principal global player. It was supposed to be state-of-the-art, top-of-the-line. The problem was that after $500 million worth of research and development, Skybolt did not work. The Air Force had nothing to show but five failed test shots. McNamara wanted to scrap the whole thing, saving $2 billion.

The unilateral decision amounted to an attempt on Macmillan's political life because the prime minister's survival depended on maintaining the polite and politic fiction that the United States and Great Britain were equal partners. The *Sunday Telegraph* in London, speculating that Macmillan was close to losing a no-confidence vote in Parliament, caricatured the "special relationship" with a paraphrasing of an old Christmas song: "On the umpteenth day near Christmas, the U.S. sent to me —12 Reappraisals, 11 Compromises, 10 Tactless statements, 9 Faint denials, 8 Fervent clichés, 7 Goodwill gestures, 6 Big bland smiles, 5 Unprintable things, 4 apologies, 3 sick jokes, 2 words of cheer, and a De-Fence Secret-tary."

After he taped the year-end television interview, Kennedy sat down with McNamara, Bundy, the U.S. Ambassador to Great Britain, David Bruce, and Undersecretary of State George Ball to work out a position before he met the next day with Macmillan in the Bahamas. Bruce argued the British case, which was simple: the trustworthiness of U.S. promises and Macmillan's survival. Ball, sitting in for Rusk, was a Francophile and he could not resist arguing that favoring the British would confirm everything President de Gaulle and other European leaders believed about "Anglo-Saxon" unity at the expense of the continental European countries. He turned to Kennedy and said that he must be careful about helping Macmillan, this could be the most important decision of his presidency.

"That we get every week, George," Kennedy responded with a smile that was certainly sardonic. He decided that he would have to offer Macmillan Polaris missiles for British submarines—and he would do the same for de Gaulle.

But it was not the same. The British had warheads to put on the missiles, but France, which had tested its first atomic bomb in February 1960, did not yet have the capability to produce nuclear warheads. De Gaulle rejected the Polaris offer. The grand Frenchman was already convinced more than ever, by the unilateral U.S. action during the Cuban crisis, that France and Europe could not count on the Anglo-Saxons to defend them against the Soviets.

On December 19, while he was with Macmillan in Nassau, the Bahamas, Kennedy received an encouraging letter from Khrushchev, who said: "The period of maximum crisis and tension in the Caribbean is behind us. We are now free to consider other international matters, in particular a subject which has long been ripe for action—the cessation of nuclear tests. . . . It seems to me, Mr. President, that the time has come now to put an end once and for all to nuclear tests, to draw a line through such tests. . . ."

The premier and the President had been moving toward this within hours of the end of the Cuban confrontation. On October 30, Khrushchev had written: "Mr. President, conditions are ripe for finalizing a treaty on cessation of tests of nuclear weapons in three environments" —the atmosphere, outer space, and underwater. Kennedy had responded then by calling in Norman Cousins, an anti-nuclear activist who was editor of the *Saturday Review,* when he read that Cousins was traveling to Moscow as a private negotiator for Pope John XXIII, who hoped to persuade the Soviets to release Roman Catholic priests interned in Eastern Europe.

"I don't know if the matter of American-Soviet relationships will come up," the President told Cousins. "But if it does, Khrushchev will probably say something about his desire to reduce tensions, but will make it appear that there's no reciprocal interest by the United States. It is important that he be corrected on this score. I'm not sure Khrushchev knows this, but I don't think there's any man in American politics who's more eager than I am to put Cold War animosities behind us and get down to the hard business of building friendly relations. Just get across one point. The point that there's no one in either party more anxious to get an agreement on arms control than I am."

That, it turned out, was what Khrushchev had been wanting to hear —and his answer was what Kennedy had wanted to hear.

"One thing the President and I should do, right away, is to conclude a treaty outlawing testing of nuclear weapons," Khrushchev told Cousins. "And then we can start work on the problem of keeping those weapons from spreading all over the world. It is not true that I am against inspection. I keep seeing newspaper stories in the United States that the Soviet Union is opposed to inspection as part of any test ban. This is not true. If the United States wants reasonable inspection, it may have it. . . . We see no reason why it shouldn't be possible for both our countries to agree on the kind of inspection that will satisfy you that we're not cheating and that will satisfy us that you're not spying."

Just before Christmas, greatly encouraged by the latest Khrushchev letter and glad to have Skybolt behind him, the President flew from Nassau to Palm Beach for the holidays, bringing along the British ambassador, David Ormsby-Gore. The two men, friends since they had met in London as teenagers, were sitting by the pool at Joseph Kennedy's house when the phone rang and the President learned that McNamara had just announced a successful Skybolt test, even though the weapon had been canceled by his own orders.

"Jesus Christ!" Kennedy shouted. "Is he crazy? Why would he do that after all this?" Kennedy could not find his Defense Secretary, who was climbing a mountain somewhere out west. Ormsby-Gore recorded the scene in his diary: "We were sitting by the pool at Palm Beach behind his house ready to have a swim when the crisis burst. He was having a manicure. . . . This wonderful sunny scene beside the pool— and suddenly this vast explosion and this violent language going out via telephone while the wretched manicurist went on cutting his nails. . . ."

Calming down, Kennedy began horsing around with his son, John Junior, who was two years old. The boy was getting out of the pool and the father pulled his trunks down below his little buttocks and pushed him gently back in.

"Naughty Daddy," said the boy, nicknamed John-John. His father did it again.

"Daddy, you are a Pooh-Pooh Head," said the boy.

"John Kennedy, how dare you call the President of the United States a Pooh-Pooh Head? You rascal, you wait till I get hold of you."

That night, while their father was at dinner with friends, John and his sister Caroline came into the dining room to say goodnight. After he walked around the table, John-John stood in the doorway and called to his father: "Pooh-Pooh Head!"

Cabinet members and other officials were coming down to Palm Beach one by one, or in small groups. Working holidays at Palm Beach had already become the oldest tradition of the New Frontier, and this time the President was taking two weeks in the sun, planning to stay until January 8.

The first round of visitors came to talk about money. Containing communism was an expensive business. When Douglas Dillon talked to him about the bill for Cuba II, Kennedy went into a litany of frustration: "The percentage of our budget which is spent for defense, and you add atomic energy and space, is, what, 59 percent or something? . . . The percentage of France, Germany, and Great Britain's . . . the Germans are 28 or 29 percent, and they're cutting back because they want to balance their budget. . . . Either they're going to have to do something or we're going to have to just try to cut it down."

The time had come, too, to keep his August promise of income tax reduction and reform. Walter Heller came to Palm Beach for questioning by the President. "What's going to be in that package?" Kennedy asked.

"We haven't got it all worked out yet," said Heller. This was six months after the first public announcements that cuts and other reforms would be announced in January 1963, but the President did not seem concerned. He was ready to move on now—to get this country moving again, he hoped—and Heller wondered whether he understood the controversy he was going to face when he announced that he wanted to cut taxes at the same time he was increasing government spending.

Next came the budget director, David Bell, and when the subject of the next foreign aid budget came up, the President told him to stop using words like "aid" and "assistance." Use "International Security" instead of "aid" and "assistance." Use "International Security" instead of "International Development," Kennedy said. "Strengthen the security of the Free World" was a phrase he liked, he told Bell—because Americans did not like the idea of foreign aid, but were willing to pay for almost anything that sounded like anti-communism.

Dean Rusk came down to Palm Beach a couple of times. On one of his visits, he was greeted at the door by Caroline. "Hello, Mr. Secretary," the five-year-old said. "I am very worried about the war in the Yemen. Please tell me what is happening in the Yemen today."

"Well," Rusk began, thinking she sounded just like her father, "I think that. . . . " Then he heard her father laughing from behind a screen.

Mike Mansfield, the Senate Majority Leader, came down to Palm Beach just before New Year's Eve, to talk with the President about Vietnam. He was taken aback a bit by the rather glamorous scene around the pool. Kennedy was trading wraparound sunglasses with a striking young woman who seemed to be Mexican. This wasn't Montana.

"Let's talk alone," Kennedy said, and the two of them left the pool crowd for a two-hour cruise on Lake Worth. The senator had been in Southeast Asia many times, beginning when he was an intelligence officer in World War II, and was an old friend and backer of Ngo Dinh Diem. He was just back from a tour of South Vietnam with members of the Senate Foreign Relations Committee—a mission Kennedy had asked him to organize.

Mansfield, it seemed, might be becoming a "dove" on Vietnam. The word, along with "hawk," became fashionable when Charles Bartlett and Stewart Alsop used both in a *Saturday Evening Post* article to describe the players in the air strike versus quarantine debate in Ex Comm during the Cuban crisis.

It was immediately obvious that the President had read every word of Mansfield's report—and was very disturbed by it.

"There is a great danger of the corruption of unbridled power," Mansfield had written of Diem's rule. The president of South Vietnam was patriotic, hardworking, and personally incorruptible, but he was tired, and the problems were becoming more complex. Power was slipping to his brother Ngo Dinh Nhu, who was more intellectual and more manipulative but had no public following. "Our planning appears to be predicated on the assumption that existing internal problems in South Vietnam will remain about the same and can be overcome by greater effort and better techniques. But what if the problems do not remain the same? . . . Possible change includes a step-up in the infiltration of cadres and supplies . . . includes the use of part or all of the regular armed forces of North Vietnam. . . . If these remedies do not work, it is difficult to conceive of alternatives, with the possible exception of a truly massive commitment of American military personnel and other resources—in short going to war fully ourselves against the guerrillas—and the establishment of some form of neocolonial rule in South Vietnam."

Kennedy's neck and face were getting redder and redder as Mansfield repeated his analysis. "You expect me to believe this?" he said.

"Yes, you sent me."

"This isn't what my people are telling me," the President said.

"Well . . . ," said Mansfield. He made the point that if we thought defending South Vietnam was essential to U.S. national security, we had better be prepared to match every escalation by the other side—and they were going to put in their lives and all their resources.

What the President was hearing from his people, more often than not, were contradictions—not only contradicting what he had just heard from Mansfield but internal contradictions about the U.S. involvement itself in report after report. The President knew the details of the effort in Vietnam—he was personally reviewing and approving air and land targets in actions more and more openly involving American personnel—but he could not choose between optimistic Defense Department data and pessimistic counterinformation from the State Department and the missions he was sending out every month or so.

There were 11,500 American military men in Vietnam at the end of 1962—almost 9,000 more men than the 2,646 in there at the beginning of the year. One hundred and nine Americans were killed or wounded in the country during the year, compared with fourteen in 1961.

When the President cited numbers, Mansfield told him to beware of them, which meant beware of McNamara. Kennedy with a penchant for facts and McNamara with a passion for data made quite a team. A reporter asked McNamara how many major decisions he had made the month before and an answer came back precisely: 629. The CIA was also trying to undermine McNamara, using some of his own numbers, issuing a year-end National Intelligence Estimate that reported:

"Various statistics indicate government progress against the Viet Cong during 1962, but these can be misleading. . . . Viet Cong casualties during 1962 were reported at more than 30,000 including some 21,000 killed in action. Yet current Viet Cong strength is estimated at 22,000–24,000 regulars, as opposed to 17,600 last June. This suggests either the casualty figures are exaggerated or that the Viet Cong have a remarkable replacement capability—or both."

A State Department appraisal, written by Roger Hilsman in mid-December, had begun: "Diem and other leading Vietnamese officials as well as many US officials in South Vietnam apparently believe that the tide is now turning in the struggle against Vietnamese Communist [Viet

Cong] insurgency and subversion. This degree of optimism is premature. At best, it appears that the rate of deterioration has decelerated. . . ."

That was how it looked from Washington at the end of 1962. Some of the optimism of the summer was beginning to fade, as Viet Cong units began to figure out how to deal with U.S. helicopters, not running from them any more but bringing some down with ground fire. And that was the line the President took in public. At his last 1962 press conference on December 12, he had been asked about Vietnam. "Mr. President, it was just a year ago that you ordered stepped-up aid to Vietnam. There seems to be a good deal of discouragement about the progress. Can you give us your assessment?"

"Well, we are making a major effort in Viet-Nam," Kennedy answered. "As you know, we have ten or eleven times as many men there as we had a year ago. We have put in an awful lot of equipment. . . . In some phases, the military program has been quite successful. . . . We don't see the end of the tunnel, but I must say I don't think it is darker than it was a year ago, and in some ways lighter."

In fact, nothing seemed to be getting much better out there, and Americans on all sides, Defense and State, U.S. Military Advisory Command Vietnam (MACV), and the press had begun to focus the blame for that on Diem and the Ngo family. Diem and Nhu were rejecting the friendly advice of the Americans who were paying the bills; it was as simple as that to those in Washington.

Hilsman's report to the President had concluded:

> The possibility of a coup at any time cannot be excluded. Many officials and oppositionists feel . . . the GVN [Government of Vietnam] is not winning the war principally because of Diem's virtual one-man rule and his failure to follow through with the political and economic measures necessary to gain the support of the peasants. . . . Under most of the foreseeable circumstances involving a coup, the role of the US would be extremely important. . . . The US could be helpful in achieving agreement among the coup leaders as to who should head the government and in restoring the momentum of the government's counterinsurgency effort.

The President, no slouch himself at telling men what they wanted to hear, left Mansfield with this thought on Lake Worth: "If I tried to pull out completely now from Vietnam, we would have another Joe McCarthy Red scare on our hands, but I can do it after I'm reelected. So we had better make damn sure that I am reelected."

He told his audience what it wanted to hear three days later in Miami, getting carried away during a ceremony in the Orange Bowl for the men of Brigade 2506, the American-trained Cuban fighters captured at the Bay of Pigs. More than a thousand of them had been released from prison by Castro in return for a ransom of $53 million in pharmaceuticals, baby food, and other goods covered by the U.S. trade boycott of Cuba. Castro called the money "indemnification." Officially, the goods were donations by American corporations—particularly the big drug companies—but they did not have to do all that much for their country. Robert Kennedy had raised the money, promising the corporations tax deductions equal to the retail price of their products.

"Whatever it takes, let's do it," the President had told Richard Goodwin, his young assistant for Latin American affairs, when he learned Castro was willing to trade the prisoners for money. "We'll give them a tax write-off." He repeated what he had said more than a year before. "I put those men in there. They trusted me. I have to get them out."

The prepared text of the President's speech to the Brigade that Sunday morning in Miami was diplomatic and cool. It was obvious that barring invasion or assassination, the United States was probably going to have to live with Castro or Castroism for a long time. Because of that, Kennedy had been warned not to go to the Orange Bowl, that the freed men and their families might boo him.

But he went and he lost his own cool when forty thousand men, women, and children in the stadium rose to cheer him as he walked with his wife toward a platform on the fifty-yard line. He was handed the Brigade flag, hidden by one of the prisoners during twenty months of captivity, and stated: "I want to express my great appreciation to the brigade for making the United States the custodian of this flag. I can assure you that this flag will be returned to this brigade in a free Havana."

On the morning of January 3, 1963, a four-page memo from the Joint Chiefs of Staff, stamped "SECRET," was hand-delivered to the President in Palm Beach.

On 2 January at 0800 local time in South Vietnam, the Government of Vietnam launched a coordinated ground/helicopter operation against the Viet Cong. Considerable press activity resulted from the operation due to initial reports of the loss of five US helicopters and damage to others.

It appears that the initial press reports have distorted both the importance of the action and the damage suffered by the US/GVN forces. Although unexpectedly stiff resistance was apparently encountered, contact has been maintained and the operation is being continued. . . .

The military, frustrated by unfavorable press coverage in Vietnam, was going into the news business itself, trying to beat *The New York Times* at its own game—a competition made easier by the fact that a printers union strike in New York meant that only the Western edition of the *Times* was being published, in Los Angeles. "VIETCONG DOWNS FIVE U.S. COPTERS, HITS NINE OTHERS . . . Defeat Worst Since Build-up Began" was the front-page headline the President saw later in the *Times* over a report of the same by David Halberstam.

Three American advisers were killed in action that day, along with sixty-one South Vietnamese regulars, in an engagement forty miles southwest of Saigon. More than 1,200 of South Vietnam's best troops had been brought in by waves of U.S. helicopters, and in M-113 armored personnel carriers, to snap an intricate military trap planned by an American Colonel named John Paul Vann, who had circled above the battleground all day in a spotter plane. The objective was to surround a Viet Cong radio transmitter in a Mekong Delta village called Ap Tan Thoi, guarded by perhaps two hundred VC troops. It was exactly the kind of engagement American military advisers had been wanting: classic warfare rather than the usual guerrilla tactics of the Viet Cong. Most of the Americans did not know that Viet Minh Communists had defeated French troops in the same place ten years earlier.

And the South Vietnamese did not know the transmitter was not at Ap Tan Thoi, but a mile away at a place called Ap Bac. Two companies of GVN paratroopers, called in by Vann to close the trap by blocking the Viet Cong's last escape route to the east of Ap Bac, had landed to the west of the village. At the end of the day, Vann reported: "We sat there all day, did not close with the enemy, did not complete an encirclement of him, and that night, of course, he slipped away, as we knew he would." Basically, the GVN commander, Brigadier General Huynh Van Cao, a Diem loyalist, would not order his men to attack; Cao had been criticized a few days earlier by Diem for producing too many casualties, politically unacceptable levels.

"A victory," reported General Paul Harkins, commander of the U.S. Military Advisory Command Vietnam. MACV reported that one hundred Viet Cong were killed, and the objective, Ap Bac, was taken— which it was, after the Viet Cong escaped the trap. The next day, January 4, on page two, Halberstam reported that only three Viet Cong bodies were found. The *Times'* military editor, Hanson Baldwin, analyzed the battle under the headline, "Copters No Substitute for Men": "More proof was provided this week—if any was needed—that the war in South Vietnam is likely to be long and hard, with the ultimate outcome in doubt."

"This was a stunning defeat," Kennedy was told by Roger Hilsman. The State Department's intelligence director was in Vietnam at the time, sent there by the President after his December report of premature optimism by American military men. Hilsman was accompanied by Michael Forrestal, a thirty-five-year-old Wall Street lawyer who had taken over Walt Rostow's spot as Bundy's assistant. He was a protégé of Averell Harriman, who had become a sort of godfather to him after his father, the first U.S. Secretary of Defense, James V. Forrestal, committed suicide in 1949 by leaping from a window of Walter Reed Naval Hospital in Bethesda, Maryland—shouting, it was said, "The Russians are coming!"

Kennedy liked young Forrestal, saw him most every day. The pairing with Hilsman was another attempt at "fact-finding" in Vietnam—there was one every couple of months or so. Kennedy was trying somehow to cut through the tangle of wires coming from Saigon around the clock, day after day after day. This time, the two reported back to the President that

> the war in South Vietnam is clearly going better than it was a year ago. ... Even so, the negative side of the ledger is still awesome. ... Intelligence estimates credit the Viet Cong with actually increasing their regular forces from 18,000 to 23,000 over this past year in spite of having suffered what the government claims were losses of 20,000 killed in action and 4,000 wounded. ... We are probably winning, but certainly more slowly than we had hoped. At the rate it is now going the war will last longer than we would like, cost more in terms of both lives and money than we anticipated. ...
>
> The real question is whether the concentration of power in the hands of Diem and his family, especially Brother Nhu and his wife, and Diem's reluctance to delegate is alienating the middle and higher level officials on whom the government must depend to carry out its policies. ...
>
> The American press in South Vietnam now has good relations with the Embassy and MACV and generally are grateful for the help that they have received. But their attitude toward Diem and the government of South Vietnam is the complete opposite, and with much justice. Diem wants only adulation. ...

The CIA was saying about the same thing as other non-military agencies. In competition now with McNamara's new Defense Intelligence Agency, it had its own statistics. A January 11, 1963, CIA memo stated: "Though the South Vietnamese government probably is now holding its own against the Viet Cong and may be reducing the menace in some areas, the tide has not yet turned. ... On 1 December 1962, 793 of

2,350 South Vietnamese villages were either physically held by the Viet Cong or subject to their control. The government controlled 1,617, and the remaining 120 were not under the effective control of either side. This represents a gain of 27 villages for the Viet Cong since 1 October 1962 and 25 for the government. On balance, the war remains a slowly escalating stalemate."

The Joint Chiefs of Staff sent its own fact-finding group out in January, a twelve-man group headed by Army Chief of Staff Earle G. "Bus" Wheeler, the general who had briefed Senator Kennedy on his "missile gap" charges in October of 1960.

"Victory is now a hopeful prospect," reported General Wheeler, whose specific task was to estimate how long the war might last. "We are winning slowly on the present thrust, and . . . there is no compelling reason to change. . . . The 'first team' is in the game." But then he noted that the North Vietnamese believed the Americans were no different from the French and inevitably would lose heart and go home. And he did advocate changes—some that startled Kennedy. The Joint Chiefs wanted to attack supply lines and storage sites in Laos and Cambodia and make "the North Vietnamese bleed . . . [with] a coordinated program of sabotage, destruction, propaganda, and subversive missions"— including commando attacks along the coastline of the Gulf of Tonkin.

Wheeler's delegation also insisted that Ap Bac was a victory, blaming the press for misleading readers, including the President: "A prime instance of the harm being done to the war effort. Press members admit that they were appalled at the flood of editorial punditry and cries of doom elicited by the first incomplete accounts of the clash. They insist defensively, contrary to the facts, that the battle was a defeat. . . . Recommendation: A series of sponsored visits to Vietnam by mature and responsible news correspondents and executives."

The chief's recommendations on covert war in North Vietnam were included in the briefcase of "Weekend Reading" that McGeorge Bundy packed for Kennedy on January 12, 1963, along with CIA cables on the doings of socialists in Italy, on the endless friction and border firefights between India and Pakistan, and on King Hussein of Jordan's views on U.S. activity in Yemen. The U.S. Air Force had moved a squadron of fighter-bombers to Bahrain near South Yemen in an attempt to deter Egypt from escalating its military involvement in a war to overthrow the Imam of Yemen—and three times that weekend the President telephoned Carl Kaysen, another Bundy assistant, telling him to maintain contact with the Air Force: "If we are going in there shooting down Egyptian bombers, I want to hear about it before we shoot."

Hilsman and Forrestal attacked both General Harkins and Ambassador Frederick Nolting in a secret addition to their report which was classified "Top Secret" to begin with—a note in the President's briefcase titled "Eyes Only Annex: Performance of U.S. Mission," to be seen only by the President:

"No one man is in charge. What is needed ideally is to give authority to a single strong executive. . . . One possibility would be to appoint the right kind of general as ambassador. A better alternative would be to appoint as ambassador a civilian public figure whose character and reputation would permit him to dominate the representatives of other departments and agencies."

The "Eyes Only" report also warned Kennedy again about Diem and his brother, Ngo Dinh Nhu, suggesting that the president of South Vietnam had lost touch with reality and his brother was a vicious drug addict. "More vigor is needed in getting Diem to do what we want," was Hilsman and Forrestal's understated written suggestion to Kennedy.

Specialist Fifth James McAndrew of Santa Ana, California, a helicopter gunner, was one of the three American soldiers killed at Ap Bac. His family had received the usual letter from the President. "It was with deep regret that I learned. . . . Mrs. Kennedy joins me in extending to you our deepest sympathy."

Two weeks later, Kennedy was shown a letter addressed to him from McAndrew's sister, Bobbie Lou Pendergrass, and a reply drafted by the Army.

> Please, I am only a housewife who doesn't even claim to know all about the international situation—but we have felt so bitter over this—can the small number of our boys over in Viet Nam possibly be doing enough good to justify the awful number of casualties. . . ? Those boys are just sitting ducks in those darn helicopters. If a war is worth fighting—isn't it worth fighting to win?
>
> Please answer this and help me and my family to reconcile ourselves to our loss and to feel that even though Jim died in Vietnam and it wasn't our war—it wasn't in vain. God Bless You.

The Army reply did not satisfy Kennedy and he wrote his own, including these thoughts:

> Americans are in Vietnam because we have determined that this country must not fall under Communist domination.
>
> It is also apparent that the Communist attempt to take over Vietnam is only part of a larger plan for bringing the entire area of Southeast Asia under their domination. Though it is only a small part of the area geographically, Viet Nam is now the most crucial. . . . Your brother was

in Viet Nam because the threat to the Viet Namese people is, in the long run, a threat to the Free World community, and ultimately a threat to us also.

James McAndrew must have foreseen that his service could take him into a war like this. . . . I am sure that he knew the necessity of such a situation, and I know that as a soldier, he knew full scale war in Vietnam is at the moment unthinkable.

Forty-five American soldiers, including your brother, have given their lives in Viet Nam. . . . I believe if you can see this as he must have seen it, you will believe as he must have believed, that he did not die in vain.

Since the end of 1962, the President was persuaded that if the United States withdrew from South Vietnam, the country would collapse "instantaneously"—he had used that word in answering questions after a December speech in New York—and he was beginning to focus more on Vietnam. That commitment was mirrored by the headline over a photo essay in *Life* magazine published on January 17, "We Wade Deeper into Jungle War," which included the first color photographs of napalm bombing, showing the effect of exploding jellied gasoline on villages below the planes and helicopters. "Sweeping low across enemy-infested scrubland," read the caption, "U.S. pilot-instructor watches Vietnamese napalm strike. Object of the bombing is to sear the foliage and flush the enemy into the open."

Michael Forrestal thought Kennedy was getting nervous, extremely nervous, that he sensed events were sliding out of control in Southeast Asia. He did not yet have much company in that concern. While the President was in Palm Beach, Secretary Rusk had testified twice in executive sessions of the Senate Foreign Relations Committee. He told the President there had been no questions about Vietnam.

A few weeks later the British counterinsurgency expert, Robert K. G. Thompson, came to Washington, spreading good news: "One year ago we were neither winning nor losing in Vietnam. Now we definitely are winning."

Thompson, who had conceived the "strategic hamlets" where more than half of Vietnamese peasants were now living or held—the CIA was telling Kennedy that the six thousand hamlets were more like concentration camps than fortified· villages of patriots—had another idea: If things continued to go well, withdraw one thousand American military personnel and make a big production of it. "This," Thompson told Kennedy, "would show that (1) RVN is winning; (2) take steam out of anti-Diemists; and (3) dramatically illustrate honesty of U.S. intentions."

Chapter 39

President Kennedy intended to change the urgent tone of his administration in his State of the Union Address on January 14, 1963. "The tide of events has been running out," he had said in his State of the Union two years earlier. Now it was time to say he had turned the tide. But the day got off to a bad start. In Paris, President de Gaulle announced that France would veto the entry of Great Britain into the European Common Market, wrecking both hopes for European integration, which Kennedy considered a historical imperative, and the substance of Kennedy's free trade initiatives. At the same time, de Gaulle formally stated that France would develop its own nuclear striking force, independent of NATO, killing American ideas of a multi-national nuclear force under effective U.S. control.

Kennedy stuck with his optimistic tone that night, telling the joint session of Congress: "For 175 years we have sailed with those winds [of change] at our back and with the tides of human freedom in our favor. Today we still welcome those winds of change—and we have every reason to believe that our tide is running strong."

It was more a domestic speech this time, and he began by saying: "One step, above all, is essential, the enactment this year of a substantial reduction and revision in Federal income taxes.

"It is increasingly clear . . . that our obsolete tax system exerts too heavy a drag on private purchasing power, profits, and employment.

Designed to check inflation in earlier years, it now checks growth instead. It discourages extra effort and risk.

"I shall propose a permanent reduction in tax rates, which will lower liabilities by $13.5 billion"—a revenue cut equal to almost 15 percent of the federal budget. "Of this $11 billion results from reducing individual tax rates, which now range between 20 and 91 percent, to a more sensible range of 14 to 65 percent. . . . Two and one half billion dollars results from reducing corporate tax rates from 52 percent—which gives the government today a majority interest in profits—to the permanent pre–Korean war rate of 47 percent."

Kennedy's economic journey was ended, but he had not gone to the limit. In the final days of White House debate over the specifics of the tax-cut proposals, he had stopped short and backed up a ways. Heller thought he had backed down. The tax-rate reductions would not take effect at one time; they would be phased in over three years. The President's contradictory public economics—endorsing both growth and balanced budgets—confronted itself in the final numbers: a full cut the first year would produce a budget deficit greater than Kennedy's limit, the $12.8 billion Eisenhower debt of 1958.

The thoughts of Heller and Samuelson were now proposed as the law of the land. John Kenneth Galbraith, more liberal than those two but further away, in India, was satisfied for the moment and he wrote a letter to Kennedy suggesting that he put a picture of "the Master," as economists called Keynes, in a private place, his bedroom or bathroom. Heller, though, felt let down by the limited triumph. The President had gone as far as he thought he could safely go, Samuelson told his protégé that night; the leader of a democracy is a prisoner. "It's not just Congress. It's the people. Kennedy feels he needs the semblance of virtue here. . . . If he thought the people would go along with the bigger deficit, with more activism, he'd have been ready to go along with it."

"Look, what I have to face here is the banker mentality," the President said in a conversation with another Samuelson protégé, James Tobin, the youngest member of his Council of Economic Advisers. "You may be right, but they would kick us in the balls. They're just waiting for the chance. We'd lose everything."

Republicans who would be President were waiting, too. The two being touted by the press, which meant they were touting themselves, were Governor Nelson Rockefeller of New York and Senator Barry Goldwater of Arizona. Kennedy told Mary McGrory of the *Washington Star* that he had seen her long page one feature on Goldwater.

"What did you think of it?" asked McGrory, flushed with the flattery.

"I didn't read it," said the President. "I don't read things about politicians who say they would rather be right than be President."

Kennedy would love to be right, but he had priorities. The first was to be reelected. The three-year schedule was not the only political disappointment for the Council of Economic Advisers. Kennedy backed off on the effective date of the first cut, changing it from July 1, 1962, to January 1, 1963. And the legislation was bound up with the tax reforms proposed by Dillon and the Treasury Department, thousands of them listed in the tiny type of a 302-page book. The fine print was too much for most members of Congress—and for journalists, too—but not for lobbyists and other analysts who pondered every word, number, and comma for effects on the income and profit of their employers and interests. "One man's reform is another man's loophole," the President said to Dillon. True, Dillon replied, but whatever you called it, reform was necessary to deflect opposition from Wall Street and other Republican constituencies. Kennedy did not argue. The emerging ideas did not quite make the revolution Heller wanted. But it was all his star pupil thought possible and prudent—it was no longer economics now, it was politics.

The two Kennedy years had not been bad—not bad at all. The mild recession of 1960–61 had ended soon after he took office, though the recovery seemed equally mild. Inflation was at 1.1 percent and GNP per capita, which rose less than 1 percent during Eisenhower's second term, was beginning to take off, climbing by almost 4 percent during 1962. But 4 million Americans were still unemployed. Now the political goal was double fours—growth of 4 percent or a little more in the gross national product, and unemployment of 4 percent or a little less, compared with the current 5.8 percent. The target date was November 3, 1964, Election Day.

That timetable, a reelection insurance policy, had not been part of the President's last presentation of his economic ideas, a year-end speech to a tough audience, the Economic Club of New York: "Our tax system," he said then, "siphons out of the private economy too large a share of personal and business purchasing power. . . . Surely the lesson of the last decade is that budget deficits are not caused by wild-eyed spenders but by slow economic growth and periodic recessions. . . . In short, it is a paradoxical truth that tax rates are too high today and tax revenues are too low and the soundest way to raise the revenues in the long run is to raise the rates now."

The President thought he had persuaded the six hundred businessmen and Wall Streeters, most of them Republicans, at the Economic Club. "I gave them straight Keynes and Heller and they loved it," he said afterward. "If I can sell it to those guys, I can sell it to anyone." Important labor leaders liked the idea, too, thinking there would be more cash around and they were bound to get some of it. But the opposition to the tax cut and a proposed fiscal 1964 budget of $98.8 million was even more broad-based. Most Americans and most of their congressmen were united on only two economic ideas: defense spending was good; deficits were bad and bigger deficits were worse. "Even as a liberal Democrat, I have doubts about the continuation of a deficit," said a senator more liberal than Kennedy, Claiborne Pell of Rhode Island. "I think we would like to see a balanced budget. This worry, I think, is throughout the country as well."

On Kennedy's right, Eisenhower, the leader of the fiscal puritans, said a tax cut was "fiscal recklessness . . . that would lead to a vast wasteland of debt and financial chaos." The former President wanted spending cuts to match the tax cuts. So did Harry Truman, who reacted to the tax-cut proposals by saying: "I am old-fashioned. I believe you should pay in more than you spend." In the left wing of Kennedy's own White House, Sorensen silently agreed with a crack that the New York speech may have been pure Heller but it sounded like pure Herbert Hoover. Galbraith could not resist responding to that by telling the President that it sounded more like William McKinley to him. Galbraith wanted more government spending rather than tax reductions to get more cash into the hands of the American people. He was an unabashed big government advocate, worried that people might like the taste of tax cuts, eventually reducing the power of government.

In the State of the Union message, the President had done what had to be done, trying to pressure the new Congress by arguing that economic policy, like everything else, was really part of national security policy. "We cannot lead for long the cause of peace and freedom if we ever cease to set the pace at home," he told the Congress that night, adding in his formal Economic Report afterward, "In a setting of full employment, these measures can help to move our growth rate to 4 percent and above, the American people toward greater abundance, and the free world toward greater security."

Eight days later, at a National Security Council meeting on January 22, Kennedy was even more direct, saying all policy was national security policy: "All of these matters—the tax program, AID, defense, etc. are all related. . . . If we just drift, we will look very bad to other nations."

The President talked about de Gaulle at that meeting, making it clear that whatever was said in public, the French leader must be dealt with as an adversary of the U.S. agenda: "De Gaulle is there and we have to live with it. . . . It is our interest to strengthen Europe [as a] concept, and de Gaulle is opposed to this. By strengthening the multilateral concept, it strengthens NATO and increases their dependence on us. This strengthens our influence in Europe and gives us the power to guide Europe and keep it strong. . . .

"In the coming months we must concentrate on how we can protect the interests of the United States. We have pursued a very generous policy. We have lost our economic power over these countries. . . . Do not think the Europeans will do anything for us even though we have done a lot for them. We must be sure our economic house is in order and use our military, political power to protect our own interests."

Foreign aid should be seen in that same context, he told NSC members: "We hope we can tie this whole concept of aid to the safety of the United States. This is the reason we give aid. The test is whether it will serve the United States. Aid is not a good word. Perhaps we can describe it better as 'Mutual Assistance.' "

Robert Frost died on January 23. He had gone into a hospital in Boston just before Christmas. It seemed everyone of import in the world had sent what they knew were final messages—Khrushchev, the pope, Robert Kennedy; but not John Kennedy. Stewart Udall asked the President to call or just to say something, but Kennedy was still angry about Frost's casting doubt on American resolve. Just before the end, Frost told Udall he still hoped to tell Kennedy about his conversations with Khrushchev, but "I know how busy he is. Those people around the President, they're. . . ."

The White House issued a statement that afternoon, saying: "The death of Robert Frost leaves a vacancy in the American spirit. . . . His art and his life summed up the essential qualities of the New England he loved so much: the fresh delight in nature, the plainness of speech, the canny wisdom, and the deep, underlying insight into the human soul. . . . He had promises to keep, and miles to go and now he sleeps."

On January 24, at a news conference, Kennedy argued that trade policy, too, was a matter of national security, urging the Congress to reconsider its opposition to "Most Favored Nation" status for two Communist countries, Yugoslavia and Poland: "We are in a very challenging period . . . to take legislative action which denies us an opportunity to exploit or to develop whatever differences in attitude or tempo which may take place behind the Iron Curtain seems to me unwise."

At that conference, Kennedy was asked about the announcements by the governments of Turkey and Italy that U.S. Jupiter missiles were being removed from bases in those countries. How did this relate to Soviet actions in Cuba? The real question was whether the removal was a secret part of the deal to get the Soviet missiles out of Cuba. Kennedy brushed off the question, saying the removal of the Jupiters was routine modernization—quite an answer considering that they had been activated for less than four months. The second part of his answer was true: the area the Jupiters covered would now be on the targeting schedules of Polaris missiles on submarines in the Mediterranean Sea.

There were a couple of questions about the exchange of Kennedy-Khrushchev letters on a possible U.S.-Soviet nuclear test ban treaty. The White House that day had released partial texts of three letters: Khrushchev's letter of December 19, Kennedy's December 28 answer, and a Khrushchev answer of January 7.

Kennedy's response to the December 19 letter he had received in Nassau had begun: "There appear to be no differences between your views and mine regarding the need for eliminating war in this nuclear age . . . I am encouraged that you are prepared to accept the principle of on-site inspections. . . ."

But principles were obviously getting lost in details. Khrushchev on January 7 had referred to a U.S. proposal for three inspections a year—an offer never made, but a number that had come up in two separate private conversations between Soviet officials and scientists and Arthur Dean, the chief U.S. disarmament negotiator in Geneva, and Kennedy's science adviser, Jerome Wiesner. "There appears to have been some misunderstanding," Kennedy said in his letter—the minimum number of acceptable inspections was eight to ten. So, the Americans had come down from twenty to eight and the Soviets up from zero to three.

There the negotiating stopped, but the secret personal correspondence between the leaders continued, often in pretty chummy terms. The President and the premier had communicated with each other every few days in the weeks following the missile crisis, usually about the details (and suspicions) involved in the removal of Soviet men and equipment from Cuba. But Khrushchev had found time to comment on U.S. election results, saying: "You managed to pin Mr. Nixon to the mat. This did not draw tears from our eyes either." Another day, the Soviet leader urged Kennedy not to aggravate Fidel Castro and other Cuban leaders at his news conferences. "They're young, expansive," Khrushchev said. "In a word, Spaniards."

The premier also complained that he had noticed the contents of some of his letters seemed to be appearing in U.S. newspapers, particularly in columns from Washington. Was Kennedy leaking them? No, no, Kennedy said, explaining:

> The competition for news in this country is fierce. A number of the competitors are not great admirers of my Administration, and perhaps an even larger number are not wholly friendly to yours. Here in Washington

we have 1200 reporters accredited to the White House alone, and thousands more in other assignments. Not one of them is accountable to this government for what he reports. It would be a great mistake to think that what appears in newspapers and magazines necessarily has anything to do with the policy and purpose of this government. I am glad to say that I have some friends among newspapermen, but no spokesmen.

He added, too, that it was a mistake for the Soviets to have tried to set up a private channel to him through a reporter, John Scali of ABC, during the missile crisis—you cannot trust them. Kennedy mentioned Georgi Bolshakov, the intelligence agent who had carried messages between them until those messages turned out to be lies. "I am sorry to learn he is being returned to Moscow," Kennedy wrote. "We shall miss him very much."

The President's proposed fiscal 1964 budget was released on January 24. Federal agency requests to the Bureau of the Budget had totaled more than $108 billion and had been trimmed to $100.4 billion before being passed on to the President early in the month. He had made it immediately clear that the final number had to be below $100 billion—that figure, a first, was too symbolic; it would just make it too easy to go after him as a big-spending Democrat. The biggest increases were in the Department of Health, Education and Welfare, up from $4.2 billion to $9.3 billion, with most of the new money for education, and in the National Aeronautics and Space Administration, up from $2.4 billion to $4.5 billion to finance Kennedy's pledge that an American would be on the moon before the end of the decade. The sooner the deadline, the more money had to be spent each year. Dillon asked Kennedy what was the real date in his mind.

"1967," the President said. "I'd rather unbalance my budget and all the rest. . . ." He was willing to take political heat on that goal, and heat he took, the hottest from Eisenhower, who said: "Anyone who would spend $40 billion in a race to the moon for national prestige is nuts."

"We'll just have to cut education back," Kennedy added, figuring Congress would not pass his education bills anyway. He had told David Bell, the director of the Budget Bureau, to go back and cut the budget to $98.5 billion—and then he would personally consider every item proposed above that figure.

The final number approved by Kennedy was $98.9 billion, more than $5 billion over the fiscal 1963 total of $93.7 billion. Eisenhower emphasized that increase in a by-lined article in the *Saturday Evening*

Post entitled "Spending into Trouble," saying: "The time-tested rules of financial policy still apply. No family, no business, no nation can spend itself into prosperity. . . . They and their children will pay and pay and pay. In effect, we are stealing from our grandchildren in order to satisfy our desires of today."

Ike's final kick was a little low. He said the new budget was bigger than the final World War II budget. It was, but Eisenhower did not bother to note that Kennedy's $98.9 billion in expenditures amounted to 15 percent of the GNP, while the 1945 budget took 47 percent of GNP—in effect, government spending in 1964 was one third 1945 spending. Like almost all congressional Republicans, and many Southern Democrats, the former President wanted any tax cut matched by spending cuts—which would serve their goal of making government smaller, but would also reduce aggregate demand in the country. Kennedy responded by noting that the projected deficit in his budget was $11.8 billion—less than Eisenhower's 1958 deficit.

The most passionate attacks on the budget, though, came from liberals, who questioned not only the economics but the morality of cuts in domestic spending, as the defense budget continued to increase to almost two thirds of government spending. Of the $98.9 in proposed spending, $55.4 billion would go directly to the military, with another $5.7 billion going for the space program and the hidden lines of CIA funding. One liberal journal, *The Nation*, editorialized:

> We behold here the climactic splendor of Western civilization. Nineteen hundred and sixty-three years after Christ died on the cross and in the third year of the Presidency of John F. Kennedy, with culture enthroned in Washington and the *Mona Lisa* on display, upwards of $55 billion— and going up, up, up—is dedicated to the sacred cause of mass slaughter. The United States has in its nuclear arsenal an estimated 30,000 megatons; 4,000 megatons is generally accepted as the amount required to destroy the Soviet Union as a social political entity. . . . The specifically military section of the budget is untouchable. . . .
>
> Truly, Mr. Kennedy has set this house on fire, and the full extent of his arson is not obvious until one considers that his almost-$100 billion proposals are coupled with a request for a tax cut, and an admitted deficit of $9.2 billion. . . .

Dillon was delegated to sell the tax bill to Congress. He appeared before the House Ways and Means Committee with 507 typewritten pages of reforms, drawing lawyers and lobbyists like flies. It was going to take the House and the Senate a long time to get to Heller's pure, quick, and permanent tax cuts as the way to getting the country moving again.

"I think you have the wrong kind of economist," James Tobin had said, when Kennedy called him at Yale to invite him to serve on the Council of Economic Advisers. "I'm an ivory tower economist."

"That's the best kind. I'm an ivory tower President," Kennedy had countered. But he was not. He might have liked to be, but he was a politician, often far more patient as a professional than as a man. Big things took timing and time, particularly when it came to dealing with Congress.

So, as his three Keynesians—Samuelson, Heller, and Tobin—taught him the dismal science of economics, Kennedy had tutored them constantly in the art of the possible. When Tobin went back to Yale after a couple of years of one-man seminars with his President-student, Kennedy was astonished. "Why go back and teach rich men's sons?" he asked. "That can't have impact for twenty years. Here you can have impact on policy now."

The specifics of the new tax policy, at least the White House version of it, were contained in "The Special Message to Congress on Tax Reduction and Reform," twenty-two closely spaced pages delivered to the Congress on January 24, 1963. Heller had brought it in for Kennedy's approval before it was printed. The President flipped through the pages and handed them back, saying, "Okay."

"My God," Heller said. "That's certainly expressing a lot of confidence in me."

"Sure, why not?"

"Don't you know I have you saying something no other President has ever said—that a deficit under certain circumstances can be a good thing; that there are constructive deficits and destructive deficits and it depends on the circumstances?"

"Well, let me take another look at that," Kennedy said, taking another minute to change a sentence. Then he handed it back to Heller, saying, "Let's go."

Walking out, Heller told Evelyn Lincoln that he had forgotten to show the President the pale blue cover of the document. "Well," he said, "he won't want to be bothered by this."

"Yes, he will," she said.

Kennedy, came out, took one look and shook his head, saying: "That's not strong enough. Get royal blue or Navy blue."

Symbols were everywhere now that the President was publicly on the line. "What Have You Done for Growth Today?" signs were printed to display on desks in the White House. Many Kennedy men had avoided the word since Richard Nixon had mocked Kennedy in the 1960 campaign by making fun of " Growthmanship." With uncharacteristic wit, Nixon had said it sounded like a childhood disease.

But bumper stickers were not symbols that moved members of Congress. Wilbur Mills was not going to let the tax bill out of his Ways and Means Committee until he had reason to believe it would pass, just as he was keeping the President's Medicare bill off the floor rather than risk rejection. The Arkansas congressman's personal ideology was little more than patience and certainty. Like the President, he knew the difference between politics and vanity. He had too much of the latter to take many chances with the former. The reforms cherished by Dillon, Mills told Kennedy, would be gnawed for months in committee.

"You might be able to get the Congress to do this if we were in a depression, if we're starting downhill, and everybody could see we're starting downhill," he said. "The Congress would go with you, I think. . . . When I become convinced that I've got a choice to make between tax reduction and increased deficit and a recession, I'm going to take the tax reduction line. . . . If I have to do something, if I have to recommend to the Congress tax reduction to keep us from going downhill, you can count on me doing it. But I'm not going to ask the Congress to create additional deficits and tax reduction until I know that I'm faced with that choice."

That was the tax-cut stand of one of his best friends on the issue. The President nodded as Mills went on, then he added his own analysis of what might happen in the Senate Finance Committee, which was chaired by Harry S. Byrd of Virginia, the seventy-five-year-old economic puritan who had three times called for the resignation of Kennedy appointees who suggested balanced budgets might be retarding economic growth: "Byrd would screw us even if you put it through the House. . . ."

There was a chance that H.R. 8363, the tax bill, would never make it to the floor even if Mills thought the House was ready for it—it still might die in committee because of the tax reforms. The opening and closing of old loopholes, each important to someone influential somewhere, was at the very center of power and representation in the Congress. As the weeks of hearings and executive sessions went on in Ways and Means, Heller showed a little less confidence, telling Kennedy: "As you know I opposed cluttering up the 1963 tax cut by inclusion of tax reforms and I never bought the argument that the vested interests, just because we fed them a high protein diet of tax cuts, would be any less venal or voracious when we kicked them in their private parts. And they're not."

The midterm elections had not changed much on Capitol Hill. The 88th Congress, particularly the House, was going to be similar to the 87th. An official caucus of seventy or so Southern Democrats and moderate Republicans still held the balance of power. They voted with the

President on defense expenditures, and against him on foreign aid and almost all domestic legislation. He had to win over forty or sixty of them each time he tried to implement the Northern liberal agenda of the national Democratic Party.

At his January 24 news conference, a reporter asked about his troubles with Congress and his thoughts about former President Eisenhower's suggestion that congressional terms should be limited. "It's . . . ," the President began, a smile moving up his face. "It's the sort of proposal which I may advance in a post-presidential period, but not right now."

He was in no rush to that post-presidency. Toward the end of January, he set aside a day for meetings with the Democratic National Committee (DNC) and a giant fund-raising gala. He reminded the DNC that, with the exception of Franklin Roosevelt, no Democratic candidate for President since 1876 had received 50 percent of the vote, and that if two more states—he mentioned Michigan and Pennsylvania—went Republican in 1964, the Republicans would be back in the White House. Then he delighted the gala, a $250-a-head affair, with up-to-the-minute family jokes collected and written by Ted Sorensen. They played on and off everything from his own aversion to high culture, to the latest Broadway hit, a musical called *Stop the World—I Want to Get Off,* and his brother Robert Kennedy's ongoing crusade to pin racketeering charges on the leader of the International Brotherhood of Teamsters union, James R. Hoffa.

"Vaughn Meader was busy tonight, so I came myself," he said, paying tribute to his best-known imitator. "I listened to Mr. Meader's record, but I thought it sounded more like Teddy than it did me—so he's annoyed. . . . If anyone here feels he was pressured by his boss into coming tonight, I know just how he feels. Jackie made me buy a ticket to the National Cultural Center dinner. . . . I was proud of the Attorney General's first appearance before the Supreme Court yesterday. He did a good job, according to everyone I talked to: Ethel, Jackie, Teddy. . . . But it does show he has broader interests, more than just 'Stop the World—I Want to Get Hoffa.' "

At a private party later that night, a dinner-dance at Douglas Dillon's home, Edward Kennedy, a senator for only a couple of weeks, complained to his brother that six hundred Massachusetts men were going to be put out of work if the Defense Department went ahead with plans to close a rifle factory in Springfield.

The President smiled and said, "Tough shit!"

Chapter 40

On January 28 and again on the 31st, President Kennedy dictated two long memos to Evelyn Lincoln under the heading: "Questions to be settled . . . in the coming months." There were twenty-seven of them: four were on the Common Market and international trade; three were on nuclear weapons; three on President de Gaulle; two on Germany. The rest were on the press, NATO, Laos, Belgium, Yugoslavia, Spain, Portugal, Africa, and the moon.

"The fact is, the President cares more about Germany than about Negroes, he thinks it's more important," said Louis Martin of the Democratic National Committee. The former newspaper publisher was one of two Negroes with regular access to the Oval Office. The other was Andrew Hatcher, a deputy press secretary. On January 31, Martin sent a memo to Kennedy reminding him of campaign promises to Negroes, and warning him that whatever his white advisers and elected officials were telling him, Negroes were on the edge of revolt: "American Negroes through sit-ins, kneel-ins, wade-ins, etc. will continue to create situations which involve the police powers of the local, state and Federal government."

Negroes, particularly the young ones, Martin said, were tired of being told to wait their turn; Kennedy had to do something for them. Martin was arguing for the introduction of strong civil rights legislation. The President responded by telling him to plan a reception for Negro leaders at the White House on Lincoln's Birthday, February 12.

Martin's job was to make up the guest list. Martin, who had more or less replaced Harris Wofford as Kennedy's sounding board on civil rights issues, was intrigued by the idea that there would probably be more people of color in the White House that day than in the preceding one hundred and fifty years. He was comfortable telling his friends that discretion was the price of invitation, all publicity would be handled by the White House. And there was to be no publicity. The event was practically a state secret. Almost all the Negroes Martin approached understood that, and they were as thrilled to be invited, as charmed by Jack and Jackie, as any other Americans.

Martin was a shrewd political operator in the Chicago style, and he had demonstrated that in a personal crusade to increase the number of Negroes in medium- to high-level government jobs. One of his tricks was calling Cabinet members with the name of a Negro who might be appointed. When their answers began: "Thanks, but we've already . . ."

"OK, I understand," Martin would respond. "I'll tell that to the President."

"Wait a minute," the official on the other end of the line would invariably say. "I never said I wouldn't take him under any circumstances."

One of the few Negroes invited to the White House who talked about it was a comedian and political activist named Dick Gregory, who was publicly chastised by *Jet* magazine: "Baby, you don't send out advance publicity on meeting President Kennedy when you're a social guest."

There were few regrets sent back when the invitations went out, but Martin Luther King, Jr., and A. Philip Randolph were among the missing. King was on the Caribbean island of Jamaica, resting and making final plans for what he called "Project C," a civil rights campaign in one of the toughest of the segregated Southern cities, Birmingham, Alabama. Randolph, the seventy-four-year-old founder of the first and most powerful of Negro labor unions, the Brotherhood of Sleeping Car Porters, let it be known that he thought the Kennedys were not doing enough for Negroes—as he had let President Franklin Roosevelt know, in 1941, that he would organize a march on Washington if Negroes did not receive their fair share of jobs in the defense industry created during World War II.

On the afternoon of February 12, Lincoln's Birthday, Kennedy accepted a 246-page report prepared by the U.S. Civil Rights Commission on a century of struggle for equality by Negroes since President Lincoln issued the Emancipation Proclamation in 1863. "A freedom more fictional than real" was the way the commission described the inheritance of modern Negroes. "The legally free Negro citizen was denied the franchise, excluded from public office, assigned to inferior and separate schools, herded into ghettoes, directed to the back of the bus, treated unequally in the courts of justice and segregated in his illness, his worship and even in his death. . . . The final chapter in the struggle for equality has yet to be written. . . . As the century draws to a close, more forces are working for the realization of civil rights for all Americans than ever before in history."

The day before the Lincoln Birthday party, the eight hundred guests had received calls and telegrams telling them to come to the Southwest Gate of the White House, rather than the East Gate specified on the invitations, so that the President and First Lady could personally greet them in the family quarters of the White House. The guests were flattered, few realizing that it was a trick to keep them away from photographers in the public rooms. Martin was pleased with his work. "Oh, man," he said. "I'm the man who got Langston Hughes into the White House. It looks like Uncle Tom's Cabin around here." Hughes, the Negro poet whose verse collections included *Montage of a Dream Deferred,* was among the guests who saw the inside of the nation's house for the first time.

But it was not Hughes the President focused on before he came downstairs to the reception, but Sammy Davis, Jr., a talented song-and-dance man whose marriage to a Swedish actress named Mai Britt was considered a scandal or worse by Americans who disapproved of all interracial marriage. Davis's name had been struck off the guest list four times by the White House, and restored four times by Martin.

"What's he doing here?" Kennedy asked. It was nothing personal. Kennedy knew Davis, who hung around with Frank Sinatra and Peter Lawford, but a photograph of the black man in the White House with his white woman could be a political disaster. "Get them out of there!" Kennedy whispered to one aide after another. Still upstairs, he told one assistant after another to tell his wife to take Mai Britt aside so that the Davises would not be together before the photographers were pushed out of the room.

Jacqueline Kennedy refused. She was so angry at the suggestion she did not want to go downstairs at all, and the formal reception began without the President and his wife. He was still upstairs trying to talk her into going down. She finally did, agreeing to sit next to her husband for a formal portrait with Vice President Johnson and his wife, Mrs. Robert Kennedy, and eleven Negro leaders. Then she stood up, said she did not feel well, and left in tears.

The group portrait appeared in the next morning's *Washington Post,* in the paper's "For and About Women" section. The Emancipation Gala was rarely and barely mentioned the next day in most newspapers around the country. The *Chicago Daily Tribune* was typical, reporting in two paragraphs that it seemed unusual for a Democratic President to honor the first Republican President, never mentioning that the guests at the White House were Negroes.

But the *Tribune* did show a rise in news about race and civil rights. There were five stories on page three alone: Under heavy guard and facing placards that said: "Save Our Republic: Impeach Earl Warren," the Chief Justice of the United States Supreme Court appeared in the South for the first time since the Court's 1954 ruling against school segregation, speaking at Georgia Tech. Abraham Lincoln's great-grand-daughter, a sixty-four-year-old woman named Mary Lincoln Beckwith, attacked "the aggression of the Federal government of forcing integration on the South." The NAACP and CORE announced they would try to prevent the opening of Aunt Jemima's Pancake Kitchen, a restaurant in a Rochester, New York, suburb, saying that the old "Mammy" image was degrading to Negroes. In Hammond, Indiana, the NAACP announced it was filing new court papers charging racial discrimination in that city's public schools.

At Lincoln Birthday dinners across the country on the nights of February 12 and 13, leaders of the party of Lincoln—the party which had retained the voting loyalty of Negroes from the end of the Civil War to the New Deal of Franklin D. Roosevelt—were attacking the President for his cool civil rights record. The Republican Kennedy feared most, Nelson Rockefeller, who had just won a majority of New York's big Negro vote as he was being reelected governor, said: "The fact is that the President, on recommendation of his brother the Attorney General . . . named at least four Federal judges in the South who were known at the time of their appointment for their segregationist views. This is a strange way to expedite civil rights action."

"Rockefeller gets away with murder, what's he doing for Negroes in New York?" Kennedy remarked the next night at a small dinner in the White House.

"He likes you, you know," said Teddy White, who had just announced to the people around the table that he planned to write another *Making of the President* book in 1964 and hoped the President would cooperate. They both assumed Rockefeller would be the Republican nominee.

"I like him, too," Kennedy said. "But that's not important. He'll get to hate me. That's inevitable."

The question of the judges came up at a press conference three weeks later and the President defended the appointments. "I think that the men that have been appointed to judgeships in the South, sharing perhaps as they do the general outlook of the South, have done a remarkable job in fulfilling their oath of office."

Then he went back to his office and called Assistant Attorney General Nicholas Katzenbach to ask about the judges he had appointed: "Is it real bad?"

The answer to his question was yes, though Katzenbach could not bring himself to say that to the boss. "Not too good," he said of one judge. "He's been sitting on a lot of things." Of another, he said: "Not impossible."

"They're all Eastland's . . . ," Katzenbach said, referring to Senator James Eastland, the chairman of the Senate Judiciary Committee, a Mississippi segregationist.

"Could you get one of your boys to get up a memo . . . ," the President said, "so I'll be able to talk about it in case it comes up again."

The Mississippi judge who was "not too good" was Kennedy's first judicial appointment as President, William Howard Cox, whose qualifications included being Eastland's roommate at the University of Mississippi. Not only did the committee have constitutional power to confirm or kill all federal judicial appointments—and it regularly used that power—but each senator had the power by unchallenged tradition personally to accept or reject appointees in their home states. The former senator from Massachusetts knew all about that. He had deferred on Judge Cox to Eastland, even after receiving a letter from Roy Wilkins of the NAACP saying: "For 986,000 Mississippi Negroes, Judge Cox will be another strand in their barbed-wire fence, another cross over their weary shoulders." Cox quickly confirmed Wilkins's judgment. In his first voting rights case, from the federal bench, Cox had characterized Negro plaintiffs as "A bunch of niggers . . . acting like a bunch of chimpanzees."

Kennedy's political rationale was that he had to trade a Cox for a Negro Federal Appeals Court appointment in New York, Thurgood Marshall, the attorney who had argued the NAACP's 1954 school desegregation case before the Supreme Court. That nomination had been held up for more than a year as Eastland simply refused to convene confirmation hearings. That was the way things were done by the Southern barons in Congress. Kennedy had long ago decided he had to live with that. Those same barons had supported him for Vice President at the 1956 Democratic National Convention because they hated Senator Estes Kefauver of Tennessee, a native son but a turncoat on segregation. Looking up from a television set as one Southern state after another had voted for him during the roll call, Senator Kennedy had said: "I'm going to sing Dixie for the rest of my life."

It was easy, Kennedy thought, for a Northern Republican like Rockefeller in a liberal state with a million Negro voters. He was free to say whatever he wanted to without hurting his party because no Republicans even ran in most Southern counties. The Democratic formula was unnatural, but it seemed stable, or it had been so since Roosevelt had won over a majority of Northern Negroes in 1932. The Freedom Rides and the Mississippi troubles were still treated as isolated incidents in the White House. Kennedy had told Negro newspaper editors in a background interview before the Lincoln Birthday festivities that he saw no serious divisions between white and Negro Americans.

The President thought he had handled the racial incidents well enough, though he was worried about the build-up of white resentment in states like Alabama and Georgia. His Southern problems, in fact, were as white as Congress. The political reality of civil rights legislation, Kennedy told Martin Luther King, Jr., was this: "If we go into a long fight in Congress it will bottleneck everything else and still get no bill."

In case Kennedy might forget the attitude and intentions of Southern Democrats, he was reminded when the Civil Rights Commission rejected his private requests to slow down and announced that it would hold hearings in Mississippi. Senator Sam Ervin of North Carolina reacted to that decision by introducing legislation to reduce the pay of the commission's director, Berl Bernhard, from $22,500 a year to $20,500.

"Pretty much at peace," was the assessment of the Negro mood given to the President at the beginning of 1963 by his new civil rights assistant. Lee White had moved from Justice to the White House after Harris Wofford, frustrated by the President's bent toward peace and quiet on civil rights, had gone to Africa as a Peace Corps administrator. Cool objectivity, pure information gathering, dispassionate analysis, a decision-making mechanism unswayed by sentiment, unmoved by subjective and moral argument—that was a point of pride to Kennedy and the hard thinkers. It was a style greatly admired at the time, by the public and particularly by the coolest of his aides, men like Burke Marshall, Bundy, and McNamara, who imitated Kennedy and were imitated by him.

Father Theodore Hesburgh, an Eisenhower appointee to the Civil Rights Commission, saw the style and did not particularly like it. The priest, who was still the president of Notre Dame University, left one meeting after another with the President thinking that Kennedy would love to do something about the painful inequities of formal and official segregation, but that he saw personal involvement in the passions of civil rights issues as a good way to guarantee that he would not be reelected. "He thinks that if he does more than he has to about Negroes, he can forget about being President for eight years," Hesburgh told Bernhard.

The initiative and action on civil rights, by Kennedy's choice, were on the edges, not at the center. Marches and sit-ins and voter registration drives were being organized locally now. There was a movement. In Greenwood, Mississippi, the year had begun with voter registration sponsored by a new group calling itself the Student Non-Violent Coordinating Committee—SNCC, known as "Snick"—and the state was reacting with mass arrests and by pushing through new anti-Negro laws. One of them gave registered voters (white people) the power to block new voters (black people) by challenging their "moral character."

On February 28, after two years in office, President Kennedy introduced his first civil rights bill, a voting rights bill. Its principal provision asserted that a sixth-grade education would be considered proof of literacy in voting matters. The idea was to get around the more outrageous Southern registrars, who enforced such literacy tests by asking Negro voters to read and interpret the Constitution of the United States, article by article.

Civil rights leaders were so disappointed that they began to threaten Kennedy with talk of alliances with urban Republicans, like Governor Rockefeller and Senators Kenneth Keating and Jacob Javits of New York. The President asked the most vocal civil rights advocate in his party, Senator Hubert Humphrey, to stop talking about a comprehensive civil rights bill. Humphrey said he could not leave the field and the speechmaking to Keating and Javits. The country is not ready, Kennedy repeated, telling Humphrey and others: "When I feel that there's necessity for a congressional action with a chance of getting that congressional action, then I will recommend it to the Congress."

In a more relaxed moment with his own aides, Kennedy was a bit more direct: "We go up there with that and they'll piss all over us."

Negroes had to wait their turn, he said. But it was too late for that, warned Louis Martin, telling Kennedy again that Negroes heard him each time he said it was time to get the country moving. They *were* moving. In a new memo, Martin wrote:

> The President stated in the campaign: "Using the full moral and political power of the Presidency to obtain for all young Americans, and others similarly affected, equal access to the voting booth, the schoolroom, to jobs, to housing and to public facilities, including lunch counters." . . . The fact that progress has been made by this administration in integrating air, bus and railroad terminals and other areas tends to focus more attentions on hotels, motels, and other public facilities which have a color bar.

The Civil Rights Commission wanted to move, too. The President and the Attorney General had pressured and persuaded the commission three separate times, beginning in February 1961, not to issue public reports on the defiance of federal law by local officials in Louisiana, and then in Mississippi, the state that had produced the most citizen complaints to the commission. But, at the Lincoln Day gala, the new chairman, John Hannah, had told Kennedy that the commission intended to prepare a special report on the situation in Mississippi. Local officials, he said, had begun trying to stop SNCC's voter registration project by cutting off federal food relief programs for poor Negroes.

"You're making my life difficult," Kennedy said. "I've read this law and I know you can do anything you want to, but I would appreciate if you didn't."

That was in private. A couple of weeks later, at a press conference, he was asked whether he thought the commission should delay Mississippi hearings and he answered: "No. . . . Any hearing that they feel advances the cause or meets the responsibility which has been entrusted to them by law, then they should go ahead and hold it."

They did that, and they showed the President a draft of their report on Greenwood, making the point that illegal and violent repression was the rule in Mississippi, not an exception. Burke Marshall and Lee White tried to rip apart such conclusions in defensive memos to the President. "Set upon by vicious dogs" was a phrase in the draft, but Marshall told him there was only one dog and one minister. White went directly to the heart of the matter: "Implicit is the suggestion that the President and the Administration have not done all that could be done in the Mississippi situation. This is, of course, manifestly wrong."

"How could this happen?" Kennedy wanted to know. Robert Kennedy told him that the new members of the commission, men like the dean of Harvard Law School, Erwin Griswold, were a different breed from the Southern governors and such appointed by Eisenhower when he had created the commission five years before.

The President was surprised again when Hannah and Berl Bernhard came in to discuss the report. It included a recommendation that the President should consider cutting off all federal aid to Mississippi— which paid a total of $270 million in federal taxes and received $650 million back in federal aid and payments—until the state "demonstrates its compliance with the Constitution and laws of the United States."

"Do you really think a President has that kind of power?" Kennedy asked.

"Yes, I do," Bernhard said.

"What was the vote on this?" Kennedy asked.

"It was unanimous."

"Griswold, too?"

"Yes sir. He was very strong for it."

"Who the hell appointed Griswold?"

"You did, Mr. President," Bernhard answered.

"Okay," Kennedy said.

Hannah and Bernhard were surprised that Kennedy did not pressure them or even ask them to change anything in the report. In fact, he said, he would like it to be released through the White House. They quickly agreed. Then the President easily drained the paper of its urgency by making it public with a letter to Hannah thanking the commission: "With regard to the incidents referred to in the Commission's report, I am advised that every case but one has been successfully resolved."

That was far from the truth, but the press bought it, and most of the public barely noticed. To make sure of that, Kennedy personally briefed reporters, questioning whether the commissioners—whose legal authority was separate from his—were serious people, emphasizing the unreality of singling out one state for punishment, radical punishment at that, the cutting off of federal funding. He had it both ways this time, seeming to support the commission but privately undermining its work. "A high administration official" was quoted across the country the next day saying more in sorrow than anger:

"I wouldn't have issued that report. It doesn't do any good. It just makes people mad."

The official was President Kennedy.

Chapter 41

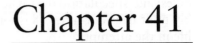

On February 13, the same day the *Chicago Tribune* published five stories on civil rights marches and demonstrations across the country, it ran twelve stories on hiking, all on fifty-mile hikes going on across the country. The lead hiking story on the front page reported on seven local Boy Scouts who hiked fifty-one miles in fifteen hours. "The latest enthusiasts—or victims—of a 50-mile hike craze which has swept westward from the White House were full of cheer," said the *Tribune*.

The fifty-mile-hike craze had started in the first week of February. The White House had put out a story that the commandant of the Marine Corps, General David Shoup, had discovered a 1908 memo from President Theodore Roosevelt ordering that all Marines be able to cover fifty miles in twenty hours, double-timing the last seven hundred yards.

Actually, it was the other way around. Someone in the White House had found the order and told the President about it. Kennedy had sent a memo to General Shoup:

"Why don't you send this back to me as your own discovery? You might want to add a comment that today's Marine Corps officers are just as fit as those of 1908, and are willing to prove it. I, in turn, will ask Mr. Salinger for a report on the fitness of the White House staff."

The news manager's little ploy worked to perfection. Half the nation seemed ready to try hiking, too. In addition to Boy Scouts, the *Tribune* that day also covered Marine hikes, congressional secretary and clerk hikes, and speculation over whether Pierre Salinger, the President's notably unfit five-foot-nine, 185-pound press secretary would be risking his life in the attempt.

"We all know and love Plucky and we think he's funny," Kennedy said. "But I wonder what the rest of the country thinks of him. I wonder if they don't think he's making an ass of himself?"

On the boss's advice, Salinger announced that he was not plucky enough to go fifty miles. But he was about the only one. Robert Kennedy did it in 17 hours and 50 minutes. Ninety-seven students at Marin County High School in California did it. A postman in Burlington, North Carolina, did it in 10 hours and 28 minutes. The President's own fifty miles were done at Palm Beach. He organized a hike that included his brother-in-law Prince Stanislaus Radziwill, Chuck Spalding, a friend from Harvard, and Max Jacobson, the amphetamine doctor, who provided some first aid for the presidential marchers along the route. They took off walking briskly and Kennedy followed in a white Lincoln convertible until he got bored. At the end of their fifty miles, he presented each with a "Medal of Honor," an inscribed tea bag.

The hikes became the national harbinger of spring. It had been a tough winter for Kennedy. His problems were summarized by a question from Tom Wicker of *The New York Times* at the March 6 news conference: "Your policies in Europe seem to be encountering great difficulties. Cuba continues to be a problem. At home unemployment is high. There seems to be more concern in the country over a budget deficit than for a tax cut. In view of all these things, there is some impression and talk in this town and country that your Administration seems to have lost its momentum. . . ."

"I've read that," Kennedy answered. "If you ask me whether this is the winter of our discontent, I would say no." But he added it could be better, and maybe it would be in the spring.

And it was. On the first day of spring, March 21, he was asked about the economy again and he began by saying, "Our prospects look good in 1963. . . ." It looked as if the gross national product had grown by more than $8 billion since the beginning of the year. Personal income was up $4 billion over the same period, reaching a record of $452 billion. New car sales were running at a record pace of 7.5 million for the year, compared with 6.9 million in 1962. New housing construction was up 17 percent; corporate profits were up 7 percent. The Dow Jones Index had reached 721, up 185.33 points since the Kennedy crash a year before.

Still, over the same three months, Kennedy's Gallup Poll job approval rate had dropped from 76 percent to 66 percent by the end of March. Cuba was the reason again. According to Gallup, only a slight majority of respondents approved of Kennedy's handling of Fidel Castro, and the number who specifically disapproved had risen from almost none after the missile crisis to 33 percent in March. Castro was still in power; there were still Russian troops and bombers on the island.

White House polling summaries confirmed to Kennedy that he had little room for political maneuver on Cuba because public opinion went in two directions: almost 60 percent of respondents to several polls thought Cuba was a serious threat to world peace, particularly with Soviet troops still on the island; but the same number and a few more were against sending United States troops to invade Castro's island. "The present tendency toward diminishing confidence in the administration is likely to continue," Kennedy was told. "Unless: (a.) Obviously strong U.S. action is undertaken—diplomatic, economic, or military; (b.) Americans conclude that no strong action is feasible; (c.) Public attention is diverted to other subjects."

Kennedy's response, in secret, was to authorize the planning of new covert action against Cuba. After the missile crisis, he had ordered the shutdown of Operation Mongoose, the $100-million-a-year project to eliminate Fidel Castro. But, on March 14, he had received and approved a memo from Robert Kennedy saying: "I think there should be periodic meetings of a half a dozen or so top officials of the Government to consider Cuba. . . . I think this kind of effort should be applied to other problems as well. The best minds in Government should be utilized in finding solutions to these major problems."

There was an asterisk after "best minds." At the bottom of the page, Robert Kennedy had written "*ME."

So the old Special Group (Augmented) with a new name, the National Security Council Standing Group, began to meet every Tuesday morning with the same old purpose—getting rid of Fidel Castro. Robert Kennedy, Sorensen, McCone, Dillon, Taylor, and Roswell Gilpatric were all members of the ten-member Standing Group, convening without staff in the White House Situation Room. McGeorge Bundy was the chairman. He reported to the President: "We agreed on the desirability of not spreading knowledge of covert operations any wider than absolutely necessary, if we are to preserve the principle of deniability." Then deniability slid into calculated lies. The numbered copies of Standing Group minutes took this line: "There was a discussion as to how to handle press inquiries about developments in Cuba such as raids from outside Cuba and sabotage actions within Cuba. It was agreed that we should flatly deny any U.S. government involvement in any of these activities."

But that was in secret. In public, no news was good news from Cuba, and a few other places. The charge and countercharge over the pace of the Soviet military withdrawal from Cuba was becoming routine. None but a few of the more tedious Republicans thought the Russians were up to much any more on the island. There were no crises at the moment in Kennedy's presidency of crises.

"President Kennedy flung wide the French doors of his office, stepped out into the spring twilight, inhaled deeply," reported *Time* magazine at the beginning of April. "The fresh scent of thick bluegrass and moist earth, the sight of grape hyacinth bordering the flower garden (which has been replanted by a new White House gardener), the hues of cherry blossoms and forsythia across the yard made him smile. Off to his right, Caroline's swings and slides lent a touch of outdoor domesticity. Said the President, with an expansive wave, 'Look at that. Isn't that great?' The President's mood seemed to reflect the nation's. . . ."

And the nation was reflecting its leader. The man who had coined the phrase "the American Century," Henry Luce, the creator of *Time* and *Life* magazines, did not particularly like Kennedy's politics, but he thought the President was focusing Americans on the things that mattered—active citizenship, the joy of life itself. He seemed to be bringing out the best in people. Kennedy seemed to be the beginning of the new, though perhaps he was just the end of the old.

The United States was beginning to burst its seams economically, technologically, culturally. Jet airliners, interstate highways, direct long-distance telephone dialing, Xerox machines, and Polaroid cameras were speeding up people and life. Air conditioning was making it possible to build new cities in swamps and deserts. New things and new words were appearing almost every day: Zip Codes, Weight Watchers, Valium, measles vaccines, transistors, computers, lasers, "the Pill," DNA, LSD. Television was becoming an environment. It was hard to get through a day of work without a couple of conversations about what happened on "I Love Lucy" or "The Beverly Hillbillies" or what the new host of "The Tonight Show," Johnny Carson, had said last night.

Catch-22, a new novel by Joseph Heller, mocked the absurdity of war. The Supreme Court ruled that prayers or the reading of Bible verses in classrooms was a violation of the Constitution's clause on separation of Church and State. It also ordered that the government must provide lawyers for criminal defendants who could not afford to pay for one themselves. *Lawrence of Arabia* won the Academy Award as best film, but another nominated picture which seemed to move America more, *To Kill a Mockingbird,* was about race and justice and hope in the South. The music of young Americans was changing from perky love songs to slightly more serious stuff. "If I Had a Hammer" and "Blowin' in the Wind" were calls for justice and freedom all over this world. Across the Atlantic, record buyers were swooning over a British group called the Beatles, singing "I Want to Hold Your Hand."

That was 1963, a year that showed a bright surface at the beginning. America was rich and its wealth was shared by many millions now. Middle-class people could buy their own homes away from the cities where they worked, send their children to the best colleges, and fly to vacations in Europe or the Caribbean. A lot of this was new, and people did not quite know what to do with it or how to act. And there were the Kennedys! Young, rich, well educated, well mannered, gaily presiding over the White House, over the world really.

There was a pattern to the stories on the Kennedy children. Most were staged when Jacqueline Kennedy was traveling. On the day his wife left for a trip to Greece, Kennedy called Laura Bergquist Knebel of *Look* magazine, saying this was the time to send a photographer for a story the magazine wanted to do under the title "The President and His Son." "This is it. We'd better get this over with quick because when Mrs. Kennedy is around things get pretty sticky."

Kennedy had married a woman with appetite and taste for finer things—and a certain distaste for what her husband actually did for a living. "Take care of this," he said to Larry O'Brien, passing along a memo from his wife that spring: "I was passing by Mrs. Lincoln's office today and I saw a man [Congressman Aspinall] being photographed in the Rose Garden with an enormous bunch of celery. I think it is most undignified for any picture of this nature to be taken on the steps leading up to the President's office or on the South grounds. If they want their pictures taken they can pose by the West Lobby. This also includes pictures of bathing beauties, etc."

Jacqueline Kennedy, exotic in the all-male White House as well as in the all-around boyishness of the Kennedy family, was, said *The New York Times*: "well qualified for the role of unofficial Minister of Culture." It was she, with the help of Pierre Salinger, who had trained as a concert pianist, who had brought the cellist Pablo Casals, the composer Igor Stravinsky, and George Balanchine, the dance master, into the White House and hung paintings by Cézanne on its walls.

"I have called for a higher degree of physical fitness in our nation," proclaimed the President. "It is only natural that I should call for the kind of intellectual and spiritual fitness which underlies the flowering of the arts." As for himself, the President preferred Sinatra and show tunes to Stravinsky. But like a boy forced to take piano lessons, he did make an effort to appear to take culture seriously. In his own way. As he told

The New York Times: "I think it is tremendously important that we regard music not just as part of our arsenal in the Cold War, but as an integral part of a free society."

Jack Kennedy was pretty much a meat-and-potatoes guy, a middlebrow. He liked movies with Kirk Douglas, *Guys and Dolls* on Broadway, comedians like Bob Newhart and Joey Bishop, James Bond novels, and British political memoirs. His heavier reading began with Churchill, whom he made an honorary American citizen on April 9, saying among other things: "Accustomed to the hardships of battle, he had no distaste for pleasure."

"This is another one Mrs. Kennedy should do," Salinger told the President one morning in the Oval Office. A delegation of Girl Scouts was coming to the Rose Garden.

"Well, Pierre," Kennedy said, "if you want Mrs. Kennedy to do something you'd better inform her in advance."

"She has been informed in advance. She said she thought this was not her problem, it was yours."

"Just give me a minute," said the President. "I'll straighten this out."

He was gone for fifteen minutes, but came back smiling. "Mrs. Kennedy is going to do it," he said. "Set it up."

"How did you do it?" Salinger asked. Mrs. Kennedy was not an easy woman.

"It cost me," Kennedy answered. "Bet you won't guess what it is."

"A new dress?" the press secretary asked.

"No," Kennedy said. "Worse than that: two symphonies."

But sitting through symphonies beat talking about them in Jacqueline Kennedy's place. He was complaining about his wife going to Palm Springs one Friday in April, leaving him to meet with music students, when Norman Cousins arrived to report on his communications with Premier Khrushchev about controlling nuclear tests.

"People want this," Cousins told the President, mentioning that strontium 90, a deadly radioactive isotope, was found in milk all over the world after the last rounds of Soviet and U.S. explosions. Kennedy said he wanted a ban, too, but he wondered about his fellow Americans. He pulled out the weekly report on White House mail. A nuclear test ban was well down the list, after questions about Caroline's horse.

"The category that leads the list again this week is requests to the Kennedy family for money," he told Cousins with a smile. The mail on nuclear testing was not for a ban, he added; it was 15 to 1 against.

"Mr. President, do you still really have any hope of arriving at a nuclear test ban agreement?" Kennedy had been asked at his March 21 news conference.

"I am haunted," he answered, "by the feeling that by 1970, unless we are successful, there may be ten nuclear powers instead of four, and by 1975, fifteen or twenty. . . . I see the possibility in the 1970s of the President of the United States having to face a world in which fifteen or twenty or twenty-five nations may have these weapons. I regard that as the greatest possible danger. . . ."

He repeated that to Cousins. "No matter what, I want you to keep at this and keep me up-to-date." He said something about the children of the world, then stood up, walked to the French doors, and looked out for a long moment before speaking.

"See those chairs?" he said. "They're for high school music students invited by Jackie. It's eleven-forty. I have to talk to them at twelve noon. What do I tell them? Do you say anything to Khrushchev about music?"

"Yes, I tell him more Americans go to concerts each day than baseball games," said Cousins, whose magazine combined serious politics and serious arts. "I tell him that more than three hundred million books were published in the U.S. last year. I tell him something about one hundred American educational television stations. . . ."

"That's great," Kennedy said. "Can you write it?" Cousins sat down with a typewriter in the Cabinet Room. The President was already beginning to strip off his shirt to head for the swimming pool. Fifteen minutes later, he was paddling around the pool, holding up Cousins's draft and reading it aloud to Kenny O'Donnell.

Kennedy used time and people well, getting what he needed and moving on. "A master of time," Janet Travell called him. The biggest gripe in the White House, as it had been in Kennedy's Senate office, was that as the boss left for the evening or the weekend, he scattered questions and chores around that ruined everyone else's plans so that he could be on top of the world on Monday morning. When he was younger, Clark Clifford and other lawyers and family retainers had cleaned up the messes, including paying off young women now and then. There was always someone—servants and friends, speechwriters and Cabinet members. Arthur Krock and Sorensen had been there when he wanted to write books. "He's an artist who paints with other people's lives," said Polly Kraft, the wife of one of the campaign speechwriters, Joseph Kraft. "He raises the spirit of a room. 'Come along with me!' he says—and we all do."

"All right, let's haul it out of here," was the way Kennedy usually phrased it to friends when he was bored with a movie. What they thought did not matter.

The second time they met, Hugh Sidey, who covered him for *Time* magazine, was walking with Senator Kennedy near the short subway that connects the U.S. Capitol with the Senate office buildings. They literally bumped into Kennedy's buddy, Senator George Smathers of Florida, who was posing for a Senate photographer with a small claque of pretty young women from his state. They pulled Kennedy into the group and he laughingly posed.

"Get hold of that photographer and destroy the negative," Kennedy said as he and Sidey waved goodbye to Smathers and the girls. And Sidey did it.

John Kennedy's life was sequential seduction and there were few complaints from the seduced. "Social flattery," it was called by Krock, who had given Kennedy his editorial skills and his valet before they became estranged when the columnist began criticizing the President in print. "I have myself been infused with the warmth of good will engendered by this courtship of a suitor of such charm and unique distinction."

"Kennedy sets the style, tastes and temper of Washington more surely than Franklin Roosevelt did in twelve years, Dwight Eisenhower in eight, Harry Truman in seven," said *Time*. "Cigar sales have soared (Jack smokes them). Hat sales have fallen (Jack does not wear them). Dark suits, well-shined shoes, avoid button down shirts (Jack says they are out of style), secure their striped ties with PT-boat clasps . . . popular restaurants in Washington are Le Bistro and the Jockey Club, which serve the light continental foods that Jackie Kennedy features. The Colony restaurant, tops during the Republican Eisenhower Administration, went broke and has closed. The C&O canal now has hikers' 'traffic jams.' The Royal Canadian Air Force exercise manual is in every office."

And the proudest boast and put-down in Washington, reported the magazine, was this: "Is your wife pregnant? . . . Mine is." Robert's wife, Ethel, was pregnant with her eighth; Ted's wife, Joan, was pregnant with her third; and on April 12, the White House announced that Jacqueline Kennedy was due late in September.

The new order in Washington was confirmed that May by the government of the District of Columbia, which rather solemnly announced a reassignment of dog licenses that week. The President's three dogs, Charlie, a Welsh terrier, Pushinka, the pup of a Soviet space dog given to Caroline by Premier Khrushchev, and Clipper, a German shepherd, would wear D.C. tag numbers 1, 2, and 3, thus dropping the Vice President's dog, Jefferson, also called Little Beagle Johnson, from number 2 to number 4, and J. Edgar Hoover's dog, G. Boy, from number 3 to number 5.

Some of the glamour of the Kennedys was faked or exaggerated, but it did seem to serve a purpose, teaching Americans how to act and spend all the new money coming their way, giving the newly prosperous some polish in a larger world. There was so much that new suburban aristocrats could learn about—custom-made suits, French chefs and wines, private schools, winter vacations and separate bedrooms, skiing, sailing, Cape Cod, Palm Beach and Palm Springs, and the Riviera, even poets and cello players. Watching the Kennedys was self-improvement.

The President tried to learn from them, too. He had grown up separated by wealth and health from ordinary lives, and he tried to make up for it by constantly asking people where they worked, how much money they made, how they lived. "I never had a feeling he had an understanding what it was like to earn money," said Sidey.

"Do you remember the Depression?" Sidey asked him.

"No," Kennedy answered. "I have no memory of it at all, really, except what I read in history books . . . my experience was the war; that's what I remember. But the Depression had no effect on me."

He learned by questioning and reading. "Poverty" became a topic in the White House that spring because of a new book, *The Other America,* a study of poverty in the United States by an American socialist, Michael Harrington. Kennedy had been shocked by the Appalachian poverty of West Virginia during his primary campaign there, but that seemed isolated, even unique. Now a book said the problem was general. Actually, Kennedy did not read the book. He saw a review by Dwight Macdonald in *The New Yorker,* who wrote:

In "The Affluent Society" (1958) Professor J. K. Galbraith states that poverty in this country is no longer "a massive affliction [but] more nearly an afterthought."

In the last year we seem to have suddenly awakened, rubbing our eyes like Rip van Winkle, to the fact that mass poverty persists, and that it is one of our two gravest social problems. (The other is related: While only eleven percent of our population is non-white, twenty-five percent of our poor are.)

The most obvious citizens of the Other America are those whose skins are the wrong color. In 1939, the non-white worker's wage averaged 41.4 per cent of the white worker's; by 1958 it had climbed to 58 per cent. . . . The least obvious poverty affects our "senior citizens"—those over sixty-five. Mr. Harrington estimates that half of them—8,000,000—live in poverty and he thinks they are even more atomized and politically helpless than the rest of the Other America.

The problem is obvious: the persistence of mass poverty in a prosperous country. The solution is also obvious: to provide, out of taxes, the kind of subsidies that have always been given to the public schools (not to mention the police and fire departments and the post office)—subsidies that would raise incomes above the poverty level. . . .

The *New Yorker* review was almost perfectly argued to get Kennedy's attention. The President, many of his men sensed, felt almost nothing but tried to figure out everything. He was not a liberal moralist—he did not call himself any kind of liberal—but rather a managerial politician. An efficiency liberal, a man, at his best, looking for the most efficient means of attaining the greatest happiness for the greatest number. He was impressed by Harrington's statistics. He wanted to do the right thing—when the nation was ready for it. Bigotry was irrational. Poverty was a problem that could be managed. Best of all, it was framed as a new problem. He intended to do something about it—when he was sure of reelection.

During a conversation in April with Senator Mike Mansfield, he said he wanted to withdraw some of the American military advisers and intelligence agents in Southeast Asia. The senator was sure Kennedy meant what he said, but he knew and so did the President that whatever he said now, the best of plans and promises depended on what was happening at the appointed time. The job was reactive. Kennedy had to respond to events unpredicted and forces unseen. That was the job. The rest was style and inspiration.

His most important role was to keep the faith and keep the faith going. The power of the presidency was that the American people believed in it—their initiative, common sense, energy, and productivity gave the man at the center the benefit of most doubts and a very large margin of error. "This is a most presidential country," Walter Lippmann said that spring in a television interview. "The tone and example set by a president have a tremendous effect on the quality of life in America. The president is like the conductor of a big symphony orchestra." If Americans backed the President by instinct, which they were inclined to do, or if he persuaded them to give him some time and room to maneuver, he had as much power as, and more resources than, any emperor in history.

What Kennedy personally brought to the center of American life and the fulcrum of the postwar world was summed up early on in his administration in a flattering Sorensen-guided article by Frederick W. Collins in the *New Republic*, required reading in the White House, called "The Mind of JFK":

A compulsive instinct for inquiry, effectively used. Utter independence. A range of concern which thrusts the Presidency far out and deep down in the government. An insistence on extracting decisions from a sum total of materials instead of from alternatives pre-cooked by staff. An ease of decision, including decision on what needs to be decided, and when. A talent for suspended judgment, strikingly described as "an ability to live with chaos." . . . There is nothing he dislikes more, it is testified, than a nice, orderly day with five appointments neatly spaced . . . he keeps filling in the gaps in the appointment list until he has guaranteed himself a 12-appointment day of continuous action. . . . Sharp, drift-free tuning which permits movement from one problem to another without overlap or confusion. . . . An unflagging intent of action. A zest which confers absurdity upon all the melodramatic and maudlin folklore about the loneliness, anguish and burdens of the Presidency.

If that was what Kennedy brought to it, what did he want from the job? One of his men, George Ball, answered: "Never to be bored, never to be frustrated, never to be alone."

When there was no one else, there was Dave Powers, a charming little Irishman who had loved and amused Kennedy since his first election in 1946. Powers was fifty-one years old on April 25, 1963. The President's gift to his friend was a silver mug, engraved with an Indian proverb that touched the irony of the most powerful man in the world: "There are three things which are real: God, human folly and laughter. The first two are beyond our comprehension. So we must do what we can with the third."

Chapter 42

"Prospects in South Vietnam" was the title of the National Intelligence Estimate that went to the President on April 17, 1963. "We believe that Communist progress has been blunted and that the situation is improving," began the consensus report prepared by all United States intelligence agencies. "Strengthened South Vietnamese capabilities and effectiveness, and particularly US involvement, are causing the Viet Cong increased difficulty. . . . Assuming no great increase in internal support of the Viet Cong, changes and improvements which have occurred during the past year now indicate that the Viet Cong can be contained militarily. . . . However, we do not believe that it is possible at this time to project the future course of the war with any confidence. Decisive campaigns have yet to be fought and no quick and easy end to the war is in sight."

The military was less equivocal. The commander of all American forces in the Pacific (CINCPAC), Admiral Harry Felt, had told a press conference in February that the war could be won in three years. Two months after that, the Military Assistance Command Vietnam (MACV) had told Kennedy: "Barring greatly increased resupply and reinforcement of the Viet Cong by infiltration, the military phase of the war can be virtually won in 1963."

American technology was beginning to be brought to bear in Southeast Asia. The counterinsurgency was beginning to look a bit more like

Kennedy's visions of Green Berets and Colonel Hillandales. When the Viet Cong lost their fear of the H-21 Shawnee helicopters and started bringing them down with ground fire, the Army came up with the H-1, the "Huey," which put the fear of God and America back into the guerrillas. The President had authorized the Air Force to use napalm. He had also approved new defoliation guidelines after checking the effects of herbicide use along 87 miles of roads and canals and the destruction of 8,000 acres of rice paddies and manioc groves, which would have produced enough food for 1,000 men for a year. On April 4, Robert K. G. Thompson, the British counterinsurgency expert, had met with Kennedy and said again that bringing home one thousand U.S. troops at the end of the year would "show that you are winning . . . and take the steam out of the Communists' best propaganda line, that this is an American war."

The trouble in Southeast Asia now was in Laos, again, only nine months after the neutrality agreement signed by fourteen nations in Geneva. It happened every spring, at the end of the rainy season. Communist forces, ten thousand Pathet Lao, were on the move against the neutralist government installed after the latest Geneva agreement, taking the great Plaines des Jarres, a high plateau in the north of the country dotted by stone jars holding the ashes of the departed. The plateau's strategic importance to all sides in Southeast Asia was that it overlooked the Ho Chi Minh Trail used by the North Vietnamese to transport men and supplies to the war in South Vietnam, in open violation of the Geneva Accords. President Kennedy responded by again moving two U.S. Army battalions in Thailand to the Laotian border and moving a carrier task force with a combat-ready battalion of Marines into the South China Sea off Vietnam. The U.S. ships' communications were uncoded, as they had been during past shows of force, so that messages concerning possible action against North Vietnam could be heard easily in Hanoi. In Washington, on April 20, the President ordered the Joint Chiefs to plan for military action against North Vietnam.

"Hello, Governor, do I have the pleasure of speaking to the architect of the Geneva accords on Laos?" said Kennedy on Sunday, April 21, when he phoned Averell Harriman, whom he had just elevated to Undersecretary of State for Political Affairs. The President was kidding, but Harriman, never noted for his sense of humor, replied that whatever happened he was ready to take the blame to protect his President.

Kennedy wanted Harriman to go to Moscow, to confront Khrushchev and demand that the Soviet Union—a co-administrator of the Laos accords with Great Britain—call off the Pathet Lao.

"There's one other thing, Mr. President," said Harriman, once again maximizing access whenever he had it. "Don't let them go overboard using your name in connection with the Clay report. . . . You must not be involved. There is a great deal of difference between money and the world's confidence in a President."

The Clay Report was an evaluation of the effectiveness of U.S. foreign aid. After General Lucius Clay's Berlin service, the President appointed him as chairman of the "Special Committee to Strengthen the Security of the Free World," trying once again to get Republicans out front on a controversial issue. Kennedy wanted to use the committee to pressure Congress not to begin cutting foreign aid. Members and, more important, their constituents were unhappy after sending more than $100 billion in aid to other countries since the end of World War II, most of it designed to block communism in Europe. But this time one of Kennedy's Republican warriors turned on him. Clay had reported back that the United States was spending too much in too many places—making Kennedy look a bit the fool.

"We are trying to do too much for too many too soon . . . ," concluded the twenty-two-page report to the President. The special committee recommended a half billion cut in Kennedy's aid requests of $4.5 billion. "We cannot believe that our national interest is served by indefinitely continuing commitments at the present rate."

The President got four Laos questions at his news conference of April 24. The last was whether or not he believed in the "Domino theory"—that one country after another would go Communist in that part of the world if there were no U.S. military presence. He said yes. "If Laos fell into communist hands, it would increase the danger along the northern borders of Thailand. It would put additional pressure on Cambodia and would put additional pressure on Viet Nam, which in itself would put additional pressure on Malaya. So I do accept the view that there is an interrelationship in these countries. . . ."

That was the public stance. In secret, the President told McNamara that he wanted to go both ways at the same time in Southeast Asia: that while they considered overt action against North Vietnam, the Joint Chiefs should also begin preparing plans to phase out the American military presence in South Vietnam. After they talked, McNamara wrote out a short note for Mrs. Lincoln to give to the boss: "The last Jupiter missile in Turkey came down yesterday."

That evening over a drink, Kennedy brought up Vietnam again with Charlie Bartlett: "We don't have a prayer of staying in Vietnam. Those people hate us. They are going to throw our asses out of there at almost any point. But I can't give up a piece of territory like that to the Communists and then get the American people to reelect me."

"He's totally out to sea about what to do in Vietnam," Bartlett said later.

Kennedy was fighting, almost day by day now, to maintain the U.S. position in Southeast Asia without a total military commitment—at least through the 1964 campaign. President Diem, according to a CIA report Kennedy saw on April 24, was considering asking for a reduction in the number of U.S. troops in South Vietnam. Diem saw more clearly than Kennedy that the two presidents were essentially in a struggle over which one would run South Vietnam. If Kennedy thought Diem's authoritarianism was hurting the effort to stop the Communists, Diem thought Kennedy's aggressiveness and American aid might bring his government down before it could save him. Three weeks later, Diem's brother Ngo Dinh Nhu, who believed the Americans were plotting against the Ngos, told the *Washington Post:* "At least 50 percent of the U.S. troops in Vietnam are not absolutely necessary in the field." By early summer, the CIA was reporting unconfirmed suspicions that Diem and his brother were trying to open secret negotiations with the North Vietnamese about the possibility of a united or federated Vietnam with no foreign advisers of any kind.

So, the happy spring of 1963 in the White House was a short season. At sea in the Pacific and frustrated by de Gaulle's tenacious opposition to Atlantic alliances, Kennedy was trying to avoid racial currents at home. This time it was Birmingham again. But the President had had some reason to believe that civil rights demonstrations had peaked by the end of 1962. "At peace," as Lee White told him. Martin Luther King, Jr.'s, "Project C" in Birmingham seemed to be having relatively little impact. The press, at least, seemed to be getting bored with the whole thing. "To many Birmingham Negroes, King's drive inflamed tensions at a time when the city seemed to be making some progress, however small, in race relations," *Time* magazine reported on April 19, quoting only one Negro by name, the richest one, A. G. Gaston, who owned a bank, an insurance company, and several other businesses serving the Negro community, including a motel. Reverend King used the Gaston Motel as his headquarters when he was in town, but Gaston was beginning to think he would prefer to have the Atlanta preacher stay home in Georgia and let Birmingham Negroes deal with their own problems.

After a month of demonstrations, fewer and fewer Negroes were coming out into the streets. King was in and out of jail, arrested twice by the city's Commissioner of Public Safety, "Bull" Connor. This was a steel town in more than one way, a hard, hardworking, Jim Crow town, where bombings and cross-burnings were just part of life. The dominant employer in town was TCI—Tennessee Coal, Iron & Railroad—a division of U.S. Steel, which had only eight Negroes among its twelve hundred white-collar employees. There were only fifteen Negroes among the two thousand legally integrated federal employees working in the city. "The most segregated city in America," King claimed.

The situation was complicated by the fact that Birmingham had two governments—or none. Bull Connor had run for mayor and been defeated, but at the same time city voters approved of a change in government from a board of commissioners to a mayor-council form. There was legal confusion over when and how the new mayor, Albert Boutwell, would take office. Meanwhile, Boutwell and Connor, the Commissioner of Public Safety for twenty-three years, were both claiming power while the Alabama Supreme Court heard evidence relating to a timetable for the transfer of power. Connor still controlled the city's policemen and firemen, and both departments were feared, for good reason, by the 147,000 Negroes who made up 40 percent of the city's population. It seemed a time for patience to Kennedy.

The Negro protests, led by King and a local minister, Fred Shuttlesworth, had begun on April 3 and seemed to be going nowhere by the end of the month. The official side, the white side, was winning its confrontation with King and the Negroes through some uncharacteristic restraint: the police were holding back, containing what action there was inside Negro neighborhoods, generally avoiding confrontations and arrests. From the beginning of the marches, the publisher of the *Birmingham News*, Clarence Hanson, had decided to try to silence the Negroes with silence itself: No front-page stories on racial events and no front-page mention of Reverend King, even when he was arrested. Play it down until it goes away. Actually, that was the President's strategy, too. He had sent in Assistant Attorney General Burke Marshall to encourage and monitor secret negotiations between Negro and white businessmen.

At the beginning of May, King organized with the little he had left after a month of disappointments: schoolchildren. He organized thousands of schoolchildren to march through the city, too many to arrest. In Washington, Robert Kennedy said King's grievances were just, of course, but . . . "The timing of the present demonstrations is open to question . . . and schoolchildren participating in street demonstrations is a dangerous business."

On the afternoon of Thursday, May 2, Bull Connor's men were overrun by children. More than a thousand Negro children, some of them as young as six years old, but most of them teenagers happily playing hooky with the permission of parents and preachers, were inside 16th

Street Baptist Church. At 1:00 P.M., in bright waves, schoolchildren began pouring out the many doors of the church—"Hurry up, Lucille," called one little girl to a friend. "If you stay behind, you won't get arrested with our group"—going through, over, under, and around the police and into downtown shopping districts, protesting the segregation of everything in the city from lunchrooms to rest rooms. By the end of the day, six hundred of them were in jail—and CBS, NBC, and ABC with their news cameras were on the way to town.

There were another thousand inside the church the next day, Friday, May 3. The police waited outside, reinforced by city firemen with hoses pointed at the doors. The kids came out and the hoses were turned on, just sprinkling them. They kept coming and the water pressure was turned up and up, until the firemen brought up a high-pressure water gun, two fire hoses feeding into one small brass nozzle, designed to knock down brick-and-mortar walls, and set it on a tripod like a cannon. A. G. Gaston was in his office on the telephone with David Vann, a white attorney. Both men were involved in legal maneuvers to force Connor out of City Hall before the new administration took over in a few weeks, when Gaston heard noise outside and went to the window.

"Lawyer Vann," he yelled, "they've turned the fire hoses on a little black girl. And they're rolling that little girl right down the middle of the street."

Still more of the young marchers came. There were already more than two thousand of them under arrest in chaotic city jails and behind fences put up around empty lots. A crowd of Negroes gathered on Ingram Square in front of the church, watching the action of the church people, and soon enough a few of them started throwing rocks and bottles at the police and fire lines. Connor brought up eight police dogs, trying to use them on the flank of the crowd outside the church, to keep the Negroes hemmed in, in a single group that could be encircled. A K-9 officer grabbed a fifteen-year-old, just a bystander, by the shirt to move him on and the dog, a big German shepherd, went for the teenager's stomach. An Associated Press photographer got the picture; so did television.

The rocks and bottles hit a couple of Connor's men—and frightened the authorities in both Montgomery and Washington, as well as the merchants and clerks in the white stores and banks a few blocks away on 19th Street. The preachers may have believed in non-violence, this crowd did not. Many of the rock throwers had come out of neighborhood bars and social clubs. Here was something new. The rocks and the hoses, the dogs and the children, were being filmed by the television cameras, shown that night and the next day all over the country. The news was all over the world. Radio Moscow was broadcasting in more than thirty languages, saying: "We have the impression that American authorities both cannot and do not wish to stop outrages by racists."

The President saw the photograph of the attacking police dog on the front page of *The New York Times* the next morning. "It makes me sick," he said during a private meeting with officers of Americans for Democratic Action. But then he said, first privately and then publicly, that there was nothing he could do. Constitutionally, the federal government had no power to intervene, this was a state matter. He sent Burke Marshall back to Birmingham on May 4, telling him, in effect, to try to negotiate a truce.

Kennedy preferred quiet negotiation. But that was impossible now in a televised America. Television. Neither Martin Luther King, Jr., nor Clarence Hanson, the publisher of the *Birmingham News,* needed an appointment to talk to the President. They talked to the cameras. "I am not criticizing the President, but we are going to have to help him," said King. "The hour has come for the Federal government to take a forthright stand on segregation in the United States." And Hanson said: "Mr. President, if these were white marches . . . we believe your Administration would have taken vigorous action to restrain them. If there is to be order, and respect for law . . . you, sir, must be the one to bring it."

Neither the President, nor the governor, nor the mayor, nor the police commissioner, nor the city's newspapers, nor the preachers had control any more of the flow of information coming from the streets and churches of that city. It was all on television—within hours, as film was developed and flown to New York or some other transmission center, then sent around the country on network cables and telephone lines. With those signals, the torch of communications was being passed to a new generation of technology, speeding up cycles of event-action-reaction-backlash, changing what people knew and when they knew it. *Time* magazine, suddenly old-fashioned, seemed perplexed by what was happening, beginning its coverage: "Birmingham's Negroes had always seemed a docile lot . . ."

The White House announced then that it was "closely monitoring events," usually a formal euphemism for "What do we do now?" It was precisely true. The President was talking to Burke Marshall a couple of times each hour during the day on May 7, while the Assistant Attorney General continued to press Birmingham's business leaders to make some concessions to integration of city businesses, in return for a truce with the Negro preachers. In Washington, the Kennedy brothers were trying to round up national business leaders who might have influence in Birmingham. The President called Eugene Rostow, the dean of Yale Law

School, and asked him to call Roger Blough, the chairman of U.S. Steel, a Yale law graduate, and try to persuade him to make the officers of TCI cooperate with Marshall. That worked. Blough was more than happy to let bygones be bygones.

At eight o'clock Tuesday evening, Marshall called the White House and got Edwin Guthman, Robert Kennedy's special assistant. Guthman took these notes: "The meeting of all the businessmen worked. Now if it holds with Negroes we're over the hump."

By 4:00 A.M. Wednesday morning, "the Big Mules," the local name for the head of TCI and a couple of other big employers, and a seventy-seven-man committee of white retail merchants called the "Senior Citizens," working first with A. G. Gaston and then with Andrew Young, an assistant to King, came to an agreement. It began with the desegregation of department store dressing rooms and moved step by step to integrated lunch counters and schools. Reasonably certain of good news, the President scheduled a news conference for the afternoon.

With eighteen months of his term left, Kennedy began to face up to the possibility that this was all there was, that he might have to run for reelection on what he had done and not done in his first thirty months. Frustrated in Europe by de Gaulle, confused in Asia, unable to satisfy anyone on Cuba, checked in Congress, at enormous risk in Alabama and the rest of the South. Maybe this was it, the record he would have to run on.

May 8, 1963, was the 2,057th birthday of Gautama Buddha, a date that meant nothing to Americans, including the American diplomats and intelligence operatives in Saigon. In the city of Hué, five hundred miles north of Saigon, Buddhists began protesting the enforcement of a law banning the flying of religious flags in the city, once the capital of a united Vietnam. Police pulled down Buddhist birthday banners, although three days before they had permitted the flying of the gold and white banners of the Vatican during celebrations of the third anniversary of the consecration of the city's Roman Catholic archbishop, Ngo Dinh Thuc, President Diem's brother.

Like many prominent Vietnamese, the Ngos were French-educated and had taken the religion of the colonialists. Catholics were a tiny minority, representing about 10 percent of the nation while more than 80 percent of their countrymen practiced some sort of Buddhism. But more than half the members of the national assembly were Catholics, as were most of the country's landowners. The tensions between the Catholics and the Buddhists went back one hundred years, to the coming of the French. But they were being made worse by the Ngos, particularly

Madame Nhu. The president's sister-in-law was using the power of government to ban polygamy, adultery, abortion, and other old mores that offended her faith. But Buddhists were offended, too, and they had been in Vietnam not for a hundred years but for a thousand.

That evening in Hué—morning in Washington—more than three thousand Buddhists gathered at the city's radio station to hear a speech by their chief monk. The station refused to let the monk speak. There was a riot and then gunfire. Nine Buddhists were killed by South Vietnamese police. "A local incident," the U.S. Embassy reported back to Washington.

Kennedy got that news from Michael Forrestal of Bundy's staff. His first question was almost pathetic: "Who are these people? Why didn't we know about them before?"

"A spectacle ... seriously damaging the reputation of both Birmingham and the country," said President Kennedy at the beginning of his fifty-fifth news conference on May 8, 1963—only a few hours after South Vietnamese security forces broke up the parades in Hué. The Buddhists were marching abroad, the Negro Baptists at home. They were linked in his mind: the Buddhists were a domestic problem because their actions, or reactions, weakened American public support for the U.S. role in Southeast Asia; and the Negroes' actions, or reactions, were hurting the image of the United States in the worldwide struggle with communism.

"I am gratified to note the progress in the efforts by white and Negro citizens to end the ugly situation in Birmingham," he said at the news conference five days after the world saw photographs and film of police-trained dogs ripping the clothes off Negro men and women, and the high-pressure hoses blasting children to the ground. "Negro leaders have announced suspension of their demonstrations and ... the newly elected Mayor has indicated his desire to resolve these problems.

"I have made it clear since assuming the Presidency that I would use all available means to protect human rights and uphold the law of the land. ... We have committed all the power of the Federal Government to insure respect and obedience of court decisions," said Kennedy, in a prepared statement at the beginning of the conference. But, he added, "There wasn't any Federal statute that was involved in the last few days in Birmingham."

"Do you think a fireside chat on civil rights would serve a useful purpose?" a reporter asked.

"Well, it might. If I thought it would I would give one," the President answered. "But I made a speech the night of Mississippi—at Oxford to the citizens of Mississippi and others. That did not seem to do much good, but this doesn't mean we should not keep on trying."

The response to Kennedy's cool analysis in the on-the-other-hand style of the press came from his appointee to the Civil Rights Commission, Erwin Griswold, the Harvard law dean. In the next day's newspapers, he was quoted, "It seems clear to me that he hasn't even started to use the powers that are available to him."

"That son-of-a-bitch!" was Kennedy's private reaction to that. "Let him try."

What powers? Send in the Marines? Kennedy quoted one of his favorite lines from Shakespeare, from Part I of *Henry IV*—where Glendower says: "I can call spirits from the vasty deep," and Hotspur replies: "Why so can I, or so can any man; But will they come when you do call them?"

"Mediation and persuasion" were the words the President had used in his statement, "and where that effort has failed, lawsuits and court actions." That was still the strategy—a small crew of Justice Department men were in the South trying to obtain and enforce voting rights orders. The plan was simple, even plausible: Win voting rights for Negroes in the segregated states and everything else would follow. But it looked pitiful played against pictures of little girls attacked by police.

A half dozen times in two and a half years, the President had turned to Kenny O'Donnell and said, "I want to clear this desk. No foreign visitors for a month. I have to concentrate on civil rights"—as if he could straighten out this damned thing in a month if he were just not so busy.

It had not happened. Now there were cables from Hué and Saigon on his desk, reporting on the May 8 Buddhist confrontations. For the first thirty hours after the killings outside the radio station, U.S. cables to Washington referred to the leader of the Buddhists there as the "Chief Bonze," using the Vietnamese word for monk, apparently not knowing his name, Tri Quang.

U.S. officials at the embassy in Saigon and the consulate in Hué reported that the Diem government was saying the riot and deaths were the work of the Viet Cong—but "this line has no credibility among population," reported John Heble, the U.S. consul. The first cables from Washington to the Saigon embassy on May 9, after Rusk conferred with Kennedy, were signed by the Secretary of State: "At your discretion, suggest you urge GVN [Government of Vietnam] take no repressive measures against Buddhists, offer sympathy and funeral expenses."

The President seemed more detached about the events in Birmingham. "Life is unfair," he had said many times. His sense of irony and his wit kept him out of corners where he might have to choose between right and wrong. He used a joke at the Gridiron dinner, a spring rite of the Washington press establishment, to dismiss demands from American conservatives that he allow a Congolese leader, Moishe Tshombe, into the United States. Tshombe was the favorite of European companies who were trying to retain control of copper mines in the former Belgian Congo. He governed the richest province and was trying, with Belgian help, to make it independent of the new Republic of the Congo. Noting that one of Tshombe's sponsors was his old mentor, Arthur Krock, a pillar of Washington's segregated Metropolitan Club, Kennedy remarked: "I am perfectly willing to offer Mr. Tshombe a visa, if Arthur Krock would give him dinner at the Metropolitan Club."

And he could be cruder than that, campaigning among Negroes in Philadelphia in the morning—for the reelection of the Democratic mayor, James Tate—then on Air Force One back to Washington turning to David Lawrence, the mayor of Pittsburgh, and telling him the current joke about Negroes moving into white neighborhoods: "Knock-Knock!" . . ."Izya!" . . ."Izya who?" . . ."Izya new neighbor," said the President.

Then he told Lawrence, who was also the chairman of the Democratic Party of Pennsylvania, that he was going to need every Northern state he could get in 1964. The way things were going in Alabama, Kennedy said, "I can kiss the South good-bye."

The deal to end the Birmingham demonstrations collapsed after only a few hours. Bull Connor's men walked up to the 16th Street Baptist Church and padlocked the doors. Then they arrested Reverend King and his second-in-command, Reverend Ralph Abernathy, putting them back into Birmingham Jail when they refused to pay bail on earlier charges. The new issue between the preachers and city officials was getting those two, and 2,500 more Negroes, out of jail. King and Abernathy were practically thrown out when A. G. Gaston, the only Negro in town with that kind of cash, came and paid their bail of $5,000. The bail for the others, more than $160,000 in cash, was quickly raised after a few telephone calls from the White House. The biggest contributors to the bail fund were three union leaders, George Meany of the AFL-CIO, Walter Reuther of the United Autoworkers, and Michael Quill of the New York City Transport Workers Union, and one rich politician, Governor Nelson Rockefeller. "Rocky" was on his honeymoon at the 15,000-acre ranch he owned in Venezuela with a new wife named "Happy" and a new political problem. He had dropped 13 points in head-to-head polling against Kennedy since his divorce, after thirty-one years of marriage, from his first wife, Mary Todhunter Rockefeller.

A Birmingham deal was finally done on Friday, May 10. White merchants and Negro preachers agreed that rest rooms and water fountains would be integrated within thirty days, lunch counters in sixty days. Martin Luther King, relieved and triumphant, went out of his way to diminish President Kennedy's role. "The President said that there were no Federal statutes involved in most aspects of this struggle," said King, during a press conference at the Gaston Motel. "But I feel that there have been blatant violations of basic constitutional principles. . . . Persons who have been arrested were arrested for going down to register to vote, and the Federal government has done nothing about that."

"When things started happening down here, Mr. Kennedy got disturbed," said King in church later that day with a touch of mockery. "For Mr. Kennedy . . . is battling for the minds and the hearts of men in Asia and Africa—some one billion men in the neutralist sector of the world—and they aren't going to respect the United States of America if she deprives men and women of the basic rights of life because of the color of their skin. Mr. Kennedy knows that."

The next night, at 10:45 P.M., with Martin Luther King back in Atlanta, two dynamite stick bombs exploded in the front of the house of his brother, the Reverend A. D. King, pastor of the First Baptist Church in the Birmingham suburb of Ensley. The second bomb exploded as he got his wife and their five children out the back of the parsonage. By midnight, A. D. King was trying to calm down a crowd of more than a thousand angry and frightened Negroes gathered around his smoking house, when a second set of bombs blew out the front of the Gaston Motel, directly below the second-floor room reserved for Martin Luther King.

That ended the power of non-violence sermons for the night, as Negro bars and social clubs emptied again into the Saturday night streets. There were bricks and bottles, fire and smoke and curses in the air until dawn. All of that was made worse by what amounted to an invasion by three hundred Alabama State Troopers from Montgomery marching into the colored section at 3:00 A.M., clubs swinging, shotguns at the ready, under orders from Alabama's new governor, George Wallace.

Mediation and persuasion had obviously failed. The President, who was at Camp David, headed back to the White House by helicopter on Sunday, May 12. He had the *Washington Post* under his arm. On the front page, the paper featured an interview with Ngo Dinh Nhu, described by the reporter, Warren Unna, as the real power in Saigon. Nhu was quoted as saying that there were too many Americans in Vietnam: "South Vietnam would like to see half of the 12,000 to 13,000 American military stationed here leave the country."

Another helicopter picked up Burke Marshall from his farm in West

Virginia. Defense Secretary McNamara, Secretary of the Army Cyrus
Vance, Army Chief of Staff Earle Wheeler, the Attorney General, and
other Justice Department officers came by car for hours of meetings
about the law and federal power beginning at five-thirty. The President's
enforcement power ranged from the overaged and undertrained U.S.
Marshals, to the paratroopers of the 82nd Airborne who were one
hundred miles from Birmingham at Fort Benning, Georgia. But, once
again, there was nothing in between except the FBI. The question for
the President now was whether to send in the Army, and how to explain
why he was doing it. Was it to restore public order, that is, control the
Negroes? Or to protect them from the police and troopers of Bull Connor and George Wallace?

"The argument for sending the troops in is what's going to happen in
the future," said the President at the late afternoon meeting. "The governor has virtually taken over the state. You're going to have his people
sticking bayonets in people and hitting people with the clubs. You're
going to have rallies all over the country . . . calling on the President to
take forceful action. . . ."

"If that agreement blows up," Burke Marshall said. "The Negroes
will be . . ."

"Uncontrollable," Kennedy interjected.

"And I think not only in Birmingham," said Marshall.

"How freely do you talk to King?" Kennedy asked Marshall.

"I talk to him freely. I'll tell you what he intends to do, Mr. President.
He intends to go to this church and call upon the people to stay off the
streets. . . ."

"Call him up, like you're just talking on your own," Kennedy told
him. He wanted to know whether King was going to be demanding that
the Army come in. No one in the Oval Office knew that King had
already told reporters he would not do that.

"I've got a battle group at Fort Benning," said General Wheeler. "It
takes six hours and thirty minutes to make Birmingham."

The President wanted to know why it would take that long, but he
dropped the subject when Marshall returned after talking to King.

"He says that if there are no more incidents he thinks he can control
his people. . . . If it causes the businessmen to go back on their
agreement, he said the game is over. And I think that's absolutely right."

As usual, the men around the President that day presented him with
three options: (1) Go all the way. (2) Talk, talk, and buy time. (3) Do
nothing.

In this case, that came down to: (1) Declare martial law. (2) Mobilize
troops, make a speech, and see what happens. Or (3) Do nothing and
see what happens. As almost always, Kennedy chose the middle option,

wondering whether the presidential statements being drafted by Burke Marshall and others went too far in taking the side of Birmingham's Negroes. Finally he decided, ordering three thousand Regular Army troops on full alert on bases around Birmingham, and putting the 2nd Infantry Division and the 82nd Airborne on alert. He ordered up the paperwork to federalize the Alabama National Guard on a moment's notice if Governor Wallace, who was legally their commander unless formally superseded by the President, attempted to use the Guard himself. The President went on television at nine o'clock that Sunday night for less than five minutes.

"I am deeply concerned about the events which occurred in Birmingham last night . . .

"This Government will do whatever must be done to preserve order, to protect the lives of its citizens, and to uphold the law of the land. . . . The Birmingham agreement was and is a fair and just accord. It recognized the fundamental right of all citizens to be accorded equal treatment and opportunity. . . . The Federal government will not permit it to be sabotaged by a few extremists on either side who think they can defy both the law and the wishes of responsible citizens by inciting or inviting violence.

"It is my hope . . . that the citizens of Birmingham themselves will maintain standards of reasonable conduct that will make outside intervention unnecessary and permit the city, the state and the country to move ahead in protecting the lives and the interests of its citizens and the welfare of our country."

Watching from behind the cameras, Burke Marshall, the most cautious of men, thought that Kennedy was betting his presidency. He was going to have to do what he most wanted to avoid, propose comprehensive civil rights legislation in his first term. And there was going to be trouble if it passed, and worse if it did not.

"To govern is to choose," Kennedy had said more than once. He had the power to send troops into Alabama or launch a nuclear strike calculated to kill 100 million Soviet citizens, at the risk of a retaliatory strike that might kill 70 million Americans. The choices were packaged in little option memos to make one seem like another, an ordinary context in which to do extraordinary things. Just check the box. The very familiarity and plausibility of rambling meetings, intelligence reports, briefing papers, talking points, memos and polls and hallway conversations could make almost anything seem normal by making it routine. Kennedy's personal style was to make it all seem like a movable feast, a floating bull session. But when the talk stopped, the President was the one who had to choose.

Choosing was using up his power. McNamara showed Kennedy a

little graph he had drawn, with the vertical axis marked "POWER" and the horizontal marked "TIME," extending out eight years. He drew a dotted line from the peak of power to the end of time, with power at the maximum at zero time, 50 percent after four years, dropping to zero at the end of eight years. "This is the way it should be," said the Secretary.

"I agree with that, Bob," Kennedy said. But he thought he should be using his power and himself up in Berlin, not in Birmingham.

Or Saigon. Asked at his news conference on May 22 about Ngo Dinh Nhu's call for bringing home U.S. troops, Kennedy was still angry, and still conflicted, trying to have this one both ways: "We would withdraw the troops, any number of troops, any time the Government of Viet Nam would suggest it. The day after it was suggested, we would have some troops on their way home. That is number one.

"Number two is: we are hopeful the situation in South Viet Nam would permit some withdrawal in any case by the end of the year, but we can't possibly make that judgment at the present time . . . I couldn't say that today the situation is such that we could look for a brightening of the skies that would permit us to withdraw troops or begin to by the end of this year."

Chapter 43

"BIRMINGHAM AND BEYOND: The Negro's Push for Equality," was the headline across the cover of *Time* magazine dated May 17, 1963. The picture underneath was not of President John Kennedy, or the Reverend Martin Luther King, Jr., but of a thirty-eight-year-old novelist, a Negro named James Baldwin, the son of a Harlem minister. Baldwin's 20,000-word essay, "Letter from a Region in My Mind," had impressed Kennedy when it was published in *The New Yorker* late in 1962. It had just been published as part of a new book entitled *The Fire Next Time*.

"Try to imagine how you would feel if you woke up one morning to find the sun shining and all the stars aflame," wrote Baldwin, whose bitter and passionate words were cast as a letter to his nephew.

You would be frightened because it is out of the order of nature. Any upheaval in the universe is terrifying because it so profoundly attacks one's sense of one's reality. Well, the black man has functioned in the white man's world as a fixed star, as an immovable pillar and as he moves out of his place, heaven and earth are shaken to their foundations. . . .

The Negroes of this country may never be able to rise to power, but they are very well placed indeed to precipitate chaos and ring down the curtain on the American dream. There is a limit to the number of people any government can put in prison, and a rigid limit indeed to the practicality of such a course. . . . A bill is coming in that I fear America is not prepared to pay.

If we—and now I mean the relatively conscious whites and the relatively conscious blacks, who must, like lovers, insist on, or create, the consciousness of the others—do not falter in our duty now, we may be able, handful that we are, to end the racial nightmare, and achieve our country, and change the history of the world.

If we do not now dare everything, the fulfillment of that prophecy, recreated from the Bible in song by a slave, is upon us: God gave Noah the rainbow sign, No more water, the fire next time!

Like Martin Luther King, Jr., Baldwin used American rhetoric to explain that Negroes were like other Americans, they were not out of the order of nature. John Kennedy did not disagree, but he was determined not to move any further than he had to until the rest of America was ready to accept Negroes as part of American nature—or were so shamed by what they saw on television that they could not resist the Negroes' cause and still call themselves Americans. Luckily for him, the agreement in Birmingham did hold. Perhaps the season was changing. The Alabama Supreme Court ruled that Commissioner Connor had to leave office. Power shifted to the new mayor, former Lieutenant Governor Albert Boutwell, a moderate segregationist who said he would meet with any Negro leaders, except Martin Luther King, Jr. The old segregationists controlling the Birmingham Board of Education made one last official attempt to break the city's Negroes, expelling or suspending the 1,081 Negro students who had been arrested during King's marches. The NAACP challenged the dismissals in Federal Court, losing in the District Court before a judge appointed by Kennedy, Clarence Allgood. But Allgood's approval was reversed by an Eisenhower appointee, Chief Judge Elbert Tuttle of the Fifth Circuit Court of Appeals in Atlanta.

King had become a national hero at the age of thirty-four, among Negroes everywhere, and among white liberals in the North. Touring triumphantly through Cleveland, Chicago, and Los Angeles, the preacher from Atlanta raised hundreds of thousands of dollars at each stop for continued struggle. Governor Wallace, who was forty-three years old, was a hero, too, to millions of others, vowing now to prevent integration of the last whites-only state university in the country, the University of Alabama.

Despite a federal court order barring interference by state officials, the governor vowed to stand in the doorway of the university to block the entrance of the first two Negroes accepted by the school, Vivian Malone and James Hood. Both were scheduled to begin summer classes early in June. Kennedy, who had told the Justice Department that he wanted the order before there was trouble, not after, said he would stand behind the law, answering without heat the first question at a news conference on May 22: "The courts have made a final judgment on this matter . . . I am obligated to carry out the court order. That is part of our Constitutional system. There is no choice in the matter. . . . We are a people of laws, and we have to obey them."

Kennedy's cool talk of law and orders was still calculated to keep him above the passions of the day. That week he traveled into the South, going to Nashville, Tennessee, for ceremonies commemorating the ninetieth anniversary of the founding of Vanderbilt University. But he devoted only a few oblique sentences to racial problems, talking again of legalism: "Certain other societies may respect the rule of force—we respect the rule of law. . . . No one can deny the complexity of the problems involved in assuring to all our citizens their full rights as Americans. But no one can gainsay the fact that the determination to secure those rights is in the highest traditions of American freedom. . . . The educated citizen has an obligation to uphold the law."

It was a standard to which many could repair, but Kennedy had been careful to apply it case by case, order by order. Wallace was in the schoolhouse door, but no one was sure yet where the President stood. In *The New Yorker* the following week, Richard Rovere argued that a moral commitment to civil rights required defiance of the laws of Alabama and a lot of other places: "For the time being, at least, he [Kennedy] lent the moral prestige of his office to a movement that seeks justice outside the law and in defiance of it. . . . Oddly, there is reason to believe that the full significance of his statement was not appreciated by the President himself when he made it. . . . It is a difficult thing for a chief magistrate to urge respect for the law as a general principle and at the same time to speak approvingly of masses who take to the streets to proclaim their disrespect for it."

In the lobbies of the U.S. Senate, many southerners believed the President was with them—another Northern politician who said what he had to say to get elected, just as they did. One of them, Senator Allen Ellender of Louisiana, a friend of the President, was telling his colleagues privately that Kennedy would be standing with them if it were not for Negroes in the politics of the North.

The next day, an assistant to Lyndon Johnson, George Reedy, gave his boss a long memo warning the Vice President, and advising him to tell the President, that they had to choose sides:

> There is a common denominator to the thinking of both the Negroes and the white supremacists. It is a belief that the United States—in the person

of the President himself—has not made a real moral commitment to the cause of equal rights and equal opportunity. Both sides realize that the courts are on the Negroes' side and that the President is prepared to use force to make the court orders effective. But the emphasis has been on compliance with the law as stated by the courts and the inference is that the President would take a different stand if the courts ruled differently. Therefore, the Negroes are uncertain that the moral force of the Presidency is on their side and the whites believe that the President is acting out of political expediency. . . . The Negroes are going to be satisfied with nothing less than a convincing demonstration that the President is on their side. The backbone of white resistance is not going to be broken until the segregationists realize that the total moral force of the United States is arrayed against them.

It's obvious that this country is undergoing one of its most serious internal clashes since the Civil War itself.

"The American Revolution of '63" was the title of a three-hour NBC documentary on the struggle against segregation. "The Negro Revolt" was *Time* magazine's headline in reporting on dozens of racial demonstrations and confrontations across the country, south and north—in Jackson, Mississippi, and Chicago; in Baton Rouge, Louisiana, and Tallahassee, Florida, and Philadelphia.

Racial confrontation was also beginning to concern the largest integrated organization in the country, the military. Air Force officers at a missile base outside Rapid City, South Dakota, called back to Washington for guidance on what to do about Negro enlisted men who wanted to go to town to join in civil rights meetings and demonstrations. The requests were kicked up to Lee White in the White House, and he decided that airmen could do anything they wanted to do when they were off duty and out of uniform. That's what the President read in *The New York Times*.

"How the hell did this happen?" the President demanded, calling White when he had read the *Times* story. "Did you know about this?"

He did, of course. Kennedy told him to call every agency that might face a similar problem and order them: "Don't do a goddamned thing until it's been cleared."

The President did have cleared-desk civil rights meetings for a couple of days, May 20 and 21, listening to his aides, led by Robert Kennedy, debate what they could do next, whether or not to introduce a comprehensive civil rights bill. The early discussion focused on trying to give the Justice Department new powers to initiate suits if Negroes complained of situations where they were being denied equal protection under federal law. Robert Kennedy and Burke Marshall were against it, saying the complaints would overwhelm the department and the courts.

"Okay, how will we get away without sending up Title III?" asked the President. Title III, of the Civil Rights Act of 1957, gave the Attorney General the power to file public school desegregation suits. It was voted down as Congress passed the rest of the act, and Senator Kennedy had joined in voting against it.

Could they persuade American business, particularly Southern business, to employ Negroes? The President answered his own question: "I called in businessmen to ask them to hire Negroes. You know what they said to me? Why should we hire Negroes? You don't hire Negroes." Then he pulled out a sheet of paper Lee White had prepared for him on federal employment in one Southern city, Nashville: "four Negroes in the 405-man Treasury Department offices; two of 249 Agricultural employees; no Negroes working in Labor and Commerce department offices. . . ."

"Hopeless, they'll never reform," Kennedy said of the southerners in Congress and local office. "The people in the South haven't done anything about integration for a hundred years, and when an outsider intervenes, they tell him to get out, they'll take care of it themselves—which they won't. . . . I don't care if they're sore. . . . We can't go around saying to Negroes you can't demonstrate—and they can't get a solution."

Robert Kennedy said he still had to court those people, and suggested a series of meetings, two or three a week, sixty or seventy people at a time, with both white and Negro leaders to begin to build local support for civil rights legislation and for hiring Negroes—before the fire next time. "You're right," the President said. Then he told his brother to make sure that Martin Luther King, Jr., was not invited. "The trouble with King is that everybody thinks he's our boy, anyway," he said. "King is so hot these days that it's like Marx coming to the White House."

By the end of May, Kennedy's attention was turned to the capital of Mississippi, Jackson. When demonstrations began there on May 28, the mayor, Allen Thompson, ordered barbed-wire enclosures built on the Mississippi State Fairground to hold up to ten thousand Negroes. City policemen stood outside Woolworth's Five-and-Ten Cent Store on Capitol Street for three hours, while white men and women charged the lunch counter and poured mustard and ketchup, sugar and salt, over three Negro students and John Salter, a white sociology professor from Tougaloo College, who were asking for service. A former policeman named Benny Oliver kicked the professor to the floor and kicked one of the students in the face again and again as other whites poured salt into the bleeding wounds.

That night, Negroes at a local church stood and applauded for twenty straight minutes when the field secretary of the National Association for the Advancement of Colored People in Mississippi, Medgar Evers, called for a "massive offensive" against Jackson's segregation.

Roy Wilkins, the executive director of the NAACP, who was almost thirty years older than King, worried that King and his makeshift organization, the Southern Christian Leadership Conference (SCLC) was displacing Wilkins's fifty-year-old, 400,000-member association as the dominant vehicle for Negro aspirations. He flew down from New York the next day for his first return to the streets in a very long time. Within hours, he was in jail himself. King, who was in Chicago, telephoned a white friend and adviser in New York, an attorney named Stanley Levison, with that news, saying, "We've baptized Brother Wilkins." Whatever he and Wilkins thought of each other—Wilkins despised King personally—the NAACP leader's arrest on the streets of Jackson was an important breakthrough. Now, King said, the movement needed a national event to pressure President Kennedy to sign an executive order banning segregation everywhere. A mass march on Washington might do it.

King sent a telegram to the White House the next day, asking for a meeting with the President to talk about Jackson. But he was pushed off —because of things he had said about Kennedy's lack of passion for civil rights to Levison the night before. The White House had the transcript of King's call within hours. The lawyer's phones had been tapped, by order of Attorney General Robert Kennedy, since March 1962. Hoover believed Levison was a secret official of the Communist Party of the United States.

Meanwhile, the President and the Attorney General were working the phones themselves, day after day, trying personally to negotiate a quiet settlement with Thompson in Jackson, as they were with governors and mayors all over the South. They were all professional politicians, Democrats, most of them, just like the President, and they wanted to get this over with as soon as possible—but without looking nigger-loving soft at home.

"I was wondering whether there's anything that we could do to make the situation less, uh, critical down there?" the President asked Mayor Thompson, in the first of several conversations they had in June.

"The Associated Press man was in this morning and I told him what a wonderful fellow you were," Thompson began. "Of course, any other things you hear about it, don't pay any attention, because I, I really think the world of you. The only thing, is that if you could some way or other ask the people in your own way—I mean, I know you've got your problems a hundredfold more than I have—but if you could just urge Congress to let the courts, I mean to go through the courts and not have marches and intimidation. . . . People listen to you and if you would just tell 'em to stay out of this because they're using these young children."

"I talked to them, there seem to be two or three things that didn't seem to me to be too unreasonable," said Kennedy, mentioning demands for Negro policemen and school-crossing guards.

"We have answered every other thing like I told 'em except the biracial committee, and I just can't do that right now."

"Reverend Smith, is he the stud duck down there?"

"R. L. T. Smith. He's not the power. Haughton, H-A-U-G-H-T-O-N, is the one that causes problems and he's real smart. . . . Now, look, Mr. President, don't get your feelings hurt in anything that comes up . . . about anything anybody says that I say."

"Okay," Kennedy said, and laughed. "I give you full permission to denounce me in public as long as you don't in private."

"You're rich. Give my regards to your wife."

"You say hello to Governor Wallace . . . I'll call you back tonight."

After a night of rioting, Mayor Thompson was not so calm in their second June conversation.

"Mr. President, we have an explosive situation here. They have just gone wild. They have got it in their system . . . and the people can't control them or anything. We are going to put some Negro policemen on. But my police just want me to shift into it without coming out and making a great big statement about it right now. . . . The commissioner in the sanitation department is already making arrangements to upgrade, uh, two, uh, people in the Negro district to put them as foremen. They went in there Saturday and the Negroes almost mobbed them. They had to come back. They're afraid to go in there. I have got to maintain my image with the white and the colored people with the police, with my employees, with everybody."

"The Negro groups are out on a limb," Kennedy responded, "so they have to look like when they call off these demonstrations that they're getting someplace. Now it should be possible in this meeting to work out some language which would save your situation and at the same time not make it look like they've all quit."

In Baton Rouge, the capital of Louisiana, Kennedy was back and forth on school desegregation in demonstrations with Governor Jimmy Davis, a country singer who had written one of America's favorite songs, "You Are My Sunshine."

"I'm going to get hurt in the thing myself, but I'm going to handle it," Davis said.

"That'll make a helluva difference," the President replied.

"I'll handle it one way or the other, but I'm not, nobody knows it but you. I hope that something happens sometime, either we have federal orders to stop some of these demonstrations, marches, and if we don't, I think it is going to spread."

"It's going to be up North," Kennedy said. "You know, this isn't any more just a Southern matter."

"When it gets up there, I'll tell you, now if, it will be black against white. Down here they have the ties that bind, I mean they're a lot of them that are very close, like that's all that I have on my farm. A colored man runs it. He sells my cows, he buys and does everything."

"It's Philadelphia, and it's going to be Washington, D.C., this summer, we're trying to figure out what we can do to put this stuff in the courts and get it off the street because somebody's going to get killed," the President said.

"It's going to be the bloodiest thing . . . that's the problem."

"Governor, I appreciate that very much. How about coming up here later on?"

"Well, I hope I can . . . I had a fellow in this room—a board member from LSU—and he said, 'I want to have a seat in the Kennedy rocker.' You know, the one you sent me. . . . How's your back?"

"These days when it rains, it's not so good, but I'm getting along pretty well."

"It's going to be a civil war," Davis had said between the small talk. That was about what George Reedy had been telling Lyndon Johnson. Sticking to a policy of not taking sides and using the Army to enforce court orders was going to lead logically to military occupation of the South. Johnson had been complaining for weeks that the President never asked for his advice. Kennedy heard about the complaints, and finally he did call Johnson in on June 3, asking whether the Vice President had any suggestions about dealing with the Congress on civil rights.

Johnson began by telling Kennedy something he did not want to hear, that the real problem was not in the Congress but in the country. They talked for a while and then Kennedy asked Johnson to repeat his thoughts to Ted Sorensen.

"The whites think we're just playing politics to carry New York," Johnson told the speechwriter. "The Negroes feel and they're suspicious that we're just doing what we got to. Until that's laid to rest I don't think you're going to have much of a solution . . . the Negroes are tired of this patient stuff and tired of this piecemeal stuff and what they want more than anything else is not an executive order or legislation, they want a moral commitment that he's behind them.

"I want to pull out the cannon. The President is the cannon. You let him be on all the TV networks just speaking from his conscience. . . . I know the risks are great and it might cost us the South, but those sorts of states may be lost anyway. The difference is if your President just enforces court decrees the South will feel it's yielded to force. He ought to make it almost make a bigot out of nearly anybody that's against him, a high lofty appeal, treat these people as Americans.

"You see, this fellow Baldwin, he says, 'I don't want to marry your daughter, I want to get you off my back,' and that's what these Negroes want. They want that moral commitment . . . saying to the Baldwins and to the Kings and to the rest of them, 'We give you a moral commitment. The government is behind you. You're not going to have to do it in the streets. You can do it in the courthouses and the Congress.'

"This aura, this thing, this halo around the President, everybody wants to believe in the President and the Commander in Chief. I think he'd make the Barnetts and the Wallaces look silly. . . . Why, he'll have as many voters on his side as these little legislators got on theirs if he tells them the truth. Because he's right, Ted."

Baldwin was being courted by Robert Kennedy. He met the writer at a Washington reception and asked him to bring together some Negro intellectuals to meet at the Kennedy family's apartment on Central Park South in New York City on May 24. It was a group of stars—singers Harry Belafonte and Lena Horne were there, along with the playwright Lorraine Hansberry. But the meeting was taken over by a former Freedom Rider named Jerome Smith, who had been on the bus that had left Montgomery on the morning of May 22, 1961. He stilled the others with angry stories of being beaten by Southern police. "I want to vomit being in the same room with you," he told Robert Kennedy; he said it made him sick to be begging for his legal rights from the man who was supposed to be enforcing them. Then the Attorney General asked him whether he would fight for his country in wartime. "Never! Never! Never!" Smith said, shouting.

"How can you say something like that?" Robert Kennedy asked. He was shocked. His mood was not helped when the meeting broke up and Clarence Jones, a Harlem attorney, shook his hand and said he was Martin Luther King, Jr.'s, lawyer, and that he had worked with Burke Marshall on the Birmingham agreement and appreciated the efforts of the Justice Department down there. "I wish you had spoken up about that," Robert Kennedy said coldly.

The New York meeting lasted three hours. The Negroes demanded a public gesture from the White House. Perhaps the President should personally escort the two Negro students waiting to begin summer classes at the University of Alabama. Robert Kennedy struck an old theme, saying that his grandfather had been a hated immigrant in Boston—"The Irish were not wanted"—and two generations later his brother was President of the United States. It just took a little patience.

"Your family has been here for three generations and your brother's on top," said Baldwin, in a rage. "My family has been here a lot longer than that and we're on the bottom. That's the heart of the problem, Mr. Kennedy."

Robert Kennedy was angry enough that, back in Washington, he made a point of telling his brother that Jones and two other men at the meeting probably were driven by guilt because they were married to white women.

Chapter 44

On the morning of Wednesday, June 5, President Kennedy left Andrews Air Force Base for a five-day tour of the West. The schedule included visits to military installations in Colorado and California, commencement addresses and fund-raising, a quick side trip to Texas, and a speech to the United States Conference of Mayors in Hawaii. There was a full-scale presidential departure, with congressmen and White House staffers waving at the President as he boarded Air Force One. John F. Kennedy, Jr., almost three, was crying because he had to stay home. Cameramen and photographers recorded it all for government archives, the evening news, and the next day's papers.

Ted Sorensen stayed in Washington to work on a commencement address that was scheduled for the morning of June 10 at American University, just an hour after the President's scheduled return from Hawaii. "The Peace Speech," it was called by the few who had been working on it for weeks inside the White House. On orders from Kennedy, they had been deliberately keeping it away from the officials in the State and Defense departments who normally passed on statements of foreign policy and national security.

Kennedy flew from time zone to time zone, editing words of peace on the plane as he went from one war show to another. He watched white ovals erupt on radar screens in the underground bunkers of the North American Air Defense Command in Colorado Springs as one American city after another was destroyed in an eighteen-minute simulation of a surprise Soviet nuclear attack. He watched Nike and Honest John missiles hitting dummy targets in the air and on the ground of the White Sands Missile Range in New Mexico. There were rocket-launched torpedoes and Sparrow missiles exploding in the sea around the U.S.S. *Kitty Hawk* as the aircraft carrier steamed into the Pacific off San Diego.

All that firepower had little to do with the real war going on as Negro demonstrations continued across the South. On the grounds of the capitol of Alabama in Montgomery, with the Confederate flag flying from its dome, Governor Wallace vowed again that he would personally prevent the integration of the University of Alabama on Tuesday, June 11. The first two Negro students were scheduled to register as the President returned to Washington to tell the world his dreams of peace.

Kennedy's last stop on the first full day of the tour, June 6, was El Paso, Texas. He stayed long enough for some direct political talk with the state's new governor. John Connally, a Lyndon Johnson protégé, had been Kennedy's first Secretary of the Navy, and had come home to win a two-year term eight months before. The Texas stop was a detour, but an important one. Kennedy's 1964 election strategy, like his 1960 strategy, depended on carrying the state. But Governor Connally, who was up for reelection at the same time as Kennedy, was trying to distance himself from a President hated by a strong right-wing establishment that included oil men and newspaper publishers.

Kennedy and Connally sat down in the Cortez Hotel with Vice President Johnson, who had flown in from Washington. "Well, Lyndon," Kennedy asked, "do you think we're ever going to have that fund-raising affair in Texas?"

"You have the governor here, Mr. President, maybe now you can get a commitment from him," Johnson said.

"Fine, Mr. President, let's start planning your trip," said Connally, trapped between his party's national leaders.

"We've been talking about this for a year and a half, so let's get on with it," Kennedy said. He wanted major events in Houston, San Antonio, Fort Worth, and Dallas. Connally promised to work out dates in October or November.

From San Diego, the President was flown out by helicopter onto the *Kitty Hawk*. He was sitting on the flight deck with California Governor Edmund "Pat" Brown as a couple of dozen photographers clicked away. The governor was pouring cream into his coffee when Kennedy leaned over to say something. Brown turned, spilling the cream onto his own lap. He jumped up, and then, noticing the photographers, he sat down again in a pool of the cream. He jumped up again.

Kennedy was laughing so hard he had trouble speaking. But finally he whispered, "Pat, with that phalanx of photographers in front of me, that steward could have poured boiling oil into my crotch and I still would have smiled."

That night Kennedy was sitting in his rocking chair on the bridge of the carrier with Admiral Robert Keith, commander of the First Fleet, watching jets catapult into the sky. "I'm afraid I can take no more," he said after a while, lifting himself from the chair, gritting his teeth. He was writhing in pain from his back, and the Navy men did not know what to do. Finally, two officers reached under his armpits, raising him and helping him to his cabin.

He had also pulled a muscle in his groin during the spring and had trouble walking. "If anyone asks," he had told Pierre Salinger, "tell them it's the back. I don't want to read anything in the papers about my groin . . . I don't want the American public thinking that their President is falling apart: 'Now he's got a bad back, now his groin is going.' The next thing the Republicans will be claiming, 'Now it's his brain.' "

On June 8, in Washington, Sorensen and Bundy showed drafts of the peace speech to the State and Defense departments for the first time. They would have almost no time to argue with the President's message, or with the President himself, who was eight thousand miles away. The message, which Defense particularly disliked, was a last attempt to get some kind of test ban agreement with the Soviets before the beginning of the 1964 campaign. Once Kennedy was openly running for reelection, there was little chance that Senate Republicans would ratify a major treaty. There was a political rhythm to being a Cold War President— talk tough to win the job, talk peace to keep it.

But perhaps this was a moment when events made it possible to consider ending the specter of mushroom clouds exploding over Pacific islands and Siberian plains. There had been the terror of the missile face-off over Cuba, and new fears over radioactive fallout, as strontium 90 and other deadly isotopes began appearing again in milk and other foods around the world. The test megatonnage of the past two years totaled more than all past explosions combined, and there was the so-bering prospect of Chinese nuclear weapons tests.

In Washington, there was also an astonished and belated realization that the Chinese Communists were pressuring Khrushchev and the Soviets to renounce talk of co-existence with the Americans. The Soviet premier, it seemed, believed that he had as much or more to fear from a nuclear China as the American President did. It now seemed possible that Khrushchev would soon have to choose between dialogue with Washington or dialectic comradeship with a belligerent Peking. The

Chinese were already on the move, involved in a border war with India in the Himalayas. Again and again, in private, Kennedy said that his greatest fear was Chinese nuclear weapons, and he had an almost romantic attachment to the idea that, somehow, the Americans and the Russians could combine to block China's nuclear programs.

It took the Americans a long time to realize the errors and cracks in their Cold War visions of a Sino-Soviet bloc, a monolithic communism encompassing the mass of China and the Soviet Union. U.S. intelligence agencies and diplomats had both missed and misread the tensions and distrust between the great Communist powers, particularly after Khrushchev had denounced Joseph Stalin at the Twentieth Soviet Party Congress in 1956. In the People's Republic of China, the style and dictates of the late dictator were still dominant. In June 1959, the Soviets had refused to give nuclear secrets to the Chinese, rejecting requests from Peking for a comradely gift of a sample atomic bomb.

The speech Sorensen was finally showing around within the higher reaches of Washington was crafted to fit that moment. The sequence of events that led to the speech had begun in early April, when Norman Cousins came to the White House to discuss meetings he was about to have with Khrushchev. That was the day he had ended up writing Kennedy's little speech on culture to high school students in the Rose Garden. The next day the President had telephoned Cousins and spelled out the message he wanted the editor to deliver to Khrushchev.

"I have no doubt that Mr. Khrushchev is sincere in his belief that the U.S. reneged on its offer of three inspections," Kennedy said, referring to the mangled communications between U.S. and Soviet scientists in December and January. "But he's wrong . . . I believe there's been an honest misunderstanding. . . . See if you can't get the Premier to accept the fact of an honest misunderstanding. There need be no question of veracity or honor and the way can be cleared for a fresh start.

"Khrushchev and I occupy approximately the same political positions inside our governments," the President continued. "He would like to prevent a nuclear war but is under severe pressure from his hard-line critics who interpret every move in that direction as appeasement. I've got similar problems. The hard-liners in the Soviet Union and the United States feed on each other. . . ."

On April 12, Cousins had delivered Kennedy's message to Khrushchev at his dacha on the Black Sea. Then he sat through hours of rambling talk from the premier. Khrushchev talked first about Mao. Peking, he said, was exploiting Moscow's embarrassments with Washington, from Khrushchev's retreat on Cuba to his naïve "soft" line on nuclear testing. Cousins had taken pages and pages of notes, and re-ported Khrushchev's remarks back to Kennedy word for word.

"People in the United States seem to think I am a dictator who can put into practice any policy I wish. Not so. I've got to persuade before I can govern. . . . You don't seem to understand what the situation is here. We cannot make another offer. . . . I was made to look foolish. . . . Frankly, we feel we were misled. If we change our position at all, it will not be in the direction of making it more generous. My atomic scientists and generals have been pressing me hard to allow them to carry on more nuclear tests. . . .

"You want me to accept President Kennedy's good faith? All right, I accept President Kennedy's good faith. You want me to believe that the United States sincerely wants a treaty banning nuclear tests? All right, I believe the United States is sincere. You want me to set all misun-derstandings aside and make a fresh start? All right, I agree to make a fresh start."

Cousins told Khrushchev that he should understand the President's problems with the U.S. Senate. Senators would never accept a treaty with only three inspections inside the Soviet Union.

"We are repeating ourselves," said the premier, pulling out his watch. "Just so there is no mistake in your mind, let me say finally that I cannot go back to the Council of Ministers and ask them to change our position in order to accommodate the United States again. . . . You can tell the President I accept his explanation of an honest misunderstanding and suggest that we get moving. But the next step is up to him."

In fact, Kennedy had taken a small step while Cousins was traveling. He had agreed to a proposal by Prime Minister Macmillan to send a joint letter to Khrushchev calling for new test ban talks. After weeks of transatlantic editing, the key sentence of the final version read: "We would be ready to send in due course very senior representatives who would be empowered to speak for us and talk in Moscow directly with you."

The President thanked Cousins for the report, then shook his head and said: "The more I learn about this business, the more I learn how difficult it is to communicate on the really important matters. Look at General de Gaulle. . . . If we can't communicate with him and get him to understand things, we shouldn't be surprised at our difficulty with Khrushchev."

On April 30, after their meeting, Cousins wrote to Kennedy with an idea. "You ought to beat Mr. K. to the punch," he said. He urged the President to speak out before the annual meeting of the Central Commit-tee of Soviet Communism, which was scheduled for mid-June. "The moment is now at hand for the most important speech of your Presidency . . . in its breathtaking proposals for genuine peace, in its tone of friendliness for the Soviet people and its understanding of their ordeal during the last war."

Kennedy was excited by the idea, though not optimistic. But he was willing to try. Talking peace while building weapons was also good politics. Demonstrations and books and scientific studies around the world were arguing that the radioactive fallout from nuclear tests was poisoning the planet. At the end of May, thirty-four U.S. senators— usually a force for more weapons, not fewer—introduced a Sense of the Senate Resolution calling for "banning all tests that contaminate the atmosphere or the ocean." The Soviet-American nuclear showdown over Cuba could be read as an indication that missiles were more valuable as negotiating tools than as weapons—that neither Kennedy nor Khrushchev was likely actually to push the button—but whether that was true or not the crisis had terrified millions of people. "We have to remember that no one who went through the missile crisis came out the same as they went in," Dean Rusk reminded Kennedy that spring.

"We Can Kill the Russians 360 Times Over . . . The Russians Can Kill Us Only 160 Times Over . . . We're Ahead, Aren't We?" ran the text of full-page newspaper advertisements across the country that spring, paid for by peace groups. The best-selling book in the country was *Fail-Safe*, a novel by Eugene Burdick, the co-author of *The Ugly American*, and Harvey Wheeler. In it an electronic glitch sends a U.S. Air Force squadron to drop H-bombs on Moscow. To forestall Soviet retaliation, the President orders U.S. bombers to destroy New York City. In Hollywood, a young director named Stanley Kubrick was making a movie from a novel called *Red Alert*, in which a crazed Air Force general named Jack D. Ripper sends bombers off to Moscow. He changed the title to *Dr. Strangelove, Or: How I Learned to Stop Worrying and Love the Bomb*.

There was one other thing: test bans, or anything else that stabilized the balance of terror, was good strategy for the United States. The Americans, after all, had more and more accurate bombs and missiles, so any kind of arms freeze tended to preserve U.S. military superiority.

On May 8, Khrushchev's answer to the Kennedy-Macmillan letter reached the White House, and it seemed to contradict everything he had told Cousins. It seemed little more than an angry restatement of Khrushchev's arguments about inspections. Kennedy happened to have a press conference that day, and one of the questions was: "Mr. President, on the test-ban issue, do you join those who feel that the prospects for a test ban are zero . . . or is there something in your private correspondence which will give you some hope?"

"No," the President answered. "I'm not hopeful. I'm not hopeful. We have tried to get an agreement on . . . the number of inspections, but we were unable to get that. . . . If we don't get an agreement this year . . . perhaps the genie is out of the bottle and we'll never get him back in again."

Macmillan was more optimistic, seizing on the fact that Khrushchev's letter ended by saying he would "receive your highly placed representatives." The British ambassador, David Ormsby-Gore, persuaded Kennedy to do the same thing he had done with Khrushchev's last missile crisis letters: answer only what he wanted to answer. So, Macmillan and Kennedy went for the one new line. They sent a joint letter to Moscow on June 1 accepting what they construed as an invitation to send representatives to Moscow that summer for more test ban talk.

Then, late on June 8, while Kennedy was in Hawaii and still working on the American University speech, Khrushchev sent a letter to Washington and London, complaining once more that the Americans and the British were determined to use test ban inspections as cover for espionage. He also accused the Americans of planning to build up West Germany as a nuclear threat to the Soviet Union. But he ended by repeating that he was willing to receive U.S. and British emissaries in Moscow and setting a time, July.

That was where things stood on Sunday, June 9, as Air Force One landed in San Francisco on the flight back from Honolulu to pick up Ted Sorensen, who had flown to the West Coast with the working copy of the peace speech. He handed it over to Kennedy to begin the final editing on the flight home.

At the same time—the morning of June 10 in Moscow—a Chinese delegation arrived, carrying a letter demanding harder-line communism everywhere in the world. The letter, addressed to world Communists, condemned Khrushchev as a weak leader seeking co-existence with capitalism, and rebuffed by war-loving America each time he begged them for such things as a nuclear test ban treaty. Khrushchev was close to having to choose whom to negotiate with: the Chinese or the Americans. That was the way the world stage was set for Kennedy's speech.

The President arrived in Washington at nine-fifteen that Monday morning, June 10. An hour later, after a steaming bath, he left the White House for American University.

"I have chosen this time and this place," Kennedy told his audience, "to discuss a topic on which too often ignorance abounds and the truth is too rarely perceived—yet it is the most important topic on earth: world peace. . . . I speak of peace because of the new face of war . . . in an age when a single nuclear weapon contains almost ten times the explosive force delivered by all of the allied air forces in the Second

World War . . . an age when the deadly poisons produced by a nuclear exchange would be carried by wind and water and soil and seed to the far corners of the globe and to generations yet unborn. . . . I speak of peace, therefore, as the necessary rational end of rational men."

That was the beginning, and it was not so remarkable; rhetoric like that rang periodically in the land, like church bells. But Kennedy's next phrases signaled change: "Some say that it is useless to speak of world peace or world law or world disarmament—and that it will be useless until the leaders of the Soviet Union adopt a more enlightened attitude. I hope they do. But I also believe that we must reexamine our own attitude—as individuals and as a Nation—*for our attitude is as essential as theirs.* . . .

"*Let us reexamine our attitude toward the Soviet Union.* . . . As Americans we find Communism profoundly repugnant as a negation of personal freedom and dignity. But we can still hail the Russian people for their many achievements—in science and space, in economic and industrial growth, in culture and in acts of courage . . . no nation in the history of battle suffered more than the Soviet Union suffered in the course of the Second World War. At least 20 million lost their lives. . . . In the final analysis, our most basic common link is that we all inhabit this small planet. We all breathe the same air. We all cherish our children's future. And we are all mortal.

"World peace, like community peace, does not require that each man love his neighbor—it requires only that they live together in mutual tolerance, submitting their disputes to a just and peaceful settlement. . . . Our problems are man-made—therefore, they can be solved by man. And man can be as big as he wants."

Kennedy closed with two announcements: The news that Premier Khrushchev had agreed to invite American and British negotiators to come to Moscow to discuss a comprehensive nuclear test ban, and that the United States would not begin a new round of atmospheric tests. "We will not be the first to resume," he said—which was news because the Soviets had completed two test series since their surprise explosion of September 1961, and the United States had countered with only one series, the twenty-four explosions from April to November of 1962.

By eleven-twenty, he was back at the White House—and another crisis at home. Robert Kennedy and Burke Marshall were there, along with Ted Sorensen and Larry O'Brien. Nicholas Katzenbach was in Tuscaloosa, Alabama, with a small crew of marshals, protecting the two Negroes who had been officially admitted to the University of Alabama, Vivian Malone and James Hood. Governor George Wallace, surrounded by state policemen in an office on the campus, had appointed himself the university's chief operating officer for the confrontation. He vowed to keep the pledge he had made in his inaugural address five months before: "Segregation now! Segregation tomorrow! Segregation forever!" Tomorrow had come. The federal courts had ordered the university to admit the two Negroes the next day, June 11, 1963.*

The President was in obvious physical pain that afternoon. He was moving awkwardly and pushing his knuckles into his cheek, then pressing them into his teeth, as he rocked back and forth, listening to strategies to get the Negroes past Wallace. Katzenbach, on the phone from Tuscaloosa, came up with the idea of approaching Wallace alone, leaving the students in a car. That way the governor could not directly violate the court order not to interfere with the students because he would never even have seen them. And that way the federal men could avoid arresting the governor and making him a white martyr across the South.

"I wonder whether you want to make a nationwide TV address," Sorensen said, as others said there was no choice any more, the President had to propose civil rights legislation as soon as possible.

"I didn't think so . . ." Kennedy began.

Robert Kennedy interrupted: "I think it would be helpful. I think there is a reason to do it, I think you don't have to talk about the legislation, but talk about employment and talk about education. . . . Giving some direction. Have it in the President's hands."

The President looked surprised. It was rare for the brothers to work things out with other people around. Normally they grunted and nodded in a fraternal language. But Robert Kennedy pressed now, trying to convince his brother that the racial situation was close to spinning out of control. There had been one hundred and sixty separate civil rights incidents during the first week in June.

"I don't think you can get by without it," Robert Kennedy said. The time had come to prepare comprehensive civil rights legislation. It was time for John Kennedy to choose sides.

"Well, I suppose we could do it," the President said. He was pounding the flat of his right hand down on his leg more and more rapidly, as if he were trying to beat the pain away.

"But is a TV address going to be helpful to the legislation?" asked O'Brien, who was going to have to push it in Congress and thought it would be better to wait until a bill was ready before going on television.

---

* In 1957, a young Negro woman named Autherine Lucy had been admitted to the university but was driven off the campus by three days of rioting.

"Yeah, it will be helpful," Robert Kennedy said. "Because I think you're going to come across reasonable and understanding and . . ."

"I think you guys have the real money on this thing on the Hill and that's when you may want to do this," O'Brien said.

The President closed the conversation: "We've got a draft which doesn't fit all these points, but it's something to work with, and there's some pretty good sentences and paragraphs. It will help us to get ready anyway, because we may want to do it tomorrow."

Through the afternoon and evening the President waited for Soviet reaction to his peace speech. There was none until midnight Washington time, when news reached the White House that *Izvestia* was publishing the full text of the American University speech. And the Soviets were turning off the thousands of transmitters used to jam signals from the Voice of America and other Western radio systems, so that translations could be heard by people from Leningrad to Vladivostok. Nothing quite like that had ever happened before. Was it the President's speech, or were the Soviets, in effect, telling the world that they would rather deal with the Americans than with their Chinese comrades?

There was also another odd, confusing piece of news for the President that evening. A Buddhist monk had burned himself to death in the middle of a busy intersection in the center of Saigon. On the morning of June 11 (at about 7:00 P.M., June 10 in Washington) a seventy-three-year-old monk named Thich Quang Duc sat in a lotus position on a small pillow while other monks poured gasoline over him, then without a word or change of expression had lit a match. A couple of American reporters had been told to be at that intersection for a Buddhist protest parade. The monk burned for almost ten minutes before his charred body toppled onto the melted asphalt. A photograph by Malcolm Browne of the Associated Press was moving around the world by wire within an hour.

The Americans at the scene were handed a statement by Thich Quang Duc: "Before closing my eyes to Buddha, I have the honor of presenting my words to President Diem, asking him to be kind and tolerant toward his people and to enforce a policy of religious equality."

President Diem had responded by sealing off the city's Buddhist pagodas behind barbed-wire barricades. His sister-in-law, Madame Nhu, said she had clapped her hands in delight at the news. Using the Vietnamese word for monk, she called it "barbecue *à bonze*," and offered to provide gas and matches to any monks or American reporters who would do the same thing.

Chapter 45

On June 11, Robert Kennedy called his brother before eight o'clock. He started to talk about Alabama, but the President interrupted him, saying, "Jesus Christ!"

The front pages of the newspapers on his bedstand showed Malcolm Browne's photograph of Quang Duc's self-immolation.

Robert Kennedy persisted, "I think we should call up the Guard now." In four hours, Nicholas Katzenbach was going to try to get Vivian Malone and James Hood into the University of Alabama. Wallace was waiting, ready to stand in the doorway of the main building on campus, Foster Auditorium. The governor, by law, was the commander of the reserve U.S. Army soldiers of the Alabama National Guard—unless or until the President of the United States chose to place the Guard under his own command. Five hundred Guardsmen, visited for a few minutes that morning by the Governor, were drilling outside the city's armory, half of them charging, throwing pine cones, and yelling, "Yankees Go Home!" as the other half moved toward them with unsheathed bayonets.

"Let's wait," the President said. "Let Wallace make the first move." Mobilizing the Guard under his own command would mean more photographs around the world of American soldiers pointing rifles or bayonets at unarmed American citizens.

Kennedy came downstairs for a breakfast with congressional leaders at nine o'clock. He talked about Saigon and about Moscow and they just nodded, waiting for him to change the focus to Alabama and to his ideas on civil rights legislation. There had to be a bill, said Mike Mansfield, the leader of the Democrats in the Senate. The government was losing control of this thing. It was a polite way of saying that the President was losing control.

"We're still talking about that," said Kennedy. He wanted a bill that would not cause southerners to oppose the tax bill and the rest of his legislative package: "The minimum we can ask for and the maximum we can stand behind."

Attorney General Kennedy had asked Governor Wallace during the weeks of guarded negotiations that ended when the Justice Department won a court order for the admission of Malone and Hood, "Do you think it is so horrifying to have a Negro attend the University of Alabama?"

"I think it is horrifying for the federal courts and the central government to rewrite all the law and force upon people that which they don't want," Wallace said. "I will never submit myself voluntarily to any integration in a school system in Alabama."

"I don't want to have another Oxford, Mississippi," Robert Kennedy said.

"You folks are the ones who will control the matter, because you have control of the troops."

"We have a responsibility, Governor, to insure that the integrity of the courts is maintained and all of the force behind the Federal government will be used to that end."

University officials had accepted the orders of the courts, deciding Malone and Hood would be enrolled like any other qualified Alabama residents. Wallace had overidden them when he appointed himself the university's temporary registrar. Now, there he stood, surrounded by one hundred state troopers commanded by Colonel Al Lingo. There were over a hundred reporters and photographers at the main entrance to Foster Auditorium. The two students would arrive on campus at noon, Washington time, President Kennedy told the congressional leaders as breakfast ended.

Now it was political theater. Standing in the doorway made Wallace a star; on television he was the same size as the President.

Kennedy was back in the Oval Office by nine forty-five for a regular morning meeting with Secretary of State Rusk. He told the President that the peace speech was being applauded everywhere in the world. So was his choice of Averell Harriman as special emissary to meet with Premier Khrushchev to discuss test ban proposals. "One of the great state papers of American history," the *Manchester Guardian* in England had reported of the speech.

The worst news that morning was from Vietnam. "The situation is deteriorating," Rusk reported. The State Department had responded to the self-immolation of Quang Duc the night before with a cable to the U.S. Embassy, approved by Harriman. It had been sent to William Trueheart, the deputy chief of mission in Saigon, and it read like the beginning of the end of American support for President Diem: "FYI— If Diem does not take prompt and effective steps to re-establish Buddhist confidence in him we will have to re-examine our entire relationship with his regime . . . [He] must fully and unequivocally meet Buddhist demands . . . in a public and dramatic fashion. . . .

"While there is no change in US policy supporting Diem," the cable continued, "we want Tho [Vice President Nguyen Ngoc Tho] to know that in event situation arises due to internal political circumstances (in which US would play no part) where Diem definitely unable to act as president and only in this situation we would want to back Tho as constitutional successor. . . . We would have to tell Tho that if word leaked we would flatly deny."

Trueheart delivered the warnings to Diem: the United States would disassociate itself from his actions against the Buddhists. He did not talk to Tho because he considered the secret message something close to a death sentence for Diem. *The New York Times,* reflecting shock at Diem's repression of the Buddhists and the immolation, said in an editorial: "If Diem cannot genuinely represent a majority then he is not the man to be President."

After Rusk left, the President met alone with the Republican congressional leaders, Senator Everett Dirksen of Illinois and Representative Charles Halleck of Indiana. They were talking again about what would be acceptable to Republicans in a civil rights bill. Robert Kennedy called during the meeting to say that Governor Wallace had just set himself up behind a podium in the doorway at the university.

In Tuscaloosa, the temperature was 100 degrees. Nick Katzenbach was coming now through a phalanx of police from Alabama and newsmen from all over the world.

"Stop!" called Wallace.

The Deputy Attorney General, who was almost a foot taller than the governor, kept coming and announced: "I have a proclamation from the President of the United States ordering you to cease and desist from unlawful obstructions. I'm asking you for an unequivocal assurance that you will not bar entry of these students and you will step aside peacefully and do your constitutional duty. Do I have your assurance?"

Wallace read a prepared statement as television cameras transmitted: "I, George C. Wallace, as Governor do hereby denounce and forbid this illegal and unwanted action by the central government . . . unwelcomed, unwarranted and force-induced intrusion upon the campus of the University of Alabama today of the might of the central government offers a frightful example of the suppression of the rights, privileges and sovereignty of this state."

" 'Central government'—like it was the Kremlin," said Robert Kennedy's special assistant, Ed Guthman, who was in the crowd, standing between two Tuscaloosa city commissioners.

"Damn him," said one of them, George Ryan, referring to Wallace. "We didn't want this."

Katzenbach walked back to his car. With cameras and reporters following, he escorted Malone and Hood to their dormitories. He had gotten the keys to their rooms the day before. "We have to check for bombs," he told the university officials. The Justice Department had learned a lot at Oxford. Four student council officers were waiting in the doorway of the men's dorm. They stepped out as Hood arrived. One stuck out his hand and said, "Welcome to the University of Alabama."

"What happens now?" Commissioner Ryan asked Guthman.

"The President will federalize the National Guard," he answered. It was at that moment that Robert Kennedy called his brother, saying: "Will you issue the proclamation now and sign it? . . . The executive order, yeah. Right now? Okey-dokey."

President Kennedy federalized the Guard at 11:34 A.M., Tuscaloosa time. Four hours later, Brigadier General Henry Graham, assistant commander of the 31st Infantry, Alabama National Guard, the same officer who had commanded the National Guard troops who had escorted the Freedom Riders out of Alabama two years earlier, marched onto the campus with one hundred Guardsmen. There were another sixteen hundred in the armory, ready to move.

At Fort Benning, Georgia, four hundred Regular Army troops, under the command of General Creighton Abrams, sat in helicopters, ready to move if there was trouble. General Graham walked to the doorway with four unarmed sergeants, saluted the man who had been his commander three hours earlier, and said: "Governor Wallace, it is my sad duty to inform you that the National Guard has been federalized. Please stand aside so that the order of the court may be accomplished."

Wallace moved two steps to the left, saluted Graham, and left in the flashing lights of a motorcade. Moments later, Vivian Malone and James Hood walked through the doorway to be registered as students of the University of Alabama. A window opened on the third floor of the building and a student waved an American flag as they passed beneath him.

In Washington, the President, watching a re-run of the Katzenbach-Wallace encounter, decided, "I want to go on television tonight."

Then he went down to the pool for twenty minutes of swimming to relieve the pain in his back before taking a nap. This, thought Sorensen, was going to be one of the two most important speeches of the Kennedy presidency, and it was not yet written. There was not even a complete first draft around. Sorensen and others began dictating phrases. Typewriters clacked from office to office.

The President came back downstairs to the office that afternoon at four o'clock. For the next three hours he sat through a series of meetings, with Harriman about the coming test ban negotiation, with Edward R. Murrow about the reporting of the civil rights troubles around the world, with James Webb about the space program.

At seven o'clock, an hour before speech time, he walked into the Cabinet Room where Sorensen, Robert Kennedy, and Burke Marshall were working. "C'mon, Burke, you must have some ideas," he said to Marshall. Flipping through the pages scattered over the big table, he realized he might have to give the speech without a full text. For the twenty minutes before air time, he sat alone with his brother in the Oval Office, taking notes. At four minutes before air time, Sorensen came in with some pages. Kennedy looked at them and began dictating changes to Evelyn Lincoln. Sorensen was dictating other changes to his secretary.

They missed the deadline. The President had only part of a speech in front of him as he sat down in front of the cameras in the Oval Office at eight o'clock. He spoke for eighteen minutes, beginning: "This afternoon, following a series of threats and defiant statements . . . the admission of two clearly qualified young Alabama residents who happened to have been born Negro. . . .

"I hope that every American, regardless of where he lives, will stop and examine his conscience about this and other related incidents. . . . When Americans are sent to Viet Nam or West Berlin, we do not ask for whites only. . . ."

He began to ad-lib then, working from a memo prepared by Louis Martin: "The Negro baby born in America today . . . has about one-half as much chance of completing high school as a white baby born in the same place on the same day, one-third as much chance of completing college, one-third as much chance of becoming a professional man, twice as much chance of being unemployed, about one-seventh as much chance of earning $10,000 a year, a life expectancy which is seven years shorter, and the prospect of earning only half as much."

Back to the text, he said: "This is not a sectional issue. . . . Nor is this a partisan issue. . . . This is not even a legal or legislative issue alone. . . . We are confronted primarily with a moral issue. It is as old as the Scriptures and is as clear as the American Constitution.

"If an American, because his skin is dark, cannot eat lunch in a restaurant open to the public, if he cannot send his children to the best public schools available, if he cannot vote for the public officials who represent him . . . then who among us would be content to have the color of his skin changed? Who among us would then be content with the counsels of patience and delay?

"We face, therefore, a moral crisis as a country and as a people. It cannot be met with repressive police action. It cannot be left to increased demonstrations in the streets. . . . It is time to act in the Congress, in your State and local legislative body, and above all, in all of our daily lives. A great change is at hand, and our task, our obligation, is to make that revolution, that change, peaceful and constructive for all.

"We cannot say to ten percent of the population that your children can't have the chance to develop whatever talents they have; that the only way they are going to get their rights is to go into the streets and demonstrate. I think we owe them and we owe ourselves a better country than that.

"I am, therefore, asking the Congress to enact legislation giving all Americans the right to be served in facilities which are open to the public—hotels, restaurants, theaters, retail stores and similar establishments. . . . I am also asking Congress to authorize the Federal government to participate more fully in lawsuits designed to end segregation in public education. . . . Other features will also be requested, including greater protection for the right to vote."

If the language was a little vague, it was because there was no bill ready to be introduced. The President was winging it. Then he ad-libbed an ending—one that was certainly close to his own thinking and even to his own disciplined feelings: "We have a right to expect that the Negro community will be responsible, will uphold the law, but they have a right to expect that the law will be fair, that the Constitution will be color blind, as Justice Harlan said at the turn of the century."

That was it. Legislation would follow, but, at last, the President of the United States had chosen sides.

"Yeah," Robert Kennedy said to him. "I think it was really good. I think it was really good, and I think it's well to have it behind us. Okay."

Four hours later, in Jackson, Mississippi, Myrlie Evers, the wife of the state NAACP secretary, was watching television with her three small children, letting them stay up, waiting for their father to come home. It was late, but the night was unbearably hot, still close to 100 degrees. And she wanted the kids to hear what their dad, Medgar Evers, thought about what they had heard the President say that night.

Evers pulled into his driveway, and picked up a bundle of T-shirts printed with the slogan: "Jim Crow Must Go!" He walked toward the house and was shot in the back by a rifleman hiding in a honeysuckle bush 150 feet away, across the road. He bled to death in front of his wife and children.

Chapter 46

"I'm sorry, Mr. President," said Carl Albert, the Majority Leader of the House of Representatives, on the telephone the next day, June 12. "We lost some of the Southern boys that we would otherwise have had. The civil rights, uh. That was it on our side."

"Hell," Kennedy said. "You know, Christ. Just events are making our problems. Christ, you know, it's like they shoot this guy in Mississippi. They shoot somebody, uh, I mean, it's just in everything. I mean, this has become everything."

Albert was reporting on the unexpected defeat in the House that day by a vote of 209 to 204 of a routine funding bill for the Area Redevelopment Administration (ARA). The agency had been created and funded in May of 1961, by a House vote of 251 to 167. That had been the first significant legislative victory of the new Kennedy administration, channeling public works money into economically depressed regions of the country, particularly Appalachia, where Kennedy had been shocked by the poverty during his primary campaign in West Virginia. Now, two years later, nineteen Southern Democrats and twenty Republicans who had originally supported ARA had switched their votes on the morning after the President's civil rights speech.

"Civil rights," the Majority Leader said. "It's overwhelming the whole program."

"How upset are the Southerners?"

"Well, uh, they're, some of them are mad. Most of them are frightened," Albert answered. "One other thing, this, this is going to affect mass transit, there's no question about that. It's gonna kill, uh . . . these farm bills."

"Civil rights did it?"

"Civil rights, yeah."

Albert Gore, the senator from Tennessee, called Kennedy with a personal story for the President: "I got a call at two in the morning from Memphis, it was some men at a bar and they said they just wanted to let me know what they felt. 'We don't want to eat with them, we don't want to go to school with them, we don't even want to go to church with them.' I said, 'Do you want to go to heaven with them?' The guy answered, 'No, I'll just go to hell with you. . . .' "

If the President had believed that his speech with its moral commitment might calm the waters parted by King and other Baptist preachers, he learned he was wrong. Headlines from *The New York Times* the next two days recorded: "N.A.A.C.P. Leader Slain in Jackson; Protests Mount" . . . "Two Seized in Gadsden, Ala., After 300 March in Protest" . . . "Marching Negroes Chant 'Freedom' in Savannah" . . . "Negroes Parade in Cambridge, Md.—Troopers on Patrol After Racist Riot and Fires" . . . "Jackson Negroes Clubbed as Police Quell Marchers" . . . "African Nationalist Urges Southern Blacks to Arm."

But the racial news was not all confrontation, either, as other *Times* headlines reported: "Alabama Campus Retains Its Calm: Two Negroes Attend Class" . . . "Moderates Take Reins in Danville: 50 Negroes Freed in Moves to Cut Virginia Tension" . . . "Schools in Atlanta Drop Color Bars—Desegregation Is Quiet" . . . "Pennsylvania Will Review Its Civil Rights Statutes" . . . "Jersey City Moves to End Segregation." And, on June 14, the *Times* reported on page sixteen that a Negro named Dave Mack McGlathery had begun classes at the University of Alabama's Huntsville Center—and nobody had paid any attention to him or to Deputy Attorney General Katzenbach, who was watching McGlathery from his car.

The racial troubles drove Kennedy's peace speech off the front pages within forty-eight hours. "Generally," said *The New York Times* in the sixth paragraph of its follow-up story on the speech, "there was not much optimism in official Washington that the President's conciliatory address at the American University would produce agreement on a test ban treaty or anything else."

Quang Duc's self-immolation got five paragraphs on page six of *The New York Times,* and the Buddhist crisis in Vietnam was sometimes twinned with religious and ethnic unrest in Iran and Iraq. In Teheran, the Shah of Iran was reported to be in hiding as more than ten thousand barefoot Muslims paraded and ran riot through the city chanting "Down with the Shah!," attacking men in Western suits and women without veils in protest against the arrest of an Ayatollah named Rouhallah Khomeini. In Iraq, the government in Baghdad was sending fifty thousand troops into the northern sectors of the country to try to crush Kurdish rebels demanding their own country, Kurdistan.

The other big foreign story was the struggle of British Prime Minister Macmillan to survive a scandal. His Secretary of State for War, John Profumo, had resigned when it was revealed that he had been having an affair with a twenty-one-year-old call girl named Christine Keeler, who was also sleeping with a deputy naval attaché at the Soviet Embassy in London.

The President's first official appointment the morning of June 12 was with Frederick "Fritz" Nolting, the U.S. Ambassador to South Vietnam, who was being cut up in the Washington way, accused of being too friendly with President Diem. Nolting was asking to be relieved after two years in Saigon, holding Rusk to a promise that he could return home because of family problems. That promise spared the President and Secretary of State from ordering Nolting home.

Kennedy was inclined to send Edmund Gullion, who was finishing a difficult tour as Ambassador to the Congo, as Nolting's replacement. He was the young consul in Saigon who, twelve years before, had told Congressman Kennedy that the United States would be driven out of Vietnam if U.S. troops moved in after the French colonial army was defeated. But Rusk was opposed to Gullion and Kennedy decided to let him have his way.

Besides, he already had another idea. At a ceremony at the Pentagon, he had run into Henry Cabot Lodge, Jr., the man he had defeated for the Senate in 1952. Lodge, the Republican nominee for Vice President in 1960, was a major general in the Army Reserve and had been doing his annual month of active duty. They had talked for a couple of minutes about Vietnam, and Kennedy remembered that when the first American combat troops had been sent there in 1961, Lodge had said he would be willing to serve as ambassador.

A couple of days later, the President asked Secretary of State Rusk to ask Lodge, unofficially, if he was still interested and available for the Saigon posting. Lodge said he was and Kennedy invited him to the White House. "Cabot," he said, "I am beginning to spend more of my time on Vietnam than anything else. The Diem government seems to be in a terminal phase. . . . I'd like to persuade you to go out there as Ambassador and as my personal representative." He would be reporting to the President rather than to Rusk. Once again, as with Lucius Clay in Berlin, Kennedy wanted a Republican in place to share the responsibility for whatever was going to happen next. That, the President told Lodge, might well be the overthrow of Diem and his family—probably in a coup by his own generals. With the Americans looking on, approvingly.

The President was shuttling now between meetings focused on two cities, Saigon to Birmingham, Birmingham to Saigon. The most important of the civil rights meetings was with the Republican leaders of Congress. Without the support of Southern Democrats, he needed the help of the two Midwestern conservatives who were the opposition's leaders in Congress, Senator Everett McKinley Dirksen, the rumbling-voiced Republican leader of the Senate from Illinois, and Charles Halleck of Indiana, the party's leader in the House. Both had generally voted against civil rights legislation over the years, but Kennedy had done some of that himself.

Kennedy's June 11 proclamation of morality was the context of their three-way negotiations. "Cloture," the parliamentary term for ending debate and calling the vote, would prevent filibusters by Southern senators determined to block any civil rights legislation. But cloture required a two-thirds vote, sixty-seven of the one hundred votes in the Senate.

"To obtain 67 votes for cloture requires, at a minimum, complete cooperation and good faith with respect to Senator Dirksen," Mike Mansfield wrote in a memo to the President on June 18. "If that does not exist, the whole legislative effort in this field will be reduced to an absurdity. . . . Any phraseology in the legislation, any parliamentary tactic or political statement which subtracts from the total of votes available for cloture is to be avoided."

In other words, there could not be a debate on civil rights in the Senate without Republican votes. Forty-eight hours later, Mansfield and Dirksen had their agreement. Rather, they had six agreements and a disagreement. The agreement was, Mansfield told Kennedy, on these titles: Title I—completion of the sixth grade would be considered prima facie evidence of literacy to vote in federal elections; Title III—empowering the Attorney General to bring suit against local boards of education to achieve desegregation of public schools; Title IV—creation of a Community Relations Service to assist local governments in handling desegregation disputes; Title V—extending the life of the Civil Rights Commission; Title VI—permitting the federal government to refuse, on the basis of racial discrimination in hiring, to fund programs or public works; Title VII—creating a Commission on Equal Employment Opportunity.

The disagreement was on Title II (Public Accommodations) of the White House proposals, which required the desegregation of hotels, restaurants, theaters, and stores open to the public. Dirksen said he himself might vote for public accommodation statutes requiring businesses to serve interstate travelers regardless of race—his state, Illinois, had a large Negro population—but he would not sponsor it. The solution was to have three separate civil rights bills submitted to the Senate Judiciary Committee: a White House bill with seven titles; a Mansfield-Dirksen bill with six; and a separate public accommodations bill sponsored by Senator Warren Magnuson, a Washington Democrat. The differences would be worked out in committee. On June 19, Kennedy introduced the White House bill. His statement began: "The time has come . . ."

That same day, across the Potomac in Arlington National Cemetery, Medgar Evers, a World War II Army veteran, was buried with honors. In his last interview before he was murdered, he had recalled his military service, saying: "If I die, it will be in a good cause. I've been fighting for America just as much as the soldiers in Vietnam." Kennedy had invited Myrlie Evers and her children to the White House after the funeral, and let her kids bounce around on the bed that Queen Elizabeth had once used.

In Montgomery, Alabama, Governor Wallace reacted to the proposed civil rights legislation by saying to the President, via television: "You're going to have to bring the troops back from Berlin if you pass that law."

At five o'clock that Wednesday, Kennedy sat down with Rusk and McNamara to discuss Vietnam and the latest turn of events in Southeast Asia. Part of their agenda was to lay out strategies that could lead to U.S. military action against North Vietnam. Their working paper was a seventeen-page memo jointly prepared by Rusk and McNamara, which began:

The root of the problem in Southeast Asia is the aggressive effort of the North Vietnamese to establish Communist control in Laos and South Viet-Nam as a stepping-stone to control all Southeast Asia. . . . We require a program for graduated increases in US political and military pressure, without setting into motion an irreversible pattern. . . . It is fully recognized that if the Communists fail to respond to lesser pressure, the third phase of this program is such as to constitute the initiation of military action against North Vietnam. . . .

The secretaries recommended what they called sequential pressures. Escalation. They asked the President to approve immediately a specific sequence of actions that stopped just short of open violations of North Vietnamese sovereignty. Kennedy approved the concept of escalation in National Security Action Memo 249, but said that he wanted to personally sign off on operations against or inside North Vietnam.

The memorandum had presented the President the usual three options: (1) To walk away and leave the Communists to have their way; (2) To allow the United States to become openly engaged anyplace or everyplace in Southeast Asia; (3) Find a middle course involving increased military aid and trainers. He chose the middle option. And, of course, those who served Kennedy knew that was what he would do. The cunning of aides was in writing the options, maximizing the chances that their staff option would become the presidential order.

After the events of Birmingham, the President, as Robert Kennedy had suggested, scheduled a series of White House meetings with groups of American leaders, hundreds of them at a time, to build a base and a consensus for both national and local action on civil rights. Clergymen, lawyers, chain-store executives, labor leaders, educators, newspaper publishers, and more, almost every one of them white, gathered weekly on the gilt chairs in the East Room of the White House to hear the President and the Attorney General and the Vice President urging them to go back home and push voluntary action against discrimination, before demonstrators and the federal government arrived to force desegregation, and before new laws were written in Washington.

One of the last of the meetings was on the afternoon of June 21. Later that day, A. Phillip Randolph and King announced that they were organizing a mass "March on Washington for Freedom and Jobs" for August 28, when the capital would be at its humid worst.

The next day, the President met with the rest of the civil rights group, this time Negroes and civil rights leaders. He told Randolph of his concerns about trouble in Washington—riots, if the streets of Washington were filled with angry Negroes. He warned that rioting or violence might set the movement back decades. "Mr. President," Randolph said, "the Negroes are already in the street. It's very likely impossible to get them off. . . . Isn't it better that they be led by organizations dedicated to civil rights and disciplined by struggle, rather than leave them to other leaders who care nothing about civil rights nor about non-violence?"

Kennedy just nodded, then moved on to discuss his proposed legislation. No Negroes had been involved in the drafting of the administration's bill. That was one of the first questions, and Kennedy's answer was that any perception that this was the work of Negro leaders, particularly if Martin Luther King, Jr., had had anything to do with it, would mean the legislation would not get out of committee.

Kennedy wanted to talk to King alone. He had asked him to come to the White House earlier that morning for a private meeting—scheduled between two other private sessions with Roy Wilkins and Walter Reuther of the United Auto Workers, the white leader of the labor union with the largest Negro membership.

While Kennedy was still with Wilkins, Burke Marshall told King that he would have to get rid of two of his advisers, Stanley Levison, the New York lawyer, and one of King's executive assistants, Hunter Pitts O'Dell. The Federal Bureau of Investigation had concluded the two men were Communists. "A paid agent of the Soviet Communist apparatus," Marshall said of Levison. King implied that he did not believe that, he asked for the government's proof. With that, King was passed on to Robert Kennedy, who asserted to him that the proof was solid, it was based on the latest technology. It would be kept secret, the Attorney General told King, because revealing the facts would reveal the sources.

The FBI had, of course, been bugging Levison's office since March 1962 with the written approval of the Attorney General. The taps had produced memos to Robert Kennedy such as this one from J. Edgar Hoover: "This Bureau has recently received additional information showing the influence of Stanley David Levison, a secret member of the Communist Party, on Martin Luther King Jr. You will recall that I have furnished you during the past few months substantial information concerning the close relationship between Levison and King. . . ."

Robert Kennedy believed Hoover; at least, he believed that even the possibility of King's being linked to Communists might bring down King and the President, too. So, he was not in the mood to argue or to confirm when he talked with King. He repeated the arguments Hoover used to avoid having to prove what he said about the secret and private activities of hundreds of well-known Americans. It was some of the best gossip in the world, channeled to a President who liked to say, "All history is gossip." In fact, Kennedy had just ordered the State Department and the CIA to send him every piece of data and dirt, unedited, that their people were sending from London on the Profumo Affair.

When it was clear that King did not believe either Marshall or Robert Kennedy, the President took over. He asked King to take a walk with him in the Rose Garden. He put a hand on King's shoulder, something he rarely did, and said: "I assume you know you're under very close surveillance." He mentioned Levison and O'Dell by name, and said: "They're Communists, you've got to get rid of them." O'Dell was the fifth-ranking Communist in the United States, Kennedy said, and Levison was above that, he was O'Dell's boss. "His handler," the President said in the jargon of spies.

"I don't know how he's got time to do all that—he's got two jobs with me," King said of O'Dell. The President did not smile. King did not believe the President, either, but he thought that John Kennedy, like his brother Robert, believed Hoover, and that he believed that his presidency was on the line.

"You've read about Profumo in the papers?" Kennedy asked. Yes, said King. "Macmillan is likely to lose his government because he has been loyal to a friend."

"If they shoot you down, they'll shoot us down, too," Kennedy said to King. "So we're asking you to be careful."

Back inside the White House, in the Cabinet Room, with King sitting on his right, the President shocked his guests by saying they should all thank Bull Connor. The room froze, as in a photograph. "After all, he's done more for civil rights than any of the rest of us."

Then Kennedy described the trouble he expected to have in getting civil rights legislation through Congress, making it clear that he did not think that a Negro march on Washington was going to help his cause.

"It seemed to me a great mistake to announce a march on Washington before the bill was even in committee. . . . We want success in Congress, not just a big show at the Capitol. Some of these people are looking for an excuse to be against us. I don't want to give any of them a chance to say, 'Yes, I'm for the bill, but I'm damned if I will vote for it at the point of a gun.' . . . The wrong kind of demonstration at the wrong time will give those fellows a chance to say that they have to prove their courage by voting against us."

King conceded that the timing of the march might be bad. "But frankly," he added, "I have never engaged in any direct action movement which did not seem ill-timed. Some people thought Birmingham was ill-timed."

"Including the Attorney General," the President said, looking over at his brother sitting against a wall with one of his young daughters on his lap.

There was some laughter after a pause, and that cut some of the tension. The President did not want a march, neither did Roy Wilkins, but obviously it was going to happen. "Okay," said Kennedy. "We're in this up to our necks. The worst trouble of all would be to lose the fight in Congress. We'll have enough trouble if we win; but, if we win, we can deal with those. A good many programs I care about may go down the drain as a result of this. I may lose the next election because of this. We may all go down the drain as a result of this—so we are putting a lot on the line.

"What is important is that we preserve confidence in the good faith of each other," the President went on. "I have my problems with the Congress. You have yours with your groups.

"One of my problems is that I am leaving for Europe tonight," Kennedy said as he adjourned the meeting. The civil rights leaders left through the front doors this time, where reporters and cameras waited for them. Kennedy went through the French doors of the Oval Office into the gardens, where a helicopter was waiting to take him to Andrews Air Force Base and then on to West Germany, Italy, England—and Ireland.

"Ireland?" said Kenny O'Donnell when the President had first brought up the subject. "There's no reason for you to go to Ireland. It would be a waste of time. If you go to Ireland, people will say it's a pleasure trip."

"That's exactly what I want," Kennedy said. "I am the President of the United States, not you. When I say I want to go to Ireland, it means that I'm going to Ireland. Make the arrangements."

Chapter 47

Air Force One took off for Germany late on the evening of June 22 after the President had stopped at Camp David for a two-hour visit with his children and his wife, who was expecting their third child in two months. The Boeing 707, cruising at 530 miles per hour, enormously expanded the personal reach and geography of its principal passenger. It was a symbol of the extraordinary fact that the American President now lived only six hours from Europe. There had been jokes that Ike had spent more time in the air than on the ground during his last year in office. Kennedy's crack was that people who said the presidency was the toughest job in the world had never flown on Air Force One.

"Is this trip necessary?" *Time* asked. The President had been invited to visit six months earlier by an Italian government that had since fallen, by a West German chancellor, Konrad Adenauer, who was retiring, and by Harold Macmillan, who might be too, involuntarily, because of continuing revelations in the Profumo scandal. And de Gaulle had made it tacitly clear that he had no interest in seeing Kennedy.

But it was de Gaulle and the Germans who were the focus of the trip. The French president was making himself, for all practical purposes, the most important adversary of U.S. policy in Western Europe—the American "Grand Design" of a unified Europe as a junior partner of the United States. He detested that design and was deliberately inflating

French nationalism—developing his own nuclear weapons, vetoing British membership in the Common Market, and undermining NATO by demanding a French voice equal to the Americans' in all political and military affairs. The greatest danger of de Gaulle's determined independence, from the American perspective, was that Germany might follow his lead.

"The Mess in Europe and the Meaning of Your Trip" was the title of the President's secret briefing paper, written by George Ball:

> Never, at any time since the war—and this is the main point—has Europe been in graver danger of backsliding into the old destructive habits—the old fragmentation and national rivalries that have twice brought the world to disaster in the past . . . de Gaulle's revival of nationalism threatens to restore the disastrous cycle that has marked modern French history. . . .
>
> Unfortunately for the West, de Gaulle has chosen the worst possible moment for reviving nationalism—just the moment when Chancellor Adenauer is relinquishing the reins in Germany. As a result we face dangerous weather with the Federal Republic. . . .
>
> A Germany not tied institutionally to the West is dangerous—and no one has offered an effective means of tying Germany to the West except through a unified Europe within an Atlantic Partnership. . . . A Germany at large can be like a cannon on shipboard in a high sea.
>
> We still have great influence with the Germans. They are closest to the firing line. Berlin is a Soviet hostage, and the German people know that their only defense is the American strength and commitment.

The depth of that American influence struck President Kennedy within minutes of stepping off Air Force One in Bonn on the morning of June 23. In the German capital, and then in Cologne and Frankfurt, the crowds were gigantic, chanting over and over again: "Kenn-ah-dee! Kenn-ah-dee! Kenn-ah-dee!" In Cologne, where the eighty-five-year-old Adenauer had been mayor before Hitler took power, every sidewalk, every square was packed with people on the route to the city's fourteenth-century cathedral, waving little paper American flags.

"Where did you get all those American flags?" Kennedy asked Chancellor Adenauer.

"The same place you get yours when you campaign in America," he replied.

In Frankfurt, Kennedy rode in an open car with Vice Chancellor Ludwig Erhard, who was slated to succeed Adenauer at the end of the year. "Let's stand and wave," Kennedy said.

"*Was?*" said Erhard, but Kennedy was already on his feet.

"Wave one arm at a time," he told the German. "You don't get as tired."

"My stay in this country will be all too brief," he said in Bonn. "But, in the larger sense, the United States is here on the continent to stay so long as our presence is desired and required; our forces and commitments will remain, for your safety is our safety. Your liberty is our liberty; and any attack on your soil is an attack upon our own. . . . The U.S. will risk its cities to defend yours because we need your freedom to protect ours. Hundreds of thousands of our soldiers serve with yours on this continent as tangible evidence of this pledge."

The Germans went wild—this was more than they expected, and from the President himself. They gave Kennedy back as much or more. Here, after the Cuban missile crisis, after the peace speech at American University, after finally taking the side of the Negroes, it was as if he were being crowned Prince of the World.

Then the President flew over East Germany to West Berlin, the half-city still under allied occupation eighteen years after the war. For four hours, over thirty-five miles, he rode through West Berlin streets. The smallest crowds he saw stood four-deep on both sides of the roadways. He went to Checkpoint Charlie, the U.S. Army roadblock across one of the few gaps in the Wall separating West and East Berlin.

"You think this is any good?" he asked during the ride to West Berlin's City Hall, showing his speech to General James Polke, the American commander in the city.

"Fifteen years ago this very day . . . ," it began, recounting the beginning of the Berlin Airlift. "Ten years ago this month a spontaneous uprising of the freedom-loving people of the Eastern Zone was repressed . . . two years ago a shameful wall was built. The story of West Berlin is many stories. . . . I will carry away from this city an inspiring picture of all I have seen."

"This is terrible, Mr. President," said the general.

"I think so, too," Kennedy said.

On the way, they made two stops to look over the Wall from guard platforms into the grayness of East Berlin. At the first one, Kennedy told his staff and the reporters following them to stay on the ground. He wanted to stand alone. There was no one on the other side, the streets had been cleared; then he saw three women, throwing open their windows and waving handkerchiefs to him. "Isn't that dangerous?" he asked Polke.

"Yes, it is."

Watching Kennedy climb slowly down, Hugh Sidey said: "He looks like a man who just glimpsed Hell."

The motorcade moved slowly—there was no choice with more than half the city's population in the streets—to the Rathausplatz, the City Hall Plaza, where 150,000 or more people had pushed their way into the square and the streets that fed into it. Those who fainted in the crush, and many did, stayed on their feet, held up by the bodies of the people around them. Kennedy, who had said very little after looking over the Wall, was putting together a new speech in his head. On a high platform built in front of the City Hall, looking out at rows of American flags on the city's lampposts, he spoke only five hundred words, rallying the ecstatic crowd into a great roaring animal, like the city's symbol, a standing bear.

"Two thousand years ago the proudest boast was 'Civis Romanus sum,' " he began, after thanking his hosts. "Today, in the world of freedom, the proudest boast is 'Ich bin ein Berliner.' "

The cheers echoed in the urban canyon. He had learned the phrase from Bundy, repeating it phonetically for days, "Ish bin ine bear-LEAN-ar."

"There are many people in the world who really don't understand, or say they don't, what is the great issue between the free world and the Communist world," said Kennedy. He paused for a beat and then leaned into the microphones in front of him and said, "Lass sie nach Berlin kommen! Let them come to Berlin.

"There are some who say that Communism is the wave of the future. Let them come to Berlin.

"And there are some who say in Europe and elsewhere we can work with the Communists. Let them come to Berlin.

"Freedom has many difficulties and democracy is not perfect, but we have never had to put a wall up to keep our people in. . . . All free men, wherever they may live, are citizens of Berlin, and therefore, as a free man, I take pride in the words 'Ich bin ein Berliner.' "

The crowd's reaction was explosive. The President was euphoric. Sorensen and McGeorge Bundy were not. In his enthusiasm, Kennedy, who had just given a peace speech and was trying to work out a test ban treaty with the Soviets, had gotten carried away and just ad-libbed the opposite, saying there was no way to work with Communists.

"Oh, Christ," Kennedy said on his way to another speech at the Free University of Berlin. He tried to straighten it out there, making it up as he went along and sounding a little like Eisenhower used to when he was deliberately trying to confuse the press. He said there that what he meant was that multi-party governments with Communist participation usually did not work well: "As I said this morning, I am not impressed by the opportunities open to popular fronts. . . . But I do believe in the necessity of great powers working together to preserve the human race."

Adenauer looked even more dour than usual after the speech. Rusk asked him what he thought about it. "I'm worried," Adenauer said, referring to the roars of the crowd. "Does this mean that Germany could have another Hitler?"

The 2 or 3 million Berliners who had come out were the largest crowds Kennedy had ever seen. He told Adenauer that he was going to leave a sealed letter for his successor with three words of advice about what to do if things were going badly at home: "Go to Germany."

Then, on the flight to Ireland at the end of the day, he told Sorensen: "We'll never have another day like this one, as long as we live."

The crowds in Ireland were the largest in that country's history, too. But it is a small place. Most of the presidential party felt a letdown. But not Kennedy. "He's getting so Irish the next thing you know he'll be speaking with a brogue," said Dave Powers, who had arranged much of the trip to the old sod. On the flight from Germany, Kennedy had told Powers and O'Donnell about his only other trip to the land of his ancestors. That was in 1947, when he was thirty years old. He had stayed with his sister Kathleen, Lady Hartigan, at Lismore Castle in County Wexford, which was owned by her husband's parents, the Duke and Duchess of Devonshire. He had driven in a borrowed car south to a place called Dunganstown, looking for the home of his great-grandfather, Patrick Kennedy, who had left Ireland during the Potato Famine of 1848.

What he found was that there were a lot of people named Kennedy in that part of Ireland. He had finally stopped for tea at one of their houses, a thatched-roof cottage with dirt floors and ducks and chickens running in and out. They might be his third cousins, he speculated, as he drove away with a friend of his sister's, Pamela Digby Churchill, a twenty-seven-year-old Englishwoman who had just been divorced from Winston Churchill's son, Randolph.

"God, it looked like Tobacco Road," she said, as they left.

"I felt like kicking her out of the car," he told Powers and O'Donnell as they flew to Ireland sixteen years later. "For me, the visit to that cottage was filled with magic. . . ."

Then, his mind back in the present, he said: "When will we be going back to see my cousins?"

"Tomorrow," O'Donnell said. The White House had even lined up a man named Robert Burrell, whom Kennedy remembered stopping to ask directions of when he had got lost looking for other Kennedys.

He came by helicopter the next day, June 27, to riverside docks in New Ross, where Patrick Kennedy had left for America. "When my great-grandfather left here to become a cooper in East Boston, he carried nothing with him except two things, a strong religious faith and a strong desire for liberty," he told the crowd gathered there. He pointed across the river to the Albatross Fertilizer Co. plant and said, "If he had not left New Ross, I would be working today over there."

Then he went on to Dunganstown for tea with his cousins, though not all the cousins favored that beverage. One of them, Jim Kennedy, filled a water glass with Irish whiskey and pressed it into the President's hand. As soon as the man turned away for a moment Kennedy passed the glass behind his back to Dave Powers, who dutifully downed it and passed the empty glass back to the President.

From Ireland, he flew to England, seeing for the first time the grave of his sister Kathleen, who had died in a plane crash in 1948. He was there for only twenty-four hours, staying the night at Birch Grove, Prime Minister Macmillan's country home. Jacqueline Kennedy had written ahead to the prime minister's wife, Dorothy, telling her she did not have to be too fancy to please her husband: "Please think of Jack as someone David Gore is bringing down for lunch—and just do whatever you would do in your own house—his tastes are distressingly normal—plain food—children's food. . . ."

The President and the prime minister, meeting without aides, handled two important pieces of business rather easily. They agreed to push as hard as they could for a nuclear test ban agreement when Averell Harriman and Lord Hailsham would go as special emissaries to Moscow in mid-July. They also agreed that it was time to end quickly talk of a European multi-lateral nuclear force. Using the MLF to persuade other NATO countries not to try to develop their own nuclear weapons had obviously failed.

"We both agreed," Macmillan wrote to Queen Elizabeth, "that the main object is not to provide more nuclear weapons for NATO (which already has too many) but to solve the German problem, now and in the future. . . ." The German problem was that Kennedy and Macmillan wanted West Germany tied as tightly as possible to the Western Alliance, but neither the Americans nor the British wanted any German to have control over the firing of any nuclear weapons.

Both leaders were shocked at how the other looked. Macmillan looked his age, sixty-nine, and more, being brought down by the Profumo Affair. Kennedy looked different to Macmillan than he did to the crowds who were cheering him along British roads. "To them, Kennedy meant youth, energy, idealism and a new hope for the world," he wrote in his diary. But Kennedy was in pain and the cortisone treatments were showing in his face. "Very puffed up, Very unhealthy." An advance team from the White House had come to Birch Grove to put in a special

bed designed to relieve pressure on the President's back. Dorothy Macmillan took one look at Kennedy lowering himself slowly into an arm-
chair and sent to town for a rocking chair that cost just three pounds.
"He suffered agony, he was a terribly brave man," her husband wrote.
"I had no idea how much he suffered. He couldn't sit very long without
getting up."

"Never has a man been so well or loyally served," the prime minister
added. He was a bit tongue-in-cheek over the dozens and dozens of men
in the presidential party. There were so many that some had to be sent
to hotels in Brighton, forty miles away. Serving Kennedy took many
forms, including drinking his whiskey and arranging the pleasures of his
nights. This time it was the Secretary of State's turn to handle the details
of a presidential liaison. Rusk and the White House's chief of protocol,
Angier Biddle Duke, were already in Italy, at Lake Como, carrying on
an unusual negotiation. They were trying to get an American couple out
of their home, a famous lakeside villa where Kennedy wanted absolute
privacy the next night.

As the European trip was being planned, the President had asked
Rusk if he knew of a beautiful and a secluded place in Italy for a private
matter. Rusk did. He had been president of the Rockefeller Foundation,
which owned Villa Serbelloni on Lake Como, once the grand vacation
home of a Milanese merchant prince. Kennedy said he wanted the villa
on the night of June 30 and he wanted it empty—no servants, no staff,
no Secret Service. Powers and O'Donnell would be there to handle any
problems, that was part of their jobs. But somebody didn't get the
message. It soon became apparent that the resident director of Rockefeller programs at the villa and his wife, Mr. and Mrs. John Marshall,
were intending to stay on the property, moving into guest quarters.

"Get them out of there," Kennedy said, and the State Department
was on the way. The Marshalls left and soon afterward a lady of some
note in Europe arrived. Rusk returned in the morning. "How was it?"
asked Rusk, who did not approve of some of Kennedy's habits.

"Wonderful," Kennedy said. "Absolutely wonderful."

The party moved on to Rome and meetings with Italian officials and
a new pope. Originally, Kennedy was to meet Pope John XXIII, whose
earthy style and whose encyclical, *Pacem in Terris,* had captured the
imagination of the world. "The two Johns," the Pope and Kennedy, had
become a banner for those around the world who yearned for change.
But Pope John had died and the President was one of the first official
visitors to the new pope, Paul VI. The press was buzzing with speculation about whether the first Catholic President of the United States
would kneel before the leader of his Church and kiss his ring. He did

not. "Norman Vincent Peale would love that," he told Powers, recalling that the prominent Protestant minister had said during the 1960 campaign that Kennedy would be controlled by the Vatican. The President and the pope talked privately for eighteen minutes about world peace. Then Paul surprised Kennedy, unpleasantly, by telling reporters he prayed for the success of the struggles of American Negroes.

In Rome, Kennedy dispatched one of the most loyal of his old friends, Lem Billings, to search the city's antiquity shops for small items to bring back home. He figured that Billings must know about such things because he had a degree in art history from Princeton. With only ninety minutes to search the city, Billings was assigned an aide to the president of Italy and a famous archeologist. The three of them raced from shop to shop, with the Italian official warning the proprietors of the consequences of selling fakes to the President of the United States. They collected twenty-seven pieces from back rooms, none of them on display, and brought them back for Kennedy's consideration. He chose two, paying $900 for a little Greek horse from the sixth century B.C. and $500 for a lifesize head, a Roman copy of Praxiteles' Hermes. The rest were sent back.

"God, I don't know why we didn't get more," Kennedy told Billings on the plane back to Washington. Billings telephoned the Italian president's office after they landed, and within a couple of days the Italian ambassador delivered a treasure of statues and jewelry. The President selected a few more pieces, giving them to his wife, then passed the collection on to Billings and other friends to make their own choices. Nothing went back to Rome this time.

President Kennedy was back in his office on the morning of July 3. He stayed in Washington through the morning of the Fourth of July—his wife and children were in Hyannis Port—to discuss a Khrushchev speech on the test ban negotiations, as well as more bad news from South Vietnam.

The State Department was still trying to piece together the text of a speech the Soviet premier had given on July 2 in East Berlin. The Soviets had not released a transcript in either Russian or English, but radio reports indicated that he had said: "The Soviet Government declares that since the Western powers obstruct the conclusion of an agreement banning all nuclear tests, the Soviet Government expresses its willingness to conclude an agreement banning nuclear tests in the atmosphere, in outer space and under water. If the Western powers now agree to this proposal, the question of inspection no longer arises."

"It seems they're offering a three-environment ban with no moratorium on underground tests," George Ball told the President. "The only question is whether they plan to insist on a NATO-Warsaw Pact Non-Aggression Treaty (or some other conditions) at the same time"—which the United States opposed because of the implication that East Germany's borders were permanent. What was the Russian really doing? The State Department was neither sure nor trusting, telling Kennedy that Khrushchev might be trying to counter the worldwide appeal of his American University speech or his ecstatic reception in West Germany. Or perhaps Khrushchev was trying to isolate China as it pushed toward nuclear testing.

On July 1, in Rome, President Kennedy had received an urgent cable from Ball and Averell Harriman, who were anxious about rumors in Saigon that President Diem planned to violate a truce that had halted Buddhist demonstrations in mid-June, and that Buddhist monks would respond with another self-immolation. "We all believe," the cable said, "that one more burning bonze will cause domestic U.S. reaction which will require strong public statement despite danger that this might precipitate coup in Saigon."

"The President was briefed on developments . . . ," began the State Department's Memorandum of Conversation of the fifty-minute meeting of July 4. Ball and Harriman reported that *The Times of Vietnam,* an English-language newspaper controlled by Diem's brother, Ngo Dinh Nhu, had begun attacking both the Buddhists and the United States. "At this point," the meeting memorandum continued, "there was a discussion of the possibility of getting rid of the Nhus in which the combined judgment was that it would not be possible. . . . Our estimate was that no matter what Diem did there will be coup attempts over the next four months."

Kennedy asked what would happen after a coup, and Roger Hilsman, now Assistant Secretary of State for the Far East, answered: "The chances of chaos are considerably less than they were a year ago." Kennedy said perhaps he should get Henry Cabot Lodge out to Saigon right away—the Massachusetts Republican's appointment as ambassador had been officially announced on June 27, when Kennedy was in Germany. Then he changed his mind and said he wanted Lodge to stay in Washington for six weeks of special counterinsurgency training.

Six days later, a special National Intelligence Estimate analyzed President Diem's problems. When he read it, Kennedy was persuaded that there was a real possibility that Diem and Nhu were considering asking the United States to remove its troops from the country, that from the perspective of the Presidential Palace, Diem could not deal harshly enough with the Buddhists to keep them in control as long as he had to keep the Americans happy.

"The GVN has always shown some concern over the implications of U.S. involvement in South Vietnamese affairs . . . ," the intelligence estimate said. "It springs from the Diem government's suspicion of U.S. intentions toward it, and from its belief that the extensive U.S. presence is setting in motion political forces which could eventually threaten Diem's political primacy . . . American criticism of the GVN has especially irritated Ngo Dinh Nhu. Above all, Nhu almost certainly doubts whether the support which the U.S. gives to his brother would be transferred to him."

The conclusions of the estimate began:

A. The Buddhist crisis in South Vietnam has highlighted and intensified a widespread and longstanding dissatisfaction with the Diem regime and its style of government. If—as is likely—Diem fails to carry out truly and promptly the commitments he has made to the Buddhists, disorders will probably flare again and the chances of a coup or assassination attempts against him will become better than even.

B. The Diem regime's underlying uneasiness about the extent of the US involvement in South Vietnam has been sharpened by the Buddhist affair and the firm line taken by the US. . . . This attitude will almost certainly persist and further pressure to reduce the U.S. presence in the country is likely.

On July 10, Kennedy received an "Eyes Only" cable from Chester Bowles, who had spent three days in Saigon before proceeding to his post as the new ambassador to India. Bowles drove another nail into Diem's future, or lack of future, with the Americans: "Many qualified observers, in and out of government, privately assert that the Diem regime is probably doomed and that while political and military risks involved in a switchover are substantial they may be less dangerous than continuation of Ngo family in present role. . . . I left Saigon with the feeling that a political explosion is likely in the foreseeable future."

President Kennedy met the press on July 17, soon after Averell Harriman had arrived in Moscow to begin nuclear test ban negotiations. He opened his news conference by announcing: "After three days of talk we are still hopeful that the participating countries may reach an agreement to end nuclear testing, at least in the environment in which it is agreed that on-the-ground inspection is not required for reasonable security. Negotiations so far are going forward in a businesslike way. . . . And for that reason I do not expect to respond to further questions on this subject."

The news conference was, in journalistic jargon, "wide-ranging." Kennedy seemed at a peak of his powers, easily handling questions on more than a dozen subjects, beginning with a firm pledge on the nature and rationale of the American commitment in Vietnam. He was asked whether the Buddhist crisis had been an impediment to the American military mission. "Yes, I think it has. I think it is unfortunate that this dispute has arisen at the very time when the military struggle has been going better than it has been going for many months. . . . I would hope this would be settled, because we want to see a stable government there, carrying on a struggle to maintain its national independence. We believe strongly in that. We are not going to withdraw from that effort. In my opinion, for us to withdraw from that effort would mean a collapse not only of South Viet-Nam, but Southeast Asia."

On his tax-cut proposals to Congress, still in committee after six months, Kennedy said: "I received a few hours ago the preliminary budget results for the fiscal year which ended June 30. The cash deficit was $4.1 billion, just half as large as we estimated some six months ago. . . . This demonstrates again the point which I emphasized in my tax message to the Congress. Rising tax receipts and eventual elimination of budget deficits depend primarily on a healthy and rapidly growing economy."

"Mr. President, do you see any indications that the Castro Government is seeking a more relaxed relationship with the United States, and, if so, are we prepared to meet them in that?"

"No. I have seen these verbal statements, but I have seen no evidence . . . the United States has indicated very clearly that we do not accept the existence of, and cannot coexist in the peaceful sense with, a Soviet satellite in the Caribbean. So I don't see that any progress is going to be made along these lines as long as Cuba is a Soviet satellite."

That was certainly true. Only a week before, the NSC Standing Group, headed by Robert Kennedy, had met to evaluate covert CIA sabotage operations against Cuba, and to hear a request from Harriman to suspend those operations while he was in Moscow trying to negotiate a test ban treaty. Harriman said the Soviet premier had already questioned whether the Americans really wanted a treaty. He had told Prime Minister Macmillan that the John Kennedy who had rallied Berliners seemed quite a different fellow from the Kennedy who had spoken so eloquently of peace at American University.

After the query on Cuba, there was a friendly question for the President on civil rights: "Mr. President, it's pretty generally acknowledged that your administration has done more for civil rights fundamental advances than any in many years. Do you find that the demonstrations which are taking place are a handicap to you, specifically the march in August?"

"No," the President answered, hiding private apprehension that the march might end up as a riot. "I think that the way that the Washington march is now developed, which is a peaceful assembly calling for a redress of grievances, the cooperation with the police, every evidence is that it is going to be peaceful. . . . This is not a march on the Capitol."

He was asked about charges by Governor Wallace of Alabama and Governor Barnett of Mississippi that Communists were behind the drive toward integration. "We have no evidence that any of the leaders of the civil rights movements in the United States are Communists. We have no evidence that the demonstrations are Communist-inspired," Kennedy said rather carefully. Then he added that it was not the Kennedys, either. "It is easy to blame it on the authorities in Washington, it is easy to blame it on the Attorney General or the President, and say, 'If they would just stop talking about these things the problem would go away.' The way to make the problem go away, in my opinion, is to provide for a redress of grievances."

"Mr. President," a reporter asked. "You used to say it was time to get America moving again. Do you think it is moving? . . . The reason I ask you the question, Mr. President, is that the Republican National Committee recently adopted a resolution saying you were pretty much a failure."

"I am sure it was passed unanimously," said Kennedy, and left them laughing.

Chapter 48

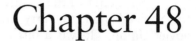

When Averell Harriman arrived in Moscow for the nuclear test ban meetings with Premier Khrushchev on July 14, 1963, he brought with him three tons of telephone and telex equipment to set up a "Hotline" between the White House and the Kremlin. The cable and telephone gaps and glitches during the Cuban missile crisis had convinced both Kennedy and Khrushchev that nuclear powers needed communications systems that could move faster than their missiles. He also carried a letter from Kennedy to Khrushchev that took note of the Russian's July 2 speech in East Berlin:

"Mr. Harriman comes with my full personal confidence and is in a position to give you my thinking. . . . We continue to believe that it will be best if we can get a comprehensive agreement . . . [but] it is sensible to reach agreement where agreement is now possible, in the area of testing in atmosphere, under water and in outer space."

Some of the American communications gear went into use almost immediately. Kennedy was in contact with Harriman three and four times a day. Spending hours in the cramped White House Situation Room, Kennedy personally edited the U.S. position, as if he were at the table himself. The Soviets were astounded when they realized that the American President had the power to make decisions on a matter like this without consulting any bureaucracy.

The big news in Moscow as the Americans and British arrived was in a four-page section of *Pravda,* beginning on the newspaper's front page, "An Open Letter of the Central Committee of the Communist Party of the Soviet Union, to Party Organizations, to All Communists in the Soviet Union." It was a bitter attack on Communist China, obviously timed as a counterpoint to the welcome given Harriman and the rest of the American and British negotiators, and a deliberate public insult to a high-level Chinese delegation in the city at the same time.

"Chinese comrades underestimate all the danger of thermonuclear war," said the letter, which defended Premier Khrushchev aggressively against Chinese charges, both public and secret, of timidity in dealing with the Americans. " 'The atomic bomb is a paper tiger; it is not terrible at all,' they contend. Some responsible Chinese leaders have also declared that it is possible to sacrifice hundreds of millions of people in war. . . . What are the Chinese leaders dissatisfied with? Is it, perhaps, the fact that it was possible to prevent the invasion of Cuba and unleashing a world war? . . ."

That the three sides were in Moscow now was probably not an accident. Khrushchev wanted to play the Americans off against the Chinese and the Americans wanted to play the Soviets off against the Chinese. In his last meeting with Kennedy before leaving, Harriman had said he thought Khrushchev had to be preoccupied with Soviet relations with China and that the Soviet leader would hope to use the United States and treaty negotiations as a lever to pry concessions from his fellow Communists. Then he had asked the President whether he could bring up the subject of Soviet-American cooperation when the Chinese developed nuclear capability—perhaps they could begin by sharing intelligence on China's nuclear program as they had shared intelligence on German battle orders during World War II.

"Yes," the President said. "By all means"—that was exactly what he wanted.

"Well, I think we ought to give them a sweetener," Harriman said.

"What do you want?"

"Throw in the MLF."

"Of course," Kennedy said, waving his hand. The American plan for a multilateral European nuclear force was dead anyway after President de Gaulle's decision that France would go it alone. "It would be a great relief to get rid of that!"

At the same time Kennedy had approved a list of ten talking points he hoped Harriman could explore informally with Khrushchev. It included exchanging intelligence on the Chinese nuclear program and these others: "Soviet concern over the economic cost of their advanced weapons program; Soviet concern over the ability of the Chinese Communists to use the racial issue to split the international Communist movement, especially in the underdeveloped countries. . . . Soviet ability to restrain the North Vietnamese."

The Soviet premier personally opened the negotiations on July 15 in Spirindonovka Palace. He called Harriman "the imperialist," jokingly, then gave the joke a sharp edge: "There are many capitalists who only deal with matters in their own country, whereas an imperialist is a capitalist who interferes in other people's affairs, as you are in South Vietnam."

The premier sat through the entire three and a half hours of the first session with Harriman and the British emissary, Lord Hailsham, before turning the Soviet file over to Foreign Minister Andrei Gromyko. He left with another joke, saying that Harriman should initial a blank page and they could fill in the details later.

At the same time, on the other side of Moscow, in the Lenin Hills, the Chinese Communist delegation, led by Party Secretary Deng Xiaoping, which had come to the city for what was scheduled as a summit meeting between the two great Communist countries, was ignored by Khrushchev until the next night. He spoke at a rally of Soviet officials on July 16 in the Kremlin's Palace of the Congresses, saying of the Chinese comrades: "What do they want? They say one should start a revolution, a war, and on the corpses and the ruins, a more prosperous society will be created. And who would remain in this prosperous society? The living would envy the dead."

In Washington, U.S. intelligence agencies began breathlessly collecting evidence of a Sino-Soviet split, but were still running far behind events and the Soviet leader's angry rhetoric. After two days, President Kennedy wrote out instructions to Harriman in longhand:

> Your report is encouraging on limited test ban . . . I remain confident that Chinese problem is more serious than Khrushchev suggests and believe you should press question with him in private meeting . . . consider that relatively small forces in hands of people like Chicoms could be very dangerous to us all. You should try to elicit K's view of means of limiting or preventing Chinese nuclear development and his willingness either to take Soviet action or accept U.S. action aimed in this direction.

The "U.S. action," as outlined in Harriman's briefing books, was classified "Top Secret." It was a discussion of an alliance between the United States and Soviet Union with the specific goal of preventing China from developing nuclear weapons, including this: "Radical steps, in cooperation with the USSR, to prevent further proliferation of nuclear capabilities. . . . Soviet, or possibly joint US-USSR, use of military forces against China"—presumably a joint air strike against China's nuclear facilities.

Even thinking such things made the moment extraordinary. After more than eight years of probing and posturing on nuclear arms agreements by both sides, with more pessimism than optimism, the table in the Kremlin was set for agreement between the Soviet Communists and the American capitalists—against the Chinese Communists. Khrushchev told Harriman he believed it would be many years before China could be considered a true nuclear threat. But Kennedy was obsessed with and depressed by the prospect. He had told André Malraux, the French minister of culture: "This is the great menace in the future to humanity, the free world and freedom on earth. The Chinese would be perfectly prepared to sacrifice hundreds of millions of their own life [for] their aggressive and militant policies."

It was clear after the first day of the Moscow negotiations that there was no real chance for a comprehensive test ban. The Soviets were not going to allow foreign inspectors near testing sites and that, the Americans believed, was the only way to surely tell the difference between underground explosions and earthquakes. "NATO spies," Khrushchev said that day, and his words were passed on by Harriman that night to Kennedy. "You're trying to tell me that if there's a piece of cheese in the room and a mouse comes into the room that the mouse won't go and take the cheese. You can't stop the mouse from going for the cheese."

After that, the negotiations focused on a limited testing ban and, for a while, on the Soviets' proposals for a NATO–Warsaw Pact non-aggression treaty at the same time. Finally, Harriman and Hailsham said their governments would consider that, but at another time. Working out the words of the limited ban, in two languages, took just ten days. On more than one occasion Harriman excused himself from the table during debates over wording or even a single word, to telephone the White House and come back in two or three minutes to say something like this: "That's fine, we'll accept word 'purpose' for 'hope' in relation to non-aggression."

On July 25, 1963, at 7:00 P.M. in Moscow, the Limited Test Ban Treaty was ready to be initialed by the negotiators. The American team telephoned the White House Situation Room. It was one o'clock in the afternoon in Washington, and Harriman reached McGeorge Bundy, who said the President was right there with him, but was on the phone with Prime Minister Macmillan. The text was read twice to Kennedy and he said, "Okay, great!" Harriman walked back into the Kremlin conference room and signed "W.A.H." on the document, which began: "Each of the Parties to this Treaty undertakes to prohibit, to prevent, and not to carry out any nuclear weapon test explosion, or any other nuclear explosion . . . in the atmosphere, beyond its limits, including outer space, or under water, including territorial waters or high seas. . . ."

Hours later, Kennedy took a bulletin from the United Press International telex in his office—"Moscow—The United States Russia and Britain today ended historic talks that diplomatic sources said sealed final agreement to end East-West nuclear tests, in space, in the atmosphere and underwater"—and wrote across it: "To Norman Cousins, with warm regards—J F Kennedy."

Even after the treaty was worked out, Kennedy repeated to Harriman: "Hope very much you will find an opportunity for private discussion with Khrushchev on China." Harriman did that, asking the Soviet leader what he would do if Chinese missiles were aimed at Russian targets. The premier changed the subject, but Harriman cabled Kennedy that it was clear that the Soviets' primary objective in signing the treaty was "To isolate Chicoms." He continued: "Therefore they place maximum importance on France's adherence to the test ban treaty. Also they will press all other countries to adhere. They want pressure on Chicoms from other countries, particularly the underdeveloped. . . ."

After their last meeting, on the afternoon of July 26, Khrushchev and Harriman walked through the Kremlin and ran into a crowd in one courtyard. They were mostly tourists from other parts of the Soviet Union, shocked to see their leader in front of them. "We just signed the test ban on nuclear bombs," the Soviet premier shouted, putting his arm around the tall American. "This is Gaspodin Harriman. I'm going to take him to dinner. Do you think he deserves dinner?"

The crowd cheered. A couple of nights before, at the closing ceremonies of a USSR-U.S. track and field meet, the Soviet leader had invited Harriman up to his box at the top of the stadium as Soviets and Americans walked arm-in-arm around the track waving the flags of their countries. There, too, the crowd had cheered the American and the Russian standing together. Harriman had looked over at Khrushchev and seen tears in his eyes.

In Peking, the official reaction was: "A big fraud to fool the people of the world. . . . The interests of the Soviet people have been sold out, the interests of the people of the countries in the Socialist camp have been sold out and the interests of all the peace-loving people of the world have been sold out." The words were more polite in Paris, but President de Gaulle also made it clear that France intended to continue to develop its own nuclear capability and to continue testing bombs in the atmosphere.*

President Kennedy began the process of submitting the new treaty, the first weapons treaty of the atomic age, to the Senate for approval. On July 24, Rusk came to the White House to confer with him before going to Capitol Hill to discuss a schedule for Senate ratification of the Test Ban Treaty. He had to wait a few minutes while Kennedy stepped out into the Rose Garden to meet a group of high school students, delegates to the American Legion's "Boys Nation" program.†

The Secretary of State came back in the afternoon to tell the President that he was surprised to find that Senator Richard Russell of Georgia, chairman of the Armed Services Committee, was friendly, saying that the treaty would be a great thing if it were workable. But, he said, there was going to be opposition, led by Senator Barry Goldwater of Arizona, who might be the Republican candidate for President in 1964, and Senator Strom Thurmond of South Carolina. Kennedy asked Rusk for his advice on when to go on television to begin building up public pressure on the Senate.

Rusk thought Kennedy should wait. "I think," he said, "that some of the Senators might feel that if you take it to the country straight away, that this consultation process is very much interfered with."

Kennedy disagreed: "We've got to hit the country while the country's hot. That's the only thing that makes any impression to these god-damned Senators. . . . We've been pretty generous with them as far as consultation. . . . They'll move as the country moves. So, I think, we've got to go to the country while there's maximum interest. . . ."

He called Harry Truman that day, the only man who had ever ordered the bomb dropped. He had sent Truman the text and analysis of the treaty. "I want to congratulate you . . . ," Truman replied. "I think it's a wonderful thing. My goodness life, maybe we can prevent a total war with it."

"I appreciate that," Kennedy responded. "We'll see what happens with China. . . ."

"I speak to you tonight in a spirit of hope," John Kennedy began his nationwide television address on the night of July 26. "Eighteen years ago the advent of nuclear weapons changed the course of the world as well as the war. . . . In an age when both sides have come to possess enough nuclear power to destroy the human race several times over, the world of communism and the world of free choice have been caught up

---

* The Chinese successfully tested their first nuclear weapon on October 16, 1964.
† One of the delegates that day from Hot Springs High School in Hot Springs, Arkansas, was seventeen-year-old William Jefferson Clinton, who would become the forty-second President in 1993.

in a vicious circle of conflicting ideology and interest. Each increase of tension has produced an increase of arms; each increase of arms has produced an increase of tension. . . . Yesterday a shaft of light cut into the darkness.

"A war today or tomorrow, if it led to nuclear war, would not be like any war in history. A full-scale nuclear exchange, lasting less than 60 minutes, with the weapons now in existence, could wipe out more than 300 million Americans, Europeans, and Russians. . . . We have a great obligation, all four nuclear powers have a great obligation, to use whatever time remains to prevent the spread of nuclear weapons, to persuade other countries not to test, transfer, acquire, possess, or produce such weapons.

"According to the ancient Chinese proverb, 'A journey of a thousand miles must begin with a single step.' My fellow Americans, let us take that first step. Let us, if we can, step back from the shadows of war and seek out the way of peace. And if that journey is a thousand miles, or even more, let history record that we, in this land, at this time, took the first step."

On the afternoon of the 28th, Harriman landed at Otis Air Force Base on Cape Cod and was driven to Hyannis Port, where the President offered him a clean white shirt to meet reporters gathered there. "Good job," Kennedy said. That was about it.

Harriman flew home to N Street in Georgetown. A crowd gathered in front of his house that night. They stood with lighted candles. When Harriman came to the door in his shirtsleeves, the people outside broke into a chorus of "For He's a Jolly Good Fellow." A woman held up a baby and called to him—thanking him, she said, for giving the child a chance for long and happy life.

Chapter 49

The Limited Test Ban Treaty was officially signed in Moscow on August 5, 1963, with Secretary of State Rusk leading the U.S. delegation, which included senators from both parties and U.N. Ambassador Adlai Stevenson, who had first proposed such a treaty during his 1956 campaign for President.

After the Kremlin ceremonies, Khrushchev invited Rusk to spend a couple of days at his dacha on the Black Sea. At the pool there, the American wore water wings, because he had never learned to swim. Later they played badminton on an Oriental rug among expensive antiques—Khrushchev won—and walked forest trails marked by blue telephone boxes, ready if the premier felt the need to talk or if someone in Moscow needed him. On their last walk, Khrushchev stopped and said, "Macmillan has told me he will not use nuclear weapons to defend Berlin. De Gaulle told me the same thing. Why should I think the Americans would use nuclear weapons if we move into West Berlin?"

It was the worst moment for Rusk. He was thousands of miles from the only American who could answer that, President Kennedy. Finally he answered: "Well, Mr. Chairman, you have to believe that we are just damn fool enough to do it."

Kennedy was further away than miles could measure. He was in the hospital of Otis Air Force Base on Cape Cod, where Patrick Bouvier Kennedy, born on August 7 at 12:52 P.M., was fighting for life.

Jacqueline Kennedy had felt labor pains, five weeks early, as she was getting ready to go riding with her daughter Caroline. The baby, four pounds, ten ounces, was delivered by Caesarean section while the President was in the air from Washington, flying in an eight-seat Air Force Jetstar because Air Force One and its back-up were being used by Rusk and the delegation in Moscow. Kennedy saw his son at 2:30 P.M., after being told the baby had been born with a lung ailment called hyaline membrane disease.

The baby was taken in an incubator to the Children's Medical Center in Boston, where doctors worked to keep his lungs open using a pressure chamber just developed for open-heart surgery. When the end came at 4:04 A.M., August 9, the President was pacing the halls of the medical center, as he had been for hours.

The funeral mass was held the next day in the private chapel of Richard Cardinal Cushing in Boston. Jacqueline Kennedy was still in the hospital on Cape Cod. Her husband was on his knees, seemingly unable to let go of the little white coffin in front of him. "Come on, Jack, let's go," Cushing said finally. "God is good."

The President had been in the Cabinet Room when the call came that his wife was in premature labor. He was with Bundy, Larry O'Brien, Fred Dutton, and several men from outside the government, including Norman Cousins and Walter Reuther, planning the formation of a citizens' committee to lobby for Senate ratification of the test ban treaty. "If there were a vote now," he said, "we would not get close to the two-thirds we need."

He returned to Washington on August 10, saying his first priority was treaty ratification. But congressional mail, like White House mail, was still running fifteen to one against any ban on testing. Millions of Americans obviously believed every word of what their leaders had been telling them for more than ten years, that the United States was in imminent danger of massive nuclear attack by the Soviet Union—and the Communists were evil liars, never to be trusted. The treaty was going to be high politics and a tough sell. The President had many audiences and many messages to deliver. He had to tell the Americans who had gathered in front of Averell Harriman's house, and people all over the world, that their leaders were in control and did care about defanging the nuclear beast. At the same time he had to reassure the U.S. military, and influential members of the country's scientific community, that the treaty would not really retard the development of more usable nuclear weapons. At the core of his job definition, after all, was the maintenance of national security, which had come to mean military advantage. And he wanted to demonstrate to allies and adversaries alike that the treaty would not sap the will or resolve of the United States. Just as Rusk had reminded Khrushchev that Americans were the only people who had ever dropped the bomb on other people, twice, and might do it again.

The first political problem the President had in the Senate confirmation fight was managing the process so that the Joint Chiefs of Staff would testify as soon as possible. He wanted their testimony to be in public before the Senate Foreign Relations Committee, chaired by Senator William Fulbright, rather than in closed session before the Armed Services Committee, or the Preparedness Subcommittee, led or dominated by senators who were opposed to the idea of the treaty.

"The reason I made such a thing about it is because, in my opinion, the Chiefs are the key," Kennedy told the Senate Majority Leader, Mike Mansfield, on August 12. "If we don't get the Chiefs just right, we can get blown out. I would like to get them on a public record before they go to the Preparedness Committee. What they will say in public would be more pro-treaty than what they will say under interrogation by [Senator Henry] Scoop Jackson with leading questions and Barry Goldwater and Strom Thurmond."

"My judgment," Mansfield said, speaking of John Stennis of Mississippi, chairman of the Preparedness Subcommittee, "is that he'll come back and say, 'Mr. President, it was my understanding that I would have Max Taylor and the Joint Chiefs of Staff.' "

"Yeah, all right, let's say he says he has Max Taylor and the Joint Chiefs of Staff," said Kennedy. "But nobody ever said that it would be first, and that we will therefore get a statement of the Joint Chiefs which will be submitted for the public record on Wednesday, perhaps Wednesday morning, to the Senate Foreign Relations Committee. Then, that would be the public record. Then they're not going to be able to leak it on us that the Chiefs have grave reservations about this treaty. Which is what I'm afraid would come out of the Stennis committee."

By moving so swiftly on the Moscow negotiations, Kennedy had politically outflanked his own military on the most important military question of the time. Khrushchev seemed to have done pretty much the same thing in the Soviet Union.

In Washington, Kennedy's man, Maxwell Taylor, without being personally committed to any disarmament initiatives, did bring younger officers into the Joint Chiefs' staffing operations, men who were at least open to considering arguments before alerting their superiors and their congressional allies that the White House was moving ahead on its own.

General Curtis LeMay, the Air Force Chief of Staff, told Senator Richard Russell of Georgia, the chairman of the Armed Services Committee, that it was only when Harriman left for Moscow that it had dawned on him that the President was really serious about trying to negotiate an agreement. In Moscow, two days after the treaty was signed, Marshal Rodion Malinovsky, Taylor's Soviet counterpart, had refused to mention that it had happened in an Order of the Day on peace initiatives.

Another problem for the President was the American nuclear scientists who wanted to conceive ever more new weapons and systems. Their most important spokesman was Edward Teller, called "the father of the H-bomb," who came to the Foreign Relations Committee to say: "The signing was a mistake. If you ratify the treaty you will have committed an enormously greater mistake."

"I think that Teller made some impression on some of the members," Senator Fulbright told the President as the Foreign Relations Committee hearings began. Teller's specific argument was that the United States needed to test in the atmosphere to begin development of an anti-missile system which would shield the country like a great umbrella. Every other scientific adviser was telling the President that a shield against hundreds or thousands of missiles, some with warheads, some decoys, coming in at 17,000 miles per hour was beyond the technical and financial resources of not only the United States but the entire world.*

"The only thing Teller had over the others is he is such an actor," Fulbright said. "I mean he's John L. Lewis and Billy Sunday all wrapped in one."

"Yeah," Kennedy answered, "there's no doubt that any man with complete conviction, particularly who's an expert, is bound to shake anybody who's got an open mind. That's the advantage of having a closed mind."

The President's best witnesses before the Senate were McNamara and Taylor. McNamara said that there was no risk to U.S. national security. One of the ways he tried to prove that was by revealing an extraordinary amount of secret information on the size and scope of the American nuclear arsenal. Using his testimony, *Time* magazine calculated: "The actual number may be reckoned with reasonable accuracy at some 33,000 warheads on station; or held, carefully stored, in ready reserve. Another 15,000 are in preparation. . . . More than 25,000 are 'tactical' —designed for short-range (mostly under 30 miles) battlefield or defensive use that could be sent on slender supersonic missiles to wipe out a company, sink a ship, or shoot down planes. The rest—over 7,000

---

* Kennedy believed an anti-missile system was not feasible, saying once that the problem was not a bullet hitting a bullet, but thousands of bullets hitting thousands of other bullets. Teller, however, continued to believe the opposite, and in 1981 he found a President, Ronald Reagan, who agreed and attempted to develop an anti-missile system he called the Strategic Defense Initiative.

warheads—are 'strategic' built to travel thousands of miles and explode deep in enemy homelands."

General Maxwell Taylor gave his Senate testimony on August 15. He said the Joint Chiefs could support the treaty with four safeguards: "(1) Comprehensive, aggressive, and continuing underground nuclear test programs; (2) Maintenance of modern nuclear laboratory facilities and programs . . . and human scientific resources to these programs on which continued progress in nuclear technology depends; (3) Maintenance of the facilities and resources necessary to institute promptly nuclear tests in the atmosphere should they be deemed essential to our national security; (4) Improvement of our capability, within feasible and practical limits, to monitor the terms of the treaty."

That morning, Kennedy had his final meeting with Henry Cabot Lodge before Lodge left for Saigon as the new U.S. ambassador. He was more than an ambassador, really. He was being sent out as a modern pro-consul, as General Clay had been in Berlin. "I particularly want you to take personal charge of all press relations," Kennedy told him, mentioning the AP photograph of Quang Duc burning himself to death. "These are the worst press relations to be found in the world today."

He gave Lodge a twenty-five-page report on the U.S. press in Saigon, written by Assistant Secretary of State Robert Manning, a former *Time* correspondent, who had just made a ten-day trip to the country. "They seem to agree to a man that the U.S. involvement in Viet Nam is a necessary free world policy," Manning said of the twelve full-time American correspondents now in the country. "But . . . the correspondents reflect unanimous bitterness toward, and contempt for the Diem government. They unanimously maintain that our Vietnam policy cannot succeed unless the Diem regime (*cum* family) is replaced; this conviction, though it does not always appear in their copy, underlies all the reports and analyses of the correspondents."

Kennedy held a news conference on August 20, in which he tried to push Congress on the Test Ban Treaty, and on his foreign aid requests. He pledged his support of the four Taylor "safeguards," which had been prepared in the White House, and laid out a plan to safeguard the safeguards—including continuing development of a new atmospheric test site on Johnson Island in the South Pacific. On foreign aid, he noted that the request, which had been scaled down from $4.9 billion to $4.1 billion after the Clay Report, represented less than seven-tenths of 1 percent of the federal budget.

That same day, the President read a long memorandum on Vietnam from Senator Mansfield that he had asked for:

"It is necessary to face the fact that either way—with the present government or a replacement—we are in for a very long haul to develop even a modicum of stability in Viet Nam. And, in the end, the costs in men and money could go at least as high as those in Korea. At this point, with the changing of Ambassadors, therefore, it is pertinent to examine this present premise of policy. . . . Have we, by our own repeated rhetorical flourishes on 'corks in bottles' and 'stopping Communism everywhere' and loose use of the phrase 'vital interests of the nation' over the past few years given this situation a highly inflated importance and, hence, talked ourselves into the present bind? In short, have we, as in Laos, first over-extended ourselves in words and in agency-programs and, then, in search of a rationalization for the erroneous initial over-extension, moved what may be essentially a peripheral situation to the core of our policy-considerations?"

Then Mansfield answered his own questions, saying yes. He pointed out that the two most respected American military men, Generals Eisenhower and MacArthur, had both, referring specifically to Vietnam, urged that the United States never send troops to a land war in Asia. Finally, Mansfield told the President that the United States was sending all the wrong signals in Southeast Asia: "Specifically, in terms of the internal situation in South Viet Nam, we might withdraw abruptly and in a matter-of-fact fashion a percentage—say 10 per cent—of the military advisors which we have in Viet Nam, as a symbolic gesture, to make clear that we mean business when we say that there are some circumstances in which this commitment will be discontinued. . . ."

At the same time, Harriman, who had no doubts about United States commitment to Vietnam, but many about Diem and Nhu, said: "I hope that Lodge will start a new era in talking about the war and cut out the word 'ugly.' . . . Who ever invented this word 'ugly'? . . . 'Ugly' conveys the impression that we are somehow ashamed of it."

Ironically, there were no questions on Vietnam that day at the President's news conference. There were questions about the Test Ban Treaty and Congress, Cuba, and Berlin, but not one about Vietnam. But, that day in Saigon senior generals called on President Diem, asking him to declare martial law to deal with the continuing Buddhist demonstrations. They were surprised when Diem immediately agreed to turn the streets over to the army at midnight the next day, August 21.

Twenty minutes after that midnight in Saigon—noon August 21 in Washington—Vietnamese Special Forces, paid by the United States and trained by the CIA for covert operations against the North Vietnamese and under the official and direct command of Diem and Nhu, raided Buddhist pagodas in Saigon and Hué and a half dozen other cities. Working from lists titled "Communists in Disguise," they arrested 1,400 people, most of them monks and nuns.

It was a night of noise and terror. The raiders came in shooting. Most were wearing regular ARVN uniforms, rather than their green berets, so that Diem and Nhu could claim it was an army operation conducted without their knowledge. Temple gongs and drums awakened the cities. People raced into the streets banging pots and pans and charging at the Special Forces, who tried to drive them back with tear-gas grenades. Thirty people were killed and more than two hundred seriously wounded around Hué's Dieu de Pagoda. In Saigon, at the Xa Loi Pagoda, soldiers went first to an altar to seize the heart of Thich Quang Duc, the monk who had burned himself to death in June. Two young monks carrying Quang Duc's ashes in a small urn scrambled to safety over the pagoda's back fence into the headquarters of the U.S. Aid Mission. The telephone and cable lines to the mission and other U.S. offices and homes had been deliberately cut as the raids began.

"Diem's regime seems determined to repress forcefully the rising Buddhist agitation, despite strong advice from U.S. representatives ... ," began the President's intelligence briefing the next morning. Kennedy's first reaction was to find Henry Cabot Lodge and get him to Vietnam. The new ambassador was in Tokyo, sleeping after a long flight from San Francisco. On the plane, quite by accident, he had sat next to Eugene Burdick, the co-author of The Ugly American, who had kept him awake with a barrage of ideas to save Vietnam from communism —beginning with "Don't trust the people in the Embassy." Lodge told Kennedy he planned to stop next in Hong Kong, but the President told him there was an Air Force Lockheed Continental warmed up and waiting to take him on the eleven-hour flight to Saigon.

The South Vietnamese capital was quiet, almost silent, when Lodge arrived at 9:30 P.M., August 22. He was greeted by the commander of MACV, General Paul Harkins, an old friend—the two men had served together in the 2nd Armored Division during World War II—and forty American reporters and photographers. Lodge had said specifically that he did not want to see reporters, but he was a politician, and he walked over to talk with them, and began arranging one-on-one lunches. Then he drove to the U.S. Embassy through silent streets lined with soldiers with their backs to him, one every few yards.

Lodge already believed that there was no chance that President Diem or the Nhus could survive. It was just a matter of time. His briefings in Washington and in Honolulu, where he had met with his predecessor, Frederick Nolting, and Roger Hilsman of the State Department, and his own understanding of Vietnamese history, had persuaded him that the country had endured one tyranny after another, with the successful tyrants ruling for eight or nine years before being overthrown. And Diem had been in power for nine years. "You can't have the police

knocking on the door at three o'clock in the morning, taking sixteen-
and seventeen-year-old girls to camps outside of town," Lodge told
Hilsman. "You can't do that in any country . . . without laying the basis
for assassination."

Lodge, correctly guessing that the pagoda raids had been timed to try
to get the Buddhists under control before his arrival, came to Vietnam
with one opinion, and two specific orders from his President. Kennedy
had told him that the Diem government was almost certainly in its
terminal phase. But he wanted the ambassador to make a last try to
persuade Diem to accept American partnership—which meant getting
his brother and Madame Nhu out of the government and out of the
country—and begin listening to the people who were paying the bills.
Kennedy also told Lodge that he was not to thwart a military coup. On
his own, Lodge had concluded that the Communists were on the verge
of taking over the entire country, either because of public revulsion with
the methods of Diem and Nhu, or because Nhu would turn to the enemy
to make a deal to push the Americans out.

Diem did not listen to Lodge, any more than he had to Nolting. It
was not a language problem. Lodge and Diem both spoke fluent French.
The President gazed at the ceiling when Lodge raised subjects he preferred not to discuss, and began long monologues on his childhood and
his interpretations of history. The ambassador decided to avoid the
Presidential Palace. Back in Washington, the Vietnamese Ambassador
to the United States, Tran Van Chuong, who was Madame Nhu's father,
resigned his post, saying that as long as his daughter's husband and
brother-in-law were in power, there was no chance to defeat the Communists.

Time magazine also switched sides that week, turning against Diem
with a vengeance:

> The chief U.S. objection to Diem is not so much that he is a dictator, but
> an inefficient dictator. The proper democratic standards of the League of
> Women Voters cannot be applied to a deeply war-torn country. . . . The
> U.S. has proceeded on the assumption that it was safer to stick with him
> than risk the chaos that might surround the switch to a new, unknown
> and unpredictable regime. But by his move against the Buddhist monks,
> who have the growing support of the country's vast Buddhist majority,
> Roman Catholic Diem may finally have shattered his own political use-
> fulness.

The anti-Buddhist campaign halfway around the globe had created
a new problem in Washington, an anti-war movement that surprised

Kennedy, making him ask once more: "Who are these people?" The Ministers Vietnam Committee was taking out newspaper advertisements and had sent the President a petition signed by fifteen thousand clergymen, some of them quite prominent, beginning with Harry Emerson Fosdick of the Riverside Church in New York; Reinhold Niebuhr, the country's best-known Protestant theologian; Episcopal Bishop James Pike; and Unitarian Donald Harrington, who was also vice-chairman of New York's Liberal Party. They endorsed a four-point statement questioning not only the commitment to Diem but U.S. policy itself, protesting:

> Our country's military aid to those who denied religious freedom;
>   The immoral spraying of parts of South Vietnam with crop-destroying chemicals and the herding of many of its people into concentration camps called "strategic hamlets";
>   The loss of American lives and billions of dollars to bolster a regime universally regarded as unjust, undemocratic and unstable;
>   The fiction that this is "fighting for freedom."

The President flew to Hyannis Port on Friday, August 23. He was both sad and angry as he left Washington. This was his first time back since the death of Patrick Bouvier Kennedy. And, on the day before, he had been humiliated in Congress. The House had unexpectedly voted, 222 to 188, to cut $585 million more from his foreign aid bill. He had asked first for $4.9 billion and had to settle for $3.6 billion. Sixty-six Democrats, most of them from the South and border states, had joined 156 Republicans, making the largest aid cut since the program began after World War II.

It was rainy and gloomy that weekend, and Kennedy, in private, was on crutches. His back pain seemed to reflect the tensions of race at home and chaos abroad. On Saturday, he was alone with the day's newspapers, reading reports of demonstrations and repression in Vietnam. Students were attacking pro-Diem professors in the universities; Foreign Minister Vu Van Mau had resigned just before he was to officially greet Ambassador Lodge, shaved his head, and said he planned to become a Buddhist monk.

"POWER SHIFT TO NHU SEEN IN VIET-NAM" was the front-page headline in the *Washington Post* over a UPI story by Neil Sheehan. Warren Unna, reporting for the *Post* from Washington, wrote: "Even before the declaration of martial law, Nhu, President Diem's closest adviser, was generally considered to be the real ruler of the country." The Washington paper also reprinted an analysis from the *Observer* in London by

Stanley Karnow, an American reporter: "It is remarkable to hear plain sedition being preached by high civil servants and important army officers. Even men close to Diem now speak calmly of a forthcoming assassination."

The President's briefcase of "Weekend Reading" was filled with the same kind of material—the same U.S. officials in Saigon and Washington were leaking to the press at the same time as they were reporting to the White House. The idea was, as usual, to get the President's attention in one way or another, and this time they were succeeding. One bundle included a cover note by Averell Harriman's protégé, Michael Forrestal:

> I attach the latest cables on the situation in Saigon. It is now quite certain that Brother Nhu is the mastermind behind the whole operation against the Buddhists and is calling the shots. This is now agreed by virtually everyone here. . . . Agreement is also developing that the United States cannot tolerate a result of the present difficulties in Saigon which leaves Brother Nhu in a dominating position.
>
> Averell and Roger now agree that we must move before the situation in Saigon freezes. I am pressing them to get John McCone's endorsement of one of several courses of action which can be presented to you at the earliest opportunity.

Forrestal called the President on Saturday afternoon to report that CIA contacts with high South Vietnamese officials during the past twenty-four hours—Secretary of State for Defense Nguyen Dinh Thuan and General Tran Van Don—had indicated that a coup might be imminent in Saigon. The army was ready to take the Presidential Palace; they seemed to be waiting for a nod from the Americans.

"Can't we wait until Monday, when everybody is back?" Kennedy asked Forrestal, who reported back that Harriman and Hilsman were eager to cable new instructions to Ambassador Lodge.

McNamara was mountain-climbing in the Grand Tetons of Wyoming. Bundy and McCone were both on short vacations. Rusk, in New York for U.N. meetings, was at Yankee Stadium watching a ball game. Harriman and Roger Hilsman, now Assistant Secretary of State for the Far East, seemed to be running the show at the moment. And Harriman was a master of office politics at the highest levels, not worrying at all about going around Rusk, because he was one of the few people who knew the President was thinking seriously about replacing his Secretary of State, perhaps with McNamara or Bundy—or perhaps Harriman.

"Averell and Roger really want to get this thing out right away,"

Forrestal told Kennedy. The "thing" was a cable to Lodge with instructions about what to do if there was a coup.

"Well, go and see what you can do to get it cleared," the President said. So far, the cable was only the work of the State Department, not including the Secretary, who was at Yankee Statium.

Kennedy's next call was from George Ball, the State Department's number-two man. Hilsman had found him playing golf at the Chevy Chase Club. Back at the State Department, Ball read the President the most important parts of the cable Hilsman had showed him.

"Okay, George," Kennedy said; "if Rusk and Gilpatric agree, then go ahead."

Right, Ball said. He was trying to track down the Deputy Secretary of Defense, Roswell Gilpatric, who could act for McNamara, and Maxwell Taylor, and the CIA's director of operations, Richard Helms, who could act for McCone. He told Kennedy that a copy of the cable was on its way to Hyannis Port.

Forrestal called the President at about nine o'clock that night, reporting that there were clearances from State, from Defense, from the CIA, from the Joint Chiefs.

"Okay, send it out," Kennedy said. DEPTEL 243, the cable's official designation, was sent to Saigon at nine thirty-six that night, under the heading: "TOP SECRET . . . ACTION: AmEmbassy SAIGON—OPERATIONAL IMMEDIATE . . . EYES ONLY—AMBASSADOR LODGE."

It is now clear that whether military proposed martial law or whether Nhu tricked them into it, Nhu took advantage of its imposition to smash pagodas with police and Tung's Special Forces loyal to him, thus placing onus on military in eyes of world and Vietnamese people.

US Government cannot tolerate situation in which power lies in Nhu's hands. Diem must be given chance to rid himself of Nhu and his coterie and replace them with best military and political personalities available. If, in spite of all of your efforts, Diem remains obdurate and refuses, then we must face the possibility that Diem himself cannot be preserved. . . .

(1) First, we must press on appropriate levels of GVN following line: (a) USG cannot accept actions against Buddhists taken by Nhu and his collaborators under cover martial law. (b) Prompt dramatic actions redress situation must be taken, including repeal of decree 10, release of arrested monks, nuns, etc.

(2) We must at the same time also tell key military leaders that US would find it impossible to continue to support GVN militarily and economically unless above steps are taken immediately which we recognize requires removal of Nhus from the scene. . . . You may also tell appropriate military commanders we will give them direct support in any interim period of breakdown central government mechanism.

(3) We recognize the necessity of removing taint on military for pagoda raids and placing blame squarely on Nhu. You are authorized to have such statements made in Saigon as you consider desirable to achieve this objective. We are prepared to take same line here and to have Voice of America make statement. . . .

Concurrently with above, Ambassador and country team should urgently examine all possible alternative leadership and make detailed plans as to how we might bring about Diem's replacement if this should become necessary. . . .

You will understand that we cannot from Washington give you detailed instructions as to how this operation should proceed, but you will also know we will back you to the hilt on actions you take to achieve our objectives. Needless to say we have held knowledge of this telegram to minimum essential people and assume you will take similar precautions to prevent premature leaks.

Ambassador Lodge replied to DEPTEL 243 almost immediately, and that answer was sent to the President in Hyannis Port on Sunday. The State Department's cable approving Lodge's reply was included at the end of the message to the President: "From: Forrestal. To: General McHugh for President. EYES ONLY."

For President's information following cable was received from Lodge in answer message of last night. Begin Text:

Believe that chances of Diem's meeting our demands are virtually nil. At same time, by making them we give Nhu chance to forestall or block action by military. Risk, we believe, is not worth taking, with Nhu in control combat forces Saigon.

Therefore, propose we go straight to Generals with our demands, without informing Diem. Would tell them we prepared have Diem without Nhus but it is in effect up to them whether to keep him. . . . I present credentials President Diem tomorrow 11 A.M.

Ball, Harriman, and Hilsman answered that one on Sunday morning, August 25: "TO LODGE FROM ACTING SECRETARY. TOP SECRET:

"Agree to modification proposed. . . . Suggest Ambassador decide best means getting word to generals."

Chapter 50

The President returned to Washington on Monday morning, August 26, 1963, to find both the city and his most important advisers in tense struggles to keep control during the days ahead. Rusk, McNamara, and Taylor were waiting inside the White House to tell him that he had been tricked into approving or ordering a coup d'état in South Vietnam. Outside, thousands of police, National Guard troops, and various federal forces, including park rangers and the FBI, were mobilizing to try to preserve public order during the Negro march on Washington scheduled for Wednesday.

"RIGHTS LEADERS REAFFIRM BELIEF THAT MARCH WILL BE ORDERLY" was the headline on the front page of the day's *Washington Post.* "The march is a living petition—in the flesh . . . a demonstration in behalf of the human rights of twenty millions of people," said a statement issued by ten march leaders, including A. Philip Randolph and Martin Luther King, Jr. "We call for self-discipline. Remember that evil persons are determined to smear the March and to discredit the cause of equality by deliberate efforts to stir disorder. . . . Let's win at Washington."

"The general feeling is that the Vandals are coming to sack Rome," said the *Washington Daily News.* The *Washington Star* said: "If this misguided pressure is to be capped by some climactic idiocy, like the proposed March on Washington of one hundred thousand demonstrators, then it will have no happy ending."

The police were estimating the number of marchers would be 140,000, most of whom they expected to arrive in the city on Wednesday morning and be on their way out by sunset. That was the basic security plan, get people in and out as quickly as possible. It had been put together by Robert Kennedy's Justice Department, which was paying much of the expenses of the march. Two thousand five hundred National Guardsmen were mobilized to assist city police, four thousand regular Army troops, code-named "Task Force Inside," were moved by helicopter to a U.S. Navy station inside the District and to Fort Myers, across the Potomac River in Virginia. Fourteen thousand men of the 82nd Airborne Division were on stand-by alert at Fort Bragg in North Carolina. All of them were ready to move on executive orders which had been prepared in advance, stating: "An extraordinary assemblage of persons constituting a threat to life and property in the District of Columbia [are ordered] to disperse and retire peaceably. . . ." The papers waited only for the President's signature.

Kennedy's Vietnam crisis was still secret for the moment, but it seemed far more dangerous to him. "My God! My government's coming apart," Kennedy told Charlie Bartlett after hearing Rusk and McNamara. The secretaries of State and Defense and Max Taylor told the President that they had not seen or cleared the Sunday cable to Ambassador Lodge in Saigon. The dispute between those who thought President Diem was the problem in Vietnam, and those who thought he was still the last best hope of the U.S. policy, was on the table now. Kennedy's anti-Diem faction, led by Averell Harriman, seemed to have taken over U.S. policy that weekend. The President angrily summoned a dozen men to come to the White House in an hour. At noon.

Meanwhile, in Saigon, Henry Cabot Lodge was just as angry, but not because of the Saturday telegram. He welcomed that, it gave him more independent power to move against Diem, power he had every intention of using. What enraged him was a Voice of America (VOA) broadcast in Saigon that morning. He threw a handful of cables, and a transcript of the broadcast, onto a table, demanding to know whether anyone on his staff knew what was going on. "Jack Kennedy would never approve of doing things this way," he shouted at them. "This certainly isn't his way of running a government."

At 8:00 A.M. Saigon time, August 26, three hours before Lodge was to present formally his credentials to Diem, the VOA practically broadcast the contents of the Top Secret Saturday cable, alerting anyone who was listening that the United States was ready to abandon Diem and Nhu, and back the generals talking of overthrowing the government. In English and Vietnamese, announcers read:

"From Washington. High American officials blame police, headed by President Diem's brother Ngo Dinh Nhu, for anti-Buddhist actions in the Vietnam Republic. The officials say Vietnam military leaders are not, repeat not, responsible for last week's attacks against pagodas and the mass arrest of monks and students.

"The new U.S. Ambassador in Vietnam—Henry Cabot Lodge—is said to be under instructions to make it clear to President Diem that the U.S. considers those measures a violation of President Diem's assurances that he would seek a peaceful settlement of Buddhist complaints against the government. . . .

"The officials indicate the U.S. may sharply reduce its aid to Vietnam unless President Diem gets rid of secret police officials responsible for the attacks."

Lodge's anger was directed at the loss of whatever element of surprise there might be in a generals' coup. Probably he was deluding himself on that one. Truck drivers at the tea stalls of Saigon usually knew more about such things than the American ambassador. The American reporters in the city were already discussing coup coverage, and were assuming that Lodge had been sent to preside over the demise of the Ngo family. But Lodge's other worry—the reaction of Diem and Nhu to the VOA declarations—was real enough. He told General Paul Harkins and his titular number two, John Richardson, the embassy's deputy chief of mission, whose real job was CIA station chief, that they should not come with him to the eleven o'clock presentation of credentials ceremony at the Presidential Palace.

Lodge thought there was a chance that he, and anyone with him, might be taken hostage by the same secret police the VOA was condemning. "If they try any funny business, it might be better if one of us was on the outside," Lodge told Harkins as he left for the palace.

After Lodge's protests, the VOA reversed itself, denying its own report on aid cuts. The first broadcast, which had been cleared by Roger Hilsman, was just one more unpleasant surprise for Kennedy when his most important advisers on Vietnam gathered at noon. There were Rusk, McNamara, Taylor, Bundy, Roswell Gilpatric, and General Victor Krulak for Defense, Richard Helms and General Marshall Carter for the CIA, and the men who had pushed, or passed along, the Saturday telegram—Harriman, Hilsman, Forrestal, and Ball.

The first order of business was to address the President's demand to know what had happened. The story was put together with denial and back stabbing all around.

Hilsman, with Harriman pushing him, had written the cable in response to CIA reports that ARVN generals were complaining about

VOA reports charging them with ordering the pagoda raids. Then the play began—"An end run," thought Gilpatric, listening to the explanations. Harriman and Hilsman said they had been determined to get the cable out as soon as possible when, reading cables from Saigon, they concluded that the pagoda raids had finally turned the people of Vietnam against Diem and Nhu.

On Saturday morning, August 24 in Washington—it was already almost midnight the same day in Saigon—Hilsman had tracked down George Ball and General Krulak, both of them on the golf course at the Chevy Chase Club in Maryland. He had asked them to sign off for Rusk and Taylor. Neither had been willing to do it on his own. Then Harriman had gone to Ball's home, but Ball had said only that he would talk to the President and Rusk. Krulak had said he would try to find Taylor.

Ball had called Kennedy in Hyannis Port on Saturday. The President had said he preferred to wait. But he had also said: "If Rusk and McNamara or Gilpatric agree, George, then go ahead."

That had begun the telephone round-robin, with Kennedy telling Ball that he could go ahead if Rusk and McNamara or Gilpatric signed off on the cable. Hilsman and Forrestal did most of the calling, leaving the impression that they were acting on the President's orders. And Kennedy had been getting the impression that everyone in Washington was on board.

Rusk, back from Yankee Stadium, had been even more cautious than usual. He was a man who assumed rooms and telephones were bugged, and he had been reluctant to talk on an ordinary telephone at the Waldorf-Astoria Hotel about plotting to overthrow allied heads of state. He had said, as always, that it was okay with him if the President approved. Gilpatric, at his farm in Maryland, had said if it was okay with Rusk and the President, then he would sign off for McNamara. At the CIA, Richard Helms, sitting in for Director John McCone, who was in California, had said he considered the cable a policy matter beyond the scope of intelligence operations. But he had offered his opinion: "It's about time we bit that bullet." Taylor said he had not seen the cable until after eleven o'clock Saturday night. That would have been an hour and a half after Forrestal made his last call to the President in Hyannis Port to tell him State and Defense were agreed on the cable and Kennedy had said, "Okay, send it out!"

"This shit has got to stop!" the President said after hearing the confused Saturday chronology. He began to poll the table—as he had done just before the Bay of Pigs more than two years before—asking each of those around him whether they stood by the cable, or whether they wanted to rescind it, or change it. "Do you want to cancel, Mr. Rusk? . . . Do you want to cancel it, Mr. McNamara? . . . Do you want to cancel it, General Taylor? Yes or no? . . ."

Each man in turn said, "No."

The August 24 cable was still U.S. policy.

"Okay, that's it," said Kennedy. "I don't want to see any of this in the newspapers."

Except for the President, Rusk was probably the most upset of the men in the room. This was coming to a moment of truth. If the situation did not improve in Saigon, he said, "We must actually decide whether to move our resources out or to move our troops in."

Taylor thought Kennedy had done the right thing, whether or not he approved of what Harriman and Hilsman had done. He thought he knew what Kennedy was thinking: "You can't change American policy in twenty-four hours and expect anyone to believe you again." There was, in fact, a rough consensus: Nhu had to go and Diem probably had to go, too. Maybe Harriman and Hilsman had moved too fast, but this had to happen sooner or later. So this was sooner. The real gripe of McNamara and Taylor was not the message to Saigon, but the last sentence of the cable: "Needless to say we have held knowledge of this telegram to minimum essential people. . . ." These were men who considered themselves essential—and they had not known.

After the meeting, Forrestal approached Kennedy and offered to resign.

"You're not worth firing," the President said. "You owe me something, so you stick around."

That afternoon, the CIA sent out a cable to its Saigon station that filled in some of the details on where the U.S. government stood that Monday:

Headquarters instruct . . . to discuss the coup with the generals, based on the August 24 cable, using the following points:
  • We in agreement Nhus must go.
  • Question of retaining Diem or not up to generals. . . .
  • We cannot be of any help during initial action of assuming power of the state. Entirely their own action, win or lose. Don't expect to be bailed out.
  • If Nhus do not go, and if Buddhists' situation is not redressed as indicated, we would find it impossible continue military and economic support.
  • It is hoped bloodshed can be avoided or reduced to absolute minimum.

The policy, or the policies, or lack of policy, was beginning to look like the approval of the CIA plan to invade Cuba with plausible deniability in the spring of 1961. President Kennedy knew more this time, but the secret debate was again focused on finding the right man to back or to eliminate. "Looking under bushes for the Vietnamese George Washington," was Taylor's description. But there were differences. This time the particulars of the debates inside the White House were being leaked to reporters—with the Harriman-Hilsman side prevailing for the moment.

Though the press still knew nothing of the August 24 cable, a news analysis by Warren Unna in Tuesday morning's *Washington Post* showed a sense of what was happening in secret. "The Kennedy Administration has now decided that the United States no longer can afford to sit on its hands and watch South Viet-Nam go down the drain, and U.S. policy with it. . . . Administration officials reportedly now are just convinced that the mandate of the Diem-Nhu regime has run out."

That was on page eight that Thursday. The front-page news in the *Post* was under an eight-column banner headline, "Leader Calls March 'Revolution.'" At the National Press Club, A. Philip Randolph was passing on the details of planning for the next day's "March on Washington for Jobs and Freedom." The *Post* estimated the number of marchers at one hundred thousand, and other stories reported a tense city. The streets of the city were lined with water tanks, first-aid stands, and portable toilets. No one seemed certain of what to expect on Wednesday—psalm singing or chaos?

The next White House meeting on Vietnam was set for four o'clock Tuesday afternoon, August 27. The Vietnam group was beginning to function as a smaller version of Ex Comm during the Cuban missile crisis. There was one new face at the table this day, Fritz Nolting, whom Lodge had replaced in Saigon. Max Taylor had mentioned to Kennedy that Nolting was in Washington and the President wanted to know why he had not been invited in by the State Department.

"His views are colored," interjected Harriman, meaning he considered Nolting too pro-Diem.

"Maybe they're properly colored," snapped Kennedy. "I want to see him."

The President questioned Nolting closely that afternoon and the former ambassador confirmed Harriman's view of him, consistently defending Diem. He said the Vietnamese president and his brother were like Siamese twins, impossible to separate. He stopped short, however, of mentioning that Americans in the embassy called brother Nhu "Bobby."

"The Vietnamese generals haven't got the guts of Diem and Nhu," Nolting told the President as Harriman listened in silent fury. "They will not be a unified group, but will be badly split. They do not have real leadership, and they do not control the predominant military force in the country."

The President was shaken by that, and by the implication in Nolting's warning that the CIA had already gone so far that there might be no turning back. "If we go back on these generals now, we will lose them," Nolting admitted, partially countering his own arguments supporting Diem. As in the Bay of Pigs planning, the CIA had left the President with a "disposal problem"—but this time it was generals rather than ordinary troops. Then Harriman ripped into Nolting for being taken in by Diem and accused him of betraying U.S. interests. "You've been wrong from the beginning," he said. "No one cares what you think."

Kennedy, predictably, wanted more information. The minutes of the meeting said: "The President said we should send a cable to Ambassador Lodge and General Harkins asking for their estimates of the prospect of a coup by the generals. They should also be asked to recommend whether we should proceed with the generals or wait. . . . The President said he thought they should also be asked whether the effect would be harmful if we decided now to cut our losses."

Rusk summarized again as the President just listened: "We should make clear to our officials in Saigon that we are not changing their existing directives on which they are already proceeding to take numerous actions." Leaving the White House, Harriman refused to ride in the same limousine as Nolting for the trip back to the State Department.

General Taylor sent Harkins a cable that evening: "Eyes Only. Reference State to Saigon 256. August 27 . . . Important White House meeting on subject message scheduled for 1200 28 August EDT, your views urgently needed on reference message and on overall feasibility of operation contemplated in CAS Saigon 0346. . . . FYI State to Saigon 243 was prepared without DOD or JCS participation. Authorities are now having second thoughts."

That "second thoughts" cable enraged Kennedy when he saw it. Taylor was obviously guiding his former assistant to undermine the State Department's maneuvering.

On his own, General Harkins, as reported by Marguerite Higgins in Tuesday morning's *New York Herald Tribune,* was saying that the war was going so well that he expected the United States to start phasing out its military presence in a year or so. Kennedy mentioned the Higgins piece at a meeting that day and Harriman went after the two U.S.

generals, saying he did not understand Harkins's return cable until he had seen Taylor's outgoing message. The President, who had seen them both and come to the same conclusion, had trouble not laughing when Harriman made his move against Taylor and Harkins. Seeing Forrestal in the hall later, he said, "Averell is one sharp cookie, isn't he?"

Robert Kennedy was not attending the Vietnamese meetings because he was overseeing the planning for the next day's march. He went to a dinner party that night at Harriman's house in Georgetown, where he was seated next to Marietta Tree, a member of the United States delegation to the United Nations. He mentioned Bayard Rustin, the man Randolph had chosen to organize the march, who had once been a Communist and had once been arrested on a sodomy charge. Leaning toward Tree, he said: "So, you're down here for that old black fairy's anti-Kennedy demonstration."

Mrs. Tree tried to deflect the Attorney General by asking what he thought of Martin Luther King, Jr. "He's not a serious person," said Robert Kennedy. She had no idea what that could mean. The Attorney General was operating on a different level, having seen transcripts produced by the FBI's taps and bugs on King's telephones and in the hotel rooms the Justice Department helped find for march leaders in Washington.

"If the country knew what we know about King's goings-on, he'd be finished," the Attorney General told Mrs. Tree.

She decided not to pursue the conversation.

Five weeks earlier, Attorney General Robert Kennedy had authorized the FBI to tap the phones of King and of Clarence Jones, the New York attorney he had first met during the angry meeting with James Baldwin. He had acted after Jones had approached Deputy Attorney General Burke Marshall on July 16, asking questions about which lines of communications were safe for King to use. To Robert Kennedy, the questions meant that King had told Jones of the President's June 22 warnings about "very close surveillance." To him, that represented both a personal betrayal of the President and a political danger at a time when Southern politicians were accusing King of being a Communist, and the Kennedys of consciously aiding Negro Communists.

The Attorney General had signed off on the Jones bugs and taps on July 22, but he had held back on an order to tap King's phones the same day. By mid-August, however, J. Edgar Hoover had provided him with tapes of King talking to Jones and others about sex on the road—by coincidence, the preacher was staying at Jones's house in New York during the planning for the March on Washington. "He's a Tom Cat," exulted Hoover, reading the transcripts of King's conversations, before editing them and sending them on to the Kennedys.

There was no great mystery in high places about what Hoover was doing. Dean Rusk, with his devotion to discretion, made a point of telling the FBI director, in front of the President, that if he ever found a tap on his telephone or a bug in his office, he would immediately resign and go public with the evidence. And that summer, when the New York office of the President's back doctor, Hans Kraus, was broken into and the records obviously searched—the same thing that had happened to all Kennedy's other doctors—White House speculation had focused on three suspects, in reverse order of probability: the Republicans, the Soviets, the FBI.

The President and the other men at the noon Vietnam meeting on Wednesday, August 28, could hear the sounds of the March on Washington through the closed windows of the air-conditioned White House. There were two hundred thousand marchers outside on the Mall from the Washington Monument to the Lincoln Memorial, the largest political gathering in the history of the country.

The meeting opened with William Colby of the CIA reporting that Saigon was quiet, pointing out that Diem and Nhu controlled at least two thirds of the South Vietnamese troops in the city itself. He said the CIA was, at that moment, trying to convince Diem that a telegram intercepted by South Vietnamese intelligence urging the immediate overthrow of his government was not a signal from the White House. It was, in fact, just a Western Union telegram to Ambassador Lodge from a citizen in Laguna Beach, California, who wanted Lodge to know he supported him.

Then George Ball summarized the situation for the President:

"One: We can't win the war against the Communists with Diem in control. The U.S. position in the eyes of the world is being badly damaged. Hence, we can't back off from our all-out opposition to Diem and Nhu.

"Two: If we merely let the generals proceed and then, if they fail to overthrow Diem, we have lost as well. . . .

"Three: We decide to do the job right. There is no other acceptable alternative. We must decide now to go through to a successful overthrow of Diem."

Kennedy listened, but said it sounded to him as if the coup forces did not have the strength to overthrow Diem.

"Then don't go," said Treasury Secretary Dillon.

The President asked McNamara whether there was a plan to build up the anti-Diem forces in the Army of Vietnam, and if there had not been then it was time to come up with one.

Harriman interrupted to say that if the coup failed, "We have lost Vietnam!"

The President sent his own messages to Saigon after that meeting, under the heading: "TOP SECRET: EYES ONLY FOR THE AMBASSADOR FROM THE PRESIDENT":

> In this personal message I want to emphasize again that I wish to have your independent judgment and also that of General Harkins at every stage. The basic policies set forth in DEPTELs 243 and 256 represented my best current judgment, but this judgment in turn is heavily dependent on your on-the-spot advice. . . . While naturally there are differences in emphasis among the many officials concerned here in Washington, Washington will act as a unit under my direction. . . . In all this, I continue to think of you as my personal representative and repose greatest confidence in you.

It was only then, after reading the President's short cable, that Lodge heard about Taylor's "second thoughts" cable. John Richardson—who had been summoned to MACV headquarters at five o'clock that morning to read the Taylor message, told Lodge that he was ordering his agents to hold off committing to anything in their meetings with Vietnamese generals.

"Why?" Lodge asked.

Richardson showed him the Taylor cable and Lodge blew up. "Why wasn't I informed of this cable?" he shouted, a question heard up and down embassy corridors.

Lodge sat down and wrote a long, lecturing cable—numbered 375—that arrived in Washington early on the morning of Thursday, August 29:

> We are launched on a course from which there is no respectable turning back: the overthrow of the Diem government. . . . There is no turning back because there is no possibility, in my view, that the war can be won under a Diem administration, still less that Diem or any member of the *familia* can govern the country in a way to gain support of the people who count, i.e, the educated class in and out of government service, civil and military—not to mention the American people. . . . I am personally in full agreement with the policy I was instructed to carry out by last [Saturday's] telegram.
>
> We should proceed to make all-out effort to get generals to move promptly. . . . If generals insist on public statement that all U.S. aid to

Vietnam through Diem regime has been stopped, we would agree, on express understanding that generals will have started at same time.

I realize that this course involves a very substantial risk of losing Vietnam. It also involves some additional risk to American lives. I would never propose it if I felt there was a reasonable chance of holding Vietnam with Diem.

At the same time in Paris, President Charles de Gaulle made a move, issuing a three-paragraph statement to "All of Vietnam"—meaning both the South and the North—saying France would cooperate with moves to rid the country of all "foreign influence." The Americans could ignore the declaration, and officially they did, but it greatly heightened suspicions that there were, or might soon be, attempts by Diem's brother Nhu to reach an accommodation with North Vietnam, an arrangement that would obviously mean the end of the American presence.

The lead headline of the *Washington Post* on Thursday, August 29, was:

Mammoth Rally of 200,000 Jams Mall
In Solemn, Orderly Plea for Equality

Tucked among pages of stories and photographs of the great civil rights march were two headlines from Saigon: "Nhu Called Real Viet-Nam Ruler," and "Vietnamese Regime Headed for Showdown with U.S."

President Kennedy's official day on Thursday began with extensive reports on the March on Washington, Lodge's cable, de Gaulle's challenge, and a telephone call to Roger Hilsman to ask about a front-page story by Tad Szulc in *The New York Times* on August 28 under the headline: "Long Crisis Seen on Vietnam Rule."

Szulc reported that high officials in Washington believed that getting rid of Nhu or of both Nhu and Diem was the only way to resolve the United States' Vietnam problems. "He seems to be getting pretty close to things," said Kennedy, asking who might be the sources of the story. Twelve hours later, after another day of meetings, Kennedy personally approved of two "EYES ONLY" cables sent from Washington to Saigon:

"Highest level meeting noon today"—cable language for the President—"reviewed your 375 and reaffirmed basic course. Specific decisions follow: . . . USG supports the movement to eliminate Nhus from the government, but before arriving at specific understandings with the generals, General Harkins must know who are involved, resources available to them and overall plan for coup. The USG will support a coup which has a good chance of succeeding but plans no direct involvement of U.S. Armed Forces. . . . You are hereby authorized to announce suspension of aid through Diem Government at a time and under conditions of your choice."

The second "EYES ONLY" cable to Lodge that night was signed by Rusk:

> The only point on which you and General Harkins have different views is whether an attempt should be made with Diem to eliminate the Nhus. . . . My own hunch based on the report of Kattenburg's conversation with Diem is that such an approach could not succeed if it were cast purely in terms of persuasion. Unless such talk included a real sanction, such as threatened withdrawal of our support, it is unlikely that it would be taken completely seriously. . . . But if a sanction were used in such a conversation, there would be a high risk that this would be taken by Diem as a sign that action against him and the Nhus was imminent and he might at a minimum move against the generals or even take some fantastic action such as calling on North-Vietnam for assistance in expelling the Americans.

There was a third cable that night, signed by President Kennedy, and classified "PERSONAL FOR THE AMBASSADOR FROM THE PRESIDENT. NO OTHER REDISTRIBUTION WHATEVER."

> I have approved all the messages you are receiving from others today, and I emphasize that everything in these messages has my full support.
> We will do all that we can to help you conclude this operation successfully. Nevertheless, there is one point on my own constitutional responsibilities as President and Commander in Chief which I wish to state to you in this entirely private message, which is not being circulated here beyond the Secretary of State.
> Until the very moment of the go signal for the operation by the Generals, I must reserve a contingent right to change course and reverse previous instructions. . . . When we go, we must go to win, but it will be better to change our minds than fail. . . . This message requires no direct answer but if you do wish to reply, your answer should be headed "For President Only, Pass White House Directly, No Other Distribution Whatever."

On Friday, August 30, Lodge, who had been in the country for only eight days, answered the telegrams from Washington, telling Rusk:

> I agree that getting the Nhus out is the prime objective. . . . This surely cannot be done by working through Diem. He wishes he had more Nhus,

not less. The best chance of doing it is by the generals taking over the government lock, stock and barrel. . . . My greatest single difficulty in carrying out the instructions of last Sunday is inertia. The days come and go and nothing happens. Here it is Friday and there is not enough to show for the hours which we have all put in. . . . I am sure that the best way to handle this matter is by a truly Vietnamese movement even if it puts me rather in the position of pushing a piece of spaghetti. I am contemplating no further talks with Diem at this time.

On Saturday morning, a week after the August 24 cable, General Harkins called in General Tran Thien Khiem, an emissary from General Duong Van Minh, the leader of the generals planning a coup. The American said: "If the generals were ready to remove Diem, the United States government would back them."

General Khiem came back in the afternoon and told Lodge that there would be no coup. Not now. They were afraid, he said, that Diem and Nhu were still backed by the United States, and that the brothers were just waiting for a coup attempt to flush out the conspirators.

"There is neither the will nor the organization among the generals to accomplish anything," Lodge cabled Washington. "If at some indeterminate date in the future some other group with the necessary strength and lust for office comes forward, we can contemplate another effort.

"I think the U.S. Government was right to instruct me as it did last [Saturday] not only because of the state of opinion in America and Free World but because the Government of Viet-Nam has acted as both liars and criminals."

Richardson of the CIA reported the same thing with a warning attached: "This particular coup is finished. There is little doubt that GVN"—Diem and Nhu—". . . aware of U.S. role and may have considerable detail."

So there was another meeting in Washington on Saturday, August 31. With the President back in Hyannis Port again, Secretary Rusk presided. He invited Paul Kattenburg, staff director of the Interdepartmental Task Force on Vietnam, to the session—the "Kattenburg" referred to in his August 29 cable to Lodge—because Kattenburg was the last American to talk at length with Diem in Saigon, for three hours on August 28.

"A garden path to tragedy," was the way Kattenburg described Vietnam policy, when he was asked to speak. He had listened for an hour, stunned by ignorance around the table concerning the present situation and Vietnamese history. Rusk, McNamara, Robert Kennedy, and Vice President Johnson glared at him after that opening. Kattenburg was flustered, but he went on. "At this juncture," he said, "it would be better for us to make the decision to get out honorably. . . . In from six months to a year, as the South Vietnamese people see we are losing the war, they will gradually go to the other side, and we will be obliged to leave."

"That's just your speculation," Rusk said to Kattenburg. "We will not pull out of Vietnam until the war is won. . . . And we will not run a coup." McNamara nodded approval as Rusk spoke, then said: "We are winning this war!" *

In one final cable to the President that Saturday, Lodge spoke of new intrigues in Saigon, and in Hanoi, the capital of North Vietnam: "I am very reliably informed that French Ambassador Lalouette was with Nhu for four hours . . . also advised by a dependable source that he wants the U.S. Government out of Viet-Nam so the French can become the intermediary between South and North Viet-Nam. . . . I am reliably advised that Nhu is in a highly volatile state of mind and that some sort of gesture through Nhu to North Viet-Nam is not impossible."

The message had gotten through to President Kennedy that the government the United States was officially supporting and financing and fighting for might be dealing secretly with the Communists—and might ask the Americans to leave.

The return cables from the White House to Saigon that day, August 31, ordered the embassy and the military mission to recall and destroy all copies of the messages received and sent during the week that began with the cable of August 24. In Washington the same orders, over the President's name, were sent to the State Department, the CIA, and the Defense Department: Destroy all coup cables.

---

* Kattenburg was never again invited to a high-level Vietnam meeting and was soon transferred to the U.S. Embassy in the new country of Guyana.

Chapter 51

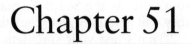

AUGUST 28, 1963

At 1:30 A.M. on August 28 there was a traffic jam in the Lincoln Tunnel between New York and New Jersey. New Yorkers in chartered buses had begun leaving the city at midnight, headed south for the March on Washington. At 8:00 A.M., one hundred buses were counted in and around the Baltimore Harbor Tunnel. At that hour, the first chartered train, from Pittsburgh, arrived at Union Station in Washington, followed by trains from Chicago, Detroit, Gary, Jacksonville. "The Freedom Train," which had left Miami at nine-thirty on the morning of August 27, was cheered by crowds of Negroes at stations and along the tracks on its way north.

More than fifteen hundred special buses arrived on the morning of the March, guided to assembly areas by military police in jeeps at intersections around the city. Army helicopters hovered above, looking for trouble spots, of which there appeared to be none. More than three thousand reporters from around the world covered the event. Live television coverage began at eleven-thirty on the three U.S. networks. One of the viewers was President Kennedy, sitting in the Oval Office with Attorney General Robert Kennedy, Burke Marshall, and Secretary of Labor Willard Wirtz. Then Kennedy began shuttling between the television and the Vietnam meetings which began at noon that day in the Cabinet Room.

The city was tense at the beginning. Robert Kennedy had negotiated the closing of Washington's bars and liquor stores, and had persuaded the American League to postpone the Washington Senators scheduled night games against the Minnesota Twins on August 27 and 28.

The most liberal of the city's newspapers, the *Washington Post*, analyzed the March in terms of what it meant to the President:

> In recent months, there have been indications that whites, especially in the North, have become disenchanted with the way Negroes seem to be nagging and protesting about less important, perhaps even picayune, aspects of discrimination. The march can serve to restore the dignity and validity of the Negro cause and refocus the Nation's attention and conscience on the big issue: that the Negro wants the breaks that other Americans have.
>
> Prospects appear dim at this time that Congress will enact a strong public accommodations provision into national law. . . . If Congress fails to act, then the President may be thrown into the spotlight, because election year or not, he may be forced to issue executive orders to carry out his civil rights program to avert racial disturbances throughout the land.

The *Post* also reported on the campaign for governor of Mississippi between Lieutenant Governor Paul Johnson and former Governor J. P. Coleman. Johnson, who had briefly stood in the doorway of the University of Mississippi when James Meredith entered in October 1962, was using advertisements that said: "Remember These Things: J. P. Coleman endorsed, spoke and voted for Kennedy for President of the United States. . . . Yes, remember J. P. Coleman would turn Mississippi over to the Kennedys—lock, stock and barrel."

The President thought he was already in the spotlight. The last Gallup Poll had indicated that 63 percent of Americans disapproved of the March, and that 38 percent thought he was pushing too fast on integration. At the same time the Harris Poll estimated that Kennedy, who had won election by roughly 118,000 votes, was currently losing 4.5 million votes because of his stands on civil rights, most of them in the South and border states, and could expect to pick up fewer than 600,000 new Negro voters, even including those allowed to register for the first time.

Washington itself was a city still clinging to Southern history and tradition. "A place of Northern charm and Southern efficiency," John Kennedy joked, reversing the local boast. The *Post* had only stopped running segregated employment and real estate advertising in 1960. But the capital was also a Negro city; Negroes accounted for 55 percent of the population in the 1960 census, as more and more white families moved to suburbs in Maryland and Virginia.

The President had tried without success to persuade A. Philip Randolph and the other leaders of the March that there was more risk than gain in this exercise. If there was violence, he said, their movement could be set back decades—and his civil rights bill would be dead. Unable to beat the March, he had chosen to join it, which meant trying to shape it as an all-American one-day rally for his civil rights bill. Above all, the President wanted no televised racial violence and no new demands for federal action to reward or compensate Negroes for the many injustices of the past. In press conferences before the March, he had had to deny insinuations from Southern officials (and FBI leaks) that King and other civil rights leaders were fronting for Communists or were all perverts, as Senator Strom Thurmond of South Carolina had charged, reading the details of Bayard Rustin's homosexuality conviction into the *Congressional Record*. At his August 20 news conference, the President had been asked whether he believed that Negroes were entitled to special government help or quotas in private employment, and he had said no.

"I don't think we can undo the past," he continued. "In fact, the past is going to be with us for a good many years in uneducated men and women who lost their chance for a decent education. We have to do the best we can now. That is what we are trying to do. I don't think quotas are a good idea. I think it is a mistake to begin to assign quotas on the basis of religion, or race, or color, or nationality. I think we'd get into a good deal of trouble. . . . On the other hand, I do think we ought to make an effort to give a fair chance to everyone who is qualified—not through a quota, but just look over our employment rolls, look over our areas where we are hiring people and at least make sure we are giving everyone a fair chance."

When John Kennedy had realized that he could not stop the March, he had given his brother the assignment of taking it over. Robert Kennedy's Justice Department had channeled hundreds of thousands of dollars to the six civil rights organizations sponsoring the event, beginning with the NAACP and King's SCLC. "The march has been taken over by the government," said Malcolm X, a spokesman for the Nation of Islam, which had refused to participate. "This is government controlled."

Six weeks earlier, one of the Attorney General's assistants, John Douglas, had been delegated to work with Randolph and Rustin. The government's first decision had been choosing the site for the closing rally, the Lincoln Memorial. No place could be more appropriate than the great sitting statue of the Great Emancipator, even if Negroes had been segregated in a separate section on the side when the Memorial was dedicated in 1922. It was also a perfect site to police and control because the Memorial was away from both residential and commercial areas, and was surrounded by water on three sides. The March itself was less than a mile, from the Washington Monument down the great Mall to the Lincoln Memorial. Jerry Bruno, the President's favorite advance man, and an expert on gathering and controlling crowds, was assigned to sit behind Lincoln's statue with a switch that could cut off the power to the sound system if the speaker got too excited. It was the best system money could rent, selected by the Justice Department. The worry was that if people at the edges of the crowd could not hear what was going on, they might begin entertaining themselves, starting trouble.

The White House had set the date for the March, choosing a Wednesday, hoping that people would come and go in one day because they had to go to work the day before and the day after. Rustin had negotiated hour by hour and point by point with Douglas and Bruno and sometimes Robert Kennedy until they signed off on a plan for a three-hour rally, rather than a protest march. The ceremonies would end by four o'clock in the afternoon, leaving enough time for the crowds to leave town before a late summer sunset. Robert Kennedy and Burke Marshall got tough with the Washington Police Department when the District's chief said he wanted to use dogs for crowd control. No dogs!

"We're in this up to our necks," the President told King before the March. Whether or not his neck was on the line, Kennedy had held his own presence back. He declined an invitation to speak, because he thought it was impossible to craft a speech that would satisfy both the crowd at the Memorial and a nation watching on live television. He also refused to meet with Randolph, King, and Roy Wilkins before the March to avoid photographs that would make him look bad if there was trouble in the streets. And he wanted to make sure that no Negro leader would give him a list of demands before the speeches and then denounce him from the Memorial if he turned them down.

One of the first problems of the day, at least for the White House, came when members of SNCC, the Student Non-Violent Coordinating Committee, mimeographed copies of the speech of their twenty-three-year-old president, John Lewis. "We will march through the South, through the heart of Dixie, the way Sherman did," Lewis planned to say. "We shall pursue our own scorched earth policy and burn Jim Crow to the ground non-violently."

The Roman Catholic Archbishop of Washington objected to those words. Patrick Cardinal O'Boyle, who had desegregated Catholic schools in Washington in 1948 long before it was either mandated or fashionable, told the men from the Justice Department that if the Sherman line stayed in, he would refuse to give the invocation at the beginning of the ceremonies at the Memorial. The President and his advisers were focusing on another Lewis line: "We cannot support the Administration's civil rights bill."

Robert Kennedy, Burke Marshall, and Randolph and King, too, worked on Lewis, a veteran of twenty-two civil rights arrests and a dozen police beatings. Finally, with the President himself doing the editing, late in the morning, Lewis finally agreed to drop the Sherman line and say: "It is true that we support the Administration's Civil Rights Bill in Congress. We support it with great reservations, however." *

Away from the internal politics of the day, thousands and thousands of marchers black and white—one out of four were white—gathered around the Washington Monument, waiting for the eleven-thirty start of their parade. The route was along two broad boulevards on either side of the Monument and the Mall, Independence and Constitution avenues. Rank-and-file marchers were prohibited from trespassing onto Capitol Hill that day as their leaders spent the morning meeting with congressional leadership. The meetings in the Capitol continued past noon. They were still talking when they got word that the crowd at the Washington Monument was getting restless in the August heat and humidity. The parade was going to begin, with or without leaders. In a scene that made the President laugh when he heard about it, the leaders ran out of the offices of the House of Representatives frantically hailing cabs. Determined to get out in front of their followers, the chiefs forgot they had limousines waiting.

Kennedy needed a laugh. He was in secret meetings, listening to plans to evacuate the four thousand American civilians in South Vietnam if a coup led to civil war. That session broke up just before 1:00 P.M.—a half hour before the speeches were to begin at the Lincoln Memorial—and was scheduled to reconvene at six. Like much of America, the President went back to the television set in his office. He was impressed. The first great cheer rose when the master of ceremonies, actor Ossie Davis, introduced Carol Taylor, who had just been hired as the first Negro airline stewardess in the United States.

The speeches were limited to seven minutes, separated by cameo appearances by Negro and white entertainers. Harry Belafonte, Marlon Brando, Charlton Heston, Marian Anderson, Paul Newman, Sammy Davis, Jr., Diahann Carroll, Joan Baez, Josh White, and Bob Dylan were there.

Randolph was the first speaker that day, and his words paralleled many a Kennedy speech on different subjects, rejecting calls for patience: "Those who deplore our militance, who exalt patience in the

---

* In 1986, John Lewis was elected to Congress from the Fifth District of Georgia.

name of a false peace are in fact supporting segregation and exploitation. They would have social peace at the expense of social and racial justice." John Lewis, symbolically a grandson of Randolph and a son of Kennedy, went one step further, saying: "To those who have said be patient and wait, we must say that we cannot be patient, we do not want our freedom gradually. We want to be free now! . . . Get in and stay in the streets of every city, every village and every hamlet in this nation, until true freedom comes, until the revolution of 1776 is completed." He was cheered fourteen times.

The flap over Lewis's speech turned out to be the most troublesome moment of the day. Not one arrest was related to the demonstration. The March was a triumph of managed protest. Reverend Eugene Carson Blake, who had been Eisenhower's pastor when he was President, spoke, then Whitney Young of the Urban League, Walter Reuther, Roy Wilkins, and Rabbi Joachim Prinz of the American Jewish Congress. Floyd McKissick spoke for James Farmer of CORE who was in a Louisiana jail. This was a church crowd dressed in Sunday best. The event ended a little after four o'clock in the afternoon with the two most famous Negro church people in the land, gospel singer Mahalia Jackson and the Reverend Martin Luther King, Jr.

"I'm going to tell my Lord when I get home," she sang. "Just how long you've been treating me wrong," sang Jackson, her voice rolling over the crowd and the country. ". . . I've been 'buked and I've been scorned, trying to make this journey all alone."

She set the mood for the last speaker. Martin Luther King had not been involved much in the planning of the rally, deferring to the seniority of Randolph and Roy Wilkins of the NAACP. The preacher from Atlanta had been the preeminent figure in the civil rights movement since Birmingham. He was committed to non-violence and he had the oratorical power to move a crowd without sending them charging into the streets. He gave white Americans, particularly ignorant northerners, a memorable glimpse of the power and Christian dramatics of the Negro church and Southern religion. Mahalia Jackson's voice and a CBS television camera on top of the Washington Monument to show the size of the crowd framed the moment, and King's voice began to fill that frame. He was supposed to speak for seven minutes, but he went on for nineteen. No one wanted him to stop.

"Five score years ago a great American in whose shadow we stand today, signed the Emancipation Proclamation. . . ," King began. Then he had a couple of false starts, talking of Lincoln's promises of freedom as a check that came back marked "insufficient funds," and of walking together with white brothers.

"There are those who are asking the devotees of civil rights, 'When will you be satisfied?' We can never be satisfied as long as the Negro is the victim of the unspeakable horrors of police brutality. We can never be satisfied as long as our bodies, heavy with the fatigue of travel, cannot gain lodging in the motels of the highways and the hotels of the cities. We can never be satisfied as long as the Negro's basic mobility is from a smaller ghetto to a larger one. We can never be satisfied as long as our children are stripped of their self-hood and robbed of their dignity by signs reading 'For Whites Only.' We can never be satisfied as long as a Negro in Mississippi cannot vote and a Negro in New York believes he has nothing for which to vote. No. No we are not satisfied, and we will not be satisfied until justice rolls down like waters and righteousness like a mighty stream.

"I say to you today, my friends, that in spite of the difficulties and frustrations of the moment, I still have a dream. It is a dream deeply rooted in the American dream. I have a dream that one day this nation will rise up and live out the true meaning of its creed: 'We hold these truths to be self-evident—that all men are created equal.'

"I have a dream that one day on the red hills of Georgia the sons of former slaves and the sons of former slaveowners will be able to sit down together at the table of brotherhood.

"I have a dream that my four little children will one day live in a nation where they will not be judged by the color of their skin but by the content of their character.

"This will be the day when all of God's children will be able to sing with new meaning 'My country 'tis of thee, sweet land of liberty, of thee I sing. Land where my father died, land of the pilgrim's pride, from every mountainside, let freedom ring.' "

"He's damned good," said the President, watching on television in the living quarters of the White House. "Damned good!" He had only seen short film clips of King's speeches before.

A half hour later, the leaders of the March, glowing with triumph, came to the Cabinet Room for their meeting with the President—and, now, photographs. Kennedy felt he had won, too. This had helped, not hurt the chances of his civil rights bill. His happiest moment that afternoon had come when he had seen, on television, several dozen senators and representatives arriving at the Lincoln Memorial. As they walked down the steps to take seats, a hundred thousand people, more, were chanting: "Pass the Bill! Pass the Bill!"

The President walked up to King and shook his hand. Kennedy nodded to him and said, "I have a dream." He nodded again. It was an appreciation, an acknowledgment. King was a star, too.

Then they got down to the business of the day, and King deferred once again to Wilkins and Randolph. "You made the difference," Wilkins told the President. "You gave us your blessings. It was one of the prime factors in turning it into an orderly protest to help our government rather than a protest against our government.

"We think," Wilkins went on, "that today's demonstration, if it did nothing else, showed that people back home, from the small towns, to the big cities, the working people, men who gave up two days' pay, three days' pay, $30, $40, $50, $100, who flew from Los Angeles at three hundred dollars round trip to come here means that they, not Martin Luther King, or Roy Wilkins, or Whitney Young or Walter Reuther dreamed up this civil rights business."

But time was running out, Randolph said. "The teenagers are dropping out of school. It is estimated that seventy-five percent of Negro children now in school will not finish high school. And not only are they dropping out of school and unemployed but they're running out of hopes. They present an alarming problem because they had no faith in anybody white, they have no faith in even Negro leadership, they have no faith in God, they have no faith in the government. They believe that the hand of society is against them."

"Isn't it possible for the Negro community," the President responded, ". . . to place the major emphasis on the responsibility of these families, even if they're split and all the rest of the problems they have, on educating their children. . . ? With all the influence that all you gentlemen have in the Negro community . . . [you] really have to concentrate on what I think the Jewish community has done on educating their children, on making them study, on making them stay in school, and all the rest."

Kennedy said he wanted to talk about the numbers in Congress. "We just made a count of how our votes look and we figure, now, in the House, we have 158 or 160 Democrats. We need 60 Republicans to get a majority. . . . That's hard to get. That means Charles Halleck has to support the administration bill. In the Senate, on the civil rights bill, our civil rights bill, we figure: right, forty-eight, wrong, forty-four, doubtful —eight. Pretty good. That's after cloture has been established."

"Mr. President," said Randolph, after Kennedy had gone through the Congress, state by state, name by name, "from the description you have made of the state of affairs in the House and the Senate, it's obvious that it's going to take nothing less than a crusade to win approval for these civil rights measures."

"I think that it would be helpful," Kennedy said.

"It's going to be a crusade, then," Randolph said. "And I think that nobody can lead this crusade but you, Mr. President."

Chapter 52

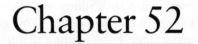

SEPTEMBER 2, 1963

The "CBS Evening News" went from fifteen minutes a night to thirty on Monday, September 2, 1963. That was Labor Day, and Walter Cronkite, the CBS anchorman, flew from New York to Hyannis Port that morning to film an interview with President Kennedy for the expanded telecast. "You might want to ask him some questions about Vietnam," Pierre Salinger had suggested to Cronkite the day before. On the short flight to Cape Cod, Cronkite read an Associated Press story saying that the President would be using the CBS interview to make his first public policy statement on South Vietnam, and on Diem's rule, since the Buddhists' first rising in May. It seemed to Cronkite that he was only a messenger, and he did not like it. When he found Salinger, he said: "You can go to hell, Pierre, I'll ask anything I want to ask."

"You'll be sorry, Walter," Salinger told him.

Cronkite began his interview with the President's prospects for reelection, asking about the effects of Negro demonstrations on the 1964 elections. More than ten minutes into the interview, he finally asked: "Mr. President, the only hot war we've got running at the moment is of course the one in Vietnam, and we have our difficulties there obviously."

Kennedy, who had rejected advice to go on television after the secret August 24 cable, had briefly hoped that he could keep Vietnam off the front pages. But he was now determined to gain control of both the war and the coverage of the war. Bundy and Sorensen had worked through the weekend at the White House, sending draft statements to Kennedy in long telegrams. He intended to play off Cronkite's questions in order to put pressure on Diem and Ngo Dinh Nhu.

"I don't think that unless a greater effort is made by the government to win popular support that the war can be won out there," he responded to Cronkite. "In the final analysis, it is their war. They are the ones who have to win it or lose it. We can help them, we can give them equipment, we can send our men out there as advisers, but they have to win it, the people of Viet-Nam, against the Communists. . . . And, in my opinion, in the last two months, the government has gotten out of touch with the people.

"The repressions against the Buddhists, we felt, were very unwise. Now all we can do is to make it very clear that we don't think this is the way to win. . . . With changes in policy and perhaps with personnel, I think it [the government] can win. If it doesn't make those changes, I would think that the chances of winning would not be very good. It is my hope that this will become increasingly obvious to the government, that they will take steps to try to bring back popular support for this very essential struggle."

The threat to Diem was clear; it was the public equivalent of the August 24 telegram. But Kennedy may have kept his options open too long. The vacuum during the weeks of White House silence and uncertainty had been filled by an odd coupling of the old boys of American foreign policy and the young reporters in Saigon—symbolized by Averell Harriman and David Halberstam.

During the week of meetings at the end of August, Kennedy had gone after Halberstam a dozen times. "Goddamit, I don't want you reading those stories in the *Times*," he said at one point. "We're not going to let the policy be run by some twenty-eight-year-old kid." For the old boys, Harriman and Lodge, often political adversaries over the years, formed an alliance, effectively creating policy and momentum that bypassed the President. Though they had never been close, the two men understood each other and shared a hard vision of the uses of power. They often communicated privately, usually by letter, such as this one from Harriman:

Dear Cabot
    . . . I can assure you that from the President on down everybody is determined to support you and the country team in winning the war . . . there are no quitters here. Photographs in the press of your shirt-sleeved walk through the market got you a lot of votes here.
    Marie joins in sending you and Emily our love. . . .

In Saigon, Halberstam, Malcolm Browne of AP, and Neil Sheehan of UPI, all in their twenties, were, like Harriman and Lodge, staunchly anti-Communist, pro-war, and anti-Diem. Halberstam particularly admired Lodge, considering him to be the right man in the right place at the right time. All three were passing along horror stories about the regime, particularly about Nhu. And they were not alone. Joseph Alsop came back from a reporting tour of Vietnam to tell the President privately that Nhu was paranoid, and that he could not be separated from his brother, even though he was now privately calling Diem an old fool. "I just don't think this is viable," Alsop said of a continuing alliance with the Ngo family.

Stories about Nhu's use of opium were so common in Washington that Kennedy asked Fritz Nolting whether Nhu was an addict. The former ambassador said he doubted it. Maxwell Taylor, too, returned from an August inspection tour of U.S. bases in Asia and told the President about a dinner with Nhu: "I think that guy is nuts. He's either nuts or he's blind."

Lodge agreed. He saw Nhu on September 6, learning that Madame Nhu would be traveling abroad for two or three months. But Lodge reported back to Washington that the usually impassive Nhu had gone on a tirade saying: "I'm the winning horse—they should bet on me. Why do they want to finish me? I want to be—not the adviser to President Diem—but the adviser to Henry Cabot Lodge. If I leave, the Armed Forces will take over the government. 'Ces grenouillards' "—which Lodge translated as "these schemers" or "these contrivers"—"of the CIA and USIS will sabotage the war effort."

With all of that in the air, many of the senior men of the press corps in Washington and New York were in a struggle with what they thought were their excitable young colleagues in far Asian fields. *Time* magazine attacked the resident correspondents: "One of the more curious aspects of the Vietnam story is that the press corps on the scene is helping to compound the very confusion that it should be untangling. The country is completely alien to their experience. . . . In the camaraderie of the Hotel Caravelle's eighth-floor bar, they pool their convictions, information, misinformation and grievances. . . . Such reporting is prone to distortions."

So now the President was answering Cronkite with the pained candor of a man worried that he was losing control, if he had ever had it. The anchorman asked four more questions on Vietnam, and Kennedy expanded on his first answer, emphasizing the country's critical importance:

"All we can do is help, and we are making it very clear, but I don't agree with those who say we should withdraw. That would be a great mistake. I know people don't like Americans to be engaged in this kind of an effort. . . . We made this effort to defend Europe. Now Europe is quite secure. We also have to participate—we may not like it—in the defense of Asia. . . . It doesn't do us any good to say, 'Well, why don't we all just go home and leave the world to those who are our enemies.' "

As soon as the thirty-minute interview ended—CBS edited it down to twelve minutes on air—the President's words were cabled to Saigon, with this attachment: "They represent the U.S. Government's attitude toward the situation and should be followed as the official U.S. public position."

But neither Kennedy's performance nor his position seemed persuasive in either Saigon or Washington. The President complained to CBS that its editing made him seem more anti-Diem than he was. In the newspapers, more than a little upset that policy proclamations were becoming television events, Kennedy was criticized again for being soft and indecisive.

"Roger? Who puts this stuff out in Washington?" said the President, calling Roger Hilsman from his bedroom four days after the Cronkite interview. "There's an article in *The New York Times* by Tad Szulc, page five. He says officials say that Nhu is trying to blackmail us. . . ."

"I've given strict orders not to talk to the press," answered the Assistant Secretary of State. "I don't know where he gets this stuff."

"We can't have people saying that U.S. officials are saying these kinds of things," Kennedy said. "If somebody is, we've got to put a stop to it. . . . Call *The New York Times*."

Another *Times* in another place, *The Times of Vietnam,* controlled by Nhu and his wife, who sometimes dictated front-page stories and headlines, led on September 6 with a banner headline across the top of its front page: "CIA FINANCING PLANNED COUP D'ETAT." Foreign diplomats in South Vietnam understood the headline, which was more true than false, better than they understood the intent of Kennedy's words. They saw Kennedy backing Diem and Nhu into a corner—for no apparent reason, some said. If there were a coup, those diplomats suggested to any Americans who asked, Saigon would be run by generals with no political credibility and less governmental talent. But there was no sense of that in the reporting from Washington. James Reston of *The New York Times* mocked Kennedy for indecision, writing that the President's message to Diem was "Change, or we'll string along with you anyway."

"He both threatened and reassured Diem," Reston wrote in an analysis of the CBS interview. "It was like the head of a foreign government announcing publicly that President Kennedy was pursuing a losing policy, was out of touch with the American people, but might make amends by firing Bobby." That needle started some tough telephone dialogue between the White House and the Times building on West 43rd Street in New York. Two days later a *Times* editorial seriously rallied around flag and President: "The lessons of the present crisis are plain. One is that the anti-Communist war in South Vietnam . . . is not only, as President Kennedy declared, 'their war' but ours—a war from which we cannot retreat and which we dare not lose."

The President was late that Friday morning for another meeting on Vietnam. The form of the meetings was the same as for Ex Comm during the Cuban missile crisis, but the mistrust, the manipulation of information, and the hidden agendas of the process were more reminiscent of the Bay of Pigs. Before going in, Kennedy had read two memos that symbolized the divergent information that was coming at him day after day from his military and civilian advisers. The first was from Maxwell Taylor, summarizing military operations during August:

"Favorable trends in all military activities, despite Saigon's preoccupation with the unstable political situation," he wrote.

> During the month of August, the Government forces conducted 166 large operations (battalion equivalents or more), a figure which compares most favorably with the 168 large operations conducted in July. Small unit actions show an increase from 10,240 in July to 15,480 in August. There were 56 large and 3211 small unit government operations in progress. . . . The latest Government of Vietnam figures indicate that 8,227 of the 10,592 planned hamlets had been completed. Seventy-six per cent, or 9,563,370 of the rural population, are now in these hamlets.

The second was a single paragraph from Lodge in response to a line in the cable from Washington that stated: "Goal is that GVN have political support at home and abroad indispensable to winning war."

"As to 'political support at home and abroad,' " Lodge told Kennedy, "I do not believe the GVN really understands this at all. They are essentially a medieval, Oriental despotism of the classic family type, who understand few, if any, of the arts of popular government. They cannot talk to the people; they cannot cultivate the press; they cannot delegate authority or inspire trust; they cannot comprehend the idea of government as the servant of the people. They are interested in physical security and survival against any threat whatsoever—Communist or non-Communist."

When the President finally came into the room, Rusk told him that he had opened the meeting by saying that, if the situation continued to deteriorate, and if American public opinion turned against Diem, the

United States would have no alternative but a massive military commitment. Robert Kennedy had asked whether the war could be won with Diem in charge and Rusk had answered no, not the way things were going.

"Then why not grasp the nettle now," Robert Kennedy said. "We have to be tough. . . . We have to tell Diem that he must do the things we demand or we will have to cut down our effort as forced by the American public." McNamara had said there just was not enough intelligence to know whether or not this was the time to have a showdown with Diem. Rusk had said he was for pressuring Diem, jawboning the government, but he added: "It is very serious to threaten to pull out of Vietnam. If the Viet Cong takes over in Vietnam we are in real trouble."

With the President settled in, Robert Kennedy now asked Taylor what American officers in the field believed. Taylor said he didn't know and suggested that General Victor Krulak should go to Vietnam and ask them. Now. The Marine General sat in the meetings now as the Joint Chiefs' director of counterinsurgency, a job created by Kennedy, who had known Krulak since 1943, when PT-109 had rescued Marines under Krulak's command in the South Pacific. Krulak had promised him a bottle of Three Feathers whiskey that day, and had delivered it to the White House eighteen years later, as an inaugural gift.

McNamara ordered Krulak to go to Andrews Air Force Base to take off immediately. The idea, unspoken, was to prevent the State Department from sending Hilsman along on this trip. But McNamara could not get around Harriman, who sent an assistant to telephone Hilsman from outside the White House, telling him to get someone out to Andrews right away. Joseph Mendenhall was their man; his job was to interview State Department and CIA officers in Saigon, Hué, and Danang while Krulak went to the provinces. Kennedy said he wanted them back in Washington in four days, on Tuesday, September 10, which meant they would spend thirty-six hours in Vietnam.

The President then said he wanted to see whether Diem could shut up Madame Nhu, because it was her talk of barbecuing bonzes that was causing most of the public relations problems in the United States. But, he asked, would the United States benefit from the removal of her husband, brother Nhu, too? Nolting said Nhu's removal might solve some problems in Washington but would not be helpful in Saigon, and that whatever was done, it would be a great mistake to present Diem with an ultimatum. Rusk said he understood that. If the United States decided to pull out, Diem should be told in advance. Then he added that a pull-out of some American military men might accomplish the goal some wanted, a military coup.

The cable sent to Lodge by the President after the meeting asked more questions about how to pressure Diem into accepting American demands and demonstrate to the world he was not running a police state:

> It is clear that at a minimum we face a major problem with world, with US Congress and with American public opinion which will require GVN to take actions include effective silencing and probably removal from country of Madame Nhu, releasing of bonzes, students, etc., along line we have discussed.
>
> What is not clear is whether these measures will suffice to restore sufficient confidence in the Diem Government within Viet Nam to permit them to win the war. . . .

That cable was backed up by another from the State Department to Lodge reporting on Hilsman's appearance before a congressional committee: "Two-hour executive session today with Far East Subcommittee of Senate Foreign Relations Committee revealed far-reaching doubts regarding not only Diem-Nhu leadership but also advisability of continued US participation in Viet-Nam war. . . . Probable introduction of resolution condemning further US support for GVN; e.g. 'It is the sense of the Senate that the American people are no longer willing to support a regime in South Viet-Nam that oppresses the people and religious sects. . . .' "

The idea of the resolution was to pressure Diem to take U.S. orders. Hilsman knew the wording well, because he had written it for the subcommittee chairman, Senator Frank Church of Idaho. In executive session, Hilsman told the President, Senator Church had accused the White House of being soft on Diem: "This mandarin. There has been nothing like him since the Borgias!"

On Monday, September 9, the President sat down for an interview with anchormen Chet Huntley and David Brinkley of NBC for that network's first half-hour nightly news broadcast, "The Huntley-Brinkley Report." The ground rules were different than for CBS the week before. This time Kennedy had approval over NBC's editing, and Brinkley began with questions about Vietnam.

"Mr. President, have you had any reason to doubt this so-called 'Domino Theory,' that if South Viet-Nam falls, the rest of Southeast Asia will go behind it?"

"No, I believe it," the President said. "I think that the struggle is close enough. China is so large, looms so high just beyond the frontiers, that if South Vietnam went, it would not only give them an improved geographic position for a guerrilla assault on Malaya, but would also give the impression that the wave of the future in Southeast Asia was China and the communists. So I believe it."

"Are we likely to reduce our aid to South Viet-Nam at this point?"

"I don't think we think that would be helpful at this time. If you reduce your aid, it is possible you could have some effect upon the government structure there. On the other hand, you might have a situation which could bring about a collapse. Strongly in our mind is what happened in the case of China at the end of World War II, where China was lost, a weak government became increasingly unable to control events. We don't want that.

"We must be patient, we must persist," said the President. "What I am concerned about is that Americans will get impatient and say because they don't like events in Southeast Asia or they don't like the government in Saigon, that we should withdraw . . . I think we should stay."

At the same time, exactly halfway around the globe, Ambassador Lodge was meeting with President Diem. His cable back to Kennedy was not encouraging:

> Hour and fifty minute conference. . . . Whenever I tried to get back either to the departure of Nhu or the lifting of the censorship of the press he would start off on something else. . . . He said that his representative proposed to show in New York that the pagodas had been turned into bordellos, that they had found a great deal of female underwear, love letters and obscene photographs. That the virgins were being despoiled there. They knew of one priest who had despoiled 13 virgins. . . . Although I stated what I intended to state many times, I did not feel he was really deeply interested. He seemed totally absorbed with his own problems here and was justifying himself and attacking his enemies. Perhaps this is all part of his medieval view of life.

The Republican Minority Leader of the Senate, Everett McKinley Dirksen of Illinois, came into the Oval Office after Brinkley left, to talk about the Test Ban Treaty, which was now on the floor of the Senate. It had been discharged by a 16-to-1 vote of the Foreign Relations Committee, but several senators who had voted for discharge had said they were reserving the right to vote against ratification on the floor. A parade of retired military men was testifying against the treaty, and Senator Barry Goldwater of Arizona argued that before the treaty was ratified the Soviets should show good faith by removing all their troops from Cuba and knocking down the Berlin Wall.

Dirksen was a big flowery man, sixty-seven years old, with a great bass voice, more *profundo* than profound some thought, but Kennedy liked him. The President listened for a minute or so while Dirksen warmed up by telling stories of the tribulations of lining up Republican votes for the two-thirds Senate vote needed for approval of the treaty. Kennedy interrupted him with a laugh.

"You got your notes?" the President asked.

"Yes, I do, Mr. President."

"Can I have them?"

Kennedy read the draft of the letter Dirksen wanted sent to himself and to the Majority Leader, Mike Mansfield.

"Okay," said the President, laughing again. "It will be done."

The letter came the next day, answering the principal public concerns of the military and of most Republicans and conservative Democrats:

> Dear Senator Mansfield and Senator Dirksen:
> Underground nuclear testing, which is permitted under the treaty, will be vigorously and diligently carried forward. . . . The United States will maintain a posture of readiness to resume testing in the environments prohibited by the present treaty. . . .
> I am glad to emphasize again that the treaty in no way limits the authority of the Commander-in-Chief to use nuclear weapons for the defense of the United States and its allies, if a situation should develop requiring such a grave decision.

Senator Dirksen walked onto the Senate floor, making small talk while the chamber was filling at the word that he was going to speak on the treaty. He began by reading a prepared statement, saying that his early doubts had been proved wrong. Then he set down his eight-page text—"I do not read a manuscript very well"—and took off in the old style:

"The whole bosom of God's earth was ruptured by a man-made contrivance we call a nuclear weapon. . . . Oh, the tragedy. Oh, the dismay. Oh, the blood. Oh, the anguish. . . . One bomb—66,000 killed, 69,000 injured. . . . A young President calls this treaty the first step. I want to take a first step, Mr. President. One my age thinks about his destiny a little. I should not like to have written on my tombstone, 'He knew what happened at Hiroshima, but he did not take a first step. . . .' "

By the time Dirksen finished, everyone in the chamber and in the country knew that the Limited Test Ban Treaty would be ratified as the first arms control agreement of the nuclear era. The Democratic Majority Leader, Senator Mansfield, stood up across the aisle, looked at his Republican adversary, and said, "I salute a great American."

That day, September 10, General Krulak and Mendenhall arrived back in Washington after their thirty-six hours in Vietnam. It turned out that they disliked each other; they did not speak on the flight back. Landing at Andrews, they went straight to the White House to meet with the President and the Vietnam group at ten-thirty in the morning.

The general spoke first, and said in the Marine way, "Can do! The shooting war is still going ahead at an impressive pace. . . . There is a lot of war left to fight, particularly in the Delta, where the Viet Cong remains strong. . . . The war will be won if the current U.S. military and sociological programs are pursued, irrespective of the grave defects in the ruling regime."

Then Mendenhall said, "I was struck by the fear that pervades Saigon, Hué, and Da Nang. These cities have been living under a reign of terror. . . ." He saw the possibility of a religious civil war or a slow turning of the South Vietnamese people to the Viet Cong. "Hundreds of students were arrested again today. Most families of government officials, civilian and military, have felt government's oppressive hands on their children, with results in attitude that can be expected. . . . Nhu must go if the war is to be won."

The President looked from Krulak to Mendenhall and back, and finally asked: "Did you two gentlemen visit the same country?"

That was the divide Kennedy saw, as if the ground were opening beneath his presidency. His Defense Department said the war was being won; his State Department said the country was being lost to any American influence. In fact, the State Department's Bureau of Intelligence was reporting: "Proliferating reports of varying credibility allege activity on the part of Ngo Dinh Nhu to negotiate with Hanoi on South Vietnam's future, with or without French connivance." Rusk brought that to the President, saying: "If we move against Diem too fast, we cannot dismiss the possibility that he might bring the Vietnamese house down around him and go to North Vietnam for assistance. . . ."

The difference between State's pessimism and Defense's optimism, General Krulak told the President, with obvious contempt for his traveling companion, was that he had been in the countryside with the troops, while Mendenhall was having tea with intellectuals in the cities. There were two men at this meeting whom Kennedy had never met. The first was Rufus Phillips, a former CIA agent who headed AID in Saigon and happened to be back in Washington on leave.

"What would you do, Rufus Phillips?" asked the President.

"Send back Ed Lansdale," said Phillips, who had once worked for him. "If anyone can talk to Diem, it's him. He's the best qualified man we have to help put together a new government."

"What about the war?"

"I'm sorry to disagree with General Krulak," said Phillips, who was thirty-three years old. "But I don't believe we're winning the war, particularly in the Delta. . . .The strategic hamlets are being chewed to pieces by the Viet-Cong. They are being overrun wholesale."

"The battle," Krulak interrupted angrily, "is not being lost from a military point of view. . . . As between General Harkins and Mr. Phillips, I would take General Harkins' assessment."

Harriman came alive then, going after Krulak, telling him to his face that he had always thought he was a damn fool. Kennedy just listened, but after the meeting he called Krulak into the Oval Office to say, "I just wanted you to know I understand."

The second new face belonged to John Mecklin, the embassy spokesman in Saigon, who had flown back with Krulak and Mendenhall, the only three passengers in a military Boeing 707 with no windows and almost no conversation. When Krulak had seen that Mecklin was carrying cans of television network news film back to the United States—which U.S. officials did routinely to help American correspondents get around GVN censorship—the general had ordered him to leave the film in Alaska, during a refueling stop at Elmendorf Air Base, and had suggested he stay there himself.

"What would you do?" the President asked Mecklin.

"Send in American combat troops," answered Mecklin. "Accept an engagement comparable with Korea . . . both to promote unseating of the regime and against the VC."

"This is impossible," Kennedy said later. Some of these people were fools, some were liars, but he did not have enough information to tell which was which.

The thing that made Kennedy angriest was a story he heard that someone in the U.S. Embassy had tipped off a photographer that U.S. AID trucks—with American markings on their doors—were being used to round up thousands of South Vietnamese students taken to jails on suspicion of criticizing Diem's government. "Why would an American do that?" he wanted to know.

The answer, of course, was to undermine support for Diem and his supporters in the United States. As if to underscore that point, Lodge sent a cable from Saigon questioning General Krulak's mission and testimony: "I question the value of the answers which are given by young officers to direct questions by generals—or, for that matter, by ambassadors. The urge to give an optimistic and favorable answer is quite understandable."

The meetings of September 10—there was another one that evening, during which Robert Kennedy and Mac Bundy insisted that the time for generalities was over and that the President needed information on specific actions—ended with Harriman and McNamara renewing the argument over whether the war could be won with Diem still in power, and with a request from the director of USIA. It was recorded this way in the minutes: "Mr. Murrow asked that he be relieved of writing press guidance until after tomorrow's meeting in view of the fact that the guidance could not be written until our policy was clear."

Cabot Lodge wanted action rather than guidance. He cabled Rusk on September 11: "The ship of state here is sinking. . . . The government is obviously cut off from reality—not looking at anything objectively but solely concerned with fighting back, proving how right it has been— and privately thumbing its nose at the US. . . . If there are effective sanctions which we can apply, we should apply them in order to force a drastic change in government. The only sanction which I can see is the suspension of aid. . . ."

At the President's September 12 news conference, a reporter asked the same question Murrow had: "Mr. President, in view of the prevailing confusion, is it possible to state today just what this Government's policy is toward the current government of South Viet-Nam?"

"I think I have stated what my view is and we are for those things and those policies which help win the war there," said Kennedy, an edge in his voice. "That is why some 25,000 Americans have traveled 10,000 miles to participate in that struggle. What helps to win the war, we support; what interferes with the war effort, we oppose.

"We have a very simple policy: We want the war to be won, the Communists to be contained, and the Americans to go home. That is our policy. I am sure it is the policy of the people of Viet-Nam. . . . We are not there to see a war lost."

Then Vietnam was forgotten for the moment. It was back-to-school time around the country and the President had begun the conference by saying, "In the past two weeks, schools in 150 Southern cities have been desegregated. There may have been some difficulties, but . . . what prevailed in these cities through the South finally was not emotion but respect for law."

After that, a reporter asked: "Dr. Gallup asked people this question: 'Do you think the Kennedy administration is pushing integration too fast or not fast enough?' Fifty percent replied that they thought you were pushing too fast. Would you comment?"

"I think probably he is accurate," Kennedy answered. "That same poll showed forty percent or so thought it was more or less right. I thought that was rather impressive, because it is change; change always disturbs, and therefore I was surprised that there wasn't greater opposition. . . . I think you must make a judgment about the movement of a great historical event which is taking place in this country after a period of time . . . after a good many years."

Then the questions went back to Vietnam. The Church Resolution, calling for an end to repression in South Vietnam, had been introduced in the Senate that morning with twenty-two co-sponsors. The President said he interpreted that to mean that the Senate was as steadfast as he in its commitment to stay there and to win the war. As more detailed questions began, Kennedy cut the reporters off: "Aside from the general statements which have been made, I would think that sort of matter should be discussed by the Ambassador—Ambassador Lodge. . . ."

Henry Cabot Lodge, against all odds, was both the President's man and his own, having the same kind of independent power that General Clay had assumed in Berlin two years earlier. A Polish diplomat who was a member of the International Control Commission established to monitor the Geneva Accords, Mieczyslaw Maneli, reported back to Warsaw that Lodge reminded him of Soviet ambassadors in Eastern Europe.

Walter Cronkite asked Kennedy about the conventional wisdom on Lodge: "Mr. President, the sending of Henry Cabot Lodge, who after all has been a political enemy of yours over the years at one point or another in your career, and his, sending him out to Saigon might raise some speculation that perhaps you are trying to keep this from being a political issue in 1964."

"No," Kennedy snapped back with some heat. "Ambassador Lodge wanted to go out to Saigon. If he were as careful as some politicians are, of course, he would not have wanted to go there. He would have maybe liked to have some safe job, but he is energetic and he has strong feelings about the United States and, surprisingly as it seems, he put this ahead of his political career. Sometimes politicians do those things, Walter."

The two politicians from Massachusetts were back and forth almost every day, sometimes several times a day. Lodge had certain advantages in his daily struggle against the Defense Department. He was fluent not only in French but in the same political language the President spoke. He told Kennedy in a cable numbered 478, received in Washington on September 11:

The evidence grows that elite is filled with hostility towards the Government of Viet Nam. Consider therefore the lieutenant in the Vietnamese Army whose father has probably been imprisoned; whose mother has seen her religion insulted, if not persecuted, whose older brother has had an arbitrary fine imposed on him—and who all hate the government with good reason. Can the lieutenant be indifferent to that? Now come the high school demonstrations and the fact that the lieutenant's younger brother has probably been dragged off in a truck (bearing the US insignia) to camping areas with the result that our lieutenant also has a deeply disaffected younger brother, if not a sister, who has been handled disrespectfully by the police.

Lodge made no effort to conceal what he was doing, which was planning a coup. In that same cable, he told Kennedy: "Renewed efforts should be made to activate by whatever positive inducements we can offer the man who would take over the government—Big Minh or whoever we might suggest. We do not want to substitute a Castro for a Batista. . . . We should at the same time start evacuation of all dependents. Both in order to avoid the dangers to dependents which would inevitably ensue, but also for the startling effect which this might have."

The President's support for that was repeated in his response the next day, September 12: "Your 478 is a major paper and has stirred a corresponding effort to concert a proper response here. . . . While we are working, I want you to know that your courageous and searching analysis has already been of great help, and that the strength and dignity of your position on the scene are clear."

Later that same day, Lodge again raised the question that most troubled the President, the possibility that Nhu and Diem would prefer making a deal with the Communist government of North Vietnam rather than bow to American pressure: "Hope some study will be given to what our response should be if Nhu, in the course of a negotiation with North Vietnam, should ask the US to leave South Vietnam or to make a major reduction in forces. This is obviously the only trump card he has got and it is obviously of the highest importance. It is also obvious to me that we must not leave. But the question of finding a proper basis for remaining is at first blush not simple."

Then, in the midst of the hour-after-hour discussions of Vietnam at the White House, the President's attention was snapped back to Birmingham. On Sunday morning, September 15, a dozen sticks of dynamite exploded under stairs leading into the city's largest Negro church, the 16th Street Baptist Church, the center of many of the events and marches of May. The congregation was inside celebrating the first integration of Alabama elementary schools six days before, when the dynamite went off at ten twenty-two in the morning. The blast killed four girls—Denise McNair, eleven; Carole Robertson, fourteen; Addie Mae Collins, fourteen; and Cynthia Wesley, fourteen. Before Sunday was over, there were Negro marches and some rock-throwing. And two more young Negroes were shot to death, a sixteen-year-old boy named Johnny Robinson, who ran away when police ordered him to stop, and a thirteen-year-old boy named Virgil Ware, who was riding on the handlebars of his brother's bicycle when a white Eagle Scout on his way home from a segregationist rally pulled out a pistol and shot him.

A Sunday in Birmingham. Six children dead. That night, white people, weeping, came to the doors of the families of the dead girls to say they were ashamed of what had happened. The President issued a statement expressing "deep outrage." Three weeks after the March on Washington, Martin Luther King, Jr., and a delegation of Birmingham's Negro ministers were back in the White House to ask Kennedy to send federal troops to Birmingham. He would not do that, he said. But he would send personal representatives to mediate disagreements between the Negro and white citizens of the city which just lived up to an old nickname "Bombingham." He chose a former Secretary of the Army, Kenneth Royall, and Earl Blaik, the former West Point football coach— but he told the Negro ministers with some irritation that the federal government was on their side but this was now the Negroes' fight, to win or lose themselves.

His words to King and the others echoed exactly what Kennedy was saying about Vietnam, before and after the domestic explosion. "I know that this bombing is particularly difficult. But if you look at any, as you know, of these struggles across the world, it's a very dangerous effort. So everybody just has to keep their nerve."

On Vietnam, it was the President's own nerve that was being tested: Was he ready yet to push aside Diem and his family? Lodge reported that Sunday, September 15, that Diem had told him Madame Nhu, who was now out of the country and no problem in Saigon, intended to come to the United States and hold press conferences to defend herself. "I told him it would have a bad effect on U.S. opinion," said the ambassador. ". . . They seem to take no interest in what other people may think, but are simply interested in expressing their own feelings and their own pride. They are non-politicians."

On Tuesday, September 17, the State Department presented the President with detailed plans for two policy tracks for Vietnam, called "Reconciliation" and "Pressures and Persuasion." The idea of the first track was simply to accept Diem as he was and get on with the war against the Communists. The obvious way to signal reconciliation, the paper said, was to send the man Diem always asked for as a liaison, Ed Lansdale. Ironically, Lodge, who was against reconciliation, also asked for Lansdale, thinking he might be able to split or remove the Ngo brothers with the least fuss and blood. He also had another motive: he wanted to get rid of CIA station chief John Richardson, whom he suspected of communicating too freely with Nhu.

"No Lansdale," said CIA Director McCone. "No," said Rusk. "No," said McNamara.

"I have no confidence whatever in the man," said McCone. He would resign before sending Lansdale into the field again, because the man was uncontrollable. "Lodge can have his way with Richardson, but I won't accept anyone from the outside."

The second track in the State Department's options paper to the President also began by trying to avoid confrontation with Diem, then escalated first to cutting U.S. aid to the South Vietnamese government (but not the Army of Vietnam), and then to the backing of coup attempts. Finally, the United States would decide between withdrawing from South Vietnam or just taking over the country:

> If the U.S. correctly has estimated civil and military readiness to overthrow Diem, an alternate government should emerge with sufficient popular support to carry on the fight against the Viet Cong while coping with Diem, if he remains in the Saigon area. If the U.S. has not correctly assessed the readiness of the military to desert Diem and he, in fact, retains control of most major forces, the U.S. would face the final decision of U.S. military intervention or complete withdrawal from Viet-Nam. In this situation, U.S. military intervention to fight a former ally could serve no useful purpose, since there would not exist a sufficient popular base of support for U.S. objectives. Inherent in all [final phase] activities is the element of extreme danger to U.S. essential personnel remaining in Viet-Nam.

In a long cable to Lodge, the President said he considered the first phases of "Pressures and Persuasion" to be a low-risk interim plan. The plan was to ask Diem one more time to implement the same list of actions he had been ignoring for weeks—call off Nhu's secret police, release jailed Buddhists and students, end press censorship, bring new blood into his Cabinet, local elections—and, finally, again, "Nhu's departure from Saigon and preferably Vietnam for at least an extended vacation."

"Meanwhile," Kennedy ended his cable, "there is increasing concern here with strictly military aspects of the problem, both in terms of actual progress of operations and of need to make effective case with Congress for continued prosecution of the effort. To meet these needs, [the President] has decided to send Secretary of Defense McNamara and General Taylor to Vietnam, arriving early next week."

Chapter 53

The McNamara-Taylor mission to Vietnam seemed to be President Kennedy's last best shot at constructing a consensus among his closest advisers. Knowing that, Averell Harriman was furious that the President was sending two men from the Defense Department on what could be the most crucial of the many Kennedy missions. "These two men are opposed to our policy," Harriman told his man in the White House, Michael Forrestal. "Our" from Harriman did not mean the U.S. government nor the President, it meant "his," the view that Diem must be overthrown.

Roger Hilsman, the President's official "action officer" on Vietnam, and Harriman's closest ally, was so upset that he followed the President into the Oval Office, still arguing, until Kennedy turned and snapped at him, "I know all this, Roger . . . I know all this. But we've got to keep the Joint Chiefs on board." He feared that the Pentagon could rip apart any Vietnam policy with leaks, true and not so true, to reporters friendly to the military. "And the only way we can keep the Chiefs on board is to keep McNamara on board and he wants to go and see for himself. . . . That's the price we have to pay to keep the government together."

Harriman wanted Hilsman to represent the State Department on the trip, but that was quickly vetoed by McNamara. Instead, the highest-ranking State Department representative on this one was William H. Sullivan, a young Hilsman assistant.

In fact, Kennedy was not rejecting the State Department's anti-Diem thrust. Far from it. He had chosen McNamara and Taylor, not because of their opinions or their titles, but because he thought they were the smartest men he had—"The brightest and the best," in a phrase he knew from a Shelley poem. He was quietly desperate about the contradictions and misinformation swirling around him. Perhaps half of what he was being told was wrong, but he did not know which half. He trusted McNamara to figure that out.

The confusion and the contradictions of the deliberations at the White House, morning after morning, afternoon after afternoon, were a joke to the few who knew. The President was one of them. Bundy showed him a wicked parody of official minutes written by another of Hilsman's assistants, James Thomson. The title was: "MINUTES OF THE *NEXT* HIGH-LEVEL MEETING ON VIET-NAM":

The Secretary of State opened the meeting, in the absence of the President, by urging that priority be given to the key question of the past thirteen hours: How did we get here, and Where do we go from here?

On the one hand, he said, it was important to keep moving forward. But on the other hand, we must deal with things as they are.

The Secretary of Defense concurred but felt that we must not permit the views of a handful of neurotic Saigon intellectuals to distract us from the major goal, which was to get on with the war. He asked General Krulak to report on his latest sampling of opinion among the trainers of Vietnamese secret police at Fort Belvoir. . . .

General Krulak responded that the American trainers had advised him to refrain from talking with the Vietnamese since their views were well known to the trainers, and conversation would distract them from the purpose at hand, i.e., to win the war.

Governor Harriman stated that he had disagreed for twenty years with General Krulak and disagreed today, reluctantly, more than ever; he was sorry to say that he felt General Krulak was a fool and had always thought so. . . .

General Taylor said that if risks were involved, "You can count me out."

The Secretary of State re-phrased the basic question in terms of Saigon's 897. What were we to do about the five hundred school-girls who were seeking asylum in the American embassy?

(At this point, the President entered the room.)

The President said that he hoped we were not allowing our policies to be influenced by immature twelve-year-old school-girls, all of whom were foreigners. He felt that we must not lose sight of our ultimate objective, and in no state was the Vietnamese vote worth very much.

The Attorney General said that it was high time to show some guts, and here was a good place to begin. . . .

The President asked that inter-agency committees be put to work on the nature of our dialogue with Diem, and he suggested that the EX-COMM meet again in a week or so. Next time, he said, he hoped there would be a good map of Viet-Nam available.

The President could laugh at that. His decision making all along on Vietnam had been designed to avoid any irreversible decision, including the one that had been on the table for the past four months, ever since the pagoda raids: What should the United States do about the brothers, Nhu and Diem?

To govern is to choose. The choices were clear enough now; the consequences were not. The State Department was telling him that the war could not be won with the Ngo family in the Presidential Palace. The Defense Department, with statistics and charts, was saying that whatever the politics of Saigon, victory was certain as long as the United States was steadfast. Kennedy certainly wanted victory. He committed himself publicly again and again to staying the course. But he did not want to commit combat troops to an Asian war. "Get General MacArthur to agree and I will, too," he said regularly now, reminding aides of the general's advice after the Bay of Pigs.

Since the middle of 1962, when the statistics from Vietnam looked best, he had pushed McNamara and the Joint Chiefs for contingency plans to withdraw troops from Vietnam. The plans were ready, but more and more men were going, not coming back. There were more than sixteen thousand American military men there now. The President had his own political-military conflict. Politically, he could not afford to look weak militarily. Whatever he truly thought and believed about the commitment of Americans on the ground in Asia, he was not ready, as he had told CBS only a month before, to be accused of losing Vietnam to the Communists, as other American politicians had only ten years before been accused of losing China to the Communists, and had been destroyed. Congressman and Senator Kennedy had been one of the accusers.

Lodge was as angry about the McNamara-Taylor mission as Harriman and Hilsman. He sent the President a barrage of cables protesting the mission, this one on September 18: "For President only. Pass White House directly. No other distribution whatever. . . . If Secretary of Defense and General Taylor come to Viet-Nam, they will have to call on President Diem and I will have to accompany them. This will be taken here as a sign that we have decided to forgive and forget and will be regarded as marking the end of our period of disapproval of the oppressive measures which have been taken here since last May."

The answer came back:

Personal for Ambassador Lodge from the President. No other distribution. I appreciate your prompt comment and I quite understand the problem you see in visit of McNamara and Taylor. At the same time my need
for this visit is very great indeed. . . .

We can readily set up this visit as one which you and I have decided
on together, or even as one which is sent in response to your own concern
about winning the war in the current situation . . . my own central concern in sending this mission is to make sure that my senior military advisers are equipped with a solid on-the-spot understanding of the situation,
as a basis both for their participation in our councils here, and for the
Administration's accounting to the Congress on this critically important
contest with the Communists. . . . I do not think I can delay announcement of the McNamara mission beyond Saturday, September 20th.

Lodge calmed down and cabled back: "Believe it would be helpful if
you could announce that I had asked McNamara and Taylor to
come. . . . " But he was still sarcastic about his visitors, as he cabled
Kennedy again the following day: "I doubt that a public relations package will meet needs of situation which seems particularly grave to me,
notably in the light of General Big Minh's opinion expressed very privately yesterday that the Viet Cong are steadily gaining in strength; have
more of the population on their side than has the GVN; that arrests are
continuing and that the prisons are full; that more and more students
are going over to the Viet Cong.

"As regards withholding of aid," Lodge continued, addressing the
new "Pressures and Persuasion" planning, "I still hope that I may be
informed of methods which will enable us to apply sanctions in a way
which will really affect Diem and Nhu without precipitating an economic collapse and without impeding the war effort. . . . It would be
one of the greatest discoveries since the enactment of the Marshall Plan
in 1947 because, so far as I know, the U.S. has never yet been able to
control any of the very unsatisfactory governments through which we
have had to work in our many very successful attempts to make these
countries strong enough to stand alone. . . ."

McNamara and Taylor left Washington for Saigon on September 23.
In the air, the Defense Secretary laid out their mandate: "The job is to
appraise the course of the war, the present and future of the Diem
government, and to determine how the US can best influence the SVN
government."

The next day President Kennedy left Washington, too, on a three-day
cross-country tour emphasizing conservation issues. For a man whose

Secretary of the Interior, Stewart Udall, was convinced he cared nothing about conservation issues other than those that affected the beaches of Cape Cod, the trip provided a chance to practice and probe before the beginning of his reelection campaign. He was going to Minnesota and Wisconsin, and to places like North Dakota, Wyoming, Montana, and Utah—states often overflown and overlooked in presidential election years. But the first stop, Milford, Pennsylvania, was more personal. He went there to officially accept as national parkland the estate of Gifford Pinchot, a former governor of Pennsylvania and National Forester under President Theodore Roosevelt. Pinchot also happened to be the great-uncle of Toni Bradlee, his friend Ben's wife, and of her sister Mary Meyer, a Georgetown artist who was the ex-wife of a CIA official, Cord Meyer. Mary Meyer flew up with the President. They had been sleeping together for several months; usually she came to the White House whenever Jacqueline Kennedy was out of town.

The President got great news that day in Pennsylvania. Larry O'Brien called from the Capitol to tell him that the Senate had just approved the Limited Test Ban Treaty by a big vote, 80 to 19. On September 25, he was at the county fairgrounds in Billings, Montana, where the crowd was bigger than the city's population of 60,000. His speech touched dutifully on Western subjects like reclamation and wetlands acquisition, matters that bored him. But both the speech and the trip took a dramatic new direction when he thanked Montana's Mike Mansfield and Everett Dirksen of Illinois for their help in the Senate on the treaty "to bring an end to nuclear tests. . . ." The crowd roared and roared; there were waves of cheering and applause.

The next night, Kennedy was in the Mormon Tabernacle in Salt Lake City, conservative and isolationist Republican country. The Utah crowd stood and cheered for more than five minutes as Kennedy appeared. He began a long and confident speech about the American role in the world:

"It took Brigham Young 108 days to go from Winter Quarters, Nebraska, to the valley of the Great Salt Lake. It takes 30 minutes for a missile to go from one continent to another. . . . That is why the test ban treaty is important as a first step, perhaps to be disappointed, perhaps to find ourselves ultimately set back, but at least in 1963 the United States committed itself, to one chance to end the radiation and the possibilities of burning. . . . We did not seek to become a world power. This position was thrust on us by events. But we became one just the same and I am proud that we did. . . . The United States has rightly determined, in the years since 1945, under three different administrations, that our interest, our national security, is best served by preserving and protecting a world of diversity in which no one power or no one combination of powers can threaten the security of the United States. . . ."

They cheered and cheered. The Washington press corps watched in astonishment. The senior member, Merriman Smith of UPI, a man not noted for his enthusiasms, walked up to Kennedy and said, "Mr. President, that was a great speech!"

Kennedy was elated. He trusted the crowd, an instrument he had learned to play well. For the first time he felt sure that he was going to be reelected. The next day, still in Salt Lake City, he pressed the button that was supposed to start the generators at a new federal dam at Flaming Gorge, 150 miles south on the Colorado River. "I never know when I press these whether it means we are going to blow up Massachusetts . . . but I am going on the assumption we are going to start up the generator. . . ."

"When the President pushes the buzzer," said a voice from the loudspeakers, "we will wait then to hear from Mr. Walton over the loudspeaker who will report on what the generator does . . ."

There was a long pause before J. R. Walton, the project engineer, said, "Mr. President, the generator is now running at full speed!"

"Now," said the announcer's voice, "you can sum up anything you want to say, Mr. President."

"This gives you an idea of how difficult the life of a President is," Kennedy said, grinning. "We do this all day."

In Saigon that day, Michael Forrestal, who was traveling with McNamara and Taylor in South Vietnam, was hand-delivering a short "Dear Cabot" letter from Roger Hilsman to Ambassador Lodge:

> I am taking advantage of Mike Forrestal's safe hands. . . . More and more of the town is coming around to our view and if you in Saigon and we in the Department stick to our guns the rest will also come around. As Mike will tell you, a determined group here will back you all the way. I think you are probably right in the judgment that no pressures—even a cut-off in aid—will cause Diem and Nhu to make the changes we desire and that what we must work for is a change in government . . . you have handled an incredibly difficult task superbly. My very heartiest and most sincere congratulations.

Half the globe apart, Harriman and Lodge plotted how to win over McNamara, the auto executive who had emerged as the President's brightest boy, charged by him with figuring out who was telling the truth in South Vietnam: Lodge or Harkins and the military. The official notes of the last meeting between Kennedy, McNamara, and Taylor included this remark: "The President emphasized to Secretary McNamara the importance of getting to the bottom of differences in reporting from U.S. representatives in Vietnam."

The principal actors in the drama met on the tarmac of Tan Son Nhut Airport. As McNamara came down the stairway of his military Boeing 707, he was met at the bottom by Ambassador Lodge, alone. Harkins was trying to move toward his bosses, but Lodge's men from the embassy pushed him away as if he were an intruder. The general had prepared the visitors' itinerary—this was officially a military mission —and during each day after being blocked at the airport he was at McNamara's side almost constantly. But the nights were Lodge's. Protocol dictated that the Secretary stay with the ambassador. And Lodge used that time well, running breakfast and late-night seminars for McNamara.

One of those nights, Lodge turned McNamara around on Diem. On September 26 he brought in Patrick Honey of the University of London to meet McNamara. The Secretary, identifying Honey as "Professor Smith," took careful notes of the conversation:

> Diem has aged terribly since 1960. He is slow mentally . . . would not last 24 hours without Nhu who handles the bribes and manipulates the power base necessary for his survival.
>
> Only a military coup or an assassination will be effective and one or the other is likely to occur soon. In such circumstances we have a 50% chance of getting something better.
>
> Through independent sources he has confirmed . . . that the North Vietnamese have approached Nhu through the French.
>
> The American government cannot do anything other than to either publicly support Diem or keep our mouths shut. If we follow the latter policy, a coup will probably take place within four weeks.

After a day of briefings in the "secure room" of MACV headquarters, McNamara and Taylor traveled the country together for four days, using Harkins's C-54, protected by T-28 fighter-bombers and UH-1B attack helicopters. It was the top-of-the-line VIP tour. Viet Cong weapons were piled at one field post, just captured, according to a captain's briefing. McNamara picked up a 57-mm recoilless rifle. "Chinese, I suppose," he said. Actually it had been made in the U.S.A. The Viet Cong mostly used weapons captured from ARVN.

General Taylor, though, who knew more about weapons, had something of an agenda of his own. During the final meeting with Kennedy, Taylor had said: "It would be useful to work out a schedule within which we expect to get this job done and to say plainly to Diem that we were not going to be able to stay beyond such and such a time with such and such forces, and that the war must be won in this time period."

The President had not commented, and Taylor had taken that as a

go-ahead. Spending his time with the military in the field, he was coming
to the same conclusions General Krulak had two weeks earlier. The war
was being won, he thought, and the Viet Cong could be reduced to
banditry within two years—by the end of 1965.

After a week in Vietnam, McNamara, Taylor, Lodge, and Harkins
met with President Diem on September 29, at the palace for three hours.
Diem spoke for the first two hours, repeating over and over again that
the war was going well. The construction of thousands of strategic
hamlets, armed and fortified against the Viet Cong, was bringing the
countryside under strong government control, he said, and attacks on
his family were unfair and inaccurate.

McNamara and Lodge were carrying a letter from Kennedy to Diem,
to be used at their discretion. The letter put Diem on notice that the
United States was running out of patience, and that if he continued his
refusal to discuss its demands, including the removal of Nhu from
power, the President was ready to withdraw American troops and everything else from South Vietnam.

"What I must make clear is the effect that recent events are having
here in the United States," Kennedy had written.

> It is a fact that unless there can be important changes and improvements
> in the relations between the Government and people in your country,
> opinion in the United States, both in the public and in the Congress, will
> make it impossible for me to continue without change the great coopera-
> tive programs which we have been pressing together since 1961. I have
> said publicly that we do not wish to cut off our aid programs at this time,
> but it would be wrong for me not to let you know that a change is
> inevitable unless the situation in Vietnam takes a major visible and credi-
> ble turn for the better.

McNamara and Lodge decided not to use the letter. They said the
same things themselves, giving both Kennedy and Diem more room to
maneuver. But Diem was not interested in moving. According to the
Americans' notes of the meeting, he listened to McNamara, and then:
"Diem ascribed all this to inexperience and demagoguery within Viet-
Nam and to misunderstanding in the United States of the real position
in Viet-Nam because of the vicious attacks of the American press on his
government, his family and himself. He said nothing to indicate that he
accepted the thesis that there was a real problem, and his whole manner
was one of rejecting outright the Secretary's representations."

The U.S. summary ended: "Diem offered absolutely no assurances
that he would take any steps in response to the representations made to
him by his American visitors. . . . His manner was one of at least out-

ward serenity and of a man who had patiently explained a great deal and who hoped he had thus corrected a number of misapprehensions."

There was little serenity in Washington where Kennedy was following McNamara's and Taylor's cables day by day, even hour by hour. One of the last he saw was a summary of a conversation with the vice president of Vietnam, Nguyen Ngoc Tho, the Americans' choice to succeed Diem if there were a coup. General Taylor, who was working on his timetable for U.S. military involvement and withdrawal, did most of the questioning. He concentrated on the high morale of the villagers he had met in the last week, contrasting it with the whining of intellectuals and politicians in Saigon.

No, Tho said, the villagers are discontented, too, but for different reasons—they feel they have to pay too much in work and rice to the government's village agents and then they have to pay again to the Viet Cong who control the fields outside the hamlets.

"But that should not happen in a well-defended hamlet," Taylor said.

"Why, General Taylor, don't you know?" Tho replied. "There are not more than twenty to thirty properly defended hamlets in the whole country."

McNamara and Taylor, who had been guided and helicoptered from one model site to the next, did *not* know. They did not know either—nor did Kennedy—that the hamlets were being built and fortified by forced labor. Villagers were being required to work for eight, twenty, even forty hours a week without pay, clearing jungle, building fences and common buildings, and stringing barbed wire. There was a silent rage against Saigon. At least it could not be heard by Americans who spoke no Vietnamese.

Parts of the McNamara-Taylor report on military progress and the security of the hamlets had already been written from the cables they had been sending back to the Pentagon, and had already been read by the President. Now, for the first time, McNamara, the keeper of the statistics, thought that perhaps he should listen to the translators and the foreigners, and even the young U.S. officers who were telling him—or trying to tip him off—that the Vietnamese officials and officers were just making up the numbers to keep the Americans happy. And Americans in the field and in Saigon were goosing even those numbers to keep him happy and the dollars flowing from Washington.*

---

* Three months later, on December 21, 1963, McNamara concluded or realized or admitted to himself that U.S. policy in Vietnam had been based on years of misinformation. He wrote a memorandum for the record that day saying: "There is no organized government in South Vietnam at this time. . . . It is abundantly clear that statistics received over the past year or more from the GVN officials and reported by the US mission on which we gauged the trend of the war were grossly in error. . . . The Viet Cong control larger

For McNamara, if there were no numbers—"Where is your data. Don't give me your poetry"—there was no way to make rational decisions. He was, above all, a rationalist, like his boss the President. But he was not inflexible. He had been shaken by the conversations with Vice President Tho and "Professor Smith." By the time he was ready to leave, McNamara was ready to join Lodge and Harriman in their conviction that Diem and Nhu had to go.

McNamara, Taylor, and William Sullivan began working on the final wording of the report even before they left Saigon. They worked on separate sections, then exchanged rough drafts. When Sullivan saw Taylor's draft on U.S. troop strength on the flight back, he jumped up to look for McNamara.

"I can't buy this. This is totally unrealistic," Sullivan told the Secretary. McNamara and Taylor had put in a timetable: The United States would begin withdrawing troops before the end of 1963, have all troops out of the northern regions of South Vietnam by the end of 1964, and have everybody home before the end of 1965. "We're not going to get troops out in '65. We mustn't submit anything as phony as this to the President."

"You're right," McNamara said. He talked to Taylor and they took out specific numbers and dates. But Taylor said he still thought the timetable was a good idea and a good way of putting visible pressure on Diem to shape up or else.

"Goddammit," Taylor said. "We've got to make these people put their noses to the wheel—or the grindstone or whatever. If we don't give them some indication that we're going to get out sometime, they're just going to be leaning on us forever. So that's why I had it in there."

"I understand that," Sullivan said. "But it's not honest. If it becomes public, people will know it's a fraud."

The mission to South Vietnam returned to Washington on the morning of October 2, 1963. Its report no longer included a timetable for United States military withdrawal, or a declaration that one thousand American military advisers would come home before the end of the year. The junior man on board, Sullivan, had prevailed by threatening to submit a minority report. McNamara had wanted the thousand-man

---

percentages of the population, greater amounts of territory, and have destroyed or occupied more strategic hamlets than expected. . . . Starting in about July, indices on progress of the war turned unfavorable for the GVN. . . . The strategic hamlet has encountered resistance in the delta because relocation removed families from their fields and locations occupied for generations. Many defections of entire villages were reported. . . . It is my conclusion that the coup came when there was a downward trend which was more serious than was reported and, therefore, more serious than realized. . . . In my judgment, there are more reasons to doubt the future of the effort under present programs and moderate extensions to existing programs (i.e., harassing sabotage against NVN, border crossings, etc.;) than there are reasons to be optimistic about the future of our cause in South Vietnam."

withdrawal in, but his first priority was a consensus paper that the President could call a policy.

They went straight to the White House, where they spent an hour going over the report with Kennedy. The bottom line, McNamara said, is: "These pressures will push us toward reconciliation with Diem or a coup to overthrow Diem."

The McNamara-Taylor Report, classified "Top Secret," was presented to the National Security Council in the Cabinet Room later the same day. The President thanked the Secretary and the general and then said: "We are agreed to try to find effective means of changing the political atmosphere in Saigon. We are agreed that we should not cut off all U.S. aid to Vietnam, but are agreed on the necessity of trying to improve the situation in Vietnam by bringing about changes there. . . . We are not papering over our differences. . . . We must all sign on and with good heart set out to implement the actions decided upon."

He insisted: "There are no differences between Washington and Ambassador Lodge or among the State and Defense Departments and the CIA."

The report summary that survived the day was entitled "Memorandum to the President." Its recommendations emphasized military progress and political uncertainty: "The military campaign has made great progress and continues to progress. . . . The Diem-Nhu government is becoming increasingly unpopular. . . . There is no solid evidence of the possibility of a successful coup, although assassination of Diem or Nhu is always a possibility. . . ."

With the President silently listening, McNamara and Taylor talked of a war being won and a timetable for disengagement. The report once again included the thousand-man withdrawal and the 1965 deadline for removing almost all U.S. personnel. "This action should be explained in low key," the summary said, "as an initial step in a long-term program to replace US personnel with trained Vietnamese without impairment of the war effort." The other principal military recommendation was for more heavily defended strategic hamlets.

The political recommendations were less definite:

"The following actions be taken to impress upon Diem our disapproval of his political program.

"*Continue to withhold commitment of funds in the commodity import program, but avoid a formal announcement. . . . Suspend approval of the pending AID loans.

"*At this time, no initiative should be taken to encourage actively a change in government. Our policy should be to seek urgently to identify and build contacts with an alternative leadership if and when it appears."

"The prospects that a replacement regime would be an improvement appear to be about 50–50," said McNamara and Taylor. "Initially, only a strongly authoritarian regime would be able to pull the government together and maintain order. In view of the pre-eminent role of the military in Vietnam today, it is probable that this role would be filled by a military officer. . . . We therefore need an intensive clandestine effort, under the Ambassador's direction, to establish necessary contacts to allow U.S. to continuously appraise coup prospects."

"Deceitful," was the private comment of William Sullivan, but he had already been maneuvered away from writing a minority report. He was helpless as the President looked around the table and said, "As of tonight, we have a policy."

McGeorge Bundy added: "Now that a policy decision had been made, we should be absolutely certain that no one continues to talk to the press about differences among U.S. agencies." He knew that McNamara and Taylor emphasized winning the war, and that State Department people would like to go further. "No, no," Harriman interrupted, the wording was fine, there is no disagreement.

It was what Harriman had wanted. Beginning with the April 24 cable, Hilsman, Lodge, and he had won the day by bringing McNamara over to their side. There were still pro-Diem dissenters, particularly in the Army and the CIA, Taylor, Harkins, and McCone among them. But these were not men who could publicly break ranks.

Kennedy said he wanted to talk further with McNamara, Taylor, and Rusk, just the four of them, to put together a short statement for the press. After fifteen minutes, as he read over their statement, he was still worried by the phrase "by the end of this year," after the announcement of the withdrawal of one thousand men. Rusk said it was needed to placate Fulbright and others in Congress who were complaining that the commitment seemed open-ended. The solution to that, according to the minutes of the meeting, was: "The draft announcement was changed to make both of the time predictions included in paragraph 3 a part of the McNamara-Taylor report rather than in the public statement as a prediction of the President."

That settled, they went back into the Cabinet Room. Other NSC members were still going over the report. Almost everyone objected to the troop withdrawal and the 1965 deadline for U.S. involvement, saying it was fantasy, or repeating Kennedy's usual line about avoiding specific numbers and dates. The President listened for a bit longer, then walked out, leaving McNamara to take a verbal pounding without letting on that he had his orders from the top. It was Kennedy who wanted the troop withdrawals announced.

Pierre Salinger came out of the press office just before seven o'clock to release the statement to waiting reporters and answer questions. He said the report was endorsed by all the members of the NSC and that what he was about to say was U.S. policy. He read slowly:

"The security of South Viet-Nam is a major interest of the United States as of other free nations. We will adhere to our policy of working with the people and Government of South Viet-Nam to deny this country to communism and to suppress the externally stimulated and supported insurgency of the Viet Cong as promptly as possible. . . .

"The military program in South Viet-Nam has made progress and is sound in principle. . . . Major U.S. assistance in support of this military effort is needed only until the insurgency has been suppressed or until the national security forces of the Government of South Viet-Nam are capable of suppressing it.

"Secretary McNamara and General Taylor reported their judgment that the major part of the U.S. military tasks can be completed by the end of 1965, although there may be a continuing requirement for a limited number of U.S. training personnel. They reported that by the end of this year, the U.S. program for training Vietnamese should have progressed to the point where 1,000 U.S. military personnel assigned to South Viet-Nam can be withdrawn."

He ended the statement by saying that the United States was still troubled by the political situation. "The United States has made clear its continuing opposition to any repressive actions in South Viet-Nam. While such actions have not yet significantly affected the military effort, they could do so in the future."

Then Salinger took questions, sort of . . . The first one was: "How many troops do we have in South Vietnam?" The answer: "I couldn't tell you that." The number was classified "Secret."

There were now over seventeen thousand Americans in uniform in South Vietnam. Most of the press, relying on leaks, was usually a little behind on the count, generally repeating "about 14,000." The reason for not officially acknowledging any numbers was that the United States was still informally bound by the Geneva Accords setting a limit of 685 U.S. military advisers in South Vietnam.

The short statement seemed to quiet almost everyone for the moment, from doubting Fulbright and questioning Mansfield to the hawks of *Time*. The magazine reported the official policy this way:

> Sensible and firm. . . . Winning the war against the Communist VietCong comes first. . . . The U.S. will continue to string along with Diem's regime, if only for the reason cited last week by The New York Herald Tribune in recalling an Al Smith quote: "You don't change barrels going over Niagara Falls."

In setting a 1965 deadline for victory in the bullet battle against the Viet Cong, the Administration was not necessarily making a military judgment. Such a judgment would be unrealistic. . . . But the apparent deadline did have a shrewd political aim. It served notice that if the Diem regime does not reform itself, the U.S. can fairly say: "You, and not the U.S., are responsible for the failure to achieve victory—and you cannot accuse the U.S. of not having given you every chance."

Two senators, Wayne Morse of Oregon and freshman George McGovern of South Dakota, were calling for total withdrawal from Vietnam, but they were more or less talking to themselves. In the press, the *Washington Post* called the report "Groundless prophecy." The *Chicago Tribune* said: "The latest of a series of guesses, none of which has been realized in the event."

In Saigon, Henry Cabot Lodge was surprised by the notion of withdrawing troops. "That's just politics," he told friends, and a Democratic President preparing his reelection campaign was not about to consult a Republican ambassador about that.

"No Nhus is good news" was one flip characterization of the policy. Politically, at least, whatever *Time* thought, the McNamara-Taylor Report was Diem's death warrant—if only because recommended reductions in U.S. non-military aid were sure to be seen by the plotting generals of ARVN as a signal that the United States was behind them. The President signed off on the secret details of the new policy late on October 5—a day when the sixth Buddhist monk burned himself to death in the streets of Saigon. On that day, AID, the United States' foreign assistance agency, was ordered to withhold or freeze $30 million in assistance to the Government of Vietnam, most of it from a $100 million Commercial Import Program (CIP), which subsidized the importing of American condensed milk, wheat flour, and cotton for civilian use—a clever choice for coercion. The suspension did not affect military spending and, because the money was generally paid four months in advance, Diem had time to reverse himself and accept U.S. demands to get the Nhus out of power and out of the country.

The other significant cut authorized by the President was funding for the salaries of "Special Forces," the Vietnamese Green Beret force that had been created in 1961. Nhu had made them into a presidential guard under the command of Colonel Le Quang Tung, an officer who answered only to the Ngos—and had led the pagoda raids of August.

The new orders were cabled "Eyes Only" to Lodge that evening:

These instructions have the President's personal approval: Actions are designed to indicate to Diem Government our displeasure at its political policies and activities and to create significant uncertainty in that government and in key Vietnamese groups as to future intentions of United States. . . .

Your policy toward the GVN of cool correctness in order to make Diem come to you is correct. . . . There are three issues at root of strained relations between GVN and US and of our judgment that victory may be jeopardized. The first concerns military effort; GVN must take steps to make this more effective. The second is crisis of confidence among Vietnamese people which is eroding popular support for GVN that is vital for victory. The third is crisis of confidence on the part of the American public and Government.

The cable made some specific demands of the Diem government, reflecting the state of relations between the governments: "Avoid divisive press attacks, e.g. Times of Viet-Nam story attacking CIA, etc. . . . Cease public statements slandering the US effort and the role of US military and civilian personnel. . . . Cease undercover efforts to discredit the US and weaken the will of US individuals to give their full support to programs, e.g. 'mendacious briefings' of GVN troops and rumors of physical danger to US families and other personnel.

"No public statement will be issued here for the present."

A preceding memo sent through Rusk had emphasized to Lodge: "The President thinks it of the greatest importance that, to the very limit of our abilities, we should not open this next stage in the press. . . . You should personally control knowledge of individual actions and tactics, and accept, as we will try to, necessary dissatisfaction of determined reporters with cryptic posture."

The information flow back to Washington from Saigon that day had an urgency. A new coup was in the works. Cables reported contacts with Vietnamese generals by Lieutenant Colonel Lucien Conein, a CIA agent who had once been a French Foreign Legionnaire and was now listed officially as a military attaché at the embassy. Conein's most important conversations had been with Duong Van Minh, "Big Minh," the Americans' local favorite:

Gen. Minh stated that he must know American Government's position with respect to a change in the Government of Vietnam . . . action to change the government must be taken or the war will be lost to the Viet Cong.

Gen. Minh made it clear that he did not expect any specific American support . . . but he stated he does need American assurances that the USG will not attempt to thwart this plan.

Minh outlined three possible plans for the accomplishment of the change of government:

    a. Assassination of Ngo Dinh Nhu and Ngo Dinh Can, keeping President Diem in office. Gen. Minh said this was the easiest plan to accomplish.

    b. The encirclement of Saigon by various military units. . . .

    c. Direct confrontation between military units involved in the coup and loyalist military units in Saigon. Gen. Minh claims under the circumstances Diem and Nhu could count on the loyalty of 5,500 troops within the City of Saigon.

Lodge attached his own recommendations for dealing with Big Minh to Conein's cable. The ambassador recommended that Big Minh be told directly that the United States would not thwart his plans and would, in fact, help make them—all except assassination details.

> 1. Assure him that US will not attempt to thwart his plans. . . . 2. Offer to view his plans, other than assassination plans. . . . 3. Assure Minh that US aid will be continued to Vietnam under government which gives promise of gaining support of people and winning the war against the Communists.

The White House answer to Lodge was:

> No initiative should now be taken to give any active covert encouragement to a coup. Urgent covert effort to identify and build contacts with possible alternative leadership as and when it appears. We repeat that this effort is not repeat not to be aimed at active promotion of [a] coup but only at surveillance and readiness. . . . This effort must be totally secure and fully deniable.

Bundy expanded on that in another follow-on cable to Lodge: "In order to provide plausibility of denial suggest you and no one else in Embassy issue these instructions orally to Acting Station Chief and hold him responsible to you alone for making appropriate contacts and reporting to you alone."

The acting CIA chief, with Richardson gone now, was David Smith, who recommended to Lodge and then to McCone that "We do not set ourselves irrevocably against the assassination plot, since the other two alternatives mean either a bloodbath in Saigon or a protracted struggle."

Alarm bells went off at CIA headquarters in Langley, Virginia. "Assassination" was supposed to be kept out of written records. As soon as McCone saw the cable, he cabled Lodge: "We certainly cannot be in the position of stimulating or approving, or supporting assassination, but on the other hand, we are in no way responsible for stopping every such threat of which we might have partial knowledge."

McCone called Kennedy and asked to come over to the White House. Robert Kennedy was with the President in the Oval Office when he arrived. McCone avoided using the word "assassination"—the President had to be able to deny ever talking about it—but, he said, he wanted to make clear his own understanding of the CIA's role: "We are collecting information on coup planning, but not attempting to direct it."

Kennedy did not respond specifically, and McCone left thinking that the President wanted Diem out, but agreed with him that the United States should not become directly involved in assassination planning. The CIA chief immediately cabled David Smith in Saigon: "McCone directs that you withdraw recommendation to ambassador under McCone instructions, as we cannot be in position actively condoning such course of action and thereby engaging our responsibility therefore."

Smith reported back the next day that he had advised Lodge and that the ambassador agreed with McCone. But Lieutenant Colonel Conein knew nothing of that exchange. Lodge, who was giving all the orders in Saigon, verbally in Conein's case, said nothing to the man who was meeting regularly with Minh and the other plotters.

On October 7, 1963, the President was pulled away from the cabled whispering to and from Saigon, and from muttering curses each time he saw newspapers with photographs of Madame Nhu, who had arrived in New York to begin a speaking tour. On that day, he completed the process of what he considered his greatest achievement. He signed the Limited Test Ban Treaty, saying: "In its first two decades the age of nuclear energy has been full of fear, but never empty of hope. Today the fear is a little less and the hope a little greater. For the first time we have been able to reach an agreement. . . ."

That same day, *The Times of Vietnam* broke the story that the United States was withholding aid to South Vietnam in an eight-column headline across the top of page one: "US FREEZES ECONOMIC AID PROGRAM."

At the end of the day, Lodge sent an urgent cable that drew the President right back into the plotting in Vietnam:

In an interview with Italian journalist . . . Nhu says in effect that he can and would like to get along without the Americans. . . . He wants VietNam to be treated as U.S. treats Yugoslavia—giving them money but not seeking to influence their system of government. . . . He said that if his father-in-law, former Ambassador Chuong, were to come to Saigon, "I will have his head cut off. I will hang him in the center of a square and let him dangle there. My wife will make the knot on the rope." . . . The above leads me to the conclusion that we cannot remove the Nhus by non-violent means against their will. . . . We should consider a request to withdraw as a growing possibility.

Two days later, on October 9, Kennedy held a press conference, spending a little more time than usual preparing. He expected the session to be dominated by questions on coup fever in Vietnam—but that did not happen. He began with an announcement that the U.S. government would not interfere with the private sale of American wheat, 150 million bushels of it, to the Soviet Union and three of its allies, Hungary, Bulgaria, and Czechoslovakia.

It seemed a tough call. The Soviets, suffering another of their bad harvests, had requested wheat in late September. The request made American farmers happy, but Kennedy's willingness to consider it was incomprehensible to many American cold warriors. "What is this? A mutual aid society?" asked Senator Barry Goldwater. A Democratic representative from Idaho, Ralph Harding, said what Kennedy should give them was surplus tobacco: "They might contract lung cancer!" Frances Bolton, a Republican congresswoman from Ohio, was one of the representatives of wheat-growing states the President called in to the White House when the offer was made. "But, Mr. President . . . ," she responded. "Aren't we at war with them?"

"I have considered it very carefully and I think it is very much in the interest of the United States," Kennedy said at the news conference. "Basically, the Soviet Union will be treated like any other cash customer in the world market who is willing and able to strike a bargain with private American merchants. . . . We have got 1 billion bushels of this in surplus, and American taxpayers are paying to keep it, and I think we can use the $200 million or $250 million of gold which will help our balance of payments."

There were coup questions after that, but the coups in question were not in Southeast Asia, they were in the Caribbean and Central America. "We are opposed to military coups, and it is for that reason that we have broken off our relations with the Dominican Republic and Honduras," said the President without a trace of irony. Nor did he seem to show a trace of concern that Alliance for Progress support for the sale of U.S. armaments to Latin American armies—mobilization against Communists—was obviously tempting generals to dispose of elected leaders, confident that their new friends in North America might look the other way as long as the coups were presented as anti-Communist.

Meanwhile, in Saigon, the CIA was picking up stories about the "Assassination Lists" of Ngo Nhu Dinh. It was said that he planned to begin with Henry Cabot Lodge. The scheme would begin with a "student" demonstration at the U.S. Embassy, allowing a killing squad to charge into the building. Whether or not they were true, the rumors were real and were raising the already high American blood pressure in the city.

On October 10, Lodge cabled Washington on those reports:

"If I am assassinated in the way indicated in above reports, the deed will in effect have been done by the GVN, however much they attempt to disguise it. . . . For Diem and Nhu even to be thinking of my assassination is so unbelievably idiotic that a reasonable person would reject it out of hand. But Nhu is apparently pleased with his raids on the Buddhist pagodas last summer and is said to be annoyed with me for having advised him to leave the country for awhile. Also he is reported to be smoking opium. . . ."

Lodge also responded to the rumors by telling the Vietnamese what he thought would happen if he were murdered: "I have instructed Acting Station Chief to have his agent tell source that if GVN mounts such an operation, American retaliation will be prompt and awful beyond description. Source will be invited to examine record of U.S. Marines in Pacific during WWII and ask himself candidly whether GVN wishes to have such a horrible and crushing blow descend on them."

On October 11, the President signed National Security Action Memorandum 263, the document that officially made the McNamara-Taylor Report national policy, with one significant change: "The President approved the military recommendations contained in Section I B (1–3) of the report, but directed that no formal announcement be made of the implementation of plans to withdraw 1,000 U.S. military personnel by the end of 1963."

The President also met with Representative Clement Zablocki, a member of the House Foreign Affairs Committee. Kennedy had urged the committee to send a fact-finding mission to Vietnam and eight members had gone in early October, led by Zablocki, a Wisconsin Democrat. On his return the congressman told the President he thought removing President Diem would be a big mistake, unless the United States had a successor in the wings.

"Remember Cuba," Zablocki said. "Batista was bad, but Castro is worse."

"I hope you'll write an objective report and not put President Diem in a favorable light," said Kennedy.

"Well, you know what the boss wants," Pierre Salinger remarked cheerfully as Zablocki left the White House.

"The boss will get what we think is right," the congressman said. "Somebody's giving the boss some bad information."

Chapter 54

President Kennedy had begun 1963 declaring that his priority for the year was his plan to reform and cut income tax rates. By the middle of October, that all seemed a long time ago. The third year of his presidency would be remembered as a tale of two cities, Birmingham and Saigon. It was not until October 15 that hearings even began in the Senate Finance Committee on the Revenue Act of 1963, which by then was no longer a tax reform bill. "They're opening more loopholes than they're closing," Walter Heller, chairman of the Council of Economic Advisers, told Kennedy one day, as lobbyists clustered outside the doors of the hearing room of the House Ways and Means Committee.

The "reforms," which began with 571 pages of pro-business testimony by Secretary of the Treasury Dillon, grew each day, as practically every industry and corporation and interest in the country appeared with a paragraph or two, or even just the right word, to exempt themselves from one regulation or another.

"Those robbing bastards," Kennedy said when Heller mentioned one of the players, the oil and gas industry. "I'm going to murder them!"

But he could not. He had enough trouble trying to sell his ideas to middle-class taxpayers. "The high wartime and postwar tax rates we are now paying are no longer necessary," Kennedy had said again during a national television address in late September. "They are, in fact, harmful. These high rates do not leave enough money in private hands to

keep this country's economy growing and healthy. . . . Here is how it
will work: A factory earner with three dependents earning $90 a week
will have his taxes reduced by a third. The typical American family, a
father, mother, and two children, earning about $6,000 a year, now
pays an annual tax of $600. This bill will cut that tax by 25 percent.
. . . A salaried employee with a wife and two children who earns $8,000
a year will receive a tax cut of more than twenty percent. . . . As these
typical families, and millions like them across our country, spend that
extra money on dishwashers, or clothes, or a washing machine, or an
encyclopedia, or a longer vacation trip, or a down payment on a new
car or a new home, that is what makes jobs."

Kennedy was more comfortable with the politics of the tax cuts than
the economics. But he had learned enough in the past three years to
realize that he now knew a great deal more about the numbers than
the congressional leaders regularly quoted as national economics
spokesmen. "He's just ignorant," the President said to Heller after another long meeting with Representative Wilbur Mills of Arkansas, the
chairman of Ways and Means.

But Mills was a reminder to Kennedy that his conversion to Keynesian economics was personal. The American people, at least the ones in
Mills's district in Arkansas, were clinging to older beliefs. "They are not
up to date on that, Mr. President," said the congressman. "I'm satisfied
100% of the people in my district would welcome tax reduction. But
when they talk about reducing taxes, they get back to this old, uh,
concept that they've grown up with: If you're gonna cut taxes . . . you
better cut your spending."

Politics was the common language spoken during the weeks of Kennedy's stroking and negotiating to get the tax cut out of Ways and
Means. Like almost everything Kennedy wanted, it finally came down
to getting more votes from Southern Democrats. There were about fifty
of them. They called themselves "the economy bloc," but everyone else
called them the "Boll Weevils."

"Let's take a fellow," Kennedy said to Mills. "A fellow who was
prone to vote for the tax bill. . . . How would they get him? I mean,
what, what would be the offer on civil rights that could get 'em?"

"Block it in the Rules Committee," Mills answered.

"Block the civil rights bill in the Rules Committee?" the President
repeated.

The conversation drifted again to business demands for tax breaks,
particularly the demands of oil men who were big contributors to congressional campaigns. "They tell me that we wouldn't get but about
three votes for the tax bill out of the entire California delegation," Mills

said, blaming one oil man for that. "I'll tell you where that's from, you know it and I know it. Ed Pauley's a big contributor in California to those campaigns, backed every one of them. . . ."

"Yeah," said Kennedy, naming a Texas oil man. "This fellow H. L. Hunt's running around the country. . . . The day's gonna come when we're gonna have the Congress and the president"—their campaigns—"financed by the government. . . . It'll be the best thing that ever happened. God you know those oil companies . . . I don't mind anybody getting away with some, but what they get away with."

He went on and on. But it was a tough sell.

"I am absolutely for the tax cut, I think you have to have it," said Representative Martha Griffiths, the Michigan Democrat, when the President telephoned her, saying that she might be the deciding vote in Mills's committee.

"I hear it's thirteen to twelve up there, so Larry O'Brien tells me. So you're the key and I'm, we really need you. I think it's the only chance we have to avoid a recession in '64. . . ."

Griffiths said again: "I assure you that on the economics of the thing, I absolutely agree that the tax cut is essential. But my problem, Mr. President, is that from my district all I receive is letters saying, 'Please stand pat.' " Americans believed in old virtues, beginning with balanced budgets. Neither a borrower nor a lender be. If you want something more, something new, save for it.

"Okay, Martha," Kennedy said. "Do the best you can, will you?"

Finally, Kennedy told Dillon that he had to drop the reforms, which were being cut or padded or mangled out of shape anyway behind the doors of the Ways and Means Committee. The tax bill became a simple tax-cut bill, H.R. 8363, when it was released after seven months by the House Ways and Means Committee and passed by the full House of Representatives at the end of September by a vote of 271 to 155, pretty much along party lines. If it could get through the Senate—not a sure thing by any means—it would reduce the existing individual income tax-rate schedule from a range of 20–91 to 16–77 percent in 1964 and then to 14–70 percent in 1965. The effective corporate rate schedule would drop from 52 percent to 50 percent to 48 percent at the same times. The rate on capital gains—the profit on investments, defined as stocks or other assets sold after being held for a year—was reduced from 25 percent to 21 percent.

The Senate hearings were scheduled to continue until November 27, the day before Thanksgiving. *Time* magazine was not much impressed with its chances, or with the President's command of Congress, saying:

"Timetable. The prospects . . . Tax cuts: Passed by the House, but locked in Conservative Democrat Harry Byrd's Senate Finance Committee, and won't even get to the Senate floor before Dec. 20, at which point the Senate plans to adjourn for the Christmas holidays until Jan. 2.

"Civil Rights Bill: Locked in House committees until the first week of December. If it gets to the Senate, it faces a filibuster.

"The betting: no tax cuts or civil rights bill this year."

And that was not all. Kennedy had had some successes in Congress, including a higher education bill providing $1.2 billion for classroom and laboratory construction at both public and private colleges. But he had been defeated again in Congress on Medicare and humiliated by the 25 percent reduction in his foreign aid requests. Heller tried to cheer him up, telling him, not for the first time, that Theodore Roosevelt got more legislation through Congress in his second term than in his first.

"It's just crazy," Kennedy said to Senator Stuart Symington, a Democrat up for reelection in 1964, who was still not committed to vote for the tax cut. "Stu, the only thing that's going to lick you is going to be a recession. It's not going to be whether you should have a $9 billion deficit or $11 billion deficit. . . . God, you want that money in circulation! Whether it's in circulation because people are spending it on themselves, or because you're spending it in a pretty good government program. The important thing is to have momentum. . . ."

The President was having conversations like that every day now, trying to win senators over one by one. A week after the House vote, he asked Larry O'Brien about Senator Albert Gore of Tennessee: "What's the problem, now. . . . Is Gore being a son-of-a-bitch about this?"

"Gore is gone," O'Brien answered.

"After we gave him that judge and everything?" Kennedy said. "Son-of-a-bitch. Albert Gore, if we get a good recession next summer, it's not going to do him much good, is it? . . . Why does he care . . . ?"

"Well," O'Brien answered, "I guess, basically civil rights. . . ."

"He's upset about civil rights?" Kennedy said. "I thought he was a great liberal."

"That's what I thought," O'Brien said, laughing. "But you told me that, I didn't really know . . ."

"I don't know why we even sent that goddamn judge up," the President said. And he was not laughing. "The district judge from Tennessee. We did that for Gore about two months ago. Goddamn it."

The civil rights bill scared O'Brien, a talented politician who followed orders, followed up, and kept his word. He worried that race and race relations were beyond politics. These were the secrets of the human heart, not easily learned or understood, much less used as political coin to trade for a judgeship or a small defense contract. O'Brien had argued against submitting a comprehensive bill after the troubles all year in Alabama, and so had Ted Sorensen, not because of what was in their own hearts, but because they calculated that the weight of the Negroes' burdens could drag down everything else Kennedy was pushing and proposing.

President Kennedy knew that better than anyone. He had no choice. He was going to have to campaign for reelection as the new champion of Negro rights. So, all things being equal, which they were not, it would be better to get the legislative debate and dealing over with before the 1964 campaign. But that was not happening. And polls were still showing him losing six or seven white votes for every Negro one he gained. So far, though, the white losses were concentrated in the states of the old Confederacy. If he picked up enough Negro votes to carry California, which he had lost by 35,000 votes in 1960, he could afford to lose a half dozen of the Southern states he had won big that year. But Electoral College politics was a tricky business, and given a choice Kennedy would have preferred to have American Negroes go into the streets in someone else's administration.

"I don't know what 1964 is going to bring," he had answered, when asked about election numbers in his news conference of September 12. "I think a division upon racial lines would be unfortunate—class lines, sectional lines. . . . Over the long run we are going to have a mix. This will be true racially, socially, ethnically, geographically, and that is really, finally, the best way."

At the same time, in private, or in secret, the President's entanglement in the webs of surveillance coming from the office of FBI Director Hoover was becoming trickier, because of the director's obsession with destroying Martin Luther King, Jr. Wiretaps on the civil rights leader's office and home phones were approved by Robert Kennedy on October 7. The FBI was also investigating a growing political scandal involving the high-living and low life of the secretary of Democratic membership of the U.S. Senate, a Lyndon Johnson protégé named Bobby Baker.

All the while, too, the FBI was continuing to build up its Kennedy files, with the newest entries including not only Mary Meyer, a regular White House visitor during the past eight months, but also a twenty-seven-year-old German woman named Ellen Rometsch, the wife of an Army sergeant assigned to the West German Embassy since April 1961. She was, it seemed, a call girl, paid by and reporting to Baker, who ran a stable of willing young women available to senators and other Washington powers. Mrs. Rometsch's clientele, the FBI discovered, included some of the most important men in the Congress, and—they were certain—the President, too.

Hoover, knowing that Rometsch had fled East Germany in 1955, assumed that she must be a Communist spy. When her double life—German Army wife and high-priced prostitute—was discovered by the FBI, she had been secretly expelled from the United States on August 21 by order of Attorney General Kennedy. That was supposed to have been the end of it. But it was not. Baker came under investigation within a month for a series of financial transactions and ventures that made it clear he was a very expensive influence peddler. Rometsch's name and her occasional friendships were just below the surface when Baker resigned in October and went into hiding rather than answer a summons to appear in private before the Senate leaders, Mike Mansfield and Everett Dirksen. Their first question was going to have been how had he become a wealthy man in just a few years on a Senate salary that peaked at $19,612 a year.

At the same time as he was implicitly threatening the President with exposure, Hoover was pushing his crusade against Martin Luther King, again asking the Attorney General for the required written permission to wiretap the telephones in King's home in Atlanta. When Robert Kennedy signed that order on October 7, he had been procrastinating on it for more than three months. The tapping order was the same one he had proposed himself on July 16, then rejected on July 25. Two weeks later, on October 21, before the home tap was in use, Robert Kennedy had signed a second order authorizing taps on the four phone lines into King's offices at the Southern Christian Leadership Council in Atlanta, this time ordering that the material collected by the tap be reviewed in thirty days, to determine whether the eavesdropping should be continued.

On October 25, the Attorney General discovered that the FBI was circulating a classified memo through military intelligence agencies, and the office of the Secretary of Defense, describing King as "An unprincipled man . . . who is knowingly, willingly and regularly taking guidance from Communists." This time Robert Kennedy confronted Hoover, calling him to ask what responsibilities he thought the Army and Navy had regarding Martin Luther King, Jr. Then he wanted to know what effect he thought a message like this would have on the chances that Congress would pass a tough civil rights bill. Hoover, of course, knew it could kill the bill, which was probably why he had sent it out.

The Attorney General then ordered him to call back the memo. The existing copies were all called back, though the document was copied and hidden by military intelligence in its own extensive files on King.

The Rometsch story broke the next day, October 26, in the *Des Moines Register,* moving on to other papers over the next couple of days. No clients were named, although there were rumors that John Kennedy was one. *The New York Times* and the *Washington Post* dealt with it at arm's length, as a local sidebar to the Profumo case in London.

"I thought of Baker primarily as a rogue, not crook," Kennedy told Ben Bradlee one night late in October. "He was always telling me where he could get me the cutest little girls, but he never did." Then he turned to the subject of Hoover: "Boy, the dirt he has on those Senators you'd never believe it." And on ex-senators, too.

The Rometsch investigations died quickly when the President and the Attorney General arranged a secret meeting between Hoover, Mansfield, and Dirksen at Senator Mansfield's house on October 28. They were stunned by Hoover's performance. The FBI director rambled through a long list of dates, times, and the names of senators from both parties, stopping occasionally to make the point that some of the girls were foreigners and some Negroes. The President was not mentioned, Mansfield reported to John Kennedy by telephone as soon as Hoover left. Ellen Rometsch was not mentioned, either, not even in closed sessions of the hearings on Baker's secret activities which began the next day.

Having pledged their silence on the Rometsch affair, Mansfield and Dirksen returned to the Capitol, and to the tangled negotiations on the civil rights bill. Kennedy's bill was in trouble in both houses. After the church bombing in Birmingham, the chairman of the House Judiciary Committee, Representative Emanuel Celler of New York, and other liberal Northern Democrats, with the encouragement of the NAACP and other civil rights groups, had added a series of tough new provisions to H.R. 7152. Basically, Celler had expanded the definition of "Public Accommodations" to include private schools, law firms, and medical associations, and to give the Justice Department the power to sue on behalf of any citizen who claimed a violation of his or her constitutional rights. On October 1, Celler had proudly pushed what amounted to a new bill through a Judiciary subcommittee, surprising and outraging committee Republicans, and the Kennedy brothers.

The new provisions fouled up a deal the President had quietly made with House Republicans, particularly Representative William McCulloch of Ohio, the ranking minority member of Celler's committee. Republicans would get equal credit for the legislation and McCulloch would have veto power over liberal amendments added to the legislation in the Senate. In return, McCulloch and the House Republican leader,

Charles Halleck of Indiana, would round up enough Northern Republican votes to offset the Southern Democrats voting against the bill in committee and on the floor of the House.

"What the hell is this?" the President had shouted at his brother when he heard about Celler's amendments. "Can the NAACP deliver sixty Republican votes on the floor? Can they? McCulloch can deliver sixty Republican votes."

"I know, I know," Robert Kennedy said. The Attorney General did his shouting at Celler, telling the chairman from Brooklyn that he had just killed any chance of passing a civil rights bill. The proof, he said, was that Southern Democrats were already saying they would vote for the Celler version in committee, knowing that it would be defeated on the floor of the House.

Finally, toward the end of October, Celler agreed to undo what he had done and worked out a plan to push back toward the original White House bill, and even to add language from old Republican civil rights proposals. For his part, Robert Kennedy said he would appear before Celler's committee and say publicly that the new version of H.R. 7152, with Republican language, was stronger and better than the original White House version. Everyone had their lines, rehearsed in advance. The motions to modify the bill and add the Republican language would be made by Representative Roland Libonati of Illinois, a sixty-two-year-old cog of the Democratic machine run by Chicago Mayor Richard J. Daley.

Libonati was a man used to taking orders. He agreed to do the public backing down, so that Celler would not be humiliated among New York liberals. At least the congressman from Chicago agreed until he turned on his television at home and saw Celler announcing that he was still for the strong bill, and had nothing to do with the compromises being worked out between the White House and Republicans.

"When I hear that," said Libonati, "I says to myself, 'Lib, where are we at here, anyway?' . . . If the chairman says he doesn't have anything to do with my motion, then certain representations that were made to me is out the window. So I withdraw my motion."

The Judiciary Committee was in chaos, and so was a lot of the rest of Washington. In the committee, on October 22, a West Virginia Republican, Representative Arch Moore, moved to discharge the tough Celler version of the bill. He had the votes to do it, too—which would have killed both Kennedy's civil rights bill and any claim to competence in dealing with Congress. But it was close to lunchtime and Celler adjourned the committee.

The President called congressional leaders to the White House that afternoon, Democrats and Republicans. "We can't let this happen," he said. "What can we do?"

Put Humpty-Dumpty together again, said McCulloch, the Republican from Ohio. "All the King's horses and all the King's men *could* put Humpty-Dumpty together again."

So, they tried, with the heavy lifting being done by the Democratic King, the President, and the Republican House Leader, Charles Halleck of Indiana, a crusty old soul with no known sympathies for Negro civil rights legislation. But it was immediately obvious that Halleck was very pleased to be brought in this way for legislative summit sessions with a President.

"The colored vote in my district don't amount to a bottle of cold piss," Halleck told Kennedy when they were alone. But then he told Kennedy a story. He said that he liked to go down to Warm Springs in Georgia, the resort town where President Roosevelt often visited and where he had died. He said that it made him mad when restaurants refused to serve his driver, who was a Negro. Kennedy looked surprised. Halleck said, "Once in a while a guy does something because it's right."

Halleck said he would get seven of the seventeen committee votes needed to get back to a compromise bill. The President then had to get ten and he had nine already. On October 28, he called Mayor Daley in Chicago.

"Roland Libonati is sticking it right up us," said Kennedy.

"He is?" Daley said with surprise in his voice.

"Yeah, because he's standing with the extreme liberals who are going to end up with no bill at all. Then when we put together a bill with the Republicans which gives us about everything we wanted, and he says, 'No.'"

"He'll vote for it," said the mayor. "He'll vote for any goddamned thing you want."

Kennedy laughed.

"Where is he?" the mayor asked. "Is he there?"

"Well, he's in the other room."

"Tell Kenny to put him on the wire here."

"Okay," Kennedy said, then thought better of it. "Or would you rather get him when he gets back up to his office? That's better, otherwise, 'cause he might think . . ."

"The last time I . . ." Daley said. "I told him, 'Now look, I don't give a goddamned what it is, you vote for anything the president wants. This is the way it will be and this is the way we want it and that's the way it's gonna be.'"

"That'd be good," Kennedy said. "Thanks, Dick."

Halleck left the White House saying he would call the next day at noon with his vote count on the motion to kill the Celler plan. But no call came, and at 12:45 P.M., Kennedy called him.

"I'm terribly sorry, Mr. President," the Republican leader said. "I had a hard time catching a couple of my fellows and I just talked to the last one. But I was just about to call you with good news—I've got you the votes to get your bill out of the committee."

They talked by phone again after the committee finally voted to kill the stronger plan, leaving the way open to consider the new bipartisan compromise.

"You did a great job," Kennedy said.

"I got a lot of mad people up here," Halleck said.

"I got a lot of 'em, too. I got a lot of mad Negroes that are ready to come and throw rocks at me, but that's all right. . . . That was terrific, Charlie. You really did what you said."

Actually, Halleck had done more than he had said he would in delivering nine votes, because there had been a Democratic defection, for which Kennedy apologized. "Well, we didn't get Roland Libonati. Daley. Evidently that Cook County machine isn't as strong as we hear," he said.*

"I got a little trouble on my side, uh, a lot of guys bitching," Halleck said. "I ain't sure they'll make me leader again, but I don't give a damn. We got to get a rule. Mr. President, uh, if I could just make a little suggestion: let a little dust settle."

"Right. Right. Right. Okay."

President Tito of Yugoslavia came to Washington in the middle of all this. The anti-Soviet Communist leader, who won power as a guerrilla leader fighting Nazi occupiers of his country, and then broke with Joseph Stalin's regime in 1948, was a proud and touchy man who had angled for years to meet with an American president. At seventy-one, the marshal saw himself as a great world figure, one of the surviving victors of World War II, the de Gaulle of the Balkans.

He got to see Kennedy by seeing Khrushchev. During the summer, he had received the Soviet leader in Belgrade, immediately triggering White House concerns about a Yugo-Soviet reconciliation. But most Americans, particularly those who had fled communism in the "captive nations" of Eastern Europe, and the members of Congress who represented those Americans, saw him as an enemy, just another Com-

---

* Six months later, Libonati was denied renomination by the Daley-controlled Cook County Democratic Organization.

munist. So, Kennedy, the first President with the courage to invite a Communist into the White House, also demonstrated his usual caution. He allowed photographers into the Oval Office, but they had to stay behind him, so all the photographs showed only the back of his head. No handshakes, rocking chairs, or children this time.

Tito felt that coolness, and he did not like it at all. At one point he looked out the window and saw American Nazis, a ragtag bunch led by a man named George Lincoln Rockwell, wearing old Nazi uniforms and waving signs calling Tito a killer. "What kind of country is this?" asked the marshal, who had fought the real troops of Adolf Hitler. "The Nazis can do anything they want and I am treated as an enemy."

Kennedy asked Tito, who had just traveled through South America, whether the Soviets or the Chinese were winning struggles for control of Latin American Communist parties. The marshal was offended again, saying: "Mr. President, you know I would never interfere in the internal politics of a host nation. I had nothing to do with the politics or political life or partisan politics in any country I visited."

"Come on . . ." said Kennedy with a smile that may have been difficult to translate, "we're both politicians. What's going on down there?"

That pleased Tito. The "we" meant that the President of the United States accepted him as an equal. "Well," he said in a man-to-man tone now, "the Soviet blocs in the Communist party are cautious and trying to be careful and conservative. It is the Chinese element, which is in a minority, that is creating the most difficulty and, frankly, is probably thrusting its way to the leadership. They're the ones that are probably going to emerge in the long run as the leaders in Latin America."

Kennedy had asked George Kennan, his former Ambassador to Yugoslavia, to accompany Tito and his wife in their travels around the United States, and to do what he could to help steer Tito away from anti-Communist demonstrators. In a way, those demonstrators had cost Kennan his job. He had gone back to teaching at Princeton University at the end of 1962, when Congress had voted to end Yugoslavia's "Most Favored Nation" status in matters of trade. In the early fall of that year, Kennan had passed along Kennedy's assurances to Tito that MFN status would be continued without public debate and the usual congressional tirades about using taxpayers' money to prop up a Communist government, even one that had taken no military aid or advice from Moscow for fifteen years. It didn't work out that way, so someone had to quit, and it was not going to be the President.

Kennan, one of the most distinguished of U.S. diplomats, was shattered by what he considered the irredeemable stupidity of the Congress and the unwillingness of Kennedy to stand up to it, but he also understood his duty. The President had invited him to the White House then, and Kennan recorded their meeting this way in his diary:

> I understood the cruelty of his choice. . . . He was terribly alone with this loneliness that is known only to people in supreme position. I realized this. When I came home and saw him there in his room—that bedroom of his upstairs in the White House—and realized the pressures that were brought to bear against him, I realized what it meant to him to take an hour out to sit down in his rocking chair and talk with me, I always was aware that I must not look at his position from the standpoint of my problems. Great as they seemed to me, these were only a tiny portion of the problems that he had. His own decency toward me, his readiness to listen, convinced me that, if he was unable to support me, it was not for lack of desire on his part; it was because he thought that, on balance, this was the politically desirable thing to do; that to him, as to every man in senior political position, politics was the art of the possible, and he could only do those things that seemed to him, on balance, correct. I had nothing but sympathy for him. I was sorry that it was myself whom he was obliged in a way to destroy.

Demonstrators met Tito everywhere. The Waldorf-Astoria Hotel on Park Avenue in New York, where he went after Washington, was surrounded by people waving placards that read "RED PIG," "MURDERER," and such. In the lobby and the coffeeshop there were more men and women, screaming and spitting on his entourage, calling the women "prostitutes." The police around the hotel seemed to be on the demonstrators' side, standing aside as they yelled and cursed. Back in Washington, Senator Barry Goldwater of Arizona made a point of comparing Tito and another guest at the hotel that night, Madame Nhu. "We are dining with our enemy," Goldwater said, "and slapping our friends in the face."

Assassins came within seconds of getting to the Yugoslav president in his room that night. Two Croatians, former secret policemen in their homeland, had been working at the hotel for months in anticipation of Tito's stay. The pair were able to walk by U.S. Secret Service guards, nodding in recognition, just before eleven o'clock and were at the door to Tito's suite on the thirty-fifth floor of the Waldorf Towers, with a key in the lock, when a New York City police sergeant stepped out of an elevator.

"What the hell is going on here?" he said, charging and tackling the men, both of them armed. News of the attempt was called to the White House, waking the President. He ordered U.N. Ambassador Adlai Stevenson, who lived in the hotel, to go to Tito's rooms and apologize immediately. But when Stevenson arrived at about 1:00 A.M., Tito and his wife were both asleep again. Kennedy also sent the State Department's chief of protocol Angier Biddle Duke to New York, telling him to stay as close to Tito as possible until the marshal left for home on the S.S. *Rotterdam* on October 25.

On the ride to the ship anchored in the Hudson River, Ambassador Duke, sitting in the back of a limousine with Tito, showed the marshal the day's *New York Herald Tribune,* which had a picture of Stevenson in Dallas the morning before to make a speech, being cursed and hit with a placard by an angry woman demonstrator.

"You see, Mr. President, you're not the only target," Duke said. "This is what we do to our own leaders."

"That could happen against a great man like Adlai Stevenson?" Tito asked, as he had before. "What kind of country is this?"

Chapter 55

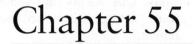

NOVEMBER 1, 1963

O n October 17, two weeks after McNamara and Taylor returned from Vietnam, President Kennedy read the Central Intelligence
Agency's weekly "Situation Appraisal," this one on South Vietnamese
reaction to his own statements and public actions since the mission. The
report concentrated on war, not between the North and the South, but
between the United States and the Government of Vietnam.

> Recent developments convey the unmistakable impression that the Diem/
> Nhu combine are prepared to dig in for a protracted war of attrition with
> the United States, resisting pressures for reform, seeking to mute these
> pressures by exploiting any differences which may emerge among Ameri-
> can policymakers. . . . Several sources in Saigon have now reported that
> the government is indeed cutting back on functionary salary payments.
> The policy may merely reflect an anticipatory GVN response to a possible
> US-initiated cutback in aid. A lesser possibility, but one which cannot be
> overlooked, is that Ngo Dinh Nhu is conditioning officials to an eventual
> full break with the United States, brought about at the initiative of the
> Diem regime.

In case anyone did not grasp that possibility, Nhu said, in an interview with European journalists published in *The Times of Vietnam*
on October 18, "People here are wondering what the United States is
doing. . . . People have lost confidence in the United States." He said

that interrogation of jailed Buddhist monks had revealed that "Day by day, CIA agents and some other employees of American civilian government agencies, urged the bonzes to stage a coup against the government."

Official Saigon was feverish with talk of conspiracy, with the American ambassador, not the president of South Vietnam, at the center. That night at a reception for U.N. observers, Lodge was approached by Diem's defense minister, Nguyen Dinh Thuan. President Kennedy saw the transcript of the conversation, cabled by Lodge, at breakfast the next morning:

"When we were seated off to one side, Thuan said: 'The President wanted me to ask you whether Washington had reached any decision regarding resumption of commercial imports.' He then continued without a pause, but with a pleasant smile, 'And I told him I believed they had not. Is that right? . . . I will tell him that's what you think.'

"After a few desultory remarks, I said that I had great hope that the time would come when I would be able to show by my actions the strong feelings I have for Viet-Nam. Thuan said: 'I have faith that all of this is going to work out that your mission will be a great success . . . I think it will be soon.' "

The advance copy of *Time* that Kennedy saw that Sunday said: "Best estimates in Saigon [are] that the South Vietnamese are holding their own militarily. It remains to be seen how they will fare in South Vietnam's second war—the political war waged by the U.S. against the Diem government."

On Monday, October 21, Kennedy had lunch at the White House with Arthur Ochs Sulzberger, the new publisher of *The New York Times*. He told Sulzberger, rather candidly, of the complexity of the problems in Saigon, many of them made worse by the gap between Asian sensibilities and the tenets of American journalism. He said he had been a young reporter himself, for Hearst, just before and after World War II, then said: "I wish like hell that you'd get Halberstam out of there."

A David Halberstam story the month before on the front page of the *Times*—"Rift with Saigon on War Tactics Underlined by 2 Red Attacks" was the headline—had set Kennedy off, and he had asked the CIA for an analysis of all of Halberstam's dispatches from June through September.

"A review indicates that he is by and large accurate in terms of the facts that he includes in his articles," the CIA reported back. "The conclusions he draws from his facts, plus the emphasis of his reporting, however, tend to call his objectivity into question. In his almost invariably pessimistic reports, Halberstam makes liberal use of phrases 'some Americans,' 'informed Vietnamese,' or 'lower (or higher) ranking Americans,' etc. Such sourcing is impossible to refute . . . optimistic sources are almost never quoted by Mr. Halberstam."

Sulzberger said he understood the problem and he would see what he could do. He called New York that afternoon and asked his editors about Halberstam. It turned out that the reporter was already preparing to come home. The editors thought Halberstam was too tired to stay in Vietnam and he was scheduled to be replaced by Hedrick Smith. At dinner that night, the publisher mentioned all of that to his Washington bureau chief, James Reston. Reston responded immediately, "Well, obviously we can't do what we were thinking of doing. We can't buckle in to that kind of stuff."

So, Halberstam was told to unpack; he would be staying in Saigon for a while longer. In Washington, Kennedy told McNamara angrily, "The only way to confound the press is to win the war."

The October 14 CIA report had also emphasized that it would be a mistake to discount the reports that Diem's government might be planning to assassinate U.S. officials, beginning with Ambassador Lodge. That same day, Kennedy had received the first "Eyes Only" report from Lodge on a secret one-on-one communications channel he had ordered set up after the McNamara-Taylor mission. Kennedy had initiated the channel three days earlier with a list of basic questions he wanted Lodge to answer each week. The first one was: "Are we gaining or losing on balance, and day by day in the contest with the Viet Cong?"

The ambassador answered: "We appear to me to be doing little more than holding our own. . . . Our presence here is a stabilizing influence in Viet-Nam and in Southeast Asia; it also keeps the GVN from being overthrown, which would undoubtedly happen if we were not here. But the U.S. cannot make the people like the Government of Viet-Nam. . . ."

"What does the evidence suggest on the strengthening or weakening of effectiveness of GVN in relation to its own people?" was Kennedy's next question.

"The evidence suggests that the Government of Viet-Nam has some of the strength which the government of a police state has, as long as the police remain strong and dependable and the government continues to control the police," answered Lodge. "Clearly Viet-Nam is not a thoroughly strong police state (much as the 'family' would like to make it one) because, unlike Hitler's Germany, it is not efficient and it has in the Viet Cong a large and well-organized underground opponent strongly and ever-freshly motivated by vigorous hatred. And its numbers never diminish—reckoned at a higher figure than it was two years ago, even though it is often said that 24,000 Viet Cong have been killed during that period."

Lodge ended by quoting from Graham Greene's *The Quiet American* on the mind-set of Vietnamese in the countryside: "They want enough rice; they don't want to be shot at; they want one day to be much the same as another."

Kennedy was persuaded that Diem had lost the peasants. Lodge argued regularly that he had lost the intelligentsia. The United States was ready to use its power to transform South Vietnam from a pseudo-democracy and ineffective police state, which it could not help or control because the wrong man was in charge, into an effective military dictatorship ready to work with the United States. The cable traffic back and forth between Washington and Saigon at the end of October, tens of thousands of words each day, focused on Kennedy's contradictory concerns. What the President wanted was a coup with plausible deniability of U.S. involvement, *and* up-to-the-minute information on the plotters, complete with assurances that they had a reasonable chance to succeed in removing Nhu and Diem.

"Control and cut-out" was the phrase McGeorge Bundy used when he transmitted the President's orders to Lodge on October 23: Kennedy wanted as much control as he could get over coup planning, but needed a cut-out in the U.S. command chain—someone passing along orders without knowing they were from the President himself. Then only Bundy would have to lie to protect Kennedy.

"I appreciate the concern expressed to you relative to the Gen. Don/Conein relationship," Lodge cabled the White House on October 25. General Tran Van Don, acting chief of staff of ARVN, was communicating plot information to the United States through Lucien Conein of the CIA, whom he had known for eighteen years. What was worrying the White House was that General Don had referred to "A Presidential directive"—as if it were Kennedy himself who was directing the conspirators. Don, through Conein, had promised Lodge that he would give the Americans forty-eight hours' notice before the first shots were fired. When the subject of assassinating Diem and Nhu had come up, Conein told Don he had been ordered not to discuss that subject. "All right, you don't like it," the Vietnamese commander said, "we won't talk about it anymore."

"We should not thwart a coup for two reasons," Lodge told Kennedy in that same cable.

> First, it seems at least an even bet that the next government would not bungle and stumble as much as the present one. Secondly, it is extremely

unwise in the long range for us to pour cold water on attempts at a coup, particularly when they are just in their beginning stages. We should remember that this is the only way in which the people in Vietnam can possibly get a change of government. . . . I applaud General Don's desire not to be a "vassal" of the U.S. But I do not think his promise of a democratic election is realistic. This country simply is not ready for that procedure.

"President wants you to know of our concern," came Kennedy's answer that same day: "We are particularly concerned about hazard that an unsuccessful coup, however carefully we avoid direct engagement, will be laid at our door by public opinion almost everywhere. Therefore, while sharing your view that we should not be in position of thwarting coup, we would like to have option of judging and warning on any plan with poor prospects of success."

On Sunday, October 27, Ambassador Lodge was surprised by an invitation to spend a day in the country with President Diem. They left Saigon by helicopter that morning, and spent most of the day at the president's villa in the hill town of Dalat.

On Monday, Lodge sent a long cable:

Diem is very likeable. One feels that he is a nice, good man who is living a good life by his own rights, but he is a man who is cut off from the present, who is living in the past, who is truly indifferent to people as such and who is simply unbelievably stubborn.

I said you wanted us to do something for you, what can you do for us? Ours is a government of public opinion. . . . The President [Kennedy] himself could not fly in the face of a totally adverse public opinion and the bad publicity coming out of Vietnam could make it hard for the President.

When it was evident that the conversation was practically over, I said: "Mr. President, every single specific suggestion which I have made, you have rejected. Isn't there some one thing you may think of that is within your capabilities to do and that would favorably impress US opinion?" As on other previous occasions when I asked him similar questions, he gave me a blank look and changed the subject.

As he was returning to Saigon that same Monday, October 28, Lodge ran into General Don at the Dalat airport. The general had one question: "Does Conein speak for you?"

"Yes, he does," Lodge answered. He asked Don when the coup was scheduled.

"I cannot give you that information," the general replied.

Cabling the President again on October 28, Lodge said he was certain the coup was inevitable now: "I do not know what more proof can be offered than the fact these men are obviously prepared to risk their lives and that they want nothing for themselves. If I am any judge of human nature, Don's face expressed sincerity and determination on the morning that I spoke to him. For practical purposes therefore I would say that we have very little influence on what is essentially a Vietnamese affair. . . ."

Late the next afternoon in Saigon, General Don questioned Conein at length about the timing and details of Lodge's plans to leave the country on October 31 for meetings in Washington. He urged Conein to tell Lodge not to change his plans, because that might tip off Diem that a coup was coming. He said also that he would give the Americans four hours' notice of the action, not forty-eight. Don also told Conein he wanted a store of U.S. cash to distribute to other generals if the coup failed and they were forced to go on the run. The CIA man collected all the money he could find in the embassy, $42,000.

After Conein reported the conversation to Lodge, the ambassador sent a cable that arrived at 8:00 A.M. on the 29th, Washington time: "It would appear that a coup attempt by the Generals' group is imminent; that whether this coup fails or succeeds, the USG must be prepared to accept the fact that we will be blamed, however unjustifiably; and finally, that no positive action by the USG can prevent a coup attempt short of informing Diem and Nhu with all the opprobrium that such an action would entail."

An hour and a half later, another cable from Lodge reached Washington. It reported a conversation with a former assistant minister of defense, Tran Trung Dung, who said General Don and "Big Minh" were the leaders of the plotting generals. Neither had been highly regarded by Americans over the years. Younger men in the U.S. mission called them dressed-up sergeants in the old French colonial army. Ed Lansdale, who knew them both, had offered the White House this assessment in late 1961: "Minh—always complaining, and doesn't take action when he has the opportunity; his plans never seem to be complete. Don—an excellent staff officer who is misplaced in combat command. The Joint General Staff—very good, as playboys."

Tran Trung Dung had told Lodge one more thing: "The generals are planning the complete removal of the Ngo family."

At four o'clock on the afternoon of Tuesday, the 29th, in Washington —five o'clock the next morning, October 30, in Saigon—the President met in the Cabinet Room with his usual Vietnam group. He began by telling them that until further notice, all departments and agencies (State, Defense, the Joint Chiefs, the CIA, and USIA) should send every single Vietnam cable to him. He wanted to see every piece of paper, every word, incoming or outgoing. He was suspending the traditional power of those agencies to communicate with their own people in the field without being monitored from above.

William Colby, who had been CIA station chief in Saigon in 1962, did a map-and-pointer show for the President. He pointed to an equal number of pro-Diem and anti-Diem units close to the Presidential Palace —9,800 on each side, another 18,000 considered politically neutral.

"Each side will ask for our help," said Rusk. "If we support Diem, then we will disrupt the war effort because we will be acting against those generals who are now fighting the war against the Viet Cong. If we support the rebel generals, then we will have to guarantee that they are successful in overthrowing the Diem government."

Kennedy said the troop balance was probably normal, that troops usually joined up when they saw a coup seemed to be succeeding. But Robert Kennedy disagreed. He could not see any difference between the situation now and back in July and August, when these same generals had proved incapable of organizing a coup. Supporting a coup, he said, meant putting Vietnam, or even all of Southeast Asia, in the hands of one man unknown to all of them. "This risks so much," he said. "If it fails, Diem throws us out."

"I know my view is the minority view," Robert Kennedy concluded. But, in fact, Taylor and McCone immediately agreed with him, saying a failed coup would be a disaster for the United States, and a successful one would slow down the war effort as new men learned new jobs.

The President wavered then, taking the argument back to where it had been weeks before, telling Rusk to check with Lodge about the balance of forces. "If Lodge agrees with this point of view," Kennedy said, "then we should instruct him to discourage a coup."

"The burden of proof should be on the coup promoters to show that they can overthrow the Diem government and not create a situation in which there would be a draw," John Kennedy said that evening at another meeting of the same group. Then he echoed Robert Kennedy's doubts: "If we miscalculate, we could lose our entire position in Southeast Asia overnight."

The cable to Lodge, which went out at 7:22 P.M. that night, was written by McGeorge Bundy: "Need urgently your combined assessment with Harkins. . . . We are concerned that our line-up of forces in Saigon indicates approximately equal balance of forces, with substantial possibility serious and prolonged fighting or even defeat. Either of these could be serious or even disastrous for U.S. interests, so that we must have assurance balance of forces clearly favorable."

General Harkins's answer arrived in Washington first, in the early morning hours of Wednesday, October 30, and it became painfully clear that Lodge had not informed him of coup intelligence clacking between the teletype machines of the embassy and the White House:

> I sat with Don and Big Minh for 2 hours during the parade last Saturday. No one mentioned coups. . . . Don is either lying or playing both ends against the middle. What he told me is diametrically opposed to what he told Col. Conein. He told Conein the coup will be before November 2. He told me he was not planning a coup.
>
> The Ambassador and I are currently in touch with each other but whether the communications between us are effective is something else. . . . In my contacts here I have seen no one with the strength of character of Diem, at least in fighting communists. Certainly there are not Generals qualified to take over in my opinion. . . . After all, rightly or wrongly, we have backed Diem for eight long hard years. To me it seems incongruous now to get him down, kick him around, and get rid of him. . . . Leaders of other under-developed countries will take a dim view of our assistance if they too were led to believe the same fate lies in store for them.

Lodge's answer got to the State Department a couple of hours after Harkins's and was delivered to the White House at seven-thirty that morning. He said: "We must, of course, get best possible estimate of chance of coup's success and this estimate must color our thinking, but do not think we have the power to delay or discourage a coup. . . .

"Don has made it clear many times that this is a Vietnamese affair," Lodge continued. "It is theoretically possible for us to turn over the information which has been given to us, in confidence, to Diem and this would undoubtedly stop the coup and would make traitors out of us. General Harkins has read this and does not concur."

Kennedy did not want to concur either. But no one would quite tell him directly, once again, that events he had set in motion were now beyond his control. The President did not like the tone of Lodge's acknowledgment that the White House intended to try to control the action in Saigon. "Thanks for your sagacious instruction," Lodge signed off. "Will carry out to best of my ability."

"He sounds amused," said Robert Kennedy. The brothers were alone in the Oval Office for a few moments. "I told you he was going to be trouble."

"You know what's terrific about you?" John Kennedy snapped back. "You always remember when you're right."

The Kennedys, and the other men forming the unofficial Ex Comm in the White House, considered one cable after another from Saigon, asking one question after another. Bundy signed the cable that was received by Lodge on the morning of October 31 in Saigon.

We do not accept as a basis for U.S. policy that we have no power to delay or discourage a coup. . . .

This paragraph contains our present standing instructions for U.S. posture in the event of a coup:

• U.S. authorities will reject appeals for direct intervention from either side, and U.S.-controlled aircraft and other resources will not be committed between the battle lines or in support of either side, without authorization from Washington.

• But once a coup under responsible leadership has begun, and within these restrictions, it is in the interest of the U.S. Government that it should succeed.

President Kennedy held a news conference that afternoon, October 31. There was one question on Vietnam, coming after a half dozen about the possibility of a United States troop withdrawal from NATO in Western Europe. A reporter asked whether there might be other withdrawals, from South Korea, or a speed-up in the withdrawal of the thousand men who were supposed to leave South Vietnam.

"Well, as you know," Kennedy answered, "when Secretary McNamara and General Taylor came back, they announced that we would expect to withdraw a thousand men from South Viet-Nam before the end of the year, and there has been some reference to that by General Harkins. If we are able to do that, that would be our schedule. I think the first unit or first contingent would be 250 men who are not involved in what might be called front-line operations. It would be our hope to lessen the number of Americans there by one thousand, as the training intensifies and is carried on in South Viet-Nam."

"Mr. President," someone else asked. "Mr. President, just shortly after the Bay of Pigs I asked you how you liked being President, and as I remember you said you liked it better before the event. Now you have had a chance to appraise your job, and why do you like it and why do you want to stay in office four more years?"

"Well, I find the work rewarding. Whether I am going to stay and what my intentions are and all the rest, it seems to me it is still a good many, many months away. But as far as the job of President goes, it is rewarding. And I have given before to this group the definition of happiness of the Greeks, and I will define it again: it is full use of your powers along lines of excellence. I find, therefore, the Presidency provides some happiness."

Eight hours later, at 12:30 P.M., Friday, November 1 in Saigon, which was 11:30 P.M., Thursday, October 31, in Washington, General Big Minh stood up during a luncheon at the Officers' Club of the Joint General Staff of the Army of the Republic of Vietnam, and announced that a coup d'état was under way. At that moment, military policemen marched through the doors, aiming machine guns at the assembled generals and colonels. Minh began extracting pledges of support from both the plotters and the few commanders still loyal to Diem.

Within the hour, troops wearing red neckerchiefs—the traditional coup symbol in Vietnam—surrounded the Defense Ministry, the headquarters of the National Police, Radio Saigon, Tan Son Nhut Airport, and Saigon's PTT, the central post office, telegraph, and telephone building. An airborne battalion attacked the headquarters of Diem's Presidential Guard, a thousand meters from the Presidential Palace. Telephone and telegraph lines were cut or shut down—except for special lines strung the day before, including one between the Officers Club and the United States Embassy.

Just after 1:00 A.M. on the morning of Friday, November 1, in Washington, the telex bells rang in the Situation Room in the White House basement. The watch officer began reading the jumping lines of a cable marked "Flash CRITIC." "Flash" meant "Essential to National Survival." The transmission, from the CIA station in Saigon where it was now two o'clock Friday afternoon, reported that a coup was apparently under way. The officer telephoned McGeorge Bundy and Michael Forrestal. They waited until just after three to awaken the President—there had been false coup alarms regularly since the August 24 telegram—and Kennedy told them to come to his bedroom at 6:00 A.M.

Bundy arrived with a small stack of CIA and military cables from Saigon. The one on top, received from Harkins at 1:44 A.M. Washington time, began: "At 1345 Hours General Don telephoned Stilwell, J-3 and stated in the clear all Generals were assembled with him at JGS HQ and were initiating a coup. Stilwell asked if timing was immediate and was told yes. I notified Ambassador at 1400. He had just received info that Marine unit had seized the PTT—Numerous troop movements reported this morning. All details later. Will keep you advised." *

The story unfolded in CIA cables. The first of the series had been received in the White House Situation Room at 2:34 A.M. It was a report on a telephone call to the U.S. Embassy by Colonel Conein. He had called on the special direct line strung the day before from coup headquarters, the South Vietnam Officers Club, where he had gone with the

---

* 1345 hours on a 24-hour military clock was 1:45 P.M. Saigon time was thirteen hours ahead of Eastern Standard Time: 6:00 P.M. in Saigon was 5:00 A.M. the same day in Washington; at 6:00 P.M. in Washington, it was 7:00 A.M. the next day in Saigon. JSG stands for Joint General Staff; AAA for anti-aircraft artillery. Colonel Le Quang Tung was the commander of the 3,400 Presidential Guards, Special Forces, and Combat Police, trained and paid by the United States and reporting directly to Ngo Dinh Nhu, rather than to the Joint General Staff. The "Chinese town" of Cholon is a section of Saigon.

$42,000 in embassy funds to be distributed among the generals' families if the coup failed.

> Generals attempting contact Palace by telephone but unable to do so. Their proposition as follows: If the President will resign immediately, they will guarantee his safety and the safe departure of the President and Ngo Dinh Nhu. If the President refuses these terms, the Palace will be attacked within the hour by Air Force and Armor.

> Received 3:40 A.M.: "Conein reports from JGS Gens firmly decided there to be no discussion with President. He will either say yes or no. . . . Observed four AD-6 fighter bombers with munitions aboard at approx 10,000 feet over Saigon. . . . JGS Gens have monitored radio broadcast from Palace to First and Second Corps and 21st Division. Can hear fighting from Embassy. Can confirm insurgents not arrested. As of 1535, fire reported Palace vicinity."

> Received 3:55 A.M.: "Conein reports from JGS that Gens have group of nationalistic, pro-Western civilian politicians with them at JGS. . . . Military hopes to turn government to the civilians within two or three days. . . . Now heavy fighting vicinity Embassy. AAA going up. Apparently duel going on between aircraft and ships in river."

> Received 4:11 A.M.: "Conein at JGS reports Big Minh called President on telephone but President allegedly not present and Big Minh spoke to Nhu. Col Tung was forced at gunpoint to announce he a prisoner. Air Force Commander did not speak. Conein believes he has been eliminated. . . . Big Minh stated to Nhu that if the President and Nhu did not resign, turn themselves over to the coup forces within five minutes, the Palace would sustain a massive airborne bombardment. At this, Gen Minh hung up . . . at 1715 Gen Minh once more called Diem and Diem hung up. . . ."

The last cable Bundy had brought to the President's bedroom was the text of a telephone call at four-thirty in the afternoon in Saigon from President Diem to Ambassador Henry Cabot Lodge at the U.S. Embassy:

> *Diem:* Some units have made a rebellion and I want to know: What is the attitude of U.S.?
> *Lodge:* I do not feel well enough informed to be able to tell you. I have heard the shooting, but am not acquainted with all the facts. Also it is 4:30 am in Washington and US Government cannot possibly have a view.
> *Diem:* But you must have some general ideas. After all, I am a Chief of

State. I have tried to do my duty. I want to do now what duty and good sense require. I believe in duty above all.

Lodge: You have certainly done your duty. As I told you only this morning, I admire your courage and your great contributions to your country. No one can take away from you the credit for all you have done. Now I am worried about your personal safety. I have a report that those in charge of the current activity offer you and your brother safe conduct out of the country if you resign. Had you heard this?

Diem: No. (And then after a pause) You have my telephone number.

Lodge: Yes. If I can do anything for your physical safety, please call me.

Diem: I am trying to re-establish order.

Diem had been lying when he said no to Lodge. Big Minh and Diem had been talking and hanging up on each other in anger. Diem paused during the call when Lodge's answers made it clear to him that the Americans were in touch with the plotters. Less than two hours later, Ambassador Lodge sent a cable received in Washington at 7:55 A.M.: "Following message is being passed to General 'Big Minh': 'Generals will be received at Embassy after coup is over.' (FYI: I expect to receive them myself.)"

It was more than two hours after that, when he came downstairs to the Cabinet Room at 10:00 A.M. Washington time, that Kennedy saw a cable from Lodge reporting on a personal meeting he had that morning with Diem. The meeting had ended only thirty minutes before the coup began. The ambassador had accompanied Admiral Harry Felt, the commander of the United States forces in the Pacific, to the Presidential Palace for a farewell visit after a quick tour of U.S. facilities in Saigon. "I know there is going to be a coup, but I don't know who is going to do it," Diem had told Lodge and Felt. The ambassador had replied that he thought Diem really had little to worry about. This cable had been held up both in Saigon and at the State Department because it had a lower priority rating than the emergency FLASH cables.

Received at White House 9:37 A.M.: "The Palace notified me early Friday morning that President Diem wanted to see me alone for fifteen minutes after the Felt interview. As soon as Admiral Felt had left the room, I said that I could assure Diem that these rumors of [my] assassination had not in any way affected my feeling of admiration and personal friendship for him or for Vietnam. I had long admired his courage before coming to Saigon and since getting to know him, I formed sentiments of friendship for him. . . . When I got up to go, he said: "Please tell President Kennedy that I am a good and a frank ally, that I would rather be frank and settle questions now than talk about them after we have lost everything. (This looked like a reference to a possible coup.) Tell President Kennedy that I take all his suggestions very seriously and wish to carry them out but it is a question of timing."

Comment: I feel that this is another step in the dialogue. . . . If U.S. wants to make a package deal, I would think we were in a position to do it. . . . In effect he said: "Tell me what you want and we'll do it."

Rusk, McNamara, Bundy, McCone, and Robert Kennedy were in the Cabinet Room. It was almost a missile crisis reunion. It had been nearly nine hours since the shooting began in South Vietnam, and the Cabinet Room had been turned into a war room. Detailed maps of Saigon and troop placements in and near the city were arranged around the big table.

The cables from Washington to Saigon began moving within an hour that Friday morning, All Saints' Day, a Catholic holy day. At 10:50 A.M., as he was leaving to go to mass at Holy Trinity Church in Georgetown, Kennedy told Rusk to send a cable to Lodge, suggesting that he reconsider immediate U.S. recognition of the coup government. "If coup succeeds, recognition problem will be urgent. Of course you would expect to deal in friendly and cooperative fashion with effective authorities from the outset but timing of our announcement might be delayed for brief period . . . recognition by United States in advance of other governments would falsely brand their action as American-inspired and manipulated. . . . We assume Generals leading coup will not call on you in large group, thus giving false impression they were reporting to headquarters."

The cables to Saigon focused not on events but on preparing an explanation of those events. The first official U.S. response to Associated Press reports of the coup was a single sentence. It was approved by the President and given to reporters by a State Department spokesman. "I can categorically state that the U.S. Government was not involved in any way."

The first instruction to Lodge, approved by the President, was sent out Saturday at just after noon, Washington time: "If coup succeeds, acceptance and understanding of its purpose here will be greatly increased if Generals and their civilian associates continue to develop strongly and publicly the conclusion reported in one of their broadcasts that Nhu was dickering with Communists to betray anti-Communist cause. High value of this argument should be emphasized to them at earliest opportunity."

At 6:05 P.M. Friday evening, the White House received word from Lodge that Diem had telephoned the generals at the Officers Club at

6:20 A.M. in Saigon, an hour earlier. He had offered to surrender, asking only safe passage out of Vietnam for himself and his brother, Nhu. Lodge did not know where the Diem call had come from, because the brothers had escaped from the palace during the night and disappeared into the city. "General Minh has accepted this," Lodge reported. But only two minutes later, the CIA sent a Flash CRITIC saying there were indications that Diem and Nhu had been captured somewhere outside the palace grounds and were in the custody of the generals.

An hour and a half after that, at 8:47 P.M. in Washington, Kennedy approved another cable to Lodge, focusing once more not on what to do, but on what to say:

> At 9:15 Washington time tomorrow morning [Saturday, November 2], President will review position and urgently ask your recommendations for this meeting. Our preliminary thinking is that if current trends are continued we should move promptly toward support and recognition, but this move will require careful justification in light of danger of misleading comparisons in Latin America.
>
> We expect to background press this evening that this is not a coup in the sense that it is merely the product of a few scheming officers, but that day's events plainly show that Diem has yielded to virtually unanimous determination of military and civilian leadership of his country. In the context of civil war, this amounts to a national decision.

Lodge answered within two hours, with a bit of self-congratulation: "Agree we should move promptly to support and recognize. Believe the very great popularity of this coup should be stressed. Every Vietnamese has a grin on his face today. When I drove to the office with a very small US flag flying, there were bursts of applause from the sidewalk, people shaking hands and waving. The tanks which were standing at the street corners were being covered with garlands of flowers and the Army was evidently immensely popular with the people."

The Flash bells in the White House rang next at just about thirty minutes past midnight on Sunday, November 2. A CIA Flash CRITIC read: "Best estimate this time is that Diem and Nhu dead. Radio announcement reports they committed suicide by poison. Bodies reported to be in JGS in armored personnel carrier or inside building. Feel with reasonable certainty that they are dead and continuing to check by what means and where now located."

The President was already in bed upstairs, and Bundy decided that there was no point in waking him up until there was verification of Diem's death. His assistant, Mike Forrestal, and Averell Harriman approved a cable to Lodge sent out at 2:55 A.M.: "News of Diem, Nhu suicides shocking here and presumably in rest of world. Generals must preserve to extent possible good reputation their actions have thus far created. Therefore important to establish publicly beyond question that deaths actually suicide if this true and it not by violence."

At 8:00 P.M., November 2, Saigon time, 7:00 A.M. in Washington, Lodge sent this cable:

> Very reliable source gives following story about death of Diem and Nhu:
> They left the Palace on Friday evening accompanied by Chinese businessman who was organizer of the Republican Youth in the Chinese town of Cholon. . . . This Chinese took Diem and Nhu to a clubhouse which he owned where they arrived at about nine o'clock. After spending the night at the clubhouse they, at eight o'clock in the morning went to church and about 10 minutes after that they were picked up by the Army and were forced to enter an Army vehicle into which they were locked. This source does not know what happened after that—whether they are alive or murdered or suicides.

That cable reached the White House shortly after 9:00 A.M. Saturday, November 2, just as the President arrived downstairs to begin the day's crisis meeting. Rusk, McNamara, McCone, Robert Kennedy, Taylor, and Harriman were there. The President nodded to them as he sat down. Mike Forrestal walked in holding Lodge's cable. He handed it to the President, who looked at it, stood up, and rushed from the room without a word, looking pale and shaken.

The others looked at each other. None of them had ever seen anything like it. Under his breath, Taylor said, "What did he expect?"

Diem and Nhu had been killed after Diem had telephoned his surrender to Big Minh. The general had sent troops to pick up the brothers at Don Thanh Church in Cholon. Soldiers had loaded them into the back of a U.S. M-113 armored personnel carrier, driven a short distance, and shot both in the back of the head. The bodies were mutilated with bayonets. The Catholic ascetic who Kennedy had helped project as an anti-Communist saint was buried in an unmarked grave in a cemetery next to the house of the American ambassador.

The generals in Saigon issued a statement saying the deaths were suicides. Within less than twenty-four hours, the Saigon CIA station cabled Washington: "Young Vietnamese Saigon businessman . . . casual source exhibited set of snapshots morning 3 Nov which showed Ngo Dinh Diem and Ngo Dinh Nhu covered with blood, apparently bullet-riddled, lying dead on floor of armored vehicle with hands tied behind them. Photos appear authentic. Source states pictures taken approx 1000 hours 2 Nov. Pictures now being offered for sale to international press in Saigon."

The generals then changed the listed cause of death from "suicide" to "accidental suicide." Part of Kennedy's apparent shock was his disbelief that Diem, a devout Catholic, would kill himself. Then he learned that the Americans probably could have saved the brothers. The generals had asked the CIA to provide Diem and Nhu safe passage out of the country and into exile. David Smith, the acting station chief, told Conein to tell Minh it would take twenty-four hours to get a suitable plane from Guam to Tan Son Nhut Airport. "We can't hold them that long," Big Minh told Conein. It sounded like a death sentence.

Pierre Salinger read a statement expressing official U.S. regrets, then fended off reporters' questions, earning a memo from Bundy: "Pierre! Champion! Excellent prose. No surprise. A communique should say nothing in a way as to feed the press without deceiving them."

Rusk cabled United States missions around the world with the official version of the coup:

> All missions, especially in Western Hemisphere, should be prepared to give full explanation this decision and sharp distinction between its basis and USG opposition to military coups against democratic regimes elsewhere. Elements of difference are these:
> (1) Diem regime had become instrument of complete personal authority of one family.
> (2) Diem regime was deeply opposed not merely by mass of people but increasingly by its own senior officials, civilian and military.
> (3) Regime was increasingly incapable of giving effective direction to national effort against Communist subversion and aggression.

The most important editorial voice in the United States, *The New York Times,* saw nothing to criticize. It said on November 2: "The only surprising thing about the military revolt in Saigon is that it did not come sooner. The inefficiency, corruption, inflexibility and growing unpopularity of the Diem-Nhu regime has been increasingly evident for the last two years. . . ."

Late on Saturday in Washington, the White House cabled Lodge, giving him the authority to tell the new government that suspended U.S. aid payments would be paid immediately, and stating: "Deaths of Diem and Nhu, whatever their failings, has caused shock here and there is danger that standing and reputation of incoming government may be significantly damaged if conviction spreads of their assassination at direction of one or more senior members of incoming regime. . . . Across the months of repression and increasing ineffectiveness, American people and government remember great services to freedom rendered by Diem over many years."

At six o'clock that Saturday evening, Kennedy flew by helicopter to meet his wife and children in their new horse-country house on Rattlesnake Mountain. At dinner there, a friend, Mary Gimbel, said of Diem and Nhu: "They were just tyrants."

"No," the President said. "They were in a difficult position. They did the best they could for their country."

There was, in fact, a certain euphoria throughout the country. The government and the press were together again, united in the handsome American conviction that ugliness and pessimism in Vietnam had been eliminated with the fall of Diem. The Americans, for all practical purposes, had taken over the country. The Vietnamese generals smiled for the cameras, but they were anxious and waiting for money and direction from Washington, the new capital of South Vietnam. They awaited the orders Diem had rejected, ready to get down to the business of winning the war!

There were notable exceptions—a few nervous senators like Fulbright and Mansfield, and angry conservative newspapers such as the *Chicago Tribune*. Columnist Frank Conniff of Hearst accused Kennedy of "Murder most foul." But the tone was set, rather fittingly, by the big voices, harmonious again, of the White House and *The New York Times*. "The loss of South Vietnam to the Communists would raise doubts around the globe about the value of U.S. commitments to defend nations against Communist pressure," said the *Times* editorially. "Fortunately, the new Vietnamese rulers are dedicated anti-Communists who reject any idea of neutralism."

"Saigon Coup Gives Americans Hope" was the headline of David Halberstam's analysis in *The New York Times* of November 4. "Americans are gratified by a sense of joy that they find in Saigon . . . hope that the repressive political climate that weighed heavily on the population and on the army has been lifted for good . . . hope that the new government will be able to rally the people and turn back the communist threat."

On Wednesday, November 6, Ambassador Lodge sent the last of his private cables to President Kennedy:

> Eyes only. Now that the revolution has occurred, I assume you will not want my weekly reports. . . .
> I believe prospects of victory are much improved, provided the generals

stay united. . . . There is no doubt that the coup was a Vietnamese and a popular affair, which we could neither manage nor stop after it got started and which we could only have influenced with great difficulty. But it is equally certain that the ground in which the coup seed grew into a robust plant was prepared by us and that the coup would not have happened as it did without our preparation. . . . People cheer the American flag; they are free to express their loathing of the "family"; and the pagodas are full of smiling people. The whole trend of the new crowd is to have warm and cordial relations with the American people and government. . . . Certainly officers and soldiers who can pull off an operation like this should be able to do very well on the battlefield if their hearts are as much in it. General Harkins concurs.

All this may be a useful lesson in the use of US power for those who face similar situation in other places in the future. The President, the State Department, the military, the AID, the USIS, and the CIA deserve credit for this result. Without united action by the US Government, it would not have been possible. . . . My thanks to you and all those associated with you for comprehending and imaginative guidance and support.

The President replied that night:

Eyes only for Ambassador Lodge from the President.
Your own leadership in pulling together and directing the whole American operation in South Vietnam in recent months has been of the greatest importance, and you should know that this achievement is recognized here throughout the Government. Your own actions made it clear that we wanted improvements, and when these were not forthcoming from the Diem Government, we necessarily faced and accepted the possibility that our position might encourage a change of government. We thus have a responsibility to help this new government to be effective in every way that we can.
With renewed appreciation for a fine job.
John F. Kennedy.

Chapter 56

On November 8, 1963, the United States formally recognized the new Government of South Vietnam, with General Duong Van Minh as president and former Vice President Nguyen Ngoc Tho as premier. The national assembly had been dissolved and the Constitution suspended. Ambassador Lodge called on the new foreign minister, Pham Dang Lam, that day. Lam told him that he had accepted the position only on the understanding that he could count on American help. Lodge assured him the Americans would be there when the new government needed them, and offered a first suggestion which he reported back to Washington that day: "A warm approach to the public . . . I thought that if ['Big' Minh] would arrange to visit some of the pagodas, if only for twenty minutes and shake hands and sign some autographs, it would fill a need all people feel, regardless of race or geography, of being courted by political leaders."

Lodge and Lam talked about Cambodia and its touchy young ruler, Prince Norodom Sihanouk. The prince, whose country had already received more than $350 million in U.S. aid from the Kennedy administration, was apparently concerned that the Americans could do to him what he believed they had done to Diem—weaken him by cutting off aid, and then kill him. Sihanouk broke off discussion of an alliance between his country and South Vietnam after Diem's assassination, and now he was talking about rejecting U.S. aid and accepting help from China.

In Washington on November 11, Veterans Day, President Kennedy went to Arlington National Cemetery for ceremonies at the Tomb of the Unknowns. John Junior stole the show, marching along backwards in front of his father and the honor guard. ". . . The President thought the whole incident was hilarious," *Time* magazine reported primly, saying, "Some folks thought a good, firm nanny might well be employed to keep a 2½-year-old out of solemn ceremonies." After a twenty-one-gun salute to the war dead, Kennedy walked among the graves of U.S. servicemen on a hill that overlooked the Potomac River across to Washington. "This is one of the really beautiful places on earth," he told McNamara. "I think, maybe, someday this is where I'd like to be. . . ." That night, though, he told Charlie Bartlett that he thought he would be buried in Boston, because that was where his library would be—if there were one. "I'm not going to have a library if I only have one term," he said. "Nobody will give a damn."

Death and defeat stayed on John Kennedy's mind for a time after the assassination of Diem. But he cheered up, as he usually did, when Red Fay was around. Fay asked what he thought he might do after he was President. He would be fifty-one years old after a second term.

"We could go back to the South Pacific and revisit those waters where we personally turned the tide of war," Kennedy said. "Then drift through the Greek islands, with our wives administering to our every wish."

"Come on."

"I'd run for the Senate."

"Isn't it quite a come-down from being the President of the United States?"

"John Quincy Adams served in the House after being President. When a man comes from the White House to the Congress, he could give a voice of judgment and authority. . . ."

"Of course, when Bobby or Teddy becomes President, then I'd probably be most useful as Secretary of State. . . . I'm just not quite sure that I would ever get adjusted to addressing Bobby or Teddy as 'Mr. President.' Let's not dwell too long on the prospect of taking orders from Lovable Bob."

First, though, Kennedy still had to get that second term, and he was starting to concentrate on 1964. He went to New York for the biennial convention of the AFL-CIO, big labor's last national meeting before the next election, and decided abruptly not to travel by motorcade into Manhattan. His limousine stopped for ten traffic lights on the way in from the airport. At the last one, a woman ran into the street for a photo, popping a flashbulb at the rear window inches from Kennedy's face. "Oh, my God," exclaimed the officer in charge of the New York Police security detail. "She could have been an assassin."

On November 13, Kennedy convened the first planning meeting for his reelection campaign. Robert Kennedy, Sorensen, O'Donnell, O'Brien, and Democratic National Committee chairman John Bailey were there, along with Richard Scammon, the director of the Bureau of the Census, and the new campaign manager, the President's brother-in-law, Stephen Smith, who had taken over the management of Kennedy money after Joseph Kennedy's stroke.

Kennedy's approval rating in Gallup polls had dropped from 76 percent to 59 percent during 1963, and he recited those numbers to dampen a certain overconfidence in the White House. That decline, Scammon said, was attributable almost entirely to civil rights. The President was losing the support of southerners who thought he was moving too fast on behalf of Negroes. One of those Southern Democrats, Governor Wallace of Alabama, had already announced he would oppose Kennedy in Democratic primaries in both the South and the North, beginning in Ohio. He was also losing the support of some Northern liberals who thought he was moving too slowly. John Roche, who succeeded Arthur Schlesinger as the president of Americans for Democratic Action, had attacked Kennedy in the current issue of *ADA World,* calling him a technocratic liberal: "JFK is totally dedicated to managerial politics . . . the end point of which is to beautify cities by replacing Negroes with trees. . . . The choice is between efficiency and justice . . . examples of that are to desegregate the armed forces, not because it is inefficient to have a segregated army but because it is wrong. The same is true with education. Good education is right, not just a device to beat the Soviets to the moon."

But the latest horse-race polls showed Kennedy with a percentage lead of 55 to 39 over the current favorite to win the Republican nomination, Senator Barry Goldwater. "This could be fun, if it's Barry," said Kennedy at the beginning of the meeting. He liked Goldwater. He also thought he was unelectable, too conservative for most Americans. "Don't waste any chance to praise Barry. Build him up a little," he said. "Don't mention the others." Then Robert Kennedy added: "Goldwater is just not very smart and he will destroy himself." But not too soon, they all hoped.

The "others" the President didn't want them to mention were Nelson Rockefeller and the new Republican governor of Michigan, George Romney. "We have to watch Romney," Robert Kennedy said, pointing out that he was a devout Mormon and had a fine business reputation earned as president of American Motors. "People buy that God and country stuff," the President said. As for Rockefeller, Kennedy had con-cluded that, beyond the political problems of a messy divorce and a new wife, the New York governor just did not have the guts to sustain a presidential run.

"Romney could be tough," the President said. "You have to be a little suspicious of somebody as good as Romney. No vices whatsoever, no smoking and no drinking. Imagine someone we know going off for twenty-four or forty-eight hours to fast and meditate, awaiting a mes-sage from the Lord whether to run or not to run.

"Give me Barry," he concluded with a laugh. "I won't even have to leave the Oval Office."

"Peace and prosperity" was the 1964 theme, Kennedy told them. He wanted to emphasize prosperity by attacking poverty. In fact, that morning he had announced a "crash program" to bring food and public works to eastern Kentucky, which he called "the most severely dis-tressed area in the country." He passed around the article from *The New York Times* that had prompted the program. "Kentucky Miners: A Grim Winter," published on October 18, told of the lives of miners put out of work by new automated mining equipment being used in the Cumberland Mountains of eastern Kentucky. "The welfare system has eroded the self-respect of the mountain people," wrote Homer Bigart, describing the miners and their families as whipped and dispirited.

It was West Virginia all over again for Kennedy. He wanted to be seen as a man of compassion in 1964. He was persuaded that his pro-grams were popular, but that he himself had been unable to make any emotional connection with the voters. He also knew enough now to compare the impoverished mountaineers and the poor Negroes in cities such as New York, Chicago, and Philadelphia. He wanted to make the important political point that most poor people in America were white. "There's a tremendous problem, I want people to see it," he told Walter Heller, who was a principal advocate of an anti-poverty program. He told Kenny O'Donnell, and Franklin Roosevelt, Jr., in the Commerce Department, that he wanted visits scheduled to create photo opportuni-ties in poor city neighborhoods with Negroes and with the white miners in the mountains.

"I wouldn't do that, Mr. President," said Richard Scammon, who was sitting with a mound of census documents.

"Why not?"

"You can't get a single vote more by doing anything for poor people. Those who vote are already for you," he said. "I was thinking of photo-graphs with policemen in the cities. Then you should go to the new shopping centers on the highways. The voters you need, your people, men with lunch pails, are moving out to the suburbs."

Kennedy was immediately hooked. This was what he prized most, information with a purpose. For two hours, he concentrated on Scammon's numbers, the results of the 1960 census and the demographics of the 1964 election. Some of it he already knew. The groups that supported him most strongly were Negroes, Poles, and Jews. "The Polish are fantastic, the best Democrats," the President said. "They never write you a letter. They never complain. They just vote solidly." The groups he was weakest with were farmers, retired people, and businessmen. As Scammon talked of a new American mobility, rural Southern Negroes coming to Northern cities and Catholic Democrats moving out to become homeowners, and worried about property taxes and storm sewers, Kennedy closed in on one question: If a Democrat started making more money and moved to the suburbs, at what level did he start to vote Republican?

"It might be less than $10,000 a year," Scammon said. "I'll try to find out."

"It's going to be a new kind of politics," Kennedy said.

"It's a new kind of country," said Scammon.

The President said he would be making two political swings in the next ten days, the first to Florida, the second to Texas. He was going to San Antonio, Houston, Fort Worth, and Dallas, the result of his confrontation with Governor Connally in El Paso in June. The goal was money more than votes, though he thought the key to winning easily in 1964 was to carry Texas and Florida to make up for any losses in other Southern states. "Massachusetts has given us about two and a half million dollars and New York has been good to us, too," he told the group. "But when are we going to get some money out of those rich people in Texas?"

"This has been very helpful," Kennedy said, as he ended the session. It was almost seven o'clock, the meeting had gone on for more than three hours. "We'll get together again when I come back from Texas."

He held a news conference, the sixty-fourth of his administration, the next morning, and the questions were almost all negative: "Mr. President, how menacing do you regard the Cambodian threat to reject our foreign aid? Can that country be slipping into the Communist orbit?" . . . "Mr. President, it now seems unlikely that you will get either your tax bill or your civil rights bill in this session of Congress. Does that disturb you?" . . . "Mr. President, there have been published reports that General Harkins may have lost his usefulness in Vietnam because of his identification with the Diem regime" . . . "Mr. President, appropriations bills are still hung up in Congress, the first time in history this late. What has happened on Capitol Hill?"

He fended them off in good humor. He said he had high hopes for the new government in Vietnam and still hoped to bring home several hundred U.S. troops before year's end. Of his congressional problems, he said: "They are all interrelated. I think there is some delay because of civil rights. . . . However dark it looks now, I think that 'Westward, look, the land is bright,' and I think that by next summer it may be. . . . Not this year, but next year. . . . This is going to be an eighteen-month delivery!"

"He has been lucky in his competition," said James Reston in *The New York Times* the next day, November 15. His record, good or bad, was not going to be the issue if Goldwater was the Republican nominee, as seemed more and more likely. Goldwater's words would be the issue. The senator from Arizona was too conservative for most voters. "A choice not an echo" was what Goldwater said he was offering, but more often than not the choice seemed to be a confrontation—with the Russians, with Negroes, with anyone who offended his vision of American righteousness.

"The Outlook for Kennedy: Victory with Tears" was the headline over Reston's column.

> A reporter who asks about him in unfamiliar and varied communities comes away with the distinct impression that the American people are going to reelect him, probably by a wide margin, but don't quite believe in him. . . .
>
> A great many people respond to questions about the President with surprise and even astonishment, as if their opinions had nothing to do with Kennedy. . . . Vietnam and Berlin are discussed as "Kennedy's problems," and one gets the impression that he can do almost anything with them he likes (provided he doesn't get into a big war), but new tax levies for schools are a matter of primary interest and concern. . . . He is admired, but he has not made the people feel as he feels, or lifted them beyond their private purposes to see the larger public purposes he has in mind.

That day in Congress, as if confirming his philosophizing in his news conference, Kennedy was just clobbered. The foreign aid bill finally got through the Senate, but in tatters. By a 12-to-2 vote, the Senate Finance Committee rejected speeded-up hearings on his tax-cut bill. And the House Judiciary Committee announced that action on the civil rights bill could not be completed in 1963.

Kennedy went to Palm Beach for the weekend; then on Monday, November 18, he began testing Florida's political waters with Senator George Smathers at his side. They argued some, with Kennedy complaining about Smathers's regular votes against administration bills.

"Goddamnit, George," Kennedy said, "you're just knocking my jock off on civil rights. Can't you take it a little easy?" The senator brought up newspaper stories speculating that Kennedy was considering dropping Lyndon Johnson as his running mate. "George, you have *some* intelligence, I presume," Kennedy said sarcastically. "Can you see me now in a terrible fight with Lyndon Johnson, which means I'll blow the South? You know, I love this job, I love every second of it. . . . Smathers, you just haven't got any sense, and if Lyndon thinks that, he ought to think about it. I don't want to get licked. I really don't care whether Lyndon gets licked, but I don't want to get licked and he's going to be my Vice President because he helps me!"

His first speech was in Tampa before the Florida Chamber of Commerce. Afterwards, he was asked about Cuba and about civil rights, and he answered carefully, starting to draft the answers that would carry him through 1964.

"There is a good deal of unfinished business in Cuba," Kennedy said. "We have not been successful in removing Mr. Castro. He still remains a major danger to the United States." But, he went on, the United States was successfully isolating the country. Cuba's trade with the United States and its allies was down 80 percent, the gross national product was down 25 percent since Castro took power. "As a symbol of revolt in this hemisphere, he has faded badly."

"Why are you pushing civil rights so vigorously?" he was asked next.

"I know this program has not gotten great support in Florida," he responded, then talked to them of his burden. "I think you gentlemen should recognize the responsibility of the President of the United States. That responsibility is different from what your responsibility may be. In this country I carry out, execute, the laws. . . . This is a matter that is going to be with us long after I have disappeared from the scene. No country has ever faced a more difficult problem than attempting to bring ten percent of the population of a different color, educate them, give them a chance for a fair life. . . . If we are going to have domestic tranquillity, if we are going to see that our citizens are treated as I would like to be treated, and as you would like to be treated. . . . That is my objective and I think that is the objective of the United States."

Back in Washington on Tuesday, November 19, the President was concerned with both Cuba and Vietnam. He met with Jean Daniel, the editor of the French socialist magazine, *L'Observateur,* a friend of Ben Bradlee's who expected to see Fidel Castro the next day in Havana. The Frenchman passed along the message that Castro had agreed to see an American official if the United States was interested in normalizing relations. Kennedy said he could not take a chance that the press might learn of a secret U.S. envoy, but he told Daniel to tell Castro that the President himself was interested in hearing what he had in mind. Two days later in Florida, Kennedy had sent a public signal, saying: "Cuba [has become] a weapon in an effort dictated by external powers to subvert other American powers. This and this alone divides us. As long as this is true, nothing is possible. Without it, everything is possible." But, at the same time, the CIA was still recruiting assassins. In fact, a ballpoint pen with a poisoned needle designed to kill Castro was scheduled to be delivered to a potential assassin on November 22 by Desmond FitzGerald, who had replaced William Harvey as director of Task Force W, the CIA unit charged with overthrowing the Castro government.

Concerning Vietnam, the President wanted to formalize post-coup U.S. policy. The details were the subject of a nine-hour conference between Rusk, McNamara, and Taylor with Lodge and Harkins on Wednesday, November 20, in Honolulu. The notes on that meeting were cabled to McGeorge Bundy, who drafted a National Security Action Memo from them. The national security adviser planned to give it to Kennedy on Sunday, the 24th, before a meeting with Lodge.

Bundy's draft began: "It remains the central object of the United States in South Vietnam to assist the people and Government of that country to win their contest against the externally directed and supported Communist conspiracy. The test of all U.S. decisions and actions in this area should be the effectiveness of their contribution to this purpose."

The particulars included both a commitment that military and economic aid would be higher than to the Diem government, and that the United States planned to stick with its intentions of withdrawing some troops before the end of the year. A secret attachment outlined plans for covert action against North Vietnam, with schemes to preserve plausible deniability. And, for the first time, the NSAM included specific authority for military operations up to thirty miles inside Laos and a statement that Cambodia was now of "first importance" to the United States.

Before he left for Texas on Thursday, Kennedy called in Mike Forrestal to discuss Prince Sihanouk's announcement the day before that he had decided to reject all U.S. aid. "You go out there and tell Sihanouk that this terrible thing has happened in Saigon," he said. "But that we still think that he is the best solution for his country.

"Wait a minute," the President said, as Forrestal got up to leave. "When you get back, after the first of the year, I want you to organize an in-depth study of every possible option we've got in Vietnam, including how to get out of there. We have to review this whole thing from the bottom to the top."

"What did he mean?" Roger Hilsman asked Forrestal later.

"It was devil's advocate stuff," Forrestal answered.

The President flew to Texas on Thursday, November 21, with his wife, who was making her first political trip since the election campaign in 1960. He dedicated the Aerospace Medical Center in San Antonio, before going to Houston for a testimonial dinner for Representative Albert Thomas. Then he went on to Fort Worth, to spend the night at the Texas Hotel in Suite 850, decorated with a Monet, a Picasso, and a Van Gogh taken from local museums for this one night.

On Friday morning, November 22, Kennedy was awakened by a tapping on the door of the master bedroom by his valet George Thomas. "It's raining, Mr. President," Thomas said. Looking out the window, Kennedy was surprised by the size of the crowd already gathering eight stories below. He crossed over to his wife's room to get a better look. "Isn't that terrific?" he asked her. He had been using the word again and again. At each stop, the crowd was larger and more enthusiastic than expected. But the headline on the front page of the *Dallas Morning News* was not so terrific: "PRESIDENT'S VISIT SEEN WIDENING STATE DEMOCRATIC SPLIT." He called in Kenny O'Donnell and told him his job that day was to make sure that Vice President Johnson and Senator Ralph Yarborough, political adversaries for decades, rode in the same car. "I don't care if you have to throw Yarborough into the car with Lyndon, get him in there." Kennedy wanted to look like the leader of a unified Democratic Party, particularly in Texas where he already had enough troubles. The Belden Poll showed that his approval rate in the state was just 50 percent, down from 76 percent in 1962. The *News* was also carrying a full-page advertisement on page fourteen, paid for by H. L. Hunt and other right-wing businessmen, asking the President twelve loaded questions, including: "Why did you host, salute and entertain Tito—Moscow's Trojan Horse . . . ?" and "Why has the Foreign Policy of the United States degenerated to the point that the CIA is arranging coups and having staunch Anti-Communist Allies of the U.S. bloodily exterminated?"

"We're heading into nut country today," Kennedy said when he saw the ad. But the reception certainly seemed friendly when he looked out the window again at the platform from which he would be speaking in a few minutes. "Look at that platform," he said to O'Donnell. "With all these buildings around it, the Secret Service couldn't stop someone who really wanted to get you."

Going downstairs, he saw his driver, Muggsy O'Leary, and told him: "Mary Gallagher wasn't here last night to help Jackie. Mary hasn't any business in motorcades. She's supposed to reach hotels before we do, and so far she's batting zero. Get her on the ball."

"Where's Jackie?" someone yelled as the President began speaking.

He turned and pointed up to the eighth floor. "Mrs. Kennedy is organizing herself," he said. "It takes longer, but of course, she looks better than we do when she does it." He talked briefly about defense, particularly the bombers and other weapons systems manufactured in Fort Worth. He said that in the next month the United States would launch the largest rocket ever built, finally getting ahead of the Soviet Union in sheer lifting power.

"That strength," he concluded, "depends upon the willingness of the citizens of the United States to assume the burdens of leadership. I know one place that they are, here, in this rain, in Fort Worth. . . . We are going forward.

"Thank you."

The White House transcripts of what the President said each day continued with this note:

"After the breakfast at the Texas Hotel in Fort Worth the President flew to Love Field in Dallas. There he acknowledged greeters for a brief period and then entered an open car. The motorcade traveled down a 10-mile route through downtown Dallas on its way to the Trade Mart, where the President planned to speak at a luncheon. At approximately 12:30 (CST) he was struck by two bullets fired by an assassin.

"The President was declared dead at 1 P.M. at the Parkland Hospital in Dallas."

Source Notes

The first citation of a work gives the author, full title, and place and date of publication of the edition used for page references. Primary sources are cited wherever possible. Major works are listed in the bibliographic essay that follows.

Unless noted below, references in the text to President Kennedy's schedule are from his daily appointments log, available at the Kennedy Library, and all references to Gallup polls are from George H. Gallup, ed., *The Gallup Poll: Public Opinion 1935–1971* (New York: Random House, 1972), Vol. 3.

ABBREVIATIONS

The following abbreviations are used throughout the notes:

BU	Mugar Manuscript Library, Boston University (Boston, MA)
CC	*Alleged Assassination Plots Involving Foreign Leaders: An Interim Report* (Washington, DC: 94th Congress, 1st Session, Report No. 94-465, November 1975) (report of the Church Committee)
CMC	Laurence Chang and Peter Kornbluh, eds., *The Cuban Missile Crisis, 1962: A National Security Archive Documents Reader* (New York: New Press, 1992)
conv	conversation (with author unless specified)
CSIA	Center for Science and International Affairs, Harvard University (Cambridge, MA)
CU	Columbia University Oral History Research Collection (New York, NY)
DDEL	Dwight D. Eisenhower Library (Abilene, KS)
DDRS	Declassified Documents Reference System (Carrollton Press, Washington, DC)
FBI	Federal Bureau of Investigation (Washington, DC)

FDRL   Franklin D. Roosevelt Library (Hyde Park, NY)

FOIA   Freedom of Information Act

FRUS   *Foreign Relations of the United States 1961–1963: Vietnam,* 4 vols. (Washington, DC: Government Printing Office, 1988–90)

Howard   Civil Rights Documentation Project, Moorland-Spingarn Research Center, Howard University (Washington, DC)

int   interview (by author unless specified)

JFKL   John F. Kennedy Library (Boston, MA)

JFKPP   *Public Papers of the Presidents: John F. Kennedy, 1961–1963,* 3 vols. (Washington, DC: Government Printing Office, 1962–64)

LBJL   Lyndon B. Johnson Library (Austin, TX)

LC   Library of Congress (Washington, DC)

memcon   memorandum of conversation

NA   National Archives (Washington, DC)

NSA   National Security Archive (Washington, DC)

NSAM   National Security Action Memorandum

NSF   National Security Files

NW   *Newsweek*

NYT   *New York Times*

OH   Oral History

POF   President's Office Files

PP II   *The Pentagon Papers,* Senator Gravel edition, Vol. 2 (Boston: Beacon Press, 1971)

telecon   memorandum of telephone conversation

Time arch   Archives of *Time* magazine

USN&WR   *U.S. News & World Report*

USVNR   *United States-Vietnam Relations, 1945–67* (Washington, DC: Government Printing Office, 1971) (Defense Department edition of the Pentagon Papers)

VDDHD   *Vietnam: The Definitive Documentation of Human Decisions* (Stanfordville, NY: Coleman, 1979)

WHCSF   White House Central Subject Files

WP   *Washington Post*

INTERVIEWS

Hundreds of interviews went into the assembly of this book, with the persons named below contributing the most significant information. Talks that were less formal than standard interviews are listed as conversations. All discussions were held by the author, except where noted.

Herbert Alexander; Susan Mary Alsop; George Bailey (conversation); George Ball; Charles Bartlett; Berl Bernhard; Richard Bissell; Georgi Bolshakov (conversation); Ben Bradlee; Jerry Bruno (conversation); McGeorge Bundy; Fyodor Burlatsky (conversation); James MacGregor Burns (conversation); Elizabeth Carpenter; Abram Chayes; Clark Clifford; William Colby; Norman Cousins; Victor de Grazia (conversation); C. Douglas

Dillon; Anatoly Dobrynin (conversation); Angier Biddle Duke; Fred Dutton; Myer Feldman; Betty Friedan; J. William Fulbright (conversation); John Kenneth Galbraith; Arthur Gelb; Roswell Gilpatric; Arthur Goldberg (conversation); Albert Gore, Sr.; Katherine Graham; Anatoly Gromyko; Edmund Gullion; Edwin Guthman; William Haddad; David Halberstam; Kay Halle; Richard Helms; George Herman; Theodore Hesburgh; Roger Hilsman; Frank Holeman; Eduard Ivanian; Ruth Jacobson (by Peter Keating); Peter Kaplan (conversation); Stanley Karnow (conversation); Robert F. Kennedy (conversation); Sergei Khrushchev (conversation with Peter Keating); Leonard Kornet; Polly Kraft; Dr. Hans Kraus; Harry MacPherson; Mike Mansfield; Burke Marshall; Louis Martin; Robert McNamara; David Michaelis; Edmund Morris; Daniel Patrick Moynihan; Richard Neustadt; Dr. James Nicholas (conversation); Paul Nitze; Richard Nixon (conversation); Lawrence O'Brien; Herbert Parmet; D. A. Pennebaker; Charles Peters; John Plank (by Peter Keating); Joseph Rauh; James Reston; Walt W. Rostow; Dean Rusk; Pierre Salinger; Paul Samuelson; John Ralston Saul (conversation); Richard Scammon; Arthur Schlesinger, Jr.; Thomas Schoenbaum; David Schoenbrun; John Seigenthaler; Jean Kennedy Smith (conversation); Stephen Smith; Ted Sorensen; Elvis Stahr (by Peter Keating); Tad Szulc; James Tobin; Marietta Tree; Sander Vanocur; Theodore White (conversation); Tom Wicker; and Harris Wofford.

Chapter 1

21 On the first Saturday night of December: Janet Travell, *Office Hours: Day and Night; the Autobiography of Janet Travell, M.D.* (New York: World Publishing, 1968), p. 354.

21 "Senator": NYT 12/7/60.

22 a certain contempt: The disregard of Kennedy's advisers for what they saw as Eisenhower's passive and bureaucratic style was well known. Clark Clifford, for example, wrote Kennedy that "President Eisenhower apparently considered the Cabinet to be in the nature of a Corporate Board of Directors. Decisions would be made and he would carry them out. . . . This is contrary to every basic concept of the Presidency and should be junked." Robert Kennedy later said his brother considered Eisenhower "very, very shallow." Clifford memo to JFK, 11/9/60, Clifford papers, courtesy of Clark Clifford; RFK OH, p. 598, JFKL.

In June 1960, Eisenhower had said, "I will do almost anything to avoid turning over my chair and the country to Kennedy," and Ike referred to JFK as "that young whippersnapper" and "Little Boy Blue." Stephen E. Ambrose, *Eisenhower the President* (New York: Simon & Schuster, 1984), p. 597. Piers Brendon, *Ike, His Life and Times* (New York: Harper & Row, 1986), p. 397; Herbert S. Parmet, *JFK: The Presidency of John F. Kennedy* (New York: Penguin, 1984), p. 72.

22 The two men had met for the first time: "As you are perhaps aware," Kennedy later wrote Eisenhower, "I have been an admirer of yours since our first meeting in Frankfurt in 1945, when I accompanied Secretary Forrestal on a trip to Europe." JFK letter to Eisenhower, 5/17/62, POF Box 29a, JFKL.

22 Their meeting on December 6: Despite the coolness between Kennedy and Eisenhower, the transition of 1961 was one of the smoothest of U.S. presidential successions. Neither side wanted a repeat of the hostilities evident when Eisenhower had assumed command from Harry Truman in 1953, and Eisenhower's staff in particular was well organized. The account of the December 6 meeting is drawn from the following sources: John Sharon and George Ball memo to JFK, 12/5/60; "Briefing Memoranda for Meeting with President Eisenhower Tuesday December 6, 1960"; "Informal List of Subjects to Be Discussed at Meeting of President Eisenhower and Senator John F. Kennedy," 12/5/60; all in POF Box 29a, JFKL. "Topics for Discussion with President-elect Kennedy," 12/6/60; Eisenhower memo, "Account of My December 6th, 1960 meeting with President-elect Kennedy"; Wilton Persons memo for the record, 12/6/60; Robert Anderson memo for the record, 12/6/60; all in Ann Whitman File, Presidential Transition Series, Box 1, DDEL; and *Time*, 12/19/60.

23 the two men had impressed each other: Eisenhower memo, "Account of my December 6th, 1960 meeting with President-elect Kennedy"; RFK OH, pp. 36–37, JFKL.

Eisenhower told Persons that he found Kennedy to be a "very personable, attractive man who appeared to be well-briefed," and had Persons call Clifford to relay his favorable impressions. Wilton Persons OH, p. 144, CU; Parmet, *JFK*, p. 73.

24   "I don't want to wake up on the morning of November 9": Kennedy said this to Clark Clifford over breakfast at his N Street home in Georgetown in August. Clifford int.

24   "Okay, girls": Benjamin C. Bradlee, *Conversations with Kennedy* (New York: W. W. Norton, 1975), p. 32.

24   But he looked tired and subdued: The armory scene is described in *Time*, 11/21/60. In photos and films taken the day after the election, Kennedy sometimes looks downcast. "We were badly disappointed, fooled by the large crowds at the end," said Larry O'Brien, who thought Kennedy would win with 53 or 54 percent of the vote. Kennedy later told Richard Nixon that Lou Harris, his chief pollster, had predicted he would win by 3 or 4 million votes. O'Brien int; Nixon letter to author, 5/22/89.

24   "The occupants of 71 to 74 positions": John J. Corson memo, Clifford papers. Corson worked for McKinsey and Company. Clifford sent his own 21-page memo to the new President-elect on November 9, after Kennedy called him from Hyannis.

25   falling asleep: Fred Dutton int. Ted Sorensen wrote that two weeks after the election, Kennedy "still seemed tired . . . and reluctant to face up to the details of personnel and program selection." The editor of the *Wall Street Journal* met with Kennedy in December and thought he was "a man who has suffered a shock in realizing the job he fought for isn't as easy as he thought it would be and who (momentarily at least) is harassed by uncertainties and doubts." Theodore C. Sorensen, *Kennedy* (New York: Bantam Books, 1966), p. 268; Vermont Royster letter to author, 8/12/88.

25   "We can learn our jobs together": Kennedy often used this verbal device, humorously putting across his disregard for experience. McNamara, for example, told Kennedy that he had discussed the job of Secretary of Defense with Thomas Gates and said, "after seeing what it's all about, I am convinced I can handle it." Kennedy smiled and replied, "I talked over the presidency with Eisenhower, and after hearing what it's all about, I'm convinced I can handle it." When prospective budget director David Bell said to Kennedy, "I've never run a large organization before," JFK responded, "Neither have I." Arthur Schlesinger accepted his job as special assistant to the President by saying, "I am not sure what I would be doing as special assistant, but if you think I can help, I would like very much to come." Kennedy said in turn "that he didn't know what he would be doing as President either but guessed there would be enough to keep us both busy." *Time*, 4/7/61; Bell OH, pp. 1–3, JFKL; Arthur M. Schlesinger, Jr., *Robert Kennedy and His Times* (New York: Ballantine Books, 1979), p. 245.

25   Robert McNamara: Robert McNamara int; McNamara OH, p. 11, JFKL; Deborah Shapley, *Promise and Power: The Life and Times of Robert McNamara* (Boston: Little, Brown, 1993), pp. 83–86; Roswell Gilpatric OH, p. 63, JFKL.

25   "Jesus Christ": Daniel Patrick Moynihan int.

25   Dean Rusk: Dean Rusk int; Thomas Schoenbaum, *Waging Peace and War: Dean Rusk in the Truman, Kennedy, and Johnson Years* (New York: Simon & Schuster, 1988), pp. 15–24. When Rusk said, "there is no way to be adequately prepared to become the Secretary of State," Kennedy smiled and repeated his joke: "The same is true for the job of President."

26   Walter Heller: Walter Heller OH, p. 73, JFKL; Parmet, *JFK*, p. 93.

27   C. Douglas Dillon: Dillon int; Heller OH, p. 120, JFKL. Eisenhower strongly advised Dillon against taking the job unless Kennedy gave him free rein in setting Treasury policy. "Dillon answered that he had such an agreement, though not in writing. . . . At week's end . . . Kennedy noted that no commitment at all had been offered to Dillon. 'A President,' said Kennedy, 'can't enter into treaties with cabinet members.' " *Time*, 1/2/61.

28   Orville Freeman: Orville Freeman int; Freeman OH, p. 6, JFKL.

28   "Paul, I have a friend of yours": Paul Nitze OH, p. 181, JFKL; Nitze int.

28   But McNamara held Kennedy to their deal: "Kennedy was embarrassed that he was unable to keep his commitment to me," Nitze concluded. "His commitment to Robert McNamara was of overriding importance." Nitze OH, p. 181, JFKL.

28   The next day: McNamara int. See also Brock Brower, "Last Chance for Junior," *Saturday Evening Post,* 7/27/63.
29   his brother: Schlesinger, *Robert Kennedy and His Times,* pp. 245–250; John Seigenthaler int.
29   "Nine strangers and a brother": Dutton int.
29   On January 19, 1961: This account is drawn from Clifford, Dillon, McNamara, and Rusk ints, and from the following sources: Transcript of Eisenhower interview by Malcolm Moos, 11/8/66, Post-Presidential Papers Box 11, DDEL. Robert Hurwitch OH, p. 4, JFKL. Persons OH, pp. 142–145, CU. Eisenhower memo to JFK, dictated over the phone by David Kendall to Evelyn Lincoln, 1/17/61; and "Memorandum of Subjects for Discussion at Meeting of President Eisenhower and Senator Kennedy on Thursday, January 19, 1961"; both in POF Box 29a, JFKL. "Topics Suggested by Senator Kennedy for Meeting January 19, 1961"; Christian Herter memo for the record, 1/19/61; and Persons memo for the record, 1/19/61; all in Post-Presidential Papers Box 11, DDEL. Clifford's handwritten notes of the meeting, Clifford papers, courtesy of Clark Clifford. JFK memo, dictated to Evelyn Lincoln, 1/19/61; Clifford memo to JFK, 1/24/61; and McNamara memo to JFK, 1/24/61; all in POF Box 29a, JFKL. Hurwitch was the desk officer who prepared memos on Cuba for both Eisenhower and Kennedy.
    See also *Washington Evening Star,* 1/19/61; *Time,* 1/27/61; Clifford memo to LBJ, 9/29/67, PP II Document 97, pp. 635–637; Clifford, "A Viet Nam Reappraisal," *Foreign Affairs* (July 1969), pp. 604–605; Schoenbaum, *Waging Peace and War,* p. 387; Hugh Sidey, *John F. Kennedy, President* (New York: Atheneum, 1963), pp. 37–38.

Chapter 2

34   Then he paused: The account of the inauguration is drawn from the following sources: Records of the 1961 Presidential Inaugural Committee, 1960–1961, Record Group 274, NA; *Life,* 1/27/61; NYT, 1/20–21/61; WP, 1/20–21/61; *Washington Star,* 1/20/61; Paul B. Fay, Jr., *The Pleasure of His Company* (New York: Harper & Row, 1966), pp. 80–93; Parmet, *JFK,* p. 82; Arthur M. Schlesinger, Jr., *A Thousand Days: John F. Kennedy in the White House* (Boston: Houghton Mifflin, 1965), pp. 1–5.
35   Angie Dickinson: Fay, *The Pleasure of His Company,* p. 89; Records of the 1961 Presidential Inaugural Committee.
35   Robert Frost: Stewart Udall int.
36   Reserved Section 1-A: Records of the 1961 Inaugural Committee.
36   "He's a master of words": Udall OH, p. 54; JFKL.
36   "Let the word go forth": JFKPP, 1/20/61.
37   "missile gap": Walter Lippmann, "Kennedy at Mid-Term," NW, 1/21/63.
37   Some calculated that Soviet police techniques: "We didn't realize until much later that many of these people didn't care about Marxist ideology. They wanted our secret police methods." Eduard Ivanian int. Ivanian, a Soviet Kennedy scholar and author, was the deputy chief of the Soviet mission to the United Nations in the early 1960s.
38   he had studied a long report: RAND Report RM-2683, Pre-Presidential Papers, Box 64, JFKL.
38   "Flexible Response": Maxwell Taylor, *Swords and Plowshares* (New York: W. W. Norton, 1972), pp. 166, 169, 180.
39   "You can't do this": Harris Wofford, *Of Kennedys and Kings* (New York: Farrar, Straus & Giroux, 1980), pp. 98–99; Wofford int.
39   thirty-one changes: WP, 1/21/61.
39   "It's a place without history": Pierre Salinger int.
40   "Look at this": John Kenneth Galbraith, *Ambassador's Journal: A Personal Account of the Kennedy Years* (Boston: Houghton Mifflin, 1969), p. 20; Stephen Smith int.
40   "There must be more we can do": Chester Clifton, quoted in Goddard Lieberson and Joan Myers, eds., *John Fitzgerald Kennedy . . . As We Remember Him* (Philadelphia: Courage Books, 1965), pp. 110–111.
40   "Call the commandant": Richard N. Goodwin, "The Art of Assuming Power," *NYT Magazine,* 12/26/76.
40   Inside the White House: The full text of Khrushchev's January 6 speech can be

found in N. S. Khrushchov, *Communism—Peace and Happiness for the Peoples* (Moscow: Foreign Languages Publishing House, 1963), Vol. 1, pp. 12–76. (Loyal Communists rejected the American spelling of Khrushchev's name.)

41   "Read, mark, learn and inwardly digest": *Time,* 2/10/61; RFK OH, p. 245, JFKL.

41   "Are you going to write that?": Arthur Krock OH, p. 21, JFKL.

41   a dramatics coach: Dutton int.

41   Churchill was his literary model: *Why England Slept,* which essentially reprinted Kennedy's senior thesis from Harvard, amounted to a thin companion volume to Churchill's *While England Slept.* Kennedy's second book was an American version of Churchill's *Great Contemporaries,* a 1922 study of world leaders at the turn of the century. "Courage," that book began, "is rightly esteemed the first of human qualities because it is the quality which guarantees all others." Three decades later, *Profiles in Courage* opened this way: "This is a book about the most admirable of human virtues—courage." It ended: "A man does what he must—in spite of personal consequences, in spite of obstacles and dangers and pressures—and that is the basis of all human morality."

41   "Kennedy Sworn In": NYT, 1/21/61.

42   The *Times* health story: The press release stated that Kennedy was completely able to meet "any obligation of the Presidency without the need for special medical treatment, unusual rest periods, or other limitations." NYT, 7/5/60; Travell, *Office Hours,* pp. 332–333.

42   Addison's disease: Confidential source interviews. In the thirty years following Kennedy's death, researchers pieced together much circumstantial evidence on Addison's disease. See, for example, Joan and Clay Blair, Jr., *The Search for JFK,* pp. 561–578, and Parmet, *JFK,* pp. 17–19, 118–124. The issue was also discussed in several articles and letters to the editor in the *Journal of the American Medical Association* (10/26/64, 2/15/65, 4/5/65), as Kennedy's official autopsy report made no mention of his adrenal glands. See also NYT, 10/6/92.

Additional proof that Kennedy had Addison's disease became available in at least three forms in 1992. First, J. T. Boswell, a principal pathologist in the Kennedy autopsy, stated for the record that no evidence of adrenal glands was found in examining JFK after his death. This fact, confirmed by Robert Karnei, who was a pathology resident at Bethesda Naval Hospital in November 1963, "is diagnostic of severe Addison's Disease." George D. Lundberg, "Closing the Case in *JAMA* on the John F. Kennedy Autopsy," *Journal of the AMA,* 10/7/92; NYT, 10/6/92.

Second, parts of the medical files of Dr. William Herbst were released. Herbst was a specialist recommended to Kennedy by the Lahey Clinic in Boston, where JFK had sought medical help since 1936, and for a decade he treated Kennedy's venereal disease problems. In 1953, the staff of the clinic wrote Herbst: "Senator Kennedy . . . has had quite a variety of conditions. The most serious of these has been Addison's Disease. . . . When he was in Boston last week, his medical condition was checked by Dr. Elmer Bartels who has been following his Addison's Disease since it was first discovered." Herbst Clinical Notes, 1950–1963, Medical File MS-83–38, JFKL.

Third, doctors who performed Kennedy's back operation in 1954, and who needed to proceed with extreme care because of the low resistance to infection caused by Addison's disease, confirmed that JFK was their patient. This, together with their description of the operation in a 1955 journal article, is discussed below.

On JFK and VD, also discussed in William Herbst's clinical notes, see Nigel Hamilton, *JFK: Reckless Youth* (New York: Random House, 1992), pp. 808–810. One effect of Kennedy's troubles with venereal disease was anxiety about possible damage to his fertility, noted by Hamilton and confirmed by one of JFK's doctors, who said that Kennedy went so far as to have his sperm count tested after his marriage to make sure he was capable of fathering children. Ibid., p. 809; confidential source int.

After John Kennedy's death, his brother Robert, acting in his capacity as Attorney General, ruled that "all correspondence which deals with a personal medical matter should be regarded as a privileged communication, and should not go to Central Files." Travell memo for the file, 12/6/63, WHCSF Box 104, JFKL.

42   cortisone injections, pills and pellets: George Burkley int; Hans Kraus int; Travell OH, JFKL; Herbst Clinical Notes, 1950–1963, Medical File MS-83–38, JFKL.

42   For emergencies: Parmet int. Kennedy's friend William Walton remembered that an aide with a special small bag followed JFK everywhere during the 1960 campaign because "he had to have medical support all the time." Parmet, *JFK*, p. 18.

42   "I'd rather be dead": Peter Collier and David Horowitz, *The Kennedys* (New York: Summit, 1984), p. 201.

42   "This is the one that cures you or kills you": O'Brien int; Lawrence F. O'Brien, *No Final Victories: A Life in Politics from John F. Kennedy to Watergate* (New York: Doubleday, 1974), p. 44.

42   The operation was described: James A. Nicholas, et al., "Management of Adreno-cortical Insufficiency During Surgery," *AMA Archives of Surgery* (November 1955).

Over the years, several researchers pursued the question of whether the third patient described in this article was in fact John F. Kennedy. In January 1961, Gannett's Washington bureau chief, Paul Martin, matched the description of the patient in this article to accounts of Kennedy's back operation, but his speculation went virtually unnoticed. In 1967, physician John Nichols made the same link, also to little effect. He wrote: "this writer believes the case cited by Nicholas et al. is that of the late President and he accepts their clinical diagnosis of Addison's Disease." John Nichols, "President Kennedy's Adrenals," *Journal of the AMA*, 7/10/67; Joan and Clay Blair, Jr., *The Search for JFK*, pp. 560–579.

In 1992, hospital officials and Dr. Nicholas, the lead author of the original article, finally confirmed on the record that Kennedy was indeed patient number three. As the authors stated flatly in 1955, JFK had suffered from Addison's disease for seven years prior to his back operation. Lundberg, "Closing the Case in *JAMA* on the John F. Kennedy Autopsy."

43   Besides all that: Kennedy also wore a small corset brace to support his lower back and a quarter-inch lift in his left shoe heel to compensate for a slight difference in the lengths of his legs. Parmet, *JFK*, pp. 119–124; Sidey, *John F. Kennedy, President*, pp. 385–386; *Today's Health* (February 1961).

43   Joining the Navy: Kennedy's willingness to conceal his health problems and his father's use of his political and intelligence connections succeeded in getting JFK into the Naval Reserve, into Midshipmen's School, and ultimately onto PT-boat service. See, for example, Hamilton, *JFK: Reckless Youth*, pp. 405–408, 489–494, 500–506.

43   In politics: At the time of his spinal operation, for example, Kennedy was reported to have undergone the operation "to clear up a wartime injury" and to have "suffered a spinal injury in action in the Solomon Islands." NYT, 10/11/54, 10/21/54.

In the years leading up to 1960, Robert Kennedy, Ted Sorensen, and Kennedy's doctors reiterated and reinforced the stories about JFK's wartime and football injuries and "minor adrenal insufficiency." In February 1961, *Today's Health*, a publication of the American Medical Association, published a "Health Profile of Our New President," which gave full expression to the Kennedy health cover-up. Young John Kennedy, it reported, returned home from the London School of Economics after graduating from Choate because of a "jaundice attack." JFK's back troubles were ascribed to "an apparent ruptured disc in the lower lumbar area" from football. The magazine is in the Arthur Schlesinger papers, Box W-9, JFKL.

43   Lyndon Johnson: NYT 7/5/60. On the Fourth of July, 1960, India Edwards, co-chair of Citizens for Johnson, told reporters that Kennedy had Addison's disease, which she referred to as "something to do with lymph glands." Doctors, she said, "have told me he would not be alive if it were not for cortisone."

JFK had baited Johnson on the health issue. In replying to Harry Truman's criticisms of his candidacy, Kennedy noted a week before the Democratic convention in Los Angeles that "during my lifetime alone, four out of our seven Presidents have suffered major heart attacks that impaired at least temporarily their exercise of executive leadership. . . . Older men may always be appointed to the Cabinet . . . but then if ill health cuts short their work, others may replace them." LBJ, then fifty-two years old, had suffered a heart attack in 1955.

43   "Tell them I don't have Addison's Disease": Salinger OH, p. 71, JFKL.

44   "Jack, the way you take that jab": Draft manuscript of Fay, *The Pleasure of His Company*, Myrick Land papers, Box 12, BU. Land edited Fay's book for Harper & Row in 1965–66. Fay cut more than two thousand words from his original draft at the

request of Robert and Jacqueline Kennedy, whose initials appear next to sections of the manuscript that each wanted deleted.

Land also handled the condensation of William Manchester's *Death of a President* (New York: Harper & Row, 1967) for *Look* magazine. Again the Kennedys intervened, sending proposed cuts through Richard Goodwin and ultimately Robert Kennedy. Manchester agreed to many of the changes but balked at others, and a nasty feud erupted. Indeed, Manchester publicly compared his experience with the Kennedy family and their representatives to an encounter with officials in Nazi Germany. Material on the Manchester edits and aftermath is in the Land papers, Boxes 8–10 and 14, BU. Now a professor at the Reynolds School of Journalism at the University of Nevada, Land preserved his notes and correspondence so that the cuts would not be lost to history.

Chapter 3

45   He quickly read the proclamation: Angier Biddle Duke int.

45   "the vital center": NYT, 1/3/60.

46   Kennedy wanted to see everything himself: Richard Helms int. Kennedy, said Helms, a top CIA official for more than twenty years, was the only president to ask for raw intelligence cables.

46   "This is going to be the worst one yet": W. W. Rostow, *The Diffusion of Power: An Essay in Recent History* (New York: Macmillan), p. 264.

46   *The Ugly American:* William J. Lederer and Eugene Burdick, *The Ugly American* (New York: W. W. Norton, 1958).

48   "We must support Diem": Lansdale's report is contained in USVNR, Book 11, pp. 1–12. Lansdale published an account of his 1950s experiences in Southeast Asia as *In the Midst of Wars* (New York: Harper & Row, 1972).

48   "Diem still presents our chief problem": Collins said that Diem had a "marked inability to understand the political, economic, and military problems associated with Vietnam." He told officials in Washington that "Diem must be replaced . . . plan of action should go into effect immediately." Memo for the Assistant Secretary of Defense for International Security Affairs, "Debriefing of General Collins," 4/26/55; Memo for the Assistant Secretary of State for Far Eastern Affairs, "Report on Collins Visit and Vietnam Situation"; both in USVNR, Book 10, pp. 937, 945.

49   "Get down here right away!": William J. Rust, *Kennedy in Vietnam* (New York: Scribner, 1985), p. 21.

49   Kennedy had an idea for Lansdale: "I would think that General Lansdale's story of the counter-guerilla case study would make an excellent magazine article for something like the *Saturday Evening Post*. Obviously, it couldn't go under Lansdale's name but he might if the Department of Defense thinks it is worthwhile and the State Department he might turn this memorandum over to them and he could check the final story." JFK memo to Bundy, 2/5/61, POF Box 62, Lincoln Dictation File, JFKL. Lansdale's story was printed, with the title "The Report the President Wanted Published," *Saturday Evening Post*, 5/20/61.

49   "I want to thank you": The January 28 meeting is detailed in Summary Record, FRUS 1961, Document 3, pp. 13–15; Rostow memo to McGeorge Bundy, 1/30/61, NSF Box 192, JFKL; Rostow OH, p. 44, JFKL.

49   "Basic Counterinsurgency Plan for Viet-Nam": FRUS 1961, Document 1, pp. 1–12.

50   The President quickly approved: FRUS 1961, note 6 to p. 15; JFK memo to Rusk and McNamara, 1/30/61, USVNR, Book 11, p. 13.

50   Back at the State Department: Notes on meeting between Rusk and J. Graham Parsons, 1/28/61, FRUS 1961, Document 5, pp. 19–20.

50   Rusk felt free: Cecil B. Currey, *Edward Lansdale: The Unquiet American* (Boston: Houghton Mifflin, 1988), pp. 228–229.

51   "President Kennedy had me in for a long talk": Lansdale letter to Ngo Dinh Diem, 1/30/61, FRUS 1961, Document 6, pp. 20–23.

51   The first time Kennedy met: Parsons OH, p. 30, JFKL.

51   *Spartacus:* Fay, *The Pleasure of His Company*, pp. 111–114.

52   "John Kennedy could not stand being cornered": "He couldn't stand boredom and he couldn't stand solitude," said George Ball. "He couldn't stand being alone. I think that had something to do with why those tarts were around." Ball int.
52   "We plan to continue": JFKPP, 2/19/61.
52   "The lines of control have been cut": Wheeler OH, JFKL. "JFK thought he could organize the presidency better," Douglas Dillon said later, "and abolish the National Security structure, and I think that led to the breakdown connecting and coordinating between the departments and the President. There was no one to prepare agendas for ad hoc meetings and there was no one to organize and coordinate actions after them. I was in overall charge of Cuba planning at the State Department under Eisenhower and the Bay of Pigs was just a plan to be evaluated. If Kennedy hadn't dismantled the security council apparatus, it never would have happened." Dillon int.
52   "These general meetings are a waste of time": NBC-TV broadcast, 4/11/61, "JFK Report Number Two." Kennedy was interviewed for the program by Ray Scherer on 3/24/61.
53   "Come on in here, Ken": Galbraith int.
53   up to fifteen hundred words per minute: Kennedy was a quick study, but reports of his speed reading were greatly exaggerated. "We called up the reading institute where he was supposed to have taken the course, but nobody could really remember him reading in that," said Hugh Sidey of *Time*, who researched the subject. "They suggested that he probably read about 700 or 800 words a minute, which was twice normal. . . . The President didn't like that one bit. . . . Galbraith had also testified that JFK had a twenty-six page memo and it had taken him just about ten minutes because he'd noted it on the clock. . . . It came out about a thousand words per minute. Well, the President still felt that was a little slow, so what I did was to round that figure out to twelve hundred. We put that in the article, and I noticed for months and years after that this became the real gospel on his reading speed." Sidey OH, p. 35, JFKL.
53   "Tell me the ten things": Wofford, *Of Kennedys and Kings*, p. 24.
53   "We're not looking for business": Joseph Kraft, "Kennedy's Working Staff," *Harper's* (December 1962). Sherman Adams, Eisenhower's chief of staff, was quoted as having said, "I count the day lost when I have not found some way of lightening the President's load."
54   "Arthur Goldberg suggests": Dutton memo to JFK, 3/14/61, POF Box 63, JFKL.
54   One set of government growth projections: Richard Bissell int; Martin Hillenbrand OH, pp. 36–37, JFKL.
54   Part of his official biography: Records at the London School of Economics stated that upon arriving at the university, Kennedy "immediately fell ill and has been obliged to return to America." Kingsley Smalley, who was slated to tutor JFK, said he never met him: "As far as I know, he never showed up." Demarest dispatch, 11/16/60, Time arch.
54   "Whatever happened to that guy": Charles Bartlett int.
54   Six days into the Kennedy presidency: Heller OH, p. 240, JFKL. Kennedy's feeling that his economic advisers needed better political education was confirmed by Dutton, John Kenneth Galbraith, Rostow, Paul Samuelson, and James Tobin ints.
55   "Mr. President": O'Brien, *No Final Victories*, p. 107.
56   "A new administration": JFKPP, 1/25/61.
56   Two days later: Heller OH, p. 240, JFKL.
56   his first State of the Union Address: JFKPP, 1/30/61.
57   "Let us move this program": O'Brien, *No Final Victories*, p. 107; *Time*, 2/3/61.

Chapter 4

58   "Kennedy Defense Study": NYT, 2/6/61.
58   "What the hell is this?": McNamara int.
58   "we are facing a gap": Kennedy gave his missile gap speech in the Senate in 1958: "There is every indication that by 1960 the United States will have lost its Calais—its superiority in nuclear striking power." John F. Kennedy, *The Strategy of Peace* (New York: Harper, 1960), pp. 33–45.
58   There was no missile gap: Earle Wheeler OH, p. 2, JFKL. Kennedy, briefed by

Wheeler during the 1960 campaign, asked if there weren't any "doubting Thomases" on the issue of comparative missile strength. Wheeler replied that that was the role of the "intelligence community"—if Kennedy wanted missile gap fiction, in other words, he might get it from the CIA but not from the military.

Maxwell Taylor wrote that as President, Kennedy "liked to look around the Cabinet Room during a military discussion and ask whimsically, 'Who ever believed in the missile gap?' " Taylor, *Swords and Plowshares*, p. 205.

59   "The bottom line on the missile gap": For a contemporaneous account, see "The Truth About a 'Missile Gap,' " USN&WR, 2/27/61. For detailed accounts of changing U.S. intelligence estimates of Soviet missile strength, see McQuade memo to Nitze, "But Where Did the Missile Gap Go?" 5/31/63; Nitze memo to Bundy, 5/30/63, Nuclear History papers, NSA; and John Prados, *The Soviet Estimate: U.S. Intelligence Analysis and Russian Military Strength* (New York: Dial, 1982), pp. 111–125, 173–181.

59   The President sent out his press secretary: Shapley, *Promise and Power*, pp. 97–99.

59   "It would be premature to reach": JFKPP, 2/8/61.

59   "Could you let me know": JFK memo to Bundy, 2/8/61, POF Box 62, JFKL.

59   Theodore Hesburgh: Theodore Hesburgh int; Hesburgh OH, JFKL.

60   "Can't you just tell the Africans": Wofford int.; see also Rusk OH, pp. 326–327, JFKL; *Time*, 5/19/61.

60   "I already have a special assistant": Wofford int; Wofford OH, pp. 103–104, JFKL.

61   Also at the February 8 news conference: JFKPP, 2/8/61.

62   "I'll tell you something about that": Moynihan int.

62   Kennedy had moved his entourage: Salinger int.

62   He had walked out of Kennedy's office: Moynihan int.

62   George Thomas: Arthur Krock, *Memoirs: Sixty Years on the Firing Line* (New York: Funk & Wagnalls, 1968), pp. 326, 331. Krock described Thomas as a "fat, good-natured Negro of high competence as a domestic. . . . The only complaint Kennedy ever made to me about George was, 'Why *can't* he learn to tie a white tie?' "

62   a single telephone call: Louis Martin int; Wofford int; Taylor Branch, *Parting the Waters* (New York: Simon & Schuster, 1988), pp. 359–369; Wofford, *Of Kennedys and Kings*, pp. 16–21; "Kennedy's Call to King," panel OH, JFKL.

62   "Well, I guess I have to start": Wofford int.

63   On February 10: Joseph Rauh int; Rauh OH, pp. 99–104, JFKL; Robert Nathan OH, pp. 22–23, JFKL.

64   Queen of the Mardi Gras: JFK appointments schedule, 2/10/61, JFKL.

64   Photographs were political coin: Aware of how much his presence meant in pictures, Kennedy would later refuse to be photographed with the president of the American Medical Association (who opposed him on Medicare); with economist Leon Keyserling (who had said that he was "as bad as Eisenhower"); and with Sammy Davis, Jr. (who had a white wife), among many others. Gilpatric OH, JFKL; Carl Kaysen OH, JFKL; Branch, *Parting the Waters*, p. 698.

64   Vel Phillips: Phillips, a Milwaukee city councilwoman, met Kennedy in 1957: "Of course, he sort of had his eye on the sparrow in a way, but I have to be honest with you and this is how we got to be very good friends. He was shaking hands, and he was sort of looking at me because I was a Negro, and he didn't know many Negroes. . . . In '60 . . . I was thoroughly . . . committed, personally in many ways, to Jack Kennedy. We had talked together and he used me in his literature and we worried because I didn't come out dark enough. . . . In terms of the color and things like that he could say to me from an honest practical point of view, you know? And we did the picture over a couple of times." Vel Phillips OH, pp. 43, 47, Howard.

Chapter 5

65   items like this in February: JFK's sporadic bursts of dictation to Evelyn Lincoln are collected in POF Box 62, JFKL. They are spicy enough to have served as the primary basis for a book called *JFK Wants to Know: Memos from the President's Office 1961–1963*, Edward B. Claflin, ed. (New York: William Morrow, 1991).

66 "Is this one of ours or one of theirs?": Rostow int.
66 "He's frightening": RFK OH, p. 191, JFKL.
67 The next call was from Red Fay: Fay draft manuscript, Land papers, Box 12, BU.
67 "Dear Mr. Chairman": Schlesinger, *A Thousand Days*, p. 343.
68 "All my diplomatic colleagues": Thompson cable to Rusk, 3/16/61, section 1, quoted in Honoré M. Catudal, *Kennedy and the Berlin Wall Crisis: A Case Study in U.S. Decision-Making* (West Berlin: Berlin-Verlag, 1980), p. 62, note 15.
68 "We must at least expect": Thompson cable to Rusk, 3/16/61, section 2, reprinted in Catudal, *Kennedy and the Berlin Wall Crisis*, p. 304.
68 a list of nineteen national security "tasks": Rostow, *The Diffusion of Power*, p. 169.
69 green berets: Parmet, *JFK*, p. 138; Rust, *Kennedy in Vietnam*, p. 36.
69 "White House ranks defense Viet-Nam": FRUS 1961, Document 16, pp. 40–42.
69 the Peace Corps: JFKPP, 3/1/61.
69 Why don't we organize American businessmen: Rusk OH, p. 60, JFKL. Bobby repeated this suggestion throughout the administration, as for example after the erection of the Berlin Wall. RFK memo to JFK, 8/17/61, Berlin papers, NSA.
69 "What do you think": Charles Peters int.
69 The CIA was training Cuban exiles: On the training of Cuban exiles prior to Kennedy's direct involvement, see Gordon Gray OH, pp. 27–34, DDEL; Haynes Johnson, *The Bay of Pigs: The Leaders' Story of Brigade 2506* (New York: Dell, 1964), pp. 25–72; Peter Wyden, *Bay of Pigs: The Untold Story* (New York: Simon & Schuster, 1979), pp. 9–87.
70 "Everybody must be prepared to swear": Memorandum of Conference with the President, 3/18/60, DDRS (1991) 3407.
70 "U.S. HELPS TRAIN AN ANTI-CASTRO FORCE": NYT, 1/10/61.
70 "Has the policy for Cuba": JFK memo to Bundy, 2/15/61, POF Box 62, JFKL. Kennedy had written Bundy on February 4: "It is my understanding that there is a sharp difference of opinion between defense and CIA on what we should do about Cuba and Berle. Can you find out if the differences of view have been settled, or if they continue I believe we should have an opportunity to have them placed before me and have them argued out again. Would you let me know right away on this?" JFK memo to Bundy, 2/4/61, POF Box 62, JFKL. Adolf Berle, a New Deal diplomat, was the head of Kennedy's interdepartmental task force on Latin America.
70 On March 11: Wyden, *Bay of Pigs*, pp. 98–101.
71 They assumed that once troops were on the ground: "We felt that when the chips were down—when the crisis arose in reality," Allen Dulles wrote later, "any action required for success would be authorized rather than permit the enterprise to fail." Lucien S. Vandenbroucke, "The 'Confessions' of Allen Dulles," *Diplomatic History* (Fall 1984).
In the mid-1960s, Dulles, irritated by accounts that pinned blame on the CIA for misleading Kennedy about the Cuban invasion, planned to publish his side of the story. Although he finished a manuscript that was accepted by *Harper's* magazine, however, he ultimately decided to maintain his silence. Background material, correspondence, and drafts of Dulles's "My Answer to the Bay of Pigs" are in the Dulles papers, Boxes 138 and 244, Seeley Mudd Manuscript Library, Princeton University.
71 The CIA was pursuing parallel assassination plans: See CC, pp. 71–74, 91–99, 125–126.
71 "Don't forget one thing": Wyden, *Bay of Pigs*, p. 101.
72 "They're not queer at State": Collier and Horowitz, *The Kennedys*, p. 264.
72 "You can't beat brains": Rostow int.
72 "You can't have him": Chester Bowles OH, p. 53, JFKL.
72 National Security Action Memorandum 31: NSAM 31, NSF Box 313, JFKL.
72 Four days later: Schlesinger, *A Thousand Days*, p. 243; Wyden, *Bay of Pigs*, pp. 101–103.
72 "the floating crap game": John Ranelagh, *The Agency* (New York: Simon & Schuster, 1986), p. 365.
72 "Mr. President, I know you're doubtful about this": Theodore Sorensen OH, JFKL.

73   the President pacing the floor: Richard Goodwin, *Remembering America* (Boston: Little, Brown, 1988), pp. 156–159.

73   "Public popularity": Lou Harris and Associates confidential study for JFK, "Public Reaction to President Kennedy During the First 60 Days of His Administration," 3/22/61, POF Box 105, JFKL.

74   "What is our position out there?" Winthrop Brown OH, pp. 14–15, JFKL.

74   "As far as Laos is concerned": Schlesinger, *A Thousand Days*, p. 332.

74   But at the same time: Rust, *Kennedy in Vietnam*, p. 31. On Laos generally, see Parmet, *JFK*, pp. 131–155; Schlesinger, *A Thousand Days*, pp. 334–338; Charles Stevenson, *The End of Nowhere: American Policy Toward Laos Since 1954* (Boston: Beacon Press, 1972), pp. 134–148. For examples of military reports from Laos, see JCS Situation Reports, 12/20/60, 1/2–4/61, and 1/7/61, DDRS (1980) 49B-C, 50A-C, and 52A.

Galbraith later wrote to Kennedy from New Delhi that "the entire Laos nation is clearly inferior to a battalion of conscientious objectors from World War I." Galbraith memo to JFK, POF Box 29, JFKL.

75   He ordered the Seventh Fleet: Rust, *Kennedy in Vietnam*, p. 31; Rostow, *The Diffusion of Power*, pp. 266–267.

75   Rostow was delegated: Rostow int; NYT 3/21/61.

75   "These three maps": JFKPP, 3/23/61.

75   In private: "Vietnam is the place": James Reston int; Collier and Horowitz, *The Kennedys*, p. 274; Rust, *Kennedy in Vietnam*, pp. 32–34.

Chapter 6

76   "What do you think": Schlesinger, *A Thousand Days*, p. 246.

76   "Do you know anything": Dean Acheson OH, pp. 2, 13, JFKL.

77   "It seems more likely than not": Acheson memo to JFK, 4/3/61, Nuclear History papers, NSA; Bundy cover memo to JFK, 4/4/61, NSF Box 81, JFKL.

77   "Kennedy respected Acheson": See, for example, Douglas Brinkley, *Dean Acheson: The Cold War Years 1953–1971* (New Haven: Yale University Press, 1992), pp. 108–109.

77   "There is no 'solution' ": Acheson memo, 4/3/61.

78   a special message to Congress: JFKPP, 3/29/61.

78   "Where are you going for the holiday?": J. William Fulbright, OH, JFKL; Wyden, *Bay of Pigs*, pp. 122–123.

78   "The invasion is an open secret": Fulbright memo to JFK, "The Cuban Memorandum," 3/29/61, reprinted in Karl E. Meyer, ed., *Fulbright of Arkansas* (New York: Robert B. Luce, 1963), pp. 194–205.

79   raw CIA reports: The information on Cuba summarized in the CIA's Intelligence Weekly Summary for the period 2/9–4/6/61 is in DDRS (1977) 10D–11C.

The board of inquiry appointed by Kennedy after the Bay of Pigs to look into the disaster cited intelligence reports that estimated that one fourth of all Cubans might have supported an invasion force. Cuba Study Group (the Taylor Report), memo 1, 6/13/61, Cuba papers, NSA.

79   On the Tuesday after Easter: Fulbright OH, p. 61, JFKL.

79   There were a dozen men: The account of the April 4 meeting is drawn from Bissell, Dillon, Nitze, Rusk, and Schlesinger ints; Fulbright conv; and from the following sources: Fulbright OH, pp. 61–63, JFKL; Goodwin, *Remembering America*, p. 175; Schlesinger, *A Thousand Days*, pp. 251–252; Wofford, *Of Kennedys and Kings*, p. 355; Wyden, *Bay of Pigs*, pp. 146–151.

82   After the meeting: Dillon int; Fulbright OH, p. 64, JFKL.

82   "If force is used": Schlesinger, *A Thousand Days*, pp. 253–256.

82   "I'm trying to make sense out of it": Schlesinger int.

83   "We seemed destined to go ahead": Schlesinger, *A Thousand Days*, p. 256.

83   The younger Kennedy: Schlesinger, *A Thousand Days*, p. 259.

83   a correspondent named Harold Handleman: Schlesinger memo to JFK, 4/1/61, POF Box 65, JFKL; Schlesinger, *A Thousand Days*, pp. 260–261.

83   John Plank: John Plank int.

83   "The attached article": Schlesinger memo to JFK, 4/6/61, Schlesinger papers, Box W-5, JFKL.
83   "Gil Harrison came through": Schlesinger follow-up memo to JFK, 4/6/61, Schlesinger papers, Box W-5, JFKL.
83   "a front-page story by Tad Szulc": Turner Catledge, *My Life and the Times* (New York: Harper & Row, 1971), pp. 261–265; Schlesinger, *A Thousand Days,* p. 261.
84   the size of the headline was reduced: For an argument that the *Times* did not capitulate on any question of importance, see Daniel Kennedy, "The Bay of Pigs and the *New York Times,*" *Journalism Quarterly,* no. 63 (1986). But while Daniel Kennedy correctly points out that the great bulk of Szulc's story appeared unchanged, he underestimates the importance of moving the piece from the top of the front page and deleting the reference to the invasion's imminence.
84   "I can't believe what I am reading": Pierre Salinger, *With Kennedy* (New York: Avon, 1966), p. 194.
84   "The unfortunate fact": "I have rechecked the details of the Tad Szulc story. . . . We have very little to argue about in the story" claim by claim, concurring with CIA judgment that "we do not have a strong case against the story as inaccurate." Schlesinger memo to JFK, 4/9/61, POF Box 65, JFKL.
84   "Crisis Commanders in Washington": Bundy memo to JFK, 4/4/61, POF Box 62, JFKL.
84   "Protection of the President": Schlesinger memo to JFK, 4/10/61, POF Box 65, JFKL.
85   approve the CIA plan: Schlesinger, *A Thousand Days,* p. 264; JFK appointments schedule, 4/6–8/61, JFKL.
85   Harold Macmillan during his state visit: *Time,* 4/14/61; Parmet, *JFK,* p. 144.
85   In fact, he had lost the papers: Alistair Horne, *Macmillan: 1957–1986* (London: Macmillan, 1989), p. 286.
85   On April 12: Sidey, *John F. Kennedy, President,* p. 113.
85   "Is there any place where we can catch them?": Sidey, *John F. Kennedy, President,* p. 122.
86   that afternoon at his news conference: JFKPP, 4/12/61.

Chapter 7

88   On April 11: NBC-TV, "JFK Report Number 2."
88   "He is not only the handsomest": Quoted in *Time,* 4/14/61.
89   He told Bissell again: Taylor Report, Memo 1, 6/13/61, Cuba papers, NSA; Schlesinger, *A Thousand Days,* pp. 267–272; Wyden, *Bay of Pigs,* pp. 168–172.
89   "My observations": Wyden, *Bay of Pigs,* pp. 168–169. "They say it is a Cuban tradition to join a winner," Hawkins wrote, "and they have supreme confidence they will win against whatever Castro has to offer. I share their confidence."
89   weekends: K. Lemoyne Billings OH, courtesy of David Michaelis; Bradlee int; draft manuscript of Fay, *The Pleasure of His Company,* Land papers, Box 12, BU. Of one Glen Ora encounter with Kennedy, Fay wrote, "He moved in from the dining room to the living room on his crutches. . . . I was winning the game, and I noticed the mischievous look in his eyes. He coughed suddenly, and the checkerboard fell onto the floor beside us. 'One of those unfortunate things, Redhead. . . . You know we don't know what the outcome of that game would have been. We'll never really know."
The oral history interview of Billings, one of Kennedy's closest but least-known friends, was done by the Kennedy Library and produced an 810-page transcript. Under the terms of his donor deed, it will remain closed at the Library until 2019, fifty years after his death. In recent years, however, copies originating from Billings and his family have entered research circulation.
90n   "Go, go, baby!": Draft manuscript of Fay, *The Pleasure of His Company,* Land papers, Box 12, BU.
90n   "He wouldn't score too well": Stuart Symington OH, JFKL.
90   a B-26 bomber: *Time,* 4/21/61. The best accounts of the invasion are Johnson, *The Bay of Pigs,* pp. 101–174; Hugh Thomas, *The Cuban Revolution* (New York: Harper & Row, 1977), pp. 577–593; and Wyden, *Bay of Pigs,* pp. 210–288.

90   Stevenson was unwittingly telling the lies in New York: Parmet, *JFK*, p. 168; Wyden, *Bay of Pigs*, pp. 186–188.
91   he telephoned Rusk: Wyden, *Bay of Pigs*, p. 170.
91   Then he called Salinger: Salinger, *With Kennedy*, p. 192.
91   By himself: Stephen Smith int.
91   The last thing Kennedy did: Parmet, *JFK*, pp. 168–169; Wyden, *Bay of Pigs*, pp. 199–200.
91   "No": Wyden, *Bay of Pigs*, pp. 205–206.
92   The invasion failed before he reached his office: *Time*, 4/28/61; Johnson, *Bay of Pigs*, pp. 118–119; Thomas, *The Cuban Revolution*, pp. 583–586; Wyden, *Bay of Pigs*, pp. 173–185.
92   Castro had a favorite fishing spot: Wyden, *Bay of Pigs*, pp. 104–107. Furthermore, the area around the Bay of Pigs was one that had benefited from Castro's takeover. Home to 3,000–4,000 charcoal burners who had once been tenant farmers, the region was a pilot for Castro's literacy and apprenticeship programs. Havana had assigned two hundred adult teachers to the area and provided slots for three hundred native children to study various trades. Also, the new regime had built three roads across the swamps around the Bay, which previously had been traversed only by two rail lines, and planned to develop tourist projects there. "It would have been hard indeed to have found a region in Cuba in which a rebellion could have been less easily inspired among the local people. But then such a thing was not part of the CIA's purpose." Thomas, *The Cuban Revolution*, p. 585.
92   "I don't think it's going as well as it should": RFK OH, p. 62, JFKL.
92   By noon the next day: Parmet, *JFK*, pp. 170–171.
92   The Cuban Revolutionary Council: Dutton int; Robert Lovett OH, p. 42, JFKL; Plank int. Plank said that "all that the Cuban Revolutionary Council really had to offer was some rhetoric and a return to the same old faces that had failed before. They weren't themselves all Batistianos by any means. Some of the fighters were, the political leaders were those who had come up in the '30s and were tired old pols."
Felipe Pazos, a prominent exile leader in Miami, told a *Time* correspondent later in April that "the invasion was a sporting event in which the boys would walk in, followed by Marines. It became fashionable to go to the camps, and the best boys from the best families did. But when the disaster came and the U.S. aid didn't come through, the boys surrendered fast and their families became hysterical. They had been playing at liberation all along—like boy scouts on an overnight hike prepared to duck into a house at the first sight of rain. The Escambray farmers lasted four months without ammunition or food. At the showdown, the yacht club boys lasted hardly a day." Arnason dispatch from Miami, 4/28/61, Time arch.
Castro's accountants later claimed that the 1,500 men of the invasion Brigade had once owned 1 million acres of land, 10,000 houses, 70 factories, ten sugar mills, five mines, and two banks in Cuba. The Brigade was in fact fairly representative of those elements of Cuban society that had opposed Castro; those elements in turn happened to be comprised of the kinds of people who owned banks and sugar mills. Thomas, *The Cuban Revolution*, p. 583.
93   "We are under attack": Johnson, *Bay of Pigs*, p. 139.
93   white tie and tails: *Time*, 4/28/61.
93   Those who had planned and sold the invasion: Bundy int; Rusk int; Schlesinger int; Stewart Alsop, "Lessons of the Cuban Disaster," *Saturday Evening Post*, 9/16/91; Schlesinger, *A Thousand Days*, pp. 277–278; Wyden, *Bay of Pigs*, pp. 269–272.
94   The unwritten plan: Lucien S. Vandenbroucke, "The 'Confessions' of Allen Dulles"; Parmet, *JFK*, p. 164; Wyden, *Bay of Pigs*, p. 270.
94   They were prisoners: Parmet, *JFK*, p. 170; Schlesinger, *A Thousand Days*, pp. 283–284.
94   "One of them is threatening suicide": Schlesinger, *A Thousand Days*, p. 278.
94   "That's a deeper commitment": Rusk int; Schlesinger, *A Thousand Days*, p. 278; Wyden, *Bay of Pigs*, p. 271.
95   "Hold his hand": Parmet, *JFK*, p. 168.
95   In the middle of a sentence: Salinger, *With Kennedy*, p. 195.

95   Kennedy was crying: Salinger int; Kenneth P. O'Donnell and David F. Powers, with Joe McCarthy, *"Johnny, We Hardly Knew Ye"* (New York: Pocket Books, 1972), pp. 316–317.

Albert Gore had the first appointment with Kennedy on the morning after the Bay of Pigs: "His hair was disheveled, he was disheveled, his tie was askew, he talked too fast, and he was extremely bitter, especially at Lemnitzer. He didn't use that word, but he felt he was framed, especially after he was asked to release jets from an aircraft carrier." Gore int.

95   "We've got to do something": Sidey, *John F. Kennedy, President*, p. 129.

95   "What matters now is this man": Schoenbaum, *Waging Peace and War*, p. 302.

Chapter 8

96   They thought they were going to Nicaragua: Parmet, *JFK*, p. 170; Schlesinger, *A Thousand Days*, pp. 279–282.

96   "We can't do any more here": Schlesinger int; Schlesinger, *A Thousand Days*, p. 283.

It was not the first time Kennedy had sent Schlesinger to deal with the Cubans. On April 13, Schlesinger and Berle had met with Miró Cardona at the Century Club in New York to tell him, among other things, that "no U.S. troops would be sent in support of the Cuban anti-Castro operations." To this, Schlesinger had noted, "Dr. Cardona displayed considerable resistance." If the movement against Castro failed, the Cuban said, the United States would be held responsible along with the Revolutionary Council. "Everyone knows," Cardona had said, "that the United States is behind the Cuban operation."

Further, Cardona had made it clear that he planned to call on American help if his forces got into trouble. "This help must come. You must understand what will happen to your interests if we lose. You must commit yourselves to full support of our efforts." Schlesinger memo to JFK, 4/14/61, Schlesinger papers, Box WH-31, JFKL.

97   Schlesinger had never seen him so drawn: Schlesinger int; Schlesinger, *A Thousand Days*, p. 283.

97   "I know something of how you feel": Plank int; Schlesinger int; Schlesinger, *A Thousand Days*, p. 284; Wyden, *Bay of Pigs*, pp. 292–293.

97   he had never seen him so impressive: Schlesinger, *A Thousand Days*, p. 284.

98   "You'll stay with the Revolutionary Council?": Plank int. Just before Plank was to depart with the exile leaders, he went to Schlesinger and said, "Arthur, I don't have a shirt and I don't have any money." Schlesinger told him not to worry and came back moments later to give him an envelope with two hundred dollars inside. Wyden, *Bay of Pigs*, p. 293.

98   The statement: Schlesinger, *A Thousand Days*, pp. 284–285.

98   Cardona emerged: This scene is drawn from confidential dispatches, Time arch.

98   "The hour is late": JFKPP, 4/20/61.

99   "It was the worst experience of my life": Richard Nixon conv; Nixon, "Cuba, Castro, and John F. Kennedy," *Reader's Digest* (November 1964); Nixon, *RN: The Memoirs of Richard Nixon* (New York: Grosset & Dunlap, 1978), pp. 234–235.

100   King's meeting with the President: Martin Luther King, Jr., OH, p. 14, JFKL; Branch, *Parting the Waters*, pp. 407, 962.

100   met with King only once: Branch, *Parting the Waters*, pp. 313–314.

100   Kennedy had told Wofford: Louis Martin int; Wofford int; Wofford, *Of Kennedys and Kings*, p. 216.

100   He had given the same instructions: "Word always went out: when Rockefeller comes down, you route him to the White House first," said Gilpatric. "The President wanted to be right on top of the situation as far as Rockefeller was concerned. Rockefeller had a house in Washington. He was down there a good deal, and there was a lot of concentrated espionage. . . . I never saw more concentrated attention given to any political subject, from the time I got to know the President well . . . through the next two years." Gilpatric OH, p. 94, JFKL.

101   By Friday morning: Schlesinger, *A Thousand Days*, p. 289.

101   "I know that many of you": JFKPP, 4/21/61.

101   "victory has a hundred fathers": Schlesinger, *A Thousand Days*, p. 289. When Schlesinger asked him where the quotation came from, Kennedy replied, "Oh, I don't know; it's just an old saying." Though Schlesinger could not source it, it is in fact a line from the wartime diaries of Mussolini's foreign minister and son-in-law, Galeazzo Ciano.

101   "What the hell do they want me to do?": Salinger, *With Kennedy*, p. 204.

101   he met with Maxwell Taylor: Ranelagh, *The Agency*, p. 377.

101   Taylor was stunned: Taylor OH, p. 9, LBJL.

102   "It's a hell of a way to learn things": Wyden, *Bay of Pigs*, p. 269.

102   lunch with former President Eisenhower: Eisenhower notes of meeting, 4/22/61, Post-Presidential Papers, Box 11, DDEL; Eisenhower memo, 4/22/61, DDRS (1980) 451F.

103   In public: NYT, 4/23/61.

103   "suggested a golf game": Eisenhower notes of meeting, 4/22/61.

103   "In a parliamentary system": Thomas Powers, *The Man Who Kept the Secrets*, (New York: Knopf, 1979), p. 115; Ranelagh, *The Agency*, pp. 365, 770. By some accounts, Kennedy said this to Dulles—it could be that he told them both.

103   He thought he would make his brother: RFK OH, p. 82, JFKL.

104   "I sat around that day": Draft manuscript, Fay, *The Pleasure of His Company*, Land papers, Box 12, BU.

104   "You see Kenny there?": Theodore White conv.

104   Of Mrs. Lincoln: Sander Vanocur int.

104   Robert Kennedy's first advice: RFK OH, p. 82, JFKL.

104   On April 27: Sidey, *John F. Kennedy, President*, p. 145.

105   a "Record of Action": National Security Council Record of Action 2422, 5/5/61, Cuba papers, NSA.

105   "Efforts should be made": National Security Council Record of Action 2425, 5/5/61, Cuba papers, NSA.

105   "Cuba means a great deal": Rusk OH, p. 208, JFKL.

105   "I put those men in there": Rostow int; O'Donnell and Powers, *"Johnny, We Hardly Knew Ye,"* pp. 316–317. Rostow said Kennedy had a "small unit commander's attitude" toward the prisoners.

106   "Last week": *Time*, 5/5/61.

106   "Kennedy: The Only Years": Schlesinger, *A Thousand Days*, p. 289.

106   "Jesus": Salinger int; Schlesinger, *A Thousand Days*, p. 292.

Chapter 9

107   "Muong Sai has fallen": Winthrop Brown cable to Rusk, 4/26/61, Vice-Presidential Security File, Box 4, LBJL.

108   "Discussions revolved": NYT, 4/27/61.

108   He blamed Franklin D. Roosevelt: James McGregor Burns conv.

108   "Our way of life is under attack": JFKPP, 4/27/61.

109   The publishers clapped politely only twice: NYT, 4/28/61.

109   the next day's editorial reaction: NYT, 4/28/61; Salinger, *With Kennedy*, p. 207.

110   "He does not feel we should intervene": JFK memo, 4/28/61, POF Box 62, JFKL.

110   twenty minutes of sex: Campbell, writing under her new married name of Exner, went public with her account of an affair with Kennedy in *My Story* (New York: Grove Press, 1977). For a time, Campbell had been romantically involved with JFK and underworld boss Sam Giancana simultaneously, and she had been questioned in 1975 by staff members of the Senate Select Committee looking into Giancana's role in CIA attempts to assassinate Fidel Castro. Her name was leaked to the press by aides to Republican senators who were incensed that the final version of the committee report referred to Exner only as a "friend of President Kennedy."

The committee's investigations revealed extensive phone contact between Exner and the White House through the spring of 1962. Exner's book combined enough information about Kennedy's schedule and evidence such as private phone numbers and photographs of invitations and notes with a naive and defensive writing style for its claims to be believable. And in 1991, newly opened White House Police Post and Gate Logs confirmed Judith Campbell's 1961 visits to the White House. See Records of the U.S. Secret Service, Record Group 87, JFKL.

It is important to note, however, that many statements Exner has made since then are not credible. Most notoriously, in the February 29, 1988, issue of *People,* she stated that she was suffering from terminal cancer and had previously lied because she had feared for her life. "Now that I know I'm dying and nothing more can happen to me, I want to be completely honest," she told Kitty Kelley, before going on to say that JFK had used her as a conduit to the mob.

Exner's new account—along with Kelley's damaging misquote of a Kennedy Library official in support of it—has been used by several authors, notably Thomas Reeves in *A Question of Character: A Life of John F. Kennedy* (New York: Free Press, 1991), but nothing exists to substantiate her story beyond the claims Exner made in 1977.

In 1993, Exner announced that she planned to write a newly definitive volume of memoirs with Anthony Summers, whose previous work includes books on the Kennedy assassination and Marilyn Monroe.

110 "This is the cork in the bottle": PP II, pp. 635–637; Clifford, "A Viet Nam Reappraisal."

111 Kennedy had also had some success: This account of Kennedy's maneuverings in Laos is drawn from Notes on NSC meeting, 4/27/61, NSF Box 313, JFKL, and the following sources: Bundy int; Rusk int; U. Alexis Johnson OH, JFKL; RFK OH, JFKL; Rudy Abramson, *Spanning the Century: The Life of W. Averell Harriman* (New York: William Morrow, 1992), pp. 582–584; Parmet, *JFK,* pp. 131–155; Rust, *Kennedy in Vietnam,* pp. 28–33; and Charles Stevenson, *The End of Nowhere: American Policy Toward Laos Since 1954,* pp. 146–148.

113 "Zero": McNamara int.

113 "The only thing to do is eliminate Castro": Goodwin, *Remembering America,* p. 189.

Fourteen years later, the Church Committee asked Goodwin about an article in that month's *Harper's* magazine which quoted him as attributing to McNamara the statement that "Castro's assassination was the only productive way of dealing with Cuba."

"That's not an exact quote," Goodwin replied. He had not said "that it was definitely McNamara, that very possibly it was McNamara." Moments later, though, he allowed as how the author had asked him "about McNamara's role, and I said it very well could have been McNamara."

Goodwin went on to say, "It's not a light matter to perhaps destroy a man's career on the basis of a fifteen-year-old memory of a single sentence that he might have said at a meeting without substantial certainty to your own mind, and I do not have that." CC, pp. 164–165, text and note 2.

Another fourteen years later, Goodwin's memoirs contained the line used in the text.

113 Kennedy rejected it: Bundy int.

113 "I hope you'll be in a good mood": Bundy memo to JFK, 5/16/61, NSF Box 287–290, JFKL.

114 Bundy's sorting of raw intelligence: The Situation Room is described in Robert M. Gates, "An Opportunity Unfulfilled: The Use and Perceptions of Intelligence at the White House," *Washington Quarterly* (Winter 1989).

115 "If the intervention involves U.S. forces": Mansfield memo to JFK, 5/1/61, Vice-Presidential Security File, Box 4, LBJL.

115 "How can I send troops to Laos": Salinger int; Schlesinger int; Nixon, *RN,* p. 234.

115 "It was rigged": "Mr. Dulles, in answer to a question, suggested that the outcome of the elections did not truly represent the popularity of President Diem, and that in essence, the elections were rigged. . . . General McGarr did not believe the elections were rigged although there was no other candidate." Arleigh Burke, Memo for the Record, 4/28/61, FRUS 1961, Document 36, p. 82.

In November, the CIA, stating that "the conditions under which the April elections were held in South Viet-Nam were such that the outcome was never in doubt," reported on the tactics used by Diem to seal his victory. One of them was that symbols were used on the official ballots to identify candidates to illiterate voters: "Quat was identified with the symbol of a water buffalo and Tan with a lotus flower"; Diem was represented by his own picture. CIA memo, 11/16/61, VDDHD, Document 73, pp. 145–146.

115   a fanfare of uncoded radio transmissions: see William Conrad Gibbons, *The U.S. Government and the Vietnam War*, (Princeton, NJ: Princeton University Press, 1986), pp. 18–33; Rust, *Kennedy in Vietnam*, pp. 28–33.

1115   Averell Harriman was sent to New Delhi: Abramson, *Spanning the Century*, pp. 582–584; Galbraith, *Ambassador's Journal*, p. 93.

116   "The cease-fire in Laos": *Time*, 5/5/61.

116   "Sons of bitches": Dutton int; Salinger int.

116   He had ticked off the reasons: Rostow int; Collier and Horowitz, *The Kennedys*, p. 274; Rust, *Kennedy in Vietnam*, pp. 32–34.

116   working paper for the meeting: "Program of Action to Prevent Communist Domination of South Vietnam," 4/27/61, FRUS 1961, Document 42, pp. 92–115.

116   "The Report the President Wanted Published": *Saturday Evening Post*, 5/20/61.

117   "A state of guerrilla warfare": "Program of Action to Prevent Communist Domination of South Vietnam."

117   The President approved more than fifty: NSAM 52, 5/11/61, USVNR, Book 11, pp. 136–137. For more on the April 29 NSC meeting, see FRUS 1961, Editorial note 40, p. 88; Draft Record of Actions, NSC meeting, 4/29/61, Vice-Presidential Security File Box 4, LBJL.

117   The Commander-in-Chief had personally overruled: On JFK and the Special Forces, see Hilsman, *To Move a Nation*, pp. 52–53, 413–439.

118   "Two minutes to launch": *Time*, 5/12/61.

118   Confidential reports to the White House: Report of the Ad Hoc Mercury Panel, 4/12/61, Sorensen papers, Box 38, JFKL. See also Sidey memo to Salinger, 4/14/61; Wiesner memo to JFK; Hornig memo to Sorensen, 4/18/61; all in Sorensen papers, Box 38, JFKL.

118   "The astronaut": *Time*, 5/12/61. See also Alan Shepard OH, pp. 1–6, JFKL.

119   "Elected officers have a code": Kenneth O'Donnell OH, pp. 24–26, LBJL.

119   "Don't worry, Lyndon": Bartlett int; Stephen Smith int; Collier and Horowitz, *The Kennedys*, p. 274.

119   "Since I took office": JFK letter to Diem, 5/8/61, NSF Box 193, JFKL.

119   "the government of Vietnam": Diem letter to JFK, 5/15/61, NSF Box 193, JFKL.

120   "For our historic task": JFKPP, 5/17/61.

120   In private talks: *Time*, 5/26/61.

120   then felt the pain: Schlesinger, *A Thousand Days*, pp. 343–344. A photo of the moment, extremely rare in its capturing Kennedy in obvious agony, is in Lieberson and Meyers, eds., *John Fitzgerald Kennedy . . . As We Remember Him*, p. 132.

120   "To prevent Communist domination": State Department Task Force on Vietnam, "Presidential Program for Vietnam," 5/23/61, Vice-Presidential Security File, Box 1, LBJL.

121   "Develop agricultural pilot-projects": "Program of Action to Prevent Communist Domination of South Vietnam."

121   He told Krock: Krock, *Memoirs*, pp. 343–345.

121   Mao Tse-tung: Schlesinger handwritten notes from conversation with Theodore White, undated Schlesinger papers, Box W-14, JFKL.

Chapter 10

122   President Kennedy found out: Schlesinger, *Robert Kennedy and His Times*, p. 317. Asked how he learned about the Freedom Riders, Robert Kennedy answered, "We read about it in the newspapers." RFK OH, p. 544, JFKL.

123   a December 1960 ruling: The new decision was *Boynton* v. *Virginia*. The buses themselves had been desegregated by a Supreme Court ruling in 1947.

123   Their goal: *Time*, 5/26/89; Branch, *Parting the Waters*, pp. 412–416; Schlesinger, *Robert Kennedy and His Times*, pp. 316–317. On the Freedom Rides more generally, see also James Farmer OH, pp. 17–23; George Leake OH, pp. 15–19; Marion Rich OH, pp. 8–9; and Fred Shuttlesworth OH, all at Howard.

123 Farmer had sent a press release: John Seigenthaler OH, p. 301, JFKL.
123 Simeon Booker: Seigenthaler OH, pp. 301–302, JFKL; Branch, *Parting the Waters*, p. 413.
124 The follow-up story: NYT, 5/16/61.
124 celebrating Mother's Day: Schlesinger, *Robert Kennedy and His Times*, p. 317.
124 "It's pretty bad down here": Seigenthaler int.
124 The President agreed with his brother's idea: Marshall int.
124 Patterson had been their man: RFK OH, p. 574, JFKL.
124 "What do you want me to do?": The account of the first Freedom Ride is drawn from Marshall int; Seigenthaler int; Marshall OH, pp. 39–40, JFKL; Seigenthaler OH, pp. 301–334, JFKL; Seigenthaler OH, Howard; Branch, *Parting the Waters*, pp. 417–430.
125 "Can't you get your goddamned friends": Wofford int.
125 "KENNEDY WEIGHS MEETING": NYT, 5/15/61.
125 "Military Planning for a Possible Berlin Crisis": McNamara memo to JFK, 5/6/61, Berlin Crisis papers, NSA.
125 he ordered five hundred more American troops: National Security Council Record of Actions, 5/5/61, Cuba papers, NSA.
125 the President had met in his bedroom: Marshall int; Marshall OH, p. 49, JFKL.
125 their grunted code: Martin int; Wofford int.
126 "Not helpful": Edwin Guthman int; Seigenthaler int.
126 "This Goddamned civil rights mess": "The new President spoke of 'that goddamned civil rights mess,' " George Ball OH, p. 165, JFKL. The President's use of the term was confirmed by Bernhard, Hesburgh, Marshall, Seigenthaler, and Wofford ints.
126 "There's going to be another bus": Marshall int.
126 "It was like talking to a brick wall": Seigenthaler int.
126 chosen to avoid appointing Harris Wofford: Schlesinger, *Robert Kennedy and His Times*, pp. 309–310.
127 Marshall laid out the law: Marshall OH, pp. 6, 7, 20, 30, JFKL; Branch, *Parting the Waters*, pp. 434–435.
127 "Hoover's on the other side": Marshall int.
127 FBI informers: Schlesinger, *Robert Kennedy and His Times*, p. 317; WP, 8/20/78. Gary Thomas Rowe, Jr., a Klan informant working for the FBI, learned about preparations for attacking the buses. The FBI, which did not give the information to the Justice Department, did forward it to a Birmingham police official known to be a member of the Klan.
127 He had criticized Eisenhower: Nicholas Katzenbach OH, JFKL.
127 He suggested creating a civilian force: Marshall int; Branch, *Parting the Waters*, pp. 434–435.
128 "Not yet": Nicholas Katzenbach OH, pp. 9–13, JFKL. For twenty-four hours, Katzenbach said, he wondered if there were "any guts behind this" operation.
128 Kennedy picked up the telephone: *Time*, 5/26/61.
128 "There's nobody in the whole country": Seigenthaler OH, Howard.
128 beaten and bloody: Seigenthaler int.
128 "very much upset": Schlesinger, *Robert Kennedy and His Times*, p. 318. Unknown to the Attorney General, George Cruit, the Greyhound superintendent, taped the call. And when Justice Department officials called Robert Kennedy from Maxwell Field in Alabama, the operator, who was married to a state trooper, tapped the conversations for Patterson. The governor passed them along to state newspapers—including a sentence in which Robert Kennedy said, "We have gone to a lot of trouble to see that they get to this trip and I am most concerned to see that is accomplished." That made it sound like the Kennedys had something to do with organizing the rides, an idea that led to some ironic laughter inside the White House but that many Americans believed after reading about the Alabama tapes. Guthman int; Marshall int; Branch, *Parting the Waters*, pp. 443–444; Schlesinger, *Robert Kennedy and His Times*, notes to pp. 318, 319.
129 He tried to rescue two Freedom Riders: Seigenthaler int; Seigenthaler OH, Howard.
129 "You did what you had to do": Seigenthaler int.
129 "My fundamental belief": Schlesinger, *Robert Kennedy and His Times*, p. 307.

130   inside the church: The account of the federal marshals relieving the church is drawn from *Time,* 6/2/61, and the following sources: RFK OH, pp. 376–380, JFKL; Marshall OH, pp. 84–86, JFKL; Branch, *Parting the Waters,* pp. 454–465; Schlesinger, *Robert Kennedy and His Times,* pp. 320–321.

During the siege, Patterson had complained to Robert Kennedy: "Your're killing me politically."

"I'd rather be dead politically," RFK snapped back, "than have those people dead inside that church." Guthman int.

130   In fact, he was making the decisions: RFK conv; RFK OH, JFKL.

130   Robert Kennedy relayed a complaint: William Orrick OH, p. 92, JFKL.

131   "Kelsey's nuts": Robert Kennedy had "Kelsey" wrong. The name came from an old Irish expression "tight as Kelsey's nuts." It means cheap.

131   "Tell them to call it off": Wofford int.

131   "Are your constituents happy?": "I grew tired," Wofford wrote later, "of his accosting me with a grin and asking me, 'Are your constituents happy?' " Wofford, *Of Kennedys and Kings,* p. 166.

132   "Who the hell was that man with Harry Belafonte?" Wofford, *Of Kennedys and Kings,* pp. 125–126.

132   "This is too much!": Wofford, *Of Kennedys and Kings,* p. 156.

132   "In Birmingham and Montgomery": NYT, 5/23/61.

133   "What gets me": Sidey, *John F. Kennedy, President,* p. 154.

133   an anti-segregation amendment: NYT, 5/23/61. See also Martin memo to Sorensen, 5/10/61, Sorensen papers, Box 30, JFKL.

133   He urged King: Marshall int; RFK OH, JFKL; Seigenthaler OH, Howard; Wofford, *Of Kennedys and Kings,* p. 297.

133   King asked Kennedy: Wofford int.

133   "They performed a service": NBC-TV broadcast, "The Kennedy Administration: Week Eleven."

134   "A cooling-off period": Schlesinger, *Robert Kennedy and His Times,* p. 321. "We've been cooling off for 100 years," James Farmer said. "If we got any cooler we'd be in a deep freeze."

134   "Wait means 'Never!' ": *Time,* 6/2/61.

Chapter 11

135   "The Constitution imposes upon me": JFKPP, 5/25/61.

136   "Jack Kennedy": *Time,* 5/26/61.

136   Kennedy read a similar warning: Thompson cable to JFK, 5/24/61, Berlin papers, NSA.

136   "He's not dumb": Sidey, *John F. Kennedy, President,* pp. 167–172.

137   Kennedy received a second warning: Thompson cable to JFK, 5/30/61, Berlin papers, NSA.

137   Georgi Bolshakov: Bolshakov conv. Years later, Bolshakov detailed his encounters with the New Frontier for a Russian magazine, *New Times,* nos. 4–6, 1989. See also RFK OH, Salinger OH, pp. 179–182, Thompson OH, pp. 46–48, all in JFKL; NW, 12/24/62.

137   "Who is he, really?": Bartlett int.

137   Holeman brought Bolshakov to the Attorney General's office: Frank Holeman int; RFK OH, JFKL; *New Times,* no. 4, 1989.

138   a total reversal in Kennedy's thinking: This account of Kennedy's initial involvement with the space program is drawn from Walter A. McDougall, . . . *the Heavens and the Earth: A Political History of the Space Age* (New York: Basic Books, 1985), pp. 309–310, and Charles Murray and Catherine Bly Cox, *Apollo: The Race to the Moon* (New York: Simon & Schuster, 1989), pp. 61–74.

139   Habib Bourguiba: Murray and Cox, *Apollo,* pp. 66–67.

139   "This country should be realistic": LBJ memo to JFK, 4/28/61, Famous Names File, "John F. Kennedy," LBJL.

139   "Are we working 24 hours a day on existing programs?": JFK memo to LBJ, 4/20/61, Famous Names File, "John F. Kennedy," LBJL.

139 "Can we beat the Russians?": Wernher von Braun OH, pp. 3–6, JFKL.
140 "The adversaries of freedom": JFKPP, 5/25/61.
140 "Executive Action": Early in 1961, probably on January 25 or 26, Bissell asked William Harvey, then chief of a foreign intelligence staff at the CIA, to establish "executive action," the means to overthrow foreign leaders by means up to and including killing them. The project to develop what the CIA called this "general standby capability" was termed ZR/RIFLE, and one agent, code-named QJ/WIN, was assigned to work under Harvey. (CIA designations of this type generally consisted of a two-letter code followed by a random word—the names were not acronyms or symbols.) Harvey studied the "problems and requirements" of assassination and used QJ/WIN to locate potential recruits for possible jobs.
Bissell told the Church Committee in 1975 that ZR/RIFLE was "internal and purely preparatory." Harvey testified that "during the entire existence of the entire ZR/RIFLE project . . . no agent was ever recruited for the purpose of assassination, and no even tentative targeting or target list was ever drawn."
Around that time, "executive action" came up in a conversation between Bissell and Bundy. Harvey testified in 1975 that Bissell had told him twice that "the White House" wanted to establish the capability to remove foreign leaders. Harvey had destroyed his notes on this matter by the time the Church Committee conducted its investigation, but a 1967 report by the Inspector-General of the CIA had quoted them to the same effect. Bundy said it was Bissell who brought it up and that his impression was that the CIA was "testing my reaction" rather than "seeking authority." Bissell first assumed that Harvey was correct, then later testified that "he merely informed Bundy of the capability and that the context was a briefing by him and not urging by Bundy."
Bissell believed Allen Dulles knew of ZR/RIFLE but said he had not provided information on the project to John McCone. McCone testified to the Church Committee that he knew nothing about it. CC, pp. 181–190.
140 three assassination plans: See CC, pp. 13–67; Richard D. Mahoney, *JFK: Ordeal in Africa* (New York: Oxford University Press, 1983), pp. 43–45, 52–53, 69–74.
140 U.S. plots against Castro: CC, pp. 71–82, 125–126.
140 Eisenhower had approved a shipment of arms: CC, pp. 196–197.
140 Kennedy had been President for only three weeks: Rusk memo to JFK, 2/15/61, NSF Box 66–67, JFKL; CC, p. 203.
141 Two days later: CIA memo, 2/17/61, NSF Box 66–67, JFKL; CC, p. 204.
141 "Get an up-to-date report": JFK memo, 5/30/61, Lincoln Dictation File, POF Box 62, JFKL.
141 "We must not run risk": CC, p. 213. On April 17, the CIA cabled its Dominican station to hold off on passing machine guns to the dissidents. Three days later, headquarters explained that this was based on "judgment that filling a vacuum created by assassination now bigger question than ever view unsettled conditions in Caribbean area." CC, pp. 205–206.
141 "We doubt statement": CC, p. 206. Essentially, as the Church Committee concluded, the dissidents had said that "this was their affair and could not be turned off to suit the convenience of the U.S. government"—a lesson that would later echo for the Kennedy administration in Cuba, Berlin, and Vietnam.
141 "The United States should not initiate": CC, p. 209.
141 "Too late": CC, p. 212. In 1975, Dearborn said that he interpreted Kennedy's May 29 cable as no change in policy, that "we don't care if the Dominicans assassinate Trujillo, that is all right. But we don't want anything to pin this on us, because we aren't doing it, it is the Dominicans who are doing it."
CIA station chief Didier, on the other hand, said that because of Kennedy's cable, he felt the final word was that the United States would withhold material support from the dissidents. On May 30, he cabled back to the CIA: "HQ aware extent to which U.S. government already associated with assassination. If we are to at least cover up tracks, CIA personnel directly involved in assassination preparation must at least be withdrawn." CC, pp. 212–214.
141 actually a family named De La Maza: CC, p. 206. See also Bernard Diedrich, *Death of the Goat* (Boston: Little, Brown, 1978).
142 "The members of our club": CC, p. 199.

Chapter 12

143   "I had the damnedest meeting in New York": Bartlett int.
144   "You know I was elected by the Jews": Bartlett int.
144   "I go as the leader of the greatest revolutionary country on earth": Schlesinger,
A Thousand Days, p. 349.
144   "It's rather like fighting": Time, 5/26/61.
144   "Why is de Gaulle screwing us?": Rostow OH, p. 100, JFKL.
144   "De Gaulle is basically solid": "President's Visit to DeGaulle," State Department
Background Papers, 5/26/61, Nuclear History papers, NSA.
145   "He was the youngest senator in the United States": Prendergast dispatch 2368
from Paris, 6/1/61, Time arch.
145   In Le Monde the day before: Coverage of Kennedy's trip to France is drawn
from Le Figaro, Le Monde, and the international editions of The New York Herald
Tribune and The New York Times, 5/30–6/2/61.
145   at Orly Airport: Time, 6/9/61; Charles de Gaulle, Memoirs: Renewal, 1958–
1962 (London: Weidenfeld & Nicolson, 1971), p. 254.
146   "Interesting": Schlesinger, A Thousand Days, p. 354.
146   but he was in terrible pain: Salinger int; O'Donnell and Powers, "Johnny, We
Hardly Knew Ye," p. 335; Sidey, John F. Kennedy, President, p. 168.
146   Even Ted Sorensen: Sorensen int.
146   amphetamines: The first form of amphetamine was synthesized in 1887 and its
effectiveness as a stimulant first noted in the 1930s. The American, British, German, and
Japanese armed forces issued oral amphetamines to their soldiers during World War II
to fight fatigue and improve endurance, and the drugs were popularly prescribed as
antidepressants and diet pills after the war. The practice of injecting amphetamines
developed sometime in the 1950s, possibly during the Korean War by American servicemen, and was picked up by doctors in San Francisco and New York.
    In the early 1960s, while President Kennedy was being treated by Dr. Max Jacobson
with injections that included amphetamine, the drug was earning the name "speed" on
the street, and an exploding number of "Dr. Feelgoods" were handing out prescriptions
to anyone who asked for them. Law enforcement authorities cracked down on dispensers
of injectable amphetamines in 1962 and 1963, and major manufacturers of amphetamine
compounds withdrew from the American retail drug market.
    But it was only later, after the use of injected amphetamines continued to rise in the
United States and led to the phenomenon of the "speed freak," that the full range of their
effects became known. Over time, as studies in 1967 and 1969 showed, the extraordinary
feelings of well-being and personal power produced by mainlining "speed" were addictive and could lead to paranoid psychosis. Federal legislation finally placed severe
limits on all production and distribution of amphetamines after their use had spread to
epidemic proportions by 1971. See Edward M. Brecher and the Editors of Consumer
Reports, Licit and Illicit Drugs (Boston: Little, Brown, 1972), pp. 278–293.
    In July 1968, and again in March 1969, Dr. Jacobson could not account for quantities
of amphetamines to the federal Bureau of Narcotics and Dangerous Drugs, and authorities seized all controlled substances in his possession. In 1975, the New York State Board
of Regents revoked his medical license. New York FBI office cable to Acting Director,
8/18/72, File 62-84930 (Max Jacobson, FBI); "Calendar No. 1,000," Report of Findings,
Determination, and Recommendation of the Hearing Panel of the Committee on Professional Conduct of the State Board for Medicine, New York State Department of Education; Jerrold M. Post, "The High and Mighty High," WP, 1/28/90.
146   Dr. Max Jacobson: material on Max Jacobson is drawn from an unpublished
memoir he wrote shortly before his death in 1979, which contains a 48-page chapter on
his relationship with President Kennedy, courtesy of Ruth Jacobson, and the following
sources: Ruth Jacobson int; confidential source int; File 62–84930 (Max Jacobson, FBI);
NYT, 12/4/72.
    Jacobson's medical records for Kennedy are not available; his widow is certain that he
destroyed them. Jacobson's FBI file, however, states that New York's Bureau of Narcotics
and Dangerous Drugs listed Kennedy as one of Jacobson's patients. New York office

cable to Acting Director, 8/18/72, File 62–84930 (Max Jacobson, FBI). Gate logs confirm that Jacobson visited the White House more than thirty times in 1961 and 1962. Records of the U.S. Secret Service, White House Post and Gate Logs, Boxes 2–12, JFKL. Also, Mrs. Jacobson possesses several minor items that corroborate stories told by her late husband in his memoir.

There is proof, morever, that he traveled with Kennedy. The protocol list of Americans who went to the Vienna summit in 1961 was processed for the White House Central Subject Files before 1972, when Jacobson's name first entered public attention, so that officials would not then have known to remove documents containing his name for privacy or "national security" reasons. Dr. and Mrs. Max Jacobson are listed as staying in Room 404 of the Hotel Kummer in Vienna. "Final List of Members of the Official American Party," 5/30/61, Department of State Office of Protocol, WHCSF Box 971, JFKL.

On the other hand, passenger manifests for White House flights, which are prepared for the FAA for all trips, have been withheld from release for the dates May 27 through June 7, 1961, which is highly unusual. These lists were processed after 1972. See withdrawal sheets, Godfrey McHugh papers, Box 18, JFKL.

147 "Evidently what the General wants": Bundy memo to JFK, POF Box 116a, JFKL.

148 The two presidents talked for almost an hour: This account of the meetings between Kennedy and de Gaulle is drawn from de Gaulle, *Memoirs*, pp. 254–259, and from the following sources: Elson dispatches 1069 and 1075 from London, 6/2/61; Prendergast dispatch 2368 from Paris, 6/1/61; Steele dispatches 2368 and 2428 from Paris, 6/1–2/61; all in Time arch; *Time*, 6/9/61; O'Donnell and Powers, *"Johnny, We Hardly Knew Ye,"* pp. 334–338; Schlesinger, *A Thousand Days*, pp. 349–354.

149 "Trujillo is dead": Salinger int; Diedrich, *Death of the Goat*, pp. 3–5, 107–110.

150 "Let's take the open car": *Time*, 6/9/61.

150 Kennedy told Rusk: Rusk int; Schoenbaum, *Waging Peace and War*, p. 371.

150 At the May 5 meeting: National Security Council Record of Actions, 5/5/61, Cuba papers, NSA.

150 He wanted U.S. Navy ships deployed: Diedrich, *Death of the Goat.*

150 they crawled across the carpet: O'Donnell and Powers, *"Johnny, We Hardly Knew Ye,"* pp. 334–335.

150 Salinger had a press briefing: Salinger int; Salinger, *With Kennedy*, pp. 225–226.

151 But Trujillo was dead: Diedrich, *Death of the Goat.*

151 Rusk also warned Kennedy: Schoenbaum, *Waging Peace and War*, p. 371.

151 At the Elysée dinner: Salinger int; Sidey int; *Time*, 6/9/61; Lieberson and Meyers, eds., *John Fitzgerald Kennedy . . . As We Remember Him*, p. 136.

152 "Let Bobby play around": David Halberstam, int.

152 "They want to send in the Marines": David Halberstam, *The Best and the Brightest* (Greenwich, CT: Fawcett Crest, 1973), p. 89.

152 Averell Harriman: Halberstam, *The Best and the Brightest*, pp. 94–95. "I've learned dealing with the White House," Harriman said later, "that you have a split second. The President looks around the room and you decide whether you're among those that agree or register their difference. You can't wait." Harriman OH, p. 121, JFKL. Looking at it from the other direction, Larry O'Brien put it this way: "In a political situation, such as a receiving line, a politician often has about ten seconds to give an impression that may last a lifetime." O'Brien, *No Final Victories*, p. 22.

153 "Pretty impressive, isn't it?": George Herman int; Mary McGrory letter to author, 7/7/89; Press Panel OH, pp. 36–39, JFKL; Sidey dispatch 2404 from Paris, 6/2/61, Time arch.

153 "My, where did you learn to speak French?": Bradlee int; Herman int.

154 It was misty: *Time*, 6/9/61.

154 "Apotheosis at Versailles": *France-Soir*, 6/4/61.

154 "What a cruel fate": André Malraux, *Antimémoires* (Paris: Gallimard, 1967), pp. 272–273.

154 "Tell her it's hurting me politically": Duke int.

155   "I'm dazzled": *Time*, 6/9/61.
155   "Stop that plane!": Duke int.

Chapter 13

156   "Rusk, you make a hell of a substitute": Schoenbaum, *Waging Peace and War*, p. 335.
156   "INNOCENTS ABROAD SAY HOWDY": Sidey, *John F. Kennedy, President*, p. 192.
156   He laughed when he read: *International Herald Tribune*, 6/5/61.
157   "Khrushchev must not misunderstand": Krock, *Memoirs*, pp. 343–345; Sidey, *John F. Kennedy, President*, p. 197.
157   The State Department had seemed to agree: State Department, "President's Meeting with Khrushchev, Vienna, June 3–4, 1961," background papers, Berlin papers, NSA. Material on Kennedy's briefings for his European meetings is also drawn from Sidey dispatch from Washington, 5/26/61, Time arch.
158   CIA psychologists: Catudal, *Kennedy and the Berlin Wall Crisis*, p. 110.
158   As a senator and candidate: During his October 1960 debates with Nixon, Kennedy had said, "I would not meet with Mr. Khrushchev unless there were some agreement at the secondary level—foreign ministers or ambassadors—which would indicate that the meeting had hope of success, or useful exchange of ideas." And before his appointment as Secretary of State, Dean Rusk was best known for a *Foreign Affairs* article in which he argued against summitry as a form of diplomacy.
158   He had been in office only three weeks: *Time*, 5/26/61; Catudal, *Kennedy and the Berlin Wall Crisis*, p. 80.
158   Dr. Max Jacobson: unpublished memoirs of Max Jacobson, "JFK" chapter, pp. 11–16; "Final List of Members of the American Official Party," Department of State Office of Protocol, 5/30/61, WHCSF Box 971, JFKL.
159   "Tell the Chairman": *Time*, 6/9/61.
159   Inside, the two leaders faced each other: JFK-Khrushchev memcon, 6/3/61, 12:45 P.M., Berlin papers, NSA.
The account given in the text of the Kennedy-Khrushchev talks is drawn from the official memoranda of conversations between the two leaders, which were released by the State Department in 1990. As historian Michael Beschloss points out, there was no adequate reason for such a wait. Records of meetings between Eisenhower and Khrushchev, which took place about two years before the Vienna summit, were released in 1982. Schlesinger and Sorensen had used the official transcripts from Vienna to write their own detailed accounts of the Kennedy-Khrushchev meetings, published in the mid-1960s, both asserting that Kennedy had held his own against Khrushchev.
162   Kennedy came out of the music room: The events and atmosphere surrounding the Kennedy-Khrushchev discussions were reconstructed from the following sources: Burlatsky conv; Dutton, Nitze, Rusk, Salinger, Schlesinger, and Sorensen ints; Thompson OH, pp. 23–26, JFKL; NYT, 6/4–6/61; *Time*, 6/9/61, 6/16/61, 1/5/62; O'Donnell and Powers, *"Johnny, We Hardly Knew Ye,"* pp. 338–346; Schlesinger, *A Thousand Days*, pp. 358–374; and Sorensen, *Kennedy*, pp. 611–620.
162   "Is it always like this?": Schlesinger, *A Thousand Days*, p. 365.
162   Thompson told his State Department colleagues: Nitze int.
163   Back inside: JFK-Khrushchev memcon, 6/3/61, 3:00 P.M., Berlin papers, NSA.
165   "Are you all right, Mr. President?": Unpublished memoirs of Max Jacobson, "K" chapter, p. 17.
165   "How did it go?": Evelyn Lincoln, *My Twelve Years with John F. Kennedy* (New York: McKay, 1965), p. 270.
166   "He treated me like a little boy": Mansfield int.
166   Hearing the gasps: Nitze int.
166   Kennedy, they realized, had barely defended himself: Nitze int; George Kennan OH, p. 108, JFKL; Martin Hillenbrand quoted in Catudal, *Kennedy and the Berlin Wall* note to p. 115.
166   Khrushchev, out at the ambassador's residence: Burlatsky conv.
166   Khrushchev's violent mood swings: Schlesinger, *A Thousand Days*, pp. 367, 373.

167   There were three thousand people: NYT, 6/5/61; Catudal, *Kennedy and the Berlin Wall Crisis*, p. 112.
167   The leaders sat down on a sofa: JFK-Khrushchev memcon, 6/4/61, 10:15 A.M., Berlin papers, NSA.
170   Dean Rusk drew in his breath: Rusk int. The text of the aide-memoire was indeed made public by the Soviets, on June 10, and was printed in *The New York Times* on June 12.
170   he had heard Kennedy was under pressure: JFK-Khrushchev memcon, 6/4/61, luncheon, Berlin papers, NSA.
170   "Why don't we do it together?": JFK-Khrushchev memcon, 6/4/61, luncheon, Berlin papers, NSA.
170   the lunch: 6/4/61, luncheon, JFK-Khrushchev memcon, Berlin papers, NSA.
171   "I'm not going to leave until I know more": *Time*, 1/5/62.
171   "This is the nut-cutter": Bradlee, *Conversations with Kennedy*, p. 126.
171   "Then, Mr. Chairman, there will be war": Rusk int. Rusk later confirmed Kennedy's use of the word "war," writing: "Mr. Khrushchev outlined what he planned to do with Berlin and said that if there were any interference from the West, there would be war. Kennedy replied, 'Then there will be war; it is going to be a very cold winter.' " Rusk letter to the author, 4/24/89.
As Rusk points out, "Khrushchev was the first one to use 'war' and Kennedy's use of the word was in direct reply to Khrushchev's statement." Nevertheless, Kennedy's reply was reported as merely saying it would be a cold winter in the official record of the conversation and in popular accounts of the meeting. JFK-Khrushchev memcon, 6/4/61, 3:15 P.M., Berlin papers, NSA; Sidey, *John F. Kennedy, President*, p. 200; Schlesinger, *A Thousand Days*, p. 374.

Chapter 14

172   "How was it?": James Reston int.
173   "If you could think only of yourself": Joe Alsop, quoted in Helen Fuller, *Year of Trial: Kennedy's Crucial Decisions* (New York: Harcourt, Brace and World, 1962), pp. 235–236.
173   He was sitting on his bed: Duke int; *Time*, 1/5/62.
173   "That son-of-a-bitch": *Time*, 1/5/62.
173   the joint statement: NYT, 6/5/61.
173   "It was just a disaster": Susan Mary Alsop int; Nitze int.
173   "I just want you to know": Alsop int.
174   Macmillan waited for Kennedy: Horne, *Macmillan: 1957–1986*, p. 303.
174   "How would you react": Horne, *Macmillan: 1957–1986*, p. 304.
174   One small slip had fallen to the floor: Lincoln, *My Twelve Years*, p. 274.

Chapter 15

175   telephoned his friend Charlie Bartlett: Bartlett int.
175   The answer came back: The number of deaths expected in 1961 from a nuclear exchange with the Soviet Union is summarized in Kaysen memo to Bundy, 7/7/61, Berlin papers, NSA.
American casualties in the Civil War in fact numbered about 364,000 deaths on the Union side and at least 165,000 on the Confederate.
175   "Goddamnit, Ros": Gilpatric int. Kennedy called Gilpatric at seven the next morning to apologize, saying, "I was just so tired."
176   He lost his temper again: Mansfield int; Joseph Alsop, "The Most Important Decision in U.S. History—And How the President Is Facing It," *Saturday Review*, 8/5/61.
176   "He's shaken": Mansfield OH, p. 7, JFKL.
176   "There are limits": Wofford, *Of Kennedys and Kings*, p. 379.
176   "We can't let Khrushchev get away with this": Dutton int.
176   "I will tell you now": JFKPP, 6/6/61.

177   "There is no reason": Richard Rovere, "Summit Diary," *New Yorker,* 6/17/61; NYT, 6/5/61. In the *Times,* Reston also used the word "shaken" to describe Kennedy.

177   CIA reports that day: USN&WR, 6/19/61.

177   "Premier Khrushchev sang": *Washington Star,* 6/7/61.

177   "If Khrushchev wants to rub my nose in the dirt": Schlesinger, *A Thousand Days,* p. 391.

177   "I question whether it's really right": Susan Mary Alsop int.

177   He was incensed: Salinger int; *New York Herald Tribune,* 6/19/61; Montague Kern, Patricia W. Levering, and Ralph B. Levering, *The Kennedy Crises: The Press, the Presidency, and Foreign Policy* (Chapel Hill, NC: University of North Carolina Press, 1983), pp. 70–71.

177   *Time* magazine: *Time,* 6/30/61.

178   "That's the drama of our age": The Lippmann interview, done by Howard K. Smith on June 15, 1961, can be found in *Conversations with Walter Lippmann* (Boston: Little, Brown, 1965), pp. 41–43.

178   *Daily Opinion Summary:* State Department Daily Opinion Summary, 6/26/61, NSF Box 81, JFKL.

178   Kennedy only stayed: Kraus int; Sidey int; *Time,* 7/14/61; USN&WR, 6/19/61; Parmet, *JFK,* pp. 118–120.

178   On the trip home from London: Rusk int.

178   On June 10: NYT, 6/12/61.

179   a one-in-five chance: Catudal, *Kennedy and the Berlin Wall Crisis,* p. 123.

179   "The only plan": Bundy int; Bundy memo to JFK, 7/7/61, NSF Box 81, JFKL.

179   "There are now 22": NSC Directive on NATO, approved by JFK on April 21, 1961, and quoted extensively in "Summary of Rowny Preliminary NATO Report Draft," 7/24/61, Taylor papers, NSA.

179   The columnist responded: Alsop, "The Most Important Decision in U.S. History."

180   "A strong program is needed": Bundy memo, "Civil Defense Meeting," 5/13/61, NSF Box 295, JFKL.

180   "I think we should ask the Civil Defense people": JFK memo to Bundy, 7/5/61, POF Box 62, JFKL.

180   Food and water were ordered: Over the eleven years prior to 1961, the Office of Civil Defense and Mobilization had spent $600 million to build just fourteen bomb shelters. In response to Kennedy's July requests, Director "Big Frank" Ellis proposed to erect large public shelters holding 5,000 persons each, make the cost of building home shelters tax-deductible, and require shelters in federally aided schools and hospitals. Ellis thought such a program would cost $20 billion in four years and "might save 50 million lives in an atomic war." NW, 7/31/61.

180   "Did you build your shelter yet?": Curtis Cate, *The Ides of August: The Berlin Crisis 1961* (New York: M. Evans, 1978), p. 112. Through July 1961, American families had in fact built about 2,000 bomb shelters and more than 300,000 swimming pools. NW, 7/31/61.

180   the Bay of Pigs investigation: Taylor OH, p. 9, JFKL; Taylor Report, 6/13/61, NSF Box 61, JFKL. The report of the Cuba Study Group consisted of four memoranda: a description of the operation; proximate causes of its failure; conclusions; and recommendations. It was sanitized in 1977 and released in full in 1984. Paul L. Kesaris, ed., *Operation Zapata: The Ultrasensitive Report and Testimony of the Board of Inquiry on the Bay of Pigs* (Frederick, MD: University Publications of America, 1981), contains the report and accounts of the Study Group's nineteen meetings, at which many of the participants and planners were interviewed. Bissell reviewed the book in *Strategic Review* (Winter 1984).

180   "The Executive branch": Taylor Report, 6/13/61, NSF Box 61, JFKL.

181   Khrushchev went on Soviet television: The speech is reprinted in Khrushchov, *Communism,* Vol. 1, pp. 162–187.

181   Flat on his back: Sidey, *John F. Kennedy, President,* p. 210.

181   On June 22: Parmet int; Kraus int.

181   Day after day: Salinger int. Economic adviser Kermit Gordon wrote of one

meeting, for example, "The following were present: The President, Martin, Dillon, Roosa, Galbraith, Turner (sitting in for Bell), Heller, and Gordon. The President was propped up in bed smoking a cigar, and we sat in a semicircle of chairs around the bed." Gordon, "Notes on Meeting with the President on Monetary Policy," 6/12/61, Heller papers, Box 6, JFKL.

181 One of his meetings: Exner, *My Story*, pp. 221, 230, 244–245. "I understood about the position he had to assume in lovemaking when his back was troubling him, but slowly he began excluding all other positions, until finally our lovemaking was reduced to this one position," Exner wrote. "Because of his back problem there were times when there was nothing else he could do. . . . The feeling that I was there to service him began to really trouble me."

181 "Walt sure uses a lot of words, doesn't he?": Schlesinger int.

181 "In these five months": Rostow memo to JFK, "The Shape of the Battle," 6/17/61, POF Box 65, JFKL.

182 wrote in his diary: Horne, *Macmillan: 1957–1986*, p. 310.

182 Kennedy had cut short a tour: Main dispatch from Washington to Parker and Clurman, 5/25/61, Time arch.

"On Laos," Roswell Gilpatric recalled, Kennedy once had "all five of the military chiefs over, and each one had a different point of view, and he just literally and figuratively threw up his hands and walked out of the room." On another occasion, "Lieutenant General [Samuel E.] Anderson of the Air Force" gave a briefing "as though it were a kindergarten class . . . he wouldn't speed it up; he wouldn't accept questions; he just stuck to his script. And finally, Kennedy got up and walked right out in the middle of it." Gilpatric OH, p. 10, JFKL.

182 Kennedy had walked out on LeMay: Gilpatric int; Gilpatric OH, p. 116, JFKL. "Every time he had to see LeMay he ended up in sort of a fit," Gilpatric said. "He would just be frantic. LeMay couldn't listen . . . outrageous proposals, proposals that bore no relation to the state of affairs in the 1960s. The President never saw him unless . . . he felt he had to make a record of having listened to LeMay. He had to sit there. He was choleric. He was just beside himself."

183 "LeMay's like Babe Ruth": Kraar dispatch, 6/1/62, Time arch. As a matter of fact, LeMay had been a batboy for the New York Yankees in his youth and had carried hot dogs and soda for Babe Ruth. Material on LeMay is also drawn from Main dispatch from Cocoa Beach to Parker, 5/3/61; Main dispatches from Washington to Parker, 5/12/61, and 5/25/61; and Alexander dispatch to Steele and Rinehart, 8/11/61, Time arch.

183 Diem estimated: Diem letter to JFK, 6/9/61, NSF Box 193, JFKL.

183 "He cannot be persuaded by eloquence": Acheson Report to JFK, "Berlin," 6/28/61, declassified by the Department of State, FOIA case number 9100042. Quoted here for the first time, the Acheson Report, which by mid-1993 was not available at the Kennedy Library, can be found in the Taylor papers, NSA.

Chapter 16

185 more than twenty thousand people: NW, 7/31/61.

186 "There's going to be a test of our nerve": JFK in campaign debate, 10/7/60, quoted in Richard Walton, *Cold War and Counterintelligence: The Foreign Policy of John F. Kennedy* (New York: Penguin, 1972), p. 76.

186 "They're fighting for New York": JFK interviewed by *Harper's*, 12/9/59, quoted in Walton, *Cold War and Counterintelligence*, p. 76.

186 "The current strategic war plan": Bundy memo to JFK, 7/7/61, NSF Box 81.

186 East Germany: For background, see *Time*, 8/25/61; WP, 11/10/89; Cate, *The Ides of August*, pp. 128–129.

187 "What action [do we] propose to take": Thompson cable to Rusk, 3/16/61, reprinted in Catudal, *Kennedy and the Berlin Wall Crisis*, Appendix IV, p. 304.

187 "The Disappearing Satellite": *The Reporter*, 3/16/61. Kennedy read the piece. George Bailey conv. Bailey later became news director of Radio Liberty, U.S. propaganda outlet and sister station to Radio Free Europe, in Munich.

188   "As a result of the stockpiling program": Lemnitzer memo to JFK, 6/14/61, NSF Box 82, JFKL. The stocks, which also included a six-month supply of brown-coal briquettes, dry milk, dehydrated vegetables, clothing, and medical supplies, were designed to meet West Berlin's needs "for a year if supplemented by an effective airlift."

188   "Look at this shit": Salinger int.

188   "There is a danger": *Time*, 7/7/61.

189   *Newsweek:* NW, 7/3/61.

189   "This shit has got to stop": Salinger int.

189   He called up J. Edgar Hoover: "The White House confirmed last week that the FBI had been asked to investigate 'leaking of secrets at the Pentagon.' Although the White House refused to specify the recipient of the 'secrets,' the FBI was investigating a story in the July 3 issue of *Newsweek* about Pentagon proposals for dealing with the Berlin crisis." NW, 7/10/61. "At no time," wrote its editors, "was *Newsweek* given any classified document, access to any classified document, or information from any document that had already been classified." See also NYT, 7/1/61; *Time*, 7/14/61; Catudal, *Kennedy and the Berlin Wall Crisis*, pp. 156–157. Catudal obtained details of the Defense Department's checking of the *Newsweek* story.

189   his usual run of morning memos: These are found in the Lincoln Dictation File, POF Box 62, JFKL.

189   "He's imprisoned by Berlin": Sidey, *John F. Kennedy, President*, p. 218; *Time*, 7/21/61.

189   "Until this conflict of wills is resolved": Acheson Report to JFK, "Berlin," 6/28/61.

190   Acheson's hard-line arguments divided: Abram Chayes OH, pp. 244–245, JFKL; Brinkley, *Dean Acheson: The Cold War Years 1953–71*, pp. 134–144; Catudal, *Kennedy and the Berlin Wall Crisis*, p. 148.

190   "If the issue is talking": Chayes OH, p. 270, JFKL.

190   "Abe, you'll see": Chayes OH, p. 246, JFKL.

190   They had a foreign ally: Horne, *Macmillan: 1957–1986*, p. 310.

190   "What do I do": Memorandum of Discussion, NSC meeting, 6/29/61, NSF Box 313, JFKL. For more on the June 29 meeting, see also Acheson OH, JFKL; Catudal, *Kennedy and the Berlin Wall Crisis*, pp. 143–152.

191   Schlesinger had the sinking feeling: Schlesinger, *A Thousand Days*, p. 386. Acheson's report was the only item listed on the agendas for NSC meetings from July 13 through July 19.

191   "Why don't you propose your own guarantees?": Schlesinger, *A Thousand Days*, p. 385.

191   "Are we not running the risk": Schlesinger memo to JFK, 7/6/61, quoted in Schlesinger, *A Thousand Days*, p. 386.

191   "Then tell me what you think": Schlesinger int; Schlesinger, *A Thousand Days*, p. 387.

192   The three men from Harvard: Chayes int; Schlesinger int; Chayes OH, pp. 245–250, JFKL; Schlesinger, *A Thousand Days*, p. 387.

192   "The paper indicates no relationship": Chayes, Kissinger, and Schlesinger memo to JFK, 7/7/61, quoted in Schlesinger, *A Thousand Days*, pp. 387–388.

192   "Well, now what can we do next?": Chayes int; Schlesinger int; Chayes OH, p. 250, JFKL.

192   They cruised: Catudal, *Kennedy and the Berlin Wall Crisis*, pp. 160–163.

192   "I want that damn thing in ten days": Sorensen int; Schlesinger, *A Thousand Days*, p. 369.

193   "If we mobilize a million men": Bundy memo to McNamara, 7/10/61, NSF Box 319, JFKL. The Joint Chiefs responded in a memo to McNamara, 7/13/61, DDRS (1991) 3040.

193   He told McNamara: Sorensen int.

193   The general handed the President a cable: Cate, *The Ides of August*, p. 86.

193   the afternoon of July 13: Agenda, Record of Actions, and Memorandum of Discussion of NSC Meeting, 7/13/61, NSF Box 313, JFKL.

193   "Official Senat refugee figures": Lightner cable to Rusk, 7/13/61, Berlin papers, NSA.

194 McNamara was ready: "The Defense Department Recommended Program Force Increases and Related Actions," 7/12/61, NSF Box 82, JFKL.

194 "Military Choices in Berlin": Bundy memo to JFK et al., 7/13/61, NSF Box 81, JFKL.

194 "Two things": Memorandum of Discussion, NSC Meeting, 7/13/61.

194 "We should not engage Khrushchev's prestige": Sorensen memo to JFK, 7/17/61, quoted in Catudal, *Kennedy and the Berlin Wall Crisis*, p. 176.

194 "Should not explicit attention be given": Schlesinger memo to JFK, 7/18/61, DDRS (1978) 301A.

195 A speech: Sorensen memo to JFK, 7/17/61; Chayes OH, p. 257, JFKL; Bundy memo to Sorensen, 7/22/61, NSF Box 81, JFKL.

195 By July 18: Catudal, *Kennedy and the Berlin Wall Crisis*, pp. 178–180.

195 "This is probably the most important": Bundy memo to JFK, 7/19/61, NSF Box 313, JFKL.

195 a one-in-five chance of war: RFK OH, JFKL.

195 "The real intent": JFKPP, 7/19/61.

196 Bowles had stalled the maneuver: Sidey, *John F. Kennedy, President,* p. 215.

196 "This is a very basic issue": JFKPP, 7/19/61.

196 Kennedy told McNamara and the Joint Chiefs: Agenda, Record of Actions, and Draft Record of Action, NSC Meeting, 7/19/61, NSF Box 313, JFKL.

196 "Gentlemen, you might as well face it": Catudal, *Kennedy and the Berlin Wall Crisis,* p. 182, note.

197 "The purpose of nuclears": T. C. Schelling, "Nuclear Strategy in the Berlin Crisis," 7/5/61, NSF Box 81, JFKL.

197 "The Berlin surcharge": RFK OH, JFKL; Dutton memo to JFK, 7/19/61, POF Box 63, JFKL; Minutes of NSC Meeting, 7/20/61, NSF Box 313, JFKL; Dillon memo to Sorensen, 7/21/61, Sorensen papers, Box 40, JFKL.

197 "If consumers and firms respond": Council of Economic Advisers memo to Sorensen, 7/18/61, NSF Box 81, JFKL.

198 Heller, Samuelson, and Harris worked up a small plot: Samuelson int.

198 "any rise of taxes": Council of Economic Advisers OH, JFKL.

198 "Can you come over here": Samuelson memo to JFK, 7/23/61, "Economics of a Berlin Tax Rate Increase," Berlin papers, NSA.

198 "You were wrong": RFK OH, JFKL.

198 "We believe Soviets watching": Rusk cable to Dowling, 7/22/61, reprinted in Catudal, *Kennedy and the Berlin Wall Crisis,* Appendix V, p. 305.

198 "Our central problem": JFK letter to Macmillan, 7/20/61, Berlin papers, NSA.

199 "Let's go swim": Sidey, *John F. Kennedy, President,* p. 213.

Chapter 17

200 "Which door will he come through?": Sidey, *John F. Kennedy, President,* pp. 229–230.

200 The pencil press pool: Salinger press briefing, 7/25/61, Salinger papers, Box 46, JFKL.

200 sweating immediately: Sidey, *John F. Kennedy, President,* pp. 223–224; Lincoln, *My Twelve Years,* p. 280; *Time,* 8/4/61.

200 "Good evening": JFKPP, 7/25/61.

202 More than a thousand telegrams: Salinger press briefings, 7/25–26/61, Salinger papers, Box 46, JFKL.

202 The mail: *Time,* 8/4/61.

202 "They are determined": NYHT, 7/27/61.

202 "It's your greatest triumph": Sorensen memo to JFK, 8/9/61, Sorensen papers, Box 36, JFKL. Sorensen did suggest finding a "TV Consultant-producer-director" to make improvements in the heat, lighting, and camera work of future broadcasts.

202 "Great speech": Harry Truman letter to JFK, 8/1/61, POF Box 33, JFKL.

202 "In a speech": NYT, 7/26/61.

202 He thought that was a signal: Catudal, *Kennedy and the Berlin Wall Crisis,* p. 192.

203   The refugees reported: *Time*, 8/18/61.
203   "Khrushchev was cordial": McCloy cable to JFK, 7/29/61; McCloy cable to Thomas Finletter, 8/2/61; both in Berlin papers, NSA; *Time*, 8/11/61.
203   "Non-communist reaction": CIA memo, "Initial Foreign Radio and Press Reaction to President Kennedy's Speech on Berlin," 7/27/61, NSF Box 82, JFKL.
204   "I hope to let every citizen know": JFKPP, 7/25/61.
204   Ordinary Americans: On the short-lived but extraordinarily intense civil defense craze, see Catudal, *Kennedy and the Berlin Wall Crisis*, pp. 171–172; Schlesinger, *A Thousand Days*, pp. 747–748; and Sorensen, *Kennedy*, pp. 691–695. Bundy still maintains that civil defense is "insurance, imperfect, but relatively cheap—a way of mitigating a possible disaster, not a way of avoiding it or making it acceptable." McGeorge Bundy, *Danger and Survival: Choices About the Bomb in the First Fifty Years* (New York: Random House, 1988), pp. 355–356.
204   "Actually": NYT, 7/26/61.
204   "I don't understand": NYT, 8/3/61. Fulbright's comments caused a firestorm of protest in West Germany and West Berlin. From Bonn, the U.S. ambassador wrote that "rarely has a statement by a prominent American official aroused as much consternation, chagrin, and anger as Senator Fulbright's recent television interview," and sent along a page of additional unfavorable West German reaction. Similarly, the American mission in Berlin cabled Washington of the "protest and indignation" Fulbright had caused. Dowling cable to Rusk, 8/3/61, and Trivers cable to Rusk, 8/2/61, both in Berlin papers, NSA.
205   "The ceding of control of access routes": NYT, 7/30/61.
205   Kennedy's "three essentials": *International Herald Tribune*, 8/4/61. These three points were first delineated by the State Department in 1958, accepted by the foreign ministers of NATO in May 1961, and listed by Acheson in his June 29 report. Catudal, *Kennedy and the Berlin Wall Crisis*, p. 145, note.
    Willy Brandt would later write, "We did not regard these formulations as wholly satisfactory . . . did the 'three essentials' mean the Russians could do as they pleased in, and with East Berlin?" Reading the "essentials," Brandt's press secretary, Egon Bahr, remarked, "That is almost an invitation for the Soviets to do what they want with the Eastern Sector." Willy Brandt, *People and Politics: The Years 1960–1975* (Boston: Little, Brown, 1978), p. 21; Hermann Zolling, et al., *Kalter Winter im August* (Oldenburg: Gerhard Stalling, 1967), p. 78. See also Dean Acheson, "Wishing Won't Hold Berlin," *Saturday Evening Post*, 3/7/59; and Marquis Childs, "The Acheson View on Holding Berlin," WP, 7/28/61.
205   "The agreements": Robert Slusser, *The Berlin Crisis of 1961: Soviet-American Relations and the Struggle for Power Within the Kremlin* (Baltimore: Johns Hopkins University Press, 1973), pp. 107–114.
205   mirrored Kennedy's "soft" line: As Thomas Hughes of the State Department's Bureau of Intelligence and Research put it: "Khrushchev's twin tactics—maintaining, even stepping up his threats concerning the consequences of failing to negotiate the Soviet proposals, and at the same time, gradually broadening the possible terms of negotiations—are clearly designed to induce the West to make a concrete and early offer to negotiate on terms close to Moscow's." Hughes intelligence note, "August 7 Khrushchev Speech on Berlin," undated, NSF Box 82, JFKL. On JFK's two-track policy, see also Hillenbrand OH, pp. 36–37, JFKL.
206   "If Mr. Khrushchev": NYT, 8/8/61.
206   "The other side": Catudal, *Kennedy and the Berlin Wall Crisis*, p. 216.
206   "If Adenauer thinks": Slusser, *The Berlin Crisis of 1961*, p. 124.
206   "Here, mine writes": *Time*, 8/18/61.
206   "The laws of war are cruel": Slusser, *The Berlin Crisis of 1961*, p. 124.
207   "The United States Government": JFKPP, 8/10/61.
207   "Gentlemen, you can rest easy": Cate, *The Ides of August*, pp. 181–183.
207   "Operation Chinese Wall": Catudal, *Kennedy and the Berlin Wall Crisis*, pp. 210–211.
207   "The governments of the Warsaw Pact": Slusser, *The Berlin Crisis of 1961*, pp. 129–130.

207   "and not a millimeter more": Catudal, *Kennedy and the Berlin Wall Crisis*, p. 209. Ulbricht is said to have turned pale as he realized Khrushchev was telling him there would be no takeover of West Berlin or its air corridors.

208   "Perhaps a wall": Rostow, *The Diffusion of Power*, p. 231. Somewhat different accounts of this quote are given in Rostow OH, p. 60, JFKL; "Ein Sonntag im August," North German TV broadcast, 8/12/76; and Schlesinger, *A Thousand Days*, p. 394. All have in common that JFK communicated to Rostow that the Soviets were about to block access to West Berlin from East Berlin and that the United States could not stop such a move. "Kennedy," said his aide, "knew this was coming down the pike."

Chapter 18

209   At St. Francis Xavier Church: Cate, *The Ides of August*, pp. 330–331; Catudal, *Kennedy and the Berlin Wall Crisis*, pp. 35–36.

209   "East German regime": Lightner cable to Rusk, 2:00 P.M., 8/13/61, Berlin papers, NSA; John Ausland, "The Berlin Wall," *Foreign Service Journal* (July 1971).

210   The troop movements: Lightner cable to Rusk, 10:00 P.M., 8/13/61, Berlin papers, NSA; John Ausland, "When They Split Berlin, Washington Was Asleep," *International Herald Tribune*, 11/14/89; Cate, *The Ides of August*, p. 304.

210   He was angry: Parmet, *JFK*, p. 199.

210   Rusk had deliberately held off: Cate, *The Ides of August*, pp. 318–320.

210   He asked first: Cate, *The Ides of August*, p. 332; Catudal, *Kennedy and the Berlin Wall Crisis*, p. 37; Schlesinger, *A Thousand Days*, p. 367.

211   "Available information": Ausland, "The Berlin Wall."

211   He was being photographed: See, for example, Catudal, *Kennedy and the Berlin Wall Crisis*, p. 34. Kennedy's appointments log made no mention of the fact that his sailing had been interrupted by the news from Berlin. JFK appointments schedule, 8/13/61, JFKL. "Go to the ball game as you had planned," he instructed Rusk. "I am going sailing." Eleanor L. Dulles, *The Wall: A Tragedy in Three Acts* (Columbia, SC: University of South Carolina Press, 1972), p. 48.

211   Monday editions: NYT, 8/14/61.

211   "Incidentally": Bundy memo to JFK, 8/14/61, NSF Box 82, JFKL. Rostow had also written that "a sealing of the East Berlin frontiers . . . is a dangerous action of a weak and insecure regime . . . but it is not an act which justifies Western military retaliation nor a breaking off of all economic or other de facto relations with the East German republic." Rostow memo to Bundy, 8/14/61, NSF Box 82, JFKL. Most American officials believed, as the CIA's Robert Amory put it, that "properly interpreted, this was an internal security measure of the East zone. This wasn't a play against Berlin." Amory OH, p. 33, JFKL.

211   "With this weekend's occurrences": JFK memo to McNamara, 8/14/61, NSF Box 82, JFKL.

212   Pierre Salinger's press briefing: Salinger press briefings, 8/15/61, Salinger papers, Box 47, JFKL.

212   "This is the end of the Berlin crisis": Cate, *The Ides of August*, p. 392. "Why would Khrushchev put up a wall if he really intended to seize West Berlin?" Kennedy asked Kenny O'Donnell. "This is his way out of his predicament. It's not a very nice solution, but a wall is a hell of a lot better than a war." O'Donnell and Powers, *"Johnny, We Hardly Knew Ye,"* p. 350.

212   the crowd booed: Ausland, "The Berlin Wall"; Eleanor Dulles, *The Wall*, pp. 68–69.

212   Murray Marder . . . Max Frankel: NYT, 8/15/61; Kern, Levering, and Levering, *The Kennedy Crises*, p. 91.

213   "Sudden fear": Dulles memo to JFK, 8/22/61, NSF Box 82, JFKL.

213   "Crisis of confidence in Berlin": Dowling cable to Rusk, 8/17/61, Berlin papers, NSA.

213   "There is a real danger": Peter Wyden, *Wall: The Inside Story of Divided Berlin* (New York: Simon & Schuster, 1989), p. 226.

213   They had rushed their film: Cate, *The Ides of August*, p. 347.

213   Brandt told a mass rally: Cate, *The Ides of August*, pp. 390–391.

214   "There has been a serious attack": NYT, 8/20/61; Brandt, *People and Politics,* p. 31; Wyden, *Wall,* p. 224.
214   "Look at this!": Wyden, *Wall,* p. 230.
214   "You're wrong": Wyden, *Wall,* p. 233.
214   "The Firebug": Bundy memo to JFK, 8/28/61, NSF Box 82, JFKL.
214   Higgins knew that already: Cate, *The Ides of August,* pp. 402–403.
214   "Why me?": O'Donnell and Powers, *"Johnny We Hardly Knew Ye,"* pp. 350–351.
214   Late that afternoon: Cate, *The Ides of August,* pp. 403–404.
215   Johnson was accompanied: The best account of Johnson's trip is Curtis Cate's *The Ides of August,* pp. 423–436. See also *Time,* 8/25/61; NW, 11/20/89; Brandt, *People and Politics,* pp. 31–34; and Wyden, *Wall,* pp. 227–234.
215   "Make it clear to him": JFK letter to LBJ, 8/18/61, NSF Box 82, JFKL.
215   "Wasn't it you who were saying": Cate, *The Ides of August,* p. 426.
216   "The new Berlin Desk Officer": See, for example, Catudal, *Kennedy and the Berlin Wall Crisis,* p. 152.
216   He had personally approved Colonel Johns: *Time,* 8/25/61.
216   "Talking to Kennedy right now": Dutton int. On Kennedy's tense oversight of the Berlin convoy, see Schlesinger, *A Thousand Days,* pp. 396–397; Sidey, *John F. Kennedy, President,* pp. 199–201; Wyden, *Wall,* pp. 229–230.
216   the President's word to his own men: Dutton int; *Time,* 8/25/61.
216   Colonel Johns's orders: Cate, *The Ides of August,* p. 420.
216   "Advise the Soviets": JCS Note, "Clearance of the First Battle Group, 18th Infantry, Convoy Through the Soviet Checkpoints at Marienborn and Babelsberg (U)," 8/29/61, Berlin papers, NSA. The movements of the Autobahn mission are summarized in "Schedule for Battle Group Movement Berlin," 8/21/61, NSF Box 82, JFKL.
217   "First unit of American Battle Group": Lightner cable to Rusk, 8/20/61, NSF Box 1, LBJ.
218   "I'm quite aware that Berlin": JFKPP, 8/20/61.
218   "The Western Powers were caught unprepared": Lippmann's column is quoted in Ausland, "When They Split Berlin, Washington Was Asleep."
218   "You were wrong, Walter!": Lippmann OH, p. 22, JFKL.

Chapter 19

219   "After having travelled": LBJ report to JFK, 8/21/61, filed with supporting documents in Vice-Presidential Security File, Box 2, LBJL.
219   "I want to take a stronger lead": JFK memo to Rusk, 8/21/61, NSF Box 82, JFKL.
220   "I read the Cyprus report": JFK memo to Bundy, 8/21/61, POF Box 62, JFKL.
220   "I would like to stay out of some of these fights": Chalmers Roberts, *First Rough Draft* (New York: Praeger, 1973), p. 203.
220   " 'Over-extended commitments' ": Parmet, *JFK,* p. 328.
220   "Security requirements": NSAM 65, 8/11/61, USVNR, Book 11, pp. 241–244, which listed decisions made by Kennedy after his review of the Staley Report. The report itself is detailed in Rusk memo to JFK, 7/28/61, VDDHD, Document 54, pp. 112–114.
221   On August 11: NSAM 65, 8/11/61, USVNR, Book 11, pp. 241–244.
221   on August 29: NSAM 80, 8/29/61, NSF Box 331, JFKL.
221   the first force would be 13,000 men: Memcon, meeting to discuss Southeast Asia, 8/29/61, NSF Box 317, JFKL.
221   "It's inconceivable to me": Memcon, 8/29/61 meeting.
221   "I would like to have you present your analysis": JFK memo to McNamara, 8/31/61, Taylor papers, NSA.
222   "These people are crazy": Gilpatric int.
223   "The planners should be told": Taylor memo, "Guidance for Berlin Contingency Planning," 8/17/61, Taylor papers, NSA. See also W.Y.S. memo to Taylor, 4/11/64, Taylor papers, NSA, for a chronology of Berlin documents involving Taylor, assembled by his staff for his Kennedy Library oral history interview.

223   Lucius Clay had agreed to return: JFKPP, 8/30/61.
223   Bundy had warned Kennedy: Bundy memo to JFK, "Issues to be Settled with General Clay," 8/28/61, NSF Box 82, JFKL.
223   he had set one condition: Wyden, *Wall*, p. 214.
223   "Fucked again": Halberstam, *The Best and the Brightest*, p. 84.
223   "The bastards": Stephen Smith int.
223   only two days before: White House Staff Reflections on the New Frontier OH, p. 93, JFKL.
223   "What are you?": White House staff OH, pp. 93–94, JFKL.
224   "What we have all feared": JFK letter to Macmillan, 8/3/61, Nuclear History papers, NSA.
224   "The President met this morning": NYT, 9/1/61.
224   "One or two weeks": Glenn Seaborg, *Kennedy, Khrushchev, and the Test Ban* (Berkeley, CA: University of California Press, 1981), pp. 87–88.
225   "I haven't had time to think about that yet": Reston int.

Chapter 20
226   "In view of the continued testing": JFKPP, 9/5/61.
226   The National Security Council had reported: During the summer of 1961, an ad hoc panel chaired by scientist Wolfgang Panofsky had looked into the issue of nuclear testing. In a report dated July 21, the panel concluded that "any decisions in the near future regarding nuclear testing can be governed primarily by non-technical considerations." George Ball, asked by Jerome Wiesner to review the report, agreed: he wrote Kennedy on August 4 that "the most advantageous course would be to defer any announcement of test resumption until at least the end of the year." In preparing Kennedy for the August 8 NSC meeting at which Panofsky presented his findings, Bundy wrote the President that "there is no one who sees much net advantage in the resumption of testing before the end of 1961." Ball memo to JFK, 8/4/61, Nuclear History papers, NSA; Bundy memo to JFK, 8/8/61, Agenda and Record of Actions, NSC meeting, 8/8/61; both in NSF Box 313, JFKL.
227   "Where would we be": Seaborg, *Kennedy, Khrushchev, and the Test Ban*, p. 31.
227   "How does the radioactive fallout": Lieberson and Meyers, eds., *John Fitzgerald Kennedy . . . As We Remember Him*, p. 147.
227   "Shit, I have no choice": Schlesinger int; Schlesinger, *A Thousand Days*, pp. 459–460; Seaborg, *Kennedy, Khrushchev, and the Test Ban*, pp. 85–86.
227   "Are you finished?": Duke OH, pp. 19–20, JFKL.
228   "President John F. Kennedy announced": JFKPP, 9/15/61; *Time*, 9/22/61.
228   "The USSR": Bureau of Intelligence and Research memo, "Assessment of Current Soviet Intentions in the Berlin Crisis: August 28–September 4," 9/4/61, Taylor papers, NSA.
228   Corona: Gilpatric int; Hilsman int; Hilsman OH, JFKL; Ranelagh, *The Agency*, pp. 324–326.
229   In addition to those missiles: See John Prados, *The Soviet Estimate: U.S. Intelligence Analysis and Russian Military Strength* (New York: Dial, 1982).
229   "Our means of delivery": Rinehart dispatch to Parker, 8/2/61, Time arch.
229   SIOP-62: "Briefing on SIOP-62," JCS 2056/281, 9/13/61, Nuclear History papers, NSA. The plan was declassified by the Joint Chiefs in 1986 and first published and discussed by Scott Sagan in *International Security* (Summer 1987).
229   "a massive, total, comprehensive, obliterating": Bundy int. Rostow called it "devastating, indiscriminately . . . orgiastic, Wagnerian." White House staff OH, p. 110, JFKL. "We became increasingly horrified," Gilpatric said, "over how little positive control the President really had over this great arsenal of nuclear weapons." Gilpatric OH, p. 76, JFKL.
230   There were 3,729 targets on the cards: SIOP-62, p. 7. This "National Strategic Target List," said the Chiefs, "was developed from a list of more than 80,000 potential targets in the Bombing Encyclopedia."
230   "the JCS will designate": SIOP-62.

230   "It must clearly be understood": SIOP-62.

230   Kennedy was tapping his front teeth: White House staff OH, p. 110, JFKL. "And brushed his hair," noted Kaysen, who also recalled that he and Rostow were "sent out of the room when things were getting too unpleasant for the kiddies to bear."

230   "Why do we hit all those targets in China": White House staff OH, p. 110, JFKL.

McNamara had been briefed on the SIOP in February. He had interrupted the presentation to say that firing multiple warheads at single targets would not only waste resources; it would generate fallout that would affect citizens all across Eastern Europe.

"Well, Mr. Secretary," replied General Thomas Power, "I hope you don't have any friends or relations in Albania because we're just going to have to wipe it out." Shapley, *Promise and Power*, p. 110.

230   "And we call ourselves the human race": Schoenbaum, *Waging Peace and War*, p. 330. McNamara later said flatly that the SIOP "was a 'plan' that [Kennedy] thought would lead to disaster if implemented." McNamara letter to author, 1/18/91.

230   an escalating arms race: From the beginning, Kennedy and McNamara worked carefully to increase civilian control and efficiency at the Pentagon. Over Air Force opposition, for example, the administration retired more than 1,200 old B-47 and B-58 bombers early in 1961, and McNamara fought production of the proposed B-70 bomber as long as he was in office, on the grounds that it was unnecessary. Ultimately, however, neither JFK nor McNamara resisted pressure to increase defense spending.

This is best illustrated by Kennedy's decision to build a thousand ICBMs just as evidence on the mythical nature of the missile gap was proving incontrovertible. In the early months of 1961, the new satellite photos plus information from Soviet defector Oleg Penkovsky placed the number of Soviet ICBMs at between four and one hundred. By autumn, all U.S. intelligence agencies (besides that of the Air Force, which would produce and deploy new missiles) had adjusted their estimates of future Soviet strength downward. The Russians were now expected to have 450 or so ICBMs by 1966, and certainly no more than 850.

While Kaysen and Wiesner suggested a force of 400 American ICBMs to Kennedy, however, McNamara recommended 1,000. "A thousand is the lowest I can go and still get it past Congress," he said; and later he estimated eventual Soviet ICBM strength at 500–1,000 to back up his decision. See Prados, *The Soviet Estimate*, passim; Shapley, *Promise and Power*, pp. 94–111. "McNamara wanted 1,000 missiles because that was the lowest figure Congress and the military would accept. The Air Force pushed for 10,000." Bundy speech at National Archives, 12/13/88.

231   a sustained arms race could break the Soviet economy: Bissell int; Hillenbrand OH, pp. 36–37, JFKL.

231   "You've made remarkable economic advances": Salinger, *With Kennedy*, p. 242.

231   sales of U.S weaponry: JFK, "Special Message to Congress on Gold and the Balance of Payments Deficit," JFKPP, 2/6/61.

"That year, McNamara began converting aid into arms sales, to reduce outlays of government defense dollars and bring revenues into the pockets of U.S. defense companies instead." Shapley, *Promise and Power*, p. 225.

In 1961, the administration created an arms sales office in the Defense Department under an International Security Affairs official named Henry Kuss. Kuss, using McNamara's management techniques, divided his staff into red, white, blue, and gray teams, each responsible for selling a quota of weapons to a particular part of the world. By the end of the 1960s, the Pentagon was selling about $2 billion of American arms annually, and U.S. arms sales to Third World nations, even excluding Vietnam, had increased 250 percent. John Ralston Saul conv; Walter LaFeber, *America, Russia, and the Cold War*, 2d edition (New York: John Wiley and Sons, 1972), pp. 219–220; Anthony Sampson, *The Arms Bazaar from Lockheed to London* (New York: Viking Press, 1977), pp. 115–118; Shapley, *Promise and Power*, pp. 225–226; Stockholm International Peace Research Institute, *The Arms Trade with the Third World* (Stockholm: Almqvist & Wiskell, 1971), pp. 5, 145–146.

231   "Strengthen the alternatives between inaction and nuclear war": McNamara memo to JFK, 9/18/61, Taylor papers, NSA.

232   "It is absolutely essential": Norstad comments, 9/16/61, attached to McNamara memo, 9/18/61.

232   "Two months": McNamara OH, p. 6, JFKL.

232   " 'Guerrillas must move among the people' ": Bradlee int.

232   "Teach them how to control mobs": NSAM 88, 9/5/61, filed with supporting documents in NSF Box 331, JFKL.

232   "There can be no successful action": Bowles memo to JFK, 9/30/61, NSF Box 331, JFKL.

233   "Bowles has volunteered": Bundy memo to JFK, 10/16/61, NSF Box 331, JFKL.

233   "If we mobilize a million men": Bundy memo to McNamara, 7/10/61, NSF Box 319, JFKL.

233   "A LETTER TO YOU": *Life*, 9/15/61.

233   "an entirely false and misleading statement": Claflin, ed., *JFK Wants to Know*, p. 107.

233   "I would appreciate receiving a weekly report": JFK memo to McNamara, 8/20/61, NSF Box 295, JFKL.

233   "Now, at last, there is such an issue": Schlesinger memo to JFK, 11/22/61, Nuclear History papers, NSA.

234   Poor people did not have backyards: "The present program is essentially a program to save the middle and upper classes," Schlesinger wrote. Schlesinger memo to JFK, 11/22/61.

Around the same time, John Kenneth Galbraith told Kennedy that it "was absolutely incredible" that civil defense pamphlets displayed "a picture of a family with a cabin cruiser saving itself by going out to sea. Very few members of the UAW can go with them." Galbraith memo to JFK, 11/9/61, Nuclear History papers, NSA.

234   "as long as you treat Peter Lawford with respect": JFK memo to Schlesinger, 9/8/61, Lincoln Dictation File, POF Box 62, JFKL.

234   he received a telephone call from Georgi Bolshakov: Salinger int; Salinger, *With Kennedy*, pp. 246–248.

234   "Good news": Salinger int; Salinger, *With Kennedy*, pp. 249–250.

235   "indicated in a number of quiet ways": NYT, 9/25/61.

235   At the United Nations: JFKPP, 9/25/61. Kennedy had scribbled the words "deep . . . slow" on his copy of the speech. The first page was photographed in NW, 10/9/61.

Chapter 21

236   "The situation gets worse": Theodore White letter to Schlesinger, 8/9/61, Schlesinger papers, Box W-15, JFKL. Schlesinger wrote White on August 25 that "our friend has carried it away to Hyannis for weekend reading."

237   "The overall aim of any counter-insurgency plan": The Thompson plan is printed in USVNR, Book 11, pp. 345–348.

237   "The Viet Cong": *Time*, 9/15/61.

237   Phouc Vinh: Rust, *Kennedy in Vietnam*, pp. 37–38.

238   a mutual defense treaty: VDDHD, Document 59, pp. 123–124.

238   the number of Viet Cong "regulars": State Department Situation Summary, 10/1/61, VDDHD.

238   "The time is now past": JCS memo to McNamara, 10/5/61, USVNR, Book 11, pp. 295–296.

238   another call from Georgi Bolshakov: Salinger, *With Kennedy*, p. 254.

239   "You and I, Mr. President": Salinger, *With Kennedy*, pp. 254–257. For more on the Kennedy-Khrushchev correspondence, see RFK OH, pp. 94, 101–102, 182–183, JFKL; Salinger OH, pp. 181–185, Beschloss, *The Crisis Years*, pp. 316–348; Sorensen, *Kennedy*, pp. 621–625. Bolshakov confirmed his role as messenger in conversations with the author in Moscow in 1987, and asked about several American friends, including Salinger. He died the following year. Bolshakov convs.

"There was a great deal of correspondence" among the allies in 1961, noted Martin Hillenbrand, the U.S. Ambassador to West Germany, "but the President did not write letters merely for the sake of writing letters. . . . He regarded such exchanges as essentially a means of assisting in the achievement of agreement in areas where disagreement existed, or as a way of accelerating agreement where agreement seemed to be slow in coming. . . . The President always went over the correspondence himself . . . and added his own stylistic touches to it. Some of it achieved a certain eloquence." Each of these observations held true for Kennedy's correspondence with Khrushchev, which eventually numbered in the dozens of letters.

"Khrushchev would always initiate the exchange," said Salinger, whom Bolshakov would call and then meet at street corners or bars in Washington, carrying envelopes hidden in newspapers. Khrushchev's letters were long, often rambling, and ranged over a wide variety of topics. Many were unmistakably personally dictated by the Soviet premier, who sometimes sent letters on separate topics almost simultaneously. Kennedy based his replies on the sections of Khrushchev's letters most palatable to American interests, and often closed by sending greetings from his family and his hopes for better relations between the superpowers. Salinger int; Sorensen int.

In January 1992, a series of Kennedy-Khrushchev letters relating to the aftermath of the Cuban missile crisis was released, and it proved highly revealing. These letters were obtained through a Freedom of Information Act lawsuit by the National Security Archive and are now available at that institution and at the Kennedy Library. But despite the passage of over thirty years, and the pleas of nearly every top living member of the Kennedy administration for the release of the rest of the letters, the U.S. State Department has kept much of the remaining correspondence secret. Many of the letters, including Khrushchev's first missive of September 29, 1961, have not even been downgraded from their original top secret classification.

239   Kennedy answered: Sorensen, *Kennedy*, pp. 622–623.

239   Gromyko came to the White House: *Saturday Review*, 1/9/71; *Time*, 10/13/61; O'Donnell and Powers, *"Johnny, We Hardly Knew Ye,"* pp. 352–353; Sidey, *John F. Kennedy, President*, pp. 261–262.

240   Ambassador Nolting: See Frederick Nolting OH, LBJL; Frederick E. Nolting, *From Trust to Tragedy* (New York: Praeger, 1988).

240   "The State Department": White letter to Schlesinger, 8/9/61.

240   "Our present policy": Nolting cable to JFK, 10/6/61, FRUS 1961, Document 147, pp. 326–328.

240   U.S. Army units were needed: JCS memo to McNamara, Plan 716-61 (SEATO Plan 5), 10/7/61, NSF Box 194, JFKL. The Joint Chiefs summarized their views in a memo to Taylor two days later. JCS memo to Taylor, 10/9/61, NSF Box 194, JFKL.

240   If North Vietnam responded: JCS Plan 716-61.

241   If China sent in troops: JCS Plan 716-61.

241   "It is somehow wrong": Rostow memo to JFK, 3/29/61, NSF Box 194, JFKL.

241   "This initial action": Alexis Johnson, "Concept of Intervention in Vietnam," 10/10/61, discussed at length in PP II, pp. 74–77.

241   one thing Kennedy did authorize: NSAM 104, 10/13/61, and Robert Johnson memo for the file, 10/18/61, both in NSF Box 332, JFKL. A Gilpatric memo for the record also summarized the decisions made at the October 11 meeting, and is quoted at length in PP II, pp. 79–80.

242   "Bear in mind": JFK memo to Taylor, 10/13/61, reprinted in Taylor, *Swords and Plowshares*, pp. 225–226. Drafts of the instructions are in FRUS 1961, Document 157, pp. 345–346, and DDRS (1991) 3298.

242   concentrate on three options: Rostow, *The Diffusion of Power*, p. 272.

242   "High administration sources": NYT, 10/15/61.

242   "As part of your appraisal": JFK memo to Taylor, 10/13/61.

242   a power struggle: The account of Kennedy's health at the end of 1961 and the clash of his doctors is drawn from the following sources: Kraus int; Parmet int; confidential source int; Burkley OH, p. 11, JFKL; Salinger, *With Kennedy*, p. 66; Sidey, *John F. Kennedy, President*, p. 209.

242   Some Secret Servicemen: Confidential source int.

242   the next painkilling step would be narcotics: Indeed, when Max Jacobson first treated Kennedy at the White House, on May 24, 1961, a concerned Jacqueline Kennedy showed him a vial of Demerol that she had found in her husband's bedroom. Later that day, she told Jacobson that a Secret Service agent had given Kennedy the drug and that

he had been dismissed. Jacobson stated that he was "in principle absolutely opposed to the use of opiates," as they were addictive and would interfere with his medications. Unpublished memoirs of Max Jacobson, "JFK" chapter, p. 10.

243 "That isn't my face": Salinger int.

243 tried to get rid of Dr. Jacobson: Jacobson wrote that in the spring of 1962, JFK told him that Robert Kennedy had demanded samples of his medication for testing by the Food and Drug Administration. Jacobson claimed that he forwarded fifteen of his vials to the Attorney General's office and that the President told him a week later that "the material had been examined, tested, and approved." Unpublished memoirs of Max Jacobson, "JFK" chapter, p. 30. His widow later mentioned RFK and Janet Travell as two administration officials particularly opposed to his ministrations. Ruth Jacobson int.

Jacobson's FBI file states that on June 4, 1962, Robert Kennedy's executive assistant "asked that certain medicine be analyzed by the laboratory for the Attorney General." Jacobson's name and address were printed on the label of the bottle received by the FBI, which was not able to analyze the medication because of the "limited quantity furnished." Cleveland memo to Martin, 8/18/72, File 62-84390 (Max Jacobson), FBI. Analogous FDA records for the early 1960s are no longer available.

244 "The President still believes": Krock, *Memoirs*, pp. 332–333.

Chapter 22

245 "There have been charges": JFKPP, 10/11/61.

245 "They don't get it": Salinger int.

246 still peppering his staff: On July 10, Kennedy had shot off a one-line memo to Sorensen: "Will we have our reorganization of Civil Defense this week?" JFK to Sorensen, POF Box 62, Lincoln Dictation File, JFKL. McNamara, noting that Kennedy had stated on August 14 that he was "concerned that we move ahead as quickly as possible on Civil Defense," reported back to the President on the Pentagon's efforts on August 16. McNamara memo to JFK, 8/16/61, NSF Box 295, JFKL.

246 He considered giving a major speech: Sidey, *John F. Kennedy, President*, p. 282. "When I get up and say those things," Kennedy remarked, "it sounds too belligerent."

246 going through the text line by line: Bundy int; Hilsman int; Hilsman, *To Move a Nation*, pp. 162–165. The Gilpatric speech is printed in *Documents on Disarmament 1961*, pp. 542–550. See also Department of Defense Report I-12087/62, undated, "What Do the Soviets Think About Strategic Policy?", DDRS (1991) 3286. Pp. 15–21 of this Pentagon report outline the Soviet nuclear stance from 1960 to 1962, including the reaction to Gilpatric's speech.

246 "These talks left us with the impression": Khrushchev's six-hour opening speech to the Twenty-Second Party Congress is analyzed in great detail in Slusser, *The Berlin Crisis of 1961*, pp. 303–324.

246 "I know that you will wish to know": Rusk news conference, 10/22/61, *Department of State Bulletin 1961*, p. 746.

247 "Our confidence in our ability": Gilpatric speech, 10/21/61.

247 "The imperialist powers": Slusser, *The Berlin Crisis of 1961*, pp. 380–387.

247 a 30-megaton thermonuclear device: NYT, 10/24/61.

248 Chou En-lai left Moscow: Chou's rough time in Moscow is detailed in Slusser, *The Berlin Crisis of 1961*, pp. 339–345, 376–377; NYT, 10/20/61.

248 the minister was stopped by East German VOPOs: Raymond L. Garthoff, "Berlin 1961: The Record Corrected," *Foreign Policy* (Fall 1991); Howard Trivers, *Three Crises in American Foreign Affairs and a Continuing Revolution* (Carbondale, IL: Southern Illinois University Press, 1972), pp. 41–42.

249 "We didn't send him to Berlin to go to the opera": Trivers, *Three Crises in American Foreign Policy*, p. 44.

249 Steinstücken: Cate, *The Ides of August*, pp. 467–469. See also Honoré M. Catudal, *Steinstucken: A Study in Cold War Politics* (New York: Vantage, 1971).

249 a replica of the Wall: Catudal, *Kennedy and the Berlin Wall Crisis*, p. 133; Garthoff, "Berlin 1961: The Record Corrected."

249 "Take your cotton-picking hands off my troops": Cate, *The Ides of August*, pp. 527–528, 469–470.

249 Clay ordered another carload of U.S. diplomats: Garthoff, "Berlin 1961: The Record Corrected"; Trivers, *Three Crises in American Foreign Policy,* pp. 45–51.
250 On Friday, another official U.S. car: Garthoff, "Berlin 1961: The Record Corrected."
250 "How are things up there?": Clay OH, JFKL; Jean Edward Smith, *Lucius D. Clay: An American Life* (Markham, Ontario: Fitzhenry & Whiteside, 1990), pp. 629–665. For more on the confrontation at Checkpoint Charlie, see Beschloss, *The Crisis Years,* pp. 333–335; Wyden, *Wall,* pp. 260–267. Beschloss's account draws from interviews with Russian sources by WGBH-TV for the television series "War and Peace in the Nuclear Age."
251 He told his brother Robert: RFK OH, JFKL.
251 Khrushchev had given the order: RFK OH, JFKL; Salinger OH, pp. 197–198, JFKL; Garthoff, "Berlin 1961: The Record Corrected."
251 their 50-megaton bomb: NYT, 11/1/61.
251 "If we don't": Notes on NSC Meeting, 11/2/61, Vice-Presidential Security File, Box 5, LBJL. For Kennedy's briefing on the meeting and a summary of the decisions made, see Bundy memo to JFK, 11/1/61; NSC Action 2440, 11/2/61; both in Nuclear History papers, NSA.
251 "This much can be said": JFKPP, 11/2/61.

Chapter 23
253 "The question": Taylor, *Swords and Plowshares,* p. 226.
253 "As we understand your position": Rostow, *The Diffusion of Power,* p. 271.
253 Kennedy told Taylor: Kennedy "recalled the situation under the French," Rostow wrote later, "as he had seen it in 1951 and studied it down to 1954. He had seen a quarter of a million military men rendered impotent because the people didn't want French rule. He said all our help, including combat troops, would be useless unless there was an underlying desire of the leaders and people to have an independent destiny in the South. . . . The most fundamental question on Kennedy's mind was this: Did the people of South Vietnam want an independent non-communist future or would they, in fact, prefer to go with Ho Chi Minh and Hanoi?" Rostow, *The Diffusion of Power,* p. 272.
254 "What have you learned here?": Edmund Gullion int.
254 "We have allied ourselves": *Congressional Record,* 1/8/52, p. HR-5879.
254 Taylor emphasized: Currey, *Edward Lansdale,* p. 226; Rust, *Kennedy in Vietnam,* p. 45; Taylor, *Swords and Plowshares,* p. 227. The eighteen pages of his memoirs that Taylor devoted to his October 1961 mission to Vietnam hold many kind words for Rostow: "He had meditated deeply on the significance of subversive insurgency as a device for Communist expansion. . . . Also, he contributed the pen of an experienced writer . . . and an agile tennis racket." Lansdale is not mentioned once.
254 "Human defoliation": Taylor Report to JFK, "Unconventional Warfare" Appendix, 11/3/61, FRUS 1961, Document 210.
255 He did not see: Currey, *Edward Lansdale,* p. 237.
255 Diem surprised Lansdale: Currey, *Edward Lansdale,* pp. 237–238.
255 "It will be necessary to include some combat troops": Taylor cable to JFK, 10/25/61, PP II, pp. 87–88. Rostow discussed the report of the mission in *The Diffusion of Power,* pp. 274–278; Rostow OH, pp. 81–84, JFKL.
255 "As an area for the operations of U.S. troops": Taylor cable to JFK, 11/1/61, PP II, pp. 90–92.
255 "South Vietnam could be a quicksand for us": Mansfield memo to JFK, 11/2/61, FRUS 1961, Document 207, pp. 467–470.
256 "It seems to me we ought to try to hold this place": Symington letter to JFK, 10/21/61, quoted in Gibbons, *The U.S. Government and the Vietnam War,* pp. 101–102, and note 61.
257 he sat himself down in the President's rocking chair: Currey, *Edward Lansdale,* p. 239.
256 "It is evident": Taylor Report to JFK, 11/3/61.

256 "Three months": Rostow int.

256 "No one action": Taylor Report to JFK, 11/3/61.

256 "I don't know": Memo for the record, meeting to discuss recommendations of the Taylor Report, 11/6/61, FRUS 1961, Document 211, pp. 532–534.

256 "There is near paralysis": Jorden memo to Taylor, 10/30/61, Appendix C to Taylor Report.

257 "a losing horse": Rusk cable to JFK, 11/1/61, PP II, p. 105.

257 "Taylor is wrong": George Ball, *The Past Has Another Pattern: Memoirs* (New York: W. W. Norton, 1982), p. 366.

257 "Indecision and uncertainty": Pelz, "John F. Kennedy's 1961 Vietnam War Decisions," p. 379.

257 "on a wide range of concerns": JFKPP, 11/8/61.

258 "The fall of South Vietnam": Rusk and McNamara memo to JFK, 11/11/61, POF Box 128, JFKL.

258 Kennedy crossed that out: Rostow int.

258 "There are some indications": Harriman letter to JFK, 11/11/61, NSF Box 195, JFKL.

258 similar small hints: In July, the CIA had relayed Soviet interest in neutralizing Vietnam. CIA report, "After Laos, South Vietnam," 7/14/61, NSF Box 231–254, JFKL. And Roger Hilsman of the State Department had written that China wanted better relations with the United States, Hilsman memo to W. P. McConaughy, "Wang P'ing-nan's Approach to Ambassador Beam," 7/7/61, NSF Box 21-27, JFKL.

258 "If we postpone action in Vietnam": Rostow memo to JFK, 11/11/61, POF Box 65, JFKL.

259 "He questioned the wisdom of involvement": Notes on NSC Meeting, 11/15/61, Vice-Presidential Security File, Box 4, LBJL. For a memo setting out Kennedy's views and questions on Vietnam just prior to the November 15 meeting, see JFK memo to Rusk and McNamara, 11/14/61, POF Box 128, JFKL.

259 the use of herbicide defoliants: The decision was formalized in NSAM 115, 11/30/61, USVNR, Book 11, p. 425. The options had been lain out for Kennedy in a Gilpatric memo to JFK, 11/24/61, NSF Box 332, JFKL.

260 "we feel we should go into Cuba, too": Notes on NSC Meeting, 11/15/61.

260 "in a sharply increased joint effort": USVNR, Book 11, pp. 400–405. The decisions made at the November 15 meeting were summarized for Nolting in a State telegram to Saigon, 11/15/61, DDRS (1976) 132C. They were formalized in Washington as NSAM 111, 11/22/61, NSF Box 332, JFKL.

260 "If this doesn't work": Rostow, *The Diffusion of Power,* p. 278.

260 "the United States would hardly be safe from the Sioux": Galbraith cable to JFK, 11/21/61, NSF Box 195, JFKL.

260 "We must make it clear to Diem": Harriman letter to JFK, 11/11/61, NSF Box 195, JFKL.

261 "the New Frontier will be measured in history": Rostow memo to JFK, 11/24/61, POF Box 65, JFKL.

261 "Get that down for the book": See, for example, Schlesinger, *A Thousand Days,* pp. x–xi.

261 "There are limits to the number of defeats": Wofford, *Of Kennedys and Kings,* p. 379.

261 "Diem is Diem": Rusk int.

261 they would make him look like a stooge: "Throughout our discussion," Nolting cabled Washington on November 25, "Diem continued to make references to the quid pro quo aspects of our proposals, claiming that they played right into the hands of the Communists. He argued that we are pressing him to give a monopoly on nationalism to the Communists." VDDHD, Document 75, pp. 148–149.

261 "Vietnam Not a Guinea Pig": Saigon telegram to State, 11/24/61, NSF Box 195, JFKL.

261 Rusk agreed: Rusk int. On Diem's intransigence, see Rust, *Kennedy in Vietnam,* pp. 56–59.

262 "They want a force of American troops": Hilsman int.

262 "Vietnam is not a great power": The exchange of letters is printed in *Depart-*

ment of State Bulletin 1962, pp. 13–14. Diem's letter to Kennedy was in fact drafted by the U.S. State Department and sent to Nolting with the other messages of November 15. State telegram to Saigon, 11/15/61, FRUS 1961, Document 257, pp. 627–628.

262   "If there is no reaction from the White House": Bagley memo to Taylor, 12/19/61, quoted in FRUS 1961, note 3 to p. 754. Lieutenant Commander Worth H. Bagley was Taylor's naval aide.

262   2,067 American military advisers: PP II, pp. 453–454.

262   James Thomas Davis: Schlesinger, *Robert Kennedy and His Times*, p. 762.

Chapter 24

263   Lansdale had thought: Currey, *Edward Lansdale*, pp. 235, 239; Rostow, *The Diffusion of Power*, p. 269. In dashing Lansdale's hopes, Kennedy also let down those of his supporters working on Vietnam. A week later, Rostow wrote the President a final memo before moving from the White House staff to the State Department: "I do not believe that all the choppers and other gadgetry we can supply South Vietnam will buy time and render their resources effective if we do not get a first class man out there . . . it is equally crucial that we free Ed Lansdale from his present assignment and get him out to the field in an appropriate position. He is a unique national asset in the Saigon setting; and I cannot believe that anything he may be able to do in his present assignment could match his value in Southeast Asia. On this matter you may have to have a word with the Attorney General." Rostow memo to JFK, 12/6/61, POF Box 65, JFKL.

263   "Drop everything else you're doing": Rust, *Kennedy in Vietnam*, p. 49.

263   "Get off your ass about Cuba!": CC, p. 141.

263   the "Special Group (Augmented)": The Special Group extended the work done on covert operations by the 5412 Committee during the Eisenhower administration. It comprised Bundy, CIA Director John McCone, U. Alexis Johnson of the State Department, Roswell Gilpatric from the Pentagon, and the Joint Chiefs' Lyman Lemnitzer. This was the group augmented at the end of 1961 by Robert Kennedy and Taylor to oversee Operation Mongoose, the administration's efforts to overthrow Fidel Castro. Lansdale was appointed chief of operations for Mongoose—his job was to coordinate the CIA's activities with the State and Defense departments. William Harvey was named to head Task Force W, the CIA unit for Mongoose, which was based in Miami, and eventually employed four hundred CIA agents and spent $100 million a year trying to topple Castro. CC, p. 140; Taylor Branch and George Crile III, "The Kennedy Vendetta: How the CIA Waged a Silent War Against Cuba," *Harper's* (July 1975); Ranelagh, *The Agency*, pp. 383–386.

263   "The Cuban problem": CC, p. 141.

264   The Attorney General's own notes: RFK memo, 11/4/62, Cuba papers, NSA.

264   "There can be no long-term living": Cuba Study Group Report, 6/13/61; CC, p. 135.

264   "Why didn't you tell me": Szulc int; Szulc, "Cuba on Our Mind," *Esquire*, (February 1975); CC, pp. 138–139.

265   "Bobby is a wild man on this": Bissell int.

265   Kennedy had asked the same questions: George Smathers OH, pp. 6B–8B, JFKL. "He was picking my brain," said Smathers. "I don't know whether he brought it up or I brought it up. We had further conversation of assassination of Fidel Castro, what would be the reaction, how would the people react, would the people be gratified."

Smathers's oral history was sanitized by an employee during her first week on the job at the Kennedy Library, and his comments on assassination were not expunged when the transcript was released. Enraged at what he considered to be a violation of the terms of the deed under which he donated the interview, Smathers vowed never to do business with the Library again. Confidential source int.

265   William Harvey: Kennedy once called Lansdale America's answer to James Bond. Lansdale suggested Harvey as a better choice, and brought him to the White House, where he checked two guns with the Secret Service just before being introduced to the President. For more on his legendary exploits—he helped uncover Kim Philby and

was in charge of building an underground tunnel from West Berlin into East Germany—see Currey, *Edward Lansdale*, pp. 242–249; Ranelagh, *The Agency*, pp. 145–153, 290–293.

265 "In confirmation of oral instructions": NSAM 100, 10/5/61, NSF Box 332, JFKL.

266 "A contingency plan": CC, p. 136.
266 "the President's interest in this matter": CC, p. 136.
266 "His loss now": CC, p. 137.
266 "We cannot, as a free nation": JFKPP, 11/16/61.
266 rendezvousing briefly: Exner, *My Story*, pp. 43–44.
266 the Dominican Republic: See Diedrich, *Death of the Goat*, pp. 193–196.
267 "Use our available assets": CC, p. 139.
267 "We are in a combat situation": Lansdale memo to SG (A), 1/20/62, quoted in CC, note to p. 142.
267 "you might as well keep going South": Goodwin, *Remembering America*, pp. 190–193.
267 "Do you know why": Goodwin, *Remembering America*, p. 192.
268 "We have made many mistakes": JFKPP, 11/18/61.
268 A flag, a visit to Washington, a steel mill from the Soviets: Duke int.
268 Jagan's interview on "Meet the Press": Salinger int; Ronald Radosh, *American Labor and United States Foreign Policy* (New York, 1979), pp. 33–34.
268 a project code-named "1290-D": Robert Amory OH, p. 101, JFKL Amory was the CIA's Deputy Director for Intelligence. The name "1290-D" derived from a 1954 National Security Council Action Memorandum, the Eisenhower equivalent of the NSAMs of the Kennedy and Johnson years. In December 1954, NSC 1290-D began an "Overseas Internal Security Program," ordering Defense and CIA to coordinate their efforts to help foreign police forces and creating a "public safety program" as part of the funding of international development. The first public safety program was established in Indonesia in 1955; twenty-seven were in place by mid-1961, including ten in Latin America and eight in the Far East. This kind of assistance was never terribly popular with Eisenhower, however, and by the time he left office, the program's budget had declined to less than $14 million per year.

By 1961, public safety had become a "peanut program," in the words of Robert Komer, a former CIA officer who advised Kennedy on intelligence matters as a member of the National Security Council staff. It was, in fact, "in the process of being dismantled" by the Agency for International Development, whose new staff "were going great guns for economic development" and "were not visibly interested in giving guns to cops or training in riot control." So "the President sent a letter to [Fowler] Hamilton [the director of AID], which said, 'Hey, let's increase our attention to [AID] programs as part of the counterinsurgency effort.'" Komer OH, p. 10, JFKL.

Declassified documents now make it clear that this increased use of international development assistance as a conduit for funding foreign police forces was just one part of Kennedy's bulking up of "internal security" efforts overseas. On September 5, 1961, following riots in Brazil, JFK asked the Pentagon to fill him in on "what steps we are taking to train the Armed Forces of Latin America in controlling mobs, guerillas, etc. . . . how many officers we are bringing up from Latin America to train here and whether we could increase the number. Also, what other steps are being taken to [ensure] intimacy between our Armed Forces and the military of Latin America." Two days later the President expanded the discussion to include State, CIA, Robert Kennedy, Richard Goodwin, and Walt Rostow, and on September 12, Bundy told Goodwin that "the President would like to get it going right away." See NSAM 88, 9/5/61, and supporting documents, NSF Box 331, JFKL.

After receiving answers to his initial questions from the various agencies involved, President Kennedy ordered a review of overseas internal security policy and programs in November 1961. The review proceeded regionally, with an interdepartmental assessment team" forwarding its first report, on ten Latin American countries, to the White House on February 20, 1962. See NSAM 114, 11/22/61, and supporting documents, NSF Box 332, JFKL. JFK's directive to AID, discussed by Komer, was issued on February 19.

NSAM 132, 2/19/62, NSF Box 333, JFKL. On March 13, JFK approved a set of counter-insurgency training objectives that stated, in part: "It is in the interest of the United States to provide counter-insurgency training to selected foreign nationals, both in the United States and in their own countries. The emphasis should be placed on countries with an actual or potential counter-insurgency problem. This training will be given in the following places: (1) In facilities operated by the Department of Defense and the Central Intelligence Agency which are available to foreigners; (2) In special facilities operated by the Department of Defense and the Agency for International Development in Panama for the benefit of foreign nationals; (3) U.S. MAAGs/missions and USOMs in countries with counter-insurgency programs." NSAM 131, 3/13/62, NSF Box 333, JFKL.

In August 1962, Kennedy created a semi-autonomous Office of Public Safety within AID and assigned it primary responsibility for the "support of local police forces for internal security and counterinsurgency purposes." NSAM 177, 8/7/62, NSF Box 338, JFKL. NSAM 177 called police assistance vital to "the freedom and stability of Third World countries." For a look at the effects of this reorganization on the forces of one country, see Gilpatric memo to JFK, "Riot Control in Guatemala," DDRS (1991) 3045.

From 1962 to 1975, when it was discontinued, OPS trained at least 500,000 foreign police overseas and about 7,500 senior officers at bases in the United States, including the International Police Academy in Washington, D.C. At its peak in 1968, OPS had 458 advisers in 34 countries and an annual budget of over $50 million. As Michael McClintock has written, "OPS advisers were in large part . . . real technicians in the more mundane skills of law enforcement, from fingerprinting to traffic control. But the worm in the apple: the CIA retained its normal use of police programs as cover for its own advisory personnel and skewed the overall impact of Public Safety by far toward the political side of law enforcement." Michael McClintock, *Instruments of Statecraft: U.S. Guerilla Warfare, Counterinsurgency, Counterterrorism: 1940–1990* (New York: Pantheon, 1992), p. 191.

Through OPS, the CIA funded interrogation centers for its Operation Phoenix, which in 1967 began trying to root Viet Cong out of the "insurgent infrastructure" in Vietnam. Phoenix was designed by Robert Komer, who earned the nickname "Blowtorch" for his efforts; it ultimately resulted in the killing of at least 20,000 Vietnamese. The CIA also ran courses in weapons manufacture and assassination through OPS at the Border Patrol Academy in Los Fresnos, Texas, which was later dubbed "the Bomb School" by the press. And it trained many future leaders of Latin American right-wing death squads, including Roberto D'Aubuisson of El Salvador and Alexander Hernández of Honduras. See McClintock, *Instruments of Statecraft*, pp. 161–196, especially pp. 188–194; Ranelagh, *The Agency*, pp. 436–441.

268   "We're going to get control of the streets": RFK OH, JFKL.
269   "Gestapo stuff": Amory OH, p. 101, JFKL.
269   "You must understand": Donald Barnes OH, JFKL.
269   an odd but significant memory trick: *San Francisco Chronicle*, 1/2/62, found in Sorensen papers, Box 36, JFKL.
269   "It's just hell": USN&WR, 2/26/62, found in Schlesinger papers, Box W-9, JFKL.
269   The only Kennedy bills of importance they supported: Stewart Alsop, "How's Kennedy Doing?" *Saturday Evening Post*, 9/16/61.
270   he had met with the Civil Rights Commission: Hesburgh int; Hesburgh OH, pp. 6–9, JFKL.
270   "It wasn't me": Marshall OH, JFKL.
270   a long options memo: Lee White memo to JFK, 11/13/61, Sorensen papers, Box 30, JFKL.
270   "It is anticipated that forced integration": Runge memo to Sorensen, 10/26/61, Sorensen papers, Box 30, JFKL.
271   "First things first": Sorensen int.
271   "We need a man on horseback": Schlesinger, *A Thousand Days*, p. 752.
271   "Civil Defense": Sorensen memo to JFK, 11/23/61, Sorensen papers, Box 30, JFKL.

271   "the present pamphlet": Galbraith memo to JFK, 11/9/61, Nuclear History papers, NSA.

272   "It is an invitation": Schlesinger memo to JFK, 11/22/61, Nuclear History papers, NSA.

272   "It would be a different world": Proposed article, 11/14/61, Adam Yarmolinsky papers, Box 26, JFKL.

272   Their father had collapsed: Parmet, *JFK,* pp. 124–126.

272   Kennedy pressured Macmillan: Horne, *Macmillan: 1957–1986,* pp. 319–326; Seaborg, *Kennedy, Khrushchev, and the Test Ban,* pp. 125–127.

273   becoming friends: Macmillan said he and Kennedy had "a very special relationship." See Horne, *Macmillan: 1957–1986,* pp. 287–330. "You know how it is when you meet someone and feel immediately as if you had known him always?" Macmillan later asked Schlesinger. "That is the way I felt with Jack. We could talk in shorthand. It was the silly things that linked us together and made it possible for us to talk about the terrible and the horrible things." Macmillan interview by Schlesinger, 5/20/64, Schlesinger papers, Box W-14, JFKL.

273   then his back went out completely: Kraus int; Parmet int; Parmet, *JFK,* pp. 122–124.

273   "I will not treat this patient": Kraus int. Burkley also "told Dr. Travell to keep her hands off the President." Burkley OH, p. 11, JFKL.

273   Secret Service technicians: Kraus int.

273   The same thing had happened: Parmet int; Parmet, *JFK,* pp. 120–121.

274   He had become convinced: Confidential source int.

274   "Who would want to read a book on disasters?": Salinger int.

274   "Sure it's a big job": *Time,* 1/5/62.

274   "Now, let's see": *Time,* 1/5/62.

Chapter 25

275   "Strengthening the Economy": JFKPP, 1/11/62.

276   two days of meetings: The account given of Kennedy's meetings with congressional leaders is drawn from Sorensen memo to JFK, "Notes for Congressional Session, January 17–18, 1962," 1/17/62, Sorensen papers, Box 36, JFKL. For more on JFK and Congress at the start of 1962, see *Time,* 1/19/62; and William White, "The Kennedy Era: Stage Two: The Coming Battle with Congress," *Harper's* (February 1962).

276   he would tell Sorensen: Sorensen int.

276   grumbling from senators and congressmen: O'Brien int.

277   "If Mike Feldman is a crook": Bartlett OH, p. 76.

277   "There has been no finding": Sorensen memo to JFK, "Notes for Congressional Session," 1/17/62.

277   "Did you understand": Myer Feldman int. See also Robert Donovan OH, JFKL.

277   "Well, that's over": Goodwin, *Remembering America,* p.119.

278   "I asked people to sacrifice": CEA OH, JFKL.

278   "Because I intend": Schlesinger int.

278   "How do you go down": Rostow int.

278   There were hundreds now: Salinger int.

279   "I'll take it out there": Chayes int.

279   "If they were for Kennedy": Smathers OH, JFKL.

280   "You have lunch with Lippmann": Bartlett int.

280   "speed-reading": Sidey OH, p. 35, JFKL.

280   "are American troops now in combat in Vietnam?": JFKPP, 1/15/62.

281   Jungle Jims: William Buckingham, Jr., *Operation Ranch Hand* (Washington, DC: Office of Air Force History, 1982), pp. 23–24.

281   The Special Group (CI): NSAM 124, 1/18/62, NSF Box 332, JFKL.

281   "Fantastic mobility": Roger Hilsman, *To Move a Nation* (New York: Delta Books, 1967), p. 444.

281   "The remarkable U.S. military effort": *Time,* 1/5/62.

282   "Why are we having so much trouble": John Mecklin, *Mission in Torment* (New York: Doubleday, 1965), pp. 103–104.
282   Binh Hoa: Hilsman, *To Move a Nation*, pp. 436–438; Rust, *Kennedy in Vietnam*, pp. 67–68.
282   "How can things like this": Hilsman, *To Move a Nation*, p. 438.
282   "You know, I like the old carbine": *Time*, 1/5/62.
282   Kennedy had approved napalm: See, for example, Hilsman, *To Move a Nation*, p. 442.
282   herbicides and chemicals: NSAM 115, 11/30/61, NSF Box 332, JFKL Documents leading up to and supporting Kennedy's decision include Gilpatric memo to JFK, 11/21/61; Rusk memo to JFK, 11/24/61; McNamara memo to JFK; all in NSF Box 332, JFKL.
283   "Operation Ranch Hand": Buckingham, *Operation Ranch Hand*, pp. 9–44.
283   "Our ultimate objective": Hilsman int. Hilsman, *To Move a Nation*, p. 432.
283   "Although General Harkins": Harkins, Commander in Chief of the Army's forces in the Pacific, had served under Taylor in the Korean War. The State Department's counterinsurgency enthusiasts had wanted a Special Forces or former OSS officer to take over in Vietnam. But Rusk deferred to the Pentagon on the matter, and Kennedy saw no need to "arouse antagonism in the top brass." Hilsman, *To Move a Nation*, pp. 426–427.
284   "We are going to win in Vietnam": *Time*, 5/11/62.
284   "They're Boy Scouts with guns": Collier and Horowitz, *The Kennedys*, p. 525.
284   "how to wire typewriters": Amory OH, p. 99, JFKL.
284   "It was mass rehearsals": Donald Duncan, *The New Legions* (New York: Pocket Books, 1967), pp. 146–148. After Kennedy learned that there were fewer than 1,000 Special Forces troops at Fort Bragg, he ordered the Special Warfare Center there to expand its operations. Its commander, Major General William Yarborough, went on to establish training bases in Panama, Vietnam, Okinawa, and West Germany. Currey, *Edward Lansdale*, p. 392.
Kennedy wanted to improve training partly because he had accepted Maxwell Taylor's advice after the Bay of Pigs that any paramilitary operation large enough to be visible should be assigned to the military, not the CIA. In June 1961, the President told the Joint Chiefs of Staff that they had "a responsibility for the defense of this nation in the Cold War similar to that which they have in conventional hostilities." NSAM 55, 6/28/61, NSF Box 331, JFKL. And at the same time, Kennedy instituted a policy that stated: "[T]he Department of Defense will normally receive responsibility for overt paramilitary operations. Where such an operation is to be wholly covert or disavowable, it may be assigned to CIA, provided that it is within the normal capabilities of the agency. Any large paramilitary operation wholly or partly covert which requires significant numbers of militarily trained personnel, amounts of military equipment which exceed normal CIA-controlled stocks and/or military experience of a kind and level peculiar to the Armed Services is properly the primary responsibility of the Department of Defense with the CIA in a supporting role." NSAM 57, 6/28/61, NSF Box 331, JFKL. These initiatives brought "the regular armed forces into the unconventional theater on a grand scale." McClintock, *Instruments of Statecraft*, p. 178.

Chapter 26

285   *Friendship 7*: This account of Glenn's successful launch and orbit is drawn from *Time*, 3/2/62, and the following sources: Salinger int; NYT, 2/21/62; *Time*, 2/23/62.
286   Younkers department store: *Des Moines Register*, 2/20/62.
286   "If only he were a Negro": Bartlett int; Collier and Horowitz, *The Kennedys*, p. 312.
287   "You've done it again": Sidey int; Sidey OH, p. 44, JFKL.
287   "On the cover of *Gentlemen's Quarterly*": The cover was shown in *Time*, 2/23/62, alongside that month's *Ladies' Home Journal*, which featured a Jackie lookalike, and *Photoplay*, whose cover showed the real Jacqueline and Caroline.
287   "A fag rag": Dutton int; Tree int.

288   It was Glenn's courage: John Glenn OH, p. 23, JFKL.
288   "He's sending me stuff on my family": RFK OH, pp. 643–644, JFKL.
288   "J. Edgar Hoover has Jack Kennedy by the balls": Confidential dispatch, Time arch.
289   caught with his pants down: O'Donnell and Powers, *"Johnny, We Hardly Knew Ye,"* p. 173.
289   "Subject: JUDITH E. CAMPBELL": Evans memo to Belmont, 3/20/62, J. Edgar Hoover Official and Confidential File 96 (John F. Kennedy), FBI; CC, pp. 129–130.
289   The FBI had discovered an illegal wiretap: See CC, pp. 77–79, 125–134; Collier and Horowitz, *The Kennedys,* pp. 292–295.
290   "Colonel Edwards advised": CC, p. 127.
290   the last of seventy telephone calls: CC, note to p. 129; p. 130.
290   dozens of other women: James Giglio has given the most succinct and fair summary of women reliably known to have been with Kennedy: "His affairs involved film stars such as Marilyn Monroe and Jayne Mansfield; would-be actresses like Judith Campbell; White House employees, including Jacqueline's press secretary Pamela Turnure and secretaries Priscilla Wear and Jill Cowan—better known to insiders as Fiddle and Faddle; socialites such as Florence Pritchett, a long-time Kennedy flame married to Eisenhower's ambassador to Cuba, Earl T. Smith, and Mary Pinchot Meyer, the artistic sister-in-law of Benjamin Bradlee and niece of conservationist Gifford Pinchot; and burlesque queens Blaze Starr and Tempest Storm. More alarming, Kennedy occasionally had affairs with casual acquaintances and virtual strangers, who surreptitiously entered the southwest service entrance of the White House as the result of solicitations of friends and aides. . . . they came during Jacqueline's frequent absences, joining the President in the pool or in the family quarters." James N. Giglio, *The Presidency of John F. Kennedy* (Lawrence, KS: University Press of Kansas, 1991), p. 267.
A few documentary fragments relating to Kennedy's extracurricular activities survive. Janet Des Rosiers, the stewardess aboard the *Caroline,* Kennedy's 1960 plane, saved a few of the notes he wrote when his voice gave out during the campaign. They include lines such as "I suppose they are going to hit me with something before we are finished," "I suppose if I win, my poon days are over," and "I got into the blonde last night." WP, 5/29/87. A memo to "Fiddle" is attached to the December 1961 JFK-Diem correspondence at the Kennedy Library. "Polly" memo to "Fiddle," 12/13/61, POF Box 128, JFKL. The FBI, which maintained extensive surveillance on Kennedy's wartime affair with Inga Arvad, kept an unfriendly eye on him in later years. The bureau's files contain myriad notations on Kennedy's sex life in addition to material on Judith Exner. These include references to "a pair of stewardesses the subject is seeing in California"; "Kennedy-Sinatra information" involving "two mulatto prostitutes in New York"; and trips Kennedy made in 1957 and 1958 to see Flo Pritchett. See File 94-37374 (John F. Kennedy); J. Edgar Hoover Official and Confidential Files 13 and 96 (John F. Kennedy); all at FBI.
Marilyn Monroe's FBI File, 105-40018-4, sometimes cited as a source for Kennedy material, in fact contains material that is almost entirely either from the public press, unsubstantiated, or heavily sanitized.
290   "I wonder how it is for you, Harold?" Horne, *Macmillan: 1957–1986,* p. 290.
291   Mary Meyer: Phillip Nobile and Ron Rosenbaum, "The Curious Aftermath of JFK's Best and Brightest Affair," *New Times,* 7/9/76; NW, 3/1/76.
291   "We're a bunch of virgins": Dutton int.
291   "Happening babes": Peter Kaplan conv. The phrase is from Lem Billings.
291   Laura Bergquist Knebel: Laura Bergquist Knebel OH, JFKL, pp. 16–17.
291   "That's just the way Jack is": Confidential source int.
292   "Is there anything you'd like to talk about?": William Haddad int.
292   "Any prosecution in the matter": CC, p. 131.
292   reactivated the Mafia plotting: CC, pp. 132–134.
292   "You just can't associate with this guy": Collier and Horowitz, *The Kennedys,* p. 295.
292   "Lido Hotel, Palm Springs": SAC, Los Angeles memo to Hoover, 3/5/62, J. Edgar Hoover Official and Confidential File 13 (John F. Kennedy), FBI.

293   "Bing Crosby's residence": SAC, Los Angeles memo to Hoover, 3/19/62, J. Edgar Hoover Official and Confidential File 13 (John F. Kennedy), FBI. Kennedy brother-in-law Peter Lawford was assigned the thankless task of breaking off Kennedy's relations with Sinatra, and watched his career plummet as a result.

Sinatra was reportedly so angry when he heard of Kennedy's change in plans that he took to the heliport that he had built for Kennedy with a sledgehammer and destroyed it.

Chapter 27

294   "Terrific!": This account of the steel crisis is drawn from the following sources: Bartlett, Bradlee, and Clifford ints; Arthur Goldberg conv; RFK OH, JFKL; Sidey OH, pp. 30–31, JFKL; Bartlett OH, pp. 94–95, LBJL; Goldberg memo, undated, and accompanying documents, Sorensen papers, Box 39, JFKL; NYT, 4/13–20/62; *Time*, 4/27/62; draft manuscript of Fay, *The Pleasure of His Company*, Land papers, Box 12, BU; and Sidey, *John F. Kennedy, President*, pp. 298–303.

294   "You can't just talk to me in abstract terms": Samuelson int.

295   "Good God": Draft manuscript of Fay, *The Pleasure of His Company*, Land papers, Box 12, BU.

296   the company wanted to raise prices: Bartlett int.

296   "I've been breaking my ass": Bradlee, *Conversations with Kennedy*, p. 77.

296   "Perhaps the easiest way I can explain": Bradlee, *Conversations with Kennedy*, p. 76.

296   "steel made a deal with Nixon": Bradlee, *Conversations with Kennedy*, p. 77.

297   "I'll never have another one of these receptions": Sorensen OH, pp. 161–162, JFKL.

297   Steel Price Emergency Act of 1962: The draft legislation is in Sorensen papers, Box 39, JFKL.

297   "The simultaneous and identical actions": JFKPP, 4/11/62.

297   "an estimated one billion dollars": JFKPP, 4/11/62.

298   "I just figured that this is the way": *Time*, 4/27/62.

298   "Oh, didn't he do a good one!": *Time*, 4/27/62.

299   "We're going for broke": RFK OH, pp. 299–303, JFKL.

299   "Gentlemen": Blough press conference, 4/12/62, transcript found in Sorensen papers, Box 39, JFKL.

300   "Who the fuck do they think they are?": Bradlee, *Conversations with Kennedy*, p. 78.

300   "Would increase GNP by (roughly) $2.8 to $2.85 billion": Cohn memo to Bell, 4/12/62, Sorensen papers, Box 39, JFKL.

300   "It's the Governor of Delaware": RFK OH, p. 299, JFKL.

300   "tell your friend I said let's make peace": Bartlett int.

301   "Blough and his people want to know": Clifford int.

301   Blough at the Hotel Carlyle: Clifford int.

301   "We have met the enemy and they are ours": The account of Kennedy on the *Northampton* is drawn from the draft manuscript of Fay, *The Pleasure of His Company*, Land papers, Box 12, BU.

302   "My God, this is fried chicken!": Draft manuscript of Fay, *The Pleasure of His Company*, Land papers, Box 12, BU. Fay went on: "Then, feeling perhaps that he had made too much of the incident or was taking out on the Chief the problems of the day, the President's face suddenly softened, and his tone changed. With a slight smile at the corners of his mouth, he said to the Chief, 'Chief, don't ever let those gunners' mates tell you that they are the only ones with hardship duty.' "

302   Hugh Sidey of *Time*: Sidey OH, p. 31, JFKL; *Time*, 4/27/62.

303   "The fucking *Herald Tribune*": Salinger int.

303   "The real remedy": Heller memo to JFK, 4/14/62, Sorensen papers, Box 39, JFKL.

303   "We may have already bit off more than we can chew": Tobin int.

303   "Are you smoking more and enjoying it less": JFKPP, 4/20/62.

304 "I was telling Patton what a son of a bitch he was": The scene is from Bradlee, *Conversations with Kennedy*, pp. 111–112.

304 dozens of wiretaps: Baldwin, the *Times'* military affairs correspondent, had attacked the administration in 1963 for tampering with the news. Norman was *Newsweek's* Pentagon correspondent. Fall reportedly was in touch with North Vietnamese officials. Lasky was a persistent critic of the Kennedys. McHugh apparently was tapped routinely. Amory was allegedly close to a European spy. Other persons tapped included civil rights activists Martin Luther King, Jr., Clarence Jones, and Stanley Levison; Michael Streulens, the American lobbyist for Congolese secessionist Moise Tshombe; and half a dozen people involved in sugar lobbying done by the Dominican Republic. "My God," Ben Bradlee said later, "they wiretapped practically everybody else in this town." See David J. Garrow, *The FBI and Martin Luther King, Jr.: From "Solo" to Memphis* (New York: W. W. Norton, 1981), pp. 63–77; Victor Lasky, *It Didn't Start with Watergate* (New York: Dial, 1977), pp. 69–82.

304 the White House had had its own taping system: WP, 2/4–5/82. See also the introduction to the Presidential Recordings collection, JFKL, which provides background information on the taping system.

Chapter 28

305 "How did it all happen?": Bundy int; Elvis Stahr int.

305 "Could it happen here?": Draft manuscript of Fay, *The Pleasure of His Company*, Land papers, Box 12, BU.

306 "The book says one of those men": Lieberson and Meyers, eds., *John Fitzgerald Kennedy . . . As We Remember Him*, p. 121.

306 "I want you to read this": Stahr int.

306 "You can't beat brains": Bradlee int.

306 "America and the West": *Time*, 4/29/63.

307 Nam Tha: Rust, *Kennedy in Vietnam*, p. 73.

307 "We are hopeful that we can bring about": JFKPP, 5/9/62.

307 "To signal Moscow": This account of the administration's policy in Laos during the spring of 1962 is drawn from Stephen Pelz, " 'When Do I Have Time to Think?' John F. Kennedy, Roger Hilsman, and the Laotian Crisis of 1962," *Diplomatic History* (Spring 1979), and the following sources: JFK-Hilsman telecons, 5/10/62; Bundy-Hilsman telecon, 5/10/62; all in Harriman papers, Box 479, LC; Hilsman memo, 5/11/62, "Thursday, Friday, Saturday," Hilsman papers, Box 2, JFKL; Hilsman, *To Move a Nation*, pp. 138–155. For more on Laos, see Bernard B. Fall, "Laos: Who Broke the Ceasefire?" *New Republic*, 6/18/62.

308 Chester Bowles: Bowles's departure had been delayed for months by the vociferous support of his liberal allies, but in November he had been sacked in what some journalists called the "Thanksgiving massacre." In the shuffle, George Ball had replaced Bowles, Harriman had become Assistant Secretary for Far Eastern Affairs, George McGhee had become deputy undersecretary, and Walt Rostow had left the White House staff to take over McGhee's former position as head of the State Department's Policy Planning Council. See Giglio, *The Presidency of John F. Kennedy*, pp. 92–94.

309 "You want to read something fantastic?": Bradlee, *Conversations with Kennedy*, p. 84.

310 "The story, I assume, is untrue": Salinger memo to JFK and JFK reply, 5/24/62, POF Box 65, JFKL.

310 "My brother feels he has been double-crossed:" RFK OH, JFKL; *New Times*, no. 5, 1989.

311 "He's a losing horse": Galbraith memo to JFK, 4/4/62, NSF Box 196, JFKL.

311 "I get a little tired": Hilsman int.

311 "We test and test and test": *Time*, 4/29/63.

311 "I am haunted by this": *Time*, 4/29/63.

312 "Whether it is Viet Nam or Laos": JFKPP, 6/6/62.

312 "Your mission remains fixed": Taylor, *Swords and Plowshares*, p. 254.

Chapter 29

313    $10 million trust fund: Stephen Smith int.
313   Kennedy rarely carried money: Bartlett int; Sidey OH, p. 32, JFKL; Smathers OH, p. 3D, JFKL. The Kennedy family "had their own comptroller," said Smathers, "and they just signed checks and sent bills, and so on, to this address in New York and that's all there was to it. . . . I'm certain that he had no conception how difficult it was to make money, nor did he have any idea of the value of money . . . he was a fellow who would frequently take off on a trip without a single penny in his pocket, never conscious of the fact that somebody had to pick up the bill."
   Hugh Sidey recalled that on a trip to Senator Robert Kerr's Oklahoma ranch, Kennedy "got wrapped up in finding out how a cowboy lived . . . who made two hundred dollars a month. . . . The manager of the ranch kept explaining to him how they gave him his milk and his electricity and that sort of thing." Sidey OH, p. 32, JFKL.
313   "Why are we giving them French champagne?": White House staff OH, p. 19, JFKL. Kennedy was "a real skinflint when it came to the budget," said Ted Sorensen. "I think he was a real skinflint about everything," replied Carl Kaysen, to general laughter.
   Eunice Kennedy Shriver once asked her brother if she could invite a group interested in mental retardation to the White House.
   "Well, Jackie isn't here," said the President.
   His sister persisted: "Well, could I still have them at the White House?"
   "Fine," said Kennedy. "Have them at the White House. Talk to Tish Baldridge about it, but don't run up a big liquor bill on me. Serve some kind of punch." Eunice Shriver OH, p. 11, JFKL.
314   "I want every zero put in there": Sorensen int.
314   "Don't ever let that story out": Draft manuscript of Fay, *The Pleasure of His Company*, Land papers, Box 12, BU.
314   "Good morning George": See Jim Bishop, *A Day in the Life of President Kennedy* (New York: Random House, 1964), *passim*.
314   entertainment by some of the biggest stars: *Time*, 6/1/61; NYT, 5/20/61.
315   A Monroe poster had filled the wall: Collier and Horowitz, *The Kennedys*, p. 204.
315   She was telling people in Hollywood: See, for example, Anthony Summers, *Goddess: The Secret Lives of Marilyn Monroe* (New York: Macmillan, 1985), pp. 259–260, 281, 285–290. Summers's account is detailed but highly speculative at times.
315   "I think I made his back feel better": Collier and Horowitz, *The Kennedys*, p. 413.
316   "See the editors": Haddad int. "He lied to me," Haddad said years later. "He used my credibility with people I knew."
316   "STOCK PRICES DIVE": NYT, 5/29/62.
316   "To think I voted for that son-of-a-bitch": Sidey dispatch from Washington to Parker, 5/30/62, Time arch.
316   "This administration is heading toward": *Time*, 6/1/62.
316   "I'm not against business": Sidey, *John F. Kennedy, President*, p. 303.
317   "chasing the dollar": Stephen Smith int.
317   "I understand your problems with Bill Martin": Council of Economic Advisers OH, pp. 194–195, JFKL.
317   "Restrain their wage demands": Parmet, *JFK*, p. 92.
318   a cut in the corporate rate: *Time*, 6/8/62.
318   "A Quickie Tax Cut?": CEA memo to JFK, 5/29/62, Sorensen papers, Box 40, JFKL.
318   the performance gap: See Walter W. Heller, "Why We Must Cut Taxes," *Nation's Business* (November 1962); Allen J. Matusow, *The Unraveling of America: A History of Liberalism in the 1960s* (New York: Harper & Row, 1984), pp. 42–48.
319   "The Republicans would kick us in the balls": Tobin int.
319   "That's vanity, Paul, not politics": Samuelson int.
319   "Do nothing. Say nothing": Robert Lovett OH, pp. 29–30, JFKL.
319   "Hold rigidly to the explanation": Galbraith memo to JFK, 5/29/62, Sorensen papers, Box 39, JFKL.

319 "It's not my department": Bundy memo to JFK, 5/29/62, Sorensen papers, Box 39, JFKL.
320 "WASHINGTON SEES MARKET REACTING": NYT, 5/29/62. Heller's articulation of the market "crash" can be found in a CEA memo to JFK, 5/29/62, "Why the Market Fell," Sorensen papers, Box 39, JFKL. See also two accompanying memos by Heller on the same day, "Differences Between '29 and '62" and "Possible Government Action," both in Sorensen papers, Box 39, JFKL.
320 climbed steadily to close at 603.96: See NYT, 5/30/61; *Time,* 6/1/61, 6/8/61.
320 boarded a helicopter: Descriptions in the text of Kennedy's chocolate cake and the flowers sent by Frank Sinatra are from Sidey dispatch from Washington to Parker, 5/30/62, Time arch.
320 "An across-the-board reduction": JFKPP, 6/7/62.
320 "It could be said now": JFKPP, 6/11/62.
321 "President Kennedy and his advisers": *Time,* 6/22/62, which also reprinted the cartoon from the *Philadelphia Bulletin.*
322 "Most big businessmen are": Sorensen memo to JFK, "The Kennedy Administration and Business," 6/20/62, Sorensen papers, Box 29, JFKL. See also Sorensen talking paper for Cabinet meeting, "The Administration and Business," 7/25/62, Sorensen papers, Box 29, JFKL.
The copy of the Sorensen memo entitled "The Kennedy Administration and Business" at the Kennedy Library is attached, apparently inadvertently, to a page discussing its declassification. The Library's reviewers voted 8–1 to release the memo, and their comments shed considerable light on their thought processes: "The discussion may be sensitive but at the policy rather than the personality level. . . . In an election campaign this would receive more press attention than its substance warrants. . . . Research value. Motive behind suggestion for Sec of Commerce is legitimate, no candidate is mentioned, and no criticism made. . . . Nothing embarrassing, dishonest, or slanderous here. . . . This might be embarrassing to Sorensen because of his current associations with business firms. . . . To shield TCS. Not originally intended for the public eye." Attachment to Sorensen memo to JFK, 6/20/62, Sorensen papers, Box 29, JFKL.
322 "I can't believe": JFKPP, 6/14/62.

Chapter 30

323 "Bobby and I smile sardonically": Bradlee, *Conversations with Kennedy,* p. 113; *Time,* 6/15/62.
324 being run from the White House: See, for example, Sorensen memo, "Edward Kennedy Meets the Press," 3/8/62, Sorensen papers, Box 35, JFKL.
324 aides were searching: Red Fay, Undersecretary of the Navy, had Eddie McCormack's wartime records searched, but no such material was used by the Edward Kennedy campaign. Draft manuscript of Fay, *The Pleasure of His Company,* Land papers, Box 12, BU. This fact caused a minor splash in Massachusetts politics when it was printed in the *Boston Globe* in 1993.
324 "Don't tell him that": Milton Gwirtzman OH, p. 32, JFKL.
324 "We haven't spent as much fucking time": Bradlee int; Robert Healy conv.
325 "Ted Kennedy Tells About": *Boston Globe,* 3/30/62; Thomas Winship OH, pp. 32–35, JFKL.
325 "as to whether there are too many Kennedys": JFKPP, 6/27/62; Bradlee, *Conversations with Kennedy,* p. 112.
325 "Mr. President, speaking generally": JFKPP, 6/27/62.
326 "I think that it is important for us": JFKPP, 6/27/62.
326 "That lighting is terrible": Bradlee int.
326 "We couldn't do it without TV": Salinger int.
327 "a stroke of the pen": See Parmet, *JFK,* p. 259; Schlesinger, *Robert Kennedy and His Times,* pp. 334–335.
327 "still haven't signed that order": JFKPP, 7/5/62. The demands of liberals were summed up by Joe Rauh in the newspaper published by Americans for Democratic Action: "We ask here and now that the President immediately issue the long overdue Executive Order ending discrimination in Federal Housing; the President issue an Execu-

tive Order ending all federal subsidies to segregated hospitals, schools and facilities of all kinds; the administration support legislation promised in the Democratic platform to end school segregation, to set up a fair employment council (FEPC) and make voting rights a reality." *ADA World,* 4/6/62.

328   "This is a most serious defeat": JFKPP, 7/17/62. On Kennedy's fight for Medicare, see *Time,* 6/1/62, 7/27/62; Sorensen, *Kennedy,* pp. 383–385.

328   "Burns and Keyserling are kicking me": CEA OH, p. 341, JFKL.

329   "Mr. President, the price of gold": Salinger, *With Kennedy,* pp. 189–190.

Chapter 31

330   "A tax cut is a massive economic weapon": Sorensen memo to JFK, 7/12/62, Sorensen papers, Box 40, JFKL.

331   "wait until we get the July figures": JFKPP, 8/1/62.

331   "So what happened in the 1950s": Rostow int; Rostow, *The Diffusion of Power,* p. 235.

331   "Our businessmen, workers and farmers": JFKPP, 5/8/62.

332   Marilyn Monroe was found dead: NYT, 8/5/62; *Time,* 8/10/62; *People,* 8/10/92; Summers, *Goddess,* pp. 305–326.

332   "This is an affront to the Congress": See Albert Gore, *Let the Glory Out: My South and Its Politics* (New York, 1972), pp. 144–147.

332   The July economic numbers: Heller memo to JFK, 8/9/62, Sorensen papers, Box 40, JFKL.

332   "I take some pride in the fact": JFKPP, 8/13/62.

332   "Everybody talks about our deficit": Bartlett OH, p. 120, JFKL.

333   odds on a new cycle of recession: Samuelson int.

333   Du Pont was operating: Transcript of Audiotape 10.1, 8/9/62, Presidential Recordings, Tax Cut Proposals, Vol. 1, JFKL.

333   "In other words, we're too restrained": Transcript of Audiotape 7.0B-1, 8/6/62, Presidential Recordings, Tax Cut Proposals, Vol. I, JFKL.

334   "A 1962 tax cut": Heller memo to JFK, 8/9/62, Sorensen papers, Box 40, JFKL.

335   "TWO SOVIET SPACE CRAFT CIRCLING": NYT, 8/13/62.

335   "We are behind and we will be": JFKPP, 8/13/62. For a good discussion of the odyssey of the tax-cut proposal over the summer months of 1962, see Bernard D. Nossiter, "The Day Taxes Weren't Cut," *The Reporter,* 9/13/62.

335   "It was a C-minus": Sorensen int; Matuson, *The Unraveling of America,* p. 50.

335   "I don't care if you paper over": CEA OH p. 412, JFKL.

335   "The United States will help the people": Lansdale memo, 2/20/62, CMC, Document 5, pp. 26–37. Operation Mongoose was first uncovered by the Church Committee in 1975. Those aspects of Mongoose relating to the killing of Fidel Castro are discussed in great detail in CC, beginning at p. 139, as the specific mandate of the committee was the investigation of alleged assassination plots against foreign leaders by the U.S. government.

"The Cuba project" also consisted, however, of gathering intelligence, executing sabotage plans, and at least considering military action against Cuba. These aspects of Operation Mongoose were recorded by Lansdale in regular memos, a number of which were declassified in 1988 and 1989 in response to a Freedom of Information Act lawsuit brought by the National Security Archive against the State Department. These include the memo cited above; Lansdale memo to SG (A), 3/12/62, "Policy Points to Consider"; SG (A) memo, "Guideline for Operation Mongoose," 3/14/62; Lansdale memo to SG (A), 7/25/62, "Review of Operation Mongoose"; Defense Department and JCS memo to SG (A), 8/8/62, "Consequences of U.S. Military Intervention in Cuba"; memo of Mongoose meeting, 10/4/62; and "Operation Mongoose: Main Points to Consider," 10/26/62; all in Cuba papers, NSA. In addition, Lansdale wrote weekly "highlights" or "progress" reports on Mongoose throughout the spring and summer of 1962, which are also in Cuba papers, NSA.

Taken together, these documents, while often heavily sanitized, show that while Mongoose was not able to topple Castro, it certainly was of a magnitude to have attracted the attention of the Cuban government—and probably to have prodded the Soviet government toward more heavily protecting its Caribbean client against invasion.

336 "the U.S. will make use of indigenous resources": "Guidelines for Operation Mongoose," 3/14/62, CMC, Document 6, pp. 38–39.

336 "including liquidation of leaders": Lansdale memo to Harvey, et al., 8/13/62, Cuba papers, NSA. Furious at the indiscretion, Harvey eliminated the four words from his own copy of the memo and got Lansdale to do the same to all other distributed copies. Harvey then put the whole thing in writing the next day in his memo to Helms.

336 "Reference is made to our conversation": Harvey memo to Helms, 8/14/62, Cuba papers, NSA.

337 "The subject you just brought up": CC, p. 166. This was the testimony of Walter Elder, McCone's executive assistant, to the Church Committee. McCone told the committee that he called McNamara to have Lansdale's memo withdrawn.

In 1967, at the request of Robert Kennedy, McCone spoke about the August 10 meeting to Jack Anderson, who was ready to implicate both Kennedys in attempts to assassinate Castro. McCone then dictated a memo to Helms, by then director of the CIA, which stated: "I recall a suggestion being made to liquidate the top people in the Castro regime, including Castro. I took immediate exception to this suggestion, stating that the subject was completely out of bounds as far as the USG and CIA were concerned and the idea should not be discussed nor should it appear in any papers. . . . Immediately after the meeting, I called on Secretary McNamara personally and re-emphasized my position, in which he heartily agreed. I did this because operation MONGOOSE . . . was under the operational control of DOD through the JCS." McCone memo to Helms, 4/14/67, Cuba papers, NSA.

The CIA's inspector general concluded in 1967 that Castro's assassination "was raised at a meeting at State on 10 August 1962, but is unrelated to any actual attempts at assassination." What that meeting did produce—despite the shocked reactions of Murrow and McCone—was Lansdale's action memo, recording that "liquidation" was generally acceptable to Mongoose's operations officers. CC, p. 161.

337 "I could get excommunicated": CC, p. 105. The seriousness of McCone's Catholicism was a perfect excuse for Helms and Harvey not to tell McCone of his own agency's plots to kill Castro. McCone did not directly ask Helms about possible assassination plots until the summer of 1963, when a *Chicago Sun-Times* article linked Sam Giancana to the CIA. Helms handed him a copy of the same CIA memo that had been given to Robert Kennedy on May 14, 1962, which falsely stated that the CIA had terminated its attempts to use gangsters to kill Castro. "Well," said a relieved McCone, "this did not happen during my tenure."

It must also be pointed out that as director of the CIA, McCone was much more heavily involved with technical intelligence such as obtaining and interpreting satellite photos than with the activities of human agents. This was due to his preferences, his talents, and the desire of the President to centralize control of covert operations under Robert Kennedy. See Ranelagh, *The Agency*, pp. 387–388, 412–417.

337 "It was made abundantly clear": CC, p. 149.

337 "Massive activity": Memo of Mongoose meeting, 10/4/62, Cuba papers, NSA; CC, p. 147. The official investigators of the Church Committee stopped short of concluding that the "activity" desired by the President and Robert Kennedy included the assassination of Fidel Castro. Robert McNamara's testimony to the committee summed up the stance of top administration officials: "I do not believe that President Kennedy gave the authority. I also do not believe that the CIA would take such action without the authorization of the President. I know that is contradictory but that is the way it is." CC, p. 144. Dean Rusk maintains that "the assassination of Castro was never discussed in my presence. I remember laughing about it when someone mentioned it in jest. If it had been said to me or McNamara we would have gone to President Kennedy. But I draw a blank on that subject. It was very bad business. It would have thrown international diplomacy onto a new level—it would have reduced international politics to a game of survival." Rusk int.

For his part, Richard Bissell said, "I've never known if JFK knew" about the assassination plots against Castro. "Allen Dulles had reason to believe that JFK knew, and there is no doubt that it was fully known to the Attorney General. It is inconceivable to me that the President didn't know, particularly considering their relationship. Inconceivable." Bissell int.

Asked in a 1989 interview about the plans for killing Castro, Richard Helms at first told the author, "I just want to leave that subject where it is, with what I have said before." But then he added: "Robert Kennedy ran with it, ran those operations, and I dealt with him almost every day. None of that, of course, is in Arthur Schlesinger's book about Robert Kennedy. I have known Schlesinger since we were in the OSS together in the war, and when he was finishing the Kennedy book I was spending a long weekend at the Harrimans', and Arthur would come over to use the pool every day and I would be there. He had me as a captive for two days and he never asked me about any of that —because he didn't want to know about any of that." Helms described the CIA, "then and now," as "a service organization for the President of the United States." Helms int.

Chapter 32

338   a dozen or more ships had come into Havana: CIA Current Intelligence Memorandum, 8/22/62, Cuba papers, NSA; State Department Official History, undated, "The Cuban Crisis, 1962" (the Sievarts Report), Cuba papers, NSA. The Sievarts Report, based on State Department documents, was written in 1963 for internal use. See also Elie Abel, *The Missile Crisis* (Philadelphia: Lippincott, 1966), pp. 183–184; David Detzer, *The Brink: Cuban Missile Crisis, 1962* (New York: Thomas Y. Crowell, 1979), pp. 32–33.

339   "The only construction I can put": CIA memo, 11/30/62, "Chronology of John McCone's Suspicions on the Military Build-Up in Cuba Prior to President Kennedy's October 22 Speech," Cuba papers, NSA; Krock, *Memoirs,* p. 352.

339   "Starfish": Seaborg, *Kennedy, Khrushchev, and the Test Ban,* p. 156.

340   "Guess what my cousin saw": Hilsman int.

340   McCone met with Rusk and McNamara: CIA memo, 11/30/62, "Chronology"; Krock, *Memoirs,* pp. 352–353.

340   "As many as 20 Soviet vessels": CIA Current Intelligence memo, 8/22/62, Cuba papers, NSA.

341   "Their appraisals of risks may change": Rusk, McNamara, McCone, and Lemnitzer memo to JFK, 8/23/62, Cuba papers, NSA.

342   "New supplies definitely": JFKPP, 8/22/62.

342   "The President has directed": NSAM 181, 8/23/62, CMC, Document 12, pp. 61–62.

343   without the direct intervention of United States troops: CC, p. 147.

344   "We've no evidence of troops": JFKPP, 8/29/62.

344   "Some of us were told the other day": JFKPP, 8/29/62.

344   the photographs were ready: Sorensen, *Kennedy,* pp. 755–756. On the U-2 flights, see CINCLANT Historical Account of the Cuban Crisis (the Dennison Report), 4/18/63, Cuba papers, NSA, pp. 7–8.

345   "18,000 SOVIET TROOPS IN CUBA": *Time,* 8/31/62.

345   "I am reliably informed": NYT, 9/1/62.

345   "Those CIA bastards": Sander Vanocur int.

346   "Mr. Kennedy is caught": NYT, 9/3/62.

346   "I wanted to acquaint you": Sidey, *John F. Kennedy, President,* p. 324.

346   Anatoli Dobrynin: Robert Kennedy, *Thirteen Days: A Memoir of the Missile Crisis* (New York: W. W. Norton, 1969), pp. 24–26.

346   "Nothing will be undertaken": Sorensen, *Kennedy,* pp. 752–753.

346   "Hello, Georgie": *New Times,* no. 5, 1989. Bolshakov, his credibility destroyed, was recalled to the Soviet Union after the missile crisis. Eduard Ivanian said of the courier, "He was picked precisely because he could be discounted if things went wrong." Ivanian int.

347   "Information has reached this government": JFKPP, 9/4/62.

348   "John's Other Wife": Bradlee int. See Bradlee, *Conversations with Kennedy,* pp. 45–49, 115–117; Parmet, *JFK,* pp. 112–114. Kennedy's name was listed in a genealogy of a family called Blauvelt; he was alleged to have married Durie Malcolm, a woman whom he and his brother Joe had dated in the 1940s. Those who seriously looked into the matter—including Bradlee and, at Kennedy's request, Clark Clifford—found several errors in the same entry of the genealogy and were forced to conclude that its elderly author had simply been mistaken.

348   "It's almost impossible to write": Fletcher Knebel, "Kennedy vs. the Press," *Look,* 8/28/62.

348   "No, he's not coming": Bradlee, *Conversations with Kennedy,* p. 117.

Chapter 33

349   KENNEDY PLEDGES ANY STEPS: NYT, 9/5/62.

350   " 'Now as to Cuba' ": Khrushchev-Udall memcon, 9/6/62, Cuba papers, NSA.

351   Ike had said privately: Memcon, 6/19/59, Staff Secretary Files, State Department Series Box 3, DDEL.

351   "tell them electric power plants": Udall did tell the press that he and Khrushchev had talked about power plants. See NYT, 9/8/62.

351   "too liberal to fight": NYT, 9/10/62. The eighty-eight-year-old Frost, fatigued by the end of his trip, felt misquoted and later tried to set the record straight, with little success. See F. D. Reeve, "Robert Frost Confronts Khrushchev," *Atlantic* (September 1963); Larence Thompson and R. H. Winnick, *Robert Frost: The Later Years* (New York: Holt, Rinehart, & Winston, 1976), pp. 437–438.

351   "Why did Frost say that?": Udall OH, pp. 55–56, JFKL.

352   "the Congressional head of steam": Bundy memo to JFK, 9/13/62, Cuba papers, NSA.

352   "I would like to take": JFKPP, 9/13/62.

352   "The press boys bobbled their lines": Kern, Levering, and Levering, *The Kennedy Crises,* p. 93.

353   "Consequences of US Military Intervention": Department of Defense and JCS memo to SG (A), 8/8/62, Cuba papers, NSA.

353   "To achieve complete destruction:" Accounts of U.S. military exercises are drawn from James G. Hershberg, "Before 'The Missiles of October': Did Kennedy Plan a Military Strike Against Cuba?" *Diplomatic History* (Spring 1990). The author utilized a draft copy of this work, courtesy of James Hershberg. A briefer version of it appeared in the *Boston Phoenix,* 4/8/88.

353   "I think": JFKPP, 9/13/62.

353   "There is not time enough": Griffiths letter to O'Brien, 9/18/62, Lee White papers, Housing/Executive Order, JFKL.

354   a new gold Thunderbird: RFK OH, p. 827, JFKL.

354   "We believe the USSR values its position": SNIE 85-3-62, "The Military Buildup in Cuba," 9/12/62, Cuba papers, NSA.

354   "Despite humiliation and deprivation": JFKPP, 9/20/62.

355   only 60,000 of the 1 million: Louis E. Lomax, "The Kennedys Move In on Dixie," *Harper's* (May 1962).

355   James Meredith: Details in the text are drawn from Guthman, Katzenbach, Marshall, and Sorensen ints; Katzenbach OH, pp. 104–123, and RFK OH, pp. 731–739, both in JFKL; in-depth accounts of the Oxford crisis found in *Time,* 10/5/62, 10/12/62; Branch, *Parting the Waters,* pp. 633–672; Walter Lord, *The Past That Would Not Die* (New York: Harper & Row, 1965), pp. 1–4, 139–232; Schlesinger, *Robert Kennedy and His Times,* pp. 340–351; Sorensen, *Kennedy,* pp. 542–548; and audiotape transcripts cited below.

355   "U.S. IS PREPARED TO SEND TROOPS": NYT, 9/26/62.

355   "THOUSANDS SAID READY TO FIGHT": *Jackson Daily News,* 9/26/62.

356   Little Rock: For background on the 1957 incident and JFK's criticism of Eisenhower, see *Time,* 10/12/62.

357   "You're making my life difficult": Berl Bernhard int; Bernhard OH, p. 29, JFKL.

357   "Negroes are getting ideas": Louis Martin int.

357   "I concur in your judgment": Sorensen memo to JFK, 9/28/62, Sorensen papers, Box 30, JFKL.

357   developing ulcers: Sorensen int.

358   "Governor, this is the President:" Schlesinger, *Robert Kennedy and His Times,* p. 344.

358   "This is not my order": Transcript of Dictabelt 4A.1, 9/29/62, Presidential Recordings, JFKL.

359   "You've been fighting a sofa pillow": Schlesinger, *Robert Kennedy and His Times,* pp. 344–345.

359   "I'd like to get assurances": Transcript of Dictabelt 4C, 9/29/62, Presidential Recordings, JFKL.

359   "Is this pretty much what Ike signed": Norbert Schlei OH, pp. 14–15, JFKL.

360   "We've got it all down, Governor": RFK OH, JFKL; Lord, *The Past That Would Not Die,* pp. 196–197.

360   Meredith was on the campus: Branch, *Parting the Waters,* pp. 661–662.

360   "Go to hell, JFK!": Lord, *The Past That Would Not Die,* p. 202.

360   "I think they've got it": Transcript of Audiotape 26, 9/30/62, Presidential Recordings, JFKL. The White House taping system recorded about eighty minutes of the evening meeting on September 30. John and Robert Kennedy were joined by Sorensen, Burke Marshall, Larry O'Brien, Ken O'Donnell in the Cabinet Room, because the Oval Office was being prepared for the President's ten o'clock speech. RFK is often heard on the phone to Justice Department officials in Mississippi.

361   "Good evening, my fellow citizens": JFKPP, 9/30/62.

362   "11:23—Marshal shot through leg": Lord, *The Past That Would Not Die,* p. 2. Lord's detailed account of the Oxford riot often reports phone calls and orders minute by minute, which he assembled from phone logs kept by the Justice Department, the FCC, and, most important, the Base Communications Center in Oxford.

362   "This reminds me a little bit": Transcript of Audiotape 26, 9/30/62, Presidential Recordings, JFKL.

362   "They are not to fire under any conditions": Schlesinger, *Robert Kennedy and His Times,* p. 347.

363   "People are dying in Oxford": Schlesinger, *Robert Kennedy and His Times,* p. 354.

363   "Mr. President, please": Transcripts of Dictabelts 4E.1 and 4F.1, 9/30/62, Presidential Recordings, JFKL.

363   "What are we going to say": Transcript of Audiotape 26, 9/30/62, Presidential Recordings, JFKL.

363   "I have a hunch that Khrushchev": Transcript of Audiotape 26A, 9/30/62, Presidential Recordings, JFKL.

364   "This one is a ball-breaker": Unpublished memoirs of Max Jacobson, "JFK" chapter, p. 34.

364   finally reached the campus: Branch, *Parting the Waters,* p. 669. While late, they kept coming: within two weeks, 23,000 troops, including members of the Air Force and Marines, were camped at Oxford.

Troops held back angry students on October 1 as James Meredith walked through the Oxford campus, still redolent of tear gas, to register for classes. It was the first time, he said later, he had ever heard Mississippi whites call him "nigger." Branch, *Parting the Waters,* p. 670.

After one semester at Ole Miss, Meredith held a press conference and announced: "After listening to all arguments, evaluations and positions and weighing all this against my personal possibilities and circumstances, I have concluded that the Negro should not return to the University of Mississippi. The prospects for him are too unpromising." As a white reporter began to cheer, Meredith went on to say, "However, I have decided that I, J. H. Meredith, will register for the second semester at the University of Mississippi." *Time,* 2/8/63. Meredith graduated in August 1963.

In 1988, Meredith announced his support of the Republican Party—"I hold this position because the greatest enemy facing the black race is the white liberal"—and eventually went to work for North Carolina Senator Jesse Helms. Helms's 1990 opponent, Harvey Gantt, integrated public universities in South Carolina, transferring from Iowa

State to Clemson without violent incident four months after Meredith had entered Ole Miss.

364   what authority he needed: RFK OH, JFKL.

364   "I am frank to say": Harris memo to JFK, 10/4/62, POF Box 105, JFKL.

365   "It is not necessary to build a model": McNamara memo to JFK, 10/5/62, NSF Box 35A–36, JFKL.

365   "Strategists consider the present": *Aviation Week*, 10/1/62.

366   "It's like this, Georgie": *New Times*, no. 5, 1989.

366   the President was extremely concerned: *New Times*, no. 5, 1989.

366   amphibious invasion exercises around Puerto Rico: Hershberg, draft manuscript of "Before 'The Missiles of October,' " pp. 42–45.

367   plans for an invasion: A great deal of activity suggesting an imminent American attack on Cuba took place in the weeks before the missiles were discovered. On October 1, McNamara met with the Joint Chiefs "to discuss intensified Cuban contingency planning. One of the decisions made then was to alert Admiral Dennison, Commander-in-Chief of the Atlantic Fleet, to be prepared to institute a blockade of Cuba. . . . To mask widespread preparations for the actions proposed, Admiral Dennison suggested that we announce our forces were preparing for an exercise. PHIBRIGLEX-62, a large-scale amphibious assault exercise, previously scheduled for the period October 15–20, provided a cover for our Caribbean preparations." Yarmolinsky report, "Department of Defense Operations During the Cuban Crisis," 2/13/63, Cuba papers, NSA. Adam Yarmolinsky was a special assistant to McNamara.

On October 4, noting "presidential interest" in the topic, McNamara sent Kennedy details of a possible strike against ground-to-air missile sites in Cuba: "The Navy plans to attack SA-2 targets at low level using 4 divisions of A-4D's (4 aircraft per division) armed with 250#, 500#, and 2000# low drag bombs and napalm. Similarly, the Air Force plans primary use of napalm and 20 mm cannon delivered at low level, and crews are proficient. Both have made detailed target studies; target folders are in the hands of crews; and crews are familiar with their assigned targets." McNamara also wrote, "I have taken steps to insure that our contingency plans for Cuba are kept up to date." McNamara memo to JFK, 10/4/62, DDRS (1991), 3042.

On October 6, Yarmolinsky noted, "further specific orders for highest state of readiness were issued," even though "Atlantic Fleet forces were already moving toward a high peak of readiness because of a schedule of training operations which were under way." Dennison directed the Atlantic Fleet to be ready to "execute the 314 and 316 [invasion] plans as well as 312 [air strike]," and "called attention to the requirement and prepositioning of troops, aircraft, ships, equipment and supplies." On October 7, the Joint Chiefs asked Dennison to expand his projections for U.S. troop involvement in Cuba to "include forces required for an extended period of military occupation" in the event of landings or an invasion. Hershberg, "Before 'The Missiles of October' "; Marine Corps Emergency Action Center, "Summary of Items of Significant Interest," 10/8/62, Cuba papers, NSA.

Admiral Dennison's 174-page account of the Cuban missile crisis was declassified in 1986 in response to a Freedom of Information Act request filed by historian James Hershberg and WGBH-TV. It describes the three OPLANs and recounts the Kennedy administration's mounting preparations for a move against Cuba in September and October 1962. The Dennison Report and related documents are in Cuba papers, NSA.

Evidence that the United States was planning to invade Cuba before the missiles were discovered was publicized at a reunion conference of missile crisis participants in early 1989. Top American officials heatedly denied that anything but contingency plans were in the works, but did admit that Operation Mongoose and U.S troop movements may have led the Cubans and Soviets to expect an invasion. "Taking memos as any indication of an impending invasion is a load of crap," said McNamara. "There were contingency plans when the first reports of the missiles came. We had no intention of invading. I have no doubt, though, that Castro thought differently." McNamara int. See also *Boston Globe*, 2/16/89; *Proceedings of the Moscow Conference on the Cuban Missile Crisis*, (January 27–28, 1989), CSIA.

367   "The positioning of bloc offensive weapons": Dennison Report, 4/29/63, pp. 41–42, Cuba papers, NSA.

367   "Nothing is to be put in writing": Marine Corps Emergency Actions Center, "Summary of Items of Significant Interest," 10/10/62, Cuba papers, NSA.

367   "Construction has begun": Kenneth B. Keating, "My Advance View of the Missile Crisis," *Look,* 11/3/64.

367   "Keating's a nut": Reston int.

367   "What is going on is something quite different": NYT, 10/12/62.

368   "These self-appointed generals": JFKPP, 10/14/62.

368   "Mr. President": Abel, *The Missile Crisis,* pp. 44–45; Beschloss, *The Crisis Years,* pp. 3–5. Bundy explained later why he waited until morning to inform Kennedy. Bundy memo to JFK, 3/4/63, Cuba papers, NSA.

369   "Dick, is it true?": Helms int.

Chapter 34

370   "We are probably going to have to bomb them": This account of the Cuban missile crisis is drawn from Ball, Bundy, Dillon, Hilsman, McNamara, Nitze, Rusk, Salinger, and Sorensen ints; the first-hand accounts of Bundy, *Danger and Survival,* pp. 391–462; Robert Kennedy, *Thirteen Days, passim*; O'Donnell and Powers, *"Johnny, We Hardly Knew Ye,"* pp. 354–397; Salinger, *With Kennedy,* pp. 312–346; Schoenbaum, *Waging Peace and War,* pp. 305–326; Sorensen, *Kennedy,* pp. 1–3, 758–809; coverage in *Time,* 11/2/62, 11/9/62; Stewart Alsop and Charles Bartlett, "In Time of Crisis," *Saturday Evening Post,* 12/8/62; Fletcher Knebel, "Washington Crisis: 154 Hours on the Brink of War," *Look,* 12/18/62; Stewart Alsop, "CIA: The Battle for Secret Power," *Saturday Evening Post,* 7/27/63; the narrative accounts of Beschloss, *The Crisis Years,* pp. 1–12, 431–545, and Raymond L. Garthoff, "Cuban Missile Crisis: The Soviet Story," *Foreign Policy* (Fall 1988); and documents and transcripts cited below.

The definitive documentary history of the missile crisis is Laurence Chang and Peter Kornbluh, eds., *The Cuban Missile Crisis, 1962: A National Security Archive Documents Reader* (New York: New Press, 1992), which also provides a fine chronology. The crisis has generated extraordinarily voluminous analytical and retrospective literature. Most of this is not considered in the text, which concerns what President Kennedy knew and did as events were actually unfolding.

.   370   "You still think the fuss about Cuba": O'Donnell and Powers, *"Johnny, We Hardly Knew Ye,"* p. 359.

370   "I'm going to see Gromyko here": Salinger int; Salinger, *With Kennedy,* p. 312.

371   "Have you been eating candy?": Rusk int. This exchange was excised from the transcript of the October 16 meeting available at the Kennedy Library, "in accordance of the deed of gift" of the Kennedy family.

371   "There's a medium-range ballistic missile": Transcript of Audiotape 28.1, 10/16/62, Presidential Recordings, JFKL; Robert Kennedy, *Thirteen Days,* pp. 30–31.

374   the Crown Prince of Libya: JFK appointments schedule, 10/16/62, JFKL.

374   "We'll have to do something quickly": John Bartlow Martin, *Adlai Stevenson and the World* (New York: Doubleday, 1977), p. 723.

375   *"I feel that you should make it clear"*: Stevenson memo to JFK, 10/17/62, CMC, Document 19, pp. 119–120.

375   "Bullfight critics": O'Donnell and Powers, *"Johnny, We Hardly Knew Ye,"* p. 365; NW, 11/12/62.

375   the 6:30 P.M. meeting: Transcript of Audiotapes 28.2 and 28A.1, 10/16/62, Presidential Recordings, JFKL.

376   "Really . . . really": Sorensen, *Kennedy,* p. 795.

376   "Sophomoric babble": Nitze int.

377   going-away party for Chip Bohlen: Susan Mary Alsop int.

377   "Take Cuba away from Castro": "Chronology of the Cuban Crisis October 15–28, 1962," 11/2/62, Cuba papers, NSA; Sorensen OH, p. 50, JFKL; Robert Kennedy, *Thirteen Days,* pp. 34–35.

377   "The following possible tracks": Sorensen memo to JFK, 10/17/62, CMC, Document 17, pp. 114–115.

378   speculation about action in Cuba: WP, 10/17/62.
378   an inexperienced fool: On Acheson, see "Dean Acheson's Version of Robert Kennedy's Version of the Missile Crisis," *Esquire* (February 1969); Brinkley, *Dean Acheson,* pp. 154–174.
378   "Pearl Harbor in reverse": O'Donnell and Powers, *"Johnny, We Hardly Knew Ye,"* pp. 367–368.
379   "How will the Russians respond?": Robert Kennedy, *Thirteen Days,* pp. 38–39; Taylor, *Swords and Plowshares,* p. 269.
379   "Can you imagine LeMay saying": O'Donnell and Powers, *"Johnny, We Hardly Knew Ye,"* pp. 368–369.
379   "Waterbury is either the easiest city": O'Donnell and Powers, *"Johnny, We Hardly Knew Ye,"* pp. 366–367.
379   "I've got problems": Bartlett int; Bartlett OH, p. 127, JFKL.
379   New U-2 photographs: Raymond L. Garthoff, *Reflections on the Cuban Missile Crisis,* 2nd ed. (Washington, DC: Brookings Institution, 1989), p. 209.
379   "He said he had a 'personal message' ": Hilsman, *To Move a Nation,* p. 166; Robert Kennedy, *Thirteen Days,* p. 27; Schlesinger, *Robert Kennedy and His Times,* note to p. 541.
380   "Can these things reach Oxford": Schlesinger, *Robert Kennedy and His Times,* p. 545. When the CIA drew up maps on October 19, it displayed various major cities as being within range of the Soviet missiles: New York, Miami, Dallas—and Oxford, Mississippi. CIA memo, 10/19/62, Cuba papers, NSA.
380   "Two big questions": Sorensen memo to JFK, 10/18/62, Cuba papers, NSA.
381   "Have you considered": Sorensen, *Kennedy,* p. 775.
381   "I have been instructed": JFK-Gromyko memcon, 10/18/62, Cuba papers, NSA; Anatolii Gromyko, *Through Russian Eyes: President Kennedy's 1,036 Days* (Washington: International Library, 1973), pp. 175–179; Sorensen, *Kennedy,* p. 779. On JFK and Gromyko, see Lippmann OH, p. 12, JFKL.
382   "Gromyko in this very room": Lovett OH, p. 50, JFKL.
382   "Dear Mr. Chairman:": Sorensen, draft letter from JFK to Khrushchev, 10/18/62, Cuba papers, NSA.
383   "A Pentagon spokesman denied tonight": NYT, 10/19/62.
383   Robert Kennedy sat on Alexis Johnson's lap: Robert Kennedy, *Thirteen Days,* pp. 43–44; Sorensen, *Kennedy,* p. 779.
384   "Blockade" was Ormsby-Gore's vote: Horne, *Macmillan: 1957–1986,* pp. 368–369.
385   "The campaign is over": Sidey, *John F. Kennedy, President,* p. 278.
385   "These are the issues of the campaign": JFKPP, 10/19/62.
385   "LESS PROFILE—MORE COURAGE": Salinger, *With Kennedy,* p. 314.
385   "Call Kent and tell him": O'Donnell and Powers, *"Johnny, We Hardly Knew Ye,"* pp. 371–372; Salinger, *With Kennedy,* pp. 314–315.
385   the men who convened at eleven o'clock: Minutes of Ex Comm meeting, 10/19/62, 11:00 A.M., CMC, Document 21, pp. 123–127.
386   a little unnerved by his open emotion: Dillon int.
387   "It was generally agreed": Minutes of Ex Comm meeting, 10/19/62.
387   He was writing only one: Robert Kennedy, *Thirteen Days,* pp. 45–47; Sorensen, *Kennedy,* pp. 780–781. For an example of Sorensen's plans had things turned out differently, see Sorensen memo, draft "Air Strike Scenario," 10/19/62, CMC, Document 22, pp. 128–132.
387   "Tell the press": O'Donnell and Powers, *"Johnny, We Hardly Knew Ye,"* pp. 371–372; Salinger, *With Kennedy,* pp. 315–316.
387   "There are 2 fundamental objections": Sorensen memo, 10/20/62, CMC, Document 23, p. 133.
388   At two-thirty: NSC Meeting 505, Record of Actions, 10/20/62, Vice-Presidential Security File, Box 8, LBJL; CIA memo, SNIE 11-19-62, 10/20/62, CMC, Document 24, pp. 134–143.
389   "Did you hear that from Dillon?": Sorensen OH, p. 65, JFKL.
390   "I guess Homer Capehart": Sorensen OH, p. 60, JFKL.

390   "We are very, very close to war": Sorensen OH, p. 64, JFKL; Sorensen, *Kennedy,* pp. 1–2.
390   Kennedy telephoned his wife: O'Donnell and Powers, *"Johnny, We Hardly Knew Ye,"* p. 375.
390   "The President outlined": Minutes of Ex Comm meeting, 10/22/62, Cuba papers, NSA.
391   "Is there a plan to brief": Clifton note, 10/22/62, POF Box 115, JFKL.
391   "MARINE MOVES IN SOUTH LINKED TO CUBAN CRISIS": WP, 10/21/62.
391   "How long do I have to sit here?": Walter Isaacson and Evan Thomas, *The Wise Men: Six Friends and the World They Made* (New York: Simon & Schuster, 1986), p. 628.
391   enlisting pledges of cooperation: Abel, *The Missile Crisis,* p. 102; Detzer, *The Brink,* p. 169.
391   "Shed no blood and start no war": Reston int.
392   "Whatever you do": Eisenhower memo, 10/22/62, Post-Presidential Papers, Box 10, DDEL.
392   "Call Operator 18, Washington": This account of Kennedy's meeting with the congressional leaders is drawn from Mansfield int; Hale Boggs OH, JFKL; Mansfield OH, p. 28, JFKL; Richard Russell notes on meeting with JFK, 10/22/62, Cuba papers, NSA; O'Donnell and Powers, *"Johnny, We Hardly Knew Ye,"* pp. 378–380; Salinger, *With Kennedy,* p. 326.
393   "If they think they can do the job": Sorensen OH, p. 59, JFKL.
393   it's all Jack Kennedy: Mansfield int.

Chapter 35

394   "A Day of Mystery": *San Francisco Examiner,* 10/22/62.
394   "There was an air of crisis": NYT, 10/22/62.
394   "Is Major U.S. Move In Store": *Miami Herald,* 10/22/62.
394   National Security Action Memo 196: NSAM 196, 10/22/62, Cuba papers, NSA; NYT, 11/1/62.
394   evacuating 2,810 women and children: JCS memo, "Chronology of JCS Decisions Concerning the Cuban Crisis," 12/21/62, Cuba papers, NSA.
394   "He looks sick": NYT, 10/23/62.
395   "I have not assumed that you": JFK letter to Khrushchev, 10/22/62, CMC, Document 27, pp. 148–149.
395   "Good evening, my fellow citizens": JFKPP, 10/22/62.
396   "Oh, I'm sorry, doctor": Kraus int.
396   a new suit and topcoat: Lincoln, *My Twelve Years,* p. 327.
396   "Operation Scabbards": CINCLANT cable, 10/23/62, Cuba papers, NSA.
397   "This is the first day": Horne, *Macmillan: 1957–1986,* p. 364.
397   "Now the Americans will realize": Horne, *Macmillan: 1957–1986,* p. 365.
397   "They're scared shitless": Helms int.
397   "Here lie the Soviet diplomats": Ivanian int.
397   "The reaction among students": Neustadt memo to JFK, 10/27/62, Sorensen papers, Box 36, JFKL.
397   "The President approved the following": Minutes of Ex Comm meeting, 10/23/62, 10:00 AM, CMC, Document 31, pp. 157–159.
398   "What the hell is the Monroe Doctrine?": Norbert Schlei OH, JFKL. Some observers, of course, felt differently. In September, *Time* magazine's editors wrote of "a solid rock upon which current U.S. action against Cuba might be based. That rock is the Monroe Doctrine." *Time,* 9/21/62 (featuring a cover illustration of James Monroe).
398   "I should say frankly": Khrushchev letter to JFK, 10/23/62, CMC, Document 30, p. 156.
398   "I want to answer this": Robert Manning int.
399   "immediate dismantling and removal": NYT, 10/24/62.
399   "I am concerned": JFK letter to Khrushchev, 10/23/62, Cuba papers, NSA.

400   the room rocked with laughter: Herman int. Among the administration's civil defense preparations were plans for the Army Corps of Engineers to search for caves and mines within twenty-five miles of populated areas to serve as evacuation centers. "This effort," said the Pentagon official responsible for civil defense, "is estimated to identify an additional 5 million spaces." Pittman memo to JFK through Bundy, 10/24/62, NSF Box 295, JFKL.

400   "You are allowed to bring one secretary": O'Brien, *No Final Victories,* pp. 141–144; O'Donnell and Powers, *"Johnny, We Hardly Knew Ye,"* pp. 375–376.

400   "It looks really mean": Robert Kennedy, *Thirteen Days,* p. 67.

401   "The unleashed American aggressors": *Pravda,* 10/24/62.

401   "We do not believe": Minutes of Ex Comm meeting, 10/24/62, 10:00 A.M., CMC, Document 35, pp. 165–166; Abel, *The Missile Crisis,* p. 143; Robert Kennedy, *Thirteen Days,* pp. 67–72; Schlesinger, *Robert Kennedy and His Times,* pp. 554–555.

402   "That's the end of Anderson": Gilpatric int. And Anderson was not reappointed. He was sent off to become Ambassador to Portugal.

402   "How can I deal with a man": William Knox OH, JFKL.

403   "An urgent appeal": NYT, 10/25/62.

403   "Shouldn't we be celebrating?": Bartlett int; Bartlett OH, p. 124, JFKL.

403   "Should I take out Cuba?": Horne, *Macmillan: 1957–1986,* p. 370.

403   "By what right have you done this?": Khrushchev letter to JFK, 10/24/62, CMC, Document 34, pp. 163–164.

404   "I got a cable from our friend": Bartlett OH, p. 124, JFKL.

404   "The aggressive designs": *Pravda,* 10/25/62.

404   "I regret very much": JFK letter to Khrushchev, 10/25/62, CMC, Document 39, p. 173.

404   "I don't want to put him in a corner": Minutes of Ex Comm meeting, 10/25/62, 10:00 A.M., CMC, Document 36, p. 167.

404   James Van Zandt: NYT, 10/26/62.

405   "The only place that is truly comparable": WP, 10/25/62.

405   Even Averell Harriman: Harriman memo to JFK, 10/22/62, Cuba papers, NSA.

405   "Do you, Ambassador Zorin": NYT, 10/24/62.

406   "Terrific": O'Donnell and Powers, *"Johnny, We Hardly Knew Ye,"* p. 387.

406   "EVERYTHING TO PREVENT WAR": *Pravda,* 10/26/62.

407   "Should these offensive military preparations": NYT, 10/27/62.

407   "We are going to have to face": Summary Record of Ex Comm meeting, 10/26/62, 10:00 AM, CMC, Document 42, pp. 177–183.

407   "The situation is very serious": Scali, notes on first meeting with Fomin, 10/26/62, CMC, Document 43, p. 184; Hilsman, *To Move a Nation,* p. 218.

408   "I have reason to believe": Scali, report on meeting with Fomin, 10/26/62, 7:35 P.M., Cuba papers, NSA.

408   "What the hell": O'Donnell and Powers, *"Johnny, We Hardly Knew Ye,"* p. 387.

408   "Boy, you were really rough": Bartlett int.

409   "This reads as if he wrote": Nitze int; Thompson OH, p. 38, JFKL.

Chapter 36

410   "Dear Mr. President": Khrushchev letter to JFK, 10/26/62, CMC, Document 44, pp. 185–188.

410   "There is considerable speculation": Transcript of Audiotape 40.3, 10/27/62, Presidential Recordings, JFKL; Ex Comm Record of Action, 10/27/62, 10:00 A.M., Vice-Presidential Security File Box 8, LBJL.

413   "How are we": Khrushchev letter to JFK, 10/27/62, CMC, Document 48, pp. 197–199.

414   to meet with a group of governors: JFK appointments schedule, 10/27/62, JFKL.

416   "Mr. Hilsman": Hilsman, *To Move a Nation,* pp. 220–222.

416   "This means war": Scott Sagan, "Nuclear Alerts and Crisis Management," *International Security* (Spring 1985), pp. 117–118.

416 "There's always some son-of-a-bitch": Hilsman int; Hilsman, *To Move a Nation*, p. 221.

416 "How should we regard this?": Khrushchev letter to JFK, 10/28/62, CMC, Document 52, pp. 226–230.

416 "I don't think there's any doubt": Transcript of Audiotape 41.1, 10/27/62, Presidential Recordings, JFKL; Ex Comm Record of Action, 10/27/62, 4:00 P.M., Vice-Presidential Security File Box 8, LBJL.

418 "Pilot killed?": On the downing of the U-2, see Hilsman letter to Jacqueline Kennedy, 3/6/64, Cuba papers, NSA; *Proceedings of the Cambridge Conference on the Cuban Missile Crisis*, October 11–12, 1987, CSIA; Abel, *The Missile Crisis*, pp. 189–190, 195–196; Robert Kennedy, *Thirteen Days*, pp. 75–77.

419 "You're going to have a big problem": Transcript of Audiotape 41.1, 10/27/62, Presidential Recordings, JFKL.

419 "We can't very well": Transcript of Audiotape 42.1, 10/27/62, Presidential Recordings, JFKL.

420 "This does not mention the missiles in Turkey": Robert Kennedy, *Thirteen Days*, pp. 108–109.

420 Dobrynin watched him pedal away: Dobrynin conv; Dobrynin speech at Georgetown University, 11/17/89.

421 "God, Dave": O'Donnell and Powers, *"Johnny, We Hardly Knew Ye,"* p. 394.

421 "I have read your letter": JFK letter to Khrushchev, 10/27/62, CMC, Document 51, pp. 223–225.

421 one more mechanism of compromise: Rusk memo, 2/25/87, Cuba papers, NSA.

421 "You do anything": Transcript of Audiotape 42.2, 10/27/62, Presidential Recordings, JFKL; Ex Comm Record of Action, 10/27/62, 9:00 P.M., Vice-Presidential Security File Box 8, LBJL.

423 *Roman Holiday*: O'Donnell and Powers, *"Johnny, We Hardly Knew Ye,"* p. 395.

423 "We Must Defend": *Pravda*, 10/28/62.

423 "In order to complete": Khrushchev letter to JFK, 10/28/62. Fidel Castro, whom Khrushchev did not consult before making his broadcast, flew into a rage when he learned of the Soviet premier's actions. Khrushchev, he spat, was "a son of a bitch, a bastard, an asshole." Castro reportedly went to the San Antonio Air Force Base in Cuba on October 28 to personally shoot down U.S. planes, but none flew over the area. Two days later, Castro publicly denounced Khrushchev as lacking "cojones." Tad Szulc, *Fidel: A Critical Portrait* (New York: Avon Books, 1986), pp. 649–650.

424 "I welcome Chairman Khrushchev's": JFKPP, 10/28/62.

424 "Tell them to stop that": Salinger int; Schoenbrun, int.

424 "The danger of war": CBS-TV News special, "The Crisis in Cuba," 10/28/62.

424 "We Must Ensure the Peace": *Pravda*, 10/29/62.

424 "You got away with it this time": Helms int; NW, 11/28/83; Schoenbaum, *Waging Peace and War*, p. 243.

425 "Plain dumb luck": "Dean Acheson's Version of Robert Kennedy's Version of the Missile Crisis"; Brinkley, *Acheson*, pp. 170–173.

425 "We lost!": McNamara int; Garthoff, *Reflections on the Missile Crisis*, pp. 58–59.

425 "Now, Herr Krapf": *Time*, 11/2/62.

425 "I think that you and I": JFK letter to Khrushchev, 10/28/62, CMC, Document 53, pp. 230–232.

Chapter 37

426 "This is the night": Robert Kennedy, *Thirteen Days*, p. 110. "If you go," Robert said with a laugh, "I want to go with you."

426 Kennedy called Tiffany's: Walter Hoving conv; O'Donnell and Powers, *"Johnny, We Hardly Knew Ye,"* pp. 396–397.

426 Kennedy's personal approval rating: *Time*, 9/28/62, 11/2/62.

427 "To our mutual satisfaction": Khrushchev letter to JFK, 10/30/62, "Letters Released During the Cuban Missile Crisis," JFKL.

427   "The administration's management": *The Nation,* 2/2/63.

427   they were not to speak to the press: "The President asked that members of the Executive Committee avoid all discussion with reporters, except with his specific approval, and approved in principle a plan being drawn up to ensure that the Departments of State and Defense and the White House give a consistent story of the Cuban crisis." Ex Comm Record of Action, 10/30/62, DDRS (1991), 3411.

427   *Proceedings of the Hawk's Cay Conference on the Cuban Missile Crisis,* March 5–8, 1987, CIA.

428   "If we have learned anything": Memo of NSC meeting, 10/30/62, Cuba papers, NSA.

428   a noticeable closeness: Salinger int.

428   "Well, are we making money?" Stephen Smith int.

428   "What about this?": Bradlee, *Conversations with Kennedy,* pp. 118–121.

429   the Democrats won: *Time,* 11/16/62, 1/4/63. A Gallup Poll taken just before the missile crisis showed 56 percent of voters planning to vote Democratic, a figure that had dropped from a high of 61 percent in March. Gallup surveys in 1958 had shown "measurably more interest on the part of Democratic voters than they now indicate for 1962," Census director Richard Scammon had written on October 24. Scammon letter to Sorensen, 10/24/62, Sorensen papers, Box 36, JFKL. For more on political expectations before the missile crisis, see Angus Campbell, "Why We Can Expect More of the Same," *New Republic,* 10/8/62.

429   longer-term trends: See, for example, "Widening Crack in the Solid South" and "Why I Won—Why I Lost," USN&WR, 11/19/62; "Trends That Are Making the Democrats Unhappy" and "How Washington Schools Are Resegregating," USN&WR, 11/26/62.

430   the 87th Congress: On JFK and Congress in 1962, see Neustadt letter to Sorensen, 9/24/62, Sorensen papers, Box 31, JFKL; *Congressional Quarterly,* 11/14/62; "What They Say About JFK," USN&WR, 9/30/62; Tom Wicker, "A Total Political Animal," *NYT Magazine,* 4/15/62; O'Brien, *No Final Victories,* pp. 128– 135.

430   the Trade Expansion Act of 1962: See *Time,* 10/12/62.

431   "I know everyone thinks I worry": Sorensen int.

431   "Kennedy men": "Widening Crack in the Solid South," USN&WR, 11/19/62.

432   "A story is told that indicates": "Washington Whispers," USN&WR, 11/4/63.

432   "I have today": JFKPP, 11/20/62.

432   she had refused to take the call: Joseph P. Lash, *Eleanor: The Years Alone* (New York: W. W. Norton, 1972), pp. 295–296.

433   "I listened during a rather long drive": Lash, *Eleanor,* p. 319.

433   a Presidential Commission on the Status of Women: See Blanche Linden-Ward, "The ERA and Kennedy's Presidential Commission on the Status of Women" and Judith Sealander, "John F. Kennedy's Presidential Commission on the Status of Women: 'A Dividing Line,' " both in Paul Harper and Joann Krieg, eds., *John F. Kennedy: The Promise Revisited* (Westport, CT: Greenwood Press, 1988), pp. 237–260.

433   Eleanor Roosevelt's funeral: NYT, 11/11/62; NW, 11/19/62; *Time,* 11/16/62. Extensive details and press coverage on the funeral are in ER Funeral, Vertical File; and Anna Roosevelt Halsted papers, Box 60, FDRL.

433   "What do you think": Gore, *Let the Glory Out,* p. 154.

434   "That was a nice story": Press Panel OH, p. 99, JFKL.

434   "Now that all the members of the press": *Time,* 11/16/62. Nixon's performance, said one typical editorial, "was a requiem for a might-have-been." *Detroit News,* 11/9/62.

435   like a couple of schoolboys: The phrase is McGrory's. Press Panel OH, p. 99, JFKL.

435   Nelson Rockefeller: Bradlee int; Bradlee, *Conversations with Kennedy,* p. 121.

435   do some checking: See, for example, Maneker memo to Dolan, "The Rockefeller Foundation," 11/2/62, Sorensen papers, Box 35, JFKL. As the 1964 election drew closer, the investigations got more overtly political. See, for instance, Moynihan memos to Sorensen, "The Chronology of the 1963 Rockefeller Tax Increase in New York State," 4/17/63; "Statistics Rockefeller," 4/22/63; and "A Note on Governor Rockefeller's Civil Rights Record," 7/23/63; all in Sorensen papers, Box 36, JFKL.

435   Kennedy sat with Roswell Gilpatric: Gilpatric int; Gilpatric OH, pp. 93–94, JFKL.
435   "How does he get away with it?": Gilpatric int.

Chapter 38

436   "After Two Years": JFKPP, 12/17/62.
436   the President himself who insisted: Herman int.
436   "Perfect": Max Ascoli, "The Reporter's Notes," *The Reporter*, 1/3/63.
436   "Well, I always said": Bradlee, *Conversations with Kennedy*, p. 128.
437   thought odd by colleagues: Vanocur int.
437   "Mrs. Lincoln!": Lincoln, *My Twelve Years*, p. 123.
437   "As you look back": JFKPP, 12/17/62.
438   Skybolt: This account of the Skybolt story is drawn from Memcon, 12/16/62, NSF Box 317, JFKL, and the following sources: *Time*, 12/28/62; Ball, *The Past Has Another Pattern*, pp. 262–266; Horne, *Macmillan: 1957–1986*, pp. 432–433; and Schlesinger, *A Thousand Days*, pp. 856–864.
The description of JFK in Nassau and several other scenes in Horne's official biography of Macmillan are drawn from the oral history interview of the late David Ormsby-Gore (Lord Harlech) conducted by the Kennedy Library. The transcript of this interview is closed to general researchers in the United Kingdom until 1995 under the terms of the Official Secrets Act. The Kennedy Library has decided to follow the strictures of this law, and will not release the oral history, even to researchers granted permission to see it by the Harlech estate, until it is available in Great Britain.
438   "On the umpteenth day": The cartoon was reprinted in *Time*, 12/28/62.
439   "That we get every week, George": Memcon, 12/16/62.
439   "The period of maximum crisis": Khrushchev letter to JFK, 12/19/62, "Letters Exchanged During the Cuban Missile Crisis," JFKL.
439   "Mr. President, conditions are ripe": Khrushchev letter to JFK, 10/30/62.
440   "I don't know if the matter": Norman Cousins int; Norman Cousins, *The Improbable Triumvirate: John F. Kennedy, Pope John, Nikita Khrushchev* (New York: W. W. Norton, 1972), p. 24.
440   "One thing the President and I": Cousins, *The Improbable Triumvirate*, p. 54.
440   "Jesus Christ!": Horne, *Macmillan: 1957–1986*, p. 441.
441   "Pooh-Pooh Head!": Draft manuscript of Fay, *The Pleasure of His Company*, Land papers, Box 12, BU. One of the editors or censors of Fay's manuscript changed this to "foo-foo head," noting in the margin: "I object strongly to 'pooh-pooh head' pooh-pooh is a kid's name for shit."
441   "The percentage of our budget": Transcript of Audiotape 58.1, 11/16/62, Presidential Recordings, JFKL.
441   "What's going to be in that package?": CEA OH, pp. 449–450, JFKL.
441   stop using words like "aid": "[T]he President again expressed his strong desire that in presenting the programs of economic and military assistance to the Congress and the country, we should use all terminology . . . which will stress U.S. security interest in these programs. . . . 'International Security' would appeal to him more than 'International Development,' " Bell memo to AID, 12/22/62, Sorensen papers, Box 28, JFKL.
442   "Hello, Mr. Secretary": Schoenbaum, *Waging Peace and War*, p. 282.
442   "Let's talk alone": Mansfield int.
442   "There is a great danger": Mansfield report to JFK, 12/18/62, FRUS 1962, Document 330, pp. 779–787.
443   "You expect me to believe this?": Mansfield int; Mansfield OH, p. 24, JFKL.
443   "Diem and other leading Vietnamese": Hilsman research memo RFE-59 to Rusk, "The Situation and Short-Term Prospects in South Vietnam," 12/3/62, PP II, pp. 690–716.
444   "Mr. President, it was just a year ago": JFKPP, 12/12/62.
444   "The possibility of a coup": Hilsman research memo RFE-59, "The Situation and Short-Term Prospects in South Vietnam."
444   "If I tried to pull out": Mansfield int; O'Donnell and Powers, *"Johnny, We Hardly Knew Ye,"* p. 16.

445   $53 million: *Time*, 12/28/62.
445   "Whatever it takes": Goodwin, *Remembering America*, pp. 185–186.
445   "I want to express": JFKPP, 12/30/62; *Time*, 12/28/62; O'Donnell and Powers, *"Johnny, We Hardly Knew Ye,"* pp. 319–320.
445   "On 2 January at 0800": JCS memo to JFK, 1/3/63, "Resume of the 2 Jan 1963 GVN Ground/Heliborne Action," DDRS (1985) 909.
446   "VIETCONG DOWNS FIVE U.S. COPTERS": NYT, 1/3/63.
446   Ap Bac: This account of the Ap Bac debacle is drawn from Marine Corps Emergency Action Center, "Summary of Items of Significant Interest," 1/2/63, Cuba papers, NSA; John Paul Vann interview in USN&WR, 9/16/63; David Halberstam, *Vietnam: The Making of a Quagmire* (New York: Random House, 1965), pp. 156–157; Le Hong Linh, Vuong Thanh Dien, and Nguyen Q.S., *Ap Bac: Major Victories of the South Vietnamese Patriotic Forces in 1963 and 1964* (Hanoi: Foreign Languages Publishing House, 1965); and Rust, *Kennedy in Vietnam*, pp. 81–83.
446   "We sat there all day": USN&WR, 9/16/63.
446   "A victory": See FRUS 1–8/1963, editorial note 1, pp. 1–3.
446   "Copters No Substitute for Men": NYT, 1/4/63.
447   "This was a stunning defeat": Hilsman int.
447   "The war in South Vietnam": Hilsman and Forrestal report to JFK, 1/25/63, PP II, pp. 717–725; Hilsman, *To Move a Nation*, pp. 453–476.
447   new Defense Intelligence Agency: See Stewart Alsop, "CIA: The Battle for Secret Power," *Saturday Evening Post*, 7/27/63.
448   "a slowly escalating stalemate": CIA memo, 1/11/63, FRUS 1–8/1963, Document 11, pp. 19–22.
448   "Victory is now a hopeful prospect": JCS report, 1/63, "Report of Visit by the Joint Chiefs to South Vietnam, January 1963," DDRS (1985) 906.
448   "Weekend Reading": Bundy memo to JFK, 1/12/63; Clifton memo to JFK, 1/12/63; both in NSF Box 318, JFKL.
448   "If we are going in there shooting": Kaysen OH, JFKL.
449   "No one man is in charge": Hilsman and Forrestal report to JFK, 1/25/63, "Eyes Only" annex, FRUS 1–8/1963, Document 19, pp. 60–62.
449   "Americans are in Vietnam because": The letters are reprinted in Lieberson and Meyers, eds., *John Fitzgerald Kennedy . . . As We Remember Him*, pp. 187–189.
450   "Sweeping low across enemy-infested scrubland": *Life*, 1/17/63.
450   Kennedy was getting nervous: Halberstam int.
450   there had been no questions about Vietnam: Rusk int.
450   "This would show": Memcon, 4/4/63, FRUS 1–8/1963, Document 77, pp. 198–200; Hilsman, *To Move a Nation*, pp. 461–463.

Chapter 39
451   "The tide of events": JFKPP, 1/14/63.
451   President de Gaulle announced: NYT, 1/5/63.
451   "For 175 years we have sailed": JFKPP, 1/14/63.
452   "the Master": Galbraith int.
452   Heller felt let down: CEA OH, JFKL.
452   "It's not just Congress": Samuelson int; CEA OH, p. 296, JFKL.
452   "Look, what I have to face": Tobin int.
452   "What did you think of it?": Press Panel OH, JFKL.
453   "One man's reform": Dillon int.
453   "Our tax system": JFKPP, 12/14/62.
453   "I gave them straight Keynes": Sorensen OH, pp. 146–148, JFKL.
454   "Even as a liberal Democrat": *Time*, 2/8/63.
454   "fiscal recklessness": Sorensen, *Kennedy*, pp. 484–485.
454   "I am old-fashioned": *Time*, 1/18/63.
454   sounded like pure Herbert Hoover: Sorensen, *Kennedy*, p. 483.
454   Galbraith wanted: Galbraith int.
454   "We cannot lead for long": JFKPP, 1/14/63.
454   "All of these matters": "Notes on Remarks by President Kennedy before the

National Security Council," 1/22/63, Nuclear History papers, NSA. The notes were taken by a CIA reporter.

455   Robert Frost died: NYT, 1/24/63.
455   "I know how busy he is": Udall OH, pp. 55–56, JFKL.
455   "The death of Robert Frost": JFKPP, 1/23/63.
455   "We are in a very challenging period": JFKPP, 1/24/63.
456   "There appear to be no differences": JFKPP, 1/20/63.
456   "There appears to have been some misunderstanding": JFKPP, 1/20/63.
456   "You managed to pin Mr. Nixon to the mat": Khrushchev letter to JFK, 11/12/62, "Letters Exchanged During the Cuban Missile Crisis," JFKL.
456   "They're young, expansive": Khrushchev letter to JFK, 11/22/62, "Letters Exchanged During the Cuban Missile Crisis," JFKL.
456   "The competition for news in this country": JFK letter to Khrushchev, 12/14/62, "Letters Exchanged During the Cuban Missile Crisis," JFKL.
457   "I am sorry to learn": JFK letter to Khrushchev, 12/14/62, "Letters Exchanged During the Cuban Missile Crisis," JFKL.
457   proposed fiscal 1964 budget: NYT, 1/25/63.
457   "I'd rather unbalance my budget": Transcript of Audiotape 27.1, 10/2/62, Presidential Recordings, JFKL.
457   "We'll just have to cut education": Transcript of Audiotape 27.1, 10/2/62, Presidential Recordings, JFKL.
458   "We behold here": *The Nation*, 2/2/63.
458   Dillon was delegated: See NYT, 1/25–2/1/63; *Time*, 2/1/63.
459   "I think you have the wrong kind": CEA OH, p. 140, JFKL.
459   "Why go back and teach rich men's sons?": Tobin int.
459   "Get royal blue or Navy blue": CEA OH, p. 305, JFKL.
459   "What Have You Done for Growth Today?": Parmet, *JFK*, p. 94.
460   "You might be able to get": Transcript of Audiotape 7.1, 8/6/62, Presidential Recordings, JFKL.
460   "As you know I opposed cluttering up": CEA OH, JFKL.
461   "It's the sort of proposal": JFKPP, 1/24/63.
461   "Vaughn Meader was busy tonight": Sorensen briefing papers for JFK, 1/17/63, Sorensen papers, Box 36, JFKL.
461   "Tough shit!": Bradlee, *Conversations with Kennedy*, p. 129.

Chapter 40

462   "Questions to be settled": JFK memos, 1/28/63 and 1/31/63, Lincoln Dictation File, POF Box 62, JFKL.
462   "The fact is": Louis Martin int.
462   "American Negroes through sit-ins": Martin memo to Sorensen, 1/30/63, Sorensen papers, Box 30, JFKL.
462   plan a reception for Negro leaders: Martin int.
463   "Baby, you don't send out": *Jet*, 3/7/63.
463   "A freedom more fictional": NYT, 2/13/63.
464   "Oh, man": Martin int.
464   "What's he doing here?": Martin int; Lee White OH, pp. 104–105, JFKL. "That was horrendous," White recalled. "The President was absolutely feathered. He didn't give a damn about all the others, but how did that guy get there? It was as though the whole thing was a flop, and you never saw more people hiding under the table because nobody, absolutely no one had anything to do with Sammy Davis getting invited. But he was there as big as life with his wife and kind of really put a pall on the whole thing."
464   "For and About Women" section: WP, 2/13/63.
465   "Save Our Republic": *Chicago Daily Tribune*, 2/13/63.
465   "The fact is that the President": WP, 2/13/63.
465   "Rockefeller gets away with murder": Bradlee int.
465   "He likes you, you know": Theodore White, "Notes on Social Gathering with the President," 2/13/63, Schlesinger papers, Box W-6, JFKL.

465   "I think that the men": JFKPP, 3/6/63.
466   "Is it real bad?": Transcript of Dictabelt 11A.5, 3/7/63, Presidential Recordings, JFKL.
466   "I'm going to sing Dixie": Krock OH, p. 16, JFKL.
467   "If we go into a long fight": Hesburgh int; Martin Luther King, Jr., OH, JFKL.
467   reduce the pay of the commission's director: Berl Bernhard OH, p. 49, JFKL.
467   "Pretty much at peace": Lee White OH, JFKL.
468   "He thinks that if he does more": Hesburgh int.
468   Greenwood, Mississippi: See Branch, *Parting the Waters,* pp. 633–634, 714–725.
468   his first civil rights bill: The decision to submit legislation was sudden; for a Justice Department analysis of the issues at hand, see Lee White memo to JFK, 2/25/63, Sorensen papers, Box 30, JFKL.
468   asked the most vocal civil rights advocate: Smathers OH, pp. 7–8F, JFKL.
468   "When I feel that there's necessity": Hubert H. Humphrey OH, JFKL.
468   "We go up there with that": O'Brien int.
468   "The President stated": Martin memo to Sorensen, Sorensen papers, Box 30, JFKL.
469   "You're making my life difficult": Bernhard int.
469   "No. . . . Any hearing": JFKPP, 3/21/63.
469   one dog and one minister: Marshall memo to JFK, 4/8/63, Lee White papers, Box 23, JFKL.
469   "Implicit is the suggestion": Lee White memo to JFK, 4/10/63, Lee White papers, Box 23, JFKL.
469   "How could this happen?": RFK OH, JFKL.
469   "Do you really think a President": Bernhard OH, p. 29, JFKL.
470   "Who the hell appointed Griswold?": Bernhard int.
470   "With regard to the incidents": JFKPP, 4/19/63.
470   "A high administration official": NYT, 4/20/63; Confidential dispatch, Time arch; Branch, *Parting the Waters,* pp. 746–747.

Chapter 41

471   "The latest enthusiasts": *Chicago Tribune,* 2/13/63.
472   "We all know and love Plucky": Bradlee, *Conversations with Kennedy,* pp. 129–130; *Chicago Tribune,* 2/12/63.
472   Kennedy followed in a white Lincoln: Unpublished memoirs of Max Jacobson, "JFK" chapter, pp. 35–39; Mark Shaw, *The John F. Kennedys: A Family Album* (New York: Farrar, Straus and Co., 1965), pp. 133–134.
472   "Your policies in Europe": JFKPP, 3/6/63.
472   "Our prospects look good": JFKPP, 3/21/63.
472   Kennedy's Gallup Poll: *Time,* 4/5/63.
473   "The present tendency": P/POS memos, "Current Popular Opinion on U.S. Cuba Policy," 3/8/63, and "Diminishing Public Confidence in Administration's Handling of Cuba Problem," 3/22/63, both in Cuba papers, NSA.
473   "I think there should be": RFK memo to JFK, 3/14/63, Sorensen papers, Box 35, JFKL.
473   "We agreed on desirability": NSC Standing Group Record of Actions, 4/16/63, Cuba papers, NSA. Other pertinent documents generated as anti-Castro planning started up again include "List of Raids [carried out by exile groups]," 4/1/63, POF Box 114a, JFKL; Bundy, "Checklist of Current Actions Against Castro Communism in Cuba," 4/24/63, NSF Box 37, JFKL; briefing papers for questions regarding Cuba at JFK press conference, 4/24/63, POF Box 59, JFKL.
    The administration also discussed what to do about raids against Cuba launched from the United States by anti-Castro exiles, which geared up independently in the spring of 1963. See, for example, the recently declassified record of the March 29, 1963, NSC meeting: "Secretary Rusk said that the hit-and-run raids against Cuba . . . will be blamed on us no matter what we say. . . . If anyone is shooting Russians, we ought to be doing

it, not Cubans who are acting beyond our control. . . . Secretary Dillon said it was impossible for us to control the raids. . . . Ambassador Thompson emphasized that we must prevent any raider plane bombing a Soviet ship. . . . The Attorney General commented that we did have a problem domestically of explaining why we were stopping the raids, but we can stop them by prosecuting those involved and making the raiders' stay in the U.S. very unpleasant. . . . The President suggested that we first tell the British and then, on a background basis, tell the press that the raiders are staging out of the Bahama Islands. . . . The President commented that these in-and-out raids were probably exciting and rather pleasant for those who engage in them. They were in danger for less than an hour. This exciting activity was more fun than living in the hills of Escambray, pursued by Castro's military forces." Summary record of NSC meeting, 3/29/63, DDRS (1991) 3325.

473   "There was a discussion": NSC Standing Group Record of Action, 7/9/63, Cuba papers, NSA.

474   "President Kennedy flung wide": *Time,* 4/19/63.

474   Henry Luce, the creator of *Time:* Luce OH, p. 42, JFKL.

475   "This is it": Bergquist Knebel OH, pp. 6–7, JFKL.

475   "I was passing by Mrs. Lincoln's office": Jacqueline Kennedy memo to O'Brien, 1/23/63, Lincoln Dictation File, POF Box 62, JFKL.

475   "well qualified for the role": Arthur and Barbara Gelb, "Culture Makes a Hit at the White House," *NYT Magazine,* 1/28/62.

475   "I have called for a higher degree": JFKPP, 12/18/62. Kennedy's remarks were published as "The Arts in America" in *Look,* 12/18/62.

476   a meat-and-potatoes guy: Bradlee int; Stephen Smith int; Jean Kennedy Smith conv; Jacqueline Kennedy letter to Dorothy Macmillan, quoted in Horne, *Macmillan: 1957–1986,* p. 513; draft manuscript of Fay, *The Pleasure of His Company,* Land papers, Box 12, BU; O'Donnell and Powers, *"Johnny, We Hardly Knew Ye,"* passim.

476   "Accustomed to the hardships": JFKPP, 4/9/63.

476   "This is another one": Lieberson and Meyers, eds., *John Fitzgerald Kennedy . . . As We Remember Him,* p. 186.

476   "People want this": Cousins int.

476   "Mr. President, do you still": JFKPP, 3/21/63.

477   "No matter what": Cousins int; Cousins, *The Improbable Triumvirate,* pp. 112, 118–120.

477   "A master of time": Travell, *Office Hours,* p. 359.

477   paying off young women now and then: Confidential source interview.

477   "He's an artist who paints": Polly Kraft int.

477   "All right, let's haul": Bradlee int; draft manuscript of Fay, *The Pleasure of His Company,* Land papers, Box 12, BU.

478   "Get hold of that photographer": Sidey OH, p. 2, JFKL.

478   "I have myself been infused": *Time,* 3/1/63. Krock wrote an article on the subject of "managed news" in *Fortune* (March 1963). See also "Can You Manage the News?" *BusinessWeek,* 3/2/63.

478   "Is your wife pregnant?" *Time,* 4/26/63. On Kennedy's trendsetting, see, for example, "The Monogram on This Man's Shirt is J.F.K.," *Esquire* (January 1962).

478   dog licenses: *Time,* 5/24/63.

479   "I never had a feeling": Sidey OH, p. 32, JFKL.

479   "Poverty" became a topic: RFK OH, JFKL; Schlesinger, *A Thousand Days,* pp. 1005–1010.

479   "In the last year": Dwight Macdonald, "Our Invisible Poor," *New Yorker,* 1/19/63.

480   a managerial politician: See Ted Lewis, "Kennedy: Profile of a Technician," *The Nation,* 2/2/63, in which Schlesinger is quoted as describing the new politics: "humane, skeptical, and pragmatic . . . has no dogma, no sense of Messianic mission, no belief that mortal man can attain Utopia, no faith that fundamental problems have final solutions." The generation of Democratic neoliberal politicians that came to prominence after Watergate and Vietnam adopted JFK's lack of ideological passion even as many were inspired by his calls to public service; William Schneider has dubbed them "Kennedy's Children."

480   he said he wanted to withdraw: Mansfield int.
480   "This is a most presidential country": Lippmann interviewed by Charles Collingwood, 5/1/63, printed in *Conversations with Walter Lippmann.*
480   "A compulsive instinct": Frederick W. Collins, "The Mind of JFK," *New Republic,* 5/8/61.
481   "Never to be bored": Ball int.
481   "There are three things": O'Donnell and Powers, *"Johnny, We Hardly Knew
Ye,"* p. 410.

Chapter 42

482   "We believe that Communist progress": NIE 53-63, "Prospects in South Vietnam," 4/17/63, FRUS 1–8/1963, Document 94, pp. 232–235.
482   "Barring greatly increased resupply": Rust, *Kennedy in Vietnam,* pp. 90–91.
483   the H-1, the "Huey": *Time,* 6/7/63.
483   "show that you are winning": Memcon, 4/4/63, FRUS 1–8/1963, Document 77,
pp. 198–200.
483   Laos: This account of the 1963 crisis is drawn from *Time,* 4/26/63, 5/6/63; Rust,
Kennedy in Vietnam, pp. 87–90.
483   "the pleasure of speaking to the architect": JFK-Harriman telecon, 4/21/63,
Harriman papers, LC.
484   "We are trying to do too much": *Time,* 3/29/63; 4/12/63.
484   "If Laos fell into communist hands": JFKPP, 4/24/63.
484   "The last Jupiter missile": McNamara note to JFK, 4/25/63, Cuba papers, NSA.
484   "We don't have a prayer": Bartlett OH, p. 30, LBJL.
485   "He's totally out to sea": Ibid.
485   considering asking for a reduction: CIA Report TDCSDB-3/654,285, 4/22/63,
FRUS 1–8/1963, Document 99, pp. 246–247.
485   "At least 50 percent": WP, 5/12/63.
485   "To many Birmingham Negroes": *Time,* 4/19/63.
485   a month of demonstrations: See Branch, *Parting the Waters,* pp. 734–755;
David J. Garrow, *Bearing the Cross: Martin Luther King, Jr., and the Southern Christian
Leadership Conference* (New York: William Morrow, 1986), pp. 241–248; Stephen B.
Oates, *Let the Trumpet Sound: The Life of Martin Luther King, Jr.* (New York: Harper
& Row, 1982), pp. 212–232.
486   "The timing of the present demonstrations": Branch, *Parting the Waters,* p. 762.
486   Bull Connor's men were overrun by children: NYT, 5/3/63, 5/4/63; *Time,*
5/10/63; Branch, *Parting the Waters,* pp. 756–768; Garrow, *Bearing the Cross,* pp. 248–
250; Oates, *Let the Trumpet Sound,* pp. 232–235.
488   "It makes me sick": Rauh int.
488   "I am not criticizing": Branch, *Parting the Waters,* p. 780.
488   "Mr. President, if these were white marches": *Birmingham News,* 5/8/63.
488   "Birmingham's Negroes": *Time,* 5/17/63.
488   "closely monitoring events": Branch, *Parting the Waters,* p. 778.
488   the Assistant Attorney General continued to press: Marshall int; Marshall OH,
JFKL; Branch, *Parting the Waters,* pp. 768–770; Garrow, *Bearing the Cross,* pp. 250–
254; Oates, *Let the Trumpet Sound,* pp. 238–239.
489   "The meeting of all the businessmen worked": Guthman int.
489   came to an agreement: Branch, *Parting the Waters,* pp. 775–778; Garrow,
Bearing the Cross, pp. 255–256.
489   the city of Hué: Mecklin, *Mission in Torment,* pp. 153–154; Rust, *Kennedy in
Vietnam,* pp. 94–96.
490   Madame Nhu: Her draconian pronouncements are detailed in *Time,* 6/7/63.
490   "A local incident": Hué Consulate telegram to State, 5/9/63, 3:00 P.M., FRUS
1–8/1963, Document 112, pp. 277–278.
490   "Who are these people?": Rust, *Kennedy in Vietnam,* p. 102.
490   "A spectacle": JFKPP, 5/8/63.
491   "It seems clear to me": *Time,* 5/17/63.
491   "That son-of-a-bitch!": Seigenthaler int.

491   "I want to clear this desk": O'Brien int; O'Donnell and Powers, *"Johnny, We Hardly Knew Ye,"* pp. 183–184.
491   "Chief Bonze": See, for example, Hué Consulate telegram to State, 5/9/63, 3:00 P.M.: "Head bonze requested crowd disperse peacefully and turn in flags." Tri Quang was identified—using the military-like designation "Chief Bonze, Central Vietnam"—in cables from Hué beginning in the early hours of May 10.
491   "this line has no credibility": Hué Consulate telegram to state, 5/10/63, 2:00 A.M., FRUS 1–8/1963, Document 116, pp. 284–285.
491   "At your discretion": Rusk telegram to Saigon, 5/9/63, FRUS 1–8/1963, Document 115, p. 283.
492   "I am perfectly willing to offer": Barbara Ward Jackson OH, p. 12, JFKL.
492   "Knock-Knock!": David Lawrence OH, p. 18, JFKL.
492   "I can kiss the South good-bye": Lawrence OH, p. 20, JFKL.
492   they arrested Reverend King: Branch, *Parting the Waters,* p. 784; Garrow, *Bearing the Cross,* pp. 257–258.
492   bail of $5,000: Branch, *Parting the Waters,* pp. 784–785; Garrow, *Bearing the Cross,* p. 258.
492   A Birmingham deal was finally done: Branch, *Parting the Waters,* pp. 785–786; Garrow, *Bearing the Cross,* p. 259; Oates, *Let the Trumpet Sound,* pp. 239–240.
493   "no Federal statutes involved": Branch, *Parting the Waters,* p. 787.
493   "When things started happening": Branch, *Parting the Waters,* p. 791.
493   the next night, at 10:45: NYT, 5/12/63, 5/13/63; *Time,* 5/17/63; Branch, *Parting the Waters,* pp. 792–796; Garrow, *Bearing the Cross,* pp. 260–261; Oates, *Let the Trumpet Sound,* pp. 241–242.
493   "South Vietnam would like to see": WP, 5/12/63.
494   "The argument for sending": Transcript of Audiotape 86.2, 5/12/63, Presidential Recordings, JFKL; Branch, *Parting the Waters,* pp. 796–799; Garrow, *Bearing the Cross,* p. 261.
494   "I've got a battle group": Transcript of Audiotape 86.2, 5/12/63, Presidential Recordings, JFKL.
494   "He says that if there are no more incidents": Transcript of Audiotape 86.2, 5/12/63, Presidential Recordings, JFKL; Garrow, *Bearing the Cross,* p. 261.
495   "I am deeply concerned": JFKPP, 5/14/63.
495   Kennedy was betting his presidency: Marshall int. "And if he didn't get the civil rights bill," Marshall said, "he was going to be a one-term president. There would be trouble if it passed and worse if it didn't."
"Until Birmingham," said Louis Martin, "civil rights in the Kennedy administration was a joke. They were scared of the Southern reaction, particularly Bobby. Kennedy knew exactly what was going on. No intelligent guy who was even half sensitive could see what was going on and not know that something had to be done about it." Martin int. Larry O'Brien agreed that Birmingham was the turning point that compelled the Kennedys to take the side of civil rights once and for all: "Birmingham, this was the ball buster. Civil rights became a commitment of the Democratic party, and twenty-five years later it had realigned the parties." O'Brien int.
496   "This is the way it should be": McNamara int.
496   "We would withdraw the troops": JFKPP, 5/22/63.

Chapter 43

497   "BIRMINGHAM AND BEYOND": *Time,* 5/17/63.
497   had impressed Kennedy: Baldwin first met the Kennedys when he came to the White House dinner for Nobel Prize laureates in April 1962.
497   "Try to imagine how you would feel": James Baldwin, *The Fire Next Time* (New York: Dial, 1963), pp. 73–86. Baldwin's "Letter from a Region in My Mind" was first published in the *New Yorker* in November 1962.
498   The Alabama Supreme Court ruled: *Time,* 5/31/63.
498   suspending the 1,081 Negro students: *Time,* 5/31/63.
498   Touring triumphantly: See, for example, Branch, *Parting the Waters,* pp. 803–806.

499   "The courts have made a final judgment": JFKPP, 5/22/63.
499   "Certain other societies": JFKPP, 5/18/63.
499   "For the time being, at least": Richard Rovere, "Letter from Washington," *New Yorker,* 6/1/63.
499   telling his colleagues privately: Henry Ellender OH, pp. 14, 40, JFKL.
499   "There is a common denominator": Reedy memo to LBJ, 5/24/63, Vice-Presidential Civil Rights File, Box 6, LBJL; Reedy letter to author, 8/15/89.
500   "How the hell did this happen?": Lee White OH, JFKL.
501   "Okay, how will we get away": Audiotape 88.4, 5/20/63 meeting, Presidential Recordings, JFKL (note that no transcript of this tape is available at the Kennedy Library).
501   "I called in businessmen": Audiotape 88.6, 5/21/63 meeting, Presidential Recordings, JFKL (no transcript of this tape is available at the Kennedy Library).
501   "Hopeless, they'll never reform": Audiotape 88.4.
501   Jackson: See NYT, 6/1/63, 6/2/63; *Time,* 6/7/63; Branch, *Parting the Waters,* pp. 813–820.
502   "We've baptized Brother Wilkins": Branch, *Parting the Waters,* p. 816.
502   King sent a telegram: King telegram to JFK, 5/30/63, WHCSF Box 363, JFKL.
502   The lawyer's phones had been tapped: Garrow, *The FBI and Martin Luther King, Jr.,* p. 46. Levison, a white lawyer from New York, had met King in 1956 as a sponsor of a civil rights organization called In Friendship. Over the next five years, he became a trusted adviser and close friend to King, whose abilities he complemented; Levison excelled at sorting out complex financial problems and writing detailed legal and public policy proposals.
FBI informants reportedly named Levison as a financial adviser to the Communist Party in the early 1950s. According to the bureau's chief mole inside the CPUSA, Levison's role peaked in 1954 as an administrator of secret Communist Party funds. Levison was kept under close surveillance by the FBI from early 1954 through the summer of 1955.
Levison's contacts with Jack Childs, the Communist official who funneled Soviet money to American party sources and who also began serving as an FBI informant in 1952, seem to have come to an end in late 1955. Childs no longer sent the bureau information on meetings with Levison, and by March 1957, the FBI's New York office removed Levison from its list of "key Communist figures." After 1956, Levison appears to have communicated with Communist Party officials only for the sake of disassociating himself from their activities. Indeed, the FBI decided in late 1959 to try to recruit Levison as an informant, an offer Levison rejected in February 1960.
Levison and the key FBI officials and informants involved in his case are all now deceased. As David Garrow has written, however, "all available evidence indicates that Levison had been closely involved in CP financial activities between 1952 and 1955, but that he ended that association sometime in 1955 and that he had no active ties to the CP once he became associated with Dr. King in 1956." *The FBI and Martin Luther King, Jr.,* pp. 42–43; see also pp. 26–30, 35–41; and Branch, *Parting the Waters,* pp. 516–517. Levison's FBI files, numbers 100-111180 (New York) and 100-392452 (headquarters), contain extensive but heavily sanitized records of surveillance of Levison in 1953 and 1954, his withdrawal from Communist Party activity in 1956, and the bureau's attempt to recruit him in 1959–60.
The FBI dropped its interest in Levison almost entirely after February 1960, until an informant told the bureau on January 4, 1962, that Levison had written a speech for King the previous month. Within four days, J. Edgar Hoover wrote to Robert Kennedy that Levison, "a member of the Communist Party, USA . . . is allegedly a close advisor to the Reverend Martin Luther King, Jr." SAC (New York) memo to Director, 1/4/62; Hoover letter to RFK, 1/8/62, File 100-392452 (Stanley Levison), FBI. From the moment the bureau linked Levison to King, it continued to name him to administration officials as a high-ranking Communist Party official. FBI officials further refused to supply evidence for the claim, stating that to do so would endanger their informants.
Hoover sent an additional memo on King and Levison to Robert Kennedy on February 14, 1962, and this time forwarded one to Kenny O'Donnell as well, for the President's

direct attention. On February 27, the same day he lunched with JFK on the topic of Judith Campbell, Hoover instructed his New York and Atlanta offices to review all files for "all information of a security nature plus complete background information" on Martin Luther King. On March 6, Hoover asked RFK to authorize a wiretap on Levison's office in New York, and the Attorney General assented. The wiretaps began functioning on March 20. Hoover memos to RFK and O'Donnell, 2/14/62; Hoover memos to SACs (Atlanta and New York), 2/27/62; all in File 100-106670 (Martin Luther King, Jr.), FBI; SAC (New York) memo to Hoover, 3/20/62, File 100-392452 (Stanley Levison), FBI; Garrow, *The FBI and Martin Luther King, Jr.*, pp. 45–46.

On March 2, before asking for the wiretap, Hoover okayed microphone surveillance of Levison's office. FBI agents broke into it and planted "bugs" on March 15. Hoover memo to SAC (New York), 3/2/62; SAC (New York) memo to Hoover, 3/16/62; both in File 100-392452 (Stanley Levison), FBI.

Under Hoover, at least through the mid-1960s, the FBI reserved to itself the right to approve microphone surveillances and to plan operations involving breaking and entering. Hoover informed Byron White, then Deputy Attorney General, of the policy early in the Kennedy administration: "Our policy . . . is based upon a memorandum from former Attorney General Herbert Brownell dated May 20, 1954, in which he approved the use of microphone surveillances with or without trespass . . . 'I recognize that for the FBI to fulfill its important intelligence function, considerations of internal security and the national interest are paramount and, therefore, may compel the unrestricted use of this technique.' " Hoover memo to White, 5/4/61, J. Edgar Hoover Official and Confidential File 14 (Microphone Surveillances), FBI. As investigators in the 1970s later found, the Brownell statement in 1954 was the sole basis for the bureau's maintenance of authority over all bugging operations.

As for "trespass," Hoover's deputy William Sullivan wrote in 1966 that "we do not obtain authorization for 'black bag' jobs from outside the Bureau. Such a technique . . . is clearly illegal; therefore it would be impossible to obtain any legal sanction for it. Despite this, 'black bag' jobs have been used because they represent an invaluable technique in combating subversive activities." Sullivan memo to DeLoach, 7/19/66, J. Edgar Hoover Official and Confidential File 36 (Black Bag Jobs), FBI.

In 1965, Attorney General Nicholas Katzenbach ordered an end to all FBI bugging. Hoover claimed in 1967 that authorization for "black bag" jobs also had ended. Hoover memo to Katzenbach, 9/14/65, J. Edgar Hoover Official and Confidential File 14 (Microphone Surveillances); Hoover memo to Tolson and DeLoach, 1/6/67, J. Edgar Hoover Official and Confidential File 36 (Black Bag Jobs). Today, court orders are required for any electronic surveillance and "black bag" jobs are forbidden at the FBI.

For more on the initial work done to get FBI material on King and Levison released, see Garrow, *The FBI and Martin Luther King, Jr.*, pp. 9–15. For more on Hoover's "Official and Confidential" files, which he kept especially sequestered and a first batch of 7,000 pages of which were released in 1983 in response to a Freedom of Information Act request by Marquette professor Athan Theoharis, see "The Secret Files of J. Edgar Hoover," USN&WR, 12/19/83.

502   "I was wondering whether": Transcript of Dictabelt 22A.4, 6/17/63, Presidential Recordings, JFKL.

503   "I'm going to get hurt": Transcript of Dictabelt 21A.1, 6/3/63, Presidential Recordings, JFKL.

504   Johnson had been complaining for weeks: LBJ was shut out of major decision making so completely that when Kennedy asked for his advice on June 1, he could only grumble, "I'm not competent to advise you." Johnson said he was able to gather information about the situation only "from what I've read in the press." Audiotape 90.3, 6/1/63 meeting, Presidential Recordings, JFKL (no transcript of this tape is available at the Kennedy Library); Audiotape 88.4.

JFK had made the Vice-President chair of the President's Committee on Equal Opportunity. His work there attracted scant interest from Kennedy until reporters and civil rights leaders—and, as the President noted, Southern businessmen themselves—began to criticize federal hiring practices. See JFK memo to LBJ, 4/17/63, Famous Names File, JFK-63, LBJ. Beginning in the spring of 1963, Johnson's Committee on Equal Opportunity also drew the wrath of the Attorney General. Five days after meeting James Baldwin in New York, Robert Kennedy attended the first meeting of the committee to be held since November 1962. He was infuriated to learn that "aside from the Post Office and a Veterans' Administration hospital, only 15 of the 2000 federal employees in Birmingham were black—less than 1 per cent in a city that was 37 per cent black." At the next meeting of the committee three weeks later, Robert Kennedy tore into NASA chief James Webb, humiliated Johnson, and left the room. These were, Kennedy said in 1964, "the sharpest disputes I had with Vice-President Johnson." Schlesinger, *Robert Kennedy and His Times*, pp. 360–362.

504   "The whites think we're just playing": Transcript of dictaphone recording, LBJ-Sorensen, 6/3/63, LBJL. Johnson followed up this talk with memos to the White House giving his advice on meeting with the civil rights leaders and introducing legislation. See, for example, LBJ memo to Sorensen, 6/10/63, Sorensen papers, Box 30, JFKL.

505   to meet at the Kennedy family's apartment: Details of Robert Kennedy's traumatic encounter with Baldwin, Jerome Smith, and their cohorts are drawn from Harry Belafonte and Clarence Jones convs; *Time*, 5/31/63, 6/7/63; Branch, *Parting the Waters*, pp. 809–813; Garrow, *Bearing the Cross*, p. 268; and Schlesinger, *Robert Kennedy and His Times*, pp. 355–360.

506   they were married to white women: RFK OH, pp. 427–429, JFKL.

Chapter 44

507   a full-scale presidential departure: NYT, 6/6/63.

While JFK was in Hawaii, he stayed in the guest house of Admiral Harry Felt, the commander of the Pacific Fleet. "The accommodations," noted Kennedy's naval aide Tazewell Shepard, "were very inferior to Felt's own quarters." Felt sent over a phonograph and some records, which were later accidentally returned to Washington. Felt asked that the records be returned, or that he be reimbursed. "JFK," said Shepard, "took pleasure in signing the check himself." Schlesinger notes on interview of Tazewell Shepard, 3/3/64, Schlesinger papers, Box W-14, JFKL.

507   "The Peace Speech": The account given of the genesis of Kennedy's June 10 speech is drawn from Bundy, Cousins, and Sorensen ints; Sorensen OH, pp. 71–72, JFKL; Cousins letter to Sorensen, 6/1/63, Sorensen papers, Box 36, JFKL; Lieberson and Meyers, eds., *John Fitzgerald Kennedy . . . As We Remember Him*, p. 192; Schlesinger, *A Thousand Days*, p. 900; and Sorensen, *Kennedy*, pp. 822–823.

508   eighteen-minute simulation: *Time*, 6/14/63.

508   "Well, Lyndon": James Reston, Jr., *The Lone Star: The Life of John Connally* (New York: Harper & Row, 1990), pp. 238–240.

509   "boiling oil into my crotch": Draft manuscript of Fay, *The Pleasure of His Company*, Land papers, Box 12, BU.

509   "I'm afraid I can take no more": This story is recounted by Alistair Cooke, who was there, in Lieberson and Meyers, eds., *John Fitzgerald Kennedy . . . As We Remember Him*, p. 196.

509   " 'Now he's got a bad back' ": Draft manuscript of Fay, *The Pleasure of His Company*, Land papers, Box 12, BU.

509   Sorensen and Bundy showed drafts: Sorensen said that, to his knowledge, neither he nor Bundy had talked about the speech to anyone else in government before springing the drafts on June 8. Sorensen OH, p. 72, JFKL. Carl Kaysen recalled that after Sorensen left the next day to meet Kennedy on the West Coast, a final draft of the speech was left "in his hands to clear with McNamara, Rusk, Max Taylor, Thompson and to 'inform' Seaborg." Schlesinger notes of interview with Kaysen, 8/6/64, Schlesinger papers, Box W-14, JFKL.

509   new fears over radioactive fallout: The Federal Radiation Council reported in May 1963 that after holding steady during the 1958–61 moratorium on nuclear testing, accumulated blasts by the atmospheric nuclear tests of all nations had skyrocketed to 511 megatons by the end of 1962. Handwritten graph, undated, Harriman papers, Box 541, LC.

510   Again and again, in private: Bundy, Dutton, and Schlesinger ints; Bundy speech,

12/13/88, NA; Boggs OH, JFKL; Rostow OH, p. 63, JFKL; Roberts, *First Rough Draft*, p. 217; Seaborg, *Kennedy, Khrushchev, and the Test Ban*, pp. 181–182, 187–188. "We've won a great victory . . . ," Kennedy told congressional leaders after the missile crisis. "We have resolved one of the great crises of mankind. . . . There will be another one—when and if the Chinese get the hydrogen bomb."

Averell Harriman knew of Kennedy's concern and made sure he was briefed on the USSR's relationship to China and nuclear weapons as he prepared for the test ban negotiations. See the State Department's analysis, Rice memo to Harriman, "Inhibiting Communist China's Making and Exploiting Nuclear Weapons," 6/21/63; and Harriman's response to the CIA's memo to him on Khrushchev's problems, Harriman memo to Cline, 7/5/63; both in Harriman papers, Box 539, LC.

510   tensions and distrust: Asked by the author what the single greatest difference was in governing America in 1962 and 1987, Arthur Schlesinger replied, "The perception that communism was monolithic. We didn't know about the Sino-Soviet split." Schlesinger int.

For more on the Sino-Soviet split in the early 1960s, see CIA Report SC 02684/66, "The Deterioration of Sino-Soviet Relations: 1956–1966," 4/22/66, Cuba papers, NSA; Richard Lowenthal, "Cracks in the Communist Monolith," *NYT Magazine*, 2/26/62; "China vs. Russia: The New Game," USN&WR, 7/29/63; James E. McSherry, *Russia and the United States Under Eisenhower, Khrushchev, and Kennedy* (State Park, PA: State College, 1965), pp. 163–178; and Adam B. Ulam, *Expansion and Coexistence: Soviet Foreign Policy, 1917–1973* (New York: Praeger, 1974), pp. 655–679.

Most American intelligence was blind to the Communist schism to a degree that seems incredible today. The State Department made barely any study of China at all in the fifteen years following its vilification by Joseph McCarthy in the early 1950s. Top Defense officials continued to refer to Communist "bloc" activities long after the Soviet Union and China had stopped coordinating their policies.

One exception was the CIA's Office of Current Intelligence, whose Sino-Soviet staff noticed significant differences between the Soviets and the Chinese as early as 1956. "This staff," said Ray Cline, its head from 1955 to 1957, "compiled the data that enabled the CIA to lead the way . . . in charting the strategic conflict . . . that was basic to the definitive split in 1960." But opposition within the CIA, particularly from Counterintelligence chief James Angleton, delayed acceptance of the split in the United States and in Great Britain for years. See Ranelagh, *The Agency*, pp. 503–505, 779–780.

510   "I have no doubt": Norman Cousins int; Cousins, *The Improbable Triumvirate*, pp. 79–80, 113–114.

511   "People in the United States": Cousins, *The Improbable Triumvirate*, p. 95.

511   "We would be ready to send": Schlesinger notes on test ban, 1963, Schlesinger papers, Box W-14, JFKL.

511   "The more I learn about this business": Cousins int; Cousins, *The Improbable Triumvirate*, p. 113.

511   "You ought to beat Mr. K.": Cousins letter to JFK, 4/30/63, Sorensen papers, Box 36, JFKL.

512   "banning all tests that contaminate": Schlesinger, *A Thousand Days*, p. 899.

512   "We have to remember that no one": Rusk int.

512   "We Can Kill the Russians 360 Times Over": Cousins, *The Improbable Triumvirate*, p. 95. Cousins brought a copy of the ad to Khrushchev, who "stared hard" at it while it was translated for him. He then lifted his hand and said, "Your figures are all wrong. We're not that far behind. But, as the ad says, what difference does it make? Nuclear war is sheer madness."

512   On May 8, Khrushchev's answer: Rusk OH, p. 222, JFKL; Beschloss, *The Crisis Years*, p. 596; Schlesinger, *A Thousand Days*, p. 898.

512   "Mr. President, on the test-ban issue": JFKPP, 5/8/63.

513   a joint letter to Moscow: Cousins int; Salinger int; Horne, *Macmillan: 1957–1986*, pp. 509–510; Schlesinger, *A Thousand Days*, p. 898; Sorensen, *Kennedy*, pp. 821–822.

513   complaining once more: Beschloss, *The Crisis Years*, p. 598; Horne, *Macmillan: 1957–1986*, p. 510; Schlesinger, *A Thousand Days*, p. 900.

513   a Chinese delegation arrived: CIA report, "The Deterioration of Sino-Soviet Relations," p. 27.

513   "I have chosen this time": JFKPP, 6/10/63. For an important explanation of the American University address, prepared with Kennedy's approval, see Bundy memo to Manning, "How We Hope the President's Speech at American University May Be Understood," 6/11/63, Sorensen papers, Box 41, JFKL. Bundy wrote, for example, that "the President's speech is an expression of a concern for peace which he feels deeply in a personal sense and which he has not had an opportunity to express in extended form in many months . . . [t]his speech should not be misunderstood as indicating any weakening in the American resolution to resist the pressures for Soviet expansion. The President is not choosing sides, in any ostentatious way, between Moscow and Peiping, but his speech is designed to emphasize the positive opportunities for a more constructive and less hostile Soviet policy."

515   in obvious physical pain: Descriptions of the events in Washington during the integration of the University of Alabama are drawn from the film *Kennedy v. Wallace: A Crisis Up Close*, and D. A. Pennebaker int. *Kennedy v. Wallace* was produced by Robert Drew, who gained extraordinary access to the White House over June 10–11, it was broadcast once in 1963 and again by PBS-TV on *The American Experience* (no. 107), 11/15/88. Pennebaker was a filmmaker for the original production.

515   "I wonder whether you want": Transcript of *Kennedy v. Wallace*, pp. 7–9.

516   Soviet reaction to his peace speech: The text of Khrushchev's reply to Kennedy's speech was released by Tass on June 14 and can be found in Harriman papers, Box 479, LC.

516   A photograph by Malcolm Browne: The photo had tremendous impact on worldwide—and Vietnamese—public opinion. "The government handled the Buddhist crisis badly and allowed it to grow," said William Colby, then head of the Far East Division of the CIA. "But I really don't think there was much they could have done about it once that monk burned himself." Rust, *Kennedy in Vietnam*, p. 98. Browne won a Pulitzer Prize for the photograph.

516   "Before closing my eyes to Buddha": *Time*, 6/21/63.

516   "barbecue à bonze": Rust, *Kennedy in Vietnam*, p. 104.

Chapter 45

517   "I think we should call up the Guard now": RFK OH, pp. 815–818, JFKL.

517   "Let's wait": Schlesinger, *Robert Kennedy and His Times*, p. 366.

518   "We're still talking about that": Mansfield int.

518   "Do you think it is so horrifying": Schlesinger, *Robert Kennedy and His Times*, pp. 363–364.

518   Now, there he stood: This account of the confrontation at the University of Alabama is derived from *Kennedy v. Wallace; Birmingham News*, 6/11/63; NYT, 6/12/63; *Time*, 6/21/63; Branch, *Parting the Waters*, pp. 821–822; Schlesinger, *Robert Kennedy and His Times*, pp. 365–368.

518   "One of the great state papers": Quoted in *Time*, 6/21/63.

519   "The situation is deteriorating": Rusk int.

519   "FYI—If Diem does not take": Rusk telegram to Truehart, 6/11/63, FRUS 1–8/1963, Document 167, pp. 381–382.

519   He did not talk to Tho: Truehart cable to Rusk, 6/13/63, FRUS 1–8/1963, Document 170, pp. 386–387. President Kennedy became aware of the warnings Truehart issued to Diem on instructions from the State Department only after the CIA summarized the situation in the President's Intelligence Checklist of June 14. "The President noticed that Diem has been threatened with a formal statement of disassociation. He wants to be absolutely sure that no further threats are made and no formal statement is made without his own personal approval." FRUS 1–8/1963, note 5 to Document 169, pp. 386–387.

519   Robert Kennedy called: Sidey, *John F. Kennedy, President*, p. 401.

520   " 'Central government' ": Edwin Guthman int.

520   "Damn him": Guthman int.

520   "We have to check for bombs": RFK OH, p. 818, JFKL.

520   "Will you issue the proclamation now": Transcript of *Kennedy v. Wallace*, p. 25.
520   Kennedy federalized the Guard: Schlesinger, *Robert Kennedy and His Times*, pp. 366–367.
520   "Governor Wallace": Sidey, *John F. Kennedy, President*, pp. 401–402.
521   one of the two most important speeches: Sorensen int.
521   Sorensen and others began dictating: This account of the minutes leading up to Kennedy's civil rights speech is drawn from Louis Martin int; Sorensen int; RFK OH, p. 432, JFKL; Marshall OH, pp. 109–110, JFKL; Branch, *Parting the Waters*, pp. 823–824; and Schlesinger, *Robert Kennedy and His Times*, p. 369.
521   "This afternoon": JFKPP, 6/11/63.
522   there was no bill ready to be introduced: For an outline of the difficult questions not yet decided by the administration regarding civil rights legislation, see Sorensen memo, "Agenda for Civil Rights Meeting," 5/31/63, Sorensen papers, Box 30, JFKL.
522   "I think it was really good": Transcript of *Kennedy v. Wallace*, p. 28.
523   Evers pulled into his driveway: NYT, 6/13/63; NW, 6/24/63; Branch, *Parting the Waters*, pp. 824–825.

Chapter 46

524   "I'm sorry, Mr. President": Transcript of Dictabelt 22A.2, 6/12/63, Presidential Recordings, JFKL.
524   "Civil rights": Transcript of Dictabelt 22A.2.
525   "I got a call at two": Gore int.
525   "N.A.A.C.P. Leader Slain": NYT, 6/13/63, 6/14/63.
525   "there was not much optimism:" NYT, 6/12/63.
525   Quang Duc's self-immolation: NYT, 6/12/63.
526   "Down with the Shah!": *Time* 6/14/63.
526   Nolting was asking to be relieved: See Frederick Nolting OH, LBJL.
526   Rusk int. to send Edmund Gullion: Gullion int; Rusk int.
526   Lodge had said he would be willing: Henry Cabot Lodge OH, JFKL; Henry Cabot Lodge, *The Storm Has Many Eyes* (New York: W.W. Norton, 1973), p. 205.
527   but Kennedy had done: Most notoriously, during deliberations on the Civil Rights Act of 1957, Kennedy had voted for a jury trial amendment that passed by a narrow margin. The provision guaranteed jury trials to officials charged with blocking voters from exercising their rights. Civil rights leaders maintained that the jury trial amendment effectively destroyed the voting rights measures of the act, as juries in the South could not be expected to convict abusers of Negro voting rights.
527   "To obtain 67 votes": Mansfield memo to JFK, 6/18/63, Sorensen papers, Box 30, JFKL. See also Baker memo to Mansfield, 6/12/63, Sorensen papers, Box 30, JFKL, an appraisal of the civil rights legislation situation in Congress written by Secretary to the Senate Bobby Baker at Mansfield's request.
The development of Kennedy's bill is outlined in Sorensen memos to JFK, 6/11/63 and 6/14/63, Sorensen papers, Box 30, JFKL.
527   The agreement: Mansfield memos, "Conference with Senator Dirksen," and "Differences Between the President's Civil Rights Bill and the Tentative Draft of the Majority Leader's Staff," 6/16/63, Sorensen papers, Box 30, JFKL; D. F. Sullivan, *The Civil Rights Programs of the Kennedy Administration* (University of Oklahoma Ph.D. thesis, Ann Arbor, MI: University Microfilms, 1965), pp. 361–362.
528   Dirksen said he himself might vote: O'Brien int.
528   three separate civil rights bills: Memo for the record, Mansfield meeting with Humphrey, et al., 6/18/63, Sorensen papers, Box 30, JFKL. The bills as finally proposed in Congress are outlined in "Civil Rights Acts of 1963," 7/5/63, Vice-Presidential Civil Rights File, Box 6, LBJL.
The introduction of separate bills aroused considerable controversy: there were "rumors in cloakrooms all over Capitol Hill," as New York Congressman John Lindsay told Robert Kennedy, "that the Administration and the leaders made a deal to scuttle public accommodations." As *Time* noted, it was not only that Mansfield and Dirksen co-

sponsored the bill without Title II; Southern Democrats had largely limited their attacks to opposing public accommodations, and Harlem Congressman Adam Clayton Powell had said that Title II "doesn't have a chance." Most observers concluded that the administration had cut a deal with the southerners, but in reality the Kennedys had taken Mansfield's advice and done everything necessary to keep Everett Dirksen aboard.

528   "The time has come . . .": JFKPP, 6/19/63.

528   Medgar Evers was buried: Branch, *Parting the Waters,* pp. 825–827; Schlesinger, *Robert Kennedy and His Times,* p. 370.

528   "If I die": *Time,* 6/21/63.

528   "The root of the problem": Rusk memo to JFK, undated, NSF Box 341, JFKL. This is a cover memo to Rusk and McNamara's fifteen-page plan for escalation in Laos and North Vietnam, which remains classified.

529   Kennedy approved the concept: NSAM 249, 6/25/63, NSF Box 341, JFKL.

529   a series of White House meetings: For an example of briefing material for one such civil rights meeting, with prominent Southern lawyers on June 21, see Lee White memo to JFK, 6/21/63, and Oberdorfer memo to RFK, 6/21/63, both in Vice-Presidential Civil Rights File, Box 6, LBJL.

A list of the first month of meetings is included in "Chronology of Civil Rights Actions by the President 1963," n.d., Sorensen papers, Box 30, JFKL.

529   Randolph and King announced: NYT, 6/22/63.

529   Negroes and civil rights leaders: This account of Kennedy's June 22 meeting with civil rights leaders is drawn from Martin int; Rauh int; Rauh OH, Howard; NYT, 6/23/63, 1/15/74; Branch, *Parting the Waters,* pp. 839–841; Garrow, *Bearing the Cross,* pp. 271–272; Oates, *Let the Trumpet Sound,* pp. 246–247; Schlesinger, *A Thousand Days,* pp. 968–971; Schlesinger, *Robert Kennedy and His Times,* pp. 375–376; and Roy Wilkins with Tom Matthews, *Standing Fast: The Autobiography of Roy Wilkins* (New York: Viking Press, 1982), p. 291.

530   "A paid agent of the Soviet Communist apparatus": Branch, *Parting the Waters,* p. 835. Administration officials had first approached King about Levison much earlier, when Robert Kennedy decided to have his top lieutenants at the Justice Department warn the civil rights leader about the dangers reported by the FBI. John Seigenthaler advised King to beware of associates with Communist pasts, and, at the urging of Burke Marshall, a reluctant Harris Wofford told King the FBI doubted Stanley Levison's loyalty. RFK-Marshall OH, pp. 30–33, JFKL; Wofford OH, pp. 143–144, JFKL; Branch, *Parting the Waters,* pp. 516–518; Garrow, *The FBI and Martin Luther King, Jr.,* pp. 44–45; Wofford, *Of Kennedys and Kings,* p. 216. At the same time, Marshall and Byron White asked the FBI for concrete evidence regarding Levison. Courtney Evans, the bureau's liaison to the Justice Department, acting on Hoover's orders, refused to pass on anything beyond the allegation that Levison was secretly a member of the Communist Party.

In January 1963, Marshall once more warned King about Levison, again at the request of Robert Kennedy. He also brought up Hunter Pitts "Jack" O'Dell, who Levison had hired to work in the SCLC's New York office, and whose past work with the Communist Party also translated into FBI allegations of secret party membership in the 1960s. Around the same time, the Justice Department again asked the FBI for corroborative information on Levison; this time, Assistant Attorney General J. Walter Yeagley wanted to prosecute him as a subversive. Hoover's agents interviewed fifteen top Communist informants, in an attempt to obtain a source against Levison besides the old allegations of Jack Childs and his brother Morris, but not one recognized Levison's name or picture. On February 12, 1963, Hoover wrote Yeagley that the FBI could not hand over its information; it came from a "highly sensitive source who is not available for interview or testimony." Garrow, *The FBI and Martin Luther King, Jr.,* pp. 58–60; Branch, *Parting the Waters,* pp. 696–697.

The account of the events of June 22, 1963, when King was told to disassociate himself from Levison and O'Dell by Burke Marshall, Robert Kennedy, and President Kennedy, is drawn from the following sources: RFK-Marshall OH, pp. 674–677, JFKL; Marshall memo to Hoover, 9/20/63, J. Edgar Hoover Official and Confidential File 24 (Martin Luther King, Jr.), FBI; Branch, *Parting the Waters,* pp. 835–837; Garrow, *Bearing the Cross,* pp. 272–273; and Schlesinger, *Robert Kennedy and His Times,* pp. 384–385.

King resisted moving against Levison and O'Dell, but was eventually prodded to do so. Levison took it upon himself in July to "induce him to break. . . . I said it would not be in the interests of the movement to hold on to me if the Kennedys had doubts." Garrow, *The FBI and Martin Luther King, Jr.*, p. 63. That month, King also decided that O'Dell had to leave SCLC—news stories, leaked by the FBI, that King's organization was being managed in New York by a known Communist were creating too much pressure. See Branch, *Parting the Waters*, pp. 850–851.

But King could not win at this game. He and Levison agreed to stay in touch through a third person—but that person was Clarence Jones, whom the FBI began wiretapping in July. And O'Dell's occasional contacts with SCLC after his firing were also used by the bureau as evidence that King had not severed his ties with Communists.

530   Kennedy had just ordered: Bradlee int.

531   "After all, he's done more for civil rights": Hearing Kennedy say this, Joe Rauh thought to himself, "Well, he's certainly done more for civil rights than you have."

In speaking to the civil rights leaders, Kennedy underscored his commitment to their joint cause by referring to a poll that showed him losing popular support because of racial issues. And among pundits, there had been "all sorts of rumors," as *Time* wrote, that the President's approval rating was about to slip below 50 percent for the first time.

In fact JFK's overall popularity remained high just before his trip to Europe, but he had lost support drastically in the South. In early May, his approval rating had been 55 percent in the South and 67 percent outside the South, or 64 percent overall. By late June, it was 61 percent nationally, but that broke down to 71 percent outside the South and only 33 percent in Dixie. *Time*, 7/12/63.

532   "Ireland?": Before leaving, Kennedy asked his staff to "check with the Library of Congress to find out what the Kennedy motto is in Gaelic." Lincoln memo to Holborn, 6/63, POF Box 62, Lincoln Dictation File, JFKL.

Chapter 47

533   Air Force One: Fact Sheet 87–25, U.S. Air Force, Office of Public Affairs.

533   "Is this trip necessary?": The phrase is from *Time*, 7/5/63. A rundown of problems with the trip was given in *Time*, 6/7/63.

534   "Never, at any time since the war": Ball memo to JFK, 6/20/63, DDRS (1990) 1574.

534   "Kenn-ah-dee!": *Time*, 7/5/63.

534   "Where did you get all those American flags?": Sidey, *John F. Kennedy, President*, p. 409.

534   "Let's stand and wave": *Time*, 7/5/63.

535   "My stay in this country": *Time*, 7/5/63.

535   "You think this is any good?": Sidey, "Present at the Construction," *Time*, 11/20/89.

535   He wanted to stand alone: This account of Kennedy at the Berlin Wall is drawn from Bundy int; Sorensen int; NYT, 6/27/63; Sidey, *John F. Kennedy, President*, pp. 413–414; and Wyden, *Wall*, pp. 568–569.

536   "Two thousand years ago": JFKPP, 6/26/63.

536   "Ich bin ein Berliner": Kenny O'Donnell wrote that Kennedy said to him on the flight to Berlin, "What was the proud boast of the Romans—Civis Romanus sum? Send Bundy up here. He'll know how to say it in German." O'Donnell and Powers, *"Johnny, We Hardly Knew Ye,"* p. 417.

Kennedy's brush with the German language was as difficult as his handling of Spanish in Alliance for Progress meetings. Ben Bradlee wrote that JFK "spent the better part of an hour" with a foreign service officer "before he could master 'Ich bin ein Berliner.' " Bundy said Kennedy "had no feeling for any foreign language. So there we were on the goddamned airplane coming down on Berlin while he repeated the phrase over and over again." Bradlee, *Conversations with Kennedy*, pp. 95–96; Beschloss, *The Crisis Years*, p. 605.

Max Jacobson first practiced medicine in Berlin and lived there from 1920 to 1934; his widow said she was "99.5 percent certain" that he coined the "Berliner" phrase for Kennedy.

536 "As I said this morning": JFKPP, 6/26/63.

537 "I'm worried": Bundy int; Sorensen int.

537 "Go to Germany": *Time*, 7/5/63.

537 "We'll never have another day": Bundy int; Sorensen int.

537 "I felt like kicking her": O'Donnell and Powers, *"Johnny, We Hardly Knew Ye,"* p. 418.

537 "When my great-grandfather left here": O'Donnell and Powers, *"Johnny, We Hardly Knew Ye,"* p. 420.

538 Dave Powers, who dutifully downed it: O'Donnell and Powers, *"Johnny, We Hardly Knew Ye,"* p. 421.

538 "Please think of Jack": Horne, *Macmillan: 1957–1986*, p. 513.

538 "We both agreed": Horne, *Macmillan: 1957–1986*, p. 516.

538 "To them, Kennedy meant youth": Horne, *Macmillan: 1957–1986*, p. 514.

539 "He suffered agony": Horne, *Macmillan: 1957–1986*, p. 514.

539 Villa Serbelloni on Lake Como: Rusk int; Duke OH, p. 64, JFKL.

540 "Norman Vincent Peale would love that": O'Donnell and Powers, *"Johnny, We Hardly Knew Ye,"* p. 432.

540 he prayed for the success: *Time*, 7/12/63.

540 They collected twenty-seven pieces: Billings OH, pp. 694–697.

540 "The Soviet Government declares": Telex printouts of Khrushchev's speech are in Harriman papers, Box 539, LC.

541 "It seems they're offering": Ball memo to JFK, "Analysis of Khrushchev Speech Regarding Test Ban and NATO Warsaw Pact," 7/2/63, Harriman papers, Box 539, LC.

541 The State Department was neither sure: INR Research Memo RSB-99, 7/5/63, Harriman papers, Box 539, LC.

Kennedy's arms control advisers saw hope in Khrushchev's address: "Then Chairman Khrushchev made a speech in East Berlin of all places . . . this was one in which he, after 10 pages, in the spirit of Rapallo, said we wanted a test ban and wouldn't it be good to have a test ban, and the Western powers have been very stubborn, obstinate, awful-awful . . . it's their fault we don't have a comprehensive test ban, but let's try a limited test ban. . . . At that point it looked like the Harriman mission might accomplish something." Adrian Fisher OH, p. 23, JFKL.

Harriman himself told Michael Forrestal, of Khrushchev's speech, that "it looks as if he is trying to make a bid." Harriman-Forrestal telecon, 7/2/63, Harriman papers, Box 581, LC.

541 "We all believe": Forrestal memo to Bundy, 7/1/63, FRUS 1–8/1963, Document 195, p. 432.

541 "The President was briefed": Memcon, 7/4/63 meeting, FRUS 1–8/1963, Document 205, pp. 451–453.

542 "The GVN has always shown": SNIE 53-2-63, "The Situation in South Vietnam," USVNR, Book 12, pp. 529–535.

542 "Many qualified observers": Bowles cable to JFK, 7/10/63, DDRS (1991) 3290. Bowles wrote a fuller report on July 19, after getting to New Delhi: "Although the risks in any political switchover are formidable, the risks of staying on dead center are, in my opinion, substantially greater . . . a new deal in Saigon appears to me an essential first step." Bowles letter to Bundy, 7/19/63, FRUS 1–8/1963, Document 231, pp. 518–521.

542 "After three days of talk": JFKPP, 7/17/63.

543 "There was a discussion": Summary Record of NSC Standing Group Meeting, 7/9/63, Cuba papers, NSA.

544 "Mr. President, it's pretty generally acknowledged": JFKPP, 7/17/63.

544 "I'm sure it was passed unanimously": JFKPP, 7/17/63.

Chapter 48

545 "Mr. Harriman comes with my full": JFK letter to Khrushchev, 7/15/63, Harriman papers, Box 541, LC.

545 the Soviets were astounded: Dobrynin conv. "Harriman would just get on the phone with Kennedy," said the Soviet ambassador, "and things would be decided. It was amazing."

546 "Chinese comrades": *Pravda*, 7/15/63.

546 Khrushchev had to be preoccupied: Seaborg, *Kennedy, Khrushchev, and the Test Ban*, p. 230. For Seaborg's notes of this last White House meeting on the test ban before Harriman's departure, see pp. 228–229. For Harriman's notes, see "Points for Discussion with the President," 7/9/63, Harriman papers, Box 540, LC.

On the state of mind of the Soviets, see also Moscow embassy cable A-301 to State Department, "Motivation for Moscow's Signature of the Test Ban Agreement," 9/6/63, State Department FOIA Release, case number 8503143.

546 "give them a sweetener": Harriman memo for personal files, 12/20/67, Harriman papers, Box 479, LC. As might be expected, certain diehards dissented from this view. Walt Rostow, for example, had written Kennedy the day before to underline "the three dangers" of the Harriman mission, including "being pressured (by the British as well as the Russians) into a cheap sell-out of the MLF." (The others were "gutting our freshly beefed up link to Bonn" and "being pressured . . . cheaply into a summit and a mood of detente.") Rostow memo to JFK, 7/8/63, Harriman papers, Box 540, LC.

546 "Soviet concern over the economic cost": "Points to be Explored with the Russians," 7/9/63, Harriman papers, Box 540, LC.

547 "There are many capitalists": Harriman-Khrushchev memcon, 7/20/63, Harriman papers, Box 541, LC.

547 Lord Hailsham: By all accounts, Hailsham, who had a propensity for daffy behavior, was not one of Macmillan's most inspired appointments. The prime minister, at that point reeling from the effects of the Profumo scandal, had wanted to send David Ormsby-Gore, but "had demurred on the grounds that it would be wiser to have someone of Cabinet rank, and who would not be considered an American 'stooge.'" Horne, *Macmillan: 1957–1986*, p. 509. See also pp. 510–511, 519–521. Background on Hailsham can be found in Harriman papers, Box 540, LC.

There is evidence that Harriman did not take his British counterpart all that seriously. On July 4, he asked Marquis Childs what Hailsham was like. "He is an odd bird," Childs replied. "He has a kind of righteousness that will make him difficult." Harriman said that "the Soviets will want to talk to us rather than the British anyway." Harriman-Childs telecon, 7/4/63, Harriman papers, Box 581, LC.

David Ormsby-Gore later recalled that Hailsham had sent telegrams to Macmillan during the test ban negotiations stating that Harriman "was making such demands on the Soviets that the negotiations . . . would fall through." Macmillan had then transmitted requests through Ormsby-Gore to Kennedy, asking Harriman to back off. "In speaking of this, of course," Harriman said, "David knew that Hailsham was grossly exaggerating the situation and had no real understanding of what was going on." Harriman memo for the files, 12/15/64, Harriman papers, Box 541, LC.

The success of the test ban negotiations propelled Hailsham into front-runner status in the struggle to succeed Macmillan in the fall of 1963. But he blew his chances with a highly unorthodox campaign, including a famous incident where he mixed baby food for his one-year-old child in front of TV cameras at London's Imperial Hotel in October. Shocked leaders of Britain's staid Conservative Party could not abide such a breach of dignity, and eventually turned to Alec Douglas-Home.

547 "What do they want?": *Time*, 7/26/63.

547 "Your report is encouraging": JFK cable 191 to Harriman, 7/15/63, Harriman papers, Box 539, LC.

547 "Radical steps": Department of Defense, "Harriman Trip to Moscow—Briefing Book," Vol. II, 6/20/63; "Briefing Book on U.S.-Soviet Non-Diffusion Agreement for Discussion at the Moscow Meeting," 6/12/63; both in NSF Box 265, JFKL. Gordon Chang has written the most thorough accounts of the possibility that the United States sought action against China at the time of the test ban negotiations: Gordon H. Chang, "JFK, China, and the Bomb," *Journal of American History* (March 1988); Chang, *Friends and Enemies: The United States, China, and the Soviet Union, 1948–1972* (Stanford, CA: Stanford University Press, 1990), pp. 217–252.

As noted below, most Harriman-Khrushchev memcons remain classified, and Harriman's comments on China were almost completely deleted from the summary record of a July 31 NSC meeting called to discuss "Chinese Communist intentions." DDRS (1991) 3324. So for now, the final word on potential strikes against China rests with a 1964 State Department memo: "A search of our records of the Test Ban Treaty negotiations in Moscow fails to reveal any Harriman proposal for a joint US-USSR effort to slow down Red China's nuclear weapons development. On the other hand the question of Chinese nuclear development came up in various Harriman/Khrushchev exchanges. . . . Khrushchev was obviously unwilling to talk at much length on the question and he tried to give the impression of not being greatly concerned. One of the reasons that the Chinese issue was raised was Harriman's theory that Khrushchev's interest in a test ban treaty flowed from his desire to isolate Red China in the international communist movement. Aside from this Harriman was also under instructions to express the President's great concern over Chinese development of nuclear weapons." De Martino memo to Read, 10/2/64, Harriman papers, Box 539, LC.

In 1988, McGeorge Bundy wrote that in 1963, "there had been talk about the possibility of preemptive action against the Chinese bomb—talk, not serious planning or real intent." Bundy, *Danger and Survival*, p. 532.

548   "This is the great menace": Malraux, *Antimémoires.*
548   "You're trying to tell me": Seaborg, *Kennedy, Khrushchev, and the Test Ban*, pp. 240–241.
548   a NATO–Warsaw Pact non-aggression treaty: Seaborg, *Kennedy, Khrushchev, and the Test Ban*, pp. 243–244.
548   "That's fine": This particular edit is discussed in Harriman cable 311 to Rusk, 7/24/63, Harriman papers, Box 540, LC. Harriman was unusually meticulous about keeping records, and his papers at the Library of Congress are a treasure trove of documents relating to the test ban negotiations. Moreover, his files were declassified en masse by an agreement between the State Department, which claimed ownership of copies of confidential cables Harriman had kept, and the Library of Congress, to which his family bequeathed his archives. The result was less sanitization than would normally have occurred of diplomatic exchanges. The cables Harriman sent from Moscow can be found in Box 540 of his papers, and those he received from Washington are in Box 541. Important Harriman documents not cited elsewhere in these notes include "Talking Points," 7/15/63 and 7/17/63; and "Personal Notes on Meeting with Gromyko," 7/25/63, all in Harriman papers, Box 541, LC.

Unfortunately, one significant collection of Harriman's test ban papers remains classified: the memcons of the meetings he held with Khrushchev and Gromyko in Moscow. Glenn Seaborg has written that "some of the most important deliberations took place at these private sessions," but despite repeated requests, and despite the fact that the Soviet Union does not even exist anymore, the State Department has not released these records as of mid-1993.

On Kennedy's intense personal involvement in the test ban negotiations, see memos of meetings, 7/18/63, 7/22/63, 7/23/63, all in NSF Box 317, JFKL; Benjamin Read OH, p. 3, JFKL; Sorensen, *Kennedy*, p. 829. Read was the executive secretary of the State Department.

Kennedy on several occasions tried to get Harriman to move faster in reporting to Washington. On July 17, Rusk cabled Harriman, "President and Secretary keenly interested full current reports on all your talks. If at all possible cable fuller report than contained Emtel 166 of July 16 meeting." The next day's hint was "suggest to speed communications that reports of conversations without your own evaluation and recommendations be sent without delay." Four days later, Harriman was again prodded: "Memcon of July 21 Harriman-Khrushchev meeting awaited eagerly here." Rusk cables 207, 219, and 265 to Harriman, 7/17/63, 7/18/63, 7/22/63, all in Harriman papers, Box 541, LC.

The President also instituted extraordinary security measures to protect the secrecy of the negotiations. All cables received from the Moscow mission were marked "BAN," handled as "Eyes Only," and immediately relayed to the White House. Two copies were made and sealed in brown envelopes; one was taken by Read to Rusk, the other filed away. Other than Rusk, only George Ball, William Foster, and Llewellyn Thompson were authorized to see the cables. The names of everyone at the Communications Center who had seen or handled the messages were written on the envelopes. Cables sent to Harriman were subject to the same restrictions, which were coordinated by Read and Bundy. "Handling of Ban Series Communications," undated, Harriman papers, Box 541, LC.

After Harriman returned from the Soviet Union, Bundy issued a memo that was required reading for all "holders of the test ban messages," cautioning that "all cables relating to the Harriman negotiations in Moscow have been very tightly held, with the unusual result that there have been almost no leaks to the press. The President desires that this record be maintained. . . . Readers of these cables are specifically warned against discussing their contents in any way, shape or form with members of the press, and discussion with non-readers within the Government should be conducted in such a way that juicy morsels are not let loose for idle gossip." Bundy memo, 7/31/63, Harriman papers, Box 542, LC.

548   "Okay, great!": Isaacson and Thomas, *The Wise Men*, p. 630.

549   "Each of the Parties to this Treaty": The full treaty, which ultimately was only eight hundred words in length, is printed as an appendix to Seaborg, *Kennedy, Khrushchev, and the Test Ban.*

549   "To Norman Cousins, with warm regards": A copy of the telex is reproduced in Cousins, *The Improbable Triumvirate*, facing p. 79.

549   "Hope very much you will find": Rusk cable to Harriman, 7/23/63, Harriman papers, Box 541, LC; Schlesinger, *A Thousand Days*, p. 829.

549   "To isolate Chicoms": Harriman cable 277 to JFK, 7/23/63, Harriman papers, Box 540, LC.

549   "We just signed the test ban": Harriman-Khrushchev memcon and draft memcon, 7/26/63, Harriman papers, Box 541, LC.

549   walked arm-in-arm around the track: Seaborg, *Kennedy, Khrushchev, and the Test Ban*, pp. 250–251.

550   he was surprised to find: Transcript of Dictabelt 23B.6, 7/24/63, Presidential Recordings, JFKL.

550   "We've got to hit the country": Transcript of Dictabelt 23C.1, 7/24/63, Presidential Recordings, JFKL.

550   "I want to congratulate you": Transcript of Dictabelt 24A.1, 7/26/63, Presidential Recordings, JFKL.

550   "I speak to you tonight": JFKPP, 7/26/63.

550   "Good job": Schlesinger, *A Thousand Days*, p. 909. Harriman's own thoughts are summarized in "Outlook for Future Discussions with USSR," 7/30/63, and draft, 7/28/63, Harriman papers, Box 541, LC. A transcript of Harold Macmillan's statement on the Test Ban Treaty and the ensuing commentary in the House of Commons is also in Harriman papers, Box 541, LC.

551   "For He's a Jolly Good Fellow": Abramson, *Spanning the Century*, p. 598; Isaacson, *The Wise Men*, p. 633; Schlesinger, *A Thousand Days*, p. 909.

Chapter 49

552   leading the U.S. delegation: See Beschloss, *The Crisis Years*, pp. 628–629; Seaborg, *Kennedy, Khrushchev, and the Test Ban*, pp. 259–260. Kennedy did not want to attract right-wing opposition to the treaty by letting Stevenson attend the signing, but eventually relented.

552   "Macmillan has told me": Rusk int. "I never pretended to know how to deal with the Soviet Union," Rusk said later. "They have different purposes than we have; they have an inborn sense of secrecy, and they are very suspicious of the outside world; they have stubbornness and pride and other attributes that make them very difficult to live with." Rusk OH, p. 160, JFKL.

552   Patrick Bouvier Kennedy: See *Time,* 8/16/63; O'Donnell and Powers, *"Johnny, We Hardly Knew Ye,"* pp. 434–438.

553   "Come on, Jack, let's go": Richard Cardinal Cushing OH, JFKL.

553   "If there were a vote now": Cousins int; Cousins, *The Improbable Triumvirate,* p. 129.

553   But congressional mail: Schlesinger, *A Thousand Days,* p. 910; Cousins, *The Improbable Triumvirate,* pp. 129–130.

554   "The reason I made such a thing": Transcript of Dictabelt 25B.2, 8/12/63, Presidential Recordings, JFKL.

554   did bring younger officers: Gilpatric OH, p. 76, JFKL. "Taylor changed personnel on the JCS staff so they would at least talk about disarmament issues."

554   it was only when Harriman left: Nitze OH, p. 191, JFKL.

555   had refused to mention: RR.

555   "The signing was a mistake": *Time,* 8/30/63.

555   "I think that Teller made some impression": Transcript of Dictabelts 26B.5 and 26C.1, 8/23/63, Presidential Recordings, JFKL.

555   "The actual number": *Time,* 8/23/63.

556   "Comprehensive, aggressive, and continuing": *Time,* 8/23/63. Thus the price the Chiefs and their congressional allies exacted for their support of a limited test ban treaty: the extinction of hope for a comprehensive ban any time soon. "When you stop to think what the advantages were to us of stopping all testing in the early 1960s when we were still ahead of the Soviets," Harriman told Glenn Seaborg, "it's really appalling to realize what an opportunity we missed." Seaborg, *Kennedy, Khrushchev, and the Test Ban,* p. 224.

For more on the push for ratification, see the Dictabelt transcripts collected as "Winning Senate Support for the Nuclear Test Ban Treaty, 1963," Presidential Recordings, JFKL; Harriman memo, "Points to Cover in Statement," 7/29/63; "Schedule of Witnesses for Test Ban Treaty," 8/14/63; "American Public Comment on Nuclear Test Ban Treaty," 8/23/63; all in Harriman papers, Box 541, LC.

556   "I particularly want you to take": Lodge OH, p. 5, JFKL.

556   "They seem to agree": Manning report to JFK, undated, FRUS 1–8/1963, Document 239, pp. 531–543.

556   He pledged his support: JFKPP, 8/20/63.

556   "It is necessary to face the fact": Mansfield memo to JFK, 8/19/63, NSF Country File: Vietnam, Box 1, LBJL.

557   "I hope that Lodge will start": Harriman memo to Hilsman, 8/10/63, Harriman papers, Box 467, LC.

557   to declare martial law: See *Time,* 8/30/63; Rust, *Kennedy in Vietnam,* pp. 104–107.

558   "Diem's regime seems determined": The President's Intelligence Checklist, 8/21/63, quoted in editorial note, FRUS 1–8/1963, Document 262, pp. 597–598.

558   The new ambassador was in Tokyo: Lodge OH, p. 22, JFKL.

558   "You can't have the police": Lodge OH, p. 12, JFKL.

559   "The chief U.S. objection": *Time,* 8/9/63, which featured Madame Nhu on its cover.

560   "Our country's military aid": Edward I. Gibbons, *The U.S Government and the Vietnam War 1961–1964: Executive and Legislative Relationships* (Princeton, NJ: Princeton University Press, 1986), p. 144.

560   had to settle for $3.6 billion: WP, 8/23/63.

560   "POWER SHIFT TO NHU SEEN": WP, 8/24/63.

560   "Even before the declaration": WP, 8/24/63.

561   "It is remarkable to hear": WP, 8/24/63.

561   "I attach the latest cables": Forrestal memo to JFK, 8/24/63, FRUS 1–8/1963, Document 278, pp. 625.

561   "Can't we wait until Monday": Rust, *Kennedy in Vietnam,* p. 114. The account of the events leading up to the August 24 cable is drawn from the following sources: Ball, Gilpatric, Helms, Hilsman, and Rusk ints; David Halberstam notes of interviews with Michael Forrestal, 1/7/71 and 6/71, Halberstam papers, BU, courtesy of David Halberstam; Gibbons, *The U.S. Government and the Vietnam War,* pp. 148–151; Hilsman, *To Move a Nation*, pp. 487–490; Rust, *Kennedy in Vietnam*, pp. 111–120; Schoenbaum, *Waging Peace and War*, pp. 398–399; and Taylor, *Swords and Plowshares*, pp. 292–294.

562   "It is now clear": Ball cable to Lodge (DEPTEL 243), 8/24/63, FRUS 1–8/1963, Document 281, pp. 628–629; PP II, pp. 734–735.

563   "For President's information": Forrestal cable to JFK, 8/26/63, NSF Box 198, JFKL; PP II, p. 735.

563   "Agree to modification proposed": Acting Secretary memo to Lodge, 8/25/63, NSF Box 198. Ball, Harriman, and Hilsman sent this unsigned cable on the night of the 25th, informing Kennedy of their response in Forrestal's cable the next day.

Chapter 50

564   Rusk, McNamara, and Taylor were waiting: Rust, *Kennedy in Vietnam*, p. 119.
564   "RIGHTS LEADERS REAFFIRM": WP, 8/26/63.
564   "the Vandals are coming": *Washington Daily News*, 8/26/63.
564   "If this misguided pressure": *Washington Star*, 8/26/63.
565   That was the basic security plan: Jerry Bruno conv; *Time*, 8/30/63; Thomas Gentile, *March on Washington: August 28, 1963* (Washington, DC: New Day Publications, 1983), pp. 144–150.
565   "My God!": Schlesinger, *Robert Kennedy and His Times*, p. 770. Robert Kennedy said it was "the only time the government was broken in two in a very disturbing way." RFK OH, JFKL.
566   "From Washington. High American officials": Hilsman, *To Move a Nation*, pp. 383–384.
566   The American reporters in the city: Halberstam int.
566   The story was put together: The account of the August 26 meeting is drawn from Memo of meeting, 8/26/63, FRUS 1–8/1963, Document 289, pp. 638–641; Hilsman memo, 8/26/63, Hilsman papers, Vietnam White House meeting memcons, JFKL; Halberstam, *The Best and the Brightest*, pp. 323–324; and the sources listed above for the genesis of the August 24 cable. The memo reprinted in FRUS was drafted by Victor Krulak; the official history cites relevant portions of Hilsman's memo in its notes to Document 281. Krulak and Hilsman often kept separate notes after the controversies surrounding the August 24 cable, as the disagreements between the military and the Harriman wing of the State Department carried over into the administration's recordkeeping.
568   "You can't change American policy": Rust, *Kennedy in Vietnam*, p. 120.
568   "You're not worth firing": Rust, *Kennedy in Vietnam*, p. 119.
568   "Headquarters instruct": Gibbons, *The U.S. Government and the Vietnam War*, p. 152.
569   "Looking under bushes": Taylor OH, LBJL.
569   being leaked to reporters: News of the August 24 cable leaked to *The New York Herald Tribune* in late September, and a week later, *Time* was reporting on the dispute over how it got sent. See *Time*, 10/4/63.
569   "The Kennedy Administration": WP, 8/27/63.
569   "Leader Calls March 'Revolution' ": WP, 8/27/63.
569   "His views are colored": Memo of meeting, 8/26/63; Taylor, *Swords and Plowshares*, p. 294.
570   "The Vietnamese generals haven't got": Memo of conference with the President, 8/27/63, FRUS 1–8/1963, Document 303, pp. 659–665. For purposes of comparison, see the sanitized version in NSF Box 316, JFKL.

Before the meeting, Harriman and Hilsman had talked. "I think I can bring Nolting around," Hilsman said, evidently underestimating the former ambassador's depth of feeling. In reply, Harriman asked if some people were getting cold feet. "I'm afraid of Maxwell Taylor," Hilsman said, adding, "We have to make this work." Harriman-Hilsman telecon, 8/27/63, Harriman papers, Box 581, LC.

570   Then Harriman ripped into Nolting: Hilsman int; Gilpatric OH, p. 31, JFKL.
570   "The President said we should send": Memo of conference, 8/27/63.

570   "We should make clear": Memo of conference, 8/27/63.
570   Harriman refused to ride: Hilsman int.
570   "Authorities are now having second thoughts": Taylor cable to Harkins, 8/27/63, NSF Box 316, JFKL.
570   the war was going so well: *New York Herald Tribune*, 8/27/63.
571   "Averell is one sharp cookie": Hilsman-Harriman telecon, 8/28/63, Harriman papers, Box 467, LC. The ever cautious Harriman marked his notes of the conversation, "No distribution: file here only."
571   "So, you're down here": Marietta Tree int; Tree OH, p. 41, JFKL.
571   Robert Kennedy had authorized the FBI: Baumgartner memo to Sullivan, 7/22/63; Hoover memo to RFK, 7/23/63; Evans memo to Belmont, 7/25/63; and Bland memo to Sullivan, 10/4/63; all in J. Edgar Hoover Official and Confidential File 24 (Martin Luther King, Jr.), FBI.
571   He had acted after Jones had approached: Evans memo to Belmont, 7/16/63, J. Edgar Hoover Official and Confidential File 24 (Martin Luther King, Jr.), FBI; Branch, *Parting the Waters*, pp. 852–856; Garrow, *The FBI and Martin Luther King, Jr.,* pp. 63–66. Robert Kennedy initiated the request for the wiretaps, as future FBI memos would rather gleefully record, but after a week of thinking things over, he approved taps only on Jones, not King.
571   "He's a Tom Cat": Branch, *Parting the Waters*, p. 861. Hoover referred to King by various names, including "no good any way," "the most notorious liar in the country," "one of the lowest characters in the country," "top alley cat," and, his favorite term, "burrhead."
572   he would immediately resign: Schoenbaum, *Waging Peace and War*, p. 280.
572   the Republicans, the Soviets, the FBI: Kraus int.
572   at the noon Vietnam meeting on Wednesday: The account given of the August 28 meeting is drawn from Memo of Conference with the President, 8/28/63, FRUS 8–12/1963, Document 1, pp. 1–6. This record was drafted by Bromley Smith, executive secretary of the NSC. Alternate accounts include Hilsman memo, 8/26/63, Vietnam White House meeting memcons, Hilsman papers, JFKL; and a Krulak memo for the record. Both are discussed in FRUS 8–12/1963, Editorial Note 2, pp. 6–9.
573   "In this personal message": JFK cable to Lodge, 8/28/63, FRUS 8–12/1963, Document 9, p. 17.
573   "Why wasn't I informed?": Rust, *Kennedy in Vietnam*, p. 124.
573   "We are launched on a course": Lodge cable to State, 8/29/63, FRUS 8–12/1963, Document 12, pp. 20–22; NSF Box 198, JFKL; PP II, pp. 738–739.
574   "All of Vietnam": *Time*, 9/6/63.
574   "Mammoth Rally of 200,000": WP, 8/29/63.
574   "Nhu called Real Viet-Nam Ruler": WP, 8/29/63.
574   "Long Crisis Seen on Vietnam Rule": NYT, 8/29/63.
574   "He seems to be getting pretty close": JFK-Hilsman telecon, 8/29/63, FRUS 8–12/1963, Document 14, pp. 25–26.
574   "Highest level meeting": State cable to Lodge and Harkins, 8/29/63, FRUS 8–12/1963, Document 16, pp. 32–33; PP II, pp. 736–737.
575   "The only point": Rusk cable to Lodge, 8/29/63, FRUS 8–12/1963, Document 17, pp. 32–33; PP II, pp. 737–738.
575   "I have approved all the messages": JFK cable to Lodge, 8/29/63, FRUS 8–12/1963, Document 18, pp. 35–36; NSF Box 316, JFKL.
575   "I agree that getting the Nhus out": Lodge cable to Rusk, 8/30/63, FRUS 8–12/1963, Document 20, pp. 38–39; PP II, pp. 739–740.
576   "If the generals were ready": Rust, *Kennedy in Vietnam*, p. 126.
576   there would be no coup: Rust, *Kennedy in Vietnam*, p. 127.
576   "There is neither the will": Lodge cable to State, 8/31/63, NSF Box 198, JFKL.
576   "This particular coup is finished": Richardson cable to CIA, 8/31/63, FRUS 8–12/1963, Document 32, p. 64; CC, p. 220.
576   the last American to talk: Kattenburg summarized his conversation with Diem in a cable to Hilsman, 8/29/63, FRUS 8–12/1963, Document 10, pp. 18–20.
576   "A garden path to tragedy": The August 31 meeting is reconstructed from the

following sources: "Meeting at the State Department," 8/31/63, USVNR, Book 12, pp. 540–544; Memo of meeting, 8/31/63, FRUS 8–12/1963, Document 37, pp. 69–74; Gibbons, *The U.S. Government and the Vietnam War*, pp. 160–161; Paul M. Kattenburg, *The Vietnam Trauma in American Foreign Policy, 1945–75* (New Brunswick, NJ: Transaction Books, 1980), p. 120. Again the separate records were drafted by Hilsman (FRUS) and Krulak (USVNR).

577   "I am very reliably informed": Lodge cable to State, 8/31/63, FRUS 8–12/1963, Document 34, pp. 66–68.

577   to recall and destroy all copies: Copies of the August 24 cable, "along with all similar cables between the period August 24–29, were recalled and destroyed by S/S [the executive secretary of the State Department] on instructions from the White House. . . . It is also understood that similar instructions were given by the White House to CIA and Defense." McKesson memo for the record, 9/24/63, Harriman papers, LC. John A. McKesson was the deputy executive secretary at the State Department.

Chapter 51

578   a traffic jam: The preparations of organizers and travelers to the March on Washington are recounted in Edward Brown OH, Howard; Norman Hill OH, Howard; Fred Shuttlesworth OH, Howard; Roy Wilkins OH, Howard; WP, 8/24–28/63; *Time*, 8/30/63, 9/6/63; Branch, *Parting the Waters*, pp. 868–876; Garrow, *Bearing the Cross*, pp. 276–281; Gentile, *March on Washington*, pp. 132–163; Oates, *Let the Trumpet Sound*, pp. 256–257; and Schlesinger, *Robert Kennedy and His Times*, pp. 375–378.

579   "In recent months": WP, 8/25/63.

579   "Remember These Things": WP, 8/25/63.

579   already in the spotlight: *Time*, 7/12/63; Wofford, *Of Kennedys and Kings*, pp. 173–174.

579   "A place of Northern charm": RFK conv.

580   to deny insinuations: On August 11, FBI wiretaps on Clarence Jones's telephone line picked up someone saying to King, "I hope Bayard don't take a drink before the March."

"Yes," King had replied, "and grab one little brother. 'Cause he will grab one when he has a drink." The bureau's New York office forwarded a transcript of the remarks to Hoover, who sent them on to Robert Kennedy in a memo the next day. SAC (New York) memo to Director, 8/11/63; Hoover memo to RFK, 8/12/63; both in File 100-106670 (Martin Luther King, Jr.), FBI.

On August 13, Hoover summarized everything he had on King and sex in a memo that he sent to Nicholas Katzenbach and that ultimately reached President Kennedy. Hoover memo to Katzenbach, 8/13/63, FBI File 100-106670 (Martin Luther King, Jr.); RFK memo to JFK, 8/20/63, Burke Marshall papers, Box 2, JFKL. Hoover's memo to Katzenbach, along with "all FBI recordings, transcripts, logs, and quotations from both the bugs and the wiretaps on King's home and the SCLC offices," was sealed away for fifty years by a federal judge in 1977. For more on the locking up of the King wiretap yields, see WP, 2/1/77; Garrow, *The FBI and Martin Luther King, Jr.*, pp. 9–15.

Also on August 13, 1963, Senator Strom Thurmond put Rustin's police record into the *Congressional Record* while attacking him for "perversion." Hoover's subordinates sought more information on Rustin for the remainder of 1963, obtaining in one case an explicit description of Rustin's sexual transgressions ten years before. Branch, *Parting the Waters*, pp. 861–862.

580   "I don't think we can undo": JFKPP, 8/20/63.

580   "The march has been taken over": See, for example, "Message to the Grass Roots," delivered by Malcolm X later in 1963, shortly before he left Elijah Muhammad's Nation of Islam: "It's just like when you've got some coffee that's too black, which means it's too strong. What do you do? You integrate it with cream, you make it weak. But if you pour too much cream in it, you won't even know you ever had coffee. It used to be hot, it becomes cool. It used to be strong, it becomes weak. It used to wake you up, now it puts you to sleep. This is what they did to the March on Washington. They joined it. They didn't integrate it, they infiltrated it. They joined it, became a part of it, took it

over. And as they took it over, it lost its militancy. It ceased to be angry, it ceased to be hot, it ceased to be uncompromising. Why, it even ceased to be a march. It became a picnic, a circus. Nothing but a circus, with clowns and all." Reprinted in *The Eyes on the Prize Civil Rights Reader* (New York: Viking Penguin, 1991), pp. 248–261.

580   to work with Randolph and Rustin: Garrow, *Bearing the Cross*, p. 280; Gentile, *March on Washington*, pp. 62–66, 146–147.

581   a switch that could cut off the power: Bruno conv; Gentile, *March on Washington*, p. 147.

581   The White House had set the date: Gentile, *March on Washington*, pp. 66–67, 133, 147.

581   "We will march through the South": Branch, *Parting the Waters*, pp. 873–874; Garrow, *Bearing the Cross*, pp. 281–282; Gentile, *March on Washington*, pp. 164–172.

581   Patrick Cardinal O'Boyle: Branch, *Parting the Waters*, pp. 874–875; Garrow, *Bearing the Cross*, pp. 282–283; Gentile, *March on Washington*, pp. 172–176.

582   frantically hailing cabs: Gentile, *March on Washington*, p. 195.

582   The first great cheer rose: This account of the proceedings of the March on Washington is drawn from Shuttlesworth OH, Howard; Wilkins OH, Howard; Wilkins OH, JFKL; WP, 8/29/63, 8/30/63; Murray Kempton, "The March on Washington," *New Republic*, 9/14/63; *Time*, 9/6/63; Branch, *Parting the Waters*, pp. 877–882; Garrow, *Bearing the Cross*, pp. 283–285; Gentile, *March on Washington*, pp. 184–253; and Oates, *Let the Trumpet Sound*, pp. 258–262. Motown released "The Great March on Washington" later in 1963; it is long out of print, but audiotapes of the March are in Martin Luther King, Jr., papers, BU, and video is available at the Kennedy Library.

584   "He's damned good": Branch, *Parting the Waters*, p. 883.

584   "Pass the Bill!": Gentile, *March on Washington*, p. 196.

584   "I have a dream": NYT, 8/29/63; Branch, *Parting the Waters*, p. 883; Gentile, *March on Washington*, p. 253.

585   "You made the difference": Audiotape 108.2, Presidential Recordings, JFKL (no transcript of this tape exists at the Kennedy Library).

Chapter 52

586   "You might want to ask him": Salinger int.

586   "Mr. President, the only hot war": JFKPP, 9/2/63.

588   In Saigon, Halberstam: Halberstam int.

588   Kennedy asked Fritz Nolting: Halberstam int.

588   "I think that guy is nuts": Taylor OH, LBJL.

588   "I'm the winning horse": Lodge cable to State, 9/7/63, FRUS 8–12/1963, Document 72, pp. 131–132.

588   "One of the more curious aspects": *Time*, 9/20/63.

589   "They represent the U.S. Government's attitude": Gibbons, *The U.S. Government and the Vietnam War*, p. 163.

589   "Roger? Who puts this stuff out": JFK-Hilsman telecon, 9/5/63, FRUS 8–12/1963, Document 61, pp. 111–112.

589   "CIA FINANCING PLANNED COUP": FRUS 8–12/1963, note 3 to p. 123; Mecklin, *Mission in Torment*, pp. 201–203.

589   "Change, or we'll string along with you": NYT, 9/4/63.

590   some tough telephone dialogue: Reston int.

590   "The lessons of the present crisis": NYT, 9/6/63.

590   "Favorable trends in all military activities": Taylor memo to JFK, undated, FRUS 8–12/1963, Document 53, pp. 98–99.

590   "Goal is that GVN have political support": Rusk cable to Lodge, 9/4/63, FRUS 8–12/1963, Document 59, pp. 108–109.

590   "As to 'political support' ": Lodge cable to State, 9/5/63, FRUS 8–12/1963, Document 60, pp. 109–110.

590   Rusk told him that he had opened: Memo of Conference with the President, 9/6/63, FRUS 8–12/1963, Document 66, pp. 117–120; Hilsman memo, 9/6/63, Vietnam

White House meeting memcons, Hilsman papers, JFKL, quoted in FRUS 8–12/1963, Editorial Note 67, p. 121.

591   a bottle of Three Feathers whiskey: Confidential dispatch, Time arch.

591   But McNamara could not get around Harriman: He almost did—he ordered Krulak to leave in ninety minutes, and Hilsman personally had to order the plane to wait until Mendenhall could get to the airport. Hilsman, *To Move a Nation*, p. 501.

592   "It is clear that at a minimum": Rusk cable to Lodge, 9/6/63, FRUS 8–12/1963, Document 70, pp. 128–129.

592   "Two-hour executive session": Hilsman, *To Move a Nation*, p. 506.

592   "This mandarin": Hilsman int.

592   "Mr. President, have you had any reason": JFKPP, 9/9/63.

593   "Hour and fifty minute conference": Lodge cable to State, 9/9/63, FRUS 8–12/1963, Document 77, pp. 140–143.

593   A parade of retired military men: *Time*, 9/6/63.

594   "You got your notes?": Mansfield int; O'Brien int.

594   "Dear Senator Mansfield and Senator Dirksen": JFKPP, 9/10/63.

594   "I do not read a manuscript very well": NYT, 9/11/63.

594   "I salute a great American": *Time*, 9/20/63.

595   they did not speak on the flight: Mecklin, *Mission in Torment*, pp. 206–207; Rust, *Kennedy in Vietnam*, pp. 134–135.

595   "Can do!": This account of the fractious September 10 meeting on Vietnam is drawn from Hilsman int; Memo of Conference with the President, 9/10/63, FRUS 8–12/1963, Document 83, pp. 161–167 (drafted by Hilsman); Memo of Conference with the President, 9/10/63, NSF Box 316, JFKL (drafted by Bromley Smith); Halberstam, *The Best and the Brightest*, pp. 339–342; and Mecklin, *Mission in Torment*, pp. 207–210.

596   When Krulak had seen that Mecklin was carrying: Rust, *Kennedy in Vietnam*, p. 83.

596   "I question the value": Lodge cable to State, 9/11/63, FRUS 8–12/1963, Document 86, pp. 171–174.

597   "Mr. Murrow asked that he be relieved": Memcon, 9/10/63, FRUS 8–12/1963, Document 85, pp. 169–171.

597   "The ship of state here": Lodge cable to State, 9/11/63.

597   "in view of the prevailing confusion": JFKPP, 9/12/63.

598   "the sending of Henry Cabot Lodge": JFKPP, 9/2/63.

598   "The evidence grows that elite": Lodge cable to State, 9/11/63. Bundy called Lodge's cable "one of his best," and told Forrestal it would "surely lead to the President calling a meeting on Vietnam during the day." Memo for the record, 9/11/63, FRUS 8–12/1963, Document 87, pp. 174–175. When JFK read Lodge's cable, he was indeed "personally inclined to think this assessment is the most powerful he has seen on this situation." Rusk-Bundy telecon, 9/11/63, FRUS 8–12/1963, Document 88, p. 176.

599   "Renewed efforts should be made": Lodge cable to State, 9/11/63.

599   "Your 478 is a major paper": JFK cable to Lodge, 9/12/63, FRUS 8–12/1963, Document 101, p. 202.

599   "Hope some study will be given": Lodge cable to State, 9/13/63, FRUS 8–12/1963, Document 102, p. 203.

599   a dozen sticks of dynamite exploded: NYT, 9/16/63; *Time*, 9/27/63.

600   "deep outrage": JFKPP, 9/15/63.

600   Kenneth Royall and Earl Blaik: NYT, 9/20/63; Branch, *Parting the Waters*, pp. 893–895. For more on Royall and Blaik's mission, see Earl Blaik OH, JFKL; Blaik memos to Marshall, 11/1/63, and to RFK, 11/18/63, both in Marshall papers, Box 18, JFKL; NYT, 10/11/63; and Branch, *Parting the Waters*, pp. 909–910. Recorded meetings held by President Kennedy after the Birmingham bombing include audiotapes 111.7 and 112.1, 9/19/63, with civil rights leaders; Audiotape 112.5, 9/23/63, with RFK and Burke Marshall; and Audiotapes 112.6 and 113.1, 9/23/63, with Birmingham civic leaders; all in Presidential Recordings, JFKL (no transcripts of these tapes exist at the Kennedy Library).

600   "I know that this bombing": Audiotape 112.1.

600   "Reconciliation" and "Pressures and Persuasion": Hilsman memo to Rusk, with plans attached, 9/16/63, FRUS 8–12/1963, Document 114, pp. 221–230.

601   "If the U.S. correctly has estimated": Attachment 2 to Hilsman memo to Rusk, 9/16/63.
601   "Meanwhile, there is increasing concern": JFK cable to Lodge, 9/17/63, FRUS 8–12/1963, Document 125, pp. 252–254.

Chapter 53

602   "These two men are opposed to our policy": Harriman-Forrestal telecon, 9/17/63, Harriman papers, LC.
602   "I know all this, Roger": Hilsman int.
603   "MINUTES OF THE NEXT HIGH-LEVEL MEETING": Schlesinger, *A Thousand Days*, pp. 993–995.
604   "Get General MacArthur to agree": O'Donnell and Powers, *"Johnny, We Hardly Knew Ye,"* p. 423.
604   "they will have to call on President Diem": Lodge cable to JFK, 9/18/63, FRUS 8–12/1963, Document 126, p. 255.
605   "I appreciate your prompt comment": JFK cable to Lodge, 9/18/63, FRUS 8–12/1963, Document 128, pp. 256–257.
605   "Believe it would be helpful": Lodge cable to JFK, 9/19/63, quoted in note 4 to FRUS 8–12/1963, Document 128.
605   "I doubt that a public relations package": Lodge cable to JFK, 9/19/63, FRUS 8–12/1963, Document 130, pp. 260–262.
605   "The job is to appraise": Memo for the record, 9/23/63, FRUS 8–12/1963, Document 146, pp. 284–287.
606   the Senate had just approved: *Time*, 9/27/63.
606   the county fairgrounds in Billings: JFKPP, 9/25/63; Mansfield int; Sander Vanocur, "Kennedy's Voyage of Discovery," *Harper's* (April 1964); Halberstam, *The Best and the Brightest*, p. 361.
606   "It took Brigham Young 108 days": JFKPP, 9/26/63; Vanocur, "Kennedy's Voyage of Discovery"; Halberstam, *The Best and the Brightest*, pp. 362–363.
607   "that was a great speech!": Press panel OH, p. 71, JFKL.
607   "I never know when I press": JFKPP, 9/27/63.
607   "I am taking advantage of": Hilsman letter to Lodge, 9/23/63, FRUS 8–12/1963, Document 144, pp. 282–283.
607   "The President emphasized": Memo for the Record, 9/23/63, FRUS 8–12/1963, Document 143, pp. 280–282.
608   pushed him away: Halberstam, *The Best and the Brightest*, p. 346.
608   he brought in Patrick Honey: Lodge, *The Storm Has Many Eyes*, p. 207.
608   "Diem has aged terribly": McNamara report on interview with "Professor Smith," 9/26/63, FRUS 8–12/1963, Document 150, pp. 293–295. "Professor Smith" is identifiable as Honey from Lodge's description of him in *The Storm Has Many Eyes*.
608   "Chinese, I suppose": *Time*, 10/4/63.
608   "It would be useful to work out": Memo for Record, 9/23/63.
609   met with President Diem: Memcon, 9/29/63, FRUS 8–12/1963, Document 158, pp. 310–321.
609   "What I must make clear": See supporting documents to the McNamara-Taylor Report, FRUS 8–12/1963, pp. 336–346.
609   "Diem ascribed all this": Memcon, 9/29/63.
610   Nguyen Ngoc Tho: Lodge transmitted a record of their conversation in a cable to JFK, 9/30/63, FRUS 8–12/1963, Document 159, pp. 321–323.
610n   "There is no organized government": McNamara to LBJ, 12/21/63, Vietnam Country File Box 1, LBJL.
611   "Where is your data": Halberstam int.
611   "I can't buy this": William Sullivan, OH 2, JFKL; Gibbons, *The U.S. Government and the Vietnam War*, p. 186.
612   "These pressures will push us": Memo of meeting, 10/3/63, FRUS 8–12/1963, Document 172, pp. 356–357.
612   "We are agreed to try to find": Summary Record of NSC meeting, 10/2/63, FRUS 8–12/1963, Document 169, pp. 350–352.

612 "The military campaign has made great progress": McNamara-Taylor Report to JFK, 10/2/63, USVNR, Book 12, pp. 554–573; FRUS 8–12/1963, Document 167, pp. 336–346.

613 "As of tonight, we have a policy": Summary Record of NSC meeting, 10/2/63.

614 "The security of South Viet-Nam": NSC Record of Action 2472, 10/2/63, FRUS 8–12/1963, Document 170, pp. 354–355; Salinger press briefing, 10/2/63, NSF Box 314, JFKL.

614 "Sensible and firm": *Time*, 10/11/63.

615 "That's just politics": Confidential dispatch, Time arch.

615 The President signed off: The meeting to discuss implementing the new policy was held on the morning of October 5. See memo for the files, 10/5/63, FRUS 8–12/1963, Document 179, pp. 368–370.

615 "These instructions have the President's personal approval": Rusk cable to Lodge, 10/5/63, FRUS 8–12/1963, Document 181, pp. 371–378. This document, classified until 1991, lays out the ways in which the administration planned to carry out the recommendations of the McNamara-Taylor Report in even greater detail than the memoranda of discussions that took place in Washington. See note 2 to p. 573, where the editors of FRUS correctly attribute several items in Lodge's instructions to Kennedy's personal concerns.

616 "The President thinks it": JFK cable to Lodge, 10/5/63, FRUS 8–12/1963, Document 180, p. 371.

616 "Gen. Minh stated that he must know": Saigon station cable to CIA, 10/5/63, FRUS 8–12/1963, Document 177, pp. 365–367.

617 "Assure him that US will not attempt": Lodge cable to State, 10/5/63, FRUS 8–12/1963, Document 178, pp. 367–368.

617 "No initiative should now be taken": Quoted in Bundy cable to Lodge, 10/5/63, FRUS 8–12/1963, Document 182, p. 379.

617 "In order to provide plausibility": Bundy cable to Lodge, 10/5/63, FRUS 8–12/1963, Document 182, p. 379.

617 "We do not set ourselves": Saigon station cable to CIA, 10/5/63, CC, p. 220.

617 "We certainly cannot be in the position": CIA cable to Saigon station, quoted in CC, p. 221.

618 "We are collecting information": CC, p. 221.

618 "McCone directs that you withdraw": CIA cable to Saigon station, 10/6/63, CC, p. 221.

618 "In its first two decades": JFKPP, 10/7/63.

618 "In an interview with Italian journalist": Lodge cable to State, 10/7/63, FRUS 8–12/1963, Document 186, pp. 385–386.

619 "What is this?": *Time*, 10/11/63.

619 "Aren't we at war with them?": Sorensen OH, p. 90, JFKL.

619 "I have considered it very carefully": JFKPP, 10/9/63.

620 "Assassination Lists": CIA Report TDCS-3/657, 250, 10/14/63, FRUS 8–12/1963, Document 196, pp. 398–401. Also, on October 9 the CIA distributed two intelligence cables, which stated that Nhu had plans to use a hundred agents in a student demonstration to kill Lodge and set the U.S. Embassy on fire. These cables remain classified. See note 2 to p. 394, FRUS 8–12/1963, Document 193.

620 "If I am assassinated": Lodge cable to Rusk and Harriman, 10/10/63, FRUS 8–12/1963, Document 193, pp. 394–395. McCone called Harriman after seeing this cable and said that all he had seen "were a few telegrams about assassination. . . . Lodge's reply seemed rather hysterical." Harriman said he would get on it. Note 3 to p. 395.

620 "The President approved": NSAM 263, 10/11/63, FRUS 8–12/1963, Document 194, pp. 395–396.

621 "Somebody's giving the boss some bad information": Gibbons, *The U.S. Government and the Vietnam War*, p. 194.

Chapter 54

622 "They're opening more loopholes": On JFK and Heller, see transcripts of Audiotapes 101.3, 7/25/63, and 110.3, 9/12/63, Presidential Recordings, JFKL; and CEA OH, JFKL.

622 571 pages of pro-business testimony: *Time*, 10/25/63.

623 "Let's take a fellow": Transcript of Audiotape 101.4, 7/29/63, Presidential Recordings, JFKL.

624 "I am absolutely for the tax cut": Transcripts of Dictabelts 25A.6 and 25B.1, 8/7/63, Presidential Recordings, JFKL.

624 he had to drop the reforms: Dillon int; CEA OH, JFKL.

624 "Timetable. The prospects": *Time*, 10/25/63.

625 Heller tried to cheer him up: Tobin int.

625 "It's just crazy": Transcript of Audiotape 101.4.

625 "What's the problem, now": Transcript of Audiotape 113.5, 9/30/63, Presidential Recordings, JFKL.

625 The civil rights bill scared O'Brien: O'Brien int.

626 "I don't know what 1964": JFKPP, 9/12/63.

626 were approved by Robert Kennedy: Withdrawal sheet for Hoover memo to RFK, 10/7/63, J. Edgar Hoover Official and Confidential File 100 (Martin Luther King, Jr.), FBI; Evans memos to Belmont, 10/10/63 and 10/21/63, J. Edgar Hoover Official and Confidential File 24 (Martin Luther King, Jr.), FBI. The first Evans memo relates Robert Kennedy's decision to tap King at his home in Atlanta, the second his approval for a wiretap on the SCLC's offices in New York.

626 Ellen Rometsch: See *Des Moines Register*, 10/26/63; WP, 10/29/63; Branch, *Parting the Waters*, pp. 911–914. Ellen Rometsch's FBI file, number 105-122316, contains many press clippings and several memos of specific interest, which are cited below.

627 he had been procrastinating on it: Just as Robert Kennedy had wavered in July, so too was "the Attorney General . . . apparently still vacillating in his position as to technical coverage on Martin Luther King and his organization" when Hoover requested authority for wiretaps in October. Evans memo to Belmont, 10/21/63.

RFK did approve the taps, on trial bases that became ongoing after President Kennedy's assassination. On its own, the bureau bugged King as well, recording "King during his travels to Washington, D.C., Milwaukee, Honolulu, Los Angeles, Detroit, San Francisco, and Savannah." In March 1964, the FBI delivered a memo to RFK summarizing the highlights of its voyeuristic coverage of King. Sullivan memo, 4/9/68, J. Edgar Hoover Official and Confidential File 24 (Martin Luther King, Jr.), FBI. Throughout 1964, the bureau attempted to discredit King by leaking information obtained through its bugs to the press—and tried to scare the civil rights leader by mailing a tape recording to him personally, along with bureau-crafted hate mail. This phase of the FBI's surveillance of King lasted until April 30, 1965. Sullivan memo, 4/9/68; Hoover memo to Mitchell, 6/10/69, J. Edgar Hoover Official and Confidential File 100 (Martin Luther King, Jr.), FBI; Garrow, *The FBI and Martin Luther King, Jr.*, pp. 101–150.

627 "An unprincipled man . . . ": Hoover memo to Tolson, et al., 10/25/63; note to Hoover, 10/28/63; both in J. Edgar Hoover Official and Confidential File 24 (Martin Luther King, Jr.), FBI; Branch, *Parting the Waters*, p. 911.

628 "I thought of Baker primarily": Bradlee, *Conversations with Kennedy*, p. 215.

628 arranged a secret meeting: See Evans memo to Belmont, 10/28/63; Hoover memos to Tolson, et al., 10/28/63 (11:11 A.M. and 3:05 P.M.); and especially Hoover memo to Tolson, et al., 11/7/63; all in file 105-122316 (Ellen Rometsch), FBI; Branch, *Parting the Waters*, pp. 911–914.

628 added a series of tough new provisions: *Time*, 11/1/63.

629 "What the hell is this?": RFK OH, JFKL.

629 Everyone had their lines: Katzenbach OH, pp. 159–169, JFKL.

629 "When I hear that": *Time*, 11/1/63.

630 "We can't let this happen": O'Brien int.

630 "The colored vote": Charles Halleck OH, pp. 9–14, JFKL.

630 "Roland Libonati is sticking it": Transcript of Dictabelt 28A.2, 10/28/63, Presidential Recordings, JFKL.

631   "You did a great job": O'Brien int.
631   President Tito: This account of Marshal Tito's visit to America is drawn from Duke int; Duke OH, pp. 43–45, JFKL; Kennan OH, pp. 83–85, 96–105, 115–119, JFKL; Schlesinger notes of Kennan interview, undated, Schlesinger papers, Box W-14, JFKL; and *Time,* 10/25/63, 11/1/63.
632   He allowed photographers: Kaysen OH, p. 99, JFKL.

Chapter 55

635   "Recent developments convey": CIA Report TDCS-3/657, 250, 10/14/63. A covering note from Forrestal to Bundy indicates Kennedy got the report on October 16 or 17.
635   "People here are wondering": Text of Nhu interview in *The Times of Vietnam,* 10/19/63, attachment to Document 204, FRUS 8–12/1963, pp. 416–418.
636   "When we were seated off to one side": Lodge cable to State, 10/19/63, FRUS 8–12/1963, Document 203, p. 414.
636   "Best estimates in Saigon": *Time,* 10/25/63.
636   "I wish like hell": Reston int; Harrison Salisbury, *Without Fear or Favor: The Story of the New York Times* (New York: Times Books, 1980), pp. 133–134.
636   "A review indicates that he is": CIA memo, "David Halberstam's Reporting on South Vietnam," 9/26/63, quoted in FRUS 8–12/1963. See also FRUS 8–12/1963, editorial note 117, p. 237, which points out that Kennedy asked McNamara about Halberstam's September 16 story: "How accurate is this[?] . . . Is there a split between our military and the Vietnamese on the strategic hamlets in this area[?]"
637   already preparing to come home: Reston int.
637   "Well, obviously we can't do": Halberstam int.
637   "The only way to confound the press": Memo for the record, 9/23/63.
637   "Are we gaining or losing": JFK's initial message and request for weekly reports is in his cable to Lodge, 10/14/63, FRUS 8–12/1963, Document 195, pp. 396–397.
637   "We appear to me to be doing": Lodge cable to JFK, 10/16/63, FRUS 8–12/1963, Document 197, pp. 401–403.
638   "Control and cut-out": Bundy cable to Lodge and Harkins, 10/24/63, FRUS 8–12/1963, Document 211, pp. 429–430.
638   "I appreciate the concern": Lodge cable to Bundy, 10/25/63, FRUS 8–12/1963, Document 216, pp. 434–436.
638   "A Presidential directive": Bundy cable to Lodge and Harkins, 10/24/63.
638   "All right, you don't like it": CC, p. 221.
638   "We should not thwart": Lodge cable to Bundy, 10/25/63.
639   "President wants you to know": Bundy cable to Lodge, 10/25/63, FRUS 8–12/1963, Document 217, p. 437.
639   "Diem is very likeable": Lodge cable to State, 10/28/63, FRUS 8–12/1963, Document 221, pp. 442–445.
639   "Does Conein speak for you?": Lodge cable to State, 10/28/63, FRUS 8–12/1963, Document 224, p. 449; CC, p. 222.
640   General Don questioned Conein: Rust, *Kennedy in Vietnam,* pp. 157–158.
640   "It would appear that a coup attempt": Lodge cable to State, 10/29/63, FRUS 8–12/1963, Document 226, pp. 453–455.
640   Tran Trung Dung: Lodge cable to State, 10/29/63, FRUS 8–12/1963, Document 229, pp. 457–459.
640   "the complete removal of the Ngo family": Lodge cable to State, 10/29/63.
640   At four o'clock on the afternoon: The account of this meeting is drawn from the following sources: Hilsman int; Bundy memo to JFK, 10/29/63, FRUS 8–12/1963, Document 233, p. 467; Memo of Conference with the President, 10/29/63, 4:20 P.M., FRUS 8–12/1963, Document 234, pp. 468–471; William Colby, *Honorable Men* (New York: Simon & Schuster, 1978), p. 216; Hilsman, *To Move a Nation,* pp. 518–519; and Schlesinger, *Robert Kennedy and His Times,* p. 778.
641   "The burden of proof": Memo of Conference with the President, 10/29/63, 6:00 P.M., FRUS 8–12/1963, Document 235, pp. 472–473.

641 "Need urgently your combined assessment": Bundy cable to Lodge, 10/29/63, FRUS 8–12/1963, Document 236, pp. 473–475.

642 "I sat with Don and Big Minh": Harkins cable to Taylor, 10/30/63, FRUS 8–12/1963, Document 240, pp. 479–482.

642 "We must, of course, get best": Lodge cable to State, 10/30/63, FRUS 8–12/1963, Document 242, pp. 484–488.

642 "Thanks for your sagacious instruction": Quoted in note 6 to p. 502, FRUS 8–12/1963, from a cable that remains otherwise classified.

642 "He sounds amused": RFK OH, JFKL.

643 "We do not accept as a basis": Bundy cable to Lodge, 10/30/63, FRUS 8–12/1963, Document 249, pp. 500–502.

643 "Well, as you know": JFKPP, 10/31/63.

644 a coup d'état was under way: Gibbons, *The U.S. Government and the Vietnam War*, pp. 200–201; Rust, *Kennedy in Vietnam*, pp. 161–167.

644 "At 1345 Hours General Don": Harkins cable to National Security Agency, 11/1/63, FRUS 8–12/1963, Document 251, p. 505.

645 "Generals attempting contact": This message and the three that follow are all in Saigon CIA station cable to National Security Agency, 11/1/63, FRUS 8–12/1963, Documents 252, 256, 257, 258, pp. 505–506, 511–512.

645 "Some units have made a rebellion": Lodge cable to State, 11/1/63, FRUS 8–12/1963, Document 259, p. 513.

646 "I know there is going to be": Rust, *Kennedy in Vietnam*, p. 162.

646 " 'The Palace notified me' ": Lodge cable to State, 11/1/63, FRUS 8–12/1963, Document 262, pp. 516–517.

647 "If coup succeeds, recognition problem": Rusk cable to Lodge, 11/1/63, FRUS 8–12/1963, Document 264, pp. 519–520.

647 "I can categorically state": NYT, 11/2/63.

647 "If coup succeeds, acceptance and understanding": Rusk cable to Lodge, 11/1/63, FRUS 8–12/1963, Document 266, p. 521.

648 "General Minh has accepted this": Note 2 to p. 525, FRUS 8–12/1963.

648 But only two minutes later: Note 3 to p. 525, FRUS 8–12/1963, referring to MACV CRITIC 5, 11/2/63.

648 "At 9:15 Washington time tomorrow": Rusk cable to Lodge, 11/1/63, FRUS 8–12/1963, Document 269, pp. 525–526.

648 "Agree we should move promptly": Lodge cable to State, 11/2/63, FRUS 8–12/1963, Document 270, pp. 526–527.

648 "Best estimate this time": Note 2 to p. 527, FRUS 8–12/1963.

648 "News of Diem, Nhu suicides": Rusk cable to Lodge, 11/2/1963, FRUS 8–12/1963, Document 271, p. 527.

649 "Very reliable source": Lodge cable to State, 11/2/1963, FRUS 8–12/1963, Document 273, pp. 531–533.

649 looking pale and shaken: See editorial note 274 to p. 533, FRUS 8–12/1963; Schlesinger, *A Thousand Days*, pp. 998–999; Taylor, *Swords and Plowshares*, p. 301.

649 "What did he expect?": Taylor OH, LBJL; Taylor, *Swords and Plowshares*, p. 233. See also Thomas Powers, *The Man Who Kept the Secrets*, p. 165; Rust, *Kennedy in Vietnam*, pp. 175–176.

649 a cemetery next to the house: Rust, *Kennedy in Vietnam*, p. 174.

649 "Young Vietnamese Saigon businessman": Saigon CIA station cable to National Security Agency, 11/3/63, FRUS 8–12/1963, Document 283, p. 545.

650 "accidental suicide": Rust, *Kennedy in Vietnam*, p. 174.

650 "We can't hold them that long": Rust, *Kennedy in Vietnam*, p. 171.

650 "Champion! Excellent prose": Halberstam, *The Best and the Brightest*, p. 51.

650 "All missions": Rusk circular cable to all diplomatic posts, 11/2/63, FRUS 8–12/1963, Document 277, p. 536.

650 "The only surprising thing": NYT, 11/2/63.

650 "Deaths of Diem and Nhu": Bundy cable to Lodge, 11/2/1963, FRUS 8–12/1963, Document 278, p. 537.

651 "They were just tyrants": Bradlee int.

651   "The loss of South Vietnam": NYT, 11/3/63.
651   "Saigon Coup Gives Americans Hope": NYT, 11/4/63.
651   "Now that the revolution has occurred": Lodge cable to JFK, 11/6/63, FRUS 8–12/1963, Document 302, pp. 575–578.
652   "Your own leadership": JFK cable to Lodge, 11/6/63, FRUS 8–12/1963, Document 304, pp. 579–580.

Chapter 56

653   "A warm approach to the public": Lodge cable to State, 11/8/63, FRUS 8–12/1963, Document 307, pp. 586–588.
654   "The President thought the whole incident": *Time,* 11/15/63.
654   "This is one of the really beautiful places": Bartlett int, McNamara int.
654   "We could go back to the South Pacific": Draft manuscript of Fay, *The Pleasure of His Company,* Land papers, Box 12, BU.
655   "Oh, my God": *Time,* 11/15/63.
655   for his reelection campaign: The account given of President Kennedy's first and only 1964 campaign meeting is drawn from the following sources: Scammon int; Stephen Smith int; Stephen Smith memo to JFK, et al., 11/13/63, RFK papers, JFKL; O'Donnell and Powers, *"Johnny, We Hardly Knew Ye,"* pp. 383–384; Schlesinger, *Robert Kennedy and His Times,* pp. 650–651; and Theodore S. White, *The Making of the President 1964* (New York: Atheneum, 1965); pp. 13–15.
     For more on the impending politics of 1964, see *Time,* 4/12/63, 6/14/63, 7/26/63, 8/2/63, 8/23/63, 9/20/63, 10/4/63, 10/25/63, and 11/1/63. A Charles Bartlett analysis of the prospects of Republican Governor George Romney, undated, is in Sorensen papers, Box 36, JFKL. Memos beginning preparation for the 1964 Democratic Convention are in Sorensen papers, Box 28, JFKL. Opinion polls organized or observed by the White House are in POF Box 105, JFKL. Barry Goldwater confirms that he and JFK briefly discussed campaigning together against each other: "We had a very brief conversation one day, when we felt we would be running against each other. The subject of campaigning across the country, out of one airplane, and having an old-fashioned debate at each stop, was brought up, but that's about as far as it ever went." Goldwater letter to the author, 8/9/88.
655   "JFK is totally dedicated": *ADA World* (October 1963).
656   "You have to be a little suspicious": Draft manuscript of Fay, *The Pleasure of His Company,* Land papers, Box 12, BU.
656   a "crash program": JFKPP, 11/13/63. For more on the administration's proposed aid to eastern Kentucky, see Sorensen memo, "Notes on a Crash Program for Eastern Kentucky," 10/30/63; Sorensen memos to JFK, 11/6/63 and 11/13/63; Franklin D. Roosevelt, Jr., memos to Sorensen, 10/25/63 and 11/20/63; and Gordon memo to Sorensen, 11/13/63; all in Sorensen papers, Box 37, JFKL. Other supporting memos can also be found in Sorensen papers, Box 37, JFKL. See also Lee White memo to LBJ, 11/23/63, Sorensen papers, Box 36, JFKL.
     On poverty, see Udall OH, p. 64, JFKL; Heller notes on meetings with JFK, 10/21/63 and especially 11/19/63; Heller papers, Box 6, JFKL; Heller memo to Sorensen, 11/20/63, Sorensen papers, Box 31, JFKL.
656   "The welfare system": Homer Bigart, "Kentucky Miners: A Grim Winter," NYT, 10/18/63.
656   "There's a tremendous problem": Heller, Notes on Meeting with the President, 10/21/63, Heller papers, Box 6, JFKL.
656   "I wouldn't do that": Scammon int.
657   "The Polish are fantastic": Transcript of Audiotape 101.4.
657   "Massachusetts has given us": O'Donnell and Powers, *"Johnny, We Hardly Knew Ye,"* p. 439.
657   "how menacing do you regard": JFKPP, 11/14/63.
658   "He has been lucky": James Reston, "The Outlook for Kennedy: Victory with Tears," NYT, 11/15/63.
658   Kennedy was just clobbered: NYT, 11/16/63, 11/17/63.

659   "Goddamnit, George": Ball int.
659   "There is a good deal": JFKPP, 11/18/63.
659   interested in normalizing relations: See William Atwood OH, JFKL; CC, pp. 173–174; Jean Daniel, "Unofficial Envoy: Historic Report from Two Capitals," *New Republic,* 12/14/63.
660   "This and this alone divides us": JFKPP, 11/20/63.
660   still recruiting assassins: CC, pp. 86–89, 170–176. The CIA Inspector-General's Report of 1967 concluded that "it is likely that at the very moment President Kennedy was shot, a CIA officer was meeting with a Cuban agent . . . and giving him an assassination device for use against Castro." CC, p. 89.
660   a nine-hour conference: See memcon, 11/20/63, FRUS 8–12/1963, Document 321, pp. 608–624.
660   "It remains the central object": NSAM-273, FRUS 8–12/1963, Document 331, pp. 637–640.
660   "Wait a minute": Rust, *Kennedy in Vietnam,* pp. 3–5.
661   On Friday morning, November 22: The events of Kennedy's final day in Dallas are recounted in Manchester, *Death of a President,* pp. 108–133.
662   "the burdens of leadership": JFKPP, 11/22/63.

Bibliographic Essay

For 150 years after the founding of the Republic, most American presidents took whatever papers they had with them when they left office. Sheer fortune dictated whether their records survived and if or when their heirs would eventually donate them to a public archive. Abraham Lincoln's papers, for example, did not become public until 1949.

Franklin Roosevelt changed things in 1939, when he had his own library built at his Hyde Park, New York, home, put his papers in it, and then gave it to the federal government to manage. Congress incorporated this model into law in 1955, passing legislation that empowered the National Archives to run presidential libraries if presidents donated their papers to them. Herbert Hoover, Harry Truman, Dwight Eisenhower, John Kennedy, and Lyndon Johnson all agreed to follow such a system, and as a result the John F. Kennedy Library is formally governed by the National Archives and Records Administration.

In 1974, Congress passed further legislation declaring all official presidential papers to be government property, in an attempt to stop Richard Nixon from destroying documents from his years in office. Nixon's papers were seized and placed under the control of the National Archives; they remain in a warehouse in Alexandria, Virginia, rather than at the Nixon Library, while the ex-President continues to battle the federal government for custody of them. Through 1993, legal decisions have favored Nixon, and the outcome is important, because Congress altered the system again in 1978 to its current state. Presidents can now send their papers to libraries, but must deposit all of their official records in such archives. The Ronald Reagan Library was the first to be covered by this law, and the definition of exactly what constitutes "official" papers hangs in the balance of the Nixon court cases.

The Kennedy Library began collecting papers before 1978, however, so the current law has no standing there. Instead, the National Archives and Records Administration is obligated to manage the Kennedy Library as an amalgam of donated papers and records of federal agencies from the Kennedy years. For researchers, this creates obstacles that can be quite intimidating upon first encounter, but which can be overcome.

For example, the Kennedy family was able to give whatever it liked to the Library, under whatever terms it wished to set. (One result: Joseph P. Kennedy, Sr.'s, papers never have been deeded to the Library.) Further, when the family have donated material, they have placed severe limitations on documents regarding all personal, family, and business affairs of President Kennedy and his relatives. The Kennedys have waived these restrictions only for a few particular researchers. When Library archivists review papers for release to all other scholars, they must therefore hold back references to John Kennedy's medical and financial records or his personal correspondence.

Kennedy Library officials are on record as supporting these restrictions. Will Johnson, the library's Chief Archivist, has said that "the President's (or any other person's) most intimate personal letters, inadvertently recorded conversations with his wife and children, certain medical and financial records, and his sex life are not legitimate matters of public examination during the lifetime of any of those involved, except to the degree that the actors themselves choose to make them so."

But while official reticence increases the time and costs involved in obtaining personal information on Kennedy, it does not seal facts away forever. Research for this work, for example, combined extensive interviews with records kept outside the Kennedy Library and accounts in newspapers and medical journals to establish JFK's Addison's disease and his connection to Dr. Max Jacobson.

Even when it comes to material not donated by the Kennedy family, the Kennedy Library, more than other presidential archives, mingles history with memorial. In 1963, Arthur Schlesinger and Ted Sorensen had discussed ideas for developing a White House History of the Kennedy years and assembling JFK's papers. After Kennedy's assassination, these plans became the building blocks for a monument to the slain President, as his men rounded up donors of materials and interviewees for an oral history project for the Library. Many of the interviews were conducted by Kennedy intimates shortly after the President's death and suffer greatly in perspective as a result. Taken as a whole, the oral history collection is invaluable, but researchers would be well advised to follow up by consulting later oral sources and conducting interviews of their own.

Further, hundreds of the Library's oral history interviews have remained unprocessed for years, as for whatever reasons of deed or paperwork the Kennedy Library does not technically own them. (At last count, 902 oral histories out of a total of about 1,100 have been opened.) Since 1990, researchers have been able to obtain a list of these interviews from the Library in order to contact the subjects directly for permission to read them, and this book has made use of dozens of the unlisted oral histories.

Scholars studying the Kennedy years must also contend with so-called national security restrictions on documents, which prevent the declassification of material on the grounds that its release would injure the vital interests of the United States. Again, these can appear overwhelming at first, but much can be overcome through dogged research.

Millions of documents are classified by the U.S. government each year, stamped "confidential," "secret," or "top secret," or with words that are themselves secret to denote a classification level above that of "top secret." The agency originating a document has the authority to decide on its level of classification, and it can then be declassified only with that agency's approval.

A basic problem with this is that it is far easier to classify than to declassify a document. Papers can be made secret for the flimsiest of reasons, including a simple desire to impress their intended recipients. On the other hand, asking an agency to reconsider its classification of a document, which is known as making a "mandatory review request," is a process that can take years, and one which grew more difficult after a 1982 executive order by President Reagan tightened secrecy controls on federal documents even further.

Moreover, while a document can be classified with a single stamp from an inkpad, agencies will almost never act in the opposite direction if it entails the release of embarrassing facts from their own past. For this reason, orders from Presidents Nixon and Carter to make declassification easier were largely ignored in the 1970s by the Departments of State and Defense and the CIA. A major controversy erupted as recently as 1990 when the State Department managed to print a *Foreign Relations of the United States* series on Iran from 1951 to 1954 without including any documents that mentioned the CIA's leading role in the 1953 coup that installed the Shah there. "Nothing personal, but they live off secrecy," said U.S. Senator Daniel Patrick Moynihan of the various intelligence agencies in May 1993. "Secrecy keeps the mistakes secret."

As a result, 325 million pages of documents are classified at the National Archives alone, and hundreds of millions more are at the 80,000 other government depositories that hold classified material. No one knows the total number of documents, or classified programs, or secrets, that are under wraps at federal agencies. Some documents have been kept secret since World War I.

Finally, documents can be censored for ridiculous reasons—there is little accountability in the world of top secrets. As one small example, when the Irish poet Brendan Behan sent President Kennedy a magazine article, he scrawled across the top, "Proud to be your lantsman." The remark was "sanitized," or blacked out, before the document was released at the Kennedy Library.

So, whether from the poor design of the classification laws, political embarrassment, overload, or the irrationality of the culture of secrecy, many historical documents are withheld on national security grounds for no valid reason. But there are ways for researchers to fight this problem.

The most important is relentless persistence in declassification requests, as most federal agencies do what they can to keep up with public demand. The State Department released Dean Acheson's 1961 report on Berlin to President Kennedy for use in this work, for instance, after months of requests to their Freedom of Information unit. Researchers are advised to join the National Security Archive, a non-profit institution in Washington, D.C., that has had marked success in using Freedom of Information lawsuits to obtain the release of classified documents from government organizations. The archive also acts as a clearinghouse, saving scholars time by coordinating the research finds of its members. This is especially important because agencies release documents to one researcher at a time, forcing those who work independently to repeat laborious procedures to obtain the same material.

Researchers should keep in mind that large government organizations handle decisions to classify and release documents, and must try to exploit various bureaucratic patterns for information breakthroughs. A few that crop up repeatedly include:

• Companion documents. Often an agency will keep a report secret but declassify a helpful attachment. For instance, a July 7, 1961, memo from Henry Kissinger to JFK on the strategic war plan remains classified, but the plan is actually described by McGeorge Bundy in a covering note that is now available.

• Irregular sanitization. If more than one agency possesses a document, each may process it differently. Bundy's memo to Kennedy of July 19, 1961, on that afternoon's Berlin meetings, for example, is available in NSF Box 81 and in NSF Box 313 at the Kennedy Library. One version has four paragraphs blacked out; the other is fully readable.

• Standard operating procedures. Agencies often obey their own habits rather than recorded orders. Thus, although President Kennedy ordered the State Department to destroy all memos from the week following the August 24, 1963, cable to Vietnam, one copy of each document was filed with the department's executive secretary anyway, and these are now available.

Finally, researchers must intensively seek documentary sources alternative to official archives. On occasion, persons interested in preserving history will have kept records that surpass those which government agencies allow to be declassified. Averell Harriman's papers, for example, provided this work with considerable detail that had been sanitized from State Department records.

On balance, then, despite various restrictions, recent research has added an enormous amount of material to the accepted history of the Kennedy years. Most significant are new documents on Berlin, Kennedy's correspondence with Khrushchev, Kennedy's health, Operation Mongoose, and Vietnam.

A split between favorable coverage by writers with access to President Kennedy and criticism by those who were suspicious of his "news management" became evident almost as soon as the Kennedy presidency began, in the aftermath of Robert McNamara's February 1961 admission and retraction of the fact that the missile gap did not exist. Nevertheless, magazine and book coverage of the President between 1961 and 1963 was on balance overwhelmingly favorable to him, as hundreds of pieces appeared on everything about Kennedy: his politics, his family, his wartime experience, even his clothing.

By far the most important of these are Theodore S. White's enormously influential *The Making of the President 1960* (New York: Atheneum, 1961), and Hugh Sidey, *John F. Kennedy, President* (New York: Atheneum, 1963), for which Kennedy provided several long interviews. The first and only sustained attack on Kennedy during his lifetime came in late 1963 with Victor Lasky's *JFK: The Man and the Myth* (New York: Macmillan, 1963), a blast at Kennedy's image that ran to nearly six hundred pages. *JFK: The Man and the Myth*, based mostly on newspaper and magazine research, became a best-seller but was panned by reviewers. It quickly went out of print after Kennedy's assassination, and holds up poorly today.

Kennedy's death was followed by a wave of reverence that created and cemented the Camelot myth. JFK was enshrined as war hero, family man, and world leader: he became a symbol of toughness and peace, hopeful idealism and realistic political sense, brilliant intelligence and compassion, grace and salty good humor, all at once. The essential works of the Kennedy canon appeared in 1965: Arthur M. Schlesinger, Jr.'s, *A Thousand Days: John F. Kennedy in the White House* (Boston: Houghton Mifflin, 1965), and Theodore C. Sorensen's *Kennedy* (New York: Harper & Row, 1965). Together, these books defined the standard history of the Kennedy administration as a story of the President's growth through crisis toward ever greater wisdom.

The twin pillars of Schlesinger and Sorensen were buttressed by a spate of books by Kennedy friends and officials throughout the decade following his death. Most of these books did not pretend to be objective, many were best-sellers, and some are still valuable for the insights they offer into particular events. These include Paul B. Fay, *The Pleasure of His Company* (New York: Harper & Row, 1966); Goddard Lieberson and Joan Meyers, eds., *John Fitzgerald Kennedy . . . As We Remember Him* (New York and Philadelphia: Courage Books, 1965), a coffee table book whose pictures are captioned with quotes from Kennedy intimates; Evelyn Lincoln, *My Twelve Years with John F. Kennedy* (New York: McKay, 1965); Kenneth P. O'Donnell and David F. Powers, with Joe McCarthy, *"Johnny, We Hardly Knew Ye"* (New York: Pocket Books, 1972); and Pierre Salinger, *With Kennedy* (New York: Doubleday, 1966).

More recent favorable accounts of the administration include Ralph G. Martin, *A Hero for Our Time: An Intimate Story of the Kennedy Years* (New York: Macmillan, 1983); Kenneth W. Thompson, ed., *The Kennedy Presidency: Seventeen Intimate Perspectives of John F. Kennedy* (Lanham, MD: University Press of America, 1985); and Irving Bernstein, *Promises Kept: John F. Kennedy's New Frontier* (New York: Oxford University Press, 1991).

The Pentagon Papers, leaked to *The New York Times* in 1971, made public for the first time how uncertainly yet deeply the Kennedy administration became entangled in Vietnam; the version that best combines clarity with a full look at the documents is the Senator Gravel edition (Boston: Beacon Press, 1971), 5 vols. And in 1975, the Church Committee of the U.S. Senate ripped the lid off covert operations of the Kennedy era, including the plots to assassinate Fidel Castro and the CIA's alliance with mobsters. The Committee's report is confusingly organized but essential for its substance, and was published as *Alleged Assassination Plots Involving Foreign Leaders: Interim Report of the Select Committee to Study Governmental Operations with Respect to Intelligence Activities* (New York: W. W. Norton, 1976). The Church Committee's investigations also led to the exposure of Judith Campbell Exner, the first woman to go public with tales of Kennedy's extra-marital sex life. Exner's book, *My Story* (New York: Grove Press, 1977), was controversial upon publication, but its essential details have been confirmed.

These sources contributed to a stream of revisionist evaluations of the Kennedy presidency. They include Henry Fairlie, *The Kennedy Promise: The Politics of Expectation* (Garden City, NY: Doubleday, 1973); Lewis J. Paper, *The Promise and the Performance: The Leadership of John F. Kennedy* (New York: Crown, 1975); Garry Wills, *The Kennedy Imprisonment: A Meditation on Power* (Boston: Little, Brown, 1982); and Peter Collier and David Horowitz, *The Kennedys* (New York: Summit Books, 1984). Benjamin C. Bradlee's *Conversations with Kennedy* (New York: W. W. Norton, 1975), featuring a Kennedy who in private was humorous but could be brutal, petty, and vulgar, was presented as a personal memoir but actually fits into this group of critical works.

In a pattern that resembles the study of many presidencies, recent Kennedy scholarship has started to move beyond strident revisionism as well as pure adulation. Balanced assessments of the administration include Herbert S. Parmet, *JFK: The Presidency of John F. Kennedy* (New York: Dial Press, 1983); Thomas Brown, *JFK: History of an Image* (Bloomington, IN: University of Indiana Press, 1988); Michael R. Beschloss, *The Crisis Years: Kennedy and Khrushchev, 1960–1963* (New York: HarperCollins, 1991); and James N. Giglio, *The Presidency of John F. Kennedy* (Lawrence, KS: University Press of Kansas, 1991).

Worthwhile memoirs and biographies of leading figures of the Kennedy administration include: Rudy Abramson, *Spanning the Century: The Life of W. Averell Harriman* (New York: William Morrow, 1992); George Ball, *The Past Has Another Pattern: Memoirs* (New York: W. W. Norton, 1982); Douglas Brinkley, *Dean Acheson: The Cold War Years 1953–71* (New Haven, CT: Yale University Press, 1992); Kenneth S. Davis, *The Politics of Honor: A Biography of Adlai E. Stevenson* (New York: G. P. Putnam's Sons, 1967); John Kenneth Galbraith, *Ambassador's Journal* (Boston: Houghton Mifflin, 1969), and *A Life in Our Times: A Memoir* (Boston: Houghton Mifflin, 1981); Richard N. Goodwin, *Remembering America: A Voice from the Sixties* (Boston: Little, Brown, 1988); Edwin O. Guthman, *We Band of Brothers* (New York: Harper & Row, 1971); Roger Hilsman, *The Politics of Foreign Policy in the Administration of John F. Kennedy* (Garden City, NY: Doubleday, 1967); Walter Isaacson and Evan Thomas, *The Wise Men: Six Friends and the World They Made* (New York: Simon & Schuster, 1986); Doris Kearns, *Lyndon Baines Johnson and the American Dream* (New York: Harper & Row, 1976); Henry Cabot Lodge, *The Storm Has Many Eyes: A Personal Narrative* (New York: W. W. Norton, 1973); John Bartlow Martin, *Adlai Stevenson and the World* (New York: Doubleday, 1977); Walt W. Rostow, *The Diffusion of Power: An Essay in Recent History* (New York: Macmillan, 1972); Dean Rusk, *As I Saw It* (New York: W. W. Norton, 1990); Arthur M. Schlesinger, Jr., *Robert Kennedy and His Times* (New York: Random House, 1978); Thomas J. Schoenbaum, *Waging Peace and War: Dean Rusk in the Truman, Kennedy, and Johnson Years* (New York: Simon & Schuster, 1988); Deborah Shapley, *Promise and Power: The Life and Times of Robert McNamara* (Boston: Little, Brown, 1993); Maxwell Taylor, *Swords and Plowshares* (New York: W. W. Norton, 1972); and Harris Wofford, *Of Kennedys and Kings* (New York: Farrar, Straus & Giroux, 1980).

Essential books by and about foreign leaders of the early 1960s include: Willy Brandt, *People and Politics: The Years 1960–1975* (London: Collins, 1978); Charles de Gaulle, *Memoirs: Renewal, 1958–1962* (London: Weidenfeld & Nicolson, 1971); Alistair Horne, *Macmillan: 1957–1986* (London: Macmillan, 1989); Harold Macmillan, *Pointing the Way: 1959–1961* (New York: Harper & Row, 1972), and *At the End of the Day* (New York: Harper & Row, 1973); and Strobe Talbott, ed., *Khrushchev Remembers* (Boston: Little, Brown, 1970, 1974), 2 vols.

On the Bay of Pigs, see Peter Wyden, *Bay of Pigs: The Untold Story* (New York: Simon & Schuster, 1979). *Operation Zapata: The "Ultrasensitive" Report and Testimony of the Board of Inquiry on the Bay of Pigs* (Frederick, MD: University Publications of America, 1981), which contains the Taylor Report and minutes of the meetings that led to it, is an essential primary source. Lyman Kirkpatrick, "Paramilitary Study—The Bay of Pigs," *Naval War College Review* (November–December 1972), is an important article reflecting the findings of the CIA's inspector-general. A good supplementary work is Trumbull Higgins, *The Perfect Failure: Kennedy, Eisenhower, and the CIA at the Bay of Pigs* (New York: W. W. Norton, 1987). Haynes Johnson, *The Bay of Pigs: The Leaders' Story of Brigade 2506* (New York: Dell, 1964), is an early, vivid account of the invasion from the perspective of the exile leaders.

The Berlin crisis is treated with great depth by Honoré M. Catudal in *Kennedy and the Berlin Wall Crisis: A Case Study in U.S. Decision-Making* (West Berlin: Berlin-Verlag, 1980). Other crucial sources include Robert M. Slusser, *The Berlin Crisis of 1961: Soviet-American Relations and the Struggle in the Kremlin, June–November, 1961* (Baltimore: Johns Hopkins University Press, 1973); Curtis Cate, *The Ides of August: The Berlin Crisis, 1961* (New York: Evans, 1978); and Peter Wyden, *Wall: The Inside Story of Divided Berlin* (New York: Simon & Schuster, 1989).

Several works not already listed contain good accounts of strategic and nuclear issues, including McGeorge Bundy, *Danger and Survival: Choices About the Bomb in the First Fifty Years* (New York: Random House, 1988); John Prados, *The Soviet Estimate: U.S. Intelligence Analysis and Russian Military Strength* (New York: Dial Press, 1982); and Scott Sagan, "SIOP-62," *International Security* (Summer 1987), which first published and discussed the nuclear war plan in effect under Kennedy.

American intelligence is detailed in John Ranelagh, *The Agency: The Rise and Decline of the CIA from Wild Bill Donovan to William Casey* (New York: Simon & Schuster, 1986). Also important is Thomas Powers, *The Man Who Kept the Secrets: Richard Helms and the CIA* (New York: Knopf, 1979). On counterinsurgency, the most important source is the collection of documents relating to Operation Mongoose that comprises part of the National Security Archive's Cuban missile crisis papers. See also Michael McClintock, *Instruments of Statecraft: U.S. Guerilla Warfare, Counterinsurgency, Counterterrorism, 1940–1990* (New York: Pantheon, 1992), and Douglas S. Blaufarb, *The Counterinsurgency Era: U.S. Doctrine and Performance, 1950 to the Present* (New York: Free Press, 1977). CIA memoirs include William Colby and Peter Forbath, *Honorable Men: My Life in the CIA* (New York: Simon & Schuster, 1978); Allen Dulles, *The Craft of Intelligence* (Westport, CT: Greenwood Press, 1977); and Lyman Kirkpatrick, *The Real CIA* (New York: Macmillan, 1968).

For civil rights, audiotapes at the Kennedy Library cover White House meetings on the integration of the University of Mississippi, the Birmingham crisis, visits of civil rights leaders, and the introduction of civil rights legislation. Transcripts exist for only some of these tapes; the others must be listened to with care.

Other sources to consult include Taylor Branch, *Parting the Waters* (New York: Simon & Schuster, 1988), a history of the 1954–63 period; Walter Lord, *The Past That Would Not Die* (New York: Harper & Row, 1965), an account of the integration of the University of Mississippi; Thomas Gentile, *March on Washington: August 28, 1963* (Washington, D.C.: New Day Publications, 1983); D. F. Sullivan, *The Civil Rights Programs of the Kennedy Administration* (Ann Arbor, MI: University Microfilms, 1965); Carl M. Brauer, *John F. Kennedy and the Second Reconstruction* (New York: Columbia University Press, 1977); and Victor Navasky, *Kennedy Justice* (New York: Atheneum, 1973).

Important biographies include James Farmer, *Lay Bare the Heart: An Autobiography of the Civil Rights Movement* (New York: Arbor House, 1985); David Garrow, *Bearing the Cross: Martin Luther King, Jr., and the Southern Christian Leadership Conference* (New York: William Morrow, 1986); Stephen B. Oates, *Let the Trumpet Sound* (New York: Harper & Row, 1982); and Roy Wilkins with Tom Mathews, *Standing Fast: The Autobiography of Roy Wilkins* (New York: Viking Press, 1982).

For accounts of the FBI's war against the civil rights movement, see David J. Garrow's *The FBI and Martin Luther King, Jr.: From 'Solo' to Memphis* (New York: W. W. Norton, 1981), and Kenneth O'Reilly, *"Racial Matters": The FBI's Secret File on Black America, 1960–1972* (New York: Free Press, 1989).

The Cuban missile crisis has generated an almost unmanageable volume of literature. Primary sources include transcripts of White House meetings on October 16 and 27, 1962, available at the Kennedy Library; the posthumously published *Thirteen Days*, by Robert Kennedy (New York: W. W. Norton, 1969), and the huge cache of material related to Cuba located at the National Security Archive and available on microfiche as *The Cuban Missile Crisis, 1962: The Making of U.S. Policy* (Washington, DC: National Security Archive, 1992). Eighty-three of the most important documents from this collection are reproduced in Laurence Chang and Peter Kornbluh, eds., *The Cuban Missile Crisis, 1962: A National Security Archive Documents Reader* (New York: New Press, 1992), which also provides a simple but extremely detailed chronology of the missile crisis.

Other key sources are Elie Abel, *The Missile Crisis* (Philadelphia: Lippincott, 1966); James Hershberg, "Before 'The Missiles of October': Did Kennedy Plan a Military Strike Against Cuba?" *Diplomatic History* (Spring 1990); David Detzer, *The Brink: Cuban Missile Crisis, 1962* (New York: Thomas Y. Crowell, 1979); Herbert Dinnerstein, *The Making of a Missile Crisis* (Baltimore: Johns Hopkins University Press, 1976); and Robert A. Divine, ed., *The Cuban Missile Crisis: The Continuing Debate* (Chicago: Quadrangle, 1971), a useful compendium of reprinted views of the crisis.

Beginning in the fall of 1987, a series of conferences reunited participants in the missile crisis, and the meetings eventually expanded to include former Soviet and Cuban officials. Transcripts of the proceedings of the conferences held in Hawk's Cay, Florida (March 1987), Cambridge, Massachusetts (October 1987), and Moscow (January 1989) are available from the Center for Science and International Affairs at Harvard University's Kennedy School of Government. Proceedings of the meeting held in Antigua (January 1991) are available from the Center for Foreign Policy Development at Brown University.

On the test ban treaty, see Glenn Seaborg, *Kennedy, Khrushchev and the Test Ban* (Berkeley, CA: University of California Press, 1981); Norman Cousins, *The Improbable Triumvirate: John F. Kennedy, Pope John, Nikita Khrushchev* (New York: W. W. Norton, 1972); and Gordon Chang, *Friends and Enemies: The United States, China, and the Soviet Union, 1948–1972* (Stanford, CA: Stanford University Press, 1990). Walter LaFeber, *America, Russia and the Cold War, 1945–1975* (New York: John Wiley, 1976); James E. McSherry, *Russia and the United States Under Eisenhower, Khrushchev, and Kennedy* (State Park, PA: State College, 1965); and Adam B. Ulam, *Expansion and Coexistence: Soviet Foreign Policy, 1917–1973* (New York: Praeger, 1974) all also contain useful information on U.S.–Soviet relations.

As of mid-1993, official Department of State History records were available for only one subject for the Kennedy years: Vietnam. The resulting document sets, *Foreign Relations of the United States* (Washington, D.C.: Government Printing Office, 1988–90), 4 vols., immediately rendered most other primary sources obsolete and are essential.

Works on Vietnam include William J. Rust, *Kennedy in Vietnam* (New York: Charles Scribner's Sons, 1985), William Conrad Gibbons, *The U.S. Government and the Vietnam War: Executive and Legislative Roles and Relationships* (Princeton, NJ: Princeton University Press, 1986), *Part II: 1961–1964;* David Halberstam, *The Best and the Brightest* (New York: Random House, 1969); Ellen J. Hammer, *A Death in November: America in Vietnam, 1963* (New York: E. P. Dutton, 1987); George C. Herring, *America's Longest War: The United States and Vietnam, 1950–1975* (New York: John Wiley, 1979); and Stephen Pelz, "John F. Kennedy's 1961 Vietnam War Decisions," *Journal of Strategic Studies* (December 1981).

For Kennedy and the press, Montague Kern, Patricia W. Levering, and Ralph B. Levering, *The Kennedy Crises: The Press, the Presidency, and Foreign Policy* (Chapel Hill, NC: University of North Carolina Press, 1983), comprehensively analyzes coverage of the administration by five major newspapers and Kennedy's interaction with the media. Besides Bradlee's and Salinger's books, first-hand accounts that contain useful information include: Marquis Childs, *Witness to Power* (New York: McGraw-Hill, 1975); Arthur Krock, *Memoirs: Sixty Years on the Firing Line* (New York: Funk & Wagnalls, 1968); Chalmers M. Roberts, *First Rough Draft: A Journalist's Journal of Our Times* (New York: Praeger, 1973); and Harrison Salisbury, *Without Fear or Favor: The New York Times and Its Times* (New York: Times Books, 1980).

Highly recommended works that do not fall into any of the above categories include Walter W. Heller, *New Dimensions of Political Economy* (Cambridge, MA: Harvard University Press, 1966); Richard D. Mahoney, *JFK: Ordeal in Africa* (New York: Oxford University Press, 1983); Allen J. Matusow, *The Unraveling of America: A History of Liberalism in the 1960s* (New York: Harper & Row, 1984); Charles Murray and Catherine Bly Cox, *Apollo: The Race to the Moon* (New York: Simon & Schuster, 1989); Gerald T. Rice, *The Bold Experiment: JFK's Peace Corps* (South Bend, IN: University of Notre Dame Press, 1985); and Charles Stevenson, *The End of Nowhere: American Policy Toward Laos Since 1954* (Boston: Beacon Press, 1972).

—Peter J. Keating

Acknowledgments

Because I worked on this book for several years, I have more than the usual number of men and women to thank for their help and encouragement in completing it. But, in addition to my family, there are two people without whom it would not have been possible: Peter Keating, my principal researcher, and Alice Mayhew, my editor.

On one of my first reporting trips to Boston in 1987, I put a small notice up on a bulletin board at Harvard. I was looking for someone to collect and Xerox documents for a few hours each week at the John F. Kennedy Library. Peter, then a junior at the college, appeared at our door one day and said he was the man for the job. He was indeed. He was two years past a master's degree at the Kennedy School of Government by the time we finished, and I suspect there are only a handful of historians who know as much about the Kennedy presidency as he does.

I had done three books with Mayhew before this one, so I knew she was good. I just did not know how good she really was. Whatever it is that makes great editors—intellect, memory, basic psychiatry, passion, and stamina come to mind—she had it all for me this time. I will be forever grateful.

I also owe a good deal to several other researchers who worked with me over those years: Michelle Barthelmy and Laurence Borde in Paris; Joan Andrews and Ari Paparo in Washington; Terry Freas in New York;

and Rosanne Landay and Allison Holmes in Los Angeles. Natalie Goldstein did the photo research in New York.

I am grateful, too, for all the help I received at libraries and archives. At the Kennedy Library: Ronald Whealan, Maura Porter, June Payne, Will Johnson, Michael Desmond, Alan Goodrich and James Cedrone. At the National Security Archive: Scott Armstrong, William Burr, and Laurence Chang. At the State Department: Margaret Roman. I would also like to thank the staffs of Widener Library, Lamont Library, and the Kennedy School of Government at Harvard, and of the Lyndon B. Johnson Library in Austin, Texas, and the Dwight D. Eisenhower Library in Abilene, Kansas. We also worked at the National Archives, the USIA Archives, the FBI Reading Room, and the Moorland-Spingarn Research Center at Howard University, all in Washington, D.C. James Ashe, director of the John Jermain Library in Sag Harbor, New York, allowed me to use that wonderful little place as the book's first workspace. We also made extensive use of the UCLA libraries in Los Angeles and the Patchogue, New York, Public Library. The *International Herald Tribune* in Paris kindly granted me access to its files.

For access to their personal papers and research, I am indebted to: Herbert Alexander, Irving Bernstein, Tom Blake, Henry Brandon, Clark Clifford, Fred Dutton, Mel Elfin, David Ellis, Betty Friedan, Ed Guthman, David Halberstam, James Hershberg, Walter Isaacson, Ruth Jacobson, Myrick Land, Robert Manning, David Michaelis, and William Shawcross.

I am personally indebted to a number of friends who helped me along the way on this book: Susan Mary Alsop, Ken Auletta, Felicity Barringer, Ben Bradlee, William Colby, Byron Dobell, Clay Felker, Katharine Graham, Millie Harmon, Lee and Berna Huebner, Tom and Mireille Johnston, Ward Just, Peter Kaplan, Patricia and Frederic Keating, William Keller, J. Anthony Lukas, Steve Meyers, Tully Plesser, Miles Rubin, Gail Sheehy, Philip Taubman, William Taubman, Amanda Urban, John Vinocur, and Patricia and Walter Wells. And to Mario Bonello, the manager of the St. Botolph Club in Boston.

Lynn Nesbit, my agent, was with me at the beginning and at the end of this book as she has been on everything I have written. I would follow her anywhere. At Simon & Schuster, I am grateful to George Hodgman and Elizabeth Stein for their help.

I never met President Kennedy. I received no help that would be considered out of the ordinary from members of the Kennedy family. Mrs. Jacqueline Kennedy Onassis agreed to answer fact-checking questions. I interviewed the President's brother-in-law, Stephen Smith, twice before his death. As a *New York Times* correspondent, I traveled with

Robert F. Kennedy and Edward Kennedy and interviewed both of them, sometimes touching on events of their brother's presidency. I asked Senator Edward Kennedy three times for interviews related to this book and he declined each time.

The years I worked on this book were times of great joy and some significant stress in our family. I could not have done this or many other things if I were not lucky enough to be married to Catherine O'Neill.

Richard Reeves
Pacific Palisades, California
June 1993

Index

PHOTO CREDITS

Richard Reeves is the author of eight books, including *American Journey: Traveling with Tocqueville in Search of Democracy in America*. He is a nationally syndicated columnist and teaches political science at UCLA. He lives in Los Angeles with his wife, Catherine O'Neill.